# Historical Dictionary of France from the 1815 Restoration to the Second Empire

**Historical Dictionaries of French History**

This five-volume series covers French history from the Revolution through the Third Republic. It provides comprehensive coverage of each era, including not only political and military history but also social, economic, and art history.

*Historical Dictionary of the French Revolution, 1789–1799*
Samuel F. Scott and Barry Rothaus, editors

*Historical Dictionary of Napoleonic France, 1799–1815*
Owen Connelly, editor

*Historical Dictionary of France from 1815 Restoration to the Second Empire*
Edgar Leon Newman, editor

*Historical Dictionary of the French Second Empire, 1852–1870*
William E. Echard, editor

*Historical Dictionary of the Third French Republic, 1870–1940*
Patrick H. Hutton, editor-in-chief

# Historical Dictionary of France from the 1815 Restoration to the Second Empire

M-Z

*Edited by*
**EDGAR LEON NEWMAN**

**ROBERT LAWRENCE SIMPSON,**
*Assistant Editor*

**Greenwood Press**
New York
Westport, Connecticut

**Library of Congress Cataloging-in-Publication Data**
Main entry under title:

Historical dictionary of France from the 1815 restoration
   to the Second Empire.

   Bibliography: p.
   Includes index.
   1. France—History—Restoration, 1814–1830—
Dictionaries.   2. France—History—Louis Philip, 1830–
1848—Dictionaries.   3. France—History—Second
Republic, 1848–1852—Dictionaries.   I. Newman, Edgar
Leon.
DC256.H57   1987      944.06′03′21      85–17728
ISBN 0–313–22751–9 (lib. bdg.: alk. paper)
ISBN 0–313–26045–1 (lib. bdg. : alk. paper : v.1)
ISBN 0–313–26046–X (lib. bdg. : alk. paper : v.2)

Library of Congress Catalog Card Number: 85–17728
ISBN: 0–313–22751–9 (set)
ISBN: 0–313–26045–1 (v.1)
ISBN: 0–313–26046–X (v.2)

First published in 1987

Greenwood Press, Inc.
88 Post Road West, Westport, Connecticut 06881

Printed in the United States of America

The paper used in this book complies with the
Permanent Paper Standard issued by the National
Information Standards Organization (Z39.48–1984).

10 9 8 7 6 5 4 3 2 1

FOR MY FATHER

# Contents

# Contributors

*Albury, W. R.*, University of New South Wales, Kensington, New South Wales, Australia

*Aldrich, Robert*, University of Sydney, Sydney, New South Wales, Australia

*Allen, James Smith*, Phillips University, Enid, Oklahoma

*Bailey, Charles R.*, S.U.N.Y.-Geneseo, Geneseo, New York

*Beach, Vincent*, University of Colorado, Boulder, Colorado

*Beck, Thomas*, Chapman College, Orange, California.

*Bertier de Sauvigny, Guillaume de*, Paris, France

*Brown, Robert*, Pembroke State University, Pembroke, North Carolina

*Caron, Jean-Claude*, Nogent-sur-Marne, France

*Castelli, Helen*, East Stroudsberg, Pennsylvania

*Chandler, David*, Royal Military Academy Sandhurst, Camberley, Surrey, Great Britain

*Chastain, James*, Ohio University, Athens, Ohio

*Collins, Irene*, University of Liverpool, Liverpool, Great Britain

*Comeau, Paul*, New Mexico State University, Las Cruces, New Mexico

*Connor, Susan*, Tift College, Forsyth, Georgia

*Cook, Bernard*, Loyola University, New Orleans, Louisiana

*Creighton, John K.*, University of Texas at El Paso, El Paso, Texas

*Crosland, Maurice*, University of Kent at Canterbury, Great Britain

*Day, C. Rod*, Simon Fraser University, Burnaby, British Columbia, Canada

*de Luna, Frederick A.*, University of Alberta, Edmonton, Alberta, Canada

*Earls, Irene*, Orlando, Florida

*Ehrenberg, John*, Long Island University, Brooklyn, New York

*Elwitt, Sanford*, University of Rochester, Rochester, New York

*Frader, Laura*, Northeastern University, Boston, Massachusetts

*Freedeman, Charles E.*, S.U.N.Y.-Binghamton, Binghamton, New York

*Fuchs, Rachel*, Arizona State University, Tempe, Arizona

*Grubb, Alan*, Clemson University, Clemson, South Carolina

*Gullickson, Gay L.*, University of Maryland, College Park, Maryland
*Guthrie, Christophe E.*, Tarleton State University, Stephenville, Texas
*Gutman, Sanford*, S.U.N.Y.-Cortland, Cortland, New York
*Harrigan, Patrick J.*, University of Waterloo, Waterloo, Ontario, Canada
*Higgs, David*, University of Toronto, Toronto, Ontario, Canada
*Johnson, Christopher H.*, Wayne State University, Detroit, Michigan
*Kaiser, Thomas E.*, University of Arkansas at Little Rock, Little Rock, Arkansas
*Kieswetter, James K.*, Eastern Washington University, Cheney, Washington
*Klinck, David M.*, University of Windsor, Windsor, Ontario, Canada
*Kors, Alan C.*, University of Pennsylvania, Philadelphia, Pennsylvania
*Kselman, Thomas*, University of Notre Dame, Notre Dame, Indiana
*Latta, Claude*, Professor of History, Lauréat de l'Académie Française
*Lehning, James*, University of Utah, Salt Lake City, Utah
*Longfellow, David*, Baylor University, Waco, Texas
*Loubère, Leo A.*, S.U.N.Y.-Buffalo, Buffalo, New York
*McBride, Theresa*, College of the Holy Cross, Worcester, Massachusetts
*McPhee, Peter*, Victoria University of Wellington, Wellington, New Zealand
*Moon, S. Joan*, California State University, Sacramento, California
*Moss, Bernard H.*, University of Auckland, Auckland, New Zealand
*Necheles, Ruth F.*, Long Island University, Brooklyn, New York
*Neely, Sylvia*, Indiana University-Purdue University at Fort Wayne, Fort Wayne, Indiana
*Newman, Edgar L.*, New Mexico State University, Las Cruces, New Mexico
*O'Brien, Patricia*, University of California-Irvine, Irvine, California
*Outlaw, Shelby A.*, Atlanta, Georgia
*Pinkney, David H.*, University of Washington, Seattle, Washington
*Popkin, Jeremy*, University of Kentucky, Lexington, Kentucky
*Porch, Douglas*, The Citadel, Charleston, South Carolina
*Rader, Daniel*, San Diego State University, San Diego, California
*Ratcliffe, Barrie M.*, Université Laval, Quebec, Quebec, Canada
*Reedy, W. Jay*, North Dakota State University, Fargo, North Dakota
*Reid, Donald*, University of North Carolina, Chapel Hill, North Carolina
*Rooney, John W.*, Marquette University, Milwaukee, Wisconsin
*Rose, Robert Barrie*, University of Tasmania, Hobart, Tasmania, Australia
*Sandstrom, Roy E.*, University of Northern Iowa, Cedar Falls, Iowa
*Schleifer, James T.*, College of New Rochelle, New Rochelle, New York
*Schmidt, Daniel P.*, Marquette University, Milwaukee, Wisconsin
*Sibalis, Michael*, Brock University, St. Catherines, Ontario, Canada
*Simpson Robert L.*, New Mexico State University, Las Cruces, New Mexico
*Smith, Bonnie G.*, University of Rochester, Rochester, New York
*Smith, Don*, Oakland, California
*Smith, Robert J.*, S.U.N.Y-Brockport, Brockport, New York
*Staum, Martin S.*, University of Calgary, Calgary, Alberta, Canada

*Strumingher, Laura S.*, University of Cincinnati, Cincinnati, Ohio
*Sussman, George D.*, Delmar, New York
*Truant, Cynthia*, University of California-San Diego, La Jolla, California
*Weber, William*, California State University-Long Beach, Long Beach, California
*Weissbach, Lee Shai*, University of Louisville, Louisville, Kentucky
*Weisz, George*, McGill University, Montreal, Quebec, Canada
*Welch, Marcelle Maistre*, Florida International University, Miami, Florida
*Zhang Zhilian*, Peking University, Peking, People's Republic of China

# Preface

The period from 1 January 1815 to 31 December 1852 began and ended with a Napoleon Bonaparte as emperor of the French. It included two major revolutions and several revolts, an experiment with parliamentary government and an independent press, the dawn of socialist ideology, the golden age of romanticism, and the beginning of the Industrial Revolution. But this was an age dominated by memories, not events.

The conflicts of the great French Revolution grew in stature as time passed. They seemed larger than life, like the ancient wars between gods and giants. The Republic and the Terror had proven that France was not ready for democracy, and the men associated with the Republic and the Terror were generally despised. The memory of Napolean, however, was more and more the one source of excitement in a lackluster world. France was a divided nation, and only the army was a truly national institution. The legend of its conquests could confer glory upon the most ordinary shopkeepers and peasants. While the surface of political life kept changing, Bonapartism remained the constant undercurrent in France during the first half of the nineteenth century. It surfaced as soon as it could. In the first democratic presidential election, which took place on 10 December 1848, the common people cast their votes for Louis-Napoleon Bonaparte. Meanwhile the memory of Napoleon and the Revolution had affected every event, every trend in literature and art, and every mind in France. Frenchmen of the nineteenth century had a sense of being dwarfs who lived in the shadow of giants. Each current event was seen as the product of the Revolutionary past. Leftists, however moderate, could be made to appear dangerous if they were presented as reincarnations of Maximilien Robespierre. The memory of Voltaire was a living force; his books were best-sellers, and his ideas were at the height of their influence. Consequently figures from the past like Robespierre and Voltaire have been included in this book because of their influence on France between the two Napoleons. And the system of cross-references, which has been used in all the volumes of this Greenwood Press series of French historical dictionaries, is especially appropriate for this one in which so many entries are interrelated.

Readers who follow the cross-references from one entry to another will become aware of the wide spectrum of viewpoints included in this book. There are more than 950 articles written by 75 scholars from countries throughout the world. Some of these scholars are conservatives, some Marxists, and some are not part of either school. Because there is no definitive interpretation of most issues, I have tried to present a balance of several prevailing viewpoints and to allow each author enough space to defend his or her conclusions. Each entry has a brief bibliography of works for further reference.

Although this book is called a historical dictionary, it is intended to serve as a useful reference guide in many fields. Several authors are specialists in literature, art, music, sociology, and other disciplines. Our goal has been to include as wide a variety as possible of academic fields and political points of view.

This historical dictionary reflects the time in which it was written: the 1980s. In addition to the standard entries on writers, politicians, kings, battles, newspapers, scientists, philosophers, generals, artists, revolutionaries, laws, and schools, there are entries that reflect the triumph of social history, the *Annales* school, and Fernand Braudel, such as: Childrearing Practices; Children, Abandoned; Children, Institutions For; Child Labor; Wet Nursing; Public Welfare; Liberty of Education; Public Instruction; Singing Societies; Domestic Servants; Silk Industry; Women's Newspapers; Worker Poets; Railroads; Banking; Jews; Coal Industry; Peasants; Popular Religiosity; Fertility; Migration; Mortality; Nuptiality; Population; Banking; and of course, Bonapartism. There is more about women, more about economic and social matters, and more history-from-the-bottom-up than there would have been in a book written twenty years ago. On the other hand, political leaders are given relatively little space, and military leaders are often left out unless they participated in a popular revolution. It was all but impossible to find somebody to write the entry on the battle of Waterloo. Everyone seemed to be working on demographics, economic and social change, and popular mentality. Just a few weeks before I wrote this preface, an angry President François Mitterand complained that schoolchildren in France know the price of wheat in 1789 but they have never heard of the marquis de Mirabeau. Indeed there are indications that historians may be responding to Mitterand's complaint and turning back to the study of great leaders and important events. In any case, this dictionary includes and cross-references both the traditional dictionary items and subjects of interest to the *Annales* school of history-from-the-bottom-up.

It includes extensive articles on the principal movements of the period. This was the Romantic age: Victor Hugo, Honoré de Balzac, René de Chateaubriand, Alphonse de Lamartine, George Sand, Hector Berlioz, Eugène Delacroix. There was an explosion of literature accompanied by the appearance of an independent press; newspapers like the *Constitutionnel* and the *Journal des débats* during the Restoration and like the *National* and the *Réforme* during the July Monarchy had a powerful influence on public opinion. Although their circulation was less than 50,000, they could launch political careers for their editors and ignite the spark of popular revolution.

French politics have never been more interesting than in the years between the two Napoleons. Only a few men could vote: there were fewer than 100,000 electors during the Restoration (1814–30) and about 300,000 electors during the July Monarchy (1830–48). Nevertheless France achieved a workable parliamentary government based on free elections, a comparatively free press, and the rule of law. The nation was learning to deal with the divisions that caused and were caused by the French Revolution without suspending its constitutional guarantees of individual freedom. All of this would be swept away after the June Days of 1848 and during the plebiscitary dictatorship of Napoleon III (1852–70), but it laid the basis for the constitutional parliamentary democracy of the Third, Fourth, and Fifth Republics.

The relative success of constitutional government in France from 1815 to 1852 was remarkable in view of the differences between the rulers and the ruled. The common people were an Anglophobic, aggressively nationalistic mass of peasants, artisans, and shopkeepers ruled by a pusillanimous élite of frightened landowners and bourgeois. Support for constitutional liberty was narrow and thin, and the liberal politicians and journalists who supported it were true heroes. They deserve the large amount of space devoted to them because of the weakness of their cause, not because of its strength.

Far stronger than constitutional liberalism were the resurgent conservative movements centered around the Bourbon monarchy and the Catholic church. Guillaume de Bertier de Sauvigny, the leading historian of the Restoration, has contributed a number of articles on these movements, which dominated life in the south and west of France and were second only to Bonapartism as a political force among the masses. The power of clericalism and conservatism in nineteenth-century France should never be underestimated. No government could stand against them and survive. This was the creative golden age of conservatism, which inspired Balzac, Alexandre Dumas, Chateaubriand, the young Lamartine, the young Lamennais, and the young Victor Hugo. The works of the great English constitutional conservative, Edmund Burke, exercised a powerful influence on French political and social thought affecting both liberals and conservatives from Pierre-Paul Royer-Collard to François Guizot to Alexis de Tocqueville. Less influential were the paternalistic clerical monarchists Bonald and de Maistre and their socialist counterpart, Saint-Simon, who insisted that the nation was not capable of governing itself. The failures of the great French Revolution had cast doubt upon the powers of human reason and upon the ability of the individual to live in freedom. The legacy of the Revolution was conservatism and self-doubt.

Of course, there were two revolutions, one in 1830 and one in 1848, during this great conservative age. These revolutions made heroes of a variety of malcontents and misfits who wrote revolutionary tracts and led revolutionary movements, and who consequently occupy a great deal of space in this dictionary. France was still divided and disorderly enough so that any loudmouthed scofflaw could hope to emerge as a popular leader. Revolutions can turn ridiculous people into powerful ones and vice-versa. The years between the two Napoleons saw the birth of socialism and the rebirth of revolutionary republicanism, and both movements have been covered here. Bernard Moss, who wrote the article on the Society of the Rights of Man, sees republicanism as a democratic and socialistic revolutionary movement that clung at first to the memory of the First French Republic and then expanded to capture the imagination and the loyalty of the working classes. Christopher Johnson's entry on socialism follows the same argument: that revolutionary socialism became the dominant ideology of the proletariat. Michael Sibalis's entry on Bonapartism also sees the popular devotion to the memory of Napoleon as essentially republican and socialistic, dominated by the tricolored flag of the democratic Republic rather than the eagle of the nationalistic and militaristic Empire. The entries by Bertier de Sauvigny, on the other hand, see the masses as concerned essentially with their own material needs, and David Pinkney's entry on the July Revolution does not see the crowd as motivated by a particular ideology. My entry on the republicans views the French people as Bonapartist and nationalist and consequently unimpressed by either republican or socialist ideas. In the end, it is crucial but impossible to know the mentality of the French people during the years between the two Napoleons. The period ended with a democratic republic in February 1848, a democratic and socialist uprising in June 1848, a massive vote for Louis-Napoleon Bonaparte in December 1848, followed by socialist electoral victories, then a Bonapartist military coup d'état, and finally a plebiscite massively endorsing that coup. The populace went through many moods, and we can only guess which of its faces showed its true inner nature.

France during the years between the two Napoleons was more disunited and disorderly than it would ever be again but more harmonious and peaceful than it had been in the past. Despite the revolutionary upheavals of 1830 and 1848–52, the wounds of the great French Revolution had begun to heal so that the nation could begin to deal with the changes that the Revolution had produced. In addition, the new means of production, especially in manufacturing and mining, and the new means of transportation like steamships and the first railroads would have to be absorbed into a nation that was still politically unstable. To its credit, France in this period coped with its problems by means of constitutional government, elected parliaments, a relatively free press, and the rule of law. Liberals, conservatives, nationalistic Bonapartists, and socialist revolutionaries each laid the groundwork for their nation's future, each hoping to pull it in a different direction. The result of their efforts has divided, confused, and enriched France ever since, through the near-miss of the Dreyfus Affair, the age of a Herculean Clemenceau, through the reforms of Léon Blum, the shame of Vichy, the napoleonic pride of de Gaulle, the dashed hopes of Mitterand, and beyond.

This book was made possible by the imagination and devotion to scholarship of the Greenwood Press and especially of Cynthia Harris, the editor of reference books. The years betwen the two Napoleons have not attracted a large number of scholars, but the high quality, style, and thoughtfulness of these entries attests to the vitality of the field. Those who took the time to contribute their work deserve, along with Ms. Harris and Greenwood Press, the thanks of everyone who will benefit from this dictionary. Finally, this volume was made possible only by the hard work and dedication of Robert Simpson, the assistant editor. He compiled the cross-references and the index, carried on the bulk of the correspondence with six dozen authors, and made my life much easier for the past four years.

Edgar Leon Newman

# M

**MACAIRE, ROBERT,** fictional character representing selfishness, materialism, and greed; the French Ebenezer Scrooge. The fictional character Robert Macaire first appeared as a highwayman in a melodrama, *L'Auberge des Adrets*, in 1823. A play, *Robert Macaire*, was produced in 1834. The caricaturist Honoré Daumier borrowed this character, dressed him as a banker, a lawyer, a journalist, and others, and thereby revealed the larceny and greed that lay beneath the respectable dress of the bourgeoisie, the *honnêtes gens* who ruled the France of the July Monarchy. Largely because of Daumier's cartoons, Macaire became part of the French vocabulary used by popular writers like Eugène Sue as a symbol of materialism and self-interest; he signified the lack of principle and humanity of the Orléans regime. As "J. Christian Sailer," a Christian socialist poet, put it:

There are no Robert Macaires in Heaven.
. . . Nowadays, it is only too notorious that men are vain,
selfish, hateful and disloyal.
They believe in nothing.

*Grand Larousse Encyclopédique*, vol. 6 (Paris, 1962); E. L. Newman, "L'arme du siècle, c'est la plume: The French Worker Poets of the July Monarchy and the Spirit of Revolution and Reform," *Journal of Modern History* 51 (1979); J.-C.Sailer, "Le positif ne vaut pas l'ideal," in *Lice chansonnière*, vol. VI-VII (Paris, 1839–1840).

*Edgar Leon Newman*

*Related entries:* DAUMIER; SUE.

**MACDONALD, JACQUES-ETIENNE-JOSEPH-ALEXANDRE** (1765–1840), duc de Taranto, marshal of the Empire and peer of the Restoration. MacDonald was born on 17 November 1765 at Sedan (Ardennes) to a Scottish family that had fled to France after the 1745 Jacobite uprising in Scotland. He enlisted as an officer cadet in 1784. When the Revolution began, he remained while most officers of his regiment emigrated. Promoted to general under the

Republic, he assisted Napoleon in the coup of 18 Brumaire. Napoleon rewarded him with a marshal's baton on the battlefield of Wagram on 7 July 1809, and he became duke of Taranto on 9 December.

MacDonald was one of the last of the marshals to accept Napoleon's abdication, which in fact he had urged. On 5 April 1814, he and Michel Ney attempted unsuccessfully to convince the czar to accept a conditional abdication. Then on 11 April he and Armand-Augustin de Caulaincourt carried the final abdication document from Fontainebleau to the Allies in Paris. The Restoration appointed him to the War Council, named him a peer, and gave him the Order of Saint Louis and the governorship of a military district. When Napoleon escaped from Elba, MacDonald went with Artois to Lyons where he tried in vain to halt the popular reception of Napoleon. Then he returned to Paris, persuaded the king to flee, and escorted him to the border. He accepted no appointment during the Hundred Days. After Waterloo the Bourbons gave him the task of disbanding the army of the Loire, which he did as gently as possible, even warning those who might be arrested. His testimony in favor of General Jean-Baptiste Drouet notwithstanding, he became grand chancellor of the Legion of Honor and was one of the four marshals commanding the royal guard. As a peer he took an active part in debates in the Chamber and presided fearlessly over an inquiry that revealed corruption in Angoulême's Spanish campaign. After the July Revolution he retired to his estate, where he died on 25 September 1840. This gentle man, whose favorite pastime was playing the violin, had spent the last fourteen years of his life looking after the veterans of the Empire and their families. His *Souvenirs* were published in 1892.

Archives parlementaires; A. G. Macdonnell, *Napoleon and His Marshals* (London, 1950); A. Robert et al., *Dictionnaire des parlementaires français* (Paris, 1889–91).

*James K. Kieswetter*

*Related entries:* ANGOULEME, L.-A; CAULAINCOURT; CHAMBER OF PEERS; CHARLES X; DROUET D'ERLON; HUNDRED DAYS; LOUIS XVIII; REVOLUTION OF 1830; ROYAL GUARD; SPAIN, 1823 FRENCH INVASION OF.

**MADELEINE CHURCH,** a large church in classic architecture, constructed 1806–42, in the eighth arrondissement of Paris; correctly called the Church of Saint Mary Magdelene. As early as the thirteenth century, a chapel dedicated to Saint Mary Magdelene existed in this vicinity on a fief of the bishop of Paris. It became a parish in 1639 and underwent several reconstructions over the centuries. In 1764 it was decided to build a new church, similar to the Pantheon and aligned on the axis of the rue Royale, to serve the expanding population of the district. Work was begun under the architect Constant d'Ivry and continued after his death in 1777 by Guillaume Couture.The Revolution interrupted construction, and the parish functions were transferred in 1802 to the Church of the Assumption. During the Revolution and early Empire, proposals were made to complete the structure and use it as a stock market, a court of commerce, a bank, a theater, a library, or something else. In December 1806, however, Napoleon specified that it was to be a Temple of Glory in honor of the Grande armée, constructed in the style of an Athenian temple. More a monument than a church, its facade was to balance that of the Palais Bourbon facing it across the Seine. Barthelemy Vignon took charge of the work, modified the structure of d'Ivry and Couture, and began additional construction.The temple was unfinished at the end of the Empire, by which time Napoleon himself had almost abandoned the temple idea in favor of a church.

The Restoration continued the work under Vignon although now changing the function to that of a church. In 1817, however, it was decided to give the structure the exterior appearance of a Greek temple while the interior was to be in Roman style—hence the fifty-two Corinthian columns around the outside and the three domes, which dominate the interior ceiling. At Vignon's death in 1828, direction of the nearly completed project was assumed by Jean-Jacques Huvé. The work was finished between 1830 and 1842 with the completion of the vaults and sculpture by Philippe-Joseph Lemaire, François Rude, Denis Foyatier, Jean-Jacques Pradier, Antoine-Louis Barye, Antoine Etex, Francisque-Joseph Duret, and François-Joseph Bosio. First, however, one last alternative was proposed: that the building should become Paris's first railway station. In the completed church, the high altar was placed in the location Napoleon had intended for his throne. The surrounding square (the place de la Madeleine) was begun in 1808 and completed in 1824.

J. Hillairet, *Dictionnaire historique des rues de Paris* (Paris, 1963); G. Poisson, *Napoléon et Paris* (Paris, 1964).

*James K. Kieswetter*

*Related entry:* BOSIO.


**MADIER DE MONTJAU, JOSEPH-PAULIN** (1785–1865), administrator of the Empire and Restoration, deputy of the July Monarchy. Born at Bourg-Saint-Andéol (Ardèche) on 11 February 1785, Madier entered the bar in 1805 and became an auditor in the Council of State in 1810. The following year he was appointed inspector general of combined duties, and in 1813 he joined the imperial court at Nîmes.The Restoration retained him in office, and he continued developing the liberal reputation he had already acquired. In 1815 he tried to curtail the excesses of the royalist reaction. He received the Legion of Honor in 1818. In March 1820 he sent to the Deputies a turgid petition denouncing ultra-royalist violence in the Midi and the existence of a secret ultra government, which was attempting to restore the Old Regime. His petition, which contained much truth, stirred considerable controversy and resulted in Madier's being censured by the Court of Cassation. But his petition was forwarded by the Deputies to Duke Armand-Emmanuel de Richelieu, an act of acceptance by the Chamber. It also established him as a leader of the liberal wing of the constitutional monarchist party.

In June 1830 the department of Aude elected Madier to the Deputies, but he was not involved in the July Revolution. He joined the conservative majority in supporting the July Monarchy, which shortly named him attorney general at Lyons. Reelected a deputy in October 1830, Madier worked to maintain the existing magisterial system. He also supported the amendment of the Charter that stated that Catholicism was the religion of the majority of the French. Later in 1830 he assisted in the prosecution of the former ministers of Charles X. Reelected again in July 1831 by the Ardèche, in December of that year he became a councillor in the Court of Cassation. He subsequently participated actively in support of conservative causes in the Chamber, such as the hereditary peerage and the Law on Associations.

Madier's neglect of his judicial functions, however, resulted in complaints by his fellow magistrates to the minister of justice. He was defeated for reelection in 1834 but was returned in a by-election when his opponent's election was annulled. Although he continued to support the ministry, his attendance in the Chamber now became so irregular that special efforts were made to ensure his presence for important votes. During the 1835 debates on press restrictions, Madier spoke harshly against both republicans and legitimists, supporting the political jurisdiction of the Peers and advocating the proposed repressive measures. In 1837 he abandoned the Chamber of Deputies but not political life. In the early 1840s he joined the opposition, writing against the authoritarian abuses of the government and recanting his previous voting record yet leaning toward the legitimist camp. In 1846 he helped found and edit *L'Esprit public*, a journal of opposition to Louis-Philippe.

Madier did not support the Second Republic. Rather, with a great deal of fanfare he resigned from the Court of Cassation on 19 April 1848 as a protest against the Provisional Government's efforts to modify the irremovability of judges. Thereafter Madier lived in retirement, although he still occasionally took up the pen. In 1849 he supported the legitimists, and he was briefly arrested during the 1851 coup. Madier died at Prés-Saint-Gervais (Seine) on 10 May 1865.

*Archives parlementaires*; A. Robert et al., *Dictionnaire des parlementaires français* (Paris, 1889–91); G. Vapereau, *Dictionnaire universel des contemporains* (Paris, 1858).

*James K. Kieswetter*

*Related entries:* COURT OF CASSATION; *L'ESPRIT PUBLIC;* PRESS LAWS; RICHELIEU; ULTRAROYALISTS; WHITE TERROR.

**MAGENDIE, FRANCOIS** (1783–1855), experimental physiologist. Throughout his career in teaching and research, Magendie waged a vigorous campaign to establish physiology on an experimental basis. Shortly after receiving his doctorate in medicine at Paris in 1808, he attacked the prevailing theories of life as empty speculation and began experimental investigations of the organic functions of the body. As his career progressed, Magendie became more and more skeptical toward efforts to systematize the results of physiological research into a coherent theory. This tendency to value the brute, empirical fact over rational understanding was later criticized by Magendie's successor and most brilliant pupil, Claude Bernard; however, in the first half of the nineteenth century, it served as an effective polemical weapon against the resurgence of metaphysical theories of life in French philosophy and medicine. Magendie, an ardent republican whose father had raised him on Rousseauean principles, was as hostile to the reactionary political overtones of such ''spiritualistic'' theories as he was dismissive of their scientific pretensions.

Magendie's *Précis élémentaire de physiologie* (1816–17) was the first physiology textbook to make a thorough and consistent use of experimentation the basis of its teaching. In 1821 he founded the *Journal de physiologie expérimentale*, the first periodical devoted entirely to experimental work in physiology, and in that same year he was elected to the Académie des sciences and the Académie royale de médecine. Shortly afterward he became involved in a celebrated controversy with the Scottish anatomist and physiologist Charles Bell (1774–1842) over the functions of the spinal nerve roots. His part in this controversy together with his reputation as a ruthless vivisector made him the object of a parliamentary outcry when he visited Britain in 1824.

The final period of Magendie's career began in 1831 with his appointment to the prestigious chair of medicine at the Collège de France. During some fifteen years of active teaching at this institution Magendie devoted his lecture courses to the public demonstration of his techniques of experimental research. Although facilities at the Collège did not permit the training of significant numbers of research students, Magendie's lecture courses and publications did much to promote the acceptance of experimental physiology as the basis of scientific medicine.

J. E. Lesch, *Science and Medicine in France: The Emergence of Experimental Physiology, 1790–1855* (Cambridge, Mass., 1984); J. M. D. Olmsted, *François Magendie* (New York, 1944).

*W. R. Albury*

*Related entries:* ACADEMY OF SCIENCES; BERNARD; COLLEGE DE FRANCE; REPUBLICANS; ROUSSEAU.

**MAGU, MARIE-ELEONORE** (1788–1860), weaver in Lizy-sur-Ourq and major worker poet of the July Monarchy. Because he was the least political of the major worker poets, Magu probably best reflected the sentiments of his class. He was not without political ideals and ideas, but his greatest interest was in his personal survival. He said in reply to a deputy who had suggested that hunger stimulates the poetic imagination:

Don't come to me praising hunger.
Victor Hugo, Turquety, Lamartine,
Chateaubriand, Reboul, and Béranger
Have written well, but not without eating.

Like most of his fellow artisans, Magu was always reasonable and often hungry.

Unlike any other major worker poet, Magu was an example of downward social mobility. He was poor only because his father, a rich cloth merchant, had squandered the family fortune to purchase a title of nobility under the Old Regime and then been ruined during the Revolution of 1789. Born in his father's house on the rue du Temple in Paris on 25 March 1788, he fled with his family in 1796 when he was eight to the village of Tancrou (Seine-et-Marne) near Lizy-sur-Ourq in order to escape the dangers of the Revolution. Magu's newly poor family could afford to send him to the village school in Tancrou for only three winters. Magu had to spend his time as a door-to-door salesman for his father and then, at the age of twenty, he became a weaver in Lizy-sur-Ourq. His failing eyesight prevented him from exercising this profession from time to time, and he would support himself and his family by selling his poetry.

Magu had taught himself poetry by reading Lafontaine, who always remained his favorite author and his model. He wrote his first poem in 1806 when, at the age of eighteen, he fell in love with his peasant cousin and began to send poetry to her. He would eventually marry her and have fourteen children with her, three of whom survived and one of whom married the socialist locksmith, poet, and deputy Jérôme-Pierre Gilland. When his eyesight failed in 1814, Magu was forced to stop weaving and sell his verse door to door, writing songs to celebrate marriages and other events and generally eking out a living as a modern troubadour. Some teachers at the collège of Meaux began to notice his talent, especially in his poem "A ma navette," a hymn of praise to his loom. The regional press began to publish his works, and in 1838 a poem addressed to King Louis-Philippe in praise of the taking of Constantine got him known in Paris. In 1839, with the help of local dignitaries and societies of the Seine-et-Marne department, he published his first book of poems. It sold out its entire press run of 2,000 copies at 4 francs each, thanks in part to the help of Abel-François Villemain, minister of public education, who bought fifty copies. Magu's *Poésies* went through five editions and sold 9,000 copies in two years. This sellout, plus a pension of 200 francs from Narcisse-Achille de Salvandy, the minister of public instruction, for which he had been recommended by Pierre-Jean de Béranger and by Villemain, gave Magu a brief period of relative financial security. It also made him a celebrity, winning him the admiration and support of literary stars like George Sand and Béranger, and the sculptor Pierre-Jean David d'Angers even made a bronze medallion of him. Magu was overwhelmed; when he visited Mme. de Feray, an admirer of his poetry who had recommended him for a government pension, he was so impressed by her magnificent rug that he refused to walk on it until after she had given him her hand and led him in. The sky was the limit, and it seemed to Magu that under the July Monarchy, resignation and hard work were the keys to success. The poor should be resigned to their fate, count their blessings, and trust in God. Such thoughts were unlikely to appeal to militant socialists like George Sand and the Saint-Simonian workers of the *Ruche populaire*. But the simplicity and charm of Magu's verse made him sought after by everyone who wanted to show the dignity and capacity of workers. Magu's poetry was printed in the *Ruche populaire*, and George Sand called him one of the "ten or twelve notable worker-poets" of the day. Perhaps Magu's generous spirit was not too far from George Sand's socialist principles; Magu frequently called upon his government and his fellow countrymen to care about the poor and to help them just as the government and the rich had helped him. Magu had every reason to feel that the July Monarchy was a socialist society, and he asked only that the government expand its socialist principles from him to the other 30-odd million Frenchmen. He knew that things were bad, but he was certain that they were getting better. In a song, "Le bon Dieu s'est moqué de moi" (God is making fun of me), written to the tune of "Chante, chante troubadour, chante" and published in 1845, Magu wrote:

I have read that God made the earth
For mankind, whom he made all equal,
That was acting like a good father.
. . .

Lord, what kind of a caprice of yours is this?
Should you have treated me so badly?
What! everything's on one side and nothing's on the other,
The division is too unequal.
I get the work and the sorrow,
My rich neighbor gets a good-paying job;
I'm exhausting my strength, he's out for a stroll,
It looks like God is making fun of me.
. . .

A voice says to me: "Patience."
It is the voice of friendship.
Daughter of Heaven, through you I feel
That I was wrong to have lacked faith;
I've found again my little portion,
God has not been making fun of me.

The 1848 Revolution was both financially and politically embarrassing for Magu. It was financially embarrassing because it cost him his pension. Politically, Magu claimed that he had been duped into supporting the July Monarchy and that he had been a republican at heart all along. During the Second Empire the old widower, once a real literary star, faded into obscurity, proudly refusing all requests that he now use his pen to praise the Second Empire as he had once used it to defend the July Monarchy. After the death of his wife in 1858, he moved into the house of his daughter, the widow of Jérôme-Pierre Gilland, in the rue du Vert-Bois in Paris and died in La Charité Hospital there on 13 March 1860.

E. Baillet, *De quelques ouvriers-poètes, Biographies et souvenirs* (Paris, 1898); E. Dolléans, *Féminisme et mouvement ouvrier: George Sand* (Paris, 1951); L. Dupille, *Etudes sur Magu et Gilland* (Meaux, n.d.); M. E. Magu, *Poésies* (Paris, 1839), *Poésies, avec une préface par George Sand* (Paris, 1845), and *Poésies nouvelles, précédées de la biographie littéraire de l'auteur* (Paris, 1842); E. L. Newman, "L'arme du siècle, c'est la plume: The French Worker Poets of the July Monarchy and the Spirit of Revolution and Reform," "*Journal of Modern History* (1980) and *The French Worker Poets of the July Monarchy*, forthcoming; E. Thomas, *Voix d'en bas; la poésie ouvrière du XIXe siècle* (Paris, 1979).

*Edgar Leon Newman*

*Related entries:* BERANGER; DAVID D'ANGERS; LOUIS-PHILIPPE; RE-PUBLICANS; REVOLUTION OF 1848; *LA RUCHE POPULAIRE;* SAINT-SIMONIANISM; SALVANDY; VILLEMAIN; WORKER POETS.

**MAISON, NICHOLAS-JOSEPH, MARQUIS** (1771–1840), general of the Empire, marshal and peer of the Restoration, minister of the July Monarchy. Born 19 December 1771 at Epinay (Seine), Maison volunteered for the army in July 1792 and rose rapidly to the rank of captain. Although he distinguished himself bravely at Jemmapes, the deputies on mission regarded him as politically suspect. He lost his commission and reverted to the ranks. Severely wounded several times, Maison was promoted to major. Under Napoleon he became a general, and in 1808, a baron of the Empire. In the campaign in Germany in 1813 he fought valiantly at Lützen, Bautzen, and Leipzig, in recognition of which Napoleon on 14 August 1813 advanced him to count of the Empire. For the 1814 campaign in France, Napoleon gave him command of the Army of the North. In spite of inadequate resources, he held down the restive Belgian population, resisted the attacks of three Allied corps, and checked the enemy on 31 March at Courtrai. He continued to fight, and, in spite of Bourbon offers of money and a marshal's baton, he was preparing an operation on the enemy flank when he learned of Napoleon's unconditional abdication. Then he accepted an armistice.

During the First Restoration the Bourbons gave Maison the Legion of Honor, the Order of Saint Louis, and the governorship of Paris and on 4 June 1814 named him a peer of France. At Napoleon's return in 1815 he retired to his estates and remained inactive until after Waterloo. The Bourbons subsequently appointed him to command the First Military Division in 1815, the Eighth Division in 1816, and the First again in 1819. As a peer he did not make himself highly evident by participating in debates. When he did speak and vote, it was usually with the constitutional royalists, especially to oppose the policies of the Villèle government. When he was appointed to the panel to judge Marshal Michel

Ney, he declared himself incompetent. In August 1817 Louis XVIII gave him the title of marquis. As governor of Paris in 1820, he may have flirted with the Bazar conspirators. Although he declined to commit himself to them, his loyalty was subsequently questioned. In 1828, over Charles X's reservations, he commanded the 15,000-man French expedition to aid the Greeks in the Morea. There he signed a convention with Imbrahim Pasha which avoided much bloodshed. Maison then settled down to occupation duty. But when the armistice terms were not promptly fulfilled, his troops seized the fortresses of Navarino and the Morea, and he successfully held the Morea against Turkish-Egyptian counterattacks. For his services in Greece, Charles X presented him with his marshal's baton on 22 February 1829.

During the July Revolution Maison's appointment to command the Paris National Guard was one of the concessions Charles X accepted to try to halt the course of events. Louis-Philippe, however, gave Maison, baron de Schonen, and Odilon Barrot the task of persuading Charles X to leave Rambouillet and France as quickly as possible. This Maison did on 3 August, albeit by grossly exaggerating the number of Parisians marching on Rambouillet. On 2 November 1830 he became minister of foreign affairs but resigned on 16 November. He then served as ambassador to Austria from 1831 to 1833 and then as ambassador to Russia until 1835. On 30 April 1835 he became minister of war. As minister he was responsible for reorganizing the commissary service, the health service, and the administration of France's African colonies. He retired as war minister on 6 September 1836 but continued to sit among the liberals in the Chamber of Peers. Maison died in Paris on 13 February 1840.

*Archives parlementaires;* V. Beach, *Charles X* (Boulder, 1971); J. L. Bory, *La Révolution de juillet* (Paris, 1972); D. Pinkney, *The French Revolution of 1830* (Princeton, 1972); A. Robert et al., *Dictionnaire des parlementaires français* (Paris, 1889–91).

*James K. Kieswetter*

*Related entries:* BARROT, C.-H.-O.; BAZAR CONSPIRACY; DE SCHONEN; IMBRAHIM PASHA; NATIONAL GUARD; NEY; VICTOR; VILLELE.

**MAISTRE, JOSEPH DE** (1753–1821), Savoyard counter-Revolutionary, writer, magistrate, and diplomat. Born in Chambéry (then part of the Kingdom of Sardinia) on 1 April 1753, the scion of a senatorial family, Maistre inherited the title of count upon his father's death in 1789. Educated by the Jesuits, he studied law in Turin and associated with the Freemasons. Helping to form a Masonic lodge in Chambéry in 1778, Maistre came under the influence of the mystical, theosophic teachings of both Martinez-Pasqualis and the *philosophe inconnu*, Louis-Claude de Saint-Martin. These left a lasting imprint on his subsequent thought.The incursion of French Revolutionary armies forced him to flee to Lausanne, where he gathered with other *émigrés.* There he began two of his most important tracts, the *Etude sur la souveraineté* (completed, though not published, in 1794–96) and the very popular *Considérations sur la France* (1796–1797). Appointed regent for the island of Sardinia in 1799, the more prominent position of ambassador to the Court in St. Petersburg was bestowed on Maistre in 1802. He and his family remained in Russia until their 1817 return to France. During that residence he composed his other major works, none of which, however, found immediate publication. These included *Essai sur la principe génerateur des constitutions politiques et des autres institutions humaines, Du Pape, Examen de la philosophie de Bacon*, and, the book that has become best known, the dialogic *Soirées de Saint-Pétersbourg*. The last did not appear until several months after his death in February 1821. But the first two (though they made him, along with Louis de Bonald and Félicité de Lamennais, one of Francophone Europe's most notable traditionalist writers) alienated Czar Alexander and Louis XVIII because of their strident Catholic ultramontanism. Here the Maistrean outlook paralleled that of the Congrégation and the Chevaliers de la foi. His counter-Revolutionary thought bore many similiarities with other reactionary publicists. Typically he castigated Protestant individualism, attacked the sophistry of Enlightenment theorizing, excoriated the anarchic violence of the Revolution, deflated the claims to superiority of man-made democracy over God-given monarchy, and criticized the pride embodied in the secular, scientific world view and the facile idea of progress it engendered. Yet in strategy, style, and rhetoric, Maistre's conservatism displayed a certain uniqueness. The illuminism of Saint-Martin marked most of his polemics with an irrational, mysterious, and even grotesque cast. Divine ways are ultimately unfathomable and sinful, mankind's activities unpredictable and perpetually liable to err. War, sacrifice, and the suffering of the good and innocent are inevitable and expiatory. The judge, the soldier, and especially the executioner are the horrible but necessary symbols and keepers of order in the chaos humanity persists in creating for itself.

Following Montesquieu and Edmund Burke, Maistre advised societies, under the sacred and renewed guidance of Rome, to preserve their time-honored organizational customs and governmental forms to achieve the maximum of earthly happiness for all. In his portrait of the uprooted, disenchanted individual bred by modernity, a French tradition of psychological analysis stretching from Pascal to Barrès was sustained. It cannot be denied that this Augustinian gloom was adaptable to the inflammatory purposes of such later right-wing propagandists as Louis Veuillot and Charles Maurras. Seen by some scholars as a precursor of literary romanticism, Maistre idealized the staid culture of the *grand siècle* with a provocative imagery that anticipates Alphonse de Lamartine, Victor Hugo, Alfred de Vigny, or Charles Baudelaire. Like Louis de Bonald, he adopted certain notions from the *philosophes* only to show the inherent flaws or disastrous practical consequences lurking within a reason bereft of Christian supervision. It is a telling fact that Rousseau, as moralist of civic virtue and solidarity, stands closer than any other eighteenth-century theorist to Maistre's orientation. Unlike Bonald, Maistre did not try to construct a science of society that would be the pious obverse of the Enlightenment's scientific panaceas. Rather, he emphasized the illusoriness of systematic ratiocination about sociopolitical life. Lacking the flexibility and moral optimism of François-René de Chateaubriand, he shared with the author of the *Génie du christianisme* a preference for an aesthetic mode of counter-Revolutionary discourse. Maistre's utopian vision of the golden age of a restored past is at once more romantic and less unrealistically rigid than the universalistic *théorie du pouvoir* of his like-minded correspondent, Louis de Bonald.

F. Bayle, *Les Idées politiques de Joseph de Maistre* (Paris, 1945); E. Dermenghem, *Joseph de Maistre, mystique* (Paris, 1946); G. Durand, "Portrait philosophique de Joseph de Maistre," *Cahiers de l'histoire mondiale* 6 (1956); F. Holdsworth, *Joseph de Maistre et l'Angleterre* (Paris, 1935); R. Lebrun, "Joseph de Maistre and Rousseau," *Studies on Voltaire and the Eighteenth Century* 87 (1972), "Joseph de Maistre, Cassandra of Science," *French Historical Studies* 6 (1969), and *Throne and Altar: Political and Religious Thought of Joseph de Maistre* (Ottowa, 1965); R. Triomphe, *Joseph de Maistre: Etude sur la vie et sur le doctrine d'une materialiste mystique* (Geneva, 1968).

*W. Jay Reedy*

*Related entries:* BAUDELAIRE; BONALD; CHATEAUBRIAND; FREEMA-SONRY; HUGO; LAMARTINE; LAMENNAIS; LOUIS XVIII; ROUSSEAU; THEOCRATS; VEUILLOT; VIGNY.

**MANGIN, JEAN-CLAUDE** (1786–1835), magistrate and prefect of police of the Restoration. Born at Metz in 1786, Mangin studied law and was admitted to the bar at age sixteen. In 1815 the Bourbon government appointed him attorney general at Metz. In 1818 he became director of civil affairs in the Ministry of Justice. Then in 1821 he was sent as attorney general to the royal court at Poitiers. There he prosecuted General Jean-Baptiste Berton in a fashion that earned him widespread public disapproval, although it satisfied his superiors. His accusations that several deputies were involved in Berton's plot stirred a storm of controversy. Jacques Laffitte, Benjamin Constant, Auguste Kératry, and Maximilien-Sébastien Foy all brought a defamation charge against him. The court rejected the case. But Mangin's action against Constant led to the latter's being sentenced to a fine and prison term. Mangin's determined prosecution of liberals earned him a place as councillor in the Court of Cassation in 1827.

At the formation of the Polignac ministry in 1829, Mangin became prefect of police of Paris. This appointment angered the Paris populace and resulted in increased importance being given to the secret police. As prefect, Mangin promulgated harsh new measures—for example, subjecting even strolling sidewalk comedians and street singers to the censorship and enforcing Sunday closing laws. He also undid some of the reforms of his predecessor, Louis Debelleyme; however, he did introduce new measures dealing with such perennial problems as stray dogs, carriage traffic, and hours of construction work. Compared with police officials such as François Franchet d'Esperey or Guy Delavau, Mangin was a man of discretion and ability. He was an able administrator, noted for his fairness toward his subordinates. In the spring and summer of 1830, however, he failed to report continuing unrest among the people. Before Charles X signed the July Ordinances, Mangin assured him that Paris would not react. Mangin then tried to enforce vigorously the ordinances' provisions dealing with the press, as well as his own measures to meet the situation. But he remained initially oblivious to the storm developing around him, perhaps misled by the falsely optimistic reports that reached him. With indecision apparently prevailing everywhere and the situation rapidly worsening, municipal police functions were virtually abandoned to the army. In spite of a threatened attack on the prefecture and its personnel, Mangin did, with the aid of troops, hold the prefecture until the night of 29 July. Then, after sending a last futile warning to the king at Saint Cloud, Mangin and his officials evacuated the prefecture when they learned of plans to replace Charles with the duc d'Orléans. He then felt it wise to seek safety abroad. Thus he fled to Brussels and later continued on to Germany. He returned to France in 1834, planning to resume his legal career, but he died in Paris in 1835.

J. L. Bory, *La Révolution de juillet* (Paris, 1972); H. Buisson, *La Police son histoire* (Vichy, 1949); F. Hoefer, *Nouvelle biographie générale* (Paris, 1852–66); J. Peuchet, *Mémoires tirés des archives de la police de Paris* (Paris, 1838); D. Pinkney, *The French Revolution of 1830* (Princeton, 1972).

*James K. Kieswetter*

*Related entries:* BERTON; CHARLES X; CONSTANT; COURT OF CAS-SATION; DEBELLEYME; DELAVAU; FOY; JULY ORDINANCES; KER-ATRY; LAFFITTE; POLIGNAC; REVOLUTION OF 1830.

**MANIFESTO OF THE SECRET SOCIETIES** (1848), a profession of republican faith signed by republicans of all types. The main part of this manifesto, which was part of the campaign for the elections to the Constituent Assembly in 1848, is a declaration of rights like that of 1793. After briefly recalling the history and role of the secret societies since 1815, especially the role of Jean-Baptiste Berton, Joseph-Augustin Caron, Jean-François Bories, and others under the Restoration, the authors proclaimed that since the political question was resolved on 24 February 1848, with the triumph of the Republic, it was time to resolve the social question.

The purpose of society was to realize the goals set forth in the motto of the Republic: liberty, equality, fraternity. Liberty of association and expression, the right to work and to have a job, the right to property, but subordinate to the interests of society and regulated by law: these were some of the rights of man. The Republic should aid the poor ("There will be no more poor under the Republic"), agriculture, and industry. There should be a progressive income tax. Education should be compulsory and gratis. ("Nobody can be denied the benefit of a public education.") Finally, every citizen has the right to justice given by those elected by the people, the only sovereign, who delegate their power to the government. Every citizen is an elector and is eligible to be a government official and a soldier. All men are brothers, and all (as in the 1793 declaration) have the right of revolution, "the most sacred of duties," against any government that violates the principles of liberty, equality, and fraternity.

The goal of this manifesto was to gather together the "fervent apostles of Democracy" and to denounce the "defenders of privilege who are today disguised as Republicans." But it was also a text designed to conciliate various shades of republican opinion, and it was signed by Etienne Arago and Pierre Leroux, Albert and Marc Caussidiére, Ferdinand Flocon and Louis-Joseph-Antoine Cahaigne.Consequently, it said little about the social question, even if in some areas (the right of association, the right to education without cost, a progressive income tax) it laid out definite ideas.

*Manifeste des sociétés secrètes.*

Jean-Claude Caron, trans. E. Newman

*Related entries:* ALBERT; ARAGO FAMILY; BERTON; BORIES; CAUSSIDIERE; CLUBS, POLITICAL; CONSTITUTION OF 1848; FLOCON; LA ROCHELLE, FOUR SERGEANTS OF; LEROUX; REPUBLICANS.

**MANUEL, JACQUES-ANTOINE** (1775–1827), opposition deputy and orator. Born in Barcelonnette (Basses-Alpes), he was the son of a notary. After study at a Jansenist school in Nimes and a brief apprenticeship in commerce, he became a soldier in 1792. Returning home after the Treaty of Campo Formio, Manuel took up the law and moved to Aix, where he became a member of the bar. He established a reputation as a versatile and eloquent lawyer.

When Napoleon exiled Joseph Fouché to Aix, Manuel became Fouché's friend. During the Hundred Days, Manuel was elected to the Chamber of Representatives by the departmental college of Basses-Alpes. Fouché could not sit in the lower chamber because of his noble title, and Manuel was generally considered to be a spokesman for his views. He supported the demand for Napoleon's resignation after Waterloo and gave a pivotal speech on 23 June that ended with the Chamber's formal (but empty) proclamation that Napoleon II was emperor by virtue of his father's abdication. Manuel argued that this choice was the only one that would unify the country, that negotiation with the foreign powers had to be carried out in the name of a head of state, and that this was the only way to protect the interests of France and to proclaim national sovereignty. On 3 July Manuel expressed his opposition to the return of the Bourbons by stating that France would justly resent any sovereign imposed by foreign powers. The happiness of France, he believed, was incompatible with the return of the Bourbons.

After the Second Restoration, Manuel settled in Paris. In 1816 he sought admission to the bar, but it was denied because of his outspoken political views. He applied again in 1818 and was once again turned down. This rejection became politically significant in the elections following the electoral law of 1817. Manuel and two men who led the opposition to his admission, the moderate royalist Louis-Ferdinand Bonnet (the *bâtonnier* of the Paris bar) and the *procureur général* Nicolas-François Bellart, were all candidates for the Chamber of Deputies for Paris. In the elections of September 1817, Manuel was one of a group of liberal candidates led by Jacques Laffitte. On the first round of voting for eight deputies, Laffitte was the only candidate to receive a majority. Manuel with 2,777 out of

6,625 voting was fourth. On the second round, he received 3,084 out of 7,030 and came in sixth. Five deputies remained to be chosen in the runoff in round three, so Manuel's chances looked good; however, the government exerted enormous pressure in support of its candidates, and Manuel was defeated. He was eighth in a field of ten, with 3,342 votes out of 7,378.

In 1818 he renewed his candidacy in Paris, which had one empty seat to fill. Three prominent liberals vied for their group's support: Benjamin Constant, Manuel, and Pierre-Paul Gilbert de Voisins. Serious division within the party was avoided only on the evening before the voting was to take place in Paris when news arrived of Manuel's surprising election in the Vendée. Out of 658 voters, Manuel received 421 votes on the first round and was elected. The liberals in the Vendée had taken advantage of the location of the election in the city of Fontenay-le-Comte at the extreme southeast of the department instead of in the much smaller town of Bourbon-Vendée, the *chef-lieu* of the department. This location made it difficult for the royalist voters from the arrondissements of Sables and Bourbon-Vendée to make the trip, and it undermined the influence of the central administration. Manuel was also elected in 1818 in Finistère. He opted to represent the Vendée. His election and that of others such as General Lafayette brought on a ministerial crisis and the fall of the Richelieu government.

Manuel immediately became one of the most prominent liberal spokesmen in the Chamber. He was one of very few deputies willing to intervene in debate without a prepared speech. Manuel was a leader as well in the political organization of the liberal opposition. He is repeatedly mentioned as part of a committee in Paris to coordinate electoral activity. Manuel had been one of the founders in 1817 of the Société des amis de la liberté de la presse, which agitated for freedom of the press and helped journalists condemned for political crimes. After the press law of 1819 relaxed restrictions on the press, the society took on the character of a political club, discussing parliamentary debates and elections. After the elections of September 1819, which elected many liberals (including the notorious abbé Grégoire), the government began its attack on the group by arresting two men who had hosted meetings of the society. Meetings were held at Manuel's home to discuss the issue.

The liberal opposition in the Chamber was in a quandary over the problem of Grégoire's election. Manuel was part of a delegation asking him to resign rather than risk the far more dangerous precedent of having the Chamber refuse him admission. Grégoire declined to resign and was excluded in the stormy session of 6 December 1819. Manuel argued on that occasion that freedom of elections would be done away with if the Chamber took upon itself to judge the character of those elected, not merely whether the elections were validly conducted. Tyranny would result.

Manuel played a prominent role in the debates over new laws on individual freedom, freedom of the press, and elections that followed the assassination of the duc de Berry in February 1820. On 1 April 1820 he was one of the signers of a manifesto seeking subscriptions to aid victims of the new laws, and he protested when the government only prosecuted those signers who were not deputies. In a speech of 29 May Manuel accused the government of violating the Charter in establishing the Law of the Double Vote. The new law, he said on 9 June, left the friends of liberty with no hope. The implication was clear that extralegal measures were justified to fight the illegality of the government.

Manuel almost certainly knew of the aborted plot of 19 August 1820 and might have been one of the deputies involved in it. There is more substantial evidence that he was a member of the *comité directeur* of the Carbonari. In spite of these activities and the government's attempt to link Manuel to the conspiracies by bringing his name up in the trials of the conspirators, he was reelected in November 1822 by the Vendée, chosen this time in the single-member district of Fontenay-le-Comte on the first round of voting with 193 out of 297 votes. The officials in the Vendée looked for a means of annulling the election but abandoned the idea.

Manuel's fame as an orator stemmed from his skill in debate and from his habit of taunting the royalists by statements of support for the Revolution and veiled attacks on the king. The members on the Right of the Chamber listened to his every word, ready to protest when he seemed to be going too far. As his speeches were interrupted by cries of protest, Manuel would wait coolly and impassively until the commotion was over and then continue his remarks. In January 1822, in a speech against a new and more restrictive press law, Manuel remarked that the people of France in 1814 had looked upon the appearance of the Bourbons with a certain "repugnance." This led to enormous recriminations against the speaker, and the term *répugnance* was hurled at him repeatedly from then on. To the Right, it appeared obvious that Manuel was preaching insurrection from the podium of the Chamber.

A chance to get even with him came on 26 February 1823 during a debate over a request for money to fund the French expedition against Spain. Manuel argued that contrary to what Chateaubriand had said the day before, such an involvement would not help King Ferdinand. He cited the case of the Stuart kings of England whose cause was hurt by French support and then said, "Do I need to add that the dangers of the French royal family became far more grave when foreigners invaded our land, and that France, Revolutionary France, feeling the need to defend herself by new forces and a new energy . . . " The rest of his sentence was drowned out by a storm of protests from deputies who accused him of justifying regicide. Prevented from resuming his speech, Manuel wrote to the president of the Chamber during the adjournment that followed that his sentence would have continued: "set in motion the masses, stimulated popular passions, and thus brought on terrible excesses and a deplorable catastrophe in the midst of a noble resistance." The session resumed after an hour's recess, but the deputies of the Right refused to listen to Manuel's explanations and demanded his expulsion. The deputy François de La Bourdonnaye made a formal proposal for Manuel's exclusion the following day. Manuel defended himself by saying that it made no sense to accuse him of preaching regicide when the whole point of his speech was to prevent the circumstances that he saw leading to it.

The vote on his expulsion was to be taken on 3 March 1823. Jean Demarçay and other deputies on the Left declared that they wholeheartedly endorsed Manuel's sentiments and that if he was to be excluded, they should be as well. The Chamber voted to exclude him and adjourned. The next day, Manuel (accompanied by the deputies of the Left, all dressed in their official uniforms) marched into the Chamber and refused to leave. A detachment of the National Guard was brought in to remove him, but they refused to carry out the order. Gendarmes then appeared to seize Manuel and carry him out of the Chamber followed by the deputies of the Left, sixty-two of whom signed a protest against this action and boycotted the rest of the session.

The defeats suffered by the conspirators in 1822 had resulted in splits within the ranks of the Carbonari. Manuel and his followers believed the time had come to be cautious, but they were also more willing to take advantage of the force and enthusiasm of Bonapartists and former imperial officers to overthrow the government than were the liberal purists grouped around Lafayette. There was, then, no united Carbonarist movement to attempt to subvert the French army as it crossed into Spain. The French exiles and conspirators failed miserably to stir the army to make a *demi-tour* as Pierre-Jean de Béranger's song suggested (''Nouvel ordre du jour'').

The liberals suffered a resounding defeat in the general election of 1824, and Manuel was one of those not reelected. His close friend the poet Béranger believed that Manuel lost because some of his former colleagues (notably Constant) wanted to get rid of the intransigent deputy and had not done enough to support him. But Manuel was accused by others of not doing enough for himself, assuming that his popularity after his expulsion would ensure success. Manuel believed that though the voters of Paris were unwilling to vote for him, they indicated their support for his stand by choosing his close associate Jacques-Charles Dupont de l'Eure as their deputy.

In the last years of his life, Manuel spent considerable time at Jacques Laffitte's estate at Maison, often in the company of Béranger. He was an avid hunter. Plagued by an illness of the bladder for some time, he died at Maisons-Laffitte on 20 August 1827. Manuel's funeral became the occasion for a large liberal demonstration. Béranger estimated 150,000 accompanied the body to the Père Lachaise cemetery where eulogies were pronounced by Lafayette, Béranger, Laffitte, and Augustine-Jean de Schönen. Béranger launched a subscription to erect a monument to Manuel by writing ''Le Tombeau de Manuel,'' but the subscription was not very successful. In 1857, Béranger was buried in Manuel's tomb.

E. Bonnal de Ganges, *Manuel et son temps, étude sur l'opposition parlementaire sous la Restauration* (Paris, 1877); J. Touchard, *La Gloire de Béranger*, 2 vols. (Paris, 1968).

*Sylvia Neely*

*Related entries:* BERANGER; CARBONARI; CONSTANT; DE SCHONEN; DOUBLE VOTE, LAW OF THE; DUPONT DE L'EURE; FOUCHE; GRE-

GOIRE; LA BOURDONNAYE; LAFAYETTE, M.-J.-P.-Y.-R.-G; LAFFITTE; PRESS LAWS; RICHELIEU; SOCIETY OF FRIENDS OF THE FREEDOM OF THE PRESS; SPAIN, 1823 FRENCH INVASION OF.

**MARCHANGY, LOUIS-ANTOINE-FRANCOIS DE** (1782–1826), lawyer and writer, government prosecutor at the trial of the four sergeants of La Rochelle. Son of a minor court official in Nièvre, Marchangy rose to fame as both a literary figure and a prominent prosecutor for the Restoration government. He worked in the court systems first for Napoleon and later for the Bourbon regime. He was named *avocat général* of the Paris appeals court in 1822.

Marchangy's most famous case was his prosecution of the four sergeants of La Rochelle, who were executed in 1822 for their part in a Carbonari plot to overthrow the government. His summary for the prosecution lasted five hours and was published as a 196-page book. In numerous other cases, he supported the repressive conservative government against the liberal opposition.

Marchangy's most famous literary work was his eight-volume *La Gaule poétique* (1813–17) a "gothic rhapsody." His writing, like his courtroom style, was verbose and flowery. Although his family was not of aristocratic origin, Marchangy always affected a "de" before his name. He was twice elected to the Chamber of Deputies (1823 and 1824) but was not allowed to sit because the amount of taxes he paid (a rough indicator of wealth) was insufficient to qualify him, as was quickly pointed out by liberal legislators.

Marchangy died in February 1826 at the age of forty-four after contracting a cold in the Basilica St. Denis during a long religious ceremony.

F. Hamm,"*Etude sur Louis-Antoine-François de Marchangy*" (thesis, University of Strasbourg, 1962); *La Grande encyclopédie inventaire raisonné* (Paris, 1886–1902); P. Larousse, *Grand dictionnaire universel du XIXe siècle* (Paris, 1873); L.-A.-F. Marchangy, *Plaidoyer de M. de Marchangy, avocat général de la Cour royale de Paris; prononcé le 29 août, 1822, de la Cour d'assises de la Seine, dans la conspiration de La Rochelle* (Paris, 1822).

*Don Smith*
*Related entries:* CARBONARI; CHAMBER OF DEPUTIES; LA ROCHELLE, FOUR SERGEANTS OF.

**MARIE, ALEXANDRE-THOMAS** (1795–1870), lawyer and politician, defender of republicans and a deputy under the July Monarchy, member of the Provisional Government, and deputy under the Second Republic. Born in Auxerre, Alexandre Marie graduated from the Paris Law School in 1819. Already an opponent of the Bourbon Restoration, he was not hired as a professor at his old school. A convinced but moderate republican (he would later oppose the socialist ideas of Louis Blanc), he was especially active defending republicans accused of plotting against the July Monarchy, including the communist Etienne Cabet and the would-be assassin Pépin, who was involved in the Fieschi plot. In 1837 he joined other republicans like Etienne Garnier-Pagès and Alexandre-Auguste Ledru-Rollin on an electoral committee. In 1842 and again in 1846, he was elected to the Chamber of Deputies from Paris. On 9 July 1847, he spoke at the famous antigovernment banquet of Château-Rouge.

On 24 February 1848, Marie was the first to speak out against a regency for King Louis-Philippe, who had just abdicated. He became minister of public works for the new republican Provisional Government, and he undertook the organization of the National Workshops, designed to reduce unemployment and to undercut the socialist projects of Louis Blanc. He was elected to the Constituent Assembly where, as a supporter of the moderate policies of the Provisional Government, he was elected to the Executive Commission.

It was he who on 22 June 1848 received Pujol and the delegation of workers from the National Workshops who were protesting their closing. Marie was firm: "If the workers won't leave, we will eject them by force." His intransigence provoked the insurrectionary violence of the June Days. He resigned his ministry, which the Assembly gave to General Eugène Cavaignac. He justified the savage repression of the June Days: "It was not a war of the Republic against the Republic; it was barbarism that dared to raise its head against civilization."

In the Constituent Assembly, he served briefly as president and then as minister of justice, and it was he who presented the law restraining the freedom of the press on 11 August 1848. He supported the prosecution of Louis Blanc and Marc Caussidière. He opposed the abolition of the death penalty, the graduated income tax, and the election of the president of the Republic by the Assembly. He opposed the politics of Louis-Napoleon Bonaparte. He was not elected to the Legislative Assembly, and so he returned to the practice of law until 1863, when he was elected a deputy from Marseilles. He was not reelected in 1869, and he died the next year.

A. Chérest, *La Vie et les oeuvres de A. T. Marie, avocat* . . . (Paris, 1873); O. Pinard, *Le Barreau au XIXe siècle*, 2 vols. (Paris, 1864–65); G. Weill, *Histoire du parti républicain en France de 1814 à 1870* (Paris, 1900).

*Jean-Claude Caron, trans. E. Newman*

*Related entries:* BANQUET CAMPAIGN; BLANC; CABET; CAUSSIDIERE; CAVAIGNAC, L.-E.; FIESCHI PLOT; GARNIER-PAGES; LEDRU-ROLLIN; NATIONAL WORKSHOPS; PRESS LAWS; REPUBLICANS.

**MARIE-AMELIE DE BOURBON** (1782–1866), wife of Louis-Philippe and queen of the French. Marie-Amélie was the daughter of Ferdinand IV, king of the Two Sicilies, and Marie-Caroline, archduchess of Austria. In 1809 she married Louis-Philippe, the future king of France. She bore five sons and three daughters. She was devoted to her family and to the education of her children and was not involved in politics. In 1848 she accompanied Louis-Philippe when he left France and then lived in England at Claremont House as the comtesse de Neuilly. After the death of Louis-Philippe in 1850, Marie-Amélie attempted to bring about a reconciliation between the Orléans family and the Bourbons.

A. Trognon, *Vie de Marie-Amélie, reine des français* (Paris, 1871).

*Gay L. Gullickson*

*Related entries:* BORDEAUX; CHARTRES; JOINVILLE; LOUIS-PHILIPPE; NEMOURS; PARIS, COUNT OF; REVOLUTION OF 1848.

## MARMONT, AUGUSTE-FREDERIC-LOUIS-VIESSE DE (1774–1852), duc de Raguse, Napoleonic general, marshal of France.

Auguste Marmont was born in Chatillon-sur-Seine (Côte d'Or) on 20 July 1774, the only son of a family of substantial Burgundian landed proprietors. He early determined to follow a military career and in 1792 entered the Royal Artillery School at Chalons-sur-Marne. A few months later in the turmoil following the overthrow of the monarchy, he was hastily commissioned a sublieutenant and posted to a regiment of foot artillery.

He participated in the siege of Toulon in 1793 and there attracted the attention of Napoleon Bonaparte, who commanded the artillery in the besieging force. He accompanied Napoleon to Italy in 1796 as an aide-de-camp and impressed the general as a particularly promising young officer. Thereafter his rise was rapid. He became a colonel in 1796 at the age of twenty-two and a brigadier general in 1798, fought with distinction in the Egyptian expedition, took part in the coup d'état of 1799, and was appointed to the Council of State. In 1798 he married Hortense Perrégaux, daughter of the wealthy and influential Parisian banker J.-F. Perrégaux. During the Empire he participated in most of the important campaigns and was rewarded by elevation to the nobility in 1808 as duc de Raguse and in 1809 by a marshal's baton.

In April 1814, in command of the VI Corps, Marmont was charged with covering Fontainebleau, where Napoleon was preparing his final military effort to save the Empire. Convinced by representatives of the Bourbons that France would be best served by an early peace, Marmont withdrew his troops to the opposite side of Paris, thus ensuring the end of the Empire.

The Bourbon government named him to the Chamber of Peers and, after the Hundred Days, when he accompanied Louis XVIII into exile, appointed him a major general of the Royal Guard. He never attained, however, the important position under the Bourbons that he thought he merited. He turned to business enterprise and speculation but succeeded only in accumulating a large debt.

He hoped for the command of the Algerian expedition in 1830 and was embittered against the Polignac ministry and the royal family when the appointment went to Marshal Louis de Bourmont. In July 1830 Polignac called on him, as major general of the Royal Guard, to maintain order in Paris after the publication of the July Ordinances. He was unable to pacify the capital or even, in the end, to hold it. After the loss of Paris, he persuaded Charles X to abdicate in favor of his grandson, the duc de Bordeaux, and urged him to withdraw into the royalist west and there carry on the resistance to revolutionary Paris in the expectation of saving the crown for the family. Charles chose not to follow this advice, and Marmont accompanied him into exile in England.

Marmont took the oath of allegiance to Louis-Philippe, perhaps hoping to return to France, but the new government offered him no encouragement, and he spent his remaining years in exile. He died in Venice on 3 March 1852.

R. Christopher, *Le Maréchal Marmont, duc de Raguse* (Paris, c. 1968); A. de Marmont,

*Mémoires du Maréchal Marmont, duc de Raguse de 1792 à 1841*, 3d ed. (Paris, 1857); P. Saint Marc, *Le Maréchal Marmont, duc de Raguse, 1774–1852* (Paris, c. 1957).

*David H. Pinkney*

*Related entries:* ALGIERS, EXPEDITION TO; BORDEAUX; BOURMONT; COUNCIL OF STATE; HUNDRED DAYS; JULY ORDINANCES; LOUIS-PHILIPPE; POLIGNAC; REVOLUTION OF 1830; ROYAL GUARD.

**MARRAST, MARIE-FRANCOIS-PASCAL-ARMAND** (1801–1852), Republican journalist and activist of the Restoration, July Monarchy, and the Revolution of 1848. Born at Saint-Gaudens on 5 June 1801, little is known about Armand Marrast's early life. After successfully completing a university course in Paris during the last years of the Restoration, he was excluded from teaching for a time because of his involvement in demonstrations at the funeral of the extreme left-wing politician Jacques-Antoine Manuel in 1827. Toward the end of the Restoration, he took up journalism, and by May 1831 he had become chief editor of the *Tribune des départemens*. He not only advocated militant republican opposition to the July Monarchy in the columns of the *Tribune* but was actively involved in seditious organizations, first the Amis du peuple and later the Société des droits de l'homme et du citoyen, a partly secret organization that sought to escape the government ban on political societies of more than twenty members by forming a network of small groups. In 1834, risings in Lyons and Paris provided the government with an excuse for prosecuting 164 known republicans, among them Armand Marrast, on charges of high treason. The trial dragged on for many months before the Chamber of Peers. This not only brought unpopularity to the government but discredited the accused, who publicly quarreled with each other. When conviction seemed certain, 28 of the accused, including Marrast and another prominent republican, Godefroy Cavaignac, managed to escape and flee to England. The rest were condemned to transportation or to lengthy terms of imprisonment. The defense of the accused had increased the number of judicial penalties heaped upon the *Tribune*; its disappearance in May 1835, followed by the introduction of the severe September Laws, virtually outlawed republican opposition from monarchical France.

In England, where he married an illegitimate granddaughter of George IV, Marrast became a great admirer of the peaceful radicalism of the Chartists. From them he came to believe that if the entire male population was admitted to the franchise, artificial divisions of class would either disappear or cease to matter, for everyone would help his neighbors in a spirit of brotherly love. His letters from England helped from 1837 on to popularize the term *radical* as a description of those deputies in the Chamber who stood slightly to the right of the republicans— a confusion in terminology increased by the fact that the republicans were prevented by the September Laws from calling themselves republican and usually called themselves democrats.

Returning from exile, probably as a result of the amnesty of 1839, Marrast resumed his journalistic career. In 1840 he acquired the chief editorship of the *National*, which had been somewhat in the doldrums since the death of Armand Carrel. Throughout the ministry of François Guizot the *National* advocated policies that would have been recognizable to the British Chartists: extension of the franchise with a view to wiping out corruption, which was vigorously attacked; criticism of the new industrial feudalism, which had come to power in 1830, but at the same time a repudiation of socialist doctrines as likely to lead to class conflict. The *National* had no wish to destroy capitalism, which it regarded as inevitable, but sought instead the improvement of working-class conditions through legislation dealing with specific abuses. Actual proposals were few and often vague, but they included the right of labor to organize, the abolition of consumer taxes in favor of a progressive income tax, and provision of free, compulsory primary education. Radicalism, or right-wing republicanism, was thus dissociated from civil war, class hatred, and the Terror. Godefroy Cavaignac, who returned from exile in 1840, broke with his former colleague Marrast for having become too moderate, denounced his alliance with Odilon Barrot and the dynastic Left, and joined Alexandre-Auguste Ledru-Rollin on the slightly more extreme *Réforme*.

In the early weeks of 1848 Marrast supported the campaign for holding a reform banquet, preceded by a procession, in Paris. On behalf of the organizing committee, he couched a manifesto outlining the arrangements for the procession and published it in the *National* on 21 February 1848. The manifesto revealed Marrast's willingness to harness mass discontent behind the moderate reform movement and followed up his past pleas for the democratization of the National Guard by assuming his own right to call out the legions. The government replied by banning the demonstration, and at a meeting at the house of Odilon Barrot the majority of deputies involved in the organization decided there was no point in going on with the arrangements. Marrast is said to have urged the left-wing deputies to resign from the Chamber in protest (an action which could hardly have furthered the campaign), and he seems not to have turned up when, in spite of the government ban, the procession formed on 23 February. The dispersal of the procession by troops caused popular anger, and on the next day barricades were built all over Paris. In the afternoon the king dismissed Guizot and tried to form a ministry under Louis-Mathieu de Molé. In the evening a crowd gathered outside the offices of the *National* seeking guidance. Marrast in a fiery speech urged them to remain armed until they had secured complete parliamentary reform under a Thiers-Barrot ministry. As the crowd proceeded down the boulevard des Capucines, they were stopped by troops, and an accidental skirmish led to the death of fifty-two demonstrators.

During the night of 23–24 February the king agreed to form a Thiers-Barrot ministry, but Marrast followed the mood of the crowd, which had now become more aggressive, and at a meeting at the headquarters of the *National* he declared that only the abdication of the king would suffice. When the king did indeed abdicate, a delegation from the *National* to the Chamber of Deputies demanded the proclamation of a republic. However, Marrast, as spokesman for the delegation, supported Alphonse de Lamartine in the decision not to proclaim a republic immediately but to set up a Provisional Government. Crowds from the Chamber of Deputies, the *National*, and the *Réforme* converged on the Hôtel de ville, and in the ensuing melée, a Provisional Government of eleven men, including Marrast and his rival editor from the *Réforme*, Ferdinand Flocon, was formed. Lamartine was soon prevailed upon by the crowd to proclaim the Second Republic.

In contemporary prints of the Provisional Government, Marrast appears as a man of moderate height with a round face, short curly hair, a wide moustache, and "chin-strap" beard. He soon attached himself to the right-wing majority while Flocon, Ledru-Rollin, Louis Blanc, and the worker Albert formed the left wing. Of the latter group, only Louis Blanc had far-reaching socialist ideas. Just as all supported the declaration of universal male suffrage, all supported the formation of the National Workshops as an expedient.

In April Marrast was elected to the National Constituent Assembly by four departments. He was not a member of the Executive Commission, which replaced the Provisional Government, but as mayor of Paris, a post to which he was appointed on 9 March, he wielded considerable patronage and power. He was suspected, rightly, of trying to diminish popular pressure (for instance, he undermined the power of the political clubs by denying them the use of public buildings for their meetings), but the accusation that used to be leveled at him by historians—that he engineered the attack by left-wing agitators on the National Assembly on 15 May in order to destroy them—seems now to have been exploded.

The rising of the workers in June, followed by severe repression, did not alter Marrast's views as to the desirability of democracy leading to social reform. Chosen as president of the Assembly on 17 July, he curbed the more conservative elements that would have denied Proudhon a hearing. Presenting the final draft of the Constitution to the Assembly, he argued that although the promise of a right to work had been omitted, fraternity required the state to help those who suffered hardship at times of economic crisis.

On 12 November 1848 Marrast presided at the ceremony in the place de la Concorde at which the Constitution was promulgated. The rain and sleet seemed to symbolize the dampened hopes of those who had greeted the formation of the Republic with enthusiasm in February. In December Marrast also presided at the meeting of the Assembly at which Louis-Napoleon Bonaparte swore an oath of loyalty as newly elected president of the Republic. On 29 January 1849 the Assembly voted its own dissolution, and this virtually ended Marrast's political career, for like many other moderate republicans, he was not elected to the more conservative Legislative Assembly chosen in May 1849. He retired to private life and lived in modest circumstances until his death in 1852.

P. H. Amann, *Revolution and Mass Democracy: The Paris Club Movement in 1848* (Princeton, 1975); A. Crémieux, *La Révolution de février* (Paris, 1912); F. A. de Luna,

*The French Republic under Cavaignac, 1848* (Princeton, 1969); G. W. Fasel, "The French Moderate Republicans, 1837–1848" (Ph. D diss., Stanford University, 1965); H. Guillemin, *La Tragédie de quarante-huit* (Geneva, 1948); I. Tchernoff, *Le Parti républicain sous la monarchie de juillet*, 2d ed. (Paris, 1905); G. Weill, *Histoire du parti républicain en France, 1814–1870*, 2d ed. (Paris, 1928).

*Irene Collins*

*Related entries:* ALBERT; BANQUET CAMPAIGN; BARROT, C.-H.-O; BLANC; CARREL; CAVAIGNAC, G.-E.-L.; DEMONSTRATIONS OF 1848– 1849; FLOCON; GUIZOT; LAMARTINE; LEDRU-ROLLIN; MANUEL; MOLE; *LE NATIONAL*; NATIONAL WORKSHOPS; PRESS LAWS; PROUD-HON; PROVISIONAL GOVERNMENT; *LA REFORME;* REPUBLICANS; REVOLUTION OF 1848; SOCIETY OF THE RIGHTS OF MAN; THIERS; *LA TRIBUNE DES DEPARTEMENS.*


**MARTAINVILLE, ALPHONSE-LOUIS-DIEUDONNE** (1776–1830), reactionary publicist and journalist; editor of *Drapeau blanc*, an ultraroyalist newspaper. Martainville was born in Cadiz, Spain, to French parents. Returning to France, he vigorously opposed the Revolution and survived only because of his contacts with a judge of the Revolutionary Tribunal. He tried working as an actor and collaborated with Charles-Guillaume Etienne on a history of the Théâtre-français, ultimately published in 1802. After the fall of Maximilien Robespierre, he became one of the most notorious of the *muscadins*, the reactionary young men who went about doused with musk and seeking physical vengeance against the Jacobins. In 1794 he published several tracts against the Jacobins, including a short-lived effort, *Journal des rieurs*. During Napoleon's reign, he was at least superficially an imperialist. Between 1802 and 1814 Martainville wrote numerous comedies and melodramas.

At the Bourbon Restoration, Martainville became a royalist. He continued to write, turning his pen from vaudeville and ridicule to staunch defense of reactionary virtues and beliefs. From 1818 to 1820 he helped edit the *Conservateur*. In January 1819 he assisted in founding the *Drapeau blanc*, which became the leading ultraroyalist newspaper, although from 16 June 1819 until 1 February 1827 the paper was extensively controlled by its manager, Eugène Destains. In the *Drapeau blanc* Martainville represented the views of the extreme ultras who opposed even the more moderate ultras led by Joseph de Villèle. Martainville used the *Drapeau* to attack practices such as the sale of national lands, referring to their buyers as revolutionaries, which landed him in court. He specifically blamed Elie Decazes for the murder of the duc de Berry in February 1820 and helped bring about the fall of the Decazes ministry. Martainville's paper became so virulent that when a new censorship measure was adopted in 1820, the *Drapeau blanc* was given special attention by the censor. Martainville replied with a pamphlet, *La Bombe royaliste*, attacking the measure and the more moderate royalists. In 1827 the government passed a new press measure, the Law of Justice and Love, which Martainville refused to defend. Consequently his paper was closed on 1 February 1827. His extremism had resulted in his paper's achieving little popularity, with a circulation of only a few thousand. From 16 May to 15 July 1829 he edited the *Démocrite*. When the liberal opposition to Charles X and his policies increased, Martainville came to the defense of the king by reviving the *Drapeau blanc* on 16 July 1829. He published it until 26 July 1830. When Martainville died in Paris on 31 July 1830, his paper perished with him.

I. Collins, *The Government and the Newspaper Press in France, 1814–1881* (Oxford, 1959); E. Hatin, *Bibliographie historique et critique de la presse périodique francaise* (Paris, n.d.) and *Histoire du journal en France, 1631–1853* (Paris, 1853); J. Popkin, *The Right-Wing Press in France, 1792–1800* (Chapel Hill, 1980); R. Rémond, *The Right Wing in France from 1815 to de Gaulle* (Philadelphia, 1969).

*James K. Kieswetter*

*Related entries:* BERRY, C.-F.; CENSORSHIP; *LE CONSERVATEUR;* DE-CAZES; *LE DRAPEAU BLANC*; ULTRAROYALISTS; VILLELE.

**MARTIGNAC, JEAN-BAPTISTE, SILVERE GAYE, VICOMTE DE** (1776–1831), political leader of the Restoration. Before 1815 he had made a name for himself in his native Bordeaux through his talent as a lawyer and by some poetry he had written. In 1821 he entered the Chamber of Deputies representing Marmande, and there he faithfully served the policies of the Villèle government, which brought him into the Council of State. In 1823 he accompanied the duc d'Angoulême into Spain as a civil commissioner of the government. In recompense for these services, he was ennobled and named minister of state and shortly afterward director of the administration of the domaines. When Joseph de Villèle lost the elections of 1827 and had to resign, he advised Charles X to bring Martignac into the new government. In this new ministry of January 1828, Martignac, minister of the interior, seemed to be the head of the government, though he was not president of the Council, because he was the government's chief spokesman before both chambers, a job he did well. He tried to construct a cautiously liberal policy that could rally centrist politicians to the crown. But the concessions that he thought he could make to the Left alienated him from Charles X. The king, after hiding his true intentions for a long time, abruptly dismissed him at the beginning of August 1829. Martignac's last political act was also his most honorable one: during the trial of the former ministers of Charles X in December 1830, he came before the court despite his own grave illness to defend Jules de Polignac, who had replaced him one year earlier.

E. Daudet, *Le ministère de M. de Martignac* (Paris, 1875).

*Guillaume de Bertier de Sauvigny, trans. E. Newman*

*Related entries:* ANGOULEME, L.-A.; CHAMBER OF DEPUTIES; CHARLES X; COUNCIL OF STATE; POLIGNAC; SPAIN, 1823 FRENCH INVASION OF; VILLELE.

**MARTIN, ALEXANDRE.** See ALBERT.

**MARX, KARL** (1818–1883), sometime resident of Paris; historian of the French Revolution of 1848 and the Paris Comune of 1871; philosopher, economist, journalist, labor organizer, and revolutionary. In developing his characteristic system uniting theory and practice, Marx was profoundly influenced by the history of the French Revolution and by early nineteenth-century French socialism, as well as by German philosophy and English classical economics. Marx derived his notion of class struggle largely from his studies of the French Revolution and his idea of the revolutionary proletariat largely from French socialist circles when he first visited Paris in 1843–44. He read extensively in primary materials on the French Revolution and even planned to write a history of the National Convention. In Paris Marx also produced his first major work, which remained unpublished until 1932 and is now known as the *Economic and Philosophic Manuscripts of 1844* or *The Paris Manuscripts*. It was here that Marx developed his famous concept of alienation.

Evicted from France in 1845 by the Guizot government, Marx moved to Brussels, where in 1847 he wrote a criticism of Proudhon, *The Poverty of Philosophy*, which contained the first published elaboration of his materialist conception of history. Marx returned briefly to Paris in 1848, shortly after the February Revolution, on the invitation of a radical member of the new republican government, Ferdinand Flocon. In the French capital Marx organized the Paris Circle of the Communist League, as well as the German Workers' Club, but contrary to what some writers have assumed, he was not a member of the French Society of the Rights of Man. After a month in Paris, Marx went to Cologne, where he edited the *Neue Rheinische Zeitung*. Following the revival of counter-revolutionary forces in Germany, Marx returned to Paris in 1849, but within three months the government of Louis-Napoleon Bonaparte forced him to emigrate once more, this time to London. There Marx produced his now-celebrated studies of the Second French Republic.

*The Class Struggles in France* (1850) was Marx's first extended application of his general materialist theory to a specific historical situation, the events from 1848 to 1850. Here Marx argued that only a fraction of the bourgeoisie—the so-called finance aristocracy—had ruled during the July Monarchy, and the February Revolution made possible the rule of the entire bourgeoisie. But the Paris proletarians, who had fought alongside the bourgeois and petty-bourgeois in February, eventually felt compelled to rise against the bourgeois democratic Republic. The insurrection of the June Days was thus "the first great battle . . . between the two classes that split modern society." Although defeated, the proletariat had gained class consciousness, had "ripened into a real revolutionary party." The election of Louis-Napoleon Bonaparte to the presidency in December 1848 signified the intervention of still another class, the peasantry. In *The Class Struggles*, Marx also for the first time analyzed still another class, the lumpenproletariat, and he first employed the phrase *dictatorship of the proletariat* as a future aspiration. In *The Eighteenth Brumaire of Louis Bonaparte*, written a few months after the coup d'état of 2 December 1851, Marx again analyzed recent French history in similar terms, now with a view to demonstrating "how the class struggle in France created circumstances and relationships that made it possible for a grotesque mediocrity to play a hero's part." Here also Marx developed his theory of the parasite or independent state. Friedrich Engels later cited *The Eighteenth Brumaire* as the best example of the materialist conception of history, and it is often regarded as Marx's most brilliant historical work.

During the 1850s while pursuing his economic studies, Marx wrote extensively on the Second Empire of Napoleon III in many articles published chiefly in the *New York Daily Tribune*. There are few comments on France in the manuscripts later published as the *Grundrisse* and the several volumes of *Capital*. French workers formed an important contingent in the International Working Men's Association formed in 1864 largely under the inspiration of Marx, and France once more was the subject of the three addresses of the International, written by Marx on the Franco-Prussian War and the Paris Commune of 1871, and republished as *The Civil War in France*. It was in exasperation with some of his French followers of the late 1870s that Marx uttered his famous remark, "I am not a Marxist." Marx's last writing on France was the 1880 preamble to the "minimum program" of the *Parti ouvrier* drawn up by Jules Guesde.

P. Amann, "Karl Marx,'Quarante-huitard' français?" *International Review of Social History* 6 (1961); L. Krieger, "Marx and Engels as Historians," *Journal of the History of Ideas* 14 (1953); J. M. Maguire, *Marx's Theory of Politics* (Cambridge, 1978); K. Marx, *The Class Struggles in France* (New York, 1964) and *The Eighteenth Brumaire of Louis Bonaparte* (New York, 1963); D. McLellan, *Karl Marx: His Life and Thought* (London, 1973); R. Price, *The French Second Republic* (London, 1972); M. Rader, *Marx's Interpretation of History* (New York, 1979).

*Frederick A. de Luna*

*Related entries:* COUP D'ETAT OF 2 DECEMBER 1851; FLOCON; GUIZOT; JUNE DAYS; PROUDHON; PROVISIONAL GOVERNMENT; REVOLUTION OF 1848; SOCIETY OF THE RIGHTS OF MAN.


**MAUBREUIL, JACQUES-MARIE-ARMAND GUERRY** (1783–1868), marquis d'Orvault, Vendéan army officer, equerry to Jerome Bonaparte, thief, adventurer, and perhaps would-be assassin of Napoleon. Jacques-Marie-Armand-Guerry was born on 26 May 1783 near Nantes in Brittany. He later took the title marquis d'Orvault from a maternal ancestor. When most of his family emigrated, he remained behind with his grandmother and joined the local *chouans* at a young age. Taking up the ways of the *jeunesse dorée* during the Directory, he adopted for himself the name de Maubreuil from the family chateau. Apparently in 1802 he made the acquaintance of Jerome Bonaparte. After Jerome became king of Westphalia and married Catherine, daughter of the king of Württemberg, he appointed Maubreuil equerry to the queen and captain of the hunt. Maubreuil, however, had an affair with Jerome's mistress, Blanche Carrera, which led to his expulsion from the court. He then joined a Westphalian army unit in Spain, rising to the rank of captain. Returning to France, he quit the army. In 1811 he attempted to join the French army, only to find he was persona non grata. Maubreuil then became involved in a scheme to sell provisions to the French army, but instead he lost his own fortune as a result of Napoleon's intervention in 1813 and was reduced to living by various expedients.

Although Maubreuil still professed to be a devoted Bonapartist, when the Allies invaded France in 1814 he volunteered to help retrieve some of the crown jewels from the fleeing Bonaparte family. But then occurred a mysterious affair that has never been completely explained. On 21 April 1814 at Fossard, Maubreuil and a troop of men robbed Jerome Bonaparte's wife, Catherine, taking her money and jewels as she returned to Germany. She recognized Maubreuil and complained to the Allied sovereigns in Paris. On 25 April he was arrested. He then claimed that his true mission had been to assassinate Napoleon and that it had been approved by Charles-Maurice de Talleyrand, the comte d'Artois, Alexander I, and Frederick William III. However, he claimed he had acted to thwart their criminal designs and appease them with the jewels, which in fact he had kept for himself and had not turned over to the government. Maubreuil did indeed possess letters for assistance for a secret mission issued by the new Bourbon postmaster, the war minister, the minister of police, the Russian commandant of Paris and a Prussian general. Some French officials, such as the prefect of police Etienne-Denis Pasquier, believed that in fact Maubreuil had been sent on an assassination mission. The government, however, decided to imprison Maubreuil without trial to avoid the outrage his claims would cause. He was released on 19 March 1815 as the Bourbons fled Paris. A court investigation during the Hundred Days also concluded there had been an assassination plot. Maubreuil was arrested again in 1816 but escaped with the aid of some known royalists and was finally retaken in June. The government was unable to avoid trying him, but it shuffled the case from one court to another until finally in December 1817 the royal court of Douai took jurisdiction. But Maubreuil escaped again on 1 January 1818, and his trial was held without him. The court sentenced him to five years in prison for jewel theft and left the conspiracy unprobed, as the government demanded.

Maubreuil did not return to France until 1823, when his sentence had lapsed. But he continued to attack Talleyrand and others he accused of betraying him, writing letters and pamphlets to justify himself. On 21 January 1827 he assaulted Talleyrand at the Abbey of Saint Denis and knocked him to the ground. Arrested, Maubreuil used his trial to try to attack his betrayers but largely failed in his effort. He was sentenced to five years' imprisonment and ten years' surveillance, the sentence reduced on appeal to two years' imprisonment. Released from jail in 1829, Maubreuil received a secret pension from the government during the July Monarchy. In the meantime, he had unsuccessfully sued Talleyrand and others, the procedure dragging on until 1833. Thereafter he remained comparatively inactive, receiving a pension from Napoleon III in 1862. In 1866 he married

Catherine Schumacher, known as Mlle. La Bruyère, a rather dubious adventuress. Maubreuil died in Paris on 17 June 1868.

E. Daudet, *Conspirateurs et comédiennes* (Paris, n.d.); M. Garcon, *La Tumultueuse existence de Maubreuil Marquis d'Orvault* (Paris, 1954); E. D. Pasquier, *Histoire de mon temps* (Paris, 1893–95).

*James K. Kieswetter*

*Related entries:* CHARLES X; HUNDRED DAYS; PASQUIER; TAL-LEYRAND.


*LE MAYEUX* (July 1831–May 1832), republican and satirical paper, thirty-two issues. Mayeux was the personification of republican France whom the 1830 Revolution had liberated by removing a demon that had long silenced him. Above the title was a vignette of Mayeux at the foot of a liberty tree. After the twelfth issue, the editors split. One launched a rival, *Le Véritable Mayeux, évangéliste populaire* (thirty-one issues, October 1831–May 1832), under a vignette of Mayeux holding a tricolor. To avoid the new laws on caution money, this paper had to change its name repeatedly—for example, to *Simon le prolétaire.* Both papers were bitterly critical of the July Monarchy, particularly the press laws, and saw themselves as filling the role played by Camille Desmoulins in 1789.

E. Hatin, *Bibliographie historique et critique de la presse périodique française* (Paris, 1866).

*Peter McPhee*

*Related entries:* PRESS LAWS; REPUBLICANS.


**MAZENOD, CHARLES-JOSEPH-EUGENE DE** (1782–1861), bishop of Marseilles. Born into a family of the nobility of the robe in Aix-en-Provence, he lived most of his childhood in various Italian cities where his father had sought asylum. They were able to return in 1802. In 1808 Eugène entered the famous Saint-Sulpice seminary in Paris. After his ordination to the priesthood, he returned to his native province, clearly determined to devote his ministry to conducting missions in neglected rural villages. For this purpose, operating under the protective authority of his uncle, Charles-Fortuné de Mazenod, bishop of Marseilles, he founded a special religious society, the Oblats de Marie-Immaculée. With a growing number of associates, he tirelessly preached in many southern provinces and even in Paris. Eventually bishops from the United States begged for his help, and his society expanded overseas. In 1837, his uncle resigned the see of Marseilles and Eugène, who had been groomed by him as vicar general, became bishop of the great commercial city, while keeping the office of superior-general of his congregation. Until his death he was a tireless pastor, developing in all imaginable forms the institutions of devotion, charity, and Christian education. In spite of his legitimist background, he supported Louis Napoleon in December 1851 and, less enthusiastically, the restoration of the imperial title. Napoleon III named him senator in 1856 and tried, albeit unsuccessfully, to have him made cardinal. At the time of Mazenod's death, his congregation numbered 6 bishops, 267 priests, 53 students, and 89 brothers, with establishments in Canada, the United States, Ceylon, and Natal.

J. Leflon, *Eugène de Mazenod*, 3 vol. (Paris, 1957–65); J.-R. Palanque, *Le diocèse de Marseille* (Paris, 1967).

*Guillaume de Bertier de Sauvigny*

*Related entries:* MISSIONS.


**MEHEMET (MOHAMMED)-ALI** (1769–1849), reforming Egyptian viceroy, political figure, and sometime French client. Méhémet-Ali was born in Kavala, Rumelia (southern Bulgaria), of uncertain, but largely Balkan, ancestry. Orphaned early, he was adopted by Ali Aga, a Janissary captain from whom he learned the intricacies of military politics in the Ottoman Empire. After making a good marriage in 1787, Méhémet commanded a detachment of 300 irregular soldiers on the Turkish expedition to expel Bonaparte from Egypt in 1799, and barely escaped the resulting disaster at Aboukir (25 August–2 September 1799). His popularity with the Albanian troops who made up a substantial part of the Turkish army helped his career, and he returned to Egypt in 1801 as co-commander of the Ottoman forces after the French withdrawal. Skillfully playing on the mutual hostilities of the Turks and the native Mamelukes, Méhémet succeeded in getting the Ottoman governor (pasha) recalled and allowed his successor to be killed in fighting with the Mamelukes by refusing to lead his Albanian levies to his aid. Méhémet's mastery of the conspiratorial and sometimes homicidal methods of Ottoman political infighting brought his recognition as pasha of Egypt (by imperial *firman* on 9 July 1809). Deftly making use of British military aid when he needed it, Méhémet broke the power of the Mamelukes and massacred their leaders in 1811 and began a campaign of political and economic reforms, imposing efficient tax collection and putting idle farmland into production. Authorized by the sultan to repress the Wahabi Islamic heresy in Arabia, Méhémet and his son Imbrahim extended Egyptian hegemony over Jidda, Medina, and Mecca between 1811 and 1818, and he brought Nubia and the Sudan under his rule. Méhémet's success was in large part due to his reorganization of the Egyptian army (the *Nazim-jidad*) along European lines after 1816, a task he entrusted to veteran Napoleonic officers, many of whom converted to Islam. Although Méhémet had supplied grain to the British Mediterranean fleet and Wellington's troops in Spain during the Napoleonic wars, the British government became increasingly alarmed at the growing Egyptian threat to British trade routes in the Red Sea and refused to assist in the construction of an Egyptian fleet. The French consul-general in Cairo (Drovetti) played on these differences, permitting Méhémet to construct ships in Marseilles.

In 1822, the sultan offered Méhémet the *pashlik* of Crete if he would put down a revolt by the native Greeks, a task the Egyptian viceroy accomplished with his new fleet and army. An opportunity to extend his power into Greece led Méhémet to commit sixty-three ships and 16,000 men (under Imbrahim) to the Turkish effort to repress the Greek war for independence, but the intervention of England, France, and Russia led to the destruction of his navy (at Navarino in October 1827) and the withdrawal of Egyptian forces. In 1829, Méhémet conducted simultaneous negotiations with the French (offering to invade Algeria on their behalf); the sultan (Mahmoud), from whom he sought a declaration that his vice-regency was hereditary; and the English, whose aid he asked in overthrowing the sultan. In 1830, Méhémet's armies invaded Palestine and Syria, and Imbrahim defeated the sultan's army at Koniah in Asia Minor (1832). Great power pressure forced Méhémet to accept the Treaty of Kutahia (February 1833), which left his conquests intact but denied him the hereditary title he sought.

While the French hoped to make use of Méhémet and offered him support, the British government sought to preserve the integrity of the Ottoman Empire and generally backed the sultan. A Turkish attempt to push Méhémet out of Syria was defeated at Nazib on 24 June 1839, at which point the Turkish fleet sailed to Alexandria and defected from the sultan, who died on 1 July. His heir, Abdul Majid, was only sixteen and immediately offered the viceroy the hereditary title. While Méhémet hesitated, Britain, Russia, Austria, and Prussia offered their support to Abdul, and the Thiers ministry in France decided not to aid any attempt to depose him. The Treaty of London (15 July 1840) confirmed Méhémet's control of southern Syria and the hereditary vice-regency but threatened military action if the offer were not immediately accepted. Still hoping for French assistance, Méhémet delayed, at which point the British landed troops in Syria, provoked a native revolt, and defeated Imbrahim's army. A British squadron blockaded Egypt, and Méhémet signed an agreement (29 November 1840) to return the Turkish fleet, give up Syria and Palestine, and accept hereditary title to Egypt alone. The sultan subsequently confirmed the terms imposed by the British and reduced Méhémet's autonomy, limiting the size of his army and navy and reimposing the annual tribute payments to Constantinople. Old (seventy-one) and defeated, Méhémet governed Egypt as a tributary state for a decade longer but suffered from intermittent bouts of mental instability after 1844. His son Imbrahim having died in 1848, he was succeeded by his grandson, Abbas-Ibrahim.

Méhémet-Ali's internal reforms converted Egypt from the Ottoman Empire's poorest and worst-administered province to its wealthiest and best governed, but his larger ambitions were thwarted by European concern for the stability of the eastern Mediterranean. Some nineteenth-century intellectuals (the Saint-Simonians among them) saw him as a Western liberal, while others found him little more than another Levantine despot. Given his real abilities and traditional Ottoman political methods, neither view seems entirely accurate.

D. Cameron, *Egypt in the 19th Century* (London, 1898); H. Dodwell, *The Founder of Modern Egypt* (Cambridge, 1931); G. Douin, *Mohammed Aly et l'expédition d'Alger* (Paris, 1930); M. Fahmy, *La Révolution de l'industrie en Egypt et ses conséquences sociales au XIXe siècle* (Leiden, 1954); S. Ghorbal, *The Beginnings of the Egyptian Question and the Rise of Méhémet Ali* (London, 1928); P. Hamont, *L'Egypte sous Méh-*

*émet Ali*, 2 vols. (Paris, 1843); P. Mouriez, *Histoire de Méhémet-Ali*, 4 vols. (Paris, 1855–58); H. Rivlin, *The Agricultural Policy of Mohammed'Ali in Egypt* (Cambridge, Mass., 1961); S. Shaw, "The Financial and Administrative Organization and Development of Ottoman Egypt (1517–1798)" (Ph.D diss., Princeton, 1958).

*David Longfellow*

*Related entries:* ALGIERS, EXPEDITION TO; IMBRAHIM PASHA; NA-VARINO, BATTLE OF; SAINT-SIMONIANISM; THIERS.

**MELUN, ARMAND DE** (1807–1877), a leader of the social Catholic movement. During the July Monarchy, Armand de Melun concentrated on private charity to alleviate the plight of urban workers. In 1845 he founded the newspaper *Annales de la charité* and became unofficial spokesman for social Catholicism for the next quarter-century. Originally a legitimist, he became convinced with the Revolution of 1848 that the state had to intervene in the social arena. Elected to the Legislative Assembly in 1849 from Ille-et-Vilaine, he sponsored a number of bills concerning housing and conditions in factories.

Potentially his most important bill was one that secured a committee of thirty to examine possibilities for public assistance promised in article 13 of the new Constitution. In that committee, de Melun argued for a "protective society," which, while permitting private property and individuality, would engage in comprehensive prevention of poverty through hospitals, schools, day care centers, orphanages, hostels, and workers' associations that could share profits with employers. All organizations were to be supervised by a committee of the Legislative Assembly in cooperation with local government and private institutions. Adolphe Thiers, a noninterventionist, was appointed reporter of that very divided committee, however, and little came of it. The Napoleonic coup that inaugurated the Second Empire ended Melun's brief experiment in politics and his return to private action. His twin brother Anatole assisted him in many enterprises and himself represented the Nord in the early years of the Third Republic.

A. de Melun, *Mémoires du Vte. Armand de Melun* (Paris, 1891).

*Patrick J. Harrigan*

*Related entries:* CONSTITUTION OF 1848; COUP D'ETAT OF 2 DECEMBER 1851; LEGISLATIVE ASSEMBLY; SOCIAL CATHOLICISM; THIERS.

*LE MEMORIAL CATHOLIQUE* (1824–1830), clericalist monthly journal. *Le Mémorial catholique* presented an ultraclerical and royalist polemic as well as literary criticism. It was founded by abbé Philippe-Olympe Gerbet and Louis-Antoine de Salinis in 1824. Its printer was Pierre Leroux, who that same year helped found the *Globe,* the *Mémorial*'s rival and antagonist. That the lofty intellectual *Globe* would deign to joust with the *Mémorial* is a tribute to the latter's chief editor, Father Robert de Lamennais. Lamennais' strict royalism and his total loyalty to the church but not to Gallicanism were tempered by an occasionally surprising breadth of intellectual spirit in philosophy, literature, and social issues. In its literary aspect, the journal promoted the Restoration battle between classicists and romantics, between old and new. When the ultra *Quotidienne* adopted a more clericalist stance in 1828 by dropping Joseph-François Michaud and others of its staff, the vacancies created were filled by writers for the *Mémorial*. Both periodicals vehemently attacked the alleged persecution of the Jesuits by the new moderate government of Jean-Baptiste de Martignac. The *Mémorial catholique* became a casualty of the July Revolution.

C. Boutard, *Lamennais*, 3 vols. (Paris, 1905–13); A. Dansette, *Histoire réligieuse de la France contemporaine* (Paris, 1948); N. Hudson, *Ultra Royalism and the French Restoration* (Cambridge, 1936).

*Daniel Rader.*

Related entries: *LE GLOBE*; JESUITS; LEROUX; MARTIGNAC; MICHAUD; *LA QUOTIDIENNE*; REVOLUTION OF 1830; ULTRAROYALISTS.


**MENNAISIAN.** See LAMENNAIS.


*LE MENTOR.* See *LA LORGNETTE*.


*MERCURE DU XIXe SIECLE* (1823–1832), quarterly magazine founded by Léon Thiéssé, who first translated Byron; by Pierre Tissot, former Collège de France professor and experienced journalist; by Henri de Latouche; by Etienne de Senancour; and by others. It was a descendant of a long line of *Mercures* beginning with *Le Mercure galant* in 1672, which combined politics and literature in a light vein. In 1724 it became *Le Mercure de France*, more literary in its pursuits and boasting such distinguished contributors as Thomas Corneille and Voltaire. It briefly bore the title *Le Mercure français* during the Revolution and was suppressed by Napoleon from 1811 until his demise. Again suppressed in February 1818, it was replaced by the *Minerve française*, which it took to court to regain its rights before it disappeared in 1820.

Reborn as the *Mercure du XIXe siècle* in 1823, its politics throughout the decade of its new life remained liberal and, at least for the first five years, dominated its pages, political convictions often influencing literary judgments. It mounted a vigorous battle against the ultras entrenched in La Société des bonnes lettres. Despite the surprisingly eclectic and impartial literary policy expressed in Tissot's initial prospectus, it staunchly adhered at the outset to traditional classical principles and especially castigated romantic excesses imported from Germany. It waged a bitter war during its first, definitely antiromantic, year against François-René de Chateaubriand and against the Deschamps group and its journal, *La Muse française*, published from July 1823 to June 1824.

Following the expiration of *La Muse*, a transformation from classicism to romanticism occurred through progressive adaptation. It confirmed that the fight for political freedom meant enough to warrant significant concessions and compromises of literary principles on the part of the editors. This gradual shift began within a few months with the appearance in the third volume in 1823 of a new prospectus. It called for literature to become involved, to be of service to society, and to present both sides on political questions. As the repressive policies of Charles X angered more and more Frenchmen, journalists became increasingly uncomfortable with the neutral policies of the *Mercure*. Henri de Latouche fomented the internal dissention that marked the *Mercure*'s existence in 1825–26. He had responded to Louis-Simon Auger's Academy-speech and launched within the *Mercure* group a campaign for romanticism. The result was an attempt to be impartial, which reduced its literary effectiveness to practically nothing. Many significant works were simply not reviewed.

The eclectic policy that a third prospectus in 1826 had implied was clearly and openly announced in still a fourth statement in 1827. Noting the intensifying struggle being waged, especially on the stage, it recognized the classic-romantic confrontation but dedicated itself to the *juste milieu*. The nonalignment was further accentuated by the absence of references to the organization of Hugo's *grand cénacle* in 1827, though the *Mercure* critics hailed his *Cromwell* preface as outstanding. The moderate policy was reaffirmed in an 1828 policy statement, which again declared adherence to neither of the two schools, stressing that a new French literature still needed to be found, with the emphasis on freedom and the truth. It was late in 1828 that it finally determined that one of Prosper Mérimée's closet dramas, *La Jacquerie*, illustrated best its major goal of a new national drama.

A sixth preface of 1829 revealed a frustration with politics and literature and announced a shift to scientific and travel articles, which in fact began to appear more frequently. But never had a preference for romanticism been more obvious than in the first volume of 1829, which published works of known romantics, especially Victor Hugo. He had become so important that the *Mercure* could no longer ignore him. His prominence caused the journal to abandon its impartiality and to favor romanticism. Favorable reviews of romantic poems, novels, and plays proliferated in the 1829 issues. Despite some attenuation in 1830 due to renewed fervor for politics, especially after the 1830 Revolution, the periodical had definitely opted for the romantics, praising *Hernani* without reservation. It had finally attained a liberal posture in both politics and literature. Its last two years, 1831–33, were strongly focused on politics. As the only periodical published throughout the Restoration, its pages offer a unique collection of liberal views of the period.

A revived *Mercure de France* was later a prominent feature of the literary scene of *la belle époque* first associated with *symbolisme* and by 1900 professing a new eclecticism supporting the efforts of all schools and writers.

C. H. Albro Jr., "Romanticism as Reflected by *Le Mercure de France (1815–1830)*" (Ph.D diss., University of Kentucky, 1955); R. Bray, *Chronologie du romantisme (1804–*

*1830)* (Paris, 1932); Ch.-M. Des Granges, *La Presse littéraire sous la Restauration, 1815–1830* (Paris, 1907).

Paul Comeau

*Related entries:* AUGER; CHATEAUBRIAND; *HERNANI*; HUGO; LA-TOUCHE; MERIMEE; *LA MINERVE; LA MUSE FRANCAISE*; ROMANTI-CISM; THIESSE; TISSOT; ULTRAROYALISTS.


*LE MERCURE ROYAL DE FRANCE* (1819–1820), royalist periodical. An occasional publication of ultraroyalists between September 1819 and March 1820, it was the royalist answer to the *Mercure de France* of Benjamin Constant and Antoine Jay, which had been suppressed in 1818 and whose staff continued in the *Minerve française*. Its subtitle was *Mémoires de l'Académie des ignorants*.

C. Ledré, *La presse à l'assaut de la monarchie* (Paris, 1960).

Daniel Rader

*Related entries:* CONSTANT; JAY; *MERCURE DU XIXe SIECLE;* ULTRA-ROYALISTS.


**MERILHOU, JOSEPH** (1788–1856), liberal lawyer and magistrate; deputy, peer, and minister of the July Monarchy. Mérilhou was born at Montignac (Dordogne) on 15 October 1788. He studied law in Paris and was admitted to the bar in 1810. Napoleon appointed him councillor-auditor in the imperial court in 1814, and the Bourbons retained him at the First Restoration. But he incurred royal displeasure by opposing the prosecution of Lazare-Nicolas-Marguérite Carnot for his *Mémoire au roi* and especially for serving as deputy prosecutor in the imperial court of Paris during the Hundred Days. Thus at the Second Restoration he was removed from office and briefly exiled from Paris. Mérilhou then returned to the practice of law in Paris, taking a prominent part for several years in defending liberals in various political trials, staunchly championing freedom of the press. In 1817 he defended the *Censeur* and in 1820 won the jury trial of the *Bibliothèque historique*. In 1825 he obtained the acquittal of the *Courrier français*. Mérilhou was a high-ranking member of the Carbonari leadership. Thus he also aided many accused of conspiracy, including General Jean-Baptiste Berton and Jean-François Bories, one of the four sergeants of La Rochelle. Mérilhou himself apparently was involved in some clandestine plotting. He participated in the anticlerical activities of the mid–1820s. He joined the Société des amis de la liberté de la presse and may have belonged to Aide-toi, le ciel t'aidera, the militant political organization. He opposed the Polignac ministry and actively protested the July Ordinances.

As a former Carbonaro and republican, Mérilhou was very much involved in the various meetings that led to the establishment of the July Monarchy. On 29 July 1830 he joined the Paris Municipal Commission and on 31 August became provisional secretary-general of the Ministry of Justice. During his two months in that office, he revoked the law on sacrilege, removed numerous judges, and made other reforms. On 20 August he was appointed to the Council of State and on 2 November became minister of public instruction and worship in the Laffitte government. Although he disappointed some liberals, as minister he suppressed the Society of Missions of France and required university degrees for certain church offices. Then on 27 December 1830 he moved to the Ministry of Justice, where he remained until 7 March 1831. He resigned in opposition to attempts to limit the press. In July 1831 he was elected to the Chamber of Deputies and usually voted with the moderate opposition. His opposition, however, was sufficiently mild that in 1832 the government offered him a place as councillor in the Court of Cassation. He had declined this post in the spring of 1831, but on 21 April 1832 he accepted. He failed to win reelection to the Deputies in 1834 but received a peerage on 3 October 1837. He participated actively in the Peers, serving as a reporter on the insurrection of 12 May 1839, assisting in the drafting of a new military code in 1842, and helping to reform the mortgage laws in 1845. On 29 March 1846 he was made a grand officer of the Legion of Honor. The 1848 Revolution resulted in his removal from the Court of Cassation, but he was recalled to the court in 1849. He died in Paris on 18 October 1856, leaving numerous articles and an encyclopedia of law.

L. Girard, *Le Libéralisme en France de 1814 à 1848* (Paris, 1967); A.Robert et al., *Dictionnaire des parlementaires français* (Paris, 1889–91); A. Spitzer, *Old Hatreds and Young Hopes* (Cambridge, 1971); G. Vapereau, *Dictionnaire universel des contemporains* (Paris, 1858).

*James K. Kieswetter*

*Related entries:* AIDE-TOI, LE CIEL T'AIDERA; BERTON; *LA BIBLIO-THEQUE HISTORIQUE;* BORIES; CARBONARI; CARNOT, L.-N.-M.; *LE CENSEUR;* COUNCIL OF STATE; *LE COURRIER FRANCAIS*; COURT OF CASSATION; LAFFITTE; LA ROCHELLE, FOUR SERGEANTS OF; LAW OF SACRILEGE; MISSIONS; MUNICIPAL COMMISSION; POLIGNAC; SOCIETY OF FRIENDS OF THE FREEDOM OF THE PRESS.

**MERIMEE, PROSPER** (1803–1870), romantic poet and novelist. Reared in a cultivated Parisian household, Mérimée studied law briefly before devoting himself entirely to literature, with Stendhal's encouragement. His early works owed much to Spanish influence clearly evident in *Théâtre de Clara Gazul*—a collection of pert closet dramas published in 1825— and *La Guzla, ou Choix de poésies illyriques*—a collection of mysterious ballads that appeared two years later. In 1830 Mérimée's historical sketch, *Chronique du règne de Charles IX*, turned an adventure story set during the religious wars into a profound psychological study. But Mérimée's real inspiration appeared in the remarkably concise style of the stories collected in *Mosaïque* and *La Double méprise*, both published in 1833. Named inspector of historical monuments in 1834, Mérimée traveled throughout France with the young Eugène Viollet-le-Duc to inventory the country's archaeological heritage. Frequent trips to Mediterranean countries as well inspired the poetry of *La Vénus d'Ille* (1837) and the novellas *Colomba* (1840) and *Carmen* (1845) in which the understated style contrasts sharply with the stories' passionate violence. He was elected to the Académie française in 1844. Favored by Eugénie de Montijo and the court of Napoleon III— Mérimée was appointed to the Legion of Honor and made a senator during the Second Empire—he continued to write historical essays and stories with a clear realistic tone right up to his death at the age of sixty-seven in Cannes. Mérimée's largely romantic literary accomplishments developed themes frequently explored in the first half of the nineteenth century, especially the interest in medieval history and historical fiction, the depiction of exoticism and local color, the evocation of violent, often fatal passions, and the taste for the fantastic and supernatural. Refusing the facilities of the pathetic, Mérimée adopted instead logical plots, precise descriptions, and characters deftly revealed by their actions, all in a highly restrained style comparable to Stendhal's. Whether ironic or dramatic, Mérimée's stories are always, as Charles-Augustin Sainte-Beuve observed, "neat, lean, alert, and drawn from life." This tendency anticipated the developments of literary realism despite the popular romantic climate in which he lived. This independence he exercised as well in his services to the Second Empire that earned him the opprobrium of his literary friends in outspoken opposition to the regime.

F. P. Bowman, *Prosper Mérimée: Heroism, Pessimism, and Irony* (Berkeley, 1962); P. Trahard, *La Jeunesse de Prosper Mérimée, 1808–1834* (Paris, 1925), *La Vieillesse de Mérimée* (Paris, 1930), and *Prosper Mérimée de 1834 à 1853* (Paris, 1928).

*James Smith Allen*

*Related entries:* ACADEMIE FRANCAISE; ROMANTICISM; SAINTE-BEUVE; STENDHAL; VIOLLET-LE-DUC.


*MESSAGER DES CHAMBRES* (1828–?), small newspaper established to support the policies of the Martignac ministry; opposed Jules de Polignac; continued in July Monarchy. *Le Messager des chambres*, "journal des villes et des campagnes," appeared as an evening paper in the official service of the vicomte de Martignac's ministry in 1828. Its editors set the tone of the regime and attempted, during this one thoroughly constitutional government of the entire Restoration, to create alliances in the opposition press. But the ultra Right scorned it, and most of the liberal journals, such as the *Constitutionnel*, were distrustful. Only the *Journal des débats* was friendly to Jean-Baptiste de Martignac and his *Messager*, but this powerful support evaporated when the *Débats*' François-René de Chateaubriand failed to win the Foreign Ministry and received instead the embassy to Rome. With the loss of the *Débats* and its 11,000 subscribers, the *Messager des chambres*, with a mere 1,200, had to promote its conciliatory programs alone.

When Martignac was dismissed and entered the Chamber of Peers, he continued to support the paper with some help from a few legitimists. The *Messager* was very critical of the ultra Polignac ministry of 8 August 1829.

After 1830, the newspaper accommodated in general to the dynastic Left, the Thiers or liberal wing of the July Monarchy, but changed its support in relation to issues and ministers. Its circulation was miniscule by the late 1840s. The paper's modest career demonstrates that the ideal of truly constitutional monarchy could win little respect or support.

E. Daudet, *Le ministère de M. de Martignac* (Paris, 1875); E. Hatin, *Histoire de la presse* (Paris, 1859–61).

*Daniel Rader*

*Related entries:* CHAMBER OF DEPUTIES; CHAMBER OF PEERS; CHATEAUBRIAND; *LE CONSTITUTIONNEL; JOURNAL DES DÉBATS;* MARTIGNAC; POLIGNAC; RESTORATION, SECOND; THIERS; ULTRAROYALISTS.

**METTERNICH, CLEMENS-WENZEL, LOTHAR, PRINCE VON** (1773–1859), Austrian statesman. His father, Count Franz-Georg von Metternich, came from an old Rhenish family, and he had entered the service of Austria. His mother, Maria-Beatrix von Kagenegg, belonged to a family that served the Empress Maria Theresa at court, and she assured her son's future by arranging his marriage with Eleonore von Kaunitz, grandaughter of the powerful chancellor of the empress. Young Clement was given an entirely French education, notably at the University of Strasbourg, and all his life he preferred to speak and write in French rather than in German. His career began in 1792 in Brussels as assistant to his mother, who had been named minister of Austria to the Estates General of Belgium, and later, in 1797, plenipotentiary to the Congress of Rastadt. He rose rapidly in the diplomatic service: minister to the king of Saxony in Dresden (February 1801), ambassador to Berlin (December 1803), and finally to Paris (August 1806). As ambassador to France, he helped to push Austria into a declaration of war on Napoleon, at the time stuck in the Spanish muddle. His country's defeat in that war served paradoxically to advance his career because the Emperor Francis chose him to replace Johann von Stadion, the minister of foreign affairs who had been held responsible for the disastrous war. The marriage of the Emperor Francis's oldest daughter to Napoleon allowed the new minister to reduce the difficulties of his country's defeat. In the events of 1813–14, which ultimately led to the fall of Napoleon's empire, Metternich played a clever game, leading his country from alliance with France to membership in the European coalition against Napoleon. After Napoleon's defeat, Metternich, who had arrived in France with his sovereign, was one of the negotiators of the first Treaty of Paris (1 May 1814). From the end of 1814 to the spring of 1815, the great powers meeting in Vienna set about reorganizing Europe; this famous Congress of Vienna was a play in which Metternich was the director, as well as one of the principal actors. He was careful to limit the ambitions of Russia, and in this he had the full agreement of the British minister, Lord Castlereagh. He thus ensured Austrian predominance in Germany and in Italy.

Napoleon's vain attempt to regain his throne brought the Allies back to Paris again. This time they stayed for several months during the difficult negotiations of the Second Treaty of Paris. Metternich played the role of mediator between the harsh demands of Prussia and the more generous policies of Czar Alexander. Here the treaty of the Quadruple Alliance was signed on 25 November 1815, creating a kind of European Directory responsible for maintaining the order established at the Congress of Vienna. That treaty would be the basis for Metternich's policies throughout the next decade; he would follow those conservative policies symbolized by the Holy Alliance. In 1819–20, Metternich concentrated principally on repressing the liberal movement in Germany, and he sponsored rigorous police measures that were adopted at the conferences of Carlsbad and of Vienna. The liberal revolution that broke out in the Kingdom of Naples in July 1820 threatened to destabilize all of Italy, so Metternich saw to it at the Congress of Troppau (October 1820) and at the Congress of Laibach (April 1821) that Austria was mandated by Europe to reestablish monarchical order. The precedent thus created came into play later when in 1822 France asked for the same right of intervention in Spain. Metternich, despite his distaste for this, found himself obliged to join in the decisions made at the Congress of Verona (October–December 1822). Shortly afterward, the Quadruple Alliance of 1815 found itself practically dissolved when England got together with Russia directly in order to intervene in the question of Greek independence, an intervention that Metternich had desperately tried to avoid. The 1830 Revolution in France, with its diverse consequences in Belgium and in the Iberian Peninsula, completed the decomposition of the conservative system and ended the preponderance of Metternich in European councils. His role henceforth was that of a commentator, a giver of advice, a keeper of the rules of the diplomatic game, sometimes as a useful mediator, as in the European crisis of 1840.

Metternich should also have had a preponderant role in the internal government of the Empire because of his position as chancellor, which he had received in 1821. But as long as Emperor Francis lived, he controlled the smallest details of all the branches of the administration, and it was the emperor, not his minister, who took responsibility for the paternalistic police state that was the Austrian government at that time. His oldest son, Ferdinand, was weak minded, so under his rule the government was exercised by a small council composed of the two archdukes, who were the uncles of the emperor, of Metternich, and of Count Kolowrat, minister of the interior, whose authority often counterbalanced that of the chancellor in the affairs of the Empire. Still, because of his ministerial longevity, Metternich had become the living symbol of the conservative order in Austria as in Europe. The popular riots of Vienna in March 1848 terrified the court and Metternich's colleagues, who convinced him to resign (on 13 March). The chancellor had to flee to escape mistreatment at the hands of the rebels. He lived in exile in England and then in Belgium, up to the moment when he was able to return to Vienna in September 1851 following the triumph of the reaction in Austria. There he lived out his life in serenity.

G. de Bertier de Sauvigny, *La Sainte Alliance* (Paris, 1972), *Metternich and His Times* (London, 1962), and *Metternich et la France*, 3 vols. (Paris, 1968–71); *Mémoires . . .*

*laissés par le prince de Metternich*, 8 vols. (Paris, 1880–84); Allan Palmer, *Metternich, A Biography* (New York, 1972).

*Guillaume de Bertier de Sauvigny, trans. by E. Newman*

*Related entries:* HOLY ALLIANCE; LONDON, TREATY OF; PARIS, SECOND TREATY OF; QUADRUPLE ALLIANCE; QUINTUPLE ALLIANCE; SPAIN, 1823 FRENCH INVASION OF; TROPPAU, CONGRESS OF; VERONA, CONGRESS OF; VIENNA, CONGRESS OF.


**MEYERBEER, GIACOMO** (1791–1864), German opera composer. At birth named Jacop Liebmann Beer, Meyerbeer was born to a wealthy Jewish merchant family in Berlin, a background strikingly close to that of Felix Mendelssohn. After studying music throughout Germany, most notably in Darmstadt with the great abbé Georg Joseph Vogler, he first distinguished himself primarily as a piano virtuoso. After the failure of his first attempts at German opera, primarily Singspiel, he moved to Italy in 1816 and in 1824 achieved a notable success with his *Il crociato in Egitto*. In 1825 he moved to Paris. He already had an international reputation as a composer of the Italian style of opera, but once in Paris he shifted to a style of musical theater based on earlier French works, and this new style became known as grand opera. He never settled with a permanent residence in Paris, and in 1842 his appointment as *generalmusikdirektor* at the court in Berlin limited his presence there even more. Yet Paris is where all his notable successes took place and where the opera genre he helped shape was based. It was quite fitting when in 1849 he was the first German composer to be granted the commandeur of the Légion d'honneur.

The term *grand opéra* had been used as early as 1780 to denote works designed on a large scale, but from the première of *Robert le diable* on 11 November 1831, it carried even sharper connotations. Socially it meant opera produced with broad commercial interests, all the way from the handling of initial investments to spin-offs of sheet music for amateur consumption. Textually it usually involved an active historical interest in the subject and realistic portrayal of events on stage in text, scenery, costumes, and in some cases even musical style. Musically it meant use of a large orchestra for powerful effect but nonetheless a focus on the principal voices for their use of the bel canto style of singing.

Meyerbeer established the genre first of all in *Robert*. He was never very productive, partly because of his own working habits but also because the problems of developing productions consumed much of his time. His second major work, on the subject of the Saint Bartholemew's Day massacre, came in *Les Huguenots* in 1836, and the third, on the Exodus of the Jews with Moses in *Le Prophète*, in 1849. His final major opera, *L'Africaine*, did not appear until a few months after his death in 1864.

J. Fulcher, "Meyerbeer and the Music of Society," *The Musical Quarterly* 67 (April, 1981).

                                                                    *William Weber*

**MICHAUD, JOSEPH-FRANCOIS** (1767–1839), historian, journalist, editor of the ultra *Quotidienne* during the Restoration. Joseph Michaud entered the journalistic arena of the Revolution in 1790, when, as a new member of the Feuillant club, he wrote editorials for their newspapers. By late 1792, when most royalists had fled Paris, Michaud gamely remained. At the very moment of the September Massacres, he dared to coedit a new royalist paper, *La Quotidienne*, which survived repeated ordeals until its suppression in 1797. Michaud's manager was executed, and he was placed on the Convention's proscribed list. Much of his activity was clandestine and dangerous. After Fructidor, when the paper was outlawed, Michaud went into hiding, a fugitive but not an *émigré*.

Returning to Paris under the amnesty of the first consul, he resumed the study of history begun in his youth. It was a devotion to this discipline that informed the sturdy principles of his later life. He was sent to the Temple for some anti-Bonapartist writing, but, upon affecting a conversion to the Empire and its glory, he was released after a short time. He was elected to the Académie in 1811, ostensibly for his historical work but perhaps also for several verses in honor of the emperor's Austrian marriage.

Michaud's deeply legitimist sentiments were at last set free with the Restoration, but they were tempered and strengthened by principles equally profound. He believed in legitimacy, the Bourbons, and the Charter, including, as a matter of necessity, a free press. He opposed revolution and sedition, which he saw in the press and polemic of the Left, but he also had little use for the Jesuits or other extreme clericalists on the Right. He was adamant in his distaste for Joseph de Villèle, whose policies he considered corrupt and harmful to the Restoration, including proposals to destroy the press. He truly believed in a dialogue with the opposition and would amiably engage any of the liberal journalists or deputies with wit and friendship.

In 1814 and again after the Hundred Days, Michaud restored the name *La Quotidienne* to journalism. Under the senior editorship of Joseph Fiévée, the new journal included also François-René de Chateaubriand, Charles Nodier, and other legitimist stars of the literary world. In January 1822, Michaud became chief editor, replacing Fiévée, and *La Quotidienne* came to reflect his guiding hand for six years. The full period of the ministry of Villèle found Michaud's personal voice denouncing that ministry in his paper.

As one of the Right's prominent scholars, Michaud was honored with the title of reader to the king. His independence was put to the test in 1824–25 when Villèle's agent offered to buy out his newspaper. Michaud, like Chateaubriand of the *Débats*, publicly scorned the offer and publicly commended his fellow legitimist of the *Débats*. Addressing Villèle, Michaud wrote, "Perhaps if you could restore my health, I would allow myself to be corrupted!'' His integrity was shown again in 1827 when he editorially ridiculed the notorious Law of Justice and Love, a proposed bill to muzzle the press, drawn up by the Peyronnet and ultra faction. Villèle was forced to request the bill's retirement, but he pressed King Charles X to dismiss Michaud as his official reader, a petty vengeance that served only to illuminate the expanding rift on the Right. Michaud, along with Chateaubriand and his *Débats*, formed the core of the "defection": legitimist but accepting the compromise of the Restoration and opposed to Villèle. Michaud once remarked that the Revolution had removed heads but not ideals, that Napoleon had provided national glory, but that Villèle's rule was all cynicism and corruption.

During the moderate Martignac ministry (January 1828–August 1829), *La Quotidienne's* directors added some members to their staff from the clerical *Mémorial catholique*, as a step toward healing the breach on the Right. At this, Michaud left his desk and insisted that his own replacement be his old colleague Pierre Laurentie, who also hated Villèle. Thus the "defection" continued in the *Quotidienne* but with only an occasional contribution from Michaud, who welcomed the Polignac cabinet with some misgivings and more resignation than enthusiasm.

In May 1830, recognizing that Charles X without Villèle was as compromising to the principle of legitimacy as he had been with Villèle, Michaud left France for a year of historical and archaeological studies in the Near East. He remained abroad until well after the revolution he had foreseen.

During the reign of Louis-Philippe, Michaud returned to historical studies, his former newspaper, under Laurentie, now a weak voice of the already divided legitimists. He died in 1839, too early to see the complete edition of his history of the Crusades (1840) in six volumes, although the first, shorter edition had already been published between 1811 and 1822. Michaud is also responsible, with his brother, for the anecdotal, generous, and balanced *Biographie universelle*, begun in 1813 and continued all his life.

Respected even by many of his political foes for his love of friendly conversation, his true nature is seen in his life-long habit of carrying a pocket edition of Montaigne for his personal consolation.

E. Hatin, *Histoire de la presse*, vol. 8 (Paris, 1859–61); P. Thureau-Dangin, *Royalistes et républicains* (Paris, 1874).

*Daniel Rader*

*Related entries:* CHATEAUBRIAND; FIEVEE; JESUITS; *JOURNAL DES DEBATS;* LEGITIMISM; MARTIGNAC; *LE MEMORIAL CATHOLIQUE;* NODIER; PEYRONNET; POLIGNAC; PRESS LAWS; *LA QUOTIDIENNE*; ULTRAROYALISTS; VILLELE.

**MICHELET, JULES** (1798–1874), romantic and nationalistic historian and author of a notable history of the French Revolution. Jules Michelet was born in Paris on 21 August 1798 to Angélique Constance Millet and Jean-François-Furcy Michelet, a printer who had just managed to eke out a precarious living during the Revolution and whose fortunes worsened considerably during the Empire. Young Jules thus grew up on the margin of poverty, nourishing a hatred for Napoleon and the First Empire. His family's poverty notwithstanding, Jules Michelet received a fine schooling, first at the pension of M. Mélot (1810–12) and then at the Collège Charlemagne (1812–17), where, after having to repeat his first year because of inadequate preparation, he won numerous prizes for scholastic excellence. An unhappy child, Michelet found compensation in the enthusiastic pursuit of knowledge. Meanwhile, his father had found employment, first in a sanitorium between 1815 and 1818 and then in the boarding house of a Mme. Fourcy; in the latter, young Michelet met his future wife, Pauline Rousseau. By the end of 1821, Michelet, following several years of study, had completed two theses for the *doctorat* (1819), and passed his *agrégation*.

During his years as a teacher of history at the Collège Sainte-Barbe (1822–27), Michelet educated himself as a historian and pursued in addition the study of the philosophy of history, reading, among others, Kant, Herder, Condorcet, and Vico and discussing his ideas with the philosopher Victor Cousin. Even at this early stage in his career, as his "Discours sur l'unité de la science" of 1825 makes clear, Michelet sought a view of history that combined the three elements of humanity, harmony, and the unity of science. Between 1825 and 1827, Michelet published three textbooks on modern European history, including *Précis de l'histoire moderne*, which began in 1453 and ended just before the outbreak of the French Revolution. About this time, Michelet also made the acquaintance of Edgar Quinet, who was in the process of discovering the lure of Herder's ideas on the philosophy of history.

For Michelet, 1827 was a landmark year. Named in February as a lecturer in philosophy and history at the Ecole normale, a position he would retain until 1838, he also published his influential translation of Giovanni Battista Vico's *Scienza nuova*. Prefaced with Michelet's "Discours sur le système et la vie de Vico," this edition of the Neapolitan philosopher's almost unknown speculations on the nature of history found reviewers in all the leading intellectual journals of the day and was mentioned by Victor Cousin in his lectures of 1828. In Vico, Michelet found attractive the notion that promethean man had an active role in the creation of civilization and that history consisted of an eternal struggle between human freedom and fatality. Michelet also prepared the entry on Vico for Michaud's famed *Biographie universelle*. Between 1827 and 1829, the young teacher continued to lecture on philosophy and history. In the Revolution of 1830 and the new government that brought many of his friends and contemporaries to high public office, Michelet took no active role; however, he did view the Revolution as a unique event, as the culmination of French history, and as a revolution that had the people as the principal actor instead of individual heroes. This conception of the Revolution of 1830 first appeared in Michelet's *Introduction à l'histoire universelle* (1831), in which the historian narrated world history from its origins in ancient India to its culmination in nineteenth-century France. After completing the two-volume *Histoire romaine* in 1831, Michelet changed the focus of his interests and centered his attention henceforth on the history of France, a study greatly facilitated by his appointment in the same year as archivist of the historical section of the Archives nationales. Using to full advantage the resources at his command, Michelet insisted on the importance of archival sources for the writing of history.

Throughout the 1830s and the first half of the 1840s, Michelet gave himself over to two principal tasks. He traveled the length and breadth of France in order to know his country and to examine the sources held in provincial archives. He also began publishing his monumental *Histoire de France*, the first two volumes of which appeared in 1833 and the sixth volume in 1844. These volumes, which bring the narrative to the end of the Middle Ages, contain two of Michelet's most memorable pieces of historical writing, the "Tableau de la France," which opened volume 2, and the essay on Joan of Arc in volume 5. In the "Tableau," Michelet viewed the emergence of the French nation, following the demise of Roman rule in Gaul, as a triumph of unity over racial and geographical heterogeneity; in the figure of Joan of Arc, Michelet perceived a symbol of the moral, religious, and political unity of the French people. The dominant theme of the *Histoire de France*, hence, was nothing less than the slow but inexorable growth of a unified French nation. In this history and indeed in the soon-to-be-started *Histoire de la Révolution française*, Michelet's goal was neither to narrate the past as Augustin Thierry had done nor to analyze it as Guizot had done, but to resurrect it, albeit lyrically and subjectively. In the midst of his work on this history of France, Michelet left the Ecole normale in 1838 to accept the prestigious chair of history at the Collège de France. In the same year, he was elected to the Académie des sciences morales et politiques.

In the early 1840s, when Michelet began to change his mind with regard to the Middle Ages and to find them and their chief symbol, the Catholic church, wanting, he came to see the Renaissance as a distinct and unique epoch in European history, an idea he would develop fully when he resumed his *Histoire de France* in 1855. Meanwhile, Michelet plunged into the religious and political controversies of his day and then devoted himself to the history of the French Revolution.

Michelet's growing antipathy toward the Catholic church, his concept of himself as the moral educator of France, and perhaps his intellectual reorientation that grew out of the personal crisis of 1842 brought him into a direct confrontation with Catholic leaders. At the heart of this conflict lay a long-standing debate over control of French education, which the church intensified in 1841 with attacks on professors unsympathetic to a religious influence in education. Michelet's personal involvement began when Louis Veuillot's *L'Univers* launched in March 1842 an attack on him, Edgar Quinet, Adam Mickiewicz, and fifteen other professors at the Collège de France and the Sorbonne, accusing them of subversive teaching. Quinet and Michelet answered their critics with first a series of simultaneous lectures on the Jesuits and then with the publication of these lectures in the summer of 1843. An instant best-seller, *Des Jésuites* sold 5,000 copies in ten days and 10,000 copies by the end of the year. In *Des Jésuites* Michelet described a subtle Jesuit conspiracy, arguing that this religious order was anti-French and hence should be excluded from any role in the French educational system. In *Du prêtre, de la femme, de la famille*, which sold some 14,000 copies in the eight months following its publication in January 1845, Michelet continued his polemical attacks on the Jesuits. By 1845, this controversy had become so bitter that it spilled over into government circles and into the legislative chambers. Michelet, meanwhile, had turned his attention to what he considered a greater threat to the unity of France: the existence of bitter class divisions within the nation. To purge France of these antagonisms and to replace them with a spirit of association and patriotism became the purpose of *Le Peuple*, written in 1845 and published in January 1846. In this book, Michelet glorified the people and called for a reconciliation of all the classes within France, especially the literate and the illiterate, which would be achieved by the teaching of love, understanding, and patriotic brotherhood in the schools. To Michelet, France was a religion, and his supreme educational goal was to bring the people and classes of France together, uniting them by a common love of France.

In 1846, Michelet undertook in his lectures to reiterate these themes, and he attracted immense audiences; between 800 and 1,200 frequently turned out to hear him. Frightened by antigovernment sentiments that seemed to be widespread among Michelet's auditors, the government suspended his courses on 2 January 1848, a move that not only failed to silence Michelet, since he published his remaining seven lectures in pamphlet form and then as *L'Etudiant*, but that also provoked large demonstrations in the Latin Quarter.

In the Revolution of 1848 Michelet avoided an active role. He resumed his lectures in March, arguing once again that education was the sole means by which national unity and harmony could be achieved. In the aftermath of the election of Louis-Napoleon as president of the Second Republic, Michelet's relations with the government worsened. On 13 March 1851, the Ministry of Education suspended his courses, and, just over a year later, Michelet, together with his comrades Quinet and Mickiewicz, was expelled from the Collège de France. Because he refused to take the oath of allegiance to the new government of Napoleon III on 4 June 1852, he also lost his post at the Archives nationales.

The years of controversy with the church, the battles over French education, the effort to end class divisions in France, and the years of political tumult between 1848 and 1851, while consuming much of Michelet's time and energy, did not prevent him from writing and publishing between 1847 and 1853 his seven-volume *Histoire de la Révolution française*. This most famous of Michelet's books was not by any standard his most popular; his polemical pamphlets of the 1840s and his essays of the late 1850s and the 1860s by far outsold it. In his passionate, vivid, and often lyrical history of the Revolution, Michelet recreated— resurrected, to use his word—the history of France between 1789 and the fall of Maximilien Robespierre. For him, because the Revolution represented all that was ideal in France, the people became its hero. Further, it meant the triumph of law, the rebirth of justice, and even the victory of ideas over brute force. The *French Revolution* became more than a work of history; it became a work of prophecy and exhortation. The first year of the Revolution, from the storming of the Bastille to the Fête de la fédération, called by Michelet the "best day of our life," represented its high point. Although Michelet found little to approve in the course the Revolution took after 1790 and little to admire in Robespierre, his book nonetheless defended and justified the whole Revolution. Even for Robespierre, condemned for his extremism and intolerance, Michelet managed to evoke some sympathy. In the *French Revolution*, the narrative comes alive because Michelet, who prided himself on his command of the archival sources and his knowledge of the oral tradition, wrote in vivid and evocative prose.

In the last twenty years of his life, Michelet published twenty-six books. He completed the eleven final volumes of the *Histoire de France* (1855–67), including the famous seventh volume in which he set forth for the first time his concept of the Renaissance as a distinct historical period, and the three volumes of the *Histoire du XIXe siècle* (1872–74). He also explored in a series of extremely popular works the themes of women and nature; these books include *La Sorcière* (1862), *L'Amour* (1858), *La Femme* (1860), *L'Oiseau* (1856), *L'Insecte* (1858), *La Mer* (1861), and *La Montagne* (1868). *Bible de l'humanité* (1864), which presented a historical view of the world's religions, including the Indian and the Persian, explored how man creates his own gods and sketched a statement of Michelet's world view.

Michelet, who lived to see the Franco-Prussian War and the horrors of the Paris Commune, ended his life in doubt and despair. He died at Hyeres on 9 February 1874. At the insistence of his wife, Michelet's coffin was moved in 1876 to Père Lachaise, where Michelet had loved to walk as a child.

A. Aulard, "Michelet: Historien de la Révolution française," *La Révolution française* 81 (1928); L. Febvre, *Michelet* (Geneva, 1946); O. Haac, *Les Principes inspirateurs de Michelet* (Paris, 1951); E. K. Kaplan, *Michelet's Poetic Vision: A Romantic Philosophy of Nature, Man, and Women* (Amherst, Mass., 1977); S. A. Kippur, *Jules Michelet: A Study of Mind and Sensibility* (Albany, 1980); F. E. Manuel, "Michelet and the Philosophy of History," *Clio* 6 (1977); J. Michelet, *Ecrits de jeunesse*, ed. Paul Viallaneix (Paris, 1959), *Journal*, 4 vols. (Paris, 1959–76), and *Oeuvres complètes*, ed. Paul Viallaneix (Paris, 1971–); G. Monod, *La Vie et la pensée de Jules Michelet* (Paris, 1923); L. Orr, *Jules Michelet: Nature, History, and Language* (Ithaca, 1976).

*Robert Brown*

*Related entries:* ACADEMY OF SCIENCES; COLLEGE DE FRANCE; COUSIN; GUIZOT; JESUITS; MICHAUD; QUINET; REVOLUTION OF 1830; REVOLUTION OF 1848; THIERRY; VEUILLOT.

**MIGNET, FRANCOIS-AUGUSTE** (1796–1884), journalist, historian of the French Revolution, academician, and archivist. François Mignet was born in Aix on 8 May 1796, the son of Jean-Alexis Mignet, a master locksmith and moderate supporter of the French Revolution. Owing to the limited resources of his artisan family, Mignet began his education in a local school, but after his intellectual promise had been noted by an inspector of the Imperial University in 1809, he entered the imperial lycée of Avignon as a scholarship student. At the end of four years at the school, which he served as sergeant-major, he completed his studies in 1814 and contemplated quite seriously a military career, a step his mother dissuaded him from taking. In 1814 and 1815, Mignet's former lycée engaged him as a history teacher, but, uncomfortable with the changed atmosphere of the school during the Restoration, he soon returned to his home. Following the Hundred Days, Mignet commenced three years of legal studies at the Law School of Aix, all the while continuing his historical investigations. At the law school, Mignet met Adolphe Thiers, and the two opened an enduring friendship that would continue until Thiers' death in 1877 separated them. The two young men, who shared ardent liberal opinions and who harbored similar literary ambitions, entered the bar in 1818 and practiced law with but moderate success for about eighteen months. Meanwhile, Thiers and Mignet began to circulate in the liberal circles of Aix.

The same path, that of success in literary prizes, carried Thiers and Mignet to Paris. The latter put to good use his historical knowledge and his literary talents between 1819 and 1821, submitting first an *Eloge de Charles VII* for a prize offered by the Académie de Nîmes and then a more sophisticated and substantial work, *De la Féodalité, des Institutions de Saint-Louis*, to a competition sponsored by the Académie des inscriptions et belles-lettres. For the essay on Charles VII, he won a gold medal and he shared with Auguste-Arthur Beugnot the prize of 1,500 francs for the study of the institutions of Saint-Louis. Mignet then sold the publication rights to *De la Féodalité*, the work in which first appeared his controversial idea of historical fatalism, for another 600 francs. With his prize money, with the money realized from the sale of his book, and with some parental assistance, Mignet, who had originally traveled to Paris in July 1821 to receive his award, settled in the French capital determined to make his fortune. A letter of introduction to the famed liberal Jacques-Antoine Manuel opened many doors to him and even helped him obtain in October a position on the staff of the *Courrier français*; his first article appeared at the end of November. Not long after Mignet took up residence in Paris, his friend Thiers joined him, and the two young provincials shared an attic room on the passage Montesquieu. Mignet's essays in the *Courrier français* soon brought him to the attention of prominent liberals, and throughout the remaining years of the Restoration he mixed freely in opposition circles. In the salons of Charles-Maurice de Talleyrand and the marquis de Lafayette, he learned much about the French Revolution from the men who had participated in it, knowledge that he would use shortly when writing his history of the Revolution. Mignet also frequented the salons of Jacques Laffitte and Etienne Delécluze. Between 1822 and 1824 he contributed articles to the ill-fated *Tablettes universelles*, the first newspaper to express in print the views of the generation of 1820. During these same busy years, he gave two highly popular courses at the Athénée; that of 1822–23 dealt with the

Reformation and the Catholic League, while that of 1823–24 focused on the English Revolution and the Restoration, topics of not only historical but also political interest during the Restoration. These lectures attracted such prominent Restoration intellectuals as Pierre-Claude Daunou and Antoine-Louis-Claude Destutt de Tracy, and they made such an impression on the audience that Charles-Augustin Sainte-Beuve recalled them with enthusiasm some thirty years later.

In the mid-1820s, no lucid and succinct narrative history of the French Revolution yet existed, and both Mignet and Thiers, who applied themselves with diligence to the formidable task of filling this lacuna, wrote very different studies of the Revolution. Thiers, in ten somewhat diffuse volumes published between 1823 and 1827, traced its history from 1789 to 1799; Mignet covered not only the same ground but also the Consulate and the Empire in just two volumes published in 1824. Written in four months, the book was nonetheless the fruit of two years of study and thought. Primarily a political narrative of the Revolution, Mignet's volumes, which seek to explain and justify the Revolution, concentrate on the events that took place between 1789 and 1794. Fully two-thirds of the *Histoire de la Révolution française* is devoted to these five years; the Thermidorean Reaction and the Directory receive about 21 percent, and the Consulate and the Empire together obtain only 12½ percent. Since printed sources available for consultation were limited both in quantity and quality in the early 1820s, none of the great document collections having yet appeared, Mignet no doubt leaned heavily on what could be learned from such participants in the Revolution as Lafayette, Talleyrand, Benjamin Constant, and others. By no means neutral in his approach toward history, Mignet clearly intended his book to be a defense of a Revolution under constant assault from royalist polemicists; he nonetheless felt no obligation to defend or justify the Terror. Among the *Histoire*'s many virtues are Mignet's extraordinary ability to reduce events of great complexity to a clear and concise narrative and his insistence that the Revolution was a logical outgrowth of French history. The rigorous logic of Mignet's prose has, in fact, led many to criticize him for his historical fatalism. The tone of the book, not surprisingly, is cool and dispassionate, too much so for some who, like the English historian Thomas Carlyle, found the *Histoire* wanting in life and color.

After 1825, Mignet took a more active role in the campaign waged by Restoration liberals against the Bourbon dynasty. At the funeral observances for his patron Manuel, an occasion for the expression of liberal discontent in 1827, Mignet participated in the demonstration that accompanied the inhumation of the body, and he wrote a biographical notice for the *Courrier français*. When the censors refused to allow this notice to appear, the electoral society Aide-toi, le ciel t'aidera published it in pamphlet form. Mignet's account of the events surrounding Manuel's funeral resulted in his indictment and trial in September 1827. Although the court acquitted Mignet, the government refused to release his pamphlet; it could only be published abroad.

Like Thiers and many other opposition leaders, Mignet failed to anticipate the Revolution of 1830. Nevertheless, when Charles X appointed the reactionary Jules de Polignac to head the ministry in 1829, Mignet cast his lot with the vocal opposition. With Thiers and Armand Carrel he founded the *National* early in 1830, and to it he contributed a large number of vigorous articles, all highly critical of the Bourbon regime. When Charles issued the July Ordinances, Mignet was among the first to protest, his name appearing among the first on the famous protest of the journalists drafted by Thiers on 26 July 1830. Although less active in the ensuing revolutionary events, Mignet joined Thiers in drafting the celebrated placard praising the virtues of the duc d'Orléans that appeared in Paris on the morning of 30 July. In the immediate aftermath of the Revolution, Mignet sought, like so many of his comrades, to claim a reward for the risks he had run, but his aspirations were intellectual rather than political.

In the heady atmosphere that followed the July Revolution, Mignet solicited and obtained the cherished directorship of the Archives of the Ministry of Foreign Affairs, a post left vacant by the death on 28 July 1830 of Alexandre-Maurice d'Hauterive. Ideal for a man of Mignet's scholarly temperament, this post, which he held until 1848, permitted him access to the documents needed for a projected history of the Reformation, a work he never completed. As director of the archives, Mignet opened the documents in his care to scholars, and he undertook the publication of several important collections; of these, *Négociations relatives à la succession d'Espagne sous Louis XIV*, published in four volumes between 1835 and 1842, contained a significant introduction and notes by Mignet. Three additional works on Franco-Spanish relations in the sixteenth century later flowed from his pen. In addition to his duties at the archives, Mignet participated actively on several committees, including the Société d'histoire de France and the Comité de l'histoire de France, founded to make historical sources and documents available to the reading public of the 1830s and the 1840s. Mignet thus had a role of major importance in making the nineteenth century the century of history in France.

Despite the active involvement of his intimate friend Thiers in the politics of the July Monarchy, Mignet made every effort to avoid taking part in French political life. His one, not particularly enthusiastic, attempt to secure election to the Chamber of Deputies resulted in failure. Only after considerable pressure did Mignet agree to undertake a diplomatic mission to Spain in October 1833. Nevertheless he remained behind the scenes as a close political confidant and adviser of Thiers, and he even served on occasion as an intermediary between Thiers and those seeking favors or an audience. Mignet clearly meant to devote his considerable energies to his duties as an archivist and to his role as an academician.

Elected to the Académie française in 1836 and to the Académie des sciences morales et politiques three years earlier, Mignet gave much of his life to the building of the latter academy, the youngest of the five academies comprising the Institut de France. Upon the death of Charles Comte in 1837, Mignet became permanent secretary, a position he would hold for forty-five years until his resignation shortly before his death. As the Academy's chief administrative officer, Mignet created for it an effective organization, arranged for the publication of the discussions and the memoirs presented to the Academy, and in general created an appropriate intellectual atmosphere for this learned society. He also took on the task of preparing the *éloges* of deceased members and, over the course of some thirty-two years, he transformed these addresses into an art form. In Mignet's four volumes may be found brilliant portraits of nineteenth-century French intellectuals, many of which still bear a close reading.

No supporter of the Revolution of 1848 or the Republic created by it, Mignet lost his post at the archives following a disagreement over the Republic's Italian policy. Despite his lack of enthusiasm for the Republic, Mignet joined with his fellow academicians and acceded to General Eugène Cavaignac's request for a series of books designed to educate a French populace that now enjoyed universal manhood suffrage; Mignet contributed *Vie de Franklin*, which he wrote between August and December 1848. Mignet was an opponent of Napoleon III and the Second Empire, which he interpreted as a backward step in the general progress of France toward liberty. Mignet helped organize and lead the opposition within the ranks of the academies, and he even used the occasion of the *éloges* to criticize the government. His *éloge* of Théodore Jouffroy sparked considerable controversy in 1853. Mignet also played a leading role in the Institut's opposition to Napoleon III's effort in 1855 to alter the rules and the statutes of the five academies. During the Second Empire and the Third Republic, Mignet continued to write and publish, although he never completed his history of the Reformation. Between 1851 and 1875, he gave to the public *Histoire de Marie Stuart* (1851), *Charles Quint à Yuste* (1854), and *Rivalité de François Ier et de Charles Quint* (1875). Although he courageously remained in Paris during the war of 1870, the siege of Paris, and the Commune, Mignet avoided having any part in the creation of the Third Republic, even refusing an ambassadorship offered by Thiers. Of the many painful events that marred the last years of Mignet's life, none was more terrible than the death of Thiers in 1877; he nonetheless participated in the many memorial services, including the dedication of the statue at Saint-Germain on 19 September 1880. While Mignet continued to work at both academies, he gave most of his time and efforts to the Académie des sciences morales et politiques, to which he read his final *éloge* (of Amédée Thierry) in 1877 and presented his final verbal report in 1881, and which he served as permanent secretary until his resignation on 23 October 1882. François-Auguste Mignet died in Paris on 24 March 1884.

Y. Knibiehler, *Naissance des sciences humaines: Mignet et l'histoire philosophique au XIXe siècle* (Paris, 1973); F.-A. Mignet, *Antonio Perez et Phillipe II* (Paris, 1845), *Charles Quint, son abdication, son séjour et sa mort au monastère de Yuste* (Paris, 1854), *De la féodalité, des Institutions de St. Louis* (Paris, 1822), *Histoire de la Révolution française* (Paris, 1824), *Histoire de Marie Stuart* (Paris, 1851), and *Pages choisies de*

*Mignet,* ed. Georges Weill (Paris, 1896); J. Simon, "Eloge de Mignet," *Mémoires de l'Académie des Sciences morales et politiques* 15 (1885).

*Robert Brown*

*Related entries:* AIDE-TOI, LE CIEL T'AIDERA; CARREL; CAVAIGNAC, L.-E.; CONSTANT; *LE COURRIER FRANCAIS*; DAUNOU; DELECLUZE; DESTUTT DE TRACY; LAFAYETTE, M.-J.-P.-Y.-R.-G.; LAFFITTE; MANUEL; *LE NATIONAL*; POLIGNAC; REVOLUTION OF 1830; REVOLUTION OF 1848; SAINTE-BEUVE; *LES TABLETTES UNIVERSELLES*; TALLEYRAND; THIERS.

**MIGRATION.** Migration was a major part of the experience of the French population in the first half of the nineteenth century, as virtually every kind of record makes apparent. Precise measurement is difficult, however, because migration was not irreversible and frequently was only temporary. Measures of migration, therefore, only begin to describe the true dimensions of the movement of the French population. They do suggest, however, that migration in this period was both from the countryside to the cities, especially the large urban centers such as Paris, Lyons, Bordeaux and Marseilles, and between rural areas. Most cities owed much of their population growth to immigration rather than natural increase, drawing population in from the surrounding countryside. Perhaps the largest amount of migration, however, was from one rural area to another.

These general statements cannot adequately cover the complex patterns of migration that existed in early nineteenth-century France. Migration may be described in terms of both the extent of the break with the migrant's place of origin and the distance moved. Much early nineteenth-century migration was temporary, as many rural residents traveled relatively short distances to nearby cities to work in industry or as domestic servants until they could establish a farm and then returned to their native village. Others followed well-established routes of migration to other rural areas to help with harvests and periods of high labor demand in viti-culture. Other temporary migrants traveled farther, however: stonemasons from the Limousin traveled long distances to Paris and other major cities for the building season and then returned home in the autumn and winter. By the middle of the nineteenth century, some 45,000 of these seasonal building workers were leaving the Limousin for urban construction sites each year but returning as construction activity ended for the winter.

These temporary migrations, whatever their distance, resulted from a number of causes: the poverty of the migrants' native villages, the lack of local resources and employment, the need for specie to pay taxes, and overpopulation in many areas. Yet they were not definitive, and even the mentality of the migrant remained that of a peasant; the difficulty of the work did not matter, and even the smallest amount of income was worth earning.

Increasingly in the early nineteenth century, permanent migration joined and superseded in importance these patterns of temporary migrations, as industrial employment in the cities became a larger part of the labor force. To some extent this definitive migration developed from earlier patterns of temporary migration. The construction workers of the Limousin, for example, began to stay longer in the cities, bringing their families to stay with them and finally remaining permanently. In many cases the experiences and contacts acquired through temporary migration made definitive rural-urban migration easier, as both types of migrants followed a kind of chain. Permanent migration followed much the same routes as temporary migration. Both drew on the populations of the Massif central in the center of France, with routes heading for Paris, the southwest Atlantic coast, and the Saone-Rhone corridor in the southeast. By the end of the period, temporary migration remained an important part of the patterns of mobility of the French population, but permanent migration had established itself as a major part as well.

A. Chatelain, *Les Migrants temporaires en France de 1800 à 1914* (Villeneuve-d'Ascq, 1976); L. Chevalier, *Laboring Classes and Dangerous Classes in Paris during the First Half of the Nineteenth Century*, trans. Frank Jellinek (New York, 1973) and *La Formation de la population parisienne au XIXe siècle* (Paris, 1950); C. H. Pouthas, *La Population française pendant la première moitié du XIXe siècle* (Paris, 1952).

*James Lehning*
*Related entries:* DOMESTIC SERVANTS; PEASANTRY; POPULATION.

**MILLET, JEAN-FRANCOIS** (1814–1875), painter. Millet came from a family of peasants and grew up on a farm. He demonstrated artistic ability early. After studying with the painter Langlois de Chevreville, he left for Paris in 1837, where he painted for two years in the atelier of Paul Delaroche, who considered him uneducated and unteachable. To earn money, Millet made chalk drawings in imitation of eighteenth-century rococo artists, as well as commercial signs and portraits. In 1840 he exhibited at the Salon for the first time, with a portrait. In 1841 he married Pauline Ono but was back in Paris by 1842. He exhibited *The Milkmaid* and *The Riding Lesson* at the Salon of 1844, the year of his wife's death. In 1845 he remarried (Catherine Lemaire) and held a successful exhibition in Le Harve. After his *St. Jerome* was rejected by the Salon of 1846, his *Winnower* was accepted at the Salon of 1848. At this time he began to win the praise of Théodore Rousseau; however, his fame was still questionable as Théophile Gautier called him "le peintre de l'ignoble." After the Revolution of 1848, Millet settled in Barbizon, where he was to spend the last years of his life painting the scenes of rural life. In 1870 the Franco-Prussian War prompted his return to Cherbourg, where he painted seascapes. In 1874 he was commissioned to execute decorations for the Pantheon, but these were never completed. During the pinnacle of his success in the later nineteenth century, his work became extremely popular and was shown by many American museums. The Louvre in Paris, however, acquired the most important examples: *The Gleaners* (1857), *The Angelus* (1858), and *Church at Gréville* (1871).

Millet always painted from memory, never from nature, and with his unusual vision he achieved a grandeur and dignity without lessening his rusticity in the least. He said of himself, "I make the trivial an expression of the sublime." In 1850 he painted his famous *The Sower* (Museum of Fine Arts, Boston), and his masterpiece *Man with a Hoe* was painted in 1862. But just as he was becoming popular, he died and left his widow poverty stricken.

The distinguishing feature of Millet's art is its simplified hero of the soil flavor and its synthetized technique, which gives his drawings, so admired by Vincent Van Gogh, the same power as his painting. In the late 1840s, after early attempts at mythological and religious subjects, Millet found his characteristic theme in the romantic veneration for rural life. Following in the tradition of the Le Nain brothers and Chardin, Millet's work may also be related to the viewpoint of Gustave Courbet, and Honoré Daumier, who frequently drew their subjects from the lower classes. Millet's work is not marked by sentimentality but rather by a deeply rooted respect for the peasants with whom he remained in close proximity. His wood-cutters, reapers, and gleaners are painted with monumental elegance. His dignified, frequently extremely religious images of peasants at work were to influence directly such important artists as Georges Seurat and Van Gogh.

Paul Bell, *Millet* (London, 1928); L. Bénédite, *The Drawings of Jean-François Millet* (London, 1906); L. Delteil, *Le Peintre-graveur illustré*, Vol. 1 (Paris, 1906); R. Herbert, *Barbizon Revisited* (Boston, 1962) and "Millet Revisited," *Burlington Magazine* 104 (July and September 1962); Moreau-Nelation, *Millet raconté par lui-même* (Paris, 1921).

*Irene Earls*

*Related entries:* DAUMIER; DELAROCHE; GAUTIER.

*MILLIARD DES EMIGRES.* See INDEMNITY BILL OF 1825.

*LA MINERVE* (1818–1820), left-wing newspaper of the early Restoration. Left-wing attacks on the moderate ministry of Elie Decazes were cleverly sustained by a nondaily journal that began in February 1818 and appeared fifty-two times a year at irregular intervals, thereby evading the police controls that fell upon the periodical press. In government records and royalist literature, the *Minerve* figures as a Bonapartist paper because it sympathized with old soldiers discharged from Napoleon's armies and because it published the poems of Pierre-Jean de Béranger. The regular contributors to the *Minerve*—Etienne de Jouy, Pierre Tissot, Charles-Guillaume Etienne, Antoine Jay, Evariste Dumoulin, Etienne Aignan, and Benjamin Constant—were all men who had held posts under Napoleon and lost them with the return of the king. This made them particularly sensitive to the rise of royal favorites. There is no real evidence that they wished to overthrow the monarchy, however. Their anti-aristocratic and anticlerical prejudices were shared by most of the left-wing press. Since the *Minerve* was not a newspaper but a review, opinions often had to be expressed in the form of literary criticism. This was most easily done by attacking romantic literature, which the *Minerve* presented purely and simply as propaganda for the glorification of feudalism. Even Benjamin Constant discarded his romantic proclivities when he wrote for the *Minerve*, where he criticized Mme. de Staël's *Considérations* for giving too favorable a view of the aristocracy. Again, however, the defense of classicism was common among left-wing critics during the Restoration.

Subscriptions to the *Minerve* rose within a year from 1,500 to 10,000, the highest figure recorded for a nondaily paper during the Restoration and higher than that of most daily newspapers. The popularity of the journal was chiefly due to a series of articles by Etienne entitled "Lettres sur Paris." Etienne's great skill lay in satirical analysis of the nature and working of bureaucracy. Often the letters were concerned with specific abuses, of which information was obtained from communes in the remotest corners of France. In this way the centralizing tendencies of the restored monarchy were brought home pointedly to thousands of readers.

The *Minerve* absorbed the writers of the former *Mercure de France*, a journal struck down by censorship in February 1818. In its turn the *Minerve* ceased publication rather than conform to the censorship law of 1820.

I. Collins, "Liberalism and the Newspaper Press during the French Restoration," *History* 46 (1961); E. Harpaz, *L'Ecole libérale sous la Restauration: le Mercure et la Minerve* (Geneva, 1968); P. D. S. Pedric, *Le Groupe littéraire de la Minerve française, 1818–1820* (Paris, 1927); L. Thiéssé, *M. Etienne* (Paris, 1853).

*Irene Collins*

*Related entries:* CENSORSHIP; CONSTANT; DECAZES; DUMOULIN; JAY; JOUY; *MERCURE DU XIXe SIECLE*; STAEL-HOLSTEIN; TISSOT.


**MIRACLE CHILD.** See BORDEAUX.


*LE MIROIR DES SPECTACLES* (1821–1823), literary and satirical review; became *La Pandore*, 1823–1828. The *Miroir*'s title continued *letters, manners and arts*, and for the most part it was a magazine of criticism, theater, and fashion. Not infrequently, however, it voiced the liberal political ideas of its editors, who included Etienne de Jouy, Antone-Vincent Arnault, Emmanuel Dupaty, and Louis Cauchois-Lemaire. Such articles, although usually veiled in allusion and allegory in the "little journals," were behind the provision of the 1828 press law to extend the caution money bond to all periodicals. *La Pandore* protested vehemently and, in spite of a large reduction in the proposed bond, was unable to survive financially. An earlier trial of *Le Miroir* had resulted in acquittal on the grounds that satirical allusions were not criminal acts.

C. Ledré, *La Presse a l'assaut de la monarchie* (Paris, 1960).

*Daniel Rader*

*Related entries:* CAUCHOIS-LEMAIRE; JOUY; PRESS LAWS.


**MISSIONS.** The Catholic church of France took advantage of the support it received from the Bourbon government to mount a major effort to rechristianize the French population by means of missions, which were similar to the revivals organized by groups like the Wesleyan Methodists in the English-speaking countries. They offered during a period of several weeks a series of sermons aimed at various groups of the faithful, some pious exercises, and some big outdoor demonstrations, such as processions and raising of crosses. A Société des missions de France, founded by Jean-Baptiste Rauzan, a priest from Bordeaux, devoted itself mainly to this work. Its headquarters were at Mount Valérien, a former place of pilgrimage at the gates of Paris. Other congregations also joined in the effort: Lazarists, Montfortains, and Oblats of Marie-Immaculée, an order founded by Father de Mazenod, which was especially active in the south of France. The results of these efforts appear to have been largely positive, despite the hostility that was reawakened in part of the French public. This was caused in part by the lack of tact demonstrated by certain preachers, the overuse of spectacular demonstrations, and the confusion too often created between religious faith and devotion to the restored Bourbons.

E. Sevrin, *Les Missions religieuses en France sous la Restauration*, 2 vols. (Paris, 1948–59).

*Guillaume de Bertier de Sauvigny, trans. E. Newman*
*Related entries:* MAZENOD; MISSIONS OF THE HOLY SPIRIT; RAUZAN.


**MISSIONS OF THE HOLY SPIRIT.** The original Society of the Holy Spirit had been founded in Paris in 1703 by a priest from Rennes, Claude-François Poullart des Places. Its original purpose had been the training of poor students for the priesthood. Toward the end of the eighteenth century, a number of its subjects had been sent as missionaries to distant colonies in the Far East, Africa, and America. Along with the other religious societies, the Society of the Holy Spirit was dissolved by a decree of the Revolutionary government (August 1792). Napoleon allowed its restoration in 1805 because of the services he expected from the missionaries as informers abroad. Louis XVIII gave legal confirmation and provided financial help for the recovery of its vast former mother-house in Paris, located on the rue des Postes. In 1840 another society was born in Amiens, designed for the special purpose of ministering to the poor Negro workers and slaves in the colonies of Africa and America; the founder was François-Marie-Paul Liberman (1802–52), the son of an Alsatian rabbi converted to Catholicism. His society, under the title of Congrégation du Saint-Coeur de Marie, grew rapidly, but it lacked legal status. Liberman, considering that his priests worked in the same field as those of the Holy Spirit Society, proposed to consolidate both of the organizations into a single body; this was done in 1848 by a decree of the Holy See. The older society provided the legal umbrella, and the younger provided an infusion of younger blood and inspiration. The delicate operation was smoothly concluded, and the *spiritains*, as they came to be called, were to become some of the most active French missionary priests during the second half of the nineteenth century.

P. Blanchard, *Le Vénérable Liberman*, 2 vols. (Paris, 1960); H. Le Floch, *Claude-François Poullart des Places* (Paris, 1915).

*Guillaume de Bertier de Sauvigny, trans. E. Newman*
*Related entry:* MISSIONS.

**MIXED COMMISSIONS**, special tribunals set up after the coup d'état of 2 December 1851. In the aftermath of the coup d'état of 2 December 1851, the prefects, military authorities, and public prosecutors of France arrested about 30,000 individuals, including not only participants in the uprisings against the coup but also "subversives" singled out for republican or socialist activity. On 29 January 1852, the minister of the interior directed the prefects to release all those who had merely been "misled," but this still left far too many prisoners to be dealt with either by the ordinary procedures of the regular courts or by courts-martial that disposed of a limited range of sentences. The government sought an administrative solution to its problem. The circular of 3 February 1852, signed jointly by the ministers of justice, war, and the interior, created in every department a sort of mixed tribunal or departmental commission comprising the prefect, the military commander, and the public prosecutor of the departmental capital. These committees, commonly called mixed commissions, were to examine every prisoner's case and to make a decision on his fate before the end of the month. The commissions deliberated in secret, considering only the dossiers submitted to them by the arresting authority; they neither interviewed the prisoner nor gave him the opportunity to respond to the charges. The commissions had full discretionary power to apply a wide range of sentences, which excluded, however, imprisonment, hard labor, or death. These were: release; trial by court-martial (for murder or attempted murder); trial by civilian court (for minor offenses); transportation to the harsh tropical penal colony at Cayenne; "Algeria plus" (transportation to an Algerian penal colony); "Algeria minus" (transportation to an Algerian town of the prisoner's choice); permanent expulsion from France; temporary exile from France; forced residence in an assigned town in France; and forced residence in a French town of the prisoner's choice.

The whole operation was highly irregular, violating all established judicial norms. The mixed commissions made arbitrary decisions based not on incontrovertible legal proof of specific criminal acts but on one-sided evidence and subjective judgments as to the moral character and political reliability of the prisoners. As the prosecutor in Nancy wrote: "Our mission was less judicial than political, . . . less a matter of sentencing the guilty than of delivering society from the pernicious elements which have been threatening to dissolve it."

The commissions handled 26,884 cases in 82 departments (all of France except Corsica and three Breton departments). An incomplete tally gives the following results: freed, 5,609; court-martialed, 315; sent before civilian courts, 1,319; Cayenne, 239; Algeria plus, 4,549; Algeria minus, 5,032; permanently expelled, 980; temporarily exiled, 640; forced residence in an assigned town, 2,827; forced residence in a freely chosen town, 5,194. Sentences tended to be harshest in regions where armed resistance to the coup had been fiercest. Alleged leaders—which usually meant those who belonged to secret societies or who had engaged in organizational and propaganda work—earned more severe penalties than ordinary participants in insurrection. The commissions, as instructed, often spared prisoners with important family connections, but they also tended to punish the middle and upper classes more than peasants and workers.

The presidential decree of 5 March 1852 issued under the powers assumed by Louis-Napoleon Bonaparte (and approved by national plebiscite) formally authorized the application of the mixed commissions' decisions. Thus, although procedures may have been illegal, as some critics protested, the legality of the penalties themselves was upheld by the court of appeals even after the fall of the Empire. The decree of 27 March 1852, which lifted martial law in France, dissolved the mixed commissions. The day before, the president had appointed three special commissioners to review the penalties; they issued commutations or amnesties in about 2,000 cases. The emperor also granted individual pardons over the following years and finally issued a general amnesty on 16 August 1859.

T. R. Forstenzer, *French Provincial Police and the Fall of the Second Republic* (Princeton, 1981); T. W. Margadant, *French Peasants in Revolt: The Insurrection of 1851* (Princeton, 1979); H. C. Payne, *The Police State of Louis-Napoleon Bonaparte, 1851–1860* (Seattle, 1966); C. Seignobos, "Les Operations des commissions mixtes en 1852," *La Révolution de 1848* 6 (1909–10).

*Michael Sibalis*

*Related entry:* COUP D'ETAT OF 2 DECEMBER 1851.


**MOBILE GUARD.** See GARDE MOBILE.


*LA MODE* (1829–1854), fashion journal of the Restoration and legitimist newspaper of the July Monarchy. Among the numerous specialized journals that appeared toward the end of the Bourbon monarchy, *La Mode*, founded by Emile de Girardin and Lautour-Mézeray, was a fashion journal catering to women. After the Revolution of 1830, however, it changed its character and became a vigorous carlist newspaper. It recruited a number of spectacular writers, including the vicomte Walsh and occasionally Honoré de Balzac. In spite of the reluctance of juries to apply the severe press laws of 1835, *La Mode* was prosecuted three times between 1835 and 1840. It nevertheless survived to take part in a great congress of legitimist journalists in 1850.

E. de Grenville, *Histoire d'un journal: "la Mode"* (Paris, 1861).

*Irene Collins*

*Related entries:* BALZAC; GIRARDIN; LEGITIMISM; PRESS LAWS; RE-VOLUTION OF 1830.


**MOLE, LOUIS-MATHIEU, COMTE DE** (1781–1855), statesman. A descendant of an old parliamentary family, Molé became an influential statesman whose political career embraced the first half of the nineteenth century. He participated in each of the three regimes of that period in important posts but never quite gained the prominence or influence of his sometime political allies, François Guizot and Adolphe Thiers. Some accused him of lacking political conviction. He preferred to see himself as a public servant seeking moderation and reconciliation in an age of political extremes.

Molé first came to the attention of Napoleon when he published at the age of twenty-five his *Essai de morale et politique*. Some accused Molé of writing this apology for despotism as a means to gain public employment. Whatever the degree of truth in this, the work seems to reflect Molé's fundamental political views whether in service of Napleon, Louis XVIII, or Louis-Philippe. In it he argued that monarchy—including an emperor like Napoleon—was the natural form of government, since order was the instinctive aspiration and object of society. Like many other admirers of England, however, he called for a mixed monarchy to include intermediary institutions and especially a powerful aristocracy to guarantee liberty and the authority of the monarch. Unlike others who revered England, however, Molé worried that too much power rested in the English Parliament and not enough in the monarch. Foreshadowing Alexis de Tocqueville, he maintained that social hierarchy and the preservation of social conventions and morés were necessary to protect against society's being reduced to a mass of individuals. Having lived through the Revolution, in which his father lost his life in 1794 on the scaffold, Molé argued that the Enlightenment and the excessive attention to human reason was partly responsible for bringing anarchy to France. Only the sword of the conqueror (Napoleon) had saved France from this, but the true principles on which morality, politics, and social order rest were yet to be restored.

Napoleon was sufficiently impressed with Molé's *Essai* to call him to serve in several important capacities: *auditeur*, *maître des requêtes* to the *Conseil d'état*, prefect of Côte d' Or, director general of *Ponts et chausées* and, finally, minister of justice in 1813. In all he was a loyal admirer of Napoleon and an effective administrator for the Empire. Seen as one of the dangerous aides of Napoleonic despotism, Molé was eliminated from political office during the First Restoration. Upon Napoleon's return during the Hundred Days, Molé was again offered a place on the Conseil d'état and was named a peer on 2 June 1815. Probably out of a combination of conviction and political good sense, Molé refused to sign the famous declaration of principles of the Conseil d'état, which called for the sovereignty of the people, and he abstained from sitting with the Conseil. With the Second Restoration Louis XVIII recognized this allegiance to the Bourbons and named him a peer of France.

In his memoirs Molé acknowledged the enthusiastic welcome given the Bourbons upon their return but also stated his own reservations. He especially feared that the Bourbons would identify too closely with the *émigrés* and the interests of the Old Regime. Significantly, he pointed out that Napoleon was disliked by the people not for his despotism but because of his wars. Napoleon had guaranteed the interests of the Revolution, but the people trusted the Bourbons less and therefore demanded a liberal constitution. This was not, according to Molé, so much for its guarantee of liberties as for its protection of those who benefited from the Revolution. He continued his advocacy of a strong role for an aristocracy but one that was based on wealth and services, as well as family lineage, and one that was dedicated to modern civilization. He worried that the peerage of the Restoration might not be able to fulfill its appointed role because it lacked historic names and its members were chosen too frequently just to please various parties rather than for their prestige and standing.

During the Restoration Molé was a strong opponent of the ultras, giving his fullest support to the Richelieu ministries. He served as minister of the navy (12 September 1817–28 December 1818) in the second Richelieu cabinet and helped to enact a law making the slave trade illegal. Afterwards he supported a moderate course after but worried that Elie Decazes and the liberals advocated too much democratization. With the assassination of the duc de Berry, Molé joined with those who sought some retrenchment from the liberal gains of the past two years, but he strenuously opposed what he saw as the Villèle ministry's reactionary innovations. He spoke out especially in opposition to the proposed law on primogeniture, which, he argued, was contrary to the spirit of the Civil Code and, more important, an affront to the new interests.

A strong opponent of the Polignac ministry, Molé was still not an enthusiastic supporter of the July Revolution. He saw 1830 as a veritable social revolution and not like England's 1688. He fought, unsuccessfully, for retaining the heredity of the peerage as the last dike braking the forceful push toward equality but despaired that an aristocracy, even a liberal one, was no longer possible in France.

Still, Molé was to play an active role in the politics of the July Monarchy. Despite his ambivalence to the 1830 Revolution, Molé rallied early to Louis-Philippe. The new king appointed him to the Ministry of Foreign Affairs, where he tried to reassure foreign powers by pursuing a policy of nonintervention in the revolutions elsewhere in Europe. But Molé soon left office to help lead those in the chambers resisting a more dynamic foreign and domestic policy. In 1836, after the fall of Thiers, Molé again took up the Ministry of Foreign Affairs, only to leave office six months later with the fall of the cabinet.

For the next three years Molé was to find himself in the middle of frequent parliamentary realignments and changes of ministries. In 1837 Louis-Philippe appointed Molé to the presidency of the Council of Ministers, hoping to take advantage of his relative independence from all parties and his attachment to order. Louis-Philippe may have also thought he could have more personal control over the government with Molé as prime minister. Unfortunately for Molé he won the jealous enmity of Guizot and the political opposition of Thiers and the dynastic opposition. Despite the fact that Guizot, on the one side, and Thiers and the dynastic opposition on the other, were caught up in debating how much power the king should have in relation to the chambers, all managed to coalesce and declare war on ''the court government.'' Molé survived one crisis in 1837, but in late 1838 a strong coalition of Guizot, Thiers, Pierre-Antoine Berryer, and Odilon Barrot called for the fall of the ministry in the name of parliamentary responsibility. Molé also created opposition to himself and Louis-Philippe by his generous treatment of the former ministers of Charles X and his attempts at rapprochement with the absolutist powers. Still, he held firm against the opposition to his ministry and survived a vote of confidence in the Chamber of Deputies by eight votes. Hoping to increase his support, he obtained from the crown a dissolution of the Chamber. But in the ensuing electoral struggle, the government lost thirty seats, and Molé sent in his resignation on 8 March 1839. During the next eight years, he remained active in the debates in the Chamber of Peers. In 1840 he was called to Académie française.

Events in 1848 again brought Molé to power, if only fleetingly. Louis-Philippe called Molé to head the government in the last days of February after the crowds in the streets had successfully gained Guizot's resignation. But events quickly eliminated Molé as an option and the Republic was proclaimed. In September 1848 he was elected as a deputy from the Gironde to the Constituent Assembly, where he first supported Eugène Cavaignac as the best guarantee for order. In 1849 he was elected to the Legislative Assembly, where he tried to bring together legitimists and Orleanists. Finally on 2 December 1851 his political career ended when he and others were arrested by Louis-Napoleon. He was soon released, but for the remainder of his life he watched the political scene as a private citizen.

A. de Barante, "Elogé de . . . ," *Bulletin de la société de l'histoire de France* (1855– 56); Lacour-Gayet, *Le Cte Molé* (Paris, 1931); L.-M. Molé, *Essais de morale et de politique* (Paris, 1806) and *Life and Memoirs*, 4 vols. (New York, 1924).

*Sanford Gutman*

*Related entries:* BARROT, C.-H.-O.; BERRYER, P.-A.; BRIDGE AND ROAD SERVICE; CAVAIGNAC, L.-E.; COUNCIL OF STATE; DECAZES; GUIZOT; HEREDITY LAWS; RICHELIEU; THIERS; TOCQUEVILLE; VILLELE.

**MOLLIEN, FRANCOIS-NICOLAS, COMTE** (1758–1850), minister of the Empire; peer of the Restoration and July Monarchy. Born on 28 February 1758 at Rouen, Mollien studied in Paris and entered the Ministry of Finance. In 1784 he became supervisor of the general farms and urged on Calonne policies that led to the construction of the octroi barriers around Paris. He left government service on 10 August 1792 and went into the cotton business. However, he was arrested in February 1794 for suspected complicity with the farmers-general. Mollien gained his freedom after the fall of Robespierre and went to England, ostensibly to study the English financial system. He returned to France shortly before 18 Brumaire.

The Consulate appointed him director of the sinking fund, established to back up promissory notes and to manage the government bond market. Napoleon consulted him on reorganizing the Bank of France, on the sinking fund, and on various taxes. In fact it was Mollien who taught Napoleon much of whatever he knew of economics. After the threatened collapse of the Bank of France in 1805, Napleon on 26 January 1806 appointed Mollien to be minister of the treasury, an office he retained until 30 March 1814. On 26 April 1808 Napoleon appointed Mollien a count of the Empire. In 1814, when the Allies approached Paris, Mollien accompanied Marie Louise to Blois and then lived in retirement during the First Restoration. When Napoleon returned in 1815, he summoned Mollien back to the treasury.

After Waterloo Mollien retired to his estate of Jeurs near Etampes. In 1818 and 1819 Armand-Emmanuel de Richelieu and Elie Decazes offered him cabinet posts, which he declined. But on 5 March 1819 he was named to the Chamber of Peers, where he frequently served on matters dealing with financial affairs. He became a leading influence in the upper Chamber, where he adopted a strong constitutional royalist position and opposed such ultra measures as the 1826 proposal on primogeniture. Mollien remained in the Peers after 1830, presiding over a project to improve Parisian commerce and serving on the High Council of Commerce and the General Council of the department of Seine-et-Oise. When Mollien, the last surviving minister of the Empire, died in Paris on 20 April 1850, Napoleon III memorialized him by naming one of the pavilions of the new wing of the Louvre for him. Although Mollien was not one of the most flamboyant cabinet ministers, he was one of the most competent and conscientious. He also was one who dared to oppose Napoleon. Mollien left his *Mémoires d'un ministre du trésor*, initially written during the 1820s and published in 1845.

*Archives parlementaires*; M. Marion, *Histoire financière de la France depuis 1715* (Paris, 1914–31); A. Robert et al., *Dictionnaire des parlementaires français* (Paris, 1889–91); R. Stourm, *Les Finances du Consulate* (Paris, 1902).

*James K. Kieswetter*

*Related entries:* BANKING; BOURSE, PARIS; CHAMBER OF PEERS; DECAZES; DOCTRINAIRES; HUNDRED DAYS; RICHELIEU; ULTRA-ROYALISTS.

*LE MONDE* (16 November 1836–1 November 1837), an unsuccessful daily newspaper founded by F.-L. Pistor. This moderate opposition journal advocated pacifism, free trade, and European union. It is noteworthy for two reasons: Félicité de Lamennais was its editor for four months, and George Sand contributed to it a series of articles on women's emancipation. Early in 1837 Lamennais needed money and seized the opportunity offered by Pistor to take over the paper and have complete freedom as to the paper's content. He was editor from 10 February to 4 June 1837, and the paper's circulation rose to just under 700. At this time Lamennais was close to Sand, who never ceased to admire the publicist and social reformer. Charles Didier (1805–64), a minor literary figure and friend of Sand, helped edit the paper, and she herself agreed to contribute articles even though the *Journal des débats* had made her a more lucrative offer. These articles were the famous *Lettres à Marcie*, six of which were published in *Le Monde*. Written in the form of a fictional correspondence, they presented Sand's views on the place of women in contemporary society and quickly became the subject of controversy in Parisian literary circles. Sand spoke out against what she regarded as the stifling of women's intellectual and emotional growth, but when she wanted to write an article in favor of the right to divorce, the misogynist Lamennais, who always defended the family, objected (he had already censored the third of the six articles Sand had published), and her collaboration ceased.

*Barrie M. Ratcliffe*

Related entries: *JOURNAL DES DEBATS*; LAMENNAIS; SAND.


*LE MONITEUR*, official newspaper of the French government for edicts, laws, debates, and presentation of administrative policy; begun in 1789 and continued under a variety of names. In September 1789, Bernard Maret (later duke of Bassano) began to publish his *Bulletin de l'assemblée nationale* at Versailles. This journal offered popular and lively coverage of current debates and soon followed the Assembly and the king to Paris. Soon, however, a competitor appeared: The *Moniteur universel* or *Gazette nationale*, the private enterprise of Charles-Joseph Panckoucke. It started publication 24 November 1789 and also recorded official decrees and debates. The *Bulletin* and the *Moniteur* merged on 2 February 1790, when Maret's columns under his paper's separate title were inserted in each issue of the *Moniteur*. Maret also won the admiration of fellow journalists by forcing the Assembly to admit newspaper reporters to its audience. The family-operated *Moniteur* was informally accepted as the government's paper. Panckoucke's family stock company continued its legal ownership even when Revolutionary changes deprived it of control.

By a decree of Nivôse VIII, the paper was formally adopted by the government. During the First Restoration, it was suppressed, appearing infrequently under the title *Gazette officielle*. Panckoucke's heirs, still holding their stock, restored it in February 1815, and this family-government relationship continued until 1868 when it was bought out by the Wittersheim family, under the aegis of the Interior Ministry, and thereafter called *Le Journal officiel*.

Beyond enlightening the public about the policies and practices of each new ministry or chamber over the decades, the *Moniteur*'s publication literally enacted the law. Rarely, the appointed editors added columns of opinion, always dictated at least indirectly by an agent of the ministry in power. *Moniteur* editors were summoned to the Tuileries, the Palais royal, or the Elysée in times of crisis and were the first reporters to know officially of wars, coups, or edicts. The paper has always been useful to historians as an available source of documents although selective and limited in those relating to judicial and legislative actions.

I. Collins, *The Government and the Newspaper Press in France* (Oxford, 1959); E. Hatin, *Histoire de la presse* (Paris, 1859–61); F. Mitton, *La Presse française sous la révolution, le consulat, et l'empire (Paris, 1945)*.

*Daniel Rader*


**MONTALEMBERT, CHARLES-FORBES, COMTE DE** (1810–1870), politician, notable, liberal Catholic. The Montalembert family, which traced its aristocratic origins back to the Crusades, emigrated during the Revolution to London, where Charles was born. Upon returning to France, he graduated from

Sainte-Barbe and then resided again for three years during his late teens outside France, when he became interested in Irish and Belgic politics (particularly the seating of Daniel O'Connell in the British House of Commons). In his youth, then, he demonstrated a combined interest in both liberal and Catholic causes, which presaged his liberal Catholicism and his leadership of the cause of liberty of education in France during the July Monarchy.

Captivated by the ideas of Félicité de Lamennais as expressed in an early issue of *L'Avenir*, whose motto was "God and Liberty" and which Montalembert read while still in Ireland, he became a junior associate of Lamennais and Henri Lacordaire within months after they launched *L'Avenir* in 1830. By advocating freedom of association, press, religion, and education, as well as demanding that the church adjust to the new social and political exigencies of time, the newspaper managed to alienate the Orleanist monarchy, conservative French bishops, and the Vatican. Responding to Lamennais', Lacordaire's, and Montalembert's appeal to the pope over episcopal sanctions against *L'Avenir*, Gregory XVI's encyclical, *Mirari Vos* (15 August 1832), condemned many of the ideas of *L'Avenir*. Although Lamennais broke with the church, Montalembert formally submitted in 1834 before retiring for a year to the family estate.

Wearied but not broken at age twenty-five by his travails, he returned to a Paris circle of liberal and social Catholics and devoted his energies to the specific cause of liberty of education: the right of private individuals (specifically clergy) to conduct secondary schools, a right that, during the July Monarchy, remained a monopoly of the state. With the demise of *L'Avenir*, Montalembert looked to a new podium and became a shareholder in the recently (1833) founded, rather scholarly, and still obscure (1,000–2,000 subscribers) *L'Univers*. With Montalembert's influence, the newspaper became more political but remained relatively moderate in tone until Louis Veuillot became first a contributor (1840) and then an editor (1842). Although they managed to collaborate on the question of liberty of education, Montalembert was calling Veuillot a devil by 1846, and his last article (1870) was an attack on Veuillot, the Syllabus of Errors, and the ultramontanism that culminated in Vatican Council I's declaration of papal infallibility.

Arguing within the spirit of classical liberalism, Montalembert insisted in an 1839 letter to the minister of education, Abel-François Villemain, that both lay public and private Catholic schools, the latter of which could be directed by a layman, should coexist. Rallying around him liberal members of the episcopacy like Bishop Félix Dupanloup and Bishop Marie-Dominique Sibour together with conservative bishops like Louis Pie and Jean-Marie Doney, the democrat Lamenais, and the reactionary Veuillot, Montalembert forged a rare unity among Catholics. After the defeat of a compromise measure by Villemain in 1844, Montalembert organized a Catholic party (Comité pour la défense de la liberté religieuse) to contest the 1846 elections on the issue of liberty of education; another newspaper, *La Gazette de France*, had made an earlier unheeded call that may have encouraged Montalembert. Newspaper agitation, the publication of about 45,000 copies of an 1843 speech by Montalembert, and the publication (1844) of his *Du devoir des catholiques dans les élections* brought some results. The issue received wide public attention; 146 elected deputies committed themselves to the principle of liberty of education, but by no means all of those had it a high priority. Montalembert would achieve his goal, however, only with the Falloux Law of 1850 that followed upon the revolutionary overthrow of the July Monarchy.

Frightened by the social turmoil of 1848 and the insurrections in the Papal States, and always preferring the corporative society of the Middle Ages to republican democracy, Montalembert supported the electoral law of 31 May 1850, which disenfranchised many working-class Frenchmen, and remained silent in the face of Louis-Napoleon's coup d'état while he served as a deputy from Doubs. He remained consistent on the principle of liberty of education, however, vigorously opposing an 1849 offer of a monopoly of education made by Thiers, who hoped the church could restore social order. The Falloux Law's dual system of education with both church and state operating schools was the incarnation of Montalembert's dream; one year later he was elected to the Académie française. He broke with the Bonapartist regime after his election to the Corps législatif in 1852, publishing that same year *Les Intérêts catholiques au XIXe siècle*. In 1855 he joined with other liberal Catholics in reorganizing the third major Catholic journal of his career, *Le Correspondant*.

His last fifteen years were frustrating ones during which he defended Catholicism against positivism and secularism but disputed reactionary and ultramontane Catholics; his bitterest rival was his old ally Veuillot. His final article, published posthumously in 1870, tried to prevent the spirit of the papacy's 1864 *Syllabus of Errors* being made articles of faith by Vatican Council I.

A. Dansette, *Religious History of Modern France*, vol. 1 (New York, 1961); E. Lecanuet, *La Comte de Montalembert d'après son journal et sa correspondance*, 3 vols. (Paris, 1895–1902); J. Moody, "The French Catholic Press in the Education Conflict of the 1840s," *French Historical Studies* 7 (Spring 1972).

*Patrick J. Harrigan*

Related entries: *L'AVENIR*; DUPANLOUP; FALLOUX LAW; *LA GAZETTE DE FRANCE*; LACORDAIRE; LAMENNAIS; LIBERAL CATHOLICISM; LIBERTY OF EDUCATION; SOCIAL CATHOLICISM; THIERS; ULTRA-MONTANES; VEUILLOT; VILLEMAIN.


**MONTALIVET, MARTHE-CAMILLE-BACHASSON, COMTE DE** (1801–1880), peer of the Restoration, minister of the July Monarchy, senator of the Third Republic. Marthe de Montalivet was born at Valence (Drôme) on 24 April 1801, the second son of Jean-Pierre de Montalivet. He studied at the Collège Henri IV and the Ecole polytechnique, preparing for a career in civil engineering. But when his father and elder brother both died in 1823, he inherited his father's title of count and his seat in the Peers. In the Chamber of Peers he advocated a constitutional course, opposed the Polignac ministry of 1829, and supported the

221 deputies who signed the address criticizing the king in March 1830. When the July Revolution broke out, Montalivet was one of the most notable supporters of the Orleanist cause among the peers.

Montalivet quickly rallied to the regime of Louis-Philippe and became a personal follower of him. In August Montalivet became colonel of the National Guard. On 3 November he was appointed minister of the interior. He was immediately confronted with the trial of Charles X's former ministers for whom the mob demanded the death penalty. To avert a riot, Montalivet collaborated closely with the marquis de Lafayette, Etienne-Denis Pasquier, and others to move the ministers to Vincennes at the close of their trial. On 21 December Montalivet himself led the troops in the successful execution of this plan. A few days later, he also handled many of the delicate negotiations that led to the resignation of Lafayette as commander of the Paris National Guard. However, when violent anticlerical riots erupted on 14 February 1831, Montalivet was not able to contain them. At the fall of the Laffitte cabinet in 1831, Louis-Philippe asked Montalivet to help form a new ministry, ultimately headed by Casimir Périer, in which Montalivet was minister of public instruction and worship. Here he accomplished some reforms in primary education. Before his death, Casimir Périer named Montalivet to succeed him as minister of the interior. Thus it was Montalivet who had to deal with the legitimist plot of 1832, as well as with a republican uprising in June 1832. He resigned from the cabinet in October 1832 after a dispute over political principles. He then became intendant general of the civil list. Montalivet returned as minister of the interior from February to September 1836 and then again in the Molé cabinet from April 1837 to March 1839. But this time his work was more closely directed by Louis-Philippe, who, having extended his influence over foreign policy, now supervised domestic policy. Thus Montalivet was criticized for subservience to the king. As minister of the interior, the conduct of elections fell under Montalivet's jurisdiction, and his opponents vigorously attacked him for the use of government influence. But he also was responsible for achieving prison reform, constructing public works, and improving the archives.

After his final resignation from the cabinet, Montalivet devoted himself to his duties with the civil list, which he continued until the February 1848 Revolution. This post involved him in projects such as expanding the Louvre museum, establishing the Museum of Versailles, and restoring other buildings. In 1840 he was elected to the Académie des beaux-arts. He ultimately seems to have supported electoral reform, and he was instrumental in convincing Louis-Philippe on 23 February 1848 that Guizot had to go. Nevertheless he remained close to the Orleanist cause. He escorted Louis-Philippe as he fled Paris and subsequently looked after the property of the Orléans family until its confiscation in 1852. He defended the July Monarchy with various writings during the Second Republic and Second Empire. Although he made no apparent effort to reenter public life for thirty years after the fall of Louis-Philippe, he was not a disinterested observer. After the fall of Napoleon III, Montalivet supported the conservative republicanism of his friend Adolphe Thiers and was critical of the attempted reconciliation between Orleanist and legitimist factions in the early 1870s. His correspondence expressing this view may have shaped the development of the Organic Laws of 1875. In February 1879 he accepted a life senatorship, which was voted to him by 153 of 154 voting. He died on 4 January 1880 in Paris. He left in print various tracts and pamphlets, letters to the *Journal des débats*, a study of Casimir Périer in the *Revue des deux mondes*, and his memoirs, *Fragments et souvenirs* (1899).

*Archives parlementaires*; T. Howarth, *Citizen-King, the Life of Louis-Philippe* (London, 1961); D. Pinkney, *The French Revolution of 1830* (Princeton, 1972); A. Robert et al., *Dictionnaire des parlementaires français* (Paris, 1889–91).

*James K. Kieswetter*

*Related entries:* ACADEMY OF FINE ARTS; GUIZOT; *JOURNAL DES DEBATS;* LAFFITTE; MOLE; PASQUIER; PERIER; POLIGNAC; PUBLIC INSTRUCTION; *LA REVUE DES DEUX MONDES*; THE 221.

**MONTBEL, GUILLAUME-ISADORE, COMTE DE** (1787–1861), ultraroyalist deputy and minister of the Restoration. Born on 4 July 1787 at Toulouse, Montbel, whose father died on the guillotine during the Revolution, became a staunch royalist and a member of the ''banner'' of the Knights of the Faith in Toulouse. He served on the Municipal Council of Toulouse and succeeded his friend, Joseph de Villèle, as mayor. In November 1827 the department of Haute-Garonne elected him to the Chamber of Deputies, where he may have been a member of the secret ''banner'' of the Knights of the Faith in the Chamber. During the Martignac ministry he defended the policies of the Villèle cabinet and attacked the liberals, seemingly without fatigue at his repeated defeats. He especially opposed freedom of the press, blaming opposition journalists for the assassination of the duc de Berry. In 1829 as a political stratagem, he supported the attack on the former ministers by Guillaume-Xavier Labbey de Pompières, a radical liberal. He opposed French involvement in the Greek rebellion. By the spring of 1829 Montbel was clearly recognized as a leader of the ultras, and he was a member of the secret cabinet that the king consulted, although Charles X regarded him as too inexperienced to be a minister.

When the Polignac cabinet was formed on 8 August 1829, Montbel received the Ministry of Ecclesiastical Affairs and Public Instruction, over some objections by Charles. During his three-month tenure he accomplished nothing significant, but he did refuse to sanction canceling the classes offered by Victor Cousin, François Guizot, and Abel-François Villemain. On 18 November he reluctantly became minister of the interior, a shift Jules de Polignac hoped would mollify the cabinet's critics. Although he appointed Jean-Jacques Sirieys de Mayrinhac, an extreme ultra, to head the police, Montbel unsuccessfully tried by repeated statements in the Chamber to improve the cabinet's popularity. During the discussions on the address to the throne in March 1830, he vigorously opposed the version the Deputies adopted. He was one of the first to suggest that Charles dissolve the Chamber and hold new elections, which he was confident they would win. But he also suggested that after the elections were held, the king should appoint a new cabinet. Albeit lacking vigor in its application, Montbel did not hesitate to use government power to attempt to influence the election, instructing the prefects to send him confidential reports on the subject. On 19 May with some reluctance, Montbel became minister of finances, where he remained until the July Revolution. Although he had reservations about the July Ordinances and even tried to resign, he was one of the ministers who signed the ordinances and backed Charles unflinchingly.

When the July Revolution began, Montbel opposed all concessions to the opposition, supported the efforts to put down the uprising, and rejected efforts at conciliation by Charles de Sémonville and Antoine-Maurice d'Argout. When Charles X left Saint-Cloud for Rambouillet, Montbel and others proposed moving the government and the Deputies to Tours. Montbel accompanied the king, urging him to resist. After the duc d'Orléans was made lieutenant general of the kingdom, Montbel returned to Paris and then departed for Switzerland and Vienna, where he continued to aid the royal family and later joined their little court in exile. He was included in the accusation by the Deputies against the former ministers on 28 September 1830. Tried in absentia by the Peers, he and the others were sentenced to civil death and perpetual imprisonment in December 1830. He was the target of a special act of sequestration against his property as a result of the 421,000 francs he had authorized on 28 July to reprovision the king's troops. Montbel published a protest against his conviction in 1831. He was amnestied, along with his fellow former ministers, by the Molé ministry on 26 November 1836. He thereupon returned to France but took no part in public affairs. He subsequently wrote his memoirs and a study of the exile of Charles X. Montbel died at Frohsdorff, Austria, on 3 February 1861 during a visit to the comte de Chambord.

Archives parlementaires; V. Beach, Charles X (Boulder, 1971); J. L. Bory, La Révolution de juillet (Paris, 1972); N. Hudson, Ultra-Royalism and the French Restoration (Cambridge, 1936); D. Pinkney, The French Revolution of 1830 (Princeton, 1972); G. de Bertier de Sauvigny, Le Comte Ferdinand de Bertier (Paris, 1948).

James K. Kieswetter

Related entries: CHEVALIERS DE LA FOI; COUSIN; D'ARGOUT; GUIZOT; LABBEY DE POMPIERES; MARTIGNAC; MOLE; POLIGNAC; SEMON-VILLE; ULTRAROYALISTS; VILLELE; VILLEMAIN.


MONTESQUIOU, FRANCOIS-XAVIER-MARC-ANTOINE DE (1757–1832), abbé and government official. Montesquiou became a priest quite young and distinguished himself by the ability he showed in the important job of general agent of the clergy in 1785. A deputy of the clergy to the Estates General of 1789, he was twice president of the Constituent Assembly. He fled to England in September 1792 but was able to return to France under the Directory, and while there he was one of the secret correspondents of the future Louis XVIII.

In spring 1814 he aided Charles-Maurice de Talleyrand as a member of the Provisional Government and was named minister of the interior by the king. He took an active part in helping to draw up the Constitutional Charter. After the Hundred Days he was given a comfortable retirement in the Chamber of Peers and in the French Academy.

J. de Boislisle, "L'Abbé de Montesquiou, ministre de la Restauration," *Annuaire de la Société d'Histoire de France* (1927).

*Guillaume de Bertier de Sauvigny*

*Related entries:* ACADEMIE FRANCAISE; CHAMBER OF PEERS; CHARTER OF 1814; LOUIS XVIII; TALLEYRAND.

## MONTLOSIER, FRANCOIS-DOMINIQUE REYNAUD, COMTE DE

(1755–1838), deputy to the Estates General, Gallican polemicist, peer of the July Monarchy. Montlosier was born at Clermont-Ferrand (Puy-de-Dôme) on 16 April 1755, the twelfth child of a poor but old noble family. Educated by the Jesuits, he developed a keen interest in history and science. In 1789 he published a study of the volcanoes of the Auvergne. He was elected an alternate deputy to the Estates General and actually took his seat in September 1789. He immediately became a staunch defender of the power and independence of the crown and opposed reforms that would curtail it. He also opposed the Civil Constitution of the Clergy. In 1791 he published in Paris a tract calling for a counterrevolution and detailing the means of achieving it. After the National Assembly completed its work in September 1791, Montlosier went to Coblentz where he joined the *émigré* army and fought with it in 1792, gaining a reputation as a duelist. He subsequently went to Hamburg and then London, where in 1796 he published a tract arguing that any monarchist restoration required the maintenance of much of the Revolutionary heritage. He also joined with Jacques Mallet du Pan, Pierre-Victor Malouet, and Gérard Lally-Tollendal in publishing the French-language paper *Courrier de Londres*. The *Courrier* adopted a moderate position and after the coup of 18 Brumaire supported Napoleon.

Montlosier learned that Charles-Maurice de Talleyrand had requested his return to France. He hastened back, only to be arrested at Calais and briefly imprisoned. Sent back to England, he returned to France again in 1803, this time to stay. He hoped to transfer his journal to Paris under the title *Courrier de Londres et de Paris*, but after a few issues the censor closed it. Napoleon, however, gave him a post at the Foreign Ministry and demanded his collaboration in the *Bulletin de Paris*, for which he wrote extremely anglophobic articles. With the establishment of the Empire, Napoleon assigned Montlosier to write a history of the French monarchy to demonstrate that its fall was inevitable. However, Montlosier, who was perhaps actually a secret agent of Louis XVIII, used the work to urge the reestablishment of the feudal system. Needless to say, the work was shelved until the Restoration published it in 1814 with the addition of a preface that viciously attacked Napoleon. The emperor then assigned Montlosier the task of informing on the opinions of those in his circle. But Napoleon carelessly left a dossier of these reports in his carriage, and Montlosier was thus unmasked. He returned to his scientific interests, going to Italy to study volcanoes in 1812.

Although Montlosier devoted himself to his estates after the fall of Napoleon, he could not stay away from politics. He gained fame for his ultraconservative views, opposing the Charter and supporting direct rule by the crown and the privileges of the aristocracy. Between 1815 and 1817, he published a work on the First Restoration, and in 1825 he became president of the academy of Clermont. But in 1824 his Gallican sensitivities were alarmed by the Jesuits, the Congrégation, and the ultramontanists. After publishing several articles in the *Drapeau blanc*, in 1826 he addressed to the Chamber of Peers a two-volume *Mémoire à consulter*, which attacked these groups as threats to society, the state, and religion. It created an instant furor in the newspapers. Although heavy with bias and conjecture, it contained a considerable amount of truth and quickly went through eight printings. In August 1826 Montlosier laid his complaint before the royal court, which declared itself incompetent. The Peers, however, ultimately forwarded his address to the president of the ministers. The Villèle government subsequently halted the pension Napoleon had given Montlosier. Thus finding himself in the opposition, Montlosier collaborated with the *Constitutionnel* in 1830, albeit still opposing the ideas of revolution just as he had in 1789. After the July Revolution he became councillor-general of Puy-de-Dôme, and in October 1832 Louis-Philippe named him to the Chamber of Peers. He proved to be a vigorous defender of the July Monarchy. At his death in Clermont on 9 December 1838, he refused the last rites of the church from the bishop who demanded as a condition Montlosier's retraction of his religious ideas. The people of Clermont, however, came en masse to his funeral. His other major writings included a two-volume history covering the Revolution through the Restoration, published in 1830, and his own memoirs, published in four volumes in 1831.

*Archives parlementaires*; A. Bardoux, *Etudes sociales et politiques: le comte Montlosier et le gallicanisme* (Paris, 1881); J. Brugerette, *Le Comte de Montlosier et son temps* (Aurillac, 1931); A. Robert et al., *Dictionnaire des parlementaires français* (Paris, 1889–91).

*James K. Kieswetter*

*Related entries:* CONGREGATION; *LE CONSTITUTIONNEL; LE DRAPEAU BLANC*; JESUITS; TALLEYRAND; ULTRAMONTANES; ULTRAROYAL-ISTS; VILLELE.

**MONTMORENCY, MATHIEU-JEAN-FELICITE, DUC DE** (1767–1826), statesman. As a young officer he had taken part in the war for the independence of the United States along with the marquis de Lafayette and, like him, he defended the most liberal ideas before the Constituent Assembly of 1789. But in 1792 he had to leave France to save his head. He found asylum for a while at the home of Mme. de Staël in Coppet. Thanks to her, he was able to return to France during the Directory. The sight of the excesses of the Revolution forced

Montmorency to reconsider his ideas and to adopt new principles based on the monarchy and the Catholic faith. His zeal as a newly converted Catholic led him to devote his time and his resources to good works. He was one of the first members of the Congrégation, which was founded by the former Jesuit Delpuits, and several years later he was one of the first members of the secret society known as the Chevaliers de la foi, of which he became grand master. Helped by this secret network of friendships, he took part in the restoration of the Bourbons and occupied an eminent position at their court, in the Chamber of Peers, and in the councils of the comte d'Artois. In 1821 he became minister of foreign affairs in the royalist government, and in that position he joined with the Allies at the Congress of Verona to prepare France's intervention in Spain. But a minor disagreement with Louis XVIII and with Joseph de Villèle forced him to give up his ministry to François-René de Chateaubriand. Charles X, who held him in high esteem, placed his young grandson, the duc de Bordeaux, in his care in January 1826, but before he could take over these duties he died suddenly while he was praying in the Church of Saint Thomas Aquinas on good Friday, 26 March 1826.

*Guillaume de Bertier de Sauvigny, trans. E. Newman*
*Related entries:* BORDEAUX, DUKE OF; CHATEAUBRIAND; CHEVA-LIERS DE LA FOI; CONGREGATION; SPAIN, 1823 FRENCH INVASION OF; STAEL-HOLSTEIN; VERONA, CONGRESS OF; VILLELE.

**MOREAU, HEGESIPPE,** pseudonym of **PIERRE-JACQUES ROULLIOT** (1811–1838), Parisian poet and sometime typographer; perhaps the best-known and most tragic figure among the French worker poets of the July Monarchy. Whereas most other worker poets gloried in their double status as workers and as poets, Hégésippe Moreau, the ''accursed poet,'' tried to make the leap from the working-class world to the literary world and died trying. He thus became *le poète maudit*, a symbol used by other worker poets and middle-class moralists alike to warn all workers against trying to change their status.

Born Pierre-Jacques Roulliot, the bastard son of a schoolteacher and a servant woman, in Paris in 1811, Hégésippe Moreau had a difficult youth. When he was four, he lost his father to tuberculosis. His mother worked first as a dressmaker and then as the servant in an inn. Her employers took charge of the boy's education, sending him to the collège of Provins and then to the seminary of Avon, near Meaux. After his mother died of tuberculosis when he was eleven, the employers continued to pay for his education. By 1826, Moreau had reached the second class in rhetoric so that his schooling was far superior to that of the other worker poets. He was apprenticed to a typographer and acquired that trade, along with the liberal and democratic political ideas of his coworkers. He fell in love with his boss's daughter, who was married but separated from her husband. At the age of nineteen he fled this situation, leaving both Provins and his profession so that he could go to Paris in search of literary glory. Once in Paris he held a series of odd jobs such as schoolmaster, corrector at the Firmin-

Didot press, and tutor in a pension for students in order to support himself while he wrote. A republican who sympathized with the Girondin phase of the French Revolution, Moreau in 1828 wrote poems opposing the Restoration Monarchy and supporting the revolution in Greece. He fought and killed a Swiss Guard in Paris during the 1830 Revolution, and he fought again in the Paris uprising of June 1832. In 1833, after the death of the regicide Revolutionary *conventionnel* Merlin de Thionville, Moreau defended the Revolution:

> What! lying accounts that are accepted out of fear
> Make the holy epoch into an accursed time!

Nevertheless, despite his revolutionary actions and beliefs, Moreau preached social peace during the July Monarchy, saying that "the weapon of the century is the pen."

Moreau's routine of days without food and nights without rest as a patron of the *goguette* Les Infernaux, a working-class singing society, left him exhausted, and he returned to Provins to convalesce. Here he tried to found a newspaper, *Le Diogêne*, in imitation of Auguste-Marseille Barthélemy's scandalously successful *La Némésis*. His association with it and his continuing relationship with Louise Jeunet made life impossible for him in Provins, and he returned to Paris. Here he lived in desperate poverty, writing pieces for vaudevilles and even accepting money to publish some verses in praise of Henri-Joseph Gisquet, the prefect of police, under a pseudonym. Finally, in 1838 he was able to publish his *Myosotis*, a volume of his collected poems. By this time he was near death from tuberculosis and exhaustion. He would attain the glory he had sought but only after his death on 19 December 1838. His funeral was attended by more than three thousand people, including Louis Blanc, Pierre Leroux, and the songwriter Altaroche. Béranger, Armand Marrast, Félix Pyat, and L.-A. Berthaud were his pallbearers. In 1913, a Comité Hégésippe Moreau was still meeting in Paris.

In 1828, a hopeful Moreau had written at the age of eighteen:

> I'm eighteen! everything is changing, and Hope
> Is guiding me by the hand toward the Horizon.
> One more day to suffer through
> And then happiness will smile on me tomorrow.

G. Benoit-Guyod, *La Vie maudite de Hégésippe Moreau* (Paris, 1945); J. Maitron, ed., *Dictionnaire biographique du mouvement ouvrier français*, vol. 3 (Paris, 1966); H. Moreau, *Le Myosotis, petites contes* (Paris, 1838) and *Oeuvres complètes* (Paris, 1861); E. L. Newman, "L'Arme du siècle, c'est la plume: The French Worker Poets of the July Monarchy and the Spirit of Revolution and Reform," *Journal of Modern History* (1980) and *The French Worker Poets of the July Monarchy*, forthcoming; E. Thomas, *Voix d'en bas; la poésie ouvrière du XIXe siècle* (Paris, 1979); J. Touchard, *La Gloire de Béranger*, 2 vols. (Paris, 1968).

*Edgar L. Newman*
*Related entries:* BARTHELEMY, A.-M.; BERANGER; BLANC; FIRMIN-DIDOT; LEROUX; MARRAST; PYAT; REPUBLICANS; REVOLUTION OF 1830; SINGING SOCIETIES; SWISS GUARD; WORKER POETS.


**MORGAN, SYDNEY OWENSON, LADY** (1776?–1859), Irish novelist, essayist, and hostess. The daughter of an actor, Robert Owenson, she drew inspiration for her first novels from Irish folktales and legends. *The Wild Irish Girl* (1806) established her fame as a romantic writer. The diminutive, lively author became a fixture of aristocratic society in Ireland and England, prized for wit and singing as well as writing. In 1809 she joined the household of the marquess and marchioness of Abercorn, who arranged her marriage in 1812 to their physician, Sir Thomas Charles Morgan. Entering marriage with some reluctance, Sydney soon grew happy with her husband whose scholarly, rational temper complemented her outgoing nature. Two years after her marriage, she published *O'Donnel: A National Tale* (1814), which championed the cause of Catholic emancipation.

Like Mme. de Staël, Lady Morgan moved from novels to travel literature. In 1816 she and Sir Charles visited France, recently reopened to English visitors. Paris society lionized the famous novelist, but she made a point of meeting people from all levels of French life. She was especially proud to have made friends with Baron Vivant Denon and the marquis de Lafayette. Her description of visiting Lafayette's country estate formed a significant part of her book of journalistic impressions, *France* (1817). The Morgans revisited France in 1818 on their way to Italy where she was to produce a similar travel book (*Italy*, 1821). Having criticized royalist circles in her earlier book, she was even more welcome in French liberal ranks, meeting such notables as Benjamin Constant and being inducted into a Masonic lodge. Excerpts from letters and diaries of this trip were published in *Passages from My Autobiography* (1859). The Morgans' last trip to France in 1829 provided material for *France in 1829–30* (1830). In 1837, the Morgans moved from Dublin to London. Sir Charles died in 1843. Lady Morgan's busy social and literary life continued until her death in 1859.

L. Stevenson, *The Wild Irish Girl: The Life of Sydney Owenson, Lady Morgan* (New York, first published in 1936); E. Suddaby and P. J. Yarrow, eds., *Lady Morgan in France* (Newcastle upon Tyne, 1971).

*Sylvia Neely*
*Related entries:* CONSTANT; FREEMASONRY; LAFAYETTE, M.-J.-P.-Y.-R.-G.; STAEL-HOLSTEIN.


**MORTALITY.** Mortality remained high in France throughout the entire period 1815 to 1851. Infant mortality (zero to one year) was especially high, and expectation of life at birth was low for men and women. By mid-century France still had not entered a strong decline in mortality levels. The period was also marked by exceptionally high mortality at certain times due to outbreaks of epidemic disease.

Mortality between birth and age one showed little change during the first half of the nineteenth century. Only in the July Monarchy was there a decline, and this proved to be temporary. For this period, therefore, between 15 and 20 percent of all infants born alive did not survive to their first birthdays. The chances were slightly better for females than males (16-17 percent versus 18-20 percent), but for both sexes rates were very high. These high rates of infant mortality were the result of the unhygienic conditions in which children were born and raised and the widespread practice of sending infants to wet nurses almost immediately after birth. Mortality among these nurslings may have been as high as 50 percent.

Once the first birthday was reached, prospects for survival improved considerably. Child mortality rates were only one-sixth of those for infants, and those in ages five to fourteen were lower by another two-thirds. Age-specific rates remained around these levels until the late forties and early fifties age groups, when they turned sharply up. This pattern by age held for both men and women and remained true throughout the first half of the century.

The high rates of infant mortality prevailing and the absence of dramatic changes in either infant or adult mortality for men or women meant that expectation of life at birth was low and improved only slightly during the period 1815–51. For men the change was from 37.6 years in 1815–17 to 41.8 years in 1850–52; for women there was less improvement—from 40.2 years to 42.7 years—but it started from a higher level. The French population, therefore, had not experienced much improvement in its chances for survival even by the middle of the nineteenth century.

Some shading must be placed on this picture, however, for there was geographic and social inequality before death in France in this period. Those who lived in the cities, especially Paris, were subject to heavier mortality than were those who lived in the countryside. Within the cities the poor and laboring classes were struck hardest by mortality. To some extent these patterns were the result of the susceptibility of the urban poor to epidemic disease. The most dangerous of these was cholera, which struck France, especially its cities, in 1832 and again in 1848–49, causing substantial increases in mortality. Smallpox also remained a significant disease, although vaccination had reduced its impact in much of the country. In Paris, however, it still produced mortality of epidemic proportions; in 1822, 1823, and 1825 the capital experienced smallpox epidemics. The conditions in which most urban laborers lived, marked by overcrowded housing and poor ventilation, helped turn infection into epidemics that spread throughout the city. Even without epidemics, urban artisans, shopkeepers, and laborers and their families found life more dangerous than did their social betters. Occupational morbidity and mortality was higher for these groups, especially those who required inside work. Consumption of the lungs and other pulmonary diseases were encouraged by the cramped posture and damp atmosphere in which many urban artisans and workers labored and lived. Their children, moreover, were frequently exposed to the dangers of wet nursing, a practice that killed large numbers of infants, because of the inability of the laboring families to spare the income of the mother.

J. Bourgeois-Pichat, "The General Development of the Population of France since the Eighteenth Century," in D. V. Glass, ed. *Population in History* (Chicago, 1965); W. D. Camp, *Marriage and the Family in France since the Revolution* (New York, 1961); L. Chevalier, *Laboring Classes and Dangerous Classes in Paris during the First Half of the Nineteenth Century*, trans. Frank Jellinek (New York, 1973) and *La Formation de la population parisienne au XIXe siècle* (Paris, 1950); C. H. Pouthas, *La Population française pendant la première moitié du XIXe siècle* (Paris, 1952); E. Van de Walle, *The Female Population of France in the Nineteenth Century* (Princeton, 1974).

*James Lehning*

*Related entries:* FERTILITY; MIGRATION; NUPTIALITY; POPULATION; WET NURSING.


**MORTEMART, CASIMIR-LOUIS-VICTURNIEN DE ROCHECHOUART, DUC DE** (1787–1875), Prince de Tonnay-Charente, general, peer, and ambassador of the Restoration and July Monarchy, senator of the Second Empire. Scion of a noble family, Mortemart was born in Paris on 20 March 1787. He was raised in England, where his family fled during the Revolution. They returned to France in 1801, and he joined the *gendarmerie d'ordonnance*. He participated in the campaigns in Prussia in 1806 and Poland in 1807, earning the Legion of Honor. In the 1809 Austrian campaign he served as an aide-de-camp to Etienne-Marie de Nansouty and in 1810 became an ordinance officer to Napoleon. His conduct during the Russian campaign, especially at Borodino, earned him the title of baron of the Empire. He also fought in the 1813 campaign in Germany and the 1814 campaign in France. He supported the dethronement of Napoleon in 1814, however.

The First Restoration appointed him a peer on 4 June 1814, gave him the Order of Saint Louis, and commissioned him colonel of the Cent-Suisses, the unit his grandfather had commanded in 1789. During the Hundred Days he fled to Ghent. In October 1815 he was appointed major general of the Paris National Guard and in November *maréchal du camp*. He later became captain-colonel of the *gardes du corps à pied* and received the Order of the Holy Ghost. Until 1828 his participation in political affairs was quite limited. But in April 1828 Charles X sent him as ambassador to Saint Petersburg, where his experience in the 1812 campaign stood him in good stead. Although he was a staunch constitutional royalist, he retained this post under the ministry of Jules de Polignac, to whom he counseled firmness but moderation. In January 1829 he was proposed as foreign minister but declined. In the midst of the Greek war, with the Ottoman Empire apparently on the verge of collapse, Mortemart asked Polignac for instructions, thereby provoking Polignac's well-known plan (September 1829) to redraw the map of Europe. On leave from this post, Mortemart returned to France in May 1830, having been promoted to lieutenant general in December 1828.

Suffering from a fever, Mortemart was preparing to leave Paris to take the waters when he learned of the July Ordinances. On 28 July he hastened to Saint Cloud and early on 29 July urged the king, in vain, to recall these measures. Later that day Charles finally realized he had to compromise. Acting on the insistence of Eugène-François de Vitrolles, Charles de Sémonville, and Antoine-Maurice d'Argout, he summoned Mortemart to offer him the presidency of the ministry. Mortemart, doubting that he could save the dynasty, objected that he was a military officer, not a politician. But he finally accepted when the king agreed to include Casimir Périer and Etienne-Maurice Gérard in the cabinet, to recall the July Ordinances, and to convoke the Chamber immediately. Detained overnight by the king, Mortemart left for Paris the next morning, 30 July, with signed ordinances decreeing these changes, which he attempted to put into effect. But he arrived on foot in Paris too late and was outmaneuvered by the leaders of the Orleanist movement. That day Auguste Bérard, a leading Orleanist, bluntly told him that the Bourbons were through. From his headquarters in the Luxembourg Palace, Mortemart tried but was unable to reach agreement with the various deputies with whom he met, in part because his age and ill health prevented him from pursuing an aggressive course in his negotiations. By the afternoon of 30 July he agreed that Orléans should become lieutenant general of the kingdom, and he sent General Alexandre de Girardin to warn Saint Cloud of an impending attack. That night Mortemart met with Orléans, who convinced him he would support Charles and his family. However, having been unable to contact or influence even one of the centers of power in the Revolution, by the morning of 1 August Mortemart realized that the Bourbon dynasty was finished. He returned to Saint Cloud where the king and his advisers, lacking any word from him, had concluded that his mission had failed.

Rallying to Louis-Philippe, Mortemart remained in the Chamber of Peers and was given various assignments, including a return to the Saint Petersburg embassy (1831–33). There he successfully convinced Nicholas I to recognize the new French monarchy. He remained in the Peers until 1848, frequently revealing a moderately liberal tendency. He retired from his active army commission in June 1848. But Louis-Napoleon recalled him to command the Nineteenth Military Division and in 1852 appointed him to the Senate. Mortemart, however, took little part in affairs of politics or the court, devoting himself instead to charity work. He died on 1 January 1875 at Néauphle-le-Vieux (Seine-et-Oise). His one significant written work was "Un Manuscrit sur les journées de juillet," published in *Le Correspondant* in December 1930.

*Archives parlementaires*; J. L. Bory, *La Révolution de juillet* (Paris, 1972); V. Beach, *Charles X* (Boulder, 1971); H. Contamine, *Diplomatie et diplomates sous la restauration*

(Paris, 1970); T. Howarth, *Citizen-King, The Life of Louis-Philippe* (London, 1961); D. Pinkney, *The French Revolution of 1830* (Princeton, 1972).

*James K. Kieswetter*

*Related entries:* BERARD; D'ARGOUT; GERARD; JULY ORDINANCES; PERIER; POLIGNAC; REVOLUTION OF 1830; SEMONVILLE; VITROLLES.

**MOTIER.** See LAFAYETTE, M.-J.-P.-Y.-R.-G.

*LE MOUVEMENT* (1831–1832), republican newspaper launched in 1831 with the subtitle *A Political Paper Covering the New Concerns.* The paper had sales difficulties throughout its short existence and finally fused with *La Tribune des départemens* (1829–35), which henceforth became *La Tribune du mouvement.*

I. Collins, *The Government and the Newspaper Press in France, 1814–1881* (London, 1959).

*Peter McPhee*

*Related entry:* LA TRIBUNE DES DEPARTEMENS.

**MUNICIPAL COMMISSION** (July–August 1830), a provisional body created after the collapse of the Bourbon government to ensure the continuation of basic public services in Paris. The Municipal Commission of Paris was a provisional committee established on 29 July 1830 by a group of liberal deputies to ensure the safety and provisioning of Paris after insurrectionary forces had obliged royal officials to abandon the city. The deputies selected five of their own number as commissioners: Casimir Périer, Georges Lobau, Pierre Audrey de Puyravault, Augustine Jean de Schonen, and François Maugin.

The commissioners established themselves at the Hôtel de ville, where they were subject to the influence of the street fighters who controlled the building and of General Lafayette, who had there set up his headquarters as commander of the National Guard of Paris. While attending to its prescribed duties, the commission moved toward the role of a national provisional government, appointing commissioners to administer the national ministries and issuing orders to the army. Two days later, when the duke of Orléans accepted the lieutenant generalcy of the kingdom, he and his advisers feared that a rival government might at any moment emerge at the Hôtel de ville, and the lieutenant general's first public act was to go there in person to seek the endorsement of Lafayette, the Municipal Commission, and their supporters. His mission did succeed, and the duke's triumph was dramatically sealed before the crowd gathered in the place de Grève by "the republican kiss of Lafayette." The duke then moved quickly to gather the reigns of power into his own hands. After 31 July the commission confined its activities to strictly municipal affairs, and a few days later it surrendered its powers to the newly appointed prefect of the Seine, Alexandre de Laborde, and ceased to exist.

P. Duvergier d'Hauranne, *Histoire du gouvernement parlementaire en France, 1814–1848*, vol. 10 (Paris, 1857–1871); D. H. Pinkney, *The French Revolution of 1830* (Princeton, 1972); L. de Viel-Castel, *Histoire de la restauration*, vol. 20 (Paris, 1860–78).

David H. Pinkney

*Related entries:* DE SCHONEN; LAFAYETTE, M.-J.-P.-Y.-R.-G.; LOBAU; LOUIS-PHILIPPE; NATIONAL GUARD; PERIER.

*LA MUSE FRANCAISE* (1823–1824), periodical devoted to publicizing works illustrating and defending the early romantic aesthetic. Through its efforts, the movement could finally be said to exist. It succeeded Victor Hugo's *Conservateur littéraire*, which had been too closely associated with the ultra politics of the Société des bonnes lettres. Founders of the *Muse*, each of whom contributed 1,000 francs, were six elite members of Deschamps' salon: Emile Deschamps himself; the two Alexandres from Toulouse: Soumet and Guiraud; Victor Hugo; Alfred de Vigny and A.-S. Saint-Valry. Its contributors numbered about twenty including Charles Nodier, Charles-Julien Chênedollé, Charles Brifaut, Pierre-François Baour-Lormian, Jacques-Argène Ancelot, Marceline Desbordes-Valmore, and Sophie Gay and her daughter Delphine. Most were poets and regular visitors at the Deschamps *cénacle* on rue Saint-Florentin. The enterprise was clearly Deschamps' idea, although the task of composing a prospectus, which appeared as an introduction in the first issue, fell to Guiraud. He established the journal's major objective: to conquer public indifference to poetry, and to restore and maintain enthusiasm for it. This meant poetry of all persuasions, as he declared with a flourish that criticism would be free and impartial. Genuine strides were made to reach that goal when one considers the diversity of aesthetic beliefs the collaborators represented and the flood of troubadour-style odes and elegies that graced the pages of the journal during its short life. One is quite startled by the eclecticism of a publication recognized as one of the promoters of romanticism.

The publisher Ambroise Tardieu produced the twelve monthly issues that spanned a year: 15 July 1823–15 June 1824. Each issue contained three parts, entitled "Poésie," "Critique littéraire," and "Moeurs," accompanied by an appropriate inspirational epigraph. One of the periodical's significant achievements was to have advanced the cause of literary renewal by publishing two of the important early manifestos. On 4 December 1823, the historian Charles-Jean de Lacretelle, at the Académie's opening session, had attacked all new literary doctrines. Former political friends of the Bonnes lettres were becoming literary enemies. Thus, Guiraud fired one of the first salvos of the classic-romantic war of the crucial year of 1824 by inserting a response entitled "Nos doctrines" in the January issue. It presented the nineteenth-century subjective inspiration as the equal of the seventeenth-century objective one and simply discarded the eighteenth as unproductive. Deschamps would include in the May issue a much bolder pronouncement, "La Guerre en temps de paix; Ourika, l'Académie" in reaction to Louis-Simon Auger's famous condemnation lecture delivered at the Académie's annual public session of 24 April 1824. With wit and logical precision, he refuted the speech's main arguments.

Economic, political and literary speculations, revolving around François-René de Chateaubriand, Alphonse de Lamartine, and Soumet, have been suggested to explain the periodical's sudden demise. The most plausible seems to be that it was sacrificed to ensure Soumet's election to the Académie. In any event, it ceased publication after the 15 June 1824 issue.

R. Bray, *Chronologie du romantisme (1804–1830)* (Paris, 1963); Ch.-M. Des Granges, *La Presse littéraire sous la restauration, 1815–1830* (Paris, 1907); H. Girard, *Emile Deschamps, 1791–1871* (Paris, 1921); L. Séché, *Le Cénacle de la Muse française, 1823–1827* (Paris, 1908).

*Paul Comeau*

*Related entries:* AUGER; CHATEAUBRIAND; DESBORDES-VALMORE; DESCHAMPS; GAY, D.; GAY, S.; GUIRAUD; HUGO; LAMARTINE; NODIER; ROMANTICISM; SALON D'EMILE DESCHAMPS; SOUMET; VIGNY.

**MUSSET, LOUIS-CHARLES-ALFRED DE** (1810–1857), the "bad boy" of French romanticism whose poetry was the epoch's purest expression of personal lyricism. The handsome and precocious Alfred excelled at the Collège Henri IV and was admitted to the *cénacle* in 1828, where his brilliance and effortless creation won acclaim while exciting jealousy. He had flirted with law, medicine, art, and music before fixing upon a literary career. Musset is ranked with Victor Hugo, Alphonse de Lamartine, and Alfred de Vigny as the four great French romantic poets, but he remained essentially independent of any school. While he expressed the romantic sensibility in the suffering and self-absorption portrayed in his lyric poetry, his impertinent imagery shocked even the romantics.

Musset was too marked by a classical education, and eighteenth-century rationalism as well, not to temper romantic bombast with irony. He affected the air and dress of the dandy, which suited him admirably. His personal tragedy was that his looks, his family, and his talent destined him to be the spoiled darling of a glittering society and released him from the necessity of effort. He personified the general malaise of the time, a melancholy known as *le mal du siècle* and which summarized for Musset the impossibility of reconciling his idealism and his hunger for an absolute with the reality of daily existence.

Musset's celebrated affair with George Sand typifies the romantic existence. He fell passionately in love when he met her in 1833. They were soon off to Venice, but the idyll was marred by infidelities and recriminations on both sides. After a definitive rupture in 1835, both artists seemed determined to have the last word in print on the episode. Musset described the experience in *Confession d'un enfant du siècle* (1836) and satirized it cleverly in *Histoire d'un merle blanc* (1842). After his death, George Sand defended her role while heaping abuse on Musset in *Elle et lui* (1859). Musset's devoted brother, Paul, retorted with *Lui et elle*, a novel that made no scruple about using oral confidences of Musset, as well as Sand's own *Journal intime*.

Musset was a victim of his own vices: laziness, self-indulgence, a facile talent, and an attraction to opium. Ironically he had begun his literary career translating Thomas DeQuincey's *Confessions of an Opium Eater* (1828). His great lyric poetry was written before 1837: *Contes d'Espagne et d'Italie* (1830), *Les Nuits*, a series of four meditations with his muse, and *Rolla*, a byronesque portrayal of the essential purity of heart of the *débauché*, which won immediate acclaim. After 1834, most of his work was published in the *Revue des deux mondes*.

Musset was a raconteur, thoroughly at ease in the short story, but his facility with dialogue and situation indicates that the theater was his genre of predilection. He published *Un Spectacle dans un fauteuil* (1832), *André del Sarto*, *Les Caprices de Marianne* and *Fantasio* (1833), and *On ne badine pas avec l'amour* and *Lorenzaccio* (1834). The last, suggested by George Sand, was the apogee, psychologically and dramatically, of Musset's talent. His theater continued the tradition of marivaudage but was too far from the romantic affectations of the day to be appreciated until long after his death.

Musset was appointed librarian to the minister of the interior in 1838. His verve and promise were beginning to fade, victims of his excessive life-style. He lost the appointment in 1848 but was reappointed in 1854. By the time he was named to the French Academy in 1852, his genius, which flowered precociously, was essentially silenced. He has survived as the image of eternal youth embodied in the romantic young man who suffers for love. He was a lucid critic who struck a delicate balance between classicism and romanticism, a rational mentality delicately dissecting the spleen of his century, born, as he said, "too late in a world too old."

C. Affron, *A Stage for Poets: Studies in the Theatre of Hugo and Musset* (Princeton, 1971); P. Gastinel, *Le Lyrisme de Musset* (Paris, 1933); D. Sices, *Theater of Solitude* (Hanover, 1974); Ph. Van Tieghem, *Musset, l'homme et l'oeuvre* (1945).

*Shelby A. Outlaw*

*Related entries:* ACADEMIE FRANCAISE; HUGO; LAMARTINE; ROMANTICISM; SAND; VIGNY.

**MUTUAL SCHOOLS.** See *ECOLE MUTUELLE*.

# N

NADAUD, MARTIN (1815–1899), the author of the best-known memoirs of a worker in the nineteenth century (*Mémoires de Léonard, ancien garçon maçon*, 1895). Nadaud's life and work are probably more important for what they represent than for their impact on French history. Born in the hamlet of La Martinèche in the arrondissement of Bourganeuf, at fifteen he followed the pathways of his ancestors, accompanying his father and a group of his colleagues to Paris where they made their *campagnes* as masons of the Creuse. The Limousin had long sent its sons to Paris, Lyons, and other large cities to work on a seasonal basis in the building industry. Small proprietors, they left the oversight, if not the financial responsibility, of their lands to their women while they plied their artisanal skills. Living in *garnis* (furnished rooms) they saved as much as possible, money that, when merged with the meager returns from the poor soil of their native country, allowed them and their families to subsist. This strategy for survival was typical of millions of other rural families in eighteenth- and nineteenth-century France. Temporary migrant work, generally by males, varied immensely (from the roughest agricultural work to unexpected activities such as itinerant schoolteaching), but each region—always poor and usually mountainous—had its own specialty and established regular connections with specific market areas. This reciprocity between advanced and disadvantaged areas, a fact of extraordinary significance in French economic development in the first half of the nineteenth century, peaked during the July Monarchy, when, according to Abel Chatelain's estimates, perhaps a third of the active population of the countryside took temporary wage work elsewhere.

Young Nadaud was quickly initiated into the secrets of his craft by working side by side with his father and learned the ruses necessary to offset abuses of the building trades' entrepreneurs and their subcontractors. Although most masons from Limousin knew French (but they communicated with one another in their own patois), Martin had the unusual advantage of an education. Like many of his compatriots, he mixed in the politics of the 1830s, though he gravitated rapidly away from his father's Bonapartism to the social republicanism of the Société des droits de l'homme, then to the secret societies of the later 1830s, and finally to the camp of Etienne Cabet's Icarian communism. His discussion in *Léonard* of Left politics and the personalities he encountered remains a classic source for the period. Nadaud's political activism, though perhaps more thoroughgoing than that of many other Creusois, underlines a reality of immense significance: temporary migrants served as living conduits by which political opinion (usually left wing) spread from city to countryside. Of necessity bilingual— if not generally as well informed as Nadaud—they carried the advanced ideas of the age into many of the remotest villages of France. Alain Corbin has analyzed the process in detail for the Limousin, but most places where rural-to-urban temporary migration was significant seemed to witness some degree of political radicalism during the Second Republic. Nadaud's life was representative in this respect, for it was the Creuse, not Paris, that sent him to the Legislative Assembly on 13 May 1849. Although his record there was undistinguished (and he was ridiculed by the Right), Nadaud linked himself with the stalwarts of the *démoc-soc* Left in defense of the Republic against Louis-Napoleon and reaction. His most notable contribution in the Assembly itself was to expose the ulterior political motives of a law of 1851 severely restricting the operations of cafés and cabarets in France. Through his experience, he understood clearly that the café was the traditional center for working-class political discussion; it was now the last bastion of Left politics, since most political organizations had been smashed. His intervention failed to stop the law's passage, but he did reveal the cynicism of the reactionaries in their alleged desire to combat the "immorality" of the café.

Outside the Assembly, Nadaud was deeply involved in another activity typical of the age, the development of a mason's worker cooperative, which reached a point where "there was no private entrepreneur in Paris who gave work to more workers or who had better materials." The success amazed all, but, as Nadaud wrote, they had discovered "the secret of suppressing mastership [*la maîtrise*] and by consequence, the exploitation of man by man" (*Léonard, maçon de la Creuse*, p. 247). The cooperative dream, like the Revolution itself, soon evaporated. Nadaud was forced into exile in England but after the amnesty of 1859 had the right to return. He sought to rejoin the Association des maçons that he had helped to found. Not only was he rejected because "our clientele will think that we dream of returning to 1848," but he also discovered that it had become little more than another capitalist enterprise, dominated by key shareholders who soon sold off much of the cooperative's essential equipment. Nadaud returned to England, to come home only after the fall of the Second Empire in 1870.

He was briefly appointed prefect of the Creuse, then came to Paris during the Commune (although he did not participate in it), and finally made his political bed with the Opportunists. In 1876, he reentered the Chamber as a deputy from Bourganeuf, remaining there until defeated by a Boulangist in 1889. In many respects he remained the quintessential revolutionary of 1848: though disillusioned, he still held out hopes for cooperation; he felt that education was the panacea by which the working class could gradually take a place of equality and carry out a gradual social revolution (his support for Jules Ferry was total); and the democratic republic would naturally pave the way to the social republic. Class interests and the realities of class conflict remained blurred, though he sided with the "people." In the end, he would even suppress the fact that he had supported Louis-Auguste Blanqui—along with Etienne Cabet and François-Vincent Raspail—in the Taschereau affair of 1848.

Nadaud, artisan and man of the people, thus invites comparison with another Gambettist who was no less an opponent of the Second Empire but who made his peace with capitalism and did so explicitly: Denis Poulot, author of *Le Sublime* (1870). Together they provide a sobering reminder of the dual inheritance of the spirit of 1848: a breathtaking affirmation of democracy to be sure, it also left the question of the exploitation of man by man largely unanswered.

A. Chatelain, *Les Migrants temporaires en France de 1800 à 1914*, 2 vols. (Lille, n.d.); A. Corbin, *Archaïsme et modernité en Limousin au XIX<sup>e</sup> siècle (1845–1880)*, 2 vols. (Paris, 1975); Jean Maitron et al., eds., "Martin Nadaud," *Dictionnaire biographique du mouvement ouvrier français, Première partie (1789–1864)*, vol. 3 (Paris, n.d.); M. Nadaud, *Discours et conferences*, 2 vols. (Guéret, 1889) and *Léonard, maçon de la Creuse* (Paris, 1977); D. Poulot, *Le Sublime* (Paris, 1980).

*Christopher H. Johnson*

*Related entries:* AGRICULTURE; BLANQUI; CABET; CLUBS, POLITICAL; ECONOMIC CHANGE; LEGISLATIVE ASSEMBLY; MIGRATION; POPU-LATION; RASPAIL; REVOLUTION OF 1848; SOCIETY OF THE RIGHTS OF MAN; WORKERS' COOPERATIVES.

*LE NAIN JAUNE* (1814–1815), satirical journal of the First Restoration and the Hundred Days. This little satirical journal, founded by Louis Cauchois-Lemaire in December 1814, appeared weekly in the form of a booklet. Its pages were devoted entirely to accusing aristocrats and priests of trying to regain their former privileges and to ridiculing the men who had come back into favor as a result of the return of "Louis le Désiré." Poems, parodies, and anecdotes were interspersed with criticisms of royalist writers, many of them obscure even at the time. Once a month there was a cartoon, sometimes in color and sometimes in black and white. Aristocrats were depicted as Knights of the Extinguisher, swearing death to enlightenment, and a nobleman and a priest were seen trampling on a Declaration of Equality. Though strangely out of date, it created something of a stir on account of its irreverence, and Elie Decazes, a councillor of the royal court of Paris at the time, thought it ought to have been suppressed. Louis XVIII, however, was said to have been amused by it. When Napoleon returned from Elba, the *Nain jaune* attributed his favorable reception in France to the fact that he had promised the people liberty. Throughout the Hundred Days the *Nain jaune* pressed for a genuine constitution, and after the defeat of Napoleon's armies at Waterloo it urged Frenchmen to support the Chamber of Representatives in resisting the Allies. The journal was understandably suppressed by the police at the Second Restoration. Cauchois-Lemaire fled to Brussels, where he published the journal from March to December 1816 as *Le Nain jaune réfugié*. Its bitterness against Louis XVIII greatly concerned Armand-Emmanuel de Richelieu, who was afraid that the Allies might obtain from it the impression that the restored monarchy was insecure in France. Eventually the British and Austrian governments persuaded the king of the Netherlands to suppress the journal.

I. Collins, "Liberalism and the Newspaper Press during the French Restoration," *History* 46 (1961); J. de Montenon, *La France et la presse étrangère en 1816* (Paris, 1933).

*Irene Collins*

*Related entries:* CAUCHOIS-LEMAIRE; DECAZES; HUNDRED DAYS; LOUIS XVIII; RESTORATION, SECOND; RICHELIEU.

**NAPOLEON II.** SEE REICHSTADT, N.-F.-J.-C.

*LA NATION* (1843–1845), moderate newspaper of the July Monarchy. In February 1843 Eugène de Genoude, the eccentric editor of the legitimist *Gazette de France*, founded another newspaper, *La Nation*, in the hope of appealing to readers who might not approve of the democratic ideas promoted by the *Gazette*. The *Nation* described itself as the "journal of the rights and interests of all," and its professed policy was to unite liberty with authority. In spite of its moderate tone and the reluctance of juries to convict editors under the harsh press laws of 1835, the editor of the *Nation* was condemned in both March and April 1844 for attacks on the existing dynasty. The paper ceased to appear in June 1845, having never acquired more than 1,600 readers.

*Irene Collins*

*Related entries: LA GAZETTE DE FRANCE*; PRESS LAWS.

*LE NATIONAL* (1830–1851), important revolutionary and republican newspaper of the Restoration, the July Monarchy, and the Second Republic. On 3 January 1830 there appeared the first number of a new daily paper, *Le National*, founded by Adolphe Thiers, François-Auguste Mignet and Armand Carrel with the express purpose of overthrowing not merely the Polignac government but the Bourbon dynasty. In spite of the preamble to the Charter of 1814, which described constitutional government as graciously granted by the king to the people, the *National* insisted that fundamental authority belonged to the people, and by comparing France in 1830 with England in 1688 the authors of the paper managed to suggest that the people had the right to overthrow a dynasty that threatened their liberty. In April the publisher who was designated as legally responsible for the paper, Auguste Sautelet, was condemned to three months' imprisonment and a 1,000 franc fine for attacking the order of succession to the throne. The charge so much preyed upon his mind that he committed suicide, but neither the condemnation nor the personal tragedy to which it led changed the tone of the *National*.

When Charles X's July Ordinances appeared in the *Moniteur* on 26 July 1830, a protest was drawn up by Thiers in the offices of the *National* and signed by forty-four journalists: "The government has today lost the character which commands obedience. We shall resist as far as it concerns us. It is for France to judge how far her own resistance should go." The *National* was among only four newspapers that continued publication despite the ordinances. The arrival of the police to put a stop to the printing resulted in clashes with the crowds outside the office, and this violence could be regarded as the beginning of the revolution, although the declaration of the journalists had carefully indicated that they did not intend to be responsible for popular disorder.

After the revolution, Thiers and Mignet retired from the editorial board, leaving the unpredictable Carrel in control. Carrel in his younger days as an army officer had taken part in republican conspiracies and had fought in Spain in 1823 on the side of the rebels. In a profession of faith published in the *National* on 30 August 1830, he declared his allegiance to Louis-Philippe but insisted with alarming vigor on the need for popular policies by the government. When Louis-Philippe appointed the conservative Casimir Périer as his chief minister in March 1831, Carrel declared stormily in the *National* that the bond between government and press had been broken. By the beginning of 1832, Carrel had become to all intents and purposes republican.

Périer inaugurated a policy designed to wear down opposition newspapers by constant prosecutions and fines. By October 1833 the editors of the *National* had appeared in the courts twelve times and accumulated over 6,000 francs in fines. Fortunately the 5,000 subscribers to the newspaper seem to have been sufficient to keep it in funds. Its fortunes were shaken by the death of Carrel in a duel in 1836, but they revived when Armand Marrast became chief editor in 1840.

Throughout the ministry of François Guizot, the *National* denounced electoral corruption with a wit and fearlessness that won readers outside the small circle of republicans. It also seized every opportunity to criticize foreign policy because the king was known to take a personal interest in directing foreign affairs. As far as positive reform was concerned, the *National* advocated gradual extension of the franchise and mild welfare measures for the benefit of the workers. This policy was too moderate for radicals such as Alexandre-Auguste Ledru-Rollin, who founded a rival newspaper, *La Reforme*, in 1843. Subscriptions to the *National* nevertheless were maintained at about 4,200. Unfortunately the managers had been obliged to lower the price of the annual subscription by 20 francs to withstand the competition of more commercial newspapers such as *La Presse*, but the *National* remained almost exclusively political in content and did not win subscribers by publishing serial stories. Hence few advertisers used its columns, and its funds were low when the Revolution of 1848 began.

On 21 February 1848 the *National* published the order of procession that the banquet committee had drawn up in readiness for its demonstration on 22 February. Marrast could not resist the temptation to make the procession sound as formidable as possible, but he had no intention of starting a revolt, and when the government was so alarmed as to ban the whole demonstration, he agreed with Odilon Barrot and other left-wing deputies involved in the organization that there was nothing to do but back out. During the chaos of the next two days, the *National* offered no leadership. Only when the news of Louis-Philippe's abdication on 24 February filtered through the barricaded city did the *National* begin to act. Armand Marrast called a meeting in his newspaper office in the rue de Richelieu and insisted that a republic must be set up instead of a regency for Louis-Philippe's little grandson. A crowd from the *National* swarmed to the Hôtel de ville, where it was found that seven men had already been chosen by the Chamber of Deputies to form a Provisional Government. The crowd accepted the seven, provided that its own editor was added to the list. Another crowd, from the *Réforme*, insisted on adding its editor Ferdinand Flocon, and also Louis Blanc and a workman Albert. While the three last formed the left wing of the new government, Marrast entrenched himself with the right wing and obtained so many official posts for friends and colleagues that an Englishman in Paris described France as being "absolutely governed by the *National!*" The newspaper was accused of indulging in as much nepotism within three months as it had denounced over the past eight years.

Throughout 1848 the *National* acted as the organ of the republican upper bourgeoisie. It condemned the rising of the workers in the June Days and supported the candidature of Eugène Cavaignac against that of Louis-Napoleon in the presidential election of December 1848. In 1851 it opposed the movement to revise the Constitution in such a way as to allow Louis-Napoleon to remain president of the Republic for ten years, and in consequence it was among the numerous journals that were obliged to cease publication shortly after Louis-Napoleon's coup d'état at the end of 1851.

I. Collins, *The Government and the Newspaper Press in France, 1814–1881* (Oxford, 1959); F. A. de Luna, *The French Republic under Cavaignac, 1848* (Princeton, 1969); C. Ledré, *La Presse à l'assaut de la monarchie, 1815–1848* (Paris, 1961); R. G. Nobécourt, *La Vie d'Armand Carrel* (Paris, 1930).

*Irene Collins*

*Related entries:* ALBERT; BANQUET CAMPAIGN; BARROT, C.-H.-O.; BLANC; CARREL; CAVAIGNAC, L.-E.; FLOCON; GUIZOT; JULY ORDINANCES; LEDRU-ROLLIN; MARRAST; MIGNET; *LE MONITEUR*; PERIER; POLIGNAC; *LA PRESSE*; *LA REFORME*; REPUBLICANS; REVOLUTION OF 1830; THIERS.

**NATIONAL ASSEMBLY,** a generic term that refers to a variety of legislative bodies. See LEGISLATIVE ASSEMBLY; LEGISLATIVE BODY; CONSTITUTION OF 1848.

**NATIONAL CONSERVATORY OF ARTS AND CRAFTS.** See CONSERVATOIRE NATIONAL DES ARTS ET METIERS.

**NATIONAL GUARD** (1789–1871), the national citizen militia, originating in Paris and organized on the local level, whose history parallels the revolutionary history of France. The National Guard was a critical presence in the Great Revolution as well as in the revolutions of 1830 and 1848, and the Paris Commune of 1871. Established by the Committee of Electors of the city of Paris in July 1789, the National Guard responded to the need for public order, conducting its first night patrols on 13 July 1789. The guard consisted of sixteen legions, sixty battalions, or 60,000 men, and the marquis de Lafayette was designated by the electors as the guard's first commandant on 15 July 1789. The original organization of the guard was formalized in 1790 and 1791, with legislation governing discipline, dress, membership, and the election of officers. During the subsequent eighty years of its history, the guard was reorganized a number of times, with the most significant changes in the areas of the election versus the appointment of officers and the nature of membership, universal or restricted.

In addition to its primary purpose of maintaining order and protecting private property, the National Guard was established to defend Revolutionary principles, and the National Assembly in particular, against an aristocratic conspiracy. Never intended as a neutral peacekeeping force, the National Guard was throughout its history a political entity identifying with bourgeois revolutionary aims. The National Guard was curtailed after 10 August 1792 and briefly reestablished between Thermidor (July 1794) and Vendémiaire (October 1795). Both the Directory and the Consulate chose to rely instead on the army as the preferred force of order.

During the First Empire, the National Guard lost its autonomous character as a citizen militia. Officers were appointed by the minister of the interior and, after the Russian campaign, the guard was mobilized as a reserve to fight a foreign enemy. With the capitulation of Paris in March 1814, the guard was placed at the disposal of the Allies and served as a transitional peacekeeping force. Although the restored Bourbons feared an armed bourgeoisie and sought to keep the guard inactive, they maintained the guard and attempted to identify with it symbolically (Louis XVIII placed the new Charter under its protection, and the comte d'Artois returned to Paris in the National Guard uniform). The guard retained its liberal leanings and, in 1827, because it publicly criticized the ministers of Charles X and supported the Charter, the legions were dissolved, although individuals were not disarmed.

The guard was reconstituted on the second day of the July Revolution of 1830. In both its creation and its collapse, the July Monarchy had a particular dependence on the National Guard as the bourgeoisie in arms. The guard did not help make the July Revolution, but under Lafayette it played a crucial role in the reestablishment of order by the revolutionaries. The support provided by the seventy-three-year-old Lafayette and the National Guard ensured the accession of the duc d'Orléans to the throne. The guard performed effectively against insurrectionary movements, most notably in 1832 and 1834. Its use in controlling riots and demonstrations waned considerably after 1841, with greater reliance placed on the army as the more effective force. The conspicuous and important posts of the Hôtel de ville and the Tuileries continued to be maintained by the guard.

During the July Monarchy, the guard was important socially for the status it conferred on the merchants and shopkeepers who filled its ranks. A law that opened membership to large numbers of disenfranchised petty bourgeois in 1837 reinforced the guard's reformist spirit but did not dilute its predominantly bourgeois identification. Guardsmen continued to pay dues and provide their own equipment. Elite units were formed that were distinguished by their more elaborate and expensive uniforms. Discipline became lax or nonexistent. Serving jail sentences of a few days for refusal to respond to the call or to perform night patrol duty was almost like a social event for artists and intellectuals, and the prison on rue de la Gare became popularly known as the Hôtel des haricots. Politically the guard maintained a liberal and reformist orientation. This, combined with poor discipline, inadequate deployment plans, and a confused chain of command, meant that on 22 February 1848 the guard was incapable of responding to the threat of revolution. Many guardsmen defected to the side of the revolution, and, without the support of the army and the National Guard, the government collapsed.

The February Revolution resulted in the abolition of tax-paying requirements for membership, and the guard was opened to all males of eligible age, more than tripling its size to 190,000 soldiers in Paris. Class antagonisms within the Paris guard erupted on 16 March 1848 with the elite troops (the *bonnets à poil*) of the guard protesting the dissolution of their companies, revolutionary reforms, and open membership. The guard was strongly divided in this period between its bourgeois and democratic elements. In April guardsmen elected an officer corps of bourgeois moderates and conservatives, many of whom were prerevolutionary incumbents. During the June Days only about 12,000 troops from the bourgeois western quarters of Paris turned out to fight under army direction against the insurgents. The National Guard was in decline. Reorganization in 1851 and 1852 weakened both the democratic election procedures and the autonomy of the National Guard. The guard, its prestige eroded, lost many of its peacekeeping functions during the Second Empire and was moribund politically and socially.

With the initial defeats in the Franco-Prussian War of 1870, the National Guard revived its old procedures of election of officers and resumed its simple uniform. It was active in the revolution of 4 September and became the means by which Paris was armed for the siege. For the first time, Guardsmen received a daily allowance (1 franc 50 centimes) for patrolling the ramparts and maintaining order in the city. The guard engaged in one bloody battle with the enemy during the siege on 22 January 1871. It was fervently patriotic and ruled Paris with the belief that the citizenry in arms was the best defense against the invader. After the armistice, the attempt by the Versailles government to disarm the National Guard resulted in the establishment of the Paris Commune (18 March 1871). Military inefficiency, lack of discipline, and administrative wrangling over central versus local control hampered seriously the guard's ability to mobilize and undermined its effectiveness as a fighting force. In the May repression, the guard was massacred, and the institution was definitively suppressed by the law of 30 August 1871.

Throughout its history, the National Guard was least dependable in periods of crisis and could pose a real danger to existing regimes. Because of this, those in power chose to rely increasingly on a modern conscript army as a more reliable fighting force in serious disorders, riots, and revolutions. This was true in the provinces as well, where the National Guard was primarily a municipal phenomenon concentrated in the large cities. Both its politics and its lack of military discipline contributed to the undependability of the National Guard as a permanent peacekeeping force. The development of a modern police after the mid-nineteenth century made the guard obsolete in this role.

More than just an armed force, the National Guard was significant as a political and social institution of the bourgeoisie. As a defender of private property and of liberal and reformist political programs, the guard embodied the development of the bourgeois revolutionary tradition. It was during the July Monarchy that the social and political contradictions in the guard's role as a defender of the state and a protector of bourgeois interests became most pronounced. The insurrections of 1848 constituted a crisis in the institution that democratization resolved by undermining its bourgeois character and emphasizing its patriotic identification. This latter aspect fueled the short-lived revival of the National Guard in 1870.

P. H. Amann, *Revolution and Mass Democracy: The Paris Club Movement in 1848* (Princeton, 1975); L. Girard, *La Garde nationale, 1814–1871* (Paris, 1964); J. M. House, "Civil-Military Relations in Paris, 1848," in R. Price, *Revolution and Reaction: 1848 and the Second French Republic* (London, 1975); D. H. Pinkney, "Pacification of Paris: The Military Lessons of 1830," in J. M. Merriman, *1830 in France* (New York, 1975).

*Patricia O'Brien*

Related entries: CHARLES X; CHARTER OF 1814; DEMONSTRATIONS OF 1848–1849; GARDE MOBILE; GARDE REPUBLICAINE; JUNE DAYS; LA-FAYETTE, M.-J.-P.-Y.-R.-G.; LOUIS XVIII; LOUIS-PHILIPPE; REVOLU-TION OF 1830; REVOLUTION OF 1848; ROYAL GUARD; SWISS GUARD.

**NATIONAL LANDS,** property confiscated during the Revolution from the church and emigrants, whose ownership remained a devisive political issue during the Restoration. For political and economic reasons the French Revolutionary governments seized the lands of several groups during the period 1789–1796. These groups included the Roman Catholic church, whose charity activities were also assumed at that time by the government, the royal family, aristocrats who emigrated from France, and convicted counter-Revolutionaries. These lands were worth up to 5 billion francs and in the economic crisis caused by the war with Allied Europe were made the backing for the French unit of currency, the *assignat*. Some of the property was sold.

When Louis XVIII was restored to the throne in 1814, he accepted a Charter that specified that "all property is inviolable and no exception is made for what is called 'national' property." Napoleon had earlier made a similar legal guarantee to the new owners and so did the new king, Louis-Philippe, in the July 1830 Revolution. Despite this guarantee and the fact that the unsold confiscated land was returned to the previous owners in 1814, the question of the national lands led to political struggle during the Restoration, both inside and outside the legislature.

The issue of the national lands was of little direct interest to the common people. Most of the previous owners were aristocrats, and most of the new owners were rich landowners, merchants and industrialists. These new owners were distrustful of the restored Bourbon regime because of its connections with the returned emigrants and tended to be in the opposition. When Napoleon returned in the Hundred Days of 1815, many of his early supporters were owners of national lands. In the White Terror following the reimposition of the Bourbons many of the victims were national land owners, including a Protestant congregation in Nîmes that had bought a former Dominican church and an Ursuline convent.

In the Chamber of Deputies, the issue came to a head in 1825 when the king's minister, Joseph de Villèle, introduced a bill to repay the former owners of the national lands by lowering the interest on state bonds. The bond-owning bourgeoisie opposed this, and the liberal deputies argued that this bill violated the Charter. One liberal deputy asked why all of France should pay for what 50,000 emigrants spurned. Another liberal felt that the seizures had been necessary to fight a war provoked by the emigrants, many of whom fought with France's enemies. The Chamber, with a majority of royalists, eventually passed the indemnification bill by a vote of 221 to 130. The actual cost turned out to be 630 million francs with 70,000 people getting an average payment of 45,000 francs.

Although the 1825 law was something of a compromise, some deputies abandoned support of the king over this issue. The idemnification law was also an issue in the 1827 elections, which returned a Chamber of Deputies that turned against the king, thus provoking the July 1830 Revolution. Ironically the new liberal king who replaced the Bourbon king was the duke of Orléans, who himself had received the largest indemnity payment, 12,704,000 francs ($2,540,000).

*La Grande encyclopédie* (Paris, 1886–1902); Larousse, *Grand Dictionnaire universel du XIX<sup>e</sup> siècle*, entries under "Biens nationaux" and "Domaine" (Paris, 1873).

*Don Smith*

*Related entries:* CHARTER OF 1814; HUNDRED DAYS; INDEMNITY BILL OF 1825; LOUIS XVIII; LOUIS-PHILIPPE; VILLELE; WHITE TERROR.

**NATIONAL WORKSHOPS,** relief in the form of payment for participation in public works projects and of doles given to the unemployed during the deepening economic crisis of 1848. The most important relief program—in terms of the numbers helped, the costs incurred, and the controversies the scheme engendered—was the National Workshops set up in the capital. The Parisian experience was repeated on a lesser scale in a number of provincial cities, especially in industrial areas most affected by the midcentury depression. Contemporaries ascribed considerable practical and symbolic importance to the National Workshops, but historians are nearer the truth in playing down both their novelty and their impact. Only one study—the now-dated 1933 work by Donald C. McKay—has been devoted to them, and it deals only with Paris.

At the time, both apologists and detractors agreed on their importance. In the euphoric early days of the Second Republic, many workers, above all in Paris, put exaggerated hopes in an institution that, along with the Luxembourg Commission, also set up late in February, seemed to announce an era that would give labor new dignity, organization, and protection. These ill-founded hopes were to be dashed in the bloody failure of the June insurrection and the closing of the National Workshops on 3 July. Karl Marx, who sharpened his analytical tools in his efforts to understand the events in France at this time, viewed the scheme as a Machiavellian bourgeois trick designed to discredit socialist ideas and to bribe workers into supporting the regime. There may be some truth in this view, since Alexandre-Thomas Marie, the first minister of public works in the new Republic, came to see the workers of the workshops as possible defenders of the regime against insurrection, and Emile Thomas, the first director of the scheme, also tried to exert restraining political control over those enrolled. However, Marx ascribed too much prescience to the Provisional Government. In the confused early days of the Republic, it established the National Workshops in Paris merely as a temporary expedient to alleviate distress. Some contemporary observers also considered the scheme a socialist experiment. In fact, despite the rhetoric that accompanied their creation, workshops were no radical innovation; the provision of public works to alleviate distress had been resorted to by previous governments. Still others, in the face of the growing popular unrest that culminated in the June Days, insisted that the National Workshops were a drain on meager government funds and, worse, a catalyst of revolt. Once again, these criticisms are exaggerated. The suppression of the Parisian workers' June insurrection cost the government five times as much as had the relief given the unemployed in the preceding four months and, in any case, less than 15 percent of those enrolled in the workshops participated in the revolt.

Part of the explanation for the importance contemporaries mistakenly attributed to the scheme is to be found in the confusion that surrounded the creation of the workshops in February 1848. The role that Parisian workers played in overthrowing the July Monarchy and the political power they now enjoyed helped put two socialists, Louis Blanc and Albert, in the eleven-member Provisional Government. And it was the power of Parisian street demonstrations and the weakness of the new government that led to the famous but notoriously vague decree of 25 February. In this decree the government committed itself "to guarantee the existence of the worker by labor," undertook "to guarantee labor to all citizens," and recognized that "workers should associate with one another in order to enjoy the legitimate fruits of their labor." The following day, the National Workshops were established.

What was the meaning of this rhetoric, and why were the workshops set up? The decree was the government's response to a demonstrators' petition—drawn up by the editors of the *Démocratie pacifique*, the Fourierist journal—that demanded a guarantee of full employment and the institution of social welfare programs. Since such programs were beyond the means of the Provisional Government, the 25 February decree hastily drawn up by Blanc was meant as a saving gesture. The fact that the relief scheme for unemployed Parisian workers announced the following day bore the title "National" also fueled false hopes among the workers by implying that the workshops would become a fundamental aspect of the new regime like the National Assembly or the National Guard. Louis Blanc's presence in the government, indeed, led many at the time and later to see the National Workshops as the implementation of proposals in Blanc's *Organisation du travail*, first published in article form in 1839, which advocated the creation of social workshops (*ateliers sociaux*), producer cooperatives to be set up with government help. The scheme, though, owed little if anything to Blanc's ideas and much to the public works relief programs to which previous regimes had resorted in times of high unemployment. The best-known instances of these charity workshops are those set up in Paris in 1788–91 and 1830–31. These had set the unemployed to work building roads and clearing waste land. At their peak, the 1830–31 relief programs had employed just under 14,000. The Provisional Government anticipated that a similar number would seek relief in the National Workshops.

Such a belief was not entirely without foundation. Though early in 1848 the capital was still in the grips of a depression, the 1847 harvest had been good, and there were signs of an imminent recovery. The political crisis from February onward, however, shattered still-fragile business confidence and led to a sharp downturn in the economy. By June between 50 and 60 percent of the nearly 350,000 workers (men, women, and children) in the capital were unemployed. By that time the workshops were giving relief to 117,000 workers, as compared with 28,350 at the end of March and 99,400 at the end of April. Such numbers quickly and inevitably put a strain on the unpaid mayors of the twelve arrondissements charged with administering the scheme. It was the appointment as director of Emile Thomas, an unknown civil engineer aged twenty-five, that saved the situation.

Thomas centralized administration and gave the workshops a military-type organization. However, even he failed to persuade government engineers to collaborate fully and provide enough public works projects to employ all those on relief, and at any one time there was never work for more than 10,000 of them. Applicants for whom work could be found were paid 2 francs a day; the others were at first given 1 franc 50 centimes a day and, from 17 March 1 franc. The inadequacy of these doles to maintain a family can be gauged from the fact that the average daily wage for male workers in Paris in 1847 was 3 francs 80 centimes (80 percent of all men earned between 3 and 5 francs). Little provision was made for women workers (who made up 33 percent of the labor force of men, women, and children), but the doles to male workers were supplemented by soup kitchens and by the provision of free medical services by a team of twelve doctors.

The establishment of the workshops in Paris was the signal for demands by workers in the provinces that public works programs already set up in the 1847 depression be expanded and payments to the unemployed increased. And central government and municipalities made some effort to meet these demands. The most important program was implemented in Rouen, where there was widespread distress. At a cost of nearly 2 million francs, between 14,000 and 16,000 workers were given aid in the first months of 1848.

Apart from the unexpectedly large numbers of workers they aided, there is a further reason why the National Workshops were a major element in political discourse in the first months of 1848: there was an unprecedented effervescence and political mobilization among Parisian workers. With the new freedom and enthusiasm after 24 February, political clubs and newspapers mushroomed (at least 200 of each were established), and workers' cooperatives expanded. Besides, the Provisional Government introduced other changes that gave credence to the belief held by many workers that this was truly a social and democratic republic, one that would solve the social problem. Thus not only were universal suffrage, the abolition of the death penalty for political crimes, and the end of slavery in the colonies proclaimed, but the Luxembourg Commission to study solutions for labor problems was set up and the first legal limitation of the working day (ten hours in Paris and twelve in the provinces) enacted. The establishing of the National Workshops, then, coincided with self-assertion and rekindled hopes among workers. Their subsequent history is a litmus paper of the decline of these hopes and the failure of radical revolution.

In late February, when the workshops were created, the government was to a large extent in the power of the Parisian revolutionary crowd. In the following weeks the moderate republicans who controlled this government gradually gained strength. In the general elections of 23 April the provinces repudiated radicals and socialists, and even Paris, while electing Albert and Blanc, rejected socialists like Armand Barbès, Etienne Cabet, and François-Vincent Raspail. The moderate nature of the new Constituent Assembly is revealed in its composition—only 26 of its 900 members could be called working class—and in the composition of the government it chose—Blanc and Albert were excluded. Both the Constituent Assembly and its government became increasingly alarmed at the increase in the number of applicants for relief in the workshops, and all the more so since workers seemed to be being drawn in from outside the capital. Fears that relief recipients would be tinder for insurrection seemed confirmed, first by the revolt at Rouen that killed fifty-nine workers at the end of April and then by the 15 May demonstration in Paris, the most important since February. Not only did the ill-organized demonstration, which disrupted the proceedings of the Assembly, fail, but leading workers' leaders were arrested and the Luxembourg Commission dissolved. This failure also affected the workshops because some of those receiving relief—Thomas calculated 14,000—participated in the events. The hope that some moderate republicans had entertained that relief recipients would become a conservative bulwark of the regime was thereby dashed.

From mid-May onward, then, it was only a matter of time before the workshops were dismantled. The government, though, was reluctant to act precipitately. An unceremonious dissolution would leave large numbers of unemployed without aid and perhaps without scruples. This explains why other plans to provide work were considered at this time. The most ambitious of these—it reached the stage of a bill presented to the Constituent Assembly—was Alphonse de Lamartine's proposal to nationalize the railroad companies that were in financial difficulties and to use Parisian unemployed in the completion of their lines. This project had the added advantage of promising to take workers out of Paris and thus helping defuse tensions in the capital. Increasing numbers enrolled in the workshops, together with signs of growing restlessness in the capital, however, persuaded the government first to remove Thomas, deemed too committed to maintaining the workshops, and then, on 21 June, to issue a decree ordering workers under twenty-five to enroll in the army and all others to be prepared to leave the capital to work on projects in the provinces.

The workers' revolt that began the following day was without clear-cut political objectives or major leaders—Marx called it the first great struggle between the proletariat and the bourgeoisie—but the threat against the National Workshops helped to provoke the insurrection, and they were dismantled when it failed. Fears that the 21 June decree signaled the imminent closure of the workshops were part of the workers' disillusion at the course of events during the preceding weeks. Once the insurrection had been suppressed, the government used the participation in the revolt of workers enrolled in the workshops as an argument for ending the scheme. The argument was only a pretext; at most one in six of those enrolled joined the insurrection. The majority refrained from doing so more out of necessity than indifference; the government continued to pay benefits throughout the June Days.

Like the February Revolution itself, the National Workshops had begun with workers' self-assertion and a widespread feeling that the new Republic represented more than a change of political regime, that it would confer on labor the dignity it deserved. When they were dismantled, there was a widespread feeling of betrayal among Parisian workers. And the workshops were closed just when the economic crisis was at its lowest point. Henceforth the authorities would avoid major public works schemes in the capital. However, they were to continue them in the provinces and, even in the capital, unemployed workers were given relief, some industries were given subsidies, and some workers' producer cooperatives given aid. In the last six months of 1848, for instance, city and central government spent almost as much on outdoor relief in Paris as they had spent in the National Workshops scheme, 13 million as against 13.5 million.

M. Agulhon, *The Republican Experiment, 1848–1852* (Cambridge, 1983); T. R. Christofferson, "The French National Workshops of 1848: The View from the Provinces," *French Historical Studies* 14 (1980); F. A. de Luna, *The French Republic under Cavaignac, 1848* (Princeton, 1969); R. Gossez, *Les Ouvriers de Paris. Livre I. L'organisation, 1848–1851* (Paris, 1967); L. A. Loubère, *Louis Blanc: His Life and His Contribution to the Rise of French Jacobin-Socialism* (Evanston, 1961); D. C. McKay, *The National Workshops: A Study in the French Revolution of 1848* (Cambridge, 1933); D. H. Pinkney, "Les Ateliers de secours à Paris (1830–1831): précurseurs des ateliers nationaux de 1848," *Revue d'histoire moderne et contemporaine* 12 (1965); R. Price, *The French Second Republic. A Social History* (Ithaca, 1972); E. Thomas, *Histoire des Ateliers nationaux* (Paris, 1848).

*Barrie M. Ratcliffe*

*Related entries:* ALBERT; BARBES; BLANC; CABET; CLUBS, POLITICAL; *LA DEMOCRATIE PACIFIQUE*; DEMONSTRATIONS OF 1848–1849; FOURIER; JUNE DAYS; LALANNE; LAMARTINE; LUXEMBOURG COMMISSION; MARIE; MARX; NATIONAL GUARD; PROVISIONAL GOVERNMENT; RASPAIL; THOMAS; WORKERS' COOPERATIVES.

**NAVARINO, BATTLE OF** (20 October 1827), a naval battle fought by a combined Allied fleet of British, French, and Russian ships against the Turkish-Egyptian fleet in the Bay of Navarino in the western Peloponnesus. The Greek War of Independence, which began in 1821, became a fashionable cause in Europe. In July 1827, following the Treaty of London, the British, French, and Russians dispatched a naval expedition whose purpose was to intimidate the sultan. The British especially were fearful of any advantages that the Russians might gain from a diminution of Turkish power. The Allied force blockaded the Turkish fleet in the Bay of Navarino. After an English officer was killed trying to counter a Turkish fireship, the Allies opened fire with their twenty-six ships. Within three hours, the sixty-four ships in the Turkish fleet had been sunk or beached. The Turks suffered over 6,000 casualties, the Allies 177. This battle broke Turkish power in southern Greece. In 1829, Greece gained independence.

P. Fleuriot de Langie, *L'Affaire de Navarin* (Paris, 1930).

*Douglas Porch*

*Related entries:* IMBRAHIM PASHA; LONDON, TREATY OF.

**NEMOURS, LOUIS-CHARLES-PHILIPPE-RAPHAEL D'ORLEANS, DUC DE** (1814–1896), second son of King Louis-Philippe and Queen Marie-Amélie. Louis d'Orléans, duc de Nemours, was born in Paris on 25 October 1814. His family, back from exile after the Hundred Days, sent him to the Lycée Henri IV, where his older brother, the duc de Chartres, was already a student. When the 1830 Revolution broke out, he played no important role and waited to enter Paris at the head of his regiment on 3 August.

Louis-Philippe thought of placing Nemours on the throne of Belgium, which had just freed itself from the Dutch yoke; indeed, the Belgian National Congress had asked for him. But the Great Powers, especially England, were opposed. Nemours consequently had to give up his aspirations to the throne of Belgium in February 1831 and sometime later to the throne of Greece. Nevertheless, he took part in the French expedition to aid Belgium and especially in the seige of Antwerp in November 1832. He also helped to maintain order in Paris in April 1834 and then left in 1836 for Algeria. After one failure (November-December 1836), a second expedition (October 1837) conquered Constantine after violent fighting that caused the death of General Charles de Damrémont. Named a lieutenant general on 11 November 1837, the duc de Nemours in 1840 married the duchess of Saxe-Cobourg-Gotha, Victoire-Auguste-Antoinette, but the Chamber of Deputies refused to vote for the dowry of 500,000 francs that the Soult ministry had proposed.

Nemours took part in a third Algerian campaign in 1841, which resulted in victory over the troops of Abd-el-Kader.

The accidental death of his elder brother in 1841 made him heir to the throne, and he made a series of trips in France and abroad, took part in the debates of the Chamber of Peers, but was never very popular. When the February Revolution of 1848 broke out, he and his wife went before the Chamber of Deputies, but he was forced to leave for exile with his family on 27 February. He went to Claremont, England, and sent to France (May 1848) his protest against the law banishing the Orléans family. During his exile, he visited the other pretender to the throne, the comte de Chambord.

Back in France in 1870 after the abrogation of the exile laws, the duc de Nemours played no important role in politics. He was a general in the reserve army but was dismissed in June 1886 under the law that deprived all members of former ruling families of their public offices. He died in Versailles on 26 June 1896. He had four children, two of them sons. One of his sons married the daughter of Peter II, emperor of Brazil, and the other married Sylvia-Augustina of Bavaria, better known as the duchess of Alençon, who would die in the fire of the Charity Bazar on 4 May 1897.

J. P. Garnier, *Le Drapeau blanc (la Maison d'Orléans de 1787 à 1873)* (Paris, 1971); J. Lebreton-Wary, *Les Orléans d'hier et d'aujourd'hui* (Maulévrier, 1979).

*Jean-Claude Caron, trans. E. Newman*
*Related entries:* BELGIAN REVOLUTION OF 1830; BORDEAUX; CHAMBER OF DEPUTIES; CHAMBER OF PEERS; CHARTRES; JOINVILLE; LOUIS-PHILIPPE; MARIE-AMELIE DE BOURBON; PARIS, COUNT OF; REVOLUTION OF 1830; REVOLUTION OF 1848; SOULT.

**NERVAL, GERARD DE** (pseudonym of GERARD LABRUNIE) (1808–1856), author of romantic poetry and prose poems, forerunner of symbolism and surrealism. Born the son of a military physician, he never knew his mother and spent his early life at Mortefontaine. His father took charge of his education in Paris and never forgave Gérard's refusal to study medicine. The youth's literary bent manifested itself in his teens, however, with a translation of *Faust*, part 1, which caused Goethe himself to remark that it revitalized his own reading of the work.

The success of *Faust* brought him into the orbit of the romantic *cénacle*, and he attended the battle of *Hernani* in 1830 with Théophile Gautier. In 1834, an inheritance from his grandfather permitted him to carry on his bohemian existence on a more luxurious scale. It was about this time that he fell passionately in love with an actress, Jenny Colon, who typified his ideal beauty. He squandered his fortune in a vain attempt to secure her love, even founding a lavish revue, *Le Monde dramatique*, to enhance her reputation.

By the time Jenny married in 1838, Gérard was financially ruined and obliged to depend the rest of his life on journalism for a hand-to-mouth existence. In order to break out of this dependence, he attempted to write several plays, only one of which, *Léo Burckart*, enjoyed success.

In 1840 his translation of *Faust*, part 2, appeared. After its publication, he had a reconciliation, or at least a meeting, with Jenny Colon in Brussels. After his return to France in February 1841, Gérard suffered his first mental breakdown, and he spent several months in the clinic of Dr. Blanche. Henceforth, he would live in the shadow of the fear of recurring madness.

After the death of Jenny Colon in 1842, he began a life of vagabondage that seemed to appease his anxiety while renewing his creative energies. The appearance of *Le Voyage en Orient*, inspired by his travels to Cairo, Constantinople, and Syria, is an artistic transposition of his experiences seen through his imagination rather than a faithful account of his travels.

Nerval continued a vicious cycle: traveling in order to write, writing in order to travel—London, Germany, Belgium, and Holland—and finally reduced to exploring the outskirts of Paris and Paris itself. He lived with the constant anguish of a relapse, and beginning in 1849 the crises became more frequent.

Gérard had always been a prolific writer, but, as though haunted by the fear that his mind would fail before he could complete his work, he alternated periods of care in Dr. Blanche's clinic with frenzied periods of writing. From these years date his greatest masterpieces in which memory and dream coalesce, mythic experiences transfused with the presence of his idealized woman. He had created a dream world inhabited by the mysterious, evanescent women who had eluded him in the real world: his mother, Jenny Colon, the beautiful baronne de Mortefontaine and her sister. Of Jenny, he said that she belonged to him more in death than in life.

It is the fusion of dream and experience that distinguish his best works: *Sylvie* (1852), *Les Illuminés* (1853), *Les Petits Chateaux de Bohème* (1853), *Contes et facéties* (1853), *Les Filles du feu* (1854), *La Pandora* (1855), and *Les Chimères*, of which three or four sonnets—"El Desdichado," "Artémis," "Erythréa"— suffice to secure his reputation among France's great poets. Life lived on the fine edge of madness seemed to inspire his pen to ever greater fluidity, and his style never lost its limpidity and purity. As his friend Théophile Gautier said, he was "reason, taking dictation from madness."

At the peak of literary life, concurrently with the publication of the first part of *Aurélia* and of *Promenades et souvenirs* and the Théatre-français production in preparation of *Misanthropie et repentir*, he was found one cold January morning, hanging from a railing in the rue de la Vieille Lanterne, the last pages of *Aurélia* in his pocket. Was his suicide the result of poverty or despair, or did his madness cause him to follow on an ultimate journey one of the mysterious phantoms who peopled his existence? His life as well as his death have been the subject of much romanticizing, but his contribution to modern poetry is incontestable and his best writing—a blend of linguistic precision and hallucinatory imagery—continues to enthral and enchant.

A. Béguin, *Gérard de Nerval* (Paris, 1945); J. Richer, *Nerval, expérience et création* (Paris, 1963); N. Rinsler, *Gérard de Nerval* (London, 1973); B. Sowerby, *The Disinherited: The Life of Gérard de Nerval* (New York, 1974).

*Shelby A. Outlaw*
*Related entries:* GAUTIER; *HERNANI.*


**NETTEMENT, ALFRED-FRANCOIS** (1805–1869), journalist and historian. He became a journalist at the end of the Restoration, but it was under the July Monarchy that Nettement made his reputation as one of the best pens at the service of the legitimist party. He wrote for all sorts of enterprises, but his principal work remains his *Histoire de la restauration* in eight volumes (Paris, 1860–72). He wrote other useful works: *Histoire de la littérature française sous la restauration* (2 vols., 1852) and *Histoire de la littérature française sous la royauté de Juillet* (2 vols., 1854).

E. Biré, *Alfred Nettement* (Paris, 1901).

*Guillaume de Bertier de Sauvigny, trans. E. Newman*
*Related entries:* LEGITIMISM.


**NEY, MICHEL** (1769–1815), duc d'Elchingen, prince de la Moskowa, marshal of the Empire, renowned commander of the Napoleonic Wars. *Le Brave des braves* (as Napoleon referred to him for his stalwart conduct during the retreat from Moscow in 1812) began the year 1815 as the servant of King Louis XVIII. His relationship with the restored Bourbons was never easy, and he spent much of his time at Coudreaux. However, on 7 March—shortly after news of Napoleon's return from Elba had reached Paris—he assured the king that he would at once take up his duties at Besançon in the Sixth Military Division (or District) and promised that he would soon return to Paris with his former master "in an iron cage."

Events proved otherwise. As more and more troops deserted the Bourbon cause, the pressure on Ney mounted, and on 12 March at Lons-le-Saunier he received emissaries from Napoleon and eventually decided to join his old master.

They met at Auxerre on 18 March and were reconciled. Napoleon duly reached Paris and in late March sent Ney to survey the frontier defenses between Lille and Landau. Although he made Ney a peer of France on 2 June, it was not until 11 June that the emperor summoned Ney to join the headquarters of L'Armée du nord, and only on 15 June—the day the campaign opened—was he given command of the two corps forming the left wing. The significant role he played during the next three days of maneuver and fighting has been the subject of some controversy—and the outcome of the Waterloo campaign is often in part laid at his door. His courage and personal example in action remained superb, but for the rest his swings of mood from rashness to inaction proved disastrous to Napoleon's cause.

Following Napoleon's renewed abdication, Ney made no attempt to seek safety in exile abroad but took refuge at the Chateau de la Bessonie (Cental). On 3 August he was arrested, and taken back to Paris. There he was arraigned before a Council of War comprising a number of former comrades in arms, but Ney insisted on his right to be tried before the Chamber of Peers. He won his point. The outcome was a sentence of death for high treason, passed on 6 December. The next day he was executed by firing squad at the Carrefour de l'Observatoire in the Luxembourg Gardens. Typically, Ney refused the offer of a blindfold and personally gave the order to fire.

H. Bonnal, *La Vie militaire du Maréchal Ney*, 3 vols. (Paris, 1910–14); H. Kurtz, *The Trial of Marshal Ney* (London, 1956); M. Ney, *Documents inedits du duc d'Elchingen* (Paris, 1833); S. de Saint-Exupery and C. de Tourtier, *Les Archives du maréchal Ney* (Paris, 1962).

*David Chandler*
*Related entries:* CHAMBER OF PEERS; HUNDRED DAYS; LOUIS XVIII; WATERLOO, BATTLE OF.


**NIBOYET, EUGENIE MOUCHON** (1796–1883), author of numerous books, translator of Charles Dickens, editor, liberal Protestant involved in feminism, social reform, and pacifism. Eugénie Mouchon was the daughter of a doctor from Montpellier and the granddaughter of a Swiss pastor. Both of her parents were of liberal persuasion and Protestant faith. Her childhood was spent in the cult of equality and Bonapartist glory that followed the Revolution. While she was studying at home, her brothers gained many honors in the Grande Armée. At the age of twenty she married Niboyet, a Protestant lawyer from an influential family.

After her marriage, Eugénie Niboyet became interested in prison reform, and her first published work, in 1836, was titled *De la Nécessité d'abolir la peine de mort*, followed two years later by *De la réforme du système pénitentiare en France*. She was equally interested in improving education for all children, writing *Des Aveugles et de leur éducation* in 1837. Niboyet viewed her work as part of the moral obligation of good Christians. In Paris, she became the secretary-general of the Société de la morale chrétienne, presided over by François La Rochefoucauld-Liancourt.

She was also attracted by some of the ideas of the Saint-Simonians who appointed her the chief of their chapter in the fourth arrondissement of Paris. She adopted some of the Saint-Simonian principles about women, especially the idea that women, far from being blamed with original sin, should be man's moral guide through life. In 1833, when she accompanied her husband back to Lyons, she started a feminist journal, *Le Conseiller des femmes*, dedicated to the advancement of all women. Niboyet believed that women's position in society must be improved so that they would be able to exercise a salutary influence on men.

The *Conseiller* was determined to start women on the road to improvement through education. It contained articles on health care— nursing, weaning, teeth cleaning, general knowledge—grammar, history, biographies of famous women; on theater for its moral lessons; on fashion with the purpose of improving taste; and on household management. A few weeks after the journal began to appear, Niboyet announced her plans to create a moral and intellectual tribune for women. The Athenée began meeting in January 1834. Members read their papers, and good work was published in the *Conseiller*.

Eugénie Niboyet was also influenced by another Saint-Simonian belief: that progress did not require guns or war but only industry. In 1844, following the International Pacifist Congress meeting in London (which she probably attended), Niboyet founded the first group of French pacifists and launched a pacifist journal, *La Paix des deux mondes*. She collaborated in her pacifist work with Emile Souvestre, Michel Chevalier, de St.-Aignan, and the Countess Oleskewitch. The goal of the thirty-two men and women who made up her organization was to attract the well-educated and intellectual leaders of society to pacifism. To that end they sponsored essay writing contests, such as: "On the possibility of universal and permanent peace, and of the influence of peace on the happiness of mankind and on the means to realize peace."

In 1863, Eugénie Niboyet summed up her philosophy in *Le Vrai livre des femmes*. In it she approved of a division of labor, with men caring for politics and commerce, while women reigned over morals and the family. The good mother would engrave her lessons on the hearts of her children and thus improve the world.

C. Moses, "St.-Simonian Men/St.-Simonian Women: The Transformation of Feminist Thought in 1830's France," *Journal of Modern History* 54 (June 1982); L. S. Strumingher, *Women and the Making of the Working Class* (Montreal, 1979).

*Laura S. Strumingher*

*Related entries:* CHEVALIER; LA ROCHEFOUCAULD-LIANCOURT; SAINT-SIMONIANISM; SOCIETY OF CHRISTIAN MORALS; WOMEN'S NEWSPAPERS.

**NINETEEN AUGUST, CONSPIRACY OF.** See BAZAR CONSPIRACY.

**NOAILLES, ALEXIS-LOUIS-JOSEPH, COMTE DE** (1783–1835), ultraroyalist deputy of the Restoration. Born in Paris on 1 June 1783, Noailles' father, Louis, emigrated, and his mother was guillotined in 1794. His aunt, the duchesse de Duras, raised him and instilled in him a devotion to religion and the monarchy. He also acquired a taste for ancient and modern literature and languages, at which he became quite fluent. As early as 1807, he was working for the restoration of the Bourbons. He joined the Congrégation and the Knights of the Faith. In 1809 Pope Pius VII launched a bull of excommunication against those who had seized the Papal States. Noailles distributed this document and other forbidden material, for which he was arrested. He was imprisoned for seven months, refusing an offer by Joseph Fouché to serve in the army as an aide-de-camp to Napoleon in return for his freedom. When he was finally freed in 1810, he was exiled to Switzerland. He journeyed on to Vienna, Russia, and Sweden, where he briefly joined Count Bernadotte's court. He tried to organize a Bourbon network on the Continent. Then he went to England in 1812 to join Louis XVIII, who sent him on a mission to Russia. In 1813 he became an aide-de-camp to Bernadotte and saw active service against the French in 1813 and 1814. He especially attempted to arrange a French popular movement in favor of the Bourbons. Noailles then joined the comte d'Artois as aide-de camp on his return to France and tried to intervene with the Allies to obtain better treatment for French royalists.

In April 1814 Noailles was named a royal commissioner to the Nineteenth Military Division, and he subsequently accompanied Charles-Maurice de Talleyrand to the Congress of Vienna. When the Allies at Vienna declared war on Napoleon on 13 March 1815, it was Noailles who carried this declaration to Louis XVIII at Ghent. He returned to France after Waterloo and was named president of the electoral college of the department of Oise, which in August 1815 elected him to the Chamber of Deputies. There he joined the ultraroyalist majority and was temporarily affiliated with the secret Société de l'anneau. He was not returned in the 1816 election. Noailles presided over the electoral college of Corrèze in 1818 and 1824, being elected to the Deputies from that department in 1824 and reelected in 1827 and 1830. He supported the Villèle ministry and was a member of the "banner" of the Knights of the Faith. Yet he occasionally voted with the constitutional royalists. Charles X appointed him minister of state, colonel of the general staff, and aide-de-camp to himself. Noailles strongly supported the Polignac ministry, but at the July Revolution he took the required oath to Louis-Philippe. However, when he sought reelection, he was defeated in 1831 and again in 1834. He then retired from public life and died in Paris on 14 May 1835.

*Archives parlementaires*; N. Hudson, *Ultra-royalism and the French Restoration* (Cambridge, 1936); T. Muret, *French Royalist Doctrines since the Revolution* (New York, 1933); R. Remond, *The Right Wing in France from 1815 to de Gaulle* (Philadelphia, 1969); A. Robert et al., *Dictionnaire des parlementaires français* (Paris, 1889–91).

*James K. Kieswetter*

*Related entries:* BERNADOTTE; CHEVALIERS DE LA FOI; CONGREGATION; FOUCHE; POLIGNAC; TALLEYRAND; ULTRAROYALISTS; VIENNA, CONGRESS OF; VILLELE.

**NODIER, CHARLES** (1780–1844), journalist, literary critic, novelist, writer of short stories and fairy tales, bibliophile, lexicographer, librarian, entomologist, and leading proponent of the romantic cause. Nodier was born at Besançon on 29 April 1780 to Suzanne Pâris, who later became housekeeper for Antoine Melchior Nodier (lawyer, later judge and mayor), and then became his wife in 1791, an act that legitimized the birth of Charles. As a boy, he was hailed by the local citizens as a child prodigy. His adolescent years were spent developing a taste for politics (through membership in secret societies such as the Amis de la constitution, Les Philadelphes, which he founded, and Les Méditateurs), for science (especially for entomology), for bibliography and lexicography as a librarian, and for literature through the publication of a few poems and the presentation of a play. As a true child of the Enlightenment, his was a natural urge to pursue knowledge in many directions.

Having moved to Paris at the turn of the century, young Nodier's major effort through the Empire period involved the writing of prose fiction and literary criticism. He had devoured *Werther* at sixteen and had identified with the hero enough to pour his deception, his melancholy, into a series of short novels: *Les Proscrits* (1802), *Le Peintre de Salzbourg* (1803), *Les Essais d'un jeune barde* (1804), and *Les Tristes ou mélanges tirés des tablettes d'un suicidé* (1806). The unfettered inspiration had tempted him even earlier when he produced his *Pensées de Shakespeare* (1801). Until 1825, his aesthetic allegiance would quite freely alternate between the classical and the romantic. In fact, by late 1812, newly elected to the Académie de Besançon, he would defend classicism quite firmly in a series of articles composed for the *Journal de l'Empire*. Having published in London a satirical ode, *La Napoléone*, in 1803, and spent more than a month in prison because of it, he just as easily shifted his loyalty to the Bourbons. Though closely watched by Joseph Fouché's agents, he dared to reveal the *Histoire des sociétés secrètes dans l'armée*, albeit anonymously, and was decorated with the *Ordre du lys*. These major pursuits in literature, criticism, and politics did not, however, stem his curiosity in other areas. By 1808, he was again diversifying, teaching a course combining philosophy, history, grammar, and literature, as well as publishing a dictionary and a handbook of entomology. He married Désirée Charve in 1808 and soon fathered a daughter, Marie, whom he took with him to Illyria (now Yugoslavia and Albania) for most of 1812, where he served as municipal librarian in Laibach (Ljubljana) and editor of the multilingual newspaper *Le Télégraphe illyrien*. In November 1812, back in Paris after the Austrian victory, Nodier became a contributor and literary critic for the *Journal de l'Empire* (soon to be *Journal des débats*), and, a year later, he established a permanent home in Paris, where his old friend Etienne de Jouy was a neighbor and where he could invite Pierre-Simon Ballanche, Charles Millevoye, Charles-Guillaume Etienne, and many others. During his tenure with the *Journal des débats*, he reviewed many poems and plays that illustrated the search for a new aesthetic. More than any other critic of the early Restoration, he defended what was to become romanticism. He even went so far as to publish an extensive detailed encomium of *De l'Allemagne*. He alone at that time sensed what the future held for French literature and dared to uphold it (though with prudent caution) in the pages of a classical newspaper. Of course, many of his *Débats* essays were political, designed to castigate the Revolution and Empire and thus to avenge his father's dismissal from the bench and death in 1808.

His early experience with wertherian prose nearly twenty years earlier had produced modest success. In 1818, a deliberate, mature decision to return to creative writing established another turning point in his life. A political shift to the royalist side was accompanied by a literary commitment to the romantic side. This time his short stories and novellas would illustrate a romantic theme. The six fantastic vampire stories appearing during the next five years—*Jean Sbogar*, *Thérèse Aubert*, *Lord Ruthwen*, *Adèle*, *Smarra*, and *Trilby*—are seen as representing the first stage of French-style romanticism. Although their depressing, macabre topics bear a striking resemblance to those of the melodramas of his friend Guilbert de Pixérécourt and of gothic novels, Nodier's style makes the telling charming enough for the reader to appreciate the superstitious Dracula-type tales of ghosts, demons, and nightmares especially in *Jean Sbogar*, *Smarra*, and the highly acclaimed *Trilby*. Thus, he created a new vogue that Victor Hugo and Honoré de Balzac would follow as they launched their writing careers. From 1818 to 1824, he also continued as a contributing editor for *Le Conservateur littéraire*, *Le Journal des débats*, *Le Drapeau blanc*, and *La Quotidienne*, wrote travelogues, and revived his interest in theater by collaborating in 1820 with two colleagues on the script of *Le Vampire*, a melodrama. After receiving *la croix de la Légion d'honneur*, as a reward for his support, he would begin that same year a crucial friendship with Baron Isidore Taylor.

In 1823, Taylor and Alphonse de Cailleux, with whom Nodier had traveled to Scotland to visit Sir Walter Scott's home before *Trilby*, had become aides to Generals d'Orsay and Jacques-Alexandre Lauriston. That year, when the librarian for the comte d'Artois' library at the Arsenal died, the two friends nominated Nodier. He was appointed and installed as director of the Arsenal Library in April 1824. Thus began the most significant period of his life. In his salon, he gathered around him many of the young writers of romanticism, thus continuing the task begun by Emile Deschamps. Assisted by his wife, Désirée, and his beloved daughter, Marie, he presided over their discussions like a father. He cultivated their friendship and encouraged their efforts in a multitude of letters, and he wrote favorable reviews of their works for the *Débats* and the *Quotidienne*. He literally became, for about five years, the apostle of romanticism, and his home became the center of Paris literary life. His status won him an official invitation to one of the key events of the period, the coronation of Charles X at Reims in late May 1825, which he attended with his protégé, Victor Hugo. He would record the event as a sort of historian, and Hugo would commemorate it with an ode as poet laureate. Just two years later, Hugo abruptly and perhaps ruthlessly dissolved the master-disciple relationship to assert his leadership by establishing his own *cénacle* at his apartment of rue Notre Dame des Champs.

As the crowning blow, he publicly welcomed his new young friend, Charles-Augustin Sainte-Beuve, as the group's new critic, thus brushing aside Nodier as the romantic authority and guide. After 1827, the romantic writers went to Hugo's to promote the cause, to discuss literature, and to Nodier's to be entertained. The rejection deeply distressed Nodier and cooled a close friendship. However, the movement needed the unity, the solidarity, and the militant leadership that Hugo could provide and Nodier could not.

The year 1830 was one of distress and misfortune, especially financial, for Charles Nodier. It began with the anguish of having to sell his cherished personal library to provide a dowry for Marie's marriage to Jules Mennessier. Also, just a few days before the Revolution of 1830, Polignac dismissed him from the Arsenal post. The revolution reversed the decision, though he was forced to accept a reduced salary. To add to his grief, he spent nearly three months in bed following the upheaval, having sustained a broken leg in an accident. To remain in Louis-Philippe's good graces, he downplayed his contacts with the previous regime, which gained him Etienne de Jouy's sympathy. Since 1824, Nodier had employed various maneuvers to be accepted into the Academy, and, by 1826, he realized that his election would require political footwork. He had to dull the royalist-romantic image that had incurred the displeasure of his one-time friend, Jouy, leader of the most powerful Institut faction. After the July Revolution, Nodier's debts made this courtship more necessary, and he pursued it with vigor until, with Jouy's sponsorhip, he became the first militant romanticist to join the august body in 1833. By so doing, however, he indirectly rejected his romanticist friends, although he had just triumphed with the greatest of his fairy tales, *Jean-François les bas bleus* and especially *La Fée aux miettes*. He composed about thirty such stories during his declining years. His life since 1830 had in fact already become an escape from a world of reality to one of fantasy, dream, and legend, belonging to those he called *les lunatiques*. As opium had provided a refuge in his youth, his own imagination became one during the last decade of his life, though he had finally earned an international reputation as an authority of the French language. Miscellaneous writings, Academy activities, and publication of the *Bulletin du bibliophile*, which he founded, filled his final years as he fought off the effects of chronic nephritis. The disease finally prevailed, and he died in January 1844. His role as a leading literary figure had been fully recognized, and he had achieved the elusive fame he had sought most of his life.

M. Held, "Charles Nodier et le romantisme" (dissertation, Université de Berne, 1949); H. Nelson, *Charles Nodier* (New York, 1972); R. A. Oliver, *Charles Nodier, Pilot of Romanticism* (Syracuse, N.Y., 1964).

*Paul T. Comeau*

*Related entries:* ACADEMIE FRANCAISE; ARSENAL, SALON OF; BALLANCHE; BALZAC; CORONATION OF CHARLES X; DESCHAMPS; *LE DRAPEAU BLANC*; FOUCHE; HUGO; *JOURNAL DES DEBATS*; JOUY; LOUIS PHILIPPE; POLIGNAC; *LE QUOTIDIENNE*; ROMANTICISM; SAINTE-BEUVE; STAEL-HOLSTEIN.

**NORMAL SCHOOLS.** See *ECOLES NORMALES PRIMAIRES*.

*NOUVEAU JOURNAL DE PARIS* (1829–1830), republican newspaper that became Orleanist under the July monarchy. The *Nouveau journal de Paris* was one of four small republican or crypto-republican newspapers that appeared in 1829, the most important of which was the *Tribune des départemens*. The new *Journal* was the creation of baron Augustine de Schonen, deputy of the Seine, and Jacques Bavoux, former imperial judge, law professor, and also a deputy. The paper's editorials were usually from the pen of Bavoux or Léon Pillet and stirred the wrath of the ultra press, leading to a personal feud in its columns with the choleric Alphonse Martainville of the ultraroyalist *Drapeau blanc*. In 1830 the paper had 1,330 subscribers, about equal to Adolphe Thiers' *National*. The editors used the strategy of urging the election of only those deputies of the far Left and opposing any votes for moderate liberals. This was to gain potential support for a future republic should the government's anticipated coup result in such an opportunity.

The 1830 Revolution saw the *Nouveau journal de Paris* defect from the staunch republicans and accept, without enthusiasm, the new regime. The paper's republicanism had always been clothed in abstractions such as a general franchise, social welfare, and greater equality. It was this softer polemic that the more ardent republicans of 1830 later denounced as the cause of their political failure.

E. Hatin, *Histoire de la presse* (Paris, 1859–61); D. Rader, *The Journalists and the July Revolution* (The Hague, 1973).

*Daniel Rader*

*Related entries:* BAVOUX; DE SCHONEN; *LE DRAPEAU BLANC*; MARTAINVILLE; *LE NATIONAL*; REVOLUTION OF 1830; THIERS; *LA TRIBUNE DES DEPARTEMENS*.

**NUPTIALITY.** French nuptiality in the first half of the nineteenth century conformed to the West European marriage pattern. Marriage was relatively late, and a relatively high percentage never married at all. For the entire population, female mean age at marriage was around twenty-four years, and about 12 percent of women never married. For men, marriage took place later, with mean age at marriage around twenty-eight years, but was more frequent. In general, these patterns of nuptiality remained constant during the period from 1815 to 1851 and appear to have been strongly influenced by long-standing local and regional traditions.

The local variations in proportions married were very strongly related to marital fertility levels in an inverse direction. Thus, areas with relatively high marital fertility (the west, north, east, Pyrenees, and parts of Provence) were also areas of relatively low proportions married, whereas the rest of the country had both lower marital fertility and higher proportions married. Nuptiality therefore tended to balance marital fertility levels, producing a relatively stable level of overall fertility. This balancing effect fits an explanation of nuptiality behavior that sees marriage as the most efficient means by which a pre-Malthusian population can control its growth. For the many rural Frenchmen of the first half of the nineteenth century, limiting marriage was the alternative to limiting fertility within marriage as a means of achieving a desired family size.

There is some limited evidence, however, that in certain circumstances, this general balancing of nuptiality and marital fertility was undercut. The extension of cottage industry into the countryside in the late eighteenth century may have reduced age at marriage by removing the necessity for inheritance of a family farm before a household and new family could be established. The result was an increase in overall fertility and population growth. This result of cottage industry has been found in the north of France and in other countries, but there is also a body of evidence that indicates that cottage industry could coexist with family farming and low proportions married.

J. Bourgeois-Pichat, "The General Development of the Population of France Since the Eighteenth Century," in D. V. Glass, ed., *Population in History* (Chicago, 1965); W. D. Camp, *Marriage and the Family in France since the Revolution* (New York, 1961); C. H. Pouthas, *La Population française pendant la première moitié du XIXe siècle* (Paris, 1952); E. Van de Walle, *The Female Population of France in the Nineteenth Century* (Princeton, 1974).

*James Lehning*

*Related entries:* COTTAGE INDUSTRIES; POPULATION.

# O

OBERKAMPF, EMILE (1787–1837), industrialist and politician. Emile Oberkampf expanded the important printed fabrics works established by his father, a German immigrant who was ennobled by Louis XVI. His factory at Jouy, near Versailles, was one of the first to integrate chemical processes with spinning and weaving. He was made a baron in 1820 and married into the Vernes family, regents of the Bank of France. Oberkampf was a deputy for Seine-et-Oise from 1827 to 1831 and was among the 221 opposition deputies in 1830.

A. Robert, E. Bourloton, and G. Cougny, *Dictionnaire des parlementaires français*, 5 vols. (Paris, 1891).

*Peter McPhee*

*Related entries:* ECONOMIC CHANGE; THE 221.

OLLIVIER, EMILE (1825–1913), republican prefect and lawyer. Emile Ollivier was indocrinated in the entire spectrum of the politics of the July Monarchy. His father, Desmosthenes, belonged to the Carbonari, was arrested for his subversive activities, and was close friends with Armand Carrel, Pierre Leroux, and Alexandre-Auguste Ledru-Rollin, while his maternal grandmother was a fanatical legitimist. Emile received the best schooling available in Provence, and when his father's business failed, Emile won a scholarship to the Lycée Saint-Barbe in Paris. He studied law in the capital and was admitted to the bar of Paris in 1846.

The young lawyer was thrust into politics by his father after the Revolution of 1848. Ledru-Rollin wanted to appoint his friend, the elder Ollivier, as commissioner-general for Marseilles. Desmosthenes, believing new men should staff the Republic, declined in favor of his son. Ollivier brought youthful enthusiasm to his new job. He preached unity to the citizens of the Bouches-du-Rhône as he attempted to plant firmly the tree of republicanism in the legitimist soil of the Midi. The young idealist, who wanted to accomplish great things, was an eloquent and powerful speaker. He had the ability to move his fellow citizens, even admirals at Toulon, to tears. His rhetorical power, however, could not compensate for his lack of political experience.

Like his hero, Alphonse de Lamartine, Ollivier had a pure vision of the goodness of the people, and Ollivier correctly saw that strident republicanism could not succeed in Marseilles. He failed, however, to understand that the fruits of victory could also not be denied his fellow republicans. He thus refused to remove all Orleanists from power, he supported the bishop, and he even favored a wide spectrum of candidates in the April elections. Although these compromising actions angered the republicans of Marseilles and Ledru-Rollin, he was nonetheless promoted to prefect of the Bouches-du-Rhône on 8 June 1848. Shortly after, Ollivier lost the support of the forces of order by his failure to prevent the workers of Marseilles from manning the barricades over their own grievances.

Although Ollivier successfully restored order to Marseilles, General Eugène Cavaignac had no tolerance for an official who put charity ahead of order. Ollivier was demoted to the prefecture of the Haute-Marne (10 July 1848). Once again, this religious socialist captured the hearts of the populace with his eloquence while also running an efficient administration. Nevertheless, soon after the election of Louis-Napoleon, Ollivier, who had voted for Lamartine, was removed from his post, despite the public outcry from the citizens of Chaumont.

Ollivier continued to express his political views based on love and fraternity, which the regime interpreted as socialism. He was arrested by the prefect of the Var, Baron Haussmann, in 1849 for campaigning for republican candidates. Acquitted by a jury and cheered in the streets, Ollivier went forth with his preaching to the citizens of Provence. His early political career ended in 1851, however. His father, who had been elected to the Constituent Assembly in April 1848 and sat with the Left, was banished from France. His brother, the editor of a republican newspaper for which Emile wrote and which was being prosecuted by the government, was killed in a duel by a legitimist. After these shocks and having lived the life of a romantic republican, Ollivier returned to the life of a lawyer.

His ability to capture the minds of people through his speeches propelled Ollivier back into the political arena as a Parisian lawyer, then as an opposition deputy to the Corps législatif, and finally as leader of the Liberal Empire in 1869. He returned with a more practical view of politics, yet one where his belief in unity over blind dedication to party would endure.

E. Ollivier, *Journal, 1846–1869* (Paris, 1961); T. Zeldin, *Emile Ollivier and the Liberal Empire of Napoleon III* (Oxford, 1963).

*Thomas Beck*

*Related entries:* CARBONARI; CARREL; CAVAIGNAC, L.-E.; CONSTITUTION OF 1848; LAMARTINE; LEDRU- ROLLIN; LEROUX; REPUBLICANS; REVOLUTION OF 1848.

**OMNIBUS COMPANY,** Parisian stage line. Although Paris had had public carriages with fixed itineraries as early as the 1660s, public transport remained largely in the hands of individual owners until the early nineteenth century. In

1828, after ten years of rejecting applications to start city-wide service, the prefect of police licensed F. Baudry (who owned a public transport company in Nantes) to start omnibus lines (*transports en commun*) in the capital. Baudry opened eighteen lines in April 1828, using stagecoach-like *diligences* with fourteen seats divided into three compartments (*coupé, intérieur, rotonde*) and an average fare of 25 centimes. Baudry mismanaged the company (L'Entreprise de l'omnibus), lost money, and committed suicide, but the service he provided was popular, and by the 1850s more than a dozen horse-drawn omnibus companies were operating. Competition, overlapping routes, traffic congestion, and poor service to outlying areas of the city led the prefect of police to order the consolidation of the various companies, and in July 1854 a contract (ratified by imperial decree in February 1855) united the nine surviving firms (Dames-réunies, Favorites, Béarnaises, Citadines, Batignolles-Gazelles, Constantines, Tricycles, Excellentes, and Hirondelles-parisiennes) as the Société générale des omnibus de Paris. The city granted the new company a thirty-year monopoly, fixed fares at 30 centimes (later lowered to 20), and approved the routes to be served.

The company initially ran twenty-five lines (covering 150 kilometers) inside the city limits and twenty-eight lines (195 kilometers) in the *banlieue*, as well as two tram lines (with the carriages on rails) from the Louvre to St. Cloud and Sèvres (18 kilometers). It owned 569 coaches (all with added open-air impériales [15 centime fare]) and 3,285 horses, carried an estimated 40 million passengers in its first nine months, and made a gross profit of more than 8 million francs. In 1860, the company received a new fifty-year monopoly (until 1910) and by 1868 was serving thirty-two routes. As electric trams became available in the 1880s, they were included in the company monopoly, and tracks were laid to handle the new vehicles, which could seat up to forty passengers. There were no fixed stops, and prospective passengers signaled the driver to stop his coach. Service in the 1870s was available from 7 A.M. until midnight.

Travelers' accounts suggest that the system was horribly overcrowded, and the growing profusion of vehicles and tracks (which accelerated after the city began licensing competing tram companies in the 1870s) soon confronted city officials with the same problems of congestion that the creation of the Omnibus Company had been designed to eliminate. Ever-larger coaches (horse drawn, electric, or with steam, hot water, or compressed air power) confined traffic increasingly to the major boulevards and further aggravated the situation. This resulted in the search for less disruptive means of transport that culminated in the decision to construct the subway system in 1895. In 1929, the remaining tram lines were replaced with motor buses.

The creation of the Omnibus Company reflected the government's continuing interest in providing the widest possible service while maintaining central direction of the system. The directors of the company, on the other hand, never entirely reconciled themselves to the necessity of servicing some routes at a loss and sought to streamline their operations and maximize profits. This conflict, like the problem of congestion, was ultimately resolved only by the Métropolitain.

N. Evenson, *Paris* (New Haven, 1979); C. Freedeman, *Joint-Stock Enterprise in France, 1807–1867* (Chapel Hill, 1979); J. K. Huysmans, *Croquis parisiens* (Paris, 1886); A. Martin, *Etudes historiques et statistiques sur les moyens de transport dans Paris* (Paris, 1894); P. Merlin, *Les Transports parisiens* (Paris, 1967); A. Sutcliffe, *The Autumn of Central Paris* (Montreal, 1971).

*David Longfellow*

**ONE HUNDRED DAYS.** See HUNDRED DAYS.

*L'OPINION DES FEMMES* (1848–1849), radical women's paper, two issues in August 1848 and six monthly issues January–August 1849, under the subtitle *Liberty, Equality, Fraternity for All Men and Women. A Publication of the Women's Mutual Education Society.* The chief editor was Jeanne Deroin, a seamstress and then teacher, and among the contributors were Olinde Rodrigues and Hortense Wild, two wealthy Saint-Simonians who sustained the paper, Désirée Gay, and Pauline Roland. Five thousand copies were printed of the January 1849 issue. It called for the elimination of all privileges of sex, race, birth, caste, and wealth, for the right to work and to subsistence, and for equal educational and job opportunities for women. However, despite its hostility toward Pierre-Joseph Proudhon, the paper accepted a certain stereotype of women as embodying justice and civilization in a pacific and nurturing role. The paper was more important as the mouthpiece of Deroin's program to unite all existing workers' associations in a socialism of production and distribution. The imposition of caution money in July 1849, requiring 5,000 francs deposit, was fatal for the paper.

L. Adler, *A l'aube du féminisme: les premières journalistes (1830–1850)* (Paris, 1979); R. Gossez, *Les Ouvriers de Paris*, vol. 1 (Paris, 1967).

*Peter McPhee*

*Related entries:* DEROIN; PROUDHON; ROLAND; SAINT-SIMONIANISM; SOCIALISM; WOMEN'S NEWSPAPERS.

*L'ORGANISATEUR* (15 August 1829–15 August 1831), four-page weekly journal published by the Saint-Simonians. After their first journal, the *Producteur*, had ceased publication in 1826, the Saint-Simonian sect spent two years in discrete discussions out of the public eye. By late 1828, however, the group was ready again to take up the challenge of public debate and transmitting their message. Since it set particular store by achieving its ends through persuasion and conversion rather than through political or violent means, it undertook an increasingly varied propaganda campaign. Lectures and discussion meetings were begun in the capital, proselytizing missions sent to the provinces and abroad, and an elaborate correspondence established with selected bourgeois in the provinces. But above all it sought to convert by the printed word. It issued a stream of tracts and pamphlets that grew to a torrent in 1831, as well as journals that were eventually distributed free to deputies and subscribers throughout the country. The best known of the latter is the *Globe*, the successful liberal paper that the sect took over in December 1830 and published for seventeen months. However, the Saint-Simonians' first intention late in 1828 had been to resurrect the *Producteur*, and it was while publication plans were being made that a member of the group, P. M. Laurent de l'Ardêche (1793–1877), was offered the editorship of a new paper to be devoted to a discussion of recent theories on education. Laurent agreed, provided that he could also deal with wider philosophical questions in the paper's columns. The journal, which took the name of the *Organisateur* (also the title of one of Saint-Simon's periodicals), quickly became an entirely Saint-Simonian publication. The intention was that this journal would make the analysis of contemporary ills and the remedies the sect was developing in its lectures in the capital available in abbreviated form for a wider public. The journal secured able editors; Charles Duveyrier (1803–66), Gustave d'Eichthal, and Hippolyte Margerin joined Laurent. Nevertheless, the new weekly enjoyed scant success and by December 1829 had secured only 150 subscribers. When, in August 1831, the sect's propaganda activities were putting too great a strain on financial resources, the *Organisateur* was abandoned in favor of the *Globe*. The *Globe*, too, proved a propaganda and financial failure.

*Barrie M. Ratcliffe*

*Related entries:* D'EICHTHAL; *LE GLOBE*; SAINT-SIMON; SAINT-SIMONIANISM.


*L'ORGANISATION DU TRAVAIL* (1848), workers' newspaper, twenty-two issues 3–23 June 1848, under the subtitle of *The Voice of the People Is the Voice of God. The Street Is the First and Most Sacred of Clubs*. Its founder was Léon-Hubert Lacollonge (alternatively La Collonge, Lacolonge), a lycée professor, founder of the Democratic Association of Schoolmasters, and president of the working-class Club des Antonins. Among the contributors were Savinien Lapointe and Charles Deslys, who wrote a satiric column "Les Prolétariennes." Up to 10,000 copies of each issue were printed. The paper was forcibly closed in June.

The paper was a major organ of the workers' movement, publishing many manifestos and statutes of associations and cooperatives, especially for wallpaper workers. On 8 and 11 June it published, with *La Réforme*, lists of the sixty leading capitalists of Paris and the eighty richest proprietors of France.

Controversy centers on whether this revolutionary and socialist paper was also Bonapartist. A founder, Clavelle d'Oisy, was a Bonapartist former banker, and the paper called for "a little bread and glory. . . . Long live whoever will give us bread!" However, Lacollonge was a leading figure in the June insurrection, heading an effective administration from the town hall of the 8th arrondissement in the faubourg Saint-Antoine, after evicting the elected mayor, Victor Hugo. The town hall was not taken until the afternoon of 25 June. Lacollonge was sentenced to twenty years' imprisonment but amnestied in 1856.

R. Gossez, "Presse parisienne à destination des ouvriers (1848–1851)," in *La Presse ouvrière, 1819–1850*, ed. J. Godechot (Paris, 1966); D. C. McKay, *The National Workshops. A Study in the French Revolution of 1848* (Cambridge, Mass., 1933).

*Peter McPhee*

Related entries: BONAPARTISM; HUGO; JUNE DAYS; LAPOINTE; *LA REFORME*; REVOLUTION OF 1848; WORKERS' COOPERATIVES.

**OUDINOT, CHARLES-NICOLAS-VICTOR** (1791–1863), duc de Reggio, general, and politician. Oudinot served as Napoleon's page at the battle of Wagram in 1809. He was commissioned into the Hussards soon after and became André Masséna's aide-de-camp in Portugal. He fought in the Russian campaign, at the battle of Leipzig (1813) and at Montmirail and Craonne (1814). Napoleon's surrender in 1814 found Oudinot a colonel. He took the oath of loyalty to Louis XVIII and remained faithful to the Bourbons during the Hundred Days of Napoleon's return from Elba. During the Restoration, he was given the task of reorganizing the cavalry school at Saumur. He resigned from the army in 1830 but returned to serve in Algeria as a lieutenant general in 1835. As the deputy for Saumur during the July Monarchy, he voted with the moderate opposition. In 1849, Oudinot commanded the French expeditionary force in Italy that captured Rome on 1 July. He earned the gratitude of the Romans for his refusal to bombard the city during the two month siege. He was arrested following Louis-Napoleon Bonaparte's coup d'état of 2 December 1851.

L. Girard, *La IIe république* (Paris, 1968); G. Six, *Les Généraux de la Révolution et de l'Empire* (Paris, 1934).

*Douglas Porch*

Related entries: CHAMBER OF DEPUTIES; COUP D'ETAT OF 2 DECEMBER 1851; HUNDRED DAYS; LOUIS XVIII; ROMAN EXPEDITION.

**OUVRARD, GABRIEL-JULIEN** (1770–1846), financier. The son of a papermaker, he got an early start in the colonial trade on which the prosperity of Nantes was based, and he had already made a sizable fortune when the Revolution and the fighting in the western provinces compelled him to seek temporary asylum in the ranks of the republican armies. After Thermidor he was safe to resume his commercial and banking activities. In 1797, he obtained from the Directory a commission as purveyor general for the French armies, to which he added the same office for the Spanish fleet, which received supplies in French ports. Among all the profiteers of the corrupt regime, he was possibly the most conspicuous, displaying the luxury of a nabob. Napoleon was both fascinated and exasperated by the wizardry and boldness of the financier; many times he had to resort to his help, borrowing heavily from him and then accusing him of swindling. Three times he had Ouvrard arrested, without being able to obtain a conviction on the charges.

After 1815 Ouvrard continued to be in the forefront of activity, producing financial plans so ingenious that public officials could not understand them and dismissed them with skepticism or hostility. In his memoirs Ouvrard boasted that he had had a decisive part in helping France to meet the financial obligations of the Treaty of Paris and thus put an early end to foreign occupation, though it is difficult to assess the validity of these claims. It is a fact, at least, that the honest Armand-Emmanuel de Richelieu trusted him enough to allow his nephew, General Auguste Rochechouart, to marry Ouvrard's daughter. The great financier had always had a special interest in Spain. Around 1804 he had conceived a grandiose plan for using the resources of Spanish America. When Spain, in 1820–21, was once again torn by internal strife, Ouvrard helped the conservative junta by floating a loan on its behalf. He went to Verona to submit his plans to the congress of European ministers that had met to consider the Spanish situation. When the French army entered Spain in the spring of 1823, it was at first hampered by the mismanagement of supplies by the military administration. Ouvrard stepped in and set up his own private operation, which succeeded in supplying the army in a way that was also satisfactory for the Spanish people. Afterward, however, doubts were expressed concerning the regularity of his actions. The matter was debated at length in the parliament, and Ouvrard was brought to court. Finally he was acquitted. But the government reneged on its obligations, and Ouvrard faced bankruptcy. Instead of trying to remove this debt, Ouvrard chose to spend five years, the maximum legal sentence, in the special prison for debtors (Sainte-Pélagie). When he emerged, his luck and importance had faded. With the emergence of the house of Rothschild, governments had other—and perhaps more trustworthy—financiers to solve their problems. Ouvrard, almost forgotten, lived his last years in Holland and England.

M. Payard, *Le Financier Ouvrard* (Reims, 1958); O. Wolff, *Ouvrard, Speculator of Genius* (London, 1932).

*Guillaume de Bertier de Sauvigny*
*Related entries:* PARIS, SECOND TREATY OF; RICHELIEU; ROTHSCHILD FAMILY; SAINTE-PELAGIE PRISON; SPAIN, 1823 FRENCH INVASION OF; VERONA, CONGRESS OF.

# P

**PALAIS BOURBON.** See CHAMBER OF DEPUTIES.

*LA PANDORE.* See *LE MIROIR DES SPECTACLES*.

**PARIS.** Although the history of the capital between 1815 and 1852 has not received as much attention from historians as the preceding and succeeding periods, Paris in this period underwent significant demographic and socio-economic change. These changes altered its economic geography, its use of urban space, and its place in France's economy and society. Administrative centralization, which had been strengthened under the Revolutionary and Napoleonic regimes, meant that Paris had some 5,000 civil servants, including over a thousand at the Ministry of Finance but excluding the 500 who worked for the prefecture of the Seine and the mayors of the arrondissements. Cultural centralization meant that Paris drew in and drew out talents and was a cultural and artistic center without rival in Europe. Heine, indeed, claimed, "Paris is actually France; the latter is only the surrounding area of Paris." Whether or not this is true, it is clear that politics and culture in Paris blend with the history of France as a whole and will not be studied here.

The history of Paris as urban history—its demography, economy, and administration—has received much less attention from scholars. The tendency has been to assume that the only significant change taking place was the unprecedented in-migration that so impressed bourgeois contemporaries and, in their wake, the historian Louis Chevalier. A number of considerations seemed to justify this assumption. Paris was still a pedestrian rather than a railway city. Its industry was still largely artisanal, was dominated by the local and luxury markets, and was structured by large numbers of small enterprises and thus little touched by change. Its prefects lacked the éclat, daring, and achievements of a Baron Haussmann. Indeed, there seemed to be little planning and, apart from the ring of fortifications built around the capital between 1840 and 1844, no extension of the administrative limits of the city. Only recently have scholars begun to realize that this neglected period of Parisian history was one of unprecedented change. The changes were only in small part wrought by decision makers in local government. They were in large part the consequence of wider, interrelated forces, of demographic and economic changes, that radically altered the size, physiognomy, and functions of the city. Paris's role as a political and cultural capital was enhanced, as was the wealth of the city and its elite. Trends like the westward migration of bourgeois and business quarters were reinforced. The economy of the Right Bank grew more rapidly than that of the Left. The peripheral quarters and inner suburbs to the north and north-east of the city saw the beginnings of remarkable development. Worries began to be expressed as to the spatial development of Paris and its shifting center of gravity.

The most obvious of these forces was the demographic. In 1801 Paris, with just over a half-million inhabitants, was already five times larger than Lyons, the second city. Fifty years later it had nearly doubled its population (to 996,067) and had grown faster than any of France's nine largest cities. As a result, Paris had 2.3 percent of French population in 1801 but nearly 3 percent in 1851, and the Paris region, which had constituted 15 percent of urban population in 1811, made up 19.5 percent in 1851. This growth is striking when it is compared with the population history of Paris in the eighteenth century. It is all the more striking because it was achieved in large measure by in-migration rather than by natural increase. Half of the city's population in this period had been born outside the Seine department. Further research is needed on the causes and consequences of this in-migration from a relatively limited catchment area. We already know, however, that it helped give the Parisian population an age pyramid that set it off from the national average; a higher proportion of inhabitants were in the productive, adult years. This demographic growth not only encouraged the spatial expansion of the city and its inner suburbs but led to rising population densities within the capital and to overcrowding in some quarters. Especially high densities (over 1,000 per hectare) were found in the Montorgueil, Marchés, Lombards, and Arcis quarters in the center Right Bank area that contained over a third of the city's inhabitants. Since provision of housing and services in these overcrowded slums failed to keep pace with population increase, death rates were high. These areas were particularly vulnerable to the cholera epidemics that periodically struck Paris and other European cities from the early 1830s. The cholera outbreak of 1832, for instance, carried off 20,000 inhabitants in the space of a few months. The July Days of 1830, by contrast, led to only 600 or 700 fatalities. These areas, then, helped give Paris a crude mortality rate of 26.1 percent as against a national average in 1851 of 23.3 percent. Fears about the effects of such unsanitary conditions on the social mores and behavior of Parisian workers were a recurring theme in the writings of hygienists and reformers, as well as in many contemporary novels.

The economy, and above all the industry, of the Paris region was also going through significant change and was of increasing importance in France as a whole. The Empire had already consecrated Paris's triumph over other regional redistribution centers like Lyons and Orléans. After 1815, however, the dynamism of the capital was all the more striking in view of the stagnation in many other regional redistribution centers and the languor of the Atlantic ports. Its business elite wielded increasing power in certain sectors of the economy: banking, investments in transport, particularly canals and railways, and in modern heavy industry. In banking, for example, the capital attracted both funds and financial talent and enjoyed the advantage of having the Bank of France, which until 1835 restricted its activities to Paris, as well as a wealthy and innovating merchant banking community. As a result, Paris enjoyed a greater supply of bank notes, better discount and credit facilities, and thus lower interest rates than the provinces.

Although the capital had 340,000 industrial workers in 1847, a depression year, 89 percent of industrial firms employed fewer than ten workers, and as many as half either had only one worker or consisted of an artisan working alone. This structure and the handicraft nature of much local industry should not induce us to believe that structures were immobile or that Paris was of no consequence in industrial growth in this period. Important innovations in products and capitalist organization took place even in sectors untouched by mechanization as, for instance, in the rise of ready-made clothing and shoes and in hat and shawl making. At the same time, large-scale and mechanized industry expanded. In 1847 over 7,000 enterprises employed more than ten workers. Chemicals, sugar refining, and, above all, machine building not only grew but were leaders in their sectors in France. That Paris was responsible for about a third of French industrial production by value is some indication of the weight of the capital in the national economy. That industrial exports from Paris tripled in value between 1820 and 1847 and, as a percentage of French exports, rose from 11 to no less than 23 percent is indicative of the capital's significance in France's foreign trade. That industrial workers and their dependents made up at least 60 percent of the city's population is some indication of the importance of industry in the Parisian economy. That the value of industrial production in the city declined by at least half between 1847 and 1848 shows the importance of fluctuations in the trade cycle—in this case, as in the early 1830s, accentuated by political disturbances—in the life of the Parisian worker.

Industrial growth was favored by in-migration and by traditions and networks of craft skills and enterprise. Large-scale enterprise was aided by relatively cheap capital, a local reservoir of skills, and improved transportation. Paris in this period remained a pedestrian city. Goods transport was still largely water-borne at midcentury. Transport to and within the capital, however, was transformed from the 1820s. Horse-drawn omnibuses made their appearance in 1828, and by 1850 there were eleven companies with a combined fleet of 300 vehicles. But they provided only a limited service and served only a middle-class clientele. The railway also came to Paris, first in suburban lines to St.-Germain (1837) and to Versailles (1839), then in trunk lines to Rouen, Orléans, the north and Belgium, Strasbourg, and Lyons. By 1850, then, there were six railway terminals in the capital; however, the railway still played a minor role in goods transport. The most important developments here occurred in water transport. Whatever its imperfections, the canal network proposed in the early 1820s and gradually completed thereafter improved the capital's links with markets and sources of supply. The Parisian canals—the St. Denis, which linked La Villette to the Seine below the capital, opened in 1821, and the St. Martin, which in 1825 completed the link by joining La Villette to the river above Paris at the new port at the Arsenal—had a major impact on the economic and spatial development of the city. Their success, together with the topographical advantages of the St. Denis plain, encouraged the development of peripheral quarters and inner suburbs to the north and northeast of the city. As a consequence and although the navigability of the Seine to and within the capital was only tardily and imperfectly improved, Paris by the 1840s was the country's largest port, handling 2.5 million tons of goods and over 21,000 boats a year. The port of La Villette alone handled as much traffic as did the port of Le Havre.

Given the unleashing of such forces and the unprecedented scale of the urban problems they created, it is not surprising that local government failed to grapple adequately with them. There is reason to believe, however, that historians have underestimated the difficulties faced by the municipal administration and unfairly dismissed its achievements. It is true that the two principal incumbents of the post of prefect of the Seine—the comte Chabrol de Volvic (1773–1843), who was prefect from 1812 to 1830, and the comte de Rambuteau (1781–1869), prefect from 1833 to 1848—enjoyed the political power to impose their wills. The Municipal Council, nominated before 1834, had no real voice in the city's administration, while the mayors of the twelve arrondissements, who were also nominated, had small staffs and few powers. What the prefects did not have and what Haussmann, their more famous successor, did were the prerequisites that would have enabled them to grapple properly with problems: money (or at least financial daring), technical know-how and personnel, and an overall plan. Municipal finances, for example, were long burdened by the cost of two military occupations of the capital in 1814 and 1815 and by the costs of relief stemming from the poor harvests of 1816–17, which together cost the city 77 million francs. The city's budget at this time was around 40 million francs a year. This burden helps explain why prefects were anxious to avoid increasing the municipal debt, though it does not excuse Rambuteau's turning the need for economy into an article of faith. It helps explain, too, why both Chabrol and Rambuteau were willing to call on private enterprise for many new projects. The new bourgeois residential quarters, like Grenelle and Tivoli, that were set up in the 1820s were created entirely by private speculators. Private companies built bridges across the Seine and had given gas lighting to half the city's streets by 1850.

Nonetheless, both prefects had achievements. Between 1815 and 1830 Chabrol spent 32 million francs on canals, over 55 million on restoring and erecting public buildings, 8 million on extending water supply and drains, and 7 million on street improvements. Far from regretting Chabrol's timidity, indeed, one recent historian (Jean Tulard) has accused him of being too audacious in his ambitions for the capital and encouragement to private enterprise and industry. No such accusation has ever been made of Rambuteau. Whatever his timidity and parsimony, however, he achieved more than Chabrol in his public works. The quays along the Seine were completed, and the rue Rambuteau was pushed through the Marais. Water distribution was improved, and there was a tenfold increase in length of pipes and volume of water distributed (though only one-sixth of this went to private houses). The length of drains in Paris increased just over threefold between 1832 and 1850, and the male Parisian gained street urinals. In the last years of the July Monarchy, Rambuteau was planning even more extensive changes, but economic crisis and political revolution prevented their execution.

Despite these achievements, neither Chabrol nor Rambuteau effectively tackled the problems posed by a burgeoning city. There was thus no attempt to establish the major arteries that would have eliminated the barriers to east-west, north-south traffic in the congested city center. Their improvements enhanced rather than reduced the social inequality in accessibility of services—drains and water—because the lion's share went to the richer quarters. In 1850, then, Paris had only sixty-eight public fountains (1 per 15,000 inhabitants) but some 5,000 water carriers, and many residents were forced to rely on impure water from river and wells. That too little had been done was also evidenced in the municipal budget; social services—hospitals and poor relief—were still the major items of expenditure.

The matrix of demographic and economic forces that formed the capital had an impact on classes and class relations and on the spatial development of the city. The gap between rich and poor widened. The wealth and status of the bourgeoisie were enhanced. One sign of this is the tax burden borne by Parisians. Making up just under 3 percent of the population, they paid nearly 7 percent of direct taxation and 12 percent of indirect in the 1830s. Another sign is the power and status the Parisian bourgeoisie increasingly enjoyed. Their behavior patterns were becoming more and more the norm, as witnessed in the growth of restaurants, of which there were over 3,000 in 1820 as against under 50 before the Revolution, the opening of shopping arcades, and the first department stores, like the Aux trois quartiers, the spread of *charcuteries*, and the rise of elegant new quarters on the Right Bank west. If it is clear the bourgeoisie was becoming richer and more influential, there are no indications that the working classes were improving their conditions. Fragmentary statistics indicate that literacy was widespread; some 80 percent of Parisians could read and write. They also indicate, however, that male workers' real wages stagnated at best. Given the marked fluctuations in the trade cycle and the spread of capitalist organization in industry, there is even reason to believe that there was a deterioration in living standards for all but a small proportion of workers. Women workers certainly saw their conditions worsen. Their wages averaged half those of male workers. Between 1837 and

1846 there were nearly 100,000 illegitimate births in the capital (some one-third of total births), and it was working-class women who bore the cost.

Just over 85 percent of industrial workers, and a similar proportion of industrial production, was concentrated on the Right Bank. Spatial development—the shifting center of gravity of the city, the traffic congestion and overcrowding of some city center areas—led to debates on the problem and possible solutions. Only under Napoleon III and Haussmann were effective solutions implemented. But even then, as earlier, there were facets of urban growth that decision makers did not control, like industrialization, working-class housing, and suburban growth. The history of the capital and the use of urban space continued to be dominated by more discrete factors such as topography, land values, and transport systems.

G. de Bertier de Sauvigny, *La Restauration* (Paris, 1977); E. Canfora-Argundona and R. H. Guerrand, *La Répartition de la population, les conditions de logement des classes ouvrières à Paris au XIXe siècle* (Paris, 1976); L. Chevalier, *Classes laborieuses et classes dangereuses à Paris pendant la première moitié du XIXe siècle* (Paris, 1958) and *La Formation de la population parisienne au XIXe siècle* (Paris, 1950); A. Daumard, *La Bourgeoisie parisienne de 1815 à 1848* (Paris, 1963); Georges Duby, ed., *Histoire de la France urbaine*, vol. 4 (Paris, 1983); M. Daumas, ed., *Evolution de la géographie industrielle de Paris et sa proche banlieue au XIXe siècle*, 2 vols. plus atlas (Paris, 1976); H. Heine, *Lutezia* (Leipzig, 1959); P. Lavedan, *Histoire de l'urbanisme à Paris* (Paris, 1975); G. Massa-Gille, *Histoire des emprunts de la ville de Paris (1814–1875) (Paris, 1973); J. Tulard, Paris et son administration (1800–1830)* (Paris, 1976).

*Barrie M. Ratcliffe*

Related entries: BANKING; CHABROL DE VOLVIC; MIGRATION; OMNIBUS COMPANY; PARIS, SECOND TREATY OF; POPULATION; RAILROADS; RAMBUTEAU.


**PARIS, COMTE DE** (1838–1894), Orleanist pretender and publicist. Louis-Philippe-Albert d'Orléans, the comte de Paris, became heir to the throne of Louis-Philippe on the death of his father, the duc d'Orléans, in 1842. When Louis-Philippe abdicated on 24 February 1848, the count's mother, Hélène of Mecklenberg-Schwerin, tried in vain to convince the Chamber of Deputies to accept the nine year old as monarch.

After the Revolution of 1848, he was brought up by his mother at Eisenach and in England. He and his brother Robert, duc de Chartres, were aides-de-camp in McClellan's federal army in 1862. After the fall of the Second Empire in 1870, the count sought fusion with the Bourbon house with the understanding that the heirless Chambord would be pretender, with the count of Paris as his successor. Chambord consistently rejected this until his death in 1883.

The count lived in Paris until expelled by the Chamber of Deputies in 1886 after attempts to establish a more obvious presence as the royal alternative to the Republic. He lived in England until his death. Among his many publications during his lengthy periods of exile is *Les Associations ouvrières en Angleterre* (1869).

*Grand Larousse Encyclopédique*, 10 vols. (Paris, 1960–64).

Peter McPhee

Related entries: BORDEAUX; CHAMBER OF DEPUTIES; CHARTRES; JOINVILLE; LOUIS-PHILIPPE; NEMOURS; REVOLUTION OF 1848.

**PARIS, SECOND TREATY OF** (1815), final treaty ending the war between Napoleonic France and the Allies. The discussions for the drafting of this treaty were more drawn out than had been those for the first treaty of May 1814. The Allies were in no haste to reach a conclusion; their armies, some 1 million men spread over the greater part of France, could enjoy living off the fat of the land. According to the procedure set in their first meeting, the ministers of the four great Allies (Austria, England, Prussia, and Russia) began by discussing among themselves the terms that would be presented in a common document to the French government. Such an accord was not easily reached. The four parties acknowledged that France would have to pay dearly for the blood and money expended to defeat Napoleon a second time and also that some precautions would have to be taken against the renewal of such calamities. But the Prussians wanted to cut out large chunks of the northeastern provinces as a buffer zone, while the Russian czar considered only financial retributions, bolstered by some temporary military occupation of French territory. The British foreign secretary, Viscount Castlereagh, and Clemens von Metternich, working hand in hand, acted as arbiters; they compelled the Prussian representatives, Karl-August von Hardenberg and Alexander von Humboldt, to desist from their extreme position. Still, the draft presented to Charles-Maurice de Talleyrand on 20 September was so harsh that the French minister rejected it outright. Three days later he resigned, and Louis XVIII appointed in his stead the duc de Richelieu. In the meantime the king had also written a personal letter to Czar Alexander stating emotionally that he would abdicate before accepting such a *diktat*. The terms were then slightly amended so that the king and his new minister could swallow the bitter pill. But it still took more than six weeks to complete the numerous secondary documents that covered all the details of the financial and military arrangements. The treaties were formally signed on 15 November 1815. France lost most of the territories it had been allowed to retain in 1814. It would have to pay a war indemnity of 700 million francs, plus all the debts incurred toward foreign private parties (which eventually were to amount to 240 million francs). Finally, there would be a military occupation of the borderland provinces by 150,000 foreign troops, the maintenance of which would also be charged to the French treasury. Part of the 700 million indemnity was to be used to build a line of fortresses along the French-Belgian (kingdom of the Netherlands) border.

G. de Bertier de Sauvigny, *Metternich et la France* (Paris, 1968); J. Cretineau-Joly, *Histoire des traités de 1815 et de leur exécution* (Paris, 1842); A. Schaumann, *Geschichte des zweiten Pariser Friedens* (Göttingen, 1844); A. Sorel, *Le Traité de Paris du 20 Novembre 1815* (Paris, 1872).

*Guillaume de Bertier de Sauvigny*

*Related entries:* HUNDRED DAYS; LOUIS XVIII; RICHELIEU; TALLEYRAND.

**PARIS FACULTY OF MEDICINE.** By abolishing universities, academies and corporations from 1791 to 1793, the Revolutionary government destroyed the system of medicine of the *ancien régime*. For a decade, liberty of practice was permitted in spite of the fact that the military need for qualified medical men led to the reestablishment in 1794 of institutions of medical education. In 1803 these became the basis for a national system of education and licensing for doctors.

Three faculties—at Paris, Montpellier, and Strasbourg—granted the doctorates of medicine and surgery that served effectively as national licenses. To supplement these institutions, towns and cities were encouraged to establish *écoles secondaires de médecine et de pharmacie* around their local hospitals. These were integrated into the medical education system from 1806 to 1809. They were permitted to teach the first two years of the four-year program for the doctorate, but their primary role was the training of low-level *officiers de santé* for practice in the countryside.

Professors at the Paris Faculty of Medicine soon constituted a powerful elite within this system. With the return of the Bourbons to France in 1814, a major challenge to the authority of the Paris Faculty was mounted by the remnants of the corporate elites of the *ancien régime*, led by the chief surgeon of Louis XVIII, Père Elisée (Marie-Vincent Talachon). In November 1815, the king appointed a special commission to examine the state of medicine, unleashing a massive pamphlet campaign against or in favor of the existing system of medicine. The commission voted by a narrow margin to dismantle the existing system of medical education and to return to a system of corporate control. The government, however, proved unwilling to act on this advice or to retreat in any way from the centralized system established under the Empire. After 1820, its relationship to the faculties deteriorated considerably as a result of the regime's drift to the right and the widespread hostility of medical students to the electoral law. But rather than transforming institutions, the government preferred to change personnel. In 1822, the government closed the Paris Faculty of Medicine, reopening it several months later without eleven professors who were dismissed from their posts and replaced by government nominees.

During the next thirty years, dissatisfaction with the system of medical education remained intense. Although it did not disappear, the idea of dismantling the medical faculties was overshadowed by debates over more specific issues like the quality of education in the *écoles secondaires*, extending by a year the program for the doctorate, overcrowding in medicine, and, in the 1860s, the need to provide formal hospital training to all students. By far the most controversial issue involved the *officiers de santé*. Almost everyone agreed that *officiers* were poorly trained. One solution was to upgrade the program and raise educational standards. This idea lay behind reform proposals introduced in 1826 and 1842. Another, vigorously promoted by the organized medical profession and inspiring reform projects in 1821, 1838, and 1847, was to eliminate the degree and to allow only doctors to practice medicine. This, however, raised the spectre of serious shortages of qualified practitioners in rural areas. The issue was debated for over thirty years but could not be resolved within the framework of legislative reforms. In 1854 the educational administration abandoned this legislative route and utilized its administrative prerogatives to raise the educational standards of *officiers*. From then on, the number of *officiers* declined steadily until the formal abolition of the degree in 1892.

A. Corlieu, *Centenaire de la Faculté de Médecine de Paris, 1794–1894* (Paris, 1896); C. Coury, *L'Enseignement de la médecine en France des origines à nos jours* (Paris, 1968); R. Fox and G. Weisz, eds., *The Organization of Science and Technology in France, 1808–1914* (London and Paris, 1980); J. Léonard, "Les Études médicales en France entre 1815 et 1848," *Revue d'histoire moderne et contemporaine* 13 (1966) and *Les Médecins de l'ouest au XIXe siècle* (Lille, 1978); G. Weisz, "The Politics of Medical Professionalization in France, 1845–1848," *Journal of Social History* 12 (1978).

*George Weisz*

**PARTY OF MOVEMENT,** a loosely knit group of reformists who wanted the Orléans monarchy to become more liberal. They wanted it to widen the franchise, to give more power to the Chamber of Deputies, and to carry out a more assertive foreign policy. While it is true that there were no political parties in the twentieth-century sense under the July Monarchy, contemporaries and historians have often seen an essential contrast between the forces of *mouvement*, almost always in opposition, and those of *résistance*. In contrast to the right center of Casimir Périer and his successors and the *Doctrinaires* (supporters of François Guizot and Nicolas-Jean de Soult), the Party of Movement included those, on the Center Left (among them Adolphe Thiers, Jules Dufaure, Charles de Rémusat, Prosper Duvergier de Hauranne, and their mouthpiece *Le Constitutionnel*) and those firmer in their opposition on the dynastic Left (Odilon Barrot, François Mauguin, Adolphe Crémieux, Gustave de Beaumont, Léon de Malleville, Edmond d'Alton-Shée, with *Le Siècle*). The term also distinguishes the monarchist opposition to the July Monarchy from those republicans who wished for a change of regime, although by the mid–1840s republicans such as François Arago, Etienne Garnier-Pagès, and Alexandre-Thomas Marie had accommodated themselves to the constitutional monarchy.

There were a number of issues over which a division of opinion between forces of change and resistance may be seen. First among these was the issue of the balance of power between Louis-Philippe and the legislature. If 1830 had been only a change of dynasty, as Casimir Périer insisted, then the political initiative should continue to lie with the king; if it had been a revolution, then the lower house should be dominant. In practice, while Louis-Philippe never refused to sanction legislation, he sought to play an active and directing role that brought him into conflict with Thiers in particular. Second, the Party of Movement was prepared to call for a cautious widening of the electoral base through a reduction of the tax qualification for voting. Duvergier de Hauranne, for example, wanted the qualification to be lowered from 200 francs to 100 or even 50 francs. Series of political banquets calling for such reform were held in 1840 and 1847–48. Third, the opposition consistently called for parliamentary reform to disqualify government officials from continuing in their positions if elected to the Chamber of Deputies. (Between 1832 and 1846, the number of such double office-holders had increased from 140 to 184 of the 459 deputies.) Barrot also called for administrative decentralization. Finally, this group generally called for a more independent and assertive stance in foreign affairs, notably disagreeing with the entente with England and the government's alleged capitulation (for example, over Tahiti).

The Party of Movement enjoyed control over policies only in the first nine months of the July Monarchy, notably during Jacques Laffitte's ministry (November 1830-March 1831). After the anticlerical riots of February 1831, following the mass at St.-Germain l'Auxerrois to commemorate the assassination of the duc de Berry, Laffitte removed Barrot as prefect of the Seine but was himself dismissed by Louis-Philippe. The ministry of Casimir Périer (March 1831-March 1832) established the guidelines of the regime to 1848, even during Thiers' two brief periods as chief minister in 1836 and 1840.

Thiers' actions when in power are among the reasons why many historians are skeptical about commitment to movement or change as a defining characteristic of the opposition to Guizot. They also point to a continuity of personnel in the ministries of Laffitte and Périer and the similar social attitudes of almost all deputies, especially toward workers and the social question; and they argue that calls for electoral and parliamentary reform were no more than attempts by those frustrated at Louis-Philippe's refusal to appoint them to ministries to seek other ways of winning power.

The 1846 elections returned supporters of Guizot, including large numbers of officials, by a majority of 291 to 168. In response to this, Charles Gauguier and Ovide Remilly again proposed parliamentary reform, and Crémieux, Barrot, and Thiers a widening of the franchise. The majority's refusal to countenance such changes prompted groups within the opposition to take their case to the electorate in a series of about sixty reform banquets. These had a limited success and, combined with the scandals that hit Guizot's government during the winter of 1847–48, resulted in the majority declining to 222 against 189 in Charles Sallandrouze's new proposal for electoral reform on 12 February.

Ultimately, however, the Party of Movement failed since the government did not make concessions on any key issue; moreover, as the loyal opposition within the regime, it was bypassed in the February Revolution by groups for whom a change of regime was necessary. In this sense the Revolution was also made against those who sought to reform the July Monarchy; Louis-Philippe's belated decision to turn at last to Barrot did not satisfy the insurgents. However, as notables who were well known in their electorates and whose opposition to Guizot gave them a claim to be progressive, the men of the Party of Movement were successful in the elections of 1848 and became part of the Party of Order that developed during the Second Republic. Barrot himself was Louis-Napoleon's first prime minister from December 1848 to October 1849.

E. d'Alton-Shée, *Souvenirs de 1847–1848* (Paris, 1879); O. Barrot, *Mémoires posthumes*, 4 vols. (Paris, 1876); D. Johnson, *Guizot: Aspects of French History, 1789–1874* (London, 1963); F. Ponteil, *La Monarchie parlementaire, 1815–1848* (Paris, 1949).

*Peter McPhee*

*Related entries:* ALTON-SHEE; ARAGO FAMILY; BARROT, C.-H.-O.; CREMIEUX; DOCTRINAIRES; DUVERGIER DE HAURANNE; GARNIER-PAGES; GUIZOT; LAFFITTE; MARIE; PARTY OF ORDER; PERIER; REMUSAT; SAINT-GERMAIN L'AUXERROIS, RIOT OF; *LE SIECLE*; SOULT; THIERS.

**PARTY OF ORDER (Parti de l'Ordre),** a monarchist organization of about 200 members that evolved from the Comité (or Réunion) de la rue de Poitiers, founded in May 1848 following a radical demonstration in Paris. There is no definite date on which the group became known as the Parti de l'ordre. In fact, some references use the two names interchangeably. More frequent use of the name begins with the December 1848 election and the accession to power of Louis-Napoleon following his defeat of Eugène Cavaignac at the polls. He immediately chose a member of the Parti de l'ordre, Odilon Barrot, to form his first cabinet. Barrot had been Louis-Philippe's last minister.

As the elected president of the Republic, Louis-Napoleon appeared anxious to work with the Parti de l'ordre, the members of which expected to dominate his ministry and crush the republicans in the National Assembly. While the military leader, General Nicolas Changarnier, proposed using force to dissolve the Assembly, Louis-Napoleon and the Parti de l'ordre opposed him. Many newspapers called for the dissolution of the Assembly. The republican deputies offered an ineffective resistance and finally agreed, on 12 January 1849, to dissolve the body and call for new elections. They had passed only two organic laws, involving elections and the Conseil d'état. In the May 1849 elections the notables in the Parti de l'ordre won a majority of about two-thirds of the 713 seats in the Assembly, ending the domination of the republicans. Even with universal male suffrage inserting an unknown quantity into the elections, results were still conservative. The Parti de l'ordre influenced elections through local committees that were beholden to conservative notables who most often selected the candidates themselves.

In his study of the election by regions, Tudesq found that the Parti de l'ordre carried the elections in the north-northwest, west, and southwest. It was especially strong in ten departments of the north, where, except for six democrats, all those elected were members of the Parti and nearly all were *grands notables*. There the Parti had submitted a list of favorite candidates, some of whom were not residents or had only slender ties to the region.

In the west the eighty-six deputies elected in five departments had the support of the Parti de l'ordre. In four other departments, there was only one person elected who had not been a deputy in the July Monarchy. Universal suffrage in this region served only to strengthen the traditional heritage.

In another group of eight departments between Indre-et-Loire and the Gironde, of the sixty-two deputies elected, fifty-eight were candidates of the Parti de l'ordre. In Charente, Gironde, and Lot-et-Garonne, all except one of the elected deputies had been backed by the Parti. In Bordeaux the great Protestant families lost their influence. In Lorraine and Champagne, fifty-two of the fifty-eight elected deputies were Parti de l'ordre candidates. In the southern part of the Parisian Basin and the middle Loire valley, the Parti also won a majority in spite of the lack of unity among the notables. The election returns in Loire-et-Cher were the least favorable to the organization. In the southeast, feelings were strong against the notables, and a spirit of independence was emerging. In Haute-Garonne and Aude, even with strong democratic opposition, the Parti de l'ordre still won all the seats.

The elections saw the *grands notables* regain their influence and dominance in two-thirds of the departments, and they represented a majority in the Parti de l'ordre, which now embarked on a reactionary course, encouraged by the elections. A majority of Orleanists, 140 legitimists, some Bonapartists, and moderate republicans combined forces in the Parti to oppose radicalism in a transitional society. The number of middle-class deputies had been sharply reduced. Opposing the Parti de l'ordre was the Montagne, a group of radical republican deputies.

Other elections in 1849 and 1850 would see a shift leftward and repressive governmental measures to stem the tide. For example, in March 1850 the *loi Falloux* was passed by the Assembly, returning more authority in education to the church and signaling the return of the church-state alliance. Its intent was to make teachers and the general population more docile and moral.

A new electoral law was imposed in May 1850 that required voters to maintain a residence for three years before being able to vote. Under the old law, a residency of only six months was required. Proof of residency would be provided by a listing on personal tax rolls and by a declaration of parents or an employer. This measure served to reduce by about 29 percent the number of voters because of the mobility of workers due to the changing job market. The percentage was much higher in some areas, especially the cities. Bearing responsibility for passage of the law was the majority of former Orleanists and legitimists, while Bonapartists either abstained or cast negative votes.

Although the Assembly, dominated by the Parti de l'ordre, seemed in the beginning to be a homogeneous group composed of mostly notables, it was not harmonious in its deliberations. The Barrot cabinet soon started to lose its influence in spite of Louis-Napoleon's initial profession of willingness to let the ministry and the Assembly govern. In October 1849 Bonaparte was able to force Barrot, vicomte Falloux, and Alexis de Tocqueville of the Parti de l'ordre to resign. By the following January, he felt secure enough in his popularity and following to say that the ministry's allegiance was to him and not to the Assembly. Favorable economic conditions in 1850 were another factor, added to a pervasive fear of a red terror. While the Parti de l'ordre candidates preached family, property, and religion, Bonapartists quietly talked about roads, canals, and railroads. Louis-Napoleon set about to eliminate parties that were dividing France and to plan for the future. By putting distance between himself and the Parti de l'ordre and winning over the masses and the church, he had destroyed the opposition before his coup d'état.

F. A. de Luna, *The French Republic under Cavaignac, 1848* (Princeton, 1969); R. Price, *The French Second Republic: A Social History* (London, 1972); R. Rémond, *La Droite en France de la Première Restauration à la Ve République* (Paris, 1968); A.-J. Tudesq, *Les Grands Notables en France (1840–1849): Etude historique d'une psychologie sociale*, vol. 2 (Paris, 1964).

*Helen Castelli*

Related entries: BARROT, C.-H.-O.; CAVAIGNAC, L.-E.; CHANGARNIER; COMITE DE LA RUE DE POITIERS; CONSTITUTION OF 1848; COUP D'ETAT OF 2 DECEMBER 1851; ELECTIONS AND ELECTORAL SYSTEMS; FALLOUX LAW; LEGISLATIVE ASSEMBLY; PARTY OF MOVEMENT; REPUBLICANS.

**PASQUIER, ETIENNE-DENIS, DUC** (1767–1862), prefect of police, deputy and peer, president of both Chambers, minister of justice, interior, and foreign affairs, chancellor of France. Pasquier was born in Paris on 21 April 1767 into a family of the nobility of the robe. His father was a councillor in the Parlement of Paris. Educated in the traditions of the robe, which greatly influenced him later, Pasquier entered the parlement in 1787. In 1790 Pasquier's father joined other magistrates in protesting the dissolution of the parlements, an act that nearly cost Pasquier his life. Fleeing Paris, Pasquier returned in November 1793 to marry Anne-Sophie Serre de Saint-Roman. On 20 April 1794 Pasquier's father was executed, and the Committee of Public Safety ordered his own arrest in June. Arrested in Amiens, Pasquier and his wife were saved by the fall of Maximilien Robespierre. Aided by Josephine de Beauharnais and Jean-Jacques de Cambacérès, Pasquier regained some of their confiscated property, including the family chateau of Coulans near Le Mans. There they spent most of the Directory period after an abortive effort in politics in 1795.

Growing restive, Pasquier finally entered Napoleon's service on 11 June 1806 as a master of requests in the Council of State. He was promoted to councillor of state in February 1810. He rationalized that it was to his interest and that of

France to serve Napoleon while awaiting the return of the Bourbons. On 14 October 1810 he was appointed prefect of police. In this capacity he diligently supervised the usual constabulary functions plus such delicate matters as helping ensure the grain supply of Paris. Although the 1812 Malet conspiracy caught him by surprise, he remained as prefect until the First Restoration. Then Louis XVIII appointed him director general of roads and bridges. Pasquier remained unemployed during the Hundred Days. He simultaneously held the ministries of justice and the interior in the Talleyrand government of 1815, using his position to oppose the excesses of the ultraroyalists.

When the Talleyrand government fell, Pasquier left these offices. But he was elected to the Deputies and made a councillor of state. As a deputy until 1821, he followed a moderate royalist path and was elected president of the Deputies in 1816. On 19 January 1817 he became minister of justice, supporting Gouvain Saint-Cyr's army law, the suppression of the provost courts, and the new election law. Resigning with the rest of the cabinet in December 1818, Pasquier returned as minister of foreign affairs under Elie Decazes in November 1819. He was retained in the second Richelieu ministry. A highly capable orator, Pasquier served as chief legislative spokesman for the second Richelieu ministry, combating the excesses of liberals and ultras alike but sanctioning various extraordinary measures on press freedom, individual liberty, and elections. As foreign minister, albeit under Armand-Emmanuel de Richelieu's guidance, Pasquier dealt with the revolutions in Spain, Portugal, Naples, and Piedmont and the congresses of Troppau and Laibach. He attempted to preserve French freedom of action and expand French influence into Spain and Italy. Appointed a peer in September 1821, Pasquier resigned as foreign minister with the fall of Richelieu in December 1821.

In the Peers from 1821 to 1830, Pasquier usually supported the moderate royalist opposition to the ultra governments of the period. He opposed primogeniture, the sacrilege law, and other conservative measures. He hoped to head a cabinet of his own. Instead in August 1830 he was appointed president of the Peers by Louis-Philippe. There he vainly strove to preserve the hereditary peerage, the last vestige of the old noble prerogatives, which was abolished in 1831. Politically Pasquier generally supported the policies of Louis-Philippe. As president of the Peers, he also presided over the trials before the upper Chamber of men such as Louis Napoleon, Fiéschi, the ministers of Charles X, and certain ministers of Louis-Philippe. On 27 May 1837 Louis-Philippe revived the title chancellor of France for Pasquier, and in December 1844 he was made a duke, with inheritance of the title going to his grandnephew, Edme-Armand-Gaston d'Audiffret, whom he later adopted. In 1842, after publishing his *Discours et opinions* (4 vols.), Pasquier was elected to the French Academy. On 24 February 1848, after the proclamation of a Republic, Pasquier closed the Chamber of Peers and soon fled from Paris, his political career at an end. He subsequently wrote six volumes of important memoirs covering the period from the Old Regime through 1830 (*Histoire de mon temps*, published 1893–95) plus a work on the Revolution of 1848. Pasquier died in Paris late on the night of 5–6 July 1862.

*Archives parlementaires*; L. Favre, *Etienne Denis Pasquier chancelier de France* (Paris, 1870); J. K. Kieswetter, *Etienne-Denis Pasquier: The Last Chancellor of France* (Philadelphia, 1977); L. M. Molé, *Le Comte Molé sa vie ses mémoires* (Paris, 1922–30)

*James K. Kieswetter*

*Related entries:* BOIGNE; BRIDGE AND ROAD SERVICE; CAMBACERES; CHAMBER OF PEERS; COURS PREVOTALES; DECAZES; DOCTRINAIRES; FIESCHI PLOT; GOUVION SAINT-CYR; LAW OF SACRILEGE; PRESS LAWS; RICHELIEU; TALLEYRAND; ULTRAROYALISTS.

*LA PATRIE,* independent newspaper of the July Monarchy and Second Republic. At its foundation in 1841 *La Patrie* supported Guizot's ministry, but in 1846 it began to adopt a critical attitude toward the government. It was sometimes said to belong to a third party, but its attitude could more accurately be described as independent and unpredictable. With 3,140 subscribers it was a considerable annoyance to François Guizot. After the Revolution of 1848 it remained devoted for a time to constitutional monarchy but supported the candidature of Louis-Napoleon Bonaparte for the presidency in December 1848, hoping that he would destroy the Republic.

R. Pimienta, *La Propagande bonapartiste en 1848* (Paris, 1911).

*Irene Collins*

*Related entries: L'ESPIRIT PUBLIC*; GUIZOT; REVOLUTION OF 1848.

*LE PATRIOTE* (1830), democratic newspaper, appearing June–December 1830. The leading individual on the paper was the lawyer Alfred Franque, a prolific writer on electoral, legal, and political reform, and previously editor of *La Jeune France*; he was to be a defense lawyer at the mass trial following the insurrection of April 1834. *Le Patriote* was the only democratic paper under the Restoration but, though it expanded its format after the July Revolution, it could sustain print runs of only forty to sixty copies in late 1830, and the reintroduction of caution money and newspaper taxes was fatal. Before its closure, it tried to create a Patriotic Press Association to buy up available printers' licenses to safeguard the republican press. It is not to be confused with *Le Patriote français* and *Le Patriote de 1830*.

E. Hatin, *Bibliographie historique et critique de la presse périodique française* (Paris, 1866).

*Peter McPhee*

*Related entries: LA JEUNE FRANCE*; REPUBLICANS.

**PEASANTS.** During the first half of the nineteenth century, more than half of all French men and women worked on the land and could generally be classified as peasants. Stratification within the peasant world was complex and based on relationship to the land and degrees of wealth. At the top of the economic pyramid were the *laboureurs* or *cultivateurs*, who owned the land they farmed. They produced crops for the market, hired other peasants to work for them, and enjoyed a relatively high standard of living, consuming wine or cider with meals, eating meat as well as bread and cheese, and owning plow teams, cows, and herds of sheep or pigs. *Laboureurs* who owned substantial plots of land gradually made a transition into the bourgeoisie, sometimes becoming absentee landlords in the process.

In northern France most of the land was owned not by the peasants but by the bourgeoisie and nobility, who rented it to peasants for a money rent. The renters, or *fermiers*, often approached the *laboureurs* in terms of well-being, but they lacked the social status of owning the land. The ranks of the *laboureurs* and *fermiers* encompassed a wide range of economic well-being and social standing. In some areas they owned or rented large tracts of land and were relatively wealthy. In other areas they owned or rented only small plots and were quite poor.

In southern France much of the land was rented to peasants not for a money rent but for a share (usually half) of the crop. These sharecroppers or *métayers* were uniformly poor. The *métayer* provided the labor on the farm; the landowner provided the land, the working capital, cattle, plow, and so on. In the *fermier* regions, the tenant farmers provided their own seed, farm capital, plow teams, cattle, and similar items. From the time of the Revolution on, *métayage* in France was in decline, gradually being replaced with rent tenancy.

Many peasants who owned or rented land had such a small holding that it would not sustain the family. In these families the men, women, and children worked during the harvest season for the wealthy *laboureurs* and *fermiers*, hoping to earn enough to stay above the subsistence line during the winter. Even lower on the socioeconomic ladder were the *journaliers*, who owned and rented no land at all but hired themselves out for the day or season. These men and women constituted a kind of agrarian proletariat, working for pay or a share of the harvest, living in villages, but owning no land or animals.

Peasant life was characterized by seasonal and sexual divisions of labor, hard work, monotonous diets, and incomes based on the earnings of all members of the family from a combination of work in agriculture and cottage industry. Agriculture remained a highly seasonal activity in the first half of the nineteenth century. The demand for workers to harvest the grain crops was high and the work season short. Farmers in commercial agricultural regions often had to rely on migrant workers from subsistence farming areas to cut and bring in the grain. During winter months there was little work in agriculture other than in viticulture regions, and peasants were largely unemployed. Many peasant families alternated summer agricultural work with winter work in cottage industry, especially the cottage textile industry. Male peasants in regions where there was little or no work available in cottage industry and where the land was of marginal quality migrated to urban areas to work as laborers during winter months.

Geographical specialization in agriculture did not occur in a major way until the second half of the century. Most regions attempted to be self-sufficient, as did most farms. On the farms there was a sexual division of labor. Peasant men were responsible for the plowing, planting, and harvesting of fields. Peasant women were responsible for gardens, barnyard animals and all produce from these animals (milk, cheese, butter, eggs), the marketing of produce, and care of the house, including the preparation of meals. During the harvest this spatial and sexual division of labor broke down temporarily when peasant women as well as men worked in the fields.

The majority of peasant families lived close to the subsistence line, and hunger was a common experience. The difficulty and cost of transporting grain before the building of the railroads and improving of the highways in the second half of the century meant that local harvest failures continued to create starvation conditions, high bread prices, and peasant unrest.

Bourgeois observers of peasant life generally viewed peasants as superstitious, dirty, uncivilized, and savage. These views were enhanced by the poor educational system in France, which left most peasants illiterate, by continuing beliefs in witches and other superstitions in much of the peasant world, by the low standard of living attained by most peasants, by the persistence of peasants in speaking various patois, by such customs as the cohabiting of animals and people in very poor regions during winter months when the heat of the animals' bodies was the major source of warmth for the family, and by the generally conservative politics of the peasants. Peasants were more likely than urban groups to be influenced by the conservative political positions of the Catholic church and when given an opportunity to vote, as in 1848, generally voted for conservative candidates, frustrating and infuriating urban workers and intellectuals. Diversity reigned within the peasant world, however, and many peasants resolutely voted Left wing and engaged in anti-government strikes. Landless peasants in southern France were devoutly republican and openly revolted against Louis-Napoleon's coup d'état in 1851.

M. Agulhon, *La République au village* (Paris, 1970); W. Shaffer, *Family and Farm* (Albany, 1982); M. Vidalenc, *Le Peuple des campagnes* (Paris, 1970); T. Zeldin, "Peasants," in *France, 1848–1945* (Oxford, 1973).

*Gay L. Gullickson*

*Related entries:* AGRICULTURE; COTTAGE INDUSTRY; COUP D'ETAT OF 2 DECEMBER 1851; MIGRATION; POPULATION; RAILROADS; REPUBLICANS.


**PEERS, CHAMBER OF.** See CHAMBER OF PEERS.


**PELISSIER, AIMABLE JEAN-JACQUES** (1794–1864), marshal of France, duc de Malakoff, professional soldier and later diplomat. After serving in the armée du Rhin in 1815, Pelissier saw most of his service in Algeria, where he gained a reputation for vulgarity and brutality. In 1845, he became the object of a national scandal when he ordered his men to asphyxiate several hundred Algerians who had sought refuge in the grottes du Dahra by building fires in the mouths of the caves. This did not compromise his career. On the contrary, in May 1855 he was named commander of French forces in the Crimea and succeeded in storming the troublesome battery of Malakoff, which guarded Sebastopol. This earned for Pelissier both a title and a marshal's baton. In 1858, he served as French ambassador to the court of Saint James, and in 1860 he was named governor-general of Algeria, a post he occupied until his death.

General Derrecagaix, *Le Maréchal Pelissier duc de Malakoff* (Paris, 1911); C.-A. Julien, *Histoire de l'Algérie contemporaine* (Paris, 1964).

*Douglas Porch*

*Related entries:* ALGIERS, EXPEDITION TO.

**PERDIGUIER, AGRICOL** (1805–1875), *compagnon* joiner known as "Avignonnais-la-Vertu," poet and songwriter, deputy to the Constituent Assembly in 1848 and to the Legislative Assembly in 1849, friend of George Sand and hero of her novels, and, according to the historian of the worker poets Edmond Thomas, the best-known worker of the nineteenth century. Agricol Perdiguier became a model of the artisan class, a true worker hero. Much of this is due to his friend George Sand's fictional account of his life in her *Le Compagnon du tour de France*, but part of it is due to his own character and work.

Perdiguier was born in Morières (Vaucluse) on 4 December 1805, the son of a joiner and a dressmaker. His father had been a soldier in the armies of the Republic, and for this the family was harassed by the royalist population of the area during the White Terror after 1815. His parents were able to give him little schooling; he spent only three years in inadequate private classes often taught by Napoleonic veterans who were barely literate themselves. Although most of his teachers were secular, he read mainly religious books like the *Imitation of Christ, Duties of a Christian, The Holy Week,* and *The Devoted Soul.* Although he had barely learned to read in his classes, he also managed to make his way through his grandfather's copy of the hair-raising folktale, *The Story of the Four Sons of Aymon,* and Aesop's *Fables.* Later he would acquire a taste for the tragedies of Racine and Voltaire and for Bossuet's *Universal History,* and much of his work would suffer from his anxiety to show his erudition; he tried to model his poetry after that of François-René de Chateaubriand, Alphonse de Lamartine, Félicité de Lamennais, and (perhaps a better model for him) Pierre-Jean de Béranger.

It was his ordinary working life, however, that first gave him a desire to become a writer. At work, he remembered, "We used to sing *compagnon* songs and sometimes songs of war. The Emperor was at the heart of our thoughts. I for my part was a Bonapartist and at the same time a republican: . . . I believed that Bonaparte was the same as freedom. All my co-workers thought the same way." Perdiguier was apprenticed to his father and then to other joiners in Avignon and from 1824 to 1828 went on his Tour de France as Avignonnais-la-Vertu, *compagnon* of the Devoir de Liberté. He went from town to town— Marseilles, Nîmes, Montpellier, Béziers, Toulouse, Bordeaux, Rochefort, Nantes,

Chartres, Paris, Chalon-sur-Saône, and Lyons—working for various skilled joiners and learning his trade. He was also learning the complex rules and bloodthirsty songs of the illegal but tolerated unions for skilled artisans, the *compagnonnages*, which protected member workers and brutally excluded nonmembers and members of rival *compagnonnages* from the towns and workshops under their control. Perdiguier noticed that this murderous rivalry among the *compagnonnages* was sapping the strength of the working class. Whereas the songs that he had learned on his tour de France called for the destruction of rival *compagnonnages*, Perdiguier began to compose songs that called for all workers to unite into a single *compagnonnage*, and he began to publish these songs in 1834. His Christian formation, with its message of charity and peace, would serve throughout his life as a framework for his socialist ideas and as inspiration for his songs. He wrote in his *Livre du compagnonnage*, first published with the help of subscriptions from his fellow *compagnons* in 1839:

Let the happier *compagnons*,
Forgetting their disastrous wars,
Be able to see and to love one another,
As friends and brothers.

The success of Perdiguier's *Livre du compagnonnage* made him a hero among his fellow *compagnons* and among the literary and political elite, especially the socialist intellectuals. In 1840 he undertook a second tour de France, this time to spread his ideas. One highlight of his trip was his invitation to dine with George Sand at her home. From this meeting and from her reading of Perdiguier's book would come her two-volume novel, *Le Compagnon du tour de France*, which was published in 1841 and whose hero, the *compagnon* joiner Pierre Huguenin, was really Agricol Perdiguier. Eugène Sue, an even more popular novelist of the time, based his character Agricol Baudouin, a poet and worker in Sue's novel *The Wandering Jew* (1844–45), on Agricol Perdiguier, whom he went to meet in Paris at Perdiguier's school of design in the faubourg Saint-Antoine. Perdiguier wrote for Vinçard's Saint-Simonian *La Ruche populaire* and became an editor of the Buchezian *Atelier*. His fame, plus the backing of Béranger, Lamartine, and George Sand, helped him to be elected to the Constituent Assembly in the elections of 23 April 1848. Perdiguier won in Paris and in the Vaucluse. Besides this, an even greater victory for Perdiguier seemed to be at hand: on 20 March 1848 about 10,000 *compagnons* from rival *compagnonnages* met at the place de la République (now the place des Vosges) in Paris and took an oath of brotherhood. A club of *compagnons* was founded to advance the interest of the *compagnons* and other workers. It wrote a *compagnonnage* constitution, which was submitted in March 1849 and, although approved in Paris, was rejected by the local *compagnonnages*. This was the beginning of the end of Perdiguier's dream.

By the time of the elections for the Legislative Assembly on 13 May 1849, France was in the midst of a conservative reaction. Perdiguier was one of the few democrats elected in Paris, while Armand Barbès, Victor Hugo, François-Vincent Raspail, Pierre Leroux, and Sue were defeated. Perdiguier opted to represent Paris rather than the Vaucluse, where he had also been elected. He joined the Left in its unsuccessful defense of the freedom of the clubs to assemble and of the newspapers to publish without first depositing a ruinously (for the small newspapers) large sum of money as a bond against future fines. He fought unsuccessfully against the exile of Louis Blanc. In a speech on 8 September 1849, which his poor health and the shouts of the right-wing majority prevented him from finishing, he cited Lamennais, the Chinese philosopher Mencius, Confucius, Socrates, Hippocrates, and many others in his defense of the 1848 law reducing the workday by one hour. He also voted with the leftist minority against the military expedition to save the pope from the revolution in Rome and against the Falloux Law, which allowed the Catholic church to take a role in French education. He was especially hostile to the growing personal power of President Louis-Napoleon Bonaparte. Meanwhile, he was working on his *Democratic History of Ancient and Modern Peoples*. The first four volumes, which concerned the Hebrews, the Assyrians, the Ethiopians, the Egyptians, the Greeks, and the Chinese, appeared in 1849, and the fifth, sixth, and seventh volumes, on the Greeks, would appear in 1850 and 1851. The book was a call for democracy and freedom.

Such ideals were becoming increasingly dangerous, and Perdiguier was among the first to be arrested and exiled after Louis-Napoleon's coup d'état of 2 December 1851. In Geneva in 1854–55 he published *Mémoires d'un compagnon*. He returned to Paris in 1856 and organized a school of design and a bookstore for the workers of his faubourg Saint-Antoine. When Bonaparte fell and the Paris Commune of 1871 detached itself from the appeasement policies of the new Third Republic, Perdiguier remained faithful to his belief in a strong, central republican government and refused to support the Commune. By the time of his death in Paris on 26 March 1875, Perdiguier's ideas and his books had lost their influence. His meteoric rise to fame had reached its apogee in 1848. The *compagonnages* were in decline, and Perdiguier was more and more out of touch with an increasingly conservative France. The "best-known worker of the nineteenth century" died in obscurity.

J. Briquet, *Agricol Perdiguier, compagnon du tour de France et représentant du peuple* (Paris, 1955); Jean Maitron, ed., *Dictionnaire biographique du mouvement ouvier français*, vol. 3 (Paris, 1966); E. L. Newman, "L'arme du siècle, c'est la plume: The French Worker Poets of the July Monarchy and the Spirit of Revolution and Reform," *Journal of Modern History* (1980), and *The French Worker Poets of the July Monarchy* (forthcoming); A. Perdiguier, *Le Livre du compagnonnage* (Paris, 1840) and *Mémoires d'un compagnon* (Paris, 1864); E. Thomas, *Voix d'en bas; la poésie ouvrière du XIXe siècle* (Paris, 1979); J. Touchard, *La Gloire de Béranger*, 2 vols. (Paris, 1968).

*Edgar Leon Newman*

*Related entries: L'ATELIER*; BARBES; BERANGER; BLANC; BUCHEZ; CHATEAUBRIAND; CLUBS, POLITICAL; COMPAGNONNAGES; HUGO;

LAMARTINE; LAMENNAIS; LEGISLATIVE ASSEMBLY; LEROUX; RAS-PAIL; ROMAN EXPEDITION; *LA RUCHE POPULAIRE*; SAINT-SIMONI-ANISM; SAND; SUE; TOUR DE FRANCE; VINCARD; WHITE TERROR; WORKER POETS.

*LE PERE DUCHENE* (1848), widely read left-wing newspaper of the Second Republic. Of the many newspapers founded during the early days of the Second Republic, the *Père Duchêne* was one of eighteen that adopted titles reminiscent of the First Republic and one of the very few to achieve importance. By June 1848 it claimed to have a circulation of 75,000, and though this figure may have been an exaggeration, the *Père Duchêne* was certainly the most widely read of all left-wing journals. It was produced almost entirely by the publisher Emile Thuillier and the chief editor Jean-Claude Colfaru, young men from moderately well-to-do families. Like its famous predecessor, its language was violent and its program indefinable, except when it played a leading part in trying to bring about the abortive Banquet of the People in June 1848. It was probably because of the latter campaign that Colfaru was arrested and deported after the June Days, there being no evidence that he had taken part in the insurrection. The *Père Duchêne* was suppressed by Eugène Cavaignac on 25 June; thereafter it reappeared for one day only (25 August 1848).

P. H. Amann, *Revolution and Mass Democracy: The Paris Club Movement in 1848* (Princeton, 1975); H. Izambard, *La Presse parisienne: Statistique bibliographique et alphabétique* (Paris, 1853).

*Irene Collins*

*Related entries:* CAVAIGNAC, L.-E.; JUNE DAYS; REPUBLICANS; REVOLUTION OF 1848.

**PEREIRE BROTHERS.** EMILE PEREIRE (1800–1875) and ISAAC PEREIRE (1806–1880) were Saint-Simonians, journalists, railway entrepreneurs, and financiers. In their time they received bad press; the spectacular rise and fall of the *Crédit mobilier* they set up in 1852 led many contemporaries to make harsh judgments on them, to see them as parvenus and speculators, typical of the gaudy, parvenue Second Empire. However, by the midcentury they already had significant achievements as both economic journalists and railway promoters and managers. Even so, they have never been the subject of a biography.

Their careers down to 1850 merit attention for four reasons. First, they were part of that generation of bourgeois Jews in Paris who faced a crisis of assimilation into Gentile society. The Bordeaux Sephardic community in which they were brought up was an open one, and there was a decline in religious observation among some members of the Jewish upper bourgeoisie in the capital, to which they came in the 1820s. Not surprisingly, the Pereires early ceased to be orthopraxis, and, though they still married within the faith, most of their children did not. Second, the Pereires played a major role in the Saint-Simonian sect. Isaac Pereire's commitment to the group and to Barthélemy Enfantin, its leader, was not only intellectual but spiritual and emotional. His brother never gave the same commitment. Both, however, accepted the Saint-Simonian diagnosis of the economic and social ills that afflicted France, and both helped develop the cures the sect proposed. Their experience in the sect, indeed, was both excitant and catharsis; it broadened their vision and confirmed their careers, enthusiasm, and ideas.

Third, the Pereires were leading economic journalists in the early 1830s. Emile wrote first in the *Globe*, a Saint-Simonian journal, and then in the *National* and the *Revue encyclopédique*. Isaac also contributed to the *Globe* as well as to the *Journal des connaissances utiles* and, from 1838 to 1846, to the *Journal des débats*. The Pereires wrote on political economy and, above all, on economic policy, domains that contemporaries believed to be of special significance when social and political problems were made the more acute by the severe depression of 1827–32. Their writings at this time are important for another reason: they show that there was a basic continuity in the Pereires' ideas on taxation and government finance, banking, and tariff reform. The criticisms they made and the solutions they proposed in the early 1830s they were to repeat and attempt to put into effect throughout their later careers. Thus they attacked indirect taxes and advocated increased land, capital gains and estate taxes, and greater recourse to loan flotations as a means of raising government revenue. They denounced the tariff policy of a regime they saw as dominated by conservative and privileged groups and proposed a gradual reduction of customs duties and the abolition of all levies and restrictions on imports of raw materials. They also criticized what they considered to be the timorous policies pursued by the Bank of France, insisting that a centralized banking system was needed to improve commercial credit, to provide long-term industrial credit, and to widen the catchment area for credit by bringing savings, large and small, into productive investment. In September 1830 Emile Pereire submitted a project for a discount bank that was seriously considered by the government. In 1848 he again proposed the creation of a commercial credit institution to alleviate the economic crises, and he helped to draw up the statutes for the *Comptoir d'escompte* that resulted.

Fourth, the Pereires became leading railway magnates, and in the 1840s Heinrich Heine dubbed Emile the "Pontifex Maximus" of French railways. Their success in this domain earned them their reputation as managers and financiers and enough wealth to be able to purchase the Crécy and Amainvillers estates from Louis-Philippe's sister. It was thus not the creation of their famed Crédit mobilier bank in 1852 that launched their careers. Their first success in railway promotion was the Paris-St.-Germain line, France's first passenger railway, planned in 1832, approved by the government in 1835, and opened in 1837. The enterprise proved an immediate success, and in the twenty years after 1832 the Pereires were to devote most of their energies to this suburban line. It was the trampoline that launched their business careers, because to build the line they secured the financial backing of a group of Parisian bankers, the chief of whom was James de Rothschild. This group backed the other railway enterprises the Pereires planned at this time.

From the beginning, they saw the 18 kilometer St.-Germain as the base from which a larger network could be created, as the first link in trunk lines to major cities and ports. Their railway imperialism, however, was only partially successful. They did build a line to Versailles that used their St.-Lazare terminus—a line that opened in 1839—and the Paris-Rouen railway, which they did not control, branched onto their line, used their station, and brought considerable financial advantage to their company. But their other projects for longer lines failed, and even their attempts to set up what was to become the western network did not succeed until 1855. In the 1840s the Pereires diversified their railway activities; they helped to build and operate the Northern Railway in 1845 and were on the board of directors of the Paris-Lyons company.

The Pereires' careers down to 1850, then, took them from relative poverty— their father had gone bankrupt under the Empire and their mother had turned to shopkeeping—through a revolt against Judiasm and the established order, to concrete proposals for changing the economy and economic policy and to business success. The Second Empire was to bring them even greater political influence and to take them to even dizzier heights of business success.

B. M. Ratcliffe, "Les Pereire et le Saint-Simonisme," *Economies et sociétés* 5 (1971), "Railway Imperialism: The Case of the Péreires Paris-Saint-Germain Company," *Business History* 17 (1976), "Some Banking Ideas in France in the 1830s: The Example of Emile and Isaac Péreire," *Revue internationale d' histoire de la banque* 7 (1973), "Some Jewish Problems in the Early Careers of Emile and Isaac Péreire," *Jewish Social Studies* 34 (1972), and "The Paris-Saint-Germain Railway," *Journal of Transport History* 1, 2 (1972–73).

*Barrie M. Ratcliffe*
*Related entries:* BANKING; ENFANTIN; *LE GLOBE*; JEWS; *JOURNAL DES DEBATS*; *LE NATIONAL*; RAILROADS; SAINT-SIMONIANISM.


**PERIER, CASIMIR-PIERRE** (1777–1832), banker, political leader, and minister. Casimir Périer was born in 1777 into a wealthy bourgeois family of the department of the Isère. His father, Claude Périer (1742–1801), had holdings in the paper and textile industries, coal mining, and banking. The father was also active in the patriot party in the early stages of the Revolution and added to the family fortune by purchases of national lands. Casimir, the fourth of seven brothers, served briefly in the army of the Republic and for a time in the imperial administration, rising to be a departmental prefect in 1810, but before he became active in national politics he was primarily a businessman. With his brother Scipion, he organized and directed the banking house of Périer and Frères in Paris, and they moved into insurance, textiles, sugar refining, flour milling, iron, and coal. Both served as regents of the Bank of France.

In 1817 Casimir won election as a deputy of Paris, and he sat in the Chamber of Deputies from that date until his death in 1832. Originally a member of the government majority, he was, after 1820, increasingly alienated by the policies of the ultraroyalists and shifted into the opposition. In the parliamentary session of 1830, he voted with the 221 for the censorious reply to the king's opening address, and during the July Days of 1830, although initially hesitant, he was among the first deputies to associate themselves with the resistance to the royal government. He continued, however, to be fearful of the possible consequences of popular violence. On 29 July he accepted appointment as a member of the Provisional Municipal Commission charged with maintaining security and ensuring the provisioning of Paris, and when it appeared that Charles X would not be able to reestablish his authority in Paris, he rallied to the support of the duc d'Orléans as a new ruler who could stop the revolution short of a republic and social upheaval. In the interregnum between Charles's abdication and Louis-Philippe's installation, he was one of Orléans' inner circle of advisers, and on 12 August he became a minister without portfolio in Louis-Philippe's first ministry.

Périer was, however, soon in disagreement with his more liberal associates in the new government. He viewed the Revolution of 1830 as no more than a change in the person of the head of state and was anxious that it go no further toward social reform or political democratization. When in November Louis-Philippe named the liberal Jacques Laffitte head of a new ministry intended to appease the growing popular hostility toward the new regime, Périer left the government. In March 1831 he accepted the king's call to head a new conservative ministry. For the next thirteen months as president of the Council and minister of the interior, he imposed his authoritarian and conservative rule on France and on his associates. He excluded the king from meetings of the ministry, denied his ministers all independence of action, restricted the political activities of civil servants, and ruthlessly suppressed popular disorders. In May 1832, exhausted by the heavy duties of office, he fell victim to the cholera epidemic sweeping France and died in Paris on 16 May 1832.

The family tradition of political activity was carried on by his son, Auguste Casimir-Périer (1811–76), who served as deputy under the July Monarchy and the Second and Third Republics and in the 1870s as Thiers' minister of the interior, and by his grandson, Jean Casimir-Périer (1847–1907), who was president of the Council of Ministers and president of the Third Republic.

P. Barral, *Les Périer dans l'Isère aux XIXe siècle d'après leur correspondance familiale* (Paris, 1964); P. Duvergier d'Hauranne, *Histoire du gouvernement parlementaire en France, 1814–1848*, vol. 10 (Paris, 1857–71); C. Rémusat, *Mémoires de ma vie*, vol. 2 (Paris, 1958–67); P. Thureau-Dangin, *Histoire de la Monarchie de Juillet*, vol. 7 (Paris, 1888–1900).

*David H. Pinkney*

Related entries: CHAMBER OF DEPUTIES; CHARLES X; COUNCIL OF STATE; LAFFITTE; MUNICIPAL COMMISSION; REVOLUTION OF 1830; THE 221; ULTRAROYALISTS.

**PERRIN, CLAUDE-VICTOR.** See VICTOR.

**PERSIGNY, VICTOR FIALIN, DUC DE** (1808–1872), ardent Bonapartist, close friend of Louis-Napoleon, minister of the interior and ambassador to Great Britain during the Second Empire. The son of a tax collector, Persigny was born

Jean-Gilbert-Victor Fialin at Saint-Germain L'Espinasse on 11 January 1808. He attended the Collège de Limoges and the cavalry school in Saumur. Graduating in 1828, he joined the Fourth Regiment of Hussars as a sergeant major. He converted to republicanism while in the army and was eventually dismissed for his extreme views (1831). However, his advocacy of republicanism did not last long, and, by the mid–1830s, he had become a Bonapartist, an attachment that remained total and unwavering for the rest of his life. Napoleon III would later state that Persigny was more of a Bonapartist than the emperor himself.

Persigny attempted to publicize his new ideology as editor of the Parisian newspaper, *L'Occident français*, but only one issue ever saw the light of day. Yet the paper did bring him to the attention of the exiled Bonaparte family and facilitated his first meeting with Louis-Napoleon Bonaparte in 1835. Soon after this first meeting, Persigny helped organize and participated in Bonaparte's abortive coup in Strasbourg in October 1836. After the attempt failed, Persigny followed Louis-Napoleon into exile, first to Switzerland and then to England, and became a permanent part of his retinue. While in England, Persigny published *Lettres de Londres* (1840), a Bonapartist propaganda tract directed at the French common people.

Later in 1840, he participated in Louis-Napoleon's second try to topple the July Monarchy at Boulogne. When this attempt also ended in failure, Bonaparte was imprisoned at the fortress of Ham, and Persigny received a sentence of twenty years in the prison of Doullens. The authorities released him from Doullens shortly after because of illness and sent him to an army hospital in Versailles. Taking advantage of the lax security at the hospital, he left France in 1846 and joined Bonaparte, who had escaped from Ham, in England.

Persigny returned to France a few months after the February Revolution of 1848 in order to help organize Louis-Napoleon's campaign for the presidency of the new Republic. Yet after Bonaparte won the election in December 1848, he did not reward Persigny with a cabinet post. The new president instead sent his loyal friend on a six-week tour of the German states and Austria. Although the government stated that the tour's purpose was only to foster goodwill among France's German neighbors, its real goal was to sound Prussia out on the possibility of implementing Bonaparte's German unification scheme, a plan that would unify Germany at Austria's expense and also provide France with additional territory along the Rhine. Persigny carried out his assignment to the letter, but Louis-Napoleon never seriously pursued the matter any further.

Persigny never received a cabinet post in the years before the coup d'état of 1851. Bonaparte did, however, give him several special projects to do and he also participated in the planning of the 1851 coup. Yet, although Persigny was one of the strongest advocates within Bonaparte's inner circle of an illegal seizure of power, the duc de Morny, who handled the overall direction of the coup, disliked him and gave him only minor tasks to perform.

The year following the coup d'état in 1852 marked the high point in Persigny's career. In this year he finally received his long-awaited cabinet position as minister of the interior, a post he resigned in June 1854 for health reasons. He was reappointed in 1860 but dismissed after the legislative elections of 1863, which Napoleon thought he had bungled. He thereupon left Paris and retired to his native department of the Loire to work on his *Mémoires* (published posthumously in 1896) and proposals for administrative reforms. But due to his disgrace at the Ministry of Interior and the implacable hatred of the empress, his views were ignored in Paris.

When the Empire fell in September 1870, Persigny, fearing reprisals from the new government, fled to England. He returned to France in July 1871 and settled at his new estate in Chamarande (Seine-et-Oise). He moved to Nice in December 1871 for health reasons and died there from a stroke on 12 January 1872.

H. Farat, *Persigny, un ministre de Napoleon III* (Paris, 1957); R. L. Williams, *The World of Napoleon III, 1851–1870* (New York, 1965).

*Christopher E. Guthrie*

Related entries: BONAPARTISM; COUP D'ETAT OF 2 DECEMBER 1851; COUNCIL OF STATE; REPUBLICANS; REVOLUTION OF 1848.

*LE PETIT HOMME ROUGE* (1848), newspaper of the Revolution of 1848. This newspaper was rather less ephemeral than some others that appeared during the Revolution of 1848 in that it ran to fourteen numbers during April and May. Each number had an engraving in red over the title. The paper described 1848 as year I of the Republic.

*Irene Collins*

Related entries: REVOLUTION OF 1848.

*PETITS-SEMINAIRES,* minor seminaries designed to provide elementary and secondary schooling prior to theological training in a *grand* (major) *séminaire* for boys intending to become priests. Recommended by the Council of Trent as a means of preventing boys with a calling to the priesthood from being contaminated by secular society, these schools became an important component of Catholic schooling in nineteenth-century France. The ordinance of 5 October 1814 permitted each diocese to operate a single *petit-séminaire* exempt from the ordinary jurisdiction of the University; newly founded ones, however, were not to be placed where they could draw students away from the public lycées and collèges. Amid a general reaction to the ultras' regime and to clerical dominance of the University, the law of 16 June 1828 restricted the number of students in them nationally to 20,000, required students fourteen years old and older to wear clerical garb, and required graduates of such schools to be ordained to the priesthood before they could receive the baccalaureat. These laws were modified by the Falloux legislation of 1850, which effectively granted bishops jurisdiction over conduct within the schools by designating the bishop as principal once the University approved the existence of such a school.

The new description—*établissement d'instruction secondaire* rather than the older *séminaire* or *école ecclésiastique*—implied a willingness to accept a social reality that the 1828 legislation had attempted to contain: that such schools were teaching a host of students who would never receive holy orders and who were intent mainly on obtaining secondary schooling. Some would lose their vocation during the ten to fifteen years between their matriculation at a *petit-séminaire* and when they reached a minimum age for ordination; others found seminaries the cheapest access to secondary schooling. If, between 1828 and 1850, the baccalaureat was officially denied graduates of the minor seminaries who did not take orders, they could take the examination after instruction by a tutor or after a single year at a lycée. No one knows how many bachelors of letters once attended a *petit-séminaire*, but both inspectors' complaints and restrictive legislation imply that these schools did more than guide lads to the *grands séminaires*, which taught theology, philosophy, and sacramental duties. In areas that lacked any other secondary school, *petits-séminaires* often served as the secondary school, with a program of studies like those of the lycées. After the Falloux Law, some bishops were admitting what they had kept hidden earlier: "our seminaries admit all the boys who want a Catholic and familial schooling; we never ask what their vocation may be" (Msgr. Parisis, *Mandements*, 1856).

Minor seminaries constituted a shadow sector of Catholic secondary schooling available to those who desired Catholic, not necessarily sacerdotal, instruction. Within regions, they often complemented each other. One diocesan seminary would direct their students to a *grand séminaire*; another would provide inexpensive, classically based secondary instruction. After the Falloux Law, a few abandoned any pretense of priestly training, expanded their staff, and advertised that their end was to prepare students for the baccalaureat. Average boarding costs were half those charged by public high schools and often adjusted according to familial finances. Archival reports indicate that enrollment in the *petits-séminaires* had surpassed the legal lid of 20,000 students by 5,000 to 10,000 by the 1860s and had exceeded it by some unknown number during the July Monarchy. No systematic study of the *petits-séminaires* exists.

P. J. Harrigan, "The Church and Pluralistic Education: The Development of and Teaching in French Catholic Secondary Schools 1850–1870," *Catholic Historical Review* 64 (April 1978); J. Leflon, "Les Petits séminaires de France au XIXe siècle," *Revue d'histoire de l'église de France* 61 (1975).

*Patrick J. Harrigan*

*Related entries:* FALLOUX LAW; PUBLIC INSTRUCTION.


*LE PEUPLE* (1829), newspaper launched in January 1829 and lasting sixteen issues. While ostensibly a review of literature and the fine arts, the paper also echoed the complaints of small producers against large entrepreneurs, noting, for example, the threat posed to small shopkeepers by large retail outlets.

E. Hatin, *Bibliographie historique et critique de la presse périodique française* (Paris, 1866).

*Peter McPhee*

*LE PEUPLE* (1830), workers' newspaper, seventeen issues from 30 September–27 November 1830 (though perhaps longer, as there is no complete edition). Its subtitle was *A General Paper for Workers, Edited by Them Alone*. The manager was Lemaire, a printing worker. On the masthead were two cornucopias, linked by a banner on which was written "Honor to national industry" and below which was a saying from Confucius on the link between respect for the people and the strength of the state.

While *Le Peuple* initially supported the new government of the July Monarchy and opposed direct action by workers, it became increasingly hostile to politicians who used the people as a ladder to power, to abuses of civil liberties, and to lack of action to protect workers from mechanization. It supported intervention on the side of revolution in Belgium, strikes, and the death penalty for Charles X's ministers, seeing the call for leniency as a Jesuitical plot.

E. Hatin, *Bibliographie historique et critique de la presse périodique française* (Paris, 1966); G. Weill, "Les Journaux ouvriers à Paris (1830–1870)," *Revue d'histoire moderne et contemporaine* 9 (1907).

*Peter McPhee*

*Related entries:* BELGIAN REVOLUTION OF 1830; CHARLES X; JESUITS; REVOLUTION OF 1830.

*LE PEUPLE CONSTITUANT* (1848), liberal newspaper published by Félicité de Lamennais. As soon as the Provisional Government of the Second Republic established liberty of the press, Lamennais made his final attempt to promote the cause of freedom by launching on 27 February 1848 *Le Peuple constituant*, for which he wrote long, erudite articles expressing sympathy for all oppressed peoples, including the Irish and the Poles. In the reaction that followed the June Days, however, the government expressed its intention of reestablishing caution money for newspapers. On 11 July 1848 the *Peuple constituant* appeared with a black border and announced that the government had decreed "silence to the poor." For this final gesture, the editor was condemned to six months' imprisonment and a 3,000 franc fine.

H. Izambard, *La Presse parisienne: statistique bibliographique et alphabétique* (Paris, 1853); R. Rémond, *Lamennais et la démocratie* (Paris, 1948).

*Irene Collins*

*Related entries:* JUNE DAYS; LAMENNAIS; PROVISIONAL GOVERNMENT; REVOLUTION OF 1848.

*LE PEUPLE SOUVERAIN.* At least three provincial newspapers existed under this name during the Second Republic. At Bordeaux, the *Peuple souverain* was founded in March 1849 for the specific purpose of supporting the most radical republican candidates for the Legislative Assembly. The paper was seized three times during the first month of publication. The editor was condemned to two years' imprisonment and a fine of 3,000 francs for inciting to civil war. The fine absorbed the whole of the caution money, and since no further deposit was available, the paper collapsed.

At Lyons, radical newspapers were a source of anxiety to the government, and in the latter half of 1848 *commissaire* Emmanuel Arago, fanatical son of the republican astronomer, persuaded the local authorities to seize two issues of the socialist *Peuple souverain* as a warning to others. In March 1849 the editor was prosecuted on a charge of publishing an article insulting to Marshal Thomas-Robert Bugeaud, commander of the troops stationed at Lyons. He was acquitted by a jury but shortly afterwards imprisoned for his part in the Lyons rising of 15–16 June. The *Peuple souverain* was suspended by decree, but a Parisian correspondent, Naquet, kept the paper alive for some time by publishing it under different titles at monthly intervals. The paper eventually disappeared early in 1850, when the printer was prosecuted and then deprived of her license.

At Marseilles a republican paper entitled *Le Peuple souverain* came into existence shortly after the Revolution of 1830. Its editor, Maillefer, was regarded as a leader of the republican opposition in the Midi: his arrest for complicity in the plot of April 1834 caused the journal to be suspended, and for twelve years it proved impossible to persuade any other printer in Marseilles to take on the production. It was revived in 1846 and sustained a precarious existence until killed off again by the press laws of 1849.

C. Bellanger et al., *Histoire générale de la presse française*, vol. 2 (Paris, 1969); T. R. Forstenzer, *French Provincial Police and the Fall of the Second Republic* (Princeton, 1981); G. Perreux, *Au temps des sociétés secrètes* (Paris, 1931).

*Irene Collins*

*Related entries:* ARAGO FAMILY; BUGEAUD; LEGISLATIVE ASSEMBLY; PRESS LAWS; REPUBLICANS.

**PEYRONNET, CHARLES-IGNACE, COMTE DE** (1778–1854), restoration minister. Peyronnet's royalist father was a victim of the Terror, and the son eagerly welcomed the duke of Wellington's army when it arrived in Bordeaux in March 1814. Although he had pursued indifferent legal studies, Peyronnet's career owed its initial success to his role as the duchess of Angoulême's escort when she left Bordeaux for England during the Hundred Days (March 1815). Under the Second Restoration, Peyronnet was made president of the criminal tribunal of Bordeaux and then *procureur-général* in Bourges. In 1821, he was called to Paris to direct the prosecution of the conspirators of 19 August 1820 before the Chamber of Peers. A deputy (Cher) in 1821, he joined the Villèle government as minister of justice, defending the use of *agents-provocateurs* against republican conspirators, and supporting harsher censorship laws by arguing that the royal authority antedated the Charter and was not limited by it. Created a count in August 1822, Peyronnet was the principal architect of the Law on

Sacrilege (which decreed the death penalty for profaning sacred vessels in Catholic churches) in 1825 and the Press Law of 1827 (which imposed delays in publication for government review, made publishers as well as editors liable for violations of the law, and permitted the government to pursue newspapers for libel even if the libeled party did not seek damages).

After defeats in legislative elections in Bourges and Bordeaux, Peyronnet was replaced at the Justice Ministry in January 1828, but he entered the Polignac ministry as head of the interior in May 1830. Peyronnet first proposed using article 14 of the Charter to suspend the legislature, change the electoral laws, and call for new elections in July 1830, and the July Ordinances were largely his work. Arrested in Tours after the Revolution of 1830, he and other ministers (Jules de Polignac, Jean de Chantelauze, and Martial-Magloire de Guernon-Ranville) were tried for treason before the Chamber of Peers, and he was sentenced to life imprisonment and loss of civil rights (21 December 1830). He was released from the prison of Ham under the general amnesty of 1836 and retired from public life.

V. Beach, *Charles X of France* (Boulder, 1971); A. Boltz, ed., *Procès des ex-ministres* (Paris, 1830); N. Hudson, *Ultra-Royalism and the French Restoration* (Cambridge, 1936); D. Pinkney, *The French Revolution of 1830* (Princeton, 1972); A. B. Spitzer, *Old Hatreds and New Hopes* (Cambridge, Mass., 1971).

*David Longfellow*

*Related entries:* ANGOULEME, L.-A.; CARBONARI; CHARTER OF 1814; JULY ORDINANCES; LAW OF SACRILEGE; POLIGNAC; PRESS LAWS; REVOLUTION OF 1830; VILLELE.


**PHILOSOPHY OF INDUSTRIALISM,** a social and economic philosophy that emerged during the Second Restoration. Industrialism, which the French historian Henri Gouhier has aptly described as an economic doctrine enlarged into a science of the social order, appeared during the early days of the Second Restoration. Primarily the work of two small groups of intellectuals, one centered on the *Censeur européen* of Charles Comte and Charles Dunoyer and the other on the philosopher-prophet Henri de Saint-Simon, Industrialism quickly passed through three stages of development: a preparatory period (1815–16), during which its founders built their new doctrine around the ideas of four influential thinkers, a heyday (1816–17), during which the two groups worked together to propagate the new doctrine, and a period in 1817 when Comte and Dunoyer and Saint-Simon abruptly parted company. Following the end of this fruitful collaboration, Industrialism developed along two quite independent paths.

The first comprehensive analysis of Industrialism, a major retrospective essay by one of its founders, appeared when Dunoyer published in 1827 his "Notice historique sur l'industrialisme" in the *Revue encyclopédique*. Asserting that this original social and economic philosophy was of recent vintage, being but ten or twelve years of age, he contended that it represented a significant break with past ideas, with the thinkers of the Enlightenment and earlier centuries who, by theorizing abstractly about types of political and social organization, had completely failed to penetrate to the essence of questions concerning the nature of society and the relationship between society and political institutions. Three authors of recent books, Dunoyer went on, had commenced an intellectual movement that not only challenged received ideas but also provided a provocative set of alternatives. Benjamin Constant, in his *De l'esprit de conquête*, had, instead of meditating endlessly on the various forms of political organization, raised a much more important issue by asking what is the purpose of modern society and, hence, of political institutions. With one word, Constant answered his question: *industry*. Despite the wish of the comte de Montlosier that his *De la monarchie française* would spark in France an aristocratic revival, this second of Dunoyer's authors clearly demonstrated how the industrious classes of society had, by slowly emancipating themselves and by rising within society, pushed the old aristocratic class aside and had shaped modern society according to their interests. Jean-Baptiste Say, the third precursor of Industrialism identified by Dunoyer, demonstrated in the 1814 edition of his influential *Traité d'économie politique* that all wealth stems from physical labor. Edward Allix, incidentally, argues in favor of a much greater influence by Say on the origins of Industrialism than Dunoyer allows him. From these three authors, then, Dunoyer recalled, the founders of Industrialism had learned that the purpose of modern society was industry, that the study of history revealed the slow but inexorable rise of the industrious classes, and that all wealth results from physical labor. Many, but by no means all, of the elements of Industrialism were present.

For a variety of reasons, the most important being perhaps the notoriety that surrounded the comte de Saint-Simon and his Saint-Simonian disciples, Dunoyer deliberately downplayed the eccentric philosopher's role in the creation of Industrialism. Of a close relationship between Saint-Simon and Comte and Dunoyer between December 1814 and the spring of 1817, there can nevertheless be little or no doubt. Not only did Comte and Dunoyer's first journal, the *Censeur*, publish works by Saint-Simon, it also reviewed or commented on his pamphlets of 1814 and 1815. Further, Saint-Simon's *L'Industrie* listed the same address for its office as did Comte and Dunoyer's *Censeur européen*. The exact extent and nature of Saint-Simon's contribution, however, cannot be established with certainty, for he contributed only one essay during the heyday of Industrialism.

Conceived during the White Terror in the atmosphere of disillusionment, frustration, and anger that accompanied the Second Restoration, Industrialism was, to a large degree, a product of the times. Comte and Dunoyer, who had vigorously advocated in *Le Censeur* a liberal position during the First Restoration, who had suffered bitter disappointment at the precipitous collapse of the Bourbon monarchy, who had resolutely opposed the Hundred Days, and who had witnessed the suppression of their paper by Joseph Fouché during the early days of the Second Restoration, spent the time between the disappearance of the *Censeur* and the founding of the *Censeur européen* engaged in serious study. Largely from their efforts came Industrialism, an imaginative social and economic philosophy that would replace, they predicted, the profitless discussions about the proper form of government with a solid and positive philosophy. The purpose of their *Censeur européen*, its new name indicating an internationalist perspective and its motto of "Peace and Liberty" reflecting two of its editors' most cherished ideals, was to disseminate Industrialism to the largest possible readership. Four essays in the *Censeur européen*, two each by Comte and Dunoyer, summarized the bulk of their contribution to the genesis of Industrialism. Other aspects of the philosophy were added in early 1817 by the essays in Saint-Simon's *L'Industrie*, in particular the lengthy *Des Nations et leurs rapports mutuels* by the young Augustin Thierry, then secretary to the elderly Saint-Simon, and by Saint-Simon's own "Lettres de Henri Saint-Simon à un Américain."

The doctrine of Industrialism rests on certain assumptions about human nature drawn principally from the ideas of the sensualist school of the eighteenth century, which had been transmitted to the early nineteenth by the *idéologues*. Accordingly, the Industrialists believed both that the fundamental law of human behavior revealed man to be motivated by the rational pursuit of self-interest and that human nature remained the same throughout history. If the reasoned pursuit of one's own interests is the basic law of human behavior, then freedom becomes an absolute necessity and any form of restraint a deplorable evil. According to the Industrialists, each man's freedom to act, to employ his native faculties, to live by work, and to obtain and enjoy the products of that work make possible human happiness, a happiness the Industrialists understood to result from the material satisfaction of self-interest. Moreover, the diligent pursuit of individual self-interest, Comte, Dunoyer, and the Industrialists believed, would result in prosperity for all. Finally, because the Industrialists held that the laws of human behavior, like all other scientific laws, could be discerned by observation, because they assumed human nature to be immutable, and because they believed that all social, political, and economic ills resulted from ignorance, they took as a moral duty the propagation of Industrialism.

If the true law of human nature was the rational pursuit of self-interest, then society must be constituted and organized so as to permit, if not actively encourage, the development of industry. Hence the Industrialists never tired of writing such phrases as "industry is the vital principle of society" or "industry is the fundamental goal of society." Exactly what the Industrialists meant by the term *industry* Dunoyer made clear when he declared industry to be human activity considered in all its useful applications; in 1817, these activities included agriculture, manufacturing, commerce, and banking. When he later expanded the concept to include all those who make useful contributions to society, Dunoyer contended that Industrialism was not the sum of a list of professions but an attitude, a way of living.

On the subject of government, which the Industrialists distrusted, suspicious of its ability to direct anything, Comte, Dunoyer, and their colleagues had much to say. They were, above all, minimalists who held not only that there should be the least possible role for government but also that it should be as inexpensive as possible. Although they professed to see no particular advantages in any one form of government, they did demand that it be composed of men drawn from the useful or industrial occupations. Government, in other words, should reflect the main forms of economic activity. Further, government should not hinder free and unlimited competition among all the professions; it had no right to intervene in private affairs, and it should be restricted to the protection of society from internal disorders and external attacks. The Industrialists believed that this virtually nonexistent and inexpensive government would be able to function because it would reflect the nature of the economic base, and it would be in accordance with the historical development of society.

Integral to the doctrine of Industrialism was a novel and important materialistic philosophy of history. By arguing in 1817 that historical change results from alterations in the method of production, the Industrialists were certainly among the first to advance this influential idea. Historical change, moreover, is progressive, and it passes through three distinct stages: the savage, the barbarian, and the industrial. According to the proponents of Industrialism, the French Revolution opened the transition to the industrial stage; unfortunately the Revolution not only went astray, but it was followed by the Napoleonic era, which was even worse. The struggle delayed by the Revolutionary and Napoleonic interlude recommenced during the Restoration, and it explains the troubled nature of the times. The Industrialists, who viewed history in terms of a class struggle, an age-old battle between the industrious and useful classes and the idle and oppressing classes, emphasized that the most notable theme in history was the progressive rise of the industrious, a rise particularly evident since the twelfth century. Each step forward by this class took society nearer human perfection.

Although the Industrialists never carefully articulated it, they cherished a vision of the future. Perceiving their own era as an uncomfortable time of transition, they looked forward to the day when social evolution would cease and when society would be made up of one harmonious class of industrious men and women. Free from war and oppression, with little or no government to hinder it and drain away its resources, this society would prosper because every member would, by acting rationally in accord with his self-interest, produce a cornucopia of useful goods. Happiness and peace would thus be the lot of mankind.

The coalition formed to propagate Industrialism collapsed shortly after the publication of the initial essays. During the late spring or early summer of 1817, the collaboration between the group of the *Censeur européen* and Saint-Simon ended, with the result that henceforth Industrialism would develop along two divergent paths. Moreover, probably as a consequence of this split, Augustin Thierry left the employ of Saint-Simon and joined the staff of the *Censeur européen*, for which he wrote prolifically until the paper's suppression in 1820. Saint-Simon quickly replaced the young historian with Auguste Comte in August 1817.

That Saint-Simon's variant of Industrialism had taken on a new emphasis, in some regard a revival of his earlier ideas, became evident when the third volume of *L'Industrie* appeared. Not only did this work launch an audacious attack on the Catholic religion, it also called for the creation of a "terrestrial morality," a morality Saint-Simon believed suitable for the nineteenth century. Although this plea cost Saint-Simon the support of his former benefactors, he continued along his chosen path, a path that would ultimately lead to the *Nouveau christianisme* and to the Saint-Simonians. Along the way, he had published in *L'Organisateur* the famous "parable of the Industrials," in which he mischievously wondered what would be the impact on France of the sudden loss of the royal family, the aristocracy, the officials of the church, the bureaucrats, and the military. Very little, he answered, for all of them could easily be replaced. But if France lost its scientists, its artisans, its manufacturers, and its merchants, the effects would be catastrophic. This *jeu d'esprit* won for Saint-Simon not only a considerable notoriety but also prosecution in court.

Meanwhile, Comte, Dunoyer, and Thierry continued the publication of the *Censeur européen* until its suppression in 1820, when these three men separated to follow different paths, only Dunoyer remaining a prophet of Industrialism. Augustin Thierry turned to the study of history, becoming shortly one of the most influential French historians of the nineteenth century. Charles Comte, who devoted his energies to the study and teaching of the law, published in 1826–27 the four-volume *Traité de législation*. Dunoyer continued to expound the doctrine of Industrialism, giving in 1825 a series of lectures at the Athénée, which he first published under the title *L'Industrie et la morale considérées dans leurs rapports avec la liberté*, and which he revised several times, the final edition appearing in 1845 as *De la Liberté du travail*.

Although when compared with some of the other great intellectual edifices of the nineteenth century it is a relatively minor system of thought, Industrialism is of importance, for it appeared at a time when many of the great ideas of the nineteenth century were beginning to ferment. Not difficult to demonstrate is the fact that Industrialism influenced the genesis and development not only of Saint-Simonianism and positivism but also of Marxism. Moreover, through the work of Thierry, it had an impact on the growth of historical thought in France during the first half of the nineteenth century.

E. Allix, "J. B. Say et les origines de l'industrialisme," *Revue d'économie politique* 24 (1910); *Le Censeur européen* (Paris, 1817–20); C. Dunoyer, *Oeuvres*, 3 vols. (Paris, 1870–86?); H. Gouhier, *La Jeunesse d'Auguste Comte et la formation du positivisme*, 2d ed., 3 vols. (Paris, 1970); S. Gruner, *Economic Materialism and Social Moralism* (The Hague, 1973); E. Halévy, "The Economic Doctrine of Saint-Simon," in *The Era of Tyrannies*, trans. R. K. Webb (New York, 1966); E. Harpaz, "*Le Censeur européen*. Histoire d'un journal industrialiste," *Revue d'histoire économique et sociale* 37 (1959); H. Saint-Simon, *Oeuvres*, 11 vols. (Paris, 1868–76); A. Thierry, *Des Nations et leurs rapports mutuels* (Paris, 1817).

*Robert Brown*

*Related entries: LE CENSEUR; LE CENSEUR EUROPEEN;* COMTE; CONSTANT; DUNOYER; FOUCHE; *IDEOLOGUES;* MONTLOSIER; POSITIVISM; SAINT-SIMON; SAY; THIERRY; WHITE TERROR.

**PICARD, LOUIS-BENOIT** (1769–1828), comic actor, author of light comedies, theatrical director, and novelist. Called the Molière of the nineteenth century by admiring contemporaries, Louis-Benoît Picard was born in Paris on 29 July 1769, the son of a lawyer at the Parlement of Paris. Despite being destined by his father for the law and despite a solid education at the Collège d'Harcourt and the Collège Louis-le-Grand, Picard developed a passion for the plays of Molière and the stage, and he abandoned the study of the law. Becoming during the waning years of the Old Regime a moderately successful actor, he also began to write plays, the first of which to be performed was a one-act *bluette* entitled *Le Badinage dangereux* (1789). During the Revolution, Picard established a considerable reputation as an actor and playwright. Of the twenty-eight plays he composed between 1789 and 1799, most, however, were hastily written topical satires aimed at pleasing Revolutionary audiences.

Picard's successes continued during the Napoleonic years. In 1801, he commenced a twenty-year career as a theatrical manager, heading, in chronological order, the Louvois Theater (1801–2), the Theater of the Empress (1802–7), the Opéra (1807–15), and the Odéon (1815–21). Picard also benefited from the patronage of the emperor, who bestowed upon him an annual pension. In 1807 Picard, who had by now retired from his acting career, became a member of the Institut; shortly thereafter he received the Legion of Honor from Napoleon. Picard's greatest success of this period was *La Petite ville* (1801); his one attempt to write a masterpiece of high comedy, *Les Capitulations de conscience* (1809), failed.

The restoration of the Bourbons brought no interruption to Picard's career, and he remained an influential theatrical manager until his retirement in 1821. Leisure brought by his retirement allowed Picard to resume his writing, and, in the seven years of life remaining to him, he wrote novels, contributions to encyclopedias and journals, and sixteen plays, many of which were composed in collaboration with younger authors. Just prior to his death in 1828, Picard reviewed the works of his Revolutionary youth, wrote a preface for each play, and prepared for publication plays banned during the Empire and the Restoration. The resulting *Théâtre républicaine* appeared in 1832.

Of Picard's Restoration plays, the best known are *Les Deux Philibert* (1816), *Vanglas* (1817), *L'Agiotage* (1826), and *Les Trois quartiers* (1827). Like his earlier plays, these works, all light and gay in tone, combine lively topical satire with piquant realism, and they may be read today as entertaining documents of social history. *L'Agiotage*, for example, poked fun at financial speculators of the early 1820s. The comic tradition represented by Picard was continued during the July Monarchy by Eugène Scribe.

L. Allard, *La Comédie de moeurs en France au XIXe siécle*, vol. 1 of *De Picard à Scribe (1795–1815)* (Paris, 1924); L.-B. Picard, *Oeuvres de L. B. Picard*, 12 vols. (Paris, 1821–32); W. Staaks, *The Theater of Louis-Benoît Picard* (Berkeley, 1952).

*Robert Brown*

*Related entry:* SCRIBE.

*LE PILOTE* (1820–1827), small liberal opposition newspaper of P. Tissot, 1820–1824; purchased by Joseph de Villèle in 1824 and suppressed in 1827. *Le Pilote*, originally a small commercial journal (1818–20), was purchased by the classicist Pierre-François Tissot in March 1820 and became a vigorous voice of the liberal opposition to the ultras and especially Villèle. Tissot was punished by the latter through press trials, although acquitted, and the loss of his academic rank. Villèle finally "amortized" or bought out the paper in 1824 and suppressed it altogether in 1827, as it had lost money while in his service.

E. Hatin, *Histoire de la presse*, vol. 8 (Paris, 1859–61).

*Daniel Rader*

*Related entries:* PRESS LAWS; TISSOT; ULTRAROYALISTS; VILLELE.

**PINEL, PHILIPPE** (1745–1826), physician and psychiatrist. Despite a lackluster early career, Pinel became one of the dominant figures in French medicine after his appointment to the Paris Faculty of Medicine established by the Convention in 1794. First named adjunct professor of medical physics and hygiene upon the founding of the school, he became professor of internal pathology in 1795 and retained that position until 1822 when he was removed by the government of the Restoration for his liberal sympathies.

Pinel made substantial contributions to the clinical training of physicians, stressing the meticulous bedside observation of patients' symptoms. His textbook of 1798, *Nosographie philosophique*, a classification of diseases inspired by the sensationalist epistemology of John Locke and Etienne de Condillac, enjoyed almost unchallenged authority for about twenty years and went through six editions during that period. Pinel's influence began to wane in 1816 when his former pupil, F.-J.-V. Broussais, published a scathing attack on his doctrines, plunging the Parisian medical world into decades of controversy.

Pinel was restrained in his therapeutics and, unlike Broussais, discouraged the use of bloodletting. In the areas of prevention and diagnostics, however, he accepted the latest innovations. The first vaccination against smallpox in Paris was administered in his clinic in 1800, and he readily adopted the new diagnostic techniques of percussion of the chest and stethoscopy, introduced by J.-N. Corvisart and R.-T.-H. Laennec, respectively.

Apart from his work in internal medicine, Pinel achieved fame for his reform of the treatment of the insane. Appointed physician at the Hospice de Bicêtre in 1793, Pinel released the inmates from their chains and instituted a more humane regime for the care of the insane. These reforms were continued at the Hospice de la Salpêtrière, where he was chief physician from 1795 until the end of his life. His principal psychiatric publication, *Traité medico-philosophique de l'aliénation mentale*, first appeared in 1801 (2d edition, 1809).

E. H. Ackerknecht, *Medicine at the Paris Hospital, 1794–1848* (Baltimore, 1967); J. Postel, *Genèse de la psychiatrie: les premiers écrits de Philippe Pinel* (Paris, 1981).

*W. R. Albury*

*Related entries:* BROUSSAIS; CORVISART; LAENNEC; PARIS FACULTY OF MEDICINE.

**PIUS IX.** MASTAI-FERRETI, JEAN-MARIE, COMTE (1792–1878), pope from 1846 to 1878. The son of a noble family of Sinigaglia (Ancona) destined for a military career, he chose theological studies after an illness and came to Rome. Ordained a priest in 1819, he spent two years in Chile and then, upon his return, was named archbishop of Spoleto in 1828 and bishop of Imola in 1832. A cardinal in 1839, he was a partisan of modern reforms and thus was wrongly seen as a liberal. When Pope Gregory XVI died, he became pope as Pius IX on 16 June 1846. He amnestied the revolutionaries who had been imprisoned after the riots of 1831–32, and his popularity was at its zenith. At the same time he authorized the Jews to leave their ghetto and to travel freely. He also reduced his expenses and took measures to aid the poor.

Although Italian liberals who wanted to unite their country pinned their hopes on him, he remained intransigent on the subject of Rome and the Papal States. He refused to support the war against Austria (March-April 1848) and remained aloof from republican demonstrations that began in Rome after the French Revolution of February 1848. On 24 November 1848 he fled from the demonstrations in Rome and took refuge in Gaeta. The Roman Republic was proclaimed in his absence on 9 February 1849. Pius IX asked for and received French aid and the French army, commanded by Charles-Nicolas Oudinot, helped him to take back his powers between July 1849 and April 1850.

His relations now became strained with the Kingdom of Savoy-Piedmont despite Camillo di Cavour's diplomatic skill. In France he supported ultramontanes like Monsigneur Pie and Louis Veuillot and was hostile to Gallicans like Bishop Dupanloup, Monsigneur Darboy, and Charles-Forbes de Montalembert, who were accused of being liberals. His encyclical Quanta Cura (December 1864) strongly condemned Gallicanism, socialism, and statism and the *Syllabus* which was part of that encyclical contained a list of things Catholics could not do.

But Pius IX was more and more isolated in Italy and, after the fall of Napoleon III, Rome was taken on 20 September 1870, and the Papal States were annexed to Italy. Confined to the Vatican, the pope exercised his functions, which were henceforth solely spiritual, until his death in 1878 after a reign of thirty-two years.

P. P. Fernessole, *Pie IX, pape, 1792–1878* (Paris, 1960); E. E. Y. Hales, *Pio Nono: A Study in European Politics and Religion in the Nineteenth Century* (London, 1954); F. Hayward, *Pie IX et son temps* (Paris, 1948).

*Jean-Claude Caron, trans. E. Newman*
*Related entries:* DUPANLOUP; MONTALEMBERT; OUDINOT; REVOLUTION OF 1830; ROMAN EXPEDITION; ULTRAMONTANES; VEUILLOT.

**POITIERS, COMITE DE LA RUE DE.** See COMITE DE LA RUE DE POITIERS.

**POLIGNAC, JULES-AUGUSTE-ARMAND-MARIE, PRINCE DE** (1780–1847), diplomat and minister. The second son of a lady-in-waiting at court who had been scandalously enriched by the favor of Queen Marie-Antoinette, he emigrated with his mother just after the fall of the Bastille. After his education had been completed, he went to London to join the entourage of the comte d'Artois, who developed a strong and unshakable affection for him. Under the Consulate of Bonaparte, Jules de Polignac and his brother Armand returned to France in secret to take part in the royalist conspiracies of Georges Cadoudal and Charles Pichegru. Arrested and given a rather short prison sentence, Jules was nevertheless kept in prison arbitrarily along with his brother until they escaped in January 1814.

Polignac, who had been among the first members of the secret society of the Chevaliers de la foi, participated in the actions that allowed the Bourbons to be restored. He was at the side of the comte d'Artois in his little group of advisers, all of whom were inspired by his reactionary ideals. In that group, Polignac was especially devoted to the reestablishment of Catholicism, since he was a member of the Congrégation as well as the Chevaliers de la foi. At the end of 1814 he was charged with a confidential mission to Pope Pius VII, who conferred upon him the title of a Roman prince on that occasion.

After the Hundred Days, Louis XVIII, whom he had followed to Ghent, raised him to the Chamber of Peers. At first Polignac refused to swear the required oath because he believed that the Constitutional Charter did not respect the rights of the Catholic church. The rise of the ultraroyalist party to power and then the crowning of King Charles X gave Polignac access to the highest responsibilities of state. But Joseph de Villèle, who feared a rival influence on Charles X, was careful to send him away by naming him as ambassador to London. In that post Polignac showed more ability than he is usually given credit for, and after Villèle resigned, Charles X fixed upon the idea that his "dear Jules" should succeed him. The king accomplished this at last by forming his doomed ministry of 8 August 1829.

At first Polignac was only minister of foreign affairs in this government, and only on 17 November 1829 did he also become president of the Council. To his credit, he handled well the diplomacy involved in conquering Algeria, despite the strong opposition of England. But Polignac bears the grave responsibility for the imprudent domestic policies that led to the fatal confrontation between the king and the majority of the legislature—which was backed by public opinion— and for the inept preparation of the coup d'état inherent in the ordinances of July 1830, when he assumed par interim the duties of the minister of war. His resignation itself was made gracefully, but it came too late to save the dynasty.

Polignac was recognized and arrested when he tried to flee the country, and he was brought before the Chamber of Peers in December 1830 along with two of his former colleagues. He was condemned to life imprisonment and to civil death, a sentence that was invented to satisfy those who wanted him to pay with his head for the blood that he had caused to flow in July. Imprisoned in the fortress of Ham, he was released in 1837 when Louis-Philippe felt that public opinion had quieted down enough to offer him an amnesty. Living in deep retirement in Versailles, he wrote a kind of apologia: *Etudes historiques, politiques et morales* (1845). The most lenient judgment that one can make of him is doubtless that of Alphonse de Lamartine: "M. de Polignac was one of those men whose crimes can be called only errors, and who exceeded the limits of their intelligence without dishonoring their names."

R. Dufourg, *Le Proces des ministres de Charles X* (Bordeaux, 1935); P. Robin-Harmel, *Le Prince Jules de Polignac* (Avignon, Paris, 1942–50).

*Guillaume de Bertier de Sauvigny, trans. E. Newman*

*Related entries:* ALGIERS, EXPEDITION TO; CHARLES X; CHARTER OF 1814; CHEVALIERS DE LA FOI; CONGREGATION; JULY ORDINANCES; LAMARTINE; REVOLUTION OF 1830; ULTRAROYALISTS; VILLELE.

*LA POLITIQUE DES FEMMES* (1848), radical women's paper, two issues 18 June and 2 August 1848, under the subtitle *Paper Published in the Interests of Women and by a Society of Women Workers*. It was founded by Désirée Gay, a working-class woman who had written for *La Femme libre* in 1832, became an Owenite after visiting England, and in 1848 was a delegate at the National Workshops. Contributors included Jeanne Deroin, Marie Dalmay, Augustine Genoux, and H. Sénéchal. The paper was openly socialist, attacking middle-class women and calling for state aid to establish cooperatives of women workers. The reintroduction of caution money in August 1848 killed the paper, but Gay remained an active writer and organizer (in the International) until her death forty years later.

E. Hatin, *Bibliographie historique et critique de la presse périodique française* (Paris, 1866); J. Maitron, ed., *Dictionnaire biographique du mouvement ouvrier français* (Paris, 1964–66).

*Peter McPhee*

*Related entries:* DEROIN; NATIONAL WORKSHOPS; WOMEN'S NEWSPAPERS; WORKERS' COOPERATIVES.

**PONCY, CHARLES** (1821–1891), socialist poet, songwriter, and mason in Toulon. Born in Toulon 4 April 1821, the son of a mason and second of four children, Charles Poncy became first a mason, then a worker poet described by Jules Vinçard as "one of the glories of our poetry," then a Saint-Simonian socialist writer and poet, then the mayor of Toulon during the Second Republic, and finally a rich real estate developer in Toulon and recipient of the Legion of Honor in 1865. His life was not typical of other French artisans of the period, but it may well have been typical of the life they wanted.

Poncy was apprenticed to his father's trade when he was nine. He had already had some schooling (he began to read and memorize prayers when he was seven), most of it church sponsored, and had been, as he recalled, "covered with laurels like Alexander" (Charles Poncy, "Au *Magasin pittoresque*," [Toulon, 1854], in *Athénée de Provence* [Marseille: Gueidon, 1855]) for his scholarly accomplishments. He continued to attend vacation classes, first at the local mutual school when he was twelve and then for eighteen months at the school of the Brothers of the Christian Doctrine, followed by three months at the communal upper school in Toulon. By reading far into the night, Poncy expanded his education to include an eclectic collection of works, such as Racine's *Athalie*, the comedies of Molière, the poems of Lord Byron, Alphonse de Lamartine, and Victor Hugo, the *Fables* of Lafontaine, and the popular *Magasin pittoresque*, a review with lots of pictures and few intellectual pretensions, which Poncy began to read in 1832. The *Magasin pittoresque* taught Poncy geography, history, and nearly every subject but politics. It was cheap (50 centimes for each monthly issue), but for a boy earning 2.75 francs a day, it was a major expense.

Poncy began scribbling poems on spare pieces of paper. His talent was discovered in 1840 when he wrote a poem on the back of a prescription from a local doctor who had come to visit his sick father. The doctor read it and recognized Poncy's talent. This was a time when each region was discovering its local worker poet, and the young Poncy could not only write poems but could write them in French, which was a second language for most Toulonais. (Poncy's older brother, Alexander, was also a poet, but he never achieved national fame because he could write only in Provençal.) Poncy's star rose quickly. In June 1840 the local doctor arranged for Poncy to read four of his poems to the Academy of Sciences and Letters of Toulon. In October 1840 François Arago came to Toulon on his way to Egypt expressly to meet the young worker poet. Poncy gave him a poem, "La Mer," which Arago published in the first number of the *Revue indépendante* (November 1841). The poem was preceded by two enthusiastic notices, one from Arago and one from "Gustave Bonnin," who was really George Sand and who became Poncy's lifelong friend, guide, and benefactor. With the help of the Toulon Academy of Sciences and Letters, a volume of his *Poésies* was published in Toulon in 1842. In 1842 a second collection, the *Marines*, was published in Paris with the help of his new protectors and of his fellow Toulonais, who in one week subscribed to 500 copies of the book. This work made him even more of a local hero in Toulon and brought him national attention from such literary giants as Pierre-Jean de Béranger. Abel-François Villemain, minister of public instruction, gave him 200 francs' worth of books for his library. Jules Vinçard, the Parisian ruler maker, Saint-Simonian *chansonnier*, and editor of the working-class newspaper *La Ruche populaire*, called Poncy "a great and holy poetic imagination" in the May 1842 number of the *Ruche populaire*.

Poncy continued to work as a mason from 5:00 A.M. to 8:00 P.M., but his life was changed. For one thing, his friendship with George Sand changed the nature of his poetry from descriptions of himself and of nature to socialist polemics. "Young as I am," he wrote in a letter dated 12 July 1842, "now that my patroness or rather my holy mother George Sand has revolutionized my poetry and made me associate pictures of the savage and sonorous sea with human thought and feeling, I am no longer satisfied with just the appearance of things." Sand would write 226 letters to Poncy; her last letter to him was dated 3 April 1876. During the July Monarchy it was hard to tell where Sand's ideas ended and Poncy's began. He was the ideal type for her to stick on a pin and add to her collection of socialist worker poets.

George Sand wrote the preface and helped to finance the publication of Poncy's second volume of poems, *Le Chantier*, in 1844. In the preface she proclaimed that the appearance of so many working-class poets was a sign that the Messiah would soon return to earth and that the proletarian poets were his messengers. Poncy echoed her thoughts in one of the poems in the volume, "L'Aspiration":

> I found, gathered together in sublime constellations,
> All the bards of the people on their knees before God!
> [And God said]: "A suffering humanity is hoping for a Messiah. . . .
> I will be that Messiah, children, and you will be
> The sacred apostles of my new faith!
> Poets, go and tell the haughty nations
> To melt down their cannons, to erase their border lines!
> Tell them that honor is tarnished by blood!
> Tell the oppressors that their reign is over!
> Go present yourselves, Bible in hand!
> Sow, sow the light everywhere on your way."

This sense of a social mission infused much of Poncy's poetry during the July Monarchy, which he called a "reign of Jews, of kings at 5 percent." He wrote:

> The rich man, who turns his mocking eye away from my workman's
>     blouse,
> Is more often than once jealous of my workman's gaiety.
> Gaiety! God always gives it
> To whomever knows how to live happily with little.
> Let your iron voice, my hammer, resound
> To glorify work and God.
> I live happy as a king.
> When a man is useful to everyone,
> He can be proud of himself

Poncy consistently sided with the underdog, even with the Bedouins who were being colonized by victorious French armies in North Africa and who, he predicted, would curse the Christians and demand vengeance in a hundred years: "The earth has been promised justice and equality." There should be no more slavery and no more wars of conquest. Women should be equal to men. Poncy was a republican and socialist who approved of the purifying destruction of the French Revolution, but he was convinced that the final revolution that would usher in the new world of equality and justice would be a peaceful change accomplished by the power of poetry, God, and steam.

> For God Himself divided the earth's treasures among everyone:
> The land to the farmers, the sea to the sailors.

This desert, which no eye could measure without fear
Will see the trails of steam engines twenty times a day.

Poncy shared the Saint-Simonian faith in the power of science to reduce human labor:

All unhealthy or repugnant jobs,
The steam engine thunders, and his hollow cry proclaims
That all people who were slaves yesterday are free today.
The blood of Christ only redeemed the soul,
But engineering genius has redeemed the flesh!

By the time he wrote this poem in praise of science, which appeared in his third volume of poetry, *La Chanson de chaque métier*, published in Paris in 1850 and dedicated to George Sand, Poncy had become part of the Saint-Simonian team. His admission to that team came in 1845 when Jules Vinçard organized and financed his triumphal visit to Paris with money collected from his fellow workers. While in Paris Poncy met Béranger, Lamartine, Lamennais, Alfred de Vigny, Etienne Arago, and other French literary stars, and he was made a member of the Lice chansonnière, the best-known *goguette*, or working-class singing society, in Paris. He also got out his mason's tools and repaired the smoking chimney of the hotel where he was staying. Arago, Autran, the satirical poet Auguste-Marseille Barthélemy, Joseph Méry, and the jurist Eugène Ortolan, who wrote the preface to Poncy's *Marines*, also encouraged him, and his poetry continued to appear in the *Revue indépendante* as well as Vinçard's Saint-Simonian socialist working-class newspapers, the *Ruche populaire* and later the *Union*.

When the 1848 Revolution came, Poncy and his friends thought they were ready. His friend Agricol Perdiguier was elected to the Constituent Assembly in 1848 and to the Legislative Assembly in 1849. Poncy, however, ran unsuccessfully for the Constituent Assembly and refused to run for the Legislative Assembly. He became secretary to the mayor of Toulon and then secretary to the Chamber of Commerce of Toulon during the Second Republic. Napoleon's coup d'état of December 1851 ended the dreams of the worker poets, but Poncy proved to be resilient. During the Second Empire he speculated on new construction in his native city and became a rich man. He continued to write poetry, but now he wrote in Provençal, and he joined Frédéric Mistral in the *félibrige* movement, becoming vice-president of the Toulon Academy of Science and Literature that had helped him start his career. He never lost his nostalgia for the days of the worker poets. In a letter to Henry Jouin, future secretary of the Ecole des beaux-arts in Paris, written from Toulon in 1884, Poncy wrote: ''The worker-poets have had their hour. Their light was snuffed out in 1848 with the proclamation of the Republic that they had desired and preached. But their republic was not of this world. Now, Béranger aside, they are forgotten and duly buried.''

Poncy died in Toulon on 30 January 1891. Solange Sand, George Sand's daughter and godmother of Poncy's daughter, remembered him as a man with a "heart of gold, an elite intelligence, and the most faithful of friends."

Dorrya Fahmy, *Charles Poncy, poète-macon, 1821–1891* (Paris, 1934); J. Maitron, ed., *Dictionnaire biographique du mouvement ouvrier français*, vol. 3 (Paris, 1966); E. L. Newman, "L'Arme du siècle, c'est la plume: The French Worker Poets and the Spirit of Revolution and Reform," *Journal of Modern History* (1980) and *The French Worker Poets of the July Monarchy* (forthcoming); E. Thomas, *Voix d'en bas; la poésie ouvrière du XIXe siècle* (Paris, 1979); J. Touchard, *La Glorie de Béranger*, 2 vols. (Paris, 1968).

*Edgar Leon Newman*

*Related entries:* ARAGO FAMILY; BARTHELEMY; BERANGER; BYRON; HUGO; LAMARTINE; LAMENNAIS; LEGISLATIVE ASSEMBLY; PERDIGUIER; REPUBLICANS; *LA REVUE INDEPENDANTE*; *LA RUCHE POPULAIRE*; SAINT-SIMONIANISM; SAND; SINGING SOCIETIES; VIGNY; VILLEMAIN; VINCARD; WORKER POETS.


**PONTS ET CHAUSSEES.** See BRIDGE AND ROAD SERVICE.


*LE POPULAIRE* (1833–1835, 1841–1851), republican and utopian newspaper of the July Monarchy and the Second Republic. When Etienne Cabet founded *Le Populaire* in July 1833, he had not yet fully developed his utopian socialist ideas. The paper was republican but less political in content than the big national newspapers. Sympathy with the workers was strongly expressed, and single issues of the paper were sold at 2 sous a copy in order to reach a clientele who could not afford to take out a yearly subscription. Hawkers were engaged—some paid, some volunteers—to sell the paper in the streets and to attract attention by shouting slogans to the passers-by. On one occasion 12,000 copies were sold in Paris alone, and the printer ran out of paper in his attempts to meet further demands. In France as a whole, Cabet claimed to sell as many as 27,000 copies. His venture was supported by the republican secret societies, whose leaders felt that it gave their propaganda an extra social dimension.

The distribution of the paper was curbed by a law of February 1834 requiring hawkers to have a license, and it disappeared in October 1835 as a result of the press laws of the previous month, which made it a criminal offense for anyone to declare himself in favor of a republic. It was refounded by Cabet on a weekly basis in March 1841. By this time Cabet had published his famous essay *Le Voyage en Icarie*, and his paper was devoted to the idea of setting up egalitarian communes. It had a particularly strong appeal to journeyman shoemakers, tailors, and the like. In 1846 the subscriptions numbered about 3,000, of which 1,000 were in the Paris area. On 9 May 1847 Cabet published in the *Populaire* his famous appeal for volunteers to go with him to Illinois to found a commune. Thereafter he was himself wholly absorbed in this project, but the *Populaire* continued publication until 1851.

P. H. Amann, *Revolution and Mass Democracy: The Paris Club Movement in 1848* (Princeton, 1975); I. Collins, *The Government and the Newspaper Press in France, 1814–1881* (Oxford, 1959); C. H. Johnson, *Utopian Communism in France: Cabet and the Icariens* (Ithaca, 1974).

*Irene Collins*

*Related entries:* CABET; PRESS LAWS; REPUBLICANS.

*LE POPULAIRE ROYALISTE* (1837–1839), legitimist newspaper of the July Monarchy. Edited by François-René de Chateaubriand, Alfred-François Nettement, and a number of other writers prominent in the royalist press, *Le Populaire royaliste* tried between 28 January 1837 and April 1839 to convince the people that they could achieve reforms necessary to their welfare only from a paternalistic monarchy such as that of the Bourbons. The first number was condemned in the law courts for contempt of the government of Louis-Philippe.

*Irene Collins*

*Related entries:* CHATEAUBRIAND; LEGITIMISM; LOUIS-PHILIPPE; NETTEMENT.

**POPULAR RELIGIOSITY,** religious beliefs and practices in France after 1815. The Restoration of the Bourbons to the French throne in 1815 led to a reestablishment of the alliance between throne and altar that had characterized the *ancien régime*. But the church's friendly relations with the state did not solve the pastoral problems that had emerged as a result of the Revolutionary and Napoleonic eras. The intermittent persecution of the church during the past quarter-century and the catastrophic decline in the number of clergy meant that large numbers of Frenchmen had received little or no religious education and no longer habitually went to Sunday Mass and received the sacraments. In the clergy's attempt to recover their authority and power, they were able to draw on popular religious beliefs and practices that had survived among most Frenchmen throughout the Revolutionary period. One of the most widely held beliefs, disseminated through almanachs, oral traditions, sermons, and religious art, was that human history was being guided by providence through distinct stages separated by catastrophic political and social events. Throughout the *ancien régime* certain individuals were judged to be capable of discerning, with the help of the books of Daniel and Revelation, the hand of God in current events. During the Restoration a revival of this prophetic tradition provided the French people with an eschatological framework for the interpretation of recent history. Prophetic publications explained and justified the recent troubles of France and the church and predicted a glorious future for these institutions. The cult of saints and shrines, after withstanding the attacks of a violent iconoclastic minority during the Revolution, was viewed sympathetically by clergymen who created new institutions designed to link popular religious needs with the political and doctrinal goals of the church.

During the Restoration a large quantity of prophetic literature appeared that imbued the Enlightenment, the Revolution, and the Restoration with eschatological significance by seeing them as part of a providential plan for the salvation of France and the world. Many of these prophecies were revised versions of tracts from previous centuries, such as those attributed to Jean Prêcheguerre, Nostradamus, the abbé Holzhauser, and Sister Nativité. Contemporary prophets also flourished, however, such as the peasant Thomas Martin, whose visions of St. Michael the Archangel inspired him to warn Louis XVIII about compromising his legitimist principles, and the comte Joseph de Maistre, whose *Soirées de St. Petersburg* (1821) included a defense of prophecies and a warning to Frenchmen not to repeat the errors of the Enlightenment. The prophetic literature of the Restoration generally identified the *philosophes* as agents of the anti-Christ whose work was continued by the Jacobins and Napoleon. The Revolution was portrayed as divinely ordained punishment inflicted by God on a France that had been seduced by the pride and arrogance of the Enlightenment. The chastisement, however, was designed only to recall France to its religious duties. The defeat of Napoleon and the Restoration of the Bourbons and Pius VII were signs that God had now forgiven France. In some of the prophecies, the returning Bourbons assume millennial significance as great kings who, in conjunction with an angelic pope, would create a world empire that would conquer Turkey, recover the Holy Land, and prepare the way for the Second Coming of Christ.

The same themes of the sin, chastisement, and redemption of France stressed in the prophetic literature were repeated in the sermons preached by the missionaries who circulated in France throughout the Revolution. During a mission preached at Migné (diocese of Poitiers) in 1827, a cross appeared in the sky at the conclusion of sermon and caused a violent emotional reaction in the crowd of 2,000, who were reported to fall on their knees and beg for mercy. Following an investigation, the bishop of Poitiers sanctioned belief in the apparition and interpreted it as a sign of hope for the future of France. The investigation and approval of the apparition at Migné established a pattern that was repeated on several occasions throughout the nineteenth century.

The prophetic tradition remained vital throughout the July Monarchy, when it was amended by two Marian apparitions that became the basis for important national cults. In November 1830 Mary appeared to Sister Catherine Labouré at the mother house of the Daughters of Charity in Paris and assured her that France retained a special place in her affections despite the recent July Revolution. The medal revealed to Sister Catherine, in which the light of divine grace flowed from her outstretched arms to France, became popular as a healing talisman during the cholera epidemic of 1832. Millions of what came to be known as Miraculous Medals were distributed by the Daughters of Charity, the largest nursing order in France, throughout the July Monarchy; their diffusion helped keep alive the idea that France had a special role to play in world history. In addition to its thaumaturgic and political functions, the Miraculous Medal also helped to popularize the doctrine of the Immaculate Conception through the prayer stamped around its circumference: "O Mary conceived without sin, pray for us who have recourse to thee." This doctrine, which asserted that Mary had been conceived without original sin in honor of her future status as the mother of Jesus, was strongly encouraged by the church throughout the nineteenth century and was officially promulgated by Pope Pius IX in 1854. The cult of the Miraculous Medal reveals the close association that existed in the first half of the nineteenth century between popular beliefs about the healing power of saints, the political mission of France, and the doctrinal authority of the church.

A second major apparition took place in 1846 when Mary appeared to two shepherd children, Mélanie Calvat and Maximin Giraud, at La Salette (Isère). Mary's message at La Salette referred explicitly to the current economic crisis, which she claimed was the result of widespread irreligious behavior, including the eating of meat on Fridays and the failure to attend Mass on Sundays. Mary promised that if the French people would convert, "the stones and rocks would become mounds of wheat." The prophecy of La Salette immediately provoked a local religious revival, and pamphlets about the miracle were being distributed throughout France within a year. Clerical sympathy for the apparition and the reports of healings at a fountain that appeared at the site of the miracle led to the creation of a shrine that grew throughout the nineteenth century and remains a major pilgrimage center in contemporary France. The success of the prophecy of Our Lady of La Salette suggests the sustained ability of the prophetic tradition to explain and justify economic catastrophes during the first half of the nineteenth century. Following the Revolution of 1848, Mary's message was reinterpreted by the clergy as a prediction of political upheaval that could be controlled only if the French followed Mary's advice and obeyed without question the laws of God and church. The pattern established at La Salette (an apparition to shepherd children, a miraculous fountain, and messages that both threaten and console) was a model for the more famous cult of Our Lady of Lourdes inaugurated by a series of apparitions to Bernadette Soubirous in 1858.

The prophetic tradition, with its use of religiously charged symbolism and its emphasis on violent and apocalyptic change, was not monopolized by the church and legitimist ideologues. Critics of the social order such as the comte de Saint-Simon, in *Le Nouveau christianisme* (1825), and Etienne Cabet, in *Le Vrai christianisme* (1846), also drew on a prophetic vocabulary and an eschatological framework. Many of the artisans who supported the Revolution in February and June 1848 also expressed their political goals with the help of language and concepts drawn from the same prophetic tradition that flowed into the royalist prophecies of the Restoration.

The sustained appeal of prophecies throughout the first half of the nineteenth century suggests that at the level of popular belief, God was still perceived to be a prominent actor in human history. But the supernatural world impinged even more immediately on everyday life through the thousands of shrines that filled the landscape of the French countryside in the nineteenth century. Following the Council of Trent in the sixteenth century, the clergy had regarded shrines with some suspicion, for they saw them as rivals to the sacramental system in providing access to supernatural graces. But the loyalty to shrines displayed by many French peasants during the French Revolution made the church more willing to tolerate and cooperate with them in the nineteenth century. Shrines dedicated to individual saints ranged from small chapels that drew pilgrims from local parishes to regional shrines such as those of St. Anne d'Auray, St. Radegonde in Poitiers, and St. Jean-François Régis of Louvesc. The development of major national shrines, the most prominent of which was Notre-Dame de Lourdes, did not occur until the creation of the railroad network in the second half of the century. But even in the first part of the century, some shrines had national reputations. The town of Ars took advantage of improved roads and specially scheduled carriages to draw thousands of pilgrims from throughout France to its parish church, where they were healed and given spiritual advice by the saintly curé d'Ars, Jean Vianney.

Pilgrimages to shrines were made for both individual and collective intentions. Individual pilgrims sought help with problems in their work, their family lives, and especially with their health. Professional pilgrims, usually older women, were frequently available for hire by those who were unable or unwilling to make the trip to the shrine personally. The choice of the shrine depended on the particular problems of the pilgrim, for saints and their shrines were frequently specialists; St. Clair was invoked for eye maladies, St. Avertine for headaches, and St. Apolline for toothaches. The Virgin Mary, however, was the most popular of all saints and could be addressed for help with all ailments. Marian devotions, including those of the Miraculous Medal and Our Lady of La Salette, were encouraged by the clergy, who saw the Virgin as a symbol of the universal church who could assist them in breaking down parochial and regional loyalties in favor of a more Roman-centered church. The rituals practiced at shrines fall into clear patterns. Pilgrims would bathe in or drink from sacred fountains, light candles before miraculous statues, and leave a gift, or *ex-voto*, in return for which they hoped for supernatural assistance. In times of collective crises, such as the cholera epidemic of 1832 or the crop failures that struck much of France in 1846, entire parishes traveled to local shrines hoping for saintly intercession on their behalf. Such collective rituals were frequently able to draw in even those individuals who had abandoned orthodox religious behavior, for trust in the power of saints was not always congruent with the attendance at Mass on Sunday or the reception of Easter Communion.

Communal processions and religious gatherings at shrines were not, however, restricted to periods of crisis. The feast days of the shrines' patrons, such as the famous *pardons* of Brittany, were annual occasions that drew together local and regional communities. The clergy were at times scandalized by the dances and feasts that accompanied these festivities, but their sustained popularity throughout this period suggests that popular religion remained to some extent independent of the institutional church.

The commitment of the French to popular religious traditions can also be seen in their continued insistence throughout this period on the religious sanctification of the crucial transitional moments of their lives. The sacraments were used universally to mark the entrance into life (baptism), the end of childhood (First Communion), the acceptance of adult responsibility (marriage), and the passing to the next world (extreme unction). Throughout the first half of the nineteenth century, the clergy made periodic attempts to limit access to the sacraments as a way of establishing control over the religious and moral behavior of their parishioners. Baptism and First Communion were at times refused to children whose parents or godparents did not attend Sunday Mass or receive Easter Communion; marriages would be allowed only after the couple had confessed and been absolved; funeral services and burial in consecrated ground was denied to those who refused to or, because of sudden death, were unable to receive the Last Sacraments. On some occasions there were also conflicts over the *casuel*, the fees charged by the clergy to administer the sacraments and over the stipends charged for Masses said for the repose of the souls of the dead.

Troubles over the reception of the sacraments and the costs of religious services became especially intense in the early 1830s when clergymen sympathetic to the royalist cause refused to bury laymen associated with the July Monarchy. On several occasions the friends and relatives of the deceased, with the support of the public officials, broke into churches and conducted funeral services on their own. The rituals associated with death and the folktales gathered by ethnographers throughout the last century suggest that most French people, at least in the countryside, continued to believe in an immortal soul that was punished or rewarded in a world beyond this one. The insistence on religious burial reveals that the intermittent anticlericalism of this era did not necessarily imply the denial of this fundamental tenet of popular religiosity. The appeal of prophecies, shrines, and sacramental life during the first half of the nineteenth century testifies to the sustained importance of belief in a God who guided human history, saints who intervened miraculously in response to both individual and collective appeals, and a soul that lived on after the life of the body and required the prayers of the living to ease its passage into the next world.

L. Bassette, *Le Fait de La Salette* (Paris, 1965); P. Boutry and M. Cinquin, *Deux pèlerinages au XIXe siècle: Ars et Paray-le-Monial* (Paris, 1981); G. Cholvy, "Le Catholicisme populaire en France au XIXe siècle," in Bernard Plongeron and Robert Pannet, eds., *Le Christianisme populaire* (Paris, 1976) and "Expression et évolution du sentiment religieux populaire dans la France au temps de la Restauration catholique (1801–1860)," *La Piété populaire de 1610 à nous jours: Actes du 99e congrès national des sociétés savantes, Besancon, 1974*, vol. 1 (Paris, 1976); C. Garret, *Respectable Folly: Millenarianism and the French Revolution in France and England* (Baltimore, 1975); T. Kselman, *Miracles and Prophecies in Nineteenth-Century France* (New Brunswick, N.J., 1983); M. Lagrée, "Religion populaire et populisme religieux au XIXe siècle," in J. Delumeau, ed., *Histoire vécue du peuple chrétien*, vol. 2 (Paris, 1979); C. Langlois, "La Conjoncture miraculause à la fin de la Restauration: Migné, miracle oublie," *Revue d'histoire de la spiritualité* 49 (1973) and *Le Diocèse de Vannes au XIXe siècle (1800–1830)* (Rennes, 1974).

*Thomas Kselman*

*Related entries:* CABET; LOUIS XVIII; MAISTRE; MISSIONS; PIUS IX; RAILROADS; REVOLUTION OF 1830; REVOLUTION OF 1848; SAINT-SIMON.

**POPULATION.** The total population of France grew from 27,349,631 to 35,783,170 between 1801 and 1851, an increase of 30.8 percent. Although substantial, this increase was relatively low compared with the rest of Europe, which was experiencing a major burst of population growth at this time. In the same period, the population of Great Britain grew by approximately 47.5 percent; that of the German states by 44.4 percent; and that of the Italian peninsula by 36.1 percent. Thus, although growing, the French population was losing its preponderant position in Europe. Its share of the European population fell from 15.7 percent in 1800 to 13.3 percent in 1850.

The strongest periods of population growth in France were the years after the Bourbon Restoration in 1815 and the period from 1831 to 1836. The first appears to reflect the recovery of the population from the wars of the Empire, as well as substantial immigration; the second corresponds to a period of strong economic development between the Revolution of 1830 and the economic crisis of 1837. In other periods, growth, although present, was not as strong, and it was particularly weak during the Empire and the Second Republic. The years of the Restoration and July Monarchy therefore appear to have been a phase of strong growth distinct from the weak growth before and after.

This growth was the result of a natural excess of births over deaths and migration into France from other countries. The largest part of the increase (88.5 percent) over the period 1801–51 was due to the excess of births over deaths, and in some intercensal periods (1826–30, 1836–40, 1846–50) the natural growth of the population outweighed substantial net emigration in order for the overall population to grow.

France was still an overwhelmingly rural country in 1851. Following the definition used in the 1846 and 1851 censuses, 74.5 percent of the population lived in communes with fewer than 2,000 inhabitants in the principal settlement. The strongest natural growth occurred in the countryside, where birth rates consistently exceeded death rates. The first half of the nineteenth century, however, did see substantial shifts of the population from the countryside to cities, and because of this migration, the most striking rates of overall population growth occurred in cities. All cities, however, did not grow at the same rates. The capital, Paris, grew much faster than other cities, and different patterns of growth in provincial cities occurred because of the different functions of cities and the extent of their participation in economic development.

The largest French city by far in 1801, Paris counted 547,756 inhabitants, 2 percent of the population of the country in that year. By 1851 it had grown to

1,053,262 inhabitants or 2.94 percent of the national population, a growth of 1.7 percent per year over the half-century. In comparison, the next largest French city, Marseilles, had 111,130 inhabitants in 1801. While the growth of Paris was considerable throughout the period until 1846, the growth from 1831 to 1846 was most spectacular, including more than half of the net gain for the entire period. Only from 1846 to 1851, marked by economic and political crises, did the city lose population.

The strong growth of Paris was due above all to an influx of migrants into the city. Over the period 1821–51, immigration accounted for 78.6 percent of the overall growth of the city. In certain periods, especially the first five years of the July Monarchy, these immigrants made up for an excess of deaths over births in the city. While it has proved difficult to identify the places of origin of these immigrants, the majority appear to have come from the northern third of France and especially the departments nearest Paris.

In comparison with immigration, the natural growth of the Parisian population furnished a limited part of the net growth of the city, accounting for only 21.4 percent of the overall growth between 1821 and 1851.

The development of cities outside of Paris took a different pattern. This was related to the economy of the particular city. Since it was rare for births to exceed deaths in any city in the early nineteenth century, growth depended above all on the ability of the city to attract immigrants. Those with expanding industry were able to do so in relatively large numbers, while primarily administrative cities found this less easy. As industrialization affected specific regions, spectacular growth could occur; cities like Roubaix and Tourcoing in the north, Mulhouse in Alsace, and Saint-Etienne in the center doubled or tripled in size between 1801 and 1851. But economic development was slow and localized in France in this period, and most major cities grew at much slower rates. Administrative cities such as Amiens, Nancy, Angers, Montpellier, and Orléans grew by only about one-third, roughly the same rate as the population of the country as a whole. Population growth in the provincial cities of France was therefore more erratic and tended to be slower than in the single large city that dominated the French landscape, Paris.

J. Bourgeois-Pichat, "The General Development of the Population of France since the Eighteenth Century," in D. V. Glass, ed., *Population in History* (Chicago, 1965); L. Chevalier, *La Formation de la population parisienne au XIXe siècle* (Paris, 1950); C. H. Pouthas, *La Population française pendant la première moitié du XIXe siècle* (Paris, 1952).

*James Lehning*
*Related entries:* FERTILITY; MIGRATION; MORTALITY; NUPTIALITY.


**PORTAL, PIERRE-BARTHELEMY, BARON DE** (1765–1845), imperial administrator; deputy, peer, and minister of the navy of the Restoration; peer of the July Monarchy. Pierre-Barthélemy Portal was born at Montauban on 31 October 1765 to a Huguenot family. He learned the trade of arms maker in

Bordeaux and by 1789 had become head of a large naval arms firm. However, the early years of the Revolution cost him his fortune, and in 1796 he had to start over. Under the Consulate, he became a judge of the Court of Commerce and president of the Bordeaux chamber of commerce. He attracted Napoleon's attention with a memoir on trade with England and was given the task of claiming restitution for merchandise from Bordeaux seized by American ships. From 1806 to 1811 he served as a municipal councillor of Bordeaux. He also was on the General Council of the department of Gironde. In 1811 Napoleon appointed him master of requests in the Council of State and considered him for the Ministry of Commerce. In 1813 he was sent as a commissioner to Marshal Nicolas-Jean de Soult's army confronting the duke of Wellington across the Pyrenees. He helped maintain order in this force until the arrival of the Duke of Angoulême in Bordeaux on 12 March 1814. Portal then fled the city but quickly found favor with the Bourbon regime, which recalled him to the Council of State.

After Waterloo the Bourbons appointed Portal to a commission to oversee supplies for the Allied armies and named him director of the colonies. In this capacity he helped negotiate the treaty settlements of 1815. The department of Tarn-et-Garonne elected him to the Chamber of Deputies where he sat among the Center Right deputies. On 29 December 1818 he became minister of the navy and colonies in the Dessolle cabinet. The appointment of a Protestant to the cabinet was intended as a gauge of the toleration of the new government. As minister of marine he earned a reputation as a competent and effective administrator. He greatly increased the appropriations for his service and succeeded in reducing the tensions between the officers and men of the Bourbon navy and those of the imperial service. Portal's ambitious naval and colonial policy marked the first improvement in the position of the navy since Napoleon. He attempted to influence the cabinet toward a *doctrinaire* position. Yet in late 1819 he advocated a conservative reform of the electoral law to favor landed property owners. On 13 December 1821 Portal resigned his ministry along with other members of the Richelieu cabinet. That same day Louis XVIII appointed him a minister of state and gave him a peerage. As a peer he voted with the moderate royalists. In 1828 he was named a regent of the Bank of France. In 1829 Jules de Polignac offered Portal a cabinet post, which he refused. After the July Revolution he supported the Orleanist monarchy and remained in the Peers until his death in Bordeaux on 11 January 1845. His memoirs were published in 1846.

*Archives parlementaires*; L. Chevalier, *Histoire de la marine française de 1815 à 1870* (Paris, 1900); B. de Gervain, *Un Ministre de la marine et son ministère sous la restauration, le baron Portal* (Paris, 1898); A. Robert et al., *Dictionnaire des parlementaires français* (Paris, 1889–91).

*James K. Kieswetter*

*Related entries:* ANGOULEME, L.-A.; *CHAMBRE INTROUVABLE*; COUNCIL OF STATE; DESSOLLE; *DOCTRINAIRES*; ELECTIONS AND ELECTORAL SYSTEMS; PARIS, SECOND TREATY OF; POLIGNAC; RICHELIEU; SOULT.

**PORTALIS, JOSEPH-MARIE, COMTE** (1778–1858), magistrate, minister, and peer of the Restoration and July Monarchy, senator of the Second Empire. Born on 19 February 1778, Portalis saw his father persecuted by the Revolution and proscribed by the coup of 18 Fructidor. Young Portalis fled with his father to Holstein, and there married the countess of Holck. After 18 Brumaire they returned to France. He served in the diplomatic corps, helping to negotiate the peace of Ameins and serving at London, Berlin, and Ratisbonne. His father became minister of worship and named young Portalis secretary general of that ministry. At his father's death in 1807, Portalis took over the ministry for a few months. He was subsequently appointed councillor of state, and Napoleon named him a count of the Empire on 9 December 1809. In 1810 he became director general of publishing. However, he incurred the wrath of Napoleon when he failed to reveal that Pope Pius VII had circulated in France various forbidden letters and bulls and that his own cousin, the abbé d'Astros, had received this material. Napoleon was especially angered at a letter of censure sent to Astros opposing the appointment of Cardinal Maury as archbishop of Paris. In the Council of State on 4 January 1811, Napoleon attacked Portalis on this subject, expelled him from the Council, and banished him forty leagues from Paris. Through the intervention of Comte Molé, however, in late 1813 Napoleon appointed Portalis first president of the imperial court of Angers.

The Restoration retained Portalis at this post and restored him to the Council of State. He served Napoleon in the Hundred Days. The Second Restoration, however, kept him on and named him councillor in the Court of Cassation on 26 August 1815. He became a staunch royalist. In the Council of State he prepared and presented laws restricting the press and repressing seditious cries. In 1818 he went to Rome to try, unsuccessfully, to negotiate a new concordat. On 5 March 1819 Portalis was appointed to the Chamber of Peers, and on 21 February 1820 he became under secretary of state at the Ministry of Justice, where he remained until the formation of Joseph de Villèle's ministry in December 1821. In August 1824 he became president of one of the chambers of the Court of Cassation. As a peer Portalis generally voted with the Center Right, for example opposing the Jesuits in 1827 and 1828. Thus when the Martignac ministry was established in January 1828, Portalis became minister of justice. As such he was instrumental in proposing measures abolishing press censorship and dealing with election fraud. He also cautioned the king against trying to appoint a cabinet without the support of the Chambers. In May 1829 he became minister of foreign affairs, remaining until the cabinet resigned in August. Nevertheless he still enjoyed the favor of Charles X, who in 1829 thought of him as prime minister. He remained on the Privy Council and was appointed first president of the Court of Cassation. He kept this judicial post throughout the July Monarchy.

Under Louis-Philippe Portalis became a vice-president of the Peers, where he continued to participate actively. He generally supported authority in his advocacy of the hereditary peerage, his opposition to divorce, and his adherence to other conservative positions. In 1832 he received the grand cross of the Legion of

Honor and later became a member of the Académie des sciences morales et politiques. He retained his judicial post even through the Second Republic. After the coup of 2 December 1851, Louis-Napoleon appointed him to the Consultative Commission and on 26 January 1852 named him to the Senate. He supported the establishment of the Second Empire. On 18 December 1852 he finally retired from the bench, retaining the title of honorary first president. In spite of his retirement, he remained active in the Senate until his death in Paris on 5 August 1858.

    *Archives parlementaires*; V. Bindel, *Histoire religieuse de Napoléon* (Paris, 1940); A. Debidour, *Histoire des rapports de l'église et de l'état en France de 1789 à 1870* (Paris, 1898); C. S. Phillips, *The Church in France, 1789–1848* (New York, 1966); A. Robert et al., *Dictionnaire des parlementaires français* (Paris, 1889–91).

*James K. Kieswetter*

*Related entries:* CENSORSHIP; COURT OF CASSATION; JESUITS; LAW ON SEDITIOUS SPEECH; MARTIGNAC; VILLELE.

**POSITIVISM.** See COMTE.

**POTHIER, EUGENE.** See POTTIER.

**POTTIER, EUGENE** (1816–1887), Parisian packer and later cloth printer, poet and *chansonnier*; composer of the "Internationale," which became the anthem of world socialism and communism. Eugène Pottier never became a well-known worker poet though he wrote what became the best-known working-class song. His father, a packer, was an avid Bonapartist and his mother a devoted Catholic. He published his first verses when he was fifteen, taking Pierre-Jean de Béranger as his "divine model." His early songs were republican, socialist, and Christian, and he looked to Jesus as the source of human fraternity, democracy, and equality of opportunity. In his *Chansons de l'atelier*, published in 1848, he wrote:

> Glory to Jesus who died on this wood!
> What we are we owe to him,
> For the Brotherhood of man,
> Is nailed to the Cross.

Thus the young Pottier combined the revolutionary spirit of his father with the piety of his mother by making Christianity a revolutionary faith. The athiest, communist, revolutionary composer of the "Internationale" began as a defender of private property who favored order, probity, vigilance, Christianity, and peace (except that he strongly favored French military aid to Poland). He published his first collection of poetry in 1832 when he was eighteen and dedicated it to Béranger. Later he was associated with the Buchezian *Atelier*. His ideas became more revolutionary with time: he participated in the 1848 Revolution and in the Paris Commune, after which he was condemned to death in absentia and forced to live in exile in England and the United States. He returned to France in 1880 and died in obscurity in Paris on 6 November 1887. Then he became famous.

J. Maitron, ed., *Dictionnaire biographique du mouvement ouvrier français*, vol. 3 (Paris, 1966); E. Pottier, *Chansons de l'atelier* (Paris, 1848), *Chants révolutionnaires* (Paris, 1887), *La Jeune muse, recueil de chansons dédiées à M. de Béranger* (Paris, 1832), and *Oeuvres complètes*, ed. P. Brochon (Paris, 1966); E. Thomas, *Voix d'en bas; la poésie ouvrière du XIXe siècle* (Paris, 1979).

*Edgar Leon Newman*

*Related entries:* L'ATELIER; BERANGER; REPUBLICANS; REVOLUTION OF 1848; WORKER POETS.


**POUMIES DE LA SIBOUTIE, FRANCOIS-LOUIS** (1789–1863), Parisian physician and memoirist. François-Louis Poumiès de la Siboutie was born on 8 June 1789 at Saint-Germain-du-Salembre in Périgord. During his youth, in which many of the vestiges of the Old Regime vanished and the Revolution peaked and declined, he devoted much leisure to reading in the municipal library of Périgueux. He studied medicine in Paris and, completing his course in 1815, remained there to seek his career. Although his competence and his polished manners gained him a wealthy clientele, he also served for more than thirty years without charge as physician to the relief committee of the tenth arrondissement of Paris. Thus he was acquainted with the great and the small of his era. When an injury forced six months of recuperation on him, he began organizing the daily notes from his diary to create his own personal history. It contained his recollections of his own youth and his medical practice, as well as of the great events of his time and the public involvement in them he had observed. After his recovery, he continued noting down his observations as a chronicle of current events. He concerned himself not primarily with his own role or with his comments on great affairs of state but rather with anecdotes and word portraits, with remarks on hospitals, the medical profession, and the sick, which he encountered in his cross-section of society from the first Empire to the second. Poumiès died at Montereau-faut-Yonne on 19 October 1863. His notes, which provide an accurate account of the common people, were compiled and published by his daughters and by Joseph Durieux.

F. L. Poumiès de la Siboutie, *Souvenirs d'un médecin de Paris* (Paris, 1910).

*James K. Kieswetter*

*Related entries:* PARIS FACULTY OF MEDICINE.


**POZZO DI BORGO, CHARLES-ANDRE** (1764–1842), Corsican political figure and Russian diplomat. The son of an old Corsican noble family, Pozzo di Borgo was educated in a Jesuit collège in Ajaccio and undertook legal studies in Pisa. Initially a moderate revolutionary, he was elected to the Legislative Assembly (1791–92) but opposed the overthrow of the monarchy and refused election to the Convention. As *procureur-général* of Corsica in 1793, he allied himself with Paoli and invited the English to establish a protectorate over the island in January 1794. Under the government of the English viceroy Gilbert Elliot, Pozzo was president of the Council of State and directed the restoration of the church lands, the tithe, the salt tax, and primogeniture on the island. With the withdrawal of English forces and the restoration of French control of Corsica (1796), Pozzo was forced into exile and entered the service of the count of Artois. Wandering from London through Italy and Austria, Pozzo joined the court of Czar Alexander I and became a Russian councillor of state in 1805. Leaving after Tilsit (1807), he returned to London until 1812, when he reentered Russian service, where he was promoted to general and named the czar's ambassador to Paris in 1814, a post he would hold until 1834. At the Congress of Vienna and in Paris, Pozzo worked to ensure the survival of the Bourbon restoration. This involved suggestions that Louis XVIII execute and confiscate the property of Napoleon's major supporters, but his advice after 1815 generally counseled moderation, and Pozzo worried that the intransigence of the ultras would alienate popular support for the regime. A confidant of Louis (who added him to his civil list and paid him more than 1.5 million francs), he was several times considered for a ministerial post and came to oppose the policies of his old patron Artois. In 1834 he became Russian ambassador to England and retired from government service in 1839.

An influential diplomat, Pozzo remained a lifelong enemy of Napoleon, a posture based as much on his Corsican experience (where the Pozzos and the Bonapartes belonged to opposing political factions) as his monarchist sympathies. After 1815, his actions and advice were often more pro-French than pro-Russian.

V. Beach, *Charles X of France and His Times* (Boulder, 1971); G. de Bertier de Sauvigny, *La Restauration* (Paris, 1955, 1963); A. Maggiolo, *Corse, France et Russie, Pozzo di Borgo (1764–1842)* (Paris, 1890); R. Palmer, *The Age of Democratic Revolution*, vol. 2 (Princeton, 1964); C. Pozzo di Borgo, *Correspondance diplomatique du Comte Pozzo di Borgo*, 2 vols. (Paris, 1890–97).

*David Longfellow*
*Related entries:* CHARLES X; LOUIS XVIII; ULTRAROYALISTS; VIENNA, CONGRESS OF.

**PRADT, DOMINIQUE-GEORGES DE RIOM DE PROLHIAC** (1759–1837), politically active cleric of the Empire and Restoration. Dominique-Georges Pradt was born to a noble family of Auvergne at the Chateau de Pradt near Saint-Flour in 1759. He entered the priesthood and became vicar general of the Diocese of Rouen in 1784. He was elected as a delegate of the First Estate to the Estates General. After having opposed reform, he emigrated in 1791. He returned to France in 1800, and due to the support of General Géraud Duroc, he was appointed chaplain to the emperor in 1804. He was appointed bishop of Poitiers, and after supporting Napoleon against the Spanish Bourbons, he was made archbishop of Malines on 18 May 1808.

He lost Napoleon's favor as the result of the failure of a mission to Poland in 1812. In 1814 he met with Charles-Maurice de Talleyrand and gave his support to the idea of restoring the Bourbon monarchy in France. Despite his active support for the Restoration, he had to abandon his archbishopric and retire to his estate in Auvergne. He received a pension from the king but nevertheless wrote pamphlets hostile to the government. He was elected as a deputy from Clermont in 1827, but in 1828, disgusted with the timidity of the liberals, he resigned. He died in Paris in 1837.

D.-G. Pradt, *Des Jésuites anciens et modernes* (1824), *Des Progrès du gouvernement représentatif en France* (1817), *Les Quatre concordats* (1818), and *Les Trois ages des colonies* (1801).

*Bernard Cook*

*Related entries:* CHAMBER OF DEPUTIES; TALLEYRAND.

*LE PRECURSEUR* (1821–1834), influential provincial newspaper of the Restoration and July Monarchy. This Lyons paper played an important role in provincial politics in the last years of the Bourbon monarchy and the early years of the reign of Louis-Philippe. Founded at a time of censorship (1821), it not unnaturally supported the royalist policies of the chief minister, Armand-Emmanuel de Richelieu. When Joseph de Villèle took office with an ultraroyalist majority, however, the *Précurseur* became increasingly hostile to the government. In 1826 a young lawyer, Jérome Morin, became chief editor, and the paper took on a definitely liberal tone, attacking the Jesuits, denouncing Charles de Peyronnet's press bill, and sponsoring a petition demanding the impeachment of the ministers. The editor was condemned to three months' imprisonment and a fine of 1,000 francs, but with the solid backing of sixty shareholders from among the business and professional classes of Lyons, the paper survived.

In 1830 the *Précurseur* won praise from François-Auguste Mignet in the *National* for its stand against Polignac. After the Revolution of 1830, the *Précurseur* moved further to the left. Without openly proclaiming itself republican, it agitated for democratic measures that would lead France toward a republic in the unspecified future. No social program was adopted to appeal to the workers, however; the *Précurseur* still relied on a mainly bourgeois readership, and its circulation during the years 1831 and 1834 was little more than 800. Meanwhile prosecutions rained down. Support from republican secret societies saved the *Précurseur* on more than one occasion, until the societies themselves were crippled by the severe measures following the insurrection of April 1834.

J. Alazard, "Le Mouvement politique et social à Lyon entre novembre 1831 et avril 1834," *Revue d'histoire moderne* (1911); R. J. Bezucha, *The Lyon Uprising of 1834* (Cambridge, Mass., 1974); G. Perreux, *Au Temps des sociétés secrètes* (Paris, 1931).

*Irene Collins*

*Related entries:* CENSORSHIP; JESUITS; MIGNET; *LE NATIONAL*; PEY-RONNET; POLIGNAC; REPUBLICANS; REVOLUTION OF 1830; RICHE-LIEU; ULTRAROYALISTS; VILLELE.

*LA PRESSE,* first low-price, high-circulation newspaper in France. In 1836 Emile de Girardin effected a revolution in the newspaper world by introducing commercialism. On 1 July 1836 there appeared the first issue of his newspaper

*La Presse*, to be sold at 40 francs a year instead of the 80 charged by other national dailies. Girardin believed that the lower price would produce an increase in sales and that a wider circulation would attract businessmen to advertise in the newspaper. His theories were derived from his knowledge of the *Times* in England. The precedent did not prove to be entirely valid, because even though 10,000 subscribers were enrolled within a short time, the income from advertisements was never as great as Girardin had hoped. Nor did cheapness in itself ensure sales. To attract large numbers of readers, Girardin abandoned the long political discussions that were the stock-in-trade of the older newspapers, and in their place he delighted his readers with gossip and fashion articles, with stunts of various kinds, with Delphine Gay's (his wife) witty and informative chronicles, and above all with serial stories.

The idea of publishing novels in installments was Girardin's most intuitive stroke of genius as a businessman. Among a new reading public, anxious to be diverted from the affairs of everyday life, wishing to be amused but unwilling or unable to concentrate for long periods, the serial story fulfilled a real demand and became at once the most popular form of literature on the market. Girardin professed to be inspired by the ideal of educating the masses, but this was probably true in a vague humanitarian sense only. Journalists with more serious democratic or socialist aims disliked Girardin's commercial attitudes. The *Presse* never wholly abandoned politics, but its affiliations reflected mainly the personal vendettas of its owner. For instance, Girardin bitterly resented an attempt by François Guizot to found a rival advertiser, and hence during 1847 the *Presse* began to discredit Guizot's government by hinting at scandalous financial transactions. In May 1847 Girardin was arraigned before the Chamber of Peers for an article suggesting that peerages had been promised in return for money; his acquittal by the Peers gave credence to his suggestions.

It was Girardin who, on 24 February 1848, entered the Tuileries and told Louis-Philippe that he ought to abdicate. Girardin hoped that the Chambers would proceed to establish a regency for Louis-Philippe's little grandson under the duchesse d'Orléans, from whom he expected to obtain social advancement. He never liked the Republic. From March 1848 the *Presse* criticized the Provisional Government for lack of a coherent social policy. It therefore figured among the newspapers whose publication was suspended and whose editors were imprisoned for encouraging the insurrection of the June Days. Girardin never forgave Eugène Cavaignac for treating him in this manner, and in December 1848 the *Presse* proved to be one of Louis-Napoleon's most vigorous supporters in the presidential election campaign. Girardin also, in 1851, urged revision of the Constitution to allow Louis-Napoleon to remain president of the Republic for ten years. However, he protested against Louis-Napoleon's coup d'état by voluntarily suspending publication of the *Presse* for ten days. For this he was exiled, but the *Presse* was allowed to continue publication.

I. Collins, *The Government and the Newspaper Press in France, 1814–1881* (Oxford, 1959); J. Morienval, *Les Créateurs de la grande presse en France* (Paris, 1934); E.

Reclus, *Emile de Girardin, créateur de la presse moderne* (Paris, 1934); A. Sirven, *Journaux et journalistes: La Presse* (Paris, 1866).

*Irene Collins*

Related entries: CAVAIGNAC, L. -E.; CHAMBER OF PEERS; COUP D'ETAT OF 2 DECEMBER 1851; GIRARDIN; GUIZOT; JUNE DAYS; LOUIS-PHI-LIPPE; PARIS, COUNT OF; PROVISIONAL GOVERNMENT.

**PRESS LAWS.** None of the constitutional regimes in France between 1815 and 1850 recognized an absolute right to press freedom. Repressive Ultra forces in the Restoration enacted a dozen laws to curtail this freedom but did not destroy it. Under the July Monarchy's Charter, freedom of the press was assured, but by 1835 a few severe laws had made it a travesty. The Second Republic tried to restore the liberty of the press but failed to maintain it in the face of growing political instability.

Three basic methods of control or regulation appear in French press legislation between 1815 and 1850. First was outright censorship, either by preliminary submission of all copy to authorities prior to issue or censorship of prohibited subject matter, such as advocacy of Bonapartist rule. Censors were either police officials or a panel selected by the appropriate ministry. Printing a censured item was a crime. The weakness of censure was that censors were overworked and not always clever enough to notice an offensive passage. Censorship also was evaded by such devices as the use of code words and phrases known to readers but innocuous of themselves. For example, *Le Constitutionnel* frequently mentioned the harmless phrase *le système*, which stood for Joseph de Villèle's corruption and chicanery. Some opposition papers survived the 1820s because of such tricks. Satire, a specialty of the French, was also used to evade censure, and we even find a certain official tolerance for it if gracefully presented.

Second, a stronger bridle for the press was the official authorization to publish, which could be revoked to penalize editors and managers of periodicals. This could include special licensing requirements for printers and vendors, thus extending the threat of total suppression. Widely and arbitrarily used from 1815 to 1820 to destroy opposition periodicals, it could be evaded by changing a journal's name and by shifting the names of the managerial staffs of papers. Louis-Philippe's government abolished preliminary authorization but was still able to suppress newspapers by statutes.

Third, specific laws defining press offenses accompanied by frequent prosecutions became the method of choice for governments of this era, especially after 1822 in the Restoration and throughout the July Monarchy. Although this method depended on pro-government legislative majorities, penalties were flexible and could be politically directed. Fines could be severe enough to destroy a journal in some cases. Because this was the least arbitrary of the three methods cited, it was the focus of much of the legislative debate and accompanying journalistic publicity. In addition, as press trials were public and direct reportage legal, press cases could become more embarrassing to the prosecuting state than the works of even the most hostile writer.

An auxiliary form of restraint, introduced in 1819, was the *cautionnement* or bond against lawsuits and fines, required from managers of certain periodicals. Although this was seen by some as preferable to censorship or arbitrary revocation, it created a hardship for poor journalists, especially the publishers of little magazines. The most hidden restraint was also fiscal. The government taxed newspapers disproportionately, the dailies paying about 30 percent of their incomes in taxes.

Most of the press laws of the Restoration were a combination of two or three of these methods, while the July Monarchy depended principally upon prosecution for statutory crimes.

Although the Charter of Louis XVIII provided for a free press subject to regulation of abuses, the law of 21 October 1814 established censorship of both newspapers and pamphlets, licensing of printers and booksellers, and preliminary authorization to publish any periodicals. In spite of its limitations, it was welcomed by such liberals as Benjamin Constant and such monarchists as the Bertins for its contrast to the arbitrariness of the imperial regime.

When Napoleon returned in 1815 as a sudden convert to liberalism, his Acte additionnel provided for an almost totally free press and helped win over many liberals to his short-lived cause. After Waterloo, the Second Restoration of Louis XVIII was accompanied by a new press law (8 August 1815) restoring censorship for newspapers only and requiring previous authorization. These functions came under the police and were somewhat capricious in practice. The Chamber amended this law by the provision of 9 November 1815, which defined press offenses more clearly but extended them to include all seditious acts of speech, printing, or artwork and placed them under the regular judiciary. This law destroyed some small journals such as *Nain jaune* and forced others to a precarious career of evasion and name changes. The *Constitutionnel* had five such title changes to escape suppression, while the *Mercure* became the *Minerve*.

In 1817 (28 February) the 1815 laws were augmented to include all magazines as well as newspapers, and on 30 December another amendment passed, a victory for liberals, to limit affected magazines to those considered political. There was no official intention to harass horoscopes, fashion journals, and scholarly works. However, many allegedly literary magazines of this period were intensely political in content and heavy with satirical allusions.

When the 21 October 1814 law lapsed in 1819, a series of new laws passed by the Chambers of 1819 (17, 26 May, 9 June) reflected the moderation of the Decazes ministry and a defeat for the extreme ultras. These laws were less ambiguous and less subject to abuse by authorities but included a novelty. The 17 May law provided for two categories of criminal press offenses and extended to speech, cartoons, and emblems as well. The first was any formal attack on the person of the king, the succession to the throne, or the authority of the king and Chambers under the Charter. Penalties could vary from three months to five years in prison and fines up to 6,000 francs. A second category included sedition of lesser gravity, defacement of public symbols of royalty, public display of illegal symbols, and attacks on freedom of religion or the inviolability of property. All of these offenses had to also include "incitement" as well as a personal expression. In addition, this law specified outrages against common decency, offenses to the royal family and ambassadors, and a rather general set of terms describing defamation and public injury, applicable to groups such as courts as well as individuals, with penalties up to a year in prison.

The 26 May law was an amendment creating the legal procedures for press prosecutions, and it also forbade any indictment under the previous laws except on the complaint of the aggrieved party or group, an important defense against judicial harassment.

The novel phase of this series of legal landmarks in 1819 was the 9 June law adding the requirement of a *cautionnement* or advance cash bond, payable by proprietors of all periodicals appearing more often than monthly and containing any political matter. This was intended as a guarantee against legal liability in case of lawsuits or fines, but it was, interestingly, also aimed at keeping the newspaper press in wealthy hands. It was largely the work of François Guizot, whose conservatism in practice often outweighed his stated liberal ideals such as press freedom. The *cautionnement* ranged from 10,000 francs per year for daily newspapers and 5,000 for magazines in the Parisian basin down to 1,500 to 2,000 francs for provincial newspapers. In addition, a proof copy of every sheet printed was to be sent to the mayor or prefecture of each appropriate jurisdiction, and secret sessions of either Chamber were closed to reportage by the press. This *cautionnement* law lasted until 1828 when it was made more flexible. Some of the difficulty it imposed on smaller periodicals was alleviated by the financial support of wealthy liberal backers.

The murder of the duc de Berry in 1820 opened a wave of reaction marked by the devious program of Villèle and escalating demands by ultra leaders. The freedom of the 1819 press laws, limited as it was, fell before a renewed campaign to suppress the opposition of journalists and writers. This campaign also greatly increased an inherent division among loyal monarchists. The laws of 31 March 1820 and 26 July 1821 were too reactionary for some royalists, who felt the Charter was the best hope of the Restoration. The 1820 law, by only a 10 percent margin, passed the Chamber after heated debate. It renewed preliminary authorization and applied it even to periodicals that appeared irregularly or as installments, designed to trap journals masquerading as books. The law also revived censorship, establishing by royal appointment a committee of twelve censors for the Paris basin and panels of three for the provincial capitals, to be selected by prefects. Moreover, violation of the censorship resulting in a trial would result in temporary suspension of the paper concerned and, upon conviction, an additional suspension of six months. This law did great damage to smaller journals and magazines, although a coalition of liberals and legitimists managed to win an amendment limiting the 31 March provisions to the current legislative year. Villèle himself objected to the independent censure committee as subtracting from royal authority. On 26 July 1821 the moderate coalition gained a concession in the Chamber, a law limiting censure regularly to coincide with the legislative session, but the ultras led by Louis de Bonald (now a censor) extended both authorization and censorship to all periodicals covered by the previous laws, whether political or not. Thus even medical journals were forced to comply, although the ultras' purpose was to entrap little or literary journals such as the *Miroir* whose prose and poetry masked a core of political satire and polemic.

Villèle, the new minister, who disliked the ultras' frontal attack because it offended prominent royalists and aided the growing schism of the Right, backed the proposal of the comte de Peyronnet for a new press law, which passed the Chamber (March 1822) by a surprising majority. It offered little encouragement to the opposition press and some ominous novelties. Authorization was no longer required for nonpolitical periodicals, and censorship was made facultative; that is, it could be invoked by royal option under grave circumstances, even during intersessions. If the courts were on vacation, the Chambers could try editors and managers of newspapers. Many specific crimes of the press were listed to cover loopholes in earlier laws. The most remarkable of these became infamous during the next six years as the Law of Tendency, providing that if the "spirit and tendency" of several articles, even unrelated, should offend "public peace" or the "state religion," the courts could suppress the offending journal.

Although the 1822 law forced the opposition press to walk on a tightrope, it did not have the desired effect. In a popular and publicized decision of the Royal Court of Paris, managers of the *Constitutionnel* and the *Courrier* were acquitted on appeal from an earlier conviction under the tendency law (3 December 1825). The king had instigated their first prosecution before the Chambers while the courts were on vacation, according to a provision of the 1822 law. Charles X was furious, while François-René de Chateaubriand's faction, opposed to Villèle, was pleased.

At the end of 1826, Villèle struck back through the ultra comte de Peyronnet, who introduced (26 December) the most extreme plan to muzzle the press of the entire Restoration. The bill was passed by the deputies after long debate and journalistic exposure, but the Chamber of Peers, led by Chateaubriand, amended it to death, and Villèle was forced to a humiliating withdrawal (17 April 1827). Had the proposal been passed, all printed matter of any kind would have been censored, newspapers and pamphlets subjected to a killing tax, with the penalties under earlier laws greatly increased.

The debates over this bill—called a "Vandal Law" by Chateaubriand and defended as a law of "justice and love" by Peyronnet—revealed how divided the royalists actually were. The ultra Joseph-François Michaud, for example, ridiculed the law in terms of overkill. Many ultra writers of this sort earnestly wanted the press to enjoy a limited freedom and saw their own destruction in the law of "justice and love."

After Villèle's downfall and the creation of a moderate constitutionalist government under Jean-Baptiste de Martignac in 1828, journalists looked toward greater freedom of the press. Their reward was the law of 18 July 1828, the most liberal of all Restoration press laws but, for political reasons, not received with enthusiasm by most liberals. Both preliminary authorization and the hated censorship with its committees were abolished. The tendency clause was also struck out as well as trial by the Chambers. The negative portion of the law was its reliance on the *cautionnement*, which was set at very high rates: 200,000 francs for dailies, 100,000 for weeklies. In addition, changes in title or periodicity had to be reported in advance in order to check the use of aliases by the smaller journals. Emphasizing these repressive aspects, liberals were lukewarm to the bill, and ultras branded it revolutionary for its latitude. Only Chateaubriand's circle steadfastly supported it in the debates and in his *Journal des Débats*. Faced with this opposition, Martignac accepted an avalanche of amendments to his bill whose final result was a maximum *cautionnement* of only 6,000 francs for large Paris newspapers. An unholy alliance of Villèlists and Leftists approved passage of the law in this form.

The 1828 law gave new life to the press. New journals sprang up in Paris and in the provinces, adding to the openness of political debate. Freedom of the press, as before, augmented the political process, while the ultras, wounded by their own factionalism, hoped for a day of reckoning.

The day of ultra revenge against the free opposition press was in Polignac's July Ordinances of 1830. Although the government rigorously prosecuted opposition papers under the 1828 law, trial court convictions were usually pyrrhic victories. Publicity of all testimony was legally printable and only magnified what the government wanted to suppress. Polignac's ministry, with the king's support, planned to suppress opposition journalism totally by invoking article 14 of the Charter, an emergency clause. Polignac moved to require authorization for all political periodicals and police seizure in case of violation, along with a revival of censorship. The successful Revolution of 1830 prevented general application of this ordinance, which may have been constitutionally legal, however foolhardy.

Louis-Philippe's new Charter of 9 August 1830 abolished censorship but reiterated the ambiguity of the 1814 Charter's guarantee of press freedom by making it "conform to the laws." Preliminary authorization was never invoked, and censorship was revived only in 1835 to deal with the problem of merciless political caricaturists such as Charles Philipon. The laws passed by the Chambers during the 1830s, however, far surpassed in rigor and scope, as well as in severity of punishment, those of the Restoration. Criticism of the legislature was equated with attacks on the royal dignity in the law of 29 November 1830. On 10 December, a preliminary declaration of responsibility was demanded of any handbill hawkers, poster affixers, or news criers who used printed matter. A companion law (14 December) upheld the stamp tax on paper used in printing and brought back the old *cautionnement* for most periodicals. Court jurisdiction and procedure were changed in a law of 8 April 1831 in order to expedite prosecutions of journalists and managers. In spite of trial by jury, more journalists, especially the republicans and some legitimists, served longer terms than were common during the Restoration.

Louis-Philippe's government also struck at the poster and broadside printers, requiring preliminary authorization to print (16 February 1834).

As in the Restoration, a political assassination attempt, that of Fieschi, was used as a pretext for a more severe repression. The September Laws (9 September 1835) drove much of the opposition press out of business or into prison. They listed more criminal offenses of the press, forbade public advocacy of a different form of government, and altered court procedures in trials to revive the concept of tendency. These laws also restored censorship, in a basic violation of the Charter of 1830, to apply to the increasingly vexatious caricatures, and doubled the *cautionnements* requiring that they be paid in cash instead of bonds as had been the previous practice. Until the 1848 Revolution, there was no true opposition press, although some journalists, such as Emile de Girardin, could afford to criticize the government as the government needed and subsidized their support.

The Revolution of 1848 brought relief from press controls, but this freedom fed a growing fear of radicalism. Dozens of new, mostly radical, journals appeared. Conservatives held these in part responsible for the bloody June Days (1848), precipitating Eugène Cavaignac's press laws. These allowed total suspensions of papers, arrests of editors (Girardin), and so heavy a *cautionnement* that Lamartine's paper was closed. As a result of Alexandre-Auguste Ledru-Rollin's radical uprising a year later (13 June, 1849), more suspensions of journals occurred, and finally, anticipating the coup d'état, the draconian law of 16 July was passed. It levied a crushing stamp tax and provided devastating fines applicable to all periodicals, even serial novels. An added feature required editors to print any criticisms sent to them.

During the violent coup d'état of 2 December 1851, Louis-Napoleon closed all opposition papers by military seizure. Throughout the year of his ensuing prince-presidency dictatorship, the mere threat of arbitrary suppression forced journalists into a virtual political silence.

I. Collins, *The Government and the Newspaper Press in France* (London, 1959); A. Germain, *Martyrologie de la presse, 1789–1862* (Paris, 1861); F. Giraudeau, *La Presse périodique de 1789–1867* (Paris, 1867); C. Ledré, *La Presse à l'assaut de la monarchie* (Paris 1960); D. Rader, *The Journalists and the July Revolution* (The Hague, 1973); A Vaulabelle, *Histoire de deux restorations*, vols. 6, 7 (Paris, 1854); G. Weill, *Le Journal* (Paris, 1934).

*Daniel Rader*

*Related entries:* ACTE ADDITIONNEL; BERRY, C.-F.; BERTIN DE VAUX, "AINE"; BONALD; CAVAIGNAC, L.-E.; CENSORSHIP; CHARTER OF 1814; CHARTER OF 1830; CHATEAUBRIAND; CONSTANT; *LE CONSTITUTIONNEL*; COUP D'ETAT OF 2 DECEMBER 1851; *LE COURRIER FRAN-*

*CAIS*; DECAZES; FIESCHI PLOT; GIRARDIN; GUIZOT; *JOURNAL DES DEBATS*; JULY ORDINANCES; JUNE DAYS; LAMARTINE; LAW ON SEDITIOUS SPEECH; LEDRU-ROLLIN; MARTIGNAC; MICHAUD; *LA MINERVE; LE MIROIR DES SPECTACLES; LE NAIN JAUNE*; PEYRONNET; POLIGNAC; REVOLUTION OF 1830; REVOLUTION OF 1848; ULTRAROYALISTS; VILLELE.

**PRIESTS OF THE MISSIONS OF FRANCE,** a society founded during the Restoration to spread the Catholic religion in France. The restoration of the old Bourbon Monarchy seemed to entail also the revival of the traditional French religion. Among the means of achieving this purpose, it appeared paramount to many that faith and devotion had to be rekindled among the people by means of intensive preaching and ceremony. Two priests, Charles de Forbin-Janson and Jean-Baptiste Rauzan, thus conceived the idea of a special society devoted to this work: the Society of the Missions of France. They received legal status from Louis XVIII (1816) who established them at an old place of pilgrimage just outside Paris, on Mont Valérien. In 1821 they were given the task of reviving the religious life of the great church of Sainte-Geneviève, which the Republic had desecrated to make into a Pantheon for the burial of its great men. The government created by the Revolution of 1830 returned the monument to its secular uses. The government's hostility toward the missions in France threatened to extinguish all of the activities of the society. Rauzan and Forbin-Janson decided then, with the pope's approval, to give a wider scope to their work, changing the society's name to Society of the Priests of Mercy. Some of these priests were later to cross the Atlantic and establish foundations in New York, New Orleans, and Saint Augustine.

P. A. Delaporte, *Vie du Très Révérend Père Jean-Baptiste Rauzan* (Paris, 1857); E. Sevrin, *Les Missions religieuses en France sous la Restauration*, vol. 1 (Sainte-Mandé, 1948).

*Guillaume de Bertier de Sauvigny*
*Related entries:* FORBIN-JANSON; LOUIS XVIII; MISSIONS; RAUZAN.

**PRIESTS OF THE SACRED HEART.** A name given to several groups of Catholics who emphasized the spiritual and emotional, as opposed to the rational, content of their religion. A sentimental devotion to the Heart of Jesus—as a symbolic expression of the Savior's love for mankind—was part of the great tide of romanticism. It also took on a certain reactionary connotation because the royalists of the Vendée had displayed the image of the Sacred Heart as a rallying emblem. It was therefore natural that a number of the religious foundations of the early nineteenth century should have chosen titles linked to an object of special devotion. Among the notable foundations of the time can be mentioned the following:

Société du Sacré-Coeur, established in 1791 by the Jesuit priest Joseph Picot de Clorivière (1735–1820) in order to maintain secretly the religious life proscribed by Revolutionary legislation. It was short-lived; the rebirth of Jesuit and other orders fulfilled its purpose much more effectively.

Congrégation des Sacrés-Coeurs de Jésus et de Marie, founded in 1800 by Joseph Coudrin (1768–1837). The rather odd name of *Picpusiens*, by which it became commonly known when it expanded its operations to foreign missions, comes from the fact that the first community house was established in a Paris suburb close to a site that had served as a mass burial place for the victims of the Revolutionary guillotine.

Pères du Sacré-Coeur, founded in Lyons in 1821 by André Coindre (1787–1826), mainly for Christian education.

Congrégation des Missionnaires du Sacré-Coeur de Jésus, established at Issoudun (near Bourges) in 1854 by Jean-Jules Chevalier (1824–1907).

Even more numerous were the religious societies of women and pious confraternities of laypersons established under the invocation of the Hearts of Jesus and Mary.

F. Norbert, *Vie du P. André Coindre* (Lyons, 1888); S. Perron, *Vie du R. P. Marie-Joseph Coudrin* (Paris, 1900); Ch. Piperon, *Le T. R. P. Jules Chevalier* (Paris, 1912); Rayez, "Clorivière et ses fondations," *Revue d'histoire de l'eglise de France*, 54 (1968).

*Guillaume de Bertier de Sauvigny*

*Related entries:* MISSIONS; ROMANTICISM.

**PRIMOGENITURE.** See HEREDITY LAWS.

**PROGRAM OF THE HOTEL DE VILLE,** reforms demanded by republicans and others who rallied around Lafayette, commander of the Paris National Guard, and the provisional Municipal Commission of Paris, established at the Hôtel de ville, July–August 1830. On the afternoon of 29 July 1830, when the last royal troops had been forced out of Paris, a group of opposition deputies, meeting at the home of the banker Jacques Laffitte, appointed a provisional Municipal Commission of five members to ensure the security and the provisioning of Paris. At the same time it approved the marquis de Lafayette's assumption of command of the revived National Guard of Paris. Later in the day the commissioners and Lafayette installed themselves at the Hôtel de ville, and around them rallied the militants, the republicans, and others who would sharply curtail or destroy the royal authority. In the next few days the commission assumed the role of a national government, appointing commissioners to head the national ministries and issuing orders to the army, and Lafayette established his control over the National Guard, the only organized armed force in the capital. The Hôtel de ville was emerging as a power base, comparable to the Paris Commune of 1792–94, threatening to the authority of the deputies and to their plans for a change of monarchs.

To defuse this threat and to win the support of "The Party of Hôtel de ville" for the replacement of Charles X by the duc d'Orléans, the deputies on July 31 issued a proclamation endorsing reforms that this loosely formed group was demanding:

We shall assure by laws all the guarantees necessary to make liberty strong and durable:

The reestablishment of the National Guard with the participation of guardsmen in the choice of officers

The participation of citizens in the formation of departmental and municipal administrations

Trial by jury for press offenses

Legal responsibility of ministers and of secondary agents of the administration

Pay and promotion of the military to be determined by law

Reelection of deputies appointed to public office

On 7 August 1830 the Chamber of Deputies approved in its revision of the Charter an article that began, "The following subjects will be provided for by separate laws within the shortest possible time." There followed, in slightly different verbal form, the program of the Hôtel de ville and two other projected reforms.

The liberal deputies' maneuver achieved its purpose. On 1 August Lafayette, the one man with power and influence to foil their plans, declared his support of the duc d'Orléans, and the Municipal Commission thereafter confined its activities to municipal affairs. Some, although not all, of the program of the Hôtel de ville was subsequently enacted into law.

G. de Bertier de Sauvigny, *La Révolution de 1830 en France* (Paris, c. 1970); A. Nettement, *Histoire de la restauration*, vol. 8 (Paris, 1860–72); D. H. Pinkney, *The French Revolution of 1830* (Princeton, 1972).

*David H. Pinkney*

*Related entries:* CHAMBER OF DEPUTIES; CHARTER OF 1830; LAFAY-ETTE, M.-P.-J.-Y.-R.-G.; LAFFITTE; LOUIS-PHILIPPE; MUNICIPAL COMMISSION; NATIONAL GUARD; REPUBLICANS; REVOLUTION OF 1830.

**PROTECTIONISM.** See FOREIGN TRADE AND TARIFF POLICY.

**PROUDHON, PIERRE-JOSEPH** (1809–1865), important socialist-anarchist theoretician and propagandist, newspaper editor and parliamentary representative during the Revolution of 1848, and major influence on the European revolutionary movement until World War I. A largely self-taught product of the Besançon peasantry, Proudhon was born during the Restoration and came to maturity during the July Monarchy. His early writings, which attracted little notice, were based on his attempt to discover the "laws of society," to solve "the social question," and to prove that equality of conditions was the "logical" outcome of history. His first major work, *Qu'est-ce que la Propriété?* (June 1840), established him as a leading ideological force on the French Left. The first rigorous, scientific analysis of bourgeois property, the book attempted to demonstrate that property (defined as the right to make use of another man's labor) was the most serious obstacle to freedom and equality. The attack on "parasitism" attempted to establish property connected with work and productivity as the foundation of a stable and just social order. Like most other socialist theoreticians of the period, Proudhon wanted to return to the producer social value equal to his contribution.

The notoriety that Proudhon's book stirred up—expressed in his famous statement that "property is theft"—continued throughout the 1840s as he produced a steady stream of attacks on traditional political economy, the Roman Catholic church, the state, and politics. Trying to establish a framework within which the autonomy of the small producer would be protected, Proudhon devoted himself to the "organization of work" and attacked concentrations of capital, the destructiveness of "free competition," idle property, and *la féodalité capitaliste*. His search for "justice" led him in an increasingly individualist and anarchistic direction during this period.

The Revolution of 1848 provided an opportunity for Proudhon to become socially and politically active. Elected to the National Assembly on 4 June 1848, he campaigned for the organization of work, a Banque d'échange to guarantee cheap credit and ensure reciprocity, and the defense of the Republic. He was also a widely read journalist and newspaper editor during this period, and was notable for his courageous defense of the June 1848 rising of the Paris workers. A fierce opposition to Louis-Napoleon Bonaparte and uncompromising attacks on the reaction led to his arrest and imprisonment from June 1848 to June 1852.

The period after 1848 saw a rapid development of Proudhon's anarchism as he identified the government as the incarnation of the principle of authority and the violator of social health. He appealed for class peace throughout this period, convinced that socialism would be good for all. Free and universal credit with guarantees for small producers and workers were the foundations of his political economy, and he appealed for an alliance of the proletariat and the petite bourgeoisie to organize a mutualist and federated structure for French society. The free exchange of equivalents, guaranteed by the preservation of different centers of production, was the basis of his "mutualist" economic order and its federalist political form. The increased production that would result would guarantee social peace as the arbitrary state was absorbed back into society and free association replaced force as the cement of society. His aim was equilibrium and stability based on the free individual conscience, the organization of work, and the protection of small property. His antipolitical orientation led his disciples to try to transform the First International into a cooperative society that would organize work, make credit available, and stay out of the workers' struggles. The ideological struggle between Marx and Proudhonism was a major factor in the history of the International and influenced the entire European revolutionary movement until the Russian Revolution, when Proudhon's direct influence was eclipsed by that of Marxism.

A. Berthod, *P. J. Proudhon et la Propriété* (Paris, 1918); C. Bouglé, *La Sociologie de Proudhon* (Paris, 1911); E. Fournière, *Les Théories socialistes au XIXe siècle de Babouf à Proudhon* (Paris, 1904); G. Gurvitch, *Proudhon* (Paris, 1965); R. Hoffman, *Revolutionary Justice* (Urbana, 1972); H. Lubac, *The Un-Marxian Socialist* (New York,

1948); A. Ritter, *The Political Thought of Pierre-Joseph Proudhon* (Princeton, 1969); G. Woodcock, *Pierre-Joseph Proudhon*, (London, 1956).

*John Ehrenberg*

*Related entries:* JUNE DAYS; MARX; REVOLUTION OF 1848; WORKERS' COOPERATIVES.

**PROVENCE, COMTE DE.** See LOUIS XVIII.

**PROVISIONAL GOVERNMENT,** the government that first replaced that of Louis-Philippe. On 22 February 1848, the people of Paris took to the streets in insurrection against Louis-Philippe, king of the French, and against his corruption-ridden government under François Guizot. Two days later, Guizot had resigned, and the king abdicated and fled to England. From a balcony of the Hôtel de ville, a group of politicians, journalists, and one poet, all active in the opposition during the 1840s, proclaimed the Republic. Below, in the place de Grève, a crowd, mostly workers, cheered the dawn of democracy; many waved red flags, which from that time forward became the symbol of social revolution. Few of those on the balcony welcomed the sight of the red flag. Although they considered themselves heirs to the republican tradition of 1792, they did not sympathize with popular demands for a democratic and social Republic. It was this conflict, manifest from the very beginning of the Second French Republic, that generated the political struggles that marked the brief life of the Provisional Government.

The men on the balcony and others had been associated with two main opposition newspapers, *Le National* and *La Réforme*. The former had liberal tendencies, the latter democratic. The eleven members of the Provisional Government were drawn primarily from their ranks and reflected the two tendencies. Seven formed the liberal wing of the government: Pierre Dupont de l'Eure, François Arago (the least conservative of the seven), Alphonse de Lamartine (the poet), Adolphe Crémieux (the first Jew to hold executive power anywhere), Alexandre Marie, Louis Garnier-Pagès, and Armand Marrast, editor of *Le National*. They all had one thing in common: resolute hostility to the various socialist currents that had been running through France during the preceding decade. Two others, Alexandre Ledru-Rollin and Ferdinand Flocon, were democrats and more or less sympathetic to socialist ideas. Both had had connections to the several secret societies that existed under the July Monarchy, but their sympathy for socialism was limited. They believed that a democratic republic, supported by universal manhood suffrage, would by itself bring an end to the social abuses of exploitation, unemployment, and poverty on which the Paris workers focused their attention. Thus, their conception of the democratic and social republic was considerably more limited than that of those whose revolt had brought them to power. Only two members of the Provisional Government, the socialist Louis Blanc and the worker-mechanic Albert (a *nom de guerre*), genuinely represented working-class interests. Their inclusion in the government was taken by the workers to be symbolic of the new regime's intention to deal with the social question; their colleagues, however, meant them to be only a camouflage for the essentially bourgeois character of the Provisional Government.

The news of the proclamation of the Republic traveled swiftly through France and brought with it the installation of republican municipal councils and considerable popular action against entrepreneurs and landowners. For the people, the establishment of the Republic signaled the start of the social and economic struggle rather than its culmination. From the point of view of the Provisional Government, however, the political victory constituted an end in itself and inaugurated the reign of republican order. For most of its members, neither socialism nor conservative reaction was acceptable, although the menace of the former threatened to push them toward the latter. Moreover, whatever the symbolism of the First Republic, they ruled out any experiments in Jacobinism.

Lamartine, who acted as foreign minister for the government, underlined the distance that the Republic had traveled. On 4 March he announced to the rest of Europe the pacific intentions of the new regime, which foreswore any support of revolutions elsewhere, not to say any thought of foreign conquest. This was a matter of principle and expediency. The republicans of 1848 had none of the missionary zeal of those of 1792–99, nor was the internal situation stable enough that they could even contemplate such adventures had they been inclined to do so. From this point on, socialism, not republicanism, became the dominant international revolutionary movement.

The workers on the barricades of February fought under the banners of the "right to work" and the "organization of labor." No mere slogans, they expressed a genuine social consciousness and the substance of demands that the Provisional Government found itself immediately forced to confront. At the same time, it could not afford to terrorize respectable bourgeois opinion that had initially supported the revolution. Nor was the government inclined to impose any restrictions on the rights of property that a full-scale social program would have entailed. Treading a narrow path between order and social revolution (but firmly committed to defending the former), the Provisional Government moved on two fronts to establish economic stability and to head off working-class radicalism.

First, two of the most conservative members of the government, Garnier-Pagès and Marie, took charge of the key ministries of finance and public works, respectively. Garnier-Pagès immediately took steps to ensure bourgeois confidence in the government's fiscal responsibility. Rather than forcing the Bank of France—run by the financial oligarchy against which the revolution was directed—to loan the state large sums of cash to finance social programs, Garnier-Pagès froze savings deposits held mostly by petty bourgeois depositors and turned them into depreciated state bonds redeemable only at the stock exchange, which was run by the same people who ran the Bank of France. In addition, Garnier-Pagès ordered the bank to expand its supply of small units of currency in order to facilitate commercial transactions.

Second, the Provisional Government created National Workshops in early March. Far from being part of an overall policy to improve the conditions of employment, the workshops were basically make-work projects to occupy the thousands of unemployed workers whose presence on the streets of Paris constituted a menace to public order and a potential recruiting ground for revolutionaries. The workshops supposedly were modeled on the social workshops that Blanc had proposed as cooperative associations of producers, which would displace capitalist production. Significantly, the workshops were controlled by Marie's ministry and run by the engineer Emile Thomas, who had no use for socialism. The workshops were financed by a 45 centime surtax on landed property that fell most heavily on peasants in the provinces. The tax had the effect of alienating peasants from the government and planting the seeds for the subsequent growth of rural radicalism. For the moment, however, it was the Right, and not the Left, that benefited from peasant disaffection.

Blanc, the one member of the Provisional Government with the most credit among the workers, could not be ignored, nor could he be unleashed. In response to workers' demands to undertake the organization of labor, Blanc became chairman of a commission to study the labor question. Known as the Luxembourg Commission from the locus of its proceedings, the commission became one of the two foci for working-class political activity—albeit under controlled conditions. Representatives of the various craft organizations worked day and night in the commission on a broad program for social and economic reform. Their recommendations were, they believed, to become the basis for the democratic and social Republic. However, the true purpose of the commission was to isolate Blanc, other socialists, and their popular following while the Provisional Government carried on its own work of political consolidation.

The other focus of working-class political activity, totally separate from the Provisional Government, was the clubs of Paris. Formed in late February and early March and numbering nearly 200 by April, the clubs had three purposes: to mobilize the citizens of Paris to exert constant pressure on the government in favor of social programs; to strengthen the political links among the popular classes; and to disseminate democratic and socialist propaganda throughout the country in competition with the government's official *commissaires de la ré-publique*. Many of the clubs had evolved from the republican secret societies of the 1840s and included bourgeois as well as working-class leaders. Such famous revolutionary names as Auguste Blanqui, Armand Barbès, Etienne Cabet, and François Raspail took active roles in the clubs. Although the clubs were the principal center of popular politics in Paris and the principal center of opposition to the government's moderate policies, they never developed a comprehensive political strategy. Thus, they remained constantly on the defensive against a government bent on containing and finally destroying the popular movement.

Only on one occasion did the aims of the Provisional Government and those of the clubs coincide. The circumstances involved purging the Parisian National Guard—the civil militia—of its elite cadres drawn from the city's wealthy neighborhoods and by far the best equipped units. Although these troops had supported the revolution in February, by mid-March they had become politically suspect, if not downright dangerous to liberals and radicals alike. Thus, the Provisional Government welcomed a mass demonstration organized by the clubs in support of the purge, which took place on 17 March. Apparently a great popular victory, the demonstration only reinforced the government's authority and was not translated into a popular political force. In effect, the clubs had done the government's work for it; their leaders made the mistake of thinking that they had gained the upper hand. Nothing was further from the truth. Furthermore, at the same time the prefect of police in Paris, Marc Caussidière—no friend of the people— recruited under his command a Garde mobile drawn from the young people who had participated in the Revolution of February 1848. The Garde mobile, a kind of militarized national workshop, was much more solidly organized and systematically drilled than was the National Guard. It became the government's shock brigade.

As each day passed, the government grew stronger and the working-class movement weaker. The clubs put another crowd into the streets on 16 April. The demonstration's purpose was to pressure the government to postpone elections to the Constituent Assembly until missionaries from the clubs could deliver the democratic and socialist message to the provinces. The Provisional Government did not want that message to get through. While it conceded the cities to the Left, it expected to rally the countryside to the moderate Republic. The 16 April demonstration was put down quickly. The government mobilized loyal national guardsmen from bourgeois neighborhoods and the Garde mobile who dispersed the crowd with chants of "Long live the Republic" and "Down with the communists." The failure of 16 April marked a turning point in the balance of forces between the Provisional Government and the Parisian workers. Henceforth, order prevailed over social revolution. From that point on, the dissolution of the clubs and the subsequent reaction became only a matter of time. In mid-May a number of club leaders were arrested and several clubs suppressed.

The results of the Constituent Assembly elections strengthened the Provisional Government's hand. Republicans sympathetic to the regime and resolutely antisocialist commanded a majority. Almost none of the radicals won election, whereas a substantial number of pre-1848 conservatives and newly minted republicans did. Following the elections, the first episodes of violence between government and workers occurred. In Rouen, the moderate list of candidates to the Constituent Assembly defeated that supported by the radical workers. The leader of the latter had been responsible for organizing National Workshops for the city's unemployed. After the election, the threatened closing of the workshops created a provocation that drove workers into the streets. The Rouen National Guard, bourgeois in composition, attacked the workers' hastily erected barricades with cavalry charges and cannon. When it was all over, several dozen workers lay dead. Similar outbreaks occurred elsewhere in late April and early May. Although not the first conflicts among those who had originally made the revolution, they were the first in which fatalities occurred and, more important for what was to come in June, in which clear class lines were drawn.

The convocation of the Constituent Assembly on 4 May marked the formal end of the Provisional Government. An Executive Commission of five was elected and a number of new ministers—all openly antisocialist—appointed. Among the latter was Eugène Cavaignac, minister of war. A man of order with good republican credentials, Cavaignac emerged as the strongman of the new government. The move to the Right became clear, and the workers of Paris made one last desperate bid to salvage their revolution. A crowd organized by the remaining clubs invaded the Assembly on 15 May, demanding a show of solidarity with revolutionaries in Poland. But whatever the initial motive for the demonstration, it looked very much like an attempt to reverse the results of the elections by force, and more than one member of the republican majority recalled the events of 31 May–2 June 1793 when the *sans-culottes* invaded the Convention and forced the purge of the Girondists. History, however, did not repeat itself. Cavaignac mobilized elements of the National Guard, the Garde mobile, and troops of the line to crush the demonstration. From that day reaction went into full swing. More revolutionary leaders were arrested and the remaining clubs shut down. Then came the ultimate provocation: the Executive Commission on 21 June ordered all men under 25 enrolled in the National Workshops into the army, and the rest to pack up for the provinces. In reaction, angry workers filled the streets on 22 June and erected barricades in the east end of Paris. For three days fierce fighting went on between troops commanded by Cavaignac and the hopelessly outgunned workers. By the morning of 26 June, the last of the barricades had been taken. Up to then, only several hundred had died, mostly those defending the barricades. It was after the revolt had been crushed that the fearsome revenge of the government was unleashed. At least several thousand workers were rounded up and summarily executed. Fifteen thousand others were deported to Algeria.

Following the class war of June, the Executive Commission resigned, and Cavaignac, who had preserved order, became chief of the executive power. His military dictatorship—but in defense of the Republic—effectively continued the Provisional Government, to be sure more efficiently.

M. Agulhon, *The Republican Experiment, 1848–1852* (New York, 1983). P. Amann, *Revolution and Mass Democracy: The Paris Club Movement in 1848* (Princeton, N.J., 1975); L. Girard, *La Deuxième république* (Paris, 1968).

*Sanford Elwitt*

*Related entries:* ALBERT; ARAGO FAMILY; BARBES; BLANC; BLANQUI; CABET; CAUSSIDIERE; CAVAIGNAC, L. -E.; CLUBS, POLITICAL; CONSTITUTION OF 1848; CREMIEUX; DUPONT DE L'EURE; EXECUTIVE COMMISSION; FLOCON; GARDE MOBILE; GARNIER-PAGES; GUIZOT; JUNE DAYS; LAMARTINE; LEDRU-ROLLIN; LUXEMBOURG COMMISSION; LOUIS-PHILIPPE; MARIE; *LE NATIONAL*; NATIONAL GUARD; NA-

TIONAL WORKSHOPS; RASPAIL; *LA REFORME*; REPUBLICANS; REVOLUTION OF 1848; THOMAS.

**PROVOST COURTS.** See *COURS PREVOTALES*.

**PUBLIC INSTRUCTION,** the system of schooling, including elementary, secondary, technical, and professional, under the direction of a national, administrative University established by the laws of 10 May 1806 and 17 March 1808. Composed of both private and public, religious and lay schools, the system remained with jurisdictional modifications throughout three political regimes.

*University and Supervision of Schooling.* The Napoleonic administrative structure, of which public instruction was one part, survived for want of an alternative. After twenty-five years, everyone assumed that public responsibility for instruction would continue. Who would take that responsibility, what they proposed, and how they intended to achieve their objectives were less clear.

Defenders of a state-supervised system contended that only a neutral state should direct education in a pluralistic society. Men like Victor Cousin searched for a notion of *éducation* (both the moral and intellectual formation of youngsters) that was short of the notion of *morale laique* asserted by anticlerical republicans during the 1870s and 1880s but that divorced morality from the teachings of any particular church. Few Catholics challenged the continuing existence of the University, for conservatives were either concentrating on political questions or attempting to shut themselves off from society at large. Liberals wanted the church to play a role within the University, and Catholics had long been accustomed to church-state alliances.

The real controversy surrounded representation within the University and its authority over components of the instructional system. Early legislation (1814–20) permitted the establishment of diocesan schools to train boys preparing for a priestly vocation but restricted the number of them, taxed private schools, and designated the state-administered baccalaureate examination as a requirement for entry into all the *grandes écoles* (professional schools); the state confirmed its monopoly of degree granting. On 27 February 1821 bishops gained the right to supervise religious teaching in the schools and to have rights of inspection equal to those of bureaucrats of the state. On 1 June 1822, a clergyman soon to be ordained a bishop, Denis Frayssinous, became chairman of the University body and two years later was appointed minister of religion and of public instruction. During his ministry, the power of the state University actually increased, along with clerical control of it. Professors and administrators thought to be anticlerical or liberal, including François Guizot (later a minister of education during the July Monarchy), and about 10 percent of the corps of secondary school teachers were purged. During this period, schooling suffered, and both the church and the Bourbon monarchy lost credit.

With the demise of the rightist Villèle ministry and the accession of Jean-Baptiste de Martignac in 1828, clerical domination of the University ended forever. Msgr. Frayssinous was dismissed, the Ministry of Public Instruction separated from that of Religion, and Guizot and Victor Cousin resumed their appointments. More important, bishops lost their power to supervise primary schools, and enrollment in the *petits-séminaires*, which had been teaching Catholic youths who had no intention of receiving Holy Orders, was legally restricted to 20,000. Although Catholic bishops vigorously opposed these ordinances in a petition to the king, Pope Leo XII refused to intervene in a matter of French politics, and Charles X signed the relevant laws on 16 June 1828.

These ordinances, combined with the overthrow of the Bourbons in 1830, inaugurated a new era in the debate about jurisdiction of the University. Some bishops, like Msgr. Devie, quickly denounced all public schools as "institutions of pestilence" and others like Cardinal de Bonald threatened to withdraw all chaplains from the schools. Other Catholics, like Félicité de Lamennais, Charles-Forbes de Montalembert, and Msgr. Affre, archbishop of Paris, became convinced that the church had to separate from the state and that the key to a future role for the church in modern society was the creation of a Catholic system of education independent from the state. They would fight their battle under the flag of liberty of education. In both the revised Charter for the July Monarchy (article 69) and the Guizot Law (1833), requirements for the opening of private schools were eased (in large part because the new regime was intent on expanding schooling for the masses and lacked the national resources to accomplish their ends quickly enough). Restrictions on private schools at the secondary and postsecondary levels remained throughout the July Monarchy, however, and may have become more contentious because of the greater administrative efficiency of the University. Whatever its legal authority, the University was a far more efficient body—whoever directed it—in 1847 than it had been in 1814.

Liberty of education became a more divisive question as attempted compromises failed in 1837, 1844, and 1845. Both Catholics and *universitaires* became more intransigent during the 1840s. Once again, the controversy would be resolved with a change of regime. The Falloux Law (1850) created a dual system of schooling, permitting public and private schools at primary and secondary levels to operate, both to receive financial support from taxes, and declaring that Catholic priests and nuns who had attended ecclesiastical schools were as qualified to teach as were lay teachers graduated from a public school. It also reduced the power of the University by giving more to local committees.

Despite all the fetters engendered by disputes among Bourbons, Orleanists, republicans, and Bonapartists, despite divisions between conservative and liberal Catholics, and between Catholics and anticlericals, public instruction made enormous advances between 1814 and 1852.

*Primary Schooling.* The grand work of the constitutional monarchies was in the area of primary instruction. The Guizot Law (1833) embodied this direction but was by no means the sole cause of it. Announced in the original ministerial circular as a charter for primary education, its purpose was to provide all Frenchmen with the basic knowledge essential for social order and progress. It envisioned a partnership between state and church with equal standing for public and private schools and with religious instruction an integral part of the curriculum. It established a minimal wage for teachers while requiring close supervision of them. The law further directed all communes to provide a primary school, all Department capitals (*chef-lieus*) of more than 6,000 to found an *école primaire supérieure*, and all departments to establish a normal school.

Its most important provisions concerned teachers. If the minimal wage was very low, it placed a national stamp of respectability on the profession and, through the normal schools, which increased from forty-seven to seventy-four in the next four years, fixed an institution for systematically training a profession. In other areas, the Guizot Law tended to affirm rather than redirect social trends. The requirement for all communes, for example, to provide a primary school had been anticipated by a law in 1816. When the Guizot Law was passed, only 15 percent of communes lacked a school; over the next fifteen years, half of those established a school. The Guizot Law wrought no revolution.

The history of primary education as a national institution begins with the establishment of schools. However mean the immediate results, with many early classes conducted in churches, lofts, and teachers' houses, the creation of a school was a significant social event. It meant a prescribed space for which commune, state, church, parents, or donors were responsible and an assigned teacher whose pay, preparation, and pedagogy could be enjoined. The creation of that school was the beginning of a competitive pressure among communes and families and the beginning of a kind of instruction of parents, taught that at a certain age their children should be sent to the care of others. The fact that learning took place away from home in a new environment had great psychological implications and was part of a larger revolution in patterns of learning. Schools gave that process an increasing regularity attached to certain hours of the day, seasons of the year, and years of childhood. To establish and expand these patterns the school itself was the central instrument, whether it was a school for boys or girls or both, private or public, whether it was taught by religious or lay teachers, by men or women.

In 1814 approximately 25,000 primary schools existed in France; that number nearly doubled by the time of the Guizot Law (45,000) and surpassed 60,000 by 1848. Enormous growth (5 percent annually to 1821) occurred in the first years of the Restoration, slowed under the ultras (1 percent), exploded in the four years preceding the Guizot Law (6 percent)—the fastest post-Revolutionary growth in French history—remained high during the next four years (4 percent), and maintained at about 2 percent for the rest of the July Monarchy. French primary schools increased in number by about 140 percent during the constitutional monarchies; they would expand by less than 40 percent during the remainder of the century. In 1850 France had three-quarters of the schools it would have at the beginning of the twentieth century. Even allowing for growth in school-age population during the century, France had achieved about half of the 1900 ratio of schools to school-age population by 1833 and two-thirds by 1850. The Guizot law and national legislation generally had a less dramatic effect on the availability of schooling than the historical literature has asserted heretofore. Because the published censuses (*Statistiques générales*) first counted girls' schools in 1837, they give an exaggerated picture of growth following the Guizot Law.

A similar pattern emerges when one looks at enrollment. Although precise national figures are unavailable prior to 1829, archival reports indicate substantial growth during the first half of the Restoration and slow growth during its second half. At the beginning of the July Monarchy approximately 1.5 million children were enrolled in school; that figure had risen to 2 million by the Guizot Law and to 3.5 million by 1850. That 2 million advance during the July Monarchy alone equaled total growth during the remainder of the century. The most rapid growth took place in the years (1829–37) immediately preceding and after the Guizot Law (6 percent), although the law did not require school attendance of anyone.

Considering enrollment in terms of the school-age cohort confirms that more children were receiving instruction and for more years than the reports of dismayed contemporaries acknowledged. Precisely half the departments had achieved an average of five years of primary schooling by 1850 (all had achieved that before the Ferry Laws would make schooling compulsory three decades later). Six years of primary schooling for all children was an impressive target; nearly a third of France's departments had reached it (or achieved it statistically by having some children in school still longer) by 1850. In these figures, the pattern for schools is repeated: a surprisingly large early start, a burst of growth in the early 1830s, steady progress for another decade, and a slight decline during the political turmoil of 1848–50.

The availability of schooling and enrollment in schools enjoyed tremendous growth during the quarter-century reign of the constitutional monarchies. Enthusiasm at the national level of policymaking burst forth also at local levels and within homes. Besides the increase in schools and enrollment, three other patterns that would describe French education for a century were set in these crucial years: steadily decreasing disparity among departments, regional variations predicting future growth, and lengthier periods of instruction, better facilities, and improved teachers.

Local initiative was the main reason for the early emergence of primary education. This sense of local initiative can be demonstrated in a variety of ways. National expenditures were the result, not the cause, of local efforts to establish primary schools. About one-fourth of all schools during the July Monarchy were in buildings specifically designed for instruction. Departments that were the first to establish schools were leaders in library books, voluntary expenditures, teachers' qualifications, and the number of students receiving diplomas (*certificats d'études*) at the end of the century. Indeed the number of schools in a department in 1829 statistically was the best predictor of enrollment over the entire century. Early leaders continued to lead late in the century, and laggards continued to lag. The foundation of a school system was laid prior to the Guizot Law.

At the same time differences among departments gradually lessened. The ratio between the maximum and minimum in enrollment per school-age population, more than twenty to one in 1829, was less than seven to one by 1840, and less than five to one in 1850. Variation among departments (coefficient of variation) declined from 80 percent to 50 percent between 1829 and 1850. The famous division of France by the St. Malo-Geneva line showed a seven-to-two advantage for the northeast in 1829; that reduced to three to two by 1850.

Early in the nineteenth century, the ages at which children attended school varied widely. Archival reports for 1829 often mentioned that they began at all ages. Indeed school-age population was defined then as five to fifteen, although officials never anticipated children completing more than six years of full schooling. Moreover, the school year was irregular, often six months or less; most rural schools shut their doors during harvest and planting seasons. Regular attendance remained a problem during this period. Nevertheless, amid a surge in enrollment, the proportion of enrolled children actually present in a classroom during the summer (and thus normally present for the full school year) increased marginally from three-fifths to two-thirds during the July Monarchy. Many children attended one-room schoolhouses for a few months over many years in order to complete a rudimentary education, consisting primarily of reading, writing, arithmetic, and religion. Steadily increasing literacy statistics reflect the success of ill-equipped schools in accomplishing their minimal goals. The Lancaster method, which was imported from England and involved older students tutoring younger ones, was one of many methods adopted in an attempt to compensate for inadequate numbers of teachers. Rather than supporting notions of social resistance to schooling, this pattern speaks to widespread social demand for schooling that surmounted social and economic constraints. Only gradually did ages six to thirteen emerge as normal years of attendance.

Distinctions among private and public schools and male and female enrollment were important during the July Monarchy (distinctions are uncertain for the Restoration). In 1837 nearly 59 percent of all enrolled students were male; by 1850 the percentage had declined to 54 percent. Although there was a clear differential by gender, it was not great at a time when male and female roles were sharply demarked. Catholic and private schools remained important cogs within the wheel of public instruction. About one-quarter of the pupils attended private schools, and about one-quarter of the remainder (especially girls) attended a public school headed by a religious. The most important of the religious orders was the Christian Brothers, who conducted 320 schools with 1,420 brothers in 1830. They and, later, female religious had been exempted from the teaching certificate by a circular of 16 March 1819. A public system of education was firmly in place by the July Monarchy, but it was one typified by diversity rather than the monolithic one that would operate under the Third Republic. The national state, as it increased its power in many areas, gradually took control of a system developed by state, church, local government, and individual effort.

*Secondary.* Secondary schooling reflected the elitist concept that dominated French pedagogical thought during the nineteenth century. With a curriculum based on the classics, most students boarding at the school, rates expensive, and enrollment limited to males, it remained entirely separate from primary schooling with elementary classes conducted within secondary schools. The baccalaureate, which crowned secondary studies, became a prerequisite for admission to higher schools. Thus secondary schools screened for elites. In an attempt to respond to demand for increased schooling while retaining distinctive tiers, the July Monarchy introduced in 1833 *écoles primaires supérieures* for the working classes. Enrollment in those schools grew rapidly, while enrollment in secondary schools stagnated until after the Falloux Law, there being fewer students in 1843 in these *collèges* than in 1788.

Teachers remained underpaid, subject to administrative tyranny, but also very conservative in both politics and curriculum matters. Most reforms, like Narcisse-Achille de Salvandy's proposal for an equal scientific track, were stillborn. Except for the *petits-séminaires*, the state retained a lay monopoly of secondary schooling between 1814 and 1850. This monopoly became a matter of intense political debate concerning "liberty of education" during the 1840s and ended with the Falloux Law of 1850, which permitted private secondary schools and inaugurated a period of growth.

*Technical.* The Restoration made significant advances in technical schooling. It inherited a base in the *écoles des arts et métiers*, which were gradually expanded and improved. Their graduates, who generally came from the lower and lower-middle classes, provided semiprofessional workers, foremen, and draftsmen for the expanding French industry of the 1840s and 1850s. They displayed remarkable social mobility and often became successful entrepreneurs.

Despite industrial advances in the 1840s, the July Monarchy left it to private enterprise to found training schools. Individual manufacturers, the Christian Brothers, and the Protestant Institution of Saint-Marcel taught a variety of practical courses, mainly in the cities. Adult education increased and the *salles d'asiles* (day care centers), which dated from the *ancien régime*, were reestablished in 1836; all of these endeavors, however, were primarily the result of private initiative.

*Higher Education.* The faculties, inherited from Napoleon, had as their purpose supervision of lower levels and certification rather than teaching or research. Although that function changed little before the Second Empire, particular lecturers in science, as well as Guizot and Cousin in history and philosophy, achieved fame. Higher education was essentially professional, based on the traditional faculties of law and medicine and the so-called *grandes écoles*— Polytechnique for engineering, St. Cyr and Samur for the army, Navale for the navy, the reestablished (1816) Ecole des mines, the newly established Chartres (1821) and Forests (1824), and the privately founded (1829) Ecole centrale des arts et manufactures. The Ecole polytechnique may have been the most prestigious scientific school in the world at that time, whose engineering graduates primarily served the state in the army or in the bureaucracy. Graduates of Centrale and the lesser *écoles des arts et métiers* entered private industry. Law and Polytechnique, which drew from the highest classes of society, served largely to preserve elites, while the other schools were agents of mobility. The basic structure of the *grandes écoles*, laid prior to the July Monarchy, and their importance in the formation of French elites remain 150 years later.

M. Gontard, *L'Enseignement primaire en France de la Revolution à la loi Guizot, 1789–1833* (Paris, 1959); R. Grew and P. J. Harrigan with J. B. Whitney, "The Availability of Schooling in Nineteenth-Century France," *Journal of Interdisciplinary History* (1983); J. Moody, *French Education since Napoleon* (Syracuse, 1978).

*Patrick J. Harrigan*

Related entries: AFFRE; BROTHERS OF THE CHRISTIAN SCHOOLS; ECOLE MILITAIRE (SAINT-CYR); ECOLE NAVALE; ECOLE POLYTECHNIQUE; ECOLES NATIONALES DES ARTS ET METIERS; ECOLES NORMALES PRIMAIRES; ECOLES PRIMAIRES SUPERIEURES; FALLOUX LAW; FRAYSSINOUS; GUIZOT; GUIZOT LAW ON PUBLIC EDUCATION; LAMENNAIS; LIBERTY OF EDUCATION; MARTIGNAC; MONTALEMBERT; PETIT-SEMINAIRES; SALVANDY; SOCIETY FOR ELEMENTARY INSTRUCTION; VILLELE.

**PUBLIC WELFARE.** The Ministry of the Interior had jurisdiction over all public welfare programs. These included public hospitals and hospices, *bureaux de bienfaisance, monts-de-piété, dépôts de mendicité*, and other public shelters. In 1849 republican legislators created L'Assistance publique (a central office for public assistance) in Paris, which henceforth had administrative responsibility for social welfare institutions and programs.

In 1815, the Ministry of the Interior included special departments for the insane, the indigent sick, aged, and incurables who could not live at home but required institutionalization, and abandoned children and poor orphans. National, departmental, and communal hospitals and hospices existed for these groups. They were governed by an administrative council of hospitals and hospices that reported directly to the Ministry of the Interior. Members of this administrative council also served on the boards of directors of *bureaux de bienfaisance* and *monts de piété*.

A Ministry of the Interior ordinance on 2 July 1816 created the *bureaux de bienfaisance*, which were municipal committees (or bureaus) of charity, and charged them with distributing home aid to the indigent in their area. Initially there were twelve committees, one in each arrondissement of Paris, but they spread rapidly to other cities in France. The committees distributed both temporary and long-term aid in the form of jobs or services (but not money) to those unable to work and deserving of aid. The committees demanded conditions of sobriety, cleanliness, vaccination, and morality; they would not aid those living in concubinage or unwed mothers. People entitled to temporary aid included the wounded, the sick, married pregnant women, and legitimate orphans. Recipients of long-term aid were the paralyzed, the blind, the incurably infirm, and the aged.

The administrative council of the hospitals and hospices, the prefect of Paris, and a committee of directors governed the bureaus. The directors included the mayors of the arrondissements, a local priest, and twelve administrators named by the minister of the interior. Nuns and philanthropic women who visited the poor (*dames de charité*) had a consultative voice. One-fourth of the directors were candidates for renewal each year. Every committee of charity had a central house used for administrative meetings, free consultations with the poor, a pharmacy, and a storeroom for linen and clothes to be given out. *Dames de charité* and nuns decided who needed aid and distributed it. Affiliated with each bureau were doctors, surgeons, midwives, nuns, teachers, and legal experts in numbers fixed by the minister of the interior upon the recommendations of the prefect and the administrative council of the hospitals and hospices. Funds to operate the bureaus came from donations and legacies, a tax on entertainment and concerts, special fund-raising drives, a donation from the king, and grants from the municipal governments.

In 1821 the Ministry of the Interior issued new administrative regulations for the *bureaux de bienfaisance*. The minister chose the administrative committee, or board, of each bureau, which henceforth consisted of five members. This committee was assisted by the newly created Councils of Charity comprised of notables such as lawyers, bishops, government officials, presidents of commercial businesses, and former justices of the peace. The administrative committee and Council of Charity, with the approval of the Minister of the Interior, determined the operating budget. Doctors, surgeons, pharmacists, nuns, teachers, and philanthropic women continued to serve. In 1828 the minister of the interior inaugurated a system of national inspection. An inspector would examine needs, resources, and the operating budget and then make recommendations to the minister of the interior.

Under the Restoration, *monts de piété* (financial lending institutions) multiplied. Funding came from the municipal government, augmented by donations, legacies, and from the same sources as the *bureaux de bienfaisance*. The *monts de piété* lent money to the deserving poor—with interest. The administration of these lending institutions, chosen by the prefect, consisted of three members of the administrative council of hospitals and hospices, two members of the administrative committee of the *bureau de bienfaisance* in the area, notables specializing in banking, and legal experts. The administrators proposed policies, programs, and budgets; the prefect gave his opinion, and the minister of the interior made the final decisions. By 1850 the *monts de piété* were a public utility. In Paris, the prefect of the city presided over its administrative board; in the provinces it was the mayor.

Departmental and communal *dépôts de mendicité* (refuges or shelters for beggars), established by a ministerial decision of 1808, were both charitable institutions and penitentiary establishments. Begging was forbidden in departments and communes where these refuges existed. The beggars placed in these institutions were, in effect, deprived of their liberty. People worked in these refuges. Half their income went to the institution; the other half was given to them when they left. The *dépôts de mendicité* were never widespread; in 1853, in all of France there were only twenty-one, housing 2,841 men and 1,932 women.

Public welfare underwent several changes during the July Monarchy. The minister of the interior judged the Councils of Charity to be unsuccessful and suppressed them in 1831. A decree of 1833 created an inspectorate to examine and verify the accountability of the provisions and services for abandoned children and poor orphans, the administration and financial arrangements of the public hospices and hospitals, and welfare establishments such as the *bureaux de bienfaisance* and *monts de piété*. The inspectors reported much disorder in all these public welfare institutions.

The minister of the interior then redefined the principles of public welfare. It had to help the indigent get out of poverty, and it had to prevent a person from falling into extreme poverty or *misère*. In so doing, it must offer people the means to better their position by their own effort, notably by working. Welfare officials gave preference to home aid but took into the hospices the indigent or sick who were without family. The minister of the interior established an administrative commission to oversee public welfare and replace the Councils of Charity. Other aspects of the public welfare administration that had developed under the Restoration remained. Nuns of the nursing orders, under the authority of the administrative commission, cared for the indigent and sick, distributed food and clothing, inspected the workhouses, taught the children in the institutions, and gave medicine when the pharmacist was absent; they were not to prepare medication. In each welfare program, all those who could work had to. They received a wage, of which they kept one-third; two-thirds went back to public welfare in repayment for care received.

In 1840 five charitable institutions of public welfare with the status of a public utility emerged: L'Hospice royal des quinze-vingts for the blind, La Maison royale de Charenton for the insane, L'Institution royale des sourds-muets de Paris for deaf-mutes, L'Institution royale des jeunes aveugles de Paris for the blind, and L'Institution des sourds-muets de Bordeaux for the insane of that area. All of these were administered under the authority of the minister of the interior and the surveillance of a council of twenty-four members chosen by the king, and a secretary chosen by the minister of interior. They had a board of directors assisted by consultative committees, which gave advice on regulations and on budget. One-sixth of the council was replaced every two years. These public utility welfare institutions were in addition to the *bureaux de bienfaisance*, the *monts de piété*, and the many public general hospitals and hospices for the indigent, aged, infirm, incurable, insane, pregnant, and abandoned. There were about twelve such hospitals in Paris alone. The larger and more famous among them were Salpêtrière for incurable, insane, and sick women; Bicêtre and La Pitié for incurable, insane, and sick men; Hôtel dieu for the sick of both sexes; Hôpital des enfants malades for sick children and Maternité for childbirth.

The Revolution of 1848 and the establishment of the Republic changed the nature and administration of public welfare. Officials believed that the Republic should protect the citizen by giving assistance to those in need, provide work to those who were without work, and give a means of subsistence to those without a family who could not work. In keeping with this ideology, on 10 January 1849 legislators created L'Assistance publique (a department of Public Assistance in Paris) as a branch of the Ministry of the Interior. Located in Paris but national in responsibility, L'Assistance publique had a director as its administrator and a general council as an advisory, policymaking, and policy-implementing board. From its inception, L'Assistance publique had primary responsibility for the insane and for abandoned children. The director of L'Assistance publique served as the legal guardian for the thousands of abandoned children of Paris. In all other departments, inspectors appointed by the central administration of L'Assistance publique were the guardians of these wards of the state by virtue of their office. The central administration gave precise instructions to the inspectors. A medical staff named by the director and general council, and approved by the minister of the interior, completed the administrative structure.

L'Assistance publique had three main activities. (1) It administered public hospitals and hospices for the abandoned, insane, infirm, and aged. (2) Through local committees and societies, it administered home aid to the needy. (3) It offered special assistance to mothers and young children. The director of L'Assistance publique delegated responsibility to individual institutions, hospitals, and hospices.

From 1830 to 1852 the number of people served by public welfare increased greatly. In 1833, nineteen *bureaux de bienfaisance* existed for each 100,000 inhabitants. In 1852 there were thirty-three *bureaux* per 100,000 people. The big increase occurred in 1850. As a result, the number of people served per bureau declined from 5,164 in the five-year period from 1833 to 1838 to 3,339 in the five-year period from 1848 to 1852. Between 1833 and 1852 the number of individuals aided by a *bureau de bienfaisance* increased from 2.25 to 2.78 per 100 inhabitants. During the same period (1833–52) the number of hospitals, hospices, houses of refuge, and public asylums for the insane declined from 1,329 to 1,324, but the average number of annual admissions increased from 471,387 in 1833 to 618,207 in 1852.

J. Dehaussy, *L'Assistance publique à l'enfance* (Paris, 1951); J. Donzelot, *The Policing of Families* (New York, 1979); R. G. Fuchs, *Abandoned Children* (Albany, N.Y., 1984);

H. Hatzfeld, *Du Pauperisme à la securité sociale* (Paris, 1971); F. Ponteil, *Les Institutions de la France de 1814 à 1870* (Paris, 1966); J. Vidalenc, *Le Peuple, des villes et des bourgs* (Paris, 1973).

*Rachel Fuchs*

*Related entries:* CHILDREN, ABANDONED; CHILDREN, INSTITUTIONS FOR.

**PUTTING-OUT INDUSTRY.** See COTTAGE INDUSTRY.

**PYAT, AIME-FELIX** (1810–1889), journalist, dramatist, and political figure. An advocate of the extreme Left, he served as a deputy in 1848, and as a member of the Paris Commune. After the amnesty he was elected to the legislature of the Third Republic.

Felix Pyat was born on 4 October 1810 at Vierzon, department of the Cher. Pyat's father was a legitimist lawyer, but when Pyat went to Paris after completing the lycée at Bourges, he was already an outspoken liberal. He fought in the July Revolution. He became a lawyer in 1831 but left the bar in order to devote all his energy to writing. He published articles in *Figaro, Charivari*, the *Revue de Paris, L'Artiste*, the *Revue démocratique*, and the *Revue des deux-mondes*. He directed the *Revue britannique* and was a founder of La Société des gens de lettres. He combated romanticism, which he regarded as a product of royalist reactionaries. When Godefroy Cavaignac founded the *Journal du peuple* in 1842, Pyat signed its socialist program along with Louis Blanc and others. He wrote several popular plays, among them *Les Deux serruriers* (1841) and *Le Chiffonnier de Paris* (1847), in which he castigated monarchism and clericalism.

With the Revolution of 1848, Pyat was appointed commissioner of the department of Cher. He was then elected to the Constituent Assembly, where he as a Montagnard sat on the extreme Left. He strenuously supported the right to work. Pyat is accused of having called for an insurrection in June but then of playing no part in it himself. His critics accuse him of a consistent lack of responsibility and courage. Pyat was a neo-Jacobin with a romantic attachment to the Terror. He never tired of calling for violence with his voice and pen but seldom exposed himself to personal danger.

Pyat was reelected to the Legislative Assembly in 1849 but had to flee to Switzerland after participating in the insurrection of 13 June 1849. He was one of the most active political exiles. With others he published the *Almanach de l'exilé*. In February 1850 he organized a secret society, La Nouvelle montagne, which was soon renamed the Comité central de la résistance. Authorities suspected that Pyat's agitation had played a large part in provoking disturbances in the valley of the Loire on 11 and 12 October 1851.

After the coup of 2 December 1851, Pyat was expelled from Brussels and went to Great Britain. In London he was the nucleus of a group of militant socialists who formed La Commune révolutionnaire, a group that advocated revolutionary violence against the Empire. It convoked the Little Dean Street meeting of exiles and appealed to American democrats for financial support. The organization disseminated Pyat's revolutionary letters among workers in France and established contact with La Commune révolutionnaire in Paris. The two groups agreed to assassinate Louis-Napoleon. The police, however, uncovered the plot, and Pyat was sentenced in absentia to ten years in prison and a 6,000 franc fine on 22 July 1852. Undaunted, Pyat published a justification of Orsini's attack on Louis-Napoleon in 1859 and was implicated in another plot in 1862.

When the First International was established in 1864, its External French Section was largely comprised of the Commune révolutionnaire, and Pyat and his associates were a constant thorn in the side of Marx and the General Council. He also played a divisive role while serving as a member of the Executive Commission of the Paris Commune. At the final meeting of the Commune on 22 May 1871, he expressed his determination to perish on the barricades but then went underground. He made his way to safety, arriving in London by 3 June. He was condemned to death in absentia on 28 March 1873.

With the amnesty of 1880, Pyat returned to France and resumed his political activity. In 1888 Pyat was elected to the Chamber of Deputies from the Bouches-du-Rhône. He sat on the extreme Left and was an outspoken opponent of Boulanger.

Pyat died on 4 August 1889 and was buried in the Père Lachaise cemetery.

*Dictionnaire biographique du mouvement ouvrier français*, vol. 8 (Paris, 1970); F. Jellinek, *The Paris Commune of 1871* (New York, 1965).

*Bernard Cook*

*Related entries: LE CHARIVARI; LE FIGARO; LE JOURNAL DU PEUPLE;* LEGISLATIVE ASSEMBLY; *LA REVUE DE PARIS; LA REVUE DES DEUX MONDES.*

# Q

**QUADRUPLE ALLIANCE,** an alliance of Austria, England, Prussia, and Russia, the four conservative great powers that defeated Napoleon. On the same day that the Second Treaty of Paris was signed with France, 20 November 1815, the ministers of the four Great Powers (Austria, England, Prussia, and Russia) also signed a secret treaty aimed at securing the execution of the obligations imposed upon France and the enforcement of the new European order established at the Congress of Vienna. Castlereagh was the inspiration for and principal author of this document. Although it referred to the earlier Treaty of Chaumont, it differed in its form. At Chaumont each of the four powers had signed a special instrument with each of the other partners, but now there was a single treaty to be signed by all four powers. Special attention was given to the possible renewal of Bonapartist or Revolutionary attempts against the established monarchy, events that would not be tolerated, and stipulations dealt with the number of troops that would be contributed if necessary. The most innovative article was the sixth; it provided for periodic meetings of heads of state or ministers to consider "great common interests and measures which would be deemed the most salutary for the peace and prosperity of the people." Thus it established in fact a kind of Directory of European Policy, a first blueprint of the Security Council of the United Nations. In its time, it was the reality behind the nebulous Holy Alliance.

G. de Bertier de Sauvigny, *La Sainte-Alliance* (Paris, 1972); C. K. Webster, *The Foreign Policy of Castlereagh* (London, 1931).

*Guillaume de Bertier de Sauvigny*
*Related entries:* HOLY ALLIANCE; PARIS, SECOND TREATY OF; QUIN-TUPLE ALLIANCE; VIENNA, CONGRESS OF.

**QUELEN, HYACINTHE-LOUIS DE** (1778–1839), Archbishop of Paris. The son of a count, Quélen chose a church career rather than military service. Growing up during the Revolutionary era, his education was interrupted several times because of changes in family residences. He studied at the Collège de Navarre, privately with several clerics, and, finally, at Saint-Sulpice Seminary. Following his parents' death in 1802 and 1803, much of his inheritance went for the construction of a boys' school.

In 1806 and 1807 Mgr. Caffarelli conferred on Quélen the four minor orders at Saint-Brieuc and named him an honorary deacon of his cathedral. The young cleric also assumed various duties at the Grand Aumonière in Paris, where he became vicar-general in 1814.

In 1812 Napoleon called in Quélen twice to discuss his plan to break with the papacy and put himself at the head of a national church. Quélen's opposition to the plan infuriated Napoleon and brought praise from the pope.

Napoleon's final campaigns sent thousands of wounded into the hospitals. Quélen gave them spiritual and material comfort despite his own serious illness. When Louis XVIII returned as king, Quélen quickly assured him of his loyalty and that of the clergy in his diocese.

In 1817 the cleric was named bishop of Samosate and appointed to the staff of the aged archbishop of Paris, Mgr. de Talleyrand-Périgord, after much wrangling over his qualifications. Cardinal Périgord in 1819 asked the king to appoint Quélen his coadjutor, with his succession in mind. With approval of the pope, Quélen was appointed and also named archbishop of Trajanopolis. He increasingly assumed the duties normally handled by the archbishop. His patron died in 1821, and Quélen succeeded him. The ambitious cleric had also hoped to succeed Périgord as *grand aumônier*, but that honor was denied him. Embittered by this rejection, he became involved in public and private disputes for years over the respective jurisdictions of the archbishop and the *grand aumônier*. Quélen was elevated to the peerage in 1822, taking seriously his duties in the Chamber of Peers, though he usually took no active part in discussions except those relating to religious matters. He became involved politically in 1824 when he opposed the conversion of government securities, contending that the measure would create hardships for small investors. In part because of his arguments, the law was not passed, and the archbishop became a popular hero while antagonizing the government.

The king died in 1824, and Quélen delivered the funeral oration in Notre Dame. That same year he was elected to the French Academy, creating something of a furor by remarks in his address praising François-René de Chateaubriand, who had just lost his ministerial office and was living in disgrace.

Following his coronation at Reims in 1825, Charles X asked Quélen to celebrate a *Te Deum* at Notre Dame. Coupled with his extravagant praise of the king, the ceremony served to improve relations between the two men and increase the archbishop's influence on the monarch. The public exhibition of the king's piety alienated many liberals who accused him of not blocking the church's attempt to restore the *ancien régime*.

When the ex-Bishop Grégoire was dying in 1831, estranged from the church, the archbishop refused him Catholic rites and interment unless he retracted his schismatic past. Grégoire did not recant, but the police insisted on and supervised the funeral rites, conducted by two priests instead of Quélen.

In June 1829 two ordinances against the Jesuits were proclaimed, bringing under University supervision some Jesuit institutions, setting forth certain requirements for teachers, and placing a limit on the number of students in church schools. Quélen headed a committee of clerics drawing up a protest against the ordinances, but the pope, in response to an appeal, said the ordinances did not violate church rights.

In July 1830 Algiers capitulated to French troops at the same time as the public was celebrating a liberal victory in the elections. A *Te Deum* for the military victory was performed by Quélen at Notre Dame, attended by the king, who was assured by the archbishop of the protection of the Virgin and urged to lead a crusade. Quélen's extravagant praise is believed by some to have been the cause of the sack of the archbishop's palace and other religious structures in 1831, the mob violence being directed as much against the church as against the monarchy. Quélen was forced to go into hiding during the July Revolution for his own safety. One newspaper reported that he had been arrested by soldiers and was taking away a million in diamonds and gold. He chose to spend this period at Conflans, his country estate. His exile was the turning point in his ecclesiastical career. Henceforth he was something of an exile in his own diocese.

On 14 February 1831 the usual requiem mass, celebrated by royalists on the anniversary of the death of the duc de Berry at Saint-Germain-l'Auxerrois, was the occasion for mob violence directed against church structures in Paris. Saint-Germain was sacked; only the bare walls were left standing. Men dressed in priestly garments paraded in the streets in mockery of religious ceremonies. The next day mobs destroyed the archbishop's palace, throwing furniture, valuable books, and sacred objects into the Seine. Neither police nor officials intervened. The orgy of destruction culminated in the looting of Conflans and the destruction of Quélen's chapel and family crypts.

Ministers, deputies, and officials refused to blame the government for the anticlerical riots. The reason given was that the archbishop was at fault for having allowed the service for the duc de Berry. He and the parish priest were accused in court of having provoked the disturbances.

Quélen had been in disguise, hiding for months in various religious institutions. Finally, in August, he was assured of police protection, but since his palace had been damaged beyond repair, he continued to live at Saint-Michel and Sacré-Coeur convents.

While he performed his ecclesiastical duties under Louis-Philippe, Quélen remained controversial in church and political affairs. He received special praise for his efforts during the 1832 cholera epidemic, especially for the care of orphaned children. His political problems centered chiefly on his bitterness over the rights of the church, the destruction of church property, and the razing of the remains of the archbishop's palace. Arguments developed over the consecration of royal appointments to ecclesiastical offices. The king later concluded it would be to his advantage to seek Quélen's advice on appointments and did so. Pope Gregory XVI tried to heal the breach by asking the archbishop to visit the king. Quélen refused to submit to pressure from all sides until an attempt on the life of Louis-Philippe in 1835 moved him to go to the palace to express his condolences. At a *Te Deum* in Notre Dame for the victims of the assassination attempt, the archbishop met his king at the portal, and a reconciliation was effected, though there continued to be friction between the cleric and the government which brought on criticism from the pope. The question of a new archbishop's palace, the greatest thorn in Quélen's side, was still unresolved when the stubborn old man died in December 1839.

T. E. B. Howarth, *Citizen King: The Life of Louis-Philippe* (London, 1961); R. Limouzin-Lamothe, *Monseigneur de Quélen, Archevêque de Paris: son rôle dans l'église de France de 1815 à 1839 d'apres ses archives privées* (Paris, 1955–57); Lucas-Dubreton, *Louis-Philippe* (Paris, 1938).

*Helen Castelli*

*Related entries:* ACADEMIE FRANCAISE; AFFRE; ALGIERS, EXPEDITION TO; ARCHBISHOPS OF PARIS; CHATEAUBRIAND; FIESCHI PLOT; GREGOIRE; JESUITS; SAINT GERMAIN L'AUXERROIS, RIOT OF.

**QUINET, JEAN-LOUIS-EDGAR** (1803–1875), historian, philosopher, and politician. Born in Bourg-en-Bresse on 17 February 1803, Edgar Quinet was the son of Jérôme Quinet, a civilian official who had served with the armies, and a devotedly Protestant mother. His bureaucratic position notwithstanding, Quinet's father was an ardent republican, and he passed on to his son a decided hostility toward Napoleon and the Empire. Young Edgar's early schooling came in the colleges of Charolles, Bourg (1815–16), and Lyons (1817–20) and from wide reading in French, Italian, English, and Latin literature. Favorites were the novels of Walter Scott, the poems of Byron, the works of Mme. de Staël, and the *Génie du christianisme* of Chateaubriand. In November 1820, Quinet departed for Paris, intended by his father first for the Ecole polytechnique and then for legal studies. The young newcomer never even took the exams for the Ecole polytechnique, preferring to enter the exciting and turbulent intellectual world of Paris in the 1820s.

While in Paris, Quinet's first great discovery was the eclecticism of Victor Cousin, a philosophy that then exercised a commanding appeal over the intellectually inclined youth of Paris. Quinet's intellectual questioning led him next to the study of the philosophy of history, from which he expected insights into the destiny of humanity, and in 1824 he sketched his *Introduction à la philosophie de l'histoire*. Already sympathetic with German ideas, Quinet traveled in England, Switzerland, and Germany, pausing to study in Heidelberg. This journey laid the foundation for Quinet's profound understanding of things German and for his enthusiasm for German culture and thought. Much taken with Johann Gottfried Herder's *Ideen zur Philosophie der Geschichte der Menschheit*, he translated the book and published it together with his essay of 1824. This work brought him into contact with Cousin and, through him, with Jules Michelet and with liberal and romantic circles. Quinet and Michelet, who would be closely associated with each other for the next fifty years, shared, among other common concerns, a lifelong faith in a vision of a renewed France and a regenerated mankind. In 1828, Quinet's adventurous spirit led him to join a scientific expedition sponsored by the Institut to Morea; from his notes, he wrote *De la Grèce moderne et de ses rapports avec l'Antiquité*, published on the eve of the July Revolution. Quinet's fervent belief in liberty, his patriotism, and his faith in the people led him to welcome the Revolution of 1830 as the dawn of a new era.

During the 1830s, Quinet pursued an astounding range of intellectual interests. From travels in Rome and Naples and from further travels in Germany, he wrote about art, literature, and religion in *Allemagne et Italie*. An interest in poetry led to *Rapport sur les épopées inédites du XIIᵉ siècle*, which occasioned a violent polemical exchange and also led to *Histoire de la poésie* (1839). Quinet wrote two epics in verse, *Napoléon* (1836) and *Prométhée* (1838), works more interesting for their philosophical and political content than for their literary value. His *Ahasvérus* (1843), written not in verse but in prose, recounted in symbolic form the history of the world and the place in it of God and doubt. A renewed interest in religion seized Quinet in the late 1830s, and he wrote a critique of David Friedrich Strauss's *La Vie de Jésus*, in which he complained that Strauss had substituted an abstraction for the historical Jesus, and, among other works, *Du Génie des religions*.

His teaching career began with an appointment as a professor of literature in Lyons (1839) and continued when he became a professor at the prestigious Collège de France (1841–45). A gifted speaker who boldly mixed politics with his scholarship, Quinet, with his friend Jules Michelet and Adam Mickiewicz, formed in the early 1840s a powerful and controversial triumvirate at the Collège de France. To help counter a Catholic revival, he and Michelet gave in 1842 a series of lectures, more polemics on the moral questions of the day than academic discourses, dealing with the Jesuits, and published them the next year. For Quinet, Jesuit teachings meant not only the destruction of all political constitutions and social organizations but also the death of the mind. The confrontation occasioned by the anticlerical polemics of Michelet and Quinet led the government to suspend their courses in 1845. Quinet, who, however, abandoned neither his interest in religion nor his belief in its importance for mankind, published *Le Christianisme et la Révolution française* in 1845. Before the 1840s had ended, he also began the publication of his first major historical work, *Les Révolutions d'Italie* (1848–51).

Quinet had a minor part in bringing about the Revolution of 1848 and in bringing it to an end. A participant in the Banquet Campaign, even to the extent of being present at the meeting of radical leaders on 21 February 1848, Quinet welcomed the February Revolution. A few months later, now a colonel of the National Guard, he led the Eleventh Legion against the insurgents of Paris during the June Days. As a deputy from the Ain, Quinet sat in the Constituent Assembly and the Legislative Assembly, concerning himself primarily with educational matters. He favored, as he explained in the *Enseignement du peuple*, a secular program of education for the people. In the electoral campaign for the presidency of the Second Republic, Quinet vigorously opposed the candidacy of Louis-Napoleon, not relaxing his opposition even after the prince's election. In the immediate aftermath of the coup d'état of 2 December, Louis-Napoleon took his revenge; Edgar Quinet was among the first exiled.

For the eighteen years of his exile from France, Quinet nourished a fierce and uncompromising hatred of Bonapartism and Catholicism. Although he turned to the study of the past, his histories of this period became vehicles in which Quinet disseminated his political, philosophical, and religious ideas. His "Philosophie de l'histoire de la France," printed in the *Revue des deux-mondes* in 1855, conceived of the central theme in the history of France as the never-ending protest of liberty against oppression, and it made the Revolution of 1789 a central event in that struggle. In 1865, Quinet devoted an entire volume to the French Revolution and, by this study of the past, sought to explain the Revolution of 1848, the failure of the Second Republic, and the triumph of a second military dictatorship. Criticizing the Revolution in its own name, Quinet also stressed its failure to replace Catholicism with a new religion. While he was in exile, two other important works by Quinet appeared: *Fondation de la République des Provinces-Unies* in 1854 and *Révolution religieuse au XIX^e siècle*.

Endowed with a profoundly religious nature, Quinet never went as far in his attacks on the church as did Michelet, and he never completely rejected Christianity. In fact, the problem of religion remained at the core of his political and historical thought, for he believed that the anticipated regeneration of mankind was linked with a religious rebirth. Within this framework, Quinet assessed the successes and failures of the French Revolution, which, despite the violent excesses of the Terror and the ultimate triumph of Napoleonic despotism, remained the high-water mark of French history. To emancipate mankind from enslavement to the Catholic church, which Quinet believed was the enemy of all freedom and of all material, moral, and spiritual progress, had been the Revolution's greatest achievement. But not only did the Revolution fail to destroy the church, it also failed to replace it with a new religion. Indeed, the Revolution had culminated in the combined triumph of what Quinet hated the most: Bonapartism and Catholicism. As a consequence, nineteenth-century men had the task of creating a new religion, one that would lay the foundation for the spiritual regeneration of mankind. As Quinet conceived of it, this new religion would be preached by the teachers of France and would stress national unity, political centralization, and patriotism. Once so educated, the people of France, in whom Quinet had a mystical faith, would make of their nation the harbinger of democracy.

Quinet, who had struggled against Napoleon III more openly than ever since 1868 and who favored a republic, found the eventual fall of the Second Empire a painful victory, for, while it rid France of the emperor, it also brought humiliation to the nation. He returned to Paris, endured the siege, and was elected a deputy in February 1871; he also condemned both the Commune and the reprisals that followed it. Although a supporter of the constitutional laws of 1875, he refused to vote for the laws creating the Senate. Quinet summarized his ideals in *La République* (1872); he favored a compulsory free and secular primary education, an appeal to women, and a number of social reforms. To those who would come after him, Quinet left two works, *L'Esprit nouveau* (1875) and *Vie et mort du génie grec* (1878), as his philosophical testament. Edgar Quinet died in Paris on 27 March 1875.

R. H. Powers, *Edgar Quinet* (Dallas, 1957); E. Quinet, *Histoire de mes idées*, ed. S. Bernard-Griffiths (Paris, 1972) and *Oeuvres complètes*, 30 vols. (Paris, 1895–1913); Mme. E. Quinet, *Souvenirs*, 4 vols. (Paris, 1868–99); H. Tronchon, *Allemagne, France, Angleterre. Le Jeune Quinet, ou l'aventure d'un enthousiaste* (Paris, 1937).

*Robert Brown*

*Related entries:* BANQUET CAMPAIGN; CHATEAUBRIAND; COLLEGE DE FRANCE; COUSIN; JESUITS; MICHELET; *LA REVUE DES DEUX MONDES*; STAEL-HOLSTEIN.

**QUINTUPLE ALLIANCE.** At the Congress of Aix-la-Chapelle (September-October 1818), the four original signatories of the Quadruple Alliance decided to include France in the future meetings provided for by article 6 of the treaty. Thus the Quadruple Alliance became, at least in appearance, the Quintuple Alliance.

*Guillaume de Bertier de Sauvigny*

*Related entries:* AIX-LA-CHAPELLE, CONGRESS OF; HOLY ALLIANCE; QUADRUPLE ALLIANCE.

*LA QUOTIDIENNE* (1814–1847), ultraroyalist newspaper of greatest importance during the Restoration when its principal editor was Joseph Michaud. It was often opposed to official royalist policies and was respected for its integrity. A legitimist organ in the July Monarchy, it ended in a merger in 1847.

There was an ancestral *Quotidienne*, upholding royalism during the Revolution, from September 1792 to September 1797. During this period of ordeal under Revolutionary persecution, its first editor was executed, the title was changed three times, and it was each time suppressed. Joseph Michaud, who joined the staff and became part owner in 1795, had been a contributor to the press of the *Feuillants* since 1790.

In 1814 and again in 1815 after Napoleon's defeat, the Restoration's *Quotidienne* was launched by Pierre Laurentie, Joseph Fiévée and Michaud. Several of the staff also wrote for the *Conservateur*. Professing taste, quality, and ultra polemics, the paper included several literary figures, such as François-René de Chateaubriand and Charles Nodier, as writers. In January 1822, reflecting a widespread distaste among some royalists for the new cabinet of Joseph de Villèle, the owners chose Joseph Michaud as chief editor. For the next six years, Michaud was to be the spirit of the *Quotidienne*, a spirit of royalist independence, loyalty to the crown and the Restoration, and outspoken enmity to the king's own minister, who was seen as both corrupt and temporizing.

*La Quotidienne* occupied a Middle-Right position among the journalistic forces supporting the Bourbons. To its left was Chateaubriand's *Journal des débats*, steadfast in its monarchism but becoming increasingly liberal in matters such as press freedom and clericalism. Beside *La Quotidienne* was the *Gazette*, Villèle's ministerial mouthpiece, somewhat larger than the *Quotidienne*, and preferred by Charles X. On the extreme Right was the blatant ultra voice of the little *Drapeau blanc* and several even lesser journals. If we exclude, as we should, the 12,000 subscribers to the *Débats* from the loyal legitimists' camp in 1830, we find the *Gazette* with nearly this number, while a mere 4,000 still subscribed to *La Quotidienne*. Yet the *Quotidienne* was perhaps the most respected member of the Rightists' press, chiefly due to the intelligence and integrity of its editor Michaud. Michaud's paper risked and lost royal favor on more than one occasion over the editor's principles. Although *La Quotidienne* was accused by the Left of ultramontanism, its columns rarely reflected this position until 1828 when Michaud, who disliked the Jesuit influence, left the staff. The paper's independence was made clear on two other occasions. In 1824, Villèle tried to buy the *Quotidienne* as well as the *Débats* and other journals. Chateaubriand grandly refused to sell out, although he had previously been willing to accept a monthly subsidy from the crown. Michaud not only rejected the proposal but even praised Chateaubriand's stand in his paper's columns. These cases of defection nourished the most serious and incurable schism among royalists in the entire Restoration.

The *Quotidienne* also editorially opposed the notorious Peyronnet press suppression bill of 1827 as being too extreme and too despotic. For this act of courage, its editor was fired from his honorary post as reader to the king.

During the moderate Martignac ministry (1828–29), the directors of the *Quotidienne*, trying to heal the schism on the Right, brought in some of the ultraclericals from the *Mémorial catholique*. The paper became more ultra in religion but remained opposed to Villèle. Michaud left his desk over this change, and the paper continued under the direction of Pierre Laurentie. During the summer of 1829, when rumors of a new ultra government under Polignac were thick in the air, the *Quotidienne* encouraged the change but warned continually that such an ultra triumph could be undermined by Villèle's partisans. Far from closing the breach in the Right, *La Quotidienne* widened it.

As Charles X and Polignac's July 1830 coup d'état took form (widely heralded in the press as the worst-kept secret of the century), Laurentie's editorial position softened. He wrote with a certain air of resignation of the impending crisis. When the July Ordinances at last appeared, he refrained from crowing as other ultra editors did and rather pessimistically stated that whatever the outcome, it was the fault of the "Revolution." Three days later, the "Revolution," had won and *La Quotidienne* reappeared, its front page encased in a thick black border and artlessly expressing amazement that the rich bourgeoisie had joined the people.

After 1830, *La Quotidienne* continued as a Bourbon legitimist paper in opposition to the July Monarchy but with a steadily declining list of subscribers (6,000 in 1831 to 3,000 in 1845). In February 1847, it merged with *La France* and *L'Echo français* to form *L'Union monarchique*.

D. Bagge, *Les Idées politiques en France sous la restauration* (Paris, 1952); E. Hatin, *Histoire de la presse en France* (Paris, 1859–61); N. Hudson, *Ultra Royalism and the French Restoration* (Cambridge, 1936); D. Rader, *The Journalists and the July Revolution in France* (The Hague, 1973).

*Daniel Rader*

*Related entries:* CHATEAUBRIAND; *LE CONSERVATEUR*; *LE DRAPEAU BLANC*; *L'ECHO FRANCAIS*; FIEVEE; *LA FRANCE*; *LA GAZETTE DE FRANCE*; JESUITS; *JOURNAL DES DEBATS*; JULY ORDINANCES; LEGITIMISM; MARTIGNAC; *LE MEMORIAL CATHOLIQUE*; MICHAUD; NODIER; PEYRONNET; POLIGNAC; ROYALIST PARTY; ULTRAMONTANES; ULTRAROYALISTS; VILLELE.

# R

**RAGUSE, DUC DE.** See MARMONT.

**RAILROADS.** The first French railroads were built by mining and metallurgical entrepreneurs in the central coal fields around St. Etienne, primarily for the purpose of moving coal from pitheads to nearby rivers. The first line, running about 11 miles from St. Etienne to Andrézieux, the city's port on the Loire River, was opened in 1828. A line from St. Etienne to Lyons began operations in 1832 and a third, between Roanne and Andrézieux, two years later. Horses provided traction except on a short segment of line out of Lyons, where steam locomotives were used from the outset.

The first French railroad built as a common carrier and for passengers as well as freight was inaugurated in 1837 between Paris and LePecq on the Seine River adjoining St. Germain-en-Laye. It used steam locomotives exclusively. The financial success of this line inspired many imitators. Two lines connecting Paris and Versailles were opened in 1839 and 1840, and construction was started on a few longer lines, including Paris-Orléans and Paris-Rouen-Le Havre. These more ambitious undertakings proved to be beyond the financial capabilities of the private companies that had undertaken them.

The problem of financing the construction of railroads became a central issue in a great national debate on railroad policy that went on for a decade after 1832. In that decade of indecision, France fell far behind Great Britain and Belgium in the pace of railway building (in 1842 Britain had 1,900 miles of railways in operation; France only 300), but by 1842, when the Chambers began consideration of a general railway law, the country's leaders had come to understand that the capital requirements of railroad construction were unprecedented in size and that the economic, social, and strategic effects of this new form of transportation would be shattering. The deputies then decided that France would have a national network serving all the country and that national interest, not the promise of private commercial return, would determine the location of lines.

The Railway Law of 11 June 1842 prescribed the construction of five main lines radiating from Paris to the national borders and one line in the south connecting the Mediterranean Sea and the Atlantic Ocean. The capital costs were to be shared, the state acquiring and preparing the right of way and permanent fixtures, such as bridges, tunnels, and stations, and private concessionaires providing the rails and rolling stock and operating the lines. The government retained the right to supervise safety and rates.

The passage of the law gave entrepreneurs and investors the reassurance they needed, and the government received scores of applicants for concessions. The first authorizations were granted in 1844 and 1845, and extensive railroad construction finally got underway. Although it was slowed by the financial crisis and depression of 1846 and 1847 and by the dislocations of the Revolution of 1848, construction never stopped, and in the 1850s it accelerated rapidly. By 1869 France had more than 10,000 miles of operating railways, and in that year they carried more than 100 million passengers and 36 million tons of freight.

In the 1850s, with the blessing of the imperial government, the many short concessions were consolidated into six large companies, each enjoying a regional monopoly in its area. They were the Nord, which connected Paris to the Channel ports and the Belgian frontier, the Est to the German frontier, the Paris-Lyons-Méditerranée to the Swiss and Italian frontiers and to the Mediterranean, the Orléans to Bordeaux and the Spanish frontier, the Ouest to Brittany and Normandy, and the Midi connecting Bordeaux and the Atlantic to Marseilles and the Mediterranean.

When the main lines were nearing completion in the 1850s, the imperial government undertook to ensure the construction of subsidiary lines that, although less profitable, were essential if the network was to serve the entire nation. By the Franqueville Conventions of 1859 the government guaranteed the interest on loans contracted by the railroad companies to finance construction of lines opened or authorized after 1857. In the later 1870s and the 1880s the government, anxious to stimulate a faltering economy and to facilitate rapid mobilization of reservists in time of war, subsidized the construction of an additional 5,000 miles of local lines. They were eventually incorporated into the systems of the six big companies, but the state at the same time tightened its controls over charges and safety.

In 1908 the state purchased the Ouest company, which had been chronically unprofitable and dependent on public aid. In 1937 it acquired the concessions, property, and all other assets and liabilities of the remaining companies and vested them, along with those of the Ouest, in a single, publicly owned operating company, the Société nationale des chemins de fer français.

F. Braudel and E. Labrousse, *Histoire économique et sociale de France*, vol. 3 (Paris, 1976); K. A. Doukas, *The French Railroads and the State* (New York, 1945); J. C. Toutain, *Les Transports en France de 1800 à 1966* (Paris, 1967).

*David H. Pinkney*

*Related entries:* CHAMBER OF DEPUTIES; COAL INDUSTRY; REVOLUTION OF 1848.

**RAMBUTEAU, CLAUDE-PHILIBERT BARTHELOT, COMTE DE** (1781–1869), politician and administrator, prefect of the Seine from June 1833 to February 1848. Like Pierre-Marie Bondy, his immediate predecessor at the Hôtel de ville, and like Gilbert Chabrol de Volvic, who had been prefect under the Restoration, Rambuteau began his career during the Empire. In 1809 he was named one of Napoleon's chamberlains, and from 1813 to 1815, in the difficult period of the collapse of the Empire, the first Restoration, and the Hundred Days, he distinguished himself as an efficient and conscientious prefect in different departments. Unlike Chabrol, however, he lost office and retired to his Burgundian estates when the Bourbons returned in 1815. Only in 1827 did he come back to public life. In the liberal election gains of that year, he was returned as an opposition deputy for the Mâcon (Saône-et-Loire) constituency. He spent the next seven years in the Chamber, and, though he was undistinguished as an orator, he was an able and hard-working member of committees. Close to General Maximilien-Sébastian Foy, Rambuteau was one of the signatories of the Declaration of the 221, supported the candidacy of Louis-Philippe in the first days of the July Revolution, and played a part in drawing up the Charter of the new regime (he was proposer of the clause that rabbis receive salaries like ministers of Christian cults, an important step in the granting of full equality to French Jews). Rambuteau now sat on the Center Right in the Chamber and was an ardent supporter of Casimir Périer. He was appointed prefect of the Seine in 1833 and made a peer in September 1835.

An appreciation of Rambuteau's achievements in this his most important post is doubly difficult. First, there is a problem of documentation. The departmental archives were burned during the Commune, and, though historians do have the memoirs he dictated in his last years, these are brief and apologetic, and no biography of Rambuteau has ever been written. Second, from the Second Empire onward he has been unfavorably compared with Chabrol, his most distinguished predecessor, and even more unfavorably with Baron Haussmann, his better-known successor. Historians have criticized his lack of vision, his failure to plan the rebuilding of Paris in general and the city center in particular, and his financial timidity. Haussmann, indeed, condemned any prudent and conservative policy as *"administration à la Rambuteau,"* and Rambuteau himself ended his memoirs with the admission that his more daring successor had accomplished more than he had, adding, however, that he had at least left the city without debts. Statistics of city expenditures seem to confirm this traditional view of Rambuteau's administration. Average annual spending on public works was no greater than it had been under the Restoration—if he spent more on street improvements, he spent less on water and drains—and yet the problems posed by industrial and demographic growth were more acute. It is, however, always easier to condemn than to understand, and there is reason to believe that his detractors have not taken into account the difficulties that beset his administration.

A number of factors hindered the implementation of a radical urban planning program such as Haussmann and Napoleon III were to introduce in the 1850s.

One was that Rambuteau's powers were not as great as either Chabrol's or Haussmann's. From 1834 on the Municipal Council, which had previously been nominated, became elective. Councillors not only acquired greater powers, especially over the budget, but increasingly came to defend the interests of the arrondissements they represented, as evidenced in the debates over the city's shifting center of gravity and the conflicts of interest between Left and Right banks. Besides, in contrast with Napoleon III, Louis-Philippe showed little interest in public works in the capital and did not encourage his prefect to innovate. The funds that Rambuteau had at his disposal were also limited. He came to office in the midst of a financial crisis: the city's debt increased by 25.5 million francs between 1830 and 1834. And it was the financial orthodoxy of the time that the city's budget should be balanced and the municipal debt reduced. This orthodoxy was based in part on the experience of the costly debt burden that had been imposed on the city by the Allied occupation and the relief given during the period of famine food prices early in the Restoration. Rambuteau also feared a repetition of the popular disturbances that the capital had witnessed in the first years of the July Monarchy. This fear had two consequences. He was reticent to embark on any large public works program that would attract large numbers of workers to Paris who, when unemployed, might become insurgents. He was also anxious not only to alleviate the lot of the Parisian poor but to promote workers' self-help through primary education and savings banks. This explains why in his memoirs he proudly gives first place in the list of his achievements not to public works but to social welfare policies. This preoccupation was reflected in the budget. Although revenues remained generally stable throughout the 1815–50 period (they averaged 50.5 million a year in the 1830s and 1840s versus 46.4 million in the 1820s), expenditures on social services showed marked increases during Rambuteau's term of office. Not surprisingly, then, he proved to be a popular, paternalist prefect.

Even in public works Rambuteau was not without modest achievements. He added 3,000 beds to existing hospitals and built a new one (the Lariboisière). The Hôtel de ville and the Palais de justice were remodeled, as was the place de la Concorde. The laying of sidewalks was accelerated, and between 1833 and 1848 their total length increased from 16 to 195 kilometers. Street lighting was encouraged by the reorganization of the Parisian gas companies. Some new streets were built, the most notable of which was the rue Rambuteau in the overcrowded and congested Marais. Rambuteau once declared his policy to be "to give Parisians water, air and shade." Thanks to his efforts, trees were planted and urinals constructed throughout the city. There were also some minor improvements to water and sanitation facilities. New pipes were laid, and the Grenelle well was dug (this proved a disappointment). The insanitary Bièvre River was completely covered, and the city dump was moved from Montfaucon, too near Paris, to the Bondy forest, farther away.

Such modest improvements, however, failed to grapple properly with the unprecedented scale of urban problems posed by the growth of the capital.

Toward the end of his term of office, Rambuteau came to recognize this. He planned to rebuild the central markets (the Halles) and the opera house and in the first weeks of 1848 proposed an 80 million franc public works program. Even had this project been implemented, it would not have been enough. Only from 1853, with the alliance (and daring) of Haussmann and Napoleon III, was the city administration to possess the political and financial power and technical expertise to meet the challenge of urban planning, and not even then were by any means all the problems solved.

P. Debofle, "Les Travaux publics à Paris au XIX$^e$ siècle: hommes et programmes (1800–1914)," *L'Administration de Paris (1787–1977), actes du colloque tenu au Conseil d'Etat le 6 mai 1978* (Paris, 1979); C. Merruau, *Souvenirs de l'Hôtel de Ville de Paris, 1848–1852* (Paris, 1875); C.-P. B. Rambuteau, *Mémoires du comte de Rambuteau, publiés par son petit-fils . . .* (Paris, 1905); A. Robert, *Dictionnaire des parlementaires français*, vol. 5 (Paris, 1891); M. Roussier, "Apercus sur le fonctionnement du Conseil municipal de Paris au XIX$^e$ siècle (1800–1870)," *Etudes d'histoire et du droit parisien. Travaux et recherches de la Faculté de droit et des sciences économiques de Paris* vol. 16 (1970).

*Barrie M. Ratcliffe*

*Related entries:* BANKING; CHABROL DE VOLVIC; CHAMBER OF DE-PUTIES; CHARTER OF 1830; FOY; HUNDRED DAYS; JEWS; LOUIS-PHI-LIPPE; PARIS; PERIER; RESTORATION, FIRST; RESTORATION, SECOND; REVOLUTION OF 1830.

**RASPAIL, FRANCOIS-VINCENT** (1794–1878), doctor, publicist and republican activist. The son of a petit-bourgeois family from Carpentras, Raspail completed a brilliant theological education before becoming a lay teacher. On leaving the Midi he survived as a tutor in Paris for several years before beginning to publish his essentially independent scientific research.

Between 1825 and 1830 Raspail published about fifty articles ranging from botany, zoology, and paleontology to microscopic anatomy, physiology, and forensic medicine. These studies were based on an early statement of cell theory, and he may be seen as a founder of microchemistry. Notable among his early publications was the *Nouveau système de chimie organique* (1833), dedicated to his teacher, the abbé Eysséric. Raspail was also a pioneer advocate of antisepsis and improved sanitation and diet. His scientific career was limited by his continued refusal to accept official positions or awards.

From the mid-1830s Raspail's scientific work became subordinate to his work as a publicist in the areas of agricultural improvement and public health. His *Manuel-annuaire de la santé* (1845) sold 195,000 copies in the first five years and was reissued until 1947; *Le Fermier vétérinaire* (1854) was reissued until 1873. Also important were his studies of prison conditions and industrial safety. From his publications and products, notably based on camphor as a guard against contagion, came a comfortable living, and his reknown made his medical practice, where advice was free, too heavy a burden.

Raspail's concern for public health and popularizing medical knowledge cannot be divorced from his political and social activism, and he was closely involved in the three great revolutionary movements of the century. He fought on the barricades in 1830 but soon became a trenchant critic of the new regime. As president of the Société des amis du peuple, he was imprisoned for fifteen months from January 1832 after a famous defense in which he openly called for democracy, a republic, universal conscription, progressive taxation, workers' associations, and wage-fixing boards. However, he consistently opposed armed conspiracy and calls for a new war of European liberation. On his release he launched the daily *Le Réformateur* (October 1834-October 1835) with the financial help of Théophile de Kersausie. He was also imprisoned for six months in 1835 for moral complicity in Fieschi's plot to assassinate Louis-Philippe.

Raspail was prominent again in 1848 and is thought to have been at the head of the crowd that forced the Provisional Government to proclaim the Republic; he also launched *L'Ami du peuple* and presided over a major club. His involvement in the *journée* of 15 May led to his detention, and he was sentenced to six years in prison in March 1849; while in prison he was elected a deputy for Paris in the September by-elections and won 37,000 votes, mainly from Paris and Lyons, in the presidential elections of December 1848.

Raspail returned to France only with the general amnesty of 1859. In 1869 he launched *La République politique et sociale* with, among others, Auguste Vermorel, Elysée Recurt, and Gustave-Paul Cluseret, and was elected as deputy for Lyons. Although inactive during the Commune, he was a deputy for Marseilles from 1876, not before having been sentenced to a year's imprisonment at the age of eighty.

G. Duveau, *Raspail* (Paris, 1948); A. Robert, E. Bourloton, and G. Cougny, *Dictionnaire des parlementaires français*, 5 vols. (Paris, 1891); S. Wassermann, "Le Club de Raspail en 1848," *La Révolution de 1848*, vol. 5, (1908–9); G. Weill, *Histoire du parti républicain en France de 1814 à 1870* (Paris, 1900); D. B. Weiner, "François-Vincent Raspail: Doctor and Champion of the Poor," *French Historical Studies* 1 (1959).

*Peter McPhee*

*Related entries: L'AMI DU PEUPLE EN 1848*; DEMONSTRATIONS OF 1848; FIESCHI PLOT; LOUIS-PHILIPPE; PROVISIONAL GOVERNMENT; *LE RE-FORMATEUR*; REVOLUTION OF 1830; REVOLUTION OF 1848.

**RAUZAN, JEAN-BAPTISTE** (1757–1847), founder of the Society of Priests of the Missions of France. Born and educated in Bordeaux, he belonged at first to the clergy of that diocese. His reputation as a popular orator grew, and he was asked to train a group of popular preachers. The suspicions of Napoleon's police curtailed this first attempt, but after 1815, with the help of his friend Charles de Forbin-Janson, who had good contacts in the royal court, Rauzan was able to establish his society. He also founded a congregation of women for the education of girls, with the title of Sainte Clotilde (the first Christian queen of the Franks). Rauzan was a powerful orator, a personable man, and a zealous priest. During the fifteen years of the Restoration, there were few dioceses where his voice was not heard.

P. A. Delaporte, *Vie du Très Révérend Père Jean-Baptiste Rauzan* (Paris, 1857).

*Guillaume de Bertier de Sauvigny*

*Related entries:* FORBIN-JANSON; MISSIONS; PRIESTS OF THE MIS-SIONS OF FRANCE.

**REBOUL, JEAN** (1796–1864), baker and poet in Nîmes and legitimist and Catholic deputy to the Constituent Assembly from the Gard Department. Born on 3 January 1796 in Nîmes, a city badly split between its royalist Catholic and liberal Protestant factions, Reboul was the son of a Catholic locksmith who died while he was still young. Apprenticed to a baker at the age of fifteen, he became a copyist in a lawyer's office at twenty and then switched back to baking because there was more money in it. He had a passion for literature and admired Horace, Corneille, Racine, and Molière; he learned to read while he was working by putting a bookstand near where he kneaded his dough and paying a boy to turn the pages, his hands in the dough and his mind on poetry. In 1823 he wrote in French (a second language for working-class people in Nîmes) a cantata on the war with Spain in which French forces had crushed the revolution and restored the monarchy. In 1828 his sentimental "L'Ange et l'enfant" was published in the influential royalist Parisian daily *La Quotidienne*. His *Poésies*, first published in 1836, went through five editions with more than 10,000 copies printed. Reboul thus became the pioneer among the worker poets, attracting the attention and admiration of François-René de Chateaubriand, Alphonse de Lamartine (who, he declared, had inspired him to write poetry in the first place), Alexandre Dumas, père, and Charles Nodier. When Reboul visited Paris during the winter of 1839, the Chateaubriands had him to dinner. Mme. Chateaubriand invited Jean-Guillaume Hyde de Neuville to come dine with "this poet, a friend of God, of the king, and of the muses."

The political tone of Reboul's poetry was strongly Catholic and royalist, but its opinions were surprisingly close to those of the socialists. Like them, he regretted that the blood spilled in the 1830 Revolution had served only to allow "Macaire to fill his cash box." Like them, he considered the selfishness and materialism of the age to be its greatest evils, and he wanted to end "this ignoble duel between the rich and the poor":

> The people, looking for material wealth
> And never looking toward Heaven,
> The earth had lost her ability to love.
> She turned her eyes toward her splendid treasure;
> But science and art could not fill up the void
> That had been left by the exile of the idea of God.

Reboul believed that only the Catholic church and the Bourbon monarchy could bring forth a society of loving kindness in which the poor would be trusting and resigned, the rich would be charitable and concerned, and everyone would share the moralizing joy and comfort of the Roman Catholic faith. Reboul criticized the poor for their lack of resignation to God's will, but he placed the main responsibility for the social problems of the July Monarchy on the selfish and materialistic *gens honnêtes* of the middle class, and in 1850 he wrote that the 1848 Revolution had been God's just punishment upon them.

Reboul was a major worker poet. The press run of his collections of poetry was 4,000, about the same as for the works of Victor Hugo and Honoré de Balzac and double that of George Sand. Locally he was a hero, and he was easily elected to the Constituent Assembly in 1849 on the strength of his reputation as a poet. He voted with Pierre-Antoine Berryer and the legitimists. By 1849 he had lost interest in politics and did not run for the Legislative Assembly in 1849. During the Second Empire he began to switch from French to his native Provençal language and joined the young Mistral and the *félibrige* movement. He died in Nîmes on 29 May 1864. The Municipal Council of Nîmes gave him a public funeral, and later a statue of him, which still stands, was placed in a public square.

M. Bruyère, *Un Poète chrétien au XIXe siècle, Jean Reboul de Nîmes, 1796–1864* (Paris, 1925); J. Maitron, ed., *Dictionnaire biographique du mouvement ouvrier français*, vol. 3 (Paris, 1966); E. L. Newman, "L'Arme du siècle, c'est la plume: The French Worker Poets of the July Monarchy and the Spirit of Revolution and Reform," *Journal of Modern History* (1980) and *The French Worker Poets of the July Monarchy* (forthcoming); C. Pitollet, "Correspondance inédite de J. Reboul et de J. Roumanille," *Revue de langues romanes* (Montpellier, 1911); J. Reboul, *Dernières poésies* (Avignon, 1865), *Lettres* (Paris, 1865), *Poésies nouvelles* (Paris, 1846), and *Poésies, préface par Alexandre Dumas, . . . lettre par M. Alphonse de Lamartine*, (Paris, 1836); E. Ripert, *La Renaissance provençal* (Paris, 1953); E. Thomas, *Voix d'en bas; la poésie ouvrière du XIXe siècle* (Paris, 1979); F. Tristan, *Le Tour de France, journal inédit, 1843–1844* (Paris, 1973).

*Edgar Leon Newman*

*Related entries:* BALZAC; BERRYER, P.-A.; CHATEAUBRIAND; DUMAS; HUGO; HYDE DE NEUVILLE; LAMARTINE; LEGISLATIVE ASSEMBLY; MACAIRE; NODIER; *LA QUOTIDIENNE*; SPAIN, 1823 FRENCH INVASION OF; WORKER POETS.

**RECAMIER, JEANNE-FRANCOISE-JULIE-ADELAIDE BERNARD**
(1777–1849), social figure, famous beauty, and mistress of a salon. Julie Récamier was born in Lyons, the daughter of J.-F. Bernard, a banker who was called to the French finance ministry by Calonne in 1784. Récamier, who had been educated in the Déserte convent in Lyons, followed her parents to Paris where, at the age of fifteen, she married forty-two-year-old Jacques Récamier, a banker, on 24 April 1793. The marriage, more social than passionate, was never consummated, but her husband's purchase of the Necker family's *hôtel* in the rue Mont-Blanc brought Récamier into contact with Mme. de Staël (who described Récamier in her *Corinne*) and other literary figures in the capital. After Thermidor, Récamier's beauty and conversational skills enabled her to conduct a popular salon, vaguely

royalist in tone, and attract a long succession of male admirers, among them Lucien Bonaparte, Generals Jean-Baptiste Bernadotte and Jean-Victor Moreau, and several returned *émigré* nobles. Récamier declined a post as one of Josephine's ladies-in-waiting under the Consulate, and her friendship with de Staël and the reputation of her salon as a center of opposition to Bonaparte brought her under police surveillance. Although Récamier was apolitical in practice, her personal sympathies lay with the Bourbons.

Récamier's husband, a regent of the Bank of France, went bankrupt during the economic crisis of 1805, and de Staël welcomed Récamier at her home in Coppet, where Prince Augustus of Prussia (Frederick II's nephew) fell in love with her. At his urging, 'Récamier began divorce proceedings against her husband (who acquiesced), but these were never finished, and Récamier's platonic affair with Augustus, and a similar relationship with the young physicist André Ampère, lasted into the 1820s. Legally forbidden to live within 50 miles of Paris under the late Empire, she returned to Lyons, where she attracted the passionate attachment of Pierre-Simon Ballanche. A trip to Rome and Naples in 1814 led to a friendship with Joachim Murat and Caroline Bonaparte at the moment the rulers of Naples were abandoning Napoleon and seeking an accord with the Allies. Récamier persuaded Benjamin Constant to petition the Allied sovereigns to permit Murat to keep his throne after Napoleon's first abdication. Under the Second Restoration, Récamier began a long (but apparently platonic) affair with François-René de Chateaubriand, which was interrupted by frequent clashes of temperament and long separations. Récamier was widowed in 1830 and never remarried, refusing Chateaubriand's proposal after the death of his own wife in 1846.

Récamier's beauty and skills as a hostess were widely admired, though she could hardly be termed an intellectual and never tried to write. Despite her ability to attract the devotion of a large number of prominent literary and political figures, it seems likely that none of her liaisons, like her marriage, was ever sexually consummated. An enigmatic figure who inspired passion without returning it, Récamier was praised in the works of Pierre-Simon Ballanche, Ampère, Constant, Chateaubriand, and de Staël and won a certain degree of immortality in her famous portrait by Jacques-Louis David.

E. Herriot, *Madame Récamier*, 2 vols. (Paris, 1926); H. Sedgwick, *Madame Récamier* (New York, 1940); *Souvenirs et correspondance tirés des papiers de Mme. Récamier*, 2 vols. (Paris, 1859).

*David Longfellow*

*Related entries:* AMPERE; BALLANCHE; BERNADOTTE; CHATEAU-BRIAND; CONSTANT; DAVID; STAEL-HOLSTEIN.

**RECURT, ADRIEN-BARNABE ATHANASE DE** (1798–1872), member of the Left opposition to Louis-Philippe, minister of the interior under the Provisional Government of 1848, and minister of public works under Eugène Cavaignac. Recurt's early concern for the social question found him caring for the poor in the faubourg St. Antoine, fighting on the barricades in 1830, and later (1833) serving on the Central Committee of the Société des droits de l'homme. Although he sat with Louis Blanc and Alexandre-Auguste Ledru-Rollin on the radical republican newspaper *La Réforme* in 1845 and 1848, Recurt sided with the more moderate *Le National* after February 1848. After serving as deputy mayor of Paris from March to April, he was elected to the Constituent Assembly from the Hautes-Pyrénées. If Recurt defended universal manhood suffrage, the representation of workers and peasants in the National Assembly, and popular membership in the National Guard, he became increasingly preoccupied with preserving law, order, and the status quo.

As minister of the interior from 11 May 1848 to 28 June 1848, Recurt ousted popular republican clubs from municipal and state-owned buildings and eventually dissolved all clubs implicated in the 15 May insurrection. Later, he first opposed and then supported Eugène Cavaignac's brutal repression of the workers' uprising in June and himself participated in the government's attack on the faubourg St. Antoine. Following the June Days, Recurt was relieved of the Ministry of the Interior by Cavaignac and made minister of public works.

Recurt's effort to maintain social peace led him to support government purchase of railroads and funding of railroad construction in order to provide employment for construction workers. In July 1848, he introduced compulsory sickness and accident insurance for workers in public works projects. Suspected as too sympathetic to the working class, Recurt was removed from the Ministry of Public Works in October and made prefect of the Seine. After the defeat of Cavaignac in December 1848, Recurt resigned and eventually left politics altogether.

P. H. Amann, *Revolution and Mass Democracy: The Paris Club Movement in 1848* (Princeton, 1975); F. de Luna, *The French Republic under Cavaignac, 1848* (Princeton, 1969); G. Duveau, *1848* (Paris, 1965); A. Robert, E. Bourloton, and G. Cougny, *Dictionnaire des parlementaires français*, 5 vols. (Paris, 1891).

*Laura Frader*

*Related entries:* CAVAIGNAC, L.-E.; CONSTITUTION OF 1848; LEGISLATIVE ASSEMBLY; *LE NATIONAL*; NATIONAL GUARD; PROVISIONAL GOVERNMENT; *LA REFORME*; REVOLUTION OF 1848; SOCIETY OF THE RIGHTS OF MAN.


*LE REFORMATEUR* (1834–1835), republican newspaper of the July Monarchy. This was a militant republican newspaper founded in 1834 by François-Vincent Raspail and Théophile de Kersausie. In June 1834 the editors were condemned to a month's imprisonment and a 10,000 franc fine for defending the men arrested for the April rising; in May 1835 a similar penalty was inflicted on them for an article described as insulting to the members of the Chamber of Deputies. With the passage of the September Laws in 1835, which made it a criminal offense to express directly or indirectly the wish, hope, or threat of the overthrow of constitutional monarchy, the *Réformateur* was clearly doomed. After three heavy penalties in ten days and with most of its editors in prison, it ceased publication in November 1835.

I. Collins, *The Government and the Newspaper Press in France, 1814–1881* (Oxford, 1959); G. Perreux, *Au Temps des sociétés secrètes* (Paris, 1931).

*Irene Collins*

*Related entries:* CENSORSHIP; CHAMBER OF DEPUTIES; PRESS LAWS; RASPAIL.

*LA REFORME* (1843–1850), important radical republican daily, appearing 29 July 1843–12 January 1850, except for a two-month suspension following the insurrection of 13 June 1849. Its founders were S.-R.-P. Grandménil, a wealthy secret society activist, and the editors Ferdinand Flocon and Eugène Baune, two radical journalists and former carbonari. The chief editor from 1848 was Charles Ribeyrolles, a former editor of *L'Emancipation* of Toulouse, regarded by contemporaries as one of the most gifted journalists of the period. The paper was founded by 250 shareholders, mostly proprietors, merchants, and professional men. Despite its undoubted importance as the focus of a radical critique of the July Monarchy, the paper rarely sold more than 2,000 copies per day before 1848, and almost three-quarters of these were provincial subscriptions.

The role of the *Réforme*, as of its more moderate rival the *National*, in opposition to Louis-Philippe and during the February Revolution was reflected in the important posts filled in 1848 by the score or so of its editors and writers. These included positions in the Provisional Government (Flocon, Louis Blanc, and Alexandre-Auguste Ledru-Rollin; Albert and François Arago had also been loosely associated with the paper); appointments of eight editors as *commissaires* of the government; the head of the Luxembourg Commission (Blanc), Paris prefect of police (Marc Caussidière), director of the post office (Etienne Arago), chief of staff of the National Guard (Joseph Guinard), and secretary of state for the navy (Victor Schoelcher). Twelve of them were elected to the Constituent Assembly in April. Among the other contributors before 1848 had been Pierre-Joseph Proudhon, Mikhail Bakunin, Friedrich Engels, Karl Marx, Constantin Pecqueur, George Sand, Savinien Lapointe, Charles Lagrange, Pierre Leroux, Jules Michelet, and Edgar Quinet.

Many of the editors, whose ages were thirty-six to forty-eight in 1848, had been involved in the Carbonari of the 1820s, the 1830 Revolution, and the risings of the 1830s. They were, and saw themselves to be, in the Jacobin tradition: they were totally committed to political democracy and saw themselves as representing the interests of workers and petits bourgeois. They stressed their affinity with the Jacobins of 1792–93, and it was this intransigent republicanism that explains the hostility of their opponents.

What distinguished them from their Jacobin precursors was their insistence on sweeping social reforms as the prime objective of political action and their interest in socialist or neosocialist theory. They insisted that the state should take the initiative in guaranteeing work, in supporting associations and producers' cooperatives, and in making rulings about hours and conditions of work. In this way they soon distanced themselves from Proudhon, Etienne Cabet, and others. However, despite Flocon's friendship with Marx and Engels, the paper urged social reforms as a way of bridging social cleavages and avoiding class war. This was to be at the heart of Marx's critique of the radicals in 1848.

*La Réforme* had a vision of foreign affairs as an extension of the struggle inside France. In language reminiscent of 1792, they called for an alliance of progressive forces against the Metternich system and carried an impressive array of reports from Germany, Italy, Poland, Great Britain and other European and American countries.

Central to radical ideology and an issue that dogged the republican movement in the 1840s, was the question of legitimate collective action. Under what circumstances could insurrection be justified by people for whom national and popular sovereignty was sacred? The paper had been launched in the aftermath of the abortive rising of 1839, which was seen in retrospect as adventurist, but at the same time it followed its predecessor, *Le Journal du peuple*, in attacking *Le National's* support for the restricted reform campaign of the parliamentary opposition. *La Réforme's* position was that an insurrection against a democratically elected government was insupportable; only a rising that was collective, spontaneous, and in defense of sovereign rights could be justified.

This explains the hesitation of the editors in February 1848 when they initially refused to call for a rising; they were convinced that it would simply offer an occasion for the government to massacre workers. It also explains the paper's criticism of the *journées* of 16 April and 15 May 1848 and why, in June, the paper felt compelled to support the Constituent Assembly and Eugène Cavaignac: although the Assembly was dominated by men the radicals detested, they had been democratically elected.

Despite this, the paper never ceased calling for radical social change. On the morrow of 15 May, it proclaimed that "being republicans, we are therefore also socialists." It was unique on the side of order in June in carrying lead articles calling for social reforms, and it castigated the hysteria of the Assembly and the press. But the civil war was a shattering experience for radicals who had always assumed that socialism was the inevitable corollary of democracy.

The paper became increasingly critical of Cavaignac after June, helping to launch the Solidarité républicaine in November 1848 and campaigning for Ledru-Rollin in December. It combined with other radical papers in the successful *démoc-soc* campaign of May 1849. However, the paper was fatally weakened when many of its writers were imprisoned or exiled after the abortive coup of 13 June 1849, for them a justifiable insurrection given that the Constitution expressly forbade a military expedition of the type Louis-Napoleon had ordered in Italy.

F. A. de Luna, *The French Republic under Cavaignac, 1848* (Princeton, 1969); L. A. Loubère, *Louis Blanc* (Evanston, Ill., 1961); K. Marx, *The Class Struggles in France, 1848–1850*; K. Marx and F. Engels, *Collected Works*, vols. 6–7 (London, 1976–77);

P. B. McPhee, "The Crisis of Radical Republicanism in the French Revolution of 1848," *Historical Studies* 16 (1974).

*Peter McPhee*

*Related entries:* ARAGO FAMILY; BLANC; CABET; CARBONARI; CAUSSIDIERE; CAVAIGNAC, L.-E.; FLOCON; *LE JOURNAL DU PEUPLE*; JUNE DAYS; LAGRANGE; LEDRU-ROLLIN; LEROUX; LUXEMBOURG COMMISSION; MARX; MICHELET; *LE NATIONAL*; PROUDHON; QUINET; REPUBLICANS; ROMAN EXPEDITION; *SOLIDARITE REPUBLICAINE*; WORKERS' COOPERATIVES.

## REICHSTADT, NAPOLEON-FRANCIS-JOSEPH-CHARLES, DUKE OF

(1811–1832), also known as king of Rome, Napoleon II, prince of Parma. Reichstadt was the only child of Napoleon I and his second wife, Marie Louise, daughter of Emperor Francis I of Austria. His birth was greeted with joy and enthusiasm in France and even beyond, for it appeared to guarantee the survival of the French Empire and the permanence of the Franco-Austrian alliance as the basis of European peace. After Napoleon's unconditional abdication on 6 April 1814, the boy left France forever on 2 May for his grandfather's court in Vienna. As Napoleon's heir, he had borne the title king of Rome. Now, the victorious Allies made Marie Louise duchess of Parma, Piacenza, and Guestalla and gave her son the rank of prince of Parma. The young prince and his mother remained in Vienna throughout the Hundred Days. After Waterloo, Napoleon abdicated in his son's favor (22 June 1815), and the Chamber of Representatives, while never officially proclaiming him, did recognize the boy as Napoleon II. The provisional government, however, ignored his claims and restored Louis XVIII.

Deprived of his beloved French governess, Mme. de Montesquiou, on his fourth birthday, the boy was turned over to Count Maurice Dietrichstein to be raised as a Hapsburg archduke. Napoleon had feared such an outcome: "I would rather see my son's throat cut than to have him brought up as an Austrian prince in Vienna." But Marie Louise was determined, in her words, "to make a German prince out of him. . . . He will have to make a name for himself, since the name he has by birth is an unfortunate one." She left for Parma in March 1816, thereafter returning to Vienna and her son for only occasional visits. The boy's grandfather and other relatives doted on him, for by all accounts he was a charming child, sweet tempered and intelligent, if somewhat introverted, reserved, and suspicious—the consequence of losing father, homeland, rank, even name and language. Family and tutors called him Francis (Franz) rather than Napoleon, spoke to him only in German, and did not discuss his father or his past life except in response to direct questions from the boy.

On 24 November 1816, Marie Louise renounced her son's right of succession to her duchies, and he lost his title prince of Parma. It would not do for a son of Napoleon to reign in Italy. His grandfather compensated him with a hereditary territory in December 1817—the Bavarian Palatinate in Bohemia—and on 11 July 1818 bestowed on him the title of duke of Reichstadt. From the age of fifteen, Reichstadt showed a keen interest in his father, whom he idolized. He wrote Marie Louise in November 1826: "For a soldier on the threshold of his career, can there be a finer and more admirable model [than Napoleon]?" While rejecting what he termed the "contemptible role" of a political adventurer, he nevertheless dreamed of future glory and restoration to his father's throne. Yet he also spoke of serving Austria and was proud to become a captain in his grandfather's army in August 1828.

The flourishing Napoleonic legend of the 1820s awakened public interest in Napoleon's heir—the "Eaglet," as he came to be known. Reichstadt was the focus of Bonapartist and nationalist hopes in France and Europe. Conspirators floated wild schemes to bring him back to France or to find him a throne in Italy, Poland, Belgium, or Greece. French peddlers hawked every kind of trinket bearing his image: prints, playing cards, tobacco boxes, scarves, dishes. Auguste-Marseille Barthélemy's poem, "Le Fils de l'homme" (1829), declared: "You are nothing more today than the Son of the Man, yet what king's son would not trade his title and future sceptre for this obscure name!" The Austrian government dared not let the duke travel abroad, and Dietrichstein allegedly remarked, "The Prince is not a prisoner, but . . . he is in a very special position."

The dreams and hopes came to nothing. The July Revolution did not turn to Reichstadt's advantage. He was, in any case, a sickly young man with, in his doctor's words, "an iron soul in a body of crystal." Already in the last stages of tuberculosis, he caught pneumonia in January 1832 and never recovered. He died on the morning of 22 July 1832 and was entombed with his Hapsburg ancestors. On 15 December 1940, the German government transferred his body to Napoleon's tomb at the Invalides in Paris as a gesture of friendship for the collaborationist Vichy government.

O. Aubry, *The King of Rome, Napoleon II, "L'Aiglon"* (Philadelphia and London, 1932); A. Castelot, *Napoleon's Son* (London, 1960); H. Welschinger, *Le Roi de Rome (1811–1832)* (Paris, 1897).

*Michael Sibalis*

*Related entries:* BARTHELEMY, A.-M.; BONAPARTISM; HUNDRED DAYS; LOUIS XVIII; REVOLUTION OF 1830; WATERLOO, BATTLE OF.

**REMUSAT, FRANCOIS-MARIE-CHARLES, COMTE DE** (1797–1875), essayist, philosopher, and politician. Charles de Rémusat was born in Paris on 14 March 1797 to Augustin Rémusat, formerly a lawyer connected with the parliament of Aix, and his young wife, a niece of the minister Vergennes. Because of their political connections, the Rémusats secured and retained important positions during the Consulate and the Empire, Augustin Rémusat becoming first chamberlain of the emperor and supervisor of theaters. Young Charles hence moved from his earliest days among the Parisian political and intellectual elite. He owed his education primarily to two sources, one formal and one informal. At the Lycée Napoléon, he proved himself a brilliant student, while discovering a taste for philosophy, especially that of Condillac. Rémusat's less formal but no less important education came in the principal Parisian salons, where he encountered, among others, the comte Louis-Mathieu Molé, the duc de Pasquier, Prosper de Barante, and Charles-Maurice de Talleyrand.

Upon leaving the lycée, Rémusat undertook legal studies, qualifying as a lawyer in 1819, a profession he never practiced. During this same period of time, he pursued his interest in philosophy and composed light verse and amusing songs. An early sympathizer with liberal ideas and an advocate of parliamentary government, Rémusat began to make his mark in French political life when scarcely twenty. He attracted the attention of François Guizot and Pierre-Paul Royer-Collard with a precocious essay on the recently published *Considérations sur la Révolution française* of Mme. de Staël, an essay Guizot published with a laudatory introduction in the *Archives philosophiques, politiques, et littéraires*. This essay and others brought Rémusat into contact with the *doctrinaires*, a group of moderately liberal political thinkers that formed around Royer-Collard in 1817 and 1818. To the Lycée français, Rémusat contributed articles on the theater, on the popular novel *Jacopo Ortis*, and on the works of Mme. de Staël; he also translated the plays of Goethe and the *De legibus* of Cicero. Following these essays came the publication of *De la Procédure par jurés en matière criminelle*, one of Rémusat's few testimonials to his legal training. In the tumultuous year of 1820, he published several political pamphlets, all under the inspiration and patronage of François Guizot.

In the early 1820s and probably after the comte de Villèle dismissed his father from his post as a prefect, Rémusat's opposition to the Restoration government became more pronounced, and he joined with Adolphe Thiers, recently arrived from Marseilles, with whom he formed a close personal relationship and whose political ideas he shared. Marriage to a niece of Casimir Périer's strengthened Rémusat's connections with the political opposition. In 1823, he joined with Thiers and with other young, talented, and ambitious men to write for Jacques Coste's short-lived *Tablettes universelles*. He also worked diligently on behalf of liberal candidates in the elections of 1824. When the *Tablettes* disappeared in 1824, a victim of a government scheme to reduce the number of opposition newspapers in Paris, Rémusat and his friends transferred their talents and energy to the newly founded *Globe* and made it during the first six years of its brief but exciting existence the leading intellectual journal in Paris. The considerable time and effort devoted by Rémusat to the *Globe* notwithstanding, he also found the leisure to write not only a refutation of the abbé de Lamennais's *Essai sur l'indifférence* and *Essai sur la nature du pouvoir* but also light poetry, political songs, and a number of dramas. On the controversial subject of romanticism, Rémusat, who wrote critical essays for the *Globe* on the poetry of Alphonse de Lamartine and Victor Hugo, favored a moderate, restrained version of the new literature. While also writing for the *Revue encyclopédique* and the *Courrier français*, Rémusat did not neglect politics. When in 1827 the Restoration government relaxed some of its restrictions on political activities, he quickly assumed a political role by serving, along with Guizot and many of his colleagues from the *Globe*, on the executive committee of the Aide-toi, le ciel t'aidera, a society formed to encourage liberal voting in the campaign of 1827.

By 1830, Rémusat's political convictions were such that, when Charles X proclaimed the July Ordinances, he was among the first to demand a public statement of protest. After hearing the lawyer André Dupin give his opinion as to the illegality of the ordinances, Rémusat hastened to the offices of the *National*, and once there he stood and watched while his friend Thiers drafted the famous protest of the journalists, which he then signed as a representative of the *Globe*. The next day, 27 July, Rémusat went further and published in the *Globe* an essay in which he described the royal ordinances as criminal. Forced temporarily by fear of arrest to seek a place of concealment, he nevertheless published on 30 July an article in which he argued that the duc d'Orléans should be called to the throne. Active from the beginning to the end of the July Revolution, Rémusat must be reckoned one of the makers of the July Monarchy.

During the eighteen years of the July Monarchy, Rémusat played a minor political role but meanwhile distinguished himself as an author. Elected in 1830 a deputy from the Haute-Garonne, he represented this department until 1848, sitting during the 1830s with the group centered on Casimir Périer, with the so-called Party of Order. Although he still professed to hold liberal ideas, by which he meant a faith in the liberty of human reason and in progress, Rémusat opposed democratic ideas. In the reaction that followed the attempt of Fieschi to assassinate Louis-Philippe in 1835, he voted for a number of restrictive and repressive laws, notably limitations on the press and on freedom of association. After serving briefly in the Ministry of the Interior in 1836, Rémusat in 1840 accepted from Thiers the post of minister of the interior; in this capacity, he had a major part in the return of Napoleon's ashes to France from St.-Helena.

Between 1841 and 1848, Rémusat, although he retained his close ties with Thiers and sat in opposition to the rule of Guizot, devoted most of his time, energy, and talents to intellectual and literary pursuits, primarily his philosophical studies. From his youthful partisanship of Condillac, Rémusat evolved into an advocate of Victor Cousin's eclecticism. Not a particularly original thinker, he nonetheless published a number of elegantly written essays, later collected in *Essais de philosophie*. He also devoted two volumes to a study of Peter Abelard and two more to a study of contemporary German philosophy. Rémusat's *Passé et présent*, important because it brought together many of his Restoration essays, first appeared in 1847. His many contributions to French intellectual life were recognized by his contemporaries, who elected him to the Académie des sciences morales et politiques in 1842 and to the Académie française four years later.

Charles de Rémusat, who regretted the fall of the July Monarchy, took but a minor part in the Revolution of 1848. Although named to the Thiers cabinet of 23–24 February by Louis-Philippe in a last-minute futile attempt to save his throne, Rémusat otherwise avoided participation in the events of February. Returned by the Haute-Garonne in May to the Assembly, he voted for the Constitution of 1848, despite his hostility to the new Republic. Indeed, on most matters brought before the Assembly, Rémusat voted with the conservatives. In 1849, he again opposed the spread of democracy and frequently supported the politics of Louis-Napoleon, elected president of the Second Republic the previous December, by giving his assent to the law of 31 May, which restricted the universal suffrage gained in 1848, and the law of 16 June, which banned public meetings. Not much time elapsed, however, before Rémusat turned against the growing despotism of Louis-Napoleon. When this nephew of the great Napoleon seized power in the coup d'état of 2 December 1851, Rémusat joined with other elected representatives to protest this event and to dismiss Louis-Napoleon from his presidency. For this audacity, Rémusat served several days in prison and found himself exiled from France; although allowed to return to his homeland shortly after, he largely avoided political activities during the Second Empire, turning once again to his writing. Rémusat appears to have returned to many of the liberal ideas of his youth, and he seems to have become willing to accept democracy. In *Angleterre au XVIII<sup>e</sup> siècle* of 1856, he favorably compared the French Revolution of 1789 with the English Revolution of 1688 and contended that he had maintained a lifelong commitment to the idea of the English system of government in French society. Other works too numerous to mention poured from Rémusat's facile pen in the 1850s and 1860s. Finally, in 1869, when political activity again became possible, Rémusat helped found in Toulouse the *Progrès libéral*, a journal opposed to the rule of Napoleon III.

In the aftermath of the debacle of 1870–71, Rémusat reluctantly gave in to the urgings of his friend Thiers and became foreign minister, thereby becoming one of the founders of the Third Republic. He died in Paris on 6 June 1875.

Of a long life that spanned the period from the First Empire to the Third Republic, Rémusat left behind an invaluable memoir. Published in five volumes by Charles H. Pouthas, *Mémoires de ma vie* are among the most important sources of the history of France during the years between 1814 and 1852.

G. de Coral-Remusat, Preface to *Mémoires de ma vie*, vol. 1 (Paris, 1958–61); P. Duvergier de Hauranne, "M. Charles de Rémusat," *Revue des deux mondes*, 15 November 1875; P. Moreau, "Charles de Rémusat, Doctrinaire et dilettant du 'Globe,' " *Revue de la litterature comparée* 42 (1968); C. de Rémusat, *Correspondance de M. de Rémusat pendant les premières années de la Restauration*, ed. Paul de Rémusat, 6 vols. (Paris, 1883–?) and *Mémoires de ma vie*, 5 vols (Paris, 1958–1961); J. Simon, "Charles de Rémusat," in *Thiers, Guizot, Rémusat* (Paris, 1885).

*Robert Brown*

*Related entries:* AIDE-TOI, LE CIEL T'AIDERA; *ARCHIVES PHILOSO-PHIQUES, POLITIQUES, ET LITTERAIRES*; BARANTE; *LE COURRIER FRANCAIS*; COUSIN; *DOCTRINAIRES*; DUPIN, A.-M.-J.-J.; FIESCHI PLOT; *LE GLOBE*; GUIZOT; HUGO; LAMARTINE; LAMENNAIS; MOLE; *LE NATIONAL*; PASQUIER; PERIER; PRESS LAWS; ROMANTICISM; ROYER-COLLARD; STAEL-HOLSTEIN; *LES TABLETTES UNIVERSELLES;* TALLEYRAND; THIERS; VILLELE.

**RENAN, JOSEPH-ERNEST** (1823–1892), philologist, historian, and philosopher, whose theological writings based on his scientific studies provoked profound controversy. He was the first to apply the method of comparative philology to the study of history, especially religious history. Although Renan was a man of many facets, the one quality that dominates and explains his life and work is his intellectual curiosity. It was responsible for his abandoning not only the church but also the cloth. It was responsible for the label of "skeptic" that contemporaries applied to his search for historical truth in biblical texts. Nonetheless, it was the cornerstone of his idealism or religion, which envisioned man striving toward the attainment of perfection: "The goal of humanity is not repose: it is intellectual and moral perfection" (*L'Avenir de la science*).

Renan himself recognized that his Celtic origins tempered his rationality with a poetic and visionary quality. Youngest of three children born to a grocery merchant at Tréguier (Brittany), he lost his father at age five and was largely raised by his sister, Henriette, twelve years his senior, to whom he was devotedly attached. Destined for the priesthood from an early age, his brilliant performance led him from the ecclesiastical college at Tréguier, to the seminary of Saint-Nicolas-du-Chardonnay, then to the seminary of Issy, and finally, in 1843, to the important Saint-Sulpice, where occurred his fateful break with the church. The crisis of conscience that prevented him from taking vows was the direct outgrowth of his philological and critical study of Semitic languages, which led him to question the divine inspiration of the Bible and ultimately the fundamental tenets of orthodox, revealed religion.

After leaving Saint-Sulpice in 1845, Renan endured considerable hardship in order to complete studies for the *aggrégation* (1848) and subsequently a doctorate (1852) at the Sorbonne. He was already a distinguished scholar of Semitic languages, recognized by the Prix Volney (1847) and his nomination to a scholarly mission investigating Semitic manuscript holdings in Italian libraries (1849), as well as by his regular contributions to *La Revue des deux mondes* and the *Journal des débats*. In 1851, he was appointed to the Manuscript Department of the Bibliothèque nationale and devoted himself chiefly to biblical studies. In 1846 he married Cornelie Sheffer. The union produced three children, Ary, Noèmi, who died in infancy, and Ernestine.

After 1861 Renan's hitherto unexceptional life changed, and he began to scandalize the society he had belonged to. His excavations in that year at Gospel sites in Syria led him to doubt the Scriptures. He expressed those doubts in his *Vie de Jésus*, published in 1863, in which he contended that Jesus had been only a divinely inspired mortal.

Renan blended the scientific mind with the soul of a poet, and his gift for lucid but radiant prose infused scholarly treatises with a rare literary beauty. He was extremely prolific, and his writings ranged from philology to history to philosophy to personal reminiscences. His first book, *L'Avenir de la science* (1848–49), published only in 1890, demonstrates the unity of his thought. He was above all a humanist in his scholarly approach and his elevated conception of the human potential.

After the revolution in 1870, the Provisional Government reinstated Renan at the Collège de France. In 1878, he became a member of the French Academy. He died at the Collège in 1892, where he had been director since 1883.

R. M. Chadbourne, *Ernest Renan* (New York, 1968); K. Gore, *L'Idée de progrès dans la pensée de Renan* (Paris, 1970); Ph. Van Tieghem, *Renan* (Paris, 1948).

*Shelby A. Outlaw*

*Related entries:* ACADEMIE FRANCAISE; COLLEGE DE FRANCE; *JOURNAL DES DEBATS*; *LA REVUE DES DEUX MONDES*.

*LA RENOMMEE* (1819–1820), liberal daily newspaper. *La Renommée*, under the direction of Benjamin Constant, shared its staff with *Le Constitutionnel* and *Le Courrier français*. Although more moderate than the *Minerve française*, it was as much a target of early Restoration censors under the laws of 1819. It ceased publication in June 1820 and merged with *Le Courrier français*.

C. Ledré, *La Presse a l'assaut de la monarchie* (Paris, 1960).

*Daniel Rader*

*Related entries:* CONSTANT; *LE CONSTITUTIONNEL*; *LE COURRIER FRANCAIS*; *LA MINERVE*.

*LE REPRESENTANT DU PEUPLE* (1848), radical newspaper of the Second Republic. Pierre-Joseph Proudhon had little faith in the Second Republic proclaimed on 24 February 1848 and for a while kept away from involvement in political life. Himself a compositor, he was eventually persuaded by a group of printers to join them in producing a newspaper, *Le Représentant du peuple*, which began on 1 April 1848. Radical journalism gave Proudhon a much wider audience than ever before and played an important part in the evolution of his ideas. The *Représentant* suspended publication voluntarily during the June Days and was suppressed by the government in August 1848. In October it was replaced by a new paper, *Le Peuple*, with much the same staff, and with Proudhon this time as chief editor. The opening manifesto demanded work for all and property for all. Although it defended the right of the people to revolt, the *Peuple* did not advocate revolution, since it was unlikely to produce results beneficial to the people.

During the presidential election campaign in December 1848, Proudhon designated Louis-Napoleon Bonaparte as the most undesirable of all the candidates and immediately after his election published two bitter attacks on him. For these Proudhon served three years in prison. The *Peuple* was suppressed, but Proudhon managed from prison to contribute articles to a successor newspaper, *La Voix du peuple*. This too was suppressed in May 1850, and Proudhon sent a few further articles to yet another journalistic venture, *Le Peuple de 1850*, which lasted from June to October of that year.

M. B. Allen, "Proudhon in the Revolution of 1848," *Journal of Modern History* 24 (1952); E. Dolléans and J. L. Puech, *Proudhon et la révolution de 1848* (Paris, 1948); R.L. Hoffman, *Revolutionary Justice: The Social and Political Theory of P. J. Proudhon* (Champaign, Ill., 1972).

*Irene Collins*

*Related entries:* JUNE DAYS; PROUDHON; REVOLUTION OF 1848.


**REPUBLICANS.** By 1815, the idea of a republic had virtually no support in France. In the political vacuum that followed Napoleon's second abdication, there were cries for an Empire under Napoleon's son, for a liberal monarchy under the duc d'Orléans or the Swedish King Bernadotte, and loud demonstrations for the second restoration of the Bourbons, but there was no evidence of support for a republic. France had tried a republic during the Revolution, and it had failed. The optimism of the eighteenth-century *philosophes*, with their faith in the natural goodness of man, had been the most important victim of the Terror. Now there was a tangible shift in the national mood. Men who had been republicans during the Revolution publicly renounced their former beliefs. Maximin Isnard, the loud-voiced regicide *conventionnel* who in 1792 had voted in the National Convention for the execution of Louis XVI, now made annual pilgrimages to the spot where that execution had taken place more than twenty years before and shouted out his regrets, asking aloud for forgiveness from God and man. The royalist writer Charles Nodier remembered that his father, a former Jacobin, had warned him to "do against [the Republic] everything I did for it. . . . I die in the hope that it will be vanquished, for it comes from Hell." According to the radical writer Edgar Quinet, many old republicans found that during the Restoration "their children had taken other opinions, most often completely contrary ones." Victor Hugo portrayed the typical republican ex-*conventionnel* living during the Restoration as a tragic figure of monumental proportions "driven out, tracked, pursued, persecuted, maligned, mocked, spat upon, accursed, and proscribed. For many years," said Hugo's *conventionnel*, "I have felt that persons believed they had a right to despise me. My face has been held accursed by the poor ignorant mob, and while hating no one, I accepted the isolation of hatred."

A police survey of ex-*conventionnels* taken in 1816 generally confirms the accuracy of Hugo's melodramatic portrayal. These men, who had once been chosen to represent their districts, were now "generally mistrusted" and had "no influence at all." Throughout the Restoration, even the political Left would avoid being tarred with the brush of republicanism. When in 1819 the abbé Grégoire was elected to the Chamber of Deputies from his native Grenoble, the liberals made no effort to stop the Chamber from voiding his election and in fact tried to persuade the old republican *conventionnel* that he should not attempt to take his seat. In 1822–23 the revolutionary carbonari refused to make any commitment to the idea of a democratic republic and was instead dominated by Bonapartists and constitutional monarchist liberals. Neither the general public nor leftist politicians nor even political revolutionaries favored a republic. During the Bourbon Restoration, there was no place for republicans in France.

And yet there were republicans. Hidden cells of these political lepers used to meet and pass on their ideas to their children. Philarète Chasles remembered that during the Restoration his republican father had shut himself up in his house in Paris "with his anger, a large dog, his Deist library containing more than a thousand volumes attacking the divinity of Christ, and educated me." Marc Dufraisse recalled that he had been "brought up, under the Restoration, in the cult of the French Revolution and in the respect for the men who made it.... To my dazzled eyes, the heroes of the *Iliad* . . . were nothing next to [the republican revolutionary Louis Antoine [de] Saint-Just."

And so republican dynasties survived the hard times of the Bourbon Restoration. Hippolyte Carnot, Godefroy and Eugène Cavaignac, and Auguste Blanqui carried on the republican ideals of their fathers, as did Jean-Baptiste-Adolphe Charras, the republican soldier. Etienne Cabet, the republican revolutionary who turned to utopian communism, had been raised by the republican regicide Prieur de la Côte d'Or. The republican conspirator Joseph-Auguste Guinard and the republican journalists Marc-Antoine Jullien and Henry Boyer-Fonfrède were also sons of republican regicides.

These republicans could keep the flame during the Restoration, but they could do little to fan it. Nevertheless, time was on their side. As opposition to the Bourbon monarchy increased, memories of the Terror began to fade. The success of the American experiment made republicanism seem less terrifying; by 1825, René de Châteaubriand could write that "the world is now becoming republican" because of the growing strength of the nation that best represented the republican ideal: the United States. The marquis de Lafayette returned from his voyage to America in that year and began with his liberal friends to publish the *Revue américaine* highly favorable to his adopted land. Also in 1825, memories of an earlier great republic were stirred by the war for Greek independence. Meanwhile, a series of memoirs and histories was beginning to change the way Frenchmen remembered their Revolution. Léon Thiéssé's *Résumé de l'histoire de la Révolution française*, published in 1826, defended the more moderate Girondin republicans like Danton. In these years a collection of memoirs relating to the Revolution was put out by two enterprising publishers, Jean-François Barrière and Saint-Albin Berville, and many of these memoirs made the heroes of the Republic both more accessible and more sympathetic to literate Frenchmen. In 1829, the *Mémoires de René Levasseur de la Sarthe, ex-Conventionnel*, described the democratic and republican Constitution of 1793 as a "gigantic monument to human wisdom." On 8 June 1829 a republican newspaper, the *Tribune des départemens*, began publication under the editorship of Auguste and Victorin Fabre and Armand Marrast. It was joined by two other republican newspapers: *Jeune France*, directed by Eugène Plagniol and the novelist Léon Gozlan, which began to publish in June 1829, and *La Révolution*, under Eugène Plagniol, Anthony Thouret, and James Fazy, which first appeared on 16 June 1829. On

15 June 1830, another new journal, *Le Patriote, journal du peuple*, proclaimed that it was both republican and democratic. The circulation for these four newspapers was surprising: *Le Pour et le contre* (*La Révolution* appeared together with a royalist newspaper in a collective format known a *Le Pour et le contre*) had a press run of 4,000 to 5,000 copies of each issue, while *La Tribune des départemens* and *La Patriote* each ran 1,000 copies and *Jeune France* ran 500 copies, compared with a press run of 4,000 copies for the Orleanist *National* and about 15,000 for the liberal *Constitutionnel*. By the time the July Revolution of 1830 broke out, republicanism, with its radical young supporters, its four Parisian and half-dozen provincial newspapers, and its growing number of history books and memoirs, could command an overflowing thimbleful of support.

"The republican party had the first hand in the Revolution and its power was immense," Lafayette wrote from Paris to an American friend on 18 August 1830. Indeed, the entire cohort of young republicans had thrown its full weight against the monarchy. On 29 July Bastide, Guinard, Godefroy Cavaignac, Thomas, and Joubert had crossed the Pont Royal to assault the Tuileries Palace, and Guinard had planted the tricolored flag of the revolution there. Despite Lafayette's (and their own) attempts to glorify their role in the 1830 Revolution, however, the republicans' participation was no more than incidental to it, and their demands that a republic be installed in place of the fallen Bourbons were easily swept aside. In fact, the revolutionary crowd had been hostile to republicans, silencing those who dared to shout "Vive la République!" and attacking the headquarters of the *Tribune des départemens*. On July 29, the National Guard had arrested the republican Godefroy Cavaignac. The crowd was strongly Bonapartist, and the liberal leadership wanted a crown and a constitution to protect their liberty and property, and so the handful of republicans, who on 30 July gathered at the restaurant Lointier, never had a chance.

They did try. On 30 July a delegation of 400 of the most violent student republicans, including Bastide, Thomas, Etienne Arago, Guinard, Trélat, Marrast, Marchais, Boinvilliers, Alexandre Chevollon, Godefroy Cavaignac, and Joseph Degousseé, all armed to the teeth, descended on Lafayette and asked him to order them to expel Charles X from France. After he refused, they went to the *National* to discuss the possibility of continuing the revolution. Here they met the Orleanist Adolphe Thiers, who brought them straight to the duc d'Orléans. Boinvilliers demanded that France at once abrogate the treaties of 1815 and march to its natural frontier on the Rhine. He asked for the abolition of both nobilities (both the legitimate and the Bonapartist nobility). Jules Bastide asked for the convocation of primary assemblies under universal suffrage to choose a new form of government for France. The duke insisted that the rump Chamber of Deputies (minus those deputies who had fled with Charles X) constituted the true representatives of the nation. Furious, on 1 August the republicans invaded the Municipal Commission at the Hôtel de ville, breaking down the door with their rifle butts. Here they received assurances from Audry de Puyraveau, but that afternoon the famous "republican kiss," which Lafayette gave to the duc d'Orléans on the balcony of the Hôtel de ville, made France a monarchy again. According to Lafayette, France had been given a "republican throne."

The republicans kept trying. They planned to provoke an insurrection for the night of 4 August but Lafayette told them that he would not tolerate such a thing, and so instead they held a demonstration in which they asked the chambers to call for a meeting of the primary assemblies. Godefroy Cavaignac was thanked on 4 August for sacrificing his republican ideals. "You are wrong to thank us; we only stopped fighting because we were too weak. It was too hard to make the people, who had fought shouting *'Vive la Charte!'* understand that their first act after their victory should be to arm themselves to destroy it."

In order to teach the people, the republicans established the Society for the Rights of Man, whose goal was to bring about a democratic and republican revolution. They had two things in their favor. First, the people had behaved well during the July Revolution of 1830; perhaps they were now educated enough and wise enough to be entrusted with their nation's government. Second, France was running out of kings, and if the Orléans monarchy should fall, France might become a republic by default.

Indeed, France became a republic after the final defeat of the republicans. The Society of the Rights of Man tried to turn the funeral of General Jean-Maximin Lamarque in 1832 into a revolutionary movement, and in that same year they tried unsuccessfully to turn the revolt of the *canuts* in Lyons into a republican revolution. They had no more success in Lyons in 1834, and their attempt to start an uprising in Paris, which resulted in the massacre of the rue Transnonain, was rather ridiculous. The conspiracy of the Society of the Seasons in 1839 was the republicans' swan song. After that date, Louis-Philippe was safe on his throne; republicanism was now a journalistic form rather than a political ideal, a fashion instead of a belief. Former republican revolutionaries like Cabet, Bazard, and Buchez were converted to various sects of socialism, a system that could be installed without a change of dynasty.

And then, after the revolutionary movement had lost its strength, came the revolution. In 1848 there was first a series of banquets, then a revolt, and then the end of the dynasty. France, lacking a king, had become a Republic.

The stock of the old republicans went up, and several of them entered the government along with Alphonse de Lamartine. Yet the French people had not been consulted, and, when they were, both Paris and the provinces voted solidly for the name of Bonaparte. The Second Republic was swept away but not before it had attempted some important social reforms and gained a foothold in the minds of the working classes.

Napoleon III did not eliminate republicanism from France, but it never threatened his hold on government. France became a Republic in 1870 because, once again, all other alternatives had been eliminated. Even then and even now, the Republic has never been completely accepted in France; there have always been those who felt that the people ought not to be entrusted with ultimate responsibility for government. The ghost of Bonaparte is made of this distrust. It has materialized

in the form of MacMahon, Boulanger, the anti-Dreyfusards, Pétain, and to some
extent de Gaulle. The ghost still lives. Republicans in France may never have
a peaceful rest.

M. Agulhon, *The Republican Experiment, 1848–1852*, trans. Janet Lloyd (London
1983); E. Eisenstein, "The Evolution of the Jacobin Tradition in France: The Survival
and Revival of the Ethos of 1793 under the Bourbon and Orleanist Regimes" (Ph.D.
diss., Ratcliffe College, 1951); T. W. Margadant, *French Peasants in Revolt: The Insurrection of 1851* (Princeton, 1979); J. M. Merriman, *The Agony of the Republic: The
Repression of the Left in Revolutionary France, 1848–1851* (New Haven, 1978); B. M.
Moss, *The Origins of the French Labor Movement: The Socialism of Skilled Workers,
1830–1914* (Berkeley, 1976); E. L. Newman, "Republicans during the Bourbon Res-
toration in France, 1814–1830 (Ph.D. diss., University of Chicago, 1969); R. Price, *The
French Second Republic: A Social History* (Ithaca, N.Y., 1972); A. B. Spitzer, *Old
Hatreds and Young Hopes: The French Carbonari against the Bourbon Restoration*
(Cambridge, Mass., 1971); I. Tchernoff, *Le Parti républicain sous la monarchie de juillet*
(Paris, 1901); G. Weill, *Histoire du Parti Républicain en France, 1814–1870* (Paris,
1900).

*Edgar Leon Newman*
*Related entries:* ARAGO FAMILY; AUDRY DE PUYRAVAULT; BASTIDE;
BAZARD; BERNADOTTE; BLANQUI, L.-A.; BUCHEZ; CABET; CARBON-
ARI; CARNOT, L.-H.; CAVAIGNAC, L.-E.; CAVAIGNAC, G.-E.-L.;
CHARRAS; CHATEAUBRIAND; *LE CONSTITUTIONNEL*; FABRE, J.-R.-
A.; FABRE, M.-J.-J.-V.; GREGOIRE; GUINARD; HUGO; *LA JEUNE
FRANCE*; LAFAYETTE, M.-J.-P.-Y.-R.-G.; LAMARQUE; LAMARTINE;
LYONS, REVOLTS IN; MARRAST; MUNICIPAL COMMISSION; *LE NA-
TIONAL*; NODIER; *LE PATRIOTE*; QUINET; REICHSTADT; *LA REVOLU-
TION*; SOCIETY OF THE RIGHTS OF MAN; SOCIETY OF THE SEASONS;
THIERS; THIESSE; THOMAS; TRANSNONAIN, MASSACRE OF THE RUE;
TRELAT; *LA TRIBUNE DES DEPARTEMENS*.

*LA REPUBLIQUE* (1848–1851), important republican daily newspaper, 25
February 1848–2 December 1851. The editor was Eugène Bareste, a prolific
writer and classics scholar before 1848 and the author of a very popular
*Nostradamus* (1840), from which came the political jibe "Barestadamus" in
1848. Among the other editors and contributors were Pierre Joigneaux (author
of a regular column, "Aux Cultivateurs"), Pierre Leroux, Paul Rochery, J.-M.
Cayla, Paul-Mathieu Laurent de l'Ardèche, Agricol Perdiguier, and Adolphe
Guéroult (the father of Pauline Roland's first child). Average sales climbed from
12,000 in March 1848 to 20,800 (August), 37,200 (October), and 43,225
(December), with a peak of 56,493 sales on 30 January 1849. The expansion
of caution money in 1849–50 seems to have reduced sales thereafter. The paper
was characterized by extensive provincial reports and published a provincial
edition until June 1848.

*La République* was the most durable and important of the radical press under
the Second Republic. Its relative caution, which earned it the nickname *La Fausse*

*république* in reference to Théophile Thoré's paper, enabled it to survive the increasing repression of these years, including the sacking of its offices by police on 13 June 1849, though Bareste was finally sentenced to six months' imprisonment in November 1851. From the outset, however, it called for the right to work and claimed that 1848 had changed only personnel, leaving structures unreformed.

Like *La Réforme*, it urged leniency in June 1848, while not supporting the insurgents, and was increasingly critical of Eugène Cavaignac. It supported both Alexandre-Auguste Ledru-Rollin and François-Vincent Raspail in December 1848 but only to protest at having presidential elections at all. It helped found Solidarité républicaine in November 1848 and the Association générale pour la propagande socialiste early in 1849. While a consistent critic of governmental repression, it always looked to electoral action, even after the law of 31 May 1850. Its target on the Left was Pierre-Joseph Proudhon, attacked both by Leroux and by Pauline Roland and Jeanne Deroin, for whom *La République* was the only sympathetic major paper. Indeed the paper was unusually supportive of women's rights in general, arguing for equal pay, though ambiguous about political rights. It shared Leroux's spiritual conception of the Republic as the march of humanity toward a Christian socialism, a process begun in 1789 and for which the socialists of 1850 were being persecuted in the same way as the early Christians.

C. Bellanger, J. Godechot, P. Guiral, and F. Terrou, eds., *Histoire générale de la presse française*, vol. 2 (Paris, 1969); *Dictionnaire de biographie française* (Paris, 1933–).

*Peter McPhee*

*Related entries:* CAVAIGNAC, L.-E.; DEROIN; JOIGNEAUX; JUNE DAYS; LEDRU-ROLLIN; LEROUX; PERDIGUIER; PROUDHON; RASPAIL; REPUBLICANS; ROLAND; SOLIDARITE REPUBLICAINE.


**RESSEGUIER, JULES DE** (1789–1862), minor poet and member of romantic salons and cénacles. Bernard-Marie-Jules de Rességuier was born at Toulouse in January 1789. For generations, family members held prominent positions in the parliament of that city. His parents having fled the horrors of the Revolution, Jules and his brother Adrien were abandoned to the care of their paternal grandmother and an aunt. A family friend, professor at the collège du bas Languedoc and prominent figure of the Académie des jeux-floraux, provided them with a solid intellectual foundation. In 1806, just a few years after the count and countess of Rességuier died in exile, Jules, at sixteen, was commissioned a *sous-lieutenant* in Napoleon's cavalry. After serving in Germany, Poland, and Spain during a five-year period, he resigned due to illness in 1811 and returned to Toulouse. In 1815, his health restored, he married Mlle. de MacMahon, with whose mother the elder Rességuier had had an affair and whose father, Colonel de MacMahon, commanded the Toulouse garrison.

During his military service, Comte Jules de Rességuier had devoted some of his leisure hours to composing poems so, after his marriage, began a lasting friendship with the two Alexandres, Guiraud and Soumet, and a long association with the Académie des jeux floraux. In fact, during those early Restoration years, he kept them and Victor Hugo, whom he had met, in touch with the activities of the Clémence Isaure group and influenced their success in Toulouse. By 1819, Soumet had definitely converted him to romanticism, but he did not move to Paris until 1820 when his very close friend, Comte Charles de Peyronnet, minister of justice, offered him the position of *auditeur* of the Conseil d'état (later *maître des requêtes*) which he accepted. The *languedocien* poet had no trouble adjusting to Paris literary society since he knew many of the romantic writers. Though welcomed into the Deschamps *cénacle* as soon as he arrived, he chose to establish an elegant *salon littéraire* of his own, on the rue du Helder and later the rue Taitbout, whose meetings were held on Saturday. Throughout the decade, the literary Rességuier would also be a prominent first-generation member of the *Muse française*, *Arsenal* and *Notre Dame des Champs cénacles* while the social Rességuier was a regular guest in the exclusive Parisian salons of the Restoration nobility, notably those of the comte de Ségur and the duchesse de Broglie. He was superbly suited to the role of *gentilhomme*, impeccably dressed, aristocratic, unpretentious, kind, and urbane, with graceful manners and a superb wit.

In June 1826, Rességuier was elected *mainteneur* of the Jeux floraux as a result of the poems he had contributed to its publications as well as to the *Annales de la littérature et des arts* and the *Muse française*. Despite some superb verses, most of his poetry on such unimposing topics as faith, the family, and friendship is of average quality. In 1828, he selected several poems for a published collection entitled *Tableaux poétiques*. By the following year, four editions had appeared, and critics unanimously praised it. The July events of 1830 devastated Rességuier, consistently faithful to the ultra cause. Despite offers, he refused to serve in Louis-Philippe's government and abandoned politics. For more than a decade, his salon thrived as a social and literary center, and he produced a novel, *Almaria* (1835), and a second poetry collection, *Les Prismes* (1838). The unnatural characters of the novel limited its success, but the poems were an improvement over those in *Tableaux poétiques*.

In 1842, their three sons, Paul, Albert and Charles now adults and the first two married, the Rességuiers decided to return to Toulouse. The turn that political and literary events had taken probably had a bearing on the decision. They retreated to the family chateau at Sauveterre in the upper Pyrenees, though maintaining contact with Paris through correspondence with several friends, especially Emile Deschamps. Through renewed activities in the Jeux floraux, he promoted the cause of poetry and continued to compose. Jules de Rességuier died a peaceful death with his faithful wife and a host of friends and relatives at his side on 7 September 1862 at the age of seventy-three. A final group of fifty-eight poems, *Dernières poésies*, was published posthumously. Though not a bright star, he deserves a measure of attention as a writer who played an important role, though less than Emile Deschamps, as a catalyst for the romantic cause.

P. Lafond, *L'Aube Romantique. Jules de Rességuier et ses amis* (Paris, 1910); L. Séché, *Le Cénacle de la Muse française, 1823–1827* (Paris, 1908).

Paul Comeau

*Related entries:* ARSENAL, SALON OF; DESCHAMPS; GUIRAUD, A.; HUGO; LOUIS-PHILIPPE; *LA MUSE FRANCAISE*; PEYRONNET; REVOLUTION OF 1830; ROMANTICISM; SALON D'EMILE DESCHAMPS; SOUMET; ULTRAROYALISTS.


**RESTORATION, FIRST** (1814–1815) the one-year period between the return of the Bourbon dynasty in April 1814 and its temporary exile in March 1815. The first abdication of Napoleon (6 April 1814) had left power in the hands of the Provisional Government appointed by the Imperial Senate, and presided over by Charles-Maurice de Talleyrand. The comte d'Artois, the king's brother, upon his return to Paris (12 April) was recognized as the head of the government, with the same ministers remaining. Louis XVIII himself arrived on 3 May. Talleyrand was kept as minister of foreign affairs. The other ministries were provided for as follows: Interior, the abbé de Montesquiou; War, General Pierre Dupont de l'Etang; Navy and Colonies, Pierre-Victor Malouet; Finances, the baron Joseph-Dominique Louis; Justice, Chancellor Charles Dambray; Royal Household, comte Casimir Blacas d'Aulps. There was no prime minister and therefore very little coordinated action. The main influence was that of Blacas, who was, since 1810, the closely trusted confidant of the king; he was therefore to become the scapegoat for all the mismanagement and faux-pas of the First Restoration.

Blacas had nothing to do with two most important events that occurred during the first few weeks of Louis' return: the signing of the first Treaty of Paris and the issuance of the Constitutional Charter of 1814. The feelings of relief and hope that had at first dominated public opinion upon the return of the old dynasty were soon dampened by a combination of unfavorable circumstances and errors of judgment. The peace treaty shearing France of all the territories conquered since 1793 humiliated the French people. The end of the commercial blockade brought a sudden flood of cheap British wares to France and provoked the failure of many industries, thus increasing unemployment. The suspension of grandiose public works undertaken by Napoleon worsened this effect. Officials of the preceding regime—many of them having lost their positions—were indignant to see the king restore useless honorific offices of the ancient court and also to witness the preference that the king and princes seemed to bestow upon the handful of *émigrés* who had returned with them. Elaborate ceremonies in honor of the victims of the Revolution seemed to contradict the intentions of forgiveness published by the king. Catholicism having been proclaimed by the Charter as the religion of the state, police ordinances were aimed at enforcing the external observation of the Sabbath. Those who had acquired nationalized estates—whether taken from the church or from *émigré* families—felt the onus of moral denunciation. All this created a dangerous fear that a return to pre-Revolutionary conditions was coming. The most dangerous discontent, however, was present within the military, now fallen from its position of supremacy. Twelve thousand officers had been shunted to inactivity on half-pay; at the same time, the king lavished attention on the newly restored ranks of his personal guard. In addition, the entire army, not just the *demi-soldes*, resented the fact that the tricolor standard had been replaced by the royal white flag with fleur-de-lys.

The growing irritation from all these sources became known to Napoleon in his exile and encouraged him to attempt his comeback. However, it would be wrong to conclude that the First Restoration was a complete failure or that its failure was foreordained. If Napoleon had not burst upon the scene, Louis XVIII might well have realized his first errors and corrected them, consolidating his regime as he was able to to do after 1815 in much more difficult circumstances.

G. de Bertier de Sauvigny, *The Bourbon Restoration* (Philadelphia, 1966).

*Guillaume de Bertier de Sauvigny*

*Related entries:* BLACAS D'AULPS; CHARLES X; CHARTER OF 1814; DAMBRAY; *DEMI-SOLDES*; LOUIS XVIII; LOUIS; MONTESQUIOU; RESTORATION, SECOND; ROYAL GUARD.


**RESTORATION, SECOND** (1815–1830), the period included between the second return of Louis XVIII (8 July 1815) and the abdication of Charles X (2 August 1830). The succession of elected chambers and governments, each responding to a change in general policies, provides convenient chronological milestones for charting the course of these fifteen years.

July–September 1815: The first formally organized ministry, under Charles-Maurice de Talleyrand's premiership, with Joseph Fouché as minister of police. It reflected a feeling of concession toward the old imperial establishment, which had been alienated by the policies of the First Restoration. This so-called Talleyrand-Fouché government had to cope with the disastrous foreign occupation and the violent stirrings of the royalist reaction in the southern provinces known as the White Terror. It initiated peace negotiations and organized the general elections in August.The unexpected result—an overwhelming majority of reactionary royalists—compelled Fouché and Talleyrand to resign.

October 1815-September 1816: A period of royalist reaction, symbolized by the *chambre introuvable*. Armand-Emmanuel de Richelieu replaced Talleyrand as president of the council and as minister of foreign affairs. In that capacity, he signed the Second Treaty of Paris. In domestic affairs he tried to appease the vengeful feelings of the majority with repressive legislation, purges of administrative and military personnel, the banishment of former regicides and by bringing to court, and having executed, a few personalities responsible for the debacle of March 1815, including Marshal Michel Ney. But the ministry was at odds with the ultraroyalist majority on a growing number of issues. Heeding the pressing advice of the Allied ministers who were in Paris as a kind of supervisory authority, Louis XVIII dissolved the unwieldy Chamber, and new elections—with changed rules—gave him a majority that would support the moderate middle-of-the road policy he wished to pursue with Richelieu.

October 1816-February 1820: The moderate liberal or constitutional experiment. The attempt to steer a course between ultraroyalism and radical liberalism was mainly inspired and led by Elie Decazes, who had entered Richelieu's administration as minister of police and won the affection of the king. He had almost a free hand in domestic policies while Richelieu concentrated his efforts on ending the Allied occupation of France. Having reached this goal at the Congress of Aix-la-Chapelle, Richelieu retired. Decazes, now minister of the interior, was then freer to step up his feud against the ultraroyalists, with the support of a figurehead, General Jean-Joseph Dessolle, as president of the Council. Eventually the progress of the liberal opposition in 1819 threatened Decazes himself, and he sought a truce with the more reasonable elements of the rightist opposition. But Dessolle, with two more of his colleagues—Laurent Gouvion Saint-Cyr (War) and Joseph-Dominique Louis (Finances)—refused this change of course and resigned. Decazes was then compelled to take the premiership. He was negotiating a change in the electoral law when the murder of the duc de Berry brought about his political demise in February 1820. During the years of Richelieu's and Decazes' stewardships, remarkable progress had been made toward economic recovery, despite a murderous famine in 1817. Also, liberal legislation had been passed for the periodical press, for the electoral systems, and for the system of promotions in the army.

February 1820-December 1821: Richelieu's second administration. Legislation was passed to curtail the liberty of the press and also to establish a new electoral system (the double vote). Royalist feelings were greatly bolstered by the birth of the posthumous son of the duc de Berry (29 September 1820). The elections of November 1820 returned a large number of ultraroyalists. Richelieu, however, still refused to include ultraroyalists in his new administration. As a result, the ultraroyalists joined with the liberal opposition to inflict a humiliating defeat on Richelieu and on his foreign policy, thus forcing him to resign from office.

December 1821-December 1827: The government of the Right. Louis XVIII, under the influence of the comtesse du Cayla, accepted the ministers chosen by his brother and heir, all of whom were members of the ultraroyalist party. At first there was no president of the Council. Joseph de Villèle, however, was soon able to establish his ascendancy. While his main possible rival, the vicomte de Montmorency, was away attending the Congress of Verona, Villèle was made president of the Council, a title he was to retain until December 1827. The new team started a thorough purge of all former imperial and liberal officials introduced or maintained by Decazes. They suppressed the subversive activities of the republican secret societies. They also tightened the restrictions on the freedom of the press. With the moral support of the conservative powers of the Continent, as obtained at the Congress of Verona, a French expeditionary force entered Spain to reestablish the absolute rule of King Ferdinand VII (1823). Villèle took advantage of the success of this difficult undertaking and called a general election

(March 1824). The leftist opposition was reduced to a score of individuals. Not long after, Louis XVIII died (16 September 1824).

The advent of Charles X, a king devoted to the ideals of the ultraroyalist party, seemed to open a new era of more systematic reaction. His solemn anointment and coronation in the cathedral of Reims (29 May 1825) signaled his desire to revive the forms and spirit of the old monarchy. The Catholic clergy was favored to the point of stimulating a strong anticlerical backlash in sections of the educated bourgeoisie whose oracle was Voltaire. Villèle's most unassailable achievement was the establishment of sound public finances. This made possible the settlement of one of the most nettlesome problems of the time, the issue of the national lands (that is, properties confiscated by revolutionary governments, sold to new owners, and again claimed by the former proprietors). An indemnity of 700 million francs in state bonds was shared among the claimants, thus extinguishing their claims and by the same stroke voiding the hostile apprehensions of the profiteers of the Revolution. Villèle was not as successful when he tried to pass legislation to strengthen the landed aristocracy or with similar efforts to tighten press censorship. In both attempts, the legislation, accepted in the Chamber of Deputies, was rejected in the Peers, which had been packed by Decazes in 1820 with more liberal-minded individuals. Among the royalist deputies themselves emerged a counteropposition group composed of people whose ambitions or convictions had been disappointed by Villèle's cautious policies. Chateaubriand, who in June 1824 had been ignominiously ousted from the Ministry of Foreign Affairs, led the campaign of public vituperation against the government. Villèle, sensing the constant erosion of his parliamentary support, tried to forestall the opposition's hopes by calling a general election (November 1827). Its disastrous result compelled the reluctant Charles X to let his trusted minister go.

January 1828-August 1829: Movement toward the Center Left. Jean-Baptiste de Martignac, a personable lawyer and brilliant orator, was given the Ministry of the Interior, and the comte de la Ferronays, a liberal-minded aristocrat and diplomat, was given that of Foreign Affairs. He cleverly managed a French intervention in behalf of Greek independence. But on the domestic scene Martignac, by his concessions to the liberal opposition, succeeded only in losing the confidence of the king.

August 1829-July 1830: The last effort of reaction. The king, disgusted by what he sensed as a dangerous drift toward a revolution, secretly prepared for the advent of an administration that in his calculations could have the support of all the segments of royalism in the Chamber, adding up to a working majority. This undertaking was to be jeopardized by the king's inappropriate choice of ministers. He chose men who would, for different reasons, antagonize public opinion: the Prince Jules de Polignac, General de Bourmont, and the comte de la Bourdonnaye. In this ill-fated ministry, appointed on 8 August 1829, there was at first no president of the Council, but in November Polignac was raised to that office, and La Bourdonnaye quit in a huff. Polignac delayed as long as possible the confrontation with the Chambers. At the belated opening of the session (March 1830), Charles gave a threatening speech from the throne. Out of 402 deputies voting, 221 responded with an address respectfully requesting a change of ministers. The king considered this to be a danger to the privileges of the crown that could alter the nature of the regime. He responded by first adjourning and then dismissing the Chamber (16 May). Elections were to be held over a period of four weeks (23 June–19 July). Charles X and his ministers hoped to influence opinion with the brilliant success of the amphibious operation that led to the capture of Algiers (5 July). But the electors returned a majority hostile to the policies of the king. He then made the fatal decision to use article 14 of the Charter to change the rules of the game. This was a clumsy coup attempt, which was to spark the Parisian revolution of July 1830 and send the Bourbons into exile.

G. de Bertier de Sauvigny, *The Bourbon Restoration* (Philadelphia, 1966).

*Guillalume de Bertier de Sauvigny*

*Related entries:* AIX-LA-CHAPELLE, CONGRESS OF; ALGIERS, EXPEDITION TO; BERRY, C.-F.; BOURMONT; CENSORSHIP; CHAMBER OF DEPUTIES; CHAMBER OF PEERS; *CHAMBRE INTROUVABLE*; CHARLES X; CHATEAUBRIAND; CORONATION OF CHARLES X; COUNCIL OF STATE; DECAZES; DESSOLLE; DOUBLE VOTE, LAW OF THE; DU CAYLA; ELECTIONS AND ELECTORAL SYSTEMS; FOUCHE; GOUVION SAINT-CYR; INDEMNITY BILL OF 1825; JULY ORDINANCES; LA BOURDONNAYE; LOUIS XVIII; LOUIS; MARTIGNAC; MONTMORENCY; NEY; PARIS, SECOND TREATY OF; POLIGNAC; PRESS LAWS; RESTORATION, FIRST; REVOLUTION OF 1830; RICHELIEU; TALLEYRAND; ULTRAROYALISTS; VERONA, CONGRESS OF; VILLELE; WHITE TERROR.


**REUNION DE LA RUE DE POITIERS.** See COMITE DE LA RUE DE POITIERS.


*LE REVENANT* (1832–1833), legitimist newspaper of the July Monarchy. This was one of many ephemeral legitimist journals appearing during the early years of the reign of Louis-Philippe. Founded by Albert de Calvimont on 1 January 1832, it was prosecuted twice for seditious libel and its editor sentenced to thirteen months' imprisonment and a 650 franc fine. It lasted certainly until June 1833 and possibly a further three months under another name.

E. Texier, *Histoire des journaux* (Paris, 1851).

*Irene Collins*

*Related entries:* LEGITIMISM; LOUIS-PHILIPPE.


*LA REVOLUTION* (1829–1832), radical Parisian newspaper. *La Révolution, journal des intérêts populaires* appeared in Paris in mid-1829 under the editorship of Jean Jacob Fazy and Anthony Thouret. A small republican journal that represented part of the rebellion of youth, it was read mostly by students on the Left Bank. Founded prior to the July Revolution, it was unable to publish during the crucial July Days. Its editors, Eugène Plagniol, Fazy, and Levasseur, however, had signed the editors' protest of the July Ordinances published in the *National* on 26 July. When *La Révolution* appeared again on 3 August, it called for a republic. Since the key decisions had already been taken, its call had no effect. For republicans, the difficulties that prevented *La Révolution* from appearing during the crucial days of the revolution were one more reason to suspect the liberals' devotion to the revolution.

For *La Révolution*, the Orleanist solution was a coup and therefore an illegal usurpation of the power of the people. The people needed to be consulted through a Constituent Assembly, not a rump of the Chamber of Deputies. During the paper's two more years of life, the editors of *La Révolution* were convicted nine times for acts against the king. The movement of politics was against *La Révolution*, and it succumbed in 1832 to the constant harassment of the government.

I. Collins, *The Government and the Newspaper Press in France, 1814–1881* (London, 1959); L. Hatin, *Histoire politique et littéraure de la presse en France* (Geneva, 1967).

*Thomas Beck*

Related entries: CHAMBER OF DEPUTIES; JULY ORDINANCES; LOUIS-PHILIPPE; *LE NATIONAL*; PRESS LAWS; REPUBLICANS; REVOLUTION OF 1830.

**REVOLUTION OF 1830,** revolution in Paris that ended the Bourbon monarchy, brought Louis-Philippe, duc d'Orléans, to the throne, and accelerated the liberalization of French political life. A conflict between crown and parliament over the responsibility of ministers created the occasion for the Revolution of 1830, but its origins lay in the unpopularity of Charles X and his first minister, Prince Jules de Polignac, in public perceptions of the government's aristocratic and clerical biases, in economic distress brought on by the depression of 1827–29 and the severe winter of 1829–30, and in the ambitions of individual political figures.

When the Chamber of Deputies assembled in March 1830 for its annual session, grievances among the deputies were sufficient to move them, in their reply to the king's opening address, to ask the king, in effect, to replace his present ministers with new men acceptable to a majority in the Chamber. Charles promptly prorogued the chamber and a few weeks later dissolved it and ordered new elections in June and July. He intended that the elections should return a majority favorable to the Polignac ministry, but in fact they added nearly fifty seats to the hostile majority.

Charles viewed the outcome of the elections not simply as a defeat for the Polignac ministry but as part of a growing and dangerous threat to the monarchy itself. He was determined, he said, not to repeat the mistake of his late brother, Louis XVI. He would not give in to the opposition. Emboldened by the success of the French expedition against Algiers in early July, he decided to use the emergency powers vested in him, he believed, by article 14 of the Charter of 1814. On 14 July he signed four ordinances. Two of them, dissolving the newly elected Chamber of Deputies and ordering new elections, were within the undoubted authority of the crown, but the other two—one instituting censorship of the periodical press and the other changing the electoral law—were of questionable legality. "The legislative power," the Charter stated, "is exercised collectively by the king, the Chamber of Peers, and the Chamber of Deputies." In issuing these ordinances, Charles exercised that power unilaterally. In justification of this action, his ministers cited the vague statement in article 14 of the Charter that the king may "issue ordinances for the execution of the laws and the security of the state."

The ordinances, prepared in great secrecy, appeared in *Le Moniteur universel* of 26 July. Journalists were the most immediately and vitally affected, and in the afternoon of 26 July a group of them issued a proclamation in which they denounced the ordinances as illegal, declared their intention to defy the censorship, and called upon the deputies to join them in resisting the ministry's violation of the laws. Less overtly they appealed for more dangerous support: "The legal regime is now interrupted, that of force has begun."

The first acts of popular violence occurred that evening when crowds broke windows in government buildings. They recurred the next day on a larger scale, and the first shots were fired. The next morning, 28 July, crowds were on the streets, and barricades were being raised throughout the center and east end of Paris.

The government had taken no military precaution before issuing the ordinances, and not until 27 July did it name a commander, Marshal Auguste de Marmont, to deal with the mounting disorders. On the morning of 28 July, he sent an urgent dispatch to the king at Saint-Cloud. "This is no longer a riot," he wrote. "This is a revolution." He attempted to pacify the city by sending three columns across it to occupy key points. They fought their way to their objectives, but with heavy casualties on both sides, and then found themselves surrounded and isolated by insurgents. Late in the evening all the columns were withdrawn to the Louvre and the Tuileries. Marmont hoped to hold the west end of the capital until reinforcements arrived, but on 29 July the defection of two regiments of the line and the Royal Guard's blundering withdrawal from the Louvre started a rout that ended in the total abandonment of the capital to the insurrectionaries. To fill the void left by the collapse of royal authority, a group of liberal deputies, meeting at the home of the banker Jacques Laffitte, appointed a provisional Municipal Commission to ensure the safety and the provisioning of Paris and approved the marquis de Lafayette's assumption of command of the revived Parisian National Guard.

The sovereign power had escaped the Bourbon government, and a struggle to capture it began among republicans, Bonapartists, Orleanists, and Bourbons. The republicans were few in number and, after Lafayette rallied to the Orleanists, lacked an effective leader. The Bonapartist heir, Napoleon's son, was far away in Vienna and unknown in France, and no prominent Napoleonic figure spoke for him. The Bourbons, humiliated by their defeat in Paris and with their armies disintegrating, lacked the means to reassert their authority. The Orleanists had a candidate for the throne, the duc d'Orléans, head of the younger branch of the Bourbon house, in Jacques Laffitte a skillful leader, and in Adolphe Thiers and François Mignet two able publicists. They presented the duke as a leader who would abide by the Charter, respect the great principles of the Revolution, and save France from the "frightful divisions" of a republic. They built up popular support for him and persuaded the deputies gathered in Paris to appoint him lieutenant general of the kingdom. On July 31 Orléans accepted the post and won the endorsement of Lafayette, a critical accomplishment, for the marquis not only controlled the sole organized armed force in the city but also was the only conceivable head of a French republic. Orléans then appointed a provisional ministry, moved to take command of the armed forces, and convoked the Chambers to meet on 3 August.

Charles, who with his court had withdrawn to Rambouillet, on 2 August abdicated in favor of his grandson and called upon Orléans to proclaim him King Henry V. Orléans ignored the order and at the opening session of parliament on 3 August simply announced the abdication of Charles X.

On 7 August the Chambers approved a number of revisions of the Charter, including specific exclusion of the power to issue ordinances "for the security of the state," and accepted a commitment to effect certain reforms, the establishment of the responsibility of ministers among them. The Chambers further declared that the throne was vacant and that "the interest of the French people calls to the throne H.R.H. Louis-Philippe d'Orléans" but only on the condition that he accept the provisions and engagements of the revised Charter. On 9 August the duke took a civil oath to observe the Charter and to govern according to the laws and became Louis-Philippe I, king of the French.

The revolution had brought France a new ruling house and raised to political power men more sympathetic with the principles of the Revolution than their predecessors. The responsibility of ministers to parliament was practically, though not legally, established. The Parisian working class rediscovered the political power of violence, and they resorted to it frequently in succeeding decades. But the events of July and August 1830 had effected no social revolution. New men had moved into the highest offices, but France was still ruled, as it had been under the Bourbons, by its well-to-do landed proprietors.

J.-L. Bory, *La Révolution de juillet* (Paris, 1972); G. de Bertier de Sauvigny, *La Révolution de 1830 en France* (Paris, c. 1970); P. Duvergier d'Hauranne, *Histoire du gouvernement parlementaire en France, 1814–1848*, vol. 10 (Paris, 1957–81); Alfred Nettement, *Histoire de la Restauration*, vol. 8 (Paris, 1860–72); D.H. Pinkney, *The French Revolution of 1830* (Princeton, 1972).

*David H. Pinkney*

*Related entries:* ALGIERS, EXPEDITION TO; BORDEAUX; CHAMBER OF DEPUTIES; CHAMBER OF PEERS; CHARLES X; CHARTER OF 1814;

CHARTER OF 1830; JULY ORDINANCES; LAFAYETTE, M.–J.–P.–Y.–R.–G.; LAFFITTE; MARMONT; MIGNET; *LE MONITEUR*; MUNICIPAL COMMISSION; NATIONAL GUARD; POLIGNAC; REICHSTADT; REPUBLICANS; ROYAL GUARD; THIERS; THE 221.

**REVOLUTION OF 1848.** The months from the February Revolution until the election of Louis-Napoleon as president of the Republic have to be understood within the context of an economic crisis that lasted from 1846 to 1852. This crisis, which varied in nature and intensity between regions and between urban and rural areas, underpins the social tensions and political mobilization of these years. Initially an agricultural crisis because of catastrophic grain and potato crops in 1846, it became an industrial crisis because of a related slump in consumer demand. While the February Revolution of 1848 occurred at a time of recovery and subsequent harvests were abundant, the fears of employers about popular participation in politics plunged the country into a new crisis of mass unemployment and depressed markets for rural produce (*mévente*).

In Paris, resentment of the foreign policy, scandals, and conservatism of the July Monarchy focused on its decision to ban a political banquet, the last of seventy organized by the parliamentary opposition. While leading republicans counseled caution, students, then workers and petits bourgeois, took the initiative and demonstrated on 22 February. Louis-Philippe's attempt to calm protests by ministerial changes failed when troops fired on angry crowds. On the night of 23 February barricades were erected all over the city, and it was evident that the middle-class National Guard had deserted the regime. Ignoring Louis-Philippe's abdication, crowds invaded the Chamber and directly nominated members of a republican Provisional Government.

The members of this government had been distinguished by their opposition to the July Monarchy, though several had been deputies. They may usefully be divided into the moderate republicans close to the newspaper *Le National* (Alphonse de Lamartine, Jacques-Charles Dupont de l'Eure, Etienne Garnier-Pagès, Alexandre-Thomas Marie, Adolphe Crémieux, Armand Marrast, François Arago) and the more radical republicans of *La Réforme* (Alexandre-Auguste Ledru-Rollin, Louis Blanc, Ferdinand Flocon, and a solitary worker, Albert). In the first months of the Republic, they introduced universal suffrage and freedom of the press and association, amnestied political prisoners, abolished capital punishment for political offenses, abolished slavery, opened the National Guard to all males, guaranteed subsistence to the unemployed, and began investigating the reorganization of work.

News of the revolution was greeted enthusiastically in the provinces, and supporters of the monarchy rushed to declare their conversion to republicanism. The collapse of authority unleashed a massive wave of direct action in towns and villages where capitalist industry and agriculture and state policies had threatened livelihood. Forests were invaded, collective practices reasserted, forges, railway lines, and machines smashed, registers of indirect taxes destroyed, and the property of moneylenders and large landowners attacked. The revolution also liberated political life, though extralegal removals of mayors varied widely, from 3 percent in the Gironde to 53 percent in the Pyrénées-Orientales.

The government, trying to reassure employers and prevent a "strike of capital" (shares in the Bank of France and government bonds plummeted in value), was also under pressure from the popular movement in Paris. Within weeks, up to 300 new newspapers appeared, together printing 400,000 copies by May; more than 200 clubs, with up to 70,000 members, were opened; and workers used trade associations and the government's Luxembourg Commission to urge state aid for producers' cooperatives. Social tension became apparent over the democratization of the National Guard and the direction the revolution should take ( *journées* of 17 March and 16 April). The government, having sent 48,000 troops to quell provincial unrest, began recalling army divisions to Paris.

The future of the Republic hinged on the elections of 23 April 1848. Political rights, hitherto reserved for about 250,000 wealthy bourgeois and nobles, were now in the hands of 9 million voters. Political clubs and newspapers proliferated, but in most areas two months was too short a time for alternative, republican leaders to challenge old elites controlling social and economic power. Voters were confused by the number of candidates, some 3,000 in all; in the Lot, 97 contested the 7 seats. The 450 delegates sent to the provinces by the Paris clubs achieved little, and the new departmental administrators (*commissaires*) primarily sought the smooth and free functioning of the poll, though 110 of them were elected.

While almost all of the 851 deputies elected in an 84 percent turnout claimed adherence to the Republic, democracy, and social justice, most of them had held elected or official positions under the previous regime. Their propaganda emphasized the virtues of existing family and property structures and was often openly supported by the church, a role facilitated by the elections being on Easter Day. The government's decision on 16 March to add a 45 percent surtax to property taxes also played into their hands. Only in specific areas of the east and south and in some cities were republicans able to win. Recent research suggests that perhaps 566 of the deputies were former monarchists of various nuances, and only 285 were genuine republicans, including 55 radicals.

In Rouen and Limoges, social tensions erupted into violence as National Guard troops attacked protests against conservative election results. In Paris, the presence of a hostile Assembly at a time of over 55 percent unemployment was explosive. The Assembly chose an executive of republicans (Arago, Lamartine, Ledru-Rollin, Garnier-Pagès, Marie) but closed the Luxembourg Commission and began to seek ways of terminating the National Workshops; by 15 May, over 113,000 workers and their dependents, by no means all the unemployed, were dependent on them. On 15 May, a demonstration to pressure the Assembly to send troops to the aid of Poland escalated into an invasion of the Assembly and an abortive radical coup.

Draconian laws prohibiting street gatherings, consequent mass arrests, and the Assembly's hostility to social reform created a situation electric with fear and anger. This was precipitated into insurrection by the Assembly's decision on 21 June to slash the rolls of the National Workshops. For four days, an unprecedented civil war tore the city in two; while some workers in the National Guard and the young veterans of the February revolution in the Mobile Guard fought for the government, the geography and social composition of the insurrection support contemporary observations that this was a class war. Both sides claimed to be fighting for the Republic: but between family, property, and religion and the social and democratic Republic lay a yawning gulf of class hostility, terror, and desperation.

The government lost about 800 troops in securing victory; at least 1,500 (and perhaps 3,000) insurgents were killed, and up to 15,000 were arrested, of whom 4,500 were imprisoned or transported. In the aftermath of the fighting, the Assembly extended the executive powers of the republican general Eugène Cavaignac voted to him on 24 June, restricted the freedom of association, tightened laws on the press, and maintained a state of siege in Paris for four months.

The Parisian radicals were opposed not only by the army and sections of the National Guard but also by waves of up to 100,000 volunteers from fifty-three departments. However, although there was minimal support for the workers in the provinces (rebellions or minor protests in Marseilles, Lyons, and twenty other cities and towns), it is evident that it was chiefly royalist landowners and urban bourgeois who flocked to Paris. After the civil war large areas of northern and western France were swept by a rural panic about fleeing Parisian *partageurs*. But in the south, the civil war had little impact; rather more important were the continuing protests against the 45 percent surtax and anger at the Assembly's reintroduction on 21 June of the indirect tax on wines and spirits that the Provisional Government had suspended on 31 March.

Between June and December,Cavaignac and his ministers were caught between a republican minority increasingly critical of continuing repression and a majority of provincial landowners, officials, and businessmen whose support for Cavaignac stemmed mainly from the efficiency with which he had suppressed the June insurrection. While Cavaignac, with justice, has always been associated with the horrors of June, there is no doubt that he and his ministers were committed to a measure of social reform. Most notable were the financial encouragement of producers' cooperatives, central to workers' demands since the 1830s, maximum hours legislation, farm schools, and cheap credit for peasants (the last defeated by the Assembly).

But Cavaignac's greatest triumph was the Constitution of the Republic, promulgated on 12 November. Given the nature of the Assembly, the Constitution was remarkably democratic and liberal and, for the first time since 1793, the state was to recognize certain social obligations. But an amendment to insert "the right to work" was rejected by 596 votes to 187, and the president was to be elected directly by the nation, not by the Assembly. Given Louis-Napoleon's increasing popularity since June, culminating in by-election victories in the Seine and five other departments on 17 September, there were growing fears on the Left that a presidency could be a stepping-stone to a monarchy or empire.

The repression of the insurrection had crushed the popular movement in Paris, but it was primarily after June that political mobilization in the countryside began to accelerate.There were sharp regional contrasts; in the local government elections of July-August, over 60 percent of July Monarchy mayors were reelected in much of Normandy and Brittany, while fewer than 30 percent were in most Mediterranean departments. The grievances endemic in most rural areas had not been met by the revolution. These problems—indebtedness, the collapse of rural industry, and exploitative rents, all aggravated by low prices for produce—were to be at the heart of rural politics for the next four years. Radical republicans, shattered by the electoral disasters of April, responded with a rural-oriented program and a new organization, Solidarité républicaine, formed in November.

It was in this situation—with a dominant but politically divided elite in the Assembly, resentment and dashed hopes in the cities, unresolved grievances in the countryside—that the presidential elections of 10 December were held. Most newspapers supported Cavaignac, though a number of influential figures (Adolphe Thiers, Louis-Mathieu de Molé, Pierre-Antoine Berryer) and papers pushed Louis-Napoleon forward, apparently as a compromise candidate of divided royalists hostile to the Republic. Both candidates sought to appeal to virtually every group in French society, though Cavaignac was inevitably judged on the basis of perceptions of his government. Only Ledru-Rollin and Raspail formulated unambiguous, radical programs, and both were pledged to abolish the presidency.

Marx described 10 December as a peasant insurrection. He was correct, but it was only the beginning of a rural mobilization of Left and Right. The 75 percent turnout gave Louis-Napoleon a staggering 74.2 percent; Cavaignac gathered only 19.5 percent and Ledru-Rollin, second in eight departments, 5 percent. Lamartine, elected by ten departments in April, won just 18,000 votes. Louis-Napoleon's lowest votes, from 24 to 54 percent, were in coastal and frontier departments with sharper memories of the privations of 1799–1815. Most urban workers, even in Paris, and particularly the rural population, had repudiated the urgings of notables to vote for Cavaignac. But the reasons for the vote were varied, even contradictory; it was not just the glory of a name.

While Louis-Napoleon could claim at the end of December to have an extraordinary mandate, the elections of May 1849 were to show that huge numbers of voters saw in him the guarantor of stability, existing property relations, and national pride, while for others he was a republican populist, a repudiation of established hierarchies, and the author of *The Extinction of Poverty*.

M. Agulhon, *1848, ou l'apprentissage de la république* (Paris, 1973) and *The Republic in the Village* (Cambridge,1982); P. H. Amann, *Revolution and Mass Democracy* (Princeton, 1975); T. J. Clark, *The Absolute Bourgeois* (London, 1973); F. A. de Luna,*The French Republic under Cavaignac, 1848* (Princeton, 1969); T. R. Forstenzer, *French Provincial Police and the Fall of the Second Republic* (Princeton, 1981); R. Gossez, *Les Ouvriers de Paris*, vol. 1: *Bibliothèque de la Révolution de 1848* (Paris, 1967); E. Labrousse, ed., *Aspects de la crise et de la dépression de l'economie française au milieu du XIXe siècle, 1846–1851* (1956); K. Marx and F. Engels, *Collected Works*, vols. 6–

10 (London, 1976–78); J. Merriman, *The Agony of the Republic* (New Haven, 1978); R. D. Price, ed., *Revolution and Reaction* (London, 1975); G. Sand, *Correspondance*, vol. 8 (Paris, 1971); W. Sewell, *Work and Revolution in France* (Cambridge, 1980); A. Soboul, *Problèmes paysans de la révolution, 1789–1848* (Paris, 1976); A. de Tocqueville, *Recollections* (New York, 1956); A.-J. Tudesq, *Les Grands notables en France (1840–1849)*, 2 vols. (Paris, 1964).

*Peter McPhee*

*Related entries:* CAVAIGNAC, L.–E.; CONSTITUTION OF 1848; GARDE MOBILE; JUNE DAYS; LAMARTINE; LEDRU-ROLLIN; LEGISLATIVE ASSEMBLY; LUXEMBOURG COMMISSION; *LE NATIONAL*; NATIONAL GUARD; NATIONAL WORKSHOPS; PROVISIONAL GOVERNMENT; RASPAIL; *LA REFORME;* SOLIDARITE REPUBLICAINE.


*LA REVUE DE L'EMPIRE* (1842–1848), Napoleonic newspaper of the July Monarchy. During the 1840s, it was fashionable in France to praise the achievements of the Napoleonic Empire in the hope of harnessing their glories to the more prosaic advantages of the July Monarchy. The *Revue de l'Empire*, founded in 1842, disappeared at the outbreak of the Revolution in 1848.

R. Pimenta, *La propagande bonapartiste en 1848* (Paris, 1911).

*Irene Collins*

*Related entries:* BONAPARTISM; REVOLUTION OF 1848.


*LA REVUE DE PARIS* (1829–1845), literary and political periodical appearing from April 1829 to June 1845, before being absorbed by *L'Artiste*. The *Revue* was founded by Louis-Désiré Véron, who was editor to 1831, followed by Charles Rabou. Politically it was consistently supportive of the July Monarchy, while its literary columns were devoted to an appraisal of ancient and foreign literature and to the encouragement of young writers. Charles-Augustin Sainte-Beuve, Alphonse de Lamartine, Casimir Delavigne, Benjamin Constant, Prosper Mérimée, and Saint-Marc Girardin were among its contributors. This publication is not to be confused with the review of the same title founded by Th. Gautier in 1851.

C. Bellanger, J.Godechot, P. Guiral, and F. Terrou, eds. *Histoire générale de la presse française*, vol. 2 (Paris, 1969).

*Peter McPhee*

*Related entries:* CONSTANT; GAUTIER; LAMARTINE; MERIMEE; SAINTE-BEUVE; VERON.


*LA REVUE DES DEUX MONDES* (1829–1944), literary and political fortnightly, published continuously from July 1829 to September 1944. During the July Monarchy, its director was François Buloz, who was consistently liberal Orleanist in sympathy, welcoming contributions from Prosper Duvergier de Hauranne, although the key political writer, Louis de Carné, was a supporter of François Guizot. In 1848, however, the shock of the June Days was enough to allow even Louis Veuillot to be welcomed to the paper, and Eugène Cavaignac was attacked because of his antipathy to monarchists.

The most important literary review of the nineteenth century, the *Revue* included among its contributors Victor Hugo, Alfred de Vigny, George Sand, Honoré de Balzac, Alphonse de Lamartine, Alfred Musset, and the Girardins. Michel Chevalier and Léon Faucher wrote economic statements of a laissez-faire nuance. Subscriptions increased from 350 in 1831 to 2,000 in 1843 and 16,650 in 1866.

C. Bellanger, J. Godechot, P. Guiral, and F. Terrou, eds. *Histoire générale de la presse française*, vol. 2 (Paris, 1969).

*Peter McPhee*

*Related entries:* BALZAC; CAVAIGNAC, L.-E.; CHEVALIER; DUVERGIER DE HAURANNE; GUIZOT; HUGO; LAMARTINE; MUSSET; VEUILLOT; VIGNY.

*LA REVUE DU PROGRES* (1839–1842), socialist newspaper. In 1839 Louis Blanc founded *La Revue du progrès* to popularize the ideas he had expressed in his book, *L'Organisation du travail*. The first number advocated a single parliamentary chamber, elected by universal male suffrage, which would control the executive power. The state would then control the economy and provide funds for socialist workshops, which would offer much greater incentives to the workers than those provided by capitalist enterprises. The journal was withdrawn by Louis Blanc in 1842, when Pierre Leroux's *Revue indépendante* proved to be more popular.

*Irene Collins*

*Related entries:* BLANC; LEROUX; *LA REVUE INDEPENDANTE*.

*REVUE FRANCAISE* (1828–1830), liberal literary, philosophical, and historical review of the Restoration. From January 1828 until September 1830, the *Revue française* appeared in Paris as the literary review associated with the *Globe*. Founded as a monthly literary and historical review by François Guizot and the comte de Rémusat, it promoted the *doctrinaires'* political and philosophical ideas. Mme. Guizot even served as the proofreader.

The staff was composed mostly of university professors. The content was not primarily political, since these same men often wrote for the *Globe*. The work of philosophers such as Abel-François Villemain and Louis Vitet, historians such as Prosper Duvergier de Hauranne and Amédée Thierry, and scientists such as André Ampère appeared in its pages. Although it had only about 100 subscribers, it reached into most Parisian intellectual circles.

Despite its mostly apolitical content, François Guizot used the *Revue* to promote his liberal ideas on politics. In the first issue, he printed a number of brochures of the liberal electoral association Aide-toi le ciel t'aidera. He also promoted the Breton Association's idea of tax resistance. In the April 1830 issue, Guizot warned that the situation might warrant a radical change in the government, "but we are nowhere near a revolution."

This smaller version of the *Globe* disappeared in September 1830 when its backers assumed the responsibilities of government under Louis-Philippe.

*Thomas Beck*

*Related entries:* AIDE-TOI, LE CIEL T'AIDERA; AMPERE; BRETON AS-SOCIATION; *DOCTRINAIRES*; DUVERGIER DE HAURANNE; *LE GLOBE;* GUIZOT; LOUIS-PHILIPPE; REMUSAT; THIERRY.

*LA REVUE INDEPENDANTE* (1841–1848), socialist newspaper during the July Monarchy. Pierre Leroux (probably the first Frenchman to call himself a socialist) founded the *Revue indépendante* with the collaboration of George Sand and Louis Viardot on 1 November 1841. Long articles expounded Leroux's ideas, which predicted conflict between the bourgeoisie and the working class but hoped to avoid it by the complete participation of the entire people in politics. To give the workers their proper weight in parliamentary affairs, Leroux advocated special representation for them. George Sand, who admired Leroux's romantic visions of reconciliation and fraternity, generously gave of her outstanding talents as a novelist to the *Revue*; both she and Leroux worked for the journal without payment. In her articles on literature, Sand did much to popularize working class poets such as Charles Poncy. The *Revue* ended in February 1848 when Sand and Leroux took up a more active role in politics.

*Irene Collins*

*Related entries:* LEROUX; PONCY; SAND.

*REVUE NATIONALE* (May 1847–July 1848), the second journal published by Philippe Buchez and his followers to spread their moderate Christian socialist theories. Their first journal, the *Européen*, had appeared in forty-seven issues between December 1831 and October 1832 and in a further eighteen numbers between October 1835 and December 1838. The *Européen* had had a small circulation, with at most a print run of 600 and only about a hundred subscribers. The *Revue nationale*, which appeared monthly until the end of February 1848, also had a much smaller circulation than the *Atelier*, another Buchezian paper published by and for Parisian workers. However, it fared better than the *Européen*, which had only appeared irregularly. The economic crisis of 1847, the February Revolution, and the effervescence of ideas and journals in the months that followed helped make the moment propitious. The journal also benefited from having a talented editorial team. Jules Bastide (1800–79), who was coeditor, was a recent recruit to Buchezism but had considerable journalistic experience, having edited the *National*, the leading moderate republican journal, for ten years after Armand Carrel's death in 1836. Another recent adherent to the school, Henri Feugueray (1814–54), who later joined the Catholic *Ere nouvelle*, also collaborated on the journal, as did Auguste Ott (1814–1903), an important theorist in his own right.

Mature Buchezian ideas were more moderate than those expressed, for example, in the *Européen*. Still, *Revue nationale* editorials at the end of February 1848 claimed that the paper had contributed to the overthrow of Louis-Philippe. In following weeks, the journal worked to turn the political into a social revolution, advocating, above all, workers' producer cooperatives, combating Louis Blanc's ideas, and stressing the social necessity of the Catholic faith. The *Revue nationale* also sought to dissuade Parisian workers from resorting to violence, particularly before the June insurrection, which it condemmed. Along with a number of other papers, it ceased publication when the government introduced more severe controls on the press. A final editorial asked subscribers to take the *Atelier* instead.

*Barrie M. Ratcliffe*

*Related entries: L'ATELIER;* BASTIDE; BLANC; BUCHEZ; CARREL; JUNE DAYS; *LE NATIONAL;* PRESS LAWS; REPUBLICANS; REVOLUTION OF 1848; WORKERS' COOPERATIVES.

*REVUE REPUBLICAINE* (April 1834–June 1835), opposition journal. The failure of the badly organized republican insurrection that followed the funeral of General Jean-Maximin Lamarque (5–6 June 1832) was attributed by opponents of the July Monarchy to insufficient attention by republican journalists and intellectuals to the problems of the lower classes. The decision to launch a serious republican review that would discuss social and economic issues reflected the improved prospects of the opposition in 1834, and the *Revue républicaine* was started by Dupont de Bussac (a member of the Society of the Rights of Man) and André Marchais (of the Association for the Liberty of the Press and a long-time friend of the marquis de Lafayette). In the introductory issue (April 1834), Dupont proclaimed that the goals of society were to preserve the well-being of the comfortable classes and to improve conditions for workers and the poor. Individual liberty and equality were impossible without fraternity and a concern for society's victims. While a thief may commit a crime, argued Dupont, an employer who impoverished his workers was an infinitely greater criminal. To achieve the proper ends of politics—moral, civil and penal reform, and true equality of means and health—universal suffrage, freedom of the press, and unrestricted access to jury duty would have to be created. A state based on universal suffrage would provide free secular education and use progressive taxation and inheritance taxes to limit inequality of fortunes. Free enterprise, which had produced such tragedies as the Lyons uprising of 1831, would be limited by government imposition of a twelve-hour day, a minimum wage, and producers' and workers' cooperatives in each canton, which would meet to fix wage levels under the supervision of departmental officials. The national and local governments should provide funds for unemployment insurance.

Dupont's article set the general tone of the *Revue*, and subsequent articles praised mechanization as a means of reducing inequality in the workplace, stressed the need for "democratic" art and literature, and described conditions in other countries. Republicans like Godefroy Cavaignac and Louis Blanc were frequent contributors; the opportunist deputies in the Chamber (led by Etienne Garnier-

Pagès) generally avoided association with the review and the secret societies to which many of its authors belonged. Stricter press laws were used to close down the *Revue* in June 1835.

I. Collins, *The Government and the Newspaper Press in France* (London, 1959); C. Ledré, *La presse à l'assaut de la monarchie* (Paris, 1960); G. Weill, *Histoire du parti republicain en France* (Paris, 1900).

*David Longfellow*

*Related entries:* BLANC; CAVAIGNAC, G.–E.–L.; GARNIER-PAGES; LAMARQUE; LYONS, REVOLTS IN; PRESS LAWS; SOCIETY OF THE FRIENDS OF THE FREEDOM OF THE PRESS; SOCIETY OF THE RIGHTS OF MAN.

**REY, JOSEPH** (1799–1855), lawyer and social reformer, revolutionary opponent of the Bourbon Restoration, magistrate during the July Monarchy, author of books on law, education, and social reform, propagandist in France for the ideas of the English socialist Robert Owen. Joseph Rey of Grenoble became interested in the social question as a young man, and throughout his life he was involved in the movement for social reform in France. As a lawyer and an *idéologue*, a follower of the *philosophe* Antoine-Louis-Claude Destutt de Tracy, he first hoped that new legislation could make mankind happy by bringing the legal system into harmony with the laws of nature. Later he realized that changes in the laws would not be enough, and so he added a demand for educational reforms to his previous call for representative government and individual liberty. Finally he saw that even new schools and new laws would have no effect if they were not accompanied by a redistribution of property. Rey hoped to accomplish his communist revolution by persuasion alone (though he was never able to convince even his wife), and he tried to orchestrate a united propaganda campaign by the followers of the Comte de Saint-Simon, Saint-Armand Bazard, Etienne Cabet, Charles Fourier, and Robert Owen that would touch the hearts of all Frenchmen and win them over.

But the more that Rey demanded, the less effective he became. At first Rey, a successful lawyer who had been disbarred during the Restoration because of his anti-Bourbon statements, had attracted powerful men to join the Union, a liberal secret society that he founded to resist the tyranny of the Restoration government. In Grenoble, where he founded the society in 1817, the original members included François Champollion, later the translator of the Rosetta Stone, and three future magistrates of the July Monarchy: Jean-Jacques Baude, Bérenger de la Drôme, and Félix Réal. In 1818, the first cell of the Union in Paris included the marquis de Lafayette (who joined because of Rey's close friendship with Destutt de Tracy) and several (fewer than thirty) young students, including Bazard, and others who would later pass into the magistracy of the July Monarchy by way of the revolutionary carbonari of the Bourbon Restoration. The reactionary events that followed the election of the abbé Grégoire in 1819 convinced the members of the Union to change their debating society into a revolutionary club. Along with the Friends of Truth, a revolutionary society masquerading as an organization of Freemasons, they plotted the so-called Conspiracy of 19 August 1820. Joseph Mérilhou, François de Corcelle, and René Voyer d'Argenson hoped to arouse discontented soldiers to make a military coup d'état that would overthrow the Bourbons. They had been promised 70,000 francs to finance the revolt if they could get Lafayette to join it. Rey acted as intermediary because both Lafayette and his son, George Washington Lafayette, were members of the Union. Rey talked to them; the Hero of Two Worlds asked, "When do I mount my horse?" and the revolt was on. But by 19 August 1820, the police had been informed. Bazard sent home the few bands of soldiers and students who had come out to begin the revolt, and the revolution was over before it had started. The government left the leaders alone, but Joseph Rey fled into exile and was condemned to death in absentia.

In Yverdun in Switzerland Rey met Johann Pestalozzi, the great educational reformer, and he became convinced that only mass education could make possible true social reform. In England in 1822, he visited infant schools in London and saw how very young children could be taught. The goal of education should be to go beyond mere professional training to a point where it could touch the moral nature of every student, turning him from selfish individualism toward human sympathy. Only through human sympathy, and never through violence, could true change be achieved.

It was, of course, violence that finally overthrew the Bourbons in the 1830 Revolution and brought Rey's friends to power in the July Monarchy. But Rey's applications for a major government job were ignored until finally, because of Lafayette's intercession, he received the minor post of judge at the Royal Court of Angers, which he kept until his transfer to the Royal Court in his native Grenoble in 1840. In Angers he established an infant school based on his theories, hoping that this model would be copied, and he pestered the government with petitions for a new system of schools that would teach all children that social interests were more important than individual interests. His *Traité complèt d'éducation physique, intellectuelle, et morale*, which he completed in 1837, did not find a publisher until 1844, and then only for the first volume. (The second volume was finally published in 1852.) His book, his petitions, and his model school went virtually unnoticed.

Meanwhile, Rey had begun to press for social reforms along the lines of Robert Owen's, whose doctrines he had absorbed while in exile in England. By 1832 he had become the departmental representative of the Saint-Simonian sect, he knew Parisian socialists like Bazard and "père" Enfantin, and he also kept in touch with the Icarians of Cabet and the Fourier socialists like Victor Considérant. Again, he insisted that only persuasion could convince people to put the interests of society ahead of their private interests, and he urged that socialists of all types should unite to win the hearts of Frenchmen to their cause. In *Des Bases de l'ordre social* (1836), Rey insisted that man is naturally good and that equality of property and education for all children could put an end to individualism and selfishness. The rich must first reform themselves and then offer their hands to the poor. Meanwhile, Rey was back in Grenoble helping to open schools and asylums for the deaf and the insane and to reform the prisons.

Rey took no part in the 1848 Revolution, but in 1849 he presented himself as a candidate from his native Isère department for the Legislative Assembly. His campaign was a summation of his life's work, calling for a redistribution of goods that would reward the worker and aid the weak, making government an expression of man's fundamental sympathy for his fellow man, using voluntary cooperation and education rather than force as a means of change. Here again (and again a summation of his life), he failed. Joseph Rey had tried to give to all society a warm family love that he had never received from his father, a prosperous confectioner, and his disinterested stepmother, and a moralizing faith that he had never found in the Roman Catholic church. His dream of a loving, godly communist world in which education and the laws would make people sympathetic and free now seems hopelessly idealistic. Meanwhile, the problems of urbanization and of the industrial revolution are being dealt with by adversarial and confrontational means rather than by the harmonious ones proposed by utopian communists like Joseph Rey of Grenoble.

R. A. Morris, "Joseph Rey of Grenoble, 1779–1855: Revolutionary—Educator—Humanitarian" (Ph. D. diss., University of Iowa, 1966); J. Rey, *Adresse à l'Empereur* (Paris, 1815), *Des Bases de l'ordre social*, 2 vols. (Paris, 1836), *Profession de foi du citoyen Joseph Rey, ex-conseiller à la cour d'appel de Grenoble* (Grenoble, 1849), and *Traité complèt d'éducation physique, intellectuelle et morale* (Paris, 1852); G. Weill, "Les Mémoires de Joseph Rey," *Revue historique*, 156 (January-April 1928) and "Un Educateur oublié, Joseph Rey," *Revue internationale de l'enseignement* 49 (January 1905).

*Edgar Leon Newman*

*Related entries:* BAUDE; BAZAR CONSPIRACY; BAZARD; CABET; CARBONARI; CHAMPOLLION; CONSIDERANT; DESTUTT DE TRACY; ENFANTIN; FOURIER; GREGOIRE; *IDEOLOGUES*; MERILHOU; SAINTSIMONIANISM; SOCIETE DE L'UNION; SOCIETY OF THE FRIENDS OF TRUTH; VOYER D'ARGENSON.

**RICHELIEU, ARMAND-EMMANUEL DU PLESSIS, DUC DE** (1766–1822), minister of Louis XVIII. A descendant of the brother of the great cardinal-minister of Louis XIII, he had been forced to emigrate at the end of 1789. He entered the service of the Russian army, and his brilliant conduct at the siege of Ismailia gained him the goodwill of the Czarina Catherine II. As a result, he became friends with her grandson Alexander. When Alexander became Czar in 1801, he called back Richelieu, who had returned to France and had refused all offers from Bonaparte. In 1803 Richelieu was named governor of Odessa and of the entire southern province recently conquered from the Turks. His administration was so benevolent that his memory is still celebrated in Odessa.

The restoration of the Bourbons in 1814 brought him back to France, where he was named a peer of France and first gentleman of the king's chamber. After

Napoleon's second defeat, the peace negotiations reached an impasse, and the Talleyrand government, which had been rejected by the electorate, was forced to resign. Louis XVIII named Richelieu minister of foreign affairs and president of the council. The friendship of Czar Alexander enabled him to moderate the early demands of the victorious Allies, and he signed the harsh Treaty of Paris on 20 November 1815. Ill at ease in a parliament and having neither the taste nor the ability for domestic politics, he left those matters more or less under the direction of Elie Decazes, minister of police and the royal favorite. But in foreign policy he succeeded, because of the confidence that his loyalty inspired, in regaining for France its rank as a European power. At the Congress of Aix-la-Chapelle in October 1818, he convinced the Allies to end their military occupation and to admit France into the concert of the Great Powers. After this he resigned. He was recalled to power in February 1820 after the assassination of the duc de Berry had brought about the fall of Elie Decazes. Under his second ministry, the reactionary laws that made it possible for the ultraroyalists to take power were enacted. When they took power, the ultraroyalists forced Richelieu to resign in December 1821, joining their negative votes with those of the left-wing liberal opposition and blaming him for a foreign policy that seemed indecisive and ambivalent. Shortly afterward he died of apoplexy on 17 May 1822.

C. Cox, *Talleyrand's Successor: Armand-Emmanuel du Plessis, duc de Richelieu* (London, 1959); J. Fouques-Duparc, *Le Troisième Richelieu* (Lyon, 1940).

*Guillaume de Bertier de Sauvigny*

*Related entries:* AIX-LA-CHAPELLE, CONGRESS OF; BERRY, C.-F.; CHAMBER OF DEPUTIES; CHAMBER OF PEERS; COUNCIL OF STATE; DECAZES; PARIS, SECOND TREATY OF; TALLEYRAND; ULTRA-ROYALISTS.

**ROBESPIERRE, MAXIMILIEN-FRANCOIS-MARIE-ISIDORE DE** (1758–1794), lawyer, deputy in the Estates General (and National Assembly), deputy in the National Convention, and member of the Committee of Public Safety. During one of the most dramatic and stormy debates imaginable in a parliamentary body, with the lives of the bitter antagonists literally at stake, the National Convention, by acclamation, ordered, even as he tried to speak, the arrest and removal from the floor of the Convention its most famous member, Maximilien Robespierre (27 July 1794). When the Commune of Paris (the municipal authorities) ordered that no prison in Paris accept Robespierre and ordered several other members expelled at the same time, the National Convention, learning that Maximilien was free, voted to place him *dehors de loi* (execution without trial after identification). Robespierre was captured at the Hôtel de ville by forces of the Convention at about 2:00 A.M. on the morning of 28 July, identified at a special session of the Revolutionary Tribunal, and executed at about 7:30 P.M. the same day. Thus ended the career of the man who probably best personifies the multifaceted character of the French Revolution from May 1789 until his death in July 1794.

Damned by those Thermidorians who had feared and destroyed him as a conspirator, scoundrel, and cowardly monster seeking to become a dictator, a step in the rehabilitation of the reputation of Robespierre was a significant development of the years between the Napoleons in French history. It was the first major phase of the process that ultimately established him as the central figure of the French Revolution.

Trained in the law at Louis le Grand and the University of Paris, he demonstrated uncommon zeal in defending the poor and the weak as a practicing lawyer in Arras. In 1789 he was elected to the Estates General as a representative of the Third Estate (from Artois) and as a member of the National Assembly (1789–91) and the National Convention (1792 until his death) he established himself in many ways as the man most representative of the various phases of the Revolution. Before assessing his impact on the Restoration era, a brief review of Robespierre's career is in order.

In reviewing hundreds of Robespierre's speeches, one is struck by the diversity of his interests and ideas and their significance then and now. In the areas of civil and human rights, Robespierre's advocacy of a host of reforms (1789–93) indicates the magnitude of his work. Far ahead of his time, Robespierre, in the National Assembly and the National Convention, supported and sponsored legislation that guaranteed freedom of speech and press, publication of the debates of the Assemblies, equality before the law, universal manhood suffrage, freedom of profession, abolition of game laws that kept peasants from hunting on their own land, popular control of the courts, unanimity of juries for conviction of criminals, and salaries for members of the National Assemblies so that those without outside income could serve. He insisted that enlisted men sit side by side with officers on court-martials, and his fear of military dictatorship meant that French generals had to be kept under civilian control. The wrongly accused should be indemnified and debtors' prisons abolished. He declared that society is obligated to provide food, clothing, and shelter for all its members. Robespierre's Republic of Virtue blazed a trail for the oppressed and underprivileged in French and European society and helped set the stage for the welfare state.

He visualized a France of small shopkeepers and small landowners in which the "right to exist" was the first of the imprescriptible rights. Maximilien (and the *sans-culottes*) never comprehended that the industrial revolution soon would bring changes that would make their dream of a society dominated by small, independent producers and distributors impossible to achieve. His advocacy of republican ideology as an instrument of foreign policy helped undermine monarchical regimes, and he was confident that Revolutionary principles such as liberty, equality, and free and compulsory public education would create the new man and regenerate humanity on a global basis. Many consider Robespierre the most creative and dynamic leader of the 1789–95 period, and his contribution to constitutional representative government has had worldwide impact. Modern politics began in France with Robespierre and the other ideologues of the Revolutionary era.

But as the leading member of the Committee of Public Safety (and the National Convention) from July 1793 to July 1794, Robespierre, in order to save the Revolution from its domestic and foreign enemies, was willing to suspend, temporarily he said, the liberties he had so brilliantly defined and defended since 1789. Robespierre's distinction between constitutional government and revolutionary government is significant. Constitutional government, in normal times, would protect individual liberties against encroachment by the state, but in a national emergency revolutionary government would protect the state from the dissidents and factions and provide the highly centralized regime necessary to meet the challenge. Robespierre's obsession with plots, conspiracies, traitors, and treason helped create the circumstances that provided the rationale for extreme measures. Blamed for the excesses of Terror by the Thermidorians who had ended his career and hated by many of the friends and sympathizers (and descendants) of royalists, *feuillants,* girondists, hébertists, *enragés,* and others who had lost their lives during the Revolution, it was not until well into the nineteenth century that serious attempts were made to defend his worldview and conduct. Criticism continued of the always controversial Incorruptible, but it was offset in part by the highest praise from a small number of political activists in France and elsewhere.

Napoleon and Louis XVIII made modest contributions to the rehabilitation of Robespierre. The count of Las Cases reported Napoleon as saying on Saint-Helena that Robespierre had "neither talent, energy, nor system but he had been made the scapegoat of the Revolution when he tried to return to a system of order and moderation" (*Memoirs*, 1:221). General Henri Bertrand quoted Napoleon as follows: "I have read the speech of Robespierre on the Supreme Being, and I don't know how one can deny his ability" (*Les Cahiers de Sainte-Hélène*, pp. 175–76). Louis XVIII, while in exile and after his return to France in 1814, said that it would be unjust to regard Robespierre as cruel and tyrannical and that he should be considered a statesman comparable to Sully and Richelieu.

The Charter of 1814, with its compromise between the institutions of the Old Regime and the institutions of the Revolutionary era, helped preserve many of the principles for which Robespierre stood. It was during the Restoration that giant steps were taken in the direction of reevaluating his role during the French Revolution. P. Paganel, in his *Essai historique . . . sur la Révolution française* (1815), praised Maximilien's high ideals and talent for influencing public opinion. An eighteen-volume collection of speeches and other documents on the Revolution (1818–21), edited by Guillaume Laurent, portrayed Robespierre in a much more positive fashion. Guillaume Lallement, in a sixteen-volume work on the Revolutionary era, was unrestrained in his praise of Maximilien. Like Filippo Buonarroti, Albert Laponneraye, Charles Teste, Etienne Cabet, Bronterre O'Brien, Louis Blanc, and others during the first half of the nineteenth century, Lallement seemed to succumb to the tendency to create an idealized version of Robespierre's role during the Reign of Terror.

In 1828 Levasseur de la Sarthe published his *Mémoires* in which, while not uncritical, he exonerated Robespierre and Saint-Just of responsibility for the excesses of the Terror. Adolphe Thiers described Robespierre as a man of integrity but also as an obstinate and bloodthirsty pontiff who "hid out on the day of danger" (*History of the French Revolution*, 4:50–51, 108). But during the first four decades of the nineteenth century, it was Filippo Buonarroti, more than any other man, who tirelessly defended the conduct and publicized the ideas of Robespierre, not only in France but in Belgium, the German Rhineland, Switzerland, and the Italian states. In 1828 Buonarroti published *Conspiration pour l'égalité dite de Babeuf*, an account of the uprising in 1796 in which François-Noel Babeuf was one of the leaders. Not only did he write in detail about the objectives and program of Babeuf, but he included a wide-ranging defense of Robespierre and the Terror.

Buonarroti insisted that the Committee of Public Safety had been not too severe but too sparing in the use of force. To restore justice and equality to a people corrupted by bad institutions, it was necessary to smite a few heads to ensure the safety of the French. In 1837 an article titled "Robespierre Jugé par Philippe Buonarroti" was published in *Le Radical*, a Brussels journal. Buonarroti described Robespierre as a temperate, modest, good, and courageous man who opposed tyranny, injustice, and immorality. He labored for social regeneration. Virtue, equality, liberty of the press, and a progressive income tax were part of his program. Unrestrained in his admiration for the Incorruptible, Buonarroti wrote: "During certain epochs there have appeared men of genius, virtue, and audacity who astounded the world and changed the course of history. Such were Moses, Pythagoras, Lycurgus, Jesus, and Mohammed, and such would have been Robespierre if he had had 50 men in the National Convention who understood and supported him" (Louis Jacob, *Robespierre vu par ses contemporains*, p. 217).

The struggle between Charles X and the Chamber of Deputies culminated in the July Ordinances and the overthrow of Charles X in 1830. During the struggle, scores of pamphlets were published by individuals and organizations eager to end the Bourbon regime. Citizen P. Rogeau of the Société des Montagnards wrote an article in the organization's newspaper, *Le Montagnard* (Bibliothèque nationale, Lb[51] 5349), and called on his fellow citizens to support the principles of the Mountain as they had been defined during the Revolutionary era. Rogeau declared that during the crises of the Revolution, "The man who distinguished himself most was Robespierre, and it was in his person that virtue reached its apogee." Robespierre, he said, overthrew the guilty king, supported Revolutionary principles, and rooted out corruption and treason. Rogeau added that no other man merits more than he the title of Incorruptible, and his fate will be that of the virtuous who sacrifice themselves in the struggle to ensure the triumph of truth. Robespierre, Saint-Just, and other members of the Mountain, with energy and courage, met the challenge presented by foreign invasion and internal revolt.

In a pamphlet entitled *Allocution prononcé à une assemblée générale de l'association pour la liberté de la presse* (Bibliothèque nationale, Lb⁵¹ 1991), Citizen Ernest demanded freedom of speech and press, election of officials, equitable taxes on the surplus of the rich, equality of rights, and the abolition of monopolies and privilege. He added that it was one of the Revolutionary assemblies that had produced the Declaration of Rights of Man and the Citizen and that the excesses of 1793 were justified by imperious necessity. He added, "Without 1793 there would have been no 1830." Pierre François Allier of the Société des Amis du peuple, when reproached for expressing his esteem for Robespierre and Saint-Just, answered in his *Lettre d'un étudiant, homme du peuple aux aristocrates doctrinaires* (Bibliothèque nationale, Lb⁵¹ 5349): "We love these great citizens and we admire all that is grand and generous in the souls of these virtuous republicans." These men, he declared, were unafraid of the hatred of their contemporaries and were satisfied to have their conduct judged by impartial posterity free of the passions of the moment.

In August 1830 the Société des droits de l'homme et la citoyen announced its Declaration of Principles. It proclaimed that Robespierre's proposed Declaration of Rights of 24 April 1793 was its platform, and members swore to support what they described as its holy principles. This republican secret society of the 1830s provided encouragement for republicans harassed by the July Monarchy and was revived as a club with the same name during the Revolution of 1848. Robespierre, one of the founders of the First French Republic, had relentlessly attacked and undermined monarchical institutions.

Albert Lapponneraye, a disciple of Buonarroti, collected and published the *Oeuvres de Maximillien Robespierre* (2 vols., 1832; 3 vols., 1840–42). While not complete, it was the first attempt to publish Robespierre's speeches and writings, and it was a significant step in the rehabilitation of his reputation. At a session of the Chamber of Deputies (6 January 1834), Marc-René de Voyer d'Argenson rose to defend Robespierre's proposed Declaration of Rights of 1793, an amended version of the Declaration of Rights of Man and the Citizen of 1789. D'Argenson spoke out not only for equality of political rights but, like Robespierre, for *égalité des conditions sociales"* (Archives parlementaires, deuxième série 1800 à 1860, LXXXV, 459). Charles Teste, a close collaborator of Buonarroti and d'Argenson, supported Robespierre's idea of a temporary Reign of Terror in which the basic freedoms might be suspended during a transition period while a republic of virtue was being established *(Projet de Constitution républicaine et déclaration des principes fondamentaux de la société*, p. 108). And Bertrand Barère, one of the Thermidorians who had helped bring Robespierre down on 27 July 1794, praised Maximilien's "integrity, love of liberty, firm principles, love of the poor and devotion to the popular cause" while criticizing his jealousy of men with talent and his relentless attacks on his enemies (*Mémoires*, 2:234–35).

Again and again Robespierrists between 1814 and 1850 referred to Maximilien's proposed Declaration of the Rights of Man, which he presented to the Jacobin

Club on 21 April and the National Convention on 24 April 1793 (*Oeuvres de Robespierre*, 9:454–59). Some of his suggestions were omitted in the draft of the Constitution approved in June by the Convention, but his proposals represent the most advanced stage of his thought. Robespierre was not a socialist, but he seemed to favor limitations on property rights, a position that appealed to some critical of the conservative Bourbon and Orleanist regimes. It was the principles he enumerated and defined in his proposed Declaration of Rights of 1793 that provided the rallying point for those who evoked his name in their efforts to establish a republic in 1830 and 1848.

Not only did Robespierre reaffirm his support for most of the principles enumerated in the Declaration of the Rights of Man and the Citizen approved in August 1789, but he addressed the social question so dear to the men who revered him during the first half of the nineteenth century. Maximilien, in article 2 of his proposed Declaration of Rights, listed the right to exist as one of the imprescriptible rights, but he did not include property as a natural right. Article 6 stated that "proprietorship is the right of each citizen to use and enjoy that portion of his wealth which is guaranteed to him by the law," and in article 7 Robespierre added that the right of property is limited, like all other rights, by the obligation to respect the privileges of others. Property rights cannot be used to threaten the safety, liberty, life, or property of others. In article 10 Robespierre declared that society is obligated to provide a livelihood for all its members, by providing either work or subsistence for those unable to work. Article 11 stated that those with a surplus must help those lacking necessities, and article 12 affirmed his support for a progressive income tax. Other articles not only reiterated his support for the principles of the original Declaration of Rights of August 1789 (equality before the law, sovereignty of the people, the right of the people to participate in their government, freedom of profession, and taxation according to ability to pay) but added the right to education and the right of insurrection. In article 38 Maximilien attacked kings, aristocrats, and tyrants, a posture that encouraged those hoping to overthrow the Bourbon and Orleanist regimes between 1814 and 1848.

Conveniently forgotten, however, was Robespierre's statement in a speech delivered to the National Convention on 24 April 1793 in which he declared: "Equality of property is an illusion and the *loi-agraire* [a proposal to redistribute land] is a ghost conjured up by the irresponsible to frighten idiots" (*Oeuvres de Robespierre*, 9:459). Later, he offended the urban masses when he helped close down the popular societies and limit the activities of the Paris sectional assemblies, as well as send leaders of the *sans-culottes* to the guillotine.

French Revolutionary studies took a giant step forward with the publication of P.-J.-B. Buchez's and P.-C. Roux's *Histoire parlementaire de la Révolution française* (40 vols., 1834–38). Speeches and articles of Robespierre are quoted at length, and Saint-Just and other Jacobins are treated sympathetically. In Russia

Alexander Herzen and Vissarion Biélinski praised Maximilien during the 1840s. Herzen described him as the truly great man of the Revolutionary era. He gave his stamp of approval not only to the Incorruptible's ideas but to his methods when he said, "He [Robespierre] walked in blood, but the blood did not tarnish him" *(Actes du Colloque Robespierre*, p. 243). Bielinski wrote that Robespierre was neither a scoundrel nor an intriguer and that a thousand year reign of God on earth would not be established by genteel idealists such as the Girondists but by terrorists such as Robespierre and Saint-Just *(Actes du Colloque Robespierre*, p. 241).

Martin Bernard called Robespierre "the new Moses who wrote on stone tablets . . . the introduction to the pact of the future" (A. Mathiez, *Girondins et Montagnards*, p. 222). Yet Auguste Blanqui described Robespierre as a hypocrite who used the guillotine to further his own ambitions *(Notes inédites de Blanqui sur Robespierre* quoted in full by Albert Mathiez, *Girondins et Montagnards*, pp. 223–35). In his four-volume popular history of the French Revolution published in 1845, Etienne Cabet defended Robespierre in terms understandable to workingmen, and his communist ideas influenced their thinking during the French Revolution of 1848. Alphonse de Lamartine praised the Girondins *(L'Histoire des Girondins*, 8 vols., 1847–48) and portrayed Robespierre as a man whose objectives were valid but one who was willing to use force and terror to achieve his goals. At about the same time, Jules Michelet *(Histoire de la Révolution française*, 7 vols., 1847–53) praised Danton while describing Robespierre as a man embodying virtue and evil who had presided over the Reign of Terror.

In England the reaction to Robespierre during the 1830s and 1840s was mixed. Bronterre O'Brien translated Buonarroti's *Conspiration pour l'égalité dite de Babeuf* and published *The Life and Character of Robespierre*. He seemed ready to elevate Robespierre to sainthood when he wrote: "Perhaps the most remarkable feature in the life and character of Robespierre is, that his career is pregnant with more of that species of instruction which is needed by reformers of the present day, than that of any other ruler, statesman, or public character that ever existed" *(Life and Character of Robespierre*, p. 397). Other Englishmen were less generous. In *Essays on the Early Period of the French Revolution* (1837), J. W. Croker had some kind words to say about Robespierre while being generally critical of the Revolution. G. H. Lewes, in *Life of Maximilien Robespierre* (1849), gave Maximilien credit for honesty and sincerity but labeled him a coward and a pedant whose legacy to mankind was nil.

In his *Histoire de la Révolution française* (12 vols., 1847–62), Louis Blanc was sympathetic in his treatment of Robespierre's role during the Reign of Terror, charging that his critics had buried him under a mountain of falsehood. Blanc, much involved in the French Revolution of 1848, maintained in *La République une et indivisible* (1851) that Robespierre was right and the Girondists were wrong when Maximilien insisted that giving authority to 3,700 primary assemblies to accept or reject acts of the National Convention would threaten the unity of the Republic.

Karl Marx, while convinced that the Jacobins had betrayed the *sans-culottes* late in 1793 and early in 1794 after using them repeatedly during earlier phases of the Revolution, saw the French Revolution in its totality as a step of the historical process in the development of the dialectic. He gave Jacques Roux and Babeuf a great deal of credit for launching what he called "the idea of the new world order" (Karl Marx and Friedrich Engels, *Collected Works*, 4:119). But he was critical of Robespierre and his colleagues: "Robespierre sees in great poverty and great riches only a stumbling block to pure democracy, not comprehending that it is the state that is the source of social ills" (*Collected Works*, 3:199). Thus, Marx is saying that Robespierre, obsessed with the political (the state), was not prepared to deal with the social problem. Marx contended that "Robespierre and Saint-Just and their party fell because they confused the ancient, realistic-democratic commonweal based on real slavery with the modern spiritualistic-democratic representative state which is based on emancipated slavery, bourgeois society" (*Collected Works*, 4:122). And Robespierre's willingness to use censorship during the Reign of Terror also was criticized by Marx. In discussing the Prussian censorship he declared: "Censorship laws are laws of terror . . . such as were invented owing to the emergency needs of the state under Robespierre" (*Collected Works*, 1:119).

During the Revolution of 1848 in France, some 200 clubs were organized that might be described as successors of the popular societies of 1792–94, which Robespierre had found too independent. Maximilien's speeches were posted on the walls of buildings and reproduced for mass distribution. The Société des droits de l'homme et du citoyen, the republican secret society of the same name in the 1830s, was reorganized in March 1848. A pamphlet it published pointed out that the proposed Declaration of Rights formulated by Robespierre in April 1793 was the basis of its principles: "In imitation of Maximilien Robespierre, we must recognize as imprescriptible the means of existence; the right to work is an obligation and idleness theft" (A. Lucas, *Les Clubs et les clubbistes*, p. 100). On 4 March 1848, at a meeting of the society, Citizen Marx (not Karl) declared: "I am a revolutionary. I want to march in the shadow of the great Robespierre" (Lucas, p. 114). The club's platform called for a strong and unified central government, universal manhood suffrage, a system of public education, more general use of jury trials, emancipation of the working classes through a better division of labor, a federation of Europe, and complete economic freedom. These demands were followed by Robespierre's proposed Declaration of Rights of 1793, which to some members of the organization seemed rather dated when its contents were compared with the rhetoric and the realities of life in revolutionary Paris in 1848.

The election of members of the Constituent Assembly was scheduled for 23–24 April 1848, and the Club of Clubs (Comité révolutionnaire pour les élections à l'assemblée constituante) was organized in March to coordinate the efforts of the many groups nominating candidates. It advertised that its platform was Robespierre's proposed Declaration of Rights of Man of 1793, and by unanimous vote the membership ordered 3 million copies of the declaration printed and distributed. The Club of Clubs voted to require its some 150 affiliated clubs "to support, apply, and develop the [Robespierre's] proposed Declaration of Rights of Man in all its democratic consequences" (Peter Amann, *Revolution and Mass Democracy: The Paris Club Movement of 1848,* p. 140). In March, during the election of officers of the National Guard, the Club Popincourt convinced the Eighth Legion (Eighth *arrondissement*) tht only candidates who had accepted Robespierre's proposed Declaration of Rights would be eligible for nomination. The *Club de l'émeute révolutionnaire,* founded in March 1848, quoted from documents written by Robespierre for his own use in 1793 and found in his room after his execution: "Where is the greatest danger? From the bourgeoisie. Who are our enemies? The rich. Will the interest of the rich be the same as the interest of the people? Never" (Lucas, p. 130).

These comments of Robespierre and the articles relative to limitations on property rights in his proposed Declaration of Rights of 1793 provide the base for extrapolation by his followers that probably goes beyond anything given his serious consideration. Generally, the neo-Jacobins of 1848 were more radical than their predecessors of the 1790s. They tended to create a Robespierre in their own image and ignore his bourgeois dedication (in theory) to a free and unregulated economy. After the June Days the government forbade citizens to "incite civil war" and comments in praise of Robespierre were placed in the forbidden category, since mentioning his name was said "to incite hatred". The unhappy fate of a number of the activist supporters of Maximilien was imprisonment or exile.

The Robespierrists of 1848, like those of the 1820s and 1830s, embraced most of Maximilien's ideas and labored not only to defend his conduct during the Revolution (1789–95) but to implement his program and world view. Although Alexandre Ledru-Rollin was no blind disciple of Robespierre, he rarely missed an opportunity to quote and praise him. Ledru-Rollin and Louis Blanc were members of the Provisional Government and were at the center of events, particularly during the early phases of the revolution. The abolition of the monarchy and the proclamation of the Second Republic by a decree of the Provisional Government (affirmed by the Constitution of 1848) were the most important goals of the Robespierrists.

With his speeches on the "right to exist" and his sponsorship of legislation which provided state financing of the minimal requirements of the poor for food, clothing, and shelter (1794), Robespierre had prepared the way for the decrees of the Provisional Government which guaranteed the right to work. But Louis Blanc's "Social Workshops" idea and the ill-fated National Workshops were part of the debate in 1848, and right to work became "fraternal assistance to the indigent . . . " in the constitution of the Second Republic. Clauses of the new constitution also incorporated other principles of the Incorruptible and his disciples: universal manhood suffrage, freedom of speech and press, free and secular primary education, taxation according to the ability to pay (the progressive income tax was discussed), the separation of powers, rejection of wars of conquest, and salaries for members of the National Assembly were among its articles and indicate that the clubs and secret societies had influenced the course of events.

During the Revolution of 1848 the French had once again been reminded of the legacy of the Great Revolution, a legacy which was to contribute mightily to the establishment of parliamentary government in the Third, Fourth, and Fifth French Republics. The Industrial Revolution with its large-scale industry and masses of workers who wanted labor unions and the right to strike had created a society which was a great deal different from the pre-industrial structure of small shopkeepers and small farmers idealized in Maximilien's description of his Republic of Virtue. The conditions of 1848 were not those of 1793.

Robespierre remains a controversial figure. His chief support has come from the left of center factions in the French political spectrum, but liberals are split and socialists (and communists) are divided on the question of his place in French history. Nevertheless, the Restoration era as a whole was one in which a great deal of progress was made in rehabilitating the reputation of Maximilien, a process which was to continue in the writings of men such as Ernest Hamel and Jean Jaurès and reach its height in the 20th century in the work of historian Albert Mathiez, who did more than any other individual to establish him as the central figure of the French Revolution.

*Actes du Colloque Robespierre* (Paris, 1967); E. B. Courtois, *Rapport fait au nom de la Commission chargée de l'Examen des papiers de Robespierre et ses complices* (Paris, 1794); J. Louis, *Robespierre vu par ses contemporains* (Paris, 1958); A. Lucas, *Les Clubs et les Clubbistes . . . 1848* (Paris, 1851); J. Madival and E. Laurent, *Archives parlementaires de 1787 à 1860*, 1st ser. 1787–99, 82 vols., 2d ser. 1799–60, 127 vols. (Paris, 1862-); K. Marx and F. Engels, *Collected Works*, vols. 1, 3, 4 (New York, 1975); A. Mathiez, *Autour de Robespierre* (Paris, 1957) and *Girondins et Montagnards* (Paris, 1930); *Oeuvres complètes de Maximilien Robespierre*, 10 vols. (Paris, 1910–67); G. Rudé, *Robespierre: Portrait of a Revolutionary Democrat* (New York, 1976); J. I. Shulim, "The Youthful Robespierre and His Ambivalence toward the Ancient Regime," *Eighteenth-Century Studies* 5 (1972); M. Slavin, *The French Revolution in Miniature: Section Droits-de-l'homme, 1789–1795* (Princeton, 1984); A. Soboul, "Robespierre and the Contradictions of Jacobinism," trans. E. Newman, *Proceedings of the Western Society for French History*, vol. 5 (November 1977); J. M. Thompson, *Robespierre*, 2 vols. (New York, 1935); G. Walter, *Robespierre*, 2 vols. (Paris, 1961); G. Weill, *Histoire du parti républicain en France (1814–1876)* (Paris, 1928).

*Vincent Beach*

*Related entries:* BLANC; BLANQUI, L.-A.; BUCHEZ; BUONARROTI; CABET; CLUB OF CLUBS; CLUBS, POLITICAL; LAMARTINE; MARX; MICHELET; REPUBLICANS; SOCIETY OF THE RIGHTS OF MAN; THIERS; VOYER D'ARGENSON.

**ROCHEFOUCAULD.** See LA ROCHEFOUCAULD.

**ROCHEFOUCAULD-LIANCOURT.** See LA ROCHEFOUCAULD-LIANCOURT.

**ROCHEJAQUELEIN.** See LA ROCHEJAQUELEIN, H.-A.-G.; LA ROCHEJAQUELEIN, L.

**ROLAND, PAULINE** (1805–1852), socialist and feminist. The daughter of a widow who directed the post office at Falaise, Pauline Roland was introduced to Saint-Simonism by a teacher and went to Paris in 1832. She lived in free unions with Jean Aicard and Adolphe Guéroult and insisted on raising her three children alone. She wrote for the early feminist papers *La Femme libre (1832)* and *La Tribune des femmes (1833)* and, while working as a teacher's assistant, wrote lengthy histories of England, France, and the United Kingdom.

After Flora Tristan's death in 1844, Pauline Roland cared for her daughter Aline Chazal, later to be the mother of Paul Gauguin. She wrote for the *Revue indépendante* (1842–47) and went to Pierre Leroux's community at Boussac, where she worked on *L'Eclaireur de l'Indre* and in the school. She did not return to Paris until late in 1848 but quickly became involved with Jeanne Deroin and Désirée Gay on *L'Opinion des femmes* and with Deroin and Gustave Lefrançais founded the Association of Socialist Teachers in 1849. Her education program was a comprehensive plan for eighteen years of learning and stressed equal educational and work opportunities for women.

With Deroin she was also prominent in establishing the important Union of Workers' Associations in October 1849. Her vision was characterized by both a commitment to producers' cooperatives and a Saint-Simonian ideal of women's mystical and divine mission. She was among the forty-six men and women arrested when the union's offices were raided in May 1850, and she was imprisoned until 2 July 1851 after an impassioned feminist speech at her trial.

The events of 1849–51 had politically radicalized her, and, despite her testimony at her trial in February 1852, she was certainly involved in the resistance to the coup d'état of December 1851. Transported to Algeria, she was released in November through the active intervention of Pierre-Jean de Béranger and George Sand but died in Lyons on her way to Paris.

L. Adler, *A l'Aube du féminisme: les premières journalistes (1830–1850)* (Paris, 1979); J. Maitron, ed., *Dictionnarie biographique du mouvement ouvrier français, (1789–1864)* (Paris, 1964–66); P. Roland, A. Ranc, and G. Rouffet, *Bagnes d'Afrique* (Paris, 1981); E. Thomas, *Pauline Roland* (Paris, 1956).

*Peter McPhee*

*Related entries:* BERANGER; COUP D'ETAT OF 2 DECEMBER 1851; DE-ROIN; LEROUX; *L'OPINION DES FEMMES*; *LA REVUE INDEPENDANTE*; SAINT-SIMONIANISM; SAND; TRISTAN; WOMEN'S NEWSPAPERS.

**ROMAN EXPEDITION** (1849), military expedition that captured Rome in 1849. The defeat of Charles-Albert, king of Piedmont, in the autumn of 1848 and the liberal revolution that chased Pope Pius IX from Rome opened Italy to Austrian intervention. A French force of 14,000 men under General Charles-Nicholas-Victor Oudinot was dispatched to Rome to prevent this. Oudinot landed at Civita-Vecchia on 25 April 1849. However, political confusion in France had deprived him of any clear orders. The Left believed that he had been sent to protect the new Roman Republic from the Austrians, while the Right wanted him to suppress the Republic and restore the pope. French diplomats hoped to negotiate a compromise between French liberals and the pontiff. However, when the republicans opened fire on French troops, President Louis-Napoleon Bonaparte, hoping to curry favor with French Catholics, ordered Oudinot to seize Rome. The siege began on 4 June 1849. Oudinot refused to bombard the city, which surrendered to the French on 1 July 1849. The restoration of Pope Pius IX placed the French Republic firmly in the camp of the counterrevolution.

A. Dansette, *Histoire religieuse de la France contemporaine* (Paris, 1965); L. Girard, *La IIe république* (Paris, 1968).

*Douglas Porch*

*Related entries:* OUDINOT; PIUS IX.


**ROMANTICISM,** a European artistic and intellectual movement, manifested most clearly in France between 1815 and 1848, that was primarily a cultural reaction to the neoclassical values and rationalistic attitudes of the eighteenth-century Enlightenment. Romanticism cannot be restricted to any one genre, country, or period; it affected literature, art, music, and even historical writing in the United States, England, Spain, Italy, Prussia, and other Western countries from as early as the beginning of the eighteenth century to as late as the post-World War II era. The movement's influence at its height in the early nineteenth century is also difficult to locate, since its clearest manifestations then were extremely varied. Rejecting neoclassical order and balance, the European romantics often embraced instead the impulsive and irrational to explore the hidden sources of self and consciousness. Their accomplishments suited the different temperaments of the individual. What the romantics had most in common, however, was an often unconscious response to the eighteenth-century *philosophes'* claims of objectivity and universality. Consequently romanticism's remarkable variety was one consequence of a largely historical subjectivity, one especially shared by artists and writers at the turn of the nineteenth century.

For France, this European artistic and intellectual phenomenon was relatively late and unenduring because of the exceptionally strong French tradition of classicism and because of the peculiar French relationship between art and politics. The first substantial evidence of romanticism in France appeared in Jean-Jacques Rousseau's *La Nouvelle Héloïse* (1761), which praised the innate virtues of rustic people and brought attention to a primitivism later developed by J. H. Bernardin de Saint-Pierre. The Revolution of 1789 effectively destroyed most interest in this aspect of Rousseau's thought; it instilled instead a fascination with classical themes and motifs reminiscent of the Roman Republic much admired by Revolutionary enthusiasts. The neoclassicism of the Revolution and its Napoleonic aftermath effectively delayed the full development of French romantic art and literature for the twenty years that the movement flourished in other European countries. Major exceptions to this were the *émigré* literati, such as F.-R. de Chateaubriand and Germaine de Staël, known as the first generation of French romantics for their deeply felt response to the Revolution's effects on French social and cultural life. While Chateaubriand's *Le Génie du Christianisme* (1804) celebrated the aesthetics of Christian ritual, Staël's *De l'Allemagne* (1808–10) introduced to France the spirit of German idealism. But only with the defeat of Napoleon, the heir to the Revolution's classicism, could the romantic movement develop fully in France.

Shortly after the Bourbon Restoration, romanticism's influence increased remarkably. Théodore Géricault's dramatic tableau, "Le Radeau de la Méduse," brought the movement to the attention of the general French artistic public in 1819. The attack on neoclassical style and subjects broadened with the publication of Lord Byron's poetic exoticism and Walter Scott's historical fiction, both of which in translation enjoyed even wider circulation in Restoration France than the lyrical emotion of Alphonse de Lamartine's *Les Méditations poétiques* (1820). Their French admirers soon undertook a more deliberate attack on eighteenth-century values by celebrating the particular over the universal, the mystical over the secular, the emotional over the rational, and the medieval over the classical. To promote their position, some writers established journals like *La Muse française* (1823–24), and others wrote manifestos like Henri Beyle's *Racine et Shakespeare* (1824). The battle lines between the romantics and the neoclassicists, especially in the traditional genres of poetry, drama, painting, and music, were thus sharply drawn for the duration of the Restoration. Whether or not they actually shared in the movement's rejection of secularism, reason, and rationality, frustrated younger writers and artists often adopted the banner of romanticism as a more general repudiation of an older generation's social and political values. Thus, it was no accident that 1830 saw the defeat of both the Bourbon regime and its neoclassical apologists; Victor Hugo's play explicitly violating the neoclassical unities, *Hernani*, was staged at the Théâtre-français just five months before the July Revolution.

While Eugène Delacroix's *Liberty Leading the People* (1831) marked the high point of romanticism in France, it also represented a crucial shift in the French movement's development. After 1830 romantic interests grew more diverse. The romantic aesthetic vision became increasingly less anticlassical and more eclectic, its politics less royalist and more socialist. The young Alexander Dumas was the only major romantic on the barricades in 1830. In 1848, both Lamartine and George Sand played leading political roles that followed logically from the moderate social-republican sympathies expressed in their writings during the July Monarchy. Others, like Hector Berlioz, eschewed this messianic interest to embrace instead an anarchistic commitment to art for art's sake. In the preface to *Mademoiselle de Maupin* (1836), Théophile Gautier defended the habits of his *petit cénacle*—distinct from Hugo's larger and better-known circle of artists and literati—to flout deliberately the social and aesthetic as well as political conventions of the Orleanist middle classes. A similar diversity appeared in romantic historical writings. The accounts of the 1789 Revolution by Adolphe

Thiers (1823–27) and Auguste Mignet (1824) stand in marked contrast to those by Lamartine (1847) and Jules Michelet (1847–53); the latter historians felt compelled not merely to defend but to exalt the Revolution. They shared in a romantic historiographic trend away from accounts of the Middle Ages to those of more recent events, a trend similar to the development of the novel of contemporary manners and mores, like Honoré de Balzac's *La Comédie humaine* (1835–50), that soon rivaled the historical novel for public attention.

By the early 1840s romanticism's growing variety of forms and interests seriously eroded its influence in France. The movement had always been extremely difficult to define, even during the Restoration, when its proponents shared a common enemy: neoclassicism. Now, after having captured the allegiance of most creative minds, the romantics had no further contribution to make other than the proliferation of careless and chaotic work. This point Alfred de Musset's "Les Lettres de Dupuis et Cotonet" made in 1838 when many other romantics were also deeply disillusioned. Their *mal du siècle* had become a *mal du système*. The movement's introspective and emotional spirit may have survived for much of the century, even to recur occasionally in the next, but its primary influence had waned significantly by the Second Republic. Then a tougher-minded naturalism in political and creative endeavor appeared, one reflected in Gustave Courbet's *Les Casseurs de pierres* (1849), which largely displaced the sentimental idealism and aesthetic diversity of the romantics. France returned to the classical values of order and realism in the arts at the same time it developed another kind of order and realism in politics—after the bloody days of June 1848 and the resounding defeat of Lamartine for the presidency of the Second Republic the next December.

J. S. Allen, *Popular French Romanticism: Authors, Readers, and Books in the 19th Century* (Syracuse, 1981); J. Barzun, *Berlioz and the Romantic Century*, 2 vols. (New York, 1969); P. Bénichou, *Le Temps des prophètes: Doctrines de l'âge romantique* (Paris, 1977); D. G. Charlton, ed., *The French Romantics*, 2 vols. (Cambridge, 1984); M. Milner, *Le Romantisme, I: 1820–1843* (Paris, 1973); H. Peyre, *Qu'est-ce que le romantisme* (Paris, 1974).

*James Smith Allen*

*Related entries:* BALZAC; BERLIOZ; BYRON; CHATEAUBRIAND; DELACROIX; DUMAS, A.; GAUTIER; GERICAULT; *HERNANI*; HUGO; LAMARTINE; MICHELET; MIGNET; *LA MUSE FRANCAISE*; MUSSET; ROUSSEAU; SAND; STAEL-HOLSTEIN; STENDHAL; THIERS.

**ROME, CONFERENCE OF** (April–July 1831). a conference called to discuss the future disposition of the Papal States. With the overthrow of Charles X in July 1830 and the accession of Louis-Philippe, liberals throughout Europe welcomed what they believed to be the beginning of the dismemberment of the legitimist order imposed upon the peoples of Europe after the fall of Napoleon in 1815. When Louis-Philippe's government denounced the right of any power to intervene in the affairs of another country and insisted that at all times the principle of nonintervention be observed, revolutionaries in the Italian states were filled with hope; they looked forward with great anticipation to the day when the yoke of Austrian occupation and the archaic rule of papal government would be lifted and replaced by rule much more responsive to the needs of the people.

Planned for many months, chiefly by the Modenese patriot Ciro Menotti, revolutionary uprisings broke out in February 1831 in Modena, quickly spread to Parma, and finally reached out and engulfed the Papal States. Within a matter of a few weeks, papal authority was maintained only in Rome and a few small enclaves in the legations. Central Italy's freedom, however, proved to be short-lived. Gregory XVI called upon the Austrian government for support so that order might be restored in the legations. Without much difficulty, the Austrians had restored order to the Italian states by the end of March 1831.

These uprisings clearly demonstrated to the European powers that the pope and his ministers were not capable of governing effectively. Moreover, the Austrians could not be permitted to remain in the legations as a force of occupation. They concluded that only by means of reform could lasting tranquility be established in the Papal States.

Baron Bünsen, Prussian ambassador to the Holy See, on 3 March 1831 proposed to the ambassadors of the Great Powers that a conference be called to discuss the reorganization of the Papal States. The idea of such a conference of the powers meeting in Rome was acceptable in principle to Austria, France, Great Britain, and Russia. Through negotiation the French government sought to achieve the immediate and complete removal of Austrian troops, total amnesty for those involved in the revolutionary uprisings, and administrative reform in the Papal States. If substantive reforms were enacted, future outbreaks of revolutionary violence on the peninsula might be prevented, thereby reducing the possibility of armed conflict between France and Austria. The British supported the French position. While not opposed to the idea of reform, Clemens von Metternich would not agree to removing Austrian troops unless papal authority could be guaranteed by all the powers. Austria enjoyed the support of the Prussian and Russian governments.

The Conference of Rome began its work on 13 April 1831. The ambassadors assembled in Rome would focus their attention on several important issues: amnesty for revolutionaries, evacuation of Austrian troops, and implementation of administrative reforms in the Papal States. As the representatives of the powers began their meetings in Rome, the pope and his ministers decided that they would be able to resolve these matters on their own. A papal edict published on 16 April attempted to address those matters under discussion at the conference. The edict established military and civil commissions to investigate the uprisings. These commissions were charged with the responsibility of distinguishing between individuals who instigated the uprisings and those merely drawn into the revolutionary movement. Amnesty and order were the objectives of the edict. Political amnesty and the promise of reform detailed in the 16 April edict did not bring an end to the problem. Austrian troops remained in the Papal States, and the powers assembled in Rome resolved to continue their meetings in the hope of bringing about a peaceful resolution to the revolutionary turmoil.

On 21 May the ambassadors presented a memorandum to the papal government. This document aimed at making the temporal power of the pope more bearable for his subjects. It called for the laity to be allowed to undertake all administrative and judicial functions, municipal councils to be elected by a popular vote, and municipal councils to select some of the members of the new supreme board of finance, which would be responsible for auditing the public accounts and supervising the public debt. This memorandum represented the only major achievement of the Conference of Rome. It would serve as the basis for the resolution of affairs just two months later.

The papal government was not favorably impressed by the memorandum. The introduction of reforms that would change the Papal States from ecclesiastical to lay, create popularly elected municipal councils, and introduce financial accountability was not acceptable to Gregory XVI and his ministers. The Austrian government remained unconvinced that the reforms proposed by the conference would bring about conditions in the Papal States that would prevent the outbreak of revolutionary violence in the future. Metternich would accept the ambassadors' memorandum only if it was accompanied by a guarantee signed by all the powers that would commit them to come to the aid of the pope should his temporal authority be challenged by revolutionary elements in the Papal States. Faced with increasing opposition at home that called for complete support for Italian revolutionaries, Louis-Philippe's government found itself in no position to accept Metternich's proposed guarantee. The French insisted that the 21 May memorandum be adopted and that Austrian troops withdraw totally from the Papal States. Without the adoption of the memorandum and the withdrawal of Austrian troops, the moderate Périer ministry, which had just come to power in March, would be certain to fall and be replaced by a much more liberal ministry, one much less willing to come to a negotiated settlement of issues.

Hoping to avoid the confrontation that might result from a change in ministries in France, the Austrian government decided to withdraw its troops from the Papal States. The papal government also agreed to the evacuation and reluctantly acquiesced to the wishes of the powers assembled in Rome. Amnesty would be accorded to all but forty individuals. Laymen would be allowed to administer one of two northern provinces, and municipal councils were to be established. By the end of July, Austrian troops had been completely withdrawn from the Papal States. By securing Austrian evacuation and the enactment of reforms, as limited as they may have been, the Conference of Rome had achieved what it had set out to do when it was called to order some two months earlier: confrontation between France and Austria had been avoided and peace ensured.

The conference completed its work by the end of July. The attention of the European powers was shifted to the north, where the Dutch were preparing to bring a forcible end to the revolutionary movement in the southern Netherlands. The conference of powers assembled in Rome in the spring of 1831 could adjourn with the knowledge that order had been maintained. However, the struggle carried on by the liberals in the Italian states to wrest power from the conservative forces of the pope and the Austrian government had not yet been completed. Within a year, revolutionary violence would return to the peninsula, and once again the competition between France and Austria for strategic superiority on the peninsula would threaten peace on the Continent.

E. Holt, *The Making of Italy, 1815–1870* (New York, 1971); N. Nada, *L'Austria e la Questione Romana della Rivoluzione di Luglio alda Fine della Conferenza Diplomatica Romana, 1830–1831* (Turin, 1953); A. J. Reinerman, *Austria and the Papacy in the Age of Metternich: Between Conflict and Cooperation, 1809–1830*, vol. 1 (Washington, 1979) and "Metternich and Reform: The Case of the Papal State, 1814–1848," *Journal of Modern History* (December, 1970); D. M. Smith, *Italy: A Modern History* (Ann Arbor, Mich., 1959); C. Vidal, *Louis-Philippe, Metternich et la crise italienne de 1831–1832* (Paris, 1931).

*Daniel P. Schmidt*

*Related entries:* BELGIAN REVOLUTION OF 1830; FOREIGN POLICY OF LOUIS-PHILIPPE; METTERNICH; PERIER; REVOLUTION OF 1830.


**ROME, KING OF.** See REICHSTADT.


**ROTHSCHILD FAMILY,** bankers and financiers. The founder of the modern Rothschild banking dynasty was Meyer-Anselm Rothschild (1743–1812), the son of a German-Jewish shopkeeper in the ghetto of Frankfurt-on-Main. Originally destined for the rabbinate, Meyer-Anselm was sent to a yeshiva in Fürth but accepted a job as a clerk in the Oppenheimer bank in Hanover on completion of his studies. He returned to Frankfurt with his savings in 1763 and opened a business firm in his own name. Dealing in antiques, rare coins, currency exchanges, and credit, he enjoyed considerable success. In 1789, his success in finding several coins for the numismatist elector of Hesse-Cassel, William I, and a friendship with Carl Bruderus, an official in the Hessian treasury, brought him into contact with the royal government. He succeeded in raising loans to finance the construction of William's palace at Wilhelmshohe and to support Hessian military operations in the wars against Revolutionary France. By 1801, he was the principal banker of the electoral regime, and in 1802 he was able to raise 10 million thalers for a loan to the Danish government. When the elector fled in the wake of the French invasion in 1806, he entrusted his personal fortune to Meyer-Anselm, who protected it from confiscation and invested it profitably.

By the early 1800s, the Rothschild bank was financing a large part of the Allied war effort, funneling funds to the duke of Wellington's armies in Spain and supplying operating capital during the Waterloo campaign, as well as a subsidy to Louis XVIII during his 1815 exile in Brussels. In the process, Meyer-Anselm, aided by his son Nathan, created the initial networks of the Rothschild courier system, which enabled the bank to move funds safely about Europe and provided reliable news of major events, which helped with speculative investments.

Meyer-Anselm married Gutta Schnapper and had ten children (five boys and five girls). His eldest son took over the family bank in Frankfurt (Meyer-Anselm de Rothschild and Sons), while the other four opened independent but affiliated banks in London, Paris, Vienna, and Naples. The family was ennobled by Francis II of Austria in 1815, and Meyer-Anselm's sons were made Austrian barons in 1822. The careers of the five sons (who all shared their father's red hair, round face, and pudgy build) and their branches of the family, are as follows.

Anselm-Meyer (1773–1855) took over the main bank in Frankfurt in 1813, became a Prussian privy councilor in 1820, court banker to Bavaria, and the Bavarian consul in Frankfurt. When he died without heirs, the bank was taken over by his nephews Karl (1820–86) and William-Karl (1828–1901). Karl was elected to the Reichstag of the North German Confederation in 1867 and became a life peer of the Prussian Landtag. Like many of the other Rothschilds, Karl married a cousin (his uncle Nathan's daughter Louise), and three of his six daughters would marry other Rothschilds.

Solomon (1774–1855) founded the Vienna branch of the family bank. He worked energetically to remove restrictions on Jews in the Austrian Empire (where they were prohibited from owning real estate and barred from the legal profession, teaching, the civil service, the officer corps, and judgeships). Solomon was instrumental in getting most of these restrictions repealed in 1843 and preventing their reimposition in 1853. He invested heavily in steelworks and charities, founding hospitals and subsidizing the Vienna water system. He was succeeded by his eldest son, Anselm Solomon (1803–74), and his third son, Albert (1844–1911).

Nathan (1777–1836) opened the English branch of the bank in Manchester in 1798, moving his offices to London in 1813. His assistance in the financial crisis of 1813 brought him close ties to the royal government. He was named Austrian consul to Great Britain in 1822. His son and successor Lionel (1808–79), who managed the London bank with his brothers Anthony and Meyer, was elected to Parliament but was unable to take his seat until 1858, when the oath was modified. Lionel's son Nathaniel (1840–1915) became a member of Parliament in 1865 and was made a baron and peer in 1885. Nathaniel married his cousin Emma Louise (Karl's daughter), and more cousinly marriages took place among his children. In addition to banking and government service, Nathaniel acquired an international reputation as an art collector.

Karl (1788–1855) established the family bank in Naples in 1820 but continued to live in Frankfurt, where he became the Neapolitan consul-general after 1829. His two eldest sons (Karl and William-Karl) took over the Frankfurt bank, and his third son, Adolphe (1823–1900), assumed the directorship of the Naples bank but eventually closed it. All four of Karl's children married Rothschild cousins.

Jacob (Jacques) (1792–1868) opened the Paris bank (Rothschild Brothers) in 1822 and served as Austrian consul in France. Jacob prospered under the July Monarchy through a personal friendship with Louis-Philippe and Casimir Périer, when his bank achieved a practical monopoly on government loans. Rothschild Brothers raised state loans in 1830, 1831, 1832, and 1844 for a total of more than 500 million francs. Jacob was made a member of the Legion of Honor in 1823 and a grand officer in 1844. Generally described as personable and open, he was a friend of Rossini, George Sand, Honorè de Balzac, and Eugène Delacroix, and he enjoyed a personal fortune of 40 million to 50 million francs. An energetic promoter of railroads, he opened rail lines from Paris to Saint-Germain (1837) and from Paris to Versailles (1839), and in 1840 he received a government concession for the Chemin de fer du Nord rail network in northern France.

As an ex-Orleanist, his influence declined under the Second Empire, and the Crédit mobilier (a joint project of his rivals Emile and Isaac Pereire and Achille Fould [Napoleon III's minister of finance] was created in 1852 partly to lessen de Rothschild's monopoly on government banking). Jacob had invested heavily in the political career of General Eugène Cavaignac in 1848 and had been disappointed by Louis-Napoleon's election to the presidency of the Second Republic and subsequent creation of the Empire. He did have the satisfaction of seeing the collapse of the Crédit mobilier in 1867, the same year in which he purchased the Chateau Lafitte vineyards in the Médoc (his cousin Nathaniel already owned the neighboring Mouton estates). Jacob had married his niece Betty (Solomon's daughter) and had four sons, of whom Alphonse (1827–1905), Edmond, and Gustave took over the bank. Alphonse was trained in the London, Frankfurt, and Vienna branches and became a regent of the Bank of France, a member of the boards of several railroads, and a noted art collector. He purchased the chateau at Ferrières (which was appropriated by Wilhelm I, Bismarck, and von Moltke during the siege of Paris in 1870) and Talleyrand's former *hôtel* on the rue Saint-Florentin in Paris. Alphonse was primarily responsible for managing the rapid payment of France's indemnity after the Franco-Prussian war.

Alphonse's brother Edmond (1845–74) became a passionate supporter of a Jewish homeland in Palestine and devoted a large part of his fortune to buying land there and encouraging Jewish emigration from Europe. Alphonse's eldest son, Edouard (1868–1949), took over the Paris bank on his father's death, and Edouard's son, Guy (1909–), and his nephews Alain (1910–) and Elie (1917–) manage it today. Guy de Rothschild fought with Charles de Gaulle and the Free French in 1943–45, and Alain and Elie served in German prisoner of war camps after the French defeat in 1940.

Intrafamily marriages, membership in the European aristocratic elite, the famous courier service, and close ties among the various banks helped preserve a sense of unity among the various branches of the Rothschild family well into the twentieth century. Their diplomatic posts and network of influential political and financial contacts enabled them to exert pressures on European governments and to lessen (or profit from) the disruptive impact of wars and revolutions. As the wealthiest Jewish financial family in Europe, the Rothschilds were frequent targets of anti-Semitic propaganda and political radicals of the Left and Right, but the unquestionable skill of generations of family members in business and banking always seemed a more reasonable explanation of their success than rumors of a powerful Jewish syndicate secretly controlling the destiny of Europe.

E. Corti, *La Maison Rothschild*, 2 vols. (Paris, 1929–30); V. Cowles, *The Rothschilds* (New York, 1973); B. Gille, *Histoire de la maison Rothschild*, 2 vols. (Paris, 1965–67); A. Muhlstein, *James de Rothschild* (Paris, 1981); S. Reeves, *The Rothschilds* (London, 1887); H. Schnee, *Rothschild, Geschicte eine Finanz Dynastie* (Gottingen, 1961).

*Daniel Longfellow*

*Related entries:* BANKING; CAVAIGNAC, L.-E.; LOUIS-PHILIPPE; PEREIRE BROTHERS; PERIER.

**ROUSSEAU, JEAN-JACQUES** (1712–1778), influential philosopher, novelist, political theorist, and composer. The son of a Geneva watchmaker, Rousseau became one of France's most controversial eighteenth-century *philosophes* whose writings exerted a profound influence on early nineteenth-century thought and literature. His importance to the generation of writers at work during the Restoration and Orleanist monarchies cannot be easily assessed. But Rousseau's publications continued to be edited and reissued, both individually and in complete collections. From 1815 to 1850, thirty-nine sets of his collected works were advertised in the *Bibliographie de la France*, the book trade's primary national commercial manual. Moreover, there were twenty-six new editions of *La Nouvelle Héloïse*, twenty-one of *Emile*, twelve of *Du Contrat social*, eleven of *Les Confessions*, eight of *Lettres sur la botanique*, and eighteen of his other works. More than forty-two books explicitly devoted to Rousseau's life, thought, or influence in France appeared in the same period, according to Quérard's 1845 analytical catalog. This significant corpus on or by Rousseau encompassed more than 1,000 volumes published from the fall of Napoleon to the coup d'état of his nephew. Edition sizes ranged from as large as 3,500 to as small as 50 copies. Nearly all the more than 100 extant catalogs of the lending libraries operating in Paris during the constitutional monarchies listed works by Rousseau. His novels especially appealed to a clientele anxious to rent books that cost at least a *journalier*'s weekly wages per volume until Charpentier's edition of the *Confessions* which sold for 3 francs 50 in 1841.

Rousseau's actual influence on nineteenth-century thinkers, however, cannot be so easily quantified. The *philosophe*'s insistence on the natural goodness of man and the depravity of the social environment, themes developed in his early work, underlie the assumptions made by the utopian socialists Claude-Henri de Saint-Simon, Charles Fourier, Pierre Leroux, and Victor Considérant. Similarly, the many surveys of the working and living conditions of the laboring poor by Antoine-Eugène Buret, Pierre Bigot de Morogues, and Louis-René Villermé, among others, explored the extent to which morality was threatened by physical misery. Perhaps even more influential was Rousseau's literary longing for closeness with nature. His awareness of the importance of the natural world to the human sensibility clearly appealed to the romantic spirit long after his death. Of all the eighteenth-century *philosophes*, Rousseau expressed most forcefully the romantic desire to overcome the split between the subjective and the objective that appeared in the work of François-René de Chateaubriand, Alphonse de Larmartine, Victor Hugo, Alfred de Vigny, and Alfred de Musset. Rousseau's doctrine of popular sovereignty also had a profound impact on French republican thought in the early nineteenth century, from the secret societies during the Restoration to the political clubs during the Second Republic. But when the revolutionary idealism of the socialists, the romantics, and the republicans failed to achieve lasting institutional form by midcentury, Rousseau's explicit influence waned rapidly, so much so that new editions of his work largely disappeared by the end of the Second Republic.

I. Babbitt, *Rousseau and Romanticism* (Boston, 1919); A. Cobban, *Rousseau and the Modern State* (London, 1934); J. Roussel, *Rousseau en France après la Révolution, 1795–1830* (Paris, 1972); J. Sénelier, *Biographie générale des oeuvres de J.-J. Rousseau* (Paris, 1958).

*James Smith Allen*

*Related entries:* CHATEAUBRIAND; CLUBS; CONSIDERANT; FOURIER; HUGO; LAMARTINE; LEROUX; MUSSET; REPUBLICANS; ROMANTI-CISM; SAINT-SIMON; VIGNY.

**ROVIGO, DUC DE.** See SAVARY.

**ROY, ANTOINE, COMTE** (1765–1847), financier and statesman. He was an able lawyer before the Revolution. Avoiding politics, he took advantage of the circumstances to build a large fortune, mainly through clever transactions on national lands. His political career began in the Chamber of Representatives during the Hundred Days, but his courageous opposition in that assembly earned him the respect of the royalist electorate of Paris, and they returned him as a deputy from the Seine in the elections of August 1815, a seat he was to keep thereafter. In the Chamber of Deputies he emerged as an expert on financial matters. Elie Decazes included him in his ministry formed in November 1819, and Armand-Emmanuel de Richelieu kept him, along with other colleagues, when he was called in February 1820 to replace Decazes. When Louis XVIII let Richelieu go in December 1821, Roy was raised to the Chamber of Peers with the title of count. He was critical of Joseph de Villèle's administration, and therefore he was a natural choice to take the Finance Ministry in the left-leaning government formed with Jean-Baptiste de Martignac in January 1828. Jules de Polignac wished to keep him in August 1829, but Roy refused. After 1830, having accepted the new regime, he kept his seat in the upper Chamber, where he continued to produce numerous reports on financial matters.

H. Castella, "Notice biographique de M. le Comte Roy," in *Notabilités contemporains* (Paris, 1846).

*Guillaume de Bertier de Sauvigny*

*Related entries:* CHAMBER OF DEPUTIES; CHAMBER OF PEERS; *CHAMBRE INTROUVABLE*; DECAZES; HUNDRED DAYS; LOUIS XVIII;

MARTIGNAC; NATIONAL LANDS; POLIGNAC; REVOLUTION OF 1830; RICHELIEU; VILLELE.

**ROYAL GUARD,** household troops created by Louis XVIII in 1815. The Royal Guard was made up of eight regiments of infantry (of which two were Swiss Guards), two regiments of artillery, and eight of cavalry. Their uniforms resembled those of Napoleon's Imperial Guard. The Royal Guard was unpopular in the army as it was seen as the most overt example of aristocratic favoritism in an officer corps composed primarily of Napoleonic veterans. Officers serving in the Royal Guard enjoyed the pay and courtesies due the next higher rank in line regiments. In the Revolution of 1830, the Royal Guards, and especially the Swiss, became the special targets of the crowd's fury. The Royal Guard was disbanded in August 1830.

D. Porch, *Army and Revolution, France, 1830–1848* (London, 1974).

*Douglas Porch*

*Related entries:* LOUIS XVIII; REVOLUTION OF 1830; SWISS GUARD.

**ROYALIST PARTY,** party seeking the restoration of the Bourbons in 1814 and advocating a second restoration in 1815; later split into ultra, moderate, and *doctrinaire* factions. A royalist party, seeking the restoration of the Bourbons, existed from the late Directory period. It included *émigrés* as well as royalists in France, both those who served Napoleon and those who had not. Some royalists engaged in various plots against Napoleon, and in late 1813 and early 1814 various schemes were tried without success. Royalist agents gathered around the comte d'Artois when he established headquarters at Nancy in early 1814. The Allies, however, were divided on a Bourbon restoration. Thus Ferdinand de Bertier led an effort to convince the Allies by arousing French opinion for the Bourbons. The royalists of Bordeaux took the lead, opening the city to the English army with Angoulême in tow. Meanwhile in Paris, Semallé, an agent of Artois, received varying tacit and overt support from municipal officials as well as from Charles-Maurice de Talleyrand. Napoleon's delays at negotiating with the Allies worked to the royalists' advantage, as did his order for Marie Louise and the regency to leave Paris, thus opening the way for royalist activity.

But even as the Bourbons returned, the royalists' ranks began to split between those who were untainted by association with the Revolution or Napoleon and those who, although royalist, had served previous regimes. The former urged a reactionary form for the new government. The latter advocated a constitutional monarchy with guarantees against royal abuses. This group, led by Talleyrand, arranged the hasty drafting of a constitution, which the Senate approved on 6 April and which recalled Louis XVIII to the throne, subject to his acceptance of that Constitution. Louis' Constitutional Charter undid some of these provisions. Yet the First Restoration generally followed a policy of conciliation, and its moderation angered many pure royalists. During the Hundred Days royalist organizations revived, urging opposition to Napoleon. A bitter royalist uprising broke out in the west, but these efforts accomplished virtually nothing. After Waterloo, the royalists did, however, figure in negotiations with Joseph Fouché for a second Bourbon restoration, and they staged a sizable demonstration when the king returned to Paris on 8 July. The pure royalists now turned on their moderate colleagues of 1814, demanding vengeance against not only those they blamed for the Hundred Days but also against the regicides of 1793. The split that had originated in 1814 now deepened.

Louis' appointment of a moderate cabinet led by Talleyrand outraged the extreme royalists. But they obtained their revenge in the legislature. In July 1815 the king removed twenty-nine peers who had rallied to Napoleon and replaced them largely with conservative ones. Then the August elections returned a huge royalist majority in the Deputies. This led to the replacement of the Talleyrand cabinet by the more conservative Richelieu government, which, however, was still too liberal to please many royalists. When the 1815 legislative session opened on 7 October, the Chambers quickly adopted a series of repressive measures and purges of the bureaucracy. Spurred by royalist committees, tens of thousands of officials were dismissed. But such harsh measures, especially the amnesty bill, caused doubts by the king, the cabinet, and many who had initially supported the repression. Thus in late 1815 began a struggle between these men and the majority in the Deputies, now called the ultraroyalists. This conflict increased in early 1816 and led to the dissolution of the Chamber in September 1816. It also led to the division of the royalist party into at first two factions, the ultraroyalists and the moderate or constitutional royalists, who in turn split into other factions later. Thus after late 1815 a monolithic royalist party no longer existed, and the various royalist factions must be considered as separate entities. The original royalist party ultimately gave birth not only to the ultra and moderate royalist factions but also the *doctrinaires* as well.

T. D. Beck, *French Legislators 1800–1834* (Berkeley, 1974); G. de Bertier de Sauvigny, *The Bourbon Restoration* (Philadelphia, 1966); P. Duvergier de Hauranne, *Histoire du gouvernement parlementaire en France, 1814–1848* (Paris, 1857–71); T. Muret, *French Royalist Doctrines since the Revolution* (New York, 1933); R. Rémond, *The Right-Wing in France from 1815 to de Gaulle* (Philadelphia, 1969).

*James K. Kieswetter*

*Related entries:* AMNESTY BILL OF 1816; ANGOULEME, L.-A.; BERTIER; CHAMBER OF DEPUTIES; CHAMBER OF PEERS; CHARTER OF 1814; *DOCTRINAIRES*; FOUCHÉ; HUNDRED DAYS; LOUIS XVIII; RICHELIEU; TALLEYRAND; ULTRAROYALISTS.


**ROYER-COLLARD, PIERRE-PAUL** (1763–1845), philosopher, deputy and *doctrinaire* royalist of the Restoration and July Monarchy. Born at Sompuis (Marne) on 21 June 1763 to a Jansenist family, Royer-Collard was educated at Chaumont and Saint-Omer. Abandoning a career as a mathematics teacher, he studied law and opened a practice in Paris in 1787. He became interested in the moderate aspects of the Revolution and was elected by the Ile Saint-Louis section to the Paris Commune, serving as its secretary until August 1792. After the fall of the Girondins, Royer-Collard returned to Sompuis, where he remained undisturbed until after 9 Thermidor. In 1797 he was elected to the Council of 500 by the department of Marne. In the Council he helped organize a royalist circle including Camille Jordan and Corbière, and he delivered a notable speech supporting freedom of worship and impartial justice. The coup of 18 Fructidor, however, annulled his election. Thereafter his devotion to monarchism, at least constitutional monarchy, became steadfast and well known, and he carried out various activities in favor of the Bourbons. He was a member of the secret royalist committee formed in Paris in February 1800. The abbé de Montesquiou, Louis XVIII's adviser, solicited him to send secret reports about conditions in France, which he apparently did in 1803. Meanwhile in Paris he devoted himself to studying philosophy. Acquainted with the great thinkers of the past from his early education, he now turned to the works of Thomas Reid, which he especially adapted to combat the ideas of Etienne de Condillac. He opposed the materialist approach and argued that consciousness and memory, not the senses, were the means of knowing the external world. He earned such a reputation in philosophy that in 1811 he was appointed to the faculty of the Sorbonne. There he achieved little success; his few notable students were Victor Cousin, François Guizot, and Charles de Rémusat.

Royer-Collard always kept his distance from Napoleon. At the First Restoration Louis XVIII appointed him to supervise the press. Although he opposed the excesses of the ultras, he did support some limitation of freedom of the press. As a councillor of state especially charged with responsibility for education, he proposed the decentralization of higher education and the creation of seventeen universities and a normal school. During the Hundred Days, as dean of the faculty of letters, he took the oath to Napoleon but sent François Guizot as his emissary to the king at Ghent. At the Second Restoration he retained these offices and was made president of the commission that took over the functions of the imperial university. In August 1815 the department of the Marne elected him to the Chamber of Deputies, where he remained until 1842, frequently being returned by multiple constituencies. In the Chamber of 1815 Royer-Collard initially supported some repressive measures. But faced with the excessive demands of the ultras, he quickly became an advocate of moderate monarchism, significantly influencing legislation and government policies. He supported the first Richelieu ministry against the ultras. He advocated a 300 franc tax qualification for voting, against the ultras' demands for a higher qualification, and they strenuously opposed his public education budget in 1817. In 1816 he became a leader of the *doctrinaires*, a constitutional royalist group. His political philosophy appeared in the *Journal général de France*. In 1819 he helped draft a liberalized press law. In spite of ultra opposition, he retained control of public education until 1819.

When he was dismissed from the Council of State in 1820, he declined the 10,000 franc pension awarded him by the king. Although he continued to view the power of the crown as the source of order and stability, he staunchly championed moderation. Thus he opposed the 1820 election law, the 1820 press law, the French invasion of Spain, and the 1825 law on sacrilege. In these debates he earned a reputation as one of the finest orators in the Chamber, as well as having unassailable integrity. In 1827 he was elected to the French Academy. In 1828 the king appointed Royer-Collard president of the Deputies. He supported the Martignac ministry and opposed the policies of the succeeding Polignac cabinet. Reelected president in 1829 and again in 1830, he had the task of presenting to the king the critical address voted by 221 deputies on 16 March 1830, an address Royer-Collard himself had helped to draft. Reelected to the Chamber at the July 1830 elections, he was at Châteauvieux during the July Revolution and took no part in it. Although he rallied to the Orleanist monarchy, his Bourbon predilections made it difficult for him to support it enthusiastically. Furthermore he was weakened by age and weary of politics. Thus he regarded his public career as finished. Yet he maintained his principles, insisting on strong government and criticizing men and ideas that weakened it. Although his interest in politics continued to decline and illness afflicted him, his department consistently reelected him until finally in 1842 he was defeated. He died on 4 September 1845 at Châteauvieux (Loire-et-Cher). His published works included his various speeches in the Chamber, a work on philosophy (1811), and a complete edition of the writings of Thomas Reid.

*Archives parlementaires*; A. Barante, *La Vie politique de M. Royer-Collard* (Paris, 1863); L. Clot, *Royer-Collard* (Paris, 1857); R. Langeron, *Un Conseiller secret de Louis XVIII Royer-Collard* (Paris, 1956); R. de Nesmes-Desmarets, *La Doctrine politique de Royer-Collard* (Montpellier, 1908); A. Robert, *Dictionnaire des parlementaires français* (Paris, 1889–91); E. Spuller, *Royer-Collard* (Paris, 1895).

*James K. Kieswetter*

*Related entries:* CORBIERE; COUSIN; *DOCTRINAIRES*; DOUBLE VOTE, LAW OF THE; GUIZOT; JORDAN; *LE JOURNAL GENERAL DE FRANCE*; LAW OF SACRILEGE; MARTIGNAC; MONTESQUIOU; POLIGNAC; PRESS LAWS; PUBLIC INSTRUCTION; REMUSAT; RICHELIEU; SPAIN, 1823 FRENCH INVASION OF; THE 221; ULTRAROYALISTS.


*LA RUCHE POPULAIRE* (1839–1849), newspaper produced by workers. During the second half of the reign of Louis-Philippe, a genuine workers' press appeared in France, which included *La Ruche populaire*, founded in December 1839 by the brothers Vinçard and directed by François Duquenne, a compositor. The journal described itself as the first weekly journal to be produced entirely by workers. This was an exaggerated claim, since the 1830 Revolution had produced a number of workers' journals, including *L'Artisan*. The latter were short-lived, however, whereas *La Ruche* survived for ten years, until December 1849.

E. Dolléans, *Histoire du mouvement ouvrier, 1830–1870* (Paris, 1936); H. Izambard, *La Presse parisienne: statistique bibliographique et alphabétique* (Paris, 1853).

*Irene Collins*

*Related entries: L'ARTISAN*; REVOLUTION OF 1830; VINCARD.

**RUE DE POITIERS, COMITE DE.** See COMITE DE LA RUE DE POITIERS.

**RURAL INDUSTRY.** See COTTAGE INDUSTRY.

# S

---

**SACRED HEART.** See PRIESTS OF THE SACRED HEART.


**SACRILEGE, LAW OF.** See LAW OF SACRILEGE.


**SACY, SILVESTRE-ANTOINE-ISAAC DE, BARON** (1758–1838), orientalist scholar. Son of a well-to-do notary of Paris, he was tutored by a learned Benedictine monk who gave him an early taste for ancient languages. At the age of twelve, the boy could already read Hebrew. Afterward he taught himself other ancient Semitic languages, as well as Persian, Turkish, and the main modern European languages. He also studied law. In 1781 he was provided a living as councillor at the Cour des Monnaies. He kept aloof from Revolutionary events, holing up in a small village and pursuing his studies. Such, however, was the reputation he had already gained by his first publications that he was called in 1795 to teach Arabic in the Ecole des langues orientales established by the Convention. In 1806 he entered the Collège de France as professor of Persian and in 1808 the Corps législatif as deputy for Paris, also receiving the title of baron from Napoleon. After 1815 he accumulated offices and titles: member of the directing board of the University, administrator of the Collège de France and the Ecole des langues orientales, member of the Chamber of Peers (1830), keeper of the Oriental manuscripts in the Royal Library, and perpetual secretary of the Académie des inscriptions et belles-lettres, among others. His innumerable publications made him the grand old master of Oriental languages and literatures. For the promotion of these, he and Abel Rémusat founded the Société asiatique.

H. Dehérain, *Silvestre de Sacy ses contemporains et ses disciples* (Paris, 1938).

*Guillaume de Bertier de Sauvigny*

*Related entries:* CHAMBER OF PEERS; COLLEGE DE FRANCE.

**SAINT-ARNAULD, ARMAND-JACQUES LEROY DE** (1801–1854), professional army officer and marshal of France. Armand-Jacques Leroy (the "Saint-Arnauld" was self-styled) was the son of a former attorney of the Parlement of Paris who had become a prefect under the Empire. He entered the army (the royal Garde du corps) in 1817, serving subsequently in several different regiments and running up heavy debts. Still a second lieutenant in 1827, he left the military and traveled widely, working as a commercial clerk and an actor. Returning to the service in 1831, he was promoted to lieutenant and helped put down the duchesse de Berry's ill-fated revolt in the Vendée in June 1832, later serving as one of her guards at Blaye. In the Vendée and at Blaye, Saint-Arnauld came under the command of General Thomas Bugeaud, who thereafter served as his patron and aided his career. Irregularities in his personal life and further problems with debts led him to transfer to the Foreign Legion in Algeria (January 1837), where he served with gallantry in the capture of Constantine and other actions. Bugeaud's appointment as governor-general of Algeria (1841–47) proved helpful, and Saint-Arnauld was a colonel by 1844.

On leave in Paris in February 1848, he was given command of a brigade and used it vigorously to repress the revolutionary disorders in Paris until Louis-Philippe ordered his troops not to resist the crowds. Unsympathetic to the Second Republic, he returned to North Africa as commander of the military district of Algiers, where his outspoken contempt for the National Assembly brought him to the attention of President Louis-Napoleon Bonaparte's agents in 1851. He was soon recruited as an officer loyal to the president, and his pacification campaign in the Petite Kabylie (May–July 1851) was loudly praised in the *Moniteur* and the Bonapartist press. Louis-Napoleon promoted him to general of division (10 July) and recalled him to Paris (26 July), where his participation in the planned coup d'état against the Assembly was secured in return for making him minister of war (27 October). As a member of the president's inner circle, Saint-Arnauld was responsible for the military preparations that helped ensure the success of the coup (2 December 1851). He supervised the repression of Parisian resistance on 4 December and was made a marshal on the first anniversary of the seizure of power (2 December 1852).

Saint-Arnauld served as minister of war until 12 March 1854 when, despite declining health (cardiac problems), he was given command of the French expeditionary forces for the Crimea (war on Russia was declared on 27 March). He cooperated effectively with the British commander, Lord Raglan, and shared credit for the first Anglo-French victory at the River Alma (20 September). As the Allied army marched on Sebastopol, Saint-Arnauld contracted cholera, which further weakened his heart, and he left for France in late September aboard the steamer *Berthollet*, turning over command of the French army to General Canrobert. He died en route to France on 29 September and was buried in the Invalides.

One of many Orleanists who rallied to Louis-Napoleon, Saint-Arnauld gave repeated proofs of his personal bravery and leadership ability in the course of his career, but his political views seem inseparable from his ambition and polished skills as a military careerist.

L. A. de Saint-Arnauld [brother], *Lettres du maréchal de Saint-Arnauld* (Paris, 1855); L. Bertrand, *Le Maréchal de Saint-Arnaud* (Paris, 1941); L. de Charbonnières, *Une Grande figure, Saint-Arnauld* (Paris, 1954); J. Dinfreville, *L'Effervescent maréchal de Saint-Arnauld* (Paris, 1960); B. Jerrold, *The French under Arms* (London, 1860).

*Daniel Longfellow*

*Related entries:* BERRY, M.-C.; BUGEAUD; CANROBERT; COUP D'ETAT OF 2 DECEMBER 1851; *LE MONITEUR*; REVOLUTION OF 1848.

**SAINT-CHAMANS, ALFRED-ARMAND-ROBERT DE** (1781–1848), professional soldier and royalist. Despite his royalist inclinations, Saint-Chamans served in the Napoleonic armies as an aide-de-camp to Marshal Nicholas Soult (who became minister of war under the First Restoration, 1814–15). Still a lieutenant in 1818, Saint-Chamans noted the tensions in the Royal Army between royalist and Napoleonic officers, observing that the two groups messed and worshipped separately. In 1830, Saint-Chamans was one of three generals Marshal Auguste de Marmont directed to repress the street disorders in July. His column of infantry, cavalry, and artillery was ordered to clear the faubourg Saint-Antoine, but the heavily equipped troops were soon exhausted by the 95° heat, and the successful storming of barricades merely saw resistance move to the roofs and windows of neighboring houses. After a day of street fighting on 28 July, Saint-Chamans withdrew his troops to the Tuileries, where they dispersed in the general panic that overtook the royal forces the next day.

Saint-Chamans later maintained that the real causes of the Revolution of 1830 were economic and not political and that had his artillery been loaded with gold coins rather than powder and ball, he could have pacified the faubourg without loss of life. His memoirs are a valuable source of information on the problems of the Restoration army.

J. Bory, *La Revolution de Juillet* (Paris, 1972); D. Pinkney, *The French Revolution of 1830* (Princeton, 1972); D. Porch, *Army and Revolution* (London, 1974); A. de Saint-Chamans, *Mémoires* (Paris, 1896).

*David Longfellow*

*Related entries:* MARMONT; REVOLUTION OF 1830; SOULT.

**SAINT-CYR.** See ECOLE MILITAIRE (SAINT-CYR); GOUVION SAINT-CYR.

**SAINTE-AULAIRE, LOUIS-CLAIR DE, BARON** (1778–1854), politician and diplomat. Although his father, a military officer, had emigrated, he himself was too young to suffer the fate that befell many other relatives of *émigrés*, and he was able to study with distinction at the newly founded Ecole polytechnique. Napoleon, seeking to attract to his service members of the old aristocracy, made him chamberlain (1809) and then prefect of the department of the Meuse (1813).

He was prefect of Haute-Garonne in March 1815 when he refused to serve Napoleon. Saint-Aulaire was elected as a deputy from the Gard in August 1815 but could not be reelected in October 1816 because of the age requirement. In 1818, however, when he turned forty he was able to recover a seat in the Chamber. In the meantime, his daughter had married the upcoming Elie Decazes and Sainte-Aulaire defended vigorously the liberal policies of his son-in-law. In the election of March 1824 he was among the many deputies of his persuasion who were defeated, but he reentered the Assembly in December 1827. In February the death of his father caused him to be raised to the Chamber of Peers. He rallied willingly to the July Monarchy and served it in three important embassies: Rome (1831), Vienna (1833), and London (1841–48). He was the author of a number of books, among which is his valuable three-volume *Histoire de la Fronde*.

P. de Barante, *Etudes historiques et biographiques*, vol. 2 (Paris, 1857).

*Guillaume de Bertier de Sauvigny*

*Related entries:* CHAMBER OF DEPUTIES; CHAMBER OF PEERS; DE-CAZES; ECOLE POLYTECHNIQUE; HUNDRED DAYS; REVOLUTION OF 1830.

**SAINTE-BEUVE, CHARLES-AUGUSTIN** (1804–1869), influential novelist, poet, literary historian, and critic. Born to an aristocratic family in Boulogne-sur-Mer, Sainte-Beuve traveled to Paris in 1818 and began studying medicine five years later. Like many other literati, he soon gave up professional study to write for *Le Globe* in 1827. Befriending Victor Hugo and his wife, Sainte-Beuve became involved in the romantic movement, especially with his reviews in literary journals and lyrics in *Vie, poésies et pensées de Joseph Delorme* (1829) and *Les Consolations* (1830). His affair with Adèle Hugo from 1830 to 1837, portrayed in *Volupté* (1834), soured his relations with Hugo and the romantic's work. In 1840 Sainte-Beuve was made director of the Mazarin library when the first of his three-volume apology of the seventeenth century, *Port Royal* (1840–59), appeared. This work on Jansenism and its society he considered his most important contribution. Elected to the Académie française in 1844, Sainte-Beuve continued to write reviews published regularly after 1832, collected in *Critiques et portraits littéraires* (1832–39), *Causeries du lundi* (1851–62), and *Nouveaux lundis* (1863–69). In 1848 he resigned his post at the Mazarin library to teach literary history at Liège, Latin poetry at the Collège de France, and literature at the Ecole normale supérieure until 1861. Appointed a Napoleonic senator in 1865, Sainte-Beuve died in Paris four years later.

In his extensive literary criticism, Sainte-Beuve sought the psychological and intellectual character of the individual author's talent, which he classified into "natural spiritual families." This biographical approach to literature and its history was thoroughly documented, despite his belief that the scientism of Ernest Renan would never elucidate the "last irreducible citadel" of literary genius. Consequently, Sainte-Beuve often resorted to an intuitive method in keeping with his early romantic sympathies. His remarkable literary production reveals a critic of taste, learning, and passion for truth in his judgment. Although he erred in his judgments of contemporary talents—errors sometimes due to personal envy—Sainte-Beuve established professional criticism and its role in modern French literary history.

A. Billy, *Sainte-Beuve: Sa Vie et son temps*, 2 vols. (Paris, 1952); A. G. Lehmann, *Sainte Beuve: A Portrait of the Critic, 1804–1842* (Oxford, 1962); P. Moreau, *La Critique selon Sainte-Beuve* (Paris, 1964).

*James Smith Allen*

*Related entries:* ACADEMIE FRANCAISE; COLLEGE DE FRANCE; *LE GLOBE*; HUGO; RENAN; ROMANTICISM.


**SAINTE-PELAGIE PRISON,** one of the lesser prisons of the Revolutionary era; used until 1893. Founded in 1665 originally as a refuge and prison for prostitutes and other unfortunate women, the Convent of Sainte-Pélagie was located at the present 65 rue de la Clef in the fifth arrondissement in Paris. It was subsequently divided into two adjoining sections, one a genuine refuge and the other a place of forcible detention. In 1792 the Paris Commune transformed the buildings into a prison for women. After September 1793 and the adoption of the Law of Suspects, Sainte-Pélagie became a political prison for men and women. Known for its crowded, humid, and unhealthy conditions, it held over 350 prisoners during the Terror. They were kept in six-foot square cells with little bedding, reeking of excrement. Initially they were forced to purchase their food. At first kept incommunicado, they developed a system to communicate from one cell to another. Later they were allowed to walk in the corridors for four hours per day. Among Sainte-Pélagie's better-known inmates were Mme. Roland who wrote her memoirs there, the princess of Monaco, the painter Hubert Robert, Marat's mistress and his sister, the actresses of the Théâtre-français, Mme. Duplay, and Le Peletier de Rosambo of the Parlement of Paris. Most of its prisoners were ultimately executed.

From 1797 until 1831, part of the prison was used for the incarceration of young men, and the other part held debtors. On 29 July 1830 the mob forced open the gates of Sainte-Pélagie and allowed the prisoners to escape. From the early 1830s until 1895, it was used as a political prison, its captives including men such as Pierre-Jean de Béranger, Armand Carrel, Barbès, François-Vincent Raspail, Armand Marrast, Pierre-Antoine Berryer, Félicité de Lamennais, Pierre-Joseph Proudhon, Prosper Duvergier de Hauranne, Félix Pyat, and Georges Clemenceau. In 1893, however, the General Council of the department of the Seine voted to abolish Sainte-Pélagie. It was demolished in 1898, leaving no trace of its existence.

P. E. Coittant, *Almanach des prisons* (Paris, Year III); C. A. Dauban, *Les Prisons de Paris sous la révolution* (Paris, 1870); L. de Duras, *Prison Journals during the French Revolution* (New York, 1891); J. Hillairet, *Dictionnaire historique des rues de Paris*

(Paris, 1963); P. Nougaret, *Histoire des prisons de Paris* (Paris, 1797); M. Roland de la Platière, *Mémoires* (Paris, n. d.).

James. K. Kieswetter

*Related entry:* REVOLUTION OF 1830.


**SAINT-GERMAIN L'AUXERROIS, RIOT OF** (14–15 February 1831), anticlerical and antilegitimist riot. The riot was provoked by the holding of a memorial mass on the anniversary of the assassination of the duke of Berry (13 February 1820). Banned at the church of Saint-Roch, the service was rescheduled for noon at Saint-Germain l'Auxerrois (across from the east facade of the Louvre). Despite intermittent showers, a large crowd was attracted by the gathering of aristocrats' carriages, emblazoned with their coats of arms, in the street outside. The Mass proceeded in an orderly fashion, but at its conclusion a cadet from Saint-Cyr pinned a lithograph of the duke of Bordeaux (Berry's son and the legitimist heir) to the drapery of the catafalque, and witnesses claimed that four Bourbon flags (white, with fleur-de-lys, the July Monarchy having restored the use of the tricolor) were unfurled. As the congregation dispersed, they were attacked by a crowd that included workingmen and better-dressed citizens from the neighborhood. The crowd then forced open the doors of the church (which the priests had hurriedly bolted) and destroyed the windows and furnishings. While a National Guard detachment escorted the clerics to safety and the prefects of police and the Seine appeared briefly to appeal for order, no real effort was made to control the violence, and some local officials (including the mayor of the arrondissment) encouraged the crowd.

Having completed the destruction and perhaps angered by the accidental death of a bystander at the hands of a National Guard officer, the crowd then crossed the Pont neuf and assaulted the archbishop's palace at the cathedral of Notre Dame. The archbishop (de Quélen) had gone into hiding, but the building was looted, with its furnishings and the archepiscopal library being thrown into the Seine. The crowd returned on 15 February to set fires and carry out impromptu parodies of the Mass in the ruins. Other churches in the city were vandalized, stripped of Bourbon ornaments, and draped with tricolors, and in the week that followed there were other riots in Conflans, Lille, Angoulême, Dijon, and Nîmes.

The passivity of the royal government is one of the most striking features of the episode. Although the minister of the interior announced on 15 February that several of the rioters had been arrested, other ministers (including Adolphe Thiers) had witnessed the violence and ordered National Guard units not to intervene. The *Journal de débats* (the semiofficial organ of the regime) blamed the violence on the Catholics' and legitimists' decision to hold the service in the first place and implied that the crowds of bystanders had been understandably provoked. In power less than a year, Louis-Phillipe's government clearly saw some benefit in a popular demonstration of hostility to the Bourbons and their aristocratic and religious supporters.

A. Dumas, père, *Mémoires* (Brussels, 1852–56); A. Latreille, *Histoire du Catholicisme en France* (Paris, 1962); J. Lucas-Dubreton, *La Restauration et la monarchie de juillet* (Paris, 1926); P. Spencer, *Politics of Belief in Nineteenth-Century France* (London, 1953).

*David Longfellow*

*Related entries:* BERRY, C.-F.; BORDEAUX; *JOURNAL DES DEBATS*; LE-GITIMISM; NATIONAL GUARD; QUELEN.

**SAINT-OUEN, DECLARATION OF** (2 May 1814), declaration by King Louis XVIII guaranteeing constitutional liberty and parliamentary participation in government to the French. After the abdication of Napoleon (6 April) the former imperial Senate hastened to produce a constitution that subordinated the authority of the crown to that of the nation and made various guarantees to the elite groups of the fallen regime. Louis XVIII could not accept such an infringement on what he conceived as his God-given rights and duties. In Compiègne, where he stopped on his return journey from 29 April to 2 May, the king had tense discussions with Charles-Maurice de Talleyrand, who spoke for his colleagues of the Senate, and with the czar, who strongly advocated a constitutional monarchy. A compromise was reached by which the king would accept most of the features of the system wanted by the Senate but only as concessions of his own will and preexisting power. On the evening of 2 May, Louis arrived in Saint-Ouen and received the senators. A final document still had to be published before the king would make his solemn entrance into the capital. The task was turned over to three of the king's councillors: Pierre-Louis de Blacas d'Aulps, Eugène-François de Vitrolles, and Louis de La Maisonfort. Without even showing it to the king they had it printed and posted in Paris early on 3 May. In that document Louis XVIII declared that the senatorial constitution, too hastily composed, could not be implemented as it was but that he promised to have another one, more appropriate, worked out by a committee of both chambers. Meanwhile he wished to state the basis of this future system: representative government with two chambers; taxation by legal consent; freedom of the individual, press, and religion; irrevocability of the sales of national (confiscated) properties; the independence of the judiciary; maintenance of all ranks, distinctions, and debts; no reprisals for past opinions and votes.

This document reflects the balance of politcal forces of the time; it made possible the peaceful reestablishment of the Bourbon monarchy and set the basis for the necessary compromises between the traditions of the Old Regime and the irreversible changes brought into French society by the Revolution.

G. de Bertier de Sauvigny, *The Bourbon Restoration* (Philadelphia, 1966).

*Guillaume de Bertier de Sauvigny*

*Related entries:* BLACAS D'AULPS; CHARTER OF 1814; LOUIS XVIII; NATIONAL LANDS; TALLEYRAND; VITROLLES.

**SAINT-SIMON, CLAUDE-HENRI DE ROUVROY, COMTE DE** (1760–1825), social philosopher and one of the great system builders of the first half of the nineteenth century. Saint-Simon has always been a controversial figure.

In his own time and outside a small circle, he remained unknown, but even then he had both apologists and detractors. Scholars, who have shown an intermittent interest in his work, have had difficulty categorizing it. The dominant mode in intellectual history has always been individualizing and genealogical: tracing the genesis and mutation of ideas, usually through the biographical approach. Some facets of Saint-Simon's life do lend themselves to such a method. He was, as John Stuart Mill said, a "clever original," with a complex and fragile mind who spent the last twenty-five years of his life pursuing what he conceived to be his mission to help his fellows understand and master the epochal changes their society was undergoing. He was also paranoid and a megalomaniac, suffered at least one major mental breakdown, and survived a suicide attempt in 1823. Yet for three reasons his thought is particularly difficult to study in this way. First, he never wrote a major work, and his scattered writings are homiletic, repetitive, and lacking in rigor. Because he was a stirring conversationalist but a mediocre writer, he transmitted many of his ideas not by the pen but by word of mouth. He was a system builder who left no coherent corpus of writing. Second, for his ideas he drew eclectically on a wide range of contemporary thinkers. Third, his theories do not fit neatly into traditional political categories, and some of them were to be obscured by the additions made by the Saint-Simonians who after his death claimed to be his followers. Thus he has been seen as an early socialist, yet he was no egalitarian. He analyzed not capitalist but industrial society, and his concept of class was very different from, say, Marx's. Some scholars—like F. A. Hayek—have even seen him as a prototalitarian, yet he did not ascribe any major role to the state in his new order. Others—like Emile Durkheim and Georges Gurvitch—view him as one of the founders of sociology, and yet he had no formal academic training and never had an academic post or recognition. Even his originality has been denied. Since he seemed to need others to work with and since his most fertile period—the Restoration—was also the time when he secured brilliant collaborators, there have always been doubts as to his own contribution. The difficulty has been made more acute by the pronouncements of some of his erstwhile confidants. Charles Dunoyer, who was close to him in the first years of the Restoration, later refused to grant any role to Saint-Simon in the formulation of the theories known as industrialism that he and others developed between 1815 and 1817. Worse, Auguste Comte, Saint-Simon's most brilliant collaborator, was later to deny him any influence in the generation of his own ideas and even called him a "depraved juggler." And the debate has continued. In a brilliant and controversial three-volume work of Comte's early years, published between 1933 and 1941, Henri Gouhier tried to prove that Comte did not need Saint-Simon to develop his positivism and concluded that the latter was no more than a brilliant publicist.

There is, however, another way of approaching intellectual history in general and Saint-Simon in particular: to anchor ideas firmly in their time and to treat theories not as abstractions but as solutions developed for contemporary rather than later problems, as witnesses not to individual genius but to their time.

Viewed in this way, Saint-Simon's ambiguous writings reflect the ambiguity of the early nineteenth century. Thinkers of this time were forced to try to make sense of the cataclysmic changes wrought by the French Revolution and Napoleon and the profound changes that industrialization was threatening to bring about. This explains why there was a widespread awareness that this was a crucial period of transition and uncertainty and why the Restoration was a time of intellectual ferment. Nobody better expressed this turmoil of hope and uncertainty that the new generation of the Restoration felt than Alfred de Musset, who later wrote: "Behind them lay a past forever destroyed, still moving in its ruins with all the fossils of centuries of absolutism; before them rose the dawn of an immense horizon, the first glimpse of the future; and between these two worlds ... was something similar to the ocean that separates the old continent from young America, something vague and undefined, a surging sea, full of shipwrecks, crossed occasionally by some distant white sail or by some ship exuding a heavy cloud of smoke." Nobody sought to chart this sea, to guide his contemporaries, with more determination than Saint-Simon, who wrote in 1824: "Mankind's Golden Age is not behind us, it is before us. Our fathers did not see it, our children will arrive there one day. We must clear the path for them."

Not until he had reached his early forties did Saint-Simon assume his self-imposed role as guide for his contemporaries. His earlier career had been varied and largely successful. As a young professional soldier, he had fought in the American War of Independence and ended his military career as a colonel. In the first years of the Revolution, he had participated in local politics, begun speculating in confiscated lands, and, though he was imprisoned for thirteen months during the Terror, amassed a considerable fortune. The year 1802, however, was a turning point. Financially ruined, he dedicated himself to a new career as a social reformer and published his first pamphlet, *Lettres d'un habitant de Genève à ses contemporains*, the following year. It was during the Restoration, though, that he did his most important work, for it was then that he had the secretaries and collaborators who could help him put his ideas on paper. From 1813 to 1817 he had Augustin Thierry, the future historian. Between 1817 and 1823–24 the young Auguste Comte was his close collaborator, and in the last months of his life he was helped by Olinde Rodriguès and Léon Halévy who, after his death, were to found the journal *Le Producteur*, the beginning of the Saint-Simonian sect. Despite the support he had in these years, his writings are still scattered in circulars and short-lived periodicals, and some were not even published in his lifetime. The most significant of his publications are the journals *L'Industrie* (1816–18), *Le Politique* (1819), *L'Organisateur* (1819–20), and *Du Système industriel* (1819–22) and his last works, *Opinions littéraires, philosophiques et industrielles* and *Nouveau Christianisme*, both issued in 1825.

Four aspects of his work, each reflecting preoccupations among French intellectuals in the early nineteenth century, are crucial for an appreciation of his thought and his times. The first is his attempt to understand the Revolutionary and Napoleonic eras. The Revolution had been a traumatic personal experience for Saint-Simon, and it left an indelible mark on his thinking. Thus, although he sought to change French, and indeed European, society, and although toward the end of his life he grew impatient at the slow pace of change, he always eschewed violence and political revolution as a means to achieve his ends. Like others, he put his faith in the power of persuasion. It was his desire to bring about a lasting peace and a reshaping of Europe in the aftermath of long wars that led him to publish one of his better-known works in 1814. His pamphlet, *De la réorganisation de la société européenne*, was one of the many schemes that surfaced immediately prior to the Congress of Vienna. In it Saint-Simon advocated an Anglo-French alliance as the foundation of a united Europe under a common parliament. More important, at the base of his entire thinking was his recognition that the Revolution had been a historic watershed that had brought to an end not only a political regime but a social order. He thus conceived his essential task to be to discover the meaning of the Revolution by putting it in the secular perspective of the gradual decline of the feudal system and to create a new science of society—he called it social physiology—to reveal the emerging new order. This new order was the industrial scientific society that Saint-Simon regarded as the ultimate destination of historical evolution. But he had also to explain why the Revolution had not ushered in this millennium—why instead it had led to excesses and wars. His explanation was that the Revolution had been stymied by the emergence of an intermediate and transitory class of lawyers and metaphysicians who, though they did not understand the rising socioeconomic system, acquired political power and had become part of the ruling elite of the Restoration. Saint-Simon thus adapted the critique of the Revolution made earlier by Edmund Burke and taken over by conservative writers in France.

The second major aspect of Saint-Simon's thinking is the analysis he made of the new industrial order he saw emerging. Influenced by the new political economy of Adam Smith and Jean-Baptiste Say and by the industrialization that already gripped British society and was beginning to have an impact in France, he was one of the first nineteenth-century thinkers to grasp the significance of the changes taking place. There is, it is true, ambivalence in his writings, and though he became increasingly aware of working-class poverty and came to stress the need to improve the lot of those he called in a redolent phrase ''the most numerous and poorest class,'' he never developed any analysis of conflict between proletariat and bourgeoisie. Neverthless, he foresaw developments that escaped the notice of contemporaries. Thus he foresaw the importance of the technocratic elite that was to prove an essential characteristic of industrialized society whether under capitalism or under Soviet control. He attributed an important role to managers and engineers, and in the society that he envisaged, promotion would be by merit. The chief purpose of the new society was productive activity and the conquest of nature, and Saint-Simon concentrated on increasing wealth and never concerned himself with the distribution of wealth. With this as the principal goal, class conflict would be eliminated and man's aggressive urges deflected away from his fellows. It was this emphasis on productive activity, moreover, that led Saint-Simon to formulate his concept of class in Restoration society. His class analysis took him beyond the political discourse of his time, which he treated as a mere surface manifestation, and he never concerned himself with forms of government or concepts like liberty and equality that were common currency in opposition parlance. Conflict in France, he argued, was between the productive and nonproductive classes, between workers and drones. Saint-Simon even coined a term to describe the rising class of businessmen, workers, and intellectuals: the industrials (*industriels*). The idlers, composed of landowners, nobles, clergy, and the military, was a declining, decadent group that had acquired political power but fulfilled no useful function. Saint-Simon's class analysis had its best-known, but not most elaborate, formulation in his famous Parable of 1820. Here he contrasted the grave consequences that would result for the country if the 3,000 leading scientists and businessmen were suddenly to die, with the little perturbation that would result if France were to lose its 30,000 leading aristocrats, clergy, and civil servants. The publication of the Parable earned Saint-Simon prosecution and rare public attention.

His historical analysis of the emergence of modern society is the third significant aspect of his thought. His history remained resolutely Eurocentric—though he did include the United States in his scheme—and there were others during the Restoration who painted the past with large brushes and used their history for political ends. Still, Saint-Simon's teleological history, his view that class conflict was the motor of change, his belief that history would end with the advent of classless industrial society, were all to haunt the nineteenth century in modified guise through the writings of Karl Marx. Saint-Simon envisaged history as an alternation of organic and critical epochs. Organic periods were times of shared ideals and solidarity; critical moments were transitional times of conflict and doubt when old systems were dismantled. Europe had been in just such a critical phase since the fifteenth century, and the French Revolution, whatever its failings, marked an intensification of the conflict between old and new, the old being the feudal system and the new being the industrial scientific society that was gradually replacing it. The motor of change, of progress, was class conflict. Since he believed that the advent of the productive classes and the organic order marked the last stage in human evolution, history would then come to an end.

Saint-Simon shared another attribute with many of his fellow intellectuals of the Restoration: he was anxious to create a system of beliefs to replace that finally shattered by the Revolution, to fill the vacuum of contemporary disbelief. He recognized—as did his admirer Emile Durkheim at the end of the century—the importance of a common morality uniting all members of society in a common goal. He therefore rejected as insufficient the self-interest that was one of the premises of liberal individualism. "A society cannot survive," he wrote in 1821, "without common moral ideas." In his last and probably best-known work, *Nouveau christianisme*, he announced that not only did society, and workers especially, need a set of generally accepted moral principles but that Christianity no longer provided it. Since the dawn of the modern era, Christianity had stood in need of rejuvenation to help it adapt to change, but both the Catholic and Protestant churches had failed to bring about the necessary reforms. To remedy this, he proposed a return to the basic principle of brotherly love and added the injunction "to improve the lot of the poorest and most numerous class." Though there was no religious sentiment or dogma in this last work, these elements were to be added after his death by his followers, the Saint-Simonians.

Saint-Simon's breathless pronouncements, his scattered analyses of current woes, and his proposed remedies went largely unheeded by his contemporaries. Yet in his preoccupations and in his theories, he reflects the intellectual ferment of the Restoration. His thought was even to live on, albeit in transmuted form, in the writings of the Saint-Simonians, who revered him, and those of Auguste Comte, who denied him.

P. Ansart, *Sociologie de Saint-Simon* (Paris, 1970); E. Durkheim, *Le socialisme: la doctrine saint-simonienne* (Paris, 1924); G. Gurvitch, *Les Fondateurs français de la sociologie contemporaine*, vol. 1: *Saint-Simon sociologue* (Paris, 1966); F. A. Hayek, *The Counter-Revolution of Science: Studies on the Abuse of Reason* (Glencoe, Ill., 1952); C. Lemonnier, ed., *Oeuvres de Claude-Henri Saint-Simon*, 6 vols. (Paris, 1966); F. E. Manuel, *The New World of Henri Saint-Simon* (Cambridge, Mass., 1956); T. Petermann, *Claude-Henri de Saint-Simon: Die Gesellschaft als Werkstadt* (Berlin, 1979).

*Barrie M. Ratcliffe*

Related entries: COMTE; DUNOYER; ENFANTIN; FOURIER; MARX; MUSSET; PHILOSOPHY OF INDUSTRIALISM; SAINT-SIMONIANISM; SAY; THIERRY; VIENNA, CONGRESS OF.


**SAINT-SIMONIANISM,** a movement composed of young, talented, and predominantly Parisian bourgeois that between 1825 and 1832 diagnosed what it felt to be the contemporary crisis and developed radical remedies to end it. The study of Saint-Simonianism, however, is made difficult by the layers of interpretation that intellectual historians and others have imposed on its theories. At one extreme is the patronizing—and damning—label of "utopian socialists" that Marx and Engels attached to the sect. At the other, there is a series of recent interpretations that claim insight and foresight of Saint-Simonian theories that cut across those great nineteenth-century antitheses, liberalism and socialism, and anticipated twentieth-century society. They thus grappled with problems that have become our problems: the failings of the market mechanism and the need for some form of central planning, industrialization and technocracy, alienation, and sexual and women's emancipation. Even scholars critical of Saint-Simonianism, like Georg Iggers, who sees it as an early theory of what he calls totalitarianism, attribute significance to it that transcends the early nineteeenth century. Current orthodoxy, indeed, is encapsulated in the claim made by François Perroux, the French economist, "We have all become more or less Saint-Simonians." This is an ahistorical way of approaching the study of ideas in general and the Saint-Simonians in particular. Both are to be studied in their context rather than ours. The Saint-Simonians shared traits in common with many other contemporary intellectual movements. Others, too, believed they faced a crisis of unprecedented proportions, and others, too, offered daring solutions. Saint-Simonian theories were no more than the still center of a whirlpool of ideas that drew into itself numberless currents of thought, contemporary and historical, and by its centripetal force shaped them and compressed them into a momentary significance before they were flung off again into the future.

There is a second difficulty. The definition of what constitutes Saint-Simonianism, and who was a Saint-Simonian or remained faithful to its ideas after the sect's breakup, is no easy task. As Nietzsche often pointed out, only that which has no history can be defined. The sect, like other messianic sects, was subject to schisms. New adherents joined; secessionists left. Besides, the emphasis put on different facets of the doctrine and theories themselves changed over time. Thus while economic questions dominate early discussions, religious, social, and sexual issues occupied a greater place from 1829 onward.

The history of Saint-Simonianism can be divided into three phases. The first, between June 1825 and October 1826, was marked by the publication of their first periodical, the *Producteur*, and by theories that remained close to those recently put forward by Saint-Simon himself. The second was a period about which relatively little is known, because after the *Producteur* ceased publication, private discussions and discreet conversions continued out of the public eye. The third period opened in December 1828 when the group began a series of lectures in Paris to present their views to a wider audience. These lectures, published in 1830 as *Exposition de la doctrine de Saint-Simon*, constitute the fullest statement of their economic and social theories. This phase is marked, first, by their attempts to convert by organizing discussion groups, lectures, and lecture tours and by publishing pamphlets and newpapers (the *Organisateur*, 1829–31, and the *Globe*, 1830–32). The Saint-Simonians, then, sought to change society not by force but by persuasion and moral example. It is marked, second, by their most important theoretical innovations, innovations that resulted from their discussions of the social problem, the position of women, sexuality, and religion and morality in the new society. Their propaganda activity and their new theories created three problems: funds were exhausted, schisms increased, and the sect attracted the attention of the authorities. It was mainly because of financial difficulties and defections that in April 1832 Prosper Enfantin, the sect's leader, took the rump of the Saint-Simonians into celibate retreat at his residence in Ménilmontant on the outskirts of Paris. Four months later the government brought the sect's leaders to trial for propagating immoral doctrines. The retreat, the trial, and subsequent imprisonment of Enfantin and Michel Chevalier, his closest collaborator, marked the effective end of Saint-Simonianism as a movement.

How can we explain why so many of the young and the talented in the Paris of the late 1820s joined a group that professed to follow the teachings of Saint-Simon, an eccentric thinker who had proved incapable of writing a full-length work? It can be explained only by the general context of the dual revolution and the specific circumstances of the France of the last years of the Restoration and the first months of the July Monarchy. The French Revolution had marked a watershed in human history that severed nineteenth-century man from the old order, but the Industrial Revolution, which for many, including the Saint-Simonians, promised to mark another, was only in its early stages. In consequence, many of the young in the 1820s were in search of a creed, of certainty, in the face of what they conceived to be the moral and religious vacuum of their day. Their generation felt little attraction for the beliefs and ideologies that their parents held, and they were not able to play any active part in political discourse when electors had to be over thirty and deputies over forty and when 40 percent of deputies still came from aristocratic families. In such a situation alienation was heightened, generational conflict accentuated, and some found commitment and a focus for their enthusiasm in Saint-Simonianism. Similarly, the evolution of Saint-Simonian theories—and their radicalization—can be understood as a response to a deepening crisis in the later 1820s. The economic crisis which began in 1827 was prolonged by the political events of 1830. Working-class problems intensified, and discontent in Paris and in Lyons became a burning issue in debates in the 1830s. Finally, the July Days did not usher in a regime that Saint-Simonians considered to be any major improvement on that of Charles X.

The crisis they believed they were living through was thus general and deepening. The solution they elaborated was more than socioeconomic. But the starting point for their analysis was the industrialist theories that Saint-Simon had shared with others like Charles Comte and Dunoyer. They therefore expressed enthusiasm for man's industrial future as offering a solution for the problems of the ''poorest and most numerous class.'' Production—understood in its widest sense—they conceived as an individual act of creation, of self-fulfillment, and as a collective act in which all humanity participated. Work was thus the fundamental attribute of society. People found fulfillment in the effort to conquer and harness nature, and their natural aggression could thereby be turned away from their fellows and toward nature. Their valorization of labor was rich in consequences. It helps explain their conception—and critique—of the class division of society. The man who works is moral; he who does not, immoral. The dichotomy of good and evil becomes productive endeavor and parasitism, workers and drones, those who earn their living and those who gain their income only through possession of property. It explains their faith in the pacific tendencies of industry binding peoples together and in the benefits of public works and improving communications. The best known of their proposals is Michel Chevalier's article ''Mediterranean System'' (1832), which envisaged an ambitious new transport network to the Mediterranean as the instrument for reconciling Europe and the Islamic world. It also explains their view of economic crises. They considered the economy to be inefficient, riddled with class antagonism, and subject to recurring depressions. These crises were partly the result of the actions of individual entrepreneurs who, lacking any overall picture of the needs of the economy, made erroneous decisions. They were also the result of a structure wherein property relations and the inheritance system meant that men without ability had control of the means of production.

The Saint-Simonians proffered a number of remedies for this crisis. They, like Saint-Simon, were historicists who believed history was on their side, that there was a pattern of development unfolding in the past. History had a dialectic, an alternation of critical and organic epochs. Organic periods were characterized by common values and ideals that were reinforced by social institutions. Critical epochs were marked by tensions and challenges to old values and institutions. Their society, they believed, was still going through such a critical, destructive phase. The Saint-Simonians' task, therefore, was to end uncertainties and antagonisms and build new solidarities. They devised schemes whereby the power of capitalists—that is, though the term was ambiguous, owners of the means of production rather than industrialists—would gradually be diminished, and capital would pass more easily from those who held it to those who needed it. Thus they proposed a form of central planning for the economy, the chief instrument for which would be a centralized banking system with the dual purpose of being an anticyclical instrument and a means by which the power of capitalists and the interest rates they charged would be reduced. But the Saint-Simonians also went further, for they proposed the abolition of collateral inheritance and a radical increase in death duties, reforms that would eventually eliminate class divisions. They were thus led to make the most radical early nineteenth-century critique of property rights, which, they claimed, made possible the "exploitation of man by man." They also attacked government policies toward the working class, especially those of the first ministries of the July Monarchy, and moved hesitantly toward the view that the major social dichotomy was not only that between those who produced and those who did not but betweeen those who owned property, including industrialists, and those who owned only the sweat of their brow.

Early historians of the sect—like Charléty and Weill—believed that the authentic Saint-Simonianism was a socioeconomic doctrine and that so-called practical Saint-Simonians—engineers, entrepreneurs, financiers—sought to apply it in their later careers, and that the sexual and religious theories developed in the sect's final phase were an aberration that resulted from the growing ascendancy of Enfantin. This is an error. The feeling of rootlessness and the religious longing of many of the adherents led them to seek a mooring of belonging and purpose in the spiritual and emotional ambiance of the sect. And if the religious doctrine they developed—public confessions, initiations and hierarchy, and search for a female messiah—appear contrived, it should not be forgotten that in Saint-Simonian eyes their religion would help put an end to the anarchy and disbelief of their critical epoch and usher in the organic. Even their critique of patriarchy and of bourgeois marriage, though not fully developed, were important facets of their theory. In January 1832 Abel Transon gave a series of significant lectures on women's emancipation, and the sect attracted Claire Demar and Suzanne Voilquin, who in 1832 were to set up the journal *Tribune des femmes*, which became an early forum for feminist issues. Similarly, the Saint-Simonian insistence on the need to satisfy sexual drives—"the rehabilitation of the flesh"—and their recognition that there are casual and long-term sexual relationships were significant and daring ideas.

The lasting impact of Saint-Simonianism was twofold. On the one hand, their theory, while singing the praises of productive endeavor and of industry, was also an early and powerful critique not only of their society but of the basic tenets of emerging industrial capitalism. They dared to cast doubts on the efficacy of the market mechanism and laissez-faire, on the inviolability of property relations, and even on the harmony of interests between bourgeois and worker. Their discussion of spiritual and sexual anguish offers a valuable key to an understanding of the generation of 1830. On the other hand, the lasting impact of the Saint-Simonian experience on erstwhile adherents was disparate. Each was marked differently, for no one is the sum total of the influences that have formed him, and everyone is self-made. While some ex-members—like Michel Chevalier and the Pereires—were to become apologists and practitioners of French captialism, others—like Olinde Rodrigues and Jules Vinçard—were to devote themselves to fostering the cause of the working class. While Adolphe Guéroult became a liberal journalist, Gustave d'Eichthal continued a lonely search for a religious synthesis. However, every mature Saint-Simonian carried the traces of his youthful experience. Sainte-Beuve, who flirted with the sect, later said, "No one who went through Saint-Simonianism did so without being marked," and Eugène Lerminier, who was a member, confessed toward the end of his life, "Let us admit that it was the only beautiful moment in our lives."

C. Bouglé and E. Halévy, eds., *La Doctrine de Saint-Simon: exposition première année, 1829* (Paris, 1924); S. Charléty, *Histoire du saint-simonisme* (Paris, 1931); G. G. Iggers, *The Cult of Authority: The Political Philosophy of the Saint-Simonians, a Chapter in the History of Totalitarianism* (The Hague, 1958); M. L. Larizza, *Il Sansimonismo (1825–1830): un ideologie per lo sviluppo industriale* (Turin, 1976); F. Perroux, *Capitalisme et communaute de travail* (Paris, 1938); F. E. Manuel, *The Prophets of Paris* (Cambridge, Mass., 1962); Barrie M. Ratcliffe, "Saint-Simonism and Messianism: The Case of Gustave d'Eichthal," *French Historical Studies* 9 (1976) and "The Economic Influence of the Saint-Simonians: Myth or Reality?" *Proceedings of the Western Society for French History*, vol. 5 (1977); G. Weill, *L'Ecole saint-simonienne: son histoire, son influence jusqu'à nos jours* (Paris, 1896).

*Barrie M. Ratcliffe*

*Related entries:* BANKING; CHEVALIER; COMTE, A.; COMTE, F.-C.-L.; DUNOYER; ENFANTIN; FOURIER; *LE GLOBE*; MARX; *L'ORGANISA-TEUR*; PEREIRE BROTHERS; PHILOSOPHY OF INDUSTRIALISM; SAINT-SIMON; VINCARD; VOILQUIN; WOMEN'S NEWSPAPERS.

**SALABERRY, CHARLES-MARIE D'YRUMBERRY, COMTE DE** (1776–1847), right-wing politician and historical writer. Salaberry came from an old noble family from Navarre. His father, former head of the Cour des comptes, was beheaded during the Terror. This, coupled with his own experience during the Revolution, inspired a deep hostility for everyone suspected of liberal sympathies. In 1790 he emigrated, joined the army of Condé, and later participated in the Vendéen wars as captain of a noble cavalry unit in the self-proclaimed "Catholic and royal army." After 1800 he returned to France but had to reside on his land under police surveillance.

During the Restoration he was an ultra among ultraroyalists, even embarrassing his allies on occasion with his intemperate remarks. Commander of the National Guard in Loir-et-Cher under the First Restoration, he took part in the last uprising of the Vendée during the Hundred Days. In the Second Restoration, he was elected a deputy from Loir-et-Cher. An admirer of the theocratic despotism of the Ottoman Empire, he found the Restoration Charter and all the ministries of the Restoration, except that of Jules de Polignac, far too liberal. In the Chambers he called for death to all those who had taken part in the Revolution. He spoke violently against the law of military recruitment, took an active part in the expulsion of the abbé Grégoire in 1819, and frequently attacked the press, describing it as "the only plague which Moses had forgotten to strike down in Egypt." Believing that the fall of Joseph de Villèle would lead inevitably to the fall of the monarchy, he played little part in discussions after 1827. After 1830 he withdrew from political life.

N. Hudson, *Ultra-royalism and the French Restoration* (Cambridge, Mass., 1936); J. J. Oechslin, *Le Mouvement ultra-royaliste* (Paris, 1960); C. M. Salaberry, *Aux hommes de bien* (Paris, 1828–29), *Histoire de l'empire Ottoman*, 4 vols. (Paris, 1813), and *Souvenirs politiques*, 2 vols. (Paris, 1900).

*Sanford Gutman*

*Related entries:* CHAMBER OF DEPUTIES; CHARTER OF 1814; GRE-GOIRE; HUNDRED DAYS; NATIONAL GUARD; POLIGNAC; RESTO-RATION, FIRST; RESTORATION, SECOND; REVOLUTION OF 1830; ULTRAROYALISTS; VILLELE.


**SALON D'EMILE DESCHAMPS** (1820–1822), first spontaneous assembly of promoters and authors of emerging romanticism at the rue Saint-Florentin home of Jacques Deschamps, also known as the team from *La Muse française* (1823–1824). Long a literature-philosophy dilettante who had entertained writers and poets, Jacques had motivated his son, Emile, to function as host of the first salon or *cénacle romantique*. Though they shared similar tendencies, the writers formed a sort of preliminary gathering without a common doctrine. In fact, they represented a variety of political and literary views, but they were poets who recognized François René de Chateaubriand and Alphonse de Lamartine as their masters. Many had been encouraged and rewarded by the Académie des jeux floraux at Toulouse. There were elders such as Charles-Julien de Chênedollé, Pierre-François Baour-Lormian, and Charles Brifaut, but most were young. Victor Hugo at eighteen had introduced his close friend and collaborator at the *Conservateur littéraire*, A.-S. Saint-Valry. Alfred de Vigny at twenty-three had brought his two comrades in arms, comte France d'Houdetot and Lieutenant

Gaspard de Pons. The troubadour from the Jeux floraux, Alexandre Soumet, had presented two friends, the other Alexandre, Guiraud, and Jules de Rességuier. There were women—Marceline Desbordes-Valmore sponsored by Sophie Gay and her daughter, Delphine—and there were lesser lights: Hyacinthe Latouche, Michel Pichat and the critic Desjardins.

Emile Deschamps, though married, lived with his parents. As early as the summer of 1820, the rue Saint-Florentin group became a brotherhood of poets who sought a new literary direction. Mutual praise of each other's works without much regard for quality was the order of the day. The next two years of their activity reflected their predilection for reforming French theater, albeit along conservative lines by retaining and somehow reinvigorating the *alexandrin*. Their efforts were timid, and their attempts to improve form and content were unsuccessful. Restoration audiences applauded Soumet's *Clytemnestre* and *Saül*, Guiraud's *Les Machabées*, and especially Pichat's *Léonidas*, but posterity promptly forgot them. They could console themselves that the liberal prose writers led by Stendhal, who met at the salons of Etienne Delécluze, Philippe-Albert Stapfer, and Eugène Viollet-le-Duc at the very same time, were having as little success despite their primary goal of liberalizing and nationalizing the French theater.

The members of the Deschamps salon were also regulars at the Société des bonnes lettres, but their liberalism in literature, modest as it was, frightened the ultras. Thus, when publication of the *Conservateur littéraire* ended and they were deprived of a vehicle for their verses, Deschamps felt the time had arrived to found a new official periodical around which his colleagues could rally. Though the founders of *La Muse française* were the stars of the Deschamps group and numbered seven like Ronsard's *Pleiade* (Deschamps, Guiraud, Soumet, Hugo, Vigny, Saint-Valry, and Desjardins), Deschamps furnished the idea, Guiraud the prospectus, and Soumet the motivating force. Joining this elite *cénacle*, now referred to as *l'équipe de la Muse française*, was the enthusiastic team of more than twenty of the other Deschamps guests, including Charles Nodier, whose Arsenal salon, by the spring of 1824, less than a year after the appearance of the first *Muse* issue, would succeed the *équipe*. The emphasis remained on the illustration of the romantic aesthetic through the publication of members' verses and mutual admiration of each other's lyrical poems. The *Muse* poets would only, however, be able to ignore their royalist enthusiasm and their religious fervor and write strictly under the banner of romantic literature at Nodier's in 1824, a few weeks after Auger's famous Académie speech that ignited the classic-romantic battle.

R. Bray, *Chronologie du romantisme (1804–1830)* (Paris, 1932); H. Girard, *Emile Deschamps, 1791–1871* (Paris, 1921); L. Séché, *Le Cénacle de la Muse française, 1823–1827* (Paris, 1918).

*Paul Comeau*

*Related entries:* AUGER; CHATEAUBRIAND; DELECLUZE; DESBORDES-VALMORE; GAY, D.; GAY, S.; GUIRAUD; HUGO; LAMARTINE; LA-TOUCHE; *LA MUSE FRANCAISE*; NODIER; STAPFER; STENDHAL; VIGNY; VIOLLET-LE-DUC.

**SALVANDY, NARCISSE-ACHILLE DE** (1795–1856), renowned opposition pamphleteer, historian, politician, and later minister of public instruction under Louis-Philippe. Son of a *cultivateur* and descendant of an Irish family that had lived in France since the seventeenth century, Achille de Salvandy attended the Lycée Napoléon on a scholarship. While there he wrote youthful poetry, and his enthusiasm for France led him to make false announcements of French victories in Germany in 1813. He was asked to leave the school to join the army. He served in Saxony and was wounded at the battle of Brienne.

De Salvandy's enthusiasm was at heart just a reflection of his love of France. He entered the house of the king in 1814 and accompanied Louis XVIII to the northern border in March 1815 before returning to Paris. The young military officer in his pamphlet *Mémoire à l'Empereur sur les griefs et les voeux du peuple français* appealed to the emperor to lead France, not rule it. De Salvandy abandoned his military career, although he would not officially retire until 1823, for a career in law.

It was as a writer and politician that de Salvandy was to spend his life. The boldness of the twenty-year-old officer in publishing a memoir to the emperor was followed in 1816 by an even more audacious act: he condemned the Allied occupation of France in the pamphlet *La Coalition et la France*. Demanding his arrest, the Allies instead were faced with the young patriot's being rewarded. Immediately upon the termination of the occupation, de Salvandy was named a *maître des requêtes* to the Council of State.

De Salvandy, master of the pamphlet, combined a biting sarcasm with humor and information to persuade his readers. He often used everyday events in an absurd manner to make his political point while avoiding the censor's condemnation. His most notable success came in 1827 when he parodied the king's gift of a giraffe from the pasha of Egypt. By describing the giraffe's journey from Marseilles to Paris, de Salvandy was able to comment on the state of the country (*Lettres de la giraffe au pacha d'Egypte*).

Many of his writings first appeared in the newspapers of the day, especially in François-René de Chateaubriand's *Journal des débats*. De Salvandy had supported Elie Decazes but became an enemy of Joseph de Villèle and championed the cause of Chateaubriand. His constant harpooning of the government led to his resignation from the Council of State in 1821.

In the mid-1820s de Salvandy turned his efforts toward history. Beginning with an historical novel, *Don Alonzo, ou l'Espagne, histoire contemporaine*, he wrote a number of works in which he was able to comment on the politics of the day. He also did more serious historical writing in *Histoire de Pologne avant et sous le roi Sobieski* (1829). His work would later earn him admittance to the French Academy in 1835.

With the advent of the Martignac ministry, de Salvandy returned to the Council of State, only to resign when Jules de Polignac was named to replace Martignac. The *Journal des débats* owed many of its most penetrating critiques of the Polignac ministry to de Salvandy. He continued to speak out for freedom of the press in particular, as in *Insolences de la censure* (1827), and he kept up his tradition of opposing the Ultramontanism of Charles X that he had first mentioned in *Discussion de la loi du sacrilege* (1825). He was returned to the Council of State in August 1830.

De Salvandy was a religious man, a believer in liberty but not democracy, and thus he favored the Orleanist solution. He entered the Chamber of Deputies from the Sarthe in the by-elections of October 1830. Taking his seat in the Center, he supported the conservative majority and defended the ministers of Charles X from persecution. Such activity did not endear him to the electors of La Flèche, however, and they refused to renew his mandate in June 1831.

The wealthy de Salvandy, whose taxes were a robust 1,600 francs per year, was returned to the Chamber of Deputies from the Eure in a by-election (November 1833). Again he took his seat in the Center, and the electors of Evreux gave him 188 votes to 161 for Jacques Laffitte in the elections of 1834. As a solid member of the majority, de Salvandy was chosen by Louis-Mathieu de Molé to be minister of public instruction (15 April 1837). Before he could settle into office, he had to fight two elections because the electors of Evreux refused to renew his mandate. The voters of Nogent-le-Rotrou (Eure-et-Loir) were more accommodating. These electors returned him to the Chamber in 1837, 1839, 1842, and 1846. His popularity grew in these years, so that in the last three elections he was also elected in the Gers, and in 1846 he even defeated Jacques-Charles Dupont de l'Eure 339 to 232 in the Eure.

De Salvandy's tenure as minister of public instruction consisted of two periods separated by a brief and frustrating tenure as an ambassador. Amid the conflict between France and England over marriage in the Spanish royal family, the newly named comte de Salvandy was appointed ambassador to Madrid (14 September 1841). He was never permitted to present his credentials, however, and he left in January 1842. He was given the grand cross of the Legion of Honor and sent to represent France in Turin. He soon resigned this post when Louis-Philippe attacked him for not voting to censor those deputies who had gone to visit the comte de Chambord.

As minister of public instruction for Molé (15 April 1837–March 1839) and for François Guizot (1 February 1845–February 1848), de Salvandy worked to increase the role of the church in education. He emphasized authority and hierarchy in the educational system. Many liberals objected to an increased role for the church, but the benefits of a solid religious foundation in education far outweighed any threat to liberty for de Salvandy. He was also a man of letters who founded the Ecole d'Athènes, instituted chairs for foreign literature in the departmental universities, gave grants of money to men of letters, and restored the Ecole des chartes. His reconstitution of the councils of public instruction ensured the place of the curé in French education. In 1846 when he visited Algeria, he became the first minister to inspect the schools in the colonies.

Being pro-clergy and indifferent to the University, de Salvandy won no liberal plaudits. In 1845 he prevented the historian Edgar Quinet from giving his anticlerical and anti-Jesuit course, thus making his position clear to the opposition. Guizot had chosen de Salvandy to appease the Catholic believers, and he performed well. De Salvandy defended his actions on the grounds of freedom of education— in this case, freedom for the church. He wanted to made education the preserve of parents, not the state. He did not capitulate entirely to the forces of religious education, however, and like anyone else trying to follow a middle course, he was attacked from both sides. The Revolution of 1848 ended the debate for de Salvandy, who left the country. Soon, however, political control reverted to the conservatives, and the result was the Falloux Law of 1850. While de Salvandy had clearly pointed the way toward the use of the church to control the masses and perhaps even the middle classes, it took the events of 1848 to create sufficient support to enact new laws.

After his return to France, de Salvandy devoted himself to agriculture. He was president of the agricultural society of the Eure, where he had an estate. His only political activities were futile attempts to reconcile the two royal families, and in September 1850 he became the first person to have visited both the Orléans and the Bourbons. In 1871, de Salvandy's son was elected to the National Assembly, where he supported Thiers.

L. Trenard, *Salvandy et son temps, 1795–1856* (Lille, 1968).

*Thomas D. Beck*

*Related entries:* CHATEAUBRIAND; DECAZES; DUPONT DE L'EURE; FALLOUX LAW; GUIZOT; *JOURNAL DES DEBATS*; LAFFITTE; MARTIG-NAC; MOLE; POLIGNAC; PUBLIC INSTRUCTION; QUINET; VILLELE.

**SAND, GEORGE** (1804–76), pseud. of AURORE DUDEVANT, née DUPIN, romantic novelist, playwright, political essayist; supported feminist, socialist and republican causes. George Sand was born Amantine Lucille Aurore Dupin on 1 July 1804 in Paris. Her parents, Sophie Delaborde, a camp follower and the daughter of a Parisian bird-seller, and Maurice Dupin de Francuel, an aide-de-camp to Napoleon's army and heir to the family estate at Nohant, secretly married without the consent of Maurice's mother shortly before the birth of their daughter. The aristocratic and virtuous Mme. Dupin disliked her working-class daughter-in-law, who already had an illegitimate daughter. After the accidental death of her son, Mme. Dupin raised the four-year-old Aurore until she was thirteen, then sent her to boarding school at the Couvent des dames anglaises in Paris. Three years later Aurore returned to Nohant and, after the death of her grandmother, found herself mistress of the estate at seventeen. These thirteen years shaped much of Aurore's emotional, intellectual, and religious character. Rejected by the mother she loved and torn by the rivalry between Sophie and Mme. Dupin, she constantly sought a perfect love. She read avidly and eclectically, studied music, languages, even surgery. The pastoral beauty of Nohant and the austerity of the convent developed her mystical Christianity.

In 1822, to escape the guardianship of her domineering mother, Aurore married Casimir Dudevant, the natural son of Baron Dudevant, and enjoyed a brief period of domestic happiness at Nohant. After the birth of their son Maurice in 1823, Aurore, dissatisfied with her boorish husband, sought platonic, and then sexual, relationships with other men. In 1830, two years after the birth of her daughter Solange, Aurore met Jules Sandeau. The next year she arranged a separate life while maintaining the facade of her marriage: she would spend half the year in Paris with Jules, and half at Nohant with Casimir and the children.

Aurore, a republican by sentiment, found life in revolutionary Paris exciting. She and Jules formed a circle of friends with the novelist Honoré de Balzac; a medical student, Emile Regnault; the republican Alphonse Fleury; and the editor of *Figaro*, Henri de Latouche. To facilitate her movements in a man's world, Aurore adopted men's clothes and boots. To supplement her income, she began to write for journals, first anonymously and then jointly with Jules. From her first to her last publication, she wrote primarily for money, disciplining herself to produce twenty pages a night. In 1832, returning to Paris from Nohant, she brought Solange and the manuscript of her first novel, *Indiana*, which was published under the name G. Sand. Fame came overnight; critics compared her to Stendhal and Madame de Staël. She hastily finished a long short story, *La Marquise*, and two more novels, *Valentine* and *Lélia*. These early, heavily autobiographical works dealt frankly with the basic themes of woman's sexuality, the brutality of marriage without divorce, socially impossible love affairs, and the search for an unobtainable, perfect love. Her celebrity brought new friends: the critics Gustave Planche and Charles-Augustin Sainte-Beuve, the actress Marie Dorval, the writer Hortense Allart, and the poet Charles Didier.

In 1833, Sand ended her relationship with Jules. She soon had a new, younger lover—Alfred de Musset. Their stormy relationship lasted until March 1835, through a disastrous trip to Venice, Musset's illness, and her affair with an Italian physician, Pietro Pagello. Desperate for money, fighting periods of depression, she continued to write. While proceeding with a legal separation from her husband, since divorce had been revoked in 1816, she became lovers with Michel de Bourges, a republican lawyer and defender of the Lyons strikers. In May 1836, Casimir accepted a separation settlement which gave him custody of Maurice and the income from a town house in Paris; Sand received Solange and the ownership of Nohant. As her affair with Michel waned, Sand found comfort in her friends—Franz Liszt, Marie d'Agoult, Charles Didier—and in the music of Frédéric Chopin. She contributed a series of articles ("Lettres à Marcie") to Félicité de Lamennais' *Le Monde* in which she condemned free love, upheld woman's moralizing role, and advocated woman's domestic sphere. After six installments, the collaboration ended due to Lamennais' censorship. She returned to novels, writing three in eight months.

In May 1838, she and Frédéric Chopin became lovers. That summer they travelled to Majorca with her children. Her eight-year liaison with her "little chap," at first sexual, then chaste due to his ill health, was consistently maternal. The affair ended over Solange and Sand's new interest in social equality. Chopin consistently sided with Solange, whose independence and jealousy of Auguste

Brault, her "adopted" sister, angered Sand. He scorned Sand's socialist and working-class friends—Louis Blanc, Pierre Leroux, Agricol Perdiguier, Charles Poncy, Savinien Lapointe. Sand wrote three didactic proletarian novels during this period—*Le Compagnon de la Tour de France* (1840), *Horace* (1842), and *Le Meunier d'Angibault* (1844), and co-founded two journals dealing with social issues—*La Revue indépendante* (1840) and *L'Eclaireur de l'Indre* (1843).

Sand, like the rest of France, was surprised by the Revolution of 1848. Concerned about Maurice, she hurried to Paris. There she quickly aligned herself with the Provisional Government, especially with the radical faction of Alexandre-Auguste Ledru-Rollin and Blanc. She supported a socialist republic as the means to equality for both workers and women. She founded a short-lived weekly, *La Cause de peuple*, and contributed to *La Vrai république*. In her articles and tracts, she minimized class conflict and opposed violent change, but supported the legal destruction of economic inequality. She extolled the heroism of the people, admonished the middle class to set a good example, and assured the rich that communism did not threaten legitimate property or the family. But as the anonymous editor of the government's *Bulletins de la République*, she threatened that if the upcoming elections to the Constituent Assembly did not return socialist-republican candidates, then revolution was inevitable. Sand rejected her own nomination as a candidate, proposed by the feminist journal *La Voix des femmes*, and warned that demands for political equality would be equated to sexual promiscuity. Marital reform and civil rights, which only a socialist republic could assure, had to precede women's suffrage.

The moderate victory in the April elections and the subsequent arrest of the leaders of the popular demonstration in May convinced her that the cause of the socialist republic was lost to bourgeois reaction. She returned to Nohant, abandoning political writing to return to her autobiography, pastoral novels, and plays. In December 1848 she opposed Louis-Napoleon Bonaparte's presidential candidacy, and after his victory warned of ensuing unprecedented confusion. When the coup d'état came in December 1851, she was unimpressed. But distressed by the repressions, she petitioned Louis-Napoleon directly. While she failed to achieve a general amnesty, she was successful in obtaining clemency for many condemned to death or deportation. After the proclamation of the Empire in December 1852, she permanently retired from politics.

For the next ten years, Sand's life centered around Nohant. Her lover and financial adviser was Alexandre Manceau. The rivalry between Manceau and her son Maurice led to her leaving Nohant in 1863 for Palaiseau, a small village south of Paris. When Manceau died in 1865, she returned to Nohant, comforted in her loneliness by Maurice and his wife, her old friend Gustave Flaubert, Alexandre Dumas *fils*, a new chosen daughter, Juliette Lamber Adam, and two grandchildren, Aurore (1866) and Gabrielle (1868). She continued to write novels which, she admitted, were not very good.

By 1870 Sand's antipathy toward the Empire had lessened due to the reforms of the 1860s which legalized strikes and trade unions, freed the press, and permitted public meetings. But when the war with Prussia came, Sand saw it as an opportunity to change the government. After Napoleon's surrender on 4 September 1870, she enthusiastically greeted the Parisian proclamation of a Republic. But the deprivations caused by the Prussians' four-month siege of the city made her advocate surrender as the only reasonable course. She then opposed both the reactionary assembly at Versailles and the Paris Commune, arguing for love, the end of political dissension, universal suffrage, and a moderate republic. The year after a monarchist Assembly established the Republic, on 8 June 1876, George Sand died at Nohant, just short of her seventy-second birthday.

During her long life Sand wrote sixty novels, twenty-five plays, numerous essays, political tracts, volumes of letters, and an autobiography. She wrote in the romantic tradition of heroic individualism, excessive emotionalism, and sublime love. Within this framework she was a feminist, a socialist, and a republican. Sand's feminism both reflected and rejected nineteenth-century ideals of womanhood. She accepted the dominant ideas of woman's nature as characterized by self-sacrificing love and her role in the domestic sphere. She rejected, however, the idea that love was devoid of sexual passion; complete love was the unity of body, mind, and intellect. She denounced sexual promiscuity, defending her own numerous affairs as seriatim, not simultaneous. Love was best expressed in marriage and motherhood, but it could only be ensured by civil, marital, and parental equality and by the freedom to divorce and remarry. She refused to support women's suffrage, arguing that civil and marital rights must precede political rights. Just as her feminism depended upon love, equality, and freedom, her socialism required fraternal love, economic equality, and political liberty. She defined socialism, or communism, as true Christianity, based upon reconciliation of class interests, not retaliation for social injustices. The end of economic inequality, the replacing of individual wealth by what she vaguely called social wealth or national property, could not be achieved immediately or by violent revolution. The means to establish a socialist society was through a republic based upon universal suffrage, gradually and legally introducing change. She entertained a Rousseauist vision of political unanimity replacing majority will as the highest expression of popular sovereignty. To many of her contemporaries, Sand was one of the literary masters of the nineteenth century; to others she was a proponent of sexual license, the destruction of the family, and social conflict. For today's readers, her novels are ponderous, her feminism is suspect, her socialism lacking in class analysis, and her republicanism unrealistic. But she remains a good example of a generation of reformers and revolutionaries who condemned the inequalities and injustices of their age and envisioned the gradual and peaceful transformation to a new society of love, equality, and freedom.

J. Barry, *Infamous Woman: The Life of George Sand* (New York, 1977); P. Blount, *George Sand and the Victorian World* (Athens, Ga., 1978); C. Cate, *George Sand: A Biography* (London, 1975); *Hofstra University Cultural and Intellectual Studies*, I (1978) and II (1979); T. Hovey, *A Mind of her Own: A Life of the Writer, George Sand* (New

York, 1977); R. Jordan, *George Sand: A Biographical Portrait* (New York, 1976); A. Maurois, *Lélia, the Life of George Sand* (1952), translated by Gerald Hopkins (New York, 1953); *Nineteenth-Century French Studies*, 4, IV (1976); A. West, *Mortal Wounds* (New York, 1973).

*S. Joan Moon*

*Related entries:* AGOULT; BALZAC; BLANC; CHOPIN; COUP D'ETAT OF 2 DECEMBER 1851; DIVORCE, ABOLITION OF; FLAUBERT; LAMENNAIS; LAPOINTE; LATOUCHE; LEDRU-ROLLIN; LEROUX; LISZT; MUSSET; PERDIGUIER; PONCY; PROVISIONAL GOVERNMENT; REPUBLICANS; REVOLUTION OF 1848; SAINTE-BEUVE; STÄEL-HOLSTEIN; STENDHAL; *LA VOIX DES FEMMES*; WORKER POETS.

**SAVARY, ANNE-JEAN-MARIE-RENE** (1774–1833), duc de Rovigo, general and minister of police of the Empire, peer of the Hundred Days, general of the July Monarchy. Jean Savary was born on 26 April 1774 at Marcq-et-Chevrières (Ardennes). He studied at the Collège Saint-Louis in Metz. In 1791 he enlisted in the cavalry and became a sublieutenant in September. He fought under Custine in 1792 and, as a result of the numerous officer berths vacated by *émigrés*, was promoted to captain in 1793 at age nineteen. In Egypt he caught the eye of Napoleon Bonaparte, and he rose with Napoleon's star to high military and administrative posts. On 23 May 1808 Savary was given the title duc de Rovigo.

On 8 June 1810 Napoleon appointed Savary minister of police general to replace his rival, Joseph Fouché. Although Savary remained loyal to Napoleon to the end of the reign, the emperor was somewhat dissatisfied by his inability to control royalist activities. Savary was one of the last of Napoleon's officials to leave him in April 1814. Unemployed during the First Restoration, Savary immediately rallied to Napoleon during the Hundred Days and was appointed commander of the gendarmerie and made a peer. After Waterloo Savary wished to accompany Napoleon to Saint-Helena and actually went as far as Plymouth on board the *Bellerophon* before the British halted him.

Placed on the Bourbons' list of men to be court-martialed, Savary was taken as a prisoner by the British to Malta, from which he escaped on 7 April 1816. He then traveled first to Smyrna. After he was condemned to death in absentia by a French court, he went to Austria, hoping to clear his name. In 1818 he returned to Smyrna and then in 1819 went to England whence he arranged to appear before a French court. He was acquitted and restored to his civil rights and honors, although he remained on inactive military status. In 1820 he may have been involved in the so-called Bazar conspiracy. An extract from his memoirs was published in 1823, accusing Charles-Maurice de Talleyrand of having masterminded the arrest and execution of Enghien in 1804. Louis XVIII was angered and banned Savary from the Tuileries. He subsequently went to Rome to live with his family. In December 1831 Louis-Philippe made him supreme commander in Algeria, where he accomplished the capture of Bône, began a strategic road system, and fostered immigration. Ill health forced him to resign his command in March 1833. He died in Paris on 2 June 1833. His complete memoirs were published in 1828.

E. d'Hauterive, *Napoléon et sa police* (Paris, 1943); B. Melchior-Bonnet, *Savary, duc de Rovigo* (Paris, 1962); B. Saint-Edme, *Biographie des lieutenans-généraux, ministres, directeurs-généraux . . . de la police* (Paris, 1829).

*James K. Kieswetter*

*Related entries:* BAZAR CONSPIRACY; FOUCHE; HUNDRED DAYS; LOUIS XVIII; TALLEYRAND.


**SAY, JEAN-BAPTISTE** (1767–1832), economist. The son of a draper, Say came from a Protestant family that had emigrated to Geneva after the Revocation of the Edict of Nantes and returned (to Lyons) only in his father's lifetime. Say's interest in economic theory was shaped by a visit to England in 1786, his reading of the *Wealth of Nations*, and his first job as secretary to the financier Etienne Clavière (a future Revolutionary minister of finance). Influenced intially by the physiocrats (especially Pierre-Samuel Dupont de Nemours), he was also an early supporter of the Revolution, publishing a pamphlet on freedom of the press in 1789 and serving as editor of the *Courrier de Provence* (a post he received from Gabriel de Mirabeau). Say served briefly in the army in 1792 and from 1794 to 1800 was founder and editor of the journal *La Décade philosophique*. After brief service in the Tribunate (from which he and twenty other original members were removed by Bonaparte), he established a cotton-spinning mill in the Pas-de-Calais and wrote on economic subjects until his firm went bankrupt in 1814–15. A utopian novel (*Oblie*, 1800) was followed by *Traité d'économie politique* (1803), in which Say embraced the laissez-faire ideas of the English classical school and added some modifications. After 1815 he taught at the Conservatory of Arts and Crafts in Paris and in 1830 became professor of political economy at the Collège de France. His major works include *De l'Angleterre et les anglais* (1815), *Catéchisme d'économie politique* (1815), and *Cours complet d'économie politique* (1828–30), as well as successive editions of the *Traité*, in which he refined his ideas.

Say was influential in popularizing laissez-faire ideas in France and modifying the physiocratic school's sympathy for government intervention in the operation of the economy. He was instrumental in making economics an objective and descriptive science. His major theoretical contribution is Say's Law, a cluster of related propositions that argue that aggregate supply in an economic system always equals aggregate demand and that emphasize that savings and investment represent only an internal transfer and not a reduction in demand. A higher rate of savings results in a higher level of output and no loss in purchasing power, while disequilibrium in an economic system reflects only the difference between the proportions of goods produced and consumers' preferred mix of purchases, not excessive aggregate production. Say's theory was designed to allay popular fears that economic crises in early industrial society were due to inherent limits on growth or the possibility of a general glut due to overproduction. Although he modified his ideas in 1826 to incorporate short-term limits on production or mismatches of supply and demand, Say maintained that a general state of disequilibrium in the economy was impossible.

Say's theory was attacked by economists like J.-C. Sismondi, who believed that capitalist competition produced inevitable social evils that required outside regulation, and cyclical theorists like Thomas Malthus and David Ricardo. Ricardo and Say conducted a long correspondence concerning their differences over price theory (value in use versus value in exchange) and utility of goods. Say argued that the natural (or inherent) values of goods were independent of their exchange value (price in the marketplace) and therefore irrelevant in economics, one of several areas in which he departed from Adam Smith's definitions. Say was also influential in distinguishing between entrepreneurs and investors or stockholders in the process of production, a distinction that was not common in classical economics in his lifetime.

M. Bowley, *Studies in the History of Economic Theory* (London, 1973); R. N. Meik, *The Economics of Physiocracy* (Cambridge, Mass., 1963); T. Sowell, *Classical Economics Reconsidered* (Princeton, 1974) and *Say's Law* (Oxford, 1973).

*David Longfellow*

*Related entries:* COLLEGE DE FRANCE; SISMONDI.


**SCHEFFER, ARY [ARIE]** (1795–1858), painter and confidant of Louis-Philippe. Born in Dordrecht, Holland, on 10 February 1795, Scheffer was the son of Johann-Baptist Sheffer, court painter to Napoleon's brother Louis. After his father's death, Scheffer's mother took him to Paris in August 1811 to study under Pierre Guérin. There he met Eugène Delacroix, Théodore Géricault, and Hippolyte Delaroche. His first major exhibit was in 1812, and he initially concentrated on historical subjects, such as in *Death of Saint Louis* (1817), the *Six Bourgeois of Calais*, and *Socrates Defending Alcibiades* (1819). He also painted works of a more popular genre, such as *Return of the Conscript*, *Widow of the Soldier*, and *Sister of Charity*. But he returned to historical and religious subjects in the 1830s, especially subjects that were morally or ideologically didactic. The period of the July Monarchy saw the production by Scheffer of numerous biblical paintings and perhaps his most famous work, *Francesca da Rimini* (1835). In 1825 he received the Legion of Honor.

Before the July Revolution, Scheffer served as instructor to the children of the duc d'Orléans, especially Princess Marie. Involved in the liberal conspiratorial movement in the 1820s, Scheffer again found himself involved during the July Revolution. By then a family friend of the house of Orléans and a member of the Palais royal circle, Scheffer went to Neuilly on 29 July 1830 to convey news of the progress of the revolution. The following day, when Adolphe Thiers visited Neuilly to persuade Orléans to assume power, he chose Scheffer to accompany him. Through the barricaded streets of Paris the two of them galloped, Scheffer and his horse easily jumping the obstacles. But Thiers, mounted on a pony, had to be lifted, mount and all, over them. They finally arrived, dusty and sweating, at Neuilly, only to find that Orléans was not there. But their effort was not in vain, for Mme. Adélaïde essentially committed her brother to accept Thiers' offer. Scheffer's artistic efforts continued unabated during the July Monarchy, and he benefited from numerous commissions for the Museum of Versailles. In 1835 he was promoted to officer of the Legion of Honor. Some professed to regard him as the leader of the French romantic school of painting, although many disputed that attribution. He devoted himself especially to scenes of French history, as well as more contemporary portraits. He exhibited regularly until 1855. Ary Scheffer died at Argenteuil on 15 June 1858.

H. Grote, *Memoir of the Life of Ary Scheffer* (London, 1860); M. Kolb, *Ary Scheffer et son temps, 1795-1858* (Paris, 1937).

*James K. Kieswetter*

*Related entries:* ADELAIDE; DELACROIX; DELAROCHE; GERICAULT; LOUIS-PHILIPPE; REVOLUTION OF 1830; SCHEFFER, C.-A.; SCHEFFER, H.; THIERS.


**SCHEFFER, CHARLES-ARNOLD** (1796–1853), journalist and historian, brother of Ary Scheffer. Born in Holland a year after its capture by French forces, Arnold Scheffer was the son of artists, Cornelia Lamme and Johann-Baptist Scheffer. His father became court painter to Napoleon's brother Louis Bonaparte in 1808 and died in 1809. Arnold moved with his mother and brothers to Paris where he became involved in liberal politics. During the Restoration he wrote for the *Constitutionnel* and the *Censeur européen*. He established friendships with Augustin Thierry and with General Lafayette, who lent him books from his library and encouraged his writing. Scheffer's pamphlets expressed opposition to the government and suspicion of English and Russian policies. In 1817, the government seized Scheffer's work *De l'Etat de la liberté en France* as seditious and arrested him. Certainly designed to influence the elections to the Chamber of Deputies, the book urges voters to choose independent men who will preserve liberty. He lauds Lafayette and the assemblies of 1789 and the Hundred Days. He was found guilty of sedition on 24 January 1818 and condemned to three months in prison and to one year of surveillance and ordered to pay a fine of 200 francs and a surety bond of 1,000 francs. He appealed and lost. On 30 March 1818, his penalty was increased to one year of prison, five years of surveillance, a fine of 5,000 francs, and a surety bond of 2,000 francs. Instead of complying, Scheffer sought refuge in Brussels, supplied with money and letters of introduction from Marc-René Voyer d'Argenson. He was pardoned on 14 October 1819 and allowed to come back to Paris.

Scheffer wrote for *La Renommeé* and became a close associate of Lafayette in the carbonarist activity of the early 1820s. He was the liaison between the Paris leadership and groups in the region of the Midi. In the unsuccessful Belfort plot, Arnold was supposed to incite Lyons to follow Belfort as soon as it had arisen. After warning Arnold's brother Henry and others that the plot had been discovered, François de Corcelle hurried to Lyons to warn Arnold Scheffer, and they were able to escape. Scheffer continued to travel throughout France to coordinate carbonarist activity during 1822. In June he was at Dijon, in July at Lyons and in the department of the Vosges, and in September at Bordeaux.

After the defeat of the liberals in Spain in 1823, Arnold decided that the time was not ripe for conspiracies and that public opinion had to be prepared for future change. His new activities to that end now included membership in the Société de la morale chrétienne and contributions to *Le Globe*. In 1825 he published *Histoire des Etats-Unis de l'Amérique septentrionale*, which concluded with an account of the American reception of Lafayette in 1824 and 1825. He wrote several volumes in the series of short histories published by Lecointe: Flanders and Artois, the German Empire, Bavaria, and Holland. The *Catalogue général des Livres Imprimés de la Bibliothèque Nationale* incorrectly identifies Arnold Scheffer as Charles-Antoine Scheffer.

Arnold and his brothers became friends of the duc d'Orléans and his supporters in the Revolution of 1830. Arnold was soon disappointed in the new regime and was a proponent of the Party of Movement, though he did not belong to opposition clubs. His opposition was expressed through his work on *Le National*, which he helped to found in January 1830. In 1834, Scheffer was condemned to four months in prison for writing that the king was at the head of a system of corruption and counterrevolution. In the mid-1840s Arnold grew bored with politics and went into business, managing an iron factory at Vierzon. But at the same time he collaborated with Corcelle and Alexis de Tocqueville on the newspaper *Le Commerce*. After the Revolution of 1848, he ran for the Constituent Assembly from Seine-et-Oise and was a member of the Comité central pour les élections générales, which included Félicité de Lamennais and Jules Michelet among others. He lived for many years at La Marche, the estate of his wife, Joséphine Boulanger, which was located in Seine-et-Oise. She died in 1846. In 1853, when Arnold fell ill, he went to live in Paris with his brother Ary and died there shortly after.

M. Kolb, *Ary Scheffer et son temps, 1795–1858* (Paris, 1937).

*Sylvia Neely*

*Related entries:* CARBONARI; *LE CENSEUR EUROPEEN*; *LE CONSTITU- TIONNEL*; *LE GLOBE*; LAFAYETTE, M.-J.-P.-Y.-R.-G.; LAMENNAIS; MICHELET; *LE NATIONAL*; PARTY OF MOVEMENT; *LA RENOMMEE*; SCHEFFER, A.; SCHEFFER, H.; SOCIETY OF CHRISTIAN MORALS; SPAIN, 1823 FRENCH INVASION OF; THIERRY; TOCQUEVILLE; VOYER D'ARGENSON.

**SCHEFFER, HENRY** (1798–1862), nineteenth-century painter, known chiefly for his genre scenes. Born in the Hague on 25 September 1798, Henry Scheffer was the third son of Johann-Baptist Scheffer (1765–1809), court painter to Louis Bonaparte, and Cornelia Scheffer, née Lamme (d. 1839). Following the sudden death of their father in 1809, the three Scheffer brothers were taken by their mother to Paris, where Henry and his eldest brother, Ary, became noted artists, and where Arnold established a reputation as a spokesman for the liberal and republican Left during the Restoration and the July Monarchy. In 1813, Henry followed his brother's lead and undertook studies in the studio of Pierre Guérin, who, although a disciple of Jacques-Louis David and a champion of neoclassicism, proved a tolerant master. From his atelier emerged not only the two Scheffers but also Théodore Géricault and Eugène Delacroix. With his two brothers and indeed many of the young intellectual elite of Paris, Henry Scheffer circulated in prominent liberal circles during the Restoration. Despite an active part in the abortive carbonari plots, he had the good fortune to escape detection and prosecution.

As a painter, Henry Scheffer enjoyed a minor reputation in the nineteenth century; he is almost totally forgotten today. His public debut as an artist occurred at the famous and controversial Salon of 1824, scene of a major confrontation between the established defenders of neoclassicism and their upstart romantic challengers, at which he showed a large historical painting. Known in addition for large religious and allegorical compositions, Scheffer nevertheless excelled in the production of the then-popular genre picture. On these small canvases, he depicted in an emotional and sentimental manner such historical or anecdotal subjects as *Charlotte Corday Protected by the Members of the Section from the Wrath of the People*, *The Reading of the Bible*, and *The Protestant Sermon*. Among Scheffer's historical paintings may be noted *Jeanne D'Arc entrant à Orléans*, now in the museum at Versailles. His *Don Juan endormi sur les genoux d'Haydée*, a subject inspired by Lord Byron's *Don Juan*, followed a popular romantic custom, according to which artists looked to admired works of the day for their subjects. A talented portrait painter, Scheffer painted, among other notable men of his day, Armand Carrel, Augustin Thierry, and Louis Blanc. His portrait of Carrel serves as the frontpiece to R. G. Nobecourt's *La Vie d'Armand Carrel*.

After a lengthy illness, Henry Scheffer died on 15 March 1862. His daughter married Ernest Renan.

M. Kolb, *Ary Scheffer et son temps, 1795–1858* (Paris, 1937).

*Robert Brown*

Related entries: BLANC; CARBONARI; CARREL; DAVID; DELACROIX; GERICAULT; ROMANTICISM; SCHEFFER, A.; SCHEFFER, C.-A.; THIERRY.


**SCHONEN.** See DE SCHONEN.


**SCIENCES, ACADEMY OF.** See ACADEMY OF SCIENCES.


**SCRIBE, AUGUSTIN-EUGENE** (1791–1861), playwright popular with the middle-class audiences of the Restoration and the July Monarchy. A popular and immensely successful playwright, Eugène Scribe was born in Paris on 24

December 1791. His father, who kept a small shop, died in 1798, leaving his family impoverished. A scholarship allowed Scribe to attend the Collège Sainte-Barbe, where he proved himself a brilliant student, even defending a thesis before the noted philosopher Pierre Laromiguière. At the school, Scribe made the acquaintance of Casimir and Germain Delavigne. To comply with his mother's wishes, he undertook, albeit with extreme reluctance, legal studies, but by the time he had received his degree in 1815, Scribe had already collaborated with Germain Delavigne in the writing of vaudevilles, several of which were performed; none of these early works, however, won any great success. Scribe persisted, and his first major triumph, *L'Auberge, ou les Brigands sans le savoir*, came in 1812. He repeated this success the next year with the comic opera *La Chambre à coucher, ou une Demi-heure de Richelieu* and a melodrama, *Koulikan*. Scribe's successes helped transform the nature of French comedy, replacing the conventional bucolic comedies of the eighteenth century with plays like *Une Nuit de la Garde national* (1815), which drew their plots from contemporary events. Both *Une Visite à Bedlam* and *L'Hôtel des Quatre-Nations* alluded to the occupation of France by foreign troops. Scribe's popularity by 1819 was such that he earned 17,500 francs that year.

Largely indifferent to the political and social upheavals that battered nineteenth-century France, Scribe aspired both to make a name for himself as an author and to make the writing of plays financially viable. His remarkable business acumen was revealed when, after the success of *Le Solliciteur* at the Variétés in 1817, he managed to demand payment for his manuscripts and a percentage of the nightly receipts. The example Scribe set did much to improve the financial lot of nineteenth-century playwrights.

The characteristics that ensured the success of Scribe's plays in his day have all but guaranteed neglect of these same plays today. Noted for the *pièce bien faite* (the well-made play), Scribe devoted much care to plot development, to ensuring that dramatic incidents within the play had obvious, simple, and often trivial causes, to the building of tension within a scene, and to the maintaining of suspense. To style, however, he paid little attention, and his characters for the most part are shallow and his thought superficial. Nevertheless, because he portrayed with gaiety and wit middle-class foibles and problems, Scribe attracted the French bourgeois audience of the first half of the nineteenth century. By so mirroring middle-class values and concerns, Scribe's plays provide a partial portrait of the bourgeoisie of the Restoration and the July Monarchy.

During the 1820s, Scribe replaced his emphasis on vaudeville with an interest in comedy. Of his plays of the 1820s, over a hundred were written for the Théâtre du gymnase, founded by Charles-Gaspard Delestre-Poirson, who gave Scribe a contract to write almost exclusively for this theater. Scribe's popularity reached its height in the years just before 1830, when both the affluent bourgeoisie and the aristocrats of the faubourg Saint-Germain flocked to see performances of such plays as *Le Mariage d'Argent*. Because the agreement with Delestre-Poirson did not prohibit contributions to the Théâtre-français and the Opéra, Scribe also penned works for these houses. Exhausted by the effort required to meet so many demands, Scribe had to take a rest cure in 1826 and 1827.

During the July Monarchy, Scribe, whose plays fared poorly until he understood the nature of the changes produced in France by the Revolution of 1830 and wrote plays to reflect them, maintained his reputation in Paris and acquired one of international scope. Commissions and requests flowed in from aristocrats and even from kings. From these years date two of Scribe's more notable plays, *Le Verre d'Eau* (1840) and *Adrienne Lecouvreur*. Perhaps Scribe's finest five-act comedy, *Le Verre d'eau*, is set during the last of Louis XIV's wars, and it contains several dramatic devices cherished by the author. A historical drama replete with local color, the play emphasizes the lesson that even the greatest events may have the most insignificant causes, that the destinies of great states are frequently controlled by the caprices of courtly life, and that a struggle always exists between romantic passion and duty. The glass of water in the play's title ultimately brings about the fall of the duke of Marlborough and the Whigs as well as the negotiations that lead to the Treaty of Utrecht. *Adrienne Lecouvreur*, the story of the doomed love of Adrienne for Maurice de Saxe, became the vehicle for the great actress Rachel's transition from classical tragedy to modern drama. Before the 1840s ended, Scribe had also written not only a historical novel, *Piquillo Alliago* (1846–47), which revealed the influence of Walter Scott, but also a number of short stories and libretti for numerous operas, including Meyerbeer's *Robert le Diable* (1831) and Verdi's *Les Vêpres siciliennes*.

The remainder of Scribe's life, with the exception of the temporary hard times brought by the Revolution of 1848, was filled with triumphs. He visited England and, when requested, wrote an opera based on *The Tempest*; he also visited the exiled Louis-Philippe and collaborated with him on an opera (*Henry VIII*). Appointed by Louis-Napoleon to the Municipal Council of Paris, Scribe held this office until his death on 20 February 1861. Some three thousand mourners accompanied his remains to Père Lachaise. Scribe's influence remained powerful even after his death, and his work, which numbers in excess of three thousand compositions, exerted a considerable impact on the plays of Alexandre Dumas, Emile Augier, and Victorien Sardou.

N. C. Arvin, *Eugène Scribe and the French Theater, 1815–1860* (1924; repr. New York, 1967); H. Koon and R. Switzer, *Eugène Scribe* (Boston, 1980); B. Matthews, *French Dramatists of the Nineteenth Century* (New York, 1901); E. Scribe, *Oeuvres complètes*, 76 vols. (Paris, 1874–85).

*Robert Brown*

*Related entries:* DUMAS; REVOLUTION OF 1830; REVOLUTION OF 1848.

**SEBASTIANI, HORACE-FRANCOIS-BASTIEN** (1772–1851), comte de la Porta, general of the Empire; deputy of the Hundred Days, Restoration, and July Monarchy; marshal of France. Born at La Porta, Corsica, on 15 November 1772, Sébastiani fled to France and became an infantry sublieutenant in August 1789. He served in Corsica and in Italy where he fought at Arcola and was promoted to major in 1799. Pretending a family tie to Napoleon, Sébastiani assisted in the coup of 18 Brumaire. After fighting at Marengo, Napoleon in 1801 sent him to Turkey and Egypt on a diplomatic mission. On his return in 1803, Napoleon promoted him to brigadier general in August and posted him to the Boulogne camp. Sébastiani was wounded at Austerlitz and was promoted to lieutenant general. Sent as ambassador to Constantinople, he convinced Turkey to declare war on Russia and oppose England. Recalled to France in June 1807, Napoleon awarded him the Legion of Honor. He went to Spain in August 1808 and in 1809 became commander of IV Corps, participating at Talavera and Ocaña and in the conquest of Andalusia. His accomplishments earned him appointment as a count of the Empire in December 1809. Sébastiani remained in Spain until 1811, although a conflict with Joseph Bonaparte and some exaggerated reports earned him some disgrace. In the Russian campaign, he distinguished himself at Smolensk and Moscow and commanded the cavalry guard on the retreat. In 1813 he served in Germany under Eugène de Beauharnais and was seriously wounded at Leipzig. He fought valiantly in the 1814 campaign.

After Napoleon's abdication, Sébastiani rallied to the Bourbons, who gave him the Order of Saint Louis. During the Hundred Days, he was elected to the lower Chamber and commanded a National Guard unit. After Waterloo, the Chamber sent him as one of its commissioners to the Allies to demand the right for France to choose its own government. In August 1815 he left for England, returning to France in 1816. In 1819 Corsica elected him to the Chamber of Deputies, where he joined the liberals in opposing the Decazes ministry. Defeated by ministerial intervention in 1824, he was reelected in 1826 by the department of Aisne to replace General Maximilien-Sébastien Foy. He renewed his opposition to the government and the king. Reelected in 1827, Sébastiani's criticism helped force the government to withdraw a series of proposed laws on local administration and departmental elections. Already an Orleanist, he was one of the 221 signers of the Deputies' address to the king in March 1830. In June 1830 Sébastiani was reelected to the Deputies by a large majority.

Sébastiani was on close terms with Orléans, whose cause he greatly aided during the July Revolution. On 11 August 1830 he was appointed minister of the navy, which he exchanged on 2 November for the Foreign Ministry, where he advocated nonintervention in the internal affairs of other states. Reelected by two departments in 1831, he served as interim war minister in November and December 1831 and resigned the Foreign Ministry on 11 October 1832. He also served as one of Louis-Philippe's private advisers. In 1834 he became ambassador to Naples and then from 1835 to 1840 ambassador to London, where he handled such sensitive issues as the Egyptian-Turkish conflict. In October 1840 Louis-Philippe appointed him a marshal of France. He was consistently returned to the Deputies during the 1830s, and in December 1840 Corsica reelected him by a unanimous vote. His health began to crumble, and, although the electors returned him in 1842 and 1846, he took little part in political affairs. The murder of his daughter, the duchesse de Praslin, in August 1847 virtually ruined his health, and he died in Paris on 20 July 1851. He was buried in the Invalides at the order of Louis-Napoleon.

*Archives parlementaires*; J. T. de Mesmay, *Horace Sébastiani: soldat, diplomate, homme d'état, maréchal de France* (Paris, 1948); D. Pinkney, *The French Revolution of 1830* (Princeton, 1972); A. Robert et al., *Dictionnaire des parlementaires français* (Paris, 1889–91).

*James K. Kieswetter*

*Related entries:* CHAMBER OF DEPUTIES; DECAZES; FOY; HUNDRED DAYS; LOUIS-PHILIPPE; NATIONAL GUARD; REVOLUTION OF 1830; SEBASTIANI, J.-A.; THE 221.

**SEBASTIANI, JEAN-ANDRE-TIBURCE, VICOMTE** (1786–1871), army officer, deputy of the Restoration, deputy and peer of the July Monarchy. Born at La Porta, Corsica, on 21 March 1786, Jean Sébastiani was the younger brother of Horace Sébastiani. Trained at the Fontainebleau military academy, Jean became a sublieutenant of dragoons in 1806. He fought in Portugal and Spain until 1811 at battles such as Vimiero and Talavera. On the Russian campaign, he conducted himself with exemplary bravery. He fought in Germany in 1813 and was promoted to colonel at Dresden. He again demonstrated outstanding courage in the 1814 campaign in France. Rejoining Napoleon in the Hundred Days, he fought at Waterloo. He was assigned to cover the French army's withdrawal and fought one of the last actions against the Allies at Patte d'Oie. He subsequently returned to Corsica.

In 1818 Sébastiani was recalled to active duty as commander of the legion of Saône-et-Loire and later of the Corsican legion. In 1823 he was promoted to *maréchal de camp* but was quickly placed on the inactive list because of his liberal political ideas. Thus free to enter politics, he was elected a deputy by the department of Corsica in April 1828. Later that year, in command of a brigade of the French forces in the Morea, he seized and held Koroni against Imbrahim Pasha. Returning to France, he was reelected to the Deputies in November 1830 and promoted to lieutenant general by Louis-Philippe. He participated in the siege of Antwerp in 1832 and was instrumental in impeding the activities of the Dutch naval squadron. Reelected a deputy in 1831 and 1834, he was a staunch supporter of the government, which in October 1837, gave him a peerage. In 1837 he became commander of the military division at Marseilles, and in 1842 he received command of the Paris division. As a peer he continued to support the government and in 1845 received the grand cross of the Legion of Honor. He remained commander of Paris until the night of 23 February 1848 and maintained his opposition to the Revolution until the king had actually departed. Sébastiani then retired to Ajaccio and lived in retirement until his death at Bastia, Corsica, on 16 September 1871.

*Archives parlementaires*; M. Glover, *The Peninsular War, 1807–1814* (London, 1974); F. Hoefer, *Nouvelle biographie générale* (Paris, 1852–66); J. F. Michaud, *Biographie universelle ancienne et moderne* (Paris, 1854–65); A. Robert et al., *Dictionnaire des parlementaires français* (Paris, 1889–91).

*James K. Kieswetter*

*Related entries:* BELGIAN REVOLUTION OF 1830; CHAMBER OF DEPUTIES; CHAMBER OF PEERS; HUNDRED DAYS; IMBRAHIM PASHA; LOUIS-PHILIPPE; REVOLUTION OF 1848; SEBASTIANI, H.-F.; WATERLOO.

**SECOND BOURBON RESTORATION.** See RESTORATION, SECOND.

**SEMONVILLE, CHARLES DE, MARQUIS** (1759–1839), adaptable monarchist under the Restoration and the July Monarchy, officer of the Chamber of Peers. Charles Louis Huguet, marquis de Sémonville, typifies those politically adept aristocrats of the *ancien régime* who survived the Revolution and contrived to win high office in each succeeding regime. Sémonville was born into a family of the nobility of the robe, and at age nineteen he became an officer of the Parlement de Paris. During the Revolution both the constitutional monarchy and the Republic found him to be a useful diplomatic agent, and in 1799 Napoleon named him his representative in the Hague. In 1805 the emperor appointed him to the imperial Senate and four years later raised him to the imperial nobility with the title of count. He rallied to the Bourbons in 1814 and served on the commission that drafted the Charter of 1814. Louis XVIII rewarded him with appointment to the Chamber of Peers and to the office of *grand référendaire*, the keeper of the chamber's seals.

On 29 July 1830, when he saw the tide of revolution about to engulf the Bourbon regime, he made a vigorous effort to save it. Making his way to the Tuileries, he sought out Jules de Polignac, the first minister, and urgently pressed him to withdraw the offending July Ordinances and to offer his resignation to the king. Failing to persuade Polignac, he hurried to St. Cloud and there was instrumental in convincing Charles X that he must name a new first minister and withdraw the ordinances. He and two others, on Charles's request, carried word of the royal decision to the marquis de Lafayette and the Municipal Commission in Paris, and the next day he and the new first minister, the duc de Mortemart, worked out a plan for winning the provisional authorities over to acceptance of the new ministry. By that time, however, events were already passing them by, and Sémonville's personal efforts to save the regime foundered. Some days later he took the oath of fidelity to the new Orleanist monarchy and kept his seat in the Chamber of Peers and his office as *grand référendaire*. He retired from the latter office in 1834 at the age of seventy-five. He died in Paris in 1839.

*Nouvelle biographie générale*, vol. 43 (Paris, 1855–70); D. H. Pinkney, *The French Revolution of 1830* (Princeton, 1972).

*David H. Pinkney*

*Related entries:* CHAMBER OF PEERS; CHARLES X; CHARTER OF 1814;

JULY ORDINANCES; LAFAYETTE, M.-J.-P.-Y.-R.-G.; LOUIS XVIII; LOUIS-PHILIPPE; MORTEMART; MUNICIPAL COMMISSION; POLIGNAC; REVOLUTION OF 1830.

*LA SENTINELLE DES CLUBS*. See *LA VOIX DES CLUBS*.

**SEPTEMBER LAWS.** See PRESS LAWS.

**SERRE, PIERRE-FRANCOIS-HERCULE DE, COMTE** (1776–1824), deputy and minister of the Restoration. De Serre, son of a cavalry officer, was born at Pagny (Meurthe) on 12 March 1776. He attended the artillery school at Châlons sur Marne and then emigrated, serving in the army of Conde. He studied law, and in 1811 Napoleon appointed him solicitor general at Metz and later that same year first president of the imperial court at Hamburg. He supported the restoration of the Bourbons, who made him first president of the royal court at Colmar. During the Hundred Days he fled to Ghent and retained his post upon his return to France.

In August 1815 the department of Haut-Rhin elected him to the Chamber of Deputies, where he earned fame for his eloquence. As a leader of the constitutional monarchist group, also led by Etienne-Denis Pasquier and Pierre Royer-Collard, he opposed the excesses of the ultras in the *chambre introuvable*. He tried to amend the law suspending individual liberty and attempted to limit the provost courts. He defended André Masséna and opposed returning unsold church property to the clergy. Thus de Serre drew down on himself the violent wrath of the ultras. Reelected in 1816, he became an ally of Royer-Collard and a member of the *doctrinaires*. He served as president of the Deputies from January 1817 until the end of 1818. Previously having been the victim of outrageous interruptions by the ultras, as president he proposed rules to limit very strictly such interjections. On occasion stepping down from the president's chair, he supported the direct election of Deputies. But in an effort to prevent executive pressure on the Chamber, he opposed the reelection of deputies holding government offices from which they were removable. In December 1818, de Serre became the minister of justice in the Dessolle-Decazes cabinet. In collaboration with the *doctrinaires*, he proposed a major reform of the press laws, abolishing all preliminary press censorship, allowing juries to hear press trials, and accepting defense testimony against government officials. De Serre himself was largely responsible for the adoption of these measures. In June 1819 he alienated the liberals, hitherto his supporters, by denouncing a proposal to readmit those exiled after Waterloo. He specifically opposed ever readmitting the regicides. In late 1819 de Serre, along with Victor de Broglie and François Guizot, proposed a major constitutional revision, including extensive electoral reform, which would have greatly improved the government. He supported Elie Decazes during the controversy over proposed changes in the election law, which offended the liberals.

When the Decazes government was replaced by the second Richelieu ministry, de Serre remained minister of justice. But de Serre, who was one of the best orators in the Chamber, had now begun to suffer from a severe pulmonary ailment requiring trips to the south. Thus his talents were frequently absent from the ministerial bench during some of the most difficult times of the Restoration. Nevertheless, breaking with his former *doctrinaire* friends, in May and June 1820 he supported the Richelieu government's election law proposal, although he actually preferred a more equitable solution. The strong opposition of Royer-Collard led de Serre to remove him from the Council of State. He also removed Camille Jordan, Prosper Barante, and Guizot. Perceiving a serious threat from the revolutionary Left, de Serre urged the courts to deal harshly with them and himself set an example in handling the demonstrations provoked by the death of a student, shot by a Royal Guard. He also urged a lengthy extension of the recently established censorship, a move to curtail the radicals of both Left and Right. When Joseph de Villèle replaced Armand-Emmanuel de Richelieu as prime minister in December 1821, de Serre declined the ultras' request that he remain in the cabinet. Thus he resumed his functions in the Deputies, returning to his earlier moderate royalist positions such as championing jury trials for press offenses. In January 1822 he was appointed ambassador to Naples and as such attended the Congress of Verona. He was, however, defeated in the 1824 elections. With his illness worsening, he returned to Naples and died at nearby Castellamare on 21 July 1824. His death was one of the tragedies of the Restoration, for he was not only an excellent orator but also a man of keen intelligence and political ability. His correspondence was published in 1876–77.

*Archives parlementaires*; J. Crauffon, *La Chambre des députés sous la restauration* (Paris, 1908); P. Duvergier de Hauranne, *Histoire du gouvernement parlementaire en France, 1814–1848* (Paris, 1857–71); A. Robert et al., *Dictionnaire des parlementaires français* (Paris, 1889–91).

*James K. Kieswetter*

*Related entries:* BARANTE; BROGLIE, A.-L.-V.; DECAZES; DESSOLLE; *DOCTRINAIRES*; GUIZOT; JORDAN; PASQUIER; RICHELIEU; ROYER-COLLARD; ULTRAROYALISTS; VILLELE.

**SEZE, RAYMOND DE, COMTE** (1746–1828), magistrate under the Old Regime, defender of Louis XVI in 1793, peer of France under the Restoration. A brilliant lawyer who had unsuccessfully defended Louis XVI at his trial in 1793, Comte Raymond de Sèze refused to work for either the Republic or the Empire. In February 1815 the restored Bourbons named him chief justice of the First Court of Justice, and in that same year he was named a peer of France. Louis XVIII also made him high treasurer and commander of the Order of the Holy Spirit. After following the king to Ghent during the Hundred Days, he was named to the Academy in 1816, and in 1817 he received the title of count. After his death, King Charles X ordered a monument to him at the Church of the Madeleine in Paris, but his memory was, in the end, kept alive only by a street named after him. His son, Etienne-Romain (1780–1862), was also a peer of France who, after the 1830 Revolution, resigned rather than take the oath to the new Orléans monarchy.

F. R. de Chateaubriand, *Eloge du comte de Sèze* (Paris, 1861); *Nouvelle biographie générale*, vols. 43–44. (Paris, 1852–66).

*Jean-Claude Caron, trans. E. Newman*

Related entries: ACADEMIE FRANCAISE; CHAMBER OF PEERS; CHARLES X; HUNDRED DAYS; LOUIS XVIII; REVOLUTION OF 1830.

*LE SIECLE,* mass circulation newspaper of the Restoration, July Monarchy, Second Republic, and the early Second Empire. Armand Dutacq founded *Le Siècle* in 1836, the same day as his rival Emile de Girardin founded *La Presse*. Sold at the same price (40 francs a year), it was commercially more successful than the *Presse*, probably because its articles and serial stories catered to a more popular audience. By 1841 it had 37,000 subscribers compared with the *Presse*'s 13,000. At the height of its success, Dutacq sold his controlling interest in the paper to Louis Perée. The readership went down slowly, but the *Siècle* nevertheless continued to attract readers away from more serious political newspapers. Not that it wholly neglected politics. It attacked the Molé cabinet, supported Adolphe Thiers in 1840, and attacked corruption under François Guizot, earning a condemnation in the courts in 1842 amounting to one month's imprisonment for its editor and a fine of 10,000 francs. In 1848 it followed the wavering lead of Odilon Barrot in moving from the dynastic Left to moderate republicanism. In the latter half of 1848, it supported Eugène Cavaignac rather than Louis-Napoleon Bonaparte. By this time politics had begun to play a larger part in its editorial policies, and during Louis-Napoleon's presidency of the Republic, the *Siècle* kept up a lively attack on him. In 1850, prefects and police seem to have regarded it as one of the most dangerous newspapers circulating in the provinces. The *Siècle* was allowed to survive in 1852 chiefly because the duc de Morny pointed out to Napoleon III the unpopularity he would incur if he abolished a newspaper whose property was distributed among more than 200 shareholders.

I. Collins, *The Government and the Newspaper Press in France, 1814–1881* (Oxford, 1959); A. Sirven, *Journaux et journalistes: Le Siècle* (Paris, 1866).

*Irene Collins*

Related entries: BARROT, C.-H.-O.; CAVAIGNAC, L.-E.; GIRARDIN; GUIZOT; MOLE; *LA PRESSE*; REPUBLICANS; THIERS.

**SIEYES, EMMANUEL-JOSEPH** (1748–1836), abbé, author of *What Is the Third Estate?* and constitution maker of the Revolution; a political survivor. The abbé Emmanuel-Joseph Sieyès was born 3 May 1748 at Fréjus, the fifth son and sixth child of a father who held a modest government appointment as a tax and postal official. While attending the Jesuit college at Fréjus in the early 1760s, he agreed to his family's suggestion that he pursue a clerical career. Sieyès became a student at the minor seminary of St. Sulpice in Paris in 1765 and received his license in theology from the Sorbonne in 1774, the same year in which he was ordained a Catholic priest. Throughout his educational career in Paris, Sieyès was regarded suspiciously by his professors, for he supplemented his instruction in Catholic orthodoxy with an independent reading of the *philosophes*, especially Descartes, Locke, Condillac, and Bonnet. Sieyès was both unsuited for and uninterested in pastoral work; he viewed his clerical status primarily as a vehicle for pursuing a successful administrative career.

This career was blocked by his social origins, however, since Sieyès' status as a commoner meant that despite his intelligence and administrative gifts, he could not aspire to episcopal office, which was limited to aristocrats by the end of the *ancien régime*. The personal difficulties he encountered may have contributed to the resentment of privilege that formed much of Sieyès' political writings. Throughout the 1770s and 1780s Sieyès gained political and administrative experience by serving as a clerical representative at the Estates of Brittany in the 1770s and the Provincial Assembly of Orléans in 1787.

Sieyès gained national prominence in 1788 and 1789 when he published three works dealing with issues raised by the political crisis: *Essai sur les privilèges* (1788), *Vues sur les moyens d'exécution dont les représentans de la France pourront disposer en 1789* (1789), and the famous *Que' est-ce que le Tiers-Etat?* (1789).

Sieyès was instrumental in the creation of the National Guard, but his most lasting contribution was the proposal that France redraw its administrative map and replace the competing jurisdictions of the *ancien régime* with uniform administrative units defined and controlled by the central government in Paris. Sieyès' plan led to the highly centralized departmental system that remains in place in contemporary France. Although Sieyès (who was on mission when the vote to execute Louis XVI was taken) wrote a letter approving of the king's execution in 1793, he opposed both direct democracy and republican forms of government and retained a preference for a constitutional monarchy that vested power in a political elite.

During the Terror of 1793–94 Sieyès became increasingly silent, although he did publicly deny both Christianity and his priesthood at the Feast of Reason on 10 November 1793. (Later, when he was asked what he did during the Terror, Sieyès responded, "I survived.") Following Thermidor, Sieyès was named a secretary to the Convention in 1795 and was a member of the Directory's Council of 500 in 1797. Sieyès was also active as a diplomat and served as minister to Prussia in 1798. In 1799 he was named to the Directory, but by then he was concerned about the lack of a strong executive authority capable of defending the Revolution against both resurgent royalism and popular disorder. Consequently, he conspired with Napoleon Bonaparte to replace the Directory with the Consulate in November 1799.

Sieyès' reputation as an authority on constitutions and his role in the coup of Brumaire that led to the Consulate gave him substantial influence in writing the Constitution of 1799, a complicated arrangement of appointed and elected bodies that effectively checked each other's power and allowed Napoleon to become the dominant figure. Sieyès was appointed senator by Napoleon and played a major role in the naming of the other senators as well. Although Sieyès was given a comfortable stipend by Napoleon, he was denied real political power, and in 1814 he supported the Senate resolution that removed Napoleon from the imperial office. Sieyès retained his state income during the First Restoration, but during the Hundred Days, fearful of the Bourbons, he let himself be named to Napoleon's reconstituted House of Peers. With the unequivocal defeat of Napoleon in 1815 and the Second Restoration of the Bourbons, Sieyès was forced into exile at Brussels, where he lived quietly for the next fifteen years. Following the July Revolution of 1830, Sieyès was allowed to return to Paris, but his age prevented him from playing any role in the political or intellectual life of France during the July Monarchy.

Although Sieyès is not the most familiar and dramatic figure to emerge from the Revolutionary era, he had a pronounced impact on the ideas and institutions of nineteenth-century France. During the July Monarchy, Charles-Maurice de Talleyrand listed the major achievements of the Revolution as the elimination of the society of orders, the creation of the National Guard, and the division of France into departments. According to Talleyrand, "These three things belong to Sieyès." Beyond Sieyès' particular contribution lies his vigorous defense of individual rights, his conviction that a constitution must limit the power of the state, and his ideal of national unity as the necessary basis of social order and individual liberty. Sieyès' forceful expression of these ideas and his insistence that they were mutually compatible helped shape the intellectual and political climate of France throughout the nineteenth century.

P. Bastid, *Sieyès et sa pensée* (Paris, 1970); J. H. Clapham, *The Abbé Sieyès—An Essay in the Politics of the French Revolution* (London, 1912); G. Van Deusen, *Sieyès: His Life and His Nationalism* (New York, 1932).

*Thomas Kselman*

*Related entries:* HUNDRED DAYS; NATIONAL GUARD; RESTORATION, SECOND; TALLEYRAND.


*LA SILHOUETTE* (1829–1830), popular liberal magazine featuring satirical caricatures and cartoons. *La Silhouette* first popularized the devastating work of the cartoonist Charles Philipon. He was later editor of *La Caricature*, which became more than a nuisance to Louis-Philippe and the July Monarchy. Other collaborators included Honoré de Balzac, Nicolas-Toussaint Charlet, and Henri Monnier. They attacked Jules de Polignac's regime and especially ridiculed its clericalism.

C. Ledré, *La Presse à l'assaut de la monarchie* (Paris, 1960).

*Daniel Rader*

*Related entries:* BALZAC; LOUIS-PHILIPPE; POLIGNAC.

**SILK INDUSTRY.** Silk weaving was introduced in France, largely by Italian weavers, in the late thirteenth and early fourteenth centuries, and small artisanal communities (*fabriques*) were established in Paris, Poitiers, Troyes, Tours, Nimes, and Lyons. The predominance of the last of these cities was established by growing royal interest in the development of a native luxury textile industry, and the weavers of Lyons won important privileges from Francis I in 1536. In 1540, the Corporation des ouvriers en draps d'or, d'argent et de soye was chartered by the king, and Lyons was granted a monopoly on the importation of raw silk (mostly from Italy and Spain) in the same year. The exclusive right to market the industry's raw material led to the emergence of Lyons as the center of the silk trade in France, and the royal charter reflected the concern of successive French kings with the encouragement of domestic production, both as a source of export revenues and as a means of lessening costly imports.

In 1605, a Lyons weaver, Claude Dangon, perfected the loom *à grand tire* for the production of elaborately patterned fabrics (*étoffes façonnées*), which was to remain the standard unit of artisanal technology for two centuries. By 1660, the Lyons *fabrique* provided work for 3,000 master weavers and nearly 10,000 looms and had definitively supplanted the other silk weaving centers in France. In addition to the costly *façonnées* (figured taffetas, velvets, and brocades), the *fabrique* also produced lighter silk plaincloth (*unies*) and silks for handkerchiefs and stockings. Lyons silks set the European standard for luxury clothing, upholstery, and wall coverings, and in 1667 Colbert provided the industry with a new royal *Règlement*, which would, with modifications, last until the end of the Old Regime. The *Règlement* of 1667 prescribed the structure of the Communauté des maîtres marchands et maîtres ouvriers fabricants en soie and specified the content and quality (down to the exact number of warp and weft threads) of each grade of silk fabric in elaborate detail. Master weavers (*maîtres-fabricants*) and wholesale merchants (*maîtres-marchands*), who provided individual weavers with commissions and marketed the finished cloth, were full voting members of the *communauté*, and the regulations fixed the conditions of admission for apprentices and journeymen. While the total number of weavers and merchants in the eighteenth century never exceeded 7,000 (in a proportion of one merchant to approximately twelve weavers), the *fabrique* included associated guilds (stocking and hat makers, dyers, and gold and silver thread drawers) and a large wage labor force (largely female) of spinners, fullers and workshop assistants (particularly the *tireuses* and *tireurs* who helped the weaver operate the Dangon loom). In the 1780s, perhaps 35,000 of Lyons' 150,000 inhabitants worked in some facet of the industry.

While the eighteenth century saw the full flowering of the *fabrique*'s artistry and international influence, it also saw the consequences of the industry's reliance on exports and a luxury market. The silk trade was always particularly dependent on foreign consumption and aristocratic patronage, and serious recessions and business slumps due to wars, tariffs, foreign competition, and changing fashions (which favored lighter fabrics and cottons) struck the *fabrique* in 1689, 1709,

1750–53, 1756–58, 1766–67, 1771, and 1784. Hard times exacerbated latent tensions between weavers, skilled and literate artisans who saw themselves as the productive heart of the industry, and merchants, who controlled employment and sought to dominate the regulatory bodies of the *communauté*. Merchants often ignored the fixed scale (*tarif*) of piecework rates paid to individual weavers, and strikes in 1744 and 1786 (which were repressed by royal troops) failed to redress the balance in the weavers' favor. In 1787, the industry slipped into a prolonged depression, which lasted into the Empire. The outbreak of the Revolution brought merchant and weaver into bitter conflict in the moribund industry.

The abolition of the *communauté* by the Constituent Assembly in 1791, though of limited impact while the weavers were able to maintain some degree of solidarity and win continued *tarifs* in 1790 and 1793, also changed the basic character of the industry. Prosperity remained elusive, and in 1793 barely one-quarter of Lyons' 12,000 looms were working.

While improved foreign trade and sympathetic government policies brought limited recovery under the Empire, the invention of the Jacquard loom (which, while still hand powered, was partially mechanical and could be worked by a single weaver) set a new pattern for nineteenth-century production. The new loom could be operated by a less-skilled (and less well-paid) weaver and resulted in greater productivity, but it was expensive and beyond the reach of most weavers. As merchants came to own the means of production, the industry (which had been confined by law to the city limits until the Revolution) was gradually decentralized as merchants substituted women, journeymen (*compagnons*), and rural cottage weavers for trained artisans. Periodic slumps accelerated this trend and forced piecework rates steadily lower as merchants sought to cut labor costs. These changes largely account for the weaver revolts of 1831 and 1834, which failed to reverse them. By 1840, the 30,500 looms in the countryside outnumbered the 27,000 still located in the city proper.

While the seventeenth- and eighteenth-century industry had depended largely on imported raw materials from Spain and Italy, improvements in sericulture in France enabled the *fabrique* to draw on domestic sources for 50 percent of its raw silk for the first time in 1845. Overproduction and a series of epidemics that decimated the domestic silkworm population caused a steady decline, however, from a high point in 1853 (2,200 metric tons of raw silk) to about 1,100 tons in 1877. After 1870, the availability of raw silk from China and Japan at competitive prices accelerated the collapse of the domestic production of raw materials, and French sericulture virtually vanished in the twentieth century. The Lyons merchants, organized in a trade association (*Union*) in 1871, succeeded in maintaining Lyons as the central European market for imported silks (rivaled only by Milan) and the center of the French industry. The second half of the nineteenth century also saw increased foreign competition (from Germany, England, and Switzerland), which encouraged protectionism among a minority of Lyons merchants but also a growing diversity of production, particularly of mixed fabrics consisting of silk, cotton, and wool (*bourettes*).

Competition also encouraged the development of power looms. The delicacy of silk thread had made the adaptation of steam-powered cotton and wool looms difficult, but a workable design for a powered silk loom was perfected in Switzerland in the 1860s. Hand-operated Jacquard looms continued to be used for the production of the finest figured fabrics, but by 1914 more than 60,000 steam-powered looms were in operation in and around Lyons, and in 1899 a power loom capable of producing *velours façonnés* was invented. The result was a 300 to 400 percent increase in production and the need to maintain and adjust the complex machinery concentrated production in factories (the famous *usines-dortoirs*) for the first time. The application of electricity as a power source after 1920 to some extent preserved rural weaving (as electric motors could be attached to individual cottage looms) and also permitted the creation of smaller weaving establishments in the city itself.

M. Beaulieu, *Les Tissus d'art* (Paris, 1953); C. Bunt, *The Silks of Lyons* (London, 1960); P. Clerget, *Les Industries de la soie en France* (Paris, 1925); J. Godart, *L'Ouvrier en soie* (Paris, Lyons, 1899); E. Pariset, *Histoire de la fabrique lyonnaise* (Lyons, 1901); N. Rondot, *L'Industrie de la soie en France* (Lyons, 1894); J. Vaschalde, *Les Industries de la soierie* (Paris, 1961).

*David Longfellow*
*Related entries: CANUTS*; COTTAGE INDUSTRY; JACQUARD LOOM; LYONS, REVOLTS IN.

**SIMEON, JOSEPH-JEROME, COMTE** (1749–1842), legislator of the Empire; deputy, peer, and minister of the Restoration. The son of a lawyer, Siméon was born on 30 September 1749 at Aix (Bouches-du-Rhône). He studied law and entered the bar, earning a reputation for his careful, clear rhetoric. He became a professor of the law at the University of Aix in 1778, and in 1783 was appointed assessor of Provence. Unsympathetic to Revolutionary ideas, he was forced to resign his university post. He subsequently participated in the federalist movement in the Midi and fled to Italy after being outlawed in August 1793. He returned after the uprising of 1 Prairial Year III. He was soon appointed *procurer-syndic* of his department and exercised his authority with firmness and conciliation. The department of Bouches-du-Rhône elected him to the Council of 500 in October 1795. He joined the moderate royalists and became a leader of the Clichy Club, a royalist organization. He opposed the oath of hatred to royalty and supported the abolition of political clubs and the suppression of newspapers. He was president of the 500 at the time of the coup of 18 Fructidor and, protesting vigorously against the coup, was dragged from his president's chair by troops. Ordered deported, he escaped but voluntarily surrendered and was exiled to the Ile d'Oléron. He was freed by the coup of 18 Brumaire.

Under the Consulate, Siméon declined the offer of the prefecture of the Marne but accepted that of substitute executive commissioner to the Court of Cassation in April 1800. Later that same month he was named to the Tribunate. He played a significant role in the preparation of the Civil Code, which he presented to the

Corps législatif. He also prepared a report on the Concordat and later supported the establishment of the life consulate and the Empire. In June 1804 Napoleon appointed him a councillor of state and later named him to the Legion of Honor. In 1807 Napoleon sent him to help organize the new Kingdom of Westphalia, with the titles of minister of justice, of the interior, and president of the Council of State. Later Siméon went as minister plenipotentiary from Westphalia to Berlin and to the Confederation of the Rhine. In 1813 he retired because of his age.

At the First Restoration, Siméon rallied to the Bourbons, who appointed him prefect of the department of Nord in May 1814. During the Hundred Days the department of Bouches-du-Rhône again elected him to the legislature, but he did not participate and thus continued to enjoy royal favor after Waterloo. In August 1815 Louis XVIII appointed him councillor of state, and the department of Var elected him to the Deputies. As a member of the constitutional monarchist minority in the *chambre introuvable*, Siméon defended the cabinet's policies, voting for the amnesty law with its proposed amendments. The 1816 elections returned him to the Deputies. He supported the 1817 law on freedom of the press and the 1818 army recruiting bill of Saint-Cyr. Having declined the Ministry of Justice, he did receive the title of count on 3 July 1818 but not a place in the Chamber of Peers. On 7 May 1819 Siméon became inspector of law schools and then undersecretary of state at the Ministry of Justice. When the second Richelieu cabinet was formed on 21 February 1820, Siméon was named minister of the interior, remaining in the cabinet until its dissolution on 14 December 1821. His appointment was due to the fact that he was acceptable to almost all royalist factions, which also virtually guaranteed that he would not be a dynamic force in the cabinet. Nevertheless, as minister of the interior, he had the difficult task of presenting and defending the new censorship law, the law restricting individual liberty, and the Law of the Double Vote. In October 1821 before his resignation from the cabinet he received a peerage. He also was appointed a minister of state and a member of the Privy Council. As a peer he spoke consistently in defense of constitutional liberty and opposed such ultraroyalist measures as the 1826 law on primogeniture. He accepted the July Monarchy, remaining in the Peers after 1830. In 1837 he became president of the Cour des comptes, from which he resigned at age ninety in March 1839. Siméon died in Paris on 19 January 1842.

Archives parlementaires; N. Richardson, *The French Prefectoral Corps* (Cambridge, 1966); A. Robert et al., *Dictionnaire des parlementaires français* (Paris, 1889–91).

*James K. Kieswetter*

Related entries: AMNESTY BILL OF 1816; CENSORSHIP; GOUVION SAINT-CYR; HEREDITY LAWS; RICHELIEU; ULTRAROYALISTS.


**SIMON, JULES-FRANCOIS SIMON-SUISSE** (1814–1896), moral philosopher, republican politician, and theorist of radicalism; a founder of the Third Republic. One of the founders of the Third Republic, known for his role in the affair of 16 May (1877), Jules Simon's reputation in the late 1830s and the 1840s rested on his roles as teacher, philosopher, and writer. Born 27 December 1814 in Lorient (Morbihan), the son of Alexandre Simon-Suisse (1775–1843), he began his studies at the Collège of Lorient and the Royal Collège of Vannes, becoming a *maître suppléant* at the Collège of Rennes. Jules Simon then spent three years at the Ecole normale (1833–36), where he became a disciple of Victor Cousin and, following a spiritual crisis that shook his religious nature, an advocate of Cousin's philosophical spiritualism. He later summarized his views on religion in *La Religion naturelle* (1856). It was, incidentally, the influence of Cousin that led him to adopt the name Jules Simon.

Simon's teaching career began with assignments at Caen and Versailles, but soon he was called back to Paris to become in 1838 a *suppléant* and then a master in philosophy at the Ecole normale. The next year, he presented a thesis, "Commentaire de Proclus sur le Timée de Platon," for the doctorate and was chosen by Cousin to be his *suppléant* at the Sorbonne. Throughout the 1840s, Simon taught the eclectic philosophy of his master, gaining a reputation as a remarkable lecturer. In the mid-1840s, when the Catholic church launched its attack on the French educational system, Simon responded with spirited defenses of the Université and the teaching of philosophy. With Amédée Jacques, he founded in 1847 *La Liberté de penser: Revue philosophique et littéraire*. In this journal, Simon developed his own unique vision of what Philip Bertocci calls "anti-Voltairean anti-clericalism." During this same decade, Simon also published editions of several noted French philosophers, among them Descartes, Bossuet, Malebranche, and Antoine Arnauld, and *Histoire de l'école d'Alexandrie* (1844–45).

Jules Simon's first attempt at a political career failed when early in 1848 he lost a race to represent the Côtes-du-Nord in the Chamber of Deputies. Following the February Revolution, which he welcomed, Simon won election to the Constituent Assembly, where he sat among the moderate republicans. In the Assembly, he took a major role in discussions concerning education and again defended the Université and the teaching of philosophy against the attacks of Charles-Forbes de Montalembert and the ultramontanes. Failing to be reelected to the Council of State in 1850, Simon returned to his teaching, presenting a celebrated course on the comparative politics of Plato and Aristotle. The coup d'état of 1851 brought Simon's teaching career to a sudden end. Immediately after his lecture of 15 December, in which he denounced the use of force in political life, the ministry suspended his course. Because of his refusal to swear the required oath of allegiance to Louis-Napoleon, he was excluded from political life until 1863, when he finally took the oath. Elected to the Corps législatif, he became one of the Second Empire's most vocal opponents. Further, his *La Politique radicale*, published in 1868, helped provide the Radical party with its program. A vigorous enemy of war with Prussia in 1870, Simon served nevertheless in the Government of National Defense (4 September 1870) formed after the defeat at Sedan. He later became minister of education in the Thiers government and prime minister under President MacMahon; his forced resignation from the latter post precipitated the crisis of 16 May (1877), which helped define the political character of the Third Republic. Honored by election to both the Académie des sciences morales et politiques (1863), which he later served as permanent secretary, and the Académie française (1875), Jules Simon did not return to political life after this affair. He died on 8 June 1896.

P. A. Bertocci, *Jules Simon: Republican Anticlericism and Cultural Politics in France, 1848–1886* (Columbia, Mo., 1978); L. Séché, *Jules Simon; sa vie et son oeuvre* (Paris, 1887).

*Robert Brown*

*Related entries:* ACADEMIE FRANCAISE; COUNCIL OF STATE; COUSIN; MONTALEMBERT; THIERS; ULTRAMONTANES; VOLTAIRE.


**SINGING SOCIETIES (GOGUETTES).** During the Restoration and especially during the July Monarchy, working-class singing societies, or *goguettes*, sprang up in cities throughout France, especially in the working-class neighborhoods in Paris. What was special about these singing societies was the political nature of the songs. The French Revolution had given ordinary Frenchmen a taste for political songs, and many people had received their entire political education in verse. "Song was for the worker what the newspaper is today," one worker remembered. "The *goguette* was the school for us all where, lacking an academic education, we could at least find some enlightened advice and the exchange of ideas." It was, according to the ruler maker and Saint-Simonian socialist *chansonnier* Jules Vinçard, "an important school of patriotic teaching," where "workers went to imbibe the love of our glories and public liberty. It was in the beautiful epics of Pierre-Jean de Béranger that the people found again that heroic courage that made them accomplish in three days that providential revolution of 1830. . . . It was indeed the first stage of the forward march of the popular intellect."

> To the sounds of Liberty
> We saved the country,
> Song was the deity
> That made genius bloom.
> When the Frenchman broke free from his bonds,
> The *Marseillaise* had in advance
> Proclaimed to the universe
> The day of our deliverance!

These lyrics, sung at the *goguette* La Lice chansonnière in 1840, showed the confidence people had in the power of song. The greatest *chansonnier* of the time, Pierre-Jean de Béranger, was far more popular and influential than any politician or even the king. Song could reach the urban artisans and touch their hearts better than any other medium, and the workers in turn made heroes of the *chansonniers*, especially in Paris, Lyons, and Lille.

The *goguettes* prided themselves on being different from the *guinguettes*, which were disorganized and undisciplined dance halls, and from cafés, which were open and unstructured places for eating and socializing. The *goguettes* were highly organized and highly structured. Admission was granted only with the approval of the president and the elected officers, who also controlled the list of singers for the evening, the judging of the prize-winning songs, and the organizing of benefit nights.

Gérard de Nerval remembered attending a *goguette* that met once a week in a café. At the door the comptroller of the society collected an entry fee of 1.20 francs, about a third of the average skilled worker's daily wage. He went up to the second floor of the café, where the *chef d'ordre* required him to show proof that he was known to the society before he allowed him to enter the meeting room. This room was dominated by a head table magnificently draped in red where three "very majestic" officers of the society were sitting, each with his own bell in front of him. When the president called for order and announced that a young girl was about to make her debut as a *chansonnier*, both he and she received absolute silence. Other testimony confirms the formality and the good order that reigned in the *goguettes*. Always it was the words that counted; the audience strained to hear them, and if the song touched their hearts, they would be moved to tears. Most *chansonniers* wrote only the lyrics and borrowed the melody from a well-known song or from a new vaudeville. This made it possible for new songs to be printed cheaply and sold for 10 centimes. The printed sheets would give only the lyrics with an indication that they were to be sung to the tune of a certain melody.

*Goguettes* were usually decorated for their weekly meetings with tricolored flags (after the 1830 Revolution) and signs such as "Homage to the Ladies," "Silence and Respect," and "Honor to Béranger." Posted rules forbade songs about politics and religion, drunkenness, and indecent behavior. (One exception was the *goguette* Les Animaux, whose sign said, "Political signs are permitted, *on peut dire merde au roi.*") The rules forbidding political songs, which were almost always ignored, were posted more to mollify the authorities than to control the participants. The government of Louis-Philippe was almost always present in the form of a *mouchard* (police spy). The *chansonniers* would play a game with the *mouchard* to see how far they could go; they might, for example, say nothing about King Louis-Philippe but insult the pear, which everybody knew was the symbol for the king. Only the *chansonniers* enjoyed the game. "A smile on a police agent," one *chansonnier* remembered, "was as rare as sweat on a mason." But the *mouchard* sometimes had the last laugh, arresting the offending *chansonniers* and closing down the *goguette*. La Lice chansonnière was forced to move in 1832, 1835, 1836, 1841 (when an insult to the king caused the police to move it out of Paris altogether), and several times more (because the police continued to watch the *goguette* even when it met in the suburbs). Les Animaux was raided and shut down entirely by the July Monarchy in 1846 and could not meet until after the 1848 Revolution, when it held a benefit for its many members who had been killed or wounded at the barricades in February. The corset maker and *chansonnier* Charles Gille, president of Les Animaux, was arrested in the police raid of 1846 and sentenced to six months in jail. After his release, he was tailed by a plainclothes policeman. This was a source of pride to Gille, who pointed him out to friends as "my agent."

It is impossible to know how many *goguettes* there were in France or even just in Paris. One former *chansonnier* said that there had been hundreds in Paris and its suburbs by 1820, while the *Constitutionnel*, an influential Paris newspaper, said that by 1845 there were 480 authorized singing societies in Paris. In 1844 the *Atelier*, a Buchezian working-class newspaper in Paris, named 44 Parisian *goguettes* in a disapproving article that said that the *goguettes* distracted workers from their work and gave them a bad image as carousing fun seekers. In any case the *goguettes* seem to have been ubiquitous in the working-class quarters in Paris and available in Lyons and in Lille. Membership lists were secret, but Charles Gille claimed that Les Animaux had "baptized" more than 500 members between the time it opened in 1841 and its forced closing by the police in 1846. La Lice chansonnière published the works of 115 member *chansonniers* between 1834 and 1847. Total membership of the *goguettes* in Paris may have exceeded 30,000. Moreover, the *chansonniers* had influence far beyond the singing societies. They could sell their songs to publishers like Eyssautier and like Durand for 50 centimes a couplet, and these publishers would then print the songs on cheap paper and sell them for 5 or 10 centimes per copy. Song was everywhere in Paris; the streets were filled with organ grinders who punched out the latest tunes on cardboard cards and ground them out in the streets and parks. A successful song could be tried out in a *goguette* one night and then be available in thousands of workshops within a week. Songs were the newspapers of the working class in French cities of the first half of the nineteenth century.

Jules Vinçard gave a brief history of the character of the *goguette* songs in his *Mémoires épisodiques d'un vieux chansonnier saint-simonien*. During the Bourbon Restoration, most songs were about wine and women. The 1830 Revolution caused a renewed interest in political songs, which had been dominant during the Great French Revolution, and more and more artisans began to join the *goguettes*. The king of the *goguettes* was Béranger, whose nationalist tributes to the glories of French armies and to Bonaparte became the dominant theme.

The discovery of the social question in 1839–40 sent a swarm of Saint-Simonian socialist worker poets, including Vinçard, into the *goguettes* to spread their socialist ideas by means of song. There was some resistance, but gradually the habitués of the *goguettes* became accustomed to hear calls for economic and social reform among their songs of wine, women, and war. It was these themes, Vinçard concluded, that gave the 1848 Revolution a social character different from that of the purely political Revolution of 1830.

Whatever success the *goguettes* may have had in spreading democratic and socialist ideas among the people before 1848, it did not last. Louis-Napoleon

Bonaparte experienced no difficulty in closing the *goguettes* after his coup d'état of 1851 and in silencing political *chansonniers*. Charles Gille's suicide in 1856 symbolized the end of an era. The political, participatory, and amateur *goguette* was giving way to the apolitical, passive, and professional *café concert*, whose artists sought to be politically innocuous and economically prosperous. During the Second Empire one *chansonnier* wrote:

> Good-bye, militant *goguette*,
> You are giving way to the *café concert*
> Where the listener can digest his food after dessert
> without having his soul stirred up;
> Death has brought an end to your fragile fad
> And to the time when Charles Gille
> Sang *Le vin de Ramponneau*.

H. Avenel, *Chansons et chansonniers* (Paris, 1890); E. Baillet, *Chansons et petits poèmes avec Préface: Fragments de l'histoire de la goguette* (Paris, 1885) and *De Quelques ouvriers poètes, biographies et souvenirs* (Paris, 1898); P. Brochon, *La Chanson française, Béranger et son temps* (Paris, 1956); [E. Imbert], *La Goguette et les goguettiers, étude parisienne* (Paris, 1873); E. L. Newman, "L'Ouvrière, sa vie est dure mais elle se plaint rarement: The French Women Worker Poets of the July Monarchy," *Studies in Nineteenth Century Society and Culture* 3 (1977), "Politics and Song in a Paris Goguette: The Lice Chansonnière, 1830–1848," *Maryland Historian* 12 (1981), and *The French Worker Poets of the July Monarchy* (forthcoming); M. Ragon, *Les Ecrivains du peuple* (Paris, 1947); J. Touchard, *La gloire de Béranger*, 2 vols. (Paris, 1968); J. Vinçard, *Mémoires épisodiques d'un vieux chansonnier saint-simonien* (Paris, 1878).

*Edgar Leon Newman*

*Related entries: L'ATELIER*; BERANGER; *LE CONSTITUTIONNEL*; GILLE; NERVAL; SAINT-SIMONIANISM; VINCARD; WORKER POETS.

**SISMONDI, JEAN-CHARLES-LEONARD SIMONDE DE** (1773–1842), historian, economist, and man of letters. Jean-Charles-Léonard Simonde de Sismondi was born in Geneva on 9 May 1773 into a titled and moneyed family. Of Italian origin, the Sismondi family had fled from its homeland to the Dauphiné in 1524 following the defeat of the Ghibellines and converted to Protestantism; the revocation of the Edict of Nantes (1685) compelled them to flee once more, this time to Geneva. Sismondi's father, who served as a village pastor, provided his son with a fine classical education. At the age of ten, the young man showed a precocious taste for political theories, especially republican ones, and he and his playmates founded an idealized republic; Sismondi endowed it with a constitution. Encouraged by his family, Sismondi chose to prepare for a career in banking by going to Lyons and serving as a clerk in the House of Eynard. Sismondi was making great progress in his new profession when Revolutionary events in Lyons compelled him to return to Geneva in 1792. But Geneva did not provide much of a refuge; Sismondi and his father, both labeled aristocrats, were imprisoned briefly, and the family fortune suffered a considerable diminution.

Between 1793 and 1794, the Sismondis took refuge in England, and Sismondi used the stay to master the English language and to study the political system and economic life. Finding the English climate inhospitable, the Sismondis returned to Geneva, but encountering little improvement in the political atmosphere, they sold the family property and emigrated to Italy. There Sismondi lived between 1795 and 1800 on a small farm near Lucca in Tuscany. Out of his experiences came his first book, the *Tableau de l'agriculture toscane*, published in 1801 after Sismondi's return to Geneva.

Sismondi's first notable work, *Traité de la richesse commerciale*, appeared in 1803. Clearly a disciple of Adam Smith at this time, Sismondi advocated the application of the principles of laissez-faire to the French economy; he also favored freedom of trade and opposed the existence of monopolies, customs duties, colonial privileges, and legal restrictions on private property. *Traité* attracted a number of admirers, including Czar Alexander of Russia, who was impressed enough to offer Sismondi a professorship of political economy at the University of Vilna. Sismondi graciously declined. *Traité* also brought Sismondi to the attention of Jacques Necker, banker, former government minister, and father to Mme. de Staël; this acquaintance gave Sismondi an entrée to the rarified intellectual society at Coppet, where he became a close friend of Benjamin Constant. Sismondi joined Mme. de Staël for the Italian journey of 1804–5 that resulted in *Corinne*.

Sismondi, who had once entertained political aspirations and who was wisely dissuaded from pursuing them by his mother, turned next to the serious study of history. His first major work, *Histoire des républiques italiennes du moyen âge*, began to appear in 1807 and was completed in 1818 with the publication of the sixteenth volume. Meanwhile, he undertook to give in Geneva a course of lectures on the literature of southern Europe. An early effort to define Mme. de Staël's version of romanticism and to study literature in its historical and religious context, the lectures had their origins in the animated discussions of the Coppet group. By this time, Sismondi had become a French citizen, and he served as secretary to the Chamber of Commerce for the department of Leman.

Sismondi's first visit to Paris came in 1813 when he journeyed to the French capital to arrange for the publication of *De la Littérature*. Strongly influenced by the Coppet group, Sismondi revealed no enthusiasm for Napoleon and but little sympathy at his fall in the spring of 1814. His disgust with the policies and activities of the returned Bourbons, however, led him to welcome the emperor's return in 1815. Like Benjamin Constant, Sismondi viewed Napoleon as the creator of an idealized liberal empire. While Constant drafted a constitution, the Additional Act to the Constitution of the Empire, Sismondi published in the *Moniteur* a series of articles defending Constant's project; he later published *Examen de la Constitution française*. Napoleon thanked Sismondi with a private audience on 3 May 1815; Sismondi, however, declined an appointment to the Legion of Honor. With the advent of the Second Restoration, Sismondi left Paris.

For Sismondi, the year 1818 was not only busy but also important for the development of his economic thought. The completion of the history of the Italian republics accomplished, he undertook an even larger project, *Histoire des français*, which would eventually include thirty-one volumes and which he would leave uncompleted at his death. The success of these histories and his many other books brought Sismondi offers of academic chairs at the Collège de France and at the Sorbonne; both appointments he refused, preferring to retain his independence. A visit to England, also in 1818, brought home to Sismondi the misery that the new industrial revolution had visited upon the lower classes, and this realization led him to revise his economic ideas considerably, first in *Nouveaux principes d'économie politique* (1819) and then in *Etudes sur l'économie politique* (1837–38). Not only did he retract his earlier advocacy of laissez-faire, he also sharply criticized David Ricardo and Jean-Baptiste Say, the two leading advocates of the classical school.

A lifelong champion of humanitarianism and fervent supporter of the idea of liberty, Sismondi rarely missed an opportunity to speak for such movements as the liberation of the slaves, the Greek war of independence, the Italian national awakening, and the revolutions in Latin America. It is hardly surprising that he welcomed the July Revolution in France.

France honored Sismondi but not until relatively late in his life. When the Académie des sciences morales et politiques was reestablished during the early years of the July Monarchy, it elected Sismondi a foreign associate. Further, he accepted in 1841 the cross of the Legion of Honor that he had declined in 1815. Sismondi died in Geneva, where he had spent the last two and a half decades of his life, on 29 June 1842.

Best known during his own lifetime as a historian, Sismondi's posthumous reputation rests largely on his later economic writings and on his critique of laissez-faire capitalism. Both his monumental histories, the eighteen-volume *Histoire des républiques italiennes* and the thirty-one-volume *Histoire des français*, find few readers today, partly no doubt because of their length and partly because of Sismondi's pronounced biases. In the history of the French, for example, he made no effort to conceal his anti-Catholic and antimonarchical prejudices and his willingness to associate medieval towns with the development of the republican spirit he favored.

In part 3 of the *Communist Manifesto*, Marx and Engels designate Sismondi as the leader of the school of "petit-bourgeois socialism." While not particularly accurate, for Sismondi never truly advocated socialism, this label does contain an element of truth. Among the first to criticize the classical school of political economy, Sismondi outlined his views in an article for the *Edinburgh Encyclopaedia* and then elaborated them in *Nouveaux principes d'Economie politique* and *Etudes sur l'économie politique*. In these works, Sismondi revealed that the central concern of his critique focused on the social consequences of the industrial revolution. According to Sismondi, political economy should be a moral science and should, in addition to taking into account the quantitative aspects of economic behavior, include within its compass the study of history, political organization, and social institutions. The key problem of political economy is thus not the production of wealth, as the classical economists argued, but the physical well-being of mankind, and that is affected by the distribution of wealth. Sismondi also challenged other articles of economic faith cherished by the classical school, such as the idea of unrestrained competition, the willingness to overlook the misery wrought by industrialization, the oppsstition to government intervention in economic life, the infatuation with mechanization, and the facile identification of a harmony between individual and general interests. In his critique, Sismondi also explored the polarization of wealth that occurs during industrialization, and he was among the first to emphasize the growth of the proletariat as an economic class. Sismondi's humanitarianism, which made him an effective critic of the early industrial revolution, did not help him suggest workable solutions to the problems he identified. His ideal of a premechanical society of peasant and artisan workers was unattainable. Nevertheless, Sismondi remains a perceptive and influential critic of the industrial revolution.

A. Aftalion, *L'Oeuvre économique de Simonde de Sismondi* (Paris, 1899); E. Halévy, *Sismondi* (Paris, 1933); B. Réizov, *L'Historiographie romantique française, 1815–1830* (Moscow, n.d.); J.-R. de Salis, *Sismondi, la vie et l'oeuvre d'un cosmopolite philosophe* (Paris, 1932) and *Sismondi (1773–1842)* (Paris, 1938); J.-C.-L. Simonde de Sismondi, *De la Littérature du midi de l'Europe*, 4 vols. (Paris, 1813), *De la Richesse commerciale*, 2 vols. (Geneva, 1803), *Etudes sur l'économie politique*, 2 vols. (Paris 1837–38), *Examen de la Constitution française* (Paris, 1815), *Histoire des français*, 31 vols. (Paris, 1821–44), *Histoire des Républiques italiennes du moyen age*, 16 vols. (Paris, 1809–18), *Nouveaux principes d'économie politique*, 2 vols. (Paris, 1819), and *Political Economy and the Philosophy of Government* (London, 1847).

*Robert Brown*

*Related entries:* ACADEMY OF SCIENCES; ACTE ADDITIONNEL; COLLEGE DE FRANCE; CONSTANT; *LE MONITEUR;* PHILOSOPHY OF INDUSTRIALISM; REPUBLICANS; ROMANTICISM; SAY; STAEL-HOLSTEIN.

**SOBRIER, MARIE-JOSEPH** (1811 or 1812–54), socialist, revolutionary, and journalist. The date and place of Sobrier's birth are not known, but it is known that his family and he had money. While a law student in Paris, he was active in the revolutionary republican Society of the Seasons during the July Monarchy. He was one of the most active participants in the February Revolution of 1848, and consequently he became an aide to Marc Caussidière, taking the position as delegate to the Department of Police. He resigned after a few days and devoted himself to journalism, founding a Montagnard newspaper, *La Commune de Paris*, which put out eighty-seven editions between March and June 1848. Among its editors and contributors were J. Cahaigne, George Sand, and Eugène Sue.

Sobrier was one of the most ardent leaders of the clubs, especially of the Club of Clubs, which met sometimes at his house. He co-signed a proclamation to the Provisional Government on 18 March: ''We now have only the name of

Republic. We need the thing. Political reform is only the instrument of social reform."He also published two appeals for the formation of capital to be used by workers. He was chosen by the Club of Clubs as a candidate for the Constituent Assembly, but he could not campaign because on 15 May, along with Aloysius Huber, he was arrested for inciting the crowd to riot. His apartment was ransacked by the National Guard, which found among his papers a project for a forced tax on landlords and people who lived on unearned income and another project to organize work "entirely in the interests of the workers."

The High Court of Bourges sentenced Sobrier to seven years in prison for his role in the uprising of 15 May, and he was deported first to Doullens and then to Belle-Ile. By the time he was pardoned in 1853, he was becoming insane. He died 21 November 1854 in the Saint-Robert Asylum near Grenoble.

*Dictionnaire biographique du mouvement ouvrier français, 1789–1864*, vol. 3 (Paris, 1966); L. de la Hodde, *Histoire des sociétés secrètes et du Parti républicain de 1830 à 1848* (Paris, 1850); A. Longepied et Laugier, *Comité révolutionnaire, Club des Clubs et la Commission* (Paris, 1850).

Jean-Claude Caron, trans. E. Newman

*Related entries:* CAUSSIDIERE; CLUB OF CLUBS; CLUBS, POLITICAL; *LA COMMUNE DE PARIS;* CONSTITUTION OF 1848; HUBER; NATIONAL GUARD; PROVISIONAL GOVERNMENT; REVOLUTION OF 1848; SAND; SOCIETY OF THE SEASONS; SUE.

**SOCIAL CATHOLICISM,** like liberal Catholicism, an attempt to apply traditional Catholic ethics to the unique circumstances of nineteenth-century society. Social Catholicism emphasized the need to ameliorate the condition of the laboring classes and gradually promoted political democracy to achieve its end.

Its principles were based in old religious ethics of charity, social responsibility, and Christian brotherhood. It stressed protection of the weak—those in poverty, children, and women—and the institution of the family; from this followed special concern about child labor, Sunday rest, and a minimum wage for a father. It rejected materialism and the liberal political economy of the age. Its roots lay in reaction to both political economy and urban blight; it was not, however, a response to secular socialism, for it developed simultaneously, independently, and separately.

Although it denied certain liberal principles, it shared some. It emphasized self-help (the motto of one of its leading publications, *L'Atelier,* was "He who won't work won't eat") but combined that with aid for the industrious worker. Social Catholics also held a firm belief in progress and in the benefits that would accrue eventually from industrialism, while cautioning that the church had to direct society on the right path. They came to link social and political questions, viewing the political arena as the one in which social problems would be resolved.

Political perspectives varied among them. During the July Monarchy, two streams flowed. The source of one was Christian democracy, represented by

Philippe Buchez and his disciples; the other ran from more traditional paternalistic and legitimist groups who stressed the obligation of Christian charity for the upper classes. Legitimists dominated the early period; republicanism rose to the forefront at the time of the Revolution of 1848, to be followed again by political conservatism after the June Days and Louis-Napoleon's coup d'état in 1851. Although all expected the church to be the regenerative force, most accepted the idea that it would operate within a neutral state. Social Catholicism differed from socialism in its rejection of class struggle, social revolution, collectivism, and materialism, as well as in its defense of private property.

Social Catholicism was always a minority movement of individuals within the church, with only about a half-dozen bishops involved, notably Olympe Gerbet. The term itself dates from the Third Republic, but its organizations and philosophy date from the Restoration. Animated by a spirit of Christian justice and a desire to help the poor, social Catholicism moved to a larger concept of social order and Church and state roles within that order. It attempted to develop a holistic social philosophy based on a Catholic ethical response to the French and industrial revolutions, and it conceived of an organic reconstruction of society rather than mere palliatives.

Buchez, a Saint-Simonist doctor converted to Catholicism in 1829, the editors of *L'Avenir*, especially Félicité de Lamennais and Father Henri Lacordaire, and Buchez's disciples who published *L'Atelier* (1840–50) argued that democracy was a necessary means to social reform. Contemporary legitimists, notably Armand de Melun, who in 1845 began the newspaper *Annales de la charité* and became the unofficial leader of social Catholicism for the next quarter-century, and Vicomte Alban de Villeneuve-Bargemont, who wrote *Economie politique chrétienne* in 1834, stressed the difference between poverty, which was a part of the human condition, and pauperism, which was inconsistent with human dignity. The efforts of the former tended at first to the voluntary, such as establishing workers' hostels and associations. Only with 1848 did de Melun become a firm advocate of national social legislation.

Another early leader was Frédéric Ozanam, who at the age of eighteen (building upon Saint-Simon's challenge to the papacy) called for the pope not merely to preach that the poor were children of God but to use the resources of the church to "improve the moral and material conditions of the most numerous class in society." In 1833 he founded the St. Vincent de Paul Society, which has since become worldwide. Beginning as a general Catholic action group, its mission quickly concentrated on the poor. Ozanam himself advocated a combination of charitable work, workers' associations, and legislation to ensure certain "moral rights"—the minimum necessities of life, education of children, and protection for one's old age. Through men like Ozanam and Lacordaire and the newspaper *L'Avenir*, there were considerable links between liberal and social Catholicism during the July Monarchy, but those links would shatter in disputes over the Revolution of 1848.

The February 1848 Revolution gave a boost to social Catholics. Dramatically clothed in his white Dominican cassock, Lacordaire sat on the Left of the Chamber of Deputies. The newspaper *L'Ère nouvelle* (1848–49) attempted to reconcile Catholicism and socialism. In its prospectus and in the tradition of Buchez, it linked social reform with political democracy. Liberal Catholics attacked both its democratic and socialist leanings, especially after the June uprisings.

Elected to the Chamber, Armand de Melun introduced a successful bill to appoint a committee of thirty to examine possibilities for public assistance promised in article 13 of the new Constitution. In that committee, de Melun argued for a "protective society," which, while permitting private property and individuality, would engage in comprehensive prevention of poverty through hospitals, schools, day care centers, orphanages, hostels, and workers' associations that could share profits with employers. All organizations were to be supervised by a committee of the National Assembly in cooperation with local government and private institutions. Adolphe Thiers, a noninterventionist, was appointed reporter of that very divided committee, and little came of it. The Napoleonic coup that inaugurated the Second Empire ended Melun's brief experiment in politics. By then liberal and social Catholics had split, and a new period of political reaction within Catholic circles set in. Individual Catholics and local Catholic groups continued important enterprises that helped poor persons, and the church took on a major role in schooling, but demands for social legislation and reconstruction of society became a secular bailiwick, with most French Catholics responding negatively.

Many social Catholic deputies during the Third Republic, notably Anatole de Melun, Armand's brother, and Baron Chaurand, had served their apprenticeship with earlier leaders. The social Catholic movement in France had widespread influence on other countries—England, Belgium, the German and Italian states. Those movements might have developed independently, but they referred to the French example. Pope Leo XIII's encyclical *Rerum Novarum* (1891) owed a great deal not only to the social Catholic movement of the late nineteenth century but also to the fact that he was involved in social Catholic movements in the Italian peninsula during his youth.

J. Duroselle, *Les Débuts du catholicisme social en France, 1822–1870* (Paris, 1951); R. Kothen, *La Pensée et l'action sociale des catholiques, 1789–1944* (Paris, 1947); P. Moon, *The Labor Problem and the Social Catholic Movement in France* (New York, 1921).

*Patrick J. Harrigan*

*Related entries:* L'ATELIER; BUCHEZ; FALLOUX LAW; LACORDAIRE; LAMENNAIS; LIBERAL CATHOLICISM; MELUN; PUBLIC WELFARE; SAINT-SIMONIANISM; THIERS; VILLENEUVE-BARGEMONT

**SOCIETE DE LA MORALE CHRETIENNE.** See SOCIETY OF CHRISTIAN MORALS.

**SOCIETE DE L'ANNEAU.** See CHEVALIERS DE LA FOI.

**SOCIETE DE L'UNION,** a mutual aid society, also known as the *indépendants* or the *révoltés*, founded in Toulon in 1830. The Société de l'union was formed from a schism within the *compagnonnage* by a group of younger journeymen, called novices or *aspirants*. These novices rebelled against the hierarchy and privilege claimed by the older members of the *compagnonnage*. Specifically, the novices rejected the harsh initiation ceremonies of the *compagnonnage*, as well as the high fees required of them as novices. The principles of the Société de l'union, by contrast, were complete equality among all members, the abolition or modification of initiation rites and other rituals, and an orientation toward individual and political liberty.

The political atmosphere of the Revolution of 1830 and the booming economic conditions of Toulon in that period probably had as much to do with the creation of the new association as did the contemporary state of the *compagnonnage*. The news of the founding of the Société de l'union spread rapidly in the early post-Revolutionary era, and branches of the Société de l'union soon emerged in Lyons, Avignon, Marseilles, Toulouse, Nantes, and Bordeaux. The society's general headquarters were located in Lyons. Another schism in the *compagnonnage*, this time in 1832, witnessed the influx of a group of liberal and somewhat older journeymen into the growing Société de l'union.

The organizational structure of the Société de l'union aimed to implement the principles of the Revolution of 1789—liberty, equality, and fraternity—among all workers. The association maintained the interurban organization of the *compagnonnage* and many of its mutual aid features, but it did away with the rival sects that undermined the unity of the *compagnonnage*. Each trade in the Société de l'union had an office in the towns on the Tour de France responsible for the free placement of workers. The administration of these branch offices was composed of a president, treasurer, secretary, and syndic, all elected by secret ballot and by a simple majority. All were also subject to recall. To avoid the fragmentation and disunity of the local chapters, a uniform code of regulations was introduced to govern all the trades in the association.

The Société de l'union faced much opposition, both from the *compagnonnage* and from the authorities, in the years after its founding. The *compagnonnage* deeply resented the schism of the *révoltés*, as they were labeled, and the *sociétaires*, as they called themselves, constantly had to defend themselves from the attacks of their rivals. The very existence of the Société de l'union thus only worsened the already violent internecine conflicts of the *compagnonnage*. The police and other officials tended to view the Société de l'union merely as a new sect of *compagnonnage*, and not as an egalitarian, progressive, and independent entity.

How politically liberal or activist the *sociétaires* were varied with the period under investigation. Fairly active and continually pursued as a dangerous organization by the police in the 1830s and 1840s, the Société de l'union continued its democratic politics and beliefs at least into the first decade of the Second

Empire. After 1870, however, the Société de l'union became politically quiescent, apparently more content to emphasize economic rather than political goals. The Société de l'union, nevertheless, was always more involved in political movements than was the *compagnonnage*. The association, again in distinction to the *compagnonnage*, never wished to be a secret society and attempted to gain official recognition as a mutual aid society. Perhaps because of its origins, however, the authorities remained deeply suspicious of the association until the late 1860s, when official status was tentatively granted.

Despite their various setbacks, the *sociétaires* continued to view themselves as part of a politically and socially progressive movement. Pierre Moreau, a journeyman locksmith who became a member of the association in 1840 and thereafter was prominent in its affairs, worked hard to promote this image. He envisaged the Société de l'union as playing a significant role in the development of the working-class movement, rescuing workers from the internal divisions and hatreds of the *compagnonnage*, while preserving what was beneficial in the older society: its spirit of fraternity and professional artistry. Modern scholars now define the Société de l'union as a type of intermediate stage between the *compagnonnage* and the French trade union movement of the late nineteenth century.

M. Agulhon, *Une Ville ouvrière au temps du socialisme utopique* (Paris, 1970); J. Marillier, "Pierre Moreau et l'Union," *Actualité de l'histoire: Bulletin de l'Institut français d'histoire sociale*, no. 5 (Paris 1953); P. Moreau, *De la Réforme des abus du Compagnonnage* (Paris, 1843).

*Cynthia Truant*

*Related entries:* COMPAGNONNAGES; REVOLUTION OF 1830; TOUR DE FRANCE.

**SOCIETE D'ENCOURAGEMENT POUR L'INDUSTRIE NATIONALE,** an organization founded in Paris in 1789 and reorganized in 1801 to provide a forum for manufacturers, scientists, public officials, and interested amateurs. This private organization of scientists, scholars, and men with experience in science, business, and administration, like Count Jean-Antoine-Claude Chaptal, was given a charter in 1824 and was enabled to receive donations and legacies. The membership of subscribers paying annual dues was organized by a council that worked with the minister of the interior and was subdivided into six committees that distributed prizes for deserving inventions or improvements to machines or other meritorious activities. From 1802 the society published a bulletin that provided much information on technical innovation in France. The society popularized Jacquard's loom and other textile weaving equipment, spread information about research at the model farm of Sénart (Seine-et-Oise) on raising silkworm productivity, and introduced new techniques for gold and silver plating and methods of producing sugar from beets.

*David Higgs*

*Related entry:* CHAPTAL; JACQUARD LOOM.

**SOCIETE DES AMIS DE LA LIBERTE DE LA PRESSE.** See SOCIETY OF THE FRIENDS OF THE FREEDOM OF THE PRESS.

**SOCIETE DES AMIS DE L'ORDRE,** a name used by two separate organizations. It was first used by the secret royalist society established by Antoine Dandré in the early years of the Directory period. The society later became the Institut philanthropique. The name was then used by a society founded at the end of 1830 by Ferdinand de Bertier in order to rally support for legitimist activities. Its organization was modeled after that of the Society of the Propagation of the Faith. That is, it was a pyramid arrangement of groups of ten individuals, each paying a monthly contribution of 25 centimes. Little is known of its size, duration, or effectiveness.

G. de Bertier de Sauvigny, *Le Comte F. de Bertier* (Paris, 1948).

*Guillaume de Bertier de Sauvigny*

*Related entries:* BERTIER; SOCIETY OF THE PROPAGATION OF THE FAITH.

**SOCIETE DES DROITS DE L'HOMME.** See SOCIETY OF THE RIGHTS OF MAN.

**SOCIETE DES MISSIONS DE FRANCE.** See MISSIONS.

**SOCIETE PHILANTHROPIQUE EN FAVEUR DES GRECS,** Greek aid organization. The struggle of the Greeks for their independence had been dragging on since 1821. Although Philhellenic movements had been growing in the main Western European countries, their effectiveness in France had been hampered by partisan politics. The liberals had been eager to stress the revolutionary aspect of the national uprising, the very feature that would rouse the suspicion of the conservative elements in and out the government and make them hesitant to heed the calls for help. In the spring of 1825 the position of the insurgents became almost desperate with the entrance on the field of the military forces of the Egyptian Pasha Méhémet Ali. But on the domestic scene in France, the defection of François-René de Chateaubriand and friends from the bulk of the royalist majority amounted to a kind of thawing or reshuffling of political positions. He, along with other undiluted royalists, such as Edouard Fitz-James, joined hands with liberal personalities, such as the banker Jacques Laffitte, the duc de La Rochefoucauld-Liancourt, Alexandre de Lameth, and others. They established the Société philanthropique en faveur des Grecs, which proclaimed itself nonpartisan, with the dual purpose of collecting funds and influencing public opinion. The president was the great industrialist Guillaume Ternaux. Corresponding subcommittees sprouted in most important cities, and contributions came in from foreign countries. From 1826 to 1829 money and arms were sent to Greece, and the Paris committee published a news bulletin. With the decision of Charles X to send an expeditionary force to Greece to separate the Turks and the Greeks, the society had fulfilled its purpose, and it dissolved.

S. Antonopoulos, "La Société philanthropique en faveur des Grecs," *Revue d'histoire diplomatique* 6 (1892); G. Isambert, *L'Indépendance de la Grèce et l'Europe* (Paris, 1900).

*Guillaume de Bertier de Sauvigny*
*Related entries:* CHARLES X; CHATEAUBRIAND; LAFFITTE; LAMETH; LA ROCHEFOUCAULD-LIANCOURT; MEHEMET ALI; NAVARINO, BATTLE OF; TERNAUX.

**SOCIETE ROYALE DES BONNES LETTRES** (1821–1830), conservative, patriotic, antirevolutionary, antiliberal organization established to reassert political and intellectual tradition and to promote loyalty to the monarchy, the church, and classical literature. The causes of the throne, of the faith, and of letters were viewed as one. The stated goal was to resist the incursion of revolutionary ideas being spread by known liberals presenting courses and lectures at the old Athénée. Essentially political and committed to *les institutions anciennes* and *les bonnes et saines doctrines* (defined in its prospectus as the models, memories, and lessons of the past), it was copied from already influential Congrégation societies devoted to good studies and good books. Founded in January 1821, just a few months after the assassination of the duc de Berry, many of its one hundred charter members, like the vicomte de Bonald, were members of the right-wing ultra-royalist party. Louis Fontanes served as president through the first year, and his old friend François-René de Chateaubriand succeeded him in 1822. Under standably, a host of conservatives constituted the remaining membership, subscribers, and honorary members, including practically the entire community of aristocratic ultras, even Jules de Polignac, as well as prominent academicians and literary figures: Alphonse de Lamartine, Victor Hugo, Charles Nodier, and Alfred de Vigny. While many of the latter showed a propensity for the romantic style (though they really still considered themselves to be classicists), they were tolerated as *sociétaires* as long as they avoided uttering the name of Mme. de Staël.

The opening session was held on 15 February 1821. Major activities beginning in March 1821 included courses on such diverse subjects as physiology, astronomy, law, history, and literature. The last two focused especially on Spanish and French writing involving both lectures and readings mainly of poems and plays. Meetings were held three times a week from January to May. Circulating among the celebrities were a number of women, whose presence was strongly encouraged to bring dignity and charm to the gatherings. In a flight of tongue-in-cheek gallantry, Vice-President Roger even proposed as a motto in 1822: *Dieu, le Roi et les Dames.*

The society's journal, *Annales de la littérature et des arts* (an intentionally misleading title), reveals much about the group's activities. Established in October 1820 before the actual founding of the club, it merged with the Hugo brothers'

*Conservateur littéraire* in 1821. This was meant to stress the literary side of the organization's mission and to emphasize the unity of purpose of the two periodicals. The collaboration proved to be quite sporadic due to some dissatisfaction on Hugo's part; it lasted only to 1823. Although critical essays by Nodier and poems by Lamartine, Hugo, and Vigny appeared in the *Annales'* pages, these contributors were considered classical writers simply attracted to the new romantic style. Furthermore, its literary judgments were always colored by political bias. Having conceded that romanticism had won, the journal expired in April 1829.

In the wake of *Hernani* and the Revolution of 1830, the society ceased to exist.

R. Bray, *Chronologie du romantisme (1804–1830)* (Paris, 1932); C. Jensen, "The 'Romanticism' of the *Annales de la littérature et des arts*," *French Studies* 19 (October 1965); M. H. Peoples, *La Société des bonnes lettres (1821–1830)*, Smith College Studies in Modern Languages, vol. 5 (Northampton-Paris, 1923); L. Séché, *Le Cénacle de la Muse française, 1823–1827* (Paris, 1918).

*Paul Comeau*

*Related entries:* BERRY, C.-F.; BONALD; CHATEAUBRIAND; CONGRE-GATION; *HERNANI;* HUGO; LAMARTINE; NODIER; POLIGNAC; STAEL-HOLSTEIN; ULTRAROYALISTS; VIGNY.


**SOCIETY FOR ELEMENTARY INSTRUCTION** (1815), association to encourage free, nondenominational elementary schools. The society was founded by Lazare Carnot in April 1815 during his brief tenure as minister of the interior in the Hundred Days. Under the Restoration, it attracted the support of such prominent liberals as Benjamin Constant, François Guizot, and Alphonse de Lamartine and served as a moderate and respectable lobby for secular primary education. It was declared a public utility in 1831, which permitted it to raise and disburse funds and to establish independent schools. Publishing a review (*Journal de l'éducation populaire*), the society concerned itself with new methods of teaching, obtaining decent pay and working conditions for elementary school teachers, and awarding medals to outstanding instructors. Although local chapters sometimes became embroiled in disputes with Catholic schools and priests in their communes, the national society generally sought to avoid controversy in its activities. The Guizot law on elementary education (28 June 1833), which authorized the creation of communal school committees and required each village (or group of villages) to open at least one free primary school with either lay or clerical teachers, can be seen as a partial achievement of the society's goals. In the 1860s, when the association was encouraged by Napoleon III's minister of education, Victor Duruy, and supported by such liberal deputies as Jules Ferry, it lobbied for compulsory primary schooling, the teaching of French, certificates of competence (*brévets*) for all teachers, and regular state inspection of schools and teachers, and it opposed the transfer of teacher hiring from local school committees to the prefects (as had been mandated in 1854). These goals were not achieved before 1870, and the society gave way to the more militant and anticlerical Ligue de l'enseignement (1866–85), which pursued the campaign for free, compulsory, secular primary schooling under the Third Republic.

K. Auspitz, *The Radical Bourgeoisie* (Cambridge, 1972); G. de Bertier de Sauvigny, *La Restauration* (Paris, 1955, 1963); M. Gontard, *L'Enseignement primaire en France de la Révolution à la loi Guizot, 1789–1833* (Paris, 1959).

*David Longfellow*

*Related entries:* CARNOT, L.-N.-M.; CONSTANT; GUIZOT; GUIZOT LAW ON PUBLIC EDUCATION; HUNDRED DAYS; LAMARTINE.

**SOCIETY FOR GOOD STUDIES** (1828–1833), Catholic educational and study society. The Society for Good Studies was one of many lay religious associations produced by the Catholic revival and the re-establishment of the Congrégation under the Restoration. Bailly de Sarcey, the publisher of the *Tribune catholique*, organized the society in 1828 in the Latin Quarter, where it provided meeting rooms, libraries, and lectures on moral and religious subjects. Catholic students were encouraged to remain true to their faith, perform the customary observances, and evangelize their free-thinking and Protestant colleagues. In 1833, the work of the society was largely taken over by the Saint Vincent de Paul Society, a study group of law students organized by Frederick Ozanam, which wished to undertake charitable activities among the poor. Sarcey served as president of the new society from 1833 to 1844, and its members, recruited largely from the Catholic student population, visited prisons and hospitals and made regular house visits to the impoverished. Although the society lacked a comprehensive ideology, Ozanam hoped to substitute Christian charity for incitements to class warfare, and in 1845 the society received special recognition from Pope Gregory XVI. In 1851, Pius IX brought it under the supervision of the Catholic hierarchy, and chapters had appeared in most of the countries of Western Europe.

A. Dansette, *Histoire religieuse de la France contemporaine* (Paris, 1948); J. Duroselle, *Les Débuts du Catholicisme social en France* (Paris, 1951); A. Foucault, *La Société de Saint-Vincent De Paul* (Paris, 1933); H. Guillemin, *Histoire des catholiques français au XIXe siècle* (Geneva, 1947).

*David Longfellow*

*Related entries:* CONGREGATION; PIUS IX.

**SOCIETY FOR THE ENCOURAGEMENT OF PRIMARY INSTRUCTION AMONG PROTESTANTS** (1829), Protestant education and teacher-training association. The society was organized in 1829 and recognized by the Bourbon regime as a public utility (which permitted it to solicit and disburse funds) in the same year. The society was a response to the proliferation of Catholic educational and teacher-training associations that had grown up during the Restoration and endeavored to coordinate the establishment and funding of Protestant schools. Paris Protestants had established an elementary school in the capital in 1817, and a secondary school had opened in Dieulefit in 1819. The first *école normale* for Protestant girls had been founded in Sainte-Foy (Gironde) in 1818. The new society was headed by François de Jaucourt, a peer and ex-émigré who had served as Louis XVIII's minister of the navy, and a committee of directors composed of Protestant pastors and notables.

Under the society's guidance, an *école normale d'instituteurs* was organized at Courbevoie (1844) and a similar academy for women teachers at Boissy Saint-Léger (1846). *Ecoles normales* in Glay, Montbéliard, Dieulefit, and Nîmes followed, supplying instructors for 563 Protestant elementary and secondary schools by 1835 and 677 by 1840. Although the society and the schools it sponsored were affiliated with the Reformed church, admissions policies in both cases were nondenominational, and all varieties of Protestants, foreigners, and even free-thinkers and Catholics were admitted.

G. Lagny, *Le Réveil de 1830* (Paris, 1958); E. Leonard, *Le Protestant français* (Paris, 1955); D. Robert, *Les Eglises reformées en France de 1800 à 1830* (Paris, 1961); R. Stephan, *Histoire du Protestantisme français* (Paris, 1961).

*David Longfellow*

*Related entries:* JAUCOURT.

**SOCIETY FOR THE TRAINING OF CHRISTIAN SCHOOLMASTERS.** Like the better-known Society for Good Studies, the Saint-Vincent de Paul Society, the Association of Saint-Joseph, and the Catholic Society of Good Books, the Society for the Training of Christian Schoolmasters was a product of the Catholic revival under the Restoration. A charitable and educational confraternity, the society was supported by the congregations of Catholic laymen organized in Paris and provincial cities and worked to reduce what was regarded as the pernicious secularizing influence of the Napoleonic University and lycées.

G. de Bertier de Sauvigny, *La Restauration* (Paris, 1955, 1963).

*David Longfellow*

*Related entries:* CATHOLIC SOCIETY OF GOOD BOOKS; SOCIETY FOR GOOD STUDIES.

**SOCIETY OF CHRISTIAN MORALS** (1821), Christian charitable and political association. Organized on 19 December 1821, the Society of Christian Morals was intended to encourage charitable and other socially responsible activities on the part of its members. The society published a periodical *Journal* and spawned associated organizations, such as the Society for the Placement of Child Apprentices, but its members' concerns were overtly political, and the society endeavored to unite opponents of the Catholic revival, the Congrégation, and the Restoration alliance of the Bourbon regime and the Catholic church. In pursuit of this end, it welcomed liberal Catholics, Protestants, and even free-thinkers, but given its focus it fell increasingly under the control of evangelical Protestant leaders of the Réveil. Its president, Philippe-Albert Stapfer (1766–1840), was an 1820 Protestant convert, and under his leadership the society developed close ties to the Protestant Society of Evangelical Missions, which sought to replace liberal and humanist theology with a return to a strict emphasis on justification by faith and reliance on Scripture. The growing doctrinal intransigence of the majority of its members seems to have weakened the original interdenominational character of the society, and it dissolved in the early 1820s.

A. Collard, *Le Mouvement social dans le protestantisme français* (Dijon, 1909); J. Duroselle, *Les Débuts du Catholicisme social en France* (Paris, 1951); D. Robert, *Les Eglises reformées en France de 1800 à 1830* (Paris, 1961); R. Stephan, *Histoire du protestantisme français* (Paris, 1961).

*David Longfellow*

*Related entries:* LIBERAL CATHOLICISM; SOCIETY OF EVANGELICAL MISSIONS; STAPFER.

**SOCIETY OF EVANGELICAL MISSIONS** (1822), Protestant evangelical organization. The society was established in 1822 in Paris by the joint initiative of the London Missionary Society and that of Basel, Switzerland. Because it wanted to reduce the distinctions between Lutherans and Calvinists and was led by men active in the revival movement, such as Mark Wilks and Jean-Marc Grandpierre, both foreigners, the new society encountered suspicion from the clergy of both established Protestant denominations in France. It found sympathy only among some ladies of Parisian society who had been touched by the piety of the revival. Years of frustrating effort passed before the society was able to show a practical result, with the sending of three missionary pastors to South Africa, where they would find the French-speaking descendants of Huguenot *émigrés*. Three more pastors were sent in 1833. However, it would not be until 1850 that the society would be able to extend its field of action to other parts of the world.

J. Bianquis, *Les Origines de la Société des missions évangéliques de Paris (1822–1830)* (Paris, 1935).

*Guillaume de Bertier de Sauvigny*

*Related entries:* MISSIONS; SOCIETY OF CHRISTIAN MORALS.

**SOCIETY OF FRIENDS OF THE FREEDOM OF THE PRESS,** the name given to at least two Restoration societies: one of liberals active between 1817 and 1819 and one of royalists that flourished during the pivotal electoral campaign of 1827. The history of the Société des amis de la liberté de la presse of 1817–19 divides into three phases, the first of which, the informal phase, began in November 1817 and lasted until May 1818. In November 1817, a printed circular carrying the names of such distinguished liberals as Victor Destutt de Tracy, the duc de Broglie, Auguste de Staël, General Lafayette, Benjamin Constant, and Jacques Manuel proclaimed that a society had been formed to defend liberty of the press. Prompted by the trial and conviction of the liberal journalist Adolphe-Thierry-François Chevalier, who had published a letter to Elie Decazes in which he accused the ministry of violating the Charter of 1814, this informal but eminent group protested against the repressive press laws of 1817 and sought to raise by subscription funds to assist journalists threatened with fines and/or imprisonment by the government. When the legislative session of 1817–18 ended, members of this group, desiring to make a public show of appreciation for the deputies who had supported freedom of the press, sponsored a dinner on 3 May 1818. It attracted some four hundred citizens, most of them qualified voters, and drew them from all walks of life. This dinner, which gave the group much needed publicity, for soon its membership rolls swelled, opened the second phase in the history of the society.

In the summer of 1818, it adopted a formal name, compiled membership rolls, assessed dues, and began recording the minutes of the sessions. At about this time, it is probable that a permanent directing committee of twenty, the maximum permitted by article 291 of the Penal Code, of the most ardent members was formed. Taking care to avoid any appearance of secrecy, the members not only held their meetings openly, often at the home of such prominent liberals as the duc de Broglie, but they also reported them in the *Censeur européen* and other liberal papers. Of the rank-and-file membership, Charles de Rémusat recalled that it included an odd assortment of former Jacobins, out-of-favor Bonapartists, half-pay officers, lawyers, and journalists, the very groups from which opposition movements during the Restoration frequently drew their recruits. Actions taken by the society consisted primarily of issuing addresses and petitions calling for reform of laws concerning the composition of juries and the press. These efforts by members of the society and others were rewarded when, in May and June 1819, the government placed new and less restrictive press laws on the books.

Following the passage of these laws, moderate members of the society, notably the duc de Broglie, Auguste de Staël, and Benjamin Constant, viewing their original goals as obtained, diminished their participation, and control began to pass to men of a more radical persuasion. Jean-Baptiste Teste (1780–1852), for example, wanted the society to broaden its orientation and taken an interest in general political matters. Over the course of this third and last phase of the society's existence, from early summer 1819 to September 1819, such men turned more and more against the moderates in the leadership and, further, apparently involved themselves in some murky Restoration plots. The Bourbon government may have been able to link the governing committee of the society with the obscure and much-feared Comité directeur, thought by many royalists to be led by Lafayette and to be the center from which plans for a new revolution flowed. Louis XVIII, in addition, held the society in particular distaste, calling it the "infernal society." In any case, the government decided to attack it as a prelude to a more general assault on the liberal opposition, ordering it suppressed and bringing two of its leaders, Antoine Gévaudan and Colonel Charles Simon-Lorière, into court for violations of article 291 of the Penal Code. Predictably, the royalist press applauded, while the liberals, especially the *Renommée*, protested vigorously, and many of the society's original members—Benjamin Constant, Jacques Manuel, Charles Comte, Charles Dunoyer, and others—were compelled by this public controversy to reavow their support. Despite the efforts of prominent liberal lawyers, among them André Dupin and Joseph Mérilhou, and despite the publicity given the case in the *Censeur européen* and other liberal journals, the convictions, the fines of 200 francs each, and the suppression of the society were upheld by the courts on 18 December 1819. (The fines were paid by funds raised by subscription.) With this decision, the short but turbulent history of the Société des amis de la liberté de la presse, only one of many such opposition groups that flourished in Restoration France between 1817 and 1820, came to an end.

A second Société des amis de la liberté de la presse, which had no connection with the society of 1817–19, appeared briefly during the electoral campaign of 1827 when François-René Chateaubriand rallied Ultra and moderate royalists opposed to the Villèle government to protest censorship of the press and to elect deputies to the Chamber who would abolish censorship laws. Chateaubriand had become a dangerous opponent of the Villèle government in June 1824 when the celebrated writer had been unceremoniously dismissed from his post as minister of foreign affairs. The ordinances of 24 June 1827, which reimposed censorship on the periodical press, provided Chateaubriand with an opportunity for political revenge that he eagerly seized. In the latter half of July a pamphlet, entitled *Marche et effets de la censure* and bearing his name, appeared, carrying at the top of the title page the motto: "Amis de la liberté de la presse." In this essay, Chateaubriand advanced the major theme that would inform all of the society's activities: to bring an end to press censorship, he contended, a new and different Chamber of Deputies must be elected. Hence, from its inception, Chateaubriand's society had a much more overt and a much broader political orientation than did the society of 1817–19.

Chateaubriand's society, probably never more than an informal grouping, formed early in July and included royalists, *doctrinaires*, and some members of the Center Left opposition that a common opposition, often personal, to the Villèle government, outrage at the reimposition of censorship, and admiration of Chateaubriand temporarily united in 1827. Meetings of the society brought such Restoration notables as Prosper de Barante, the duc de Choiseul, the comte de Montalivet, and the baron Hyde de Neuville together with many less eminent or younger men, including Charles-François Agier, the journalists Alexis de Jussieu (of the *Courrier française*), and Louis-François Bertin de Vaux (of the *Journal des Débats*), and the ambitious young intellectuals Narcisse-Achille de Salvandy (1795–1856) and Abel-François Villemain (1790–1870). Of these men, the most active in the society's work were Montalivet, Salvandy, and Villemain, all three of whom wrote prolifically for the periodical press and produced pamphlets for distribution throughout France. Alone, Salvandy authored at least ten pamphlets, including the satiric *Lettre de la Girafe au Pasha d'Egypte* and *Explication de la nouvelle loi sur les collèges électoraux*. Also influential were Félix Bodin's *La Malle poste*, Montalivet's *Lettre d'un jeune pair de France aux français de son âge*, and Villemain's *Lettre d'un electeur de Paris*. Permeating all of these essays were three major themes. Censorship of the press, they argued, violated the Charter of 1814, and censorship, even if temporary, could become permanent if a weak and accommodating Chamber bowed to government pressure. Hence, to ensure that censorship would be abolished, deputies devoted to the principle of freedom of the press and opposed to all forms of censorship had to be elected. These pamphlets also included much-needed practical advice on how to vote in Restoration France and concluded with appeals for the friendly cooperation of all those opposed to the Villèle government. Funds to underwrite the work of the society probably came from Chateaubriand's affluent friends, from men of the liberal opposition, and from the extreme Right. Along with the more famous and influential society Aide-toi, le ciel t'aidera, the Amis de la liberté de la presse had an impact on the electoral campaign of 1827. Indirect testimony to the government's fear of the society's effectiveness lies in the policies adopted by the postal service. Because it could not be relied upon to deliver political pamphlets to provincial cities and towns, trusted friends of the society had to carry many works personally. Evidence that the pamphlets reached at least part of their intended audience may be found in police reports to prefects indicating the presence of works by Salvandy and others. Finally, the society probably helped inspire the creation of local electoral committees. The Société des amis de la liberté de la presse thus contributed to the defeat of the Villèle government in the elections of November 1827 and to its replacement by the more moderate ministry of the Viscount Jean-Baptiste Martignac.

*Censeur européen* (1818–19); P. Duvergier de Hauranne, *Histoire du gouvernement parlementaire en France, 1814–1848*, vol. 4 (Paris, 1857–71); E. Hatin, *Histoire politique et litteraire de la presse en France*, vol. 8 (Paris, 1859–61); S. Kent, *The Election of 1827 in France* (Cambridge, Mass., 1975); A. Nettement, *Histoire de la restauration*, vol. 5 (Paris, 1860–72); *Procès de la société dite les amis de la liberté de la presse* (Paris, 1820); C. de Rémusat, *Mémoires de ma vie*, vol. 1 (Paris, 1958–67).

*Robert Brown*

*Related entries:* AIDE-TOI, LE CIEL T'AIDERA; BROGLIE, A.-L.-V.; *LE CENSEUR EUROPEEN*; CHATEAUBRIAND; COMTE, F.-C.-L.; CONSTANT; *LE COURRIER FRANCAIS;* DECAZES; *DOCTRINAIRES*; DUNOYER; DUPIN, A.-M.-J.-J.; *JOURNAL DES DEBATS;* LAFAYETTE, M.-J.-P.-Y.-R.-G; MANUEL; MARTIGNAC; MERILHOU; REMUSAT; SALVANDY; VILLELE; VILLEMAIN.

**SOCIETY OF GOOD WORKS,** charitable society connected to the Congrégation. The society was established in Paris after 1815 by the leaders of the Congrégation, who felt that their charitable activities should have a distinct organization apart from the other activities of the Congrégation. Not all Congrégation members would have the time or resources to devote to the necessary works of charity, and, in addition, most such activities required a great deal of cooperation with the local clergy. Thus, while the Congrégation kept as its director a Jesuit priest, Father Ronsin, the Society of Good Works was directed by secular priests empowered by the authority of the archbishop of Paris. The head priests were, in order, the abbés René-Michel Legris-Duval, Philippe

Desjardins, and Etienne-François Borderies. The society was composed of three sections devoted, respectively, to the comforting of patients in hospitals, the visiting of inmates in prisons, and the instruction of young male chimney sweeps, who came in great numbers from Lyons to Paris.

G. de Grandmaison, *La Congrégation* (Paris, 1889).

*Guillaume de Bertier de Sauvigny*

*Related entries:* CONGREGATION; JESUITS.

**SOCIETY OF MUTUAL DUTY** (1827), a secret organization of silk workers. It was founded in Lyons in 1827 by two master weavers of the silk industry, Pierre Charnier and X. Bouvery, both Christian and royalists. It was at once a mutual aid society, a fraternity for the self-regulation of the weaving community, and a secret society of resistance against the silk merchants who exploited the work force. Their struggle against unemployment and for decent salaries led to the two famous uprisings in Lyons. The first uprising of November 1831 was motivated by labor conditions and ended in peaceful surrender, after which Charnier was even called to Paris for consultations with the government. The second uprising of April 1834 involved radical elements of the republican party and was crushed by military force.

R. J. Bezucha, *The Lyons Uprisings of 1834* (Cambridge, Mass., 1974); F. Rude, *Le Mouvement ouvrier à Lyon de 1827 à 1832* (Paris, 1944).

*Guillaume de Bertier de Sauvigny*

*Related entries:* CANUTS; LYONS, REVOLTS IN; REPUBLICANS; SILK INDUSTRY.

**SOCIETY OF THE FRIENDS OF CHILDREN,** a charitable organization. It was at first a very small and informal group established in 1828 by a small Parisian bookseller named Boblet. With the help of a handful of young friends, he was able to help provide for the needs of orphans. Armand de Melun, a Christian gentleman of high society, was brought into it by happenstance by one of his friends in 1838, and soon, through his connections and his zeal, he was able to help the society expand and regularize its activities. The so-called Amis de l'enfance provided for the schooling and the apprenticeship of their wards. For Melun it was the starting point of a number of other charitable undertakings, most of them connected with childrens' welfare and workers' protection. The original foundation remained in existence at least until 1870 but as a secondary concern for Melun.

A. d'Andigne, *Armand de Melun: Un apôtre de la Charité, 1807–1877* (Paris, 1961); J.-B. Duroselle, *Les Débuts du catholicisme social en France* (Paris, 1951).

*Guillaume de Bertier de Sauvigny*

*Related entry:* MELUN.

**SOCIETY OF THE FRIENDS OF TRUTH** (1818?), Parisian Masonic lodge, carbonarist front, and liberal opposition society. The Friends of Truth was probably organized in September 1818, possibly as the Société diablement philosophique.

Government spies reporting on the society in 1820 termed it the Vengeurs de Lallemand (a student martyr in antigovernment demonstrations in June of that year), and the final name may have been borrowed from the Friends of Truth of 1789, a political club that included Desmoulins, Condorcet, Brissot, and Roland. Its organizers were Philippe Buchez, J. T. Flotard, Nicholas Joubert, and Saint-Armand Bazard, the first a medical student and the other three law students at the University. The four young men also worked together as clerks in the *octroi* bureau of the prefecture of Paris, and several were already Freemasons in 1818. The lodge was intended to serve as a cover for liberal student opposition to the Bourbon regime, using traditional Masonic rituals and rules of secrecy to permit political discussion and organization. The society actively recruited University students (particularly from the law and medical faculties), government and commercial clerks, junior and noncommissioned army officers, journalists, and lawyers. Strict Masonic membership requirements and rules governing visitors (only members and Freemasons belonging to other lodges could attend meetings) permitted the society to maintain a certain degree of secrecy. Police crackdowns on student activism in 1819–20 (when law students and a professor were arrested, the medical faculty briefly closed, and Victor Cousin's class at the Ecole normale supérieure terminated) helped to swell attendance. When the lodge was recognized by the Grand Orient on 21 August 1821, between 400 and 1,000 people were attending its meetings at 19 bis rue Saint Honoré, though it reported an official membership of only forty-five.

The Friends of Truth soon became a center of youthful opposition (its oldest member in 1822 was only twenty-eight) to the regime and an umbrella group for other student and opposition societies. The lodge helped organize the antigovernment demonstrations after M. Lallemand's death in June 1820 and at the funeral of *doctrinaire* opposition deputy Camille Jordan, and it supported the publication of clandestine pamphlets and newspapers (Corréard's *Aristarque français*). Revolutionary societies like Joseph Rey's *Union* and the *Bazar français* (composed mainly of half-pay army officers) also met under the cover of the lodge. Many of the student members dressed as National Guardsmen for the planned military uprising of 19 August 1820, and though none were arrested when the government uncovered the plot, several (including Buchez and Bazard) left the country briefly. When Buchez returned by way of Naples in early 1821, he brought with him the constitution and organizational model of the Neapolitan carbonarists, which were soon adopted by the Friends of Truth. The first French carbonarist *vente* (twenty-member cell) was established in the lodge on 1 May, and its Masonic imagery soon included the symbolism (fires, ladders, fasces) of carbonarist ritual, though its Catholic mysticism was largely ignored by the anticlerical students.

The Friends of Truth probably included most of the members of the carbonarists' directorate (the *vente suprême* and the *haute vente*) in early 1822, and plans were devised for a military uprising, possibly approved by prominent liberals like the marquis de Lafayette and Marc-René de Voyer d'Argenson. Although the student leaders of the lodge were largely republican, the plotters recruited liberal monarchists and Bonapartists as well. The resulting conspiracies (of Belfort, La Rochelle, Colonel Caron, and others) were probably loosely coordinated by the society; Sergeant Bories (of the four sergeants of La Rochelle) was a member, and Buchez traveled repeatedly to Belfort and eastern France in early 1822. The ministry uncovered the various plots in midyear, and a series of arrests, trials, prison terms, and executions ended the carbonarist threat. The Friends of Truth and its leaders survived the government actions, and the society became more seriously Masonic and less revolutionary after 1822, though it remained a stronghold of republican and anticlerical opinion in the capital. Buchez drifted into positivism and, with Bazard, became a prominent Saint-Simonian after 1825. He would serve as president of the Constituent Assembly after the Revolution of 1848.

The Friends of Truth served as a central network for young liberals and radicals in the early 1820s, though some historians feel its members were largely manipulated by more experienced revolutionaries like Joseph Rey, popular intellectuals like Victor Cousin, or the liberal deputies in the Chamber. Its large membership and relative security as a center for opposition to the regime of Louis XVIII probably meant that it harbored a variety of political persuasions at any one moment. In its later liberal-Masonic phase, the lodge was still active under the July Monarchy.

G. de Bertier de Sauvigny, *La Restauration* (Paris, 1955, 1963); F. Isambert, *De la Charbonnerie au Saint-Simonisme* (Paris, 1966); *Paris révolutionnaire*, 4 vols. (Paris, n.d.); A. B. Spitzer, *Old Hatreds and Young Hopes* (Cambridge, Mass., 1971).

*David Longfellow*

*Related entries:* BAZARD; BUCHEZ; BORIES; CARBONARI; CARON; FREEMASONRY; JORDAN; LALLEMAND; LA ROCHELLE, FOUR SER- GEANTS OF; REY; SAINT-SIMONIANISM.

**SOCIETY OF THE PROPAGATION OF THE FAITH,** Catholic missionary organization. It started on 3 May 1822 in Lyons with the initiative of a pious young woman, Pauline Jaricot (1799–1862). Until then there had been a number of agencies or persons attempting to collect funds for French missionaries abroad; Jaricot conceived the idea that it would be more effective to have one single collecting organization, which would share its resources with the various missionary institutions or posts. Furthermore, she devised an ingenious collection system. It was based upon groups of ten people, each person contributing 1 sou a week; one group would receive the funds from nine other groups, and so on, thus creating a structure that resembled a pyramid. This idea won the support of many influential members of the Congrégation of Lyons; they formed a council of twelve members and adopted the title Société de la propagation de la foi. But when they wished to expand the operation to the entire country, they needed the protection of higher personalities in the royal entourage and the government. Contacts and discussions resulted in 1822 in the establishment of a two-tier governing structure; two separate councils, those of Lyons and of Paris, were, respectively, in charge of collections in the southern and northern halves of the country. Above them was a superior council, presided over by the grand-aumonier of the crown, who acted as coordinator and protective cover in regard to the episcopate and the secular authorities. The society expanded out of France, at first to Belgium and then to most other European countries with a Catholic population. A large share of the collections, in fact some 42 per cent of the money collected from 1822 to 1932, went to Catholic bishops in the United States.

E. J. Hickey, *The Society for the Propagation of the Faith* (Washington, 1922); D. Lathoud, *Le Secret des origines de la Propagation de la foi* (Paris, 1937).

*Guillaume de Bertier de Sauvigny*

*Related entries:* CONGREGATION; MISSIONS.

**SOCIETY OF THE RIGHTS OF MAN** (1832–1834, 1848–1849), a major revolutionary republican organization in Paris, Lyons, and the provinces; its full name was the Society of the Rights of Man and of the Citizen. The society was the main instrument of socialist republicans who attempted to organize workers around a program of political and social democracy and build a mass organization capable of overthrowing the July Monarchy. It was apparently founded at the end of 1831 by the radical rump of the Amis du peuple. Finding an audience for their egalitarian philosophy among Parisian workers, they enrolled them in local neighborhood sections that adopted Maximilien Robespierre's Declaration of the Rights of Man and of the Citizen as their creed. Each section, containing fewer than twenty members in order to circumvent the law on political associations, elected a chief and three quinturions to keep members in a state of revolutionary alert. Weekly meetings were devoted to the reception of new members, collections for propaganda, and political education (the oral reading and discussion of the Declaration and various Robespierrist commentaries circulated by the society). Membership expanded after the abortive uprising set off by the funeral of General Jean-Maximin Lamarque on 5 June 1832 exposed the organizational weakness of the republican movement. By 1834 the society had about 3,000 members organized in 162 Parisian sections, with affiliates in Lyons and provincial towns in the east of France.

The organization combined democratic election with centralized command. In September 1833 section chiefs elected a central committee of eleven, including Godefroy Cavaignac, brother of the future general; Marc-René de Voyer d'Argenson, socialist aristocrat and deputy; Guillard de Kersausie, a Breton aristocrat and former cavalry officer; and student radicals Napoléon Lebon, Camille Berrier-Fontaine, and Jean-Jacques Vignerte. The committee appointed commissioners for each arrondissement and quarter who transmitted directives, circulated literature, and conducted weekly orientation meetings with section chiefs.

While the leaders were middle class in composition—mostly young university students—the sections were made up almost entirely of skilled workers—tailors, jewelers, painters, makers of luxury articles, shoemakers, and joiners—young unattached men in their twenties with high rates of literacy and permanent residence in Paris. Recruiting in wine shops and workplaces, the sections often brought together workers of the same trade. As a result, members of the society were able to provide leadership for the strike movement that broke out in autumn 1833 involving the first attempts to set up a federation of trades and producers' cooperatives.

The significance of Robespierre's Declaration, chosen as the official credo, was that unlike the actual Constitution of 1793, it contained a Rousseauist definition of property as the product of social convention rather than an inalienable right. Robespierre had drafted the Declaration for the Jacobin Club in April 1793 in response to the rising popular movement for price control. It allowed for a modification of property rights, particularly by way of progressive taxation, in order to attain greater equality of wealth and position and ensure the common welfare. Like the Constitution of 1793, it recognized the sovereign right of the people to choose their government and to take up arms against one that violated their rights, as well as the obligation of society to provide education and welfare to all citizens. Socialist and even communist implications were drawn from these precepts. Distrusting the individualism of middle-class republicans, the society tried to instill a collective social consciousness. As the touchstone of working-class republicans, the Declaration served as the expression of an emerging class consciousness.

The aim of the society was less to foment an uprising than to channel and coordinate the spontaneous mass rebellion thought to be inevitable. Awaiting the outbreak of street fighting, it alerted its members during several confrontations with the government in 1833 and 1834. A more impetuous faction, led by Kersausie, set up an action committee to take the revolutionary initiative. Subjected to continuous police harassment and arrests, the society was ill prepared for the showdown with the government that came with the passage of a new law barring political associations in April 1834. Despite the fact that the society was only reluctantly drawn into the worker uprising in Lyons and was largely absent from skirmishes in Paris, it was officially blamed for the April insurrection. Its leaders, victims of preventive detention, were tried and convicted before the Chamber of Peers for plotting the overthrow of the state. After dissolution of the society in April, its cause was immediately taken up by Auguste Blanqui, who, together with several former members, organized the secret society Les Familles along the lines of Kersausie's action committee.

The society reappeared in March 1848 as one of the leading forces in the club movement. Led by Armand Barbès, Léopold Villain, Aloysius Huber, and Lebon, it dispatched emissaries to the provinces and helped to coordinate activity of the clubs during the elections of April and June. As the government turned to economic liberalism and political repression, it began to reorganize its revolutionary sections. Urging restraint and cautioning against a premature uprising, it did not, contrary to some accounts, participate as a directing force in the June Days, which arose as a spontaneous worker protest against the threatened dissolution of the National Workshops.

The society made its last appearance in June 1849 during the constitutional crisis provoked by the French attack on the Roman Republic. On 11 June it urged radical deputies to lead an armed uprising against Louis-Napoleon. On 13 June it was standing armed and ready along the quays, awaiting the outbreak of fighting, when radical deputies were dispersed by the troops of General Nicolas Changarnier. Following 13 June the society gave way for the last time to the clandestine secret societies that continued resistance to the Napoleonic regime.

The society represented a transitional phase in the development of a working-class party during which the ideology and leadership of the movement came from middle-class democrats. When workers reemerged as a political force under the Liberal Empire, they would have their own workingmen's association, the First International. But it was not until 1880 that the first working-class political party was formed in France.

P. H. Amann, *Revolution and Mass Democracy* (Princeton, 1975); Cours de Pairs, Affaire du mois d'avril 1834, *Rapport fait à la cour par M. Girod de l'Ain*, 4 vols. (Paris, 1834); A. Faure, "Mouvements populaires et mouvement ouvrier à Paris (1830–1834)," *Mouvement social*, no. 88 (1974); B. H. Moss, "Parisian Workers and the Origins of Republican Socialism, 1830–1833," in *1830 in France*, ed. J. Merriman (New York, 1975); G. Perreux, *Au Temps des sociétés secrètes* (Paris, 1931); G. Weill, *Histoire du parti républicain en France de 1814 à 1870* (Paris, 1900).

*Bernard H. Moss*

*Related entries:* BARBES; BLANQUI, L.-D.; CAVAIGNAC, G.-E.-L.; CHANGARNIER; CLUBS, POLITICAL; HUBER; LAMARQUE; REPUBLICANS; ROBESPIERRE; VILLAIN; VOYER D'ARGENSON.

**SOCIETY OF THE SEASONS (Société des saisons)**, the revolutionary organization of Blanqui and Barbès that conducted an unsuccessful insurrection in May 1839. The Society of the Seasons was the brainchild of that consummate revolutionary Auguste Blanqui. He had been imprisoned for his revolutionary activities of 1834 but was released in the amnesty of 1837. Blanqui then immediately set about to create a new organization designed to promote the revolution he believed France needed. He, Armand Barbès, and Martin-Bernard, all vaguely Babeuvists who believed in popular insurrections, created the society on strict hierarchical principles. All knowledge of the organization was limited to those at the upper levels. At the summit was the *agent révolutionnaire*, who headed an *année*. In theory, the society had three *années*; in reality, the movement was limited to a few hundred members in Paris. Each *année* was composed of four *saisons* led by a *printemps*. Keeping with the seasonal motif, a *saison* included three *mois* led by a *juillet*, and each *mois* had four *semaines* commanded by a *dimanche*. Six individuals completed a *semaine*. With full membership, each *année* had 357 members. Blanqui had already reached his conception of revolutionary cadres that would carry out the revolution, a line of thought he doubtless derived from Filippo-Michele Buonarroti.

Like all other secret societies of this era, the Society of the Seasons had elaborate initiation rituals. Weeks were spent examining prospective members. Obedience of members to the leader was essential, and the dedication of members was tested by holding rehearsals for the uprising on Sundays or holidays. Efforts to eliminate infiltration by the police were successful. The police had no hint of the coup, although they did have general knowledge of the group's existence. The attention of the police was focused upon the radical newspapers *Homme libre* and *Moniteur républicain* and upon the previous activities of many of the members of the Society of the Rights of Man and the Society of the Families.

With the governmental crisis over, the replacement of the Molé ministry going into its third month, with economic hardships stemming from the financial crash of 1837 in the United States still affecting the working person, and with the notables of Paris busy enjoying themselves at the Champ de mars' Sunday races, the Society of the Seasons implemented its plans for the overthrow of the bourgeois monarchy of Louis-Philippe. According to the rehearsed plans, the 600 to 700 members of the society met in their small groups at 2:00 P.M. on 12 May 1839. They met in the quartier Saint-Martin and took their arms. One group, with Barbès, the apostle of Christian socialism, at the head, marched on the Palais de justice. Another group, led by their commander-in-chief Blanqui, the heir of Babeuf, headed for the Hôtel de ville. Blanqui and company took the Hôtel de ville, but Barbès and his group failed to overwhelm the prefecture of police on their way to the Palais de justice. Troops were called, barricades erected, and about seventy insurrectionists and thirty soldiers were killed. The leaders of the three divisions of the society—Blanqui, Barbès, and Martin-Bernard, a logician and admirer of Robespierre—had declared the government disbanded because it scorned starving millions, betrayed the nation, and massacred the people, and they were to have formed a provisional government with Marc-René de Voyer d'Argenson, abbé Lamennais, Albert Laponneraye, and Prosper-Ricard Dubosc. It never took power.

The entire affair was a fiasco. Voyer d'Argenson, by 1839 a long-retired veteran of republican politics, and Lamennais knew nothing of their place in the proposed government. Laponneraye and Dubosc were in prison. The masses did not respond to the call for revolution. Middle-class republicans were appalled at this resort to violence, and the National Guard responded to the call to duty. The rebels were arrested. Barbès and eighteen others were tried before the Cour des pairs. Fifteen were found guilty and Barbès received the death sentence, later commuted to life imprisonment. Blanqui was later arrested as he tried to slip out of France. Tried in January 1840 along with thirty others, he received the same treatment as Barbès. After the failure of this attempt to overthrow the monarchy violently, the republican movement would lie dormant for nearly a decade.

The society's attempt at revolution failed for two fundamental reasons. One, its hopes were based on the idea that once the opponents of the regime were armed, the revolution would occur spontaneously. Two, the moment for revolution had not arrived as Blanqui believed. He had overestimated the effect of the economic crisis on the working class of Paris, and he completely ignored the fact that seizing Paris might be insufficient to overthrow the government. The society had no plans, or apparently even members, in the provinces, despite police fears to the contrary. Finally, the squabble between François Guizot, Alphonse Thiers, Odilon Barrot, and Louis-Mathieu de Molé for the position of first minister was taken as a sign of a deep split within the ruling class, when in fact it was only a surface dispute over personal rule. When a real threat to the government arose, as it did with the outbreak of violence on 12 May, the deputies took only a few hours to resolve their differences.

The existence of the society demonstrated a deep dissatisfaction on the part of some members of society, yet in 1839 none of the necessary conditions for a fundamental shift in politics was present. The route to a social republic could not come about through a revolutionary dictatorship without a high degree of dissatisfaction toward the regime, and by 1839 the bourgeois policies of Louis-Philippe had not yet angered many middle-class supporters, nor were the laboring classes and peasants in a state of unusual hardship. No one seemed to act instinctively in politics, at least not in the manner envisioned by the republican revolutionaries of the Society of the Seasons.

The Society of the Seasons collapsed with the failure of the insurrection of 12 May. The regime could feel confident in its ability to control discontent, yet it had to be concerned that a group of disaffected citizens could raise the barricades in Paris. Barbès might be a Creole from Guadaloupe with extreme ideas, but Blanqui was from a respected middle-class family. His brother was a prominent economist. Of course, the republican journalists never disappeared, and radicalism was not dead. The policy of a *juste milieu* indeed had an extreme Left to play against. Regardless of the failure of 1839, Blanqui and company would be back, and the attitude of the officials of the July Monarchy indicated that they never doubted it.

S. Bernstein, *Auguste Blanqui and the Art of Insurrection* (London, 1971).

*Thomas Beck*

*Related entries:* BARBES; BARROT, C.-H.-O.; BLANQUI, L.-A.; BUON-ARROTI; GUIZOT; LAMENNAIS; MOLE; REPUBLICANS; ROBESPIERRE; SOCIETY OF THE RIGHTS OF MAN; THIERS; VOYER D'ARGENSON.

**SOLIDARITE REPUBLICAINE** (1848–1849), republican electoral and propaganda organization. By the fall of 1848, reaction to the events of February to June had once again made it difficult for persons of radical opinions to meet and propagate their views. The dissemination of information by the republicans was seen as essential to any hopes for a true republic. At the end of October 1848, a number of devoted republicans formed a new organization, Solidarité républicaine, to further the ideals of a social and democratic republic. The mason Théodore Bac, the representative of the Creuse, Martin Nadaud, the editor of

*La Révolution démocratique et sociale* Charles Delescluze, and such representatives of the Montagne as Félix Pyat, Germain-Marie Sarrut, and Alexandre-Auguste Ledru-Rollin came together to further the goals of "setting on a firm footing the great party that works for a Democratic and Social Republic." To avoid prosecution, they registered as a campaign organization on 4 November 1848.

Martin-Bernard was president, while Delescluze acted as secretary-general. Membership was by invitation from two current members because police infiltration was a constant concern. The preamble to the constitution made their purpose clear: that in times of danger, all republicans should unite "to assure by all legal means the pacific and regular development of social reforms, development which should be the goal and consequence of democratic institutions." They backed the right to work without rejecting the right to property. With central offices in Paris, Solidarité républicaine spread to towns throughout France. It represented the basic party organization of the Montagnards, if any existed. The executive committee in Paris did have thirty-two Montagnard deputies on it.

In addition to working to promote the democratic and social Republic in the presidential election of 1848, Solidarité républicaine distributed pamphlets, supported journals such as the *Révolution démocratique et sociale*, and tried to find positions for unemployed workingmen. Such broadbased activities did not endear the organization to the government. At the conclusion of the presidential campaign (10 December 1848), the new government of Louis-Napoleon moved to suppress the group.

The Parisian headquarters was raided on 12 December as an illegal assembly, and the club was closed. Later it would come to the light that this raid was actually against another group using the same facilities, but the revelation did not alter the government's course. On 10 January 1849 Minister of Interior Léon Faucher wrote to the prefects declaring the club Solidarité républicaine to be illegal on the basis of the raid and ordered all their meetings to be prohibited. Another raid on the Parisian headquarters took place on 29 January after the publication of Faucher's order in the *Moniteur* on 27 January. The heated objections to these actions by Ledru-Rollin in the Assembly fell on deaf ears.

The prefects engaged in systematic repression of Solidarité républicaine during the spring of 1849. The national leaders were arrested in October 1849 and convicted of conspiracy on 12 April 1850. Thus, by January 1849 Solidarité républicaine had been broken as a vehicle of republican propaganda and activity. While nervous prefects continued to worry over its rumored activities, this potential national republican political organization had been neutralized at the outset of the reign of Louis-Napoleon.

A. Calmon, *Ledru-Rollin and the Second French Republic* (New York, 1922).

*Thomas Beck*

*Related entries:* CLUBS, POLITICAL; DELESCLUZE; LEDRU-ROLLIN; *LE MONITEUR*; NADAUD; PYAT; REPUBLICANS; YOUNG (NEW) MOUNTAIN SOCIETY.

**SOULT, NICOLAS-JEAN DE DIEU** (1769–1851), Duke of Dalmatia, general of the revolution, marshal of the Empire, peer of the Hundred Days and the Restoration, war minister. A brave, crude, effective, and corrupt Napoleonic general, at the start of the First Bourbon Restoration Soult became a royalist and was appointed minister of war in September 1814 after briefly commanding in Brittany. He was instrumental in the confiscation of the Bonaparte family property and in the prosecution of General Remi Exelmans. He was also responsible for commissioning returned *émigrés* to high rank in the army. Although dismissed shortly after Napoleon returned to France, he rallied to Napoleon, who appointed him a peer. He served, not very competently, as Napoleon's chief of staff at Waterloo but vigorously attempted to rally the remnants of the army after Waterloo to halt the invaders.

Exiled by the Bourbons, he lived until 1819 in the Grand Duchy of Berg where he had fled after Waterloo. Allowed to return to France, Soult was restored to his marshal's rank in 1820, appointed to the Order of the Holy Ghost in 1825, and named a peer in 1827. The July Revolution ousted him from the Peers, but he quickly rallied to Louis-Philippe and was reappointed on 13 August 1830. Soult may have dabbled with the legitimist faction. But in November 1830, in spite of his reputation for ignorance of parliamentary practice and his crude language, he became war minister and in October 1832 president of the cabinet. He retained these functions until July 1834. His ministry carried out a significant reform of the army, invaded Belgium, and dealt harshly with repeated worker and republican uprisings. In 1838 Louis-Philippe sent him to represent France at Victoria's coronation. His prestige thus somewhat restored, in May 1839 he returned as prime minister, also holding the Foreign Ministry. He was forced to resign in March 1840 due to his handling of the Egyptian problem and a scandal involving the duc de Nemours, but he returned as war minister in October. He resigned the War Ministry in November 1845 but remained as figurehead president of the Council until 1846. In September 1847 Louis-Philippe appointed him marshal general of France. With the February Revolution of 1848, he declared himself a republican. He lived thereafter in retirement until his death on 26 November 1851 in his chateau of Soultberg (Tarn). His memoirs were published in 1854.

G. de Bertier de Sauvigny, *Le Comte Ferdinand de Bertier* (Paris, 1948); M. Glover, *The Peninsular War, 1807–1814* (London, 1974); T. Howarth, *Citizen-King: The Life of Louis-Philippe* (London, 1961); A. G. Macdonnell, *Napoleon and His Marshals* (London, 1950); A. Robert et al., *Dictionnaire des parlementaires français* (Paris, 1889–91).

*James K. Kieswetter*

*Related entries:* BELGIAN REVOLUTION OF 1830; CHAMBER OF PEERS; COUNCIL OF STATE; FOREIGN POLICY OF LOUIS-PHILIPPE; HUNDRED DAYS; JOURDAN; LOUIS-PHILIPPE; MARMONT; REVOLUTION OF 1830.

**SOUMET, ALEXANDRE** (1786–1845), minor poet, playwright, dramatist. Soumet belongs to the Nodier, Stendhal generation, the group born just before the Revolution with vestigial loyalties to classicism but with a nearly irresistible attraction to romanticism. Their lot was a flexible, vacillating literary and (in the case of Soumet and Charles Nodier) political personality. Louis-Alexandre-Antoine Soumet was born at Castelnaudary, southeast of Toulouse, on 29 January 1786. His mother died when he was an infant. When his father, Jean Soumet, became *contrôleur général* of the Canal du Midi in 1795, the household moved to Toulouse. A natural melancholy as an adolescent made him want to seek the freedom of the countryside where he could daydream at will. His early schooling was rather unsuccessful despite the efforts of the nephew of Dom Calmet, the famous Benedictine monk. For practical reasons, Jean Soumet discouraged his son's efforts to write poetry and to study the classics. Despite a forced two-year preparation, he failed, at seventeen, the examination for the Ecole polytechnique. A brief attempt to study law was no more successful, but the experience produced a lifelong friendship with another poet, Alexandre Guiraud from Limoux, and freed him to compose his verses. Soon after the Jeux Floraux Academy of Toulouse had honored his idyl *Le Vieux Chêne* in 1807, the twenty-one year old and his friend Guiraud, sharing with Jules de Rességuier and others a desire to inject new life into French poetry, founded a militant group, royalist in politics and classical in literature, though they seriously pondered Mme. de Staël's ideas.

In 1808, Soumet moved to Paris where imperialist fervor, expressed in hyperbolic pieces, soon erased any lingering royalist sentiment. The effort earned him, in 1810, the position of *auditeur* to the Conseil d'état, whose functions were somewhat vague. From a liaison with Mme. Blondel de la Rougerie was born, in 1814, a beloved daughter, Gabrielle, who inspired his only truly successful and original poem about a motherless child: "La Pauvre fille." By 1815, having awarded Soumet five *fleurs*, the Toulouse *Académie* named him maître of the Jeux floraux. He had even obtained first place in two Institut competitions. All this spread his fame as a poet, though most of his pieces lacked quality and originality and followed closely the Millevoye vein. This does not mean that he was deprived of aesthetic awareness for, in 1814, he criticized Mme. de Staël for being too timid in *Scrupules littéraires de Mme. la baronne de Staël*. The collapse of the Empire forced him to return to Toulouse for several years. During that exile, his prestige grew, and he became a full member (*mainteneur*) of the Jeux Floraux in 1818.

Having just begun a friendship with Victor Hugo and rekindled his royalist sympathies, he was able to return to Paris by the summer of 1820. His immediate goals were to seek a political post and to succeed as a dramatist. (He had produced his first tragedy, *Cléopâtre*, several years earlier and had just finished *Clytemnestre*.) He achieved both goals in 1822, becoming librarian at Saint-Cloud and having *Clytemnestre* premiere at the Comédie-francaise in November. *Saül* also played at the Odéon the same year. Hugo and his contemporaries hailed the triumph of his tragedies, his fame spread, and the king named him a chevalier of the Légion d'honneur. His new friendship with Emile Deschamps made him a regular at his salon where romantic ideas were beginning to take root. His enthusiasm was such that he joined an elite group of the Deschamps salon to become co-founder of *La Muse française* in the summer of 1823. Although Guiraud wrote the prospectus, Soumet's affable personality and fame attracted many founders and collaborators. Yet it is highly probable that his burning ambition to occupy a chair in the Académie française spelled the doom of the *Muse*, which ceased publication in July 1824. He deserted it and very likely, with the help of Deschamps and Rességuier, engineered its demise to please the *classiques*. In any event, upon his election on 29 July, he incurred the wrath of his romantic colleagues, sacrificed their friendship, and returned in literature to the *bonnes et saines doctrines*. The traditionalists had lured one of the stars away from the opposition and gained a victory.

Despite his defection, Soumet could not quite abandon the romantic muse. He pursued his dramatic career despite the failure of his tragedy *Cléopâtre* at the Odéon in early July 1824. The following spring, Mlle. Georges made *Jeanne d'Arc*, classical only in form, a resounding success. In 1826, he turned briefly to opera. *Pharamond* was only briefly acclaimed, but *Le Siège de Corinthe* was performed 105 times. Convinced by friends to return to tragedy, *Emilia* and *Elisabeth de France* did not do well, but he scored a great triumph with *Une Fête de Néron* which premiered at the Odéon late in 1829. Despite the romantic drama's recent great victories, Soumet had modest success with *Norma* in 1831. His final gasp as a playwright came in 1841 with two plays that did not survive.

Soumet's most cherished goal as a poet had, for years, been to produce the French epic poem, which had eluded Ronsard and Voltaire. Although he still composed poetry and plays, the last period of his life was almost entirely devoted to his attempt to equal *Paradise Lost* by completing his lofty poem *La Divine Epopée*. Though it sold many copies, it would be eclipsed by Hugo's *Légende*. Alexandre Soumet succumbed to a year-long illness on 30 March 1845. He had played an equivocal but important role in the development of French letters.

A. Beffort, *Alexandre Soumet, sa vie et ses oeuvres* (Luxembourg, 1908); R. Bray, *Chronologie du romantisme (1804–1830)* (Paris, 1932); J. Dedieu, "Alexandre Soumet," *Revue des Pyrénées* (1913); L. Séché, *Le Cénacle de la Muse française, 1823–1827* (Paris, 1908).

*Paul Comeau*

Related entries: ACADEMIE FRANCAISE; DESCHAMPS; ECOLE POLY-TECHNIQUE; GUIRAUD; HUGO; *LA MUSE FRANCAISE*; NODIER; RO-MANTICISM; SALON D'EMILE DESCHAMPS; STAEL-HOLSTEIN; STENDHAL.


**SPAIN, 1823 FRENCH INVASION OF,** the French incursion into Spain, with the backing of Austria, Prussia, and Russia, designed to restore King Ferdinand VII to his full rights and to crush the revolutionary (constitutionalist) forces in that country. King Ferdinand VII, on his return from Napoleonic captivity in 1814, quickly repudiated the liberal Constitution of 1812, along with many of the progressive acts created by the Cortes during his long absence. In response to Ferdinand's brutally regressive regime, revolts occurred in 1814, 1815, 1816, 1817, and 1819. All of these abortive uprisings resulted from a combination of officer discontent, thwarted ambition, and liberal principle. Finally, faced with the prospect of embarcation to the Americas to fight in an unpopular war against revolutionaries in the colonies, army mutinies sprang up across Spain. Within three months, on 7 March 1820, the king consented to the restoration of the Constitution of 1812. Like Louis XVI, however, Ferdinand was never committed to constitutional government and for the following three years plotted against the constitutional system. Political stability depended on executive-legislative cooperation, but the king had no desire to make constitutional government work. By early 1822 the king, citing the rising chaos in Spain, began to appeal to the members of the Holy Alliance for their intervention in his behalf.

Constitutionalist rule in Spain was uncertain and unstable. The king had become a virtual prisoner. In response to Ferdinand's continued pleas, on 6 January 1823 the French, Russian, Prussian, and Austrian ambassadors presented notes to the Spanish foreign minister, stating that Spain must restore Ferdinand to his full rights as king or face the consequences. A satisfactory reply was not forthcoming, and on 23 January 1823 the ambassadors demanded their passports and returned home.

Despite the efforts of Great Britain, the Right under François-René de Chateaubriand triumphed, and on 7 April 1823 a French army under the command of the duke of Angoulême—the One Hundred Thousand Sons of Saint Louis—crossed the frontier into Spain. For the first time in thirty-four years, French forces marched to a foreign conflict under the Bourbon lilies. Unlike the Peninsular Campaign of 1808–14, Spanish resistance was sporadic and weak. French forces now marched to save the traditional Spain and to vanquish revolutionary Spain. Most Spaniards greeted the invading forces warmly or with indifference.

The Constitutional government retreated, along with an unwilling Ferdinand, to Seville on 20 March 1823. Madrid fell to the French on 24 May 1823; one of Angoulême's first acts was to put guards around the houses of known Constitutionalists in order to protect them from the attacks of Spanish absolutists. On 12 June 1823 the Constitutionalists retreated farther to Cádiz, forcing Ferdinand to accompany them. The French army appeared before Cádiz on 16 August 1823 and fought the one serious battle of the invasion when they stormed the Trocadero defense works on 31 August 1823. The siege of the city continued for one month more until the king, agreeing to lenient terms for the Constitutionalists, was allowed to join Angoulême at Puerto Santa María on 1 October 1823.

Ferdinand quickly broke his promises of leniency and embarked upon a campaign of outright repression. Disenchanted by the king's excesses, Angoulême withdrew to France by November. Some 45,000 French troops, however, remained in Spain, at Ferdinand's request, until 1828, guarding against further rebellion on the part of the king's restive subjects.

J. D. Bergamini, *The Spanish Bourbons* (New York, 1974); R. Carr, *Spain, 1808–1939* (Oxford, 1966); R. M. Smith, *Spain* (Ann Arbor, Mich., 1965).

*Robert L. Simpson*

*Related entries:* ANGOULEME, L.-A.; CHATEAUBRIAND; VERONA, CONGRESS OF.

**STAEL-HOLSTEIN, ANNE-LOUISE-GERMAINE NECKER, BARONESS DE** (1766–1817), novelist, literary critic, and political thinker, one of the most interesting and famous women of her time. Mme. de Staël, as she was known, was born Germaine Necker at Paris in 1766. Her father was the famous financier and minister to Louis XVI. Her mother, Suzanne Curchod, was almost equally famous as the mistress of one of the most popular salons of Paris and as the former lover of Charles Gibbon. Mme. Curchod was an educated and handsome woman who belonged to a distinguished Protestant family from Lausanne, Switzerland. Germaine was to be profoundly influenced by both her charming father, who provided her with wealth, as well as a social and political setting in which to develop her ideas, and her mother, who educated her and provided the stimulating environment for Germaine's precocious mind. She loved her father but was to rebel against her mother's rigid emphasis on the life of the mind to the exclusion of nature and the emotions.

An opportune marriage with a Swedish nobleman and diplomat, Eric Magnus, baron de Holstein, enabled Germaine to engage her romantic interest in nature and physical pleasures fully. Seventeen years her senior, he was neither learned nor spirited enough to hold her attention. Although they remained married until he died, Germaine de Staël was given the freedom to develop her intellect and pleasures with other men. She literally and figuratively became mistress to an age. Attracting men of wit and power to her salon and to her bed, her lovers included the statesman Charles-Maurice de Talleyrand, the novelist Benjamin Constant, the historian Simonde de Sismondi, and the critic and poet August Wilhem von Schlegel. The relationship between Constant and Mme. de Staël was to be the longest, and the mutual effects on politics and literature to be the most far-reaching.

The other great influence on her life was the French Revolution. When the Revolution broke out, Mme. de Staël was living in Paris. Although married she was still close to her father, who was finance minister to the king and the Estates General. His dismissal was in part cause of the storming of the Bastille on July 14, 1789. His recall to power under the urging of the National Assembly afforded Mme. de Staël a privileged position from which to watch the events of the day. It is to this early period, until Necker's forced resignation in 1790, that she would look nostalgically in her celebrated work on the Revolution.

De Staël watched the remainder of the Revolution with much less enthusiasm and usually from a greater distance. She returned to Coppet (an estate on Lake Geneva purchased by her father upon his first dismissal in 1781) in 1792, immediately after the September Massacres. Although a vigorous supporter of the Constitution of 1791, she deplored this "second Revolution," which had radicalized the country and arrested her friends. Liberal, constitutionalist France now seemed to be under mob rule. She watched the ensuing war and Jacobin Terror, the end of Jacobin domination, and the establishment of the Directory from Coppet. Mme. de Staël hoped that this new government would bring stability to France while consolidating the Revolution, and therefore she returned to Paris hoping to reenter political life. In the next several years, her life was to alternate between political influence and residence in Paris and exile in Coppet. This was an important period of her life, especially because of her relationship with Constant, but in 1803 Napoleon banished her. For ten years, beginning in 1804, she was exiled from her beloved Paris.

Personal and political reasons brought her into opposition to Napoleon. Her own preference, and that of those attending her salon in Paris, for a moderate republic or constitutional monarchy annoyed Napoleon and helped lead first to the elimination of Constant from the Tribunat and, later, her exile to Coppet. Napoleon, however, also personally disliked this bold, forward woman who dared criticize him and give him advice. For the next several years, she and Napoleon would carry on their verbal duel.

Although miserable because of the death of her father in 1804, and less so for that of her husband in 1802, Mme. de Staël made Coppet into a salon of politics and literature. During these years she traveled frequently throughout Europe, and both on her travels and at Coppet she came into contact with many of the leading intellectuals of her day. It was also during these years that she published most of her important works: The novel *Delphine* in 1802, *Corinne* in 1807, and *De l'Allemagne* in 1813. The last had to be published in England because the third volume failed to pass Napoleon's censors. This was probably due to its favorable portrayal of Germany and German thought and a provocative letter she sent to the emperor criticizing the delay of the censors. Because of the repressive measures of an infuriated emperor, from 1810 Mme. de Staël was able to live only intermittently at Coppet. She returned to Paris and Coppet in 1814 only in the wake of the Allied victory. But she had little time to enjoy her security and freedom. She died in 1817, leaving two of her most important works to be published posthumously, *Considérations sur les principaux événements de la Révolution française* (1818) and *Dix années d'exil* (1821). The latter is a fascinating and surprisingly fair-minded portrait of this crucial period of her life and of the great contemporaries who were her enemies and friends.

Although her life and works were spent and written largely before 1815, Mme. de Staël's literary and political writings were to have a pronounced influence on the generation coming to age in the Restoration. Her works reflect a sociological and historical perspective that was to become increasingly important in the nineteenth century and a normative emphasis on freedom. The first theme is already made apparent in her *De la Littérature considérée dans ses rapports avec les institutions*. As the title implies, the work relates literature to other institutions in society and views it as part of an organic whole. Each age, each climate, each political system contains its own peculiar literature. The north, given to innovation and melancholy, is romantic; the south, more intent on form and illuminated by the Mediterranean light, is classical. Whatever its superficial generalizations and occasional factual errors, this work paved the way for a social history of literature and a literary history of society. The work also expressed her most cherished political views, proclaiming the superiority of reason over illusion and freedom over tyranny.

*De l'Allemagne*, an exhaustive survey of German customs, literature, philosophy, and religion based on her long travels in Germany, also reflects her sociology of literature and love of freedom. Much to the chagrin of Napoleon, romantic Germany appeared superior to classical France. In France, everything had stiffened into rule and custom; in Germany everything was in ferment, full of new life and hope. In France, society dominated; in Germany, there were no tyrannical rules of conduct governing language or poetry. Writers created for their own satisfaction, not for public opinion; the individual reigned supreme. Whatever the accuracy of these depictions, the message was clear: France needed to take heed of German ideas, which could filter into France only with political freedom.

Mme. de Staël's two romantic novels, *Delphine* and *Corinne*, suggest another aspect of her search for freedom and authenticity. Delphine, the heroine of the first novel, kills herself when her lover is shot. The novel has a latter-day feminist message. It is, in Christopher Herold's words, "a ferocious attack on marriage unsanctified by love, a satire on Catholic bigotry, a brief for divorce, and a plea for the rights of women." The heroine of *Corinne* may be seen as an idealized portrait of the author. She is half northern, half southern, an enthusiast and a poet given to an inner struggle between coldness and passion, between the formal restriction of the city and the greater freedom of nature. Both attributes have their value and may complement one another, but the latter must win. In these two novels, de Staël thereby explored the tensions and frustrations of women of her age in search of freedom of emotional expression. Little wonder that Napoleon was enraged by these libertarian works which challenged his attempts to legitimize his reign by imposing a more conventional morality.

Mme. de Staël's *Considérations* most fully develops her views on political liberty. Part apology for her father, part panegyric on England, part celebration of the great aristocratic families of France, part history and philosophy of history, it prompted more reaction from the Left and the Right than almost any other political work of the Restoration. For her, the French Revolution was no historical accident and certainly not the responsibility of some action taken or not taken by her celebrated father. Rather, the Revolution was an essential part of human progress toward liberty and the establishment of representative government. This march had its origins in the feudal aristocracy's independence from royal power and reached to the *parlementaires'* attempts to limit royal despotism at the end of the Old Regime. Although recognizing the self-serving nature of many of the acts of the great aristocracy, she was far more troubled by royal attempts at arbitrary rule. Such limitations on despotism by the great aristocracy had led to the Great Revolution in England in the seventeenth century and culminated in France in the Revolution of 1789.

Unfortunately, the Constituent Assembly refused the advice of her father, Jacques Necker, who advocated using the English constitution as a model to adapt to French circumstances. This, coupled with the emigration of the nobility, destroyed the possibility of creating a liberal, rational, constitutional monarchy balancing monarchical, aristocratic, and democratic forces. With the failure of the moderate Revolution, the Revolution was radicalized by the ignorant masses and destroyed its former friends. Recovering somewhat under the Directory, France then fell prey to Napoleon. An egocentric genius, he reduced every Frenchman into dependence on him. Rejecting the notion that Napoleon was either a son of the Revolution or a constitutional monarch, Mme. de Staël worried that the principles of the Revolution would be confused with those of the imperial government. *Considérations* ends with a panegyric to England, a country whose institutions best represented the author's political sentiments.

*Considérations* appeared at a crucial time in the Restoration. After two years of ultraroyalist and conservative control, liberals had come to power. They wished at once to shape the Charter in their own image and discredit once and for all those forces that appeared to want to restore the tripartite influences of throne, altar, and privileged nobility. De Staël's work threatened to split the liberal coalition because it suggested that revolution against a reforming king might reoccur. Therefore, some of these liberals responded to Mme. de Staël by arguing that although the Revolution was no accident, the target was not the reforming monarchy but rather the selfish and useless nobility. Both the feudal aristocracy and the *parlementaires* had pursued their own interests and had not helped the cause of liberty. Napoleon, on the other hand, though a threat to individual liberty, still did further the social and political interests of the Revolution, without which liberty was an illusion.

Thus, this last work of Mme. de Staël ensured her the legacy of notoriety and controversy under whose shadow she had lived most of her life. Even in her death she remained mistress to her age.

E. Cappadocia, "The Liberals and Madame de Staël," in *Essays*, ed. R. Herr and H. T. Parker (Durham, N.C. 1965); R. J. Forsberg, *Madame de Staël and the English* (New York, 1967); H. Guillemin, *Madame de Staël, Benjamin Constant and Napoleon* (Paris, 1959); G. E. Gwynne, *Madame de Staël et la Révolution* (Paris, 1969); J. C. Herold, *Madame de Staël et l'Europe. Colloque* (Paris, 1970) and *Mistress to an Age* (Indianapolis, 1958); G. A. Kelly, "Liberalism and Aristocracy in the French Restoration," *Journal of the History of Ideas* 26 (1965); E. de Nolde, *Madame de Staël and Benjamin Constant. Unpublished Letters* (New York, 1907); G. de Staël, *Considerations*, 3 vols. (Paris, 1818), *Corinne*, 2 vols. (Paris, 1807), *De la Littérature*, 2 vols. (Paris,

1800), *De l'Allegmagne*, 3 vols. (London, 1813), *De l'Influence des passions*, 2 vols. (Lausanne, 1796), and *Dix années d'exil* (Paris, 1904).

*Sanford Gutman*

*Related entries:* CHARTER OF 1814; CONSTANT; RESTORATION, SECOND; SISMONDI; TALLEYRAND; ULTRAROYALISTS.

**STAPFER, PHILIPPE-ALBERT** (1766–1840), Swiss diplomat and Protestant salonist and publicist. Born in Bern on 23 September 1766, Stapfer was ordained a Protestant clergyman in 1789. After the 1798 French invasion of Switzerland, he helped negotiate the recognition of Swiss neutrality. As minister of public instruction, he was instrumental in assisting Pestalozzi and in defending the rights of the clergy. As a diplomat in 1802, he successfully resisted French efforts to annex the Valais. A champion of Swiss unity and liberty, in February 1803 he signed the act of mediation that governed Switzerland until 1814. Having negotiated this agreement, he then left public office but remained in France, retiring to the country to pursue his studies of Kant, Socrates, philosophy, and religion. He returned to Paris in 1817.

During the Restoration, Stapfer hosted a famous Protestant salon in Paris, where he championed religious and political liberty, freedom of conscience, and separation of church and state. He was of significant influence on the Reformed church in France and abroad, especially through his efforts to combine German ideas with French religious spirit. He was a leading member of the Société de la morale chrétienne, a moderate group that opposed both religious reaction and anticlericalism. He also assisted in several other Protestant organizations. Although he proselyted actively for the Reformed church and opposed Catholic reactionaries, he earned wide respect for the objectivity of his writing, the breadth and depth of his knowledge, his keen sensitivity and fresh imagination, and his thorough research.

In addition to Stapfer's religious interests, he published numerous biographical articles, especially in the *Biographie universelle*, and critical articles in newspapers. As an editor of the *National*, Stapfer opposed the policies of Charles X and was one of the signers of the journalists' protest during the July Revolution. In politics as in all else, he sought to apply the Christian liberalism that dominated his outlook. Although he regarded Kant's system as the formula for philosophical thought, he considered Christianity to be the main source of humanity and the standard by which human action should be evaluated. In addition to his religious and political affairs, Stapfer found time to write extensively on other subjects. He produced a biography of Kant, translated Goethe's *Faust* and other dramatic works, wrote a history of the city of Bern, and prepared a description of the Bernese Oberland.

Stapfer suffered from rheumatism and other ailments in his later years. Nevertheless, he remained active in religious affairs as long as possible. He died in Paris on 27 March 1840. Selections from his correspondence were published in 1891.

E. Guillon, *Napoléon et la Suisse, 1803–1815* (Paris, 1910); J.-F. Michaud, *Biographie universelle ancienne et moderne* (Paris, 1854–65); P.-A. Stapfer, *Aus Philipp Albert Stapfer's Briefwechsel* (Basel, 1891), *Bonaparte, Talleyrand et Stapfer* (Zurich, 1860), and *Mélanges philosophiques, littéraires, historiques et religieux* (Paris, 1844).

*James K. Kieswetter*

*Related entries:* CHARLES X; *LE NATIONAL*; REVOLUTION OF 1830; SOCIETY OF CHRISTIAN MORALS.

**STENDHAL** (1783–1842), pseud. of HENRI BEYLE, genius of the modern psychological novel and leader of the liberal faction of romanticist writers. Marie-Henri Beyle was born 23 January 1783 to Henriette (Gagnon) and Chérubin Beyle on the rue des Vieux-Jésuites (today rue Jean-Jacques Rousseau) in Grenoble. Despite its breathtakingly beautiful natural setting, Grenoble was always a source of unhappy memories for Beyle. He detested the city and the bourgeois conformity and conservatism of its inhabitants. His father, a well-to-do lawyer, shared their status and material aspirations, coveting noble rank and wealth. Henri's temperament was that of an independent, rebellious child with a strong dislike for bourgeois ways and ideas and a quick temper, already bearing the mark of the political liberal he was to become. Contact with the depressing, somber, overbearing personality of his father was to a large degree a factor. From the start, he harbored an inordinate amount of affection for his mother and of hate for his father. Such emotions were strong factors in the development of Henri's character and in his irresistible impulsion to mask his true feelings. Throughout his life, he rejected the Romantic propensity for describing emotions with a flourish; there was more truth, more integrity, in understating and dissimulating them. As much as he truly detested his father, he extended to his vivacious, charming mother a consuming, almost incestuous, affection. The same contrast prevailed in the relationship with his sisters. Pauline was a close friend to share his joys and woes, and Zénaïde-Caroline was an enemy to be distrusted and shunned. Throughout his life, he would deliberately acknowledge the side of his personality owed to the sensitive, lively Gagnons and ignore that obtained from the stern, stubborn Beyles.

Henri was understandably devastated when his adored mother died in childbirth in 1790. His reaction was to withdraw even more within his own romantic imagination and to lose himself in the usually erotic books he secretly borrowed from his grandfather's library. *La Nouvelle Héloïse* particularly enchanted him. His only other refuge was the home of his maternal grandfather, Dr. Henri Gagnon, Grenoble's most prominent physician. Dr. Gagnon, his sister Elisabeth, and his valet, Vincent Lambert, compensated with their warm friendship for the hostility and persecution of Henri's aunt, Séraphie Gagnon, who after Henriette's death had become Chérubin Beyle's constant companion. To Dr. Gagnon, disciple of Fontenelle and Voltaire, was owed the limited early schooling Stendhal received, since the efforts of his official tutor, the abbé Jean-François Raillane, a supposedly despicable, ultraconservative Jesuit, went for naught as his pupil dreamed of playing an active role in the republican upheaval.

Young Beyle was enthralled by the Revolutionary happenings that were transforming Grenoble. Another strong influence in his early life was his uncle, Romain Gagnon, the antithesis of his straitlaced sister, Séraphie. Romain was a Grenoble lawyer who preferred and led the life of a notorious playboy. Charm and wit combined with selfishness and a love of pleasure involved him in innumerable affairs. It is not surprising that one of his favorite diversions was the theater. He took little Henri at the age of six to his first play, and the stage henceforth became his passion. Its fantasy world captured his soul and kindled a burning ambition to become a playwright of Molière's caliber. His fascination extended to the people he saw and triggered romantic affairs and pseudo-affairs with a number of actresses, beginning with Virginie Kubly when Beyle was only in his early teens. At the age of thirteen in 1796, Henri Beyle, along with several other youngsters of Grenoble's social elite, was enrolled in the newly founded École centrale which for the first time stressed science and mathematics. His discovery of LeTourneur's translation of Shakespeare during his four-year stay there, however, strengthened his love for free poetic form and his resolve to become a writer. Although his rational mind made him brilliant in mathematics, his love for the discipline was not sincere. He never appeared for the École polytechnique entrance examination since the trip to Paris in November 1799 represented only his long-planned escape from Grenoble. He was heeding the parting advice of his uncle, Romain, that women and not numbers led to success in the world.

Beyle, still the innocent provincial adolescent at sixteen, appropriately arrived in Paris the day after the coup d'état that gave birth to the Napoleonic era on 9 November 1799, but his mind was focused on a literary career and romantic intrigue. He did not even register at the École polytechnique as he intended to do but set out to discover Paris. He could finally attempt to give vent to the passionate side of his nature. From a small garret, however, where loneliness and illness plagued him during his first weeks in the capital, he was suddenly rescued by Noël Daru, the wealthy aristocratic cousin of his grandfather Gagnon, who restored him to health and took him under his wing. The boy's lofty dreams had been whisked away by harsh reality. He had been thoroughly disillusioned, unable to penetrate the world of the dandies and their ladies in low-cut, diaphanous dresses. The Darus, though high-ranking bureaucrats in General Bonaparte's Consulate Government, were kind and sympathetic toward their unattractive relative, whose illness had robbed him of his hair and forced him henceforth to wear a wig. Pierre Daru, Noël's son, though only thirty-three, had managed to reach the prestigious post of secretary general to the Ministry of War. It was he who played a crucial role in Henri's life. He gave him a job as a clerk in his ministry and took him to the theater, to parties, and even to literary meetings. It is to his credit that though they were at opposite poles in their ideas, feelings, and attitudes, out of family loyalty he launched his cousin on the road to success in the world. Thoroughly bored and even miserable reproducing letters in the War Office, Beyle's life for three months was dismal. Fortunately, another Daru, Martial, Pierre's younger brother (twenty-six in 1800), made his situation tolerable. His occupation and his diversions were fully as glamorous and exciting as those of Romain Gagnon, whom he now replaced as romantic tutor for young Henri. He was a career officer in Bonaparte's expeditionary forces and a handsome, experienced Paris dandy who kept a record of his sexual exploits. His dress, savoir-faire, looks, and popularity with the ladies were impressive to Henri Beyle, and he became a role model. This marked the beginning of character self-training to compete successfully in Parisian social circles, of the development of an external, social, intellectual person to complement the internal, private, emotional one.

When First Consul Bonaparte decided to take an army across the Great Saint Bernard Pass into Lombardy to recapture northern Italy and drive out the Austrians, Pierre and Martial Daru were included as administrative officers. In May 1800, they invited their cousin Henri to join them. He eagerly accepted. Paris was a disapppointment, and he could hardly contain his excitement at the possibility of finding love and adventure in the land of his dreams. Soon his cousins had transformed him, at seventeen, into a second lieutenant of the dragoons, and his military career was launched. During the next two years in Milan and surrounding areas, he took a giant step toward maturity through exposure to battle, which he barely tolerated, to Italian opera, whose music he loved, and to Italian women, whom he diligently pursued, especially one Angela Pietragrua. Milan was a growing center of political, intellectual, social, and aesthetic freedom that greatly appealed to the Latin or *espagnolisme* side of Beyle's nature, and he symbolically renounced his French origins to become a citizen of that city. One evening at La Scala, he met and conversed with Choderlos de Laclos, author of *Les Liaisons dangereuses*, a novel he reread in Milan for "romantic guidance." Beginning in April 1801, he began to record his experiences in the Po Valley in his famous *Journal* to conquer his boredom during recurring bouts with venereal disease. In February 1801, he served for a time as aide de camp to General Claude Michaud, commander of the Third Cisalpine Division, but he was already planning to forsake his military career for literature and other aesthetic pursuits. He spent many hours sketching dramatic scenarios while studying the great classical plays. At the end of 1801, he left for France on a long-sought convalescent leave, stopping for three months in Grenoble before resettling in Paris to begin his quest for literary fame by beginning to jot down philosophic thoughts and ideas gleaned from his readings in a collection of *Pensées*, which he called *Filosofia Nova*. Developed from 1802 to 1805, they were the foundation of an attitude, an outlook he termed *le beylisme*.

At twenty, his greatest ambition was still to become a great poet, which meant an accomplished playwright who could expose the psychology of his characters with the finesse and mastery of Molière. His great passion for more than fifteen years would thus be the stage and its actresses. Much of his effort was an apprenticeship, dissecting the plays of Molière, Beaumarchais, Corneille, and Racine. He studied English to read and analyze Shakespeare's works. Success as a playwright eluded him, however, because he insisted on verse and had no talent for it. From 1802 to 1817, however, from that study of plays, he gained an in depth knowledge of human psychology, which he would apply in his novels. Henri Beyle's second stay in the capital lasted nearly three years. Napoleon's creation of an Empire in 1804 perplexed the liberal Beyle, but his adulation for Bonaparte was such that he rationalized and accepted it. He resigned his commission in July 1802 and assumed the life of a salon dandy, despite his limited income. He learned to dance but preferred to haunt the theaters. Still a victim of his own insecurity with women, his passionate affairs were still largely confined to his imagination, just as his relationship with Angela in Milan had been. It was from an erotic relationship with Madeleine Rebuffel, related by marriage to the Darus and the Gagnons, and her daughter Adèle, both of whom lived in the Daru mansion, that he finally learned to involve his senses rather than his heart in his amorous endeavors. In late 1804, through his acting tutor Dugazon, he met an actress three years his senior named Mélanie Guilbert, whose stage name was Louason. They were soon involved in an intimate love affair. When she accepted an engagement at the Grand Théâtre in Marseilles, he was able to follow her and share adjoining rooms in the same boarding house because a Grenoble classmate found him a position with Meunier and Company, a food importing firm. Through the summer of 1809, Henri and Mélanie shared a satisfying life, but his dislike for the city and its inhabitants, and a deteriorating economic situation, caused it to sour. The British blockade ruined Meunier's business and forced the Grand Théâtre to close down. The lovers returned to Paris separately in spring 1806 to redirect their lives independently.

To ensure his economic survival, Beyle compromised his revolutionary principles by accepting the emperor and his court and seeking once again the support of Pierre Daru, now one of the most important men on Napoleon's staff. At first hesitating for fear of being frustrated again by his young cousin, Daru finally became convinced of his sincerity. In the fall of 1806, Beyle was assigned to assist Martial Daru, *intendant des finances* of the duchy of Brunswick, and to accompany him to Berlin. They arrived ten days after Napoleon's victory at Jena (16 October 1806) and witnessed the emperor's triumphant arrival in Berlin. Two days later (29 October), Beyle was officially given the title of provincial deputy war commissar under Martial's orders. In July 1807, after Tilsitt, he became war commissar and in January 1808 *intendant* of the conquered imperial domains in Westphalia. He stayed in Brunswick two years and studied German with little enthusiasm. Beyle was finally an important man (now Monsieur de Beyle) who performed his duty with talent and skill, but Germany and the Germans, despite their hospitality, soon bored him, and he longed for a warmer climate and the arms of Angela Pietragrua, the only woman whose vision haunted him. In May 1808, he felt a deep sense of relief when his beloved sister Pauline, in whom he confided in his letters, finally married a Grenoble businessman at the age of twenty-two. As the Austrian campaign was launched in the spring of 1809, Beyle was ordered to Austria. Within a few months, his responsibilities for supply and billeting had provided a thorough initiation to the horrors of war, but he performed with dedication and valor as Wagram and Vienna were being conquered. The fall of 1809 in Vienna was perfect for music and love. Beyle ardently pursued his cousin's wife, Countess Alexandrine Daru, who considered him a close friend.

In January 1810, Henri Beyle was back in Paris where he again courted the countess. In August, his ambitious efforts to rise in the administrative ranks bore fruit; a decree named him one of the 300 auditors of the prestigious Council of State, and shortly after he became inspector of the accounts of the imperial real property. He lived to the hilt the existence of a dandy with all its trappings. As usual, he craved a more physical relationship than he had with Alexandrine Daru, and a mistress was almost a necessity for a man of his position. This time, he chose Angélina Bereyter, an opera singer who promptly shared his lodgings. There was no depth in the liaison; she merely fulfilled a need. When the countess again rebuffed his advances in August 1811, he requested and received a leave to visit Milan. It proved to be a refreshing and restful hiatus in his heady career, combining passionate encounters with the finally accessible Angela and delightful artistic excursions in Milan and surrounding towns. In November, his leave expired, and he was back in Paris. He discovered that he had acquired new superiors and a reputation for unreliability. Having resumed his arrangement with Angélina, he spent the winter and spring of 1812 working on his *Histoire de la peinture en Italie*. Wanting to share the glory of Grande armée's Russian campaign, he was allowed to resume active duty, and the Empress Marie-Louise charged him with delivering a personal letter to Napoleon already leading the march to the East. In midsummer, 1812, he had reached the headquarters in Poland and was absorbing as a surprisingly detached observer the sounds and sights that would find their way into *La Chartreuse de Parme*. He entered Moscow with the "conquerors" on 14 September, sadly witnessed the burning of the city, and, as newly appointed commissioner of war supplies, was dispatched to Smolensk to prepare logistics for the retreat as the threatening winter began. His good spirits and resourcefulness helped him survive as he faced appalling suffering, death, and devastation during the chaotic return trip. Having just turned thirty, he set foot in Paris on 31 January 1813, proud that he had passed the test of hardship and matured in courage.

By April, he was back at the front in Germany, but his body soon succumbed to the many trials he had suffered and he found himself in September on convalescent leave in Milan. The climate of his beloved city and the tender arms of Angela Pietragrua hastened his recovery. After passing through Grenoble to pay his last fond respects to Dr. Gagnon, recently deceased, Beyle was back in Paris in December 1813. Disillusioned with war, he resumed his exhaustive analysis of French classical theater, though only briefly, since a last assignment to assist the comte de Saint-Vallier in planning the defense of Grenoble and the

Dauphiné was forced on him. For several weeks, he performed exceptionally well, but the physical and mental strain again caught up with him, and he was compelled to return to Paris in time to view the Allies' triumphal entry and the emperor's sad departure. With the collapse, Henri Beyle's world folded, and instant insolvency ensued. With remarkable restraint, he sold everything and moved into a single room and remained philosophical at having barely missed becoming a prefect and a member of La Légion d'honneur. Paris no longer pleased him, and he purged himself of the capital with its foreign troops as he planned his exile to Italy. As he waited, he composed and published, at his own expense, complete with unabashedly "borrowed" passages, a biography of Haydn, Mozart, and Metastasio. Though it appeared under one of his many aliases and failed to sell, it marked a major turning point in Beyle's life. He could now call himself a writer.

Henri Beyle arrived in Milan for an extended residence of nearly seven years (1814–21), though he would travel to Paris and England. He restored his ties with Angela and happily became a man of letters, though, as a retired official on half-pay, he could afford few luxuries. He balanced an existence with Angela, which had become stormy and stressful, with visits to museums, art galleries, and theaters. Even the hopes rekindled by the Hundred Days did not stir him. The whole experience awakened his aesthetic sensitivity to a point where he could compose a history of Italian painting, which he published at his expense in 1817. It was filled with the judgments of others, but he also included some of his own ideas. That same year appeared a book of travel notes and comments on Rome, Naples, and Florence, which gave a critical view of the people in those cities. For the first time he used the pseudonym Stendhal, borrowed from Stendal, a small Prussian town. His long affair with Angela finally ended in 1815, and his natural instinct for love was not aroused again until he met Métilde Dembowski in the spring of 1818. He became completely overwhelmed with passion for her almost immediately. She proved to be the great love of his life, the ideal woman whom he adored but could never possess, and the depth of his feelings for her nearly drove him to suicide. She was an authentic lady of the wealthy upper bourgeoisie of Milan endowed with great beauty and intelligence. Her association with the carbonari movement increased Stendhal's admiration of her. She had all the qualities he desired in a woman. Unfortunately, though she tolerated his friendship, she consistently rejected his advances; she did not trust him and ostensibly never loved him.

The following two years were filled with disappointments. Stendhal's father passed away in the summer of 1819, leaving a mountain of debts. Forced to satisfy his sexual needs, he also had another bout with syphilis. Finally, despite a past decision to live permanently in exile in Milan, the Austrian police noted his association with political and literary liberals and viewed him as an undesirable, a radical. Although the hypocrisy and the mediocrity of Restoration society disgusted him, he had to accept the inevitable and return to Paris in the summer of 1821.

His stay in Restoration Paris would span the rest of the decade. One of his first actions was to see to the publication in 1822 of his curious essay, *De l'Amour*. The image of Métilde as love personified was directly responsible for its composition. In it, he dwells not on the physical aspects of love but on its psychological forms and complexities as he experienced them with Métilde. He depicts the various stages that finally lead to the famous "crystallization" stage, which endows the loved one with perfection. His first months in Paris were a true emotional upheaval brought on by his loss of Métilde and of his beloved Italy, and, at the age of thirty-eight, he seriously contemplated suicide. Slowly his depression left him, and his instincts for secrecy, for concealment, for mystery enabled him to accommodate to life in Paris and even to its loathsome politics. His wit nurtured by Montesquieu and Voltaire was decidedly a factor, and he soon acquired a reputation as a lighthearted, entertaining conversationalist and storyteller. As such he was welcomed in the leading salons and was able to acquire close friends, many acquaintances,and a variety of interests. He knew a mixed group of the prominent cultured Frenchmen of his day, notably Benjamin Constant, Alphonse de Lamartine, Honoré de Balzac, Alfred de Musset and Charles-Augustin Sainte-Beuve among the writers, and he was most often seen in the liberal salons of Constant and Etienne Delécluze, where he met Prosper Mérimée, the short story writer, who remained his closest friend to his death and who understood the true Stendhal better than anyone else. Thus, Stendhal became active and very visible in the artistic and literary life of the 1820s. He became a prominent participant in the great classical–romantic war of words and played a key role in the promotion of a national, historical drama free of the fetters of classical rules. He was especially qualified due to the fact that dramatic theory was central to the debate, and he had always maintained a special interest in the theater. Thus, though deprived of position and success, he could live a tolerable life in the literary world where petty bourgeois values and intrigues could be ignored.

One of the *salons* where he was most often seen in the early 1820s was that of Countess Beugnot, where he had often appeared during his tenure as one of Napoleon's *auditeurs* as early as 1810. Her beautiful daughter Clementine, whom Stendhal always called Menti, had married Count Curial, who was notoriously unfaithful. Henri was slow to approach her as he found Métilde hard to forget, but Menti finally seduced him. By early 1824, she was his mistress. Theirs was a stimulating intellectual and physical relationship. It was just before this affair that he decided to make a tangible contribution to the romantic cause by composing the first version of what was to become one of its important manifestos: *Racine et Shakespeare*. It studied and criticized French comic and tragic theater and attempted to define romanticism as classicism for the moderns. Still loyal to Racine, it praised the boldness of Shakespeare. The second version, a response to Louis-Simon Auger's famous April 1824 French Academy speech, issued a strong call for freedom in the arts and letters, especially in drama. It appeared in March 1825 and established him as the elder statesman of the liberal wing of romanticism. Memories of La Scala rekindled, that same year he produced *Vie de Rossini*, whose famous William Tell libretto was the work of Etienne Jouy, a staunch foe of the romantics. After two years he was forced, while touring England in the summer of 1826, to accept the hard truth that the fickle Menti had severed their relationship. Shortly after his forty-third birthday earlier that year, he had begun to compose his first romantic novel, a tale of the sexual impotence of Octave de Malivert and his tragic love for his young cousin, Armance de Zohiloff. Despite its formalistic innovations and compelling psychological insight, it was greeted with indifference partly because of its natural, no-frills style. Work on it in late 1826 and early 1827 served as a cure for the loss of Menti. During the next two years, Stendhal's time was again occupied with the pursuit of ever-younger women, notably Alberte de Rubempré (nicknamed Madame Azur because she lived on the rue Bleue) and Giulia Rinieri (whom he offered to marry). In September 1829 a second travel book appeared, *Promenades in Rome*.

The year 1830 marked another milestone in the life of Stendhal. It was the year of his great masterpiece *Le Rouge et le noir*, the novel of energy as a major element of human behavior applied to life's situations, especially the romantic ones. The author had at last conceded, at forty-seven, that he could not write plays. The story of Julien Sorel (originally entitled *Julien*), the outsider in contemporary Restoration society, was not hyperbolic enough to impress the romantics of 1830, so Stendhal stood alone with the ''Happy Few,'' as he called the readers he considered his accomplices. The July Revolution erupted as he corrected the proofs. The hope of democratic government filled him with anticipation. As a child, he had witnessed the events of the first Revolution in Grenoble, and now he was again a spectator as Parisians manned the barricades. He was overjoyed when the people prevailed. One week after Louis-Philippe's accession on 7 August, Stendhal was volunteering his services in foreign affairs. Within a few weeks, a royal edict appointed him consul at Trieste. He was so anxious to return to Italy that he charged his publisher Levasseur with putting the final editorial touches on *Le Rouge et le noir* and agreed to its publication. Furthermore, Austria, to which Trieste belonged, had not yet approved the appointment when the jubilant new diplomat arrived in Trieste on 25 November. Unfortunately for him, the Austrians remembered his carbonari sympathies in Milan and were aware that his writings contained liberal religious and political views. Clemens von Metternich promptly sent word that Henri Beyle was not acceptable, and the news reached him on Christmas eve. On 11 February 1831, Louis-Philippe finally nominated him as consul at Civitavecchia, a small port near Rome in the Papal States, and Pope Gregory XVI consented, though aware of Beyle's radical views. After side trips to Venice and Florence, Stendhal arrived at his less important post in mid-April, resigned to accepting a salary reduced by a third. Life at Civitavecchia was quiet and soon boring. Though he made a number of friends, he escaped to Rome as often as possible to join the French ambassador's social gatherings, which included Turgenev and Horace Vernet, the painter. As the months dragged by, he missed the exciting intellectual and literary life of the Paris salons and fought his loneliness by pursuing literary projects. In fact, it was only in 1832 that he definitely abandoned his ambition to be a playwright and chose the novel as a medium that could better handle the content of contemporary reality. He sought the middle way between the historical in Walter Scott, whom he avidly read, and the psychological in Constant. Concurrently he was jotting down his private thoughts in *Souvenirs d'égotisme*. After a short vacation in Paris and a chance meeting with Musset and George Sand, Stendhal almost reluctantly returned to Civitavecchia, where his spirits were lifted by the award of the Légion d'honneur as a literary figure. To counteract the boredom of his duties, he began *Lucien Leuwen* in the spring of 1834 but left it unfinished. He probably thought it unwise to attempt to publish a story critical of the July Monarchy. In the fall of 1835, his natural inclination toward autobiography, reflected in his novels and in *Souvenirs*, led him to undertake the *Vie de Henry Brulard*, which he hoped would reveal the complexities of the identity of a man then in his fifties. Because a leave he had long desired was granted in March 1836, he abruptly abandoned his personal story at 1800, the point when he arrived in Milan at seventeen. Adolphe Thiers had intended that his stay in France be short, but his successor, Count Molé, extended it. He spent three years in Paris recovering from various ailments, mainly from venereal disease and obesity, and recapturing the full life he had once known with a group of old and new friends. Despite his age, he still fantasized a life with the woman of his dreams. Rejected by Baroness Lacuée and Mme. Gaulthier, an old friend who inspired *Lucien Leuwen*, he filled the void with a platonic family-type relationship with the Spanish Countess Montijo and her two daughters, Paca and Eugenia. The latter would become the wife of Napoleon III in 1853. In 1837, he wrote a few chapters of *Le Rose et le vert*, a novel he never finished. Between 1837 and 1839, the *Revue des deux mondes* published his series of translated stories, *Chroniques italiennes*. In 1838, perceptive accounts of his extensive travels in France were finally collected and published in *Mémoires d'un touriste* and *Voyages dans le midi de la France*. Toward the end of that year, he conceived the idea of transforming one of the Italian chronicle sixteenth century manuscripts into a fictionalized short story. Reset in the nineteenth century, the story rapidly became a novel composed in fifty-two days and offered for sale in Paris in April 1839. *La Chartreuse de Parme*, a powerful tale of Italian passion and intrigue, is considered Stendhal's masterpiece, a triumphant expression of his *espagnolisme*. In the summer of 1839, it was time to return to Civitavecchia. Resettled in August, he soon resorted again to trips to relieve the tedium. Another outlet was a new novel project entitled *Lamiel*, whose protagonist, like *Le Rose et le vert*, was an emancipated woman. Begun in October 1839, it was never finished, though it had the qualities of another masterpiece. He turned his attention to a final romantic fling with the attractive Countess Guilia Cini, which lasted only a few weeks in the winter of 1840. By then his health was appreciably deteriorating, and on 15 March 1841, a stroke left him exhausted. Although determined to carry on, he finally had to return to Paris in the fall. During the ensuing year, he gradually seemed to regain much of his physical and mental stamina, but suddenly, on the evening of 22 March 1842 during an evening stroll, a final massive stroke felled him. His funeral and burial in Montmartre Cemetery were quiet and private. His life and his writings had been consistently out of step with his contemporaries, but posterity would ensure his recognition for the new elements he introduced in prose fiction. He is widely acknowledged as a master and a pioneer of the modern historical-psychological novel.

R. Alter and C. Cosman, *A Lion for Love: A Critical Biography of Stendhal* (New York, 1978); H. A. Baatsch, *La Neige ou le bleu. Une vie de Stendhal* (Paris, 1983); M. Bardèche, *Stendhal romancier* (Paris,1977); E. Chabrun, *Stendhal, écrivain du XIX* *siècle, 1783–1842* (Paris, 1972); F. Cruciani, *Stendhal* (Paris, 1972); V. Del Litto, *La Vie de Stendhal* (Paris, 1965); M. Guérin, *La Politique de Stendhal* (Paris, 1982); S. Jameson, *Speaking of Stendhal* (London, 1979); H. Levin, *Toward Stendhal: An Essay* (Philadelphia, 1978); G. May, *Stendhal and the Age of Napoleon* (New York, 1977); J. Richardson, *Stendhal* (London, 1974).

*Paul Comeau*

*Related entries:* AUGER; BALZAC; CONSTANT; DELECLUZE; ECOLE PO-LYTECHNIQUE; JOUY; LAMARTINE; MERIMEE; METTERNICH; MOLE; MUSSET; *LA REVUE DES DEUX MONDES*; ROMANTICISM; SAINTE-BEUVE; SAND; THIERS; VERNET.


**STERN, DANIEL.** See AGOULT.


**SUE, MARIE–JOSEPH** (1804–1857), popular novelist and social reformer; known as Eugène. Born in Paris the son of a naval surgeon, Sue studied and also practiced medicine in the navy until he came into a modest inheritance that freed him from a professional career. He went to sea briefly as a naval surgeon, however, before adopting the life of a dandy and salon social climber. An admirer of James Fenimore Cooper's adventure stories, Sue made his literary debut with novels based on his travels. The appearance of *La Salamandre* in 1832 established his reputation, which he exploited in subsequent novels depicting contemporary French social manners and mores. Although his *Mathilde* was poorly received by the faubourg Saint-Germain when it appeared in 1841, it explored the possibilities of the serial novel form, which he developed later with great success. *Les Mystères de Paris* (1842–43), *Le Juif érrant* (1844–45), and *Les Sept péchés capitaux* (1847–49) earned Sue a substantial fortune and an equally brief international reputation. On the strength of his literary calls for social reform, Sue was elected to the Legislative Assembly in 1850 but left for exile in Savoy after Louis Bonaparte's coup d'état in 1851. He died in Annecy six years later.

Despite Sue's ephemeral career, he exercised substantial influence on his contemporaries. The remarkable success of his serial novels probably was owed to the sensitivity with which they expressed middle-class attitudes and values of the period, especially concerning the social problem of insistent urban poverty and crime. Sue's apparent sympathy for the laboring poor, however, was undermined by his naive moralizing narratives and by his calls for conservative paternalistic reform of the social system. With their often accurate portrayal of the Parisian working classes and underworld—the extravagant melodrama notwithstanding—Sue's works contributed to the development of French literary realism culminating in Victor Hugo's *Les Misérables* (1862) and Emile Zola's Rougon-Macquart series (1871–93).

N. Atkinson, *Eugène Sue et le roman-feuilleton* (Nemours, 1929); J.-L. Bory, *Eugène Sue: Le Roi du roman populaire* (Paris, 1962); P. Chaunu, *Eugène Sue et la seconde république* (Paris, 1948); J. Moody, *Les Idées sociales d'Eugène Sue* (Paris, 1938).

*James Smith Allen*

*Related entries:* COUP D'ETAT OF 2 DECEMBER 1851; HUGO; LEGIS-LATIVE ASSEMBLY.

**SWISS GUARD,** troops of Swiss nationality serving in the military household of the king from the fifteenth century until 1830. The term *Swiss Guards* actually applied to two units: the Hundred Ordinary Swiss Guards of the king (the Hundred Swiss) and the regiment of Swiss Guards. The use of Swiss mercenaries in French service originated with Louis XI, who employed several thousand. In 1496 Charles VIII reduced their number to a company of one hundred and placed them under a French captain. They became especially attached to the person of the king, and their duties included mounting guard at royal palaces and serving as bodyguards of the king. The Regiment of Ordinary Swiss Guards, established by Louis XIII in 1616, consisted of sixteen companies of 160 men each. They enjoyed precedence immediately after the Gardes françaises, and their duties included guarding the royal family.

The Swiss Regiment defended the Tuileries on 10 August 1792 and was subsequently massacred by the mob. Both Swiss units were disbanded by the Revolution. The Hundred Swiss were reestablished in 1814 and reorganized in 1815. The Swiss Regiment was reestablished in 1815. During the Restoration, the Swiss Guards were the object of extensive popular hatred. Violence between them and French civilians was not uncommon in the late 1820s. Furthermore their preferential treatment was the source of much enmity with the French regulars. Guard officers, Swiss as well as French, held rank one grade higher than the equivalent position in a line unit, and their pay was much different. A Swiss Guard sub-lieutenant received 2,500 francs, while a French line regiment sub-lieutenant received 1,300. A Swiss Guard colonel received 15,000, while his French line counterpart earned only 5,000. Swiss line units also enjoyed preferential pay. This favoritism was one factor in the French army's lack of enthusiasm for the Bourbons by 1830. During the July Revolution, it was in part on the Swiss that Charles X initially relied to hold Paris. The abandoning of the Louvre by the Swiss on 29 July was the signal for disintegration among other French units hitherto loyal to the crown. Furthermore, the Swiss, whose barracks became the special target of public anger during the Revolution, began to desert by 29 July. The government subsequently gave them safe conduct passes to return to Switzerland and thus avoid public vengeance. Some of the Swiss were recruited into legitimist *chouan* ranks. For its part, the government of the July Monarchy dismissed the Swiss units later in August and amended the Charter to provide that no foreigner could serve in the French forces unless specifically allowed by law.

A. Maag, *Geschichte der Schweizertruppen in französischen Diensten während der Restauration und Julirevolution, 1816–1830* (Biel, 1899); D. Pinkney, *The French Revolution of 1830* (Princeton, 1972); D. Porch, *Army and Revolution, France 1814–1848* (London, 1974).

*James K. Kieswetter*

*Related entries:* CHARTER OF 1814; REVOLUTION OF 1830; RESTORATION, SECOND.

*LA SYLPHE,* (1829), satirical and liberal perodical of literary salons. *La Sylphe* was one of the more sprightly of those Restoration *littéraires*, satirical and literary reviews, appearing weekly or monthly. Started by Louis Desnoyers, an author of children's fairytales, *Sylphe* featured a liberal polemic but stressed amusing critical reviews and gossip and news of the salon. The proposed press law of 1828, although granting relief from censorship and suppression, was a threat to such small journals by requiring a bond or *cautionnement* against damages from suits. *Sylphe* could not afford the proposed 50,000 franc assessment, so Desnoyers printed a different fairyland name on each masthead: a *Trilby*, a *Gnome*, a *Lutin*. Amendments by liberal deputies greatly reduced the caution money for such magazines, but the law foiled the *Sylphe's* method of evasive rechristening. During the July Monarchy, Desnoyers was more successful as coeditor and critic for *Le Siècle*, largest daily newspaper of the period.

D. Rader, *Journalists and the July Revolution* (The Hague, 1973).

*Daniel Rader*

*Related entries:* PRESS LAWS; *LE SIÈCLE*.

# T

LES TABLETTES UNIVERSELLES, a calendar of events, 1820–1823; then a liberal journal, 1823–1824; bought out by Villèle, January 1824; ceased publication, March 1824. When Jacques Coste purchased the *Tablettes universelles* in January 1823, he turned a mere calendar of entertainments and spectacles into a major liberal journal, employing many bright fresh minds on his staff. The *Tablettes* was unique in that it became a spawning ground for three groups of young liberal intellectual journalists known collectively as *doctrinaires*. These were University professors sacked in the post-1820 reaction, including Paul-François Dubois, Théodore Jouffroy, Victor Cousin, and François Guizot; *philosophes* of the *doctrinaire* salons, including Charles de Rémusat; and a pair of provincial activists who became a political force of themselves, Adolphe Thiers and François-Auguste Mignet. The paper's political editorials reflected Thiers' growing impatience with the polemic of the occasionally docile *Constitutionnel*.

The popularity and circulation of this lively journal were still growing when, in January 1824, Coste succumbed to the bribery of Joseph de Villèle's agent Sosthenes de la Rochefoucauld and sacrificed the publication for 300,000 francs. This enormous sum, among the largest paid by Villèle in one lump, was drawn from a secret appropriation in the king's own civil list. The shock to the liberal ranks was intense. Thiers, Rémusat, and Mignet announced in disgust they would quit the world of journalism, and Coste was castigated, to the amusement of the ultra press. François-René de Chateaubriand, whose hands were not entirely clean because of an earlier official subsidy, took Coste to task in the *Journal des débats*. In this massive buy-out of newspapers, however, the *Débats* had stood firm with great publicity.

Under new management and staff, the *Tablettes* lost its subscribers and died in ignominy two months later, with the blessing of Villèle. One unforeseen product of the newspaper's prostitution was the impetus to create new journals on the intellectual and *doctrinaire* Left. The influential *Globe* and the *Revue française* grew up in the wake of the *Tablettes* and used the talents of several of that journal's former contributors.

E. Hatin, *Histoire de la presse française*, vol. 8 (Paris, 1859–61); A. Germain, *Martyrologie de la presse* (Paris, 1861).

*Daniel Rader*

*Related entries:* CHATEAUBRIAND; *LE CONSTITUTIONNEL*; COUSIN; *DOCTRINAIRES*; DUBOIS; *LE GLOBE*; GUIZOT; *JOURNAL DES DEBATS*; LA ROCHEFOUCAULD; MIGNET; REMUSAT; *REVUE FRANCAISE*; THIERS; ULTRAROYALISTS; VILLELE.


**TALLEYRAND-PERIGORD, CHARLES-MAURICE DE** (1754–1838), politician, diplomat, and survivor of the vicissitudes of the French Revolution. Charles-Maurice de Talleyrand-Perigord was born on 2 February 1754. His first career was that of an ecclesiastic, one in which he rose rapidly to become bishop of Autun. He took an active part in the French Revolution. In the fall of 1789, he proposed the confiscation of the church lands, and in July 1790 he voted for the Civil Constitution of the Clergy. Unlike the majority of French clergymen, Talleyrand took the required oath of allegiance to the Civil Constitution. On 24 February 1791, he consecrated two Constitutional priests to be bishops; then, resigning the episcopate, he devoted his full time to politics.

Disgusted with the execution of Louis XVI in 1793, he became an *émigré*, preferring voluntary exile to unbridled radicalism. He lived first in England and then in Philadelphia.

Finding the political climate more to his liking in 1794, he returned to France to serve the Directory as foreign minister. After the coup d'état of 18 Brumaire, Napoleon retained his services. Within a few years relations between the two men soured, and Talleyrand retired from the foreign office, remaining only a privy councillor and senator.

Napoleon's disastrous Russian campaign resulted in catastrophic consequences for France. Driven back across Europe by the armies of the Fourth Coalition, the broken emperor abdicated in favor of his son, the king of Rome. This act was not honored. Seeing France faced with possible dismemberment by the Allies, Talleyrand emerged to serve his country.

In March 1814, Czar Alexander I triumphantly entered Paris as conqueror and arbiter of Europe. It was Senator Talleyrand who sumptuously hosted the czar at his palatial residence on the rue St. Florentin. There he convinced Alexander that the interest of Europe, as well as France, would be better served by invoking the principle of legitimacy. Louis Stanislaus Xavier (Louis XVIII), brother of the beheaded Louis XVI, Talleyrand noted, was the "legitimate" king of France. The czar accepted the argument; the Senate agreed; Louis was proclaimed and graciously issued the constitutional Charter. As foreign minister, Talleyrand proceeded to Vienna to represent France at the assembling congress.

At Vienna Talleyrand's negotiating skills reached their epitome. He noted that Austria, Great Britain, Prussia, and Russia habitually referred to themselves as the Allies and excluded France from their inner circles. Napoleon, Talleyrand insisted, was the enemy, not Louis XVIII. Henceforth the Allies included France in their deliberations.

At the congress, Talleyrand consistently sided with Clemens von Metternich and Viscount Castlereagh to constrain the growing power of Prussia and Russia. This is best exemplified in the Polish-Saxon affair. Russia wished to extend its western boundary to include all of Poland, and Prussia wished to increase its territories to include all of Saxony. Talleyrand, Castlereagh, and Metternich rejected these pretensions. The French foreign minister argued that Saxony's legitimate ruler, Frederick Augustus, no more than Louis XVIII, should be robbed of his lands without his consent.

To crystallize his objective, on 3 January 1815 Talleyrand negotiated a secret alliance among France, Great Britain, and Austria. These new allies agreed to joint military action if the Prussians and Russians insisted on pressing their plans for Poland and Saxony. In February the situation was resolved at the conference table by compromise. Saxony lost two-thirds of its territory to Prussia. A reduced "Congress" Poland was created with the czar as king. Prussia retained Posen; Austria kept Galicia. Saxony retained its legitimate king and one-third of its former territory.

Despite his success at Vienna, shortly after his return to Paris Talleyrand was dismissed by Louis XVIII. During the Hundred Days, Napoleon had found and sent to Czar Alexander a copy of the secret treaty of 3 January 1815. Upon Alexander's second entry into France, the furious czar told Louis XVIII that he would never again be a friend to France or oppose revived Prussian plans for France's total dismembement if Talleyrand was not dismissed and the duke of Richelieu was not named foreign minister and premier. The terrified Louis acceded, and Talleyrand began his fifteen-year retirement, spending his winters on the rue St. Florentin and his summers at the chateau de Valencay, his country estate. As grand chamberlain, he appeared frequently at court in a nonpolitical capacity. Talleyrand's public career appeared ended.

Unexpectedly, in July 1830 the aged gentleman received yet another call to serve his country. At the height of the July Revolution, Charles X abdicated in favor of his grandson, the young duke of Bordeaux, appointing his cousin Louis-Philippe to be regent and lieutenant general of the realm. Immediately Talleyrand liberalized several ambiguous sections of the Charter and with the marquis de Lafayette, the proverbial republican, urged Louis-Philippe to accept the crown, swear an oath on the revised Charter, and assume the title king of the French. When Talleyrand was informed that the foreign ambassadors were leaving Paris as they had in 1793, he went personally to Pozzo di Borgo, the Prussian ambassador, and Sir Charles Stewart, the British ambassador, and convinced the diplomats to remain. This act gave the appearance of further legitimacy for the new government, though neither ambassador's government as yet recognized Louis-Philippe. Grateful for his action, backing, and counsel, Louis-Philippe offered to appoint Talleyrand as his foreign minister. The prince, now seventy-six, declined but accepted the post of ambassador to Great Britain. In London

Talleyrand worked closely with Lord Palmerston to draw the two constitutional monarchies closer together. For four years, the aged sage's hand directed many of the protocols of the Conference of London on Belgian affairs. Permanent neutrality for Belgium was his idea. He was also intimately involved in the destruction of some of the fortresses on France's northern frontier. From his London vantage point, he dealt with the revolutions in Greece, Belgium, Poland, and Italy and the civil strife in Spain and Portugal. Frequently bypassing the French foreign minister and writing directly to Louis-Philippe, he advised his sovereign on all aspects of foreign and domestic affairs. In fact he became a prime minister in absentia.

Talleyrand retired from public life in 1834 and died on 17 May 1838. He was the consummate professional diplomat, the cosmopolitan man of the eighteenth century imbued with the nationalism of a man of the nineteenth.

J. F. Bernard, *Talleyrand* (New York, 1973); G. Lacour-Gayet, *Talleyrand*, 2 vols. (Paris, 1946, 1947); J. W. Rooney, Jr., "Richelieu and France's Fulfillment of the Treaties of 1815" (master's thesis, University of Louvain, 1957); D. P. Schmidt, "The Foreign Policy of Louis-Philippe, 1830–1832, A Study in International Diplomacy" (Ph.D. diss., Marquette University, 1976).

*John W. Rooney*

*Related entries:* BELGIAN REVOLUTION OF 1830; BORDEAUX; CHARTER OF 1814; LAFAYETTE, M.-J.-P.-Y.-R.-G.; METTERNICH; POZZO DI BORGO; REICHSTADT; RICHELIEU; VIENNA,CONGRESS OF.


**TALMA, FRANCOIS-JOSEPH** (1763–1826), tragic actor. Talma was born into a family of successful dentists and studied for that profession in London (where his father practiced after 1770) and in Paris, where he attended the lycée Louis-le-Grand and the Medical School of the University, beginning his practice in 1784. Although his later accounts of his early life were notoriously unreliable, he seems to have acquired an early love of acting and entered the Ecole royale de déclamation (later the Conservatoire) in 1786, where he was instructed by distinguished alumni of the Théâtre-français (today the Comédie française) like René-François Molé. He entered the company (then performing at the Odéon on the Left Bank) as a *pensionnaire* (salaried junior actor) in 1787 and made his dramatic debut in Voltaire's *Mahomet* on 21 November. Heavily influenced by neoclassicism and a friendship with Jacques-Louis David, Talma cultivated a heroic acting style and campaigned for accurate costuming in the classical dramas (Corneille, Racine) that were the staples of the French repertoire in the 1780s. While actors customarily performed in wigs and eighteenth-century dress, Talma's appearance onstage in Roman garb in Voltaire's *Brutus* (January 1789) caused a sensation. Encouraged by David, Antoine-Jean Gros, and Anne-Louis Girodet, Talma studied old prints, medallions, coins, and vases for classical models and became a full *sociétaire* (partner) in the Théâtre-français in April 1789. The resentment of his older colleagues and the hierarchical structure of the company confined him to minor roles, however, until his fortuitous appearance in the lead of Marie-Joseph Chénier's *Charles IX* (a role the senior actors refused) propelled him to prominence. The play's attack on religious intolerance and royal misgovernment complemented Parisian interest in the opening events of the Revolution, and Louis XVI's suspension of the play was withdrawn after public outcries. A similar suspension of Talma from the company for Revolutionary views was overruled by the Commune of Paris (September 1789).

Talma joined a new theatrical company (the Théatre de la nation [later, République]) in the rue de Richelieu (the present site of the Comédie française) when the National Assembly ended his old company's monopoly on the classical repertoire (law of 1 January 1791), and he could play the classical leads that were his specialty. Parts like Brutus, Le Cid, and William Tell, with their stirring pleas for liberty, were seen as statements of the Revolutionary creed, though Talma avoided direct political involvement. Neoclassical playwrights (Marie-Joseph de Chénier, Jean-François Ducis, Népomucène Lemercier) wrote dramas with Talma in mind. Talma's marriage to Julie Careau was a civil one, despite his pleas to the Assembly to permit actors to be married within the church, and his wife's salon brought him into frequent contact with Girondist politicians. David's friendship probably saved him from the Jacobins' arrest of the *sociétaires* of the Théatre-français in September 1793, but theater attendance declined during the Terror, and Talma's company went bankrupt by January 1799. The Théatre-français was reorganized in the same year, moving to the rue de Richelieu (the theater at the Odéon having burned in March), and Talma rejoined his old troupe.

Greatly admired by Napoleon, Talma enjoyed successes in Ducis' adaptations of *Macbeth* and *Hamlet* and Antoine de Lefosse's *Manlius* under the Empire. He performed privately for the emperor at Saint Cloud and in the Tuileries and presented productions for Napoleon and Czar Nicholas I at Erfurt in 1808 and Francis II of Austria at Dresden in 1813. Talma's personal life was marked by a nervous breakdown in 1809, almost constant indebtedness, and, despite his second marriage (to the actress Caroline Vanhove) in 1802, numerous love affairs, including one in 1812 with Pauline Bonaparte (Borghese). With the Restoration, Talma performed for Louis XVIII but remained a Bonapartist, refusing to act on the anniversary of the emperor's death after 1821. His last triumphs were in Lebrun's version of Schiller's *Maria Stuart*, Jouy's *Sylla* and Pichald's *Léonidas*. He died on 19 October 1826 and was buried in Père Lachaise (with more elaborate tombs in 1827 and 1837). His heart is preserved in a small casket at the Comédie française.

Talma was the outstanding neoclassical tragedian of his day. His innovations in costuming were widely copied, and though the parts he presented would seem stilted to many in a modern audience, he was praised in his lifetime for his portrayal of emotion and tragic grandeur. Germaine de Staël (*De l'Allemagne*) found his acting at once noble and natural, and he seems to have mastered techniques of breath control and declamation that were rare in the early nineteenth century. Though seen by many as a dramatic spokesman of the Revolution and, later, the Empire, his political interests seem to have stemmed largely from personal friendships and professional grievances against the theatrical system of the Old Regime.

H. F. Collins, *Talma* (London, 1964); A. Copin, *Talma*, 2 vols. (Paris, 1887); J. B. Regnault-Warin, *Mémoires sur Talma* (Paris, 1904, 1927); F.-J. Talma, *Quelques reflexions sur Lekain et sur l'art théâtrale* (Paris, 1826).

*David Longfellow*

*Related entries:* DAVID; GROS; LOUIS XVIII; STAEL-HOLSTEIN; VOLTAIRE.


*LE TAM-TAM REPUBLICAIN* (1835–1846), short-lived newspaper. A literary review, *Le Tam-Tam* led a precarious existence throughout the years 1835 to 1846. On 2 March 1848 the paper was revived with the claim to have become republican. It tried to become the spokesman for the many popular clubs founded in Paris at this time but failed to last more than a few months.

*Irene Collins*

*Related entries:* CLUBS, POLITICAL; REPUBLICANS.


**TARIFFS.** See FOREIGN TRADE AND TARIFF POLICY.


**TELEGRAPHY, AERIAL,** a means of sending messages by coded signals. Aerial telegraphy was invented in 1792 by Claude Chappe (1763–1805), a former priest and amateur scientist. The system employed a series of semaphores erected on hilltops and located approximately 10 kilometers apart. Each structure had a central movable axis with an indicator mounted on each end; pullies and ropes were used to change the position of the indicators, and each position indicated a specific letter or number. After refinements of the code in 1795 and 1829, the system could transmit 45,000 different signals. Only certain operators had possession of the code, so the system could send secret information. Approved for military use by the Convention in 1793, aerial telegraphy was limited to government transmissions until 1851, when it was opened to private use. Telegraphic links were established between Paris and Strasbourg in 1794 and between Paris and Brest two years later. A network of semaphores reached from Paris to Lyons in 1805, to Marseilles and Toulon in 1821, and to Bordeaux in 1823. The system was also adopted in Belgium, Italy, the Netherlands, Germany, and Algeria. The major handicap was the impossibility of transmitting signals at night or when bad weather limited visibility. The invention of the electric telegraph in 1838 gradually made aerial telegraphy obsolete, and it was last used during the Crimean War in 1856.

"Claude Chappe," *Grande Encyclopédie Larousse*, vol. 5 (Paris, 1973); E. Jacquez, *Claude Chappe* (Paris, 1893); R. Triger, *Claude Chappe et le centenaire du télégraphe* (Paris, 1892).

Robert Aldrich

**LE TEMPS** (1829–1842), liberal daily newspaper founded by Jacques Coste and François Guizot in October 1829; active against the Polignac government during the Restoration; Center-Right during the July Monarchy. *Le Temps* was created by François Guizot, who acted as chief editor, and Jacques Coste, who supplied some of the financing and directed the enterprise. From its start on 15 October 1829 *Le Temps*, spoke militantly against the newly chosen reactionary Polignac government and with greater freedom and hostility than the leading liberal journal, *Le Constitutionnel*. Although *Le Temps* received support from such diverse opposition sources as the marquis de Lafayette and the duc de Broglie, it came to reflect the Orleanist program of François Guizot, whose *doctrinaire* journal, *Revue française*, had provided a limited forum for similar ideas since January 1828.

What made *Le Temps* unique and influential was that it was owned by seventy-four shareholders,all of whom were deputies of the Left, including some with great fortunes, like Casimir Périer and General Emile Oberkampf. Guizot and Coste had launched an elector's newspaper, aimed directly at those most concerned with the increasingly pivotal Chamber of Deputies of the Polignac period. The new *Temps* was literate and bold and kept up a relentless assault on clericalism, Jules de Polignac's cabinet, and ultra attempts to stifle the press and to corrupt elections. Above all, the paper's editorials repeated warnings of a forthcoming coup by the king's ministers and suggested more and more pointedly the merits of an Orleanist alternative. In the Orleanist cause, Adolphe Thiers' rival *National* was more deeply involved than the *Temps*, largely because so much space in the latter was devoted to propaganda for or against certain candidates for the Chamber.

*Le Temps* also emphasized facts and statistics, and its files provide valuable data on such topics as crime, foreign tourism, education, and the number of titled deputies. The paper also exposed all of the secret agonies of the schism on the Right, in both the government and the ultra press. When liberal journals were prosecuted, *Le Temps* offered full accounts of the trials. The paper strongly supported and publicized the tax-refusal scheme of the alleged Breton Association with repeated allusions to legal resistance in the face of a coup, and it educated its readers about the Hampden case in England and the Glorious Revolution of 1688.

*Le Temps* appeared on 27 July 1830, flouting Polignac's edicts and advocating resistance to "illegal" laws. The next day, although hopeful for an Orléans solution to the crisis, the paper expressed its bourgeois fear of revolutionary excesses and called on the National Guard to mobilize.

Because Guizot and many of the deputy owners of the *Temps* had supported Louis-Philippe, the paper continued its loyalty to that monarch in the new regime. The newspaper now found itself in the Center Right, among those loyal to the much-abused Charter of 1830, and rigidly opposed to the republican and socialist Left. As part of the conservative establishment, the paper began to lose its appeal. Having risen to 4,000 subscribers in 1830 and 10,000 by February 1831, *Le Temps* had only 1,500 at the time it ceased publication in June 1842.

E. Hatin, *Histoire de la presse française*, vol. 8 (Paris, 1859–61); D. Rader, *The Journalists and the July Revolution* (The Hague, 1973).

*Daniel Rader*

*Related entries:* BROGLIE, A.-L.-V.; BRETON ASSOCIATION; *LE CONSTITUTIONNEL*; *DOCTRINAIRES*; GUIZOT; LAFAYETTE, M.-J.-P.-Y.-R.-G.; *LE NATIONAL*; OBERKAMPF; PERIER; POLIGNAC; *REVUE FRANCAISE*; ULTRAROYALISTS.

**TENDENCY, LAW OF.** See PRESS LAWS.

**TERNAUX, GUILLAUME-LOUIS, BARON** (1763–1833), textile manufacturer, deputy of the Restoration and July Monarchy. Born at Sedan (Ardennes) on 8 October 1763, Ternaux inherited and greatly expanded his father's textile manufacturing business. Although he initially supported the Revolution, he opposed the *assignats* for commercial reasons. Ternaux was elected to the municipal government of Sedan but was involved in the royalist plot led by the marquis de Lafayette, and after 10 August 1792 he emigrated. He lived first in Germany and then in England, where he carefully studied methods of textile manufacture. He returned to France during the Directory and greatly expanded his textile business, establishing factories in the departments of Maine and Eure and branches abroad. He also served on the General Council of Manufacturing. Although Ternaux opposed the life consulate and the Empire, he was decorated by Napoleon for his commercial achievements.

Ternaux welcomed the restoration of the Bourbons because he felt it meant peace. During the Hundred Days, he followed the Bourbons to Ghent and after Waterloo was named to the General Council of the department of the Seine, a post he held until 1822. In 1818 he tried unsuccessfully to establish in France varieties of sheep and goats he had imported from Tibet to aid in the manufacture of cashmere shawls of a type he created, known as *cachemere de Ternaux*. He also developed the digging of silos for grain storage. In October 1818 the department of the Seine elected him to the Chamber of Deputies, giving him more votes than Benjamin Constant, albeit with government support. This support did not, however, mean to him government tutelage. He did not hesitate to vote against the 1820 exceptional laws and against the revised electoral law. Indeed he became well known as one of the leaders of the liberal plutocracy, and his salon served as a gathering place for the Center Left. Nevertheless, in November 1819 Louis XVIII gave him the title of baron. In 1822 he was reelected to the Deputies. But he incurred the government's wrath by opposing the war in Spain, which damaged commerce, and in 1824 he was defeated for reelection. In 1825 he helped found a Saint-Simonian corporation that published a journal, *Le Producteur*. The elections in November 1827 once again returned him to the Deputies from the Seine. He now quickly allied with the liberals. Ternaux was one of the 221 who voted for the Deputies' address to the throne of March 1830. Reelected in the summer of 1830, he took an active part in the July Revolution. But shortly after he abandoned politics because of financial difficulties, and he did not stand for reelection in 1831. His political career thus came to an end. He did, however, manage to satisfy his creditors before his death in Saint-Ouen (Seine) on 2 April 1833.

*Archives parlementaires*; L. Girard, *Le Libéralisme en France de 1814 à 1848* (Paris, 1967); F. Hoefer, *Nouvelle biographie générale* (Paris, 1852–66); A. Robert et al., *Dictionnaire des parlementaires français* (Paris, 1889–91).

*James K. Kieswetter*

*Related entries:* CHAMBER OF DEPUTIES; CONSTANT; ELECTIONS AND ELECTORAL SYSTEMS; HUNDRED DAYS; INDEPENDENTS; LOUIS XVIII; REVOLUTION OF 1830; SAINT-SIMONIANISM; SPAIN, 1823 FRENCH INVASION OF; THE 221.

**THE 221,** the 221 deputies who on 16 March 1830 adopted a reply to Charles X's address, a reply criticizing the king and his cabinet. On 2 March 1830 Charles opened the 1830 legislative session with the customary speech from the throne. Its contents, however, were not customary, for Charles clearly indicated his willingness to overthrow the Charter to achieve his goals, warning he would not accept rule by the Chambers. Both Chambers then prepared their replies to this address. The Peers' address, adopted without controversy and presented on 9 March, indicated with great tact some dissatisfaction with Charles' address. The Deputies, presided over by Pierre Royer-Collard, appointed a committee, composed entirely of opposition deputies, that deliberated for several days before presenting its work on 15 March to a packed Chamber. Royer-Collard himself had intervened to make sure the draft maintained a sufficient level of dignity.

In secret session, debate and discussion began immediately. After some heated general debate and ministerial opposition, the first four paragraphs were adopted that day without much specific opposition. On 16 March as debate and voting progressed paragraph by paragraph, opposition developed to specific items. But all were adopted by a large majority, albeit with some minor amendments. Paragraph 12, however, generated heated debate, for it contained the statement that the cooperation (*concours*) Charles had demanded did not in fact exist. Louis-François de Lorgeril proposed an amendment, actually drafted by Jean-Baptiste de Martignac, which contained the same idea but was worded less bluntly. This amendment, however, was supported by no more than thirty votes. The twelfth paragraph was adopted without amendment, and the Chamber quickly approved the remaining paragraphs. The entire address was then adopted by a vote of 221 in favor and 181 opposed.

In fact the king's defeat was even greater, for the 30 who had supported the Lorgeril amendment had voted with the 181, although they supported the essence of the address. Thus Charles and his ministers had in fact only 151 real supporters in the Deputies. The royalist press immediately attacked the 221, the *Quotidienne* accusing them of issuing a manifesto to revolution. Polignac and his colleagues promptly offered their resignations, which Charles rejected. On 18 March Royer-Collard and 46 deputies presented their address to the king. He received it calmly but indicated that his resolution was inalterable. On 19 March he prorogued the Chamber.

In some circles the 221 were traitors, but in others they were heroes. On 2 April they were honored by a great banquet in Paris, attended by Center-Right monarchists as well as by the liberal Left. In the provinces the electors feted them, and medals were struck to honor their accomplishment. Charles X, however, removed those of the 221 who held government offices, including those who would have presided over electoral colleges when the dissolution of the Chamber was announced on 16 May. The reelection of the 221 became the goal of the opposition. When the election results were known, 202 of the 221 had been reelected, while only 99 of the 181 were returned. The 221 may have been overly precipitate in refusing to support the king and his cabinet, for they did not yet know precisely what the king's intentions were. But the events of July confirmed that Charles was not content to share government with the Chambers in any meaningful fashion, and thus their only alternative to complete submission to the royal will was the course they adopted, which, as the *Quotidienne* accused, was a summons to revolution.

*Archives parlementaires*; V. Beach, *Charles X of France* (Boulder, 1971); J. L. Bory, *La Révolution de juillet* (Paris, 1972); P. Duvergier de Hauranne, *Histoire du gouvernement parlementaire en France, 1814–1848* (Paris, 1857–71); D. Pinkney, *The French Revolution of 1830* (Princeton, 1972).

*James K. Kieswetter*

*Related entries:* CHAMBER OF DEPUTIES; CHAMBER OF PEERS; CHARLES X; JULY ORDINANCES; MARTIGNAC; POLIGNAC; *LA QUOTIDIENNE*; REVOLUTION OF 1830; ROYER-COLLARD.

**THEOCRATS,** counter-Revolutionary, Catholic writers from the mid-1790s until 1830 who stressed the role of a divine regulatory force in human affairs. During the course of the fierce political battles in France of the mid-1820s, the ultraroyalists and their allies in the Catholic clergy were charged by their liberal opponents with attempting to bring France under the heel of theocracy. And ever since, the term *theocratic* has been applied to the early counter-Revolutionary intellectuals, including Joseph de Maistre (1753–1821), Louis de Bonald (1754–1840), Félicité de Lamennais (1782–1854), and Pierre-Simon Ballanche (1776–1847). The starting point for theocrats was their fear of the modern liberated individual, the heir of Descartes and the dream of eighteenth- and nineteenth-century liberals: a man free to act in the world and perhaps even to conceive of the world, according to his own lights. To theocrats this was nihilism, or as they called it, individualism: destructive of all truth and reality. In order to counter the attraction of individualism, theocrats set themselves the task of demonstrating the existence of universal objective laws and of grand, all-embracing universal systems of relationship. Frequently theocrats identified their universal laws with a basic set of laws and institutions common to all peoples in all ages and most clearly expressed in passages of Scripture such as the Decalogue. Theocrats could envisage their systems as being ultimately mathematical: ternary or tripartite systems. Much of Bonald's writing is devoted to demonstrating that human reason, language, and all forms of human association function in terms of ternary or trifunctional relationships: cause-means-effect, power-minister-subject, religious society-political society-domestic society, and so on.

If theocrats blamed the Protestant Reformation for having originated individualism and the *philosophes* and the Enlightenment for having encouraged it further, they blamed the French Revolution—to their mind, the most important historical event since the birth of Christ—for having made individualism the dominant force in early nineteenth-century Europe: a force penetrating the mentality of the period and shaping the laws and institutions that had issued from the French Revolution. In the face of this seemingly overwhelming evil, theocrats were driven to make extreme statements about the presence of a divine power or force present in human affairs, keeping ever-rebellious man within the divine scheme of relationships. All nations, even Revolutionary France, could only go for a short spell, and then at the cost of much suffering, against Maistre's providence or Bonald's nature. Theocrats saw the hand of justice in the sufferings resulting from the violence and the dramatic upheavals of the Revolutionary era. Such misery was a form of expiation preparatory to the appearance of a new era of order, which, theocrats confidently predicted, was about to appear. Theocrats equated the appearance of the new era of order with the reestablishment of France's natural constitution. Supposedly this consisted of institutions that had existed from the time of Charlemagne or from the early Middle Ages until 1789: divine right monarchy; an authoritarian Catholic church dominating the spiritual, intellectual, cultural, and educational life of the nation; organicist and corporatist institutions such as the guilds; and feudalism. It would be a mistake to take the theocrats at face value. Their thought had its roots within the Enlightenment and not apart from it in some separate Catholic and royalist milieu. The real origins of their thought lay in the *inquiétude* of the eighteenth-century: in the fears of modern liberated man shared by religious conservatives, by romantics and by the *philosophes* and their liberal heirs before 1789 and after. Theocrats' authoritarian remarks notwithstanding, men such as Maistre and Bonald had welcomed the first, aristocratic, liberal phase of the French Revolution (1787–88). Such liberalism would remain entrenched though obscured in Maistre's and Bonald's thought, and it would flower spectacularly in the thought of Ballanche and the later Lamennais (from 1830 on). The theocrats' natural constitution shows the impact of Revolutionary liberal ideas, for it involves doing away with bureaucracy, reducing the monarchy to a symbolic moral force with little effective power, and in reality accepting the disappearance of feudalism and the guilds. The theocrats' concept of a cosmic force owes much more to the naturalism and romanticism of their era than to traditional Christianity. Behind the theocrats' grand schemes and their dogmatic assertions lay doubts, hesitation, searching, and that existential anguish common to most modern intellectuals.

D. Bagge, *Les Idées politiques en France sous la restauration* (Paris, 1952); F. Baldensperger, *Le Mouvement des idées dans l'émigration française* (Paris, 1924); N. E. Hudson, *Ultra-Royalism and the French Restoration* (Cambridge, Mass., 1936); S. Lukes, "The Meaning of Individualism," *Journal of the History of Ideas* 32 (1971); R. Rémond, *The Right Wing in France from 1815 to de Gaulle* (Philadelphia, 1966).

*David M. Klinck*

*Related entries:* BALLANCHE; BONALD; LAMENNAIS; MAISTRE.


**THEORY OF CLASS STRUGGLE.** See CLASS STRUGGLE, THEORY OF.


**THIERRY, AMEDEE-SIMON-DOMINIQUE** (1797–1873), historian of Gaul and Orleanist prefect. Like his famous brother, Augustin, Amédée Thierry undertook a career in education. He occupied himself with writing, was tutor to the grand-nephew of Charles-Maurice de Talleyrand, and contributed to the liberal journals of Paris during the later years of the Restoration. Writing for the *Globe* and its literary offshoot *Revue française*, Thierry supported the constitutional party.

After the appearance of his *Histoire des Gaulois* (1828), Jean-Baptiste de Martignac appointed him to the chair of history on the faculty of Besançon. His courses were too liberal for Jules de Polignac, however, who removed Thierry from his post. The liberal journal *Impartial* then took up the cause of the young historian. In Besançon, the suggested return of the *ancien régime* as represented by the appointment of Polignac was real, or so said the *Impartial*.

Thierry lived by his journalism until August 1830. As an enthusiastic supporter of the July Revolution and of Louis-Philippe, Thierry was not only returned to his position on the faculty of Besançon but was named prefect of the Haute-Saône. He continued as prefect until 1838, when he was named *maître des requêtes* to the Council of State. On the Council of State, he served each regime in succession until Napoleon III named him to the Senate (18 January 1860). He was awarded the Legion of Honor (1846), officer rank (1856), and the Grand Cross (1868).

For his work as a historian, Thierry was elected to the Institute (Académie des sciences morales et politiques) in 1841. Thierry based his work on an examination of the documents and the use of reason to determine cause and effect, and thus he was part of the nineteenth-century foundation of modern historical scholarship. Thierry published numerous works on the history of France during the Roman period and the fourth and fifth centuries.

*La Grande dictionnaire universel du 19e siècle* (Paris, 1866–90).

*Thomas Beck*

*Related entries:* ACADEMY OF SCIENCES; COUNCIL OF STATE; *LE GLOBE*; LOUIS-PHILIPPE; MARTIGNAC; POLIGNAC; REVOLUTION OF 1830; *REVUE FRANCAISE*; TALLEYRAND; THIERRY, A.

**THIERRY, JACQUES-NICOLAS-AUGUSTIN** (1795–1856), narrative historian and leader in the movement to revive and reform the writing of French history during the first half of the nineteenth century. Augustin Thierry was born in Blois on 10 May 1795, the first of three children born to Jacques Thierry, a minor civil servant and devoted Catholic. He received his early education at the Communal School and the collège de Blois, where he discovered in 1810 his future vocation as an historian while reading François-René de Chateaubriand's *Les Martyrs*. Admitted to the prestigious Ecole normale in 1811, he spent two years there, taking a special interest in eighteenth-century thought, particularly in the works of Montesquieu, Voltaire, and Rousseau. Assigned following his graduation in the fall of 1813 as a teacher to Compiègne, Thierry had to flee the town in January 1814, along with other public officials, at the approach of the invading Prussians, never to return to teaching.

Thierry became in 1814 the secretary to Henri de Saint-Simon (1760–1825). Over the course of the approximately thirty months that he stayed with this eccentric but brilliant nobleman turned philosopher, Thierry published, in collaboration with Saint-Simon or under his own name, several essays and one major work. Their *De la Réorganisation de la société européenne* (1814), in which the elderly count and his young secretary advanced an ambitious plan for perpetual peace in Europe, a sketch for a European parliament, a proposed constitutional union of England and France, and an evolutionary theory of European history, ended with a celebrated passage that placed the golden age of humanity not in the vanished past but in the near future. Thierry also assisted Saint-Simon in writing two anti-Napoleonic pamphlets and an essay highly critical of the coalition of 1815. Toward the end of his collaboration with Saint-Simon, Thierry worked on his mentor's new project, the journal *L'Industrie*, to which he contributed a major essay, "Des Nations et de leurs rapports mutuels"(1817), one of the first comprehensive statements of the nascent philosophy of industrialism.

After breaking with Saint-Simon, Thierry joined the *Censeur européen*, a celebrated liberal journal published by Charles Comte and Charles Dunoyer, to which he made numerous contributions over the course of the next three years in a continuing effort to develop and disseminate industrialism. Among these works may be found the four-part "Vue des révolutions d'Angleterre," in which Thierry advanced an interesting six-stage theory of revolution that he used to make telling analogies between England in the seventeenth century and France in the early nineteenth. At this point in his intellectual development, Thierry utilized history, particularly the study of oppressed peoples, to justify his political liberalism. When the *Censeur européen* became a daily in 1819 and 1820, the young publicist devoted most of his essays to issues of immediate political or social concern. While a major contributor to the *Censeur européen*, Thierry moved in fashionable political circles, especially in the one centered around the venerable marquis de Lafayette, which opposed the Bourbon regime, and many of his friends, publicists like Charles-Arnold Scheffer, became the target of government persecution.

Between 1820 and 1822, when the opposition to the Bourbon Restoration turned momentarily violent, Thierry took a part, albeit a minor one, in both the demonstrations of June 1820 and the Carbonari plots of 1821–22. Meanwhile, and of much greater importance for his intellectual development, he contributed in 1820 to the *Courrier français* a series, "Lettres sur l'histoire de France." Appearing at a crucial point in the renaissance of historical studies in France, these letters called for reform in the manner that French history was studied and written. In his "Lettres," Thierry criticized such well-known historians as François-Eudes de Mézerai, Louis-Pierre Anquetil, the abbé Velly, and those of the philosophical school, contending that history should be written as a narrative enriched with local color, just as Walter Scott wrote his novels, and that future historians of France should stress the development of liberty and the hitherto neglected heroic role of the French nation. This bold campaign in favor of a new French history aroused so many enemies that the *Courrier français* prudently discontinued Thierry's "Lettres."

Beginning in 1821, Thierry devoted four years to researching and writing his magnum opus, *Histoire de la conquête d'Angleterre*, published in 1825. To the preparation of this work, Thierry devoted monumental energy, undertaking such exhausting original research that he damaged his health and his eyesight, the result being that he had to employ a series of secretaries; of these, the first was Armand Carrel, later to win fame as one of the editors of the *National*. Influenced by both David Hume, from whom Thierry borrowed the idea of interpreting English history as the outgrowth of the Norman conquest, and Walter Scott, Thierry explained that his purpose in tracing the history of England from the establishment of the Britons to the execution of the last Saxon rebel in 1196 was to reveal the national struggle between the conquering Normans and the conquered Saxons that followed the Norman invasion and that persisted until the two peoples had so mixed that there existed in England only one people, one language, and one set of laws. This racial interpretation of history as a struggle between oppressor and oppressed, an idea that became one of the most controversial aspects of Thierry's historical thought, was later applied to French history. Thierry's sympathies lay so evidently with the conquered Saxons that the *Conquête* has been justly called an "epic of the vanquished." Although so exhausted by the work he devoted to the *Conquête* that he had to take a rest cure in 1825 and 1826, Thierry must have been pleased at the almost universal praise accorded his two volumes by the French people and the press.

Upon his return to Paris in 1826, Thierry began work, in collaboration with his brother Amédée and François Mignet, on a collection of documents on medieval history to be called *La Grande chronique de France*. When the project was abandoned, Thierry turned to a revision and enlargement of his "Lettres" of 1820. As before, the historian exhausted himself in preparing two editions of *Lettres sur l'histoire de France* for publication in 1827. To his earlier themes, Thierry added a notable new emphasis on the emancipation of the medieval communes.

Between 1828 and 1835, Thierry lived remote from Paris, spending most of his time with his brother, appointed prefect of the Haute-Saône after the Revolution of 1830, at Vesoul. During the early years of the July Monarchy, Thierry, who had married in 1831, hoped in vain for a government appointment similar to those received by many of his friends and contemporaries. He did, however, receive in May 1831 a seat in the Académie des inscriptions. Meanwhile, he collected some of the essays he had published in the *Censeur européen* and the *Courrier français* and published them, together with an important autobiographical preface, as *Dix ans d'études historiques*. Finally, in May 1834, François Guizot arranged to have the now-blind Thierry named to a commission charged to assemble and publish documents pertaining to the history of the Third Estate; he was also named librarian to the duc d'Orléans. Happily returned to Paris, Thierry continued his work on a series of essays collected in the popular *Récits des temps mérovingiens* of 1840, to which he added an important preface, "Considérations sur l'histoire de France." These episodes, derived largely from Gregory of Tours, which imaginatively brought to life the brutal realities of the Merovingian era, emphasized one of Thierry's favorite themes, the conflict between Gallo-Roman civilization and Frankish barbarism. In "Considérations," he argued that the heart of the French nation was Gallo-Roman in origin. Although the death of his beloved wife in 1844 brought him much mental anguish, Thierry nevertheless continued his studies of the Third Estate and published from time to time excerpts from his work.

The Revolutions of 1848 produced a crisis not only for France but for Thierry's thought, for he had long believed that the government of the July Monarchy was the providential culmination of French history. At this late point in life, perhaps as a result of this blow to his beliefs, perhaps as a result of his long physical sufferings, Thierry turned back to the religion of his youth, and, when he completed a final revision of *Conquête*, he had removed passages particularly offensive to the church. During these final years, the historian published "Essai sur l'histoire de la formation et des progrès du Tiers Etat" and the first three volumes of *Recueil des monuments inédits de l'histoire du Tiers Etat*. In these mature works, Thierry largely abandoned his emphasis on the conquest theory and wrote rather about the gradual rise of the Third Estate in France and the concomitant fall of aristocratic barriers. Augustin Thierry died in Paris on 22 May 1856.

Of the themes that run through Thierry's historical works, several merit special emphasis. From his earliest writings in the *Censeur européen* and the *Courrier français* to his last works, Thierry consistently defended the idea of liberty, and he usually identified it with the people. His conception of liberty nevertheless evolved over time, a trend clearly evident in the historian's changing treatment of the Catholic church and the absolutist state. In the "Lettres" of 1820 and the first edition of *Conquête* (1825), Thierry wrote harshly of the church, and he considered the state as an institution of oppression imposed on the people by military conquest. By the end of his life, the historian had softened considerably his position on both church and state, as is evident in the final version of *Conquête* (1856). Between 1814 and 1822, when Thierry took an active role in the various political movements opposed to the Bourbon Restoration, he showed considerable enthusiasm for a second theme, a constitutional government on the English model, and for republicanism. By the end of the Restoration, he had retreated from these youthful opinions, and after 1830 he considered the July Monarchy as the providential conclusion of French history.

Thierry frequently revised his writings, an awareness that should always be present in the mind of the modern reader. Throughout his long career as a historian, from his 1820 essay "Jacques Bonhomme" to his monumental works on the Third Estate, many of Thierry's themes did not change, and one of these is a profound sympathy for the common people. In his historical writings, he sought to resurrect their lives and to fill the gap occasioned by their exclusion from traditional French historical writing. The concern with the people led, at least in part, to his controversial racial interpretations of French and English history. Finally, in all of his works, Thierry sought a new method of historical writing, one that combined imaginative art and scientific erudition. Undertaking voluminous research in original sources, Thierry presented the results of his studies by blending together local color, a compelling narrative, and engaging character studies. To the enduring popularity of his works, the recent publication of an English translation of the *Récits* bears eloquent testimony.

A. Augustin-Thierry, *Augustin Thierry d'après sa correspondance et ses papiers de famille* (Paris, 1922); E. Engel-Janosi, "Augustin Thierry's Road to History," in *Four Studies in French Romantic Historical Writing*, (Baltimore, 1955); L. Gossman, "Augustin Thierry and Liberal Historiography," *History and Theory* 15 (1966); C. Jullian, "Augustin Thierry et le mouvement historique sous la Restauration," *Revue de synthèse historique* 13 (1960); B. Reizov, *L'Historiographie romantique française (1815–1830)* (Moscow, n.d.); R. N. Smithson, *Augustin Thierry: Social and Political Consciousness in the Evolution of a Historical Method* (Geneva, 1973); A. Thierry, *Oeuvres complètes*, 10 vols (Paris, 1846–56).

*Robert Brown*

*Related entries:* CARBONARI; CARREL; *LE CENSEUR EUROPEEN; LE COURRIER FRANCAIS*; DUNOYER; GUIZOT; LAFAYETTE, M.-J.-P.-Y.-R.-G.; MIGNET; *LE NATIONAL*; REVOLUTION OF 1830; REVOLUTION OF 1848; SAINT-SIMON; SCHEFFER, C.-A.; THIERRY, A.-S.-D.

**THIERS, LOUIS-ADOLPHE** (1797–1877), journalist, historian, and politician who occupied a central position in French political life between the early 1820s and the 1870s. Born on 18 April 1797 to Marie-Madeleine Amic and Pierre-

Louis-Marie Thiers, Adolphe Thiers entered life in a proper bourgeois milieu, although his wastrel of a father promptly deserted his infant son. Raised by his mother and an aunt, Thiers received the bulk of his early schooling at the lycée of Marseilles, where children no longer received a traditional classical education but one decreed by the Emperor Napoleon that emphasized Latin, mathematics, topography, geography, and history. During his years at the lycée, Thiers realized that he lacked suitability for a military career; perhaps fortunately for him, the Napoleonic wars ended before he completed his teens. Leaving the lycée in September 1815, Thiers moved to Aix-en-Provence to commence legal studies, and there he made the acquaintance of François Mignet (1796–1884), destined to be his lifelong friend. While a student in Aix, Thiers revealed, by his expressed admiration for the Roman Republic and by penning a tragedy on the subject of Tiberius Gracchus, an early propensity for liberal opinions. He also won the friendship of two local notables, and to them Thiers spoke of his admiration for Danton. Both Thiers and Mignet completed their studies in 1818, gained admittance to the local bar, and began to practice law.

The ambitious Thiers, ever alert for an opportunity to enhance his reputation, learned that the Academy of Aix had offered a prize for the best essay on Vauvenargues, an eighteenth-century moralist. Thiers won the prize in 1821 but not before he and his patrons resorted to a clever deception that concealed from the judges, biased against Thiers on political grounds, the identity of the winning essay's author. In September 1821, Adolphe Thiers, aged twenty-four but possessed of a local reputation, set out to conquer Paris; he thus joined Mignet, who had arrived in the French capital some two months earlier. The two young provincials found cheap lodgings and began their campaign.

Between 1821 and 1830, Adolphe Thiers worked diligently in a number of fields, among them journalism, the writing of history, and the cultivation of the powerful; within nine years, he had placed himself near the center of French political life. Provided with a letter of introduction to the notorious liberal Jacques Manuel, Thiers quickly gained admittance to important opposition circles. In November 1821, he succeeded in impressing Charles-Guillaume Etienne of the *Constitutionnel* and received a position on the staff of this large and influential opposition newspaper. The diminutive Thiers—he stood just over five feet tall—made the most of his opportunities, showing both an extreme self-confidence and an immense capacity for study and work. His typical day began at five and included six hours of study in the morning, afternoons in the offices of the *Constitutionnel*, and evenings in the fashionable liberal salons. During 1822, Thiers wrote widely, publishing articles on politics, literature, history, and even art. Late in that year, an opportunity arose, and Thiers used it to build his reputation. As a consequence of the great political controversy centered on the decision of the government, and approved by the European powers at the Congress of Verona, to dispatch troops to suppress a revolution in Spain, the *Constitutionnel* sent Thiers to report on the situation. For three months (October–December 1822), Thiers traveled, and, upon his return to Paris, he published *Les Pyrénées et le Midi de la France pendant les mois de novembre et decembre 1822*, a book that revealed Thiers' careful attention to detail and his powers as a descriptive writer. Indications of Thiers' growing fame as a spokesman for the liberal opposition came from the fact that the police maintained a careful surveillance of the young traveler. As Thiers' reputation grew, he attracted the attention of rich, powerful, and influential men; from their sponsorship, the young man's career as a journalist and historian greatly benefited. He won the favorable notice of Charles-Maurice de Talleyrand in 1822, and then he attracted the eye of the Baron Cotta, an influential and well-known German publisher. For Baron Cotta, Thiers wrote articles for the *Gazette d'Augsbourg*; in return, Cotta provided Thiers with the money necessary to become a voting shareholder with a voice in determining the policies of the *Constitutionnel*. Meanwhile, Thiers was hard at work on yet another project, one that would bring him public recognition, lasting fame, and considerable wealth.

Adolphe Thiers undertook, the first member of the generation that had not personally experienced the Revolution to do so, to write a long and serious narrative history of the French Revolution. On 22 February 1822, he signed a contract with Lecointe and Durey, noted publishers of popular histories, for just such a history; the first two volumes appeared just twenty months later in September 1823. Published near the end of the reign of Louis XVIII, at a time when both nobles and monarchy were enjoying a resurgence under the Villèle government and when liberals and other opposition groups had chosen the extreme path of revolutionary conspiracy, and coming from the pen of a man with a nascent reputation as an outspoken critic of the Bourbon regime, Thiers' *History* could hardly escape being a work with a content as much political as historical. Particularly evident in the first two volumes, this political message combined a vigorous defense of the early Revolution and the Constitution of 1791, a condemnation of the excesses of the Revolution and Maximilien Robespierre, and a deep-seated suspicion of the popular crowd. In the later volumes, the tenth and final of which appeared in 1827, which carried the history of the Revolution to 18 Brumaire, Thiers took greater care with this research. Since extensive published sources pertaining to the Revolution were lacking in the mid-1820s, Thiers consulted men and women who had witnessed or studied the Revolution; for military affairs, he turned to the great Antoine-Henride Jomini and to General Maximilien-Sébastien Foy; for financial matters, he consulted the baron Louis; and for diplomatic concerns, he turned to Talleyrand. This work rewarded Thiers handsomely, for not only did publication of the *History* greatly enhance his reputation, it also brought him considerable financial reward, perhaps 57,000 francs by 1830.

Thiers' historical writings provide some clues to his political opinions during the Restoration era; from his journalism, more can be gleaned. He favored, first and foremost, a constitutional monarchy, and he steadfastly opposed the idea of legitimacy. Despite opinions that aligned him with the opposition to the Bourbons, Thiers never became a conspirator or a revolutionary, for inseparable from his profound love of liberty was an abiding love of system and order. Not until 1830 were Thiers' convictions tested, and not until 1830 did it become clear what action Thiers would undertake when compelled to defend his beliefs.

Between 1824 and 1829, Thiers worked harder than ever. He published essays on art in the *Globe*, and he wrote, with Talleyrand as his behind-the-scenes source, the political bulletins for the *Tablettes universelles*. Further, for the influential banker Jacques Laffitte, Thiers wrote *Réflexions sur l'état de la rente et sur l'état du crédit*. Prior to finishing the *Révolution français* in 1827, he undertook plans for not only a history of the Consulate and the Empire but also for a universal history. Thiers' decision to depart in 1830 on an around-the-world cruise changed suddenly when the moderate Martignac ministry fell and was replaced by the reactionary government of Jules de Polignac.

The advent of the Polignac ministry convinced Thiers and others of similar convictions of the need for a vigorous campaign of opposition to the government. Unable to persuaded his colleagues at the *Constitutionnel* to take this bolder line, Thiers, with the assistance of François Mignet and Armand Carrel (1800–1836) and with the probable backing of wealthy opposition leaders, founded the *National* late in 1829. The first issue of the new paper appeared on 3 January 1830, and, over the course of the next seven months, the *National* stood at the forefront of the ever-stronger opposition to the government of Charles X. With its bold and sensational criticism of the existing regime, Thiers and the *National* proposed to educate France. The paper demanded a true constitutional monarchy on the English model, true ministerial responsibility, and the right of the lower house to refuse a budget. Thiers insisted on the parallel between the situation in France in 1830 and that of England in 1688, even suggesting that Charles X could be replaced by the duc d'Orléans and that such a change would not be revolutionary. Finally, he proclaimed his famous definition of the role of the king in an ideal constitutional monarchy: "Le roi regne et ne gouverne pas."

The July Ordinances of Charles X, two of which threatened the existence of newspapers like the *Constitutionnel* and the *National*, if they caught Thiers by surprise, converted him from a man who had opposed the Bourbon regime with his pen into a man of action. On 26 July, when angry journalists gathered in the offices of the *National* to discuss a response to the ordinances, it was Thiers who persuaded his colleagues that only a signed statement of protest would be an effective response. He promptly drafted a document in which he denounced the ordinances as illegal and called on Paris to resist. During the remainder of that day and most of the next, Thiers tried to rally opposition to the government while counseling against mob action and bloodshed. Late in the evening of 27 July, after he was warned that a warrant had been issued for his arrest, Thiers, accompanied by Mignet and Carrel, fled Paris, not returning until the early morning hours of 29 July. Fearing that events might get completely out of hand and that a republic might be proclaimed, Thiers spent Thursday trying to convince deputies and other liberal leaders that the only way to avoid a republic was to make the duc d'Orléans king. During that afternoon, Thiers and Mignet drew up the famous poster that extolled the virtues of Orléans and that called on Frenchmen to make him their king. The next day, the deputies assembled at Laffitte's house dispatched Thiers to Neuilly to ascertain the duke's position. Orléans being prudently absent, Thiers spoke with his sister and entreated her to convince the duke of the need to accept the crown. Thiers returned to Paris and the waiting deputies with a vague promise of the duke's acceptance. In short, while avoiding the fighting of the Three Glorious Days, Thiers both helped ignite the Revolution of 1830 and bring it to an end. He would soon have his reward.

Like many of his generation, Thiers received ample recompense for the risks he had taken during the July Revolution. Between 1830 and 1848, he held several important ministerial portfolios and served twice as chief minister. Named to the Council of State immediately after the Revolution, he also obtained a minor post in the Ministry of Finance; by his customary hard work, Thiers soon advanced and became an undersecretary. Elected to the Chamber of Deputies in 1830, he served there throughout the July Monarchy. In these offices and the others he held during the early days of the Orleanist regime, Thiers contributed much to the consolidation of the new monarchy. Twice Thiers served as minister of the interior, once in 1832 and again in 1834–36, and in this position he proved to be a formidable enemy of disorder, whether emanating from the Right or the Left. He pursued the duchesse de Berry and her legitimist followers with a vigor equal to that with which he persecuted the republicans. In 1834, after supporting the law of 10 April 1834 designed to restrict political activity, he mercilessly crushed rebellions in Paris (during which took place the infamous massacre of the rue Transnonain) and the uprising in Lyons. After the attempt by Fieschi on the life of Louis-Philippe, Thiers forcefully argued for the repressive September Laws. While minister of public works between 1833 and 1834, he strove to make Paris a great and beautiful city, completing, for example, the Arc de triomphe. He also contemplated plans for the fortification of the French capital. Thiers' first ministry, which lasted but six months in 1836, accomplished little, for he lacked both a coherent policy and a clear majority. In foreign affairs, Thiers tried to curry favor with Austria, Prussia, and Russia. When, however, plans for a marriage between the son of Louis-Philippe and a Habsburg archduchess collapsed, Thiers turned against the Austrians and even suggested military intervention in Spain to vex Habsburg ambitions there. Louis-Philippe repudiated this policy, and Thiers resigned. His second ministry (March–October 1840) was hardly more successful. In the complex Eastern question, Thiers backed Méhémet Ali and thus brought France close to war with England. Louis-Philippe again undercut his minister, bringing down Thiers' government. Thiers' ministry was memorable, however, because he arranged to have the mortal remains of Napoleon returned to France for burial in the Invalides. Thiers, it should not be forgotten, also participated in the notorious coalition with François Guizot and Odilon Barrot that caused the collapse of Molé's ministry in 1839.

Between 1840 and 1848, Thiers was out of office and, as the leader of the Left-Center, in perpetual opposition to both the foreign and domestic policies of Guizot's various governments. Thiers' differences with Guizot, while partially personal, centered on opposing interpretations of the Revolution of 1830. To Thiers, it signified the beginning of a slow evolutionary process that would eventually broaden the base of the Orleanist monarchy by giving the vote to the middle and lower bourgeoisie; to Guizot, the revolution brought a settlement that required no significant modifications. Because of his virtual exclusion from the center of political life, Thiers frequently absented himself from public affairs and worked on *History of the Consulate and the Empire*, which he had begun in 1838 or 1839. The first two of this massive work's twenty volumes appeared in 1845, the last some seventeen years later in 1862. But Thiers could not remain separated for long from political life. Toward the end of 1845, he and Odilon Barrot united the Left-Center and the dynastic Left in an electoral compact that pledged both men to demand electoral and parliamentary reforms. In 1847, the two men temporarily joined with the republicans in support of the Banquet Campaign. Thiers remained prudently in the background while Barrot did the speaking. The Revolution of 1848, which he had unintentionally helped bring about, caught Thiers unprepared. At the very last minute, shortly after midnight on 24 February, Louis-Philippe summoned Thiers and charged him and Barrot to form a ministry. This effort to save the July Monarchy floundered, and Thiers found that events in the streets were far beyond his control. Thiers had miscalculated in 1848, for he helped bring down a regime with which he largely agreed by his attacks on the king's exercise of power and his foreign policies.

During the troubled years of the Second Republic, Thiers became more conservative as he changed from a reluctant supporter of a moderate republic to a backer of Louis-Napoleon. Not surprisingly, the Provisional Government of 1848 found no place for Adolphe Thiers. Returned to the Constituent Assembly in June, Thiers spoke frequently, often to the applause of the conservatives, of his opposition to communistic ideas and to notions of universal manhood suffrage. In August 1848, he ardently defended the idea of private property against proposals made by the anarchist Joseph Proudhon. To strengthen his position, he also published *De La Propriété*, a book written in the remarkably short span of three months. During the debates over the proposed Constitution of 1848, Thiers attacked both the clause guaranteeing to all the right to work and the one that called for universal conscription. Despite the urging of some of his political backers, Thiers not only refused to run in the presidential elections of 1848 but also gave his support, albeit at the last minute, to Louis-Napoleon. Like so many others, Thiers misread the character of this prince; he had believed that his election would produce a weak executive and open the possibility for the return of the Orléans family. Although Thiers did not enter Louis-Napoleon's government, he frequently backed the government's positions between 1849 and 1851. In 1850, allied with Louis-Mathieu de Molé and Charles-Forbes de Montalembert, Thiers helped amend the electoral law to take the franchise from some 30 percent of the population, to remove, to use his words, the "vile multitude" from the voting lists. He also supported the Falloux Law (1850), which greatly strengthened clerical control over French education; Thiers now saw the church as a bulwark of the social order. These essentially conservative positions notwithstanding, Thiers astutely perceived the threat posed to France by Louis-Napoleon. In a speech of 17 January 1851, he warned that the slow but steady increase of presidential power would end in the creation of a new empire. Thus identified as an opponent of Louis-Napoleon's aspirations, Thiers was among the first to be arrested early on the morning of 2 December 1851. Although released from prison four days later, Thiers was banished from France and forced to leave his homeland for a temporary exile of two years.

Adolphe Thiers again served France following the disasters of 1870 and 1871. Although he had at first supported war with Prussia, Thiers later changed his mind and escaped blame for this fiasco. In the creation of the Third Republic, he played a major role, becoming its first president in 1871. He also used brutal force to suppress the Commune. Having resigned the presidency in 1873, Thiers joined the republican opposition. He died on 3 September 1877.

J. M. S. Allison, *Thiers and the French Monarchy* (London, 1926; reprinted, 1968); R. Christophe, *Le Siècle de Monsieur Thiers* (Paris, 1966); H. Malo, *Thiers, 1797–1877* (Paris, 1932); R. Marquant, *Thiers et le Baron Cotta. Etude sur la collaboration de Thiers à la* Gazette d'Augsbourg (Paris, 1959); C. H. Pomaret, *Monsieur Thiers et son Temps* (Paris, 1948).

*Robert Brown*

*Related entries:* ADELAIDE; ARC DE TRIOMPHE DE L'ETOILE; BANQUET CAMPAIGN; BARROT, C.-H.-O.; BERRY, M.-C.; CARREL; *LE CONSTITUTIONNEL*; FALLOUX LAW; FIESCHI PLOT; FOREIGN POLICY OF LOUIS-PHILIPPE; FOY; *LE GLOBE*; GUIZOT; JULY ORDINANCES; LAFFITTE; LOUIS, J.-D.; LYONS, REVOLTS IN; MANUEL; MARTIGNAC; MEHEMET ALI; MIGNET; MOLE; MONTALEMBERT; *LE NATIONAL*; POLIGNAC; PROUDHON; SPAIN, 1823 FRENCH INVASION OF; TALLEYRAND; *LES TABLETTES UNIVERSELLES*; TRANSNONAIN, MASSACRE OF THE RUE; VERONA, CONGRESS OF; VILLELE.

**THIESSE, LEON** (1793–1854), liberal publicist and prefect of Louis-Philippe. Son of an *avocat au parlement de Normandie* who was elected to the Council of 500 (1797) and sat in the Tribunate (1800–1802), Léon Thiéssé was an *homme de lettres*. He was educated in the lycée of Rouen before he moved to Paris. Although he was admitted to the bar of Paris, Thiéssé's true interest was literature. A classicist, he was an editor of the works of Voltaire and wrote *Essai sur Etienne*, and in 1814 he shared the Tissot prize. In 1816, Thiéssé became the first to translate into French the work of Lord Byron (*Vierge d'Abydos*).

As a moralist with deep political convictions, Thiéssé became a liberal harpooner of the regime of Louis XVIII. His journal, *Lettres normandes*, founded in 1820, wavered between liberalism and Bonapartism. One of his most celebrated pieces was a satire on the 21 January remembrance practiced by the ultras. This satire drew the attack of François de La Bourdonnaye and was ordered destroyed by the courts (17 March 1820). Through his contributions to the *Constitutionnel* and such works as *Manuel des braves ou Victoires des armées françaises* (1817–19), Thiéssé became one of the best-known publicists of the Restoration.

His devotion to liberalism earned him the prefecture of the Deux-Sèvres and then that of the Basses-Alpes under Louis-Philippe. After serving the regime faithfully until 1841, Thiéssé retired to his studies. His major work was the *Ouevres* of Etienne published in 1853. Thiéssé's son served the third Republic as a deputy of the Center Left (1876–89).

*Le Grand dictionnaire universel du 19e siècle* (Paris, 1866–90).

*Thomas Beck*

*Related entries:* BYRON; *LE CONSTITUTIONNEL*; LA BOURDONNAYE; *LES LETTRES NORMANDES;* LOUIS XVIII; LOUIS-PHILIPPE; ULTRA-ROYALISTS; VOLTAIRE.

**THOMAS, PIERRE-EMILE** (1822–1880), civil engineer and director of the National Workshops (March–May 1848). At the age of twenty-six, Emile Thomas achieved a position of power for a period of three months. He lived the remainder of his life in obscurity. A former student at the Ecole centrale des arts et manufactures, imbued with a devotion to his school, a supreme self-confidence, and a talent for organization, Thomas seized one of the rare opportunities that revolutions sometimes produce to have an immediate impact on events. On 3 March 1848 the young civil engineer of the Bridge and Road Service submitted a plan to the new Provisional Government of France for organizing the laborers of Paris in the newly founded National Workshops. His enthusiasm for a military-type organization captivated Alexandre-Thomas Marie, the minister of public works, and Etienne Garnier-Pagès, the mayor of Paris. Two days later Thomas won over the mayors of the twelve arrondissements of Paris, and after asking for four days to get organized, he took over as the director of the National Workshops.

The Chateau Monceau, now the Parc Monceau, became the headquarters of this effort to solve the unemployment problems of the capital. Designed to provide food and a wage in return for work on national projects, the National Workshops soon enrolled 100,000 men, although the early estimates predicted only 10,000. Thomas thus became the commander of a potential army of 100,000 workers in a time of turmoil and political uncertainty. Unfortunately the politically inexperienced Thomas had no ability to produce the jobs that he was expected to supply. To Thomas's credit, he had made it clear from the beginning that his plans could succeed only if the men had work. Nevertheless, Marie told him to enroll everyone regardless of the cost, while supplying only about 10,000 jobs. Even the jobs that were available were not well suited for most of the men. The jobs were most often of a menial nature, and the majority of the men were skilled artisans. Thus, the workshops became a dole, which angered these proud men and many others as well. The workers wanted real jobs, and the taxpayers hated to pay "the socialists" for doing nothing.

Thomas set up the workshops with ten-man squads and an elected leader. Five squads composed a brigade, and four brigades made up a lieutenance; both levels elected their own commanders. At the next level of organization, the company, composed of four lieutenances, the leadership was provided by students from the Ecole centrale des arts et manufactures. The top of the hierarchy was a service, which was composed of three companies and also led by a student engineer of the Ecole centrale. This highly centralized system was supposed to be held together by the moral force of the students. Surprisingly enough, it worked fairly well through March and April. Some disputes, especially over who made technical decisions, developed, however, between the students of the Ecole centrale and their traditional professional rivals from the Ecole polytechnique, who controlled most government projects through their hold over the Bridge and Road Service.

Politically Thomas was a moderate. He opposed Louis Blanc and the men of the Luxembourg Commission, yet Thomas was no monarchist. He defended order and did his best on 17 March and 16 April to keep his men away from the antigovernment demonstrations. He used the wages of the workshops to prevent his men from joining socialist clubs, and he even set up his own workers' club, the Réunion centrale des ateliers nationaux, on 30 March. The Réunion was organized like a workers' parliament, and Thomas was often the main speaker. It failed, however, to have a significant impact on the workers.

In the elections of April, Thomas received 28,166 votes from the citizens of Paris, far from enough for election. Thomas, however, had supported the moderate republicans and had not campaigned for himself. In fact, he had used the men of the workshops to promote the moderates. Some workers were paid to distribute handbills, and others were encouraged to disrupt meetings of the opposition.

The victory of the monarchists in April placed Thomas in a precarious position. The majority of the Assembly wanted not just order in the streets but also a return to obedience on the part of the laboring classes. Thomas, as commander of 100,000 workers, was in a position to lead the workers against any attempt to abridge the rights of the working classes. The potential conflict became real on 15 May, when despite Thomas's orders many men from the workshops participated in the invasion of the Assembly. The moralizing of student engineer commanders was wearing thin for men without work. The government lost its faith that Thomas would or could maintain the workers' support for the government.

In May the Labor Committee of the new Assembly created a subcommittee composed of Charles Beslay, Victor Considérant, and Alfred-Frédéric de Falloux to review the National Workshops. Falloux dominated the proceedings. Thomas was given just half an hour to defend his work, and the committee recommended the abolition of the workshops rather than follow Thomas's suggestion to make the workshops independent of the Ministry of Public Works. Ulysse Trélat, the new minister of public works, took Thomas's suggestion as a threat, and on 26

May Trélat dismissed the director. Rather than allow Thomas to become the focus of worker discontent, Trélat ordered Thomas to undertake an inspection of conditions in Marseilles immediately. Thomas was not even allowed to inform his mother of his departure, which followed directly after his evening meeting with Trélat. The mysterious disappearance of the still-popular Thomas caused alarm among the workers, and once the facts were known, the action was condemned by nearly everyone. Trélat wanted Thomas out of the way until the by-elections of 4 June were completed. Trélat thus created the first irreparable split between the workers and the government.

Thomas was kept occupied in the provinces while the threatened dissolution of the workshops led to the bloody June Days in Paris. During the Second Republic, he wrote for *Dix décembre* and after the coup d'état of 2 December 1851 Thomas returned to his career as a civil engineer.

E. Thomas, *Histoire des ateliers nationaux considérés sous le double point de vue politique et social* (Paris, 1848, Oxford, 1913).

*Thomas Beck*

*Related entries:* BESLAY; BLANC; BRIDGE AND ROAD SERVICE; CONSIDERANT; DEMONSTRATIONS OF 1848–1849; ECOLE CENTRALE DES ARTS ET MANUFACTURES; ECOLE POLYTECHNIQUE; GARNIER-PAGES, ETIENNE; LUXEMBOURG COMMISSION; MARIE; NATIONAL WORKSHOPS; REPUBLICANS; TRELAT.

**THREE GLORIOUS DAYS.** See REVOLUTION OF 1830.

**TISSOT, PIERRE-FRANCOIS** (1768–1854), classical scholar, historian, journalist, lawyer, and politician. A student of the classics, Tissot studied the law to support himself and rose to become a prosecutor in the Châtelet court. At his leisure, he continued his studies, which focused on classic poetry and the history of Louis XIV's age. With the Revolution he joined the Cordeliers and got a job in the War Ministry after marrying the sister of Jean-Marie Goujon of the Mountain faction. The coup of Thermidor led to a death sentence for his patron Goujon, but Tissot escaped harm because he knew Paul de Barras and Jean-Lambert Tallien. In the Year VI, he was elected deputy, but the Chamber expelled him. He was almost implicated in the Nivôse conspiracy, but again his connections, now including Joseph Fouché, saved him. He held some lucrative academic posts in the Consulate and Empire and was able to help several writers and poets by hiring them in the bureaucracy.

In 1810 he entered journalism as one of Napoleon's special editors, appointed to supervise the *Gazette*. With the Restoration of 1814, he was dismissed and reentered academic life. Tissot returned to journalism in 1820 when he purchased *Le Pilote*, a small commercial journal, and created a new voice of opposition against the increasingly reactionary program of the ultras. Tissot was prosecuted in 1823 for his editorials and, as his own lawyer, successfully defended himself. The Villèle ministry, however, abolished his academic tenure and in 1824 "amortized," or bought out, *Le Pilote*. Tissot wrote articles for several other opposition newspapers and magazines, as well as popular historical accounts of the Revolution and Empire and a preface to a new edition of Voltaire's works.

After the 1830 Revolution, Tissot regained his professorship at the Collège de France and was elected to the Academy in 1833, ostensibly for his translations and commentaries on Virgil, first published in 1822.

F. Michaud, *Biographie Universelle* (Paris, 1859–61).

*Daniel Rader*

*Related entries:* ACADEMIE FRANCAISE; COLLEGE DE FRANCE; FOUCHE; *LA GAZETTE DE FRANCE*; *LE PILOTE*; RESTORATION, FIRST; REVOLUTION OF 1830; ULTRAROYALISTS; VILLELE; VOLTAIRE.

**TOCQUEVILLE, ALEXIS DE** (1805–1859), social and political theorist, historian, observer of America, and political figure during the July Monarchy and Second Republic. Tocqueville was born into an aristocratic family of strong royalist sympathies. He was tutored by the abbé Lesueur, a man of traditional Catholic faith and morality, who gained the profound affection of his charge and helped to instill in Tocqueville a lifelong respect for religion and matters of faith. As a young man he also served as secretary to his father, Hervé comte de Tocqueville, an able prefect under the Restoration. Tocqueville began early, however, to exhibit a more independent and liberal point of view. Adolescent reading had led to a rejection of much of Catholic dogma. By the late 1820s he was critical of the reactionary policies pursued by Charles X. At this time, François Guizot's lectures on the history of France and Europe also attracted his attention, introducing him to the seminal concept of the rise of the middle classes. Trained as a lawyer and appointed in 1827 as *juge auditeur* at Versailles, Tocqueville's fledging career was interrupted by the 1830 Revolution. Despite the disapproval of his family and members of his aristocratic circle, he swore an oath of allegiance to the new regime.

In 1831 Tocqueville and his friend and fellow lawyer, Gustave de Beaumont, secured permission for a government-sponsored mission to the United States, then at the forefront of prison reform, for the purpose of studying the U.S. prison system. From May 1831 to February 1832 Tocqueville and Beaumont traveled in the United States, visiting all areas of the country (including the frontier) and meeting a great number of ordinary and leading Americans, both Jacksonians and Whigs. The two companions completed a thorough examination of prisons, but the true purpose of their journey was to observe the young Republic. They were fascinated by the United States as the society of the future and as a possible source of lessons for Europeans. Tocqueville and Beaumont hoped to write something about the United States that would be useful to France and would help to advance their political careers.

Out of that voyage came two of Tocqueville's books. The first, coauthored with Beaumont, was their official report, *Du Système pénitentiaire aux Etats-Unis et de son application en France* (1833), which quickly became influential in prison reform circles throughout Europe. The second book was Tocqueville's masterpiece, *De la Démocratie en Amérique*, published in two parts (1835 and 1840), which immediately established Tocqueville's reputation and fame. Tocqueville at age thirty was acclaimed by some as another Montesquieu. In 1841 he was elected to the Académie française.

A key element in the significance and originality of the *Democracy* is its character as a systematic study of the United States. For the first time, Tocqueville's countrymen had a thorough and informative portrait of the United States to replace vague impressions. So concise and astute was Tocqueville's analysis of the Constitution and political institutions of the United States, for example, that throughout much of the nineteenth century it was used to teach American schoolchildren.

The *Democracy* is more than a book about the United States. Written during an eight-year period of reflection, it is a profound and provocative work of social and political theory. A multifaceted study, it offers no single, systematic political philosophy and is at times marred by elusive definitions and overly elaborate deductions. But it presents ideas that would remain essential to all of Tocqueville's subsequent thinking and writing. It introduces his great theme of advancing equality and its possible results, beneficial and harmful. By way of the example of the United States, Tocqueville attempted to show how to foster the former and prevent the latter. In the book, he clarifies the tension between equality and liberty and explores the complex ways in which *démocratie*, centralization, and *individualisme* are linked. Advancing equality, he warned, could easily lead to a new tyranny of the masses and a new despotism of the bureaucratic state. To avoid these threats, Tocqueville urged respect for the freedom and dignity of the individual (civil and political liberties), widespread participation in public life, and heightened moral values that would counteract the selfish and materialistic tendencies of democratic society. The 1840 portion of his book in particular examines the broader cultural and social implications of equality; there especially Tocqueville shows himself as a social theorist of the first rank.

The *Democracy* also carries an explicit message for Tocqueville's compatriots. Although he often expressed his distaste for politics and for the leading political figures of the July Monarchy, Tocqueville was a man of intense political ambition. The pages of his book therefore offer a political program for France centering on a revival of responsible political participation at the local level. His attention also turned increasingly during the late 1830s to the issue of the French revolutionary condition and its possibly chronic nature. So he attempted as well, in the *Democracy*, to distinguish between the effects of advancing equality and the consequences of the revolutionary spirit that so marked his own nation during the nineteenth century.

Tocqueville twice visited England during the writing of the *Democracy* (in 1833 and 1835), where he became increasingly aware of the deleterious effects of industrialization, not only as an avenue to a possible new aristocracy of manufacturers but also as a cause of the increasing poverty and brutalization of the urban working classes. England revealed as well for him more of the hidden links between centralization and democracy. As England joined France and the United States in his thinking, he moved increasingly from a two-way to a three-way point of comparison, a shift in intellectual methods that is particularly apparent in the 1840 part of the *Democracy*. In 1836 Tocqueville also married an Englishwoman of modest background, Mary (Marie) Mottley, whom he had known for several years. For the rest of his life, his personal and intellectual ties led him to regard himself as belonging to three countries: France, England, and the United States.

After an unsuccessful campaign in 1837, Tocqueville's political career began in 1839 with his election to the Chamber of Deputies as representative from Valognes. As a member of the moderate opposition, he argued for expanded suffrage, for greater freedom of the press and associations, and especially for increased local responsibility and independence (limited decentralization). He was also concerned about the materialism, lack of ideals, and decline in public participation that he felt marked the July Monarchy. A strong nationalist, he urged a high profile for France in foreign affairs. In addition, he spoke and wrote against slavery and for prison and other reforms. At the beginning of 1848 he delivered a speech sharply critical of the regime, which warned of coming revolution. His remarks proved remarkably prophetic.

During the Second Republic Tocqueville served in several important capacities: as a member of the Constituent Assembly; as one of the committee charged with drafting a constitution; as a representative to the Legislative Assembly; and, for a few months in 1849, as minister of foreign affairs in the cabinet of Odilon Barrot. Tocqueville later recounted the tumultuous events of 1848 and 1849 in the form of memoirs in his *Souvenirs*, published posthumously. This book, with its firsthand accounts and candid sketches of leading political figures, clearly reveals Tocqueville's antagonism toward the revolutionaries of the June Days and the socialist theories that inspired them.

Louis-Napoleon's coup d'état (1851) led to Tocqueville's brief imprisonment (with other members of the Assembly) and to his withdrawal from public affairs. He turned his attention once again to the themes of centralization and revolution and began archival research on his other great book, *L'Ancien régime et la révolution*, the first part of which appeared in 1856. The project remained incomplete at the time of Tocqueville's death, but his social and intellectual analysis of eighteenth-century France and his fresh interpretation of the French Revolution as heir to the centralizing tendencies of the old regime were important historiographical contributions.

Tocqueville's reputation waned in the closing years of the nineteenth century, but interest revived during the late 1930s and has since increased steadily. Today he is regarded not only as a political theorist and an astute observer of the United States but also as a pioneering sociologist of modern mass culture. He is seen as well as a moralist of imposing stature who, above all else, valued the integrity and freedom of the individual.

J. P. Mayer, ed., *Oeuvres, papiers et correspondances d'Alexis de Tocqueville*, 17 vols. to date (Paris, 1951– ); G. W. Pierson, *Tocqueville and Beaumont in America* (New York, 1938); J. T. Schleifer, *The Making of Tocqueville's "Democracy in America"* (Chapel Hill, 1980); Yale Tocqueville Manuscripts Collection, Beinecke Rare Book and Manuscript Library, Yale University, New Haven, Connecticut.

*James T. Schleifer*

*Related entries:* ACADEMIE FRANCAISE; BARROT, C. H. O.; CHAMBER OF DEPUTIES; CHARLES X; CONSTITUTION OF 1848; COUP D'ETAT OF 2 DECEMBER 1851; GUIZOT; JUNE DAYS; LEGISLATIVE ASSEMBLY; REVOLUTION OF 1830; REVOLUTION OF 1848.

**LE TOUR DE FRANCE,** a practice whereby journeymen artisans traveled to various towns and cities in France seeking employment in order to complete their professional training, to learn regional trade secrets and techniques, and to broaden their local perspectives. The Tour de France became a generally accepted custom for workers in many of the skilled trades in France from at least the fifteenth century to the mid-nineteenth century. There were approximately fifteen to twenty major stopping places on the Tour, including Dijon, Lyons, Avignon, Nîmes, Marseilles, Toulouse, Bordeaux, and Nantes. The cities of northeastern France and the city of Paris (until the late eighteenth century) were rarely noted as stops on the Tour. The traditions and description of the journeymen on the Tour varied from trade to trade. Usually, however, young, unmarried journeymen between the ages of eighteen and twenty-five would travel from town to town on foot, alone or in small groups, finding work on their own or being placed by some official agent in a master's workshop. The journeyman would generally stay with one master from a few weeks to several months before moving on. Although the Tour de France existed in many trades, it was most prevalent in the building trades (where the practice may have originated) and in the metalworking trades.

The duration of the Tour was flexible but was intended to last as long as it took the journeyman to perfect his skills and to amass enough capital to purchase a mastership. Ideally the journeyman was to visit and work in all the major towns on the Tour, but there was no formal regulation that he do so. Originally, and under optimum circumstances, this period of training was to last from three to four years. As the price of masterships rose sharply in the late seventeenth and eighteenth century, however, accession to masterships became extremely difficult for the average journeyman. Consequently the Tour in this later period was probably used less to groom journeymen for eventual masterships than to help young, skilled workers find jobs throughout France.

The Tour as practiced by individual journeymen had no formal institutional structure, but it was highly developed and organized by the *compagnonnage*. The loyalty of these journeymen to their particular sect of *compagnonnage* was well known. Each sect within *compagnonnage* established a network of lodging houses and a system of mutual aid for members on the Tour de France. Such journeymen waged frequently successful campaigns to control their own placement and their payment in workshops on the Tour. The police, masters, the public, and unaffiliated workers feared the violence these journeymen of the *compagnonnage* provoked, whether over labor demands or for more personal grievances.

The Tour de France, nevertheless, always had a peaceful and productive side. This aspect of the Tour was described with enthusiasm by the noted journeyman joiner and legislative representative (in 1848), Agricol Perdiguier, in his many works on *compagnonnage* and the Tour de France. Perdiguier traveled to and worked in twelve cities on his Tour de France; he began in Marseilles at the age of nineteen in 1824 and completed his route in Lyons in 1828. Perdiguier stressed the solid training and sense of artistry he and other journeymen gained on the Tour as they worked for different masters and on their own masterpiece. This masterpiece of *compagnonnage* was required of each member before he finished his Tour de France. At the end of the Tour de France, many journeymen of the *compagnonnage* commissioned elaborate and colorful oil paintings featuring the members of the society assembled in the main square of the town in which their years on the Tour ended. Such paintings celebrated and commemorated the good fellowship and professional experience acquired while on the Tour de France. A number of such paintings now hang in the Musée du compagnonnage in Tours.

E. Coornaert, *Les Compagnonnages en France du moyen age à nous jours* (1966); E. Dolléans and G. Dehove, *Histoire de travail en France; mouvement ouvrier et législation sociale* (1953–55); A. Perdiguier, *Mémoires d'un compagnon* (1854–55, new edition, 1964).

*Cynthia Truant*

*Related entries: COMPAGNONNAGES*; PERDIGUIER.

**TOURRET, CHARLES-GILBERT** (1795–1858), moderate republican and minister of agriculture and commerce in the Cavaignac government of 1848. Tourret's political career began in the Chamber of Deputies where, from 1837 to 1842, he represented his native department of the Allier and allied with the Left opposition to Louis-Philippe. After the February Revolution of 1848, Tourret was named *commissaire* of the Provisional Government for the Allier. In April, he was elected to the Constituent Assembly and was appointed to the committee charged with drawing up a constitution for the Republic.

After the June Days, Tourret was appointed minister of agriculture and commerce by Eugène Cavaignac. In this office he wavered between innovative social reform and moderate republicanism. Notably, he attempted to broaden worker participation in the *chambrées consultatives des arts et manufactures* and was a vigorous supporter of workers' cooperatives to which he tried to make available preferential interest rates and a revolving fund of state loans. The latter proposals were treated as socialist in the Assembly and were never adopted. As minister, Tourret created a special commission to investigate ways of increasing employment, and under his influence the Cavaignac government granted funds to provide direct loans to unemployed cabinetmakers and bronze workers in Paris in August 1848.

He succeeded in establishing a short-lived program of agricultural education, but his proposals for creating chambers of agriculture similar to the Chambres de commerce and a program of cheap credit for farmers were not implemented.

The more cautious side of Tourret's republicanism is seen in his support for the prosecution of Louis Blanc and Marc Caussidière after the demonstrations of 15 May 1848, his vote against the principle of the right to work, and his vote in favor of reestablishing caution money for newspapers. After the election of Louis-Napoleon, Tourret resigned his ministerial post and withdrew from politics.

J. Dautry, *1848 et la II*ᵉ *République* (Paris, 1957); F. A. de Luna, *The French Republic under Cavaignac, 1848* (Princeton, 1969); A. Robert, E. Bourloton, and G. Cougny, *Dictionnaire des parlementaires français*, 5 vols. (Paris, 1891).

*Laura Frader*

*Related entries:* BLANC; CAUSSIDIERE; CAVAIGNAC, L.-E.; CHAMBER OF DEPUTIES; CHAMBERS OF COMMERCE; CONSTITUTION OF 1848; JUNE DAYS; LEGISLATIVE ASSEMBLY; REVOLUTION OF 1848; WORKERS' COOPERATIVES.

**TRACY.** See DESTUTT DE TRACY.

**TRANSNONAIN, MASSACRE OF THE RUE** (13 April 1834), republican insurrection. Following the repression of the uncoordinated uprising that followed the funeral of General Jean-Maximin Lamarque (5 June 1832) and the legitimist insurrection in the Vendée led by the duchesse de Berry (June 1832), whose subsequent arrest (in November) and well-publicized pregnancy weakened right-wing opposition, the July Monarchy enjoyed a year of relative tranquility. The death of Napoleon's son, the duke of Reichstadt, on 22 July removed another possible candidate for Louis-Philippe's throne, and the new ministry of the duc de Broglie (11 October 1832) soon took a hard line against the remaining vestiges of public opposition to the regime.

Liberal and republican opposition was centered largely in the press and secret revolutionary societies. Newspaper attacks from Armand Marrast's *Tribune* and Armand Nicholas Carrel's *National* met with regular prosecution in the courts (the *Tribune* was charged 114 times between 1831 and 1834 and fined a total of 150,000 francs). The secret societies tried to forge closer links between middle-class republicans and Parisian workers, believing that the absence of such efforts was largely responsible for the 1832 revolt's failure. The Society of the Rights of Man (1831–34), whose members included Auguste Blanqui, Armand Marrast, Jean-Jacques Vignerte, and deputies like Marc-René de Voyer d'Argenson, committed itself to universal suffrage, free public education, and the worker's right to form associations. The Friends of the People (1830–34), led by Godefroy Cavaignac, François-Vincent Raspail, and Ulysse Trélat, preached the right of insurrection and the principles of 1793, naming its local chapters after Maximilien Robespierre, Louis de St. Just, Jean-Paul Marat, and François-Noël Babeuf. Both societies sought to evade the existing restrictions on the size of political clubs (article 291 of the penal code) by confining the membership of each chapter to fewer than twenty.

The activities of the clubs and a strike by silk weavers in Lyons in February 1834 moved the ministry to action, and a February law restricting the activities of street criers in Paris was followed by a proposal in the Chamber (10 April) to modify article 291 and bring affiliated clubs of fewer than twenty members under government surveillance. Penalties would be fixed at two months to a year in prison and fines of 150 to 1,000 francs, and doubled for a second offense. The new law provoked a renewal of the weavers' insurrection in Lyons (where it was seen as a threat to mutualist societies) on 10–13 April, and though this revolt was speedily crushed, it inspired a similar uprising in Paris. On Sunday, 13 April, the Rights of Man called its members to arms, and barricades were erected in the traditional revolutionary strongholds of the Temple and Marais districts (the third and fourth arrondissements). The army and the Interior Ministry (Adolphe Thiers) were prepared for this eventuality, and more than 40,000 troops and National Guardsmen under General Thomas-Robert Bugeaud had been massed in and near the capital.

Street fighting lasted through 14 April. Though about 100 people were killed, popular attention was focused on an incident in the rue Transnonain on 13 April. After barricades in the street had been cleared, a shot from a window of the house at number 12 killed a popular officer. His infantry company entered the building and massacred the inhabitants, killing twenty men, women, and children. In the aftermath of the fighting, the Chamber banned the possession of arms and appropriated 14 million francs to enlarge the regular army to 360,000 men. Those arrested (initially more than 2,000) were to be tried by the Chamber of Peers rather than the criminal courts. The marquis de Lafayette's death (20 May) and funeral provoked no demonstrations, and a trial of 121 leaders of the revolt took place in the Luxembourg palace in the same month. Twenty-eight of the prisoners (including Cavaignac and Marrast) escaped before proceedings opened, and the trial was disorderly, though the president of the Peers (duc de Pasquier) banned the attempt to use a collection of liberal luminaries (Félicité de Lammenais, Auguste Comte, Alexandre-Auguste Ledru-Rollin, Jules Favre, and Blanqui) as defense attorneys. Sentences for prison or deportation were handed down, though a general amnesty in 1837 lifted these.

The government's experience with the trial, followed by Fieschi's attempt to kill Louis-Philippe with an "infernal machine" on 28 July, led to further repressive legislation on 4 August. Assize courts were authorized to try suspects in absentia and to expel unruly prisoners from proceedings, and juries would vote secretly and convict by majority vote. Surveillance of the press as tightened, fines were raised, newspapers were required to post higher deposits, and no caricatures or drawings were to be published without government approval. Thereafter armed resistance to the regime largely ended, but republicans organized new societies to carry on their opposition.

The rue Transnonain took its name from a Parisian red-light district (it was formerly the rue Trousse-nonain, Trace-putain, and Tasse-nonain) and consisted of approximately one-third of the present-day rue Beaubourg. Number 12 was still standing in 1857. Bugeaud became known as the "butcher of the rue Transnonain," and Honoré Daumier immortalized the massacre six months later in a powerful lithograph that shows a father, in nightcap and gown, lying with the bodies of his slaughtered wife, father, and child.

L. Chevalier, *Classes laborieuses et dangereuses* (Paris, 1958); J. Girard, *La Garde Nationale, 1814–1871* (Paris, 1964); J. Hillairet, *Dictionnaire historique des rues de Paris* (Paris, 1963); C. Ledré, *La Presse à l'assaut de la monarchie, 1815–1848* (Paris, 1960); J. Lucas-Dubreton *Bugeaud* (Paris, 1931); P. Philbeam, "The Emergence of Opposition to the Orleanist Monarchy," *English Historical Review* (January 1970); D. Porch, *Army and Revolution* (London, 1973); *Procès des accusés d'avril devant la cour des Pairs*, 4 vols. (Paris, 1835); I. Tchernoff, *Le Parti républicain sous la monarchie de juillet* (Paris, 1901); P. Thoreau-Dangin, *Histoire de la monarchie de juillet*, 8 vols. (Paris, 1888); P. Vigier, *La Monarchie de juillet* (Paris, 1969).

*David Longfellow*

*Related entries:* AIDE-TOI, LE CIEL T'AIDERA; BERRY, M.-C.; BROGLIE, A.-L.-V.; BUGEAUD; DAUMIER; FIESCHI PLOT; LAMARQUE; LYONS, REVOLTS IN; *LE NATIONAL*; REICHSTADT; SOCIETY OF THE RIGHTS OF MAN.

*LE TRAVAIL* (1842), democratic newspaper, twelve issues January–September 1842, under the subtitle *Paper of the Moral and Material Interests of the Working Classes.* It was in fact typical of a number of other short-lived papers in this period, which, although theoretically aimed at workers (the subtitle was copied from *L'Atelier*), were in fact vehicles for the complaints of young *déclassé* intellectuals that they were being reduced to proletarians of the mind and that society was thus threatening its own survival. Etienne Cabet's *Le Populaire* was bitter about the divisive and competitive influence of *Le Travail* and other similar papers.

R. Gossez, "Presse parisienne à destination des ouvriers (1848–1851)," in J. Godechot, ed., *La Presse ouvrière, 1819–1850*, "Bibliothèque de la Révolution de 1848," vol. 23 (1966).

*Peter McPhee*

*Related entries: L'ATELIER*; CABET; *LE POPULAIRE*.

**TREATY OF LONDON.** See LONDON, TREATY OF.

**TREILHARD, ACHILLE-LIBERAL** (1775–1855), Napoleonic prefect and Restoration liberal; the son of Jean-Baptiste Treilhard, a deputy to the Revolutionary assemblies, member of the Tribunate and the Council of State under Napoleon (who made him a count of the Empire), and prominent jurist, who was buried in the Pantheon on his death in 1810. The elder Treilhard facilitated his son's entry into government service during the Empire, when

Achille-Libéral became an *auditeur* to the Council of State (1806), secretary to the prefect of the Seine (1809), and subsequently prefect of Catalonia (when that province was annexed as a French department), the Gers, and the Haute-Garonne (this last under the Hundred Days). A career bureaucrat, Treilhard was denied a post under the Second Restoration and joined the liberal opposition. At the beginning of the Revolution of 1830, he presided over the meeting of liberal deputies at the offices of the *National* on 26 July when the decision to resist the July Ordinances was taken. Treilhard was named prefect of police in Paris after the Revolution and worked to maintain order in the city, sharing liberal fears that the National Guard would be unable to control the lower classes in the aftermath of Charles X's abdication. Having prevented popular outbursts during the trial of Jules de Polignac and his ministers in December, Treilhard resigned his post at Louis-Philippe's request on 26 December 1830, urging the new king to implement a more liberal electoral law and reform the Chamber of Peers.

L. Bergeron, *L'Episode napoléonien* (Paris, 1972); D. Pinkney, *The French Revolution of 1830* (Princeton, 1972).

*David Longfellow*

*Related entries:* ELECTIONS AND ELECTORAL SYSTEMS; JULY ORDI-NANCES; *LE NATIONAL*; NATIONAL GUARD; POLIGNAC; REVOLUTION OF 1830.


**TRELAT, ULYSSE** (1798–1879), doctor, political conspirator, minister in 1848, and director of Saltpêtrière. The son of a *notaire*, Ulysse Trélat studied medicine in Paris and took part in the campaign of 1813 as a surgeon's aide. He survived typhus, and as a medical student he helped defend Paris in 1815. He received his medical degree in 1821. While employed as a doctor at Charenton, Trélat had his name appear in the police files, where he was listed as a friend of Philippe Buchez. Like many others in his profession, Trélat was devoted to the new ideas of liberty. He belonged to the Society of the Friends of Truth and also became involved in the carbonari, though no evidence exists that he took part in the insurrections of Samur or Belfort in 1822.

In 1827 Trélat became one of the founding members of the liberal electoral organization Aide-toi, le ciel t'aidera. It is therefore not surprising to find Trélat on the barricades in July 1830. As an advocate of the interests of the laboring classes, he fought for something more than an Orleanist monarch; he soon became a leader of the Society of the Friends of the People.

After spending the early 1830s in Clermont-Ferrand, where he wrote for the *Patriote du Puy-de-Dôme*, he returned to Paris at the request of the defendants of the insurrection of 1834. Not only did he fail to gain these republicans their liberty, but his antagonistic remarks to the Chamber of Peers earned him a place in prison. He had the audacity to remind some of the Peers that they had been colleagues in secret societies but now were ''my political enemies, not my judges.'' He was freed by the amnesty of 1837.

Trélat continued to express his views, usually in the *National*, and he became a doctor at Saltpêtrière. A man marked by smallpox but blessed with a warmth that he communicated to his troubled patients, Trélat was one of the first persons to mix social ideas with political concerns. He did not accept the many socialist theories being put forth, but his advanced ideas recommended him to the Provisional Government in 1848. He was named commissioner-extraordinary to the Puy-de-Dôme, Allier, Creuse, and Haute-Vienne. At the same time, the citizens of Paris elected him as colonel in the National Guard and mayor of the twelfth arrondissement.

In April 1848 the citizens of the Puy-de-Dôme sent him to the Constituent Assembly, fifth of their fifteen representatives. The Assembly elected Trélat one of the six vice-presidents, and despite his lack of experience in public affairs, on 12 May the new executives selected him as minister of public works. Having advanced social views without political convictions to sustain them, Trélat was an excellent choice for a government trying to walk a tightrope between the workers of Paris and the monarchists in the Assembly. Unfortunately, Trélat had to face immediately the question of the National Workshops, and here his indecisive nature caused a problem.

The invasion of the Assembly on 15 May caused Trélat to decide that the youthful director of the National Workshops, Emile Thomas, could no longer control the workers of Paris. Thomas's supervision of 100,000 workers was too dangerous, especially when Thomas was urging the Labor Committee of the Assembly to give him independence from the authority of the Ministry of Public Works. When the committee recommended the eventual dissolution of the workshops, Trélat decided to take immediate action. On the evening of 26 May, he called Thomas to his office. Not only did he dismiss the director, but he also sent him on a government mission to Marseilles without even allowing Thomas to inform his mother. Trélat wanted Thomas, who was quite popular with the workers, removed from Paris until after the by-elections of 4 June. By spiriting Thomas out of the city under cover of darkness, however, Trélat united all factions in condemnation of such tactics. Although Thomas was gone, the workers for the first time took a definite step toward a break with the government. Trélat, who actually tried to defend the interests of the workers, resigned on 18 June over the manner in which the National Workshops were to be dissolved.

After the June Days, Trélat took a moderate position in the Assembly. He voted for the banishment of the Orléans family, for the prosecution of Louis Blanc and Marc Caussidière, and against the sanctioning of the Constitution by the people. Yet he also voted for the abolition of the death penalty and for the progressive income tax, and he opposed the developing power of Louis-Napoleon. The voters of the Puy-de-Dôme did not return him to the Legislative Assembly in 1849.

Trélat's concern for people was in evidence in his work on colonization. He headed the commission that hoped to relieve the plight of the workers by resettling them in the colonies. Over 13,000 workers were sent to Algeria and elsewhere by the commission. Such schemes had little chance to solve the basic socioeconomic problem of the artisanal class, but the good doctor was too much the idealist to see that reality.

Awarded the rank of chevalier of the Legion of Honor in 1849, Trélat returned to his post at the Salpêtrière. He continued his work on insanity and published in 1861 *La Folie lucide*, an important work in the history of mental illnesses. Trélat was in Paris for the Commune and served on the municipal council of Paris from 1871 to 1874.

A. Robert and G. Cougny, *Dictionnaire des parlementaires français* (Paris, 1889–91).

*Thomas Beck*

*Related entries:* AIDE-TOI, LE CIEL T'AIDERA; BLANC; BUCHEZ; CARBONARI; CAUSSIDIERE; *LE NATIONAL*; NATIONAL WORKSHOPS; REPUBLICANS; SOCIETY OF FRIENDS OF TRUTH; THOMAS.

**TRIBUNAL DE CASSATION.** See COURT OF CASSATION.

*LE TRIBUN DU PEUPLE* (1848), left-wing newspaper. This socialist newspaper, which began as the "voice of the workers" and then in its fifth and final edition became the "voice of the Mountain," was founded and edited by A. Constant, the so-called abbé Constant. Sold cheaply at 5 centimes, it sought to bring to the ordinary worker the principles of the most radical socialism: the socialism of Alexandre-Auguste Ledru-Rollin. It asked for a highly centralized government ("All divided authority is weak; we need a Republic with one head in times of danger") that would act vigorously. Yet Constant praised a wide range of politicians from Alphonse de Lamartine to the phalansterians to Etienne Cabet.

Constant saw society as divided into two classes: the exploited and the exploiters. Yet he recommended that the workers refrain from any demonstration of hostility to the rich, counting on the "sincere devotion of the rich, which will give the poor reason to be patient." This Christian notion gives some insight into the thought of a socialist who put the name of God close to that of socialism in his newspaper.

Constant was also the president of the Club de la montagne, whose meetings were reported in the *Tribun du peuple*. The vice-presidents of the club, A. Esquiros and A. Legallois, were also editors and founders of the *Tribun du Peuple, organe de la Montagne* (which lasted only for one number: 30 March 1848). This last number of the newspaper was also the most insistently Christian in tone, emphasizing the resurrection of freedom and the commandments of the Republic, which were to replace those of the Catholic church.

E. Hatin, *Bibliographie historique et critique de la presse périodique française* (Paris, 1866); H. Izambard, *La presse parisienne, statistique bibliographique et alphabétique de tous les journaux, revues et canards périodiques, nés, morts, resuscités ou métamorphoses à Paris depuis le 22 février 1848 jusqu'à l'Empire* (Paris, 1853).

*Jean-Claude Caron, trans. E. Newman*

*Related entries:* CABET; ESQUIROS; FOURIER; LAMARTINE; LEDRU-ROLLIN; REPUBLICANS.

*LA TRIBUNE DES DEPARTEMENS* (1829–1835), the most influential republican newspaper of the Left. It voiced republicans' opposition to the monarchy before and after the Revolution of 1830. It was suppressed in 1835. Its chief editor before May 1831 was Auguste Fabre, and after May 1831 it was Armand Marrast. Republicanism during the later Bourbon Restoration was distinguished by the youth and idealism of its proponents—this despite the fact that the movement's emblem, the marquis de Lafayette, was an old man and a lukewarm idealist. The first republican paper in these years appeared every five days under the title *Jeune France*. Started in January 1829 by Louis Barbarin, Armand Marrast, and Léon Gozlan, its vague ideology was announced more in terms of social equality than of political revolution. A tendency to hyperbole, which limited its acceptance, is seen in the headline announcing formation of Jules de Polignac's cabinet: "Another Blood-Bath!" Less strident, and thus more respectable, was the *Tribune des départemens*, first published in June 1829 by Auguste and Victorin Fabre, who had been active in the Aide-toi electoral society's republican left wing. The aberrant spelling of the paper's title was to avoid confusion with a small provincial opposition journal published in Niort.

Like *Jeune France*, the *Tribune* stated its position in rather imprecise terms, but a decentralized federated republic, broad suffrage, and involvement of the working class were proposed. Auguste Fabre set three goals: to advocate democratic republicanism as theory; to warn against an ultra conspiracy, especially after Polignac's ministry was formed; and, finally, to discredit the rising Orleanist propaganda and scold the liberals for their bourgeois values. All the while, the Fabres disclaimed revolutionary intentions. In October 1829, one of the subsidizers, Ascension Montgolfier, cancelled his support, and the paper folded. On 28 April 1830, the *Tribune* reappeared as a daily paper. Along with Marrast and the Fabre brothers, editorial support was added by the University-based club Friends of Truth. A new spokesman from this group, Robin Morhéry, who later helped to establish gynecology as a medical specialty, focused the paper's policy against a betrayal, by this time anticipated, on the part of the increasingly liberal Orleanist coterie. The revived *Tribune* also had the credential of old Lafayette's support, although the "hero of two worlds" was never an avid backer of lost causes. By 1830, republicanism was represented by three papers besides *Jeune France* and the *Tribune: La Révolution, Le Patriote*, and the *Nouveau journal de Paris*. All of these papers were staffed by unpaid writers, mainly medical and polytechnique students, and had fewer than 3,000 subscribers. When the July Revolution at last confirmed the *Tribune*'s prediction of a national betrayal, the paper denounced the new monarchy and, claiming that France deserved better, avowed its new policy of opposition to Louis-Philippe. The *Tribune*'s young staff had prepared for and took part in the July combat. Auguste Fabre commanded at the barricades, Victorin Fabre led some some attackers against the Babylone barracks, Godefroy Cavaignac's troops besieged the Panthéon, and Jules Bastide was among those who cleared the Pont royal for the assault on the Tuileries.

In the July Monarchy, the *Tribune*, now a major organ of republican opposition, became more influential. The paper advocated radical social reform as the path to democracy but did not adopt the socialists' program. In May 1831, the Fabrists split with Armand Marrast's faction over republican purity and left the paper with bitter feelings. The *Tribune* was singled out by Jean-Charles Persil, Louis-Philippe's chief prosecutor, for judicial prosecution even more often than Carrel's newly republican *National*. At last it was completely suppressed, even before the September Laws. The *Tribune*'s last issue appeared on 11 May 1835, after having endured, in four years, 114 trials and 23 convictions that amounted to 49 prison-years for its managers and editors, and 159,000 francs in fines, or an average fine of 7,000 francs, enough to destroy even a journal with wealthy backers. Polignac and his ultras had never approached such severity in press trials.

A. Fabre, *La Révolution de 1830 et le véritable parti républicain*, 2 vols. (Paris, 1833); D. Rader, *The Journalists and the July Revolution* (The Hague, 1973); G. Weill, *Histoire du Parti Républicain en France* (Paris, 1928).

*Daniel Rader*

*Related entries:* AIDE-TOI, LE CIEL T'AIDERA; BASTIDE; CARREL; CA-VAIGNAC, G.-E.-L.; FABRE, J.-R.-A.; FABRE, M.-J.-J.-V.; *LE JEUNE FRANCE*; LAFAYETTE, M.-J.-P.-Y.-R.-G.; MARRAST; *LE NATIONAL*; *NOUVEAU JOURNAL DE PARIS*; *LE PATRIOTE*; POLIGNAC; PRESS LAWS; REPUBLICANS; *LA REVOLUTION*.


**TRISTAN, FLORA** (1803–1844), feminist and initiator of national and international workers' organizations. The daughter of a French *émigré* and a Peruvian nobleman, Flora Tristan experienced directly the social position of poor women and children born out of legal wedlock. This was heightened by a fruitless trip to Peru to claim her inheritance, retold in her *Pérégrinations d'une Paria* (1833–34), later burned on a public square in Arequipa by enraged landowners. Her feminism was the result, too, of an unhappy marriage with the owner of an engraving factory where she had worked, the violent end to which inspired her to launch petitions for the reintroduction of divorce (1837) and the abolition of the death penalty (1838), and which inspired her posthumous *L'Emancipation de la femme ou le testament de la paria.*

In 1839 she went to England and described her impressions in the remarkable *Promenades dans Londres*. But her great work was *L'Union ouvrière* (1843), based on the idea of a national and international union of workers to ensure education, work, and social welfare. She sought to make this a reality by a checkered Tour de France in 1844, from Auxerre down the Rhône to Marseilles and through the Midi to Bordeaux, where she died. Her socialism was of an eclectic kind, influenced by St. Simonianism, Charles Fourier, Robert Owen, Louis Blanc, and active workers such as Pierre Moreau and Agricol Perdiguier, particularly the last's *Le Livre du compagnonnage* (1839).

George Sand described Tristan as sincere, active, and courageous, but also as overly proud, condescending, even ridiculous. Her writing, however, is full of insights—for example, about the links between the nature of work, violence, drunkenness, and the position of women. On 22 October 1848, a column was erected to her memory in the cemetery at Bordeaux with the inscription "To the memory of Madame Flora Tristan, author of *L'Union ouvrière*, from grateful workers. Liberty, Equality, Fraternity, Solidarity."

D. Desanti, *Flora Tristan. Oeuvres et vie mêlées* (Paris, 1973); C. N. Gattey, *Gauguin's Astonishing Grandmother* (London, 1970); J. Maitron, ed., *Dictionnaire biographique du mouvement ouvrier français*, part 1 (1789–1864) (Paris, 1964–66); S. Michaud, *Flora Tristan: Lettres* (Paris, 1980).

*Peter McPhee*

*Related entries:* BLANC; DIVORCE, ABOLITION OF; FOURIER; PERDI-GUIER; SAINT-SIMONIANISM; SAND.

**TROCADERO.** See SPAIN, 1823 FRENCH INVASION OF.

*TROIS GLORIEUSES.* See REVOLUTION OF 1830.

**TROPPAU, CONGRESS OF** (1820–1821), called to deal with the future of Italy. The liberal and constitutional government that had been established in the Kingdom of Naples in July 1820 by military force gravely menaced Austrian domination in Italy. Clemens von Metternich, encouraged by the English government, wanted to intervene quickly and alone. But Czar Alexander I insisted that this intervention could be made only by a formal mandate from the European alliance. Consequently the sovereigns of Austria, Russia, and Prussia, along with their ministers, met at Troppau in Silesia in October and November 1820. The French government was of two minds: on one hand it feared the revolutionary contagion as much as Austria and did not want to displease the Czar, but on the other hand, it did not want to be associated with the suppression of a regime that claimed that it had been inspired by Restoration France. Also, France could not be pleased by the intrusion of an Austrian army into territory ruled by a Bourbon monarchy. So France imitated Great Britain in that it allowed itself to be represented at Troppau only by ambassadors who had no power to make decisions. These ambassadors could do no more than report the text of the agreement between Metternich and the Czar for an Austrian military operation in Naples and the proclamation of a general principle of intervention against all revolutionary movements. In January 1821 the Congress moved to Laibach to receive the representatives of the Italian states, and especially the king of Naples, who had been allowed to leave by the revolutionaries so that he could plead the cause of the Neapolitan constitution. But as soon as he arrived, Ferdinand IV repudiated his oaths and allied himself with the measures set forth by Austria.

While Austrian forces were on the march against Naples, the Piedmontese carbonari issued a military pronouncement in Alexandria and Turin designed to impose a liberal constitution on the Kingdom of Sardinia-Piedmont and to arouse all Italy against foreign domination. This movement, however, was quickly snuffed out by the Austrian army, while the Allied sovereigns, meeting in Laibach, reaffirmed the right of intervention against revolutionary movements. In this way the European Alliance emerged from the twin Congress of Troppau-Laibach transformed in substance and form. Instead of the Quadruple Alliance of 1815, which had been directed only against France and in order to ensure the execution of the Treaty of Paris, this had become a conservative alliance to maintain all monarchical governments. Because England had refused to join in these policies, the alliance was reduced essentially to the three absolute monarchs who had first signed the Holy Alliance.

G. de Bertier de Sauvigny , *Metternich et la France*, vol. 2 (Paris, 1970); M. Bourquin, *Histoire de la Sainte Alliance* (Geneva, 1954); W. Schroder, *Metternich's Diplomacy at Its Zenith* (Austin, 1962).

*Guillaume de Bertier de Sauvigny, trans. E. Newman*

*Related entries:* HOLY ALLIANCE; METTERNICH; PARIS, SECOND TREATY OF; QUADRUPLE ALLIANCE; QUINTUPLE ALLIANCE.

**TROUVE-CHAUVEL, ARISTE-JACQUES** (1805–1883), liberal businessman and government official of the Second Republic, a man of order who led the workers of La Suze (Sarthe) in their resistance to Louis-Napoleon Bonaparte's coup d'état of 2 December 1851.

Trouvé-Chauvel was born at La Suze, near Le Mans (Sarthe), to René Trouvé, a simple wage earner who built up a major tannery in the village. He studied law in Rennes and Angers and commerce in Paris and worked for various commercial houses in Le Hâvre and the British Isles. In 1833 he established himself as a textile merchant in Le Mans. He married Justine-Louise Chauvel in 1834. As was the custom among business families in the province, he added her family name to his own. In 1840 he founded and became first director of the Caisse de la Sarthe, a bank that played a key role in the region's economic development. Trouvé-Chauvel was a municipal councillor (1833–48) and served one term as mayor (1840–43). An outspoken liberal, he caused a scandal in 1843 by criticizing government policy when welcoming the duc de Nemours to Le Mans. He had definite republican tendencies, yet he doubted the political capacity of the working class and mistrusted universal suffrage. He reportedly told Alexandre-Auguste Ledru-Rollin in 1848: "I am a republican in the fashion of Rome and Sparta; you are a revolutionary republican."

The Provisional Government named Trouvé-Chauvel commissioner for the Sarthe on 28 February 1848 and extended his authority over Maine-et-Loire and Mayenne on 20 March. In April the Sarthe elected him to the Constituent Assembly. Named prefect of police for Paris (17 May–19 July 1848), his prime concern was to maintain order as the necessary precondition for economic prosperity. He opposed both Bonapartism and socialism, allying himself with Eugène Cavaignac. He then served as prefect of the Seine department (19 July–25 October

1848) before succeeding Michel Goudchaux as minister of finance in Cavaignac's government. He pursued a policy of strict economy and a balanced budget. When Louis-Napoleon Bonaparte became president, Trouvé-Chauvel returned to Le Mans. He abandoned politics after a stunning defeat in the elections of May 1849. His bank was failing, and he lost the directorship in December 1850, partly because of pressure from government officials who distrusted his political views. He withdrew to La Suze and the family tannery.

On the morning of 5 December 1851, Trouvé-Chauvel led the tanners of La Suze in an insurrection against the coup d'état of 2 December. It was an uncharacteristic action for a man so devoted to order. He hoped to spark a general uprising in the Sarthe, but the venture collapsed within twenty-four hours. He fled abroad, returning only after a pardon in August 1854. He lived in obscure retirement in Paris until his death. In old age, he claimed that he had "respected and defended at all times and in all circumstances, order and liberty, religion and equality, work and fraternity, family and property."

Archives de la Préfecture de Police de Paris, dossier E/a 164–3; Archives nationales, carton F1b I 174/13, dossier Trouvé-Chauvel; F. Lemeunier, *A. J. Trouvé-Chauvel, banquier et maire du Mans, Ministre des finances de la deuxième République (1805–1883)* (Le Mans, 1953).

*Michael Sibalis*

*Related entries:* BONAPARTISM; CAVAIGNAC, L.-E.; CONSTITUTION OF 1848; COUP D'ETAT OF 2 DECEMBER 1851; GOUDCHAUX; LEDRU-ROLLIN; NEMOURS; PROVISIONAL GOVERNMENT; REPUBLICANS.

# U

**ULTRAMONTANES,** a derogatory designation for those who favored the authority of the pope over that of the local clergy or that of the heads of national states. It meant that they looked "beyond the mountains" (the Alps) for leadership and inspiration. The expression had been used in the seventeenth and eighteenth centuries in the controversies raised by Jansenism. In the early nineteenth century, it was hurled at writers like Joseph de Maistre and Félicité de Lamennais when they wrote against submission of church authorities to secular power. The debate over ultramontism versus gallicanism was particularly bitter after 1850.

*Guillaume de Bertier de Sauvigny*

*Related entries:* LAMENNAIS; MAISTRE.

**ULTRAROYALISTS,** extreme right wing of the royalist movement, led by the comte d'Artois. The ultraroyalist faction was the first distinct group to form within the monolithic royalist party in late 1815. Its members were convinced that the policy of compromise of the First Restoration had led to the disasters of the Hundred Days, and they desired to distinguish themselves from the questionable loyalty of the men of the Revolution and Empire who had converted to royalism. They were accused, in some cases accurately, of wanting to restore the Old Regime. But basically they sought a clerical-monarchical government derived from ideas developed among *émigré* circles and within the Catholic-romantic revival. Many were members of the Congrégation. By late 1815 they had established their headquarters at the home of a deputy named Piet (the *réunion Piet*) where they met to plan strategy. The organization they built there soon became a potent force in the Chambers. The ultras, who controlled the Deputies in 1815–16 and again from 1821 to 1827, dominated the cabinet from 1821 to 1827 and from 1828 to 1830.

The debates on the 1816 amnesty bill led to the establishment of the ultra faction in opposition to the king and the Richelieu government. In fact the ultras quickly championed parliamentary authority against the crown because they then controlled the Deputies. They also vigorously demanded the death of Marshal Michel Ney. Their political unity in the Deputies was furthered by the founding of a "banner" of the Knights of the Faith within the Chamber at the beginning of the 1815 session. Some of their spokesmen openly opposed the Charter. In the Deputies their parliamentary leader was the relatively moderate Joseph de Villèle, aided by Jacques-Joseph Corbière. In the Peers their leaders included Jules de Polignac, François de La Bourdonnaye, Mathieu de Montmorency, and until the early 1820s François René de Chateaubriand. The real leader of the ultras was the comte d'Artois, aided by Polignac, Eugène-François de Vitrolles, and others. Although Artois frequently preferred to exercise his role discreetly, he actively supported ultra candidates in election campaigns. Furthermore, when in 1815 he was made colonel general of the National Guard of France, he purged its ranks of nonultras and thus turned it into an ultra military force.

Among the newspapers the ultras used were the *Gazette de France*, Joseph Fiévée's *Correspondance*, and the *Quotidienne*, whose editor, Joseph-François Michaud, championed the union of throne and altar. Until the mid-1820s they also utilized the *Journal des débats* guided by Chateaubriand. From 1818 to 1820 they controlled the *Conservateur*, and in 1819 they acquired the *Drapeau blanc*. In decline from 1817 to 1819, many leading ultras were involved in the 1818 Conspiracy at the Water's Edge, a plot to force a change of cabinet. One consequence of this plot was the dismissal of Artois as commander of the National Guard and the elimination of ultra elements in it. One ultra, Vitrolles, even wrote a memoir in 1818 urging the Allies to delay the evacuation of France. In late 1819 the ultras began to revive, and they were a factor in the fall of the Decazes cabinet. The 1820 elections gave them enough seats that they gained symbolic places in the second Richelieu cabinet. To influence Louis XVIII, they made use of his favorite, Mme. du Cayla. Breaking with Armand-Emmanuel de Richelieu, especially over foreign policy, they forced the fall of his cabinet in December 1821.

The ultras then installed their own ministry led by Villèle. In 1824, with the backing of the landowning voters, they won a large election victory. During the 1820s they supported tightened press restrictions, increased power for the church, and intervention in Spain. They passed the Sacrilege Law, a law to compensate the *émigrés*, and the Septennial Law. The 1824 elections had strengthened the extreme right wing of the ultra faction, yet simultaneously they began to disintegrate. Dismissed as foreign minister in 1824, Chateaubriand went into opposition. Then the gallican-ultramontane controversy split the ultras. The dissolution of the Knights of the Faith "banner" in 1826 further cost them cohesion. Thus the ultras were unable to obtain legislative adoption of measures such as primogeniture and a new censorship law. The 1827 elections ended their control of the Deputies and brought into office the Martignac ministry, which they subsequently helped to bring down. The Polignac cabinet was a triumph for the extreme ultras but generated opposition among their more moderate members. After the July Revolution, those ultras who remained loyal to their ideals became legitimists, urging the restoration of the Bourbons in the person of the duc de Bordeaux.

G. de Bertier de Sauvigny, *Ferdinand de Bertier* (Paris, 1948), and *The Bourbon Restoration* (Philadelphia, 1966); J. Cabanis, *Charles X roi Ultra* (Paris, 1972); P. Duvergier de Hauranne, *Histoire du gouvernement parlementaire en France, 1814–1848* (Paris, 1857–71); J. Fourcassié, *Villèle* (Paris, 1954); N. Hudson, *Ultra-Royalism and the French Restoration* (Cambridge, 1936); T. Muret, *French Royalist Doctrines since the Revolution* (New York, 1933); J. J. Oechslin, *Le Mouvement ultra-royaliste sous la restauration* (Paris, 1960); R. Rémond, *La Droite en France de 1815 a nos jours* (Paris, 1954).

*James K. Kieswetter*

*Related entries:* AMNESTY BILL OF 1816; BORDEAUX; CHATEAU-BRIAND; CHEVALIERS DE LA FOI; CONGREGATION; *LE CONSERVA-TEUR*; CONSPIRACY AT THE WATER'S EDGE; CORBIERE; DECAZES; *DOCTRINAIRES*; *LE DRAPEAU BLANC*; DU CAYLA; FIEVEE; *LA GAZETTE DE FRANCE*; HEREDITY LAWS; INDEMNITY BILL OF 1825; INDEPEND-ENTS; *JOURNAL DES DEBATS*; LA BOURDONNAYE; LAW OF SACRI-LEGE; LEGITIMISM; MARTIGNAC; MICHAUD; MONTMORENCY; NEY; POLIGNAC; PRESS LAWS; *LA QUOTIDIENNE*; RICHELIEU; ROYALIST PARTY; SPAIN, 1823 FRENCH INVASION OF; ULTRAMONTANES; VIL-LELE; VITROLLES.

**UNION.** See SOCIETE DE L'UNION.

*L'UNIVERS.* See MONTALEMBERT.

*L'UNIVERSEL* (1829–1830), ministerial newspaper that supported Jules de Polignac before and after his appointment as minister. *L'Universel* appeared on 1 January 1829 as the voice of the Polignac wing of the ultra Right, and its very existence reflected the serious factionalism among even the more extreme royalists in the reign of Charles X.

While the opposition papers in 1829 were repeatedly predicting an ultra coup against the Charter, the ultra Right press was seriously divided. The *Gazette* hoped for a return of Joseph de Villèle, and the others were much too blatant in calling for a royal showdown with the "Revolution." The tiny *Universel* (circulation 1,000) attempted to promote an orthodox and unifying ultra line: no toleration of revolution, no elections of revolutionary deputies, and no coup or violation of the Charter. With the elevation of Jules-Armand de Polignac to chief minister on 8 August 1829, the paper became defensive, denying that a coup was being considered and avowing the government's benign intentions. On a few occasions, Polignac's paper revealed the true face of its owner. During the heated reelection campaign of the 221 deputies in 1830, the editor praised a provincial mob that had stoned and beaten a victorious liberal deputy. Earlier

Polignac himself had written in the *Universel* that the king would never yield in his royal prerogative, a remark taken up by his enemies as the battle cry of a coup. The *Universel* ceased publication on the first of the July Days.

D. Rader, *The Journalists and the July Revolution in France* (The Hague, 1973).

*Daniel Rader*

*Related entries:* CHARLES X; CHARTER OF 1814; *LA GAZETTE DE FRANCE*; POLIGNAC; REVOLUTION OF 1830; THE 221; ULTRAROYALISTS; VILLELE.

**UTOPIANISM.** See CABET.

# V

**VAUBLANC, VINCENT-MARIE VIENOT, COMTE DE** (1756–1845), member of the Legislative Assembly, the Council of 500, the Corps législatif, and the Chamber of Deputies of the Restoration; minister and councillor of state. Vaublanc was born on 3 March 1756 at Fort-Dauphin, Santo Domingo, the son of a minor noble and army officer. In France he studied at the Collège de la Flêche and then the Ecole militaire. Commissioned a sublieutenant in 1774, he returned to Santo Domingo where he rose to brevet lieutenant colonel. Back in France he settled near Melun, where in 1789 the members of the Second Estate elected him their secretary. He presided over the departmental administration of Seine-et-Oise in 1790. In September 1791 the department of Seine-et-Marne elected him to the Legislative Assembly, which chose him its president in November. He voted with the constitutional party, opposing measures against the nonjuring clergy and *émigrés* but also denouncing the *émigrés* gathered on the frontier. Vaublanc did not hesitate to defend unpopular causes. Thus he supported the marquis de Lafayette in August 1792. He also sponsored an accusatory decree against Jean-Paul Marat and summoned Jérôme Pétion and Pierre-Louis Roederer to account for their conduct on 20 June when the people invaded the Tuileries. Vaublanc himself was saved on 10 August through the efforts of the future General Henri-Gratien Bertrand, but he was forced into hiding during the Terror.

Vaublanc reappeared after the fall of Robespierre and became the leader of the royalists of the Paris section of Poissonnière. On 17 October 1795 Vaublanc was elected to the Council of 500 by the department of Seine-et-Marne. Two days later he was sentenced to death in absentia. His legislative seat was denied him until Fructidor, Year VI, when his conviction was annulled. In the 500 he voted with the reactionary Clichy group until the coup of 18 Fructidor. Then the club was closed, and some of its members, including Vaublanc, were ordered deported. He fled to Switzerland and Italy, not returning to France until after 18 Brumaire. He quickly became a staunch supporter of Napoleon and in

December 1800 was chosen to represent the department of Calvados in the Corps législatif. He supported the life consulate and the Empire. In November 1803 he was named to the Legion of Honor, and in February 1805 he became prefect of the department of Moselle, where he demonstrated considerable administrative competence. Napoleon created him a baron in December 1809. When the sick and wounded of the army of the Rhine fell back on Metz in late 1813, bringing with them an epidemic of typhus, Vaublanc repeatedly visited the hospitals and contracted a nearly fatal case of the disease himself.

He welcomed the restored Bourbons, who maintained him at his prefecture. During the Hundred Days he did his best to keep his department loyal to Louis XVIII. Unsuccessful, he fled to Ghent. After Waterloo Louis XVIII named him a councillor of state and made him prefect of Bouches-du-Rhône on 12 July 1815. When the Richelieu ministry was formed in 1815, Vaublanc became minister of the interior, a concession by Armand-Emmanuel de Richelieu to Artois and his followers. Vaublanc assiduously cultivated the ultraroyalists, purging the staff of his ministry, reorganizing the National Guard, which he allowed Artois to control, and abolishing the Ecole polytechnique, as if trying to atone for his imperial service. He even consulted with Artois about reorganizing his ministry. His excessively royalist ministerial policies and his sharp tongue, however, alienated his colleagues in the cabinet. He resigned from the ministry on 8 May 1816; Richelieu had demanded that the king fire him. The department of Calvados elected Vaublanc to the Chamber of Deputies in November 1820, and he remained there until 1827. He unsuccessfully led a group of dissident ultras in opposition to the second Richelieu ministry in 1820 and had a role in the fall of the ministry in 1821. The Deputies elected him a vice-president in 1821. In the Chamber he voted with the Right, supporting measures such as the Septennial Law, although he opposed the Villèle cabinet. Charles X appointed him to the Council of State in July 1830, but the July Revolution definitively ended his public career. He then devoted himself to literary pursuits and died in Paris on 21 August 1845.

*Archives parlementaires*; V. Beach, *Charles X of France* (Boulder, 1971); P. Duvergier de Hauranne, *Histoire du gouvernement parlementaire en France, 1814–1848* (Paris, 1857–71); N. Richardson, *The French Prefectoral Corps* (Cambridge, 1966); A. Robert et al., *Dictionnaire des parlementaires français* (Paris, 1889–91).

*James K. Kieswetter*
Related entries: ECOLE MILITAIRE (SAINT-CYR); ECOLE POLYTECH-NIQUE; LAFAYETTE, M.-J.-P.-Y.-R.-G.; NATIONAL GUARD; RICHE-LIEU; ULTRAROYALISTS; VILLELE.


**VAULABELLE, ACHILLE DE** (1799–1879), historian. A republican journalist under the July Monarchy, Vaulabelle sat in the Constituent Assembly of 1848 and was minister of public instruction in the government of General Eugène Cavaignac. In 1844, he began publishing the eight volumes of his *Histoire des deux restaurations*, which painted the Bourbon monarchy as an oppressive and unpopular regime imposed upon France by the victorious Allies and subservient to the reactionary nobility and clergy. This work was reedited at least seven times and contributed greatly to the unfavorable image of the Restoration that has dominated French historiography for so long.

*Guillaume de Bertier de Sauvigny, trans. E. Newman*

*Related entries:* CAVAIGNAC, L.-E.; CONSTITUTION OF 1848; REPUBLICANS; RESTORATION, FIRST; RESTORATION, SECOND.


**VAUQUELIN, NICOLAS-LOUIS** (1763–1829), chemist. Vauquelin's involvement with chemistry began in Rouen where he was apprenticed to a pharmacist in the 1770s. Moving to Paris, he became associated with the celebrated chemist Antoine-François Fourcroy (1755–1809), with whom he published a large number of joint experimental studies after 1790.

During the Revolutionary period, Vauquelin served as a pharmacist and also worked on the production of saltpeter for gunpowder. These two areas of interest largely characterized the remainder of his career, with most of his official positions involving either pharmacy and medical chemistry or else technical and industrial applications of chemical knowledge. The two posts he held the longest were the directorship of the Ecole de pharmacie, to which he was appointed on the school's foundation in 1803, and the professorship of applied chemistry at the Muséum d'histoire naturelle, which he obtained in 1804.

Apart from these two long-term appointments, Vauquelin held a series of other posts, which he vacated after a few years. These included positions at the Ecole centrale des travaux publics (later renamed the Ecole polytechnique), 1794–97; the ecole des mines, 1795–1801; the Collège de France, 1801–4; and the Faculté de médecine, 1811–22. In the case of the Faculté de médecine, however, Vauquelin's departure was involuntary, since he was dismissed by the Bourbon government along with a number of other professors suspected of liberal or Bonapartist sympathies.

While at the Ecole des mines, Vauquelin published a handbook on practical assay techniques, *Manuel de l'essayeur* (Paris, 1799). This text was immediately successful and was translated into German (1800) and Spanish (1826). It was reprinted in France during Vauquelin's lifetime (1812) and republished after his death with revisions by another hand (1836).

Other practical enterprises included the establishment of a chemical manufacturing business in partnership with Fourcroy in 1804. Vauquelin retained his connection with this company until 1822. Also in 1828 he entered the Chamber of Deputies as a member from his native district in Normandy.

Despite these practical activities, Vauquelin had a prolific output as an experimental chemist. By the time of his death in 1829, he had published over 300 contributions of his own and over 70 in collaboration with other authors.

E. Pariset, *Histoire des membres de l'Académie royale de médicine* (Paris, 1850); W. A. Smeaton, *Fourcroy, Chemist and Revolutionary* (Cambridge, Eng., 1962).

*W. R. Albury*

Related entries: CHAMBER OF DEPUTIES; COLLEGE DE FRANCE; ECOLE POLYTECHNIQUE; PARIS FACULTY OF MEDICINE.

**VERNET, EMILE-JEAN-HORACE** (1789–1863), painter and graphic artist. The young Vernet received his early artistic training from his father, Antoine-Charles-Horace Vernet, and his grandfather, the etcher Jean Moreau, and enjoyed enormous success as a painter of seascapes and battle scenes. Emile served for a time in the army, and from these experiences, as well as from those of his father and grandfather, he derived his lifelong passion for military subjects. In 1814, when the Allies were closing in upon Paris, he fought in defense of the Barrière de Clichy and for his bravery received the Legion of Honor on the battlefield from the emperor himself. Later he submitted *The Defense of the Barrière de Clichy* (Louvre) to the Salon, and when it was refused for political reasons, he exhibited it in his own studio with overwhelming success. A loyal supporter of the Empire producing propagandist lithographs and sketches, he was slow to support the Bourbon restoration. After 1820 it became advisable for him to leave France, and he traveled to Rome, where he painted his famous *Course des Barbari*. Upon his return to Paris in 1825 his popularity and output increased. Charles X, in view of Vernet's popularity, showered him with honors, including membership in the Institut de France (1826) and the directorship of the French Academy in Rome. In 1833, he left for Algeria. After his return to France, he collaborated with his friend Louis-Philippe in the creation of the military museum to the glories of France at Versailles. It was there that Vernet painted his most popular works. He made several paintings depicting the victories of French armies under the command of the Emperor Napoleon (for example, *Napoleon at the Battle of Wagram*), and the African campaigns (*Capture of the Smalah of Abd-el-Kader*, 1845), for the Versailles Museum, and he broadened his repertoire to include portraits and Oriental subjects. In 1842–43 Vernet traveled to Russia and painted the imperial couple and several subjects from Russian military history (*Battle of Wola*; Leningrad, Hermitage). As a graphic artist his output was large. He did more than 200 lithographs, mostly depicting military subjects, and contributed to the woodcut illustrations for Laurent de l'Ardèche's *Histoire de Napoléon* (1839). Later, for a few years before his death, he became the official painter of the Second Empire. His battle scenes are absurdly large, but at the same time they succeeded in glorifying the victories of French arms.

H. Béraldi, *Les Graveurs du XIXᵉ siècle*, vol. 12 (Paris, 1892); A. Daytot, *Les Vernet: Joseph-Carle-Horace* (Paris, 1898); J. Rees, *Horace Vernet and Paul Delaroche* (London, 1880).

*Irene Earls*

**VERON, LOUIS-DESIRE** (1798–1867), entrepreneur, publicist, and political figure. A qualified doctor who made a fortune from his *pâte Regnault*—a chest liniment—Véron left medicine for journalism while still in his twenties. He worked initially for *La Quotidienne* and then founded *La Revue de Paris* in 1829 before leaving in 1831 to become director of the Paris Opera. In 1835 he became publisher of *Le Constitutionnel*, and after sales had slumped from 9,000 in 1836 to 3,600 in 1844, he emulated *Le Siècle* and *La Presse* with their cheap subscriptions, large format, and serialized novels. Véron paid 100,000 francs for Eugène Sue's *Le Juif errant* and boosted sales to almost 25,000 by 1846. He also published novels by Honoré de Balzac and George Sand, despite a heated dispute with the latter.

Politically, Véron used *Le Constitutionnel* to support Adolphe Thiers and the liberal opposition to François Guizot, but his support for Louis-Napoleon in 1848 was such that Thiers broke with the paper. Though made an officer of the Légion d'honneur in 1852, Véron himself tried to assert the paper's independence from the empire. He finally sold it to the banker Mirès, the owner of the pro-government *Le Pays*, for 1.9 million francs.

Véron was elected to the Corps législatif in 1852 and 1857 as the official candidate for the arrondissement of Sceaux. His *Mémoires d'un bourgeois de Paris* (6 vols., 1853–55), which were brought up to 1863 in a later volume, are an important source for the history of politics and the press. Véron also published a novel and pamphlets on children's and workers' health.

C. Bellanger, J. Godechot, P. Guiral, and F. Terrou, eds., *Histoire générale de la presse française*, vol. 2 (Paris, 1969); A. Robert, E. Bourloton, and G. Cougny, *Dictionnaire des parlementaires français*, 5 vols. (Paris, 1891); G. Sand, *Correspondance*, vol. 6 (Paris, 1969).

*Peter McPhee*

*Related entries:* BALZAC; *LE CONSTITUTIONNEL*; GUIZOT; LEGISLATIVE BODY; *LA PRESSE*; *LA QUOTIDIENNE*; *LA REVUE DE PARIS*; SAND; *LE SIECLE*; SUE; THIERS.

**VERONA, CONGRESS OF** (1822), the largest and the most elaborate assembly of its kind since the Congress of Vienna in 1814–1815. It was preceded by an informal meeting of the ministers of the Quintuple Alliance held in Vienna during the last three weeks of September 1822. The Congress itself opened on 20 October and lasted until 14 December. Verona was chosen as the site because of the first official purpose of the meeting, which was to consider the situation in Italy following the repressive policies begun at the Congress of Laibach in 1821. Also, because Verona was in Austria's Italian dominion, Clemens von Metternich, as minister of the host power, could act as the direct master of the social and external activities of the congress and as the scriptwriter for the diplomatic activities. Thus the sovereigns of Austria, Prussia, Russia, and the Italian states (the pope excepted), other lesser princes, ministers, ambassadors, high society personalities, solicitors from all quarters, artists, and actors were gathered. The British representative should have been Viscount Castlereagh, but his unexpected and tragic death (12 August) compelled the new foreign secretary, who did not want to go himself, to send in his stead the duke of Wellington. The French minister of foreign affairs, Mathieu de Montmorency, came alone to the preliminary talks in Vienna and then moved to Verona with the other ministers. He stayed in Vienna only until 22 November. Having settled in principle the main problem—that of Spain—he returned to Paris, leaving the French representation to a troïka of plenipotentiaries: Victor-Louis de Caraman, François-René de Chateaubriand, and Pierre de La Ferronnays, who were, respectively, ambassadors to the courts of Vienna, London, and St. Petersburg. The other problems to be considered at the Congress were the question of the Negro slave trade; the pending conflict between Russia and Turkey over the Danubian provinces, a problem connected with the struggle of the Greeks for their independence; and the fate of the Spanish colonies in America, with the secondary problem of piracy in those troubled areas. Regarding the situation in Italy, the main decisions were to establish a timetable for the withdrawal of Austrian troops from Piedmont and the reduction of Austrian forces of occupation in the kingdom of Naples.

But the most momentous problem on the agenda was that of Spain. The situation there had gone from bad to worse; conservative forces in the northern provinces had risen against the liberal government established with the pronunciamento of January 1820. The future of the monarchy and the safety of the royal family were in jeopardy. The French conservative government, which had taken power in December 1821, contemplated a military intervention to save the Spanish Bourbon monarchy. The British were strongly opposed to French interference, and so the French needed the support of the great continental powers to forestall any hostile action by Great Britain. Metternich, contrary to what was often believed, viewed with apprehension the possibility of a French intervention in Spain. It might fail, and then liberal revolution might engulf France itself; or, if it did succeed, the French might try to establish in Madrid a constitutional monarchy similar to the one in Paris, a prospect anathema in the eyes of the Austrian chancellor. On the contrary, the Russian autocrat, Alexander I, thirsted for the strongest possible action against the Spanish revolution; he was even eager to commit his own armies, sending them marching through the Austrian empire and southern France. Metternich and Montmorency dissuaded him from this project, arguing that it would outrage French national pride. But the Austrian chancellor realized that the czar needed some show of force in the West to silence the critics in Russia who felt he had showed much too much restraint in the East, with the Turks. The argument that Metternich used to prevent that conflict from erupting into war was that it was necessary to preserve the union and the strength of the conservative alliance of 1815 in order to eliminate the threat of revolution in Western Europe. After much groping, the main partners settled upon the following formula: France would intervene alone in Spain and would decide how and when to intervene. The three continental allies would eventually provide some assistance, in circumstances spelled out in a document dated 19 November. This was called the minute of proceedings (*procès-verbal*) in order to avoid the more solemn format of a treaty or a protocol. In the meantime the Allies would show their united resolve by sending threatening notes to Madrid, which were very likely to bring a severance of diplomatic relations. Wellington had steadfastly refused to countenance these decisions and left Verona in a huff. Thus the Congress of Verona marked the final breakup of the great alliance of 1815.

The French had gotten essentially what they wanted: freedom to act alone in Spain, with a guarantee of help if needed. However, France could not avoid the impression that its actions in Spain bore the stamp of an enterprise commissioned by the Holy Alliance. The Russian czar had been skillfully maneuvered into accepting purely formal satisfactions for any of his contemplated actions in the East as well as in the West. As for Metternich, the price paid for maintaining a semblance of accord, and forestalling any rash actions by Russia, was the creation of the French intervention that he feared. In addition, the special understanding that he had maintained with Great Britain since 1814 was destroyed, making Austria even more dependent upon the whims of the Russian czar. Therefore it may well be said that the Congress of Verona, where Metternich appeared to be at the zenith of his influence as the "coachman of Europe," was also the starting point of his decline.

G. de Bertier de Sauvigny, *Metternich et la France*, vol. 2 (Paris, 1970). F.-R. de Chateaubriand, *Le Congrès de Verone* (Paris, 1838); I. C. Nichols, *The European Pentarchy and the Congress of Verona* (The Hague, 1971); Paul W. Schroeder, *Metternich's Diplomacy at Its Zenith* (1962).

*Guillaume de Bertier de Sauvigny*
*Related entries:* CHATEAUBRIAND; HOLY ALLIANCE; LA FERRONNAYS; METTERNICH; MONTMORENCY; QUADRUPLE ALLIANCE; QUINTUPLE ALLIANCE; SPAIN, 1823 FRENCH INVASION OF; TROPPAU, CONGRESS OF; VIENNA, CONGRESS OF.

**VEUILLOT, LOUIS** (1813–1883), conservative Catholic journalist and author. Born at Boynes-en-Gatinais (Loiret) on 11 October 1813, Veuillot, the son of a poor cooper, was placed in a solicitor's office at age thirteen. But he quickly developed an interest in literature, the theater, and political polemics. Self-taught, he began as a journalist on the ministerial paper *L'Echo de la Seine-Inférieure* in 1832 and quickly became known for his acerbic writing and his duels. In late 1832 he went to Périgueux as editor of the *Mémorial de la Dordogne*, and in 1837 he returned to Paris to work on a short-lived government paper, *La Charte de 1830*. He next became editor of *La Paix*, a *doctrinaire* journal that disappeared in December 1837, perhaps best known for its attacks on Adolphe Thiers. Thus far Veuillot was known for his witty, biting style. But he was devoid of any dedication to political or religious principle. However, in 1838 he went to Rome during Holy Week. There, in the midst of the pomp and ceremony, he underwent a conversion, becoming personally and journalistically a devout Catholic.

Veuillot returned to Paris and devoted his pen to the defense of Catholicism, producing several religious works in the early 1840s. During his stay in Périgueux, he had met General Thomas-Robert Bugeaud. In 1842 Bugeaud took Veuillot to Africa as his secretary. This contact apparently was seminal in the development of Veuillot's view of the soldier as one of the foundations of a Catholic social order. Returning to France, he served for a year and a half as senior clerk of the Ministry of the Interior before joining the staff of *L'Univers religieux*, the Roman Catholic newspaper, in 1843. He quickly became the driving force behind this paper, which he used to propagandize a violently ultramontane variety of Catholicism and simultaneously turned the paper into a significant force in public opinion. He attacked the July Monarchy so viciously on the school issue and the University that he was imprisoned for a month in 1844.

He initially welcomed the 1848 Revolution but quickly became disillusioned. As managing editor of *L'Univers* later in 1848, he briefly supported Alfred-Frédéric de Falloux and Charles-Forbes de Montalembert, whom he found to be too moderate. Then, especially from 1851, he supported Louis-Napoleon as the best hope for the church until the latter's Italian campaign of 1859 endangered the papacy. Meanwhile, in addition to editing the *Univers*, Veuillot produced a series of pamphlets attacking socialists, professors, and philosophers from 1848 to 1852. His journal openly opposed liberty, science, progress, and liberal Catholicism. He next became involved in a controversy over the Latin and Greek classics, whose use he ardently opposed. Veuillot did not hesitate to attack prelates who disagreed with him and was censured by the archbishop of Paris. But he appealed directly to Pope Pius IX and was absolved, although *L'Univers* was banned in several French dioceses.

During the 1850s his advocacy of papal power and papal infallibility became so excessive that even Pope Pius IX rebuked him. Napoleon III closed his newspaper in 1860. The fall of Napoleon in 1870 gave him the freedom to call for a Bourbon restoration, which he believed would be best for the Catholic church in France. His newspaper was suspended by the Third Republic in 1874. Failing health curtailed his activity from 1878, but his influence remained until his death in Paris on 7 March 1883. His collected works were published in thirty-seven volumes between 1927 and 1938.

I. Collins, *The Government and the Newspaper Press in France, 1814–1881* (Oxford, 1959); E. Hatin, *Bibliographie historique et critique de la presse périodique française* (Paris, n.d.) and *Histoire du journal en France, 1631–1853* (Paris, 1853); G. Vapereau, *Dictionnaire universel des contemporains* (Paris, 1858).

*James K. Kieswetter*

*Related entries:* BORDEAUX; BUGEAUD; *DOCTRINAIRES*; LIBERAL CATHOLICISM; MONTALEMBERT; PIUS IX; PUBLIC INSTRUCTION; REVOLUTION OF 1848; THIERS; ULTRAMONTANES.

**VICTOR, CLAUDE-VICTOR PERRIN BELLUNE, DUC DE** (1764–1841), marshal of the Empire and peer of the Restoration. With the First Restoration in 1814, Victor welcomed the Bourbons, who gave him the Order of Saint Louis and command of the Second Military Division. During the Hundred Days he journeyed to Ghent with the king and attended him at the *Te Deum* celebrating the French defeat at Waterloo. Louis named Victor a peer in August 1815 and appointed him one of the four major generals of the Royal Guard. Victor also served as president of the commission to investigate the conduct of officers during the Hundred Days to determine if they should be proscribed from the army. He carried out these duties with extreme severity and voted for the death of Michel Ney. In January 1816 the government gave him command of the Sixteenth Military Division, and in 1821 he was made commander of three divisions. A favorite of the ultras, on 14 December 1821 he became war minister in the new Villèle cabinet, where he remained until 10 October 1823, although he had little administrative talent. For example, he ordered each infantryman in Spain to carry 800 cartridges. He served briefly as major general of the French army in Spain but was removed at the insistence of the duke of Angoulême. He resigned from the ministry as a result of the criticism of Angoulême and the scandal that erupted around the war contractor Gabriel-Julien Ouvrard. But he remained as major general of the Royal Guard until 1830 and in 1825 became commander of the camp at Rheims. The July Revolution brought an end to his career. Indeed, he so opposed the new regime that he was accused of being a legitimist, and he escaped arrest only because of a warning from his fellow marshal, Nicholas-Jean de Soult, who was now war minister. He lived henceforth in retirement until his death in Paris on 1 March 1841.

M. Glover, *The Peninsular War, 1807–1814* (London, 1974); R. Humble, *Napoleon's Peninsular Marshals* (London, 1973); A. G. Macdonnell, *Napoleon and His Marshals* (London, 1950); A.Robert et al., *Dictionnaire des parlementaires français* (Paris, 1889–91).

*James K. Kieswetter*

*Related entries:* ANGOULEME, L.-A.; HUNDRED DAYS; NEY; OUVRARD; REVOLUTION OF 1830; ROYAL GUARD; SOULT; SPAIN; ULTRAROYALISTS; VILLELE; WATERLOO.

VIENNA, CONGRESS OF (1814–1815), congress called to rearrange the affairs of Europe following the first deposition of Napoleon. The Allied powers, after their victory over Napoleon, neither desired, nor were they able, to restore Europe to its pre-Revolutionary political and territorial structure. The new order that they wanted to establish needed the authority of a general congress, where they could at least give the appearance of having consulted the interested parties. Clemens von Metternich was the director of this grand play that was given in Vienna from October 1814 to June 1815. While festivities of all sorts were taking place, diplomacy was being carried out in the hallways in private conversations between the representatives of the Great Powers. Their agreements were then drawn up by specialized commissions like the Commission on Statistics, which was to estimate the value of sought-after territories according to their population and the amount of taxes that they paid. Finally, these agreements were concluded in separate treaties. These documents taken together, and united by the general preamble, constituted the final Act of the Congress of Vienna (June 9, 1815).

Charles-Maurice de Talleyrand, the representative of Louis XVIII, presented himself as the champion of right against might and defended the principle of legitimacy, under which "sovereignty cannot be acquired by military conquest alone, nor can it pass to the conqueror if the legitimate sovereign does not cede it voluntarily." As a result of his personal prestige, Talleyrand was able to get the Allied ministers to admit him to their preliminary conferences. Conflicts of interest among the victors even gave him the chance to sign a secret treaty of alliance among England, Austria, and France and to brag to Louis XVIII that he had broken up the Allied coalition. But all of this was only a maneuver by the English minister Viscount Castlereagh, whose goal was to force through his own policies. The final compromise was far from favorable to France because it placed a powerful and hostile Prussia on the Rhine frontier.

The Allies divided up territories according to two ideals: they wanted to ensure an equilibrium of power in Europe "by a wise distribution of power" among the victors, and they wanted to prevent future adventurism by France by surrounding themselves with a cordon of substantial secondary states. Consequently (1) they created the kingdom of the Netherlands, composed of Belgium and the former Republic of the Netherlands, whose government was vested in a prince of the house of Orange; (2) they reconstituted the Swiss confederation, whose neutrality was guaranteed by the Great Powers; and (3) they resurrected the kingdom of Piedmont-Sardinia and appended to that kingdom Savoy, Nice, and the former Republic of Genoa.

The victors divided their territorial booty in the following manner. Russia kept Finland and most of Poland, which formed an autonomous kingdom. Prussia got Swedish Pomerania, the north of Saxony, and, a more important acquisition, Westphalia and the former ecclesiastical principalities of the valley of the Rhine, one of the most advanced and prosperous regions of Europe. Austria, which had given up its hope to get Belgium back, was recompensed in northern Italy with Milan and Venice, which made up a kingdom of Lombardy-Venetia, in which the emperor would be represented by a viceroy. England kept some of the colonies conquered from France and Holland, including some important naval bases, the Cape on the route to India, Malta, and the Ionian Islands. Finally, Bernadotte, regent of Sweden and soon to be king, got the right to annex Norway in compensation for territories across the Baltic that were ceded to Prussia and to Russia. As for Germany, the Allies, especially Austria, did not want to bring back the old Holy Empire, with its 360 sovereign states, nor did they want to create a large, unified Germany, the dream of some German patriots. Their solution was the German Confederation, an association of thirty sovereigns and of four free cities. The only federal body, the Diet, which sat in Frankfurt, would be a kind of permanent assembly of ambassadors with no power of coercion over its members. The emperor of Austria, although he was by right president of the confederation, would have only one vote, just like the other sovereigns. Italy would also remain divided into seven sovereign states and would have no federal organization, although it was dominated by Austria because members of the Hapsburg family reigned in Tuscany, Modena, and Parma, because the pope depended on the Austrians to defend him, and because the king of Naples, Ferdinand de Bourbon, also needed Austrian help to keep him in power. The remarkable stability established by the Congress of Vienna, which lasted for about a half-century, is due not only to the judicious equilibrium of power established by the division of territory but also to the fact that it had come about by the free consent of the interested governments and was based on generally recognized principles of international law. But the sovereigns and the diplomats of the congress had given little recognition to the national aspirations of the peoples involved—Italians, Germans,and Poles, among others—and this failure would finally destroy their work.

K. Griewank, *Der Wiener Kongress und die Neuordnung Europas* (Leipzig, 1942, 1954); J. L. Klüber, *Akten des Wiener Kongress*, 8 vols. (Leipzig, 1815–19); C. K. Webster, *The Congress of Vienna* (London, 1934).

*Guillaume de Bertier de Sauvigny, trans. E. Newman*
*Related entries:* HOLY ALLIANCE; LOUIS XVIII; METTERNICH; QUADRUPLE ALLIANCE; QUINTUPLE ALLIANCE; TALLEYRAND.

**VIENNET, JEAN-PONS-GUILLAUME** (1777–1868), man of letters, champion of Classicism, member of the French Academy, and politician during the Restoration and July Monarchy. Known today as an opponent of romanticism and as the man elected to the French Academy instead of Benjamin Constant in 1830, Jean-Pons-Guillaume Viennet was born in Béziers on 18 November 1777, the son of Elisabeth Guibert and Jacques-Joseph Viennet (1734–1824), soldier of the Old Regime, deputy to the Legislative Assembly, member of the Convention, where as a moderate he opposed the trial and execution of Louis XVI, and deputy to the Conseil de anciens. Intended before the Revolution for an ecclesiastical office, most likely as successor to his uncle as curé of the parish of Saint-Merry, Viennet had the course of his life altered by the Revolution, and he embarked in the 1790s on a long career that eventually would combine military service, literature, and politics.

Appointed a gunnery officer in 1796,he was captured a year later and imprisoned for some months in the hulks at Plymouth. Upon his release, he resumed service, and a sentimental novel he began in captivity remained unfinished. During the Consulate and the Empire, Viennet exhibited an independent and ambiguous, if not contradictory, attitude toward these Napoleonic regimes, a stance, one that he would often repeat later in his life, that seriously hindered his prospects for advancement in the military. Owing to democratic sentiments, which he soon abandoned, Viennet first opposed the creation of both the Consulate for Life and the Empire; a reassessment of the course events were taking led to a change of mind and the composition of *L'Austerlide* (1808) and other works that celebrated in verse French military achievements. After transferring to the army, Viennet served in the campaign of 1813, winning the cross of the Légion d'honneur. Captured at Leipzig, he returned to France only after the Restoration.

Having welcomed the First Restoration with enthusiasm, Viennet became an aide to General Gaspard-Gabriel de Montélégier, an aide-de-camp to the duc de Berry. The emperor's return for the Hundred Days elicited a cautious response from Viennet: he chose not to follow the royal family to Ghent, and he voiced his opposition to the Additional Act with two pamphlets, one of which bore the title *Opinion d'un homme libre sur la constitution proposée*. His failure to support wholeheartedly the royalist cause prevented Viennet from returning to his position, and he drifted toward the liberal opposition, finally joining the staff of the *Constitutionnel*. Hardly one of François-René de Chateaubriand's legion of admirers, Viennet attacked one of his pamphlets with *Lettre d'un vrai royaliste à M. de Chateaubriand sur sa brochure intitulée "De la monarchie selon la charte"*; of Chateaubriand, Viennet wrote, "His popularity will pass and I doubt if he will be read in fifty years." In 1818, he returned to military service as an officer attached to the general staff, a position he held until his dismissal for political reasons in 1827.

An uncommonly prolific man of letters and one able to write facilely in a number of genres, Viennet published his first work in 1802 and his last one over sixty years later. His works are largely unknown today, and his literary notoriety stems from his ardent participation on the side of the classicists in the now-legendary literary battles of the 1820s. Defending the tradition of Corneille, Racine, and, above all, Voltaire, he joined with Charles-Jean de Lacretelle, Louis-Simon Auger, and others in launching a series of brazen assaults on the young writers of the romantic movement in such essays as "Aux Muses sur les romantiques" (1824) and "Préface sur les classiques et les romantiques" (1825), which he added to his poem "Le Siège de Damas." Although Viennet's literary opinions never earned him much popularity, largely because of the satiric form in which he cast them, he persisted in expressing them throughout his life, and he continued to write in accordance with the canons of the eighteenth century. A candidate for the French Academy in 1830, Viennet won election over Benjamin Constant; this decision, a grave affront to the dying Constant, has long been considered one of the great injustices committed by the Academy. Of Viennet's many works, a few deserve mention, including the tragedy *Clovis* (1820), the poem "La Philippide" (1828), which celebrated Philippe-Auguste, the novel *La Tour de Montlhéry* (2 vols., 1833), and his many *Fables* (complete edition, 1865).

From the first years of the Second Restoration on, Viennet sided with the liberal opposition on the major political questions of the day, often expressing in personal letters his opinions on such timely issues as the role of the Jesuits in France and the Greek struggle for independence. Although he found tolerable the policies of Louis XVIII, Viennet, like many of his liberal colleagues, became in the waning years of the Restoration a vociferous critic of Charles X and his repressive and reactionary policies. Owing to the publication of his *Epître aux chiffonniers sur les crimes de la presse* (7 eds., 1827), an epistle highly critical of the proposed "law of justice and love" that would have drastically curtailed freedom of the press, Viennet was dismissed from the military. Now more active than ever in the liberal struggle, he became in 1828 a representative for Hérault to the Chamber of Deputies, where he sat with the Orleanist faction. Having voted for the Address of the 221, he was reelected in June 1830. In the Revolution of 1830, Viennet had a minor but conspicuous role. On 31 July, just before General Lafayette and the duc d'Orléans stepped out on the balcony of the Hôtel de ville, Viennet read to the crowd the proclamation of the deputies that named the duke as lieutenant general of the kingdom. Rewarded by the new government, Viennet returned to the general staff of the army, retaining his post there until his retirement in 1836.

For the first seven years of the July Monarchy, Viennet served in the Chamber of Deputies, where he regularly voted with the ministerial majority. A personal friend to the king, he attacked opponents of the Orleanist regime with such vehemence that he not only became immensely unpopular but also was viciously caricatured in the popular press. Writing in 1856, some twelve years before Viennet's death, Eugène de Mirecourt called him "le Napoléon de ridicule." Made a commander of the Legion of Honor in 1836, Viennet was elevated to the peerage in 1839. Following the Revolution of 1848, although he ceased to be active in French political life, he regularly attended the sessions of the French Academy and, as grand master of the Scottish Rite, Viennet repeatedly opposed interference by the government in Masonic affairs. At the time of his death on 11 July 1868 at the age of ninety, Viennet left behind voluminous memoirs, only excerpts from which have been published.

P. Jourda, "Les Romantiques jugés par un classique," *Revue des deux mondes*, 1 July 1929, and *Un Ennemi du romantisme: Viennet* (Paris, 1935); E. de Mirecourt, *Viennet* (Paris, 1856); J.-P.-G. Viennet, *Journal de Viennet, 1817–1848*, ed. duc de Force (Paris, 1955), *Oeuvres diverses*, 4 vols. (Brussels, 1827), and *Souvenirs de la vie militaire de Jean-Pons-Guillaume Viennet, 1777–1819*, ed. A. Depréaux and P. Jourda (Moulins, 1929).

*Robert Brown*

*Related entries:* ACADEMIE FRANCAISE; ACTE ADDITIONNEL; AUGER; BERRY, C.-F.; CHATEAUBRIAND; CONSTANT; *LE CONSTITUTIONNEL*; FREEMASONRY; PRESS LAWS; ROMANTICISM; THE 221.


**VIGNY, ALFRED-VICTOR, COMTE DE** (1797–1863), romantic poet, novelist, and playwright. Born at Loches (Indre-et-Loire) on 27 March 1797 to a noble family,Vigny was raised in the traditions of the old nobility. He joined the army in 1814 but quit, disillusioned after fourteen years, to seek a career in literature. He had written poetry as early as 1815, but his first published poems did not appear until 1822. There followed a steady succession of verse, reflecting a fascination with both the sensual and the platonic. In 1826 Vigny published his first prose work, the novel *Cinq-Mars* dealing with the era of Louis XIII and the cardinal de Richelieu. In subsequent works such as the drama *Stello* (1832) and *Chatterton* (1835), Vigny reflected his own bitterness toward the materialism and philistinism of those in power. Such works also reflected the nostalgia for the past that he had acquired as a boy. His work showed the great care and sensitivity he devoted to it. His insights into human nature and the human condition helped earn him the reputation of a philosopher-poet. Although he was regarded as an early leader of literary romanticism, his lack of productivity after 1835 resulted in his being relegated to comparative obscurity. He was awarded the Legion of Honor and in 1845 was admitted to the French Academy.

Vigny was a keen and often prophetic observer of political events, especially from 1830 on, but he apparently had no political ambition. Although he was allied with no one political faction, by perhaps 1840 he had come to accept the ideas of Auguste Comte and the mutual aid movement, possibly as a result of his own sensitivity to the torments of human existence. Vigny died in Paris on 17 September 1863. Various editions of his works have appeared, and his diary (*Journal d'un poète*) was first published in 1867.

F. Baldensperger, *Alfred de Vigny* (Paris, 1929); P. G. Castex, *Vigny* (Paris, 1957); B. de La Salle, *Alfred de Vigny* (Paris, 1963); E. Lauvrière, *Alfred de Vigny, sa vie et son oeuvre* (Paris, 1946).

*James K. Kieswetter*
*Related entries:* ACADEMIE FRANCAISE; COMTE; ROMANTICISM.

**VILLAIN, LEOPOLD-J.** (?–?), revolutionary president of the Club of the Rights of Man in 1848. Villain was among the 164 accused in the trial of republicans that took place in April 1834. A member of the secret societies, he participated in the Revolution of 1848 and became president of the Society of the Rights of Man, which met daily in the Conservatory of Arts and Crafts (Conservatoire des arts et métiers). He was also a member of the Club of Clubs and participated actively in its founding and was a candidate for the Constituent Assembly.

*La Commune de Paris* (March–May 1848); A. Longepied *Le Club des Clubs* (Paris, 1850).

*Jean-Claude Caron, trans. E. Newman*
*Related entries:* CLUB OF CLUBS; CLUBS, POLITICAL; CONSERVA-TOIRE NATIONAL DES ARTS ET METIERS; CONSTITUTION OF 1848; REVOLUTION OF 1848; SOCIETY OF THE RIGHTS OF MAN.

**VILLELE, JOSEPH, COMTE DE** (1773–1854), statesman, ultraroyalist, head of the longest ministry of the Restoration era. He was born 14 April 1773 at Toulouse; his father was a member of the landed nobility of the province of Languedoc. Villèle spent the first seven years of the Revolution as a French naval officer before resigning his commission. There followed several years as a colonial landowner in the Caribbean, marriage, and a family. Villèle returned to France in 1807 and assumed management of the family estates. He remained a royalist during the Empire period and in 1815 was elected to the Chamber of Deputies of the Restoration government, where he rapidly emerged as leader of the ultraroyalists. At the end of 1821, he became minister of finance and the real head of the cabinet. In 1822 Louis XVIII named Villèle president of the Council, a position he retained until his resignation in 1828.

In domestic affairs, Villèle's most important achievement was putting France on a stable financial basis that survived the Restoration and lasted throughout the nineteenth century. Another major success was the Indemnification Law of 1825, which provided an indemnity to *émigrés* whose land had been confiscated during the Revolution and left holders of nationalized land secure in their ownership. Less successful was the Law of Sacrilege passed in 1825 by a strong majority of ultraroyalists. This act, establishing a scale of punishments, including death, for the desecration of sacred vessels, was never enforced, but it did strengthen anticlerical feeling and spurred fears that Charles X intended to restore the institutions of the Old Regime. Toward the end of his ministry, Villèle suffered increasing attacks from liberals and extreme ultraroyalists, especially over the government's attempt to establish a severe press law. Elections in the fall of 1827 gave the opposition a majority, and Villèle resigned in January 1828.

During Villèle's ministry, France regained prestige in foreign affairs. In 1823, French troops were sent into Spain to restore Ferdinand VII to his throne. The successful campaign strengthened France's ties to European conservative forces, and, despite Villèle's reluctance to support the intervention, his position as head of government was strengthened. Villèle remained cautious over the Greek insurrection against the Turks. Growing French support for the Greek cause, however, led Villèle to ally France with England and Russia in an effort to resolve the conflict. The climax came in October 1827 when an Allied naval force virtually destroyed a Turkish-Egyptian fleet inside Navarino harbor. The elation the Villèle government shared with the nation was short-lived; the ensuing election signaled the end of the Villèle ministry.

Villèle never again participated in public affairs. No doubt he was the ablest of the Restoration statesmen. His administrative and financial abilities were considerable, but he was unable to keep an extreme ultra wing of the royalists in line, and he failed to keep in touch with public opinion.

G. de Bertier de Sauvigny, *The Bourbon Restoration* (Philadelphia, 1966); J.Fourcassié, *Villèle* (Paris, 1954); J. de Villèle, *Mémoires et Correspondance du Comte de Villèle* (Paris, 1888–1904).

*John K. Creighton*

*Related entries:* CHAMBER OF DEPUTIES; CHARLES X; INDEMNITY BILL OF 1825; LAW OF SACRILEGE; LOUIS XVIII; NAVARINO, BATTLE OF; PRESS LAWS; RESTORATION, SECOND; SPAIN, 1823 FRENCH INVASION OF; ULTRAROYALISTS.

**VILLEMAIN, ABEL-FRANCOIS** (1790–1870), professor and politician. Born in Paris, Villemain enjoyed an illustrious career as an academic; appointed professor of French Literature at the Sorbonne in 1816 at the age of twenty-six, he became a member of the French Academy at thirty-one. His lectures drew large audiences, and he was counted, along with François Guizot and Victor Cousin, as one of the three great professors during the Restoration. At first a *doctrinaire*, he became a staunch liberal after he was revoked as a *Maître-des-requêtes* on the Conseil d'état by Joseph de Villèle in 1827 for having defended freedom of the press. Elected a deputy from the Eure in July 1830, he welcomed the Revolution of 1830 and was rewarded by appointment to the Conseil d'instruction publique (1830), which exercised surveillance over the Université, and elevated to the Chamber of Peers (1832) after he lost his seat in the lower chamber.

He served as minister of education first in the Soult ministry (1839–40) and later in Guizot's government (1840–44) at a time when the monopoly of the Université over higher education was under increasing attack from Catholics. Although a defender of the Université, of which he was a member, Villemain presented a government bill to the Chamber in 1841 reflecting the moderate views of Guizot and the king, which was intended as a compromise. Although the bill recognized the freedom to open secondary schools, it provided that private schools must conform to certain degree requirements for their teachers and submit to state inspection, a move that would extend the authority of the state over the petits-séminaires, ostensibly training colleges for the priesthood but in fact operated as secondary schools for a large number of bourgeois and aristocratic youth. After strong criticism of the bill by Catholic bishops, it was withdrawn during the parliamentary recess. As the campaign for freedom of education under Charles-Forbes de Montalembert's leadership gained momentum, Villemain tried to prevent members of the Université from replying. In 1844, Villemain presented a new bill to the Chamber of Peers, similar to that of 1841 but slightly more favorable to Catholics, where it passed by only a narrow margin because of Catholic opposition. The bill was also opposed by anticlericals. In the Chamber, Adolphe Thiers' committee report strongly endorsing the bill embarrassed the moderate Guizot. By this time Villemain was seriously ill from strain and overwork—his enemies alleged he saw Jesuits everywhere—which gave Guizot the opportunity to dump him in favor of the pro-clerical Narcisse-Achille de Salvandy, who subsequently allowed the bill to die. After his recovery, Villemain joined the opposition against Guizot. The Revolution of 1848 ended his political career.

A prolific writer, Villemain published over thirty volumes of literary criticism, history, biography, and some political tracts, including *Cours de littérature française*, 5 vols. (1828–29), and studies on Oliver Cromwell (1819), François de Fénelon (1824), François-René de Chateaubriand (1857), and Pindar (1859).

G. Vauthier, *Villemain, 1790–1870, essai sur sa vie, son rôle et ses ouvrages* (Paris, 1913).

*Charles E.Freedeman*

*Related entries:* ACADEMIE FRANCAISE; COUSIN; *DOCTRINAIRES*; GUIZOT; LIBERTY OF EDUCATION; MONTALEMBERT; PETITS-SEMINAIRES; PUBLIC INSTRUCTION; SALVANDY; SOULT; THIERS; VILLELE.

**VILLENEUVE-BARGEMONT, JEAN-PAUL-ALBAN, VICOMTE DE** (1784–1850), administrator and sociologist. The son of a provincial noble family, Villeneuve-Bargemont entered the prefectoral administration under the Empire. After the Bourbon Restoration of 1815, he was successively prefect of Tarn-et-Garonne, Charente, the Meurthe, the Loire-Inférieure, and the Nord. While he was serving in this last post, he became aware of the serious problem posed by the poverty of the new class of workers in the big textile factories. After the Revolution of 1830, he abandoned government service and devoted himself to the creation of his great *Traité d'économie politique chrétienne* (Treatise of Christian Political Economy) in 1834, which is rightly considered to be the first work of the nineteenth century to set forth the thinking of social Catholicism.

Sister M. E. Ring, *Villeneuve-Bargemont, Precursor of Modern Social Catholicism* (Milwaukee, 1935); A. Théry, *L'Oeuvre économique de Villeneuve-Bargemont* (Nancy, 1911).

*Guillaume de Bertier de Sauvigny, trans. E. Newman*
Related entries: RESTORATION, SECOND; REVOLUTION OF 1830; SOCIAL CATHOLICISM.

**VILLERME, LOUIS-RENE** (1782–1863), physician and sociologist. After his medical studies in Paris, Villermé became an army doctor and got his doctorate in 1814. Soon, however, he gave up his medical practice in order to devote himself entirely to his works on medical and social statistics. The fame that he thus acquired allowed him to enter the Académie des sciences morales et politiques (Academy of Moral and Political Sciences). His best-known work, which is still being used, is *Tableau de l'état physique et moral des ouvriers dans les fabriques de coton, de laine et de soie* (View of the Physical and Moral State of the Workers in Cotton, Wool, and Silk Factories), published in 1840 in Paris in two volumes.

E. H. Ackerknecht, "Hygiene in France," *Bulletin of the History of Medicine* (March–April 1948); E. Mireaux, "Un Chirurgien sociologue, Louis-René Villermé," *Revue des deux mondes* 2 (1962).

*Guillaume de Bertier de Sauvigny*

**VINCARD, JULES** (1796–1879?), known as Vinçard l'aîné. Parisian ruler maker, worker poet, songwriter for Saint-Simonian socialism, and founder and editor of the Saint-Simonian working-class newspapers, *La Ruche populaire* and *L'Union*. Vinçard was the most loyal of all the worker poets to the Saint-Simonian church, so much so that the socialist Flora Tristan referred to him as a "real Saint-Simonian sheep." But she misunderstood the man; Vinçard would always maintain his intellectual independence from the movement. He was a liberal egalitarian democrat and opposed all aspects of Saint-Simonianism that set up an elite, that stopped people from choosing their own professions, or that stood in the way of popular government. In the end, he remained faithful to both the movement and his differences with it.

Vinçard was born in Paris on the Ile de la Cité on 30 July 1796, the eldest of three children. His father was a worker who had recently purchased a small factory where he made rulers, and his mother darned and washed silk stockings. Vinçard claimed in his memoirs that his mother taught him to read even though she could not read herself, but it seems more likely that one of his father's employees taught him. He was thirteen years old before his father, in three months, taught him to write. He early acquired a passion for literature, especially Molière, and for song, singing his own songs in the *goguettes*, or singing societies, that flourished in Paris with the coming of the Bourbon Restoration in 1815. When he joined the Saint-Simonians in 1831 he was able to put his talent as a *chansonnier* at the service of the movement. He never accepted the antidemocratic and antiliberal aspects of the faith, such as the infallibility of its leader, "Father" Enfantin, the call for "classifiers" who would assign everybody to a job, and the appointment of an elite committee of managers to run the state. But when the Saint-Simonian leaders ran afoul of the police, Vinçard supported them, and their departure for Egypt in search of the female messiah left him free to practice his own democratic and liberal version of Saint-Simonianism. In 1839 he organized a coalition of socialists—Saint-Simonians, Fourierists, communists, Owenites, and others—to edit a newspaper, *La Ruche populaire* ("The People's Beehive"). Its motto, printed on its masthead, was one of Vinçard's songs:

> What difference does the banner, the party, or the color make,
> Are we not brothers in shame, in poverty, in sadness?

It turned out, however, that the banners did make a difference. The Fourierists took over the *Ruche populaire* in its fourth year, and Vinçard and his Saint-Simonians founded a new working-class newspaper, *L'Union*, in 1843.

The new journal continued to preach Vinçard's lifelong belief in the primacy of the producer and in the need for change through peaceful progress under the direction of a benevolent God. He was certain that this change was inevitable, and he wrote:

> Soldiers of industry, on guard! Line up!
> No more strife!
> Proletarians of all lands
> No more aggressors
> Nor oppressors,
> Let us join both our voices and our hearts together;
> It is God who is revealing to us
> His decrees for the future,
> It is He who is coming to unite us in a new faith.

The revolution in society would be based on an inner revolution in people's hearts. Selfishness and greed must give way to a spirit of generosity and fraternity. This revolution of the heart had already occurred among two groups of people: workers and women. Vinçard said: "God is in the heart of the people and of women." Selfishness, on the other hand, dominated in the hearts of the rich who lived on their unearned income and in England, which he called "egotism's native land." All people must be organized into producers' cooperative associations, every able-bodied person should work, and people should be paid according to the value of their labor. It was God's will as Jesus had preached it to establish a single democratic socialist republic for all the world. To spread God's word would be enough to make it happen; progress would do the rest.

Thus the *chansonnier* would be the key figure in the coming revolution, and Vinçard organized an invasion of the *goguettes* in Paris. There, *chansonniers* had copied Pierre-Jean de Béranger in singing of wine, women, and war: *les lauriers, les guerriers, la gloire,* and *la victoire.* Vinçard sang of the social question and working-class pride. In his song, "Le Prolétaire," written in 1843, Vinçard sang:

> It is he who gives out crowns,
> It is he who founds states,
> Who makes and unmakes thrones,
> Heros and potentates;
> Yet he is humble, and the crowd
> Of fortunate rich people who owe everything they have to
> his great-heartedness
> Insult him, and often crush under their feet
> The sweetest fruits of his labor.
> But then once the dear voice
> Of the universal nation
> Has sent forth its cry of liberty,
> He will come out of his obscurity.

And again in a song he wrote in 1836 and reprinted after the 1848 Revolution:

> You alone are king.
> Awake!
> Producer, impose your law!

The 1848 Revolution gave Vinçard (despite his belief in peaceful progress) a chance to realize his ideals, and he suggested that a declaration of Saint-Simonian principles be posted throughout Paris. He ran as a candidate for the Constituent Assembly but lost the election, and the posters were never made. He was forced by financial crisis to close his business, and he found that even wealthy Saint-Simonians refused to hire him for fear that his ideas would demoralize their workers.

Vinçard sustained himself with an obscure newspaper job and then finally started up his business again during the economic recovery of the Second Empire. Around 1860 some rich Saint-Simonians gave him a pension and a house so that he could work full time managing a mutual aid society. He published in 1865 a mutualist newspaper and helped producers' cooperative societies in Paris. He was a member of such a cooperative. He also tried and failed to write a history of the French people, a project that he admitted was beyond his energy and talents. He died after 1878, possibly in 1879. He never lost faith in equality, in democracy, and in progress, and he always believed that the day was at hand when people would find their salvation in their own hearts.

P. Brochon, *La Chanson française, le pamphlet du pauvre, 1834–1851* (Paris, 1957); J. Maitron, ed., *Dictionnaire biographique du mouvement ouvrier français*, vol. 3 (Paris, 1966); E. L. Newman, "L'Arme du siècle, c'est la plume: The French Worker Poets of the July Monarchy and the Spirit of Revolution and Reform," *Journal of Modern History* (1980), and *The French Worker Poets of the July Monarchy* (forthcoming); M. Ragon, *Les Ecrivains du peuple* (Paris, 1947); J. Rancière, *La Nuit des prolétaires* (Paris, 1981); E. Thomas, *Voix d'en bas; la poésie ouvrière du XIXe siècle* (Paris, 1979); J. Touchard, *La Gloire de Béranger*, 2 vols. (Paris, 1968); J. Vinçard, *Mémoires épisodiques d'un vieux chansonnier saint-simonien* (Paris, 1876).

*Edgar Leon Newman*

*Related entries:* CONSTITUTION OF 1848; ENFANTIN; FOURIER; REVO-LUTION OF 1848; *LA RUCHE POPULAIRE;* SAINT-SIMONIANISM; SINGING SOCIETIES; TRISTAN; WORKER POETS; WORKERS' COOPERATIVES.

**VINCENT, LOUIS-CHARLES-MARIE, BARON DE** (1792–1872), soldier and political figure. Born at Cap François (Haiti) to a career army officer eventually ennobled by Napoleon, Vincent studied at the military college of Saint-Germain, entered the cavalry, and served in a series of historic campaigns: Russia (1812), Germany (1813), France (1814), Waterloo (1815), and Spain (1823–24). After the July Revolution, the government stationed him in Paris where, in his own words, he fought against "anarchy," meaning the street disturbances of the early 1830s. Already a *chevalier* of the Legion of Honor since 1814, he was made an *officier* in 1831, eventually becoming *commandant* in 1850.

Vincent served as mayor of the village of Mézières (Seine-et-Oise) from 1829. He was one of France's minor notables, with a wife and two children, and a modest income of 12,000 francs a year from *rentes*. He entered on a civilian career as subprefect of Toul (Meurthe) in November 1835. Evaluations by his superiors noted that he had vague but presumably liberal political opinions, a taste for social life, and little aptitude for desk work; he administered "zealously" but "superficially." They ignored his repeated applications for promotion, and he was still at Toul when the February Revolution removed him from office.

Career frustrations under Louis-Philippe, memories of past military glory, and distaste for the mob made Vincent a likely recruit to Bonapartism. The political reaction after June 1848 opened new career opportunities, and he took an active part in the repression of republicanism and socialism. Named in quick succession to the subprefectures of Aix (15 July 1848) and Le Hâvre (23 July 1848), he was then appointed, in turn, prefect of the Lot (24 April 1849), Jura (22 August 1849), Seine-et-Marne (9 March 1851), and, finally, France's second department, the Rhône (30 October 1851). This last was a prestigious post, but his authority was limited because Lyons had been under martial law since June 1849. Thus, when in the aftermath of the coup d'état of 2 December, which he enthusiastically supported, he summoned the citizens to rally "around me," General Espirit-Victor de Castellane reprimanded him for posting proclamations without military approval. Vincent resigned his post in early 1852, subsequently becoming a member of the Council of State (19 April 1852) and then the Senate (15 August 1859). He died in Paris in 1872.

Archives nationales, carton F1b I 176/15, dossier Vincent; T. Forstenzer, *French Provincial Police and the Fall of the Second Republic* (Princeton, 1981); P. Montague, *Le comportement politique de l'armee a Lyon sous la Monarchie de Juillet et la Seconde-Republique* (Paris, 1966).

*Michael Sibalis*

*Related entries:* BONAPARTISM; CASTELLANE; COUNCIL OF STATE; COUP D'ETAT OF 2 DECEMBER 1851; LOUIS-PHILIPPE; REVOLUTION OF 1830; REVOLUTION OF 1848; SPAIN, 1823 FRENCH INVASION OF; WATERLOO, BATTLE OF.

**VIOLLET-LE-DUC, EUGENE-EMMANUEL** (1814–1879), scholar and architectural theorist, best known for his restorations of medieval monuments. Advocate of medieval architecture, restorer of many of the greatest medieval monuments of France, and author of a controversial theory of historical restoration, Eugène-Emmanuel Viollet-le-Duc was born in Paris on 27 January 1814 to Emmanuel Viollet-le-Duc (1781–1857) and Eugénie Delécluze. His father, an official at the Tuileries Palace, was also a scholar and a great collector of sixteenth-century French literature. His mother belonged to the Delécluze family, and young Eugène passed his childhood in the family home at 1, rue Chabanais, which the Viollet-le-Ducs shared with, among others, his uncle Etienne-Jean Delécluze (1781–1863), a painter and one-time pupil of Jacques-Louis David, who had exchanged his brush for the pen and, as the art critic for the *Journal des débats*, was a major figure in Restoration intellectual circles.

Viollet-le-Duc's formal schooling began at the Institut Morin at Fontenay-aux-Roses and ended at the collège Bourbon on the eve of the July Revolution. Perhaps of more consequence, his informal education gave him an easy entry into an intellectual world of considerable vitality. To his uncle he owed a debt for occasional lessons in drawing. Further, since the Delécluze home served as the setting for two weekly salons, young Viollet-le-Duc came into early proximity with many of the leading artists and intellectuals of the generation that came to maturity during the Restoration. Of these salons, the Sunday gatherings of his uncle were of the greatest consequence, for there came Stendhal, Charles-Augustin Sainte-Beuve, Prosper Mérimée, Paul-Louis Courier of the *Globe*, Ludovic Vitet, Auguste Sautelet, the architects Jean Huvé and Achille Leclère, and others, many of whom would play roles of importance in Viollet-le-Duc's later life and career.

Young Viollet-le-Duc and his father were absent from Paris when the July Revolution broke out. When the two returned on 29 July, they found themselves in the midst of the rebellion. An attractive legend describes Viollet-le-Duc's small contribution to this revolution. Observing rebels erecting a poorly constructed barricade at the corner of his street, he lent his talents and helped improve the barricade's design. With the July Revolution came a change in fortune for the Viollet-le-Duc family. Emmanuel Viollet-le-Duc regained his position at the Tuileries, and, within a year, his entire family took up residence, at the request of Louis-Philippe, in the palace. Young Viollet-le-Duc was thus in a position to catch the French monarch's eye and to benefit from his occasional patronage.

Viollet-le-Duc, who evinced a precocious talent for drawing and aspired to a career as an architect, purposely avoided the Ecole des beaux-arts, a bastion of neoclassicism conducted by the Académie royale des beaux-arts, and the usual choice for such schooling. Instead, because he wanted to learn the craft of the builder, he worked in the shops of Jean Huvé and Achille Leclère, completing his education by reading the great books on architecture and by traveling. Between 1831 and 1837, Viollet-le-Duc made six annual trips, the first five devoted to the southern and western parts of France. The sixth journey, lasting over seventeen months, took the young man to Italy for extensive travels and a residence in Rome of nine months. These same six years were also important for his personal life. His beloved mother died in 1832 during the cholera epidemic that swept France, and, within the year, he had met and married Elisabeth Tempier. Finally, Viollet-le-Duc began to achieve recognition as an artist, winning medals for watercolors exhibited at the Salon. In 1834, he was appointed *suppléant* for the Course of Composition and Ornaments at the Ecole de dessin of Paris, a position he retained until 1850. And he acquired the patronage of Louis-Philippe, who financed the Italian trip by the purchase of a watercolor.

By 1837, when Viollet-le-Duc was but twenty-three, he judged himself ready to embark on his career. While continuing to deliver lessons at the Ecole de dessin, he responded to a request from the Baron Taylor, already famed for his *Voyages dans l'ancienne France*, and provided him with nearly 250 drawings between 1837 and 1844. More important, Viollet-le-Duc was named in 1838 to the Conseil des bâtiments civiles as an assistant to his old master Leclère, now the inspector general, and then *sous-inspecteur des travaux de l'hôtel* of the Archives du royaume. The next year, he was sent to Narbonne to study a project for the completion of the Gothic cathedral of Saint-Just. Although certainly important, all this activity was but mere preparation.

For Viollet-de-Duc, 1840 became the most important year of his life. Owing to a new interest in preserving France's great architectural heritage, a movement that owed something to a contemporaneous movement in England, to the work of men like Arcisse de Caumont, to the popularity of works like the *Génie de Christianisme* of François-René de Chateaubriand and the *Notre-Dame de Paris* of Victor Hugo, and to the growing interest that men and women of nineteenth-century France took in history, the July Monarchy moved quickly to preserve France's medieval legacy, much of which was in a sad state of repair. Mérimée, who succeeded Vitet as *inspecteur-général des monuments historiques* when he became chairman of the Commission des monuments historiques, acted on a suggestion made by Delécluze and appointed Viollet-le-Duc in February 1840 to undertake the restoration of the abbey church of Vézelay. Viollet-le-Duc's brilliant work in rescuing this Romanesque church made his reputation.

The restoration of Vézelay reveals much, not just about the condition of medieval monuments in France in the first half of the nineteenth century but also about Viollet-le-Duc, his methods of working, and his developing ideas on historical restoration. The fine twelfth-century church located on a picturesque hill in Burgundy belonged to the once wealthy monastery of Vézelay, which had fallen upon hard times long before the 1840s. Although the decline had begun during the thirteenth century, Vézelay's misfortunes had multiplied during the French Revolution; in 1796, the abbey buildings were sold as national lands and razed to the ground, and the church became a parish church. By 1834, when Mérimée visited Vézelay on his first trip as inspector of monuments, the extremely poor condition of the church made the danger of collapse real. Although funds for the restoration work had been voted between 1835 and 1838, work had yet to begin because no architect willing to undertake the delicate task had been found. When approached, Viollet-le-Duc accepted and immediately set to work. He first conducted a meticulous survey of the building and then, between 1840 and 1842, propped up or restored the parts that threatened to collapse. Although certainly careful and often brilliant, Viollet-le-Duc's work aroused controversy. While restoring the nave, for example, he discovered that the last four vaults had been previously redone in a Gothic style. In the process of restoration, he had three of them removed, replacing them with vaults modeled on the Romanesque originals. The fourth vault he permitted to retain its Gothic character, for it provided a transition from the Romanesque nave to the Gothic choir. Viollet-le-Duc also added a small wall to the exterior of the choir. Both of these undertakings clearly reveal Viollet-le-Duc's willingness not just to restore but to remake buildings, a predilection that involved him in a lifetime of controversy and that has made his work still controversial.

Success at Vézelay established Viollet-le-Duc's reputation and brought him new and even more important projects, twelve alone between 1842 and 1845. Of these projects, the most important was the restoration of Notre Dame Cathedral in Paris, a task Viollet-le-Duc undertook with the aid of Jean-Baptiste Lassus (1807–51). Completed between 1845 and 1864, the work involved construction of a sacristy, rebuilding the spire at the crossing of the transepts and the nave, restoring the choir, and reworking the nave. Just as at Vézelay, Viollet-le-Duc's ideas provoked controversy, especially the decision to return the nave walls to their twelfth-century appearance; critics charged that this reworking produced a clash with the elevation of the nave, which dated from the thirteenth century.

Nevertheless, Viollet-le-Duc used this nineteen-year project to train the architects and the workers who would undertake much of the medieval restoration work in France.

Endowed with independence of character and a strong faith in his own ideas, Viollet-le-Duc did not allow criticism of his work to prevent him from undertaking numerous other significant projects in the 1840s and later. These included repair and restoration of the abbey church of Saint-Denis (1847), the reconstruction of the fortifications of Carcassonne (1849), and the restoration of Amiens Cathedral (1849). During the Second Empire, Viollet-le-Duc continued his work, becoming an inspector general of the *édifices diocésains* in 1853 and undertaking such major projects for the Emperor Napoleon III as the imaginative and controversial rebuilding of the chateau of Pierrefonds. For a brief and unfortunate period of time, he held the professorship of art and aesthetics at the Ecole des beaux-arts, the school he had scorned in the early 1830s. During the siege of Paris, Viollet-le-Duc participated in the defense of the French capital; during the Commune, however, he fled to Pierrefonds. Having become an ardent republican in the 1870s, he served on the Municipal Council of the Faubourg-Montmartre. On 17 September 1879, he died in his home near Lausanne.

Viollet-le-Duc's posthumous fame rests equally on his reputation as a preserver and restorer of medieval edifices and on his many published writings, most of which appeared during the Second Empire and the Third Republic. Some early theoretical articles, however, appeared in the *Annales archéologiques*, a highly partisan journal edited by A.-N. Didron (1806–67). Worthy of particular note are those published between 1844 and 1847 under the general title "De la Construction des édifices religieux en France depuis le commencement du Christianisme jusqu'au XVIe siècle," for in them Viollet-le-Duc sketched the rudiments of theories he developed more fully in the famous *Dictionnaire raisonné de l'architecture*, which summarized all of Viollet-le-Duc's vast knowledge of medieval architecture. He championed a rational, scientific study of Gothic architecture that emphasized the function of the structural aspects of a building. Medieval architects built soaring naves not to express religious ideas in stone but to allow light and air to fill the church. The various elements of a Gothic edifice—the pointed arch, the ribbed vault, the flying buttress, and the pinnacle—all had a specific function in the balanced and complex interplay of conflicting forces that kept a cathedral standing. All the parts of the cathedral were hence integral aspects of a totality, each serving to resolve a particular structural problem. Second, Viollet-le-Duc viewed Gothic architecture as an expression of thirteenth-century French society, and, as he made clear in the *Dictionnaire*, that society was the secular world of the medieval town. Third, Viollet-le-Duc sought to expound a theory of architecture, one derived from his studies of the medieval, that would serve as the basis for the renewal of French architecture in the nineteenth century. He hoped to find for his century an architecture as harmoniously expressive of the state of French society as the Gothic had been of the thirteenth. Finally, Viollet-le-Duc sketched some of his ideas on the problem of historical restoration. In addition to making the important point that a restorer had to understand the technical aspects of the building profession, he argued that the restoration of a building does not consist of just preserving, repairing, and remodeling it but of returning it to a complete state that it may never have had at any one moment. It was this latter theory, when applied to Vézelay, Notre Dame, and other medieval monuments, that roused such a storm of protest. Despite the many controversies he raised and despite some questionable restorations, Viollet-le-Duc's name remains inextricably linked with French medieval architecture.

The praise accorded Viollet-le-Duc's great *Dictionnaire* should not completely obscure his many other works. In a series of lectures, collected and published under the title *Entretiens sur l'architecture*, Viollet-le-Duc posed a question— Will the nineteenth century have an architecture expressive of it?—and not only answered it in the affirmative but sketched his ideas concerning the character of that architecture. He also published the six-volume *Dictionnaire raisonné du mobilier français*, in which he discussed French furnishings, decorative arts, and armor from the Carolingian period to the Renaissance. Among Viollet-le-Duc's other works are a number of monographs on various monuments, including the abbey church of Vézelay and the city of Carcassone.

P. M. Auzas, *Viollet-le-Duc, 1814–1879* (Paris, 1965); J. Dupont, "Viollet-le-Duc and Restoration in France," *Historic Preservation Today* (Washington, D.C., 1966); P. Gout, *Viollet-le-Duc: Sa vie, son oeuvre, sa doctrine* (Paris, 1914); R. D. Middleton, "Eugene-Emmanuel Viollet-le-Duc," *The Macmillan Encyclopedia of Architects*, vol. 4 (New York, 1982); N. Pevsner, "Viollet-le-Duc and Reynaud," in *Some Architectural Writers of the Nineteenth Century* (Oxford, 1972); J. Summerson, "Viollet-le-Duc and the Rational Point of View," in *Heavenly Mansions* (London, 1949); E. Viollet-le-Duc, *Dictionnaire du raisonné mobilier français de l'époque carlovingienne à la Renaissance*, 6 vols. (Paris, 1858–75), *Dictionnaire raisonné de l'architecture française du XIe au XVIe siècle*, 10 vols. (Paris, 1854–69), *Entretiens sur l'architecture*, 2 vols. (Paris, 1863–72), and *Monographie de l'ancienne église abbatiale de Vézelay* (Paris, 1873).

*Robert Brown*

*Related entries:* ACADEMY OF FINE ARTS; CHATEAUBRIAND; DELE-CLUZE; HUGO; *JOURNAL DES DEBATS*; MERIMEE; REVOLUTION OF 1830.

**VITROLLES, EUGENE-FRANCOIS-AUGUSTE D'ARNAUD, BARON DE** (1774–1854), ultraroyalist politician. After Vitrolles fought in the army of *émigrés*, he returned to France under the Consulate and even accepted a minor post in the imperial administration. With his bold character and lively eloquence, he took an active part in the events of the spring of 1814, serving as a liaison agent between Charles-Maurice de Talleyrand and the Allied ministers meeting in Chatillon. He made himself useful to the comte d'Artois when he re-entered Paris and continued to serve as his counselor. When Napoleon returned to France in March 1815, Vitrolles was placed in charge of the movement to organize royalist resistance in the south of France, for which he was imprisoned by Joseph

Fouché. Fouché later saved his life in order to use him as an intermediary between himself and the king, who was exiled in Ghent.

Following the Second Restoration, Vitrolles was a deputy from the Basses-Alpes in the *chambre introuvable* of 1815, and while there he was one of the strongest members of the ultraroyalist party, which was violently hostile to Elie Decazes. But when the ultraroyalists came to power at the end of 1821, Vitrolles was kept from office because of Joseph de Villèle's distrust. In 1824, however, Charles X gave him the title and pension of a minister of state that had been taken away from him in 1818, and in 1827 sent him as a minister from France to Tuscany. In January 1830 he entered the Chamber of Peers but took no part in preparing the ordinances of July 1830, and, during the Revolution of 1830, he tried in vain to save the crown.

Vitrolles left some interesting memoirs, but they must be read with an awareness of the excesses that his imagination, the prisoner of his vanity, led him to from time to time.

E. Forgues, *Correspondance inédite entre Lamennais et le baron de Vitrolles* (Paris, 1886).

*Guillaume de Bertier de Sauvigny, trans. E. Newman*
Related entries: CHAMBRE INTROUVABLE; DECAZES; FOUCHE; TAL-LEYRAND-PERIGORD; ULTRAROYALISTS; VILLÈLE.


**VIVIEN, ALEXANDRE-FRANCOIS-AUGUSTE** (1799–1854), renowned legal theorist, politician, and councillor of state. Although Auguste Vivien was the son of an *avocat*, he was originally destined for a military career. With the demise of the Empire, Vivien switched to the law. In 1820 he was admitted to the bar of Amiens, and he returned to Paris in 1826. The publication of *Traité de la législature des théâtres* (1830) began his distinguished career in jurisprudence. The new government of Louis-Philippe returned Vivien to Amiens as the new *procureur-général* in 1830.

Believing the July Revolution had brought the correct solution, Vivien became a partisan of the Party of Order. He subdued local riots in Amiens, and for his efforts the government brought him back to Paris to be prefect of police. From 21 February to 17 September 1831, Vivien faced republican-inspired riots on 15–16 April, 11–17 June, and 14 July. Each time he managed to maintain order without severe repression. His efforts pleased few, but this success was sufficient to gain him appointment to the Council of State.

It was as a councillor of state, especially in his leadership of the section on legislation founded in 1839, that Vivien made his mark. His *Etudes administratives* (1842–44, revised 1852) was a pivotal work, and it established Vivien as one of the greatest legal theorists of the mid-nineteenth century. Many of his ideas were expressed in the pages of the *Revue des deux mondes*; especially notable was his belief in laws on expropriation for the public utility. In 1845 he was elected to the Institute (Académie des sciences morales et politiques).

In addition to serving on the Council of State, Vivien was a deputy and minister under Louis-Philippe. Elected to the Chamber of Deputies for the first time in the by-elections of 1833 from St. Quentin (Aisne), he served until the Revolution of 1848. Vivien, who identified himself to the electors as a councillor of state, a *propriétaire*, a *rentier*, and an *avocat*, was a *grand notable* by virtue of his 1,000 franc tax payments. Initially he sat with the Third Party, whose members kept aloof both from the Party of Order on the right and the Party of Movement on the left, but he moved toward the dynastic opposition after his stint as minister of justice under Adolphe Thiers (1 March–28 October 1840). His popularity with the voters of St. Quentin was overwhelming; in the elections of 1837, 1839, and 1846 he received over 93 percent of the vote. In 1842 his percentage of the vote was somewhat lower.

The electors under universal suffrage were not quite so enamored with Vivien. Nevertheless, the voters of the Aisne sent him to the Constituent Assembly sixth among their fourteen deputies. He sat on the commission to write the Constitution, where his basically conservative ideas often prevailed. An Orleanist, Vivien was brought into the cabinet of General Eugène Cavaignac as minister of public works on 13 October 1848 in the general's attempt to broaden his base of support. He was active in attempts to promote work for the artisans of Paris. The face of the Louvre was restored, and he supported workers' cooperatives. His efforts to gain the money for a railway line to Avignon, however, were not successful. The election of Louis-Napoleon brought an end to Vivien's tenure as minister of public works.

As a deputy in the Assembly, Vivien was the reporter on the law to reorganize the Council of State. When he was elected to a position on the Council, he resigned as deputy (20 April 1849). Once again on the Council, he led the section on legislation. Although he believed that the administrative apparatus of prefectures and police should be used to control public order and even the status quo, Vivien saw Louis-Napoleon's use of the prefects and the police in the coup d'état of 2 December 1851 as a clear violation of the law. Consequently he resigned from the Council of State and returned to his legal studies.

A. Robert and G. Cougny, *Dictionnaire des parlementaires français* (Paris, 1889–91).

*Thomas Beck*

*Related entries:* ACADEMY OF SCIENCES; CAVAIGNAC, L.-E.; COUNCIL OF STATE; PARTY OF MOVEMENT; PARTY OF ORDER; RAILROADS; *LA REVUE DES DEUX MONDES*; THIERS; WORKERS' COOPERATIVES.

**VOILQUIN, SUZANNE** (1801–1877), feminist. Suzanne Violquin was born in Paris, the third daughter of Raymond Monnier, a hatmaker and Revolutionary. She attended school at the Sisters of St. Vincent for four years and remained religious for many years.

In 1821, Suzanne's mother, who had been ailing for many years, died of a cancer that she had hidden from her doctor out of modesty. Suzanne wanted to become a doctor in order to treat women, but medical school was closed to women. She fell in love with Stanislas, a medical student, who promised to marry her but instead seduced and abandoned her.

In 1823, Suzanne's father's affairs having failed, Suzanne and her younger sister, Adrienne, became day laborers. Two years later Adrienne married Charles Mallard, a typographer, and, encouraged by the newleyweds, Suzanne married Voilquin. The four lived together and became part of the Saint-Simonian family.

In 1823, Suzanne helped edit *La Femme libre*, a Saint-Simonian newspaper started by two women workers. The main purpose of this paper was to launch a new, peaceful crusade against the belief in the inferiority of women. Six months later Voilquin announced his desire to leave Suzanne to go to the United States with a new wife. Suzanne wrote in the newspaper: "A man's name seems to my independent spirit too heavy to carry. I have put it down."

Suzanne began sewing lingerie to cover her cost of living and continued to edit the newspaper. Leon Simon and P. Curie (Saint-Simonian friends) discovered the homeopathic method of Dr. Hahnemann and began to teach classes in this method to women in Suzanne's flat.

In 1834, Suzanne left Paris for Egypt, following the Saint-Simonian group that had left earlier in search of a female messiah. Suzanne became a launderer for the group to earn her keep. When the plague broke out, many of the group died, and others fled. Suzanne stayed on and took lessons from Dr. Delong and Dr. Dussap and found her true vocation in medicine.

In 1835, the Grand Pasha promised to build a hospital for women in Cairo. Suzanne prepared to become the hospital midwife by taking more classes in a military hospital. Disguised as a man, she took classes from Professor Esmengard. Suzanne herself gave birth, but the baby died within three weeks.

Suzanne left Cairo because the hospital was not built, but she took with her a certificate stating that she was an accomplished midwife. Back in Paris, she took more classes in homeopathy to perfect her knowledge. Suzanne now had to look for patients because she had to support herself, her father, and an adopted niece (one of her deceased brother's girls). She was not able to make enough money and decided to go to Russia to work.

During the seven years she spent in St. Petersburg, she wrote frequent letters to her sister, Adrienne, who had emigrated to the United States in 1833. These letters comment on the despotism of the Russian court and on her frequent illnesses due to the extreme cold. Upon returning to Paris, Suzanne continued to practice as a midwife in the Marais area. She tried unsuccessfully to establish a center for wet nurses in 1847. A year later she contributed articles to *La Voix des femmes*, edited by Eugénie Niboyet.

In September 1848, Suzanne left France with her father and a niece for New Orleans to care for her dying sister. Suzanne remained in the United States for ten years, returned to France for a year, and then went back to New Orleans for two to three years.

The remainder of her life was spent in France in various nursing homes. In 1865, she published *Souvenirs d'une fille du peuple ou la Saint-simonienne en*

*Egypte*, and in 1977 a collection of her letters, *Mémoires d'une saint-simonienne en Russie*, was edited by Maïté Albistur and Daniel Armogathe.

C. Moses, "St. Simonian Men/St. Simonian women: The Transformation of Feminist Thought in 1830's France," *Journal of Modern History* 54 (June 1982).

*Laura S. Strumingher*

*Related entries:* NIBOYET; SAINT-SIMONIANISM; *LA VOIX DES FEMMES*; WET NURSING; WOMEN'S NEWSPAPERS.


*LA VOIX DES CLUBS, JOURNAL QUOTIDIENNE DES ASSEMBLEES POPULAIRES* (1848), newspaper during the early Second Republic that attempted to speak for part of the club movement. At the beginning of the Second Republic, police restrictions on political societies were lifted, and the result was the formation of some 200 political clubs. Many ran newspapers that consisted chiefly of reports of their own meetings. Some tried to get a wider circulation by expressing the views of several clubs. One of the earliest of these was the *Voix des clubs*, which produced fifteen numbers during March 1848 and then changed its name to *La Sentinelle des clubs*. Its editor, Victor Bouton, was a former police spy. After proclaiming "Liberty, equality: each for all and all for each," the paper went on to suggest that rich men such as Emile de Girardin and the banker Rothschild should be made to contribute their fortunes to the public treasury.

P. H. Amann, *Revolution and Mass Democracy: The Paris Club Movement in 1848* (Princeton, 1975); C. Bellanger et al., *Histoire générale de la presse périodique française*, vol. 2 (Paris, 1969).

*Irene Collins*

*Related entries:* CLUBS, POLITICAL; GIRARDIN; PROVISIONAL GOVERNMENT; ROTHSCHILD FAMILY.


*LA VOIX DES FEMMES* (1848), radical women's paper, forty-six issues 19 March–20 June 1848, under the subtitle *Political and Socialist Paper: Organ of the Interests of All Women*. The paper was founded by Eugénie Niboyet, an experienced journalist from a wealthy, Bonapartist, and Protestant background who had been the first to translate Dickens into French. Among its contributors were Désirée Gay, Jeanne Deroin, Suzanne Voilquin, Anais Ségalas, Gabrielle Soumet, Adèle Esquiros, and Hortense Wild. After the first issue, 400 women, mainly workers, congregated at Niboyet's home and formed a political club. There were correspondents in Brussels, London, Turin, and thirteen provincial cities.

The extensive manifestos by women workers, especially domestic servants, midwives, and laundresses, published in the paper are a valuable source for labor history. The paper's concerns were very wide ranging, but tensions emerged over Niboyet's somewhat didactic tone, the primacy of education or immediate social change, women's suffrage, and in particular Niboyet's conservative stance over social conflict and direct action. This and at times violent male intimidation, which gave the police the pretext to close the associated club, led to the collapse of the paper.

L. Adler, *A l'Aube du féminisme: les premières journalistes (1830–1850)* (Paris, 1979); Bibliothèque de l'Arsénal Jo 224/225 bis; E. Sullerot, ''Journaux féminins et lutte ouvrière (1848–1849),'' in J. Godechot, ed., *La Presse ouvrière, 1819–1850*, ''Bibliothèque de la Révolution de 1848,'' vol. 23 (1966).

*Peter McPhee*

*Related entries:* DEROIN; DOMESTIC SERVANTS; NIBOYET; VOILQUIN; WOMEN'S NEWSPAPERS.


**VOLNEY, CONSTANTIN-FRANCOIS CHASSEBEUF DE BOISGIRAY, COMTE** (1757–1820), *idéologue*, ethnologist, geographer, moralist, historian, Orientalist, senator (1799–1814), and peer (1814–1820). Born into a family of lawyers and local notables near Angers, the young Chassebeuf adopted the pseudonym Volney (*Voltaire* plus *Ferney*) by 1785, after his return from Syria and Egypt. Even after 1815, he was renowned principally for three major works. *Voyage en Syrie et en Egypte* (1787) was the product of three years of observation, possibly on a secret diplomatic mission, of physical and political conditions in the two Ottoman provinces. *Les Ruines, ou méditations sur les révolutions des empires* (1791) was a withering attack on despotism and superstition (including the derivation of Christianity from solar myths) and a hymn of praise to Revolutionary natural rights and human perfectibility. *La Loi naturelle ou catéchisme du citoyen* (1793) was a government-inspired effort to formulate a natural moral code (in which deism tempered Volney's personal atheism) and to derive liberty, property, and equality before the law from human nature.

Less well known were Volney's history lectures at the Ecole normale (1795) that outlined critical historical methods. Another major effort to construct a new science of physical and human geography appeared in *Tableau du climat et du sol des Etats-Unis* (1803), based on a three-year visit to America (1795–98). A staunch opponent of Rousseau's noble savage, Volney deflated all mythology of the virtuous Indian (though he borrowed much from Robertson), just as he had punctured the myth of a virtuous republican Rome in his history lectures.

From 1820 to 1846, there were two major editions of Volney's collected works and at least four editions of the most famous individual works. During the Restoration, Volney worked primarily on chronology and Oriental languages. Both studies allowed him to vent his anticlerical and antibiblical skepticism. His concordance of chronologies of Herodotus and other ancient calendars (1813–14) included attacks on credulous biblical scholars. His favorite project of transcribing Arabic and other Eastern languages in European characters won little approval from the Orientalist establishment, including his Institute colleague Silvestre de Sacy. Equally unheeded were Volney's ambitious plans (posthumously published in 1821) for educating French diplomats and translators in Oriental languages. An enduring legacy is the Institute Prix Volney for the ''philosophical study of language.''

Volney kept his status as a peer and his seat in the Académie française due to his inactivity during the Hundred Days. However, his boycott of the Peers revealed as great a discontent with the Bourbons as with Bonaparte. His pamphlet of 1819 on Samuel and the biblical rite of anointing kings was meant to discourage Louis XVIII from consenting to such a ceremony. A man of political courage and strong principles, Volney inspired many other nineteenth-century writers, including Jules Michelet and Ernest Renan. His religious and political views were still so controversial in 1898 that a statue in his honor at his birthplace became the pretext for attacking his convictions.

G. Chinard, *Volney et l'Amérique* (Baltimore, 1923); J. Gaulmier, *L'Idéologue Volney, 1757–1820* (Beirut, 1951; reprint Geneva, 1980) and *Un Grand témoin de la Révolution et de l'Empire, Volney* (Paris, 1959); S. Moravia, *Il Pensiero degli Ideologues* (Florence, 1974); C.-F. Volney, *La Loi naturelle, Lecons d'Histoire*, ed. J. Gaulmier (Paris, 1980) and *Oeuvres complètes*, ed. A. Bossange, 8 vols. (Paris, 1820–22).

*Martin S. Staum*

*Related entries:* ACADEMIE FRANCAISE; CHAMBER OF PEERS; HUNDRED DAYS; *IDEOLOGUES*; LOUIS XVIII; MICHELET; RENAN; ROUSSEAU; SACY; VOLTAIRE.

**VOLTAIRE.** The nature of Voltaire's influence in France during the first half of the nineteenth century is an important and complex subject. It is important because the mere mention of Voltaire's name could and did stir controversy throughout the entire century. It is complex because not only did Voltaire influence different people in different ways but the nature of his influence changed over time as different groups emblazoned his name on their respective battle flags. Making matters more difficult is the question of Voltairianism, a label widely used as both a mark of opprobrium and a badge of pride but rarely defined. And, finally, because Voltaire's works were such an integral part of the French literary heritage, the *philosophe* exercised a subtle and pervasive influence on much of French thinking and writing in the nineteenth century, and this influence cut across the lines dividing contending political and religious groups and helped shape the writing of drama, light verse, and history.

Voltaire's most important role in the first half of the nineteenth century was to serve liberals, republicans, and, above all, anticlericals as a symbol of their cause and to provide journalists and polemicists enlisted in various crusades with both an almost inexhaustible supply of anticlerical subject matter and a satiric and mocking style. Popular interest in Voltaire reached high points whenever these movements came under attack from either an aggressive legitimism or a resurgent church, or from both, as during the Restoration. A convenient, simple, and striking index of the waxing and waning of Voltaire's popular appeal in the nineteenth century can be compiled by counting the number of complete editions of his works undertaken within a given period of time. According to Gustave Lanson, who put together one such list, nineteen complete editions of Voltaire appeared before 1778, eight between 1778 and 1815, twenty-eight between 1815 and 1835, none between 1835 and 1852, and five between 1852 and 1870. A second list, derived from the entries in J.-M. Quérard's *La France littéraire*, gives a slightly different set of figures but one not so different as to alter the general pattern. Quérard lists three editions for the 1780s, three more for the years 1789 to 1799, two for the period 1799 to 1814, and twenty-three for the sixteen years of the Restoration. From these two sets of figures emerges a pattern that shows an overwhelming interest in Voltaire during the Restoration, a sudden decline in the 1830s and the 1840s, and a modest revival after the proclamation of the Second Empire.

Additional figures confirm the powerful presence of Voltaire during the Restoration. In 1824, the *Mémorial catholique* lamented the fact that between 1817, the year when the first collected edition of Voltaire to appear during the Restoration was begun, and 1824, some 1,603,000 volumes of Voltaire had appeared, not to mention some 556,500 volumes of Rousseau and some 339,900 volumes of other Enlightenment thinkers. Of this total of almost 2.5 million books, 64 percent were by Voltaire. During this same seven-year period, twelve complete editions of Voltaire were commenced by various publishing houses. What makes this figure significant is the fact that a typical edition of Voltaire contained over seventy volumes and cost more than several hundred francs. Several publishers also issued limited editions printed on special paper and illustrated with costly engravings that sold for up to 1,000 francs. That so many publishers and printers were prepared to take the substantial risk of issuing these massive and expensive sets indicates the existence of a sizable and affluent market for the works of Voltaire.

The ubiquitous presence of Voltaire during the Restoration was primarily due to the complex political, religious, and even cultural struggle that took place in France during these sixteen years. The name of Voltaire became a symbol adopted by both those who supported the restored Bourbons and their allies in the church and by those who opposed this alliance of throne and altar. Opponents of the Restoration monarchy saw Voltaire as an emblem of the Enlightenment, the Revolution, and anticlericalism. On the whole, they appear to have decided to allow Voltaire to speak for himself, for although hundreds of thousands of copies of Voltaire's books circulated, few authors devoted either biographical or critical studies to him. In 1817, for example, the year of the first collected edition, there appeared only twenty-five works on Voltaire; this figure represents the largest number of such studies published during a single year between 1814 and 1830. Instead, opposition groups made every effort to disseminate Voltaire's works and those of the other *philosophes*, especially those of an anticlerical tendency. Hence, although Voltaire's political beliefs were probably of little value to Restoration liberals, his anticlericalism, as Lanson observes, served them well. Finally, liberal journalists like Paul-Louis Courier found in Voltaire's writings both a mocking and ironic style that could be imitated and an ample storehouse of facts and opinions.

If the liberal and anticlerical opponents of the Restoration made Voltaire into a hero, their royalist and clerical foes portrayed him in satanic terms. The abbé Frayssinous, appointed grand master of the University in 1822, not only denounced Voltaire for his impiety and asserted that because of him good society lived in fear, he also blamed Voltaire for causing the French Revolution, the Terror, and the recent assassination of the duc de Berry. "To admire Voltaire is the sign of a corrupt heart," wrote the influential Joseph de Maistre in his *Soirées de Saint-Petersbourg*, "and if anybody is drawn to his words, then be sure that God does not live for such a one." To legitimists and churchmen, then, Voltaire symbolized the Enlightenment, the French Revolution, and indeed all else that had gone wrong in the world since 1789.

But the reduction of the influence of Voltaire to a symbol praised by the opponents of the Restoration and condemned by its supporters distorts the complex nature of Voltaire's place in the history of French thought and writing after 1815. For, if this image is correct, what explains the twenty-four editions of the *Henriade*, Voltaire's paean to the founder of the Bourbon line, a number that included a special edition dedicated by the famed publishing firm of Didot to the comte d'Artois? Supporters of the monarchy appear to have found useful at least some of Voltaire's works. Further, as Lanson has pointed out, the literary legacy Voltaire left greatly influenced the writing of tragedy, light verse, philosophical history, and journalism and the writing of polemics. But most important, the example of Voltaire helped shape the way a large number of Frenchmen thought and wrote. Associated with Voltaire was a typically French style of expression, one that placed a premium on clarity, fluidity of expression, lightness, and wit and that called for the avoidance of the striking or the bizarre. Voltaire's style thus remained a standard for those writers who cultivated a purely intellectual style.

With the overthrow of Charles X in the July Revolution of 1830 came a sudden decline in interest in the works of Voltaire. The number of complete editions of his works available from publishers dropped markedly. Perhaps the market was glutted, but a more likely explanation lies in the fact that both legitimism and clericalism were in a temporary retreat. However, when the Catholic church commenced its offensive against the French educational system in the early 1840s, the interest in Voltaire and Voltairianism returned.

Under the guise of a plea for freedom of education, the church launched a campaign in 1840 to break the government's monopoly on education, an assault that soon became notorious for the violence and intemperance of its language. To defend the University, one of the focal points of the Catholic attack, Jules Michelet and Edgar Quinet gave in 1843 their celebrated course of lectures, later published as *Des Jésuites*. In the process of defending the University, the two professors appealed to Voltaire in their condemnation of the church and the Jesuit order. Voltaire, Quinet exclaimed, was the "destroying angel sent by God against the sinful church." Elsewhere he spoke of the *philosophe* as "an act of Providence, an overwhelming of the unfaithful church by the very weapons of the Christian spirit, humanity, charity, brotherhood, the instrument of the vengeance of God, the living voice of humanity in the eighteenth century." His colleague Michelet, whose early opinion of Voltaire had been unfavorable and who had just recently painted a romanticized portrait of the Middle Ages, suddenly rediscovered Voltaire and proclaimed that he now embraced the "true France of Voltaire and Rousseau." On the occasion of Michelet's second polemical work on the Jesuits, *Du Prêtre, de la femme et de la famille*, Emile Saisset wrote in the *Revue des deux mondes* that Michelet had launched a renaissance of Voltairianism. This Voltairianism, reborn during the 1840s, found its mature expression during the Second Empire in the pages of *Le Siècle, L'Avenir national*, and Michelet's polemics. It developed into a bitter and ascerbic anticlericalism that scorned not only the church but Christianity itself. For the remainder of the century, the name of Voltaire would figure prominently as Frenchmen continued to wrestle with the religious question.

Since nothing illustrates more clearly the complex and controversial place of Voltaire in French history than the story of the changing fortunes of his tomb, it will provide a fitting conclusion for this account of Voltaire's influence during the nineteenth century. The story begins with Voltaire's death on 30 May 1778 and with the refusal of the archbishop of Paris to permit his burial; hence Voltaire's nephew, the abbé Mignot, had the *philosophe's* body clandestinely removed to an abbey in Champagne and buried there. (The abbey's prior lost his position for permitting the burial to take place.) Thirteen years later, in the second year of the French Revolution, the men of the Revolution had Voltaire's remains returned to Paris, and, with great celebration, they were placed in the Panthéon, the former church of St. Geneviève that had been dedicated on 4 April 1791 to the great men of France. Rousseau's body joined Voltaire's on 11 October 1794. When the Catholic faith was restored under Napoleon, the Panthéon was closed, not to be reopened until 1822, when the archbishop of Paris consecrated it. Throughout the nineteenth century, as regimes rose and fell in France, the building alternated between Panthéon and church. About 1885 a rumor began to circulate in Paris stating that the tombs of Voltaire and Rousseau were empty, that royalists had removed their bones in 1814 and had dumped them on a rubbish heap. Not until a government commission ordered the tombs opened and their contents verified was this story laid to rest. Although Voltaire's tomb was not vandalized during the Restoration, it was pushed into a side corridor when the church was consecrated. Only during the July Monarchy was the tomb restored to its traditional place. Even in death, Voltaire continued to be a center of controversy in France.

P. Bertocci, *Jules Simon. Republican Anticlericalism and Cultural Politics in France, 1848–1886* (Columbia, Mo., 1978); O. Chadwick, *The Secularization of the European Mind in the Nineteenth Century* (Cambridge, 1975); G. Lanson, *Voltaire*, trans. R. Wagoner (New York, 1966); J.-M. Quérard, *La France littéraire*, 10 vols. (Paris, 1827–

39); J. Vercruysse, "Bibliographie des écrits français relatifs à Voltaire, 1719–1830," *Studies on Voltaire and the Eighteenth Century* 60 (1968).

Robert Brown

*Related entries:* ANTICLERICAL CAMPAIGN; BERRY, C.-F.; COURIER; FRAYSSINOUS; JESUITS; MAISTRE; *LE MEMORIAL CATHOLIQUE*; MICHELET; QUINET; *LA REVUE DES DEUX MONDES*; ROUSSEAU.

*LES VORACES,* A workers' association that played an important role in Lyons in 1848. The *voraces* from Lyons belonged to a secret society of "brotherhood" journeyman origin. The name was given to them in 1846 by disgruntled wine merchants whom they had forced to continue to sell wine by the liter and not by the bottle. The spread of republican and socialist doctrines among them made them a political society. When the Republic was proclaimed in February of 1848 their existence came to light. They were run by a commission sitting at the Croix-Rousse, the hill overlooking Lyons occupied by the *canuts* (silk workers). Organized along military lines, they wore, as their special insignia, red armbands and sashes. They declared their allegiance to the "social and democratic Republic."

The initial days of the Republic in Lyons had been unsettled. The crisis had deeply affected the city and the authorities feared an uprising: the memories of the *canut* revolts of 1831 and 1834 remained vivid. Emmanuel Arago, commissioner of the provisional government, agreed to allow the *voraces* to collaborate in maintaining order. The *voraces* stepped in to insure the security of individual persons and contributed to relieving guard posts. Still, conservative groups were alarmed by these patrols of armed workers.

In March 1848 the *voraces* organized an expedition to "liberate the Savoy region." This province, situated near Lyons, belonged to the Piedmont kingdom but was a French-speaking area. Two thousand workers set out for Chambéry, the provincial capital. By 3 April 1848 they were in control of the city and they proclaimed the Republic. However, the venture was stopped in its tracks due to resistance from the peasants who had been frightened by the *voraces'* reputation as revolutionaries. The legitimate Piedmont authority was restored and many *voraces* were imprisoned.

The legislative elections of April 1848 awarded a victory to the moderate republicans. A revolutionary day, organized in Paris for 15 May, was a failure. Incidents in Lyons between the *voraces* and those responsible for public order (conservative officers and police who had served the previous regime) increased. On 13 May seven workers were arrested; the *voraces* demanded that they be freed. Their detention was upheld by the appeals court, against the advice of the new government commissioner, Martin Bernard. The Croix-Rousse hill was dotted with barricades.

Martin Bernard, because of the prestige stemming from his revolutionary past, was able to negotiate with the *voraces*. Despite the court's decision, he ordered that the arrested workers be freed, and he succeeded in restoring peace and quiet. The *voraces* even allowed themselves to be integrated into the National Guard. Their sense of responsibility and Martin Bernard's skillful leadership had avoided a civil war in Lyons. The *voraces* presented in 1848 a rare case of "worker power." The authorities were forced to deal with them, but their civic spirit made them accept integration into the new administrative establishment.

F. Dutacq, *Political History of Lyon during the Revolution of 1848* (Paris, 1910); J. Godart, *In Lyon in 1848: the Voraces* (Paris, 1948).

*Claude Latta, trans. Paul Comeau*

*Related entries:* ARAGO FAMILY; *CANUTS*; LYONS, REVOLTS IN; NATIONAL GUARD; REVOLUTION OF 1848; SILK INDUSTRY.

**VOYER D'ARGENSON, MARC-RENE-MARIE** (1771–1842), leading deputy of the extreme Left and participant in secret societies. Marc-René Voyer d'Argenson came from one of the great noble families of Touraine. His grandfather was minister of war to Louis XV, his great-grandfather was lieutenant general of police for Louis XIV, and his great-great-grandfather was ambassador to Venice for Louis XIII. Prior to the Revolution, Voyer d'Argenson served in the army as an aide-de-camp to General Lafayette. With the fall of the monarchy, he retired to Paulmy, which his family had owned from time immemorial. During the Revolution, he married the widow of Prince Victor de Broglie and devoted himself to the development of artificial prairies and to breeding one of the first herds of merino sheep in France.

He entered politics as president of the electoral college of Vienne in 1803. He served Napoleon as prefect of Deux-Nethes from 1809 until 1813, when he resigned over the government's illegal attempts to seize his inherited lands. Holder of the Legion of Honor (1810) and an officer of the Legion of Honor (1811), he refused an offer of the prefecture of the Rhône from Louis XVIII.

With the advent of true electoral politics, Voyer d'Argenson began his long parliamentary career in the elections of May 1815 when he was elected to the Chamber of Representatives of the Hundred Days from Belfort. Committed to the ideals of representative government, he protested the Allies' lockout of the Chamber on 8 July. At the Second Restoration the voters of Belfort again selected him as their deputy. Voyer d'Argenson is therefore one of the few men to have been elected in both May and August 1815. Possibly his combination of support for the Revolution, being one of the wealthiest men in France, and being a noble won him such broad support.

Voyer d'Argenson took his seat among the opponents of the ultras. He was the only deputy to speak out against the creation of the *cours prévôtales*, and he raised a storm of protest from the ultras when he denounced the assassinations in Nîmes. His position on the extreme Left of the Chamber was approved by the electors of Belfort in October 1816 after Louis XVIII had dissolved the uncooperative *chambre introuvable*. With the new electoral law of 1817, he became the deputy of the Haut-Rhin in the elections of 1817. Believing in republican government (kings were fine as figureheads) and being a prominent spokesman for the defense of individual liberty and freedom of the press, he was one of the leaders of the Left along with Benjamin Constant, Jacques-Charles Dupont de l'Eure, Bernard-François de Chauvelin, Lafayette, Jacques-Antoine Manuel, and General Maximilien-Sébastien Foy. He was also the first deputy to transcend purely political issues, as he opposed the tariff bill of 1819 on the grounds of its adverse effect on the standard of living of the working class.

The turn to the right of the government after the assassination of the duc de Berry in 1820 caused Voyer d'Argenson to become involved in conspiracies to overthrow the monarchy. In 1821 he was part of the *vente suprême* of the Paris carbonari. His involvement was eagerly sought by the student radicals because his wealth and status could give their efforts credibility. He was also well connected to the Protestant textile wealth of Alsace through his friend Jacques Koechlin. In 1821, Voyer d'Argenson used his home in Overbruck as the staging site for the attack on Belfort that began the insurrection. A man of individual courage but with an indecisive nature, Voyer d'Argenson was late for the rendezvous of 30 December 1821. His tardiness was a major contribution to the failure of the carbonari's attempted coup.

Voyer d'Argenson was not caught at the scene, but when General Jean-Baptiste Berton was captured with documents naming Voyer d'Argenson to the new provisional government along with Lafayette and Manuel, these three opposition deputies were implicated. They were saved from prosecution by their parliamentary immunity, which was not lifted thanks to the dedicated work of Voyer d'Argenson's stepson, the duc de Broglie, in the Chamber of Peers. Voyer d'Argenson allowed the furor to dissipate while he spent some time in London.

The voters of Alsace continued their support of Voyer d'Argenson in the elections of 1822, but he failed to survive the royalist landslide of 1824. During the years of the Villèle ministry, he wrote on social justice. He returned to the Chamber of Deputies in the by-election of April 1828 replacing Dupont de l'Eure as deputy from Pont-Andemer (Eure), but he could not adjust to the ineffectiveness of the Chamber to represent the will of the people in opposition to Charles X, so he resigned his seat in 1829.

Although he was not directly involved in the events of the July Revolution, the electors of Chatelleraut (Vienne) returned him to the Chamber of Deputies in the by-elections of October 1830. He again took up his familiar seat on the Left. The electors of Vienne failed to reelect him in 1831, but the voters of Strasbourg (Bas-Rhin) elected him in the by-elections of October 1831. He signed the *compte-rendu* of 1832, and he helped found the Society of the Rights of Man. His belief in equality and the sovereignty of the people was too advanced for the electors of Alsace, who generally became supporters of Louis-Philippe. After being prosecuted for his republicanism in 1833, he was not reelected in 1834, and his parliamentary career came to an end.

His career in politics was handicapped in the world of the *censitaire* monarchy. His republicanism was anathema, and after he met Buonarroti in 1828, Voyer d'Argenson adopted even more radical ideas than he had held earlier, even to the point of believing that a redistribution of all landed property might be necessary. Yet like so many other revolutionaries of the period, he had a horror of acting with the vulgar masses and a skepticism of humanity. Nevertheless, Guizot describes Voyer d'Argenson as having a passionate commitment to social progress combined with an aristocrat's wit. In his final phase of activity, Voyer d'Argenson provided a personal link between Buonarroti and Blanqui, and he was included in the projected provisional government of the Society of Seasons' insurrection of May 1839.

H. Bounias, *Discours prononcé sur la tombe de Voyer d'Argenson, le 4 août 1842* (Paris, 1842); H. Dourille, *Notice sur Voyer d'Argenson* (Paris, 1842); M.-R. Voyer d'Argenson, ed., *Discours et opinions de Voyer d'Argenson*, 2 vols. (Paris, 1845–46); G. Weill, "Voyer d'Argenson et la question sociale," *International Review of Social History* 4 (1939).

*Thomas Beck*

*Related entries:* BERRY, C.-F.; BERTON; BLANQUI, L.-A.; BROGLIE, A.-L.-V.; BUONARROTI; CARBONARI; *CHAMBRE INTROUVABLE*; CONSTANT; *COURS PREVOTALES*; DUPONT DE L'EURE; FOY; LAFAYETTE, M.-J.-P.-Y.-R.-G.; MANUEL; REPUBLICANS; SOCIETY OF THE RIGHTS OF MAN; SOCIETY OF THE SEASONS; ULTRAROYALISTS; VILLELE; WHITE TERROR.


*LA VRAIE REPUBLIQUE* (1848–1849), republican and socialist daily newspaper, 104 issues 26 March–21 August 1848 (suspended 25 June–9 August) and 77 issues 29 March–13 June 1849 as *Le Journal de la vraie république*, with the subtitle *Without a Social Revolution, There is No True Republic*. Its chief editor was Théophile Thoré, and among its other editors were Armand Barbès, George Sand, and Pierre Leroux. One of the most militant and popular of the socialist papers in 1848, *La vraie république* was selling 15,000 copies by 2 May and 20,000 by 17 June.

In its first issue the editors called for the full political and social consequences of the Republic: universal suffrage, a single Chamber, civil liberties, free and compulsory education, state organization of agricultural, industrial, and intellectual work, and the gradual socialization of the means of production. More specific proposals about the transition to socialism were rare, however. Politically, the paper adopted a position of critical support for the Provisional Government, but the elections of April convinced it that civil war was inevitable.

The paper is an important source for material from the workers' movement in 1848. Though few workers wrote for the paper, it published many proclamations about associations and cooperatives and continued to be a mouthpiece for workers' delegates after the closure of the Luxembourg Commission. It was one of ten papers forcibly closed in June 1848, and Thoré's involvement in the insurrection of 13 June 1849, after which he fled to Switzerland, marked the end of the paper.

B. N. LC² 1748; E. Hatin, *Bibliographie historique et critique de la presse périodique française* (Paris, 1866); G. Sand, *Correspondance*, vol. 8 (Paris, 1971).

*Peter McPhee*

*Related entries:* BARBES; JUNE DAYS; LEROUX; LUXEMBOURG COMMISSION; REPUBLICANS; SAND; WORKERS' COOPERATIVES.

# W

**WAR INDEMNITY,** the indemnity of 700 million francs that the Second Treaty of Paris required France to pay to the Allies. The first Treaty of Paris (30 May 1814) had treated France leniently and required no indemnity. The peace that followed Waterloo was much different. The small states and the Prussians, especially the Prussian general staff, insisted on revenge and demanded huge annexations and an indemnity of 1.2 billion francs. Viscount Castlereagh, however, urged a moderate peace to maintain the integrity of France and proposed only minor losses, reducing France to its 1790 borders. For five months, debate raged between these two extremes. Castlereagh ultimately made concessions, agreeing that artworks were to be returned to their owners, France would support an occupation army of 150,000 men for five years, and France would pay an indemnity of 700 million francs. These terms were incorporated in the Second Treaty of Paris, signed on 20 November 1815. Armand-Emmanuel de Richelieu, the new French prime minister, signed for France, although Charles-Maurice de Talleyrand, his predecessor, had done most of the negotiating.

Of the indemnity, 137 million francs were to be used to construct fortresses on the French border to prevent another French outbreak, and 60 million were to help build fortresses on the Dutch border. The article providing for the indemnity and stipulating the amount was part of the treaty itself. A separate convention, signed that same day by the five powers, governed the method of payment. The total sum was to be paid in fifteen equal installments over a five-year period by bearer bonds drawn on the French treasury. The first installment was due 31 March 1816, with the others following at four-month intervals. The precise details of the transfers were spelled out, and France was relieved of interest charges during the five-year period. France was, however, required to establish a fund to cover possible delinquencies, and 5 percent interest was to be charged on such overdue payments. Provision was also made for early payment in order to advance the evacuation of the Allied occupation troops.

By 1817, indemnity payments and Allied occupation costs, coupled with economic decline, had resulted in a sizable French deficit. Richelieu, determined to meet the payment schedule, had to resort to borrowing from the Dutch banking firm of Hope and the British firm of Baring Brothers on terms that in essence resulted in France's paying an interest rate of 9.5 percent and provided the bankers with the opportunity to make a capital gain of nearly 100 percent. Hope and Baring made a second loan in 1818 on terms considerably more favorable to the French. To this was added a domestically floated loan for 14.6 million francs that was oversubscribed by twelve times. With other foreign loans, France thus had the resources to pay off the indemnity entirely, albeit only after an Allied reduction of the remaining payment from 286 million francs to 265 million. This arrangement, accepted at the Congress of Aix-la-Chapelle, resulted in the immediate withdrawal of all foreign troops by 30 November 1818.

G. F. von Martens, *Nouveau recueil de traités d'alliance, de paix, de trève* (Gottingue, 1817–41); A. Nicoll, *Comment la France a payé après Waterloo* (Paris, 1929); P. Renouvin, *Histoire des relations internationales, le XIXe siècle* (Paris, 1954); H. Sée, *Histoire économique de la France* (Paris, 1942).

*James K. Kieswetter*

*Related entries:* AIX-LA-CHAPELLE, CONGRESS OF; PARIS, SECOND TREATY OF; RICHELIEU; TALLEYRAND.

**WATERLOO, BATTLE OF** (15–18 June 1815), the decisive battle of the Hundred Days. The climacteric military events of the Napoleonic wars took place in Belgium over a four-day period. Attempting to drive the armies of the Duke of Wellington and Field Marshal Gebhard von Blücher apart, L'Armée du nord fought two considerable engagements at Quatre Bras and Ligny on 16 June, but the Allies and Prussians retreated north to Mont St. Jean and Wavre, respectively, and thus proved capable of cooperating two days later at the double battle of Waterloo and Wavre. The outcome doomed Napoleon to renewed abdication and ultimately to exile on the island of St. Helena.

Following his return to Paris on 20 March, Napoleon attempted to secure international recognition of his fait accompli, announcing pacific intentions. The European powers participating in the Congress of Vienna, however, declared him an outlaw and set up the Seventh Coalition to encompass his fall. By July it was planned to mass 550,000 troops against Napoleon and invade France at three points simultaneously. While continuing his diplomatic peace offensive, the emperor was aware that it must come to a fight, but owing to his unwillingness to reimpose the hated conscription on the French population until late April, he would be seriously outnumbered. Consequently he faced a strategic dilemma: he could trade space for time and build up his forces near Paris in preparation for a renewed struggle of the type fought on French soil in 1814, or he could seize the initiative at the earliest possible moment by attacking the first enemy armies to come within range of the frontier. By late May this meant the Anglo-Dutch army of 106,000 men commanded by the duke of Wellington and the

Prussian army (some 128,000 strong) of Field Marshal Blücher, drawn up around Brussels and Namur, respectively, on the northeast frontiers of France. Anxious to spare his subjects a renewed war within France's borders and hopeful that a quick success in Belgium might confer important political advantages, Napoleon opted for the bolder course and in great secrecy began preparations for gathering 128,000 men and 366 guns (over half his available manpower) in the L'Armée du Nord to the north and east of Paris. The remainder of his forces he disposed in small armies to watch the remaining frontiers and to suppress a pro-Bourbon rising in the Vendée. His main field army comprised soldiers of great experience, as few conscripts were yet available from the depots. This army, however, had one dangerous flaw: it was made up of both ardent, die-hard Bonapartists, and of troops who had deserted the tricolor after the first abdication in April 1814 and taken service under the Bourbons before returning to their original allegiance eleven months later. The two elements distrusted one another.

To command this hybrid, if experienced, force Napoleon made some questionable appointments. As Louis-Alexandre Berthier was dead, Nicolas-Jean de Soult was made chief of staff. Louis-Gabriel Suchet would have been better. To command the two corps of the left wing, which would be facing Wellington, Napoleon ultimately chose Michel Ney (albeit only on 15 June). This was a popular and also a politic choice, but Ney's performance was variable, and Soult would have been a better choice, given his good record against the Anglo-Spanish army amid the Pyrenees in late 1813 and early 1814. To command the two corps of the right wing, which would be facing Blücher, the emperor appointed Emmanuel Grouchy, a skilled leader of cavalry but with little experience of command over an all-arm force. Not only was he resented by his corps commanders, but a far abler marshal—much feared by the Prussians—was available in Louis-Nicolas Davout, military governor of Paris. Napoleon, who retained personal command over the reserve— comprising the Imperial Guard and Count Georges de Lobau's VI Corps—also expected Grouchy to oversee the four corps of reserve cavalry. Clearly the emperor intended to conduct a virtuoso performance.

Despite their overall numerical superiority, Napoleon's forthcoming opponents possessed certain weaknesses. Although Blücher's chief of staff, August von Gneisenau, and the four corps commanders under his immediate command (Hans von Ziethen, George von Pirch, Johann von Thielemann, and Friedrich von Bülow), were highly experienced officers of proved worth, many of the troops under their command were young conscripts with little service. Blücher himself was in his seventy-third year with a full half-century of military service behind him. His rash bravery was more noteworthy than his strategic ability, but he was popular with the troops who nicknamed him *Alte Vorwärts* ("Old Forwards"), and Gneisenau's cool intellect compensated for the deficiencies of his chief. Wellington—aged, like Napoleon and Ney, forty-six—was near the peak of his military reputation. His army was multinational, only one-third being British, the remainder comprising Dutch, Belgians, Hanoverians, Brunswickers, and Nassauers of varying experience, some, indeed, having seen service in the armies of the Empire. Most of his generals were men of proved ability, including Viscount Hill, the Earl of Uxbridge, and Thomas Picton; others were unknown quantities, such as the twenty-one-year-old prince of Orange (the "Little Frog") commanding the Allied I Corps. The British contingent comprised one peninsular division (Picton's Fifth), but the rest were mainly second battalions, as the greater part of the veteran formations were currently over the Atlantic fighting the United States. The Allied army, as Wellington was well aware, was thus something of an unknown quantity. Consequently, at a meeting with Blücher at Tirlemont on 3 May, the duke pressed the need for caution. Time must be won for the Austrian and Prussian armies to mobilize, and so it was agreed that the Allied and Prussian armies would defer an attack into France until 12 July. This plan was to be overwhelmed by events, as Napoleon moved first.

It was ever the emperor's wont to seize the initiative. His plan in 1815 was to advance into Belgium to strike the junction between his two adversaries as a preliminary to defeating them in detail. The central position achieved, the two wings of L'Armée du Nord would engage their respective opponents (albeit at a local numerical disadvantage) while Napoleon marched with the reserve to reinforce each wing in turn, achieving local superiority thereby, to win two battles and open the road to Brussels beyond. He hoped that such an abrupt success would gain him the psychological advantage and persuade his foes to seek a negotiated accommodation that would leave him recognized as the de facto ruler of France. For such a plan to have a chance of success, it was clearly necessary to forestall the arrival of Austrian and Russian forces on the Rhine. Accordingly, Napoleon ordered the closure of France's frontiers from 7 June and began a rapid concentration of his corps around Beaumont from a wide dispersal area—this preliminary move being completed by 14 June. Brilliant success was achieved, and it was only late on 13 June that Prussian patrols gained any inkling of troop movements to their front, while Wellington spent that day attending a cricket match. Napoleon thus gained initial surprise, although some of his formations were thrown into confusion early on 15 June as they advanced through the darkness to cross the Sambre around Charleroi and launch their offensive into Belgium.

The initial impact fell on Ziethen's advance troops at Thuin. French progress was not consistently even, but by late afternoon Napoleon and Dominique Vandamme were masters of Charleroi, Etienne-Maurice Gerard's IV Corps was over the Sambre at Chatelet, and Honoré Reille's II Corps, heading the left wing's advance, was in the possession of Marchienne. Ziethen's Prussians meanwhile fell back toward Fleurus, while Blücher ordered his three remaining corps to advance to Sombreffe to join him. Wellington's first reaction was to dismiss the French attack as a feint, and suspecting Napoleon of attempting to cut his army off from the Channel ports, he ordered his formations to concentrate south and west of Brussels, away from the inner flank. Such a miscalculation could have proved fatal, but fortunately for the Allies the newly appointed Marshal Ney failed to take the key road junction at Quatre Bras, constituting the only real link with Blücher's army, as a result of the intelligent disobedience of orders by the nearest Allied formations, which put up the semblance of resistance at Frasnes and to the south of Quatre Bras that fooled Ney into believing that Wellington's main force was close by and that caution was necessary. This check to the emperor's plans gave Wellington time to realize his earlier mistake, and late at night while attending the duchess of Richmond's ball in Brussels, the duke issued new orders for his troops to march at full speed for Quatre Bras.

Two battles took place on 16 June. Napoleon and the Imperial Guard joined Grouchy's two corps at Fleurus just short of Ligny during the morning, having decided that Blücher's concentrating forces constituted more tempting targets than Wellington's still-distant formations. At 2:30 P.M. the battle of Ligny opened, and soon a bitter fight was raging along the stream and around the ten villages on its banks. Napoleon intended to pin Blücher's 84,000 men and 224 guns frontally with his own 68,000 troops and to bring up Jean-Baptiste Drouet d'Erlon's corps—a further 21,000 men—along the road from Quatre Bras to outflank the Prussian position. However, Marshal Ney still had not occupied the vital crossroads, believing that Napoleon intended to join his wing of the army on 16 June, and when he realized that imperial aides had ordered his reserve corps to move east, he lost no time in recalling Drouet d'Erlon forthwith to support Reille in the battle of Quatre Bras, which had tardily opened at 2 P.M.. This delay proved the salvation of Wellington. Although only 8,000 Allies were in position when the fighting opened, more formations arrived in rapid succession to bolster the line until 36,000 were in position by early evening. As a result, Ney and Reille were held to a drawn battle by nightfall, losing 4,000 casualties to Wellington's 4,800. The Quatre Bras crossroads was still in Allied hands.

Had Drouet d'Erlon's I Corps been present at either Quatre Bras or Ligny, the result would have been a decisive French victory. As it was, the formation maneuvered between each battlefield without participating at either. Napoleon had delayed launching his critical attack at Ligny for two hours to wait for Drouet d'Erlon, whose approach along an unexpected axis caused further confusion before his recall by Ney. At 7:30 P.M., despairing of the I Corps' arrival, the emperor launched the guard into the attack. Blücher's defenses crumbled, the old general was pinned beneath his horse amid a cavalry action, and the Prussians reeled back defeated, losing 25,000 casualties to the 11,000 inflicted on the French. The advent of night and the firm belief that the Prussians were retreating to the east persuaded an ailing Napoleon that there was no need to pursue that night. In fact, however, Gneisenau in the absence of his chief ordered the battered corps to retreat north overnight toward Wavre. This meant that the Prussians were not moving away from Wellington as Napoleon believed. Nevertheless, Ligny was a substantial French victory.

Learning what had befallen the Prussians early the next morning—and also that Blücher had been restored to his command, battered but unbowed, and was determined to support his Allies—Wellington ordered a retreat toward Brussels as far as the ridge of Mont St. Jean just south of Waterloo village. A lethargic

Ney did not notice the Allies thinning out from their positions. Napoleon also delayed launching Grouchy after the Prussians until 11 A.M., affording them time to break contact and head for Wavre 7 miles east of Mont St. Jean. The emperor then suddenly realized that there was no sound of firing from Quatre Bras where he presumed Ney to be pinning Wellington down to await Napoleon's arrival with the Guard from Ligny to administer the coup de grâce. Galloping over to the left wing, he galvanized Ney into movement at 2 P.M., but it was too late to catch Wellington. Amid thunder and rain, the emperor led the pursuit, but although Wellington's rearguard was in action several times, the Allies maintained their long start and by evening were in position at Mont St. Jean. Napoleon set up his headquarters at Le Caillou farm 2 miles to the south, and his weary troops bivouaced in the rain. Meanwhile, farther to the east, Grouchy had eventually discovered the true Prussian line of retreat and had halted south of Wavre on the Dyle. Wellington spent the night at Waterloo, cheered by assurances from Blücher that he would march at least two corps from Wavre to his assistance.

Although 18 June dawned fine, the wet ground persuaded Napoleon to delay opening the battle until 11:30 A.M. The emperor deployed 72,000 men and 246 guns astride the Charleroi-to-Brussels highway but only belatedly thought to issue an order to recall Grouchy near Wavre. That officer—despite the pleas of his corps commanders—insisted on carrying out his last orders (to engage the Prussians where found) received on 17 June, and as a result Blücher was able to set out for Waterloo with 72,000 men during the morning, leaving Thielemann's 17,000 to contain Grouchy's 33,000 Frenchmen. Napoleon's delay gave Wellington adequate time to position his 68,000 men and 156 guns along the ridge of Mont St. Jean, with advance posts stationed at Hougoumont, La Haie Sainte, and Le Haie-Papelotte in front of his line. A further 17,000 men were posted to the West toward Hal, as Wellington believed that Napoleon might attempt an outflanking attack; the weight of the Allied army was placed on the right, for the duke was relying on Blücher's arriving to strengthen his left flank. The troops were placed in cover behind the ridge, apart from one brigade in the center.

In fact Napoleon's plan was to smash a gap through Wellington's left center, preparing the way for the infantry of Drouet d'Erlon's I Corps with the fire of a massed battery, while Reille used part of his II Corps to mount a diversionary attack on Hougoumont. Marshal Ney was given overall command of the battle. The emperor clearly discounted the worth of his adversaries and spoke confidently of dining in Brussels that evening.

At 11:30 A.M. Reille sent Prince Jérôme Bonaparte's division to assault Hougoumont. The British Guards' light companies holding the chateau beat off attack after attack and continued to do so all day with minimal reinforcement, but more and more troops of the II Corps were drawn into the action in direct contravention of Napoleon's intention. The chateau was eventually set on fire, but the French proved incapable of driving its stalwart defenders from either the buildings or the orchard. Meanwhile, by 1 P.M. the 84 guns of the massed battery were firing at Wellington's center. A. Bylandt's exposed brigade took heavy casualties, but the effect on the formations behind the ridge's crest was minimal owing to the wet ground. After thirty minutes' fire, Drouet d'Erlon's four divisions were preparing to attack when Napoleon's attention was drawn to a mass of distant troops to the east, advancing through the Bois de Paris from the direction of Wavre. Although patrols soon identified these as Prussians, the emperor was confident that he would win the main battle before the newcomers could intervene and ordered the attack. Drouet d'Erlon mishandled this badly—two of his divisions adopted the wrong formation— and a combination of the strong defense of the farm of La Haie Sainte by Major George Baring's men of the king's German Legion in the center, and the tough quality of Picton's Fifth Division holding the ridge, repulsed the French, whose withdrawal was turned to rout by the well-timed charge of Wellington's two brigades of heavy cavalry. Unfortunately the Union Brigade—including the North British Dragoons (who captured a French Eagle standard)—exploited their success too far and charged the grand battery beyond, whereupon they were attacked in flank by French lancers and suffered heavy losses. Nevertheless Wellington's line had survived the first major attack, and Prussian aid was drawing closer. Already Napoleon had sent off Lobau's VI Corps from central reserve to form a line facing east.

After a brief lull at about 3 P.M., Ney renewed his attack against La Haie Sainte. Despite long odds, Baring held his position, receiving reinforcements from the ridge. But Ney misconstrued the movement of a convoy of wounded to indicate that Wellington was abandoning his position, and without checking this impression, the marshal sent urgent orders to Edouard Milhaud's and Charles Lefebvre-Desnouëttes' massed squadrons of the right wing to charge home immediately. Without infantry or proper artillery support, this attack came to naught against the twenty fire-fringed squares of Wellington's right center. By 4 P.M. all of 5,000 cavalry were involved, but the squares repulsed twelve consecutive attacks on a half-mile sector. To rescue the survivors, Napoleon had unwillingly to send in all of François Kellermann's and Claude Guyot's horsemen from his left wing, doubling the stakes, but Wellington's center, although battered, continued to hold firm, aided by Lord Uxbridge's light cavalry brigades. The emperor strongly criticized Ney's rashness. Since 4 P.M. Napoleon's main attention had been directed toward Plancenoit village in the east, where Lobau was under heavy attack from Bülow's and then Pirch's Prussians. Lobau lost ground rapidly, and to stabilize the position, Napoleon had to send over the Young Guard and then part of the Old, effectively his last reserves.

For Wellington the great crisis of the day came at about 6 P.M. At that hour, Ney at last captured La Haie Sainte from Baring, who was out of ammunition, and the French soon had a battery pounding the center of the Allied line from point-blank range. Some Allied batallions began to waver, and the duke had few reserves to bring up. Sensing the opportunity—correctly this time—Ney sent an urgent request to Napoleon for the Imperial Guard. This elite formation was, however, still engaged on the Plancenoit flank against Blücher, and it took over an hour to collect part of it back into reserve. Wellington in the meantime drew infantry from his right and cavalry from his left to extemporize some support for his wavering center, while the senior Prussian liaison officer brought up Ziethen's I Corps to strengthen the Allied left.

Napoleon decided to misinform his tiring troops about the identity of the latest newcomers, announcing that they were part of Grouchy's command, and handed over the battalions of the Middle Guard to Ney for one last, all-out attack. Wellington waited on the ridge, keeping his men lying down among the corn. The columns of the Guard mounted the slope to find themselves suddenly faced by the British Guardsmen of Peregrine Maitland's brigade. A short, sharp fight, and the French Guard was in retreat. Wellington ordered the whole line to charge. The morale of Napoleon's army broke as the rumor spread that Grouchy's troops had defected to the Allies. Covered by the Old Guard, L'Armée du nord fled toward Quatre Bras and Charleroi, accompanied by their master. At about 9 P.M. Wellington met Blücher near the farm of La Belle Alliance and entrusted the pursuit to the Prussian cavalry. The last fighting died out around Hougoumont, although it continued until dark at Wavre, where Thielemann had held off all of Grouchy's attacks, and indeed repulsed the last one on the morning of 19 June, losing and inflicting some 2,500 casualties.

To win Waterloo itself cost Wellington and Blücher 22,000 men. To lose it cost Napoleon 41,000 men, most of them irreplaceable veterans. The emperor also forfeited his reputation, and although Grouchy's wing carried out a skillful retreat and a last army might have been created to fight outside Paris, Napoleon's cause was doomed. Ahead of him lay renewed abdication, flight to the coast, surrender to the Royal Navy, and ultimately exile on St. Helena.

A. F. Becke, *Napoleon and Waterloo*, 2 vols. (London, 1941); A. Brett-James, *The Hundred Days* (London, 1964); D. G. Chandler, *Waterloo—The Hundred Days* (New York, 1981); H. Houssaye, *1815—Waterloo* (Paris, 1893); W. Siborne, *The Waterloo Campaign, 1815* (London, 1900).

*David Chandler*

*Related entries:* DAVOUT; GERARD; HUNDRED DAYS; LOBAU; NEY; SOULT; VIENNA, CONGRESS OF.


**WATER'S EDGE, CONSPIRACY AT THE.** See CONSPIRACY AT THE WATER'S EDGE.


**WET NURSING,** the commercial nursing of newborns widely practiced in France during the eighteenth and nineteenth centuries, particularly for urban babies placed with rural wet nurses. Throughout the eighteenth and nineteenth centuries, wet nursing was the predominant form of infant feeding for families in older, generally preindustrial cities like Paris, Lyons, Marseilles, and Bordeaux. During the first half of the nineteenth century, at least half of the babies born in the major cities of France were placed in the country with wet nurses for the first year or so of their lives.

The organization of wet nursing reflected the parents' social class. At the bottom of the scale, abandoned children were placed by the local hospital administration with distant, ill-paid nurses. Shopkeeper and artisan families, who were the major component of the wet-nursing business, placed their babies with rural nurses who lived somewhat closer to the city and afforded better care for better pay. In Paris, artisans and shopkeepers traditionally procured nurses through the municipal placement bureau, but during the nineteenth century poorly supervised private bureaus competed successfully with the municipal bureau, which was left with mostly charity cases. Well-to-do families, who in the eighteenth century had generally placed their babies with rural nurses obtained through private connections, tended after the Revolution to hire rural women who would move into the parents' homes where they could be more closely supervised as live-in nurses. Mortality of the nursing babies varied inversely with their parents' social position and the nursing arrangements they could afford to make.

The major reason why parents continued to place their babies with rural wet nurses in the nineteenth century was the necessity for women, especially of the shopkeeping and artisan class, to be fully employed in the family shop. Bottle feeding was an impractical and unsafe alternative to maternal breastfeeding before pasteurized milk, rubber nipples, and modern feeding bottles became available at the end of the century. Nevertheless, bottle feeding spread rapidly, especially in newer factory districts, from about midcentury.

One reason for the spread of bottle feeding in the nineteenth century was the dwindling supply of rural wet nurses caused by the declining birthrate and rural migration to the cities. The development of the railroad network extended the area of recruitment temporarily. Nevertheless, by the 1860s mortality and public concern mounted sharply as the number and quality of nurses declined. In 1874 the National Assembly enacted the Roussel Law, the first national regulation of the wet-nursing business.

F. Fäy-Sallois, *Les Nourrices à Paris au XIXe siècle* (Paris, 1980); G. D. Sussman, *Selling Mothers' Milk: The Wet-Nursing Business in France, 1715–1914* (Urbana, 1982).

*George D. Sussman*

*Related entries:* CHILDREARING PRACTICES; CHILDREN, ABAN-DONED; MIGRATION; MORTALITY; RAILROADS.

**WHITE TERROR** (1815–1816), the name given to the royalist excesses in 1815–1816, including mob action in the south of France, primarily directed against former supporters of Napoleon, liberals, and Protestants. Also considered as part of the White Terror are the instances of government repression and the purge of officials. The name comes from the Bourbon royal color.

Shortly after the Restoration of the Bourbons, Napoleon returned from exile for the Hundred Days. Following his final defeat at Waterloo, the early days of the Second Restoration saw royalist mobs taking their revenge on those who had served Napoleon and on groups associated with liberalism. This reign of terror was strong in the south of France, whose main seaports, Marseilles and Bordeaux, had suffered during the blockade of the Napoleonic wars. This area had also seen its textile industry decline during the wars. In addition, deserters and draft evaders had hidden in the mountains of southern France.

The first major outbreak of violence occurred at Marseilles. On 24 June 1815 a royalist committee moved into the city to seize control from the Napoleonic General Verdier. In the next two days up to 250 people were killed, including Napoleonic officers and government officials, informers, profiteers, police officers who had been overzealous in tracking draft evaders, and several Egyptian soldiers brought there by Napoleon. Royalist gangs were still pillaging in the area during October. Similar activities began in Toulon on 24 July 1815 and lasted through August.

In Avignon the assassin of a Bonapartist was released from jail by a mob of 300. In the same town Napoleonic Marshal Guillaume-Marie Brune was killed by a mob, and his body was thrown into the Rhône River. In Toulouse during July, two sets of officials claimed power, one appointed by the government and the other made up of local royalists associated with the secret Knights of the Faith. On 17 July 1815 a semiofficial battalion of royalist volunteers mobilized in Toulouse. Wearing green, the color of the king's reactionary cousin the duke of Angoulême, they searched houses and made arrests on the slightest pretext. The son of the prefect appointed by Paris called them ''a band of hired ruffians commanded by criminal agents.'' General Jean-Pierre Ramel, who had supported Napoleon during the Hundred Days, was put in charge of the National Guard by the authorities in Paris. Ramel was wounded trying to disperse a mob that included fifty royalists in green uniforms. He was later fatally stabbed in his bed.

In another area, the department of the Gard, the White Terror was aimed at Protestants. Nîmes, the largest city in the department, was one-third Calvinist, with this wealthy Protestant minority controlling industry and commerce. Just before the 1789 Revolution, the Old Regime had removed most of the restrictions on Protestants except for the right to hold public office. During the Revolutionary and Napoleonic periods, Protestants won this right and controlled the local municipal offices of Nîmes under the Empire. During the Hundred Days, the duke of Angoulême had raised 2,000 anti-Napoleon troops in the area, only six to ten of whom were Protestants. Also, at the same time numerous secret societies were formed. The ultraroyalist societies were almost entirely Catholic, while those Protestants who joined such groups predominantly joined Bonapartist ones.

On 17 July 1815 the duke of Angoulême's delegates took over in Nîmes. On 28 July the Paris-appointed prefect appeared but was prevented from taking office until 16 August. Meanwhile royalist bands pillaged 300 homes in the area, all but six of which belonged to Protestants. Another 2,000 Protestant families were victims of extortion by these groups. In the most bizarre incident of the White Terror, forty Protestant women were attacked by mobs, which lifted their skirts and beat them with a paddle embellished with a fleur-de-lys of spikes. Two to nine of the women died. In all about 100 people were killed, most of them Protestants from Nîmes. Between July and October 1815 some 2,500 Protestants fled Nîmes, creating a commercial and industrial crisis.

In November 1815 violence broke out again when a Catholic mob surrounded a packed Protestant church. The mob was dispersed by the National Guard but not before the officer in charge was wounded by one of his own troops. The guardsman who wounded the officer was a friend of the police commissioner and was never convicted of the crime.

There was a legal aspect of the White Terror as well. When the Bourbons were restored for the second time, the king issued a general amnesty, except for the "instigators and authors of the horrible plot" (the Hundred Days). On 7 December 1815 Marshal Michel Ney, who had gone over to Napoleon during the Hundred Days, was executed. Others indicted were those who had supported Napoleon before Louis XVIII fled (23 March 1815) and after he returned (8 July 1815). The ultraroyalist-dominated legislature in the 1815–16 session came within nine votes of passing a law that would have condemned 850 people to exile or death. Those regicides who had "relapsed" and supported Napoleon during the Hundred Days were not given amnesty. Several military leaders were executed, and many suspects were placed under surveillance, which included reporting to the police at regular intervals and not leaving town without police permission.

On 9 November 1815 a stringent sedition law was passed making illegal any speech or writing menacing to the life, authority, or person of the king or the life or person of any other member of the royal family. It also made it a felony to yell, "Down with the king." It was made illegal to display the tricolor flag.

On 20 December 1815 a law was passed reintroducing the provost courts. These courts, which had been abolished during the Revolution, were each presided over by a military colonel and could arrest, accuse, and convict. There was no jury and no appeal. Sentence, including the death penalty, could be carried out within twenty-four hours. The provost courts had authority to try for sedition, armed rebellion, smuggling, and some other crimes. In their first two and one-half years 9,000 persons were condemned in these courts, but most of these cases were not political. In one political case, a peasant was deported for passing around a parody of the Lord's prayer in which the king replaced the Lord. The courts were most active after the Didier conspiracy in Grenoble in May 1816. Didier had led 1,000 rebels in a march on the city, which was quickly dispersed by the army. In two days, sixteen were tried and executed.

Another repressive government act just after the Hundred Days was a massive purge of employees. Fifty thousand to 80,000 government job holders, or about 30 percent of the total, were replaced in 1815–16. There had not been a comparable purge after the First Restoration in 1814 or after Napoleon returned for the Hundred Days.

The White Terror did irreparable damage to the political future of the Bourbon royal family. Ironically, Louis XVIII was himself a moderate. Most of the repression was carried out by ultraroyalists "more royal than the king," and most of the mob violence was due to criminals more interested in looting than in defending the royal family at the opposite end of the social scale from themselves.

D. Resnick, *The White Terror and the Political Reaction after Waterloo* (Cambridge, 1966).

*Don Smith*

*Related entries:* ANGOULEME, L.-A.; BRUNE; CHEVALIERS DE LA FOI; *COURS PREVOTALES*; HUNDRED DAYS; LAW ON SEDITIOUS SPEECH; LOUIS XVIII; NATIONAL GUARD; NEY; RESTORATION, FIRST; RESTORATION, SECOND; ULTRAROYALISTS.

**WOMEN'S NEWSPAPERS.** The years after the outbreak of the Revolution of 1848 were unprecedented for the proliferation of women's newspapers of a political rather than fashionable type. Most of these twenty papers were politically radical, though some were evidently male satire of the women's movement. The most important of them, *La Voix des femmes, L'Opinion des femmes*, and *La Politique des femmes*, were published by women printers and drew links between women's rights and workers' rights by concentrating on women in the paid work force. They remain a valuable source for the movement for associations and workers' cooperatives and for the role of Saint-Simonianism and Fourierism in the history of the women's movement.

Among the themes of these papers are an emphasis on work as liberating, collective action, internationalism, antiracism, antislavery, religious toleration, radical politics, and women's equality in education, civil rights, and divorce. A key issue was the election of 1848: the papers supported progressive males (Etienne Cabet, Pierre Leroux, and Victor Schoelcher but also Pierre-Joseph Proudhon) and proposed the election of George Sand, but most leading politicians and papers were hostile, and Sand herself repudiated her candidacy.

Women's newspapers, like the women's movement itself, remained energetic until the press restrictions of July 1849 dealt them a mortal blow. By 1852, the movement was in disarray, with Pauline Roland dead, Jeanne Deroin in England, Suzanne Voilquin in the United States, Désirée Gay in Belgium, and Eugénie Niboyet publicly regretting her political role in 1848.

L. Adler, *A l'aube du féminisme: les premières journalistes (1830–1850)* (Paris, 1979); G. Sand, *Correspondance*, vol. 8 (Paris, 1971); E. Sullerot, "Journaux féminins et lutte ouvrière (1848–1849)," in J. Godechot, ed., *La Presse ouvrière, 1819–1850*, "Bibliothèque de la Révolution de 1848," vol. 23 (1966).

*Peter McPhee*

*Related entries:* DEROIN; FOURIER; LEROUX; NIBOYET; *LA POLITIQUE DES FEMMES*; PRESS LAWS; PROUDHON; ROLAND; SAND; VOILQUIN; *LA VOIX DES FEMMES*; WORKERS' COOPERATIVES.

**WORKER POETS.** There was a long tradition of workers writing poetry in France. The seventeenth-century joiner Adam Billaut, called "Maître Adam," had written poems and songs that every child knew. The French Revolution added to this tradition two new elements: a habit of using song to transmit political ideas and an interest in the working class. The Revolution of 1830 reconfirmed the desire of urban artisans to take a hand in French politics. During the July Monarchy, there were many educated Frenchmen who placed their hopes in the proletariat and many more who feared it, but nobody was disinterested. The rapid pace of change and the dislocations caused by the industrial revolution made Europeans wary of the workers. The so-called socialist flowering of 1839–40 created several constellations of intellectuals anxious to show that they understood the true spirit of the working classes and even more constellations of conservatives anxious to show that in truth it was they who understood the workers. Both sides were willing to finance the publication of poems and songs by working-class authors who agreed with their point of view. Consequently the socialist flowering of 1839 was accompanied by a bumper harvest of working-class poetry and song. Pierre-Jean de Béranger, the hero and model of many of the worker poets, wrote:

> The people are speaking; yesterday they were babbling.
> From the height of the throne men are shouting, worried,
> Here are the voices from below that are rising up.

"It is to the proletariat, to the people in the true sense of the word," wrote Mme. Amable Tastu, "that now belongs the creative and primary role of poetry; up to the seventeenth century poetry and literature were exclusively the portion of the nobility; then it was the magistrature and the high bourgeoisie who made their entrance, then the middle class; at present it is the turn of the people. As a harmonious phrase in some work of Beethoven's goes through the orchestra repeated in turn by each instrument, so the gift of poetry passes through all the classes of society." And George Sand, in her preface to the mason Charles Poncy's *Le Chantier*, a collection of his poems that appeared in 1844, wrote: "Since the first civilized societies, the people have been the Messiah promised to the nations; it is they who are doing Christ's work. . . . The spirit of the people will give birth to a great social religion. . . . Let's go, worker poets, let's get to work! Sing your songs of truth!"

Not all critics looked upon the worker poets as a collective messiah come to save mankind. François-René de Chateaubriand said that most worker poets were neither workers nor poets, and Alphonse de Lamartine said that he did not believe in democracy in art because "we do not believe in nature except when it is cultivated by education; we have never tasted with false enthusiasm those rhymed mediocrities that these artisans, who are so out-of-place in the world of letters, use too often without genius or facility to try to enrapture their century." Jules Michelet, who was more sympathetic, complained that the worker poets were too imitative and urged them to use the rough speech of their everyday lives in their poems, and George Sand also urged the mason Charles Poncy to write so that people could see the plaster on his hands.

Such criticisms were just. Most worker poets did not write good poetry, and the poetry they did write was split between those who imitated Béranger and those who imitated Lamartine. Both the style and the content of their verses was copied from their betters. Some of Poncy's poems, for example, were nothing more than letters sent to him by George Sand set to rhyme. It could be concluded, then, that the French worker poetry of the July Monarchy is both worthless as literature and useless as a source of insight into working-class mentality.

But not all worker poets followed their masters so slavishly. Jules Vinçard, a ruler maker in Paris, was a loyal Saint-Simonian socialist, but he never accepted the antidemocratic and antilibertarian aspects of the Saint-Simonian faith. Jean Reboul, the baker from Nîmes, was a faithful legitimist and Catholic, but in his poetry, royalism and religion became surprisingly similar to the socialism of Poncy and Vinçard. In other words, there does seem to be something like a universal working-class mentality underlying the songs and poetry of the French worker poets. Whatever their point of view, they demanded basic changes in their society so that the worker would be assured a decent job at decent pay and the idler would no longer get rich from the worker's sweat. Most worker poets had been educated as, and still remained, Christians, and they invoked the image of the carpenter-Messiah Jesus to support their point of view. They were all political and all revolutionary. People who took the trouble to understand the worker poets got a sense of working-class mentality and realized that the enrichissez-vous regime of Louis-Philippe and François Guizot could not last.

The worker poets were all revolutionaries. Some were revolutionaries of the Right, some of the Left, and some of the Center. The revolutionaries of the Center, like the weaver Magu of Lizy-sur-Ourq and the barber Jasmin of Agen, saw the July Monarchy as a revolutionary regime that was changing the lives of Frenchmen. They had good evidence for their beliefs; both had been granted pensions by the government, and it seemed to be only a matter of time before the government would extend its largesse to their 30 million or so fellow countrymen. Thus they counseled patience and hard work to the proletariat and charity and reform to the government. They knew that they had the ear of the king and some of his ministers. They believed that all they had to do was to speak the truth in order to change France.

Here again, their beliefs made sense. Europe had been a dull place since the end of the Revolution and the Empire, and people were now forced to rely on the power of imagination and memory for their adventures. The writer had become the new hero; as the worker poet Hégésippe Moreau put it, "The weapon of the century is the pen." The writer shaped ideas, and ideas (as Hegel had shown) moved the world. There seemed to be no doubt that Béranger had been responsible for the 1830 Revolution. After the 1848 Revolution, the Parisian brushmaker and *chansonnier* Gustave Leroy wrote:

Welcome, welcome august Republic,
Come give us the rule of law,

In my songs I've carried out a political guerrilla war,
For ten years I've fought for you.

In a world where literary giants like Lamartine and Victor Hugo could be more powerful than kings, it seemed logical that lesser writers could also hope to have some political influence.

It seems remarkable that there were not more worker poets on the legitimist Right, given the increasingly populist stance that the legitimists were beginning to take. Most legitimists claimed that the masses were really royalist and Catholic at heart. They were not alone in claiming that their system would be best for the French people; the socialist shoemaker and poet Savinien Lapointe wrote that the people had been better off back in the days when the chateaux took care of the cottages. This was essentially the message of the baker Jean Reboul, whom Chateaubriand, Lamartine, and Alexandre Dumas père accepted as a true poet. His message was that the poor should be submissive and pious and that the rich should be charitable and caring. His enemies were selfishness and materialism, the same Robert Macaire personality-type so hated by the socialist cartoonist Honoré Daumier:

While the peoples were seeking worldly goods
And never looking toward Heaven,
The earth had lost her power to love.
She turned her eyes toward her splendid treasure;
But science and art did not fill up the void
Left by the exile of the idea of God.

Reboul was the only legitimist among the major worker poets, but his following was almost as large as that of all of the other worker poets combined. The press run for his books was 4,000 copies, the same as for Balzac and Victor Hugo. He contributed to the royalist *Quotidienne*, an important Parisian newspaper, hobnobbed with local aristocrats, and was visited in his bakery by Lamartine, Chateaubriand, and Alexandre Dumas. Like the socialist worker poets, he lamented that the main result of the 1830 Revolution had been "to allow Macaire to fill up his cash box," and he saw the 1848 Revolution as God's punishment for the wicked men of the *juste milieu*. He was elected to the Constituent Assembly from his native Gard department in 1848 and voted with Berryer and the legitimists. When he died in 1864, the city of Nîmes gave him a public funeral. Clearly legitimism was a major force, and it made the legitimist worker poet Jean Reboul an important figure in French literature.

The socialist worker poets had a following about the same size as the legitimists, and there were a lot more of them to share it. They enjoyed the strong financial backing of wealthy socialists like Olinde Rodriguès, whose *Poésies sociales des ouvriers*, published in 1841, gave many worker poets their first exposure to a national audience. George Sand also helped poets like the joiner Agricol Perdiguier and the mason Charles Poncy to publish their poetry. In addition, socialist working-class newspapers like *La Ruche populaire*, *L'Union*, and *L'Atelier* printed poetry and song. The funding and the opportunity to publish created more socialist worker poets than any other kind, but this does not indicate that the artisans in France were inclined toward socialism. It does, however, indicate that certain issues concerned thoughtful artisans of all political persuasions. All were upset by the July Monarchy's emphasis on individualism and material gain and by the fact that the old nobility had been replaced by a selfish and greedy plutocracy. All had had a fundamentally Christian education and looked to the Sermon on the Mount as the source of social reform. All hated what Reboul called "this ignoble duel between the rich and the poor" and wanted France to become a caring and just nation. Most important, all were proud to be workers. Reboul was asked after he had become famous whether he still saw himself as a member of the working class; he replied: "Yes, of course, and I consider it an honor." The socialist worker poets would go even further and turn the world upside down, contending that the poor do the nation's work, create its wealth, and fight its wars. The poor are honorable: they marry for love rather than money and act out of friendship rather than self-interest. The poor are even better educated since their hearts are not frozen by years of Latin and Greek but are open to nature, beauty, and feeling. Like Rousseau, the worker poets contended that the person closer to nature and closer to God was superior to the cold, formally educated *honnêtes gens* of the July Monarchy. In short, they turned the world upside down:

> See how ingredients that are good and fat, good and
> succulent, boil up in a stew pot,
> The meat is hardly cooked
> When it goes directly
> To the bottom of the pot.
> That is the image of the century in which we live:
> Merit stays at the bottom,
> It is the scum that floats to the top.

The proof of the workers' superiority of heart and feeling was to be that they could write better poetry than the rich.

The socialist worker poets were as opposed to revolutionary violence as their conservative colleagues. They hoped to use the power of their verse to appeal to their rulers. Progress, the steam engine, and God would combine to create a more just society. They also advocated a variety of economic reforms such as confiscatory death duties, a graduated income tax, a requirement that all able-bodied people work, and equal wages for women. Their principal economic goal was the creation of producers' cooperative associations, which would give the workers control over the means of production. In politics the socialist worker poets tended to be republicans and democrats. They welcomed the 1848 Revolution but were not revolutionaries. The Parisian shoemaker Savinien Lapointe, for example, had abandoned revolutionary republicanism when he became a socialist.

After the 1848 Revolution, several of the worker poets were elected to represent Paris, and their districts throughout France (for worker poets had become local heroes both in Paris and in the provinces) in the Constituent Assembly in 1848 and the Legislative Assembly in 1849. There was a sudden outpouring of worker poetry; the Second Republic from February to June 1848 was their moment of glory. Louis-Napoleon's coup d'état in 1851 silenced them all. Some like Perdiguier were forced to flee, others simply stopped writing, and some like Charles Poncy grew rich. In 1867 Poncy looked back on the worker poets. "The celebrities of the age gloried in becoming their patrons, and their appearance gave rise to so many political and philosophical theories. Great and generous spirits had gone so far as to found their hopes for social renewal upon them. They were, alas, quickly deceived."

J. Maitron, ed., *Dictionnaire biographique du mouvement ouvrier français* (Paris, 1966); E. L. Newman, "L'Arme du siècle, c'est la plume: The French Worker Poets of the July Monarchy and the Spirit of Revolution and Reform," *Journal of Modern History* (1980) and "L'Ouvrière, sa vie est dure mais elle se plaint rarement: The French Women Worker Poets of the July Monarchy," *Studies in Nineteenth Century Society and Culture* 3 (1977), and *The French Worker Poets of the July Monarchy* (forthcoming); M. Ragon, *Les Ecrivains du peuple* (Paris, 1947); J. Rancère, *La nuit des prolétaires* (Paris, 1981); E. Thomas, *Voix d'en bas; la poésie ouvrière du XIXe siècle* (Paris, 1979); J. Touchard, *La Gloire de Béranger*, 2 vols. (Paris, 1968).

*Edgar Leon Newman*

*Related entries: L'ATELIER*; BERANGER; BERRYER, P.-A.; CHATEAU-BRIAND; DAUMIER; DUMAS; ECONOMIC CHANGE; GUIZOT; JASMIN; *JUSTE MILIEU*; LAMARTINE; LAPOINTE; LEGISLATIVE ASSEMBLY; LEGITIMISM; LEROY; MACAIRE; MAGU; MICHELET; MOREAU; PERDIGUIER; PONCY; *LA QUOTIDIENNE*; REBOUL; REPUBLICANS; *LA RUCHE POPULAIRE*; SAND; SINGING SOCIETIES; VINCARD.


**WORKERS' COOPERATIVES,** the principal objective of the early French labor movement. The French labor movement from its origin in the aftermath of the July Revolution through the 1870s had as its principal objective the establishment of workers' or producers' cooperatives. This cooperative socialism was engendered by middle-class social republicans, who gave ideological direction to the workers' experience, but the workers' experience and the structure of their trade organizations in turn gave a particular form to the socialist perspective of the middle-class republicans.

Especially after 1830, skilled workers were being proletarianized by the advance of industrialization, which was manifested in France at this time not so much by the introduction of large factories or machine production but by changing attitudes toward productivity and profit. Skilled workers had experienced an erosion of their traditional status, income, and security. In search of a solution for the deterioration of their condition, skilled workers came in contact with middle-class republicans in the Société des droits de l'homme and the Société des amis du peuple. As a result of these contacts between workers and republicans, projects were drawn up for producers' cooperatives by workers and by the middle-class theoretician Philippe Buchez.

In this new vision, the establishment of producers' cooperatives was, as more and more production came under their sway, gradually to usher in a cooperative trade socialism. After the failure of the Third French Republic to provide support for cooperatives, the notion of a gradual collectivization of the economy through a peaceful expansion of cooperatives was replaced by a revolutionary trade socialism, which looked for a revolutionary overthrow of bourgeois society and the supplanting of the capitalist system with a collective economy. The ultimate goal, however, was the same: a federation of skilled trades that would collectively own the means of production.

The call for producers' cooperatives was raised in the midst of the labor struggle unleashed by the Revolution of 1830. The revolution, which had occurred at a time of industrial depression, roused expectations of improvement. The demands of workers for improvements in wages and hours, government-provided employment through a public works program, and laws to restrict the introduction of new machinery, however, were opposed by business and the new government. In the face of this hostility, workers turned to the producers' cooperative.

Printers, who stood out among the trades because of their education, wages, and traditional solidarity, were unique in their ability to overcome the barriers against unionism. Their craft and solidarity enabled them, despite the illegality of strikes, to force their employers to bargain collectively. It was the printers, however, who first turned to the idea of workers' cooperatives as the solution for the deterioration of the conditions of skilled workers.

At the end of September 1830, the printers, who published L'Artisan, journal de la classe ouvrière, went beyond the demands of the other trades. To them exploitation was the source of the workers' problems, and they advocated workers' or producers' cooperative associations as the means for escaping exploitation. To the editors of L'Artisan, workers were the producers of all wealth. A levy was being imposed on their labor by parasitical capitalists. Machinery, the printers argued, was not evil, only its use by capitalists to further exploit the workers. According to L'Artisan, workers should join together in cooperative associations, purchase machinery, and by taking complete control of the workplace and work process free themselves from the system of capitalist exploitation.

During the 1830s, proposals for producers' cooperatives were advanced in many towns and were actually initiated in Marseilles by hatters, turners, shoemakers, and stonecutters. Most of the cooperative efforts that were launched, however, were suppressed by the government, which was antagonistic to their collective, anticapitalist character and their republican sympathies. One society, however, the Association des ouvriers bijoutiers en doré, modeled on Buchez's plan, was organized in Paris in 1834 and endured until 1873.

Buchez's plan, elaborated in 1830 and 1831, included the concept of inalienable capital, a collective nondivisible capital fund, which would be accumulated by the cooperative and would enable new members to join without having to buy their way into the cooperative. The fund of inalienable capital could never be claimed or parceled out by the workers individually or even as a group. This fund would give the cooperative an independent and collective existence.

During the 1840s the most influential advocates of workers' cooperatives were Louis Blanc, whose *Organisation du travail* was published in August 1840, and the working-class disciples of Buchez, who published *L'Atelier*. Much has been made of the differences between Blanc and *L'Atelier*. To a large extent, however, the difference was one of emphasis. Although both Blanc and *L'Atelier* expected a republic to provide credit for the establishment of cooperatives, Blanc emphasized the role of the state, while *L'Atelier* placed more emphasis on the workers' emancipating themselves. The most significant difference was that Blanc called for a single large cooperative to monopolize each trade, while *L'Atelier* advocated a number of competitive cooperatives within each trade.

The February Revolution in 1848 roused the hopes of the cooperativists that their plans for the emancipation of the workers might be implemented. The moderate republicans who constituted a majority in the Provisional Government, though unwilling to undertake a total renovation of society that would threaten the small capitalists, in general had expressed their support for the concept of associations through which workers would receive the legitimate profit of their labor.

The majority of the moderate republicans in the Provisional Government only reluctantly agreed to the principle of the right to work, which to them smacked of socialism. They preferred to foster voluntary cooperatives through state credit and merely accepted the establishment of the National Workshops as an expedient imposed by the circumstances. They relegated Louis Blanc and his socialist followers to the supposedly innocuous Commission du governement pour les travailleurs, or the Luxembourg Commission. The Luxembourg Commission in fact became such a rallying point for the coordination of strikes and political activity and the promotion of the type of universal trade associations favored by Blanc that it was dissolved in the reactionary aftermath of the April election.

Even the withdrawal of governmental recognition from the Luxembourg Commission and the decision to abolish the National Workshops, which the moderate republicans viewed as a costly club of insurrection, did not mean an immediate end to the hope for government support for cooperatives. On 23 June, after the threatened closure of the National Workshops had provoked the June Insurrection, Claude-Anthime Corbon, the chairman of the government's Committee on Labor, proposed the establishment of a Conseil d'encouragement pour les associations ouvrières to provide 3 million francs in government credit to workers' cooperatives. Although the proposal was timed to undercut support for the insurrection, Corbon's proposal mirrored the approach he had advocated as a member of the Buchezian *L'Atelier*.

Nothing came of Corbon's proposal until after the insurrection had been suppressed. On 3 July, Michel Goudchaux, the minister of finance who had regarded the National workshops as politically dangerous but who hoped to use the Republic as an instrument of social improvement, announced government support for state aid to cooperatives. Corbon introduced a new bill on 4 July to provide government encouragement through 3 million francs in credit to cooperatives consisting of workers or workers and employers. The proposal was approved on July 5 without opposition. To many conservatives in the Assembly, the law was viewed as a cynical means to discredit the idea of cooperation by an inadequately financed program, which they believed was foredoomed to failure. The Cavaignac government, however, did genuinely support the law, and it was regarded as a positive victory not only by Buchez and *L'Atelier* but also by Blanc.

Men of known sympathy for workers' cooperatives, including Corbon and several other Buchezians, were appointed to the council which was to administer the program. Though the Buchezians were able to gain the inclusion in the model statutes the council drew up of an article calling for the development of an indivisible fund, this attempt to make Buchez's notion of inalienable capital an essential element of the cooperatives was ignored in practice. Doctrinal disputes and a basic difference in orientation, in which the non-Buchezians favored employer-employee associations, led to the resignation of the Buchezians in November and December, 1848. After that, the council utilized its funds principally to provide credit to employers who allowed their employees to share in profits.

In addition to the government credit program, cooperativism had its independent propagators in the now-unofficial Luxembourg delegates. They established the Chambre du travail to provide mutual credit for cooperatives, and began a promising association with Proudhon's Bank of the People, until his fear of socialism led him to liquidate it. In November, 1849, the Union des associations united 104 workers' cooperatives in an effort to provide mutual credit and exchange. It, however, was dissolved in May 1850 by the government, which was concerned about a possible resurgence of republican socialism. The cooperative movement and continued attempts at organization nevertheless persisted until they were suppressed in the antirepublican repression following Louis-Napoléon's coup.

Between the February Revolution and the coup, 300 cooperatives were organized by 120 trades in Paris, and 800 were organized in the provinces. Whether independent or provided with some government credit, however, most of the workers' cooperatives organized in the aftermath of 1848 failed after a short time as a result of insufficient credit or managerial inadequacies. Fewer than half of the state-sponsored cooperatives survived four years. Of the forty-nine trades that initiated cooperatives in 1849, only twenty-six still had operating cooperatives in 1851. Despite their difficulties, however, cooperativism still had vitality until it was suppressed by governmental action. New cooperatives were continually formed until the coup, and in 1851 there were 200 workers' cooperatives in Paris alone. Workers were continually drawn by the cooperative vision of emancipation from wage slavery and the vicissitudes of the market. Although temporarily repressed they would re-emerge as the goal of the French workers' movement.

F. A. de Luna, *The French Republic under Cavaignac, 1848* (Princeton, 1969); R. Gossez, *Les Ouvriers de Paris* (La Roche-sur-Yon, 1967) and "Pré-syndicalisme ou pré-coopération," *Archives internationales de sociologie de la cooperation,* no. 6 (1959); E. Heftler, *Les Associations coopératives de production sous la deuxième république* (Paris, 1899); F.-A. Isambert, "Aux Origines de l'associationnisme buchézien," *Archives internationales de sociologie de la coopération,* no. 6 (1959); Bernard H. Moss, "Parisian Producers' Associations," *Proceedings of the Western Society for French History* (1974) and *The Origins of the French Labor Movement, 1830–1914: The Socialism of Skilled Workers* (Berkeley, 1980).

*Bernard Cook*

*Related entries:* L'*ARTISAN;* L'*ATELIER*; BLANC; BUCHEZ; CAVAIGNAC, L.-E.; ECONOMIC CHANGE; GOUDCHAUX; LUXEMBOURG COMMISSION; NATIONAL WORKSHOPS; PROUDHON; REPUBLICANS; SOCIETY OF THE RIGHTS OF MAN.

# Y

**YOUNG (NEW) MOUNTAIN SOCIETY.** Also called the Club of the Sorbonne, it was a part of the radical club movement in the ferment of 1848. This club was founded in March 1848 and met in the amphitheater of the Sorbonne, the university of Paris. It was one of the eight clubs in Paris to use the word *Mountain* or *Montagnard* in its title. It became important as a result of its location in the Latin Quarter, where the students lived. Its president, Juin d'Allas, published under the pseudonym of Michelet five numbers of a newspaper, *La Souveraineté du Peuple*. But when Juin d'Allas, an escaped prisoner, was discovered and sent to jail, the club collapsed. Its democratic and socialist ideals were by then out of touch with the growing conservative spirit in France.

A. Lucas, *Les Clubs et les clubistes*, 2nd ed. (Paris, 1851).

*Jean-Claude Caron, trans. E. Newman*

*Related entries:* CLUBS, POLITICAL.

# Chronology,
# 1815–1852

## FIRST BOURBON RESTORATION, May 1814–March 1815

### 1815

The population of France is 30 million. About 72 percent are peasants. Among the men, about 47 percent are literate. Among the women, about 29 percent are literate. There are fewer than 500,000 Protestants and about 60,000 Jews.

Wheat is 19.53 francs per hectoliter.

Publication of Pierre-Jean de Béranger's (1780–1857) *Chansons I* and Benjamin Constant's (1767–1830) *Adolphe*.

Publication (through 1822) of Jean Lamarck's (1744–1829) *Histoire naturelle des animaux sans vertèbres*. Augustin Fresnel's (1788–1827) research on the diffraction of light.

February 27. Napoleon (1769–1821) escapes from the island of Elba.

March 1. Napoleon lands on the southern coast of France with about 1,500 men and pushes north, carefully picking his route to avoid royalist areas like Marseilles. As he moves north, the common people seem pleased by his return, but only the soldiers take an active role in this strictly military coup d'état.

March 13. The allies declare war on Napoleon. Marshal Michel Ney (1769–1815), who had promised Louis XVIII (1755–1824) that he would bring back Napoleon "in an iron cage," joins Napoleon's army. His troops probably would not have fought Napoleon anyway.

March 19. Louis XVIII leaves Paris. His cold reception by the garrison at Lille, where he arrives on March 22, convinces him to leave France. He arrives at Ghent on March 30 and spends the rest of his exile there.

## NAPOLEON'S RETURN FROM ELBA: THE HUNDRED DAYS, March 20–June 29, 1815

March 20. Napoleon enters Paris. Start of what would later be called the Hundred Days: March 20–June 29.

March 24. Napoleon's decree suspends censorship.

March 25. Austria, Britain, Prussia, and Russia conclude a new alliance against Napoleon and invite all the other European nations to join. Most do.

April 3. Royalist forces in the south of France under the duc d'Angoulême (1775–1844), nephew of Louis XVIII, take Valence, opening up the way to Lyons for the royalists.

April 8. The duc d'Angoulême surrenders his royalist army in the face of superior Bonapartist forces and agrees to leave France.

May 1–August 7. *L'Indépendant*. Changing names to dodge the censors, this liberal newspaper is called the *Courrier général* from August 26 to October 23, when it becomes the *Constitutionnel*, the name by which it is best known. From July 1817 to May 1, 1819, it is called *Journal du commerce*. After May 1819 it is once again the *Constitutionnel*. Its enormous press runs of 16,250 per issue in 1824 and 23,333 in 1831 make it the most popular newspaper of the age. After its circulation falls during the July Monarchy, when its unchanging political stance makes it seem a bit stuffy compared to the radical press, it makes a comeback by publishing Eugène Sue's (1804–57) *Le Juif errant* in installments in 1844.

May 12. Francois-René de Chateaubriand (1768–1848), now serving as minister of the interior to the exiled Louis XVIII in Ghent, publishes his *Report to the King* in his newspaper, the *Journal universel*, defending the liberal and constitutional policies of the First Restoration. The king's brother, the comte d'Artois (1757–1836), heir to the throne, had been blaming Louis XVIII's failure on his liberal policies and had called for the abolition of the Charter once the Bourbons returned to power.

June 1. Napoleon issues the Additional Act to the Constitutions of the Empire.

June 4. Death in battle of the royalist leader Louis de la Rochejaquelein (1775–1815), who was fighting against General Jean-Maximin Lamarque (1770–1832) and 20,000 French soldiers whom Napoleon needed in the east.

June 9. Final agreements of the Congress in Vienna.

June 18. Napoleon is defeated at the battle of Waterloo. News of this French defeat will cause a 5 percent rise in the value of French bonds on the Paris stock exchange from 56.20 on June 14 to 59.25 on June 26.

June 22. Napoleon's second abdication in favor of his son, the king of Rome (1811–32).

Louis XVIII reenters France.

## SECOND BOURBON RESTORATION, 1815–1830

June 25–26. Royalist uprisings and massacres of Bonapartists, Protestants, and supporters of the revolution in Marseilles signal the start of the White Terror.

June 28. Louis XVIII issues the Declaration of Cambrai.

July 6. Louis XVIII, at the insistence of the duke of Wellington (1769–1852), accepts a new ministry with the regicide Joseph Fouché (1763–1820) as minister of police and the clubfooted Charles-Maurice de Talleyrand (1754–1838) as foreign minister. As Talleyrand and Fouché come forward to present themselves to the king, Chateaubriand notes that it is "vice leaning on the arm of crime."

July 8. Louis XVIII returns to Paris to the cheers of royalist crowds but "in the baggage train of the Allies."

July 24. A royal ordinance condemns fifty-seven men seen as dangerous to the monarchy. The list was drawn up by Joseph Fouché, the Jacobin regicide turned Napoleonic minister turned royalist minister of police. Lazare Carnot (1753–1823), one of the fifty-seven, asks Fouché, "Where do you want me to go, traitor?" Fouché replies: "Wherever you want, idiot."

July 25. Royalist mobs in Marseilles drive out the garrison and massacre former Jacobins and *fédérés* (members of the Revolutionary Federations) as the White Terror continues. Royalist gangs in Avignon kill Marshal Guillaume-Marie Brune (1763–1815). Riots in Nîmes. Riots in Toulouse, where General Jean-Pierre Ramel (1768–1815) is killed by royalist mobs.

August 8. Napoleon is banished to the island of Saint-Helena, where he will be a prisoner of the British until his death in 1821.

August 8. A royal ordinance imposes censorship on all periodicals and forbids the printing of any newspaper without prior approval.

August 14–22. The first elections under Louis XVIII's Charter, using the voting laws left over from Napoleon's Hundred Days, produce an ultraroyalist Chamber of Deputies "more royalist than the king," which Louis XVIII sarcastically called his *chambre introuvable*. 48,000 out of 72,000 eligible voters cast votes, seven times more than had voted for the Chamber of Representatives during Napoleon's Hundred Days. The king, who had tried in vain to get moderates elected, would later use his authority to dissolve the *chambre introuvable* on September 5, 1816, to the cheers of the liberal opponents of royal power.

September 21. Resignation of the Talleyrand-Fouché ministry.

September 24. A moderate new cabinet is organized under the duc de Richelieu (1766–1822).

September 26. Signing of the Holy Alliance.

October 29. The Law of General Security is signed by Louis XVIII.

November 9. A new press law defines seditious acts and hands press crimes over to correctional tribunals.

November 20. Second Peace of Paris takes away territory from the north and east, leaving France with its boundaries of January 1, 1790, and imposes an indemnity of 700 million francs on France. France is to be occupied by 150,000 foreign troops on its northern and eastern frontiers for three to five years and must pay the 150 million franc annual cost of maintaining them.

Austria, Prussia, Russia, and England sign the Quadruple Alliance, agreeing to work together in the future to preserve order in Europe.

October 29. The *chambre introuvable* passes the Law of General Security permitting arrest without trial of anyone plotting against the royal family or against the security of the state.

November 9. The *chambre introuvable* passes the Law on Seditious Speech and Publications, which calls for the arrest and fining of anyone who threatens the government or the life of the king, who shouts "Long live the emperor!" or who puts up a tricolored flag.

November 20. The Second Treaty of Paris is imposed upon France by the Allies.

November 21–December 6. Trial of Marshal Ney before the Chamber of Peers.

December 7. Execution of Marshal Ney, Napoleon's "bravest of the brave."

December 20. The Cours prévôtales are created.

The right-wing royalist *Quotidienne* publishes from 1815 to February 1847. Circulation is 5,800 in 1824, 5,833 in 1831.

## 1816

Crops are spoiled by a cold winter as the skies are black following the previous year's volcanic eruption in the East Indies. Wheat costs about 30 francs per hectoliter.

Joseph Niepce (Nicéphore) (1765–1833), a French physicist, invents the bicycle.

René Laënnec (1781–1826), a French physician, invents the stethoscope.

Port au Salut cheese is made for the first time by Trappist monks in northern Touraine.

The ship *Medusa* sinks.

French government bonds of 100 francs face value are selling at 40 francs.

January 12. The *chambre introuvable* passes the Amnesty Law, which excludes from the king's declaration of amnesty all regicides who had "relapsed" and served Napoleon or voted for the Additional Act to the Constitutions of the Empire during the Hundred Days.

February 10. The occupying powers (Britain, Austria, Prussia, and Russia) agree to the first reduction in the number of occupation troops in France.

February 29. A royal ordinance creates cantonal school boards, each chaired by the local priest, and gives them control of cantonal primary schools. All teachers other than Brothers of the Christian Schools and other members of religious orders must get a certificate of good conduct signed by their local priest or mayor before they can teach.

March 21. A royal ordinance revamps the Institute.

May. Leftist Didier conspiracy in Grenoble.

May 8. Divorce abolished.

September. Publication of Chateaubriand's *La Monarchie selon la Charte*, which is quickly suppressed.

September 5. In a royal coup d'état, Louis XVIII dissolves the Ultraroyalist Chamber of Deputies and calls for elections under the old Napoleonic electoral law slightly modified. (The right-wing royalists had wanted to liberalize the election law in order to counterbalance the influence of the rich middle class.) Dismissal of Chateaubriand from the Council of Ministers.

October. New elections bring victory to the moderates and liberals in the Chamber of Deputies. The moderates elect 146 Deputies, the Right 92.

## 1817

Wheat is at 46.50 francs per hectoliter, and in June it is 67 francs per hectoliter in Lyons and 75 francs in Bourg. Bread prices rise to 1.25 francs per pound. The government spends about 49 million francs for food relief.

Publication of Félicité de Lamennais' (1782–1854) *Essai sur l'indifférence en matière de religion.*

French government bonds of 100 francs par value are selling at 45–52 francs.

January 17. Reopening of the Ecole polytechnique.

February 8. A new electoral law limits the franchise. Only men at least thirty years old who pay taxes of 300 francs a year can vote in elections for the Chamber of Deputies, and only men forty years of age who pay taxes of 1,000 francs can become deputies. About 92,000 of 26 million French people can vote, and of those about 15,000 are eligible to serve as deputies. The new one-stage elections favor those who live in the principal cities of each department. (Under the Napoleonic system, elections had been held in each arrondissement; the new law held elections only in the administrative center of each department.) Each deputy is elected for a five-year term, with one-fifth of the Chamber to be renewed each year.

April 1. Allied occupation forces are reduced by one-fifth, or 30,000 men, as a result of the diplomatic efforts of the duc de Richelieu.

June 8. Insurrection in Lyons under the tricolored flag. Eleven rebels are condemned by the provost courts and guillotined. Colonel Charles-Nicholas Fabvier (1782–1855), sent to investigate the affair, blames it on police *agents provocateurs*, on the prefect of the Rhone, the comte de Chabrol (1771–1836), on General Simon de Canuel (1767–1840), the regional military commander, and generally on the royalist Right.

July 17. Pope Pius VII (1742–1823) ratifies the accord with France of the previous month cancelling his Concordat of 1801 with Napoleon. Later the French ministers ask the legislature to ratify the treaty in a way that would change its meaning so that, for example, bishops would be appointed by the king and not by the "full and free authority" of the pope. This is not enough to win the approval of the Deputies, but it is too much for the pope, who rejects the French bill and carries the right-wing deputies with him. The treaty is abandoned in a flurry of anticlerical and anti-Revolutionary rhetoric.

September 20. Elections. The Right loses 12 seats to the ministerial moderates, who themselves lose 12 seats to the antiministerial independents of the Left, who now control 25 of the 262 seats.

## 1818

Paris has 713,000 people (versus 622,000 in 1811 and 800,000 in 1830).

French government bonds of 100 francs face value are selling at 67 francs.

Publication of Pierre-Claude-François Daunou's (1761–1840) *Essai sur les garanties individuelles.*

Publication (through 1820) of Benjamin Constant's (1767–1830) *Cours de politique constitutionnelle.*

Posthumous publication of Mme. de Staël's (1766–1817) *Considérations sur la Révolution française.*

Publication of the vicomte de Bonald's (1754–1840) *Recherches philosophiques sur les premiers objects des connaissances morales.*

February 1818–March, 1820. Publication of *La Minerve française*, a liberal newspaper, whose contributors include Benjamin Constant.

March–April 1820. *Bibliothèque historique,* a liberal-Bonapartist periodical published by Louis-Auguste-François Cauchois-Lemaire (1789–1861).

March 12. The Gouvion-Saint-Cyr Law, named for the minister of war, Marshal Laurent Gouvion Saint-Cyr (1764–1830), provides France with a national conscript army. Substitution is permitted, and for about 700 francs a draftee can get someone else to go in his place. The term of service is seven years (raised to eight in 1824).

May. The French government issues 14.5 million francs in bonds to help pay its war debts. The French public subscribes to 163 million francs, ten times the offering.

June. The Conspiracy of the Water's Edge, supposedly a right-wing conspiracy to impose a new ministry on Louis XVIII and to assassinate him if he refuses to cooperate, is discovered. The minister of police, Elie Decazes (1780–1860), a moderate liberal and a favorite of the king, uses this alleged conspiracy to discredit the royalist Right.

August. French bonds of 100 francs face value are selling for 80 francs.

September 30. Allies open the Congress of Aix-la-Chapelle and agree to withdraw all foreign troops from France by November 30, 1818.

An exceptionally good wine harvest is called "departure wine."

October. Elections. The Right loses fifteen seats, the ministerial Center loses four, and the left-wing independents win about twenty. The marquis de Lafayette (1757–1834) and Jacques Manuel (1775–1827) are among the leftist deputies elected.

October 1818–March 1820. *Le Conservateur,* a right-wing royalist periodical, is published by Chateaubriand, Louis-Gabriel-Ambroise de Bonald, Pierre-Antoine Berryer (1790–1868), and others. Its press run is 7,000 to 8,000.

November. Allied troops evacuate France largely as a result of the efforts of the French foreign minster, the duc de Richelieu.

December 26. Armand-Emmanuel de Richelieu resigns. A new, more liberal cabinet is formed under Elie Decazes and General Jean-Joseph Dessolle (1767–1828). The new cabinet blames the government's unpopularity on the royalist Right, which had threatened revenge in 1815. Decazes sets out to "monarchize the nation and nationalize the monarchy." In a "slaughter of prefects," Decazes replaces sixteen prefects and forty subprefects. Many *émigré* army officers are put on inactive service. Fifty-two regicides and many others exiled in 1815–16 are allowed to return to France. The king appoints fifty-nine new peers to shift the political balance in the Chamber of Peers toward the liberals. New laws offer a jury trial for press offenses and end censorship. True to the liberal tradition of giving preference to people with money, the new press laws require that newspaper owners must put up a large sum of caution money as a guarantee against future fines for press offenses before they can publish.

## 1819

The corn laws of 1819 and 1821 make cereal imports into France virtually impossible.

Wheat is at 18.42 francs per hectoliter. In July, new tariffs try, in vain, to protect French grain prices, which are declining due to domestic overproduction.

France's annual budget is 896 million francs (versus 1,104 million in 1828) and in balance. (It would show a deficit only in 1823, 1825, and 1827.)

Publication of Victor Hugo's (1802–85) *Odes.* Hugo is granted a royal annuity.

Publication in Paris of Antoine-Louis-Claude Destutt de Tracy's (1754–1836) *Commentaire sur L'Esprit des Lois de Montesquieu*, which had already been published in the United States.

Publication of Joseph de Maistre's (1853–21), *Du Pape*, written several years earlier.

Théodore Géricault (1791–1824) paints *Le Radeau de la Méduse* (*The Raft of the Medusa*).

January. Alphonse-Louis Martainville (1776–1830) founds the extreme Right newspaper *Le Drapeau blanc*, which publishes until the 1830 Revolution. Its average press run in 1824 was 1,900.

Out of the fifty-five seats in the Chamber of Deputies at stake in the elections, the left-wing opposition wins thirty-five. The Right loses ten seats, and the supporters of the ministry lose fifteen. In the Isère department the abbé Grégoire (1750–1831), generally considered to be a regicide, is elected by an unholy alliance of the left-wing and right-wing opponents of the government. The election of Grégoire convinces the king and Decazes to abandon their attempt to liberalize the monarchy.

May–June. New press laws suppress censorship, narrow the definition of seditious acts, and take press crimes out of the correctional tribunals but continue to require prior notice of all political publications, even if they are not periodical, and add the posting of a bond against future fines by all publishers of political periodicals appearing more than once a month.

June 21. The Center-Right *doctrinaires* launch *Le Courier*, whose prestige far exceeds its small circulation.

## 1820

The comte de Villèle (1773–1854) buys up the shares of the royalist newspaper *La Gazette de France*. A royalist journal during and since the Empire, it remains legitimist throughout the July Monarchy, the Second Republic, and the Second Empire. Its average press run is 2,300 in 1824 and 11,200 in 1831.

Publication of Alphonse de Lamartine's (1790–1869) *Méditations poétiques*.

Publication of André Ampère's (1775–1836) *Laws of the Electrodynamic Action*.

Publication of the chevalier Jean-Baptiste de Monet de Lamarck's *Système analytique des connaissances positives de l'homme*.

Eugène Scribe (1791–1861), at twenty-eight years of age, creates the vaudeville *L'Ours et le pacha*, one of his 250 works.

January. Revolutionary coup in Spain.

February 13, 11:00 P.M. the duc de Berry (1778–1820), son of the comte d'Artois and second in line for the throne, is assassinated by a journeyman saddler named Louvel (1783–1820). The royalist journalist Charles Nodier (1780–1844) reflects his party's feeling when he writes in the *Journal des débats*: ''I saw Louvel's dagger, and it was a liberal idea.'' Soon afterward, Decazes is dismissed and replaced (February 20) by Richelieu. A new press law reestablishes censorship, and the Law of General Security allows the government to arrest political criminals and hold them without trial for three months. The birth of Berry's son, the ''miracle child'' (1820–83), on September 29, 1820, seven months after his death, seems to lend divine support to the Bourbon monarchy.

February 21. Formation of the second Richelieu cabinet.

March 31. A new press law imposes censorship on all political periodicals and drawings and requires prior authorization for all political periodicals.

April–May. The brochure campaign against the ministry evades the laws controlling the periodical press.

June 3. A liberal student named Lallemand is killed in a scuffle with the Royal Guard outside the Chamber of Deputies, where a crowd is agitating against the new election laws being debated. On 5 June, Lallemand's funeral causes demonstrations and but for a sudden rainstorm might have caused a riot.

June 12. The Chamber of Deputies passes a new election law, which adds 172 seats to the 258 seat Chamber of Deputies. The additional 172 deputies will be chosen by the top 25 percent of the taxpayers (about 22,000 men), who would thus be voting twice. This new election law is consequently called the Law of the Double Vote.

July. Liberal revolution in Naples.

August 19. A conspiracy to overthrow the Bourbon Restoration is foiled by the police. None of its leaders—Lafayette, Marc-René de Voyer d'Argenson (1771–1842), Manuel, Jacques-Charles Dupont de l'Eure (1767–1855), Claude Tircuy de Corcelle (1768–1843), Joseph-Mérilhou (1788–1856), Joseph Rey (1799–1855) of Grenoble, the old Bonapartist military men of the Bazar, and the republican students of the lodge of the Friends of Truth—is captured.

September 29. Birth of the comte de Chambord, the "miracle child," son of the assassinated duc de Berry.

October 23–December 17. The Allies confer at Troppau and then move their meeting to Laibach.

November 4 and 13. First elections under the Law of the Double Vote are a defeat for the Left and a victory for the far Right, which now has 160 supporters among the 430 Deputies. The comte de Villèle of the extreme right secret society, the Chevaliers de la foi, Jacques-Joseph Corbière (1766–1853), and Joseph-Louis-Joachim Lainé (1767–1835) are added to the cabinet as ministers without portfolios.

## 1821

The population of France is 30.4 million, versus 20.8 million in Great Britain, 18 million in the Italian states, 26 million in the German states, and 12 million in the Hapsburg Empire.

French wheat is at 16.22 francs per hectoliter.

French government bonds paying 5 percent interest on their face value of 100 francs are selling for 85.50 francs.

Founding of the Ecole de chartes for historical studies in Paris.

Publication of the comte de Saint-Simon's (1760–1825) *Du Système industriel*.

Publication of Georges Cuvier's (1769–1832) *Discourse on the Revolutions of the Globe*.

Publication of Joseph de Maistre's *Les Soirées de Saint-Pétersbourg*.

January 12–May 12. The Allies confer at Laibach.

February 27. A royal ordinance puts the secondary schools under the supervision of the bishops, and church schools get the right to confer the same degrees as state universities. Opening prayer, daily Mass, and monthly confession become compulsory.

March. National uprising in Greece against the sultan.

March. Liberal and national insurrection in northern Italy.

March. Riots in Grenoble.

May 1. First French carbonari lodge established.

May 5. Death of Napoleon Bonaparte on Saint-Helena.

July 26. Censorship imposed on all newspapers and periodicals whether or not they are political in nature. Prior authorization is required of all newspapers and periodicals.

October. Elections slightly erode the government's seats in favor of the Left.

December 12. Richelieu resigns.

December 14. Joseph de Villèle becomes finance minister.

## 1822

Victor Hugo publishes *Odes*.

Charles Nodier publishes *Trilby*.

Stendhal (Marie-Henri Beyle, 1783–1842) publishes *De l'Amour,* which sells seventeen copies in eleven years.

Alfred de Vigny (1799–1863) publishes *Poèmes*.

Auguste Comte (1797–1863) publishes *Système de politique positive*.

Charles Fourier (1722–1837) publishes *Traité de l'association domestique-agricole*.

Jean-François Champollion (1790–1832) deciphers Egyptian hieroglyphics using the Rosetta Stone.

Niepce (Nicéphore) develops a photographic image on a light-sensitive plate.

Louis-Jacques-Mundé Daguerre (1789–1851) and Charles-Marie Bouton (1781–1853) invent the diorama.

A.-J. Fresnel perfects lenses for lighthouses.

Jean B.-T. Fourier (1768–1830) publishes *Théorie analytique de la chaleur*.

The mathematician J.-V. Poncelet (1788–1867) publishes *Traité des propriétés projectives des figures*.

Eugène Delacroix (1798–1863) paints *Dante and Virgil Crossing the Styx*.

Abbé Lowenbrück, with the help of the abbé Félicité de Lammenais (1782–1854), founds the Association of Saint Joseph to find jobs in Christian workshops for workers and give them other help. It enrolls over 7,000 workers.

The chef to François-René de Chateaubriand (now serving as ambassador to the Court of Saint James's in London) names the end of the beef tenderloin in honor of his master.

February 24. The attempt of the French carbonari to overthrow the Bourbon monarchy breaks out. General Jean-Baptiste Berton (1769–1822) seizes Thouars and on February 25 marches on Saumur. He is stopped and later arrested and, in October, executed, along with Colonel Augustin-Joseph Caron (1774–1822), a carbonarist conspirator in the east of France. Other carbonarist conspirators, the so-called Four Sergeants of La Rochelle, are captured and executed without revealing the extent of the carbonari conspiracy or its true leaders: Lafayette, Manuel, Voyer d'Argenson, Corcelle, Augustine-Jean de Schonen (1782–1849), Félix Barthe (1795–1863), François Mauguin (1785–1854), Mérilhou, Nicolas Koechlin (1781–1852), and Colonel Fabvier.

March 17. New press laws forbid newspapers to have a tendency to undermine religion or the royal authority. No more jury trials for press offenses. Censorship, although suppressed by this law, can be introduced by simple royal decree. (It is imposed from August 15 to September 29, 1824, and from June 24 to November 5, 1827.)

June 1. Bishop Frayssinous (1765–1841) becomes grand master of the University, thus effectively establishing clerical control over higher education. Frayssinous has the right to appoint the personnel of state universities and to determine their curricula. By 1827, sixty-six of the eighty-eight professors of philosophy in the state universities are priests, and by 1830 about one-third of the professors in French state universities are priests.

October 20–December 14. The Allies meet at the Congress of Verona and give France permission to intervene in Spain if the Spanish king, Ferdinand VII (1784–1833), is deposed.

## 1823

Alphonse de Lamartine publishes *Nouvelles méditations poétiques*.

Stendhal publishes *Racine et Shakespeare*.

Publication of Adolphe Thiers' (1795–1877) *Histoire de la Révolution française* (through 1827).

Publication (–1824) of the comte de Saint-Simon's *Catéchisme des industriels*.

Eugène Scribe's *Le Menteur veridique*, one of sixteen of his comedies produced in 1823 (as against only eleven in 1822), is produced.

February. Expulsion of Jacques Manuel from the Chamber of Deputies. The leftist Deputies refuse to take their seats for the remainder of the session.

April 7. French troops invade Spain to put down the revolution there. Bonapartist soldiers waving the tricolored flag and singing the "Marseillaise" try to get them to stop, and Béranger writes a song inviting them to execute an about-face, but under the command of the duc d'Angoulême, the king's nephew, they win a quick victory in a nation that Napoleon had never conquered.

May 24. French armies under the duc d'Angoulême enter Madrid.

August 30. The seizing of the Trocadero gives French forces final victory in Spain, thus adding luster to the Villèle ministry and the Bourbon monarchy.

## 1824

French wheat prices are at 16.22 francs per hectoliter.

French 5 percent bonds with a par value of 100 francs are selling for more than par.

The circulation of the *Journal des débats*, linked with Chateaubriand, is 13,000.

Delacroix paints *Les Massacres de Chios* and *La Barque de Dante*. Jean-Auguste-Dominique Ingres (1780–1867) paints *The Vow of Louis XIII*.

Publication of Alfred de Vigny's *Eloa*.

Publication of Victor Hugo's *Nouvelles odes*.

Publication of François Mignet's (1796–1884) *Histoire de la Révolution française*.

Sadi Carnot (1796–1832) publishes *Puissance motrice du feu* on thermodynamics.

The newspaper *Le Globe* begins publishing in Paris for the *doctrinaire* party.

Founding of the Catholic Society for Good Books, which distributes 800,000 volumes by the end of 1826.

January 15, 1824–1830. Félicité de Lamennais and others publish *Le Mémorial catholique*.

February 26 and March 6. Elections crush the liberals, who lose 91 of their 110 seats. Lafayette, Voyer d'Argenson, and Manuel are defeated, and the result is a *chambre retrouvée* similar in personnel and attitudes to the *chambre introuvable* of 1815–16.

April. The bishops get the sole authority to issue teaching certificates to elementary school teachers.

April 14. First reception at the Arsenal gathers together the principal romantic writers.

April 24. Louis-Simon Augur attacks the romantics at the Académie française.

June 6. Chateaubriand dismissed as foreign minister, thereby causing a break in the solidarity of the royalist Right.

June 7. Chateaubriand's *Journal des débats* joins the opposition.

August. Creation of the Ministry of Ecclesiastical Affairs and Public Instruction, placing education under the control of a clergyman, Bishop Frayssinous.

August 15. Reimposition of censorship.

September 15. *Le Globe* founded by Pierre Leroux (1797–1871). From January 1831 to April 1832, it was the journal of the Saint-Simonian doctrine.

September 16. Louis XVIII becomes the last French king to die on the throne. The comte d'Artois, younger brother of Louis XVIII, becomes Charles X.

## 1825

Publication of Lamennais' *De la Religion considérée dans ses rapports avec l'ordre politique et civil*, for which Lamennais is fined and the book seized.

Publication of Augustin Thierry's (1795–1856) *Histoire de la conquête de l'Angleterre par les Normands*.

Publication of the comte de Saint-Simon's *Nouveau christianisme*.

Publication of Anthelme Brillat-Savarin's (1755–1826) *Physiologie du goût*. ("Tell me what you eat and I will tell you what you are.")

April 15. A new law sets the death penalty for sacrilege. If a person should profane either the sacred host or a vessel containing the host, his hand would be cut off (the penalty for parricide) before he was beheaded. This law would never be enforced.

April 27. The Indemnity Law sets aside a billion francs to indemnify those whose lands had been confiscated during the Revolution.

May 24. A law gives the government the right to authorize new female congregations. The number of nuns in France increases from 12,400 in 1815 to 25,000 in 1830.

May 29. Coronation of Charles X in Rheims.

The government brings charges against two liberal newspapers, the *Constitutionnel* and the *Courrier français*, for attacks on the state religion. Both are acquitted.

October 8. Riots in Rouen.

## 1826

French wheat prices are 15.85 francs per hectoliter.

Louis-Christophe François Hachette (1800–1864), founds Hachette et Cie., publishers, in Paris.

Victor Hugo publishes *Bug-Jargal*.

Vigny publishes *Cinq-Mars* and *Poèmes antiques et modernes*.

André Ampère's work on electrodynamics is published.

Eugène Delacroix paints *Greece in the Ruins of Missolonghi* and *Execution of the Doge Marino Falieri*.

Louis Daguerre joins J. N. Niepce, inventor of the bicycle, to advance the photographic process discovered by Niepce.

January 15. *Le Figaro* is founded by Etienne Arago (1802–92) and others. It publishes through May 1842 with a circulation of about 2,000.

April. Defeat of the Greeks by the Turks at Missolonghi.

April 2. Opening of Auguste Comte's public lectures on positivism.

April 8. The government withdraws its proposed law to restore some degree of primogeniture, which the Chambers had called an attempt to destroy the social reforms of the Revolution.

December 29. A law to reestablish censorship of all printed matter is introduced to the Chamber of Deputies. Despite the combined opposition of both the extreme Right and the extreme Left, this Law of Justice and of Love passes the Chamber of Deputies, only to be blocked by the Chamber of Peers.

## 1827

An economic crisis produces famine and a government deficit of 38 million francs.

Eugène Delacroix paints *The Death of Sardanapalus*.

Completion of the Paris Stock Exchange Building after nineteen years of construction.

February. Publication of Victor Hugo's *Hymne à la colonne*. Hugo, once a royalist, is now in the liberal, nationalist camp sympathetic to the Revolution and the Empire.

April 29. Charles X reviews the Paris National Guard, some of whose members shout "Long live the liberty of the press!" and "Down with the ministers! Down with the Jesuits!" That night the king dissolves the Paris National Guard.

June 24. Censorship is reimposed. Bonald is appointed chairman of the press surveillance committee. Chateaubriand founds the Society of the Friends of the Freedom of the Press, and François Guizot (1787–1874) organizes Aide-toi, le ciel t'aidera (God Helps Those Who Help Themselves) to organize the defeat of the government in the coming elections.

July 6. Signing of the Treaty of London.

October 4. The French begin hostilities against Hussein, dey of Algiers (1773–1838).

October 20. Naval battle of Navarino. The Allied British and French fleets defeat the Ottoman fleet.

November 17 and 24. The elections go against Joseph de Villèle, and the defeat of the government leads to celebrating and then to rioting. Barricades are raised in Paris for the first time since the *fronde* of 1648–52. Soldiers kill several of the rioters.

December. Publication of Victor Hugo's *Préface de Cromwell*. Hugo has identified romanticism as liberalism in art. Thus, where once the romantics had sided with the political Right and liberals had preferred the classical style, now there are growing bonds between romanticism and liberalism.

December 3. Opening of Eugène Scribe's *Le Mariage d'argent* at the Théâtre-français, Paris.

## 1828

Crop failures raise the price of wheat to 21.55 francs per hectoliter.

Founding of the Association for the Defense of the Catholic Religion.

Opening of the first railroad line in France.

Publication of the vicomte de Bonald's *Démonstration philosophique du principe constitutif de la société*, which advocates the need for a strong authority.

Publication of Saint-Armand Bazard's (1791–1832) *Exposition de la doctrine Saint-Simon*.

Publication of Alphonse de Lamartine's *Harmonies poétiques*.

Gérard de Nerval's (1808–56) translation of Goethe's *Faust*.

Ingres paints *L'Apothéose d'Homère*.

The first romantic landscapes are painted by Jean-Baptiste Corot (1796–1875).

Daniel-François Esprit Auber's (1782–1871) *La Muette de Portici* is introduced at the Paris Opéra.

Hector Berlioz' (1803–69) overtures, *Francs-Juges* and *Waverly*, are completed.

January 3. Resignation of the Villèle ministry.

January 5. A more moderate caretaker ministry, more or less under the vicomte Jean-Baptiste de Martignac (1776–1831), takes office.

February 10. Public instruction is detached from the Ministry of Ecclesiastical Affairs.

April. Opening of omnibus lines in Paris.

April 21. A royal ordinance takes away from the bishops some of their power over primary schools and gives it to a departmental committee composed of three ecclesiastics and six other members chosen by the prefect and the rector of the local academy.

June 16. The king reluctantly signs ordinances that have the effect of expelling Jesuit teachers from French schools.

July 18. A new press law ends censorship and the crime of tendency but keeps press trials in the correctional tribunals (where there are no juries), keeps the requirement of caution money as a guarantee against future convictions, and keeps the requirement of prior authorization for all newspapers.

July 19. The London Protocol by Britain, Russia, and France allows France to intervene in the Morea on behalf of Greek independence.

## 1829

The Trois Quartiers department store is founded as a small shop.

The military budget for an army of 225,000 men and 47,000 horses is 214,366,000 francs, or about 21 percent of the total budget.

Honoré de Balzac's (1799–1850) *Les Chouans* is published.

Alfred de Musset's (1810–57) *Contes d'Espagne et d'Italie* is published.

Ecole centrale des arts et manufactures in Paris opens.

Prosper Mérimée's (1803–70) *Chronique de Charles IX* is published.

Anonymous publication of Charles Sainte-Beuve's (1804–69) *Joseph Delorme*.

Victor Hugo's drama *Marion Delorme* and his novel *Le Dernier jour d'un condamné* are published.

Publication of François Guizot's *Histoire de la civilisation en France*.

Lamartine is elected to the Académie française.

The first sewing machine is developed by Barthélemy Thimmonier (1793–1859). Eighty of his new machines are destroyed by a mob to protect the livelihood of French tailors.

March 22. The Treaty of London creates an independent Greece.

June 8, 1829–May 12, 1835. A republican daily, *La Tribune des départemens*, is published by the Fabre brothers, Auguste (1792–1839) and Victorin (1785–1831), and later by Armand Marrast (1801–52), with a circulation of around 600 in 1831.

August. *La Revue des deux mondes* begins publication.

August 3. Gioachino Antonio Rossini's (1792–1868) opera *Guillaume Tell* opens at the Paris Opéra.

August 6. Dismissal of the Martignac ministry.

August 8. A royal ordinance announces the formation of the right-wing ministry under Jules de Polignac (1780–1847). Soon after, Aide-toi, le ciel t'aidera begins to organize a campaign to defeat the government in the coming elections, and the newspaper *Le Journal du commerce* calls for people to resist the government by refusing to pay taxes. In the new government, the ministries of Public Instruction and Ecclesiastical Affairs are again combined.

September. French forces land in Greece.

November. Auguste Comte begins to bring out his *Cours de philosophie positive* (–1842).

## 1830

The population of France is 32.4 million.

Paris has 800,000 people (versus 713,000 in 1818).

French government bonds at 5 percent interest on a face value of 100 francs are selling at 109 francs.

The public debt of France is 204 million francs.

There are 572 steam engines in France (versus about 200 in 1818).

Founding of the medical journal *Annales d'hygiène publique et de Médicine légale*.

Initial publication of the popular-priced illustrated *Magasin pittoresque*.

Balzac begins his *Comédie humaine*.

Théophile Gautier's (1811–72) *Poésies* is published.

Lamartine's *Harmonies poétiques et religieuses* is published.

Stendhal's *Le Rouge et le noir* is published.

Camille Corot paints *Chartres Cathedral*.

Daniel-François-Esprit Auber's *Fra Diavolo* is introduced at the Opéra comique in Paris.

French naturalists Georges Cuvier and Gouvion Saint-Hilaire (1799–1853) argue over Saint-Hilaire's theory of the unity of nature's plan and the fixity of the species.

Men begin to wear stiff collars, and women wear shorter skirts.

Hector Berlioz's *Symphonie fantastique* and *Damnation de Faust* are performed.

Publication of Lamennais' *Des progrès de la Révolution et la guerre contre l'église*.

January. Founding of a republican society among the students of Paris. Its newspaper, *Jeune France*, is founded by Armand Marrast.

January 3. Founding of the Orleanist newspaper *Le National* by Adolphe Thiers, Francois-Auguste Mignet, and Armand Carrel (1800–36) to oppose the senior branch of the Bourbons and favor the interests of the Orléans branch. After Carrel's death on July 24, 1836, Armand Marrast edits the *National*. Its circulation is over 3,000 in 1831.

February 25. Opening of Victor Hugo's *Hernani* at the Comédie-française, Paris.

March 2. Charles X opens the legislative session.

March 16. The Chamber of Deputies by a vote of 221 to 181 drafts a reply to the king's address that calls for the dismissal of the Polignac ministry.

March 19. Charles X prorogues the Chamber of Deputies.

April. Lamartine is admitted to the Académie française.

May 16. A royal ordinance dissolves the Chamber and calls for new elections to be held on June 23 and July 3. The oppositions of the Left and Right mobilize around the 221 deputies who had voted in March to ask the king to dismiss the ministry, while the king and the clergy ask for obedience to the will of the nation's father.

June 14. French troops disembark on the Algerian coast.

July. The results of the elections are known. 174 opposition Deputies and 143 government Deputies were elected. 201 of the original 221 were reelected.

July 4–5. Capture of Algiers by French forces.

July 26. The four royal ordinances appear calling for censorship of the press, dissolving the Chamber of Deputies, and changing the election laws in favor of the wealthiest landed voters by excluding the business license taxes and the door and window taxes from consideration for voter qualification. Martial-Magloire de Guernon-Ranville (1787–1866), minister of public instruction and ecclesiastical affairs, had suggested that the king might get more support if he broadened the suffrage rather than narrowed it, but this suggestion had been rejected by the king and by the other ministers.

July 26. A group of liberal journalists meets in Paris and calls for resistance to the royal ordinances.

July 27–29. The Three Glorious Days of the July Revolution of 1830. The Paris garrison under Marshal Auguste Marmont (1774–1852) is defeated by the Parisians, especially the skilled artisans,who have the strategic advantage of being able to hurl paving stones and other missiles down onto the exposed troops from their windows. On July 29, a confusion of military orders leaves the Louvre Palace undefended. Its fall at about noon brings the Bourbon monarchy down. The tricolored flag now flies in Paris.

July 30. A proclamation by Thiers and Mignet of the *National* calls for power to be given to the duc d'Orléans (1773–1850), and a rump session of about sixty Deputies invites the duc d'Orléans to come to Paris as lieutenant general of the realm.

July 31. Lafayette, recognized as leader by the republican students and by other opponents of an Orléans monarchy, dramatically wraps himself and the duc d'Orléans in the tricolored flag on the balcony of the Hôtel de ville to the wild cheers of the crowd in the square below.

August 2. Charles X abdicates in favor of his grandson, Henry V, the "miracle child," and appoints the duc d'Orléans lieutenant-general of the realm.


## JULY MONARCHY, 1830–1848

*La Révolution de 1830, journal des intérêts populaires*, a republican newspaper, is founded. It prints until 1832, with press runs of about 500.

August 2. The duc d'Orléans says his power comes from the representatives of the people only, thus denying that his cousin, the former king, Charles X, has the authority to appoint him lieutenant general of the realm.

August 3. Charles X, ex-king of France, leaves Rambouillet with his family to go into exile.

August 7. A few liberal deputies meet in Paris and call the duc d'Orléans to the throne as Louis-Philippe I, king of the French. (Each Bourbon king had called himself king of France.)

August 9. Louis-Philippe, king of the French, swears to uphold the Charter. Censorship is suppressed and, under the terms of the Charter of August 9, liberty of the press, "in conformity with the laws," is granted.

August 14. Modification of the Constitutional Charter in France, which now allows for the initiation of legislation in the Chambers, suppresses censorship, and no longer calls Roman Catholicism the state religion. Furthermore, the Charter is now the permanent constitution of France and not granted by a divine right king. The franchise is later extended to those who pay 200 francs in direct taxes, thus increasing the electorate from about 92,000 men to about 241,000, or 2.8 percent of the adult male population, 90 percent of whom were landowners and only 10 percent from commerce, industry, and the professions in this so-called bourgeois monarchy. (The Restoration had granted the vote only to those who paid 300 francs in direct taxes.) Censorship (but not prosecution of authors, which would actually be more severe under the July Monarchy than it had been under the Bourbon Restoration) is abolished forever by the Charter. The tricolored flag of the Revolution and the Empire is restored as the flag of France, replacing the white fleur-de-lys of the Bourbons. Later, a mixed ministry of liberals, Bonapartists, and Orleanists takes office, and there is a political massacre in which nobody is killed but nearly everybody—20 of 38 members of the Council of State, 76 prefects, 196 subprefects, 65 of the 75 army generals—loses his job.

August 16. Charles X, still flying his white banner, sails from Cherbourg past the tricolored flags of the town.

Delacroix's *Liberty Leading the People* celebrates the July Revolution of 1830.

August 25. A revolution starts in Belgium after a performance of Auber's *La Muette de Portici* in Brussels.

October 17, 1830–November 15, 1831. The Catholic and liberal newspaper *L'Avenir* is founded by Lamennais. Its masthead reads: "God and Liberty."

November 2–March 13, 1831. The ministry of Jacques Laffitte (1756–1844).

November 29. An insurrection begins in Poland against Russian domination caused in part by the efforts of Czar Nicholas to march Polish forces into Belgium and France to crush the revolutions there.

November 29. A new press law prohibits attacks against the dignity and rights of the king and the Chambers.

December. Trial of the former ministers of Charles X. They receive light sentences, which infuriates the mob.

December 10. A new press law calls for all salesmen of books, newspapers, and drawings to register with the government.

December 14. A new press law establishes the payment of bond money by all periodicals and raises the stamp tax on printed matter.

## 1831

Coal production: 2,571,000 tons for France; 30 million for the United Kingdom.

Honoré de Balzac's *La Peau de chagrin* and *Le Chef-d'oeuvre inconnu* are published.

Victor Hugo's *Notre-Dame de Paris* and a book of poems, *Les Feuilles d'automne*, appear.

Henri Barbier's (1805–82) *Les Iambes* is published.

The Barbizon school of artists, including Jean Millet (1814–75) and Pierre Rousseau (1812–67), gives its first exhibition.

February 3. The Belgians elect the duc de Nemours (1814–96), third son of the French king, Louis-Philippe, as their king, but Louis-Philippe bows to British pressure and forbids his son to accept the Belgian throne.

February 14. A mass at the Church of Saint-Germain-l'Auxerrois in Paris to mark the anniversary of the assassination of the duc de Berry provokes anticlerical riots in Paris, which end with the sack of the archbishop's palace and library.

March 13. The Casimir Périer (1777–1832) ministry in France (–May 16, 1832). Reorganization of the National Guard follows the forced resignation of Lafayette and limits the Guard to those who pay direct taxes. The government is taking a turn to the right.

April 19. New electoral law reduces the tax rates necessary to vote.

July. Elections produce a conservative Chamber, strengthening the hand of Casimir Périer.

August 20. French troops enter Belgian territory and force the Dutch, who had invaded Belgium on August 2, to withdraw.

September 8. Fall of Warsaw to Czar Nicholas I.

October. Mass demonstrations by the Lyons silk weavers win an increase in the *tarif*, the fixed rate paid for piecework, but the merchants refuse to abide by this agreement.

November. Revolts by the Lyons silk weavers are put down by French soldiers.

November 21. Giacomo Meyerbeer's (Jacob Liebmann Beer, 1791–1864) *Robert le diable* opens at the Académie royale de musique, Paris.

December. suppression of the hereditary peerage. The Chamber of Peers is now a house of royal nominees.

## 1832

A cholera epidemic spreads through France and the rest of Western Europe.

French industry uses 525 steam engines, which develop a national total of 900 horsepower.

Louis-Philippe establishes the Foreign Legion to help control France's new colonies in Africa.

Honoré de Balzac's *Contes drolatiques* is published.

George Sand (Amantine Lucile Aurore Dudevant, née Dupin, 1804–76) publishes *Indiana*.

Théophile Gautier proclaims the doctrine "art for art's sake."

Eugène Delacroix paints *A Moorish Couple on Their Terrace*.

Honoré Daumier is arrested and sentenced to six months in prison for cartoons attacking Louis-Philippe in the newspaper *La Caricature*.

Victor Hugo's drama *Le Roi s'amuse* appears.

Ballet *La Sylphide* opens.

French chemist Pierre-Jean Robiquet (1780–1840) isolates codeine from opium.

French shipbuilder Pierre-Louis Frédéric Sauvage (1785–1857) patents a screw propeller for steamships.

March 12. Opening of G. Donizetti's (1797–1848) opera *L'Elisir d'amore* at the Théatre de l'Académie royale de musique, Paris.

April 10. French law excludes the families of Charles X and Napoleon from France.

June. Attempt of the duchesse de Berry (1798–1870) to rouse the Vendée on behalf of the Bourbons.

June 5. Insurrection in Paris following the funeral of General Jean-Maximin Lamarque.

July. Trial and conviction of Barthélemy-Prosper Enfantin and two other St.-Simonian leaders on charges of immorality.

July 22. Death of the duc de Reichstadt, son of Napoleon, also known as the king of Rome, Napoleon II, or *L'Aiglon* ("little eagle"), born 1811.

August 15. The papal encyclical *Mirari Vos* is issued.

October 11. Marshal Nicolas Jean Soult (1769–1851) forms a ministry (–July 15, 1834) following the death of Casimir Périer, who died of cholera on May 16. This ministry, which includes the duc de Broglie (1785–1870), Thiers, and Guizot, passes new laws to repress political associations.

December 1. Founding of *Le Charivari*, satirical newspaper with cartoons by Honoré Daumier.

December 23. French troops take Antwerp. Holland is forced to recognize the independence of Belgium.

## 1833

A statue of Napoleon (in civilian dress) is placed atop the Vendôme column in Paris.

Balzac publishes *Eugénie Grandet*.

George Sand publishes *Lélia*.

Alfret de Musset publishes *André de Sarto* and *Les Caprices de Marianne*.

Jules Michelet's (1798–1874) *Histoire de France* (–1867) appears.

Frédéric Chopin (1810–49), now living in France, finishes *Twelve Etudes*, opus 10.

June 28. The Primary Education Law, or Guizot Law, provides for the establishment of local primary schools. Each commune or group of communes is to have a primary school, and each department or group of departments is to have a normal school to train elementary school teachers. There is to be a secondary school in the chief town of each department and in all towns with more than 6,000 inhabitants. The teachers must have certificates from a normal school unless they are members of a religious order, in which case they do not have to be certified. This law by a Protestant gives considerable authority over education to the Catholic church.

July 3, 1833–October 8, 1835, and March 1841–1851. The communist Etienne Cabet's (1788–1856) newspaper *Le Populaire* is published.

November 14. Opening of Eugène Scribe's *Bertrand et Raton, ou l'art de conspirer* at the Théâtre-français, Paris.

## 1834

Louis Braille (1809–52), blind since age three, perfects a system of characters for the blind to read.

Lamennais' *Paroles d'un croyant* links his Catholicism with political liberalism and democracy.

Honoré de Balzac's *La Recherche de l'Absolu* and *Le Père Goriot* appear.

Delacroix paints *Algerian Women at Home*.

Ingres paints *The Martyrdom of Saint Symphorian*.

February 16. New press law requires preliminary authorization to print posters.

April 9. Revolt of the silk workers in Lyons after the cloth merchants again refuse to pay the agreed-upon rate for piecework. The revolt spreads to other French cities, especially to the Marais district of Paris, where it results in the massacre of the Rue Transnonain.

April laws prohibit associations.

May 20. Death of the Marquis de Lafayette

June 1834–May 1842. Publication of the leftist *Journal du peuple*. Godefroy Cavaignac (1800–1845), Louis Blanc (1811–82), and Audry de Puyravault (1773–1852) are among the contributors.

October 9, 1834–October 27, 1835. François-Vincent Raspail's (1794–1878) radical newspaper *Le Réformateur* is published.

**1835**

Alfred de Vigny's play *Chatterton* and his *Servitude et grandeur militaires* appear.

Théophile Gautier's *Mademoiselle de Maupin* espouses art for art's sake and denounces bourgeois philistinism.

Béarnaise sauce with tarragon and vinegar originates at the Pavillon Henri IV, a restaurant outside Paris.

Alexis de Tocqueville (1805–59) publishes the first volume of *De la Démocratie en Amérique* based on his 1831 trip to the United States.

Simon Poisson (1781–1840) publishes *Théorie mathématique de la chaleur*.

Corot paints *Homer in the Desert*.

January 25. Vicenzo Bellini's (1802–35) opera *I Puritani* is introduced at the Théâtre des italiens, Paris.

February 23. Jacques Halévy's (1799–1862) opera *La Juive* with a libretto by Eugène Scribe, is introduced at the Paris Opéra.

March 12. The duc de Broglie (1785–1870) forms a conservative ministry (–February 1836).

April 26. First performance of Frédéric Chopin's *Grande polonaise brillante* at the Paris Conservatory.

May. Beginning of the trials of the 1834 rebels from Lyons and Paris. The coverage of the trials in the press gives the republicans a forum for their ideas despite the July Monarchy's repressive press laws.

July 28. A Corsican named Joseph-Marie Fieschi (1790–1836), with the help of some members of the Society for the Rights of Man, tries to assassinate Louis-Philippe.

September 9. The September Laws suppress radicalism and increase the government's control over politics. For example, the press law of September 9 doubles the amount of caution money that must be paid against future fines for violations of the press laws and introduces censorship of drawings. The prohibitions are numerous and include public adherence to any other form of government (such as a republic or an empire). The judicial process is speeded up and acquittal made more difficult.

## 1836

The Guizot Law is made applicable to girls.

The Communist League is formed in Paris.

The first Prix du Jockey Club horse race is run in Paris.

Alphonse de Lamartine's *Jocelyn* appears.

Charles de Musset's autobiographical *Confessions d'un enfant du siècle* is published.

Victor Considérant's (1808–93) *Destinée sociale* (–1838) appears.

Completion of the Arc de triomphe in Paris.

February 22. First ministry of Adolphe Thiers (–September) following the fall of the Broglie ministry.

February 29. Opening of Meyerbeer's (1791–1864) opera *Les Huguenots* at the Paris Opéra.

July 1. Foundation of Emile de Girardin's (1806–81) *La Presse*, a cheap, popular, conservative newspaper (press run is 22,409 in 1845).

July 1. Foundation of *Le Siècle*, a popular newspaper of the dynastic Left, which has a press run of almost 35,000 by 1845.

July 22–24. Duel between Armand Carrel and Emile de Girardin results in the death of Carrel.

September 6. Fall of the Thiers government after Thiers proposes that France invade Spain. Formation of a new ministry under the comte de Molé (1781–1855) that is really led by the king.

October 30. Louis-Napoleon Bonaparte (1808–73), nephew of the great Napoleon fails to create a revolt among the garrison of Strasbourg. Instead of seizing power in France, he is arrested and exiled to the United States.

November 6. Death of Charles X in exile.

November 26. The Molé ministry amnesties the former ministers of Charles X.

## 1837

The first passenger railroad in France opens.

Honoré de Balzac's *Les Illusions perdues* and *Le Curé de village* appear.

Alphonse de Lamartine's epic poem, *La Chute d'un ange*, is published.

Thomas Carlyle (1795–1881) writes *The French Revolution*.

Poisson publishes *Recherches sur la probabilité des jugements*, which establishes the science of mathematical probability.

Henri Dutrochet (1776–1847), French physiologist, recognizes that chlorophyll is necessary to photosynthesis.

Hector Berlioz's *Grande messe des morts*, opus 5, is completed.

Auber's *Le Domino noir* opens at the Opéra comique, Paris.

April 15. Formation of the second Molé ministry.

June 19. Eugène Scribe's *La Camanderie, ou la courte échelle*, opens at the Théâtre-français, Paris.

December 5. Hector Berlioz's *Requiem* premieres at Les Invalides, Paris.

**1838**

The French navy has forty-nine ships of the line, versus ninety for Britain, fifty for Russia, and fifteen for the United States.

J.-B.-H. Lacordaire (1802–61) revives the Dominican Order in France.

A.-A. Cournot (1801–1877), French economist, publishes *Researches into the Mathematical Principles of the Theory of Wealth*.

François Arago (1786–1853), French physicist, presents the Daguerre-Niepce method of photography to the Académie des sciences and the Académie des beaux-arts, Paris.

Charles Cagniard de la Tour (1777–1859), French physician, shows that fermentation is dependent on yeast.

Eugène Delacroix paints *Medea*. Delacroix is rejected for membership in the French Institute.

The composer Frédéric Chopin's liaison with George Sand, which would last until 1847, begins.

The actress Rachel (Elisa Félix, 1820–58) makes her debut as Camille in Corneille's *Horace* at the Théâtre-français. She establishes a new and more natural style of acting and revives French classical drama in the middle of the so-called romantic age.

September 10. Hector Berlioz's opera *Benvenuto Cellini* opens at the Paris Opéra.

November 8. Victor Hugo's *Ruy Blas* opens at the Théatre de la Renaissance, Paris.

November 30. Mexico declares war on France after the French occupation of Vera Cruz on November 27, an attempt to force Mexico to compensate French victims of civil disturbances in Mexico.

**1839**

The Arab chief Abd-el-Kader (1808–83) begins attacks on French settlements in Algeria. Despite the presence of a French army of 88,000 men under General Thomas-Robert Bugeaud (1784–1849), he would not be defeated and captured until 1847.

Louis Blanc's *Organization du travail* demands the right to a job as a basic human right and calls for labor to be organized in government workshops, thus ending capitalist exploitation. "To each according to his needs, from each according to his ability."

Louis Blanc founds the socialist newspaper *La Revue du progrès*, which continues to publish until 1842.

January 1 and 2. Riots at La Rochelle.

Stendhal publishes *La Chartreuse de Parme*.

George Sand publishes *Spiridion*.

March. Louis Daguerre perfects the process for producing a silver image on a copper plate and produces the first daguerrotype portraits.

March. Louis-Mathieu de Molé resigns.

Frédéric Chopin's *24 preludes*, opus 28, is completed.

March 9. French forces withdraw from Mexico after the Mexican government agrees to compensate French victims of civil disturbances in Mexico.

April 19. Treaty of London guarantees the independence of Belgium.

May 12. The uprising of the republican secret Society of the Seasons produces riots in Paris. The second Soult ministry is formed.

November 24. Hector Berlioz's dramatic symphony *Romeo and Juliet* opens at the Paris Conservatoire.

Elections bring about the fall of the Molé ministry.

December 1839–December 1849. The monthly *La Ruche populaire*, a working-class newspaper founded by the Saint-Simonian ruler maker and worker poet Jules Vinçard (1796–1879?). Its press run was about 500.

## 1840

France has 497 kilometers of railway lines.

Pierre-Joseph Proudhon (1809–65), a working printer, publishes *Qu'est-ce, Que la propriété?* in which he says that property is theft.

Etienne Cabet, a former carbonarist revolutionary turned communist pacifist, publishes *Voyage en Icarie*, a description of a utopian communist society.

Augustin Thierry's *Récits des temps mérovingiens* is published.

Prosper Mérimée's short story "Columba" is published.

Louis Blanc founds the *Revue du progrès*, in which his *Organisation du travail* is to be published.

Corot's painting *The Flight into Egypt* is completed.

Delacroix's painting *The Entry of the Crusaders into Constantinople* is completed.

Théodore Chasseriau's (1819–56) painting *Christ au jardin des oliviers* is completed.

The French instrument maker A. F. Debain (1809–77) constructs the first harmonium, patented in 1842.

February 11. G. Donizetti's opera *La Fille du régiment* opens at the Opéra comique, Paris.

February 26. Adolphe Thiers forms his second ministry (–October 28).

May 12. A law is enacted to make possible the return of Napoleon's remains from Saint-Helena.

August 6. Louis-Napoleon Bonaparte's second failed coup d'état, this one in Boulogne. He is sentenced to life imprisonment at the Fortress of Ham.

September 1840–July 31, 1850. *L'Atelier*, a working-class newspaper edited by Philippe Buchez (1796–1865) and featuring his version of Saint-Simonian socialism, appears. Its press run was about 1,000.

October 28. After urging French support for Méhémet Ali (1769–1849), who had just been defeated by Turkish and British forces in Syria, Thiers is dismissed as minister for foreign affairs and replaced by François Guizot. Marshal Soult becomes president of the Council.

November 17. Eugène Scribe's *Le Verre d'eau, ou les effets et les causes* opens at the Théâtre-français, Paris.

December 15. The Emperor Napoleon's remains are brought back to Paris in triumph and laid to rest at Les Invalides as the Orléans monarchy attempts to curry favor with the Bonapartists.

## 1841

The population of Paris is 935,261, versus 2,235,344 for London, 356,870 for Vienna, 312,710 for New York, and 300,000 for Berlin.

Coal production is 4,078,500 tons for France, versus 40 million for Great Britain.

Iron production is 1,247,000 tons for France, versus 1,350,000 for Great Britain.

Victor Hugo is elected to the Académie française.

Louis Blanc attacks the Orléans monarchy in his *Histoire de dix ans*.

Lamennais' *Le Livre du peuple* criticizes the exploitation of the working class and calls for liberal democracy.

Olinde Rodriguès (1794–1851) edits *La Poésie sociale des ouvriers*, which calls attention to the worker poet movement in France.

The first laws for the protection of workingmen and children are passed in France, but they are practically unenforceable and have little effect on the lives of French industrial workers.

Arc lamps are demonstrated for use in Paris streets.

Honoré de Balzac's *Une Ténébreuse affaire* appears.

Delacroix's painting *Jewish Wedding* is completed.

Théodore Chasseriau's painting *Père Lacordaire* is completed.

Rossini's *Stabat mater* is first presented, Salle Herz, Paris.

June 28. The ballet *Giselle ou les Wilis* opens at the Théâtre de l'Académie royale de musique, Paris, with music by Adolphe Charles Adam (1803–56), choreography by Jean Coralli (1779–1854), and libretto by Théophile Gautier.

July 13. France joins the alliance of Russia, Britain, Prussia, and Austria concerning Turkey.

November 1, 1841–February 24, 1848. The democratic *Revue indépendante* is edited by Pierre Leroux and George Sand.

## 1842

An *entente cordiale* develops between Lord Aberdeen (1784–1860), the British foreign secretary, and Guizot, the French foreign minister.

France has about sixty sugar beet factories producing two pounds of sugar per person per year.

Publication begins of Balzac's *La Comédie humaine*.

Eugène Sue's *Les Mystères de Paris* is a best-seller.

Dancing the polka is in fashion.

May 8. A train from Paris to Versailles jumps the track and catches fire, trapping the passengers.

June 11. The first French railway laws call for nine main lines, of which seven will start from Paris. The government is responsible for the construction of roadbeds, bridges, tunnels, and stations. The French railway mania will last for five years: 1842–47.

July 13. Death of the duc d'Orléans (1810–42), eldest son of Louis-Philippe and heir to the throne.

## 1843

Jules Michelet and Edgar Quinet (1803–75) publish *Des Jésuites*, the anticlerical courses that they had taught at the Collège de France, as Catholics and anticlericals fight for control of education.

Flora Tristan (1803–44) publishes *L'Union Ouvrière*, which calls for working-class unity.

The world's first night club, Le Bal des anglais, opens in Paris.

May 12 and 30. Opening of the railroads from Paris to Rouen and from Paris to Orléans.

July 29, 1843–January 1850. The radical newspaper *La Réforme,* more radical than Armand Marrast's *Le National*, is edited by Ferdinand Flocon (1800–66) with Alexandre-Auguste Ledru-Rollin (1807–74), Louis Blanc, and others. Its press run in 1845 was 1,698, versus 4,062 for the *National*.

August 1, 1843–November 30, 1851. Victor Considérant edits the Fourierist socialist newspaper *La Démocratie pacifique*, a successor of the *Phalanstère* and the *Phalange*.

September 2. State visit of Queen Victoria to France.

## 1844

Alexandre Dumas, père, *Les Trois mousquetaires* and *Le Comte de Monte Cristo*, are immediate best-sellers.

F. Marbeau opens the first crèche in Paris to provide day care for infants.

Eugénie Niboyet founds the first group of French pacifists and launches a pacifist journal, *La Paix des deux mondes*.

Reforms make Judaism more responsive to the regional consistories.

Balzac's *Les Paysans* appears in *La Presse*.

Hector Berlioz's *Traité de l'instrumentation et d'orchestration modernes* is completed.

Eugène Sue's *Le Juif errant* (–1845) is published.

Karl Marx (1818–83) meets Friedrich Engels (1820–95) in Paris.

February 3. Berlioz's overture *Le Carnaval romain* opens in the Salle Herz, Paris.

July 19. Morocco attacks the French in Algeria.

August 6. The French, under the duc de Joinville (1818–1900), son of Louis-Philippe, move in force against Morocco.

September 10. The French war in Morocco ends with the Treaty of Tangier.

September 12. State visit of Louis-Philippe to England.

September 24. 450 Frenchmen are massacred at Sidi Brahim, Algeria.

George Pritchard (1796–1883), an English missionary, is expelled from Tahiti by the French, thereby infuriating the British.

Edgar Quinet's anticlerical lectures are suppressed.

## 1845

First submarine cable is laid beneath the English Channel.

The French inventor Joshua Heilman (1796–1848) patents a machine for combing cotton or wool.

Thiers' *Histoire du Consulat et de l'Empire* (–1865) is published.

Alexandre Dumas père completes *Vingt ans après*, a sequel to *Les Trois mousquetaires*.

Prosper Mérimée's *Carmen* appears.

Ingres paints a portrait of the comtesse d'Haussonville.

The architect Jean-Jacques-Marie Huvé (1783–1852) completes the Church of the Madeleine, Paris.

Notre-Dame in Paris is restored in pseudo-gothic style by a commission headed by Eugène-Emmanuel Viollet-le-Duc (1814–79).

Odilon Barrot (1791–1873) and Thiers call for electoral reform and for the replacement of the Guizot ministry.

1845–48. *La Fraternité de 1845*, a self-proclaimed communist newspaper, is published.

## 1846

Bad harvest. Potato blight. Agricultural and industrial depression in France.

Revolts in Poland.

Dubonnet is introduced in France.

Proudhon, *Philosophie de la misère*, is published.

Jules Michelet, *Le Peuple*, is published.

Balzac, *La Cousine Bette*, is published.

George Sand, *La Mare au diable*, is published.

January 2. The French, who suffer heavy losses, defeat the Algerian rebels.

Electric arc lighting is introduced at the Paris Opéra.

Delacroix decorates the library of the Luxembourg, Paris, and paints *The Abduction of Rebecca*.

April 16. Attempt on the life of Louis-Philippe in Paris.

May 25. Louis-Napoleon Bonaparte escapes from the Fortress of Ham and flees to London.

June 15. The election of Cardinal Mastai-Ferretti (1792–1878) as Pope Pius IX arouses great hopes among liberals.

October 10. Princess Luisa Fernanda (1832–97), sister of Queen Isabella II (1830–1904) of Spain, marries the duc de Montpensier (1824–90), youngest son of Louis-Philippe. This violates Guizot's 1843 understanding with Lord Aberdeen, the British foreign secretary, and thus threatens relations between Britain and France. Consequently Aberdeen is replaced by Lord Palmerston (1784–1865) at the British Foreign Office, ending the Anglo-French entente between Aberdeen and Guizot.

Elections produce a governmental majority of 248 to 84 in the Chamber of Deputies. Guizot responds to demands for electoral reform by saying that the time for universal suffrage will never come.

December 8. Berlioz's oratorio *The Damnation of Faust* opens at the Opéra comique, Paris.

## 1847

Economic depression.

France produces 5,130,000 tons of coal and lignite.

French industry uses 4,853 steam engines, which develop 62,000 horsepower.

Louis-François Cartier opens a jewelry shop in Paris.

The French protectorate over Tahiti is recognized.

Karl Marx attacks Proudhon's *La Philosophie de la misère* (The Philosophy of Poverty) in *The Poverty of Philosophy*.

The first volume of Louis Blanc's pro-Revolutionary *Histoire de la Révolution française* (–1862) is published.

The first volume of Jules Michelet's *Histoire de la Révolution française* (–1853) is published.

George Sand's *Le Péché de M. Antoine* is published.

April 15. French expedition to Cochin China.

July 4. Adolphe Thiers holds the first reform banquet in Paris and demands a wider franchise. This is the start of a series of political banquets organized by the opponents of the ministry.

September 14. Guizot, following his electoral triumphs, is made premier of France.

November 26. Alfred de Musset's *Une Caprice* opens at the Comédie française, Paris.

December 31. Death of Madame Adelaïde, sister of Louis-Phillipe.

## 1848

Paris has nearly 65,000 industrial undertakings, of which only 7,000 employ more than ten workers.

France has 1,921 kilometers of railways (versus 3,424 in Prussia and 6,349 in Great Britain).

Louis Blanc's *Le Droit au travail* is completed.

Balzac's *La Comédie humaine* (complete edition, 100 volumes) is published.

Chateaubriand's *Mémoires d'outre-tombe* is published.

Alexandre Dumas, fils (1824–95), publishes *La Dame aux camélias*.

January. The Guizot ministry prohibits banquets. The *National* and the *Réforme* urge the people of Paris to struggle against the government.

January 2. Suspension of Michelet's history lectures.

February 22. Popular demonstrations in Paris associated with the prohibited banquet of the twelfth arrondissement. Louis-Philippe calls out the National Guard, which supports the demonstrations. Louis-Philippe asks for the resignation of Guizot and replaces him with Molé and puts General Bugeaud in command of the army.

February 23. Troops guarding the Ministry of Foreign Affairs (Guizot's ministry) fire on good-natured crowds, and a riot starts, ending in eighty dead and wounded. The dead are carried through the city, and barricades go up.

February 24. The king replaces Molé with Thiers and withdraws the troops. The crowd captures the Hôtel de ville and advances on the Tuileries, the royal palace where the king lives. Louis-Philippe abdicates in favor of his grandson, but this is not accepted. Instead, a Republic is proclaimed. A Provisional Government is established under the romantic poet and liberal politician Alphonse de Lamartine. Elections for a Constituent Assembly will be held with universal manhood suffrage.

The revolutions spread from Paris to Vienna, Venice, Berlin, Milan, Parma, and Rome.

## SECOND REPUBLIC, 24 February 1848–1 December 1852

February 25. The government recognizes the right of everyone to a job.

February 27. National Workshops are established in France as part of Louis Blanc's plan to provide relief to unemployed workers and eventually to supplant capitalism.

February 27–July 11. Lamennais' newspaper, *Le Peuple constituant*, is published.

February 28. The Luxembourg Commission is set up to consider questions involving labor.

March 2. The workday is set at ten hours for Paris, eleven in the provinces.

March 14. The elite companies of the National Guard are dissolved.

March 16. The wealthy units of the National Guard, the *bonnets à poil* or Bearskin Buskins, demonstrate. A 45 centime surtax on property is levied.

March 17. A leftist counterdemonstration is organized by the political clubs to force a delay of the elections so that the Left could have time to educate France's rural population, now under the influence of conservative priests and notables.

March 17. The 5 percent bonds, which had been at 116.60 francs on February 18, are at 69. On April 6 they reach their low point of 50. Bank of France shares, 3,195 on February 18, are at 1,300 on March 17.

March 20. About 10,000 compagnons meet at the place de la République and take an oath of brotherhood.

March 25. A demonstration by armed workers forces the Provisional Government to decree that all have a right to work and that labor should have the right to organize.

April 16. Another demonstration of club members and workers in Paris fails to win a delay of the elections. National Guardsmen, many of whom are workers, shout at the demonstrators: "Down with the communists! Down with Cabet! Down with Blanqui!" (referring to radical leader Auguste Blanqui, 1805–81).

April 23. Election by universal manhood suffrage of a Constituent Assembly to write a constitution for the Republic. The result is a clear victory for the antisocialist conservatives. The *démoc-soc* supporters of Louis Blanc get fewer than a hundred seats, while the moderate supporters of Lamartine get perhaps 500, the legitimists about 100, and the Orleanists about 200. Neither Blanqui nor Raspail is elected.

April 25–26. Riots break out in Rouen to protest the election results. The riots are brutally suppressed.

April 27. The Constituent Assembly abolishes slavery in all French colonies.

May 4. Convocation of the Constituent Assembly and end of the Provisional Government.

May 15. Leftist mobs march through Paris, take over the Constituent Assembly, and demand aid for the Polish rebels and domestic social reforms. The conservatives, alarmed, resolve to react. Auguste Blanqui, Aloysius Huber (1812–?), Armand Barbès (1809–70), and Albert (1815–95), leaders of the Left, are arrested.

June 2. Partial elections to the Constituent Assembly. The moderates lose to the two extremes, and the radicals Marc Caussidière (1808–61), Pierre Leroux, and Proudhon are elected.

June 7. New law forbids demonstrations.

June 21. The demise of the National Workshops, where more than 100,000 "pretorians of revolt" are working, is imminent.

June 22. Alfred de Musset's *Il ne faut jurer de rien* opens at the Comédie-française, Paris.

June 22–26. June Days. Workers in the east end of Paris, angered by threat to close the National Workshops, rise in revolt. They are crushed by General Eugène Cavaignac (1802–57) at a terrible cost. Cavaignac is given control of the government.

July–August. New laws curtail the freedom of the press, suppress secret societies, and control the clubs and political associations.

August 10. Musset's *Le Chandelier* opens at the Théâtre historique, Paris.

September 17. By-elections result in the election of Louis-Napoleon Bonaparte in the Seine and five other departments.

November 4. A republican Constitution is promulgated with universal manhood suffrage, a single legislative body of 750 members elected for three years, and a strong president elected for four years.

November 21. Musset's *André del Sarto* opens at the Comédie-française.

December 10. Louis-Napoleon Bonaparte is elected president of France, defeating General Eugène Cavaignac and several other candidates. Bonaparte gets 74.2 percent of the vote in France and 55 percent of the vote in Paris, with his biggest majorities in Paris coming from the working-class districts.

December 20. Louis-Napoleon Bonaparte takes the oath as president of the Republic and appoints a ministry under the Orleanist Odilon Barrot.

## 1849

Alphonse de Lamartine's *Histoire de la Révolution de 1848* is published.

Proudhon's *Confessions d'un révolutionnaire* is published.

Armand Fizeau (1819–96), French physicist, measures the velocity of light.

Claude Minié (1814–79) develops a rifle.

Gustave Courbet (1819–77) paints *After Dinner at Ornans*.

Delacroix paints the ceiling of the Salon d'Apollon in the Louvre.

Charles Sainte-Beuve begins his "Causeries de lundi" series in the *Constitutionnel*.

Jean-Baptiste Alphonse Karr's (1808–90), *Janvier,* which contains the phrase "Plus ça change, plus c'est la même chose" (the more things change, the more they stay the same), is published.

Eugène Scribe's *Adrienne Lecouvreur* is published.

February 9. Proclamation of the Roman Republic.

March 7–April 2. Trial of those arrested in the Paris demonstrations of May 15, 1848.

May 13. Ledru-Rollin gets 2 million votes in the elections for the Legislative Assembly as the radicals do much better than they had expected.

April 25. A French military expedition lands in the Papal States to help Pope Pius IX repress Italian nationalism.

May 26. The Legislative Assembly takes over from the Constituent Assembly as France begins to function under its new republican Constitution.

June 13. Leftist *démoc-soc* demonstrations in Paris engineered by Ledru-Rollin against the Roman expedition are easily put down, and repressive legislation is passed.

June 15. Riots in Lyons. Paris and Lyons are placed under siege.

July 3. The French enter Rome after defeating the Italian nationalist forces under Giuseppe Garibaldi (1807–82) and restore Pope Pius IX.

October 31. Dismissal of Odilon Barrot, who is replaced by General Alphonse Henri d'Hautpoul (1789–1865), with Eugène Rouher (1814–84) as minister of justice. The new cabinet is entirely dominated by President Bonaparte.

## 1850

France has 3,080 kilometers of railway lines.

Old age insurance is established in France.

Corot paints *Une Matinée*.

Courbet paints *The Stone-Breakers* and *Burial at Ornans*.

January 9. A government bill places school teachers under the control of the departmental prefects and thus under the president.

March 10. By-elections are won by the radical left in 21 out of 31 elections.

March 15. The Falloux Law, prepared by the Catholic legitimist vicomte de Falloux (1811–86), allows departments to substitute Catholic schools for lay schools and provides for freedom of education so that every child can enter the school of his choice, whether Catholic or state run.

April 12. Pope Pius IX revokes the Constitution in the Papal States. French troops garrison Rome.

May 31. Universal suffrage is restricted. A voter must have resided in his district for three years as attested by a tax receipt or an employer's affidavit, and thus he must either own property or have a job. The electorate is reduced by about 33 percent.

June 9. Political clubs and public meetings are forbidden, leftist civil servants are dismissed, homes of leftists are searched, and leftist newspapers are sued and fined.

July 16. Passage of a draconian press law that severely restricts the press

August 2. France signs the Treaty of London with Britain, Russia, Denmark, and Sweden on the fate of Schleswig-Holstein.

August 26. Death of Louis-Philippe. The comte de Paris (1838–94) becomes the Orleanist pretender to the French throne.

**1851**

The French population is 33 million to 36 million, versus 34 million in the German states, 20.8 million in Britain, and 23 million in the United States.

Proudhon's *Idée générale de la révolution au XIXe siècle* is published.

Corot paints *La Danse des nymphes*.

Charles-François Gounod's (1818–93) opera *Sappho* opens in Paris.

June 14. Musset's *Les Caprices de Marianne* opens at the Comédie-française.

July 19. The proposal to revise the constitution so that Bonaparte can succeed himself as president gets a majority in the Legislative Chamber but not the three-quarters needed to change the constitution.

August 14. Eugène Labiche's (1815–88) *Un Chapeau de paille* opens at the Théâtre de la Montansier, Paris. Labiche would have six of his plays produced in 1851, versus nine in 1850 and twelve in 1852.

October 30. Musset's *Bettine* opens at the Théâtre du gymnase, Paris.

December 2. President Louis-Napoleon Bonaparte carries out a coup d'état to change the Constitution so that he can be reelected. The Assembly is dissolved and universal manhood suffrage restored. Two hundred deputies who meet and proclaim the dismissal of the president are arrested. Riots against his coup break out in Paris the next day but are easily suppressed in the massacre of the Boulevards of December 4.

December 5–10. Resistance in the provinces. About 3,000 are arrested.

December 21. Plebiscite in France supports Louis-Napoleon, who wants to draw up a new constitution, by a vote of 7 million to 640,000. In the protests against Napoleon, about 20,000 are arrested and sentenced, about half of them to transportation to Algeria.

**1852**

The Société aérostatique, the first aeronautical society, is founded in Paris.

Aristide Boucicaut (1810–77) joins the Bon marché in Paris and institutes its policy of small markups.

Théophile Gautier's poetry is published in *Emaux et Camées*.

January 14. The new French Constitution gives kingly power to President Louis-Napoleon Bonaparte. He commands the armed forces and makes war and peace; he alone can initiate laws and choose the governing Council of State and the Senate, both of which meet in secret. The elected Legislative body can, like the Senate, accept or reject laws but, again like the Senate, it cannot initiate legislation or amend bills. According to the Constitution, "The emperor governs by means of the ministers, the Council of State, the Senate, and the Legislative Assembly."

January 22. The Orléans family is banished from France by presidential decree.

February 2. Alexandre Dumas, fils', *Camille* opens at the Théâtre du vaudeville, Paris, It had been published in 1848, but production had been held up by the censors.

February 17. Repressive measures, including censorship of the press. Every newspaper must get government permission to publish, and put up a bond of 50,000 francs. The minister of the interior can suspend any newspaper at any time.

February 28. The government authorizes the formation of joint stock banks issuing long-term credit, including the government-subsidized Crédit foncier, which lends at 5 percent. The Pereire brothers, Emile (1800–1875) and Isaac (1806–80), found the Crédit mobilier.

February 19–March 14. Elections to the new Legislative body, in which only seven members of the opposition gain election.

March 28. The state of siege is lifted.

September. President Bonaparte makes a triumphal tour of the provinces. The economy is improving, and the Bank of France has reduced its interest rate to 3 percent.

November 21. A plebiscite supports the establishment of a new empire in France by a vote of 7.8 million to 250,000.

December 1. Louis-Napoleon Bonaparte proclaims the establishment of an empire and becomes Napoleon III, emperor of the French. The 5 percent bond, selling at 91.6 on December 1, is up to 100.9 on December 16.

# Index

I compiled this index for many uses. Local historians will find the birthplace of each biographee, when it is known, listed alphabetically by town and by department (except for Paris). This cross-listing shows, for example, that Bensançon produced a wide variety of notable Frenchmen, including the romantic writers Victor Hugo and Charles Nodier, the socialists Charles Fourier and Pierre Proudhon, and the conservative magistrate Jean Courvoisier. The schools attended by the biographees are also noted, and the list of those educated at the Ecole polytechnique is especially long. I paid particular attention to ideologies: romanticism, classicism, republicanism, socialism, feminism, legitimism, Bonapartism, communism, ultraroyalism, anticlericalism, industrialism, ultramontanism, the right to work. There is a long list of page references to Imprisoned Persons, which reveals the perils of political life in this revolutionary period. A separate listing of convicted persons refers to those who were convicted but not caught.

"Chamber of Deputies" and "Chamber of Peers" list the references to members of those parliamentary bodies as well as the activities of each chamber. "University" and "Collège de France" do the same for those educational institutions, and there are other references to the various lycées, collèges, military schools, and faculties of law and medicine. Honorary institutions—the Legion of Honor, the Académie française, the Institute, the Order of the Holy Ghost—also command long lists of references to their members. The list of references to the Chamber of Deputies is the second longest in the Index.

One of the longest is the entry on England. England was the sanctuary of choice for political refugees from France, and it was the model cited by constitutional liberals. It was also "Perfidious Albion," the ancient enemy in a thousand-year war. (See, for example, the references to Joan of Arc.) The French were just beginning the long transition from the thousand-year war with England to the Entente cordiale, a transition that is still not complete.

Other changes in France are pointed out by the references to special groups, like Protestants and Jews; these references note both the activities of the groups and instances of Anti-Semitic and anti-Protestant feeling. (There is a separate heading for references to Anti-Semitism.) There are, of course, long references to the revolutions, revolts, insurrections, riots, and conspiracies that this century of revolutions is remembered for. Fields like education, banking, industry, and science are extensively indexed and cross-referenced as are literature, art and architecture, and the press. These fields were changing rapidly during the period 1815–52.

As Stendhal pointed out in *The Red and the Black* the people mentioned in this dictionary represent different colors from those in the previous period, which was the period of the Napoleonic Empire. There is still red, but now it is the red of revolutionary politics, not military uniforms. There is black, some from the priestly garments of men like Forbin-Janson and the Missionaries, but most from the inkstained hands of the journalists, novelists, playwrights, and poets who, along with black-robed judges and lawyers in their black frock coats, dominate these pages as they dominated their age. The generals most often mentioned in this Index won their battles in the Chamber of Deputies, the courtroom, and the press, not on the battlefield. This was an age of the pen, not the sword. In the Introduction I characterized the period as one dominated by Romanticism, revolution, constitutional liberalism, parliamentary government, and industrialization. Conservative elements fought against each of these changes, and the arenas in which the contending forces clashed were the newspapers, the law courts, and the Chamber of Deputies. Their weapons were words. This Index alphabetizes them.

Edgar Leon Newman

*The Dressmaker*

# CHERBOURG, FRANCE
## APRIL 10, 1912

Tess pulled at the corners of the sheets she had taken straight from the line and tried to tuck them tight under the mattress, stepping back to check her work. Still a bit bunchy and wrinkled. The overseer who ran this house was sure to inspect and sniff and scold, but it didn't matter anymore.

She glanced out the window. A woman was walking by, wearing a splendid hat topped with a rich, deep-green ribbon, twirling a bright-red parasol, her face lively, her demeanor confident and sunny. Tess tried to imagine

herself stepping forward so confidently without someone accusing her of behaving above her station. She could almost feel her fingers curling around the smooth, polished handle of that parasol. Where was the woman going?

She gazed back at the half-made bed. No more fantasizing, not one more minute of it.

She walked out into the central hall and stopped, held in place by the sight of her reflection in the full-length gilded mirror at the end of the hall. Her long dark hair, as always, had pulled out of a carelessly pinned bun, even as the upward tilt of her chin, which had so often registered boldness, remained in place. But there was no denying the shameful crux of what she saw: a skinny young girl wearing a black dress and a white apron and carrying a pile of dirty linens, with a servant's cap sitting squarely and stupidly on the top of her head. An image of servitude. She yanked the cap off her head and hurled it at the glass. She was not a servant. She was a seamstress, a good one,

and she should be paid for her work. She had been tricked into this job.

Tess dumped the soiled linens down the laundry chute and climbed the stairs to her third-floor room, untying her apron as she went. Today, yes. No further hesitation. There were jobs available, the dockworkers had said, on that huge ship sailing for New York today. She scanned the small room. No valise—the mistress would stop her cold at the door if she knew she was leaving. The picture of her mother, yes. The money. Her sketchbook, with all her designs. She took off her uniform, put on her best dress, and stuffed some undergarments, stockings, and her only other dress into a canvas sack. She stared at the half-finished ball gown draped over the sewing machine, at the tiny bows of crushed white velvet she had so painstakingly stitched onto the ballooning blue silk. Someone else would have to finish it, someone who actually got paid. What else? Nothing.

She took a deep breath, trying to resist the echo of her father's voice in her head: Don't put on airs, he always

scolded. You're a farm girl, do your job, keep your head down. You get decent enough pay; mind you don't wreck your life with defiance.

"I won't wreck it," she whispered out loud. "I'll make it better."

But, even as she turned and left her room for the last time, she could almost hear his voice following her, as raspy and angry as ever: "Watch out, foolish girl."

------

The rotting wood planks beneath Lucile's feet were spongy, catching her boot heels as she made her way through the crowd on the Cherbourg dock. She pulled her silver-fox stole snugly around her neck, luxuriating in the plush softness of the thick fur, and lifted her head high, attracting many glances, some triggered by the sight of her brilliantly red hair, others by the knowledge of who she was.

She glanced at her sister walking quickly toward her, humming some new song, twirling a red parasol as she

walked. "You do enjoy playing the blithe spirit, don't you?" she said.

"I try to be an agreeable person," her sister murmured.

"I have no need to compete; you may have the attention," Lucile said in her huskiest, haughtiest voice.

"Oh, stop it, Lucy. Neither of us is impoverished on that score. Really, you are cranky lately."

"If you were presenting a spring collection in New York in a few weeks, you'd be cranky, too. I have too much to worry about with all this talk of women hiking their skirts and flattening their breasts. All you have to do is write another novel about them."

The two of them started squeezing past the dozens of valises and trunks, brass hinges glowing in the waning light, their skirts of fine wool picking up layers of damp dust turned to grime.

"It's true, the tools of my trade are much more portable than yours," Elinor said airily.

"They certainly are. I'm forced to make this crossing because I don't have anyone competent enough to be

in charge of the show, so I must be there. So please don't be frivolous."

Elinor closed her parasol with a snap and stared at her sister, one perfect eyebrow arched. "Lucy, how can you have no sense of humor? I'm only here to wish you bon voyage and cheer you on when the ship departs. Shall I leave now?"

Lucile sighed and took a deep breath, allowing a timed pause. "No, please," she said. "I only wish you were sailing with me. I will miss you."

"I would like nothing better than to go with you, but my editor wants those corrected galleys back by the end of the week." Elinor's voice turned sunny again. "Anyway, you have Cosmo— such a sweetheart, even if he doesn't appreciate poetry."

"A small defect."

"He's a dear, and his best gift to you has been a title. Is that too crass? But it is true that he has no literary appreciation." Elinor sighed. "And he can be boring."

"Nonsense."

"You know it as well as I do. Where is he?"

Lucile was scanning the crowd, searching for the tall, angular figure of Sir Cosmo Duff Gordon. "This delay is maddening. If anybody can get things operating efficiently and on time, Cosmo can."

"Of course. That's his job."

Lucile glanced sharply at Elinor, but she was looking elsewhere, an innocent expression on her face.

------

Up the hill, away from the shipyard, amid the sprawling brick mansions on the bluffs of the Normandy coast, Tess was marching downstairs to the parlor. Waiting for her was the mistress, a prim Englishwoman with lips so thin they seemed stitched together.

"I want my pay, please," Tess said, hiding the canvas sack in the folds of her skirt. She could see the envelope waiting for her on the corner table by the door, and began edging toward it.

"You haven't finished my gown for

the party, Tess," the woman said in a more querulous tone than usual. "And my son could hardly find a towel in the hall closet this morning."

"He'll find one now." She was not going back upstairs. She would never again be backed into that linen closet, fighting off the adolescent son's eager, spidery fingers. That was her envelope; she could see her name written on it, and she wasn't standing around to hear the usual complaints before it was doled out. She moved closer to the table.

"You've said that before, and I'm going upstairs right now to check." The woman stopped as she saw the girl reaching out for the envelope. "Tess, I haven't given that to you yet!"

"Perhaps not, but I have earned it," Tess said carefully.

"Rudeness is not admirable, Tess. You've been very secretive lately. If you pick that up before I give it to you, you have burned your bridges with me."

Tess took a deep breath and, feeling slightly dizzy, picked up the envelope

and held it close, as if it might be snatched away.

"Then I have," she said. Without waiting for a reply, she opened the heavily ornate front door she would never have to polish again and headed for the docks. After all her dreaming and brooding, the time was now.

------

The dock was slippery with seaweed. Heart pounding, she pressed into the bustle and chaos around her and sucked into her lungs the sharp, salty air of the sea. But where were the signs advertising jobs? She accosted a man in a uniform with large brass buttons and asked in hesitant French and then urgent English who was in charge of hiring staff for cleaning and cooking on that big new ship.

"You're too late, dear, the service-people have all been hired and the passengers will soon be boarding. Bad luck for you, I'm afraid." He turned away.

It didn't matter how brightly she smiled; her plan was falling apart. Id-

iot—she should have come down earlier. What now? She gulped back the hollow feeling of not knowing what came next and tried to think. Find families; look for young children. She would be a good nanny. Didn't having seven younger brothers and sisters count as experience? She was ready to go, no trouble at all; all she had to do was find the right person and say the right things and she could get away. She would not, she would *not* be trapped; she would get out.

But no one paid her any heed. An elderly English couple shrank back when she asked if they needed a companion for the trip. When she approached a family with children, offering her services, they looked at her askance, politely shook their heads, and edged away. What could she expect? She must look desperate, tangled hair and all.

------

"Lucy, look at that girl over there." Elinor pointed a delicate, polished finger

at the frantic Tess. "My goodness, she's a beauty. Gorgeous, big eyes. Look at her running around talking to people. I think she's trying to get on the ship. Do you think she's running away from something? Maybe the police? A man?"

"I wouldn't know, but I'm sure you'll weave a good story out of it," Lucy said, waving to Cosmo's approaching figure. He looked, as usual, somewhat detached from his surroundings. Cool eyes, a calm demeanor; always in charge. Following him, at his heels, was a timid-looking messenger.

"Lucile, there is a problem—" Cosmo began.

"I knew it," Lucile said, her jaw tightening. "It's Hetty, isn't it?"

"She says she is unable to come. Her mother is ill," the messenger said. He bent forward almost in nervous homage—as well he might, because Lucile was furious now.

"Tell that girl she can't back out just before we sail. Who does she think she is? If she doesn't board with us, she's fired. Have you told her that?" She glared at the man.

"I have, Madame," he ventured.

Tess heard the commotion and stopped, arrested by the sight of the two women. Could it be? Yes, one of them wore the same grand hat with the gorgeous green ribbon she had spied from the window; she was right here, idly tapping the ground with that same red parasol.

The other woman's sharp voice jolted her attention away.

"A miserable excuse!" she snapped.

Someone hadn't shown up for the trip, some kind of servant, and this small person with the bright-red hair and crimson lipstick was furious. How formidable she looked. Her strong-boned, immobile face admitted no compromise, and her wide-set eyes looked as if they could change from soft to hard in seconds. There was no softness in them now.

"Who is she?" Tess demanded of a young man attached to the clustered group. Her voice was trembling. Nothing was working out.

"You don't *know*?"

She looked again at the woman, not-

ing how people slowed as they passed, whispering, casting admiring glances. Yes, there was something familiar.

"Oh, my goodness," she gasped. "That's Lucile Duff Gordon."

"Of course. *Couture,* you know. And the other woman is her sister, Elinor Glyn. She's from Hollywood, writes novels. Some quite scandalous, actually."

Tess barely heard him. This personage bristling with anger was the most famous designer in the world, someone whose beautiful gowns she had seen in the papers, and she was standing only a few feet away. Her chance—this was her chance.

"Lady Duff Gordon, I can't believe I'm actually seeing you," she burst out, pushing forward. "I admire you so much—you are so talented. I've seen pictures of your gowns that set me dreaming." She was babbling, but she didn't care. All she wanted was Lucile's attention.

The designer ignored her.

"I would love to work for you," she pleaded. "I know goods. I am a dress-

maker, I do very good work; I could be a great help to you." She thought wildly—what to say next? "I'm very good at buttonholes—anything you need done. Please—"

"She's desperate, I told you so," murmured Elinor with a giggle as she straightened her elaborately fashionable hat.

Lucile turned toward Tess. "Do you know what the job *is*?" she demanded.

Tess hesitated.

"It is as my personal maid. *Now* are you interested?"

"I can do that." Anything, anything to get on that ship. To be working for Lady Lucile would be an unbelievable opportunity.

"Where do you work now? What do you do?"

"I—work in a home in Cherbourg. And I do dressmaking. I have very satisfied clients."

"A servant of some sort—not a surprise," Elinor murmured.

Lucile ignored her. "Your name?"

"Tess Collins."

"Tessie. Ah, I see."

"No. *Tess.*"

"As you wish. Can you read and write?"

"Of course!" Tess was indignant.

Lady Duff Gordon's eyes turned appraising at this flash of temper. "References?"

"I'll have them mailed. Anything you need."

"From the middle of the Atlantic?"

"There's always a marconigram." Tess had read about them and hoped she was saying the right thing.

Lucile suddenly tired of the back-and-forth. "I'm sorry, I know nothing about you," she said. "It won't do." She turned away to talk to Cosmo.

Desperate, Tess had an idea. "Look, please look," she said, pulling open the collar of her dress. "I made this. I tried to copy the collar of one of your dresses that I clipped out of the newspaper. It's a poor copy, of course, but—"

"Not bad," murmured Elinor, peering at the collar. It was deftly turned—a crisp linen designed to be worn open or closed, requiring careful stitching.

"Very intricate. Unusual for a servant girl."

Lucile cast another look in Tess's direction, then fingered the proffered collar. It was one of her best designs. The girl had cut it in perfect proportion to her dress and stitched it by hand; there was not a wrinkle in the fabric. "You are saying you made this?" she demanded.

"Yes, I did."

"Who taught you to sew?"

"My mother, who is very skilled." Tess drew herself up proudly. "I'm known throughout the county. And I cut my own patterns."

"Everyone *cuts*, my dear. That just requires a pair of scissors. You mean *design*, I presume." Lucile reached out without a by-your-leave and lifted the sleeve of Tess's dress, noting the skill of the girl's inset work.

"Yes. I design and I sew. I do everything."

"Does your employer pay you?"

"Not for dressmaking. But I am good, and I deserve to be paid." Maybe this

was too boastful. She drew in a deep breath and gave it her all. "I want to work for you. You are the best designer in the world, and I can't believe my good fortune in meeting you. Your gowns are an inspiration—who can design like you? Please give me a chance. You won't be sorry."

Lucile stared at the girl, her expression unreadable. Something stirred in her eyes as the aides around her fell silent, waiting for what would come next.

"She's probably a bit too independent for you," Elinor said quietly in an aside. "You never know. She might not be quite what she purports to be."

Lucile's expression didn't change, even as a small smile curved her lips. "Perhaps. But then I could keep my jewelry locked in the ship's safe, couldn't I?" She turned back and addressed herself to Tess. "You are content with being a maid? I'm offering nothing else."

"I will do whatever you wish—I just want a chance to prove myself, and work for you." Yes, yes, she would do

anything. She wouldn't daydream or bunch up the sheet corners; she would work and learn and change everything. Tess was having trouble breathing. She felt the hinges of fate creaking, a door opening—or was it closing? Let her like me, she prayed.

"Anything?"

Tess pulled herself straight. "Anything respectable, none other," she said.

Lucile's appraising eye traveled the length of the girl's figure, taking in her dark tousled hair, her high, flushed cheekbones and upturned chin, her shabby boots with one broken lace.

"They're going to board us soon. Are you prepared to leave in the next hour or so?" she demanded.

"Yes, I can go immediately." Tess cut her words sharp and tight. Only one chance, she thought, don't squander it.

The little group around Lucile seemed to be holding its collective breath. Lucy hesitated one last second. "All right, you're hired," she said. "As a *maid,* you understand."

Elinor shot her a surprised glance. "Isn't that a bit impulsive, Lucy?"

Her sister didn't answer, just kept gazing at Tess as if she were peering, unfocused, into the middle distance.

"Thank you—you will never regret it," Tess said shakily, trying not to wither under Lucile's steady gaze.

"You will need to be dressed for the job, whether you are educated or not." Lucile was on firm ground again. "You are to call me Madame. And you'll need a cap." She nodded toward Cosmo. "My husband, Sir Cosmo, will take care of the details."

Tess smiled warily at the tall, thin man with the large, well-tended mustache who stepped forward to talk to her. After asking Tess a few questions, he held a murmured conversation with a White Star Line official. This was, of course, passage only for a servant, so no passport was required. Surely no problem there? They completed their chat with a firm handshake. Tess exhaled so deeply she was dizzy. Yes, the door was opening.

------

She held on to the rail, following Lady Duff Gordon down slippery steps to a tender that looked grubby and a bit frail. An officious man in a White Star uniform had told them all that the ship was too large for the shallow Cherbourg harbor, so into the tender they were to go. How big was it, that it had caused another vessel to snap its mooring lines on the way from Southampton? Tess peered into the thin gray fog, eager for her first look.

The fog lifted. And there it was, looming so high, so proud and separate, it seemed to rule the sea, not the other way around. Four huge smokestacks reaching gracefully toward the sky. Nine decks, and Tess felt her neck aching from the effort as she counted them. No wonder it was called *Titanic.* The people scrambling to hook the tender to the ship were all out of proportion, like busy ants.

A sailor reached out a hand to Tess, coaxing her onto the gangplank. She stepped up, concentrating now on putting one foot in front of the other. It was happening—no going back now. Good-

bye to Sussex, goodbye to the prune-
faced mistress and her randy son,
goodbye to all. Even to home, to mother,
to the brothers and sisters she might
never see again. Her heart quivered;
she firmly took the next step.

She was at the top. A couple up
ahead, a man with a beautifully sculpted
chin and a woman wrapped in a white
fur cape, took one step onto the ship
and paused to embrace. How nice, how
spontaneous. The man—his veined
hands showing that he wasn't as young
as he had at first appeared—suddenly
twirled the woman in a deft movement
that ended in her swooning, laughing,
into his arms. The two skipped lightly
away to scattered applause. Were they
entertainers?

Right in front of her was a man with
a handsome, restless face dominated
by a strong, molded chin and a slender
aquiline nose. His hands were jammed
into the pockets of an immaculate tan
cashmere coat. His eyes seemed
clouded. By unhappiness? His hair was
graying at the temples; probably in his
forties, she guessed. A man of busi-

ness, constantly checking his watch. He seemed enveloped in fog, and did not react to the small performance in front of him, just stood a moment watching the happy pair with what she imagined was a certain wistfulness.

"Hurry along, miss." The man behind her had a hard, impatient voice. A quick glance back; he looked very important.

"Welcome, Mr. Ismay," said an officer, reaching past her to shake the man's hand. "It's an honor to have the chairman of White Star on board. I can promise you a speedy trip to New York."

Ismay mumbled something; Tess thought he looked like nothing so much as a tall, bony crane. She quickened her step to get out of his way.

Still on the tender, Lucile and Elinor watched the girl ascend. "I don't think you have servant material there, Lucy," said Elinor with a chuckle. "She didn't even wait for the great Lady Duff Gordon to precede her. I love that."

"I'll put her to work on hems and buttons. If she doesn't do a proper job, she'll be gone the minute we get to New York."

"You've got some ulterior motive—I know you," Elinor said, giving her sister a brief hug. "Keeps things interesting. I'll keep writing about illicit passion and you keep designing the clothes a kept woman would wear."

"Elinor—"

"Oh, I know, they're for dignified women and stars of all sorts. Wasn't I good to come out to the ship to see you off?"

"You just wanted to see the *Titanic* up close." Lucile smiled, returning the hug. She frowned. "You're much too thin—I can count the bones in your rib cage. You haven't had any surgically removed, have you?"

"Such nonsense. You know as well as I do that only a few crazy women have done that, and I'm not among them."

"You aren't wearing a corset."

"Well, there you are. I've given up whalebone. Good luck in New York, and hurry back." Elinor's voice went from gentle to teasing. "Madame."

"It gives me the proper respect," Lucile retorted.

"Just don't start believing it."

"I suppose." Slightly abstracted, Lucile gazed up at the hurrying figure of the young housemaid, who was now at the top of the gangplank.

"You're focusing on that girl, dear. Say goodbye to your loving sister."

"Oh, hush." Lucile laughed and planted a bright-red kiss on Elinor's cheek, then turned to go.

-------

Tess resisted staring too closely at the array of important people moving to their cabins in first class; Mother would be mortified. She had been taught manners, after all. Don't gape. But oh, what a fantasy this was. Peek sideways at the gloriously attired women—how she wished she could stroke some of the crunchy silks, examine the design of the intricately woven shawls—and at the men in high collars who looked like rulers of the world. Act like this was all nothing new, just life as usual. Pretend to belong.

"Most of the first-class passengers

have no reason to be on this particular crossing, other than to be able to boast that they were on the *Titanic*'s maiden voyage," Madame said as Tess helped her unpack. "But it gives them a lovely little tidbit to drop at a New York dinner. It hints at a flexible, even adventurous spirit." She smiled. "As long as the faucets are gold-plated, which they are."

Tess started to reply, but Lucile's finger had flown to her lips. "Listen," she commanded.

And Tess heard for the first time the slow rumble, the vibration, of a great ship's engines gathering momentum far below where she stood. Could they watch the departure? she asked timidly.

"There's nothing special about it, I'm afraid." But Lucile led Tess back outside, where they watched the land recede. One more stop in Ireland, and the *Titanic*'s first voyage out onto the vast sea would truly begin. Madame pointed out a young woman with careful, tiny curls framing her pale skin and a strikingly handsome man attached to

her side, the two of them in a seemingly joyful bubble. A couple due soon to be married; a very important society wedding was planned in Newport Beach, she said.

"But then you have people like that," she said, pointing a delicate finger at a cheerful, round woman waving heartily toward the shore. "Mrs. Brown. Her money comes from a place called Leadville, in Colorado. Gold-mining interests. No breeding." She peered downward at the sound of shouts and cheers from steerage. "Poor uneducated souls—they've sold everything and are heading for what they think are new lives in America. Not likely, unless they learn to wash up."

Later, when Tess took her satchel down into steerage, hunting for the cot that had been assigned to her, she paused, hunching down under the low ceiling, looking around the crowded room. The air was close—a mixture of smells pungent with garlic, sliced tongue, smoke, and even urine. A man in gray pants was shaving, two children watching him. An old woman with thin-

ning hair sat rocking back and forth, moaning about her stomach. Two boys, tossing a ball to each other. Women gossiping, babies crying. The girl on the cot next to hers gave a friendly smile and offered an apple. All this life, and few would see the upper decks. Nor would those on the upper decks ever see them. But they *were* headed for new lives, just as she was.

She made her way back upstairs as quickly as she could. If she could, she'd take them all with her, but this was her time now. She would stay down here only to sleep, not one minute more. Only when the voices and sounds of crying children faded into murmurs curling up through the decks and polished brass of this amazing ship did she pause and breathe.

------

Everything was dazzling. Warming to Tess's eagerness, Lucile continued the next day to point out quite casually the stellar passengers: here, an owner of a railway; there, an aide to the United

States' President Taft; oh, and there, a famous theatrical producer—she knew them all. Together they strolled among the huge reception rooms, with their elaborately carved chairs, rich mahogany tables, and gilded mirrors, until Lucile announced that she was bored and ready for a nap. No need, then, to iron or clean or run errands? Tess asked quickly if she might wander about a little on her own.

"Go ahead, I'll be on deck at teatime. Good luck with your exploring; even the ship's stewards don't seem to know where everything is."

Alone now, Tess peeked in the doorway of a large room with mahogany walls and strange machines that looked like mechanical horses. She had heard of them; they were exercise animals, run by electricity. She glanced back and forth. There was no one around. She shouldn't venture in, but this was all so intriguing. She tiptoed inside, wandering the room, touching the horses sheathed in steel plate, debating whether she had the nerve to pull herself up onto one of them. They

looked so shiny and cold. What would it be like? She saw the switches. She could even turn one on if no one was here to see.

Then she saw the camel. A camel! She had always wondered what it would be like to ride one. Cautiously, she hoisted one foot into a stirrup, grabbed her skirt, and pulled herself onto the machine. She reached for the switch, then froze.

"Well, I see you are ready for a little exercise." It was a man's voice. "Women are far too shy about using athletic equipment, which is such nonsense." She looked up and saw the handsome man with graying hair she had observed on the gangplank. He seemed more energetic now. He was wearing a blue turtleneck sweater, and although he looked less somber, she suspected that the shadows she saw beneath his eyes never disappeared entirely.

"I hope I'm not doing any harm, but I've not seen machines like this," she said, flustered as she realized what a sight she presented. Her legs straddled the contraption like those of a simple

trollop. Good Lord, what if Madame wandered in here right now. But she wouldn't, surely. And the man didn't seem shocked enough to order her out.

"Nor have most of us," he said. "Now, take this electric camel you've become so fond of. What does it need humps for to store water, with the wonders of electricity? Shall I turn it on?"

Tess stared down at him, saw the amused light in his eyes, and tightened her grip. "All right," she said a bit breathlessly.

He flicked the switch. Suddenly she was moving back and forth, then up and down, and she couldn't help laughing at the absurdity of it all as she tightened her legs against the camel's sleek flanks of polished oak.

"Is it like riding a real horse?"

"Oh no, nothing like it. I love riding at home."

"That kind of saddle?"

"Bareback. It makes me feel free." A sudden flash of galloping along the back roads at home made this venture suddenly seem silly. "How is this exercise?"

"Your heart and lungs benefit from the movement—that's the theory, anyway."

Someone was sure to come in soon. "Turn it off now," she said.

"It can go faster. Do you want to go faster?"

"No, no." She glanced at his face, a little alarmed. "Don't tease me, please."

He smiled and turned off the camel, then reached out his arms. "May I help you down?" he asked.

"No, thank you, I can do it myself." Quickly, before he could say anything more, she slid off the machine, smoothing her skirts.

"You're totally proper now, don't worry," he said. "Would you like a little tour?" He offered his arm quite naturally, as if it were a perfectly ordinary thing to do. His mood had lightened, and it was infectious. How good it felt to laugh. Here was the squash court; do you play? And here the Turkish baths, and over there—he pointed— the fanciest of swimming pools. "A necessity when surrounded by water,

wouldn't you say? Nothing too good for the upper classes."

"I'll get there someday," she burst out.

"Are you sure you want to?" he asked with what seemed a hint of true curiosity.

She felt brave enough to give a true answer. "I'll work hard—it's easy in America." Embarrassed now, she glanced at him and then away. "Thank you for this," she said.

"You've done me the courtesy of being here, and I am delighted to be your guide."

The men she knew never talked that way. "You know I'm not supposed to be here, don't you?"

"I've seen you with Lady Duff Gordon," he said gently. "I'm an American, from the very brash city of Chicago, and not as respectful of British social niceties as I should be. I enjoyed it."

"So did I," she said.

"I hope you have a pleasant trip."

She glanced quickly at a clock. She was late. "I've got to go," she said and

hurried out, scrambling by the machines, almost tripping. The tea, the tea. She mustn't forget the cream. As she rushed to the ship's kitchen, she found herself thinking about the man's strong hands and wished she had let him lift her down. She would have liked to feel them. Idiot, what a thought to have. One of these days, she decided, she would find out what squash was—and learn to play it. Lord, what was his name? How could she not have asked?

------

Lucile watched as the girl moved quickly toward her across the deck, precariously balancing on a silver tray a Limoges teapot, a delicate porcelain cup, a small pitcher of cream, and a white sugar bowl.

"It's a miracle you made it," Lucile said as Tess deposited the tray in front of her. "These are the thinnest china cups, as I asked?"

"Yes, Madame. I made sure." In truth, she had almost forgotten in the busy ship's kitchen.

"Tea tastes like dishwater in anything else."

Tess poured a cup and handed it to her, still a bit flushed.

"How were your explorations?"

"Oh, very nice. I saw so much. There's an exercise room."

"So I heard. No self-respecting woman would indulge in such non-sense."

Tess flushed deeper.

"Take all this." Lucile waved at the tea service. "I've had enough. I want you to return to the cabin and iron the blue gown I left out for dinner tonight. Be back in a quarter of an hour, and we'll walk the promenade again."

Tess nodded eagerly, gathering the silver and loading the tray. Strolling the promenade with Lady Duff Gordon was as close as she could get to the designer's rarefied world, and to see such people as John Jacob Astor—the richest man on board, a multimillionare—smiling and chatting with Lucile was a not-to-be-missed experience. She must hurry. She began making her way

across the deck, slightly distracted by the sight of two polished men in knickers pushing wood tiles across a painted board. A game of some sort—what was it? Was it squash?

A child's ball rolled in her path. She tripped, tried to right herself, and went crashing, cream flying from the silver pitcher, small cubes of sugar skittering across the deck, still-hot tea burning her fingers. Women seated nearby jumped up, pulling back their skirts from the mess.

"I'm so sorry," she said, appalled. Somebody tittered.

Madame was standing now, looking down at her coldly. "Get this cleaned up and get back to my cabin. Immediately." She turned and walked away.

Tess took the linen napkins on the tray and started mopping up the cream. She'd done it now.

"Nasty piece, that woman. Never mind, if you'll let me, I'll take care of it."

She looked up and saw a sailor frowning down at her. He was about her age, with a strong, tanned face and

sturdy arms. He was gripping a mop. His eyes were kind, and as blue as the sea.

She put everything back on the tray, stood and brushed herself off. "That's very kind of you," she said, holding her head high. She wouldn't be humiliated—no more of that. She would stop those titters, and none would see tears from her.

"That's the girl, show them who you are," the sailor said gently.

And who might that be, Tess thought. The way out of this was to put on her mask, achieve some semblance of invisibility. She wanted to glance back at the sailor, to thank him silently, but she resisted the impulse. Yet she felt his respect as she walked away.

-------

"Your clumsiness was inexcusable." Lucile's voice was like a hammer hitting iron.

"I know it was, Madame, and I am sorry. I picked it all up—nothing was

broken, though there was a chip in the cup—"

"If we were on land, I'd fire you on the spot."

"It will never happen again, I promise."

"You promised competence, and I'm not seeing any. But I can't just throw you overboard, can I?"

"I hope not."

The side of Lucile's mouth twitched.

"The truth is, I would've done anything to sail with you," Tess said. "I've admired you for a long time, and you've done things I only dream about. If you had needed a chimney sweep, I would've found a way to be one."

"I wanted a maid."

"I'm not a good maid; I don't want to be a maid." Oh God, she could hear her father telling her to shut her mouth, be obedient. But she might as well get on with it and share the plain truth. "I went out to service early and I hated it, and all I wanted to do was sew. I'm sorry, I admire you enormously. I just don't know how—"

"To do your job properly," Lucile finished sharply. She stared at Tess. "Isn't that right?"

"With all proper respect, it depends on the job." Tess prayed that her words didn't come across as insolent.

Another twitch of the mouth. "You don't want to be a maid? Here—" Lucile beckoned Tess over to the desk, where she had laid out the cut pieces for a wool jacket. It wasn't an important piece; if the girl messed it up, it would not be a significant loss. "Prove yourself. Assemble these without a pattern. The stitching must be hand-done. I will be back in an hour to see how you are doing."

"Yes, Madame." Tess picked up a piece of the wool as Lucile left the room. It was loosely woven, a delicate plaid of copper and green—quite fine material, better than she had ever worked with. She must be careful. No, she *would* be careful; this was no stupid teacup. Her head bent forward; her fingers began their precision work. She was breathing better now.

------

Lucile picked up the completed jacket and held it at arm's length, a frown on her face. She studied it carefully as Tess nervously bit her lip.

"Well, you're obviously determined to prove yourself," she said finally, fingering the jacket. Tess had tucked the darts perfectly, which wasn't easy to do on a patterned fabric. "This is a reasonably good job. Meticulous stitching." She cast a studying glance at Tess, then folded the jacket and tucked it into her trunk. "Perhaps you have the makings of a seamstress. You might not be dusting bureaus all your life."

Just the hint of a promise, that's all. But it sent a shiver of relief down deep in her heart. Lord, thank you. If there had been any more talk of dumping her over the side of the ship, she would have jumped on her own.

Lucile glanced at a small jeweled clock on her dressing table. "That's enough talk about sewing for the moment. Get my dress out, will you, dear? It's almost time for dinner."

Tess flew to obey as Lucile began rummaging in her jewelry box. "Did I

not bring them?" she murmured fret-
fully to herself. "Where are they?"

"Can I help, Madame?" Tess asked.

"Ah, here they are." Lucile pulled out
a small bag of midnight-blue velvet,
opened it, and shook its contents onto
the dressing table. Earrings. She picked
up one and held it to her ear, facing
Tess. "Beautiful, aren't they?"

"Yes, they are." Tess was fascinated.
She had never seen anything quite like
these. Three pale-blue stones, one below the other, all shimmering with inner
light, separated by tiny diamonds and
what she thought were sapphires.
"What are they?" Tess asked shyly.

"Moonstones from Ceylon, very fashionable." Lucile fastened the earring in
her ear and gently moved her head.
The stones danced and glowed. "They
call this the traveler's stone," she said.
"It's supposed to protect against the
dangers of travel, which is total nonsense, of course. But it sells jewelry, I
suppose." She fastened the second
earring, then reached for her ever-present lipstick.

This was her cue to go. "Good night,

Madame, I hope you have a nice dinner," Tess said as she turned to leave, pulling the door closed behind her.

------

That night, back down in the claustrophobic quarters of steerage, amid the whimpers of children and the snores of their parents, she slipped into restless sleep, the kind where memory flowed like water through her dreams.

**The gravel was crunching under the landlord's heavy step as he circled her.**

**"How old?"**

**"Twelve," her father said, twisting his cap in field-weathered hands. The cow had died yesterday. Diseased. No milk now for the younger children.**

**"Her teeth?"**

**"They're good."**

**"I can chew with no problem, sir."**

**"Don't speak unless spoken to, girl."**

"Yes, sir."

"You'll do housework. Hard work. Ready for that?"

"Yes, sir."

Her dream was getting foggy, but her mother's crying from inside the house had become louder. Her father's hands were almost tearing the cap apart.

"She'll do."

Then her mother was there, grabbing her by the arm, pulling her back into the house. "She's not a horse," she shouted.

They were together now, in the bedroom. Her mother grabbed a threaded needle by the bedside and folded it into her hand.

"You see this? Maybe you have to go out to service right now, but I have taught you to sew. It will be your way out of here. Stand straight, be proud."

Tess awoke with a start. In reality, there had been no fog. And how differ-

ent the messages from her mother and father.

------

"I hear your little maid took a tumble on the deck today," Cosmo said as he and Lucile prepared for bed after dinner. "Caused a dreadful mess. Some sailor came to her rescue?"

Lucile shrugged. "Yes, ridiculous. But I rather like her."

"May I ask why?"

"I don't know if you would understand."

"Try me."

"It isn't important. Maybe there's something there, maybe nothing."

"You haven't pushed her wearing a cap."

"She's terrible as a maid. I don't know why I should bother."

"So you're applying that famous costuming eye of yours to a new blank canvas?"

"My dear Cosmo, she jumps to do my bidding, whatever it is. If the cost of

that is forgetting a servant's cap, that's fine with me."

"Something's going on in your head. To be continued, I presume." He yawned, hoisting himself into bed, his silk pajamas making a swooshing sound as he slid between silk sheets. "When you're ready, of course."

Lucile said nothing, leaning closer to the mirror above the vanity, dabbing cold cream onto her lips, removing her crimson lipstick with a steady hand.

------

"Tess, find my gold silk in that jumble and press it for dinner, please." Lucile pointed to one of her larger trunks when Tess reported for duty the next morning. "You can do that without scorching it, I trust?"

"I would never harm your gowns, Madame," Tess answered, flushing. She opened the lid of the trunk and gently began pulling out the clothes— the shimmering, beautiful fabrics that filled the massive trunk in Stateroom A-20. She plunged her hands in deeper,

shivering at the light silky touch of the fabrics. How could she describe it? They were the consistency of foaming cream. Fabrics she had never seen— delicate as cobwebs, silvery, gold, some as blue as the deepest water, all artfully twisted and looped and draped. This was heaven!

"You seem a bit overcome," Lucile said, amused.

"They look so floaty and simple. But the structure is wonderful."

"I make them to mold to a moving body. You can see that, can you?"

"Oh, yes."

"So your mother taught you to sew?"

Tess nodded, and spoke proudly. "We worked hard together, cutting, piecing, sewing."

"What did you make?"

"A shirt for a landowner, a dress for a wedding. A child's christening gown. All things."

"Quite admirable. But it didn't free her, did it?"

"There were many babies."

"Ah, the universal trap. And how did you avoid it?"

"We were excited about a seam-stress job in Cherbourg; we had friends there. Mother wanted me to escape the village boys." And her father had known all along it was a servant job; she was sure of it.

Lucile smiled, and, tentatively, Tess smiled back.

"A smart woman, your mother."

"I promised her when I got my chance I would make the best of it." She was setting up the iron now, testing it. Not too hot; this was familiar work. The gold gown caressed her fingers, slipping gently onto the board.

"And that's what you're doing now."

"Yes, ma'am."

"Madame."

"Yes, Madame." Remember this, she warned herself silently. Truly, if Lady Duff Gordon wanted to be called Your Highness, she would happily do so.

Lucile gazed at her thoughtfully. "My dear, here is lesson number one for using opportunity: waste no time on false humility. Tell the world about your achievements; don't wait for someone else to do it. Did you know I was the

first designer to use live models for fashion shows?"

"No, Madame," Tess replied. The gown was done. Carefully, she hung it on a silk-covered hanger, a bit dazzled by Lucile's relaxed, almost confiding tone.

"Well, now you do," Lucile said. "You gain confidence by doing what no one else has done. Or what no one else wants to do."

Tess couldn't help it; the words slipped out. "Like dropping teapots?"

Lucile laughed. "I think you and I will get along fine. Now I'd like you to write a letter for me so I can check out your penmanship."

"It's very good," Tess said with a cautious smile.

"Good girl. You've absorbed today's lesson."

------

By noon, Tess was free to seek out the fresh air of the deck. A fine morning all around. She found herself making a mental report to her Mother: I got past

yesterday's disaster, Mother, and Madame and I are actually *talking.* Surely that's a positive sign. Her reverie was interrupted by shouts from the boys playing tag on the deck and the girls giggling nearby, jumping rope.

"Miss?"

Startled, she realized that a sad-faced man in a rumpled black suit was addressing her. Holding each of his hands was a small, wiggling boy.

"My son, here"—he pushed forward one child—"has something to say to you. Edmond, speak up."

The child looked at Tess with imploring eyes. *"Je suis désolé,"* he whispered.

"My sons don't speak English," the man said apologetically. "But Edmond knows his ball was what made you stumble yesterday, and he is sorry. His favorite toy, his spinning top, was lost over the side of the ship and he was trying something new. You do speak French, I hope?"

Tess nodded, touched by his courteous formality. This was Mr. Hoffman,

someone had said. A widower with two small boys. He kept to himself but was devoted to his children.

*"Ce n'est pas grave,"* she said to the child, and saw the look of relief in his eyes. Edmond smiled at her as his brother wrapped himself around his father's pants leg, peeking at her. Mr. Hoffman nodded approvingly, and seemed at a loss for what to say next. "Edmond and Michel, they are usually good boys," he said. "Again, please, we are sorry." And then he turned on his heel, the children hurrying at his side, vanishing into the ship.

------

Teatime, again.

"The tea isn't quite hot enough, Tess." Madame's voice held a touch of testiness. "And the cake is dry."

Tess instantly reached for the cup. "I'll get that fixed right now," she said.

"Also, tell the kitchen crew to send out some fresh cakes."

"Yes, Madame."

"And if there aren't any, what will you do?"

Tess hardly missed a beat. "Bake them myself," she said.

Lucile smiled. "That's the spirit. Forget the tea. Let's walk the promenade."

------

"I see you watching me, Tess," she said casually as they strolled. "What do you see?"

Tess flushed. "You seem regal sometimes."

Lucile laughed and started to respond, but abruptly stopped walking. Advancing toward them was a small group of chattering men and women, all focused on a small, slender brunette in their midst, a striking young woman wearing a casually cut shirtwaist of white linen and a bright-red jersey skirt that swung briskly back and forth. On her head was a small cloche hat. People turned and stared, some whispering.

"What is *she* doing on this ship?" Lucile muttered.

"Who is she?" Tess asked as they walked by. She did not miss the frozen smiles the two women exchanged.

"Another one of those milliners who design ridiculous costumes and think they know couture. She's trying to get attention for something she calls sportswear, which is just slapping together mismatched outfits like the one she was wearing." Lucile was walking more rapidly now, heading back to her stateroom. Tess rushed to keep up.

Lucile pushed open the stateroom door, letting it slam against the wall, startling Cosmo, who had been sitting peacefully in a chair, smoking his pipe.

"That woman upstart from Manchester who steals my ideas is on the ship," she said.

"No need to get upset," Cosmo replied. "She hasn't even a crown at her disposal to open a shop. She's no competition—"

"No competition? She's working this crowd for all the attention and contacts she can get. Just like that other upstart, the one they call Chanel." Lucile pulled

off her bracelet and threw it onto the dressing table, barely missing the mirror. The diamonds hit with a clatter that made Tess wince.

Cosmo remained calm. He took a long puff on his pipe. "Lucy, you are top quality," he said. "You are *the* Lady Duff Gordon, and everyone on this ship knows no other designer can touch you. Now calm down."

Only then did Lucile seem to remember Tess's presence. "Sorry for this peek behind the veil, my dear," she said. "Even the regal can get blindsided. There are always people out to get you in my business, something you might as well learn now as later. I've fought for what I have—" She glanced at Cosmo. "With the support of my dear husband, of course."

"My wife, as usual, is being a bit flamboyant," he said evenly. "Really, dear, you are much too agitated."

It was as if they were exchanging familiar lines, like actors in a play, and Tess was their audience.

"Of course. I'm a successful woman,

with everything I've ever wanted. And I intend it to stay that way."

"Nicely said." Cosmo put his pipe down in the ashtray. "Now I'm going to check and see if we are at the captain's table tonight. That would please you, I'm sure."

Lucile gave him a bright smile. "Lovely, dear."

The tense atmosphere in the room was easing, and Tess felt that she could breathe again. She stood silently as Cosmo smiled in that serene, detached way of his, pecked his wife on the cheek, picked up his glasses, and left the room.

"You have to humor them, you know." Lucile sighed lightly as the door closed. "Men can be boring, but they are necessary. One needs to learn to work around them. Don't you think so?"

There was no casual answer, not with the gap between their stations. Tess stayed quiet.

Lucile walked over to the dressing table, picked up her bracelet, and casually tossed it into her jewelry box. "You didn't answer me," she said.

"I wouldn't know, Madame," Tess finally said.

"Why not? Are you saying you've had no experience with men?"

"Not much."

"Oh, come now, Tess. What about those village boys your mother warned you away from?" Lucile was opening a gold compact filled with powder, and Tess could see her hand shaking slightly.

"I'm sorry about the other designer," she said. "Surely she's no threat to you."

"Everybody, at some point or another, is a threat," Lucile said, patting powder lightly across her nose and cheekbones. "That's why I must keep them all on their toes. It's an act, Tess. And it has worked so far." She looked up, her eyes suddenly almost watery. "I know what you want, and I'm going to try to help you get there. But it takes more than talent."

"Thank you," Tess said.

"So when will I get those references you promised?" Lucile asked abruptly, turning back to her dressing table,

reaching now for a bottle of crimson nail polish.

"References?" Tess could only imagine the anger of the mistress of the house she had fled in Cherbourg, who would certainly have nothing good to say about her. References? There were none. Surely Madame had sensed that.

Lucile looked up from dabbing lacquer onto her nails and laughed. "You should see your face, Tess. Don't worry, I'm not interested in references—I was just playing with you. Tell me more about your life. I'm curious—not many a young woman would have jumped to leave her country on a minute's notice as fast as you did. Why?"

"I actually planned it. For a long time."

"Were you running away from something?" Lucile asked lightly.

"Just cleaning closets and toilets. And not getting paid for my real work."

"Any regrets?"

"Absolutely none." Tess said this with such fervor that Lucile laughed again.

"Well, that's good, because my brain is busy cutting you into pattern pieces.

What do you think of that? We're going to stitch a new Tess Collins together. Maybe we'll find a way to hone those sewing skills of yours."

"I will do my best, truly."

"I'm quite sure you will." Lucile covered a yawn with her hand. "Now if you don't mind, as soon as this polish dries I'm going to take a short nap."

------

Tess couldn't stop thinking about their exchange afterward, examining her memory for holes. Had she read Madame correctly? It seemed a promise had been made; surely she hadn't let her own hopes read too much into Lucile's words. But she felt it; it was there, a benevolent mood. And when Madame informed the purser that she wanted Tess's room moved up from the E deck to the A deck? It was to keep her available for longer hours, of course, but what a thrill it was to hear the news. She ran down the stairs to steerage, to the narrow bunk—only one of many

crammed together—where she had tucked her few possessions under the mattress. She squeezed past a man coughing thickly into a dirty handkerchief and shut her ears to the high-pitched bickering of two women fighting over a blanket. She inhaled deeply, defiantly. She was breathing in the rank odors of this dark, windowless place for the last time.

"You're leaving us?" the girl in the next cot said, a hint of disappointment in her tone. "Didn't see much of you, but you're my age and I thought we could talk every now and then. I'm going to my uncle's in a place called the Bowery. Know anything about it? I'll work in his saloon, but he says it's respectable in America. I've still got some apples. Share one?"

Tess shook her head and smiled. "I can't now, but maybe later."

"Oh, I don't think once you go upstairs you'll ever come back down here."

It was true, of course. Tess felt warm color in her cheeks. "Goodbye," she said. "Maybe we'll meet in New York."

-------

# APRIL 14, 1912

The day was glorious. Madame was napping again in the late afternoon, and Tess luxuriated in her new access to the first-class deck. She was allowed to sit on Madame's deck chair and watch the promenade of privileged people as they strolled by, laughing and chatting, people whose names she should learn. She had never been in a place where everyone seemed on holiday, and if she wanted to stay in their world she had to educate herself.

And then, strolling toward her, she saw John Jacob Astor and his wife. Such an elegant pair! The long, tapered fingers of Mrs. Astor's left hand rested gently in the crook of her husband's arm and her face was tipped toward the lowering sun, as if basking in its light. Tess couldn't take her eyes off them, mesmerized by this first look at what shipboard clothing was for the very, very rich. He wore immaculately creased trousers and a mohair cardigan over a crisp shirt and tie. She, on the other hand, gave little quarter to

such casualness—her pale-green gown of cord silk, so perfect with her glowing skin and soft chocolate-brown hair, drew envious glances from other women strollers. The men passing by nodded greetings, some casting equally envious glances at Mr. Astor. "He bagged quite a trophy out of that messy divorce scandal," one murmured to another.

Some time later, in the first glow of what was clearly going to be a spectacular sunset, she copied their stroll across the deck, trying to imitate Mrs. Astor's swanlike glide. The other passengers had all disappeared back into their staterooms to prepare for the evening. How had that lucky woman floated so effortlessly? Tess tried, but couldn't quite rein in her own hurried stride.

She heard a chuckle and glanced over her shoulder. A sailor was watching. And, yes, he was the same one who had quietly mopped up when she spilled the tea. Tall, about her own age, somewhat thin, even with those sturdy shoulders. His hair was unruly, but swept aside with careless confidence.

And his eyes were just as warm and alert as she remembered—the kind of eyes that didn't miss much. They were indeed as blue as the sea.

"Not bad, but you'd do best walking your own way," he said. "Don't want to fall on your nose, do you?"

Tess lifted her chin high. "No chance of that," she said, adding, "I do thank you for cleaning up the mess I made the other day."

"You handled it well. Walked away quite proper, and no giggles in your wake."

"My mother's advice was always to hold my head up."

He nodded. "First time you let it hang, somebody hammers it down further. Don't be fooled by these people; they're just rich show-offs."

"Mrs. Astor has true grace," Tess countered.

"Maybe she does, but so do you," he said gently, studying her face. "You just don't know it." He stepped forward and crooked his arm. "Shall we stroll?" he asked, half teasingly.

With only an instant of hesitation, she

accepted the invitation. They walked a few paces, alone on that deck as the brilliant sky turned orange and gold, and then, laughing, he coaxed her into a skip. A bubble of pleasure filled her throat. She could release herself for this, for just a few seconds, couldn't she?

Only a moment, a quick moment. When they stopped, he put a finger to his lips. "Good day, ma'am," he said, his voice lively with humor. "See? You can play, too. And I'll never tell." He headed back to work, whistling as he bent to pick up a heavy coil of rope, then throwing it over his shoulder.

He's a village boy, Tess told herself as she leaned against the railing and watched the dance of light on the water. A seagoing version, with a more jaunty spirit than most. And quite beautiful eyes.

She stood there for a long time, mesmerized by the expanse of limitless water reaching to a fiery red horizon. She was filled with yearning—for what, she wasn't sure. But if she listened she could still hear the seductive, melan-

choly whistle of the trains that had wound their way out of the valley and off to the larger world when she was a child. She had always wanted to be on one of them. Most people had pursed their lips, either disapprovingly or angrily, when she talked about going away. Thank goodness she realized early, somehow, that they were mostly afraid. And never, never was she going to let herself be afraid.

Tess ate dinner alone in her cabin, listening to the faint music of the ship's orchestra as the musicians played in the first-class dining saloon. Around ten, she went out on deck for a stroll under the stars, enjoying the solitude, although unable to resist peeking into the dining room. How huge it was, the width of the entire ship, she had been told. The walls and the graceful pillars were a creamy white; the dining chairs covered in a sumptuous emerald-green velvet. Wineglasses sparkled in the glow of the slender white lamps on each table, their light reflected back again through the tall, arched windows that opened onto D deck. How beauti-

ful it was. All those confident, wealthy men and women, most of them in evening dress, laughing, lifting glasses filled with brandy. She found herself trying to piece together their stories.

There was that couple that had boarded ahead of her, sitting by themselves, heads close, murmuring. They were dancers, Madame had told her—Jean and Jordan Darling—yes, lithe, beautiful, coming home to New York for a Broadway play and, everyone said, genuinely in love. "A little past their prime," Madame declared matter-of-factly. "I've dressed her for several shows, but I suspect she can't afford me anymore." And there was that handsome man in the tan coat she had met in the gymnasium. In evening dress, he was just leaving the captain's table, which meant that he, too, must be important. His name, Madame had told her when describing the more important personages on board, was Jack Bremerton. "A Chicago millionaire. No one quite knows how he made his fortune," she said. "In banking, or some-

thing equally shady. Several wives; rumor is, he's leaving the current one."

A dining-room steward carrying a tray of glasses suddenly shoved past Tess, pushing her off balance. He stumbled, the tray falling from his hands with a tremendous clatter. At that moment the chairman of the White Star Line strode around the deck corner, head turned to talk to one of the ship's officers. In evening dress, he looked more like a bony crane than ever. The tray crashed to the floor, splattering brandy onto Bruce Ismay's clothes as the glasses smashed into fragments on the deck.

"It was her fault, sir," the steward said, thinking fast, pointing to Tess. "She splatted a whole tea service on deck the other day."

"That was clumsy of you, young woman," snapped the officer. "Good Lord, you *are* the one who made that mess. Why weren't you looking where you were going?"

"I'm sorry," Tess said in surprise.

"You need to apologize to Mr. Ismay, who is, in case you don't know, the

chairman of this shipping company," the officer said. "You're Lady Duff Gordon's maid, aren't you? Surely you've been trained better than that."

"I'm not apologizing, sir, for I've done nothing wrong. I'm sorry the accident happened, but I wasn't the cause."

"You're not getting away with this, young woman. I'm going to have to talk to the Duff Gordons about your manners."

"I did nothing," Tess said, growing dismayed.

A voice cut through from the dark near the rail. "Actually, her manners are far better than yours, and I suspect her sense of balance is, too. I believe the apology is due to *her,* Officer. Are you in the habit of berating young women— or just those in service?"

Flustered, the officer turned on the steward. "Go get a towel and clean this up," he ordered. As the steward scurried away, the officer and Ismay walked on, and Tess heard him say, "These last-minute hires, you know . . ."

"That was a nice scene, wasn't it?"

Tess looked behind her and saw the

mysterious Mr. Bremerton. He had left the captain's table and was standing by the teak railing, polished and handsome in his evening clothes.

"Officious little men with power—one of the plagues of the world." He shook his head. "Good lesson, though—position doesn't make a gentleman. Or evening clothes, for that matter. But you know that, I hope."

She did, but it might not be wise to say that right now. "I really don't want any trouble," she said.

"You didn't cringe. That took some backbone."

"I needed to defend myself."

"Or what?" He looked at her keenly.

"Or it would just happen again." And again and again. No use trying to explain.

He bowed slightly. "Very wise. I'm glad to see you—I kept wishing after our time in the exercise room that I had asked your name. May I now?"

She couldn't help smiling. He must think she had been undone by riding that camel. "My name is Tess Collins."

He peered closely. "Of course. Since

we seem to keep meeting, let me introduce myself. I'm Jack Bremerton, and I
have no business judging others, to tell
the truth. What do you think of your
voyage so far?"

"I've loved it, Mr. Bremerton," she
said, walking over to the rail where he
stood. "It's a feast for the eyes and the
hands."

"The hands?"

"I love touching the draperies and
the silk tablecloths and all the beautiful
fabrics, and thinking about where I
would put them, how I would cut and
tuck them."

"You sound like you want to be a designer yourself."

"I'm going to be, someday." Just the
fact of saying it to this stranger made
her move up a notch in believing it.

"A lady who is willing to stand up for
herself has a dignity that will take her a
long way. By the way, please call me
Jack."

"I don't feel comfortable doing that,
Mr. Bremerton." She tried the word out
in her mind. *Jack.*

"I accept that, Miss Collins." He

smiled. "Hope you change your mind at some point. Isn't it a great night? Just look at those stars."

"They are splendid." They were standing so close, she could smell the faint musk of his shaving lotion. Was this really happening? Was this impressive, powerful man actually talking to her?

"It's a pleasure to be watching them with you." He glanced back in the direction of the dining room. "It's all very stuffy in there, you know. I left after the duck breasts; don't like figs. Or oyster martinis. It looks beautiful from out here, but nothing glitters quite as much when you get close up."

"You know I can't go in there, don't you?"

"So they say." He seemed to be thinking it over. "Do we agree?"

"What do you mean?"

"That a coterie of snobs can deny you entry into this stiff-backed saloon?"

"They can make the rules they want to make; it's not for me to decide."

"Well, I disagree."

She shivered. Was there a way to tell

him that in her heart, tucked away quite privately, she had the same rebellious thought?

He held out his arm, his eyes watchful but revealing nothing. Before she knew it, he was guiding her through the glass doors and right into the magical dining room. With one careless hand, he swept the room. "Here you are, Miss Collins. Shall I signal a waiter for two glasses of champagne?"

Oh, the carpet was soft. And now she could reach out and actually touch one of the velvet chairs. She could inhale the aroma of many perfumes, see the gold-crusted dining plates filled with exotic food, hear the light talk and laughter that rippled across the well-behaved room, laughter as sparkling as the sea. So much, all at once. White-clad waiters moving solicitously among the tables; diamond rings flashing each time a glass was hoisted; men hovering close to women in low-cut gowns. She didn't recognize the music the orchestra was playing, but she loved it and knew she would never forget it.

And then she spied Cosmo and Madame. *What if they saw her?*

She turned quickly and walked back toward the door. "I can't stay here," she said, a flush burning deep into her cheeks.

Bremerton made no objection, just followed her back out to the deck. "I'm a betting man, Miss Collins," he said quietly as they stood again beneath the stars. "After watching you stand up to that oaf tonight, may I make a prediction? Once you get to America, you won't be closed out of any dining rooms again. And you won't be carrying a serving tray for very long."

"Maybe I'll be busy learning how to play squash," she said, suddenly encouraged.

He laughed. "Well, it's not so popular in my country. I'm certainly glad to be going back. No offense, but I get tired of Europe. Too stodgy. Moves too slow."

"What sort of work do you do?" she ventured tentatively.

"Right now I'm setting up branches to sell the Model T."

He saw her puzzlement. A motor car,

he explained. But, more than that, it was *the* automobile in America. A masterpiece for the masses, actually, and Henry Ford, the man who thought of it, was a genius. He had plans for an assembly line, and soon he would be producing an automobile every ninety minutes.

"Amazing." She knew she should leave soon, but she didn't want to go.

"You've got me talking tonight," he said reflectively, looking into the black sea. "Maybe it's the stars. Is there a young man waiting for you in New York?"

She shook her head. "No, I don't need that. Madame will help me get work."

"My money is on you. By the way, I don't play squash, either. Have a nice evening, and I think we should find the opportunity to chat again." He reached out a hand and touched hers lightly, briefly. Then he gave her a salute and walked off.

She headed back to her cabin, stopping, turning, looking back. Jack had also stopped.

"Good night again," he said.

"Good night." She could think of nothing else to say. Taking one more deep breath of the crisp night air, she headed for her cabin. She had actually carried off a conversation with a gentleman who wasn't snapping his fingers for service or groping up her skirts. Someone with polish and manners who treated her as if she were an equal. Surely rich. What would it be like to be rich? Oh yes, she hoped they would talk again. He was obviously cultured; he would know so much more than she about books and music and plays. Still, she would have been tempted to linger longer with him just now if it hadn't felt faintly improper. And why did she have the excited thought that he felt the same?

She hurried down the stairs, consoling herself with the anticipation of a singular pleasure ahead—for in her cabin was one of the most beautiful gowns she had ever imagined, let alone owned.

Just before leaving for dinner, Lady Duff Gordon had lifted a beautiful silk

dressing gown wrapped carefully in tissue paper from her trunk and handed it to Tess. It was made of fabric as billowy as smoke, an artful weaving of one deepening color, starting from a bodice of palest lavender to a skirt of regal purple. "Here, dear, something elegant and pretty for you," she had said.

Tess was stunned. "For me?"

Lady Duff Gordon, looking pleased with herself, was already heading out the door, leaving behind a rich aura of perfume. "Why not?" she sang out over her shoulder.

Tess took the gown to the light, examining its worksmanship with awe. Such artful seaming. Then she wrapped herself in her fairy tale. She put on her lovely gown and twirled to the music, pretending that she, too, was on the dance floor, with Jack Bremerton, wishing only that her mother could see her now, this minute, here on the cusp of a new life filled with immense possibility. She must write home as soon as they arrived in New York. She had scribbled down her family address at the Cherbourg dock for one of Madame's em-

ployees, asking him to tell her parents where she was going, but his attitude had been slightly disdainful and Tess, drifting off into sleep shortly before midnight, wondered if the message had ever been sent. . . . Her eyes closed. Time enough to think about that in the morning.

## 2

It wasn't much of a jolt. More like a slight bump, that was all. Nothing alarming. At first, the hum of the ship's engines continued. Then a sudden silence; they had stopped.

Tess lifted herself up on one elbow, instantly drawn out of a deep sleep. Strange, when you knew something was wrong. Her skin tingled; her muscles tensed. Once before, the night her mother's last baby died, she had awakened like this, already fully sick at heart. Then it had been a thin, tired wail that warned her; tonight, a bump. She

jumped from bed, fully awake, and dressed quickly. Whatever was happening, she had better be ready for it.

A few cabins away, Bruce Ismay stiffened at the sound. He knew the rhythms of most ships, and there was something not quite right about that bump. It was nothing, probably, but he didn't like it. He checked the time on his pocket watch. They certainly didn't need any delays, not at this point. He decided to go on deck and hunt up Captain Smith, just to make sure all was in order.

Jean Darling shook her husband awake. She had been cold, shivering in a terrible dream where she was running somewhere and slipping, and something was chasing her, and then came that jolt, as if the ship were shivering, too. Jordan put his arm around her and tried to draw her down with him into the warm pillows, but she pulled back.

"Jordan, let's get up," she whispered.

"Why?"

"I want to be dressed properly if something is happening."

He laughed. "Now that's a novel way

of telling me you're intimidated by the presence of Lucile Duff Gordon on this ship."

Jack Bremerton felt it and didn't care. He sat at the desk in his cabin, poring over the pile of business documents he had brought with him, already impatient for the crossing to be over. He wanted nothing more than to immerse himself in the Ford Company's details and get to California, away from the sticky mess of his personal life, which probably proved the truth of his soon to be ex-wife's accusation that he was always running away. He was giving her plenty of money with his apologies, which was more than the pompous ass who scolded that young maid tonight had managed to muster. Interesting woman—hard to forget the abundance of soft hair framing her lively eyes and luminous skin. And such determined ways. Probably worth more than most of the pretenders on this ship, though she didn't know it. So fresh and young. She made him uncomfortably aware of his own advancing middle age.

Lucile felt it as she leaned across her

dressing table to remove her moonstone earrings after returning from dinner. She saw the liquid in her perfume decanter shiver and then calm. She would have pointed it out to Cosmo, but he was already in bed. How did he fall asleep so quickly? She so hated his snoring. She hesitated, fingering her earrings, waiting to see if there would be another bump. All seemed fine. Not knowing herself why she did it, she slipped the earrings into their velvet drawstring bag and tucked them into her shoe.

------

First, a discreet knock at the Duff Gordons' door.

"Ma'am, we've had a small accident," the steward outside said quickly to Lucile. "Nothing to worry about. We bumped into an iceberg, but all is well. However, you might want to come on deck."

Lucile was not fooled for a minute. The steward knew nothing—he was just prattling a reassuring line.

"Get dressed, Cosmo," she said, shaking her husband's shoulder. "And put your life belt on. I'm going to wake Tess."

She was lacing up her life belt, muttering about its clumsy design, when Tess knocked urgently on the door. "We should hurry," Tess said as the door opened. She made no attempt to smooth away the troubled frown on her face. It wasn't fitting for her to be urging speed on the Duff Gordons, but social conventions seemed not to matter right now.

"It's Cosmo who is taking his sweet time," Lucile snapped.

The hallway was filling fast with people in nightcaps and pajamas, looking comically like stuffed teddy bears in their life belts; there wasn't a silver cigarette holder in sight. Stripped of their grand clothes, they looked quite ordinary, Tess thought fleetingly.

Cosmo finally appeared, stuffing his shirttails into his trousers.

"This way," Tess said, beckoning them to the stairs. Cosmo and Lucile followed her without objection, joining

a good-naturedly grumbling crowd making its slow way to the upper deck. Most of the chatter was relaxed, if a little fretful. Some passengers were complaining they'd never get back to sleep after this silly drill, or whatever it was. Such a bother. When an English surgeon asked Lucile politely if she had watched that smashing poker game in the drawing room after dinner—so exciting—she murmured something pleasant. He turned to his companion, a man still in full evening dress: "Say, are we on for the gymnasium after breakfast? Hope they serve those pancakes again—the children loved them."

Just behind Lucile was the woman she had disapprovingly called the "coarse Mrs. Brown," the one who had turned a place named Leadville into a fortune in gold. She was laughing at the sight of her fellow passengers in various stages of dress. "Can't tell a viscount from a duke in this crowd!" she boomed. "Everybody's britches look the same!"

Nobody else laughed, although there

were a few titters. Much of it, it seemed to Tess, at Mrs. Brown's expense.

They were at the top of the stairs.

At first, things seemed calm. People were clustering on the deck, shivering and chatting nervously. "We hit an iceberg," a boy said to no one in particular, holding out a large chunk of ice in his hand, as if making an offering. "See? I grabbed a piece as we passed by. We all did, down below. We were playing."

As the minutes passed, with no one seeming to know what to do, Tess realized that crew members were struggling to untangle ropes and canvas covers, slipping on the deck, shouting to one another.

**Lifeboats. They were launching lifeboats.**

As if by signal, people began bumping one another and scrambling toward the railing, shouting as they looked down into the sea. Suddenly there was an acrid, sweaty smell of human fear in the salt air.

Minutes passed. A shiver worked its way through Tess's slender body—this was no drill, no joke. This was real. Her

heart beat painfully fast as she tried to think. Sailors, jackets open, eyes wild, red in the face—a couple of them aimlessly waving guns—began shouting orders at the growing crowd of passengers. Tess heard a shot, which started people screaming. Children were wailing as mothers began lifting them into the lifeboats, flimsy contraptions swaying high above the water. One by one, the lifeboats were disappearing over the side for their descent, crowded with passengers.

Tess looked into the distance and saw, drifting far astern, retreating into the darkness, a tower of jagged ice, sullen and cold. If there had been in her mind any doubt before, it was gone now; they had to get into a lifeboat. She glanced around wildly, realizing with a sinking heart that the lifeboats on this part of the ship were already gone.

"I'll check the bow," she said to Lucile and Cosmo, both of whom looked stunned. Lucile screamed some instruction over the noise of the crowd, but Tess paid no attention, running as fast as she could, sliding on the deck,

stumbling and dodging people in her way.

If anything, the chaos was worse at the bow. The unlaunched boats she saw there were full. A woman struggling for a place began screaming as the boat swung out and began descending without her.

"She's crazy, I'm not getting in that rickety-looking thing," exclaimed another woman, pulling her coat tight around an evening gown of emerald silk. "This ship is unsinkable; my husband told me so. He knows all about this kind of thing." It was too hard to look into her eyes.

Tess watched in horror as the scene grew worse. Jean and Jordan Darling, holding on to each other, were arguing with one of the seamen loading a lifeboat. "Only women allowed!" he bawled, pushing Jordan away. There was panic now; there were no rules. Somehow everyone seemed to realize at the same time that the ship was tipping alarmingly and there weren't enough lifeboats for the milling crowd on the deck. People were running from stern to bow and

back again, desperate to find a place. Tess saw Bruce Ismay calmly stepping into a lifeboat, keeping his head down, ignoring the stares of those who had been denied the last seats. But no one challenged his exercise of privilege. And then she saw Jack Bremerton passing a flailing, crying child into the eager hands of a woman in one of the lifeboats. He did so carefully, almost tenderly; his demeanor calm, his eyes somber.

"Mr. Bremerton!" she screamed.

He turned and saw her, his eyes widening. "Get in a boat now!" he yelled. "Go starboard!" The crowd surged, and she lost sight of him.

"Calm down, there are rescue ships on the way!" yelled a seaman.

"I told you," said a woman eagerly to her husband as she shivered in the cold. "They'll come for us, we're safer here than in those boats. That's right, isn't it?" He wrapped his arms around her, not answering as, one by one, the lifeboats started down to the water.

Tess turned around and ran back; if

there was any chance now of getting off the ship, it had to be from the stern.

By the time she got back up the slanting deck, Lucile had taken action. She had grabbed a rope holding what looked like a huge, ragged piece of collapsed canvas. It seemed dangerous and fragile, but it was the only thing resembling a lifeboat that had not yet been launched. Tess ran to help her hold it steady.

"Here's a boat—why aren't you launching this one?" Lucile yelled at the officer nearest to her.

He didn't answer. Lucile looked furious. There was no order now. Everyone was running and screaming, families were being separated, and the harried seamen shouting to one another did not seem to know what they should be doing.

"Officer, do you hear us? You're the one in charge here, aren't you?"

The officer, whose name was Murdoch, jerked around and saw her. "Yes, ma'am," he said. His forehead was glistening with sweat and his eyes were almost popping from his head.

"You've got a perfectly good boat here and I want to get in it," she declared. Even here, in this chaos, she was an imposing figure.

"Lifeboat One? It's a collapsible, a weak one at that," he said.

"Nonsense, it will float, won't it? Isn't that the *point* here?"

He hesitated. Then, "Sullivan, get that boat ready for Lady Duff Gordon!" he yelled to a tall sailor with pock-marked skin. "I'm putting you in charge of the damn boat!"

Lucile climbed in first, motioning Tess and Cosmo to follow. Tess hoisted herself up onto the deck rail and looked around. Two women were hurrying toward them, one draped in a floor-length shawl.

"Get in, you two," Murdoch said. They crawled aboard, and only when the smaller of the two looked up did Tess see that it was Jean Darling, the dancer. "Any more women?" yelled Murdoch.

There was a hesitation, and then a sudden, unruly scramble of seamen jumped into the boat.

"You bastards, can any of you row?" yelled the exasperated officer. "Bonney, you can row, get in there!"

"I've got work to do here, send somebody else!" the man named Bonney shouted as he untied the lifeboat's ropes.

Tess caught a quick glimpse of him— it was the sailor who had promenaded her across the deck only hours before.

"Do as I tell you, that's an order!"

Bonney hesitated.

"I said *move!*"

Bonney jumped. Landing on all fours, he straightened, saw Tess teetering on the deck rail, and reached out his hand. "For God's sake, quick—" he said.

The ship was settling more rapidly, tipping downward, bow first.

"Will you get on with it?" Lucile gasped angrily. "Launch this thing—I'm feeling quite ill!" She clutched her stomach as the boat rocked back and forth, her face pale.

"Yes, ma'am," said the officer. "Launch the damn boat," he yelled. *"Now!"*

"Wait, miss!"

Tess, about to jump in, turned and

saw Mr. Hoffman stumbling toward her with his two sons, their legs flailing, one under each arm. "Take my children—save them, please." His hair was damp, glued by the sea spray across his forehead. His eyes were imploring.

She reached for the children. Michel clung to his father, crying. With great effort, Hoffman broke the child's grip and handed him to Tess. She had both boys now and turned to jump into the boat.

Too late. She looked down at Lifeboat One as it plunged seaward, almost empty, lurching violently back and forth. All was unfolding like a dream. Below her, the sailor named Bonney was yelling at her, his arms outstretched.

"Jump! Jump!"

She teetered, now holding two frightened boys; it was too late. The lifeboat had already descended some fifty feet. She looked down into Lucile's upturned, shocked face. It was over, wasn't it? It was over. . . .

"Don't stand there staring, get in that one." Murdoch shoved her in the direction of a boat already partially launched,

but with its ropes tangled. "You've got a few seconds before they get it going again."

Tess slid and stumbled across the deck, managing to hold on to the boys. The boat was crammed with women and children.

"No room, no room!" shouted a sailor.

"Of course, there is." The buxom Mrs. Brown pushed him out of her way and reached up to Tess. "Pass the children to me and jump!" she commanded.

Tess obeyed. Two wild tosses; one jump, eyes closed. The boat began its seventy-foot descent from the listing ship, swinging and shuddering as they passed the crowded second- and third-class decks. People stared at them blankly, their faces white with shock, as if survival were part of another world far away.

But as the boat swayed and lurched past them, they began shouting.

"Take my little girl, take her!" yelled a man holding a small child in his arms.

"You are leaving us!" screamed a woman, pointing an accusing finger.

Tess could have touched some of

them as the boat lurched back and forth. *Why wasn't she with them?* She saw a flash of hope in the eyes of the man holding the child. Their gaze caught. He was young, worn-looking, maybe a farmer. Blue eyes, an unkempt beard. The child had a sloppy yellow ribbon in her hair, hanging lopsided now over one eye; she kept pushing it back. Her eyes were big with fright.

"For the love of God, take her!" the father screamed, holding the girl up, still looking at Tess.

Tess told the boys to hug each other, then leaned forward and stretched her arms out as far as she could. The child's hands were like small, plump peaches, soft and round.

"Watch out," yelled Murdoch above, peering over the side. "Push away, don't let any of them grab you or you'll buckle!"

A sailor thrust his fist hard against the side of the ship, sending the life-boat swinging. The chance was gone. Tess covered her face as they descended into the black waters below.

She expected a jolt. But the lifeboat

hit a surprisingly calm sea, settling in gently, and began drifting slowly away from the ship. Music was still rising into the cold, still air from the A deck. Tess had glimpsed the musicians—somber, playing steadily, braced against deck chairs to keep their balance—during the boat's turbulent descent.

"Praise God, we made it," cried one of the seamen.

It took a few moments for them all to realize that no one was rowing, a few moments more before the crew members began shouting at one another.

"Who's taking the oars?" yelled one.

"I'm not an oarsman, and who put you in charge anyway?" said another.

"Someone has to row, you bloody fool," a hoarse voice responded. "The officer on deck put me in charge, so get to the oars."

"Never done it," the other yelled back. "Jesus, are we going to sink?"

"I can't row—nobody ever showed me how," said a third seaman. Even here on the water his clothes reeked of tobacco and sweat.

"Oh, for God's sake." Scrambling for-

ward, Mrs. Brown grabbed an oar and pointed Tess to the one on the other side. "Let's show these cowards what it means to do your job!"

Tess grabbed the oar and heaved it forward. She had rowed enough times across the pond below the manor house; she could do this. "Get the back oars!" she yelled at the seamen.

One of the crewmen fumbled with the back set of oars, swearing softly. "Damn things weigh a ton," he mumbled. "But we've gotta get out of here or the ship will suck us under."

Tess looked back at the *Titanic*. The huge ship was tipping upward, its stern slowly rising into the air—a sight beyond belief. Tess could see human forms, not faces now, rushing back and forth on the decks and bodies jumping into the sea.

"*Row!*" she gasped. She wielded her oar, pulling as hard as she could, sure the muscles of her back were shredding apart. Suddenly, a tug—she looked down at the sea and into a human face.

A woman, skirts ballooning around

her, was holding on to the oar with one hand, clutching what looked like a bundle of rags with the other. "We've got to help her!" Tess screamed, dropping the oar and throwing herself flat, grabbing the woman as the boat began rocking violently.

"Hang on, I've got her!" It was Mrs. Brown, reaching out into the water with surprisingly strong arms. Together they hauled the woman in, the added weight forcing the boat deeper into the water. They were overfull as it was, dear Lord, would this sink them? But the boat stabilized and Tess grabbed her oar again.

The ship was now almost perpendicular to the starlit night sky, a straight vertical slash, hovering like a dancer on point. The electric lights in the cabins and on the decks were still blazing, and a strange green glow from the still lit lights of the submerged part of the ship illuminated the black sea. It was, oddly, an incredibly beautiful sight.

"It's going down—move, move, or it'll take us with it," yelled a voice from the stern of the lifeboat. The seamen

scrambled for the back oars, no complaints now.

"Oh, God!" screamed a matronly woman with white hair, a spiraling wail that spoke for them all. The ship, bow first, was slowly sinking into the water. People began tumbling like broken dolls from the decks, flopping, flailing into the sea. There was a huge cracking sound—and then the *Titanic* disappeared, swallowed in one huge gulp by the sea, taking with it all light, leaving the survivors in total blackness relieved only by the cold twinkling of the stars.

No sucking whirlpool—how had they escaped that? The lifeboats floated on still waters. The sea was so smooth, it reflected the stars above.

"It is two-twenty in the morning," a sailor said hoarsely. "April fifteenth." Strange, that someone would at that moment have the foresight to check his watch.

Then, rising from the water, an unforgettable, keening sound. It resembled the wail of a bitter wind curving around a snug house, the eerie sound that

makes one shiver in bed, grateful to be inside.

"Not this," wailed the woman with white hair. "My husband is out there, he must be."

"Not just yours," said another voice quietly.

Helpless, no one spoke. They barely dared to move for fear of sinking themselves.

Tess turned her attention to the still form of the woman in the bottom of the boat. Since being pulled from the sea, had she moved? Gently trying to turn her over, Tess saw that she held not a bundle of rags but a baby in a blanket—one that had perhaps been safely asleep in a cradle only an hour before. The child must be freezing. She took off her jacket to use as a wrap, even as the truth seeped into her brain. The baby was dead.

Tess stared at the small face, with its crown of silky hair. A boy or a girl, she didn't know. She looked now to the mother, realizing that she wasn't stirring, and felt a sense of relief when she saw that the woman, too, was dead,

and would be spared the pain of mourning for her baby. Tess wrapped the baby in her jacket, put it in its mother's arms, and tried to weep, but no tears would come.

# 3

## CITY ROOM, *NEW YORK TIMES*
## NEW YORK CITY
## APRIL 15
## 1:20 A.M. EST

A late-night quiet had descended over the newsroom. All the yelling and running and staccato typing that swelled to its usual climax before deadline was over. Carr Van Anda, a gruff, paunchy man with no peer in his ability to pull a story together on deadline, was not one to waste time on stray observations. But now, surveying his domain, the *New York Times* editor was struck with the thought that this grubby place looked as exhausted as he felt.

Cigarette butts on the floor. Papers crumpled, tossed in the general direc-

tion of wastebaskets, scattered like dirty snowballs everywhere. Only a few deskmen left hunched over the city desk. He had a fondness for the night crew; they tended to keep bottles of bourbon in their half-open file drawers at which they nipped leisurely through the night. He hadn't been averse to the offer of a nip or two himself on some of these long night shifts. The bourbon had vanished in the stepped-up pace of the past twenty-four hours, at least among the veterans. No one could afford to lose his edge on a primary night. Now the returns were in, and the morning edition was locked up. It was going to be a great fight. So Roosevelt won Pennsylvania tonight. But Taft had plenty of tricks up his sleeve and the two men hated each other. They were going to split the Republican vote, which meant a great opportunity for the Democrats, no question. Lots of good stories ahead.

He eyed a bottle propped discreetly in the desk drawer of his city editor, leaned back in his chair, and savored

the anticipation of lighting up a fresh cigar. His job was done. He could relax.

"Mr. Van Anda, this just came in." The night copyboy, his face a shade paler than usual, thrust a wireless bulletin into the editor's hand. Van Anda scanned it rapidly, noting that it was from the Marconi station in Newfoundland.

"You read this?" he asked.

"Yes, sir," the copyboy said, speaking tentatively. "It's the biggest ship in the world, sir. How could the *Titanic* hit an iceberg?"

"Son, anything can happen at any time." Some of these green kids never quite seemed to understand that was *why* there was a news business. "Now get me everything we've got in the archives on that ship. And"—he stopped him with a raised hand—"bring me anything we've got on iceberg collisions."

The bulletins in their metal cylinders began tumbling down the chute from the wire room above, clattering one after another into the *New York Times*

city room, each one adding details to the escalating crisis. The front page of the early edition was opened; reporters were writing fast and the Linotype operators were back in business, waiting for orders.

Van Anda lifted his head after reading one report and listened. The chute was silent.

"Is that all?" he asked.

Nobody answered.

He stared down at the report in his hands: a scrambled transmission from the *Titanic* had come in at 12:27, asking for help, but it cut off abruptly in midsentence.

"Almost an hour ago," he muttered as he read through the morgue files, listening for the clatter of a cylinder. He paid special attention to the specifications for the *Titanic,* counting and recounting the official number of required lifeboats. No matter what scenario might unfold, he realized, there weren't enough. Stupid bastards—a fancy ship without enough lifeboats.

Van Anda paced. How could there

be total silence for a full hour from the *Titanic*? He strode over to the reporter writing the original story. "We're changing the lead," he said. "Forget the 'worrisome reports' angle. Say the ship has sunk."

"Are we sure?" asked the reporter, mouth agape.

Van Anda sighed. He had been in the business a long time, and he not only trusted his instincts; he saw no need to defend them.

"I am," he said, and started to trudge back to his desk. It was time for that cigar. He turned back with another thought. "Call Pinky Wade. If there are any survivors, I want her on this story. Full-time."

"She won't like that," the reporter said.

She would be furious, Van Anda knew that. But she was the best human-interest reporter he had, even if it meant taking her off the mental-asylum story.

"I know, not enough danger for her. Call her anyway."

-------

ATLANTIC OCEAN
APRIL 15
2:45 A.M. EST

Time had disappeared, floating away on the currents. It was cold, so cold; biting deep into her bones, leaving fragments of ice under the skin of her fingertips and ears. The cold was so impossible, it hurt to breathe. The lifeboat felt as if it bobbed on a bubble of air, as if they were somehow in the sky, not on the black water. Where was the horizon? No one bothered to row anymore. With great effort, Tess tried to bail the frigid water seeping through the floor of the half-sunken boat, even as the pleas for help from the water grew fainter and fainter. She looked at Mrs. Brown, and they shared with their eyes a somber reality. They were low in the water, precariously balanced. Any sudden shifting of weight and they would sink. She stopped bailing as the last cries ended; now the lifeboat moved lazily in circles. A crewman started whistling a mournful tune. She pulled Edmond and Michel close to her, mas-

saging their arms in an effort to impart warmth.

*"Merci,"* Edmond whispered.

"Maybe it'll help a little," she replied. Their clothing had frozen to their bodies.

All across the black sea she could see blurs of white. What was she seeing? The faces of the dead, she realized. Faces above the water. They hadn't drowned; they had frozen. It was a graveyard; their faces were the tombstones.

One by one, the bodies began to vanish, sinking down. Those that still floated stared at the sky with sightless eyes. Finally, nothing. The sea was totally calm, a virtual mirror, reflecting the brilliant stars above. The lifeboat floated on the reflected stars, creating an almost magical suspension, as if plucked from a child's dream.

She could not erase from her mind the face of the man holding out the child with the yellow ribbon in her hair. Another few seconds and she could have done it. She had strong arms and hands; she would have lifted the baby

up, held her tight, and brought her into the boat. The child would have held on, arms around her neck, and she and the father would have looked at each other; there would have been relief on his face and she would have promised him, without words, to protect and endure. . . . She replayed this scenario, over and over, through the long night. Was that child now, with sightless eyes, looking up at the stars?

------

## WASHINGTON, D.C.
## APRIL 15
## 7 A.M. EST

The rising sun filled the eastern sky of Washington with hues of orange and gold, thrusting into silhouette the graceful lines of the U.S. Capitol. Had the founding fathers understood precisely how beautiful this sight would be on a soft spring morning? William Alden Smith, a Michigan man of small stature, whose kinder colleagues considered him a rough-edged, somewhat

naïve product of the Midwest, asked himself that as he stood staring out the window of his fourth-floor office in the Senate Office Building. Soon enough, he would be back to the legal problems of building railroads in Alaska. He liked giving specific attention to detail, something many of his colleagues could not abide. But it was the sight of the Capitol just past sunrise that stirred his soul. Strolling past the guards, wishing them good morning, getting attention back from them—no competition, this time of day—it gave him confidence that he held a niche in this place of power.

A hurried, sharp knock; his door opened before he gave permission. "Senator, did you hear the news?" It was an aide, holding up a copy of the *New York Times* as if it were a shield. "The *Titanic* is supposed to have sunk."

Smith grabbed the paper, scanning the headline.

"The White Star Line is denying the *Times* story," the aide said, glancing quickly down at his scrawled notes. "They're saying everybody is safe and the ship is being towed to port. The

*Syracuse Herald* is going with that, and most of the other papers are jeering at the *Times.* But there hasn't been a word from the ship since twelve-thirty last night."

"They're fools," Smith said sharply. He knew the reputation of Van Anda— if the managing editor of the *New York Times* said the ship had sunk, the ship had sunk. His eyes traveled down the passenger list, riveted by the famous names. Astor, Guggenheim—my God, even Archie Butt, Taft's White House aide. Who survived? "Bring me every bulletin," he ordered.

The aide disappeared and Smith walked to the window, catching his own reflection in the glass. Maybe he wasn't the most imposing legislator in this town, certainly not the most glamorous, but he knew damn well the country would want something more than speeches out of Washington after this catastrophe. There would be a scramble now—everybody in Congress would be grandstanding and orating and introducing addled legislation that would

do nothing. The usual harebrained response.

He stared out his window at the Capitol, drawn as usual to the bronze Statue of Freedom crowning the glistening white dome. He felt his indignation rising. This was a disaster, a moral outrage; it should not be happening. Hearings. There had to be hearings, where the tragedy could be dissected and understood. If he moved fast, he was the man to lead them.

------

## ATLANTIC OCEAN
## SUNRISE, APRIL 15

Lord, the cold. Tess could not feel her feet or her fingers now. There was nothing, nothing, not even a groan or a complaint from the others; they floated between sea and sky.

Then a hoarse cry—a sailor, the darkness lifting, had spied a ship. Tess peered in the breaking dawn and saw other lifeboats for the first time. People began to shout to one another, women

shrieking names of husbands and children. Are you there? Please answer, please be there! One voice, over and over: "Is my Amy in your boat? Amy, Amy, answer your mother." Tess waited to hear a child's answering shout, but there was none.

And then, yes, there was a ship emerging from the dark, coming directly toward them. Tess squinted, barely making out the name on the ship's hull—*Carpathia*. It wasn't a fantasy. "We've made it," Mrs. Brown said quietly. Tears of relief fell, then froze on her cheeks.

They were the second load of survivors brought on board. Canvas bags were lowered into the jammed first lifeboat, and mothers began stuffing struggling, frightened children inside them, trying to console them, then trusting them to the sailors above. Tess put Michel and Edmond in one bag at their insistence, wishing she could comfort them with her halting French. The exhausted women were next. They hung limply, dangling from ropes looped

around their waists, as they were slowly hauled upward.

When it was Tess's turn, she fastened the loop around her waist, tightened the rope, and turned to the sailor who had first helped row. She nodded in the direction of the still figures at the bottom of the boat. "Help me, please," she said. "Don't let them be dumped over the side of the lifeboat."

"Bring them up only to be buried at sea?" he said, surprised.

"Yes."

"That's a bit balmy. I'm not doing it."

"Yes, you are," she said calmly, not flinching. "I don't want either of them abandoned. You'll make sure that doesn't happen, won't you?"

He hesitated. "I'll send them up last," he promised.

Tess began rising in the air, swinging a few times against the hull of the ship, looking up to see dozens of people watching her progress, many with mouths gaping. How good it felt to look at them, to see their faces, their quick movements, their *aliveness*. Then, swinging free, up and onto the deck.

When her numbed legs began to buckle, a woman in a moleskin coat grabbed her.

"There, dear," she murmured. "You'll be all right—we're so happy our captain got here in time. These are your children? But they speak no English, just French." She nodded at Edmond and Michel, clinging to her skirts.

"They aren't mine, and I fear their father didn't make it."

"I'm French—I'll take care of them, dear." She looked past Tess and pointed curiously at the next boat now bumping against the ship's hull. "The other boats were terribly crowded, but that one is almost empty. Odd, isn't it? How did that happen?"

Tess glanced down at the sea, and felt her heart leap. There it was, the lifeboat holding the Duff Gordons—they were safe. A sailor was helping Lucile into one of the slings, and soon she would be on board. Tess trembled with relief.

And there was the sailor, the one named Bonney; he was safe, too. He glanced upward, and their gazes

caught. She waved, and he broke into a grin. She saw Jean Darling; was that her husband with her? Cosmo was holding on to a sailor's shoulder, trying to steady himself. Lucile was on her way up, swaying back and forth in the sling. They were all saved; Madame was saved. Tess waved again, still dizzy with relief. As Lucile stepped onto the *Carpathia,* Tess rushed forward, hugging her impulsively.

"Oh, my dear," gasped Lucile, patting her lightly on the back and quickly stepping away.

More lifeboats were unloading—more people were swung up high in the slings, then deposited onto the deck of the ship. Tess looked in vain for some sign of Jack Bremerton. Nothing. Just sad, stunned strangers who huddled together or stood apart. There was a stillness to them all, a loss of purpose.

Suddenly Lucile began clapping her hands, almost as if a particularly dramatic performance had just come to an end. "We've made it to safety, and we're going to celebrate," she announced to the small band from Life-

boat One. She called to the captain of the *Carpathia* and issued a blithe order. "Captain, I'm sure you will do me this *essential* favor, won't you? This is something I must have. Will one of your men take a photograph of those of us who were in my lifeboat? You have a camera, don't you?"

Taken by surprise, the startled captain nodded, beckoning to another officer. "The ship's surgeon will help you, Madame," he said.

Cosmo, looking gaunt and weary, murmured to Tess. "Lucile wants a little ceremony to celebrate our survival, and she wants you in the picture, too," he said. "Put your life belt back on, will you?"

Tess stared at Cosmo and then at the sodden vest she still held in her hand. Put it on again? She looked over his shoulder and saw Madame beckoning, her eyes bright and smiling. But there was also something else. What? A tinge of panic? No, not Madame.

"I know it's a shivery old thing, but put it on—it will be a wonderful picture," she said. "Come, dear, this will

be for the history books. Our stalwart little crew deserves remembrance."

Lining up next to Lucile were the crewmen who had been in her boat, all of them standing stiffly in their life vests. The tall, wiry one with bad skin, the one named Sullivan, who was in charge of Lifeboat One, was boasting of his own bravery, but none of the others were listening.

Tess glanced at the seaman named Bonney. He was standing to the side, observing the scene with a stony, unreadable expression. Deliberately, watching Lucile, he undid the ties of his vest and tossed it into a refuse bin.

"I'll not be a party to this vain celebration, not when so many died," he said in a strong voice that carried across the deck.

Lucile's smile faded. "Your rudeness is surpassed only by your arrogance," she snapped.

"No, that's your territory."

"How dare you say that to me?"

"You know what I'm talking about."

Lucile turned away, her eyes glittering now with hard determination. "Tess?"

She beckoned to the girl to join the huddled, wary-faced crew, some of whom were looking uncomfortably sheepish about Lucile's mandate.

"Go ahead," Tess said quickly. "I wasn't in your boat, after all."

"Very well." Lucile turned away, taking her place at the center of the group. The surgeon of the *Carpathia,* with some diffidence, but out of respect for the famous Lady Duff Gordon, stood now, holding a camera. A silence fell over those on the deck as they watched.

"Now, everybody—smile," Lucile ordered.

The camera clicked—a harsh, loud sound. His job done, the ship's surgeon quickly hurried away.

Sir Cosmo spoke then with each crewman in turn, murmuring, walking down the line, a slap on a shoulder here, a handshake there. Gratitude, solidarity, of course. Small murmurings to each man.

"He thinks it's his personal rowing team," muttered a man from the watching crowd. "Gentry, managed to snare a private boat." Tess turned in the di-

rection of the voice, but it had merged into the crowd's murmuring sighs.

Lifeboats were still arriving, and the crowd on the deck was growing, a potpourri of survivors. The shabby and bedraggled, the famous and glamorous, and somehow they all looked alike to Tess right now. Their faces were as pasty and blank as hers, she was sure of that. She looked for Jack Bremerton. A man as confident as he would have found a way to get off that ship. And then again, perhaps not.

Peering over the side, she saw Mrs. Astor, looking faint and ill, her hair loose and snarled, swinging back and forth in a boatswain chair. Sailors were cutting life belts off some of the almost comatose passengers, and stewards were passing out mugs of hot coffee and brandy. The *Carpathia*'s passengers looked at them all in some horror, but mostly with pity, as mothers clung to the side of the ship, crying, hoping with each unloaded lifeboat that a missing child or husband would emerge.

One woman stood very still, without tears, her face strong and hard. She

was the wife of one of the *Titanic's* cooks, someone whispered. "There is another lifeboat," she said calmly to whoever was listening. "My children are on it." Refusing warm clothes, refusing a hot drink, refusing food, she stood rigid, watching the horizon.

Tess slumped down on the deck, exhausted. She did not want to talk with anyone. The world she inhabited yesterday was gone. There were no beautiful clothes to unpack or iron. No silver tea service, no strolling on the promenade—none of the vanities that had seemed to matter so much. Was it only yesterday?

A shadow fell between her and the light.

"I don't even know your name," Bonney said quietly.

Startled, she glanced up and, for the first time, really looked at this man who had shared the last carefree moment of her life. A rough, dark stubble covered his face, deepening every line and crevice, making him look much older than the village boy she had met on deck yesterday. He wore a dry flannel

shirt but no sweater, as if scorning the cold, and he was smoking, drawing on a cigarette with concentrated ferocity. She was struck by the uncompromising, hard set of his chin. How different he looked. There was no lighthearted grin, no easy set of the shoulders, but then they were both different people from the pair who had met on the *Titanic*'s promenade.

"Tess Collins. And yours?"

He flicked a long ash off the cigarette in his right hand and gazed down at her a bit uneasily. "Jim. Jim Bonney. I was afraid you weren't going to make it off the ship last night."

"Me, too," she said, smiling bleakly.

"Something I have to ask—"

"Yes?"

"A sailor from your lifeboat says he hauled up a couple of dead bodies for you. You want to speak over them, is that it?"

"I just want to see them."

"All right, come with me."

She scrambled to her feet, too stiff and cold to stand straight.

------

A room had been set aside for the dead. Across the floor were the shrouded forms of a dozen people, all waiting now for a few quick words from the captain, then a quiet sliding into the sea. Bonney pointed at one figure. "I put the baby back in her arms," he said.

"Good. That's where it should be."

"I can't help you pray or anything. I'm not a religious man."

"You cared enough to come get me for this."

"Are you going to pray? If you are, I'll leave."

"I just want to say goodbye. I've helped bury a sister; I know how to do this." Her lip trembled. She was so cold, so tired, so close to tears.

"I'll help with that," he said more gently.

"It's just that no one who loves them will ever be able to."

"I'll start if you want."

She nodded.

He cleared his throat. "We wish you well and would give you life if we could. But at least you're both together for whatever journey lies ahead."

"That's close to a prayer," she said, looking gratefully at his set face.

"Your turn."

"I turn my face to the rising sun," Tess whispered, the words coming from somewhere in the recesses of memory. "O Lord, have mercy."

The room was dark; more bodies from the lifeboats would be brought in soon. Bonney turned to go.

"Wait." Tess knelt down by the woman's body, folding back the towel draped over her face. Plain, strong features, long, dark eyelashes.

"We should—"

"I want to remember her face."

They stood together for a quiet moment more, then turned and left the room, closing the door tightly behind them. Bonney's hand, in a gesture of awkward tenderness, briefly cradled her shoulder.

------

A muddled, drifting order was settling over the survivors on deck. They were breaking into clusters, like tribes, all

adhering to their own. Voices muttering, sobbing—recounting close calls and instant decisions.

A hoarse chuckle from Jim Bonney. "Now the accounting begins," he said.

"What do you mean?"

"We'll see how it plays out. Nothing to do about it. I'm glad we met again, though not like this." And then he strode away as Lucile approached, casting him a malevolent glance.

Uncertain, Tess stood watching, then moved to Lucile's side.

Jean and Jordan Darling had drawn away from the cluster of survivors, huddling together by themselves, all light-hearted gaiety stripped away. Jean reached out as Lucile passed by. "Lucile, please," she said, putting a hand lightly on her arm. "What would you have done?"

Lucile gave her a hard-edged smile. "I certainly wouldn't have tossed a tablecloth over my husband to disguise him as a woman. You are a cheat, and your husband is a coward."

Jean Darling covered her face with her hands as heads began to turn. Tess

was first shocked, then flooded with pity at the sight of her suffering.

"And yours was not?" Jean managed.

Lucile was giving no quarter. "There was no pretense. Don't you understand the difference?" she demanded.

Jean Darling lowered her hands and looked directly at Lucile. "He would be dead and I couldn't bear losing him," she said.

"Really, your behavior is pathetic." Lucile turned away.

"And what about your actions?" Jean Darling challenged.

"And what *about* me, my dear Jean?" Lucile said calmly. "Are you criticizing the fact that you and that husband of yours are both alive because of me? You are, you know." She turned to Tess, who couldn't take her eyes off Mrs. Darling's stricken face. "Tess, I'm sure you can roust up some crew member to get us a little tea. You'll do that now, won't you?"

The rules still applied. "Yes, Madame," Tess said. She was being sent away so as not to hear the rest of this.

But something had happened on that lifeboat, the shape and truth of which she might never know. And this made her uneasy.

------

The cook's wife took her eyes off the horizon long enough to grab at Tess's clothes as she passed. "My daughter is ten," she said. "She's very spirited and well able to take care of her brother. He's five. They're coming soon. I'm very happy about that."

Tess squeezed the woman's hand, but knew there was no solace she could give. She kept walking.

------

The day grew warmer as the sun rose higher in the sky. Tess served a make-shift tea with two forlorn teacups and a shabby pot of tepid water to Madame, but there were no complaints. After-ward, she slipped behind a smokestack and curled herself tight, hoping not to be noticed, hungry to be alone with the

sun. Her thoughts flashed back to Jack Bremerton, remembering his calm demeanor as he handed that child into a lifeboat, looking up at her, clearly caring that she was still in peril. How could he be gone?

"I hear you were good with the oars."

She looked up and saw Jim Bonney. "I learned, living on a lake," she said.

"You worked them hard, I'm told. I'm not surprised."

"Why not?"

He glanced down at her. "Your hands. They've seen plenty of sun. Have you worked on a farm?"

Instinctively, Tess tugged the sleeves of her sweater down over her fingers.

He spoke quickly. "Nothing to be ashamed of. May I join you?"

Tess nodded, and he sat down beside her. "If you're not a seaman, what are you?" she said.

"A coal miner—at least, I was," he said, taking a long drag on his cigarette. "Until three years ago. We went on strike—the big one, remember?" He looked at her expectantly.

She did remember, though some-

what hazily. It was all politics, her father used to say at the dinner table. Malcontents trying to get money out of the government. They should be grateful for their jobs and not make trouble. He would slam his spoon against his plate, repeating this, staring at Tess. The message was aimed at her; she was the troublemaker, the one who wanted to get away.

"I remember," she said.

"I was an organizer," he said. "Management gave in and we got better wages for the men. Organizing—that's what I want to do."

"Why in America?"

"Because it works. And people care about it." Bonney kicked at a piece of debris blowing across the deck, then— with a quick, expert movement—flipped his cigarette over the side. "There's a lot to be done with the unions in the States, especially in the West. Also"— he looked at her with a sudden smile— "a man can do what he wants, live the life he makes for himself. There's no bloody class system holding you down."

"Are you one of these—what are they called—Bolsheviks?"

"No," he said. "But I don't dismiss them. There's this bloke, Vladimir Lenin." He looked at her hopefully. "Russian. Have you heard of him?"

Tess shook her head, annoyed with herself. There was way too much she should know that she didn't.

"So what about you? Why were you leaving?"

"I hate feeding cows and pigs and I hate doing rich people's laundry, and I never want to do any of it again."

He let go with a laugh. "So we share that. What will you do?"

"I don't know yet," she said. "It depends on Madame."

"Why do you call her that?"

Tess hesitated. Because she was told to, that was the answer. But she wasn't about to say so.

"It's just for the trip."

"What happens then?"

"I don't know," she admitted. "But I think she'll give me work in her showroom. I love to sketch and sew."

"You're good at it?"

"I'm very good," she said, scorning modesty.

"Good luck. She's an arrogant one." His voice stayed even.

"She's been good to me."

"She's what's wrong with the English class system." His voice was suddenly sharp and angry.

"Why would you say that? She made it on her own, working hard."

"Marrying into the titled class. That helped. Gave her license to be cold about other people's lives."

"I know how arrogant she can be, but there is more to her than that." She pushed aside the memory of Jean Darling's face, just for the moment. She would think about that later.

Bonney studied her for a moment, then glanced down to light another cigarette, cupping the flame against the wind. "Why did you stay out of the picture she wanted?"

"It felt wrong," she said slowly.

"She'll not let you get away with independent thinking."

"It's the only kind that comes easy to

me." Brave words; she wanted them to be true.

"Don't fool yourself."

Tess felt suddenly very tired, not quite ready for his determined opinions. "I'm trying to do my job, whether you think that is worthwhile or not. I don't want to argue with you."

"I'm not trying to undermine you. I'm mad at myself."

"Why?"

"For what happened in that lifeboat. I should have fought harder against her."

"What did she do?"

"Did you notice how empty our boat was? Do you know why? She wouldn't let us pick up survivors."

"Oh, my goodness." This time Tess was the one covering her face with her hands.

"Pretty despicable, right? We could've easily saved people."

"Maybe you were in danger of being swamped; we almost were."

"You pulled that mother and her baby into the boat, didn't you? That's more than she would've done."

"But—" She thought of how fearsome the dark water had been, how that had frightened everybody. Surely Madame wasn't excluded? "There must have been good reason—are you sure? The officer on the ship said, I remember, he said the boat was unstable before it was launched. Couldn't that be why?" She felt herself pleading. "I can't believe what you're saying."

He gave her a hard look. "Are you so gone you defend her? I could tell you things."

"Well, you haven't—nothing that condemns Madame for anything. Everybody did the best they could."

"There it is, 'Madame' again. All right, I see where this is going." He spat out across the railing into the sea.

She hated it when men spat. "Well? What did you see?"

"Nothing I can talk about."

"Then you're making an ignorant denunciation." Her heart was beating too fast.

His jaw stiffened, his mouth tightening. "Could be," he said. "I see where you are. She's your meal ticket."

"What a dreadful thing to say," she blurted angrily. Tears began to trickle down her cheeks, the first she had shed since boarding the *Carpathia.*

He crushed his cigarette out on the deck and slapped one fist into the other. "I'm angry and too blunt. I don't—"

"Look!" Someone was yelling and pointing from the bow. "We're going by the damn thing! That's where we went down!"

"Oh, my goodness," a passenger from the *Carpathia* said, almost gaily. "I've always wanted to see an iceberg!"

Without a word, Tess and Jim scrambled up and hurried to the railing. Why am I drawn to this, Tess thought fleetingly. I don't want to see it, but I can't resist.

And there was the iceberg—huge, towering much higher than the ship. A beautifully shaped, evil thing formed by nature. Truly a ghastly work of art, with the sun's rays pierced deep into its shimmering green core.

"Look over there," someone shouted.

To the right of the iceberg was a wide

circular stain of muddy brown water, so distinct it almost looked painted over the blue of the sea. It took a moment to realize what it was.

The wreckage of the *Titanic* lay before them, densely packed, a compost of intimate pieces of lost lives. A baby's bonnet intertwined with a long white woman's glove. Pieces and bits of unrecognizable matter curled and wound together. Chairs floating upright, stools and elaborately carved tables on their sides and upside down, boxes, stray articles of clothing, including a bright-red silk scarf coiled over the surface of the water like some sea serpent—all manner of floatable debris that had formed a tight field, torn free of the *Titanic.* Please, God, no yellow ribbon.

"I'm sorry for what I said about you," Jim muttered. "Please forgive me."

With hardly a thought, Tess cupped her hand over his on the rail. He made no move away, then turned his hand and curled his fingers into hers. Neither spoke as the ship moved on by.

------

"What can you tell me about them?"

The Frenchwoman nodded toward the two boys asleep under a blanket near the captain's quarters.

"Their father is a widower, Mr. Hoffman."

"He didn't make it, I'm afraid. Somebody said they saw him handing the boys to you—that they heard him shout, 'Tell my wife I love her.'"

"But he's a widower."

"Well, then, they are orphans now," the woman said sadly. "We'll have to wait until we reach land to try and find their family. But thank you—at least we know their names."

"I saw them playing with tops," Tess said, touching Michel's face. "Are there any toys for the children?"

"I don't think anything like that survived."

"I'll find something," Tess said. Here was a task worth doing.

The long day dragged on. Tess searched the decks, peering at every face, wanting Jack Bremerton to be alive. Finally she mustered the nerve to go to the wheelhouse and ask to see

the official survivors list. She scanned it quickly, then more carefully. His name was not on the list. Jack Bremerton had not survived; that's how it was. He was gone. Without even closing her eyes, she could see his handsome profile, hear the warmth in his voice, as they talked that last evening on the *Titanic.* She could almost feel his closeness now. Could he truly be dead?

She handed the list back, turned, and walked out of the wheelhouse.

------

"You'd do best to come in, Tess. I think my wife wants to talk to you," Cosmo said. His look had turned almost pitying as he gave a slight bow, opening the door to the room the captain had given to the Duff Gordons.

Madame's stare was alarmingly baleful as Tess walked in.

"So, what do you have to say for yourself?" she demanded.

"Pardon me?"

"Don't feign innocence. I wanted you

in that photograph. Why did you so rudely refuse me?"

"I didn't mean to be rude. It wasn't my place to be there."

"Nonsense. You work for me. If I say you belong there, then you do."

"It seemed a bit out of place—maybe too soon." It was precisely the wrong thing to say; she could see it immediately in Lucile's eyes.

"You're questioning my judgment?" Lucile's voice lashed out, sharp and hard. "Just who do you think you are? You're a little servant girl from a farm until I make you something more, and don't you forget it. You do as I tell you, do you hear?"

"Yes, Madame. I didn't know how important it was to you." She could hardly stammer the words out.

"It's not for you to know, it's your job to *obey.* That is, if you want employment with me."

She mustn't say the wrong thing again. "I want that very much," she said. "And I will work hard."

Lucile gave a sharp laugh. "Your refusing me in front of all those people

was intolerable, Tess. Do you understand that?"

"I'm sorry," Tess said again.

Lucile's shrewd eyes surveyed the
girl's stiff figure, something flickering
across her face. "So you're not telling
me you will disobey at will?"

"No, Madame. Never."

"And who defines your duties?"

"You do." Tess held her breath. She
hated the shiver of needed subservience sweeping over her; at home she
would be genuflecting. No more of that.
But her own inner pride quavered,
mixed with shame.

"What did you hear about our boat?
Something you didn't like? Is that why
you refused to put on a life vest for the
picture?"

"No, of course not. I didn't know
what happened, I wasn't there."

Lucile's voice curled around her like
a whip. "I saw you talking with that
sailor. He was no friend of ours in the
lifeboat, Tess. And don't you forget it.
He's a liar out to make a fortune on a
lurid story."

Then, stunningly, the clouds parted

as fast as they had formed. Lucile dismissed her with a quick wave of her hand. "I'm exhausted. Will you bring me some tea? Hot, this time? The captain, I think, knows now who I am."

"Yes, of course," Tess said, both astonished and relieved.

"Yes, *Madame*." Lucile gave her a brilliant smile. "Go, go, my dear. And stop looking as if I'm biting your head off. And I hope you'll be less cranky tomorrow."

------

The hours, the days, ticked by. When Lucile allowed her free time, Tess began teaching the other women how to stitch together shirts and coats from tarps for the children. Too many of them were still huddled in shirts and jackets scratchy with dried seawater. Some of the children who had been rushed from their beds and into the lifeboats were without shoes. "I can't feel my toes," one whimpered to Tess. She kneeled down and massaged his small feet, try-

ing to warm them, hoping to see them turn pink again.

And yet, somehow, there was some laughter, some play.

On the second day, Tess found Jim on deck, surrounded by a cluster of the younger children, carving small figures for them from discarded pieces of wood.

"You're good," she said, leaning down to inspect his work. What long, deft fingers he had. Not the fingers of a coal miner, surely.

"Thanks. Got my instructions from an uncle who was a wood-carver, but I couldn't make enough money at the work." He smiled up at her. "Want to join us?" His manner was easy and gentle, which was clearly why the children were gravitating to him.

Impulsively, Tess sat down with them. He was taking orders from the children. Who wants a giraffe? An elephant? "Ah, the giraffe wins," he said to a small girl with a sad, pinched face. The child brightened, and his audience watched in silence as a small giraffe almost magically began to emerge from the

smooth wood under his fingers. "What do you think?" he said to the child. "Is this a worthy giraffe?"

She said nothing, just grinned, her eyes round and dark, as he deposited it carefully in her hand.

"It's now your good-luck charm," he said quietly. Then, to Tess after a pause, "Did she come after you?"

"Yes, she was furious. You were right."

"She's building her defense."

"Why?"

"Because she has to."

For more than an hour they sat there. Each time a small figure was completed for a child, Tess reached out and touched the smooth, newly carved wood. "You're adding the magic," Jim said with a grin. And she laughed, loath to leave this sunny little island of pleasure he had created amid so much grief.

"Can you carve a spinning top?" she asked eagerly.

"Sure. For you?" His eyes danced.

"For two small boys who need to play."

He asked no more. "Give me a few hours," he said.

------

All were chilled now by the sight of the cook's wife. Time after time, someone would gently guide her to a cabin, but she would get restless and distraught, drifting soon back to the railing, fastening her gaze again on the horizon. "They're coming soon," she said softly. "My children are in a boat. They are rowing a bit slowly." Her face was almost radiant now. Her eyes glittered in a strange way.

------

"That woman obviously has a weak character," Lucile said at one point as Jean Darling trudged past them on the deck, carrying a basket of bread for her husband. "She's certainly burned her bridges with *me,* not that the same thing won't happen with everybody else when her husband's deception becomes public." Lucile brushed a few

shriveled raisins from the biscuit crumbs on her plate onto the deck.

Automatically, Tess bent to pick them up and throw them over the railing, watching them loft into the air and then down to the sea. She was getting better, she hoped, at keeping her thoughts to herself. But she had always done that, and why had this servile gesture come so automatically? Perhaps to hide those thoughts. She wondered at the vigor of Lucile's contempt for the Darlings.

------

Too many dreams—dark ones filled with wailing. It was late when she knocked at Lucile's door the last night. Cosmo was up with the radio operator, sending telegrams, including one that she had given him for her mother, so Lucile would be alone. "I've brought you an extra blanket in case you're cold," she said as the door opened.

"That's not necessary," Lucile said crossly. "I'm tired, and I don't want any more blankets or anything else right

now." She was wearing a battered old sweater over a flannel gown that had been donated, a combination that made her look strangely vulnerable. "Go to bed. Why aren't you asleep?"

"I can't," Tess said.

"Why is that?"

"I keep dreaming about the ship going down."

"It's over, and we survived. That's all best put behind us," Lucile said firmly. But her gaze flickered. "Oh, come in, then," she said, opening the door wider.

Tess stepped in. The tiny room, so stark and bare. Something more than luxury had been stripped away.

"Aren't you still a little—afraid?" she whispered.

Lucile went still. Her face seemed to break, then quickly reconfigure itself. "I'm always afraid," she said.

"You are?"

"Of water," Lucile quickly amended. She sat down, clasping her hands in front of her. "I almost drowned when I was ten," she said abruptly. "People were on the shore, watching. None of them tried to rescue me. I screamed, I

cried. No one came." She could have been reciting a grocery list, her voice was so matter-of-fact.

"What happened?"

"A boy had the common sense to climb out on a rock and throw me a line. I managed to hang on and he pulled me in. I don't talk about this. I do hope you know I don't want it repeated."

"That must have terrified you," Tess said quietly, imagining the fear of a drowning child.

"No, I wouldn't allow it. Sit down." Lucile patted the lumpy, narrow bed.

Tess lowered herself next to Lucile. They were sitting so close, she could smell vestiges of Lucile's favorite jasmine perfume, now at the bottom of the sea.

"You will learn to move on," Lucile said, almost gently. "You will, Tess. I've learned not to show fear, to take charge, to stand up and be strong. Isn't that what you want, too?"

"Yes."

Lucile reached out and took Tess's hand, squeezing it so tightly Tess al-

most jumped. "Don't allow anyone to make you suffer, dear. We need to be thinking about what comes next, not about the past." She hesitated for a second, and then said, "I have something for you."

She reached into the pocket of her baggy sweater and pulled out the velvet drawstring bag. "Take these," she said. "My gift for your future."

Tess opened the bag and gasped as Lucile's moonstone earrings—sparkling with light even in this dense, windowless space—tumbled into her hand. "I can't take these," she stammered.

"Think of them as salvage, my dear. They've already saved my life, and I have plenty more at home. Jewelry can be soothing, you know."

It was so oddly offhanded, Tess was at a loss. She gently put them back on Lucile's lap. "I don't need these—I just wanted to tell you I feel altered somehow," she said. "I just needed to know you understand—that maybe you have nightmares, too. And you have comforted me. That's all I want." She

searched Lucile's face in confusion. Was she insulting her?

"Are you afraid I'll change my mind and demand them back?"

"No, not at all."

"Well, then, perhaps for another time." Lucile slipped the earrings back in their velvet pouch and then into her pocket. "And, as for how we deal with fear, we are who we are. I think that's enough for tonight."

Tess didn't want to leave. She didn't want their short moment of intimacy to slip away. "When did you decide that you wanted to sew, to be a designer?" she asked impulsively.

Lucile blinked, as if startled at the question. "I sewed clothes for my dolls," she said after a pause.

"My mother made me a rag doll and I sewed for her, too."

But Lucile wasn't interested in any more shared experiences. "Really, dear, we were all children once. Now go to bed and come back early. We have work to do."

-------

Tess sat down at Lucile's desk the next morning, looking as efficient as possible as she opened a drawer and pulled forth a notebook and a pen. If she had expected the intimacy of the night before, it was certainly not there now.

Lucile was pacing, talking about the messages being sent and received from her various showrooms in London, Paris, and New York. There were showings of her spring line scheduled *everywhere,* she said with satisfaction. So much needed to be coordinated, and remaking the gowns lost on the *Titanic* would take time. Nothing must cast a pall over the New York opening. She talked rapidly, firing off instructions as Tess scribbled them down on notepaper. Clients had to be notified, courted, rounded up. Was Mrs. Wharton still planning to purchase the coral tea gown she adored in London? What about the models? Were they all assembled and ready to go or not? And if not, why not?

"Actually, I believe the publicity from this disaster might help," she said, her voice trailing off as she looked at Tess

writing silently. She began to drum her lacquered nails against the table.

"My dear, I've noticed you spending a fair amount of time with that odious seaman. Since your mother isn't here, I just want to warn you—you can do better."

Tess's cheeks began to burn. She opened her mouth to answer, but Lucile cut her off.

"Second, we might as well get to this. We need to talk about your future. I don't need a maid in New York; I have two."

Her voice had hardened, businesslike, and Tess, shocked, braced herself. Now came the dreaded repercussions of her disobedience.

"But, I thought—"

"Yes, I know, I mentioned something about working in my shop. And I know you're good with buttonholes." Lucile sighed again, paced the room for a few moments.

"I can do much more than that," Tess said with a rush. "I'm good, I can be a true help to you, I—"

"Oh, Tess, you should see your face.

Don't worry, I'm just teasing. I'll find a place for you. You're quick and intelligent. I will try you out in the shop—we'll start from there. Why are you looking at me that way?"

"I'm bewildered. It's as if, sometimes, a game is being played."

"Game? *Game?* Oh, for heaven's sake." Lucile's light laughter bounced through the air. "Now sit down for a moment—I want to give you an idea of what we're going to face when we dock tonight. We are all celebrities now, you know."

Tess wasn't quite sure what that would mean. Only gradually had she realized that the fate of the "unsinkable" *Titanic* had drawn worldwide attention, that newspapers were clamoring for details, that inquiries were being planned, that the U.S. Congress would be involved. Radio messages had been flying back and forth between the *Carpathia* and the shore. Somehow it had seemed to her to be the private tragedy of the survivors, which she saw now was absurd.

"It's going to be a circus," Lucile

warned her. Tess should try to avoid the reporters; they were jackals and would crawl all over anybody unfamiliar with their deceits. She and Sir Cosmo would do the talking. There would be drivers from her New York office with cars at the dock to whisk them off to the Waldorf-Astoria hotel, so she was to stay close and not wander off. On second thought, they might stop at her salon; Madame was quite sure all the models would be there. "And wait until you see this hotel, dear," she said cheerfully. "You will *die.*"

Tess winced at that. "I'll make sure everything is ready," she said, preparing to leave the room.

Lucile must have caught the shadow that flitted across her face.

"By the way, I've forgotten the name of the family you were working for in Cherbourg," she said. "Who were they, dear?"

"We haven't talked about them." They both knew she had never named them.

"Perhaps not." Madame surveyed her thoughtfully. "But then . . ."

Why this cat-and-mouse game? She could say nothing. No, she would take a chance. "Thank you for your kindness last night," she said. "You comforted me, and I am grateful for that."

Once again, that sudden shift of expression on Lucile's face. "It isn't what I do," she said after a pause. "But you brought it out of me."

A short silence. And then it ended.

"Oh well, I know about made-up worlds. Do be sure you understand about the one we are entering—and that's the last time I'll ever remind you." Madame smiled, her eyes dancing. "So prepare yourself. We're about to go through Alice's looking glass."

------

PENNSYLVANIA STATION
NEW YORK CITY
APRIL 18
7:00 A.M.

Pinky Wade sat hunched in her seat, staring out a grimy window as her train

pulled slowly into the tunnel below the new Penn Station, that vast edifice of soaring arches and splendid skylights held up by magnificent pink granite columns. She jumped slightly as the conductor strode into the railcar and bawled out, "New York City, end of the line!" Quickly she gathered her belongings, which consisted of a small satchel with an extra shirtwaist and toiletries. Pinky Wade was proud that she always traveled light.

She stepped from the train and started to mount the stairs, looking up toward the skylights expectantly. Yes, the light was bursting through, dancing off the heads of hurrying passengers and shimmering over every polished surface. Usually she loved this elegant passage from the train to the waiting room, loved stepping onto the gleaming travertine marble floors, imagining that she was in some kind of grand palace. She had no heart for it today, though. Weary and cranky, she was still smoldering over the *Times*'s demand for her presence. She

made a halfhearted attempt to straighten out the mess of stringy hair pinned carelessly on top of her head, then glanced down at her shoes. Van Anda would probably make a few cracks about the length of her skirt, which now skimmed a few more inches above the top of her ankles. What did he expect her to wear when she was working?

She walked past a huge, gold-framed mirror and stopped, staring at her reflection. Well, surprise, she looked as cross as she felt. How could Van Anda have pulled her off the mental-hospital investigation to stick her with survivor interviews? It made her uneasy. He was a good boss, backed her up on most of her assignments. But in the end he was just like any other man in the newspaper business: when you've got something pathetically sentimental, bring in a woman reporter; that's what they're good for. If she had been booked on the *Titanic*—now that's a story that would have been worthwhile. Now she was stuck with the too-easy job of

wringing human-interest accounts out of survivors.

She walked on, indignation rising. Sometimes she wondered why she kept reporting. Would her father ever admit to being proud of her? She had grown up hearing from him how smart she was, but then there were the little sharp-edged asides: most women are married by your age; what about a family? Pinky stopped again, scrambling in her bag for taxi money. She had more freedom to do what she wanted to do than most women, and maybe he hadn't liked sharing with her the guilty joy of the job. When she was exposing abuse at an orphanage or forcing reform in a mental hospital, she felt powerful. The truth was, she could still be yanked off an important story as quickly as a child being pulled away from a candy box.

She sighed as she hurried out of Pennsylvania Station and joined a line of people waiting for taxis. At least they didn't have to put up with horse-drawn hansoms anymore.

------

## CITY ROOM, *NEW YORK TIMES*
## NEW YORK CITY
## APRIL 18
## 10:00 A.M.

Van Anda had hardly slept in three days, not that it mattered. Every other paper in the country was eating humble pie. Only the *Times* had had the nerve to print the story of the *Titanic*'s sinking before the White Star people finally stopped lying and confirmed it. This was the coup of his life, and there was no way he was going to lose that lead now. The *Carpathia* was due this evening, and he was almost ready. A whole floor at a local hotel had been reserved for his reporters, and they were ready to go. A dozen phones had been installed, with direct access to the rewrite desk. "We were first, and we're going to stay first," he crowed to the excited reporters in the city room.

"Hello, Carr."

He looked up to see Pinky Wade standing in front of him, her arms crossed, a frown on her face. He smiled, noting that her skirts had inched up

again. She was pretty enough—rosy skin, bright eyes, and a laugh that always had a bounce to it. Also something of a chameleon, which helped on undercover assignments. Plenty of courage and strong opinions. If it weren't for her smart mouth, she might even get away with pouring tea in one of those mansions on Fifth Avenue. She always gave the impression that she held enormous amounts of energy bottled inside her ready to burst out at any moment. No one loved a good story more than Pinky.

"You're to be down on the dock when the ship pulls in," he said without preamble. "Get steerage as well as first class. Quick takes—we'll piece it together. Did they see the iceberg, when did they realize what was going on. The more detail the better; get some near-miss stories. Get me—"

"Hello, Carr."

Van Anda could see that she was really angry this time.

"Hello, Pinky."

"Why me?" she asked.

"Because you're the best human-in-

terest reporter I know. And I'm sorry you don't have to risk your life for the story. I'll try to rectify that later."

She couldn't help but smile. He did have a sense of humor.

"I want to get on the ship before it docks," she said.

"Great. You find a way; I'm happy."

------

WASHINGTON, D.C.
APRIL 18
3:30 P.M.

Senator Smith barely made the train pulling out of Union Station, swinging himself up on the lower step as it began to move, a briefcase stuffed with papers tucked precariously under one arm, two aides scrambling up after him.

"You're impressing those reporters," one of them said, pointing at a swarm of men holding cameras and notebooks, now rapidly being left behind on the platform.

Smith was secretly pleased to hear his aide's somewhat awed, breathless

report. He'd shown them audacity all right, and it hadn't taken long. His position on the Commerce Committee had helped, of course. His resolution to set up an investigation, with himself chairing, had gone through the Senate like a hot knife through butter; now, there was a good old midwestern expression. And he was going to start the hearings in New York instead of Washington—right there in midtown at the Waldorf hotel. He'd snag more witnesses there, and get to them faster. Tomorrow morning, the show would begin.

The senator settled himself into a seat and checked his watch for the twentieth time. "We've got to get on the *Carpathia* before it docks," he said to the aides. "Those White Star people will vanish if we don't slap subpoenas on them right away. Especially that slippery Ismay."

"You think they planted those phony messages saying the ship hadn't sunk?" asked one.

"Absolutely." It made him angry, thinking of all the people who had set off for Halifax to greet friends and fam-

ily members after being reassured that the *Titanic* was safe. A brutal, cowardly lie, and for what? To gain more time for White Star officials to save their hides?

He frowned and leaned back in his seat. Yes, he had played his cards right. No one in Congress had thought faster than he. This, he told himself, staring out at the passing landscape, would crown his career as a public servant. If he made it in time.

------

Slowly the *Carpathia* inched forward, steaming ever closer to New York Harbor. By five o'clock people had begun lining the railings, straining for a glimpse of land. The evening would be brisk, and Tess pulled her sweater close. She watched the cook's wife, who had now taken to wandering the deck, grabbing at people's arms. "Have you seen my children? Are they eating dinner?" she kept repeating. "Please tell them I'm waiting. If they don't come soon, I have to go find them."

Jim was standing by himself, smok-

ing a cigarette, staring ahead where land would soon appear.

Tess looked around swiftly; Lucile was nowhere near. "Will you be met?" she asked shyly, joining him at the rail, feeling awkward. Most likely, reaching land would make them strangers to each other again.

"Nobody here for me." He said it with a light shrug. "White Star says they're bunking us down somewhere for the inquiry. We'll see; Ismay has other ideas." He looked down at her, seeming to search her face for something. "I heard some U.S. senator is coming aboard soon to start interviewing the officers and crew," he said.

"The captain says the government hearings begin tomorrow."

Jim let out a short laugh. "That means the politicians take over. Sorry, but I figure it will be one more dance of greedy businessmen finding excuses for their mistakes. No one gets blamed— that's what usually happens. None of them care about all the poor blighters in steerage or the men down in the

boiler room. The stokers—they never had a chance."

"You knew someone down there?" she guessed.

"A friend. A good man. We were going West together. He was stoking the boilers when we hit the iceberg. Sometimes I think I should've been down there shoveling coal with him, but I was sick of coal; told him nothing was going to get me within a mile of the stuff again."

"I'm sorry."

It was inadequate, but he didn't seem to mind.

"None of those men stood a chance, you know. The rest of us, we get to live and find out things. Nobody on that shore will care about them or remember them. I should've been with them, gone down with the ship."

"They needed you on that lifeboat—you were the only one who knew how to row and what to do," Tess said quickly. "You were just doing your job. I know it feels wrong to be alive when all those people died. I feel that, too."

He smiled slowly. "It's all right, Tess.

I guess there's enough pain and sadness on this ship without wishing for more of it."

"And your carvings comforted the children," she said quietly. "I admire you for that."

"I didn't do much," he said. "The girl I made the giraffe for? Both parents lost; she hasn't spoken a word since she told someone in the lifeboat her name. She followed me around all the time. Watched me carve for hours."

Tess breathed deeply, wishing she could expel the anguish. Who would understand, other than those who were there?

"The children made this whole bloody time bearable. And so did you." He seemed embarrassed, hesitated, and then reached into his pocket, pulling out something that he put in her hand, gently closing her fingers over it.

"This is for you—maybe not a memento you want, but it's what I found myself making. It's just whittling." He smiled. "Welcome to America, Tess. I hope we see each other again. Goodbye."

"Jim—" It was the first time she had spoken his name.

But he put his finger to his lips, the gesture she remembered from their promenade on the deck of the *Titanic,* and walked away.

Tess opened her hand. She was holding a carefully carved wooden lifeboat. Peering at it in the waning light, she saw two tiny figures inside—each holding what looked like an oar. When she looked up to thank him, he was gone.

And so was the cook's wife. What happened? One moment there she was, standing on the deck. And now gone in search of her children; slipped into the sea.

**4**

## THE *CARPATHIA*
## THURSDAY, APRIL 18
## 9 P.M.

It wasn't as difficult as Pinky had anticipated. It took just a little chatting-up of a friendly dockworker to discover that a tugboat was set to go out to the *Carpathia* before the ship docked—an important senator from Washington wanted to get on and talk to people. That had to be William Smith, the senator from Michigan, who was slated to chair a congressional investigation. Starting tomorrow morning. What a show *this* would be.

Then it was a matter of being in the right place at the right time, wearing a

pair of pants cajoled from a copyboy, her hair tucked under a cap, looking like a dockworker, when Senator Smith came hurrying up, sweat on his brow from the race from the train station. A little bustle, some hellos, some "welcome, sir"s, some shouts to crew members, all in a flurry, and Smith and a couple of officious-looking aides stepped into the tugboat. The important thing always, Pinky knew, was to act like you belonged where you were forbidden to go. Hesitation was the mark of an amateur.

Whistling, she jumped onto the tugboat in the dark. Maybe this would be worthwhile after all.

The tugboat captain cut his engine and slowly approached the *Carpathia.* Pinky looked up and saw clusters of people huddled in sodden knots at the rail, hunched forward like mourners on a funeral ship. Not even a child's shout or wail broke the silence from the deck above; for a moment, the soft lapping of waves against the tugboat stern was the only sound. Then, unexpectedly,

thunder began to roll and lightning crackled in the sky.

She considered trying to sneak closer to the aides surrounding Smith for a better idea of what they were about, but she couldn't take her eyes off those still figures on the ship. The tugboat inched forward; they were almost touching the hull.

Suddenly there was an explosion of flashing lights, revealing the presence of several more tugboats approaching the *Carpathia.* Flashpowder. Shouts.

"Hello, up there!" bellowed a voice through a megaphone. "Are you the survivors? Any of you want to talk? Jump in, we'll take care of you!"

Pinky smiled. She knew who that was, holding the megaphone—a *World* reporter, full of strut and swagger and few brains. How could he think making all that noise would persuade anyone on *this* ship to jump into the sea? Had it not occurred to him to sneak on and scoop everybody else? This would make her job easier.

Within minutes, as her rivals kept shouting up to the silent watchers on

the deck, she was climbing a rope ladder behind Smith and his entourage, slipping onto the deck and stepping back into the dark. She was sure no one saw her.

------

Tess was watching the newcomers climb aboard when she saw a shadowy figure break from the group and dodge behind a smokestack. She made her way across the deck for a closer view, wondering why someone was trying to hide. She saw a woman in dungarees, mumbling to herself as she tried to shove long, thick hair under the cap on her head.

"Could you help me with this? My hair won't stay in place," she said impatiently as Tess approached.

"Who are you?" Tess asked.

"An impostor, obviously. Please?"

Maybe it was the casual cheerfulness of her request. For whatever reason, Tess found herself lifting the back of the cap and tucking in Pinky's way-

ward locks, resisting an impulse to laugh. "You look silly," she said.

"Well, so would you if you were disguised as a man. I should've cut this whole mess off."

"So who are you?" Tess asked again.

"I guess I'm stuck with explaining, aren't I? I'm Sarah Wade, but everybody calls me Pinky."

"Why are you hiding in the shadows?" Tess stepped backward to get a better look at this rather bizarre creature, and stumbled over a coiled rope. Jim's carving flew from her pocket, hit the deck, and skittered toward the edge. With a sharp cry she reached for it.

Pinky was faster. She dived and caught the piece of wood just before it went over the edge and into the sea. Silently she stood and handed it back to Tess, squinting at it through the meager light.

"A boat?" she said, curious.

"Yes. Thank you." Tess's hand was much quicker this time as she took the carving and shoved it back into her pocket.

"Okay, to answer your question, I'm a reporter. I want to talk to *Titanic* survivors, and this outfit made it easier to get on the ship. Did I alarm you?"

"Hardly, sorry."

Pinky looked almost comically crestfallen. "Oh, right. You think I look silly."

"A little. How did you keep from being found out on the boat that brought you out here?"

"Men aren't too observant, in my experience."

"Unless you're wearing a skirt," Tess said.

"Oh, right. Then they just want to get their hands underneath."

Tess laughed. She liked this cocky little person. "Are pants more comfortable than a skirt?" she asked.

"Of course, kind of freeing—like bloomers but better," Pinky said. She peered at Tess's sloppy, worn sweater, something obviously out of a ragbag. "I'm guessing you were on the *Titanic*. Am I right?"

"Yes," Tess said, her smile vanishing. The question was coming from another

world—a safe world, one she hadn't inhabited for days.

"It must have been dreadful."

"Yes," Tess repeated. She felt itchy now. Unwilling to stand still.

"Will you tell me about it?"

"Tell me about you first."

"I work for the *New York Times.* It's one of the good papers, not a scandal sheet. Everybody says so." She quickly amended her words. "Well, almost everybody."

"I don't think I can take your word for that," Tess said, thinking of the newspapers she had seen in Europe.

"You would be a bit naïve if you did. Lots of people say we're obnoxious and deceitful, and sometimes it's true. Look, I just want to hear your story. I don't know who you are, but I'm glad you survived. I assure you, that is not a deceitful statement. What's your name?"

"Tess Collins, and please don't call me Tessie."

Someone that immediately touchy was probably a servant. "How did you end up on the *Titanic*?" Pinky asked. She tried not to make her voice hur-

ried, but she couldn't waste time if she was going to get more interviews before Smith and his crowd caught her.

"I was hired as a maid for the trip, and I was lucky."

"Why were you lucky?"

"Because I had a cabin in first class, where the lifeboats were."

Pinky waited again. She got her best information that way.

"People died because they weren't able to get on the boats," Tess said.

"There weren't enough, right? That's what we're hearing." Pinky pulled a notebook and pencil from her pocket and began scribbling. "How did you escape?"

"I made it into one of the last lifeboats, with two children; their father asked me to take them."

"Did he make it?"

"No."

This would be good color. "Whose maid are you?"

Tess stiffened. "I'm only that for the journey."

"Sorry." It took time to be adroit, time she didn't have. "So who—"

"I work for Lady Lucile Duff Gordon."

"The designer?"

"Yes."

"Was she in your boat?"

"No. Look, you can get better stories from other people." It suddenly occurred to Tess that she was disobeying Lucile, getting herself into more peril. She didn't want to talk about anything more. She just wanted this reporter to go away.

"I'm sorry, it must be brutal to get questions fired at you so fast." But Pinky wasn't through. "If all the lifeboats were on the upper deck, then mostly first-class passengers survived?"

Tess saw again the faces from steerage. "I think so," she said. "Most of the others couldn't get to the boats in time."

"Then you were doubly lucky." Pinky scribbled faster. Here it was, that whole rotten class-division thing again. This was going to be one more story, she was sure of it, of the rich getting preferential treatment over the poor. She didn't have the count yet, but she was certain many more first-class than steerage passengers survived. What a

corrupt world it was. She stopped, pencil poised. "Why weren't you in the boat with Lady Duff Gordon?"

"It was launched before I could get in."

"Why? Was it full?"

Tess hesitated. "No. I don't know why."

"How many people in it?"

"About twelve or so."

The pieces were fitting together amazingly fast—on her first try. The imperious Lucile Duff Gordon, the not-too-nice doyenne of the fashion world— this world-famous rich woman saved herself in an almost empty boat. Pinky closed her notebook. She wanted to ask more questions, but she had to catch other passengers before Senator Smith finished handing out his subpoenas. If she didn't go back on that tender with him, she'd get stuck in the crowd at the disembarking.

"Thanks, you've been helpful," Pinky said, shoving notebook and pencil into her pocket. "It was nice to meet you." She turned to go, then stopped. "Good

luck," she said, reaching out a hand. "Maybe we'll meet again on shore."

"Thank you for saving my carving," Tess said suddenly.

"Sure," said Pinky. "Maybe you'll tell me the story behind it next time."

"Story?"

"There's always a story," Pinky said as she turned away, dodged behind a smokestack, and disappeared into the crowd.

------

The ship moved on slowly, and soon those on board found themselves staring at what looked like thousands of people on the pier who, in their silence, seemed almost a mirror image of themselves. Bundled in heavy, dark coats and bowler hats with rain dripping onto their collars, the families waiting on the dock stood in lines arranged alaphabetically under large posters. It was a forlorn effort to somehow organize the reunion of survivors and families without chaos, doomed to failure.

Hoarse voices began crying out

names, hoping to hear answering shouts. Women began to cry. People pushed forward as the gangplanks were hoisted into place, many groaning in frustration when they realized that first-class passengers would be first to disembark. Doctors in white coats and nurses in starched caps moved among the waiting men and women, armed with smelling salts and cold compresses for those who might faint or suffer heart attacks when they learned the worst. It was coming for many of them, a snaking live wire of dread traveling through the crowd.

------

Senator Smith stood on the bridge of the *Carpathia,* looking out past the black sea at the crowd on the dock, his stomach roiling. He hated ships, hated the sea. His hands felt sticky with salt water. He had a strong urge to wash them, but perhaps that urge was primarily to wash away the memory of the frozen-faced Brit he had just interviewed. How could the man be so stiff

in the face of what had happened? All Ismay was worried about was saving his own hide. Smith grabbed the railing as the ship suddenly rocked sideways, pushing down the bile in his throat. He had to get off this thing. But his instinct had been right. He was glad he had come on board and caught Ismay before the wily fellow had a chance to hop a returning ship, escaping any accounting to the people of the United States. His resolve to see this through, to pursue every angle, was strengthening. It wasn't just about making a name for himself in Washington anymore. Didn't those people down below him, watching the ship come closer, knowing their lives were forever altered—didn't they deserve to know the truth of *why* that bloody ship went down? They were close enough now—he could see their faces: a woman with hands clasped in front of her mouth as if in prayer; the man next to her peering upward in obvious anguish, hoping to catch a glimpse of a familiar face. A wife? A child? He swallowed hard. He could do this. He *would* do this, follow every

lead, no matter what, for if he was anything he was a righteous man.

And that Brit, with his flat, expressionless eyes, would be the first witness, whether he liked it or not.

------

Lucile hesitated at the top of the gangplank as she looked down on the faces turned in her direction, jolted by the sheer nakedness of emotion they displayed. She shuddered, clutching at Cosmo's arm.

"Walk quickly, dear," Cosmo said. "These people don't want to see us." He held on to her firmly as dockworkers began clearing a route for the first-class passengers through the crowd and to their waiting automobiles. With Tess following close behind, the Duff Gordons made their way to the parking area and their Packard Victoria. And standing there, talking to the driver, a long coat hiding her pants, was Pinky Wade.

"Welcome back to New York, Madame Lucile," she said cheerfully, not

looking at Tess. "I'm Pinky Wade of the *New York Times.*"

"No interviews now," Cosmo said gruffly.

Lucile paused as she started to enter the car, scanning Pinky's face. "Any relation to Prescott Wade?" she asked.

"My father," Pinky said shortly.

Lucile's eyes widened slightly. "I knew your father. Long after he became famous covering the Beecher trial, of course. A very gallant adventurer, as I recall. Climbed mountains, and other things."

"Well, he did get around." As usual, Pinky looked down when her father's name was dropped into a conversation.

"We must go," Cosmo said. "No interview, please." He opened the front door and nodded to Tess to climb in next to the driver.

"Of course not, you've all been through a terrible experience." Pinky shut her open notebook with a snap. "But life goes on, and I'd like to talk to you later—about the ship and, well, I'm not much into fashion, but I'd be inter-

ested in how you're planning to market your spring collection."

Lucile nodded. "That can be arranged," she said, getting into the car.

"I know this sounds terribly inappropriate, but it's always a bounce for the social set here when you arrive," Pinky said with a grin, thinking fast. Anything to keep this woman's attention. "And I hear your sister is ready to shock Hollywood again with her latest novel— can we talk about that, too?"

This time Lucile laughed. "I'm having a dinner tonight at our hotel—why don't you join us?"

"No, that's not a good idea," objected a startled Cosmo.

"Oh, for heaven's sake, I knew her father," Lucile said impatiently. "Well?"

"I'd be delighted," Pinky said. Even she was a little shocked. With pain and sadness wrecking the lives of the people still on the dock behind them, this woman was planning a fancy dinner? She had better get back to the newsroom and write fast. This was too good to miss.

"I know what you're thinking," Lucile

said before vanishing into the car. "But you put it well, Miss Wade. Life must go on. Dinner is in an hour."

------

Tess glanced back at the figure of Pinky Wade standing on the curb as the car drove off, wondering if she should mention their encounter on the ship. But Lucile and Cosmo had launched immediately into an argument.

"You're too careless with your invitations," Cosmo began.

"Nonsense," Lucile said. Cosmo was entirely too cautious. That girl's father had been a delightful man, very responsible, not just a grubby reporter; surely this Pinky woman knew she had a legacy to live up to. There were so many more important things to think about! There were dozens of things to do in preparation for the New York spring show; thank goodness they were staying at the Waldorf. Tonight would be lovely: no more terrible shipboard food; good friends, gracious dining. . . . How could he want to spoil her fun?

"Tess, you're invited too, dear," she said.

Slumped in her seat, Tess dozed, letting herself enjoy the feel of the soft leather cushion caressing her head. She had never been in so luxurious an automobile. Outside, scraps of a new, busy city slipped by, too quickly for her brain to absorb. She would face its demands and energy tomorrow. Right now, all she wanted was a room alone, with clean sheets and a soft pillow. She closed her eyes and, with a sting of melancholy, her thoughts drifted to Jack Bremerton. He was gone, and with him her silly fantasies about seeing him again. A brave man, gone. Her thoughts turned to Jim, reliving their moments of goodbye on the *Carpathia*—his blue eyes, his kindness, his serious intensity. She could no longer dismiss him as just a village boy. Not that it mattered, because she would probably never see him again, which deepened her melancholy. By the time the sleek black Packard in which they rode pulled up at the Waldorf, she was in a hazy, deep sleep.

------

Stepping into the private upstairs dining room of the Waldorf later that night
was like stepping into a red velvet–lined
jewel box. It was the most elegant room
Tess had ever seen. Her feet—shod
now in borrowed shoes—immediately
sank deep into the carpet. Waiters hovered. Tentatively, Tess pulled a chair up
to the table, inspecting the ironing job
on the elegant white linen tablecloth
with a practiced eye. She knew the difficulties of ironing linen and lace, and
this was meticulous work.

"Does it meet your standards, Tess?"
Lucile said, apparently amused at the
girl's inspection. "We are on land now,
no rolling deck beneath our feet. Tonight, I intend to enjoy myself. The ordeal is over. Isn't that right, dear?"

Tess was spared an answer as several friends of the Duff Gordons came
bursting through the door, all descending with lavish cries and hugs and
kisses. She fingered the wispy chiffon
gown Lady Duff Gordon had pronounced that she should wear, feeling oddly naked. What was she doing

here under these glittering chandeliers, watching waiters pour champagne into thin-stemmed crystal glasses? Back in Cherbourg, she would be waiting on this table, not sitting at it.

"I feel we are welcoming you back to the land of the living," said one woman in a low, tremulous voice as she planted a moist lipstick kiss on her friend's cheek. "Dearest Lucile, we are so grateful you were saved. Look—" She reached back with her hand and pulled forward a dignified-looking gentleman with a very dark mustache. "We brought Jim Matthews to celebrate with us!"

Lucile had already taken a few sips of champagne, enough to bring a hovering waiter to refill her glass, and her color was high. She reached out her hand. This was one of her favorite, most sycophantic fashion writers—a man who always touted her designs. "My dear friend, I'm delighted to have you here, even though you refuse to take my advice and leave that awful newspaper business."

"But then where would New York be able to read the best coverage of the

latest Lucile designs?" the man asked with a smile, bending to clasp her hand.

Everyone laughed, though Tess noted Sir Cosmo's eyes narrowing. He became intent on lighting his pipe when he saw her looking at him. With the match lit and the pipe in place, Cosmo was staring disapprovingly at the door. Tess followed his eye.

Pinky Wade was standing there, surveying the scene with interest. She obviously wasn't intimidated by her surroundings. She wore a nondescript dress that was much too short and stained on the bodice, and her boots were shabby. She had a huge, floppy bag tossed over her shoulder.

"Welcome, my dear, are you staying for dinner?" Lady Duff Gordon swept her with a critical eye. "The girl is a walking clothes disaster," she murmured to a nearby friend. "Why do women do this to themselves?"

Pinky seemed oblivious. "Absolutely. It's free, isn't it?" She smiled brightly at the gathered crowd and plunked down in an empty seat. Spotting Tess across the table, she waved.

"You know her?" Cosmo said, lookly sharply at Tess.

"I met her on the *Carpathia*."

"That wasn't a good idea." His voice was cool.

"We spoke only briefly," Tess said quickly.

"I understand. But Lucile *did* advise you not to talk with reporters."

"Quite a dinner you're having," Pinky said, cutting in. She beckoned to one of the waiters holding a cheese plate, scooped up a silver spoon, and began helping herself, pleased with the way things were going. Van Anda had been deliriously happy with the material she had picked up on the ship. Her stock was so high in the *Times* newsroom that he told her she could follow the *Titanic* story from any angle she wanted. Which was exactly what she was doing tonight. She glanced at Tess, and felt even more confident of her decision to keep collecting string on Lifeboat One rather than dumping it into her first story. There was more to learn, she was sure of it, and getting this invitation had been a major stroke of luck. She spread

a healthy scoop of Camembert onto a small roll, appreciatively munching away as she looked around the room, not wanting to seem too focused on Lady Duff Gordon. This stuff was good— salty and buttery. She'd try the Fourme d'Ambert next.

Why, Pinky asked herself, was there such a mystique around this flashy woman with the pretentious last name? For someone who loomed so large in the gilded world of the New York rich, she looked very small with her flaming, almost defiantly red, hair. A curious package altogether.

"My dear, I do hope you like the cheese, but we must save room for the delicious filet mignon the chef is pre-paring for us right now," Lucile sang out across the table. Her laughter rip-pled through the dining room—lighter, more girlish than Pinky had expected.

Pinky reached for the Fourme d'Ambert, cutting herself a thick slice. "I certainly will," she said cheerfully. "So are you going to tell us all about your experience, Lady Duff Gordon?"

"Yes, what happened, Lucy?" im-

plored a woman with a boa wrapped around her shoulders. "Oh, Lucy, tell us from start to finish! How did you survive?"

Lucile cleared her throat, casting a triumphant glance at Cosmo. "My dears, looking down from the deck, hearing the screams of the poor souls below, I won't deny that I feared those black waters," she said, her naturally husky voice descending an octave. "It was the most incredible adventure of my life, and it took every ounce of resolve to cheat fate."

"Just how did you do that?" Pinky asked quietly.

"By keeping my head when others lost theirs," Lucile replied coolly.

For the next five minutes, she held her audience enthralled. She lamented the incompetence of the ship's crew, the flimsiness of the canvas lifeboat, the coldness, the fear. She described how, even with the ice water of the sea seeping up through her toes to her ankles, she managed to hold off the hysterics of the other survivors . . . and then, in a broken, almost breathless

whisper, told of the awful moment when the *Titanic* plunged to the bottom of the sea. "Women and men were clinging to bits of wreckage in the icy water, and it was at least an hour before the awful chorus of shrieks ceased," she said.

Cosmo cleared his throat, putting a cautionary hand on his wife's arm. She shook him off.

"I remember the very last cry, a man's voice calling loudly, 'My God, my God—'" Lucile's voice broke off. Her hands, quickly hidden, had begun to shake.

By now the small roomful of people had been reduced to tears. Even the waiters were riveted in place, listening, eyes wide, holding plates in midair. Swept away by her own account, Lucile lifted her face to the shimmering light from the crystal chandelier, not even attempting to wipe away the tears trickling down her cheeks.

Tess looked down at her own clenched hands beneath the tablecloth. She could almost taste the salt, the anguish; almost grab on again to the

rough, wet sides of her own boat, the telling was so vivid. She glanced up at the faces of the well-dressed men and women leaning forward under the glittering chandeliers, oohing and aahing, tossing in questions at Lucile's dramatic pauses.

"Oh Lucy, how fortunate that you had the intelligence to devise your escape," murmured one of the guests. "How brave you were."

"People were deluded, scoffing that the ship couldn't possibly sink." She seemed briefly to be somewhere else, dreaming. The room went quiet. There was palpable relief when she regained her normal authoritative tone. "I saw them pull back from the lifeboats, refusing to board. I hate to say this, but they were idiots. They didn't use their heads. Those who stayed calm had the best chance to survive."

"How many in your boat, Lady Duff Gordon?" Pinky asked abruptly.

"We were in the captain's boat, and we might have been able to take a few more if the crew hadn't been so disorganized," Lucile replied.

"Who gave the order to launch prematurely?"

"It wasn't premature—the ship was sinking, for heaven's sake."

"We weren't the only half-full boat, Miss Wade," Cosmo cut in, his words clipped tight. "We've heard that the loading of passengers was botched across the ship."

"But yours was the emptiest—makes one wonder," Pinky said. Her tone was non-accusatory, and her eyes lit up as waiters began serving thick cuts of filet mignon on pink china rimmed in silver. "Wonderful meal," she said with a nod to Lucile. "Thank you for inviting me." She began cutting into her meat, as rosy and tender as any she had ever eaten, chewing happily as the others shifted uneasily and played with their forks.

"Are you criticizing me after what I endured?" Lucile demanded.

Pinky wiped her mouth with an impatient sweep of her white linen napkin. "I'm not criticizing you, I'm stating a fact," she said. "If I understand cor-

rectly, you even called the shots in the lifeboat."

"That's quite enough on this tragic event," Cosmo said, cutting quickly into their exchange. "My wife remains distraught, as do I. We hoped you were joining us tonight to share our celebration of life, not to attack."

With hardly a sound in the room, Pinky put her fork down on the edge of her plate and looked up, gazing steadily first at Lucile and then at Cosmo.

"It's not enough to celebrate survival," she said calmly. "There are people downstairs in the hotel lobby, down at the docks, in the tenements on the East Side, who lost husbands and wives and sisters and children, and they have nothing to celebrate. People like you always survive. You owe more."

Again, silence.

"This isn't the usual rich-versus-poor story you like to tell," Jim Matthews said, glaring at Pinky. "Lucy, you've told an incredible story, and your behavior was heroic, that's my opinion. I know Mr. Hearst will want your account for

the *Sunday American.* Can we use it? With your signature?"

"I think not—" Sir Cosmo started to say, but Lucile interrupted him with a decisive shake of her head. She would not be cowed by this rude girl.

"Of course you may," she said.

Pinky pushed her chair back from the table and rose. Somehow she had managed to clean her plate. "That's definitely brave of you," she said. "I hope you'll fill out more details about what went on in your lifeboat. I'm hearing some tales. Good night, all."

She glanced at Tess, silently answering her surprised look. Yes, she had been talking to others about Lifeboat One.

Tess's eyes followed Pinky as she threw her bag over her shoulder and marched out the door. No one else here seemed to be paying attention. Lady Duff Gordon was already in animated conversation with one of her friends, and a thin vein of laughter had begun to ripple around the table, clearly at Pinky's expense. It was as if they were behind glass, safe from the anger of

others. Overdressed, caked in makeup. Lipsticked cigarettes in crystal ash-trays, smelling sour. Tess slipped out of her seat and hurried after Pinky.

"Wait," she said.

Pinky paused at the opening elevator doors. "What are you doing, trying to get your head chopped off? You shouldn't be following me. She'll fire you in an instant."

"You're right about it not being enough to survive. I wanted to tell you that."

"Be careful, those are dangerous words. You work for pompous, privi-leged people who never learn anything. I still don't know why you're risking your job. Go back and eat the fancy des-serts she's providing."

"I'm not hungry." It was true. The meal tonight might as well have been sawdust.

"What's taking away your appetite?"

"It's too soon. And it's too much." She could say it—she had to say it, whether it was disloyal to Lucile or not.

"Of course, these people don't

change. Did you think it would be different?"

Tess drew a deep breath. "Yes," she said simply.

Pinky peered curiously at Tess. For someone who had been a servant in America for no more than a few hours, she was taking some big chances. But her own anger was turning to chagrin. She was an idiot. She could have learned more about what happened on Lifeboat One instead of taking an easy shot at a puffed-up designer who could see a major disaster only through the prism of her own experience. She should have kept her wits and listened, asking questions, not making stupid speeches.

"I'm not angry at you, I'm the one who made a mess of things. I should have shut my mouth and listened."

"But you spoke up."

"So, okay, will you talk to me?" Pinky challenged.

"What is it I can tell you? Everybody did the best they could." She had said this before, somewhere.

"Oh, I see. Back in the employ of the

fabulous Lady Duff. Okay, see you later."

Pinky stepped into the elevator, letting the doors close behind her.

Flushing, Tess turned to go back to the dining room. She had been dismissed, just dismissed, as if she wasn't worth anything. She stopped. Lucile, arms folded in front of her chest, was standing at the end of the hall.

"If you do not like my food, I can make other arrangements," she said in an icy tone. "Is that what you want?"

"I wasn't hungry," Tess managed.

"That woman insulted me. Blatantly. And you apparently admired that. That's why you followed her out here."

"No, not like that . . ." Tess tried to say more, but no words came out. Lucile stared at her, an impenetrable gaze. But Tess saw again something elusive flitting back and forth in Madame's eyes. And then it disappeared.

"You may—let me put it differently— you are *ordered* to return to your room." Lucile turned on her heel, pausing to add, "Get some sleep, in a decent bed, finally." She marched back to the din-

ing room, not waiting for Tess's response.

------

Pinky stared at her image in the gilt-framed mirror at the back of the elevator as it descended. Women preened and primped in front of this thing every night, pinching their cheeks for a rosy glow, adjusting their hair, stroking their diamonds. But right now she was looking at herself, and she looked grubby. Sharp-eyed, sharp-tongued, and grubby.

She shouldn't have turned her back on Tess; she could have said something more. Why did she always feel that it was up to her to correct the unfairness of the world? Her father scolded her often enough. Lose your coolness and you'll lose your journalist eye; that's what he said.

The elevator doors parted and she stepped out into the Waldorf's lobby, where preparations were already under way for the beginning of the U.S. Senate's *Titanic* inquiry. It was a smart de-

cision to move fast, before the survivors became restive to go home. More people were gathering, probably afraid they wouldn't get seats in the morning. Even she was nonplussed at the increased intensity of the scene. Women in shabby clothes sat unheedingly on the rich brocade chairs, some of them crying and wiping their eyes. Men in tweed caps, eyes haunted, milled about, talking to one another, holding themselves apart from this alien environment. Pinky glanced down at her notebook: 706 survivors out of some 2,223 people. Sixty percent of the first-class passengers survived, most of them women. No surprise there. And only twenty-five percent of those in steerage.

Young men in stiff collars carrying boxes into the hotel were hurrying back and forth through the lobby, vanishing into a huge ballroom lit with crystal. Pinky's gaze traveled back to the center of the room, where the action seemed concentrated around a slight man in a black coat. His mustache was so big it almost swallowed his face.

So now she could meet William Alden Smith legitimately. No use keeping out of his way; he surely knew she had sneaked onto the *Carpathia*—that is, if he and his aides had read her survivor interviews in the late edition. But maybe not. Notebook out, Pinky wedged her way closer, scribbling down everything she could hear. "Hello, Senator Smith," she said with a big smile. "I'm Pinky Wade, from the *New York Times*. What—"

"Yes, Miss Wade, I think we've traveled together. Am I right?" His eyes were quick, more intelligent than she had expected.

"Yes, sir."

"Were you the one in the cap, whistling?"

Pinky felt a slight blush creep up her neck. She nodded.

"I thought so. It's a good song, 'Good Night, Ladies.' But it isn't a sailor's tune."

"Next time I'll choose a better one," she said. "Can I ask a question now?"

He smiled and nodded. He had

thrown her off balance for a second or two; that felt good.

"Who's your first witness tomorrow?"

"Bruce Ismay." No reason not to tell her. He knew her reputation; this was a reporter to cultivate.

"Is it true he was trying to set a speed record?"

Smith blinked, startled. "Who told you that?"

"I've got my sources, Senator. You can read all about it in the night edition of the *Times.*"

"I have no comment," he said stiffly.

"Okay, but it sounds like the focus of your inquiry is on White Star's culpability, right?"

"*Alleged* culpability. We will cover everything, Miss Wade. Including the fact that there weren't enough lifeboats."

"My editor figured that out first. Be sure to ask Ismay how many people were in his. There were a lot of places in those lifeboats that went begging. Especially in Lifeboat One."

"I know that," he said, annoyed. This woman was getting on his nerves.

Pinky grinned. "Thanks, Senator. See you tomorrow morning."

She turned, satisfied; at least she had a fresh top for the earliest morning edition. She headed for the door, then stopped. Sitting in a corner of the lobby, half hidden by a monster elephant-tree plant, was one of the sailors she had talked with on the *Carpathia*. He looked depressed, almost as if he was deliberately hiding himself.

Pinky edged through the crowd toward the man. "Hello again," she said, pushing back the huge leaves of the plant. "It's me, Pinky Wade. What's wrong?"

Startled, he looked up at her. "What are you doing here?"

"Oh, just a little more reporting. We didn't talk too long on the ship. Anything else you want to tell me?"

"No." He slumped back down in his seat.

"Are you going to have to testify?" she asked.

"I hope not."

"I would sure like to know what happened in that lifeboat."

He looked up at her again, more thoughtfully this time. Assessing her usefulness to him, she figured. "Maybe you will," he said.

"Now?"

"Now."

Pinky pulled up a chair.

------

It must have been long past midnight, but Tess couldn't sleep. The first night of her life in a bed with a thick, luxurious mattress that felt heavenly, covered in the smooth crispness of fine percale sheets, and she could not close her eyes. The Duff Gordons were arguing with each other, their voices rising and falling in the next room, gaining energy as the hours passed. Only when they shouted could she hear the words. "I'll say what I want to say, and no one will stop me, not even you," Madame railed at one point. Tess threw an arm across her brow. She knew enough about marital fights—she had certainly lived through many of these late-night sessions between her parents.

She rose, moving silently across the room, wary of making any noise. She stopped before a handsome mahogany dresser and poured herself a glass of water from a fragile porcelain pitcher, staring into the mirror. Only a few days ago, she wanted nothing more than to *be* the fabulous Lucile. All that she had dreamed about and hoped for had been delivered to her. She had moved into the orbit of the woman she most admired.

But things were tipping, turning sideways. That one warm moment on the ship—Lucile understanding the pain, sharing this awful experience—what a wonderful thing. To know that she cared, that she understood what it was like to try and break free and move upward—overwhelming. Yet those flashes of—say it plain, no one was listening—*cruelty* . . . What was there to say about them? Sometimes the fabulous Lucile didn't seem quite so fabulous anymore. But at other times she seemed to be reaching out, in need. How could Tess not offer solace?

And yet she couldn't shake the feel-

ing that there was something else going on that she didn't understand.

Pinky was right—it wasn't enough
just to survive. And maybe Jim was,
too: maybe she was trying too hard to
hold on to her meal ticket in this new
country.

She bowed her head, weary at being
faced once again with conflicting emotions. Stand up, challenge, do what you
want. Yes. That's what had got her off
the farm, got her fleeing Cherbourg,
got her on the *Titanic*. No. Be careful,
be loyal, challenge nothing. Why had
she survived? Why not all those poor
souls praying and pleading in the water? Why not Jack Bremerton? She
owed a debt, but it wasn't clear to
whom—or how it was to be paid.

She fingered the carving of the lifeboat she had placed in front of the mirror, moving her finger gently around its
curves and crevices. Impulsively, she
dipped a finger into a jar of cold cream
and drew the outline of her face on the
mirror, then stepped back. Odd—the
size of the image didn't change even
as she retreated. Shouldn't it be shrink-

ing? She moved forward; it stayed the same. She was no larger, no smaller.

She drained the glass, grateful for the cool water, then returned to bed. She fell into a restless sleep with one last conscious thought: whatever was to come next would not be the glamour of strolling the deck of the *Titanic*. That was gone forever, if it had ever existed.

**5**

## WALDORF-ASTORIA
## APRIL 19

Tess knocked lightly on the Duff Gordons' door the next morning, not sure what to expect. Lucile answered almost immediately, looking wan and listless. There was no sign of her husband. Silently, she pointed to a copy of the *American* on her bed.

Tess picked up the paper. "MY HARROWING EXPERIENCE ESCAPING THE TITANIC" was the headline, followed by a first-person account of Lucile's near-death adventure, enhanced with lurid prose. So melodramatic, it took her breath away.

"Did I say all that last night?" Lucile asked. Her voice was subdued.

"Some of it. But it's been embellished; it's not fair."

"I feel terrible. Cosmo is furious."

Lucile looked so fragile, her face crumpled and tired, that Tess, impulsively, took her hand. "It's just someone's idea of a way of selling newspapers," she said. "The same way it's done in England."

"But not with me as the victim." The older woman sank down on the silk-covered sofa next to the window. "Cosmo says I've put myself front and center of this disaster and we will pay dearly for it. That everybody will go after us now, making up all sorts of stories. Why are they mocking me?" She snatched the paper and threw it to the floor. "Did you read some of those sentences?" She quoted, in a mincing voice: " 'I said to my husband, we may as well get into the boat, although the trip will be only a little pleasure excursion until the morning.' I never said that! Did I?"

"No, you didn't—you weren't at all

flippant." There was no use reminding Lucile of how much she *had* said last night. "You were just telling your story."

"Thank you, dear. You understand." Lucile seemed genuinely comforted. "There's nothing about me in the *New York Times,* fortunately," she said. "The Wade girl wrote about the failings of the ship's captain and the muddled response of White Star, and threw in a few narrow-escape stories—the full front page. She didn't write about my dinner. Probably realized she owed us something for that good meal she gobbled down." Lucile glanced sideways at Tess, her only acknowledgment of their confrontation the night before.

"What a scruffy lot, these reporters," she continued. "Now help me get ready, dear. I have to get to my shop. Thank goodness I shipped most of the dresses for the show ahead of time. It would have been truly dreadful if they had all gone down. The—"

"What about the inquiry?" Tess asked, surprised.

Lucile looked at her sharply. "After this story? Tess, if I go down there I will

be inundated with reporters. You know what the bellman who brought up the papers this morning said? He said people downstairs were talking about the 'millionaires' boat.' How can I go down and be subjected to that mockery?" She waved her hand dismissively, looking less wan and more determined. "You go and find out what happens. You had your dress sent to the hotel laundress last night, didn't you? I'm going to my salon."

Tess had her hand on the doorknob when she turned back. She had to ask. "Did anything terrible happen in your lifeboat?" she asked softly.

"Are you trying to condemn me, too?" Lucile's voice was suddenly fierce.

"No, of course not. But—"

"Nothing happened, for heaven's sake. Absolutely nothing. And all this talk about our boat being huge is ridiculous. It was quite small. Aside from the Darlings' deception, there was nothing happening. Now do you feel better?"

"Yes." But she didn't. Lucile's smile was too hard at the edges.

At nine o'clock, Tess made her way to the hotel's already crowded East Room. She could hardly breathe as she pushed her way in. The room simmered under the full voltage of five huge crystal chandeliers, made all the more stifling by the hundreds of people pushing their way in, many of them—especially the ones in shabby dress—jammed up against the walls. She felt sweat building under her arms and wished she had something lighter to wear. Cosmo had slipped an envelope with her pay in American dollars for the first week under her door last night, but she could not imagine spending it on anything as frivolous as clothes. It was all she had.

A large woman slipped her ample girth into one of the last remaining seats behind Tess and leaned forward to chat. It was Margaret Brown.

"Well, hello again, my fellow oarsman, I do declare." Her face was so round and motherly. "Your lady certainly made the news this morning, didn't she?"

"Unfairly," Tess said quickly.

"She didn't give the interview?"

"Well, she did, yes."

"Ah, too bad. Though it's not quite fair to call their raft the 'millionaires' boat,' I'd say. There were plenty of millionaires on all the boats. But getting singled out isn't good. There might be a hard time ahead for the Duff Gordons."

"She was just trying to tell her story."

Mrs. Brown looked kindly at Tess. "You are a loyal young woman, I see. If she's lucky, Lady Duff Gordon will be spared any further attention. This very proper Senator Smith doesn't plan to call any women to testify. He says we're too delicate to be put through such a public trauma. Isn't that ridiculous? Here's what I think. These men don't want to hear anything critical *about* us or *from* us."

"Do you think—" Tess began. But her attention was suddenly caught by a woman in a shabby coat shouting from the back of the room. "Why do you all hate me? What did I do except save my own life?" the woman yelled.

A moan swept the room, an almost inaudible wash of sound.

"Ah, there we are," murmured Mrs. Brown. "Some man in first class probably gave her his lifeboat seat. Everything's still raw."

"These hearing are beginning too soon."

Mrs. Brown leaned close. "Honey, Neptune was exceedingly good to us," she whispered, her eyes warm and kind. "We made it out of those waters, and now we bear witness."

Indeed. That gave Tess momentum. She stood, pointing to the woman being elbowed against the wall. "Someone give that woman a place to sit down," she shouted as loudly as she could. "Don't you see, she's one of us. Shame!"

Silence fell across the room. Tess made no move to sit down. Let the merely curious onlookers laugh or disapprove, she didn't care; she could feel the fear and pain around her.

There was movement at the doorway. A chair was offered and the woman sat down. A sigh rolled through the

room, releasing the tension. Tess took her seat again, stunned at her own fury, and now fully conscious of the stares directed her way.

"Good for you, honey," Mrs. Brown said heartily, patting her on the back. "You stood up and hit them between the eyes."

"I may get in trouble."

Mrs. Brown's eyes widened in astonishment. "Trouble? Everybody gets into trouble in America—that's what it's about. People don't like being scolded with the truth, and they damn well need to be sometimes. You stood up for someone. What's wrong with that? I'd rather hear truth being defended than all the gossip and rumors people are passing around. I'm not even sure the rumor about that amnesiac being dumped in the hold is true."

Tess straightened up. "What amnesiac?" she asked.

"Some poor soul from steerage whose brain got addled somehow. Nobody's claimed him, they say."

"Are you sure he was from steerage?"

Mrs. Brown looked at her curiously. "I don't know who you were hoping it would be, dear, but no first-class passenger would be unidentified by now."

Tess lowered her head, knowing this to be true.

"Now, here's a story for you—you know those small boys you saved?" Mrs. Brown said, changing the subject.

"Are they all right?" Tess said quickly, her heart skipping a beat. It had been hard to say goodbye to Michel and Edmond. "Have the authorities located any family?"

"You might say so." Mrs. Brown's face turned sorrowful. "It turns out Mr. Hoffman's real name was Michel Navratil. He was kidnapping his sons. Their mother is very much alive and frantic to claim them."

"Oh, my goodness." If that sad-faced man on the *Titanic,* who clearly loved his boys, had been stealing them, was anybody who he appeared to be?

"So many stories." Mrs. Brown nodded in the direction of a coolly beautiful woman dressed in black sitting nearby, fanning herself with vigor. Her hair was

luxuriously abundant, her face pale as a porcelain teacup.

"Now there's Mrs. Bremerton, one of the wealthier widows. She's undoubtedly here to figure out whom to sue. Turned me down when I asked for a donation for the Survivors Committee. Some people just want their money for themselves. Take the stuff too seriously, in my opinion."

Tess stared at the woman Mrs. Brown had pointed out, mesmerized by her calmness. She could hardly believe it; this was Jack Bremerton's wife. "She must be devastated," she whispered.

"Given the fact that everybody knew he was going to divorce her, probably not." Tess gasped, and Mrs. Brown shot her a curious glance. "Was he a friend of yours, dear?"

She was trying to think of an answer when there was a sudden stir at the door. Grateful for the diversion, she turned to watch. The senator who had stalked the decks of the *Carpathia* was making his way down a narrow aisle. He was about in his late fifties, she guessed, with a huge mustache on a

face so strongly sculpted it could grace a monument. Striding past Tess and Mrs. Brown, he made his way to the head of a table positioned against the back wall, which was already filled with members of the investigating committee. He wore a black coat with a velvet collar, which he threw off the moment he claimed his chair.

Senator Smith banged his gavel for silence in the room.

"Order, please!" The hearing was about to begin.

-----

Pinky nodded to her photographer to move closer as she stared at Bruce Ismay, wondering why it was that rich, important men never seemed to know that it was a big mistake to look *too* rich at a public inquiry. The elusive manager of the White Star Line wore a dark-blue suit with a navy silk scarf threaded through his high collar, and everything—down to the linen handkerchief in his breast pocket—oozed privilege.

"You should've taken off that diamond ring, Ismay," she murmured to herself. She signaled the photographer to shoot just as Ismay put his hand up, the huge diamond glittering in the light from the chandeliers. The flash went off with a sharp explosion.

"Get those photographers out of here!" Senator Smith roared. "You have a statement, Mr. Ismay?"

A seemingly rattled Ismay cleared his throat and tugged at his cuffs. "I would like to express my sincere grief at this terrible catastrophe," he began. "We welcome this inquiry by the U.S. Senate and we have nothing to hide. Absolutely no money was spared in the construction of the *Titanic*."

"So why were you urging the captain to go fast through that ice field?" shouted a man by the door.

Smith banged his gavel, repeatedly this time. Would he be able to keep this crowd under control? Perhaps the hearing should have waited a few days. No, Ismay would have escaped the witness chair. Smith banged again, more urgently.

"What were the circumstances of your departure from the ship?" asked Smith when the room quieted down.

"The boat was there," Ismay replied. "There were a certain number of men in the boat, and the officer called out asking if there were any more women, and there was no response, and there were no passengers left on the deck."

A few people moved restlessly, looking at one another. No passengers left on the deck? Nonsense.

"What was the full complement of lifeboats for a ship of this size?" Smith asked.

"All I can tell you is, she had sufficient boats to obtain her passenger certificate," Ismay said firmly. "She was fully boated, according to the requirements of the British Board of Trade."

Smith leaned back in his chair. Fully boated? What did that mean? Ismay knew there weren't enough boats. And he knew they weren't filled properly, but he was never going to admit it.

The questions kept coming from Smith, and the other members of the board of inquiry, for the next two hours.

The air in the room became so stifling, even Senator Smith was wiping his face with a large white handkerchief. Finally he banged his gavel to announce a recess, accepting the fact that Ismay had managed to artfully dodge every question that would impugn the White Star Line. But what Ismay hadn't done was clear himself of the stain of his cold behavior. That cheered Smith up. The next witness, he declared to the room, would be Arthur Rostron, the captain of the *Carpathia*. An honorable man; a good contrast.

------

Tess made her way through the crowd to the lobby, eager for some fresh air. People began pushing one another with urgency, jostling to get out, and she suddenly felt a stab of the same panic that had gripped them all on the *Titanic*. She started to push, to squeeze through, then forced herself to take a deep breath. This was not the deck of that doomed ship; this was a room, that was all—a crowded room. She took

another deep breath; she was almost to the door. It would be a long time before she felt comfortable in a crush like this.

She spied Pinky by the elevators, looking directly at her, a small, inquiring smile on her lips as she approached, the same large bag she had carried last night slung over her shoulder. The strap was extra long, causing the bag to flop about below her waist, hitting against other people exiting the room. A few irritated glances were shot in her direction, but she seemed impervious to them. "Oops," she said once, after stepping on a fragile toe.

"You're getting people mad at you," Tess said.

"Nothing new about that," Pinky said with a shrug. She hesitated. "I'm sorry I turned my back on you last night. I made a mess of the evening."

"No, you didn't. You said what you had to say, and I admire that."

"I mean, I didn't stick around to get enough information. Will you answer a few questions now?"

Tess nodded. "If I can help, but I don't know if I can."

"I'm hearing Lady Duff Gordon refused to let the crew go back for survivors when it would have been easy to bring more into the boat. What do you think?"

"How could I know? I wasn't there."

"Nice dodge. Well, that's what I hear from a sailor on the lifeboat." Pinky abruptly changed course. "I also hear from a Mrs. Brown that it was the women who took over the rowing in your boat, and that you were one of them."

Tess nodded, then laughed. "The sailors were impossible. I don't think the ones in our boat ever had an oar in their hands in their lives."

"That's a good quote," Pinky said, scrambling in her bag for her paper and pencil. "Think of how many times women have to step up when men turn cowardly. And the pompous cretins won't even let us have the vote—"

"You're a suffragist?"

"Of course." Pinky was amused at the instant curiosity on Tess's face.

"And you will be, too, if you stay here." Then, in one of her abrupt transitions, "Which sailor gave you the carving of a boat?"

"That doesn't matter—it was just a carving." Why this seemed to be information she didn't want to give, she didn't know. Maybe because Pinky seemed to want to know everything and could spring surprises too easily.

"Oh." Pinky allowed herself a disappointed look, but she had her answer. Maybe a romance on board? That would make a nice sidebar. Or, perhaps—oh, forget it. She folded the retrieved notebook and stuffed it back into her bag. She liked Tess. No need to peel any more layers. At least, not now.

The chandelier began to blink, signaling the resumption of the hearings. "It's time to go back to the hearing room," Tess said, bracing her shoulders.

Pinky caught the movement. "They're morons, to hold these hearings so soon," she said quickly. "You must think we're ghouls."

"I see ghouls everywhere today," Tess said. "Nobody looks real."

"It's kind of a dance, you know? It's not to be taken personally. At least, not all the time."

"You know it can hurt," Tess replied.

"I do. And I'm not out to hurt you." They exchanged swift, unguarded glances. For just a second, Tess let herself believe that Pinky understood the conflicts between head and heart.

------

Captain Rostron was an unusually tall man, something Tess had noticed from the first moment she saw him on the deck of the *Carpathia*. She remembered how his bald head had shone under the morning sun.

The room fell quiet as he began his testimony. There was a daunting distance of fifty-eight miles between the *Carpathia* and the *Titanic*, and if he hadn't moved fast when he got the distress call time would have run out. He posted extra lookouts and ordered emergency gear brought on deck and

bedding prepared for the survivors. He ordered all hot water on the ship to be turned off so that every drop of water could be converted into steam. And, icebergs or not, the ship would travel at full speed.

"Captain, could you describe the *Titanic* lifeboats that carried the survivors?" Senator Smith asked at one point. "How many can they hold?"

Tess closed her eyes, waiting for the answer.

"The collapsible boats could hold sixty to seventy-five comfortably," he replied.

------

The next witness was Charles Lightoller, the second officer of the *Titanic,* the highest-ranking officer to survive. It was clear immediately that Lightoller realized that Senator Smith was no expert in maritime affairs. Smith's first questions about technical matters were clumsy, obviously uninformed. Each time Lightoller patiently explained some detail, as if to a child, he would give a

little smile and tilt his head, as if to let others in on the joke. He seemed almost cocky as he slumped back in the witness chair, fielding questions about the proximity of icebergs, the speed of the ship, the absence of warnings.

Then, unexpectedly, a direct question. "You were in charge of loading the lifeboats, sir. Why were so many not filled to capacity?"

"I was afraid that fully loaded boats might collapse on the way down to the water," Lightoller said smoothly.

"But weren't people clamoring to get on?"

"Some were, some weren't."

Tess thought of the chaos, of people being shoved into boats or pushed away from them, of the shouts and screams and total confusion of those last hours.

"Would you do it differently if you could?"

"No, I handled it the best way possible."

Glances were exchanged in the room: indignant ones accompanied by exclamations; furtive ones darting back and

forth with lips sealed. Tess stared at the man in the witness chair. She had seen smooth liars before. Just say something calmly and convincingly and there will be those who believe you.

"They're going to close ranks," a man behind her muttered. "Nobody gets the blame."

Tess was left to sit and stare and wonder at her own naïveté.

------

Lightoller's testimony—without a breath of criticism for his employer—continued for hours but was finally over, and a clearly weary Senator Smith adjourned the hearing for the day. Some in the audience went up to shake his hand, with polite murmurs of praise. But many just filed out, talking among themselves.

Smith collected his papers. Ismay, Lightoller—their testimony came as no surprise. They knew damn well they were in trouble if there was a ruling of negligence. They knew Americans could sue them, even if they were Brit-

ish. And they knew they would face a British inquiry when this one was over.

Shoulder on, he told himself. One thing he had accomplished: none of the Britons were going anywhere for a long time.

------

Pinky pushed herself back from her desk at the *New York Times,* the broken wheel of her chair catching once again on the pine boards of the newsroom floor. Tonight, she didn't care. Today's testimony would be in everybody's stories tomorrow. Not hers. Her story was juicier—written fast, headlining the early night edition—and it was more than a good story; it dug into the world of the entitled rich. What idiots they were. So the Duff Gordons hadn't done anything worse than anyone else? She didn't believe it. They deserved to be brought down. They were foils for the real story: mostly poor people died, and mostly rich people were saved; that was the fact of it.

She wadded up her discarded copy

sheets into tight little balls and threw them, one after another, into a box mounted against the far wall. It was a good way to let off steam after a deadline, and she was one of the best shots in the newsroom. And oh, it felt good to have won an argument with Van Anda. How could she name the man who had given her the information? He would immediately be fired or deported; that's what they did with those sailors. "Okay," he had finally said. "You're opening up things here, so be ready for what comes next." Tomorrow she'd talk to some suffragists who felt that it was a scandal to save women and children first. *That* would raise some hackles.

Van Anda's amused voice cut through her concentration. "Good job, Pinky," he said. "Smith will be mad as hell that you got this on your own instead of waiting for testimony. Do you have to keep showing up your fellow reporters? Go home, you've got those hearings tomorrow."

"In a minute."

"Yeah, I know."

A slow rumble began beneath their feet. The presses were running.

"You can go now," he said gently. Where did she go? he wondered. Not for the first time, he marveled at his star reporter's single-mindedness; her refusal to share anything about a private life that he suspected centered around a hot plate in a lonely rooming house. The women in this business were a strange lot.

Pinky sent one more wadded ball sailing across the room and leaned over, heaving her canvas bag up over her shoulder. She gave Van Anda a mock salute and strode out of the newsroom, kicking at an orange peel on the floor. Why was this place always so filthy? Somebody should write the shocking story of poor housekeeping at the *New York Times.* She smiled to herself as she took the stairs, two at a time. She could have tap-danced down tonight. Once again, that lovely feeling of twirling under the stars, beholden to no one, standing clear and tall on a bold byline that thousands would see,

and if that wasn't enough, then nothing was.

------

Tess stepped outside the revolving doors of the Waldorf-Astoria, breathing in the sharp, cold air. It felt wonderful. She wondered if Lady Duff Gordon was back yet from her shop. Surely she was, it was already sunset, and the street before her—filled with a noisy mix of horse-drawn clattering carts and automobiles—was bathed in a rosy glow.

But she didn't want to go upstairs to find out. Not yet. There was a park nearby, a hotel doorman told her, quite a nice park, right here in the middle of the city. He was astonished that she hadn't heard of it.

"Tess." It was a calm, familiar voice.

Jim Bonney stood on the sidewalk, hands shoved into the pockets of baggy pants held up with a knotted belt missing a buckle. If anything, he looked shabbier than before. She saw the disdain in the eyes of the doorman, who

was dressed in a navy-blue uniform with glittering brass buttons. She had seen that look today in the eyes of many of the Waldorf's bellboys and waiters as steerage survivors crowded past them.

"Jim," she said, astonished at her own rush of pleasure. "I was afraid I wouldn't see you again."

"I wanted to check up on you. I figured, well, she's over in that fancy hotel and my two feet can get me there—find out how we do on stable ground."

"Well, nothing is moving beneath us."

"No waves, no dipping horizon, no creaking decks."

"No water." She shivered slightly. "Going for a walk feels like—freedom."

"Can I keep you company?"

She felt wary. "Did you read about Lady Duff Gordon?"

"Yes." His smile came quickly, then vanished. "It's amazing what she manages to do to herself."

"I am still working for her, you know."

"Yes, I know. We could walk and talk at the same time, couldn't we?"

The light in his eye was too engaging to resist.

"Yes, we can," she said. She cast a glance at the doorman, whose eyes traveled the length of Jim's unprepossessing figure in obvious disapproval.

Jim's eye followed her glance. "Don't let him bother you," he said with a shrug. "He's probably only months or a year removed from wearing clothes like mine. That's too close for comfort. I'll be the guy saving his job one of these days. And you'll be sweeping by him in ostrich feathers." Jim spoke with such good-humored confidence, she couldn't help laughing as they walked away from the hotel.

"Were you there for the testimony today?" she said.

He nodded.

"What did you think?"

"I was proud of the girl who spoke up."

Tess colored, pleased. "Thank you, but the testimony?"

"We're lucky we had a man like Rostron bent on saving us," he said soberly. "He's brave. Lightoller? Just another

corporate man, being careful to use a whitewash brush, that's what I think." He paused. "I saw you talking with that woman reporter, or I would have come over at the recess."

"Have you met her?" Tess was surprised.

"Sure. She was on the *Carpathia* running in every direction, collaring sailors to get them to talk," he said. "Full of bounce and energy. Not a bad sort. Just doing her job, the way we all are."

"Did you talk to her?"

He shrugged. "For a few minutes, like the others."

"I like her," Tess said hesitantly. "But she still makes me uneasy."

"She's got her facts straight, Tess."

"But she wants villains. Every detail has to lead to something darker."

He sighed, running his fingers through his hair. It was brown, with flecks of gold, something she hadn't noticed before. It kept falling in his eyes, and he kept flipping it back; she had a sudden impulse to smooth it back for him. "Well, you know how I feel about that," he said.

"I do. But the newspapers made a mockery of Lucile this morning; it wasn't fair."

He gave her a startled look. "Fairness has nothing to do with it. She was no heroine in that boat. And if I'm called to testify I have to tell the truth."

"You would drag her through the mud?"

"That's not how I see it."

"I know she orders everybody around and wants things done her way—oh Jim, we're not going to spoil our walk with another argument, are we?"

"You think I'm too judgmental."

"Stubborn. I like that word better."

"That's kind of you. 'Harsh' is more like it."

"Yes, I guess it is."

"Look, I haven't told you everything."

Tess pulled her coat closer against the evening chill, but also as a shield. She didn't want to talk about this anymore; there was no way of explaining Lucile. She was still piecing it together herself. But those small glimpses of someone different underneath—they were real, she was sure of that. She

wasn't being dutiful; this was standing up for someone who needed loyalty. She pressed her lips together, resisting a sudden throbbing in her head. She wouldn't dwell on it, not now. "I see more to her than you do," she said.

"Okay." He took a deep breath. "Maybe at some point you might have to choose who you believe."

"I don't want to have to do that."

"I'll not put you in that position," he said slowly.

The tension eased. He took her arm. "No, Miss Collins, I am not going to spoil our walk. Your escort"—he bowed elaborately—"may be a stubborn, clumsy sailor, but he isn't about to wreck his few precious moments with you."

She laughed, relieved. He might be only a sailor, but she felt pleasure in his company, and she wanted no quarrels. How good it felt to hear his words dancing teasingly in the air now, not like blunt instruments.

They walked slowly up Fifth Avenue, inhaling the sights and sounds of the largest city Tess had ever seen. A street

market was closing down, and they stopped to watch two grizzled puppeteers dismantle a cardboard stage and pack up their puppets, ignoring a group of children clamoring for more performances. A woman in a wrinkled apron offered Tess an apple, and she realized suddenly how hungry she was. But at that moment a street vendor's pushcart pulled up next to her.

"Hot dog?" Jim said, pointing to the basket of steaming sausages in the man's cart.

"Dog?" Tess asked, puzzled.

*"Frankfurter,"* he said, rolling his eyes. She reddened, then nodded. She remembered what they were now, but such a strange name.

Hot dogs in hand, they continued their walk, drinking in the wonders of New York. They passed a splendid hotel that looked like a French château, and stopped to watch all the elegant carriages pulling up to its doors, depositing and picking up men and women in resplendent evening garb. Silk top hats on the men; lush, low-cut gowns on the women. Some even wore

diamond tiaras that sparkled in the light. Which ones might be clients of Lady Duff Gordon? Probably several, Tess thought, feeling a twinge of pride.

The park loomed ahead, a leafy enclave of winding paths and grassy lawns. Together they crossed the street and entered, choosing a path flanked by towering elm trees, watching as the golden light filtering through their leaves began to fade. She lifted her face, comforted by the soft glow of twilight. There were only a few people scattered across the rolling lawns, mainly children—getting in one last toss of the ball before going home for dinner. Jim did most of the talking, at first somberly, telling her about his friend who had died in the ship's boiler room. Then about the American West, especially California, which he described as a paradise with such fervor that Tess found herself growing interested. All she had ever thought of was getting to this country, not how large and diverse it was. New York alone was overwhelming.

"Think you'd ever want to go there?" he asked.

"Maybe, someday. But not now."

"You'll do well in this city," he said, surveying the lush terrain of Central Park. "I can see it offers what you want."

"I hope so," she said. "I can learn design from Lucile—that's the best part. Meeting her is the biggest stroke of luck I've ever had."

"I might say that about meeting you," he said quietly.

She felt a second shiver of surprised pleasure.

"I mean," he continued, flushing slightly, "maybe you can teach her a few things, too." He looked down at her with such a warm, open expression, she almost believed what he said next. "Our worlds aren't that different, you know."

Oh, but they were. An astonishing thought—already? Only days ago it would have been true. And somehow, because of that, perhaps, she felt suddenly free to act on impulse. She took his arm.

"Shall we?" she asked. "Just to prove we can still do it?"

"Why not?" he said, breaking into a grin.

And for just a moment, for a few, brief skips, they were back on the deck of the *Titanic* in the glow of that golden setting sun, before everything changed forever.

------

They walked slowly back to the Waldorf, walking close, not touching, Tess listening to his droll commentary on their surroundings. He wasn't intimidated by the gathering theater crowds, the furs, the marvelous black carriages, brass fittings glittering, clattering by. The gas lamps were lit now, their glow rivaling that of the vanished sun. Even the horses in Central Park had their noses in the air, he said. She laughed, deciding on his dare to stroke a lush mahogany beauty, and was delighted when the mare nuzzled at her jacket.

"She wants a treat," Jim said playfully. "Or maybe she wants you to 'turn' her collar. Isn't that what you do?"

"Well, I've never worked in leather—we'd both have to be patient."

He acknowledged her small joke with a generous laugh. They moved on, Tess acutely aware that his tall, muscular figure and strong features—in spite of his shabby clothes—were drawing attention as they walked.

"I've never thanked you for my carving." They were in sight of the hotel. He would be gone soon.

"I wanted to make something for you that marked what happened, what we shared," he said, slowing his step.

"I wish we had been in the same lifeboat."

He took a deep breath, answering in a low, suddenly impassioned tone. "When I saw you teetering on the edge of the rail, holding those children, I knew you wouldn't abandon them. And I knew you couldn't make it into the boat—you wouldn't have time to jump. I wanted to climb back up the ropes and grab you. It would've been impossible, but the sight of you standing there, doomed, never left my thoughts that night."

They both fell silent. They were almost at the hotel. "So, once more, goodbye," Jim said. He stopped, then tipped her chin up gently with his hand. His face was so close. Was he going to kiss her? No. But she felt his breath as he said, "Next time, I'm taking you for a ride throught the park in one of those carriages. If you'll let me."

"Yes," she murmured, pushing all thoughts of his being a village boy out of her mind for the moment. Then quite quickly he was gone, whistling striding west.

Slowly she walked toward the hotel, enveloped in a pleasant haze. She would heed her mother's warnings later, not now.

Ahead of her, a crowd had formed around the hotel. Did this city ever get sleepy? The streets were even more of a scramble here, almost a duel between the cars and the carriages, with drivers shouting at one another, the horses, the people dodging them as they zigzagged, crossing the street.

She saw the center of attention. A newsboy at the door of the Waldorf,

clusters of people around him, stood waving the early edition of the next morning's *New York Times*. Tess hurried past, not ready. But a bellboy who recognized her at the elevators thrust a copy of the paper into her hands. "You'll want to see this," he said.

Tess took a deep breath and stared at the headline.

DID COWARDLY BARONET AND HIS
WIFE BRIBE SAILORS NOT TO GO BACK
FOR DROWNING? EYEWITNESS SAYS
YES AND HINTS AT MORE

Underneath, the byline: Sarah Wade.

The elevator doors opened and she stepped in, head down. No one else entered with her. The doors closed. For just one fleeting moment, she would be enclosed in a protective box of steel and cable that was impenetrable. How wrong she had been to trust Pinky. Who told her those things? Somebody who hated the Duff Gordons, of course. Was it Jim?

All she knew right now was that when she emerged she would be faced with

the ordeal of trying to comfort the woman who only days before was the most invulnerable woman she had ever met. She longed for a slow ascent.

6

Lucile threw a towel over the lit lamp, ignoring Cosmo's complaint about the danger of fire. Right now, she declared, she couldn't stand any more light than necessary. She couldn't stand to have anyone see how swollen from crying her eyes were, and the ugly blotchiness of her skin.

"I was right, wasn't I? Cosmo, tell me I was right."

"Lucy, you took charge and made a sensible decision to save the lives of the people in our lifeboat. No one can fault you on that."

"Well, they have. I've never been attacked like this." She flung herself into the sofa's abundance of silk pillows, her hair matted and disheveled.

Cosmo picked up their copy of the *Times* and threw it into a wicker basket. He sat heavily on the sofa next to his wife. "It'll be all right," he said.

"Those men turned on us."

"All it took was one."

Simultaneously, they turned toward Tess.

"What decision are you talking about—" she began.

Lucile leaped to her feet, her swollen eyes blazing. "Who talked to this woman?" she demanded, kicking at the wastebasket, knocking it over and sending newspaper pages skittering across the room.

"She spoke to many people," Tess said.

"I see. And did that 'many people' include *you*?"

"Yes."

"What did you say?"

"I told her people in steerage couldn't get to the boats in time."

"What else did you prattle on about?"

"She asked why your boat was almost empty and I said I didn't know."

"Ah, yes. That started it. Then there's that sailor friend of yours. He's the one out to get us, that's who; he's the one filled with all the innuendos and lies. Not much of a mystery, is it?"

"Jim isn't a vindictive man," Tess said quickly.

"Oh, now it's '*Jim.*'" Lucile was furious. "Not vindictive? Whose side are you on? He managed to disappear when I gathered people for the photograph. Is he why you didn't join us? And where was he when Cosmo so generously thanked the crew for keeping us safe? Not vindictive? Oh, for God's sake, he's obviously an ignorant product of his class and has no judgment. He's self-righteous, through and through. You had better tell me everything, right now."

"Lucy, calm down," Cosmo interjected. "Our accuser is anonymous. This isn't testimony, it's just malicious gossip."

"Who else would have called us cow-

ards?" she said, staring at Tess. "And *bribery*? For paying those poor men a little money to get them started again? Who else?"

"Lucy, I said calm down!" Cosmo snapped.

"Maybe it was Jean Darling. No, she wouldn't dare."

"Perhaps." He pulled a cigarette from a silver cup on his dressing table and lit it, a slight tremor in his hand prolonging the task.

"The newspapers are trying to ruin me," his wife said, ignoring Tess's pale, set face.

"I'm the one described as a 'cowardly baronet,' you might recall."

Lucile sank down on the sofa. "At this moment, I need all the support you can give me. How can you be thinking of yourself? I know I shouldn't have talked for that article; I knew that the moment I walked into the shop and heard the fabric cutters whispering. Oh, they all said the interview was wonderful, that they were so happy I had survived. But the tone was dutiful, not like

last night in the dining room when my friends hung on my every word."

"You did keep them enthralled," Cosmo said dryly.

"All right, I put myself in the spotlight at just the time when the newspapers were clamoring for scapegoats. So too many rich people survived, and all that—why do *I* have to pay a price?"

She glanced at Tess. "What are you standing there for?" she demanded.

"I'm waiting for your permission to leave."

"Well, I haven't given it."

"I would like to go, please." No, at this moment she would like to run. So they *had* paid money to the sailors.

"You disobeyed me. You talked to that reporter. I should fire you."

No begging, Tess told herself. She was beyond that.

A silence. Then, in a calmer tone, Lucile said, "You look ridiculously bedraggled. Dear Tess, we must get you some decent clothes."

Tess blinked. Another sudden shift from anger to—to what?

"I can go, then?" she asked.

"Go, go, for heaven's sake. But I want you to come with me to the shop to-morrow morning. Someone else can report back on the inquiry. Now please go tell the hotel switchboard we will be taking no calls from reporters anymore, no exceptions, and I will meet you downstairs at eight-thirty. My driver will be waiting; his name is Farley. And, Tess?"

"Yes?" Tess stepped back, away— anything to get away from this volatile woman. She wanted out of here. Oh, how she wanted out of here.

Lucile suddenly stood and cupped both of Tess's hands in her own. "Now don't get upset," she said. "I know you wouldn't betray me. I have a terrible temper, and surely you won't take this too personally." She leaned closer and kissed Tess's cheek, the sweet scent of her floral perfume wafting into the air. "I'll make up for this, dear."

Tess nodded, slightly dazed. She opened the door, murmured good night, and left the room. Lucile had apolo-gized—sort of—to *her*. This thing about the money would be straightened out;

it wouldn't be bribery. Lavish tips were part of their way of life. It had to be Jim who gave Pinky that story. Who else cared? Not the sailors who lined up for pictures, she was sure of that. He must have known it was coming, or guessed it, or something. And he hadn't said a word on their walk, just let it hit her full in the face. Don't jump to conclusions, you don't know, she told herself. Her hands were shaking; she couldn't stop them.

And she couldn't quite forget the word *prattle*.

------

"You really whipped into her, Lucy. For God's sake, what are you trying to do?" Cosmo said as the door closed behind Tess. "Be your mother?"

"That awful woman? For heaven's sake, no."

"You seem to be treating this girl as if you were, my dear."

"I don't want her to—"

"To what? Take control, defy you?"

"I don't care what she does, Cosmo, for heaven's sake. There's no use scolding her for her friendship with that sailor; she looked sufficiently stricken as it was. In fact, she looked *too* stricken."

"Perhaps she's going to be a constant reminder of that terrible crossing."

Lucile paused, absorbing this. "She didn't call me Madame. Have you noticed?"

"Yes," Cosmo replied.

"That's required for her job."

"It's too late," Cosmo said simply.

"She doesn't give you proper deference, either."

"I rather like not being *Sir* Cosmo."

"You are impossible. Please don't make me sad." Lucile swept a hand over her eyes and fell back into the comforting folds of the sofa cushions. "I'm much too tired, and none of this is worth an argument. Tomorrow I'll do battle."

"My dear, we have to face facts. That story will stir an outcry on both sides of the Atlantic, and we are in deeper than I thought we would be. This diligent

Senator Smith will soon focus on us, I'm afraid."

"They wouldn't dare. And if they do I won't allow it."

Cosmo walked over to the lamp and flicked the overheated towel to the floor. The edges were already singed.

------

## WALDORF-ASTORIA
## SATURDAY MORNING, APRIL 20

"So you're the new fetch-and-carry girl? All the way from England or France or somewhere? Kind of silly—Lady Duff's got her pickings here. Well, pile in. She'll be issuing me orders the second she comes out the door."

The man gesturing Tess into the waiting black car outside the Waldorf the next morning had large, full lips and a sardonic grin that annoyed her. He had no higher status than she did, other than that conferred by a driver's license.

"I'm not a fetch-and-carry girl," she retorted.

"My dear, you are whatever she wants

you to be," he said affably. "You're joining her crew of minions—the slavering,
trembling minions that work for the
mighty Madame. I'm one of them—I'm
Farley."

Tess had barely settled herself in her
seat when Farley jumped to attention,
opening the door for Lady Duff Gordon,
slamming it quickly in the faces of a
handful of reporters who rushed up to
the automobile. He shoved the car into
gear and roared into the Fifth Avenue
traffic. Tess slumped, glancing cautiously at Lucile, whose face was more
heavily powdered than usual. No mention of their encounter last night; there
would certainly be none from her.

------

The workrooms for Lucile Ltd. were in
a dingy building just below the Flatiron
Building, on Twenty-third Street. "It's
the pride of New York," Farley said to
Tess, pointing to the Flatiron. "Does
look like an iron, don't you think?"

Maybe it was her general sense of

apprehension, but it didn't look like an iron to Tess; it looked ominous, more like the prow of a ship.

A cluster of people waiting for an elevator scattered like sparrows as Lady Duff Gordon entered the building. "Nobody's allowed to take the elevator when Madame is here; she won't share it," Farley whispered to Tess.

"Don't whisper around me, Farley," said Lucile. She stepped into the elevator and beckoned Tess to follow. Her loft, on the top floor of this building, was her sanctuary—the kingdom she had created and ruled. No one went there without her permission.

The elevator doors opened onto a vast workroom that took Tess's breath away. Everywhere there were worktables heaped with sumptuous brocades, richly hued woolens, and fragile laces. Seamstresses were bending over dressmaker's dummies, their mouths filled with pins, shaping, draping, pinning, while slender-figured women in gray crêpe kimonos lounged against the wall, waiting to be called for fittings.

The place bristled with activity and excitement.

"Wonderful, isn't it?" Lucile called out over the hum of sewing machines and chatter.

Tess nodded vigorously, looking around, openmouthed. She followed Lucile as she threaded her way past the tables, alternately smiling and frowning as she inspected a seamstress's work, picked up a bolt of fabric here, another there, testing their heft and crushability while calling out to various employees—here, finally, was the woman she had been so in awe of on the *Titanic*.

At the back of the vast workroom was Lucile's glass-walled office. The room was bursting with an abundance of flowers—roses, peonies, daffodils—every kind imaginable, perched on every available surface, including the floor, all adorned with what must be congratulatory notes.

"All my clients and friends were happy I survived," Lucile said wryly as she stepped into the room. "We'll soon see if they still are."

Waiting just inside the door, clustered together as if for comfort, a group of men and women with dutiful expressions jumped to attention.

"Good morning, Madame," said one.

Lady Duff Gordon plucked a pair of horn-rimmed spectacles from her handbag, put them on, and stared at each person in turn.

"The runway must be put in place today," she said. "And the draperies closing it off from the workroom must be hung. I don't see anyone working on that out there."

"We need the workroom space for another few days," said a woman in what looked like a white baker's coat. "All the last-minute—"

"There is always last-minute work to do," Lucile said, cutting her off. "Move the work benches closer together. We have to get that runway up early. If there are problems with it, we don't have time to correct them and we have a full house of clients coming. Do I make myself clear?"

"Yes, Madame."

Lucile turned her attention to a young man with thinning hair. "James, where are we on the wedding gown? I don't see my beaders working out there."

"They'll be in this afternoon," he replied hastily.

Lucile began pacing, her voice rising. "Why aren't we further along?" she demanded. "Why aren't the gowns being shaped on the models yet? They're standing out there with nothing to do, and time is running out! The wedding gown is the centerpiece of the show— the beading must be perfectly done, and it needs to be started *immediately*. I said all this yesterday—why isn't it happening?"

"Everyone is working at top pace—" began James, looking nervous.

"I've been alone in the ocean, struggling to survive, and nobody here is making sure the gowns for the show are ready?" Lucile waved her hand, taking in the lush array of flowers filling the room. "My friends are my clients, and my clients are my friends. They cannot be subjected to incompetence."

Tess saw a couple of people in the room exchange glances. One arched an eyebrow and rolled her eyes. This, then, was standard behavior; obviously Lady Duff Gordon knew showmanship.

Unexpectedly, the designer pointed at Tess. "Now here's someone who knows something about competence," she declared. "May I introduce Tess Collins, my fellow lifeboat survivor?" She grabbed a silk dress from the arms of one of the seamstresses, shook it out, and held it up. "Tess, what do you think? Should this have been cut on the bias or not?"

All eyes were on Tess. She studied the dress, wondering what she was expected to say. No matter, the weight of the heavy silk gave her the correct answer. After all those years sewing with her mother, she knew something about fabric. She could do this.

"No," she said firmly. "The draping will sag with one wearing."

Lady Duff Gordon triumphantly tossed the dress back into the arms of the seamstress and turned to the balding

young man who had spoken first. "James, if you're not careful, I will replace you," she warned. "Take Tess to the drawing table—let's see her draw this design the way it should be cut."

· Tess wasn't sure of her drawing abilities; she had always done rough sketches, holding the patterns in her mind, not on paper. She told James this the minute they moved out of the room, which was obviously a great relief to James, who then more kindly began to initiate her into the eccentricities of Lady Lucile.

"She likes to throw out little challenges that make people scramble, which is usually fine. But we'll do anything to keep her diverted this morning." He sighed. "Everyone showed up with a copy of the morning *Times* today, and it was hard to get them to work. I told them to be sure they stuffed them into the waste bins before she came. Nobody's talking about anything else around here. That's why things started slow today." He glanced at Tess soberly. "Haven't told her yet we've had

some orders canceled. Important ones. She'll be furious."

"I don't know what I'm supposed to do here," Tess confessed.

"Madame likes to keep new hires off balance," he said. "I'll start you on the presser."

The shop was magical. When she wasn't ironing gowns, Tess wandered among the tables, fingering the wonderful fabrics, watching the skilled seamstresses sew. At one table an elderly man sat painstakingly sewing buttonholes, separately knotting each stitch and pulling each one exactly as tight as the last. She was riveted when the fittings began. Watching as the pinning and tucking of one of Lady Duff Gordon's floating creations on a human body brought it to life. And staring at the feet of the seamstresses on the pedals of their Singer sewing machines was like watching an intricate dance. She wished her mother could see this. The memory of her—those nights beside the fire, sewing aprons and shirts for her children, the needle flashing in

and out of the goods—gave Tess a fleeting stab of pain. She was totally, hopelessly, in love with this place and all that was in it—every sound, every smell, every morsel of light and movement.

------

Through the glass walls of her office, Lucile watched Tess carefully, allowing herself a measure of satisfaction. The girl's eyes were round as melons. So she was swept up in the glamour of it all, which was precisely what should happen when all was fresh and new. It had been wise to pull Tess away from the censorious carnival taking place back at the Waldorf.

At that moment Tess glanced up. For an instant their gazes locked. And Tess saw the triumph in Lucile's eyes.

**This is what you want, and I have it to give.**

Tess felt a sudden chill. She turned away first.

------

# WALDORF-ASTORIA
# SATURDAY MORNING, APRIL 20

It was only nine in the morning, but Pinky could feel the sweat turning her hands sticky as she waited for the second day of hearings to begin. Chairs were jammed into every corner of the room, and the air was thick and sour with the smoke of dozens of cigars. Every newspaper had extra editions out on the street now, all filled with stories of bravery and cowardice and death, but the hysteria of the reporters was getting funny.

The room was filling rapidly. She half expected the Duff Gordons to send somebody to launch a counterattack, maybe get their friends to freeze her out. But everyone was picking the story up. Just put together the words *bribery* and *millionaires' boat* and there were stories for a week of good sales. She didn't see Tess, either, but that was no surprise. Lady Duff would have made sure to steer her away from today's hearing. She took her handkerchief and pressed it against her forehead, grati-

fied by the glances of envy from her colleagues. It wasn't just getting a good story—all the free-floating anger over who lived and who died on that ship now had one more big focal point. A coup, of course, but she knew how things worked in this business. Today Lady Duff was the villain; tomorrow someone else would be. Already the men who survived were apologizing, cringing almost. How good could it get?

"Well, young lady, what are you grinning about this morning?" Senator Smith had walked into the room and paused by her chair.

"Being here, Senator," she said, recovering quickly from her surprise. "You know it's the only place in town."

Smith smiled and let his starchy demeanor drop for just a second. He rather liked this feisty woman. "Of course, it is."

"Did you read my story about the Duff Gordons bribing sailors not to go back? Any comment?"

His smile faded. "I would prefer you had waited for the testimony."

"Does that mean you're going to call the Duff Gordons to testify?"

"I'm not on a witch hunt."

"Well, are you going to subpoena them?"

"That hasn't been decided." Smith turned away and took his seat at the witness table, quickly gaveling the hearing to order.

The first witness was the only surviving telegraph operator, Harold Bride. Deathly pale and surprisingly young-looking, Bride was in a wheelchair, wincing as he maneuvered his left foot—heavily bandaged—through the crowd.

Smith started his questions gently, and Bride's responses grew stronger as he talked. He and the second wireless operator had tried to raise help from other ships. At one point, he said, he had advised the other operator to use SOS instead of CQD. "It's the new call, and it may be your last chance to send it," he joked. The two men had laughed; he remembered that.

The room grew still when Bride was asked to describe how he managed to

survive. "I fell overboard, holding on to one of the collapsible boats, and then I slipped under it, into some kind of air pocket," he said. "I freed myself from it and cleared out of it. There was a big crowd on top when I got on. I was the last man they invited on board."

A tremor swept the room. *Invited?*

"Were there others struggling to get on?"

"Yes, sir."

"How many?"

"Dozens," Bride said. The word seemed not only to wrench the last shred of energy from his testimony but to strip the official proceedings of their detachment. There was a restless moving, the sound of sniffling and nose-blowing. The anguish in the young man's voice was seeping through the room.

"Dozens," Smith repeated. "In the water? With life preservers on?"

"Yes."

"The word *invited* seems somewhat unrealistic," a panel member interjected.

"That's the way I put it. And that's all I have to say on that."

"What about the boats with room for more? Were people afraid of being sucked under with the ship?"

Bride stayed steady. "I estimate I was within a hundred and fifty feet of the *Titanic*," he said. "I was swimming when she went down. And I felt practically no suction at all. Some of the boats should have come back and helped."

So much for *that* excuse for not going back. Pinky scribbled furiously, thoroughly satisfied. Her pencil hovered at one point as a sudden, surprising thought stopped her hand. Was she angry at the whole bloody lot of them?

------

During a break in the late afternoon, Pinky spotted a familiar figure breaking away from a group of sullen-looking *Titanic* crewmen and walking toward her.

"You really took on the Duff Gordons this morning," said Jim Bonney.

"So I did good?"

But his gaze had shifted; he was looking around, eyes darting from one

spot to another, a worried frown on his face.

"You're probably not the best person to ask, but I'm looking for someone; she works for the Duff Gordon woman."

"You mean Tess Collins?"

"Yes," he said, a little startled.

"I haven't seen her today."

"I have to see her," he said. "Talk to her."

"My guess is Lady Duff took her down to her studio. Sorry, I may be a reporter but I don't know everything."

He seemed to be trying to decide how much to say. "Look, the whole crew is being shipped out to Washington tonight. I have to see her before we go."

She knew that Senator Smith was preparing to move the hearings to his home base, but she hadn't thought it would happen this quickly. "When?" she asked.

"Late, but I guess you knew." Distracted, he shoved his hands into his back pockets, still scanning the room.

No, she hadn't, but she wasn't about to say so or be closed out of the story.

Maybe that's why Smith had been so affable. He thought he was going to shake her and the New York tabloid reporters off his back. "Lady Duff has a reputation as a hard taskmaster," she said cheerfully. "You probably won't see Tess around here until evening. So much for romance." It was a shot over the bow, but it was always fun to see what happened when she took a chance.

He hardly seemed to hear. "Can you reach her?"

"Sounds like something important."

"Look, you seem like a decent sort. If you see her, tell her I'm leaving, will you?"

"Sure. If you'll talk to me again," she added quickly.

"Okay, but not now. Later."

Maybe he even meant it. "You're very talented, by the way. I liked that lifeboat you carved." Another shot over the bow.

"She showed you?" His eyes lit up.

"Something like that."

"Thank you," he said, and turned to go.

"Aren't you going to say goodbye?"

He was good-looking; it was hard not to tease.

He wasn't unaware, casting her an amused look. "Well, I'll be seeing you, I suspect. You're the one covering this show, right? See you in Washington." He turned away and strode off, leaving Pinky feeling quite pleased as she stared after him. She had confirmed not only who made Tess's carving of a lifeboat but why it mattered. That was good. It was always delicious to know more about people than they thought you knew.

------

Lucile calmly surveyed her workroom as her cutters, seamstresses, and pattern-makers packed up their things and began making their way home. The fading light outside cast a wash of gold over the tables and the sewing machines, even reaching the almost finished runway at the far end.

"Tell me now. How many order cancellations?"

James glanced down at the sheet of scribbled notes in his hand. "About ten, Madame," he said.

"Did anyone have the courage to say why?"

"Other obligations," James replied weakly.

"What about reservations for the show?" She stared out at the racks of folding chairs stacked at the end of the room, ready for placement.

"A few cancellations, not many."

"Mrs. Wharton?"

"She sends her regrets; she is unable to come."

"James, I am aware of how many copies of the *Times* were stuffed into the trash bins. I'm sure it was on your orders."

James, his face gray, gave a funny little bow. "Yes."

"Thank you. Good night."

James glanced at Tess, who stood at the door of the office. "Miss Collins will do well here," he said unexpectedly. Then, "Good night."

His footsteps echoed through the

empty loft as he walked away, and now it was only Lucile and Tess.

"We should have a delicious meal waiting at the hotel," Lucile said, pulling on her gloves. She held her head high. "Their chef is absolutely the best, and the three of us will dine in our suite."

Tess followed Lucile to the elevator, trying to hold down the euphoria this wonderful place had aroused in her. How could she ever have envisioned something as good as this? Just holding the fabric, watching the meticulous work of elegant stitching and beading—it had been a day unlike any other. She didn't know how she would fit in here, but she knew that she could. She knew, more than anything, that she wanted to.

The cables pulling up the elevator groaned, louder because of the emptiness of the building. It seemed to take forever to reach the top floor. Tess and Lucile stepped in and the elevator creaked downward with a slight swaying motion that made Tess nervous. When the doors opened on the first

floor, they were instantly confronted by a mob of reporters.

"Did you bribe the sailors?" shouted one.

"Why was your boat so empty?" screamed another.

"How do you defend rowing away from the dying?" bellowed a third.

"Where is Farley?" Lucile said under her breath, ignoring the shouts, the many other questions, pushing her way to the street with Tess close behind.

And then there he was, muscling reporters out of the way, guiding them with a steady hand into the car—the blessed, safe automobile. Tess jumped in, and Farley tried to close the door.

A face poked in—the blotchy face of a man with stale tobacco breath that made Tess cringe. "We've got reports that a man was in your boat masquerading as a woman," he shouted. "Can you confirm that?"

"I won't deny it," Lucile said.

"Was it the dancer Jordan Darling?"

The door was swinging closed. Lucile held it briefly and leaned forward

with a wintry smile. "I won't deny that, either," she said.

The door slammed, Farley jumped behind the wheel, and they shot out into the street, heading uptown through the streets of New York, passing vegetable stands and churches with needle-shaped spires and polished carriages pulled by proud prancing horses, while all the while, beneath the concrete, in the dark depths of the subway, the trains rumbled and roared, hurtling their invisible occupants forward to unseen destinations.

-----

Cosmo stood at the front desk in the Waldorf's lobby, frowning over the stack of mail the clerk had just handed him. "Is this all?" he asked.

"Yes—sir," the clerk said, hesitating. Obviously he was an American who wasn't sure how to address British nobility, which made Cosmo impatient. He turned to go.

"Oh, sir, there is a message for a

member of your party," the clerk said quickly. "Do you want to take it up?"

"Yes, of course." Cosmo reached out for the proffered slip of wrinkled paper, glancing at it as he headed for the elevator. A message for Tess? What was this about? Just one line, scrawled hastily in pencil:

**Will you meet me at the south entrance to Central Park tonight? Please.**

No signature. Cosmo stared at the message for a long moment, then, slowly, he crumpled it in his fist, throwing it into a trash receptacle by the elevator. Now fully annoyed, he punched the elevator button. Obviously that infernal reporter was out to pump Tess for more information. No use telling Lucy about it—she'd just throw another fit. Just a bit of luck he had stopped and managed to intercept it in time. There was enough turmoil in their lives right now; they didn't need more.

*NEW YORK TIMES*
SATURDAY NIGHT, APRIL 20

Pinky didn't dance down the stairs of the *Times* building tonight; she was too tired. She had to get some groceries, pick up her father's medicine—and have another go-around with Mrs. Dotson, that fleshy, constantly disapproving nurse's aide who had never forgiven her for not melting into the role of a surrogate daughter. Mrs. Dotson wanted more money. Every night she complained of how hard it had become to care for Prescott Wade—his incontinence, his anger—all in a long-suffering, resigned tone as Pinky sat at the table, trapped in a narrow corner of reality that she escaped as often as she could. But it wouldn't work tonight.

She hated asking herself the kind of blunt, direct questions that had shaped her reputation as a reporter. She had no answers for the ones that affected her own life. How long would he live? How much could she afford to pay for his care?

The streets, as usual, were deserted

as she made her way home under the flickering streetlights. Whenever she saw a figure in the shadows, she straightened her shoulders and strode forward, determined to show as much confidence as a man. She would not shrink from facing the streets of this city. The first time she did, she would end up in a puddle, a failure; of that she was sure.

It would help if her father smiled once in a while. She never knew for sure if he refused to do so out of stubbornness or because he simply couldn't. After all, he was Prescott Wade, revered, lionized—and he must know that no one came around anymore. Most people thought, like Lady Duff Gordon, that he had died—not that they remembered taking note of such finality. It was easier to assume a kind of hazy, comfortable slide into nonexistence—painless, of course—so that when actual death came they could cluck and reminisce but shed no tears. That's what a life of celebrity brought. Who would remember her? What would she be? A package of bylines, mouldering in a

folder in the *New York Times* morgue.
She tossed *that* thought into a bin of
rotting tomatoes as she headed for the
meat counter of the neighborhood del-
icatessen.

Mrs. Dotson had her coat on already
when Pinky turned her key in the lock.
"He didn't have a good day," she announced as the door opened.

"He never does, Mrs. Dotson."

"Well, it's hard on me, with you traveling and all."

"This is what I do, Mrs. Dotson. This
is how I pay the bills." She pulled packages of beans and chicken from her
canvas bag and put them on the coun-
tertop, wishing this woman would go
home now, without the usual complaints.

"I know you work hard, dear." The
older woman's tone had turned ingrati-
ating. "But, you know, he's slipping
more every day. I hope you won't be
traveling much. What a shame if you
weren't here when his time comes. If I
have to stay overnight more, I'm going
to need some extra money; it's only
fair. You've been gone a lot. Not that

you shouldn't be for your work, of course."

It wasn't unreasonable. What would she do without Mrs. Dotson? Put her father in one of those hellish institutions she had been investigating? "We'll work it out," Pinky said.

"Five dollars more for night work."

"Three."

"Four—and a half." Mrs. Dotson had become braver.

"Four—that's all I can afford."

"All right."

They stared at each other. The negotiations were actually complete.

"I liked your write-up today, dear. I read it to your father, though he didn't seem to care much."

What a hurtful thing to say, and Pinky didn't believe it for a moment. Mrs. Dotson, she wanted to say, we are not friends. We don't like each other. Let's not pretend otherwise—just take care of my father, go home when you're done, and don't be chatty. I hate chatty.

Instead, she said, "Thank you." She shoved her hand into her bag and came up with a fistful of bills. She peeled off

several and handed them silently to Mrs. Dotson, who grabbed them and left quickly, with the usual promise of being back early tomorrow morning.

Pinky pulled out a knife and started cleaning the chicken, then paused. She should check on her father first.

The room was dark, not that it mattered. She flicked on the light.

"Well, it's about time you got home." His eyes were closed, and his voice seemed more raspy than usual. She could see stubble on his chin, which meant that Mrs. Dotson hadn't found the time to shave him today.

"I have deadlines, you know that."

"Out to knock the pins from under the gentry, right?"

"Just like you did."

"Right. Past tense."

"Can I get you anything?"

"My life, maybe. And, if you're not too busy, my dinner."

She had long ago vowed not to let him make her cry. This towering figure of a man she had adored and emulated lay like a lump of sodden clay on the bed, and she couldn't help him. There

was nothing to investigate or fight for here—all there could be was endurance. She turned to leave the room.

"Baked chicken?" he said.

"Yes."

"You make good baked chicken."

She walked back to the kitchen, feeling better. She knew an apology when she heard it.

------

The park had receded into the gloom of night. Still Jim stood by the 59th Street entrance, as late as he dared, peering down the street for some sign of Tess. Each time he saw a slim woman approaching with a brisk stride, his hopes went up. And each time he was wrong.

"Not your lady, huh?" A carriage driver, a jovial-looking man with drooping wattles and a badly faded cap, smiled sympathetically. "Well, there's always next time."

Jim tried to smile back. He rubbed the nose of the sleepy mahogany mare hitched to the carriage, remembering

the sight of Tess's graceful hand stroking her mane. Only yesterday?

Finally he gave up. "Thanks for your company," he said to the driver, then strode away, his pace quickening with every step.

7

A weary Senator Smith leaned back against the coarse weave of his seat as the train south to Washington gained momentum. Finally, a respite from the hysteria. His own bed tonight; a civilized hearing on Monday, surely.

"Senator, you wanted me to take some notes?" An aide had approached, his voice gently prodding.

Smith straightened in his seat. Dictating his thoughts helped him sort things out. "My primary job, of course, is to find out *why* that ship went down. Are you writing?"

"Yes, sir."

"It could have been a series of small mistakes fatally aligned, but people don't want to hear that; they want one reason, not many reasons. They don't want to examine the moral and practical decisions we're contending with." He sighed. Was it too overwhelming for them all—himself included—in this age of progress to see a product of the best minds and the most modern equipment so spectacularly punish its creators?

"You've seen the papers, Senator?"

"Indeed. They are clamoring for villains."

"Especially this British couple. Are you going to bring the Duff Gordons to the witness stand?"

"Why are you asking me? I'm tired of being hammered about that."

The aide was clearly taken aback. "Sorry, Senator. I just thought—"

"To answer your question, I'd rather not; it would anger the British too much." He slumped back in his seat. "And they're already mad at me. Did

you see this?" He pointed to a story in the *American*. "Henry Adams—you know who he is?"

"Yes, sir."

"The man's an admirable historian. He says we're running on our own iceberg, that we're a society cracking apart. He says the entire fabric of the nineteenth century is foundering, do you hear? And all of us, friend or foe, will go with it."

"Maybe we should do this later?"

"Yes, I think that would be better." Ah, home. He could impose order better there. That damn fellow Ismay was furious that he had to stay, and well he should be. This thought gave Smith a moment of satisfaction. He felt a righteous yearning for justice. He would follow this investigation wherever it might lead. And at least now he wouldn't have the New York tabloids on his back every moment. Reason enough to postpone wading into the sticky business of interrogating British nobility.

# NEW YORK CITY
## SUNDAY MORNING, APRIL 21

This was usually the most restful day of the week. Jean Darling sat with the Sunday-morning paper in her much loved breakfast room, with its bay of encircling windows that diffused the golden light. She was wearing her favorite dressing gown, the one with fox cuffs and collar bleached to a pure white; Jordan liked to see her in this on Sundays. The most restful day.

Usually she sipped her coffee, enjoying the lush panorama of Central Park spread out before her, across the street and three stories below. How exciting it had been when she and Jordan, swept up in a wave of glory after their first Broadway play, were able to walk through these elegant rooms and know that they, two minor English vaudeville players, could hold up their heads and say, "Yes, we will take this." How long ago? Years.

But she didn't lift her cup to her lips. She simply held herself still, staring at the translucent, fragile china filled half-

way. She could perhaps have been a statue, almost carved from stone. But a statue would feel no pain.

Next to the cup was her morning copy of the *New York Herald.* And there was the story she had feared would find its way into the caterwauling agony of mistakes and suffering sweeping the country since the sinking of the *Titanic.* "Dancer's Shameful Disguise," read the headline. "Dressed as a Woman to Save Self in Millionaires' Boat." Directly beneath was a photograph of Jordan, looking into the camera, a half smile on his lips. So vulnerable.

She skimmed the story. It was what she expected, a mocking screed on the man "who abandoned women" to save himself. Her eye stopped only on one sentence. "Asked to confirm this new information on the despicable happenings in the Millionaires' Boat, Lady Duff Gordon said, 'I won't deny it.'"

Such cruelty. Her dear husband, a man of courage and integrity, ruined. Their professional lives were over, of course. By tomorrow morning, all their bookings would be canceled.

What would she change? If she hadn't insisted, Jordan wouldn't have pulled that cloth close around his shoulders and head and run with her to the lifeboat; if the boat hadn't been almost empty, he would have refused to board. She knew it to be true. He wasn't a coward, he was simply trying to live. Was that wrong? Had anyone died for Jordan to live? No.

She stared now through the window out onto the winding paths and foliage below, which had imbued her on so many peaceful mornings with a sense of well-being. All she wished for now was an absence of pain.

Jean heard Jordan's footsteps approaching from the hall. Carefully she folded the newspaper and tucked it inside a bottom cabinet of the lovely old hutch they had bought on their honeymoon. That wonderful honeymoon. The trip to Morocco when they first danced as partners. They were in step from the very beginning, flowing through routines of magical grace, embracing the cheers of their audiences, and going home to each other. She smiled, look-

ing up, waiting for his cheerful face to light up the room. How many women had such a precious gift of love? Why, why should she have given him up to death?

Jordan walked into the room, giving her his usual funny little bow of greeting. "And how is my lovely wife this morning?" he asked. "How is our world today?"

She lifted two fingers to her lips and blew him a kiss. "Wonderful," she said. She stood and walked over to him, curving one arm around his shoulder, reaching with the other for his hand. She would shed no tears. A barely discernible web of fine lines appeared around her eyes as she smiled again. "It should start with a dance, don't you think? This is, after all, the most restful day."

-------

Lucile paced the length of her empty loft, frustrated by the silent sewing machines. Things should be humming and buzzing, but she didn't dare insist on

Sunday work in New York anymore, not since the Ladies' Garment Workers' Union began bullying shops like hers. It was outrageously unfair. She didn't operate some sweatshop like the Triangle people had, for heaven's sake. She paid her workers well, and none were under fourteen years old; she could have fattened their purses if they had worked today. She sighed, trying to relax. She was always nervous just before a show. But seeing her name smeared once again all through those stories about Jordan Darling posing as a woman was unnerving. All she did was answer a question, and she wasn't sorry to see Jordan Darling exposed. But attaching *her* name to the story so prominently was ridiculous. She hadn't confirmed *anything,* and that reporter who wrote the story knew it. But Cosmo wouldn't listen. He had thrown the paper into a trash basket and walked out of the room this morning, saying nothing.

Lucile slowed her pace, studying the newly constructed models' runway at the end of the long room. It looked fully presentable, sleek and polished, and

her mood lifted. It was such a thrill just before a show—the anticipation, the excitement. She loved it all. She stepped up onto the runway, pulled herself straight and began strolling, head high, in the manner she had taught her models every season here, in London, and in Paris. She turned with a practiced grace and walked back, impatient now for Monday. This was her domain, and she wanted it busy with life. She wanted what she knew, and she wanted to forget the *Titanic.* Surely all this would blow over soon; surely there would be no more cancellations. The elegant women of New York loved her designs. They wouldn't take flight. She wanted to feel safe again.

She suddenly became aware of movement in the shadows at the far end of the loft. It must be Farley, with a message. She stepped off the runway and walked toward the figure, partly alarmed, but mostly indignant. No one had permission to be up here without her consent. No one.

"Who is there? And what do you want?" she demanded.

"You always were the bossy one," a woman's voice said with a giggle. "Don't you recognize your own sister?"

Lucile gasped. "Elinor?"

"And why are you so surprised? I booked myself on the first ship out after we heard of the sinking, and got your telegraph from the *Carpathia*. Did you think I wouldn't come?"

"Oh—" Lucile could hardly speak as her sister stepped out of the shadows, that silly red parasol on her arm. Had she thought that? Had she wondered if Elinor would twirl past even the worst of happenings in her usual manner, never quite connecting?

"I should have known you would come—you always were the impulsive one."

"That trait has paid off splendidly." Elinor's voice was brisk. "I needed a new screenplay anyway. This time Hollywood will have to wait."

"Thank you. You don't know how much I need you." Something was bursting inside.

Elinor tossed her parasol onto a cutting table and extended her arms.

"From what I've seen in the papers, I have a fair idea," she murmured.

Their embrace lasted only a moment, but in that fraction of time Lucile felt the first true comfort she had experienced since the sinking of the *Titanic*.

------

Sunday morning. Tess lay in bed in her hotel room, staring at the intricate molding that joined the walls and ceiling. She stretched out her toes, at the same time winding her fingers through the bars of the brass headboard, pulling tired muscles straight. She had stood for so long yesterday, her back still ached, and it felt good to lie here in leisure, even though she couldn't erase her troubled thoughts. She didn't want to be thinking of Jim, turning over reason after reason why she hadn't heard from him. Surely he would have some explanation; she *wanted* him to, but his silence seemed to say it all. Had he been reluctant to tell her what was coming, and then ashamed to admit his role in it?

She pushed him firmly from her mind. Today was hers. Lady Duff Gordon had announced quite magnanimously last night that she would not be required to work on Sunday. Courtesy of the union rules in New York, she was free to enjoy the Sunday street markets. And Tess had seen the look of pleasure on her employer's face when she, Tess, was actually disappointed by the news. Yes, Lucile, she said to herself. I love that magical place. Your seduction is working.

------

Pinky slung the market basket over her shoulder and began to tiptoe out of the apartment, ignoring the unwashed dishes. Nothing was noisier than the clatter of dishes being washed. He was asleep, and she wanted to get out before he woke again. She didn't want any more demands this morning. She had shaved him earlier, a routine he usually enjoyed, but not today. So okay, some days were better than others.

She was getting tired of telling herself that.

"Where the hell are you going?" he yelled from the bedroom.

"Out to the market. It's Sunday, remember? I'll get some fruit, some bananas? You like those. I'll get the papers, too."

"Come here, Pinky."

Damn. Pinky put down the basket and walked into her father's bedroom. She felt a thud in her heart. He looked so ashen.

"They don't pay you much, do they." It wasn't a question.

"Oh, it's all right."

"You can't kid me—I heard you bargaining over money with that fat excuse for a nurse last night."

She smiled in spite of herself. "Maybe you can talk her into losing weight, then she won't need so much money."

"Very funny." His voice was raspy but gentle. "When are they going to give you a raise?"

Her own question, of course. "I'm getting some good stories, and next

week I'm covering the suffragist parade. I'll get one soon. They need me."

"Don't believe your own press notices. Big mistake."

There it was again, more advice on how to do her job. Pinky shifted her weight, edging back toward the door. "Look, I've got to go or all the best stuff will be picked over. Okay?"

He nodded. "Sarah—"

She stopped. He never called her Sarah.

"I'm sorry, kid."

She almost went back to kiss him on the forehead. But she couldn't trust the stinging in her eyes.

------

Tess saw Pinky first. Chatting with a vendor, her hair blowing across her face, looking as totally comfortable in this market, with its colorful awnings and boxes of lettuce and peaches and children playing around the skirts of their mothers, as she did at the hearings. Looking benign and cheery, as if

she weren't out to destroy lives and reputations. Tess started to turn away.

Too late. "Tess?" Pinky was approaching. "So Lady Duff gave you a day off? You've come to a great Sunday market." Her voice was relaxed but tentative. She was braced.

"Why did you do it?" Tess hadn't known what she would say the next time they met, but there it was.

Pinky started. "What?" she said.

"*Cowardly* baronet? *Bribing* the sailors to go back? It's not true."

"I didn't make it up," Pinky said quickly, taken aback.

"But you took somebody's word for it. Somebody who didn't have the character to put his name behind his charges. Who was it?"

"Look, Tess, I don't like being attacked. I had sources from the ship—"

"A sailor?" Tess said, dismayed.

"Yes, if you have to know."

"Not Jim Bonney." Please, not Jim Bonney.

"You mean the sailor who's sweet on you? The one who carved that lifeboat

of yours you weren't hanging on to too tightly?"

It was Tess's turn to be taken aback. "Yes," she said.

"Well, you're some friend. And I don't have to tell you anything." It was her day off. She needed fruit and vegetables for dinner; maybe she would make a stew for her father. He loved onions; she hated them. She didn't have to stand here and be attacked.

"All you want to do is get a good story. You don't care about ruining lives."

Pinky slammed her basket down on the ground, ignoring the glances from shoppers around her. She was too tired for diplomacy. "All *you* want to do is be like those self-involved, self-satisfied people you work for, looking down their noses at everyone else. So I'm wrong? What's your story? Do you know what happened in that boat?"

"You're not pulling me into that. No, I wasn't there, but Lucile swears that nothing bad happened." She was having trouble catching her breath. "Why do you hate them? You've got a privi-

leged life yourself. Look at the freedom you have! You have so much power. Why don't you use it more kindly?"

"What do you think America is?" Pinky said with mystification. "Some Nirvana where everybody is as rich as the Duff Gordons? So you come here and eat off a table filled with crystal and china the very first night and you think that's what it's all about? And that people should be free to ignore or harm other people if they can get away with it? And then you get mad at me, when I'm just trying to tell the truth?"

"You throw out one self-righteous pronouncement after another. And I don't think you care about the truth."

"Look, I work hard to find out things and I try to be a good reporter. You're the one who's self-righteous. Are you absolutely positive the Duff Gordons *weren't* trying to bribe the sailors not to go back?"

Tess responded as slowly and calmly as she could. "They gave the crewmen money, but not as a bribe—it was to *thank* and *help* them. Why is that so

hard for you to believe? Why does this make them bad people?"

"Tess, loyalty can make you blind."

"So can running after headlines."

"Could you be wrong?"

"Could you?"

They stared at each other. Pinky took charge of what came next.

"So I'm privileged—want to see where I live?" She reached out and grabbed Tess's hand. Market forgotten, Tess allowed herself to be marched down the street, turning finally onto a narrow, twisted road lined with shabby walk-ups. Pungent smells wafted from the windows, cabbage and stew meat and onions; children cried and dogs barked. Lines of laundry between the buildings flapped in a gentle wind. Pinky pointed upward.

"Fourth floor. With my father. He's sick. No pension. Not that anybody else should care. How's that for a self-righteous pronouncement?"

Tess stood silent for a moment.

"Are you saying you're poor? Is that it?"

"I'm saying I have a great job that

doesn't pay a lot of money, and it gets frustrating. Especially"—Pinky took a deep breath and tried to speak calmly— "when I'm told I am both privileged and self-righteous."

"From my perspective, you are"— Tess took a deep breath of her own. "Some of both."

"Maybe I am. I see people shoved into institutions and left to die by the rich people who attend balls and don't give a fig for anybody other than themselves."

There was no use ramming her head against such absolutes. "Can't you look at the good things, too? Lady Duff Gordon employs people and pays them decently and . . . treats them well." She blushed at her own exaggeration. "Doesn't that count for something with you?"

"You Brits, with your titles," Pinky retorted. "She's doing what works for her."

"She isn't a terrible person, Pinky."

"Okay, but I know what I believe. I think you're trying too hard to please

that woman, and her kind can't be pleased."

"She could have left me on my own after we got here, but she didn't. Do you know how important that is to someone like me?"

"You don't have to bow too deeply, Tess."

The words stung. "I don't understand why you use your power the way you do."

"I try to fight a few battles that get attention. And I try to change things a little. But I get riled, because I can't change things a lot."

They stood again in silence for a few moments.

"I might as well tell you," Pinky said reluctantly. "I got my story about what happened in your lifeboat from a sailor named Tom Sullivan. Creepy guy, but he was there."

Tess felt a wash of relief. It wasn't Jim. "How can you trust him?"

"He didn't get the amount of money he thought he would get from Lady Duff, so he's mad. They got stingy on the payout. Works for me."

"Can you possibly admit that you might be wrong?"

"Only if she denies it under oath. Even then, I'm not so sure. Why did you think Bonney was my source?"

At that moment, a boy in a green cap weaved past on a wobbly bicycle, forcing them both to step aside. Tess was grateful for the time to frame her reply. "I didn't think it. I feared it," she said slowly. "Do you understand?"

"Oh, sure." Pinky mentally scored one for her instincts yesterday, but it didn't give much satisfaction. "What do you say we go back to the outdoor market? I can introduce you to the best apples you'll ever taste," she said, a touch of cheer back in her voice.

Tess started to shake her head.

"I'm not a bad sort," Pinky said quickly. "I like you. You'll do all right here, Tess."

It was the same thing Jim had said. "I'm not sure how to think of you. Whether I should be wary of you or think of you as a friend."

A friend. Pinky liked that. "I do my job. Nobody likes reporters."

"You are too sure of yourselves."

"Unlike Lady Duff?"

Tess was silent.

Pinky sighed. "Okay, would it help if I told you that my father thinks I'm a raging harpy sometimes?"

Tess couldn't help smiling. "I guess it does. For now, anyway."

Silently, in mutual consent, they walked back the way they had come. Soon the brilliant awnings and over-flowing carts of the outdoor market came into view. Tess shaded her face from the sun, comforted by its warmth, thinking of Jim. She felt her spirit relax. For one day, surely, it was all right.

------

The sun was high when Tess made her way back from the outdoor market to the Waldorf, a small basket of apples under her arm. Pinky had done much of the talking as they wandered the stalls together, chattering away about New York, offering advice on where to buy cheap shirtwaists and the best places to buy decent tea. There was

going to be a suffrage march starting from Washington Square in a few days, she said, a big one, the biggest yet, and it was the kind of story she loved covering, because it was about oppression and women's rights. The leader would be a woman mounted on a white horse. A splendid, huge white horse. There would be banners and babies and even men—a few, anyway. What kind of existence did women lead anyhow, all trussed up in corsets and suffering through childbirth while their husbands spent nights in brothels? Marriage was a trap.

It all flowed out so passionately. There were suffragists in England; Tess had read about them, even seen them marching once, carrying banners they waved back and forth. But it was always something that happened far away. Suffragists? Women declaring independence? They were strangers, from some privileged planet. Women with the time and the energy to do something besides change bed linens and clean toilets.

"Well, they won you the vote, didn't they?" Pinky said.

"It did me no good. It took enough energy to fight off the son of my employer in Cherbourg. He figured he had license to grope."

"You see? You had no power to stop him."

"I don't see how my being able to vote could have kept his hands where they belonged."

Pinky looked at her with the impatience of a schoolteacher facing the slowest of pupils. "It might have meant you had a voice and could influence the politicians who want to stay in power enough so maybe someday there would be a law sending gropers like that to jail."

"I would love to see that day."

"Then come to the march. I'll tell you a secret," Pinky said.

"A secret?"

"It's just the most exciting thing. I'm covering the march, and they've agreed to let me ride the white horse before the march begins. I can't tell you how

much that means to me." Pinky spoke
with the reverence of an acolyte.

"You can ride?"

"Of course." She laughed. "You know
one of the best things? Women gathering, marching, doing anything together
makes a lot of men go crazy. They yell
and scream and taunt and shake their
fists. You know why? They're scared.
They're scared we'll actually gain power
and force them to change." Her eyes
brightened with the mischievousness
of a child. "That's fun to watch."

"I know men like that," Tess said. It
hadn't taken much for the officer on the
*Titanic* to blame her for a man's clumsiness. And she was used to it—would
that horrify Pinky? Probably. It felt good
to be walking along, talking about
women and voting and power and white
horses. And oh, the sun felt so good
on her skin. Pinky was chattering away
about her next *Titanic* story as Tess
only half listened. It was all quite peaceful.

"We've got reports that there were a
few survivors who didn't get counted,

probably because they were steerage and didn't speak English," Pinky said. "The funny thing is, one rich guy was missed because he was unconscious at first and wearing a ragged jacket."

Tess stopped dead. "Do you know who it was?"

"A Chicago guy named Jack Bremerton."

"He's alive? He's all right?"

"Yes." Pinky shot her a quick glance. "You know him?"

"We met on the ship."

"He's quite the important person, I'm told. The very famous Henry Ford came to see him, and he's already back in his office and working again. Sounds to me like he's still delirious." She giggled. "By the way, I've talked my editor into sending me to Washington tonight for tomorrow's hearing."

"Washington?"

"Smith decided to continue in his home territory. The whole crew was sent down there yesterday. Any message you want to give your sailor?"

"He's not my sailor." It flustered her to hear the tease in Pinky's voice. And

now she couldn't ask any more about Mr. Bremerton.

"Well, I've talked to you both, and each of you lights up at the mention of the other. Doesn't mean a thing, of course."

Tess was only half listening, remembering the handsome, smiling man with gray hair on the *Titanic.* He was here. Here in this city, now, and as far away as the moon. She wished she could see him. Oh, this was ridiculous—she was harboring a schoolgirl's crush. In the real world, what she fantasized was impossible. And Jim—Jim was gone, without a word to her.

"Tess? I'm leaving. Any message for Jim?" Pinky raised an eyebrow, waiting.

"No, no message."

**8**

## WALDORF-ASTORIA
## SUNDAY EVENING, APRIL 21

Lucile was chattering away, looking very happy as Cosmo buttoned up the back of her beautiful tea gown. "Come in, come in," she called gaily as Tess entered the suite. "We're going to have a lovely evening because the most wonderful thing has happened. My sister is here!"

"That's the first time you've ever called me wonderful," an amused voice called out from the other room. And then there she was, the handsome woman Tess remembered twirling a parasol on the dock in Cherbourg,

stretching out her hand. "Hello, Tess," she said with a smile. "I'm Elinor Glyn— I don't think we managed a proper introduction before. I hear you turned out to be anything but a proper maid— thank goodness for that."

"How did you get here so quickly?" Tess asked, surprised.

"Well, dear, my ship didn't sink."

She said it with such light casualness. So there was still, after all, an ordinary world where jokes could be made. Tess liked her immediately.

"Elinor says we're eating dinner in the Palm Room tonight, no more taking meals up here, like people guilty of something," Lucile said, pulling away from Cosmo's hands and twirling around. "It's the Darlings that need to keep their heads down now. Did you see the story about his shameful masquerade?" She pulled on white kid gloves and twirled in her long, slender gown of raspberry silk. "Isn't this the loveliest dress? Maybe I will model it myself at the spring show. Wouldn't that be different?"

"You are the best model for all your gowns, dear," said Cosmo promptly, almost automatically. He glanced at his watch and urged his wife to hurry. Their reservation downstairs was in ten minutes.

"Tess, you must join us," Lucile said. "I have a gown ready for you in the next room."

It wasn't really an invitation, of course, more like an order. But Elinor's arrival had improved Lucile's mood with astonishing speed. Tess caught her breath when she saw the gown hanging on a closet door. It looked amazingly similar to the one Lucile had given her before the *Titanic* went down. The same colors, the same cut. Had she chosen it on purpose? It slid off the hanger, floating on her fingertips, as flimsy and ethereal as passing time.

-----

The Palm Room—cupped under a magnificent domed ceiling—was filled with the easy formality and discreet

murmurings of well-dressed diners. The maître d' lifted the red velvet rope to admit their party, giving all a deferential bow, including Tess. No gaping, she told herself. Don't act like a servant girl. All around her, mirrored walls reflected a mixed glow of crystal, amber marble, and candlelight that created an almost bewildering swirl of dancing images. Beautiful.

"Head up, Tess," murmured Elinor. "You're dressed like a queen. Enjoy the fact that everyone is looking at us."

"I don't feel like one."

"Pretend, for heaven's sake."

Patrons were indeed taking note of their arrival, whispering as they walked past. But there was an edge, a sharpness to their voices, like the sound of a knife swiftly cutting through air.

"They don't wish us well," Tess said.

"A mix of envy and malice—the usual thing. Look at my sister; that's how to do it."

Lucile, her hand resting in Cosmo's crooked elbow, was not simply walking but sweeping into the room, as if any

moment applause would break out and she would take a triumphant bow. Her face was flushed. To Tess, she looked like a sunflower reaching for light.

------

"Now, Tess, I have to know. Are you staying or ready to run?"

Seated now, Elinor asked the question in a relaxed, quiet voice, but her eyes were cool. A bottle of champagne was being uncorked by the sommelier, and waiters were hovering, one behind each chair.

"I have no plans to leave," Tess said, startled.

"Lucy seems to think you may have talent. You've got an opportunity to prove yourself, a bigger one than you realize. But things aren't going to go well here for a while."

"I know."

"My sister keeps putting her foot in her mouth. This latest jab at the Darlings was idiotic."

Tess stirred uncomfortably, not sure

if she was expected to agree or simply to wait in silence.

"I'm not trying to test you; I put no value on discretion. On the contrary, I've found that strutting one's stuff gets a woman ahead—at least in the movie business."

"It's not quite the same in the servant business," Tess murmured.

Elinor laughed. "You're not in it anymore," she said. "Look, I can't stay here very long. Much as I want to support my sister, I have to get to Los Angeles." She tapped an ash from the end of her cigarette into an ashtray, the silver of her delicately slender cigarette holder catching the light. "So let me put it to you plainly. Lucile needs eyes and ears at the shop right now. And you're the obvious person at the moment. Cosmo found an apartment for you today down near the Flatiron Building, not far from Lucile's loft. You can't stay here—the hotel wants your room. This won't last too long, but Lucy can't go home until she gets through her spring show and knows for sure that she won't have to testify at the inquiry. Then you can do

whatever you want. You'll have references."

"What does that mean, to be her
eyes and ears?"

Elinor shrugged and smiled. "Oh,
you'll know." Her smile faded as she
looked at Lucile chattering away to a
silent Cosmo. He was sipping his champagne, his face a study in blankness.
"Lucy had better watch out," she said
softly.

"For what?"

"A great many unpleasant things
could happen."

Carefully, Tess picked up a silver fork
to eat the salad now before her. Delicate greens, white asparagus, and ham
cut into small pieces—but the stuffed
olives were most tempting. A quick
glance at Elinor assured her that she
had chosen the right fork. "Do you think
she'll have to testify? Senator Smith
isn't calling women before the commission."

"I know; any female who went through
that experience is too delicate to speak
of it. Such hooey. But Smith might feel

forced to. Lucy is deluged with criticism, and it's her own fault. His, too, for that matter." She rolled her eyes, glancing at Cosmo. "*Bribing* the crew not to go back? My goodness."

The maître d' approached. "A message for Lady Duff Gordon," he murmured.

"Later, not now," Lucile said, waving him away.

The maître d' leaned closer, whispering something in Cosmo's ear, then handed him the note. Cosmo scanned it quickly, his expression frozen.

"You aren't listening to me," Lucile said impatiently. "Must you be reading while I'm talking to you?"

Cosmo pushed his chair away from the table and stood. "I think we'll finish our meal upstairs," he said pleasantly to the maître d'. "Send the menus and a waiter up to our suite as quickly as possible."

"For heaven's sake—"

"Be quiet, Lucy. Let's go."

"But—"

"Hush," Elinor murmured. She grabbed

her sister's arm. Asking no questions, Tess followed them out of the restaurant, feeling the eyes of the other diners on them once again. She kept her head up, this time with effort.

------

Cosmo shut the door of the suite and faced them, lips tight and drained of color. "Jordan Darling has hanged himself," he said, keeping his eyes on Lucile. "His wife found him a few hours ago."

A shiver—where did it begin, her stomach, her legs?—spread, cold and uncontrollable, through Tess's body. Her hands began to shake.

"Who is the note from?" Elinor asked.

Cosmo stared at the paper in his hand as if it might explode at any moment. "His wife. It's for Lucile."

"I don't want to see it," Lucile said. The flesh beneath her chin was trembling.

"You will have to hear it, then." Cosmo passed the note to Elinor, who read

aloud one scrawled sentence at the end of the message, the letters in wavery purple ink.

**Why were you so cruel?**

Lucile sank into a chair with a moan, covering her face with her hands.

"She's distraught—you didn't do this," Elinor said quickly.

The shiver had subsided, but Lucile's denunciation of Darling on the *Carpathia* scratched at Tess's brain. No, no, Lucile didn't kill him—no, that was horrible.

"But I did play a part," Lucile said slowly.

Only then was Tess able to release her pity and desire to comfort by speaking up. "I'm so sorry," she whispered.

Lucile looked up, her eyes grateful. "Thank you," she said.

"Don't leave this suite tomorrow, Lucy," Cosmo said. "Pull back. I will tell everyone you are in mourning. Do you hear me? And, for God's sake, do not talk to any reporters."

## WALDORF-ASTORIA
## NEW YORK CITY
## MONDAY, APRIL 22

The sun was barely up when Tess left the hotel, glancing anxiously around as she made her way out to Farley in the waiting car. Good, no reporters yet. What a dark night it had been, haunted with dreams of throwing herself onto railroad ties, trying to protect Lucile from an oncoming train; walking into a room and seeing Jordan Darling's body hanging from a silk drapery sash—from what had her fevered brain created *that*?

The reality of today would be even more frightening. It was now her job to hold things together at the shop, Elinor had said late last night, after an almost catatonic Lucile finally fell asleep. She didn't have to know everything; she just needed to be there as a calming influence. There was no way Lucile's presence outside this room wouldn't result in more terrible stories. She could do it.

With her stomach turning cartwheels? Impossible. "I've only been in the shop

once," Tess protested, trying not to panic. "I don't know anything about how the place is run."

"You're going to learn some quick lessons tomorrow, but remember, you have James to help you. He knows a lot," Elinor said soothingly. "This is just for a couple of days. Life is an act—most of it, anyway. Get out there today and pretend you're in charge, for goodness' sake. Do you hear me? Lift up your head and *pretend*." A flicker of a smile passed over her face. "It's the secret to everything."

As she left to go to her own room, Cosmo handed her a set of keys on a small steel key ring, folding the cold metal into her hand with a scribbled address on a piece of paper. "For your flat, Tess," he said quietly. "It will be ready on Tuesday. The bed will be made, towels there. Some food. Let me know what you need." His face had been pinched tight as a withered plum—her first realization that he, too, was suffering. He looked not at all like the polished, calm man she had first met on the dock at Cherbourg. That,

surely, had fed the turbulence of her dreams.

There was no grin on Farley's face this morning, but, rather, something of a watchful, wary look. "So no Lady Duff today?" he asked, opening the door for her.

"No, she's resting."

He pulled the car out into the street and did not speak for the duration of the trip. Tess stared down at the notes she had taken from Elinor: Check the runway, inventory the gowns for the show. Make sure the embroideries and the finishing details were being done properly. Check the final fittings on the models.

This was crazy, impossible.

"I'm not the person to put in charge of this. Why don't you go?" she had protested.

"The press would love that," Elinor said, rolling her eyes. "They'll have Lucy's name smeared all over their stories on Darling's suicide. No, I'm keeping my head down, too; I don't need that sort of attention. You're the one to do this, Tess. Nobody's after you."

The sound of buzzing sewing machines reassured Tess as she stepped off the elevator and walked into the loft. A few glances came her way as she walked back to Lucile's office, but no questions. It took her a moment to realize that there were fewer people than there had been on Saturday.

James was waiting in the office, looking nervous. "Where is Madame?" he said.

"She's been working too hard and is taking a rest today." Tess looked around at the many bouquets of wilting flowers, her nose wrinkling slightly at the sickish smell of decaying blossoms, and hoped she sounded matter-of-fact enough.

"We know what that's about, don't we?" he said. "Nobody wants a death on their hands. On top of everything else that's toppled her reputation."

"I think it's up to us to get done today what needs to be done," Tess said, hoping her voice held a shred or two of confidence.

James turned his back to the glass wall, and Tess realized that he didn't

want the seamstresses to see his face. "I've got bad news," he said. He walked over to a long table and pointed. A creamy gown covered with intricate beading lay on the table—the wedding dress, the centerpiece of the show.

"It's beautiful," Tess said, reaching out to lift it up. To her horror, the skirt slipped away from her fingers. It had been slashed open and only half of it remained attached to the bodice.

"What happened?" She could not believe it. All this beautiful work, destroyed.

"Somebody hates Madame," he said. "It's monstrous. Nothing like this ever happened before." He didn't look at Tess, just stared down at the gown as if at a dead body. "Nobody liked what they were reading in the papers; she wasn't sounding too nice, but still—"

"We have to remake it."

He shook his head. "There's no time for that. And there's no way to mend it—it's too fragile."

"Who knows about it?"

"The beader—she left in tears. She said she couldn't work here anymore.

Everybody out there knows what happened now."

Tess fingered the ruined silk and the broken bead strings, remembering a stitch her mother had taught her for mending torn curtains: two loops and a twist; the trick was in the twist. If that wasn't enough, she could try gathering the fabric in with tiny bits of elastic.

"James, could you bring in a seamstress, someone you trust?"

"Yes, ma'am."

"I think I can fix this, but I need your help with everything else. I can't run this shop. I don't know how."

"Nobody can, except Madame. It's a lot of smoke and mirrors, you know. But you can count on me to help."

Tess gave him a shaky smile of gratitude. "Maybe we should tell everybody that the dress will be repaired and the show will take place as scheduled, and not pretend that nothing happened."

"Sounds good to me." He looked relieved. He started out the door and stopped when she spoke again. "What else?"

"Choosing which model wears which dress?" she asked uncertainly.

"Sounds good."

"And maybe somebody could clear out all the wilted flowers; they look too sad."

"Will do."

It was a few minutes before she realized, bending over the torn dress, that James had called her "ma'am."

------

## SENATE OFFICE BUILDING
## WASHINGTON, D.C.
## MONDAY, APRIL 22
## 5 A.M.

Pinky sat on the steps of the Senate Office Building, watching the early glow of sunrise and feeling a bit stupid for being there so early. The hearing wasn't scheduled to start until 10 A.M., but where else could she wait? Van Anda wasn't about to pay for any more nights in a hotel than he had to, so that had meant a midnight train, which put Mrs. Dotson in a tizzy. Only an extra fifty

dollars had bought her benevolent services. She'd just have to tell Van Anda she could come down only on day trips after this. Pinky rubbed her aching forehead. She debated going to the Continental Hotel, where White Star was putting up the crew, and waking a few of them; maybe they'd tell her their complaints about being cooped up without any money in a strange city. But it seemed like too much effort.

She pulled her coat closer against the chill. Maybe she should have stayed in New York and followed up on the Jordan Darling suicide. Truly, though, she had no appetite for going after Lady Duff Gordon again, even though the silly woman had brought the latest round of criticism on herself. Tess was too loyal—more than Pinky would have been, job or not. On the other hand, Darling was the one who hopped on the boat wrapped in a tablecloth; he did it to himself. She rubbed her forehead again. Sometimes this *Titanic* story made her weary. Couldn't someone come along and open the blasted

building? She wished she had worn a heavier coat.

"Hello there, young lady. I recognize you!"

A woman's voice, hearty and full, coming from a long, sleek black car that had pulled up in front of the building. Pinky stepped closer and peered through the window. Peering back at her was the beaming face of the woman from Colorado who had rowed one of the lifeboats. Margaret Brown—that was her name. Very quotable.

"Come on in, honey, and get warm. We're here for the same reason, that's pretty obvious. You're working, but I'm just curious to see how the esteemed senator handles this on his home ground." Mrs. Brown opened the door and beckoned Pinky in, immediately offering her a cup of steaming hot coffee from a thermos passed back by her chauffeur. Gratefully, Pinky jumped in and curled her cold fingers around the cup. She'd get an interview out of this, for sure.

"You're the girl with the funny name who works for the Times, right? Brash,

like me—that's what I hear. So how do you like Washington at sunrise?"

"It's quiet," Pinky said.

"Not for long. What's the latest news from the city?"

"A suicide. One of the people in Lifeboat One."

"Ah, poor Jordan Darling. Yes, I heard that back at the hotel. A fatal masquerade. The humiliation must have been too great," Mrs. Brown murmured. "Any good news?"

"The French-speaking orphans—their mother is coming for them."

"Ah, yes. I heard that, too—poor little things. At least the father did his best to save them. Preparing to die has a way of clarifying the mind."

"What did it clarify for you?" Pinky asked.

Mrs. Brown laughed. "Told me to keep doing and saying what I damn well please, and not be bamboozled by anyone. Life is short—no mulling things over for a dozen years or so. What about you?"

"I wasn't on the ship."

"A nice reporter dodge, dear. You'll

have your choices to make, too, in due time." She smiled, big and comfortable. "This Senator Smith—I'd like to shake the stuffing out of him. He won't call me to testify, and I want things to go on the record. Especially how the women had to take over from the male cowards."

"Tell them to me," Pinky said quickly. "My paper is the paper of record, you know."

"Yes, I read your masthead." Mrs. Brown's eyes were sparkling. "You know I ran for the U.S. Senate a few years ago? I'm going to do it again first chance I get."

Pinky was fumbling in her bag for her notebook. "Can I write that?"

Mrs. Brown folded ample white arms across an equally ample stomach. "Honey, you can write down anything I say. After being brined, salted, and pickled in mid-ocean, I am now high and dry."

"What about the Duff Gordons? Should they testify?"

"I think that's what you're hoping for, isn't it?"

"I'm just a reporter."

"No, you're not. I read your story, and I think you care about what happened in that boat."

A second of hesitation. "Well, you caught it," Pinky said.

"Poor old Smith doesn't want to, but he'll get himself in trouble either way. We'll see. He won't call me because I won't be polite and do it his way. He's afraid if he brings in the British upper class they'll figure out how to run the show. Good chance they will, too." She peered out the window and up at the Senate Office Building. "Everything swishing about, to and fro—do you feel it? It's like we're all in a seltzer bottle that's ready to blow. Or maybe it already has and we don't know it yet."

------

"Who's complaining *now*?" Senator Smith glared at the aide standing in the doorway of his office in the Senate Office Building.

"Daughters of the American Revolu-

tion, sir. They're worried about national morale."

"Why? We didn't build the damn ship, and we certainly didn't sink it!"

"No, sir. It's just—everybody seems so whipped up. The dancer's suicide—he was quite a favorite."

"I know, I know." Smith shoved the mountain of mail before him to the edge of his desk, not caring that several dozen letters fell to the floor. He had been up most of the night, poring over maritime books, reading up on the dangers of ice. To find out that all his plans for the day might be upended by more scandal was too much.

Smith strode out of his office, walking toward the Caucus Room, spirits glum. Charges, countercharges—whom to believe? That sailor who claimed that the lookout had been asleep in the crow's nest—any credibility to that? Not likely; the man was suspect. Smith had the crew, and he had Ismay for a while longer. But survivors were scattering already; they would have to be subpoenaed quickly or their testimony would be lost. And that meant he was

going to have to go back to New York, which did not improve his mood.

The guards pushed open the doors to the Caucus Room with effort, and Smith saw to his chagrin that hundreds of people had jammed into the huge room, including—right up front—that irritating woman from the *Times.* And right next to her was that clamorous Mrs. Brown. This most definitely would not be an easy day.

------

"Quiet, please!" Smith banged his gavel repeatedly, exasperated at how difficult it was proving even to get the hearing under way. He was already hoarse. "Our first witness will be Fourth Officer Joseph Boxhall, a principal navigator on the *Titanic,*" he announced.

A small man with black hair and a mouth that worked nervously was guided to the witness chair. Pinky glanced over at the door he had come through. With no official witness list, did Smith have all the crew members

waiting back there? Getting interviews with them might be hard.

Smith began the questioning. Boxhall took obvious pride in his navigational abilities. He had also been in charge of collecting all warnings of icebergs from other ships, and then charting the *Titanic*'s course. And who gave those warnings to him? The captain of the ship, of course. Had he gotten any warning of ice in the *Titanic*'s path? No. What was the weather like? Clear and calm.

Another member of the panel cleared his throat. "How do you account for the fact that you could not see the icebergs, if the night was so clear?"

Boxhall screwed up his face and shook his head. He couldn't—sorry.

"Are they more difficult to see at night?"

"Not always. But the water that night was in an oily calm. One little ripple on the water, we would've had a very good chance of seeing that iceberg in time to miss it."

An "oily calm": strange expression. But a time-waster to explore. Instead,

Smith decided to show off some of his new knowledge, pointing out—with Boxhall nodding eagerly—the differences between the smaller chunks of low-lying ice known as growlers and large expanses of surface ice known as field ice.

"These formations are more frequent in the latitude of the Grand Banks, I understand. And is it customary to be particularly careful in that vicinity?"

"Oh yes, sir."

"Well," pressed Smith, "how did it happen that in that identical vicinity it was not thought necessary to increase the lookout?"

Boxhall paused. "I do not know."

Enough. Smith banged his gavel and declared a recess.

Speed and stupidity, that's what did it, Pinky told herself as she elbowed her way through the crowd to the door. Same old story—she'd heard it dozens of times. It was all politics in the end. She was hungry for fresh air.

She escaped the crowd—no one seemed to want to stray too far from the vicinity out of fear of losing a place—

and made her way down the marble corridor to the entrance hall. And there, on a corner bench, she spied Mrs. Brown, talking with great enthusiasm to a sailor. Pinky moved closer and saw that it was Jim Bonney.

"Pinky, come over here," Mrs. Brown called. "Look at this man's work!"

Jim looked up, his face breaking into a slow grin when he recognized her. He looked tired and rumpled but somehow at ease. He was holding a small, curved knife and a piece of wood in his hands— large hands, Pinky noted for the first time, with strong, slender fingers.

Mrs. Brown scooped the wood from him and held it aloft. "Look at the detail," she marveled. It was a carving of the U.S. Capitol, done with impressive intricacy and skill.

"I've seen your work," Pinky said to Jim with a smile. "You're good."

Jim reached for the carving. "I'm not done, actually. Nothing much else to do around here until they call me to testify." His eyes flickered up to Pinky's with a question. What could she say? Tess had sent no message.

"Well, I'm enormously impressed," Mrs. Brown said. She looked at Jim shrewdly. "I've got a job for you if you want it, young man. Can you make a replica of that unfortunate ship we were on?"

"The *Titanic*? Sure, I can."

"With all the details on it—you know, ladders, ropings, crow's nest, that sort of thing?"

He paused, his brow furrowing. "I'd do better with a set of the plans," he said. "And I don't know if I have the time."

"I can get the plans for you," Mrs. Brown said with a wave of her hand. "You aren't planning on sitting around like a vegetable after you've testified, are you?"

A smile pulled at the corners of Jim's mouth. "No, ma'am, I'll find a job."

"You have one," she said with elaborate patience. "I am commissioning this carving of the ship. Which means I will pay you very generously. You, sir, are very talented, and now you are in my hands. I'll bring you business; I'm good at that. And, in case you don't know it,

I'm very rich." She sighed. "Mines in Colorado—that sort of thing."

Pinky watched Jim's face change. He seemed stunned at first. Then he looked down at his hands, as if seeing them for the first time.

"It's a deal," he said.

------

## NEW YORK CITY
## MONDAY NIGHT, APRIL 22

Tess wandered aimlessly around her hotel room, giddy with the knowledge that tomorrow she would be freed of the glances of curiosity from hotel staff and guests; the whispers in the wake of moving through the grand lobby to this small cubicle of privacy. Tomorrow she would be in her own place.

She sat down on the bed, enjoying the silence at first. Then a twist of loneliness. What was happening in Washington? Pinky would have a story tomorrow, surely. Had she seen Jim, talked to him? Was he all right?

Slowly she prepared for bed. There

was no use pretending to herself that she didn't miss him. She closed her eyes, conjuring up his face, the easy lope of his walk as they had made their way back to the hotel from the magical Central Park. Only two days ago.

She pulled back the covers and sank into the silky percale sheets. This was no time for foolish meanderings. She had managed to repair the dress, but tomorrow would be a hard and challenging day.

She drifted off to sleep, fingers curled tight around the comforting presence of the metal keys clutched in her fist.

## 9

### WALDORF-ASTORIA
### NEW YORK CITY
### TUESDAY MORNING, APRIL 23

"Did you see the funeral notice in the paper?" Elinor said as she pulled back the heavy drapes, letting in the morning light.

"Yes, of course I did." A hovering dust, exposed by the light, hung in the air. Lucile coughed, then moaned, clutching a handkerchief to her face.

"Oh stop it, Lucy," Elinor said impatiently. "You've played the victim long enough."

"How can you talk to me that way?"

"Because I know you, and you're too good at indignation and self-pity—

that's why. What's done is done, and the sooner we can get you out of here and back to England the better."

"My note to Jean Darling had no self-pity in it, grant me that."

"It was fine. The best you could do under the circumstances." Elinor reached for her cigarette holder and began to insert a cigarette.

"Must you? I'm so tired of the smell of your cigarettes."

"Worse than the tea and the tarts?" Elinor lit the cigarette and inhaled, staring out the open window. "You called them 'abominable' last night."

"Please, I'm trying."

Her sister's expression softened. "All right." She pinched the cigarette out and dropped it into an ashtray.

"I know you're cross with me, and clearly Cosmo is. Jordan Darling's suicide was dreadful, and I wish I had never opened my mouth to those reporters. But it is grossly unfair to blame me for what he did. He survived, why couldn't he leave it at that? What is wrong with being a survivor?"

"Quite a lot, perhaps."

Lucile compressed her lips, annoyed. "You're going to say something deep and complicated, and I'm going to want to run out of this room."

"Well, this time I've got you cornered." Elinor's voice was casual. "Aren't we the pair?"

"What's that supposed to mean?"

"Look at the two of us. I've been writing stories since I was fifteen. You, my dear sister, put your head down to the needle and sewed your way out of a miserable marriage. Then you came up with the idea of draping clothes over live models and voilà! Success. Helped along, of course, by marrying a title. Now, don't you agree that we're quite the pair?"

"You're setting the scene for something more, I know you."

"Of course. Maybe we're too used to making our own rules."

"And what does that have to do with being a survivor?"

"We're not particularly nice people, Lucy. We're both a bit careless, wouldn't you agree?"

"I'm not interested in playing your

games." She didn't have to listen to this—it was just the same old teasing that Elinor enjoyed so much.

"And self-absorbed?"

"That's what Cosmo says."

"Well, putting your dear husband aside for the moment—and, by the way, he was quite clumsy with his generosity on that lifeboat of yours. Well, you've got your answer."

Lucile lifted an eyebrow. "What is it, dear sister?"

"It's simple. The careless and self-absorbed manage to survive. Aren't we lucky?"

A silence fell over them both. Only after a long moment spent staring at the teapot on its silver tray sitting before her did Lucile respond.

"I thought you came here to comfort me."

"And to wake you up, Lucy." Elinor's voice was calm. "We're self-made women; there aren't many like us, wouldn't you say? But we can't afford to believe the fantasies we build about ourselves. Now a question—I hear that sailor who claims you stopped him from

rescuing survivors is testifying. What are you doing about it?"

"I don't know what we can do. Deny it, of course."

"I can imagine how that will go."

"It will go fine, I'm sure. And as far as believing in my own 'fantasies,' as you put it, all I have ever wanted is to be successful at what I do best, which is designing. I have done that, and I intend to enjoy it."

"It can evaporate in a minute, you know."

"Well, if either of us had stayed focused on that we'd never have got anywhere."

"Probably not even out of childhood."

"Mother was impossible."

"Oh say it, Lucy. She was mean as dirt."

They sat in silence for a moment.

"We managed," Lucile said in a different voice. "Together."

"Dear Lucy, you took the brunt of it."

"But I mastered the skill of throwing a phenomenally good tantrum."

"Which you continue to perfect," murmured Elinor, eyes dancing.

"Well, of course."

Again, silence between them—a more comfortable one this time. Lucile nibbled at a tart and sipped her tea. "Surely these terrible newspaper stories will soon wind down. I can't stand another day of hiding out in this place," she said finally. "I'm their scapegoat, but they'll get bored with me; they always do. They'll hunt for fresh ones, don't you think? I've heard of some awful behavior, particularly by the more excitable people in steerage."

"Don't count on it. You have too good a career and too high a reputation for them to leave you alone."

Lucile leaned back and closed her eyes. "I have to get back to my shop. It's my life and I don't want anyone else in charge, and certainly not Tess, who has no competence for business." Her eyes flew open; she frowned. "She was a bit vague on how things went yesterday. Did you talk to her? Is she holding something back?"

Elinor watched her sister closely. "If I tell you she was, you must promise not to get hysterical."

"Oh, dear Lord."

"Promise? If you don't, I will walk out of here and get on a train for Los Angeles right now."

Reluctantly, Lucile agreed. She sat in horrified silence as Elinor told her about the slashed wedding gown. How Tess had set about to repair it; how it had worked.

"Who would do such a thing?"

"She doesn't know. But the absence of your general manager's assistant was suspicious."

"She didn't tinker with my design, did she?"

"She did what she had to do."

"That means she did. And she was afraid to admit it."

"I said, she did what she had to do. And you seem prepared to berate her. Why did you send her in your place, then?"

"I had no choice."

"What does Cosmo say?"

"He actually thinks I'm feeling maternal. Which is nonsense."

"Trying *not* to feel maternal is more like it," Elinor said

The weight of an old, unspoken hurt descended between them.

"I'm not asking anything."

Lucile turned her head away before answering. "Mind you don't," she said.

The muted sounds of the city—horses clattering along the street, the chugging of motorcars and children calling to one another—floated through the open window, the only sounds in the silence that followed.

Elinor sighed, reaching over to pat her sister's hand. "Well, back to your spring show. I've struck a bargain with a young woman who is going to be a star in the movies, but right now she needs money."

"What kind of a bargain?"

"We give her one of your gowns and she promises to wear it here and in Hollywood, extolling your virtues as a designer."

"What is the bargain?"

"We pay her a thousand dollars."

"My Lord, that's insane! *She* should be paying *me*!"

"Lucy, she'll be a big customer very

soon. Haven't you heard of Mary Pick-ford?"

"I've read about her. I don't need such cheap advertising. No, I won't hear of it."

Elinor settled back in her seat and reached once again for her cigarette holder, taking time to again light a ciga-rette. "My dear sister, you can't afford to pass this one up," she said.

------

On Tuesday morning Tess slipped out of the hotel with a small valise, avoiding Lucile's suite. It was a relief, knowing she would no longer be a pretender to these lavish surroundings. Cosmo and Elinor surely had no inkling of how much having a place of her own meant to her. She brushed her hair away from her face, hoping she didn't look as tired as she felt.

The night had been filled with more dreams, the Darlings entwined through them all. She couldn't get them out of her mind. That affable, happy man, he and his wife the embodiment of fan-

tasy—gone, vanished. Yesterday she had pushed her thoughts into a tight corner, knowing they would be waiting for her later. And now they were hammering to be heard. *Cruelty.* The word Jean Darling had used. But Lucile didn't kill her husband—no one could say that. How ironic that a man could be cowardly and then muster the courage—or did it take only shame?—to take his own life. She skimmed the *Times* in the hotel's lobby, reading Pinky's story about yesterday's testimony. No mention of Jim; nothing about the Duff Gordons. A picture of Jordan Darling and one of his weeping wife.

And no way to offer them comfort. None, certainly not from anyone working for Lady Duff Gordon. Jim must know what happened by now. What did he think?

She climbed into the waiting car, her heart heavy. She must pull herself together. Today, just one step at a time. The shop would be frantic; the show—how could it matter in the face of such tragedy—was only days away. Last night James had ticked off all the things

that needed to be done, and she felt enormous gratitude that he had so quickly rallied to her side. He was ordering the canapés and the wine. He had even arranged for reminder cards to be hand-delivered to Lucile's patrons today. What else? She tried to focus on her concern about the models. Yesterday one of them had seemed restless and bored, unwilling to stand for final pinnings—and she was the one slated to wear the centerpiece wedding gown.

Tess rubbed her eyes; oh, she was tired, and the day had barely begun. "Lucile, come back soon," she whispered quietly. "This is more your world than it is mine." She pulled her purse close, comforted once again by the weight of the keys inside.

------

"There's a problem," James said as she came in the door of Lucile's office. His bald head glistened with sweat. "The tucks in the wedding gown made it too tight for the model."

"I can fix that with a piecing of silk, I

think," Tess said, trying to appear con-fident.

He shook his head wearily. "She pulled it off and tore it again. Said she'd never seen such a mess before a show. Then stomped out, probably with a job offer from this woman Chanel already in her back pocket."

"Bring me the dress. And another model—I don't care who."

James nodded and hurried from the room.

------

Her hands trembled as he handed her the gown and she saw the tear. She would have to change the line of the bodice, and that meant the skirt would need to be reconfigured. Lucile would be upset, but there was no choice. As Tess pulled out the seams and retucked the material—why did it need that un-derskirt?—she felt something totally unexpected and startling: a sense of euphoria. She could do this. She could salvage Lucile's creation.

The model, a tall, slender girl of about

eighteen, stared straight ahead as Tess worked, not seeming to care about or to question anything. Engrossed in the cutting and refitting, Tess worked in silence. The underskirt had bunched under the torn material; it had to go. Scissors poised, she hesitated. Would it be too sheer, or would it just give a hint of the wearer's legs? Anything else would be disastrous. She knew it would work, she was sure of it; the beading would soften the transparency and the entire gown would float much better. Sharp and sure, her scissors began cutting away the underskirt.

Just as she finished, James came bursting in, his eyes alight. "Miss Glyn called," he said. "Isadora Duncan says she will attend the show. That helps make up for Mrs. Wharton backing out, I'd say."

Tess lifted her eyes from the fabric, her breath catching. "My goodness!" she said.

"Madame has made her some beautiful clothes," James said, anticipating her question. "And she doesn't have to buy anything. She just has to *be* here.

Come quick, see the carpet—they're laying it now."

Tess peered through the door and caught her breath again. From the entrance near the shabby elevator to the back of the loft, a sweep of rich, thick purple carpet was being unrolled and hammered down. The seamstresses and fitters were watching and giggling. This factory they labored in every day, crammed with sewing machines and billowing reams of silk and soft wools, was being transformed. Chiffon curtains were being arranged around the stage, creating a silvery cloudlike setting; a workman was fiddling with the lights, dimming them to a soft glow. The effect was magical.

"Lucile knows how to do this, doesn't she?" James murmured. "Such a sense of drama. Amazing woman, as maddening as she is."

"Yes," Tess said. Could she, too, do all this someday? Maybe, she thought, letting herself slip back to the night on the *Titanic* and Jack Bremerton's unexpected vote of confidence in her. She would probably never see him again,

and his faith in her that night had been unearned at the time. But what she knew for certain was how much she wanted to try.

------

## TERRITORIES CONFERENCE ROOM
## WASHINGTON, D.C.
## TUESDAY, APRIL 23

Pinky had trouble dragging herself to the new hearing room on Tuesday morning. That cheap Van Anda had put her up in a hotel filled with boisterous late-night partygoers, and no amount of banging on the walls or shouting down the corridor had stopped the noise. She had tried to talk with Bonney yesterday, but Smith's people spotted him in the entrance hall and hustled him away with the rest of the crew. Too many witnesses and contradictions; that had left her cranky. A leather-goods man said crew members shot pistols in the air to keep panicked men from filling the boats, while a Brooklyn cleric insisted that there was complete deco-

rum on the ship, no panic at all. She had worked until her early-edition deadline, distracted by anxiety about her father. There was a neighbor "looking in" on Mrs. Dotson, hopefully with some delicacy, so the woman wouldn't guess that Pinky didn't completely trust her. She probably knew it anyway.

She slipped into a seat near the front, glad she had again come early. She missed the presence of Mrs. Brown—the eminently quotable Mrs. Brown—but that ebullient lady had returned to New York, making lavish predictions for Jim's future as an artist—all a bit over the top, in Pinky's view. But then rich people always made making money look easy.

People were clamoring outside, angry that the hearing had been moved to a room with better acoustics. They didn't care about acoustics; they just wanted to be there and hear all the sad, enraging stories that patch together any disaster, making it tasty and satisfying. God, what an awful thing to think, she told herself. How cynical am I, anyway?

The first witness to take the stand was the lookout in the *Titanic*'s crow's nest—Frederick Fleet, a shabbily dressed man fumbling with a ragged cap. His eyes kept darting nervously in the direction of Bruce Ismay, which was no surprise. How could Smith expect to get complete candor from men whose livelihood depended on White Star?

"Mr. Fleet, your job was to report any danger ahead, is that correct?" asked Smith.

"Yes, sir. They told us to keep a sharp lookout for small ice. And, well, I reported an iceberg right ahead—a black mass."

"How long before the collision, or accident, did you report ice ahead?"

"I have no idea." Again, a nervous glance in Ismay's direction.

"About how long?" Smith pressed.

"I reported it soon as ever I seen it."

"You are accustomed to judging distances, are you not, from the crow's nest? You are there to look ahead and sight objects, are you not?"

"We are only up there to report any-

thing we see," Fleet responded. "I'm not so good at judging distance."

A titter spread through the room. The lookout for the largest, grandest ship in the world couldn't judge time or distance.

"Were you given glasses of any kind?" Smith asked.

"We had nothing at all, only our own eyes, to look out. We asked for them in Southhampton, and they said there was none for us."

"On this ship, the largest in the world, there was not one set of binoculars?"

"That's right."

Pinky wrote out the two words in block letters in her notebook: "NO BINOCULARS." This would lead her story.

---

"So how do you think it's going?" she asked Smith at the lunch break.

"You again," he said shortly, walking away.

She followed him. "Senator, all I'm asking is, how is this testimony affecting you? I know how it's affecting me."

"And how is that?" he said, coming to a stop.

"It's worse than sad. It's a mess of inept people and bumbled jobs and selfishness—that's what it seems to me."

Smith allowed himself a small smile. "We're trying to put together a puzzle, Miss Wade. There are a lot of pieces not yet in place. I think we may come across more honorable stories than you expect. But remember, human nature is not necessarily courageous."

Impulsively, Pinky threw in another question. "It's as much about what some of the survivors did as what White Star did, right?"

"I know where you're going with that," Smith said, and once again turned away.

"The British are mad at you, sir," she said hurriedly. "They're calling you stupid and narrow and—"

"I know, I know—I had a report this morning." His voice turned testy. "Anything else?"

It was worth a shot. "You have the crew members sequestered until they

testify, Senator, but can I talk briefly with one of them, Jim Bonney? For background, you know. I won't write anything until you're done with him."

"Tomorrow," he said. "After the day's testimony."

"When does Bonney go on the stand?"

"Thursday."

"And when are you calling the Duff Gordons to explain themselves?"

Smith turned on his heel and walked away.

Pinky watched him go, satisfied. If she kept up the pressure, maybe she could make him do it.

------

## NEW YORK CITY
## TUESDAY NIGHT

Tess stopped in front of a modest building not far from the Flatiron Building, looking down at the crumpled piece of paper in her hands. Yes, this was the address. Eagerly she stepped up to the front door and pushed one of the two

keys into the lock. It wouldn't turn. She felt a second of panic before realizing the obvious. The other key must be for the front door of the building; this one was for her upstairs flat.

She inserted the right key and the door swung open. She took the stairs quickly, saw the right number, and inserted the second key. Again, miraculously, the door swung open. And, for the first time in her life, Tess Collins walked into a place that was all her own.

She spread her arms wide and danced slowly around the modest space. A tiny kitchen, but with an iron stove. A somewhat battered pair of oak chairs, but solid, with legs that would not collapse the minute she sat down. A bed with a cheerful quilt of red and green; a small table with an electric lamp. It was hers; all hers. Whom could she tell? Whom could she share this with? She suddenly wished Pinky were there. She had a feeling that Pinky would understand.

"I will earn it," she said out loud, a

little startled at the sound of her own voice. "And I will keep it."

------

## TERRITORIES CONFERENCE ROOM
## WASHINGTON, D.C.
## WEDNESDAY, APRIL 24

The man was not going to give an inch. A disgusted William Alden Smith watched Bruce Ismay step down from the stand. Twice up there, and still only defensive haughtiness from the cold face of the White Star corporate world.

No, he had not urged the captain to increase the speed of the *Titanic* past the point of safety. Yes, he had heard of the possibility of ice, but their speed was not excessive.

"Would you not regard it as an exercise of proper precaution and care to *lessen* the speed of a ship crossing the Atlantic when she had been warned of the presence of ice ahead?" a puzzled committee member had asked.

"I have no opinion on that," Ismay had said. "We employ the very best

men we possibly can to take command of these ships, and it is a matter entirely in their discretion."

And now there he was, back in his chair with arms folded, looking smug. You're not home free yet, Senator Smith thought grimly. I'll let you hightail it back to England only when I'm good and ready.

He looked down at his witness list. Next up was Harold Lowe, the ship's fifth officer, a man of reputed bravado and colorful language, and probably the seaman most qualified of the lot of them.

"You helped load the lifeboats, is that right?" Smith began.

Lowe nodded vigorously.

"Did you know any of the men who assisted you?"

"No, sir, not by name." He hesitated, but only for a second. "But there is a man here, and had he not been here I should not have known that I had ordered Mr. Ismay away from a boat."

A stir in the room. "You ordered Mr. Ismay away from a boat?" said Smith with surprise.

"I did, because Mr. Ismay was over-anxious and he was getting a trifle excited. He said, 'Lower away! Lower away!' I said—"

"Give us what you said."

Lowe ran fingers through his hair, clearly considering whether he should be discreet. His blunt nature won out. "I told him, 'If you will get the hell out of that I shall be able to do something. You want me to lower away quickly? You will have me drown the whole lot of them.'"

Senator Smith allowed himself a moment to enjoy Ismay's flustered demeanor. Quite satisfying, really.

Lowe was at ease now. He told of shouting down at sailors to get the plugs in the collapsible boats before they hit the water, or they'd sink, and watching as the more inept struggled with oars.

"Was there no training before the ship set sail?" asked Smith incredulously.

"There was one drill, but only two boats," Lowe said. "We were brand-

new to the ship, just the same as everybody else."

Smith let a silence fall. A collective sigh for what might have been, for what should have been, filled the room.

"So you helped load boats. Tell us what happened when you were in the water," Smith said finally.

"I got my boat near four others, herded them close—five boats altogether. Then I roped them—figured we'd be seen better by a rescue ship. Then I emptied the passengers out of my boat into the other four."

"Why did you do that?"

"So I could go back."

The room went very still. Pinky waited, her pen poised. Senator Smith leaned forward.

"So you could go back to rescue people?"

"Yes, sir. Of course, I had to wait until the yells and shrieks had subsided—for the people to thin out—and then I deemed it safe to go among the wreckage."

"You waited until the drowning peo-

ple had quieted down?" Smith's voice had a slight wobble.

"Yes, sir." Lowe was obviously not a man about to sugarcoat his story. "It would not have been wise or safe for me to go there before, because the whole lot of us would have been swamped and then nobody would have been saved. When the cries subsided, I rowed off to the wreckage and I picked up four people. Three others were dead."

"What did you do with them?"

"I thought to myself, I am not here to worry about bodies; I am here for life, to save life, and not to bother about bodies, and I left them."

"You could have saved more if you hadn't waited."

Lowe looked straight at Smith, his voice resolute. "I made the attempt, sir, as soon as any man could do so, and I am not scared of saying it. If anybody had struggled out of the mass, I was there to pick them up. But it was useless for me to go into the mass."

"You mean for anybody?"

"It would have been suicide."

The crowd stayed quiet as the seaman's words sank in. Confused glances were exchanged; Pinky sat still, staring at her notes. No one yet had so vividly put the safe, insulated courtroom observers of this tragedy out there on the water themselves, making them face the question of what was right and what was wrong. Where were the niches and holes in which to hide their proper indignation; no, to hide themselves from a key question: *What would they have done?* Her pen slowly began to move on the page.

Jim was waiting for her on the steps of the Senate Office Building after the hearing recessed for the day. Hands jammed into back pockets, he walked restlessly back and forth, jacketless, seemingly oblivious of the cool evening air of early spring. He looked up as Pinky hailed him.

"I'm told I can talk to you today," he said. "But not for a story, right?"

"For background. I'll use it after you testify tomorrow. You see, I have a hunch that you're going to put Lady

Duff back on the front pages. Am I right?"

"All I can say is I'm going to truthfully answer the questions I'm asked."

Together, they began strolling down the hill.

"Were you in the hearing room?" Pinky asked.

Jim nodded.

"What did you think of Lowe's testimony?"

"He's an honest man, and a brave one."

"Seems to me he took his time going back, wouldn't you say?"

"Are you trying that idea out on me, or do you really believe it?"

That wasn't the reply she'd expected; she hesitated.

"Well?"

"I don't know," she said.

He looked toward her, his voice tense and serious. "Think of it, will you? Lowe was scared. We all were—what the bloody hell is wrong with saying it? He did what he felt he had to do, and those smug people exchanging shocked glances in the conference room have

no idea what it was like. Sorry for cursing, but there it is."

"I've heard worse," Pinky said cheerfully. "You should spend some time in a newsroom—we're all sailors there."

"I can't quite picture you spewing out curse words; I'll bet you don't even know the ones I know," he said with a faint smile.

"Will you come to dinner with me?" she asked impulsively.

"Sure. As long as it isn't at that dingy hotel we're stuck in."

------

They found a table in Ebbitt's saloon, far back from the heavy mahogany bar, lit with a single, flickering votive candle. Pinky felt herself sink into the coziness of the booth, relaxing. She wasn't in working mode, although she knew she should be. What was it about Jim that left her feeling unguarded and even a bit softer? Anyway, he was probably thinking only of Tess.

"What are you going to say tomorrow?" she asked finally.

"You've asked me that before," he said, spearing a piece of potato on his fork. "My answer is the same. I'll tell them what happened, if they ask."

"Do you feel differently now about Lady Duff stopping you from going back? After hearing Lowe's testimony?"

He looked startled. "What do you mean?"

"Well, Tess defends her, saying what she did was no different from anyone else. Says she's being made a scapegoat for everybody's sins."

"I know." He said it quietly, almost tenderly. "We don't feel the same. But I can't tell her everything."

"I'm sorry I didn't have a message for you yesterday."

He looked a bit embarrassed at her candor. "I was hoping, but I wasn't expecting one."

"I kind of think you were."

He looked away, saying nothing.

Maybe now she could get to what was bothering her. "Would you have waited until—how did Lowe put it?— the mass in the water *thinned out*? I'm

not defending Lady Duff, but Lowe was pretty cold-blooded, too."

"Is that what you're going to write?"

Was she? She didn't know, but she wasn't about to say so. She had to file at the telegraph office in a few hours; she could think it through.

Jim leaned forward, folding his hands on the table, his face close to hers. "That isn't the story," he said. "Your story is: *he went back.* Look, we had choices. Yes, I would have gone right back, and maybe I would have been crazy and responsible for killing everyone in my boat. And maybe not. Maybe Lowe wishes he hadn't waited so long to go back with an empty boat that could hold sixty people. But he told his story straight. He's not to trying to smooth out the kinks, like Lightoller saying there was total calm on the ship and no screams in the water. Why clean it up?"

"If it was right for him to go back, then everybody should have rowed back. And they should have done it right away."

"I'll speak to what I know. The ones

who should have gone back were the ones sitting with me in a huge and shamefully empty boat." He wrapped both hands around his beer, staring into the froth. "The Duff Gordons are used to getting their way with money. Worked well this time."

"I just feel—" She stopped. She didn't want the conversation to go this way. Maybe if Jim had rowed back and capsized he would have killed people, not saved them. And maybe there was nothing noble about that, and maybe there was. She wanted firmer ground.

"You're going up against a tough pair, Jim."

"I have to. She ruled that boat, and she set the tone. It wasn't just not going back. She let things happen."

"Like what?"

He was struggling with something. "I can't talk about it."

"And Cosmo did bribe the sailors to keep quiet about it all?"

"You got that from Sullivan, right? And he probably told you he refused the bribe. The real story? I think the Duff Gordons hinted at much more

money than they eventually gave out, and he's angry." Jim laughed sharply. "Look, I'll just say what happened. I'm not going to varnish anything. I wish I could, for Tess's sake. I didn't fight Lady Duff hard enough—you think I'm proud of that? And I'm the first to shake Harold Lowe's hand, no matter what gets said about him, because he went back."

"I think I know why you don't want to testify."

Jim picked up the mug of beer in front of him and took a long, slow swallow. "Yeah, I think you do," he said.

"You know"—one of her shots in the dark—"this isn't a criminal court. And you only have to answer the questions they ask."

"They'll ask," he said.

# 10

## TERRITORIES CONFERENCE ROOM
## WASHINGTON, D.C.
## THURSDAY MORNING, APRIL 25

Another night of little sleep. Pinky, this time crouched down in front of the folding chairs jammed up to the committee's meeting table, could hardly stop yawning. The stories on yesterday's testimony were all over the map. Some reporters were appalled at the "coldness" of Lowe holding back; others pointed out what Jim had insisted was true: the man was the only person who actually had saved anyone. Staring at the ceiling last night, she had decided that Jim was right. For readers of her

story in the *Times* this morning, Lowe was a hero—a real one.

Out of the corner of her eye, she saw two men holding black leather briefcases on their laps, sitting still by the far wall, staring straight ahead. No hustling about the room, shaking hands, conferring—all those restless things congressmen and their aides did. One wore horn-rimmed glasses settled low; the other looked pale as milk. They were too well dressed to be legislators. And right in front of them, twisting uneasily on his chair, was Sullivan. Was he here to back up Jim's story? Not likely. Her gaze traveled to Jim. He was wearing a more formal jacket today, one obviously borrowed, and his wrists jutted out from too-short sleeves as he stepped up to the witness chair. He looked resolute but vulnerable.

She suddenly realized what was going on. But it was too late to warn Jim.

------

Senator Smith, squinting through the haze of cigarette smoke, banged his

gavel. "We hope today to gather information about what happened in the water and in the lifeboats," he said. "Seaman James Bonney is our first witness. A first-time seaman, I understand, who escaped on Lifeboat One. Will you take a seat, Mr. Bonney?"

The questions began. In a steady, almost toneless voice, Jim told of helping to load five different boats before moving to the starboard side, where one collapsible boat hung, caught in a tangle of ropes. Of Officer Murdoch shouting for them to get this boat ready for Lady Duff Gordon. Of rushing forward, helping other sailors clear the ropes to release the emergency boat known as Number One. Yes, he said. Seaman Sullivan was put in charge of the boat.

"Why was it launched with so few people in it?"

"Because Lady Duff Gordon insisted."

"Are you accusing her of abandoning people on the deck?" Smith asked.

"No, sir. I'm accusing her of thinking only of herself."

"When the ship sank, did you look for survivors?"

"No."

"What was the capacity of your boat, and how many were in it?"

"We could have held fifty or more. There were twelve of us, that's all."

"I believe your boat holds the notoriety of having been launched with the fewest souls in it, am I right?"

"Yes, sir."

A murmur swept the crowd, a muttering that made the back of Pinky's neck tingle.

Then one of Smith's colleagues spoke up. "Now let's get to the crux of this. With the most room of anyone, did you not go back to pick up anybody at all?"

Jim's voice was flat. "Nobody at all," he said.

"Why not?"

"The others did not want to go back."

"Did you?"

"Yes. No one agreed."

"Who was it objected to pulling back?"

"Lady Duff Gordon refused to let

anyone pick up an oar. She was afraid to go back for fear of being swamped."

"Was there, as far as you know, any danger of the boat being swamped if you did go back?"

Jim did not hesitate. "It would certainly have been possible. But we were in a big boat that wasn't full."

"How would it have been dangerous, considering that you had a crew of seven in the boat, to go among the people who were screaming for help in the sea?" barked Senator Bolton, another member of the panel. He was clearly still brooding over Lowe's testimony of the day before. "Did you hear the screams?"

"Of course I did," Jim shot back. "We all heard them. I told you, I proposed going back and they would not hear of it."

"Did you say it to anyone personally?" pressed Smith.

"I called it out to everybody."

"The man to decide whether the boat should go back was Sullivan, was it not?" Smith glanced over at his next

witness, sitting slumped in his chair, eyes darting about.

"Yes," Jim said with barely concealed contempt. "He was the man in charge. At least he was supposed to be."

"And he said no?"

"That's correct."

"Was his attitude due to the protests of the Duff Gordons?"

"Yes." This time he looked directly at Sullivan, who looked away.

"Are you sure of that?"

"I only know about my one boat. I should have overridden him."

"With what authority?"

Jim was silent.

"You say you heard cries? Agonizing cries?"

"Yes."

"And the Duff Gordons said it was too dangerous to go back to save lives?"

"Yes."

One of the committee members, a senator with a round ruddy face, leaned forward, his voice dripping sarcasm.

"Then am I to understand that be-cause two of the passengers said it

would be dangerous you all kept your mouths shut and made no attempt to rescue anybody?"

"That is right, sir." Jim straightened his shoulders, taking the blow.

Smith switched focus. "Were you promised any money by Sir Duff Gordon in the lifeboat?" he asked.

"Yes."

The room was now buzzing with whispers. The bribe, people were saying; there was a bribe.

"And was that an arrangement with the other members of the crew, to do a certain thing for a certain price? In other words, not to go back?" It was the man with the ruddy face again.

Pinky held her breath. Jim looked very tired.

"It was not proposed that way."

"What does that mean? He didn't declare it a bribe? Wouldn't that have been a bit strange? Did you think it was a bribe?"

"Yes, I did."

"I'm wondering what else this so-called bribe was meant to silence. Did

anyone in the water try to get into your boat?"

Pinky waited, holding her breath.

"Yes. There were people all around us. More than one tried to climb in."

"And what happened?"

Silence. Jim's eyes looked bleak.

"Some slipped away."

"And others?"

Again, a silence. "It was dark and hard to see," he said finally.

"Do you think anybody was forcibly pushed away?"

"It could have been."

The crowd stirred; whispers began.

"That's quite a charge, Mr. Bonney," said Senator Bolton. "A very black charge. Are you making a specific accusation?"

"I'm wary of accusing anyone I didn't clearly see, sir. But this is what I believe."

"Do you have more to say?" Senator Smith asked.

"No, sir."

"You may step down," Senator Smith said. He looked out across the room, his heart heavy. Get on with it. Next up

was the bony sailor with the pock-marked skin who had supposedly been in charge of Lifeboat One. He sat slumped in his chair, as if bored by the proceedings, even as his eyes darted back and forth across the room.

"Mr. Tom Sullivan, I understand you were the ranking seaman in charge of Lifeboat One. Will you please take the stand?"

Stunned, Pinky watched Jim step down and take his seat. So this was what he had been holding back. An attack was surely coming now. Why hadn't he told the committee that he turned down the bribe? *Because they hadn't asked.* But he had done what he said he would do—just told the truth plainly, without embellishment. They would chew him up.

------

"Tom Sullivan, is that your name?"

"Yes, sir." Sullivan pulled himself up in the witness seat, hands clasped in front of him, clutching his cap. Her source for the original bribery story. His

eyes were furious, close to burning a hole in Jim's departing back. But his face took on a mask of gravity as he turned directly to his questioner.

"Let's get your story of what happened on Lifeboat One. You were in charge, right?" Senator Perkins was doing this round of questioning, and he was impatient to be done with it.

"Yes, sir, I sure was. I was master of the situation."

"How many people were in your boat?"

Sullivan didn't hesitate. "Oh, fourteen to twenty," he said.

"We were told by the previous witness that there were twelve occupants, and you could have held up to fifty. Is that correct?"

"Well, we took who we could."

"We also understand from Mr. Bonney's testimony that you did not return to where the ship sank."

Sullivan shook his head so vigorously that his collar almost came undone. "No, sir, we came back after the ship went down and saw nothing. Thank you for the chance to correct the record."

Smith and the other panel members exchanged looks of surprise.

"You did go back?"

"Of course we did," Sullivan said indignantly. "I'm sorry to say this, but Jim Bonney is a shifty sort; he's got an ax to grind, for something."

"Did you rescue anyone in the water?"

"No, sir, nobody was alive. Didn't hear anybody." The sorrowful tone was back.

"When did you go back?"

"Soon as we could." Sullivan waved his hand vaguely.

"Then what did you do?"

"We rowed around." He glanced quickly at the two men with briefcases, a glance Pinky caught. She stared at the pair.

"Was there any confusion or excitement among your passengers?"

Sullivan seemed totally comfortable now. "No, sir, I never saw it. It was just the same as if it was an everyday affair."

An everyday affair? The silence in the room told him he had gone too far.

A few murmurings and glances were exchanged. He began picking at his fingers, his eyes once again darting toward the men with briefcases. "Not totally that, of course. But we were pulling together, you know? It was a sad time."

"Is there any other incident that you wish to state that would be of interest to the public? Anything about the actions of the passengers, the Duff Gordons?"

"No, sir, not that I know of."

"Did they refuse to go back?"

"No, sir. They are fine people."

"Did they offer you a bribe?" Senator Smith cut in.

"No, sir. Mr. Bonney is wrong on that one, too. He has problems. And I have no more to say."

Perkins leaned back in his chair, his brow furrowed. "Thank you, Mr. Sullivan. You are dismissed," he said, glancing at his watch.

"Could I say one thing more, sir?" Sullivan said.

"What would that be?"

"Sometimes people don't think right

in bad situations, and then try to cover up their own behavior. If anybody could push people away, it would be Bonney. He's got a bad reputation—he could've pushed people off, you bet. He's the bastard in this room."

Pinky stared at Sullivan. Loathsome, lying toad, trying to save his own skin by switching stories. She should have published his name. Here he was, playing the humble seaman, just a sturdy man trying to do his job; good show. The Duff Gordons had been more generous this time. She watched as the two men with briefcases slipped out the door and saw one of them give Sullivan a quick nod as he exited.

Who were they? She scrambled after the pair, following them through the exit door, shutting it in time to step in front of one of them. He looked neither startled nor displeased, just indifferent.

"Wait, I need to know—who are you?" she asked.

"That's really no business of yours, Miss Wade," he said.

So he knew her name. "I'll bet you're a lawyer. What firm are you with?"

He gave a thin smile. "Miss Wade, there are many lawyers in this room. Some, as you know, get elected to Congress. Are you so surprised that a lowly seaman might have representation? I'm afraid you aren't well versed in the law. Good day." He started to walk away.

"Wait a minute—who's paying you?"

He ignored her and kept walking.

------

Senator Smith barely looked up as he called the last witness of the morning. One more from Lifeboat One.

"Mr. Albert Purcell, please take the stand."

A burly, weathered man with large ears and thinning hair settled his bulk into the witness seat. The questioning began, covering the same ground as before—where he was on the ship, what he did.

"After the ship went down, did you hear any cries?"

"Not that I recall." He sneaked a quick look at Sullivan.

"Did anybody suggest that you should go back in the direction of the people in the water?"

"Not to my knowledge."

"Nobody said *anything* about going back?"

"No, sir." Purcell was almost beaming.

"Mr. Bonney said he did. Is that correct?"

"No, sir. He's puffing himself up."

Senator Harbinson broke in. "All right, do you remember hearing anything said about presents or about money?"

"Yes, I do, and I will explain how it came about." Purcell had his details ready, and he was anxious to spill them out. "Well, you see, Lady Duff Gordon said something like 'There is my beautiful nightdress gone,' and I said, 'Never mind about that, as long as you have got your life,' and I said we had lost everything and then Sir Duff Gordon said later he'd give us a little something to start over. That's all I heard."

"How long after the *Titanic* went down did you first hear mention of this money?"

"About three-quarters of an hour."

"Did you consider it a bribe?"

"Oh no, sir. Just a generous offer from generous people."

"Did it occur to you at all that you ought to go back?"

Purcell responded in lofty fashion. "No, it was not my place. I was not in charge of the boat; if that had been said, I would certainly have gone back."

"You were ready and willing?"

"Quite willing."

"Were you not surprised that somebody else did not suggest it?"

"Yes, I was," he said, with what he clearly hoped was indignation.

"I don't understand your frame of mind," Senator Harbinson suddenly snapped. "You were surprised that no one made the suggestion but you were not surprised that you did not make it?"

"We were half dazed at the time," Purcell stammered, casting another glance at Sullivan, who was glaring at him.

"Can you offer any explanation at all as to why your boat didn't try to pick up people?"

Purcell hesitated, trapped, then plunged on. "Yes, well, we would have been swamped if we had gone back; that is my opinion. There were so many people in the water—you could hear that by the cries."

"Ah, so you heard cries and *didn't* go back? Even to find *nothing*? And, by the way, Mr. Sullivan says you *did* go back under his direction?"

Purcell looked at Sullivan hopelessly; he had stepped into it. "No, sir. Yes, sir."

"Did anybody say it was dangerous?"

The coaching he had clearly received reasserted itself. "No, sir. Nobody said anything like that."

"Did anyone say you might be swamped?"

"No, sir."

"Does it not occur to you that you might very well have gone back with a good chance of picking up some stragglers from outside the swarm?"

"Yes, if they were outside, I guess."

Harbinson was weary. They were all weary. "It did not occur to you that you might have unloaded your passengers

by getting some of the other boats to take some of your passengers, and then gone back with a practically empty boat to pick up some of the poor people in the water?"

"No, sir."

"Enough of this," said Senator Smith. All in the room were obviously remembering the forthrightness of Harold Lowe. And Pinky, twisting about, kept hoping that she would see Jim. Sullivan surely had been brought down by this inept fool who couldn't keep his lies straight. Wouldn't everybody see it now?

------

Jim was standing alone by the front door of the Senate Office Building, drawing hard on a cigarette through pressed lips, staring at the Capitol. Deep furrows had etched their way into his strong-boned face.

"Who—" Pinky began as she joined him.

"Don't ask, because I won't answer. None of it brings back the dead."

"Look, those two were lying—anyone could see that. You came out ahead."

"Don't be so sure. You saw those men with the briefcases? Who are they?"

"I'll find out. If they're lawyers, Purcell should have been briefed better. Relax, Jim. Purcell ruined their story."

"That woman won't give up easily. You know as well as I do she's got something up her sleeve."

"Lady Duff?"

"Of course."

She paused. But she couldn't stop trying to console him. "What can she do now? The others in your boat know the truth. What is she going to do, silence them all? Somebody will back you up."

"Who? Besides those dancers and the Duff Gordons, there were only crew members in the boat. And, believe me, they have every one of them in their pocket. They know what they're doing." He dropped the cigarette to the ground, and immediately lit another. "What does it matter, anyway? Nobody's going to

jail over this. I know it happened in the other boats. I just want the damn thing to be told true. And I want Tess to believe me."

"I think she will."

"When it's between me and the woman she thinks is her lifeline?"

"She won't be fooled by a lie." Why did she speak with such conviction? How did she know what someone in Tess's situation would think? But it was hard to imagine someone not trusting Jim, especially Tess.

"I want to see her, Pinky."

"I figured I was going to be the go-between," she said good-naturedly. "Are you sure?"

"More than you can possibly know."

There was enough fervor in his words to strike her silent for the moment. There was even more fervor in what he said next.

"The thing is, right now what Sullivan said is what people *want* to believe. It's a clean lie that makes everybody feel better." He drew deeply on the cigarette and tossed it to the ground, grind-

ing it with his foot. "You know what I mean? Brave sailors and passengers go back on a rescue mission, but all those screaming people in the water have conveniently died. It's stitched up nice and neat. No wrestling with the choice of one man to wait until most of the people died; no having to believe another sailor who can't muster up a hero for them, not even for himself. Sullivan fills the bill. What people want is a steady type who did the right thing. Whatever that is."

He turned away. "I'm sorry, I've got to get out of here." He stalked away, striding off down the hill. Pinky didn't try to hurry after him. She simply followed him with her eyes.

------

And from a window in the conference room looking out on the steps, hands clasped behind his back, so did Senator William Alden Smith.

A tall man, that Bonney, striding away, looking quite somber and determined. The man was probably telling the truth,

even though there was obviously bad blood between him and Sullivan. Purcell was a joke.

How far did he want to push this? He knew in his heart, no matter what the newspapers said, that there were survivors out there having a hard time living with themselves because they acted out of fear, not courage. Was it worth it to hunt them down and expose them? Look at this man Darling. A good man, from all reports, who did one weakwilled thing, now dead by his own hand. Did he need to drag this arrogant British designer and her husband into the hearings? Weren't they getting whipped about enough in the newspapers?

He stared after Bonney and made his decision.

------

Twilight was deepening as Pinky climbed on the train and headed back to New York, exhausted from arguing with Van Anda. So maybe it looked like a story about two sailors who hated each other and one idiot. And, yes, her

source for the earlier bribery story had turned his story inside out. But Bonney had confirmed it, so it wasn't wrong. He was by far the more believable on the stand, with much to lose. Why would he say that he thought people were pushed off unless it was true? Watch out, you're trying too hard to make Bonney a hero, Van Anda said. Keep the focus on the fact that he and Sullivan were calling each other liars. Are you sure you saw lawyers? Prove it. Follow up tomorrow, and get home and get some sleep. "The Lowe piece was great," he threw in before hanging up. She slumped back into her seat, worried. Was she losing perspective? She had to quit thinking about who got hurt and who didn't. Her job was to report the facts, even when her instincts intervened. But it wasn't always easy to choose between the two.

Pinky tucked her bunched-up coat under her head and closed her eyes. Van Anda was right; she'd better get some rest. She had a job to do, and it didn't include worrying about Bonney. She had to get some groceries as soon

as she got home, and if she was late tonight the long-suffering Mrs. Dotson would have her hand out again for more money.

## II

## FLATIRON DISTRICT
## NEW YORK CITY
## THURSDAY MORNING, APRIL 25

No reporters were hovering at the entrance as Lucile and Elinor walked quickly through the front door to the elevator. Lucile punched the up button with relief.

"I can't stay long—I have an appointment with my hairstylist," Elinor said as they rumbled up to the top floor. "I don't know why you wanted me here today, anyway."

"Your hair is more important than my business? Really, Elinor."

"Your timing is good, I'll say. Right in the middle of Jordan Darling's funeral."

"Exactly. All the reporters are there. I've been away from here long enough; I can't afford to hide anymore. Thank goodness I didn't have to walk through the usual hordes. You can leave anytime you want; I'm back on familiar ground now."

"Madame," said James in surprise, lifting his head from a worktable filled with a jumble of hats and gloves and jewelry—all necessary accessories for the show. Next to him was Tess, her mouth filled with pins, on her knees fitting a skirt on a model.

"Well, I see you two are keeping busy," Lucile said with a bright smile. "James, get rid of that awful green concoction." She pointed a finger at one of the hats. "The color is atrocious. Looks like bile."

"Yes, Madame. Good to have you back, Madame."

Tess had managed to remove the pins from her mouth as she stood up. "It's good to see you," she said warmly.

"How is your new flat, dear? Didn't Cosmo move quickly?"

"It's wonderful, and I'm very grate-

ful." Grateful? Thrilled, was more like it. That wonderful, tiny flat on Fifth Avenue—so sparse, so plain, but hers alone. A pot, a couple of cups, and two dishes on the tiny kitchen counter; the first thing she had done was make herself some tea. She was on the payroll now, being paid for her work, and soon she would be paying for that flat. And then she would bring Mother over from England and they would make curtains together and she would begin to be part of a world she could call her own.

"Where is the wedding gown?"

Lucile's voice snapped her back to reality. "Over here, on the table—I've finished the repairs," Tess said. Lucile began inspecting the gown, and Tess felt a flutter of fear in her stomach. James was stepping back; two of the models were watching Lucile warily. The seamstress on the nearest sewing machine had stopped work.

Lucile lifted the skirt with two fingers, holding it at arm's length, eyes narrowed. "Where is the underskirt?" she demanded.

"It was torn and I took it off; this makes the skirt flow better," Tess said.

"And what have you done to the bodice?"

"It had to be changed—it was torn, too." She was stumbling, speaking too fast.

First, silence, as Lucile turned the dress over and stared at the bodice.

*"What have you done?"* she finally said. Her hoarse, throaty challenge carried through the shop. "I have a major show in the offing—and *you* have tampered with my showpiece design, the one that would have been the talk of the town. And now, *now*—" She dropped the dress back onto the table. "Now it is just the amateur work of a beginner who might be good at stitching up torn garments but who knows *nothing* about the aesthetics of design!"

Tess grabbed the edge of the table to steady herself, afraid she might fall. Her voice was shaky and thin. "I did what I thought needed to be done to salvage your wonderful gown. There were only a few necessary changes,

but I tried to stay true to your vision. Let the model put it on and you'll see."

Lucile glared at her. "Don't give me that nonsense. You took a Lucile creation and made it your own."

"What are you complaining about?" Elinor murmured, touching Lucile's sleeve. "You can see the girl salvaged a badly damaged gown—what else could she do? Watch out, the mood here isn't as deferential as usual. Haven't you noticed?"

Lucile shrugged off her sister's hand. "Here"—she nodded at one of the models and handed her the gown—"put this thing on so I can see the extent of the damage." She stalked over to the runway, pointing a finger at James. "When she's buttoned in, tell her to walk this way," she directed.

James went running to give the instructions to the model, pausing as he passed Tess. "You did a good job," he whispered. "Whatever she says."

It was a timid endorsement, but Tess was grateful. She watched Lucile's expression as the model walked toward her, the gorgeous gown swirling and

floating around her legs. It was still true to the basics of Lucile's design. But Lucile said nothing, and her stony expression didn't change. Of course, she wouldn't like it; there was no way she could cede that to Tess.

"Why didn't you reverse the side seams, for heaven's sake?"

"I didn't think of it."

"It no longer qualifies as the centerpiece of my collection, I'm afraid."

Tess's cheeks burned scarlet. She might have the staff's sympathy, but that would not get her through this.

"You still have quite a bit to learn, you know."

"I don't deny that."

"Don't try anything this audacious again."

Again, that odd, poised feeling of being on the brink of something. Tess held her breath.

Lucile suddenly stood, brushing off her skirt briskly. "It will have to do. Tess, do something you're capable of doing. Start steaming the nettings on the hats, will you? They are dreadfully wrinkled."

"Yes, Madame."

"Only a few days to the show, every-body," Lucile called out, clapping her hands as she marched into her office. "Let's get busy!"

------

"Lucile, can we talk?" Tess said as the two women stepped out onto the side-walk at the end of the day.

"I am much too tired from fixing the damage around here for idle chatter." Lucile would not so much as look at her.

"I did my best to help. I'm sorry it wasn't good enough."

Lucile stared at the waiting car, her jaw held stiffly. "Be at the shop by eight in the morning," she said. *"And do not call me by my first name."* With that, and with a blank-faced Farley holding the door, Lady Duff Gordon stepped in without looking back.

------

Tess jiggled the key in the door of her apartment, desperate for it to open. It

had been a day of not only steaming hat nettings but pressing hems, mopping up spills, discarding baskets of fabric scraps—anything that did not involve picking up a needle, cutting patterns, or adjusting fittings. Nothing beyond what a maid would do. All this, to prove to everyone in Lucile's loft that Madame was still in charge, that she was the designer—as if anyone doubted that. Tess had tried her best, tried to salvage a great design, and her work was wanting. Would she always be wanting?

The key turned. Miraculously, the door opened as it was supposed to, and Tess stepped into her refuge. Turn on a light; close the door. With relief, she leaned against the doorframe. She had worn her servant mask today, and, oh, how hard it was to breathe through. Once, she had looked up from picking fabric scraps off the floor and seen Lucile staring at her with that unreadable expression in her eyes she had seen before. Something different from anger, something she had briefly hoped would make her employer reachable.

Tess walked over to the cupboard, smoothing her hand over the rough-hewn surface of the table as she passed. No word yet from Jim. Let it go, let it go. Surely he would have managed to contact her by now if he had wanted to. She was on her own.

She took a deep breath and looked around. If she wanted this, if this small flat was truly to be a route to a new independence, she had to figure out what it was that Lucile intended for her. Everyone around her molded themselves to whatever shape she demanded in the moment. How could you know who you were, what you could do? Was Lucile's shop a place of promise or just another form of servitude? Was she slipping into the same artful dodging of those who fawned over the great Madame? She felt suddenly bone-weary. She would work hard and well; that was all she could do. Her thoughts wandered back to Jim. Where was he on this dreary night? If she closed her eyes she could imagine herself with him in a horse-drawn carriage, feel his arm holding her close. She wished now that she

had sent a message, and wondered why she hadn't.

A pot of water on to boil. A bit of tea, sipped by the window, looking out on the street. She began to calm down. Enough, in fact, to realize that she had no food for her meal. There was a market down the block that she had passed coming home. That was worth one more trip out. Tess finished her tea and picked up her purse, feeling a little better. At least right now this was her haven, and she had the key.

------

The butcher at the meat counter held up a limp-looking chicken and a leg of mutton. "Which one?" he said. They were apparently her only choices, and Tess pointed to the mutton, hoping the oven in her flat worked. She wandered over to the vegetable bins and picked up a few potatoes, then some bread. It felt good to be getting her own supplies. Some fruit would be nice, but the apples looked a bit shriveled and she

hesitated, her hand hovering over one of them.

"Try an orange. They look better."

A familiar voice, a shockingly familiar voice. She looked up into the face of a man standing on the other side of the heaping baskets of fruit. A half-healed scar had left a thin slash of red that ran from his forehead to the tip of his ear, but it had done nothing to diminish his smile. His gray hair was neatly combed, his suit polished and smooth, and he looked much as he had that last night on the *Titanic.* In his hand he held out an orange.

"Mr. Bremerton." She could barely say his name.

"Hello, Miss Collins." He glanced down at the mutton in her bag, the smile twitching at the corners of his mouth. "Looks tasty."

"What are you doing here? How—"

"I found ways to look you up. Are you doing well?"

Was he really standing opposite her, talking in that relaxed, confident manner? "I can't believe I'm seeing you,"

she said, still somewhat breathless. "I heard you had survived."

"Well, I can only hope you're as pleased as I am at seeing you."

"I am. I am, yes." She could almost smell the salt air of that last night when the two of them had stood together on deck. Hearing his voice again brought it all back to pulsating life. "But why are you here? You don't live down here, surely." She imagined him in a grand home farther up Fifth Avenue—not here, not in this modest neighborhood of business lofts and small flats like hers.

"I have an office in the Flatiron Building. But now that I've found you, I have a proposal. As good as this mutton looks, would you consider doing me the honor of sharing dinner with me?"

"I would enjoy that very much," she managed.

"On one condition," he said gently. "You must call me Jack."

"Well—"

"Not yet? I understand."

What a gentleman he was. She put down the mutton and potatoes, leaving

them on top of the apples, and together they walked out, past the startled grocer. Or perhaps she was sleepwalking. Later, Tess was not sure which it was.

-------

The restaurant was called Sherry's, at the corner of Fifth Avenue and Forty-fourth Street, and, to Tess's eye, it was grander than the Waldorf. High, ornate ceilings, sparkling crystal sconces and chandeliers; tables covered with pristine linen cloths; the murmurs of waiters bowing deferentially to diners who looked like full-dressed chandeliers themselves. She made no pretense of not being impressed, and stared about with unconcealed delight.

"We love excess in America, Tess," Jack said gently. "And we love copying the British."

"I can't imagine why. We all want to copy you." She cradled a delicately bowled glass and then let the first martini of her life slip softly down her throat. It felt strangely dry, leaving a faint taste

of herbs that vanished almost immediately on her tongue.

He laughed. "You do say what you're thinking, don't you?"

"Not always, but I am now."

"You have much to talk about, I wager. Ah, here are our lobsters."

The plate set smoothly in front of her held a brilliantly red crustacean, claws arched forward, tiny beaded eyes frozen in mid-boil. She stared at it, wondering what came next.

"Let me show you," he said gently. Deftly, with a nutcracker, he twisted off the claws, exposing the meat. With a long, slender utensil she did not recognize, he pulled forth an offering and held it up to her. Unhesitatingly, Tess took it. It was delicious. Another sip of the martini and she was telling him about her trials with the mercurial Lucile. She, who tried to weigh every word in this new country, realized that she felt not a qualm about talking to Jack.

"You keep asking about me, but say nothing about yourself," she said finally.

"I'm your standard American self-made man," he said with a shrug. "I sit

through my share of operas, but if you want to hear all about Ford's Model T, I'm the man. Brilliant automobile, soon to boast a speedometer and a horn."

"That sounds interesting," she said shyly.

"Progress is wonderful," he said. "The world is changing, and if you don't change with it you're gone."

The evening slipped by—thrilling, dazzling. She took tiny sips from her second drink, wary of the dizziness that seemed to make the room glow. She was on a glittery, floating stage, but the best thing was that the man next to her was actually listening, truly listening, when she talked.

And yet not once, not even glancingly, did they talk about the sinking of the *Titanic* and Jack's experience on the *Carpathia.* Only as they rose to go did that strike Tess as strange.

------

"I would like to see you again," he said outside her building.

"I would like that, too," she said.

They stood close, both silent.

"I kept hoping to find you on the *Carpathia*," she said.

"That matters greatly, that you cared."

"I couldn't believe you had died. I didn't want to." She felt a catch in her throat.

"Some might have felt it a convenient development."

Tess's thoughts flew to Jack's wife. How could that woman not have mourned this man?

"I can't say I remember the time I was out of my head on the *Carpathia*. But if I had known, that last night on the *Titanic,* what I know now, I wouldn't have been so polite. I would have kissed you, Tess. I would have taken you in my arms and kissed you."

For a moment, there was nothing but the sound of their mingled breathing.

"May I do that now?" he finally asked.

"Yes."

He pulled her close, searching for her lips with his. There was no need for Tess to say anything, just to go on tiptoe and kiss him back.

------

Late into the night, Tess lay in bed and stared at the ceiling, remembering the sound of him murmuring her name. Husky, intimate—she could not sleep. She sat up in bed and stared out the window. How could it be that a gentleman like Jack Bremerton was interested in her? He was much older than she was, probably in his forties. So calm and assured. She had never met anyone like him, and he had held her and kissed her. No demands, no fumbling, no skittery fingers. And he wanted to see her again. What could she dare dream about now? Who was he, and who was *she,* given the thoughts she was having?

And there was Jim. She buried her head in the pillow, trying, just for the moment, to block him out of her thoughts, but it wasn't working. He was there; she could sense him by her side. She pushed off the thought angrily; there was no reason to feel torn. She wasn't betrothed, for heaven's sake. There was no reason to feel guilty. Two men, so very different. Jim was more than a village boy, much more, but Jack

was a man of the world. Exciting, in a
new way. And yet—oh Lord, why hadn't
Jim contacted her? Where was he—
had he forgotten her? Her thoughts
flashed back to the shared moment of
offering their halting prayers over the
dead mother and baby; of his kindness
as with swift, deft fingers he carved
toys for the children. She felt again the
taste of delight as they skipped together through Central Park. Was she
just dazzled by the glamour of Jack's
life? If so, where was Jim?

Enough. She pounded the pillow angrily. There would be no sleep tonight.

------

## NEW YORK CITY
## FRIDAY MORNING, APRIL 26

The newsboy outside the grocery store
ran back and forth, hollering out the
news that was bringing him an abundance of nickels and dimes from passersby to stuff into his pocket this sunny
morning. Read all about it, the latest
bombshell about the Millionaires' Boat

from the *Titanic* hearings in Washington. Sailors face off against each other, battling over the truth! Extra, extra!

Tess fumbled for change, taking copies of the *Tribune* and the *Times* to the back of the store. "WERE DROWNING PEOPLE PUSHED OFF LIFEBOAT ONE? SAILORS EXCHANGE CHARGES," screamed the *Tribune* headline. Two photographs, one of Jim and the other of the man named Sullivan. And then a subhead: "WHO IS THE LIAR?" The headline of Pinky's story was quieter: "CONFLICTING ACCOUNTS BY LIFEBOAT ONE SEAMEN, BACKUP WITNESS STUMBLES."

She read quickly, hands shaking as she turned pages still sticky with ink. Jim, Jim, are you sure—what did you see? Who are you accusing? She lifted up her head, the sidewalk looking washed with rain, but it was viewed through tears. Not going back could be cold, cowardly, sensible, fearful. All those things. Pushing people away? Cruelty, panic? But it was so dark that night, hard to see anybody, even in her boat, which was jammed with survivors. He hadn't tried to accuse the Duff Gordons. It was so like the man she

already instinctively knew. He told what he saw when asked; there was no vilification. And in all of this, who was most vulnerable? He was.

She threw the paper in a bin outside the store and headed for work, trying to remember the sound of Jim's voice. But it had slipped from her somehow. Gone into the air.

Lucile was in the loft, calmly pinning new layers of tulle under the wedding gown, replacing the ones Tess had cut away.

"Good morning," she said evenly. "Have you seen the papers?"

"Yes."

"I was right about your sailor friend. Obviously he *was* the source for the first story, so now he thinks he has us, I suppose. Well, we're not through fighting. Mr. Sullivan's support was helpful. And the other one did his best—not too intelligent a man, perhaps."

She couldn't stay silent. "Sullivan was the source for the first bribery story, not Jim. Pinky Wade told me. And I don't believe anything he says."

"Oh, don't you? Then whom do you

believe—this sailor of yours? That there was bribery? An actual murder? What? Are you blaming me for all that?"

"I don't know what happened in your boat."

Lucile shook out a bolt of tulle, slamming it on the table, cutting through it with a pair of very sharp scissors. "I'd advise you to figure it out fast. This Bonney creature is trying to destroy us, and don't you dare deny it."

There was no stopping now. "He had to testify—he had no choice but to answer their questions."

"Oh come, Tess." Lucile stopped, shears in midair. "His *intent* was obvious. Your sailor comes off as somewhat intense and bitter, wouldn't you say? I wouldn't be at all surprised if he turned down our little gift because he planned to angle for more. Blackmail, very obviously. Think what the newspapers would do with that."

"He's not a blackmailer," Tess said as calmly as she could.

"Will you stop defending him? We did nothing wrong. Sullivan and Purcell spoke for themselves. And Bonney is

making us pay for his own scrupulous conscience."

"I don't believe he is."

"I am saying that in the heightened—and heated—circumstances we've all been living in since that infernal ship went down, it's easy to judge in black and white. Look at how the press has treated us." Her eyes turned mournful. "Do you believe we're evil people? That we did terrible things? Yes or no?"

"No," Tess said heavily. "You are not evil. But sometimes—"

"Thank you, dear. I am deeply relieved." Lucile's mood changed quickly to bright exuberance. "I have an idea, a job for you that I'm hoping you'll want to take on. During the show. I want you to be the face of this company. You will be my vendeuse! Who better than you? You know every gown in the show, and you can introduce them all by name. I was going to have you serve the tea and biscuits, but someone else can do that. This will get you an incredible amount of attention."

Tess barely heard her. "I know how frightening it all was. What I can't un-

derstand is fear so great that people would be pushed away."

"Of course, that would be murder, my dear. So, what do you say?"

"To what?"

"My offer to make you my vendeuse. Aren't you listening?"

"Oh my, that's generous, but—"

"Then everything is settled. Now, let's put all this behind us and move on."

Before she could answer, a voice broke in.

"Tess."

Elinor was in back of them both, leaning against a cutting table, hair piled fetchingly on her head, arms crossed. "Sorry to interrupt, but it seems like the right time. Shall you and I go pick up the table linens for the show? A little shopping would do us both some good. At least, it would do *me* good. I'm getting sick of hotel rooms and fabric and sewing machines."

Tess glanced at Lucile. She had put her head down and was smoothing out the length of tulle she had cut, her red nails bright against the creamy gauze.

There was no more to say. For the moment.

"All right," Tess said.

Farley held the car door open as Elinor slipped in, and Tess followed, leaning back into the soft leather seat. A short while ago she had been awed by the magnificence of this smoothly running, polished machine, with its sumptuous upholstery. A short while ago? A lifetime ago.

"Herald Square, Farley," Elinor instructed before collapsing back into the soft cushions and turning to Tess. "Good thing I was there," she said without preamble. "You and Lucy were heading for a nasty little fracas. You know that, don't you?"

"I've admired her from the first day we met, but not today. I don't know what's true, but I know Jim is not a liar." The words were surprisingly easy to say. It was like that with Elinor.

"I know, but you need to understand her better."

"Whenever I think I do, she manages a surprise."

"I warned Lucy you weren't going to

remain meek and eager to sit at the feet of the goddess for very long." Elinor laughed. "May I be totally frank with you?"

Tess nodded mutely.

"My sister's world is shaky, and she doesn't even know it. It's not just this *Titanic* thing and all the bad publicity. It's—God, I need a cigarette, and I'm sure I don't have any." She set to rummaging furiously in her bag, and let out a cry of pleasure—she had found one slightly bent cigarette, compressed tobacco leaking out of one end. She lit it quickly. "What was I saying?"

"It's more than the *Titanic.*"

"Yes, of course. You see, anyone who goes around in this day and age saying a woman's knees are ugly is out of touch with fashion. Short skirts will come, there's no doubt about it. And Lucy won't stop sneering at them. My poor sister considers herself an irreplaceable brand, and she's so wrong. All that lace and tulle—and actually *naming* her dresses, for heaven's sake."

"I wondered yesterday if she was afraid."

"Maybe. You also felt that she treated you like a slave. Correct?"

Tess nodded, not trusting her voice.

"Well, you were right. You salvaged that wedding gown of hers, and you were given shabby treatment. So you're angry. Am I right on that, too?"

"Yes."

"I thought so. But don't forget, she can teach you a lot about this business. You're talented, and you know you have a future in it if you want. And I think you do want it."

"I'm not going to deny it—of course, I do."

"But you're beginning to get restive, right?"

Tess turned away, staring out the window. "I'm sorry—I told you, I'm having trouble admiring her anymore." And figuring out what was true, she added silently.

"Oh, for heaven's sake, you were never going to be one of her lapdogs. Please understand. She's struggling, and she won't face what's happening. Look, clients are dropping out; Lucy thinks it's all because of the negative

publicity, but I'm not so sure. We had more cancellations yesterday; I'm trying to hold on to Mary Pickford, but she's acting a bit vague. If Lucy's show is a disaster here in New York, it will harm her dreadfully in Paris and London, and she isn't prepared for that." She reached for Tess's hand. "Have some compassion, Tess. I know she has been ungrateful and critical of you. But she needs you."

"How could she possibly need *me*?"

"Well, things get complicated."

"I feel a great loyalty to her," Tess said slowly. "But I fear she's trying to make me into something I'm not. On the ship? She talked about cutting me into pieces, like a bolt of fabric, and putting the design together again in a different way."

"And that troubles you?"

"It didn't then. It does now."

Elinor laughed. "Don't you see, dear? She is your Pygmalion."

"I don't know what you're talking about."

"Never mind—it's an old myth of

sorts. Now, to another subject—how important is this sailor to you?"

The question caught her by surprise. "We are friends, or at least I thought we were," she said, taken aback by her own reserve. It sounded stiff, uncaring, distant. It wasn't enough. "And I don't want anything bad to happen to him. He's an honorable man."

"Well, rest easy. Honorable men survive." Elinor tapped sharply on the glass with a red polished fingernail. "Farley, drop us at Macy's." She turned brightly to Tess. "This is a wonderful store— you'll like it. It's owned by the Straus family, you know."

Tess looked at her blankly.

"Mr. and Mrs. Isidor Straus, dear. They went down on the *Titanic*."

When they returned several hours later, the car was filled with boxes of fine linen napkins and tablecloths. For Tess, the experience of wandering the huge store had been amazing. Acres and acres of space filled with clothes, dry goods; lively, laughing people promenading; clerks pulling wonderful garments out of storage rooms, young girls

trying on gloves heaped up on counters; women in crisply cut, simple jackets and skirts, walking around, skirts flipping up to show their calves. . . .

"See what I mean?" Elinor said at one point, nodding toward a quite nicely turned-out matron trying on hats. "She's no client of Lucile's. Everything you see in this place is ready-to-wear. This is the future, not floating chiffon."

In the flurry of unloading their packages, it took Tess a few minutes before she caught sight of Pinky standing in front of Lucile's building, looking as thrown-together as always, the same drooping bag swinging from her shoulders.

"They won't let me up," Pinky announced cheerfully, without preamble. "Lady Duff says she isn't talking to reporters anymore."

"Oh, she's just busy," Elinor replied airily, pushing open the door with her arms filled. "Come on up—you can talk to Tess."

"You're her spokesperson now?" Pinky asked, looking at Tess, eyes widening. Stranger things happened. One

minute someone was on one side; the next, on the other. Expediency.

"Of course not," Tess said quickly.

"No, no, she's just the one who knows what's going on to prepare for the show. You are here to write about that, aren't you?"

They were already in the elevator. She had got this far, Pinky told herself. No use pretending. "You're her sister, aren't you?" she said to Elinor as the doors closed. "I don't think we've met. I'm Pinky Wade, and I'm covering the *Titanic* hearings."

"Ah, I see. Then you're here to make my sister apoplectic. It isn't a good idea at the moment." The doors opened into the loft and Elinor stepped out, holding them open, and said in genial fashion, "Tess, just put your bundles on the table, then maybe you could escort Miss Wade downstairs again. Would you?"

Tess obeyed, but the elevator had already descended.

"Well, I guess this is the closest I get to the great designer's secret haven," Pinky said, peering around at the busy loft.

"Did you know what Jim was going to say in advance?"

"No. But I know it was hard for him."

"Your story was the best."

Pinky gave her a quick, grateful glance. "Glad you think so. Balancing things out isn't easy, especially when I know what I really believe and which way I want a story to tip."

"Is he all right?" Tess asked. It was a bit of a naked question, but it could be asked; she and Pinky were on the same side.

"I think so. But who wants to be called a liar? Sullivan and Purcell didn't help themselves by contradicting each other. And I'm writing tomorrow about the lawyers in the hearing room. Imagine, they're from the firm that takes care of the Duff Gordons. Coincidence, huh?" Her eyes were still traveling around the room. "I think the Duff Gordons tried to fix the inquiry testimony. Can't prove it yet, but I think they did."

The elevator doors opened behind them, and they both stepped in. Pinky was rummaging in her bag. "Sorry, I didn't get much sleep last night and I'm

a mess, more than usual." She pulled out a comb with some teeth missing and ran it randomly through her hair. "It's like Jim said—people choose whatever they want to believe and declare it true, I guess. I need proof. Anyway, that's what I'm working on. There's more, and I'll find it."

"I want you to be wrong," Tess said slowly. "But maybe you're not."

"Tess, you're a real grown-up."

Tess smiled at this. "You need a new comb," she said. "And I'm glad you are back."

Pinky looked at the implement distractedly. "Maybe that's why I never look different." She tossed it back into her bag; it was time to convey her most important message. "Jim wants to see you. Very much."

"Then why didn't he come before he left for Washington? He vanished without a word," Tess said quickly. The sting of that had not eased.

"But he did try to see you," Pinky replied. "He left a note at the hotel. You didn't get it?"

"No, I didn't." So he had not forgotten her.

"You're not angry with him for testifying?"

"For having the courage to go up there and say what he thought? No. How could I be?"

"You were a pretty good defender of Lady Duff, you know. He thinks you won't want anything to do with him now."

"I couldn't feel that way," Tess said. "I don't want him hurt."

"I think he's coming off better than the other crew members. I'm positive the Duff Gordons had their big-shot lawyers coaching Sullivan. You're kind of stuck in the middle, aren't you?"

"It isn't like that," Tess said quickly.

"Will you see him when they let him come back to New York?"

"Yes, of course." She hoped Pinky, with her sharp senses, hadn't caught her instant of hesitation. For if she had there was no way to tell her the true reason for it. She turned away from the curiosity in Pinky's eyes. "I have to go back up now."

"Guess I won't get invited," Pinky said. Her eyes began to dance. "Unless I get assigned to cover the fashion show."

------

Tess stepped out of the closing elevator, almost bumping into Lucile, who beckoned her into the office.

"I realize from what Elinor reports that I'm going to have to tell you, quite definitely, that I value you and want you to be happy here." Lucile's hands were folded in front of her, and her voice was matter-of-fact. "And that if I don't mean it you will leave. Is that right?"

"Yes, that's right," Tess said, knowing that it was.

"You would give up your future here, and your apartment?"

"I would find another way to make my future, if I had to."

"Ah, a spark of bravado, Tess? Depending on the circumstances, I suppose. But, I assure you, what I'm saying is true. I do value you, and I'm not

out to damage your sailor, even though I think you can do much better."

Imperious and conciliatory at the same time. They stared at each other, and Tess realized that her knees were still. A good sign.

"With one caveat."

Tess waited.

"You must promise you will do nothing to damage *me*."

"Of course," Tess said.

"Well." Lucile seemed somehow at a loss how to continue.

"I should get back to work," Tess said gently, and turned to go.

"By the way, you're too skinny. You aren't in training to be a model, you know."

Now it was Tess's turn to be at a loss for words. Somewhat awkwardly, she shifted from one foot to the other, her hand on the doorknob. "I haven't had much of an appetite lately," she said finally.

Lucile's mood suddenly became exuberantly playful. "Well, I think we are through a rough patch. So now I want to tell you about a challenge that I think

you will love. Maybe it's not possible, but you'll learn a great deal from taking it on. Can you sketch a design, cut, sew, and fit a dress between now and the show?"

"Oh—" Tess caught her breath. "My goodness, what . . . how . . ."

Lucile laughed. "Tess, I love seeing your surprise."

Tess colored, flustered. Then she grew wary. "I don't have the talent for that yet. . . . I'm not experienced enough. Why—"

"Answer my question. Well, can you?"

"Yes. I can, I think I can. At least"— and all the years of hoping and dreaming were in her answer—"I want to try."

"Then that's your job, dear." Lucile smiled broadly. "And if it's good—mind you, it has to be good—I will introduce your work at the show. You and I, we need to get on with life, don't you think?"

Together they walked out of the office, stopped almost immediately by the sight of a strange man in a delivery cap waiting for them. Cosmo, his lips pulled tight, stood beside him.

"Who is this man, and who let him up here?" Lucile said as, expressionless and with a quick tip of his cap, he thrust a white envelope into her hand.

"Brace yourself, Lucy." Cosmo stepped forward. "And, for God's sake, don't get hysterical. Senator Smith has issued you a subpoena."

Lucile stared at the envelope. "How dare he?" she whispered.

"Too much gossip swirling in the air, I suspect. He couldn't resist," said Cosmo.

Lucile swayed slightly and went pale, then turned toward Tess with an oddly triumphal look. "Too bad, Tess. You may have to choose sides after all," she said.

Cosmo took his wife's arm, guiding her into her office. He closed the door on Tess.

"Before you say a word, please note that I am not screaming and crying."

"Duly noted," he said with the ghost of a smile.

Lucile brushed the sleeve of her jacket, irritated by a smudge. This city was so dirty; you couldn't wear any-

thing without some cleaning disaster. She took off the jacket and threw it to the floor.

"Lucile. Sit down."

"I don't want to talk about that impossible, strutting senator and what he's trying to do to me!"

"Sit down."

His somber face warned her not to object. Reluctantly, she sat down on the sofa. "Can't you make this awful thing go away?" she pleaded. "All I want to do is put on my spring show and get out of this terrible place and home to England."

"It's not going to go away. I thought we had Smith's assurance that we wouldn't be dragged into this, but you can't trust a politician. They move where the wind blows."

"When do I have to testify?"

"Next week. He's moving the hearings back to New York for a few days, so people like you and me can't scatter. And, believe me, the place will be packed." Cosmo was pacing, not looking at her. Keeping his distance.

"I'll answer what I want to answer!"

"You will stick, word for word, with what our lawyers tell you to say. You will not say one extra word, do you hear me?" His voice, hard and even, was that of a schoolmaster.

Lucile was startled at his intensity but rallied quickly. "Don't underestimate me, Cosmo. I can orchestrate this. I'll dress for the occasion. A very large, black hat with plenty of powder. I can look very pale if I have to. By the time I'm done, the whole country will see how victimized I've been."

"Good girl." His smile flickered again, more tiredly this time. "All Smith will get out of this is anti-British rhetoric. But I have more bad news. There will be an inquiry in Britain as well, and both of us are going to be under subpoena to testify. I've not been able to do anything to stop it. The mood there is that we're an embarrassment to the country. Certainly, my reputation has been destroyed." His voice turned bitter. "You think the newspapers here have been bad? My dear, wait until you see what happens there. We are heading into a maelstrom."

At home? Impossible. Her reputation was unassailable, yet nothing seemed to be holding fast. "What are we going to do?" she asked.

"I am pulling every string I can. There will be no compromise on putting us both on the stand. Perhaps we can find a way to orchestrate that."

"Of course, we can. It's tragic, treating us this way."

"You'll have to do more than rehearse your performance."

"What do you mean?"

"That sailor will probably be testifying in England, too."

"The one called Bonney?"

"Yes."

"That's completely unacceptable."

"I don't think it's up to you."

"We'll see about that."

Cosmo regarded her almost coolly. "The investigating panel in Washington found him quite believable, I'm told. At least here you won't have to testify with him in the room, waiting to deny your story. England will be worse. I would suggest that from this point on you do not speak of the sinking or anything of

what has happened here to anyone, do you hear me?"

"Why don't you just say it?" she demanded, furious. "You think I'm the one who got us into this muddle, isn't that right?"

"Can't you answer that yourself? Do you really need me to do so?"

"Don't forget you were on that boat, too."

"And what is that supposed to mean?"

"My dear husband, you were no hero." She turned away, taking a deep, steadying breath. "I will not let them tear me apart in some courtroom. I'll think of something."

## 12

Almost a week of hard work gone by already. Tess's hand ached. She was holding the pencil too tightly—the sign of an amateur. She leaned closer over the drawing board, softening her strokes. She could sketch in the tucked sleeves she had designed in Cherbourg; that would work. Think of the fabric. Don't think of the subpoena. Don't think of Jim. She looked at the skirt she was drawing. It should be in a stiff but moldable fabric; stay away from chiffon.

She sat back, eyeing her design critically. Hopefully. All these long hours,

sketching and resketching, determinedly keeping her mind away from the feeling that everything was crumbling. Lucile would have to testify the day before her show, and the tension in the shop was spiraling upward.

But at the end of each day she would rise from her drawing board, bid the workers good night, and walk out into another world. Jack's world.

There he would be, at her door, tipping his hat, offering his arm to take her to yet another elegant restaurant where the light shimmered and everything was beautiful. Bit by bit, she had pieced together some information about him. Mrs. Brown was right; he was going ahead with a divorce—which, he said, wasn't his first. "Don't make it a black mark—I'm a slow learner," he had said good-humoredly, and she had smiled, not quite sure how she felt about that.

Then later, at home, staring at the ceiling: where was Jim? Would he show up for Lucile's testimony? Or was he already heading West, having forgotten

her? She had to face the possibility that because of the mislaid note, left unanswered, she might not see him again.

Come morning, she would be back at her drawing board, pushing both men out of her thoughts, concentrating on the most exciting challenge she had ever known.

And now the end of the fourth day. A stab of pain; she rubbed her fingers. She was doing it again, clutching the pencil too tightly.

------

"She's taking this seriously," Elinor said to her sister as they watched from Lucile's office.

"She'd better, after what that sailor friend of hers did to me."

"Don't take it out on her; she's caught between the two of you."

"Her design isn't half-bad, so far."

Elinor raised one eyebrow, studying Lucile. "You know, I actually think you mean it."

"Why wouldn't I?"

"In another mood, dear sister, you

might have given someone this opportunity to see how quickly they would fall on their face. And then come crawling back to the invincible Madame."

"And what do you think now?"

"I think you want her to succeed."

Tess glanced up at just that moment and saw the two women looking at her. Lucile acknowledged the eye contact with a brisk nod, but Elinor was smiling.

They think I can do it, Tess thought. And I can.

------

It was late. Her feet hurt as she stepped out onto the sidewalk; why not hop onto one of the streetcars heading toward home? One was coming her way now, bell clanging, people crowded inside and jammed on the steps, holding on to whatever they could grasp. How did you do this? She hoisted her skirt with one hand, jumped on, and grabbed for a post with the other, almost falling off as the car lurched forward.

"You need some training," said a girl, giggling, as she hung on to her hat.

A woman holding a bag of apples was running for the streetcar. "Slow down!" she yelled. Now the woman was hoisting her skirt, grabbing for the post. She tripped on the skirt, and Tess held her breath. But the driver, with an angry shout to hurry up, had slowed enough for the woman, breathless, to pull herself on.

"That was dangerous," Tess said to the passenger next to her.

"Dangerous? Honey, we do it all the time," the woman replied.

"She could move faster in a shorter skirt."

The woman snorted. "Shorter skirts? Not respectable."

·······

Tess jumped off the streetcar at her stop, hoping for a soothing cup of hot tea before Jack arrived—something to bridge the two worlds in which she was living. She would not brood over what was going to happen at the inquiry; she

could call this a good day. And tomorrow—her heart skipped a beat—tomorrow she would cut the gown.

"Miss Collins?"

A man in a bowler hat was approaching her, the sound of his heels clicking
against the pavement. She had been
so engrossed in her thoughts that she
hadn't seen him.

"Please, an introduction. I'm Howard
Wheaton, Mr. Bremerton's secretary."
He tipped his hat, looking uncomfortable as he thrust his arm forward; only
then did Tess see the bouquet of flowers. "He asked me to deliver these to
you with his note, and with his apologies for not delivering them in person;
he had important business downtown."

Nobody had ever given her flowers.
Tess took the fragrant bouquet, inhaling the heady fragrance of lilacs and
roses.

"The note?"

"Of course." She flushed as she
opened the small envelope tucked into
the flowers. "Sherry's at 10:30?" it read.

"Your response?"

"Please tell Mr. Bremerton I will be there," she said.

"Thank you; he will be pleased. A car will pick you up."

She nodded and, somewhat giddily, watched the dutiful Mr. Wheaton walk away.

------

This time it was a private room, fragrant with the smell of leather-bound books lining the walls. "I want to spend every evening with you," Jack said, rising from a chair near the door as he shoved papers back into a briefcase. He had a slightly distracted look, but it vanished as Tess came closer. "Forgive me for not bringing you the flowers myself. Work intervened, I'm afraid."

"Mr. Ford's automobile?" she asked.

"I don't want to bore you with business."

"But I learn things."

"You're feigning interest, and I adore you for that." With ease and naturalness, he leaned over and gently kissed her ear.

"Won't a waiter come in?" she asked nervously.

"They have my orders. Not until I ring the bell."

Jack leaned forward, holding her hand and stroking it. His face looked weary; there was a furrow in his brow she hadn't noticed before that made him look older. But his touch was contained, steady. So sure.

"I have to go to California," he said.

"Are you coming back?" she asked, her heartbeat quickening.

"Yes, but it might not be for quite a while. I don't like being away from you." He cupped her chin and turned it toward him. "You could come with me."

Tess drew in her breath, shocked. "That's impossible."

"Are you sure?"

In the silence that followed, she could hear a clock on the wall ticking. Then his hand tightened on hers. It dawned on her, the realization, yes—there was a possibility of a different answer. She didn't want him to go away. She hesitated.

He smiled, leaning back. "I know,

Tess, you aren't that kind of girl. But wouldn't it be a lark? I could show you a wonderful life out there."

"I'm sure, but—I have work here."

"All right, forget that idea. I'm an impulsive man, I suppose. Or so any number of people have told me. But this is different. I knew you were extraordinary from the moment you tiptoed into the *Titanic*'s gym. I wanted to lift you down from that silly camel, but you wouldn't let me. It was all I could do not to kiss you." He laughed. "I knew right then that you were the one to change my wandering ways."

Was he teasing? "I need to go home soon, it's very late," she said, hoping she didn't sound priggish. Looking around the room—the books, the flickering candlelight, the privacy—she realized that he was pulling her closer, but it didn't feel inappropriate.

And then they were together on a velvet sofa, all pretense to interest in dinner gone. He began smoothing her long dark hair, twining it around his fingers, rubbing it against his cheek, look-

ing baffled when he tried to insert the comb that held it up in place.

"I'll do that. I can't leave this restaurant not looking respectable."

"My preference? Your long hair would clothe you—nothing else."

She closed her eyes. A man had just said that to her—a man like no other, a man whom she didn't have to immediately slap and denounce, a man whom she could or could not give permission to say such things. She had that choice, and it was delicious. What was it about this man? His assuredness. There was safety here—is that what it was? No worries, a haven. She closed her eyes and let him kiss her.

------

So little sleep. Her back ached as she bent over the cutting table the next morning, a pair of scissors poised in her hand. The muslin version of her dress had worked. The slant of the bodice basting needed to be adjusted, but it looked good. Still, she hesitated. Lying flat before her on the table was

the beautifully moldable cream silk she had chosen—a fabric that, cut correctly, would be both soft and substantial. One of the most luxurious bolts of fabric from Lucile's generous stock. She could not make a mistake.

"Would you like one of the cutters to do this part?" James said gently.

Tess looked up and saw that a handful of Lucile's workers—seamstresses, cutters, trimmers—had gathered around the table to watch. Several of them smiled tentatively.

She glanced in the direction of Lucile's office, wondering where she was. She had hurried in and out earlier, murmuring something about a meeting with her lawyers, obviously distracted. Everything was happening at once. She was on her own here, the way it had been when she repaired Lucile's wedding gown, and that made her apprehensive.

"Thank you, but I think I can do this," she said. She willed her hand to be still. "Here we go."

Tess cut into the fabric with a firm motion, allowing the scissors to glide

along the pattern lines with only a few stops for adjustments. The fabric was separating beautifully, cleanly. Her confidence grew as she cut the sleeves. She had to trust that she had left enough material for the elaborate tucking she envisioned.

As she cut the last piece, the silence around the table erupted into clapping. "Great job," James said, beaming. "Takes nerve, the first time you cut fabric like this."

It did, it did. It was like being on top of a mountain, standing here, still holding the scissors, as the seamstress she had chosen began carefully basting the gown.

"Tess—" James beckoned her over to the other side of the table. "Look at this." He held up a small curiously made metal contraption.

"What is it?"

"It's a hookless fastener. Watch." He pulled at a flat piece of metal, exposing what looked like interlocking teeth, then pulled it back up, magically closing the space with the teeth alternately connected. "The salesman said you can

sew the cloth edges into things like money belts and life vests. What do you think?"

Tess turned the fastener around in her hand, charmed by the ease with which it worked. Would it add bulk to a gown? Hard to tell. It might work, though. She ran her fingers over the tiny rectangular teeth, fascinated.

James's eyes danced. "Knew you'd be interested," he said.

It was hours later when Lucile burst from the elevator, marching in with a flower consultant who was busy scratching notes as she threw out instructions. "The flowers must look beautiful under blue lights; bring in *nothing* that turns green or sallow, do you understand?" she said. "I won't tolerate it. Do not forget the urns; they must be five feet high, no shorter, and— yes?" She glanced impatiently at Tess's expectant face.

"My gown is cut and basted—would you like to see it?" Tess asked.

"Lovely," Lucile said with a hasty wave of the hand. "I'll look later. You've worked hard, dear. Take tomorrow off."

And, with that, she and the consultant disappeared into her office.

It was oddly deflating, as if she had somehow been dismissed. Tess straightened her shoulders and beckoned to the model who had just wiggled into the carefully basted dress. "Walk toward me," she said.

She couldn't help holding her breath. Yes, the gown moved just as she had envisioned it would—the creamy silk breaking into varying hues, as subtle as a wave breaking on the sand. The sleeves needed extra tucking, but that wasn't a problem; the material was there. Yet something bothered her.

"How do you feel, walking in this dress?" she asked the model.

Obviously surprised, the model stammered an answer. "I like it—I don't feel caught up in gauze and lace." She immediately colored, clearly horrified at her criticism of Lucile's style.

"That's all right," Tess said gently. "I know what you mean."

"Just one thing, if you're asking."

"Yes?"

"It's a dress for daytime, just right. But I'd hate to catch it in a train door."

Tess stared at her creation, remembering her ride on the streetcar. She reached over to the table and picked up the scissors. No need to think it through; she knew what she wanted. Within minutes, it was done—eight inches of precious fabric cut from the hem. She'd take ten if she dared.

"It's going to be ready for the show— I can hardly believe it," she said to James.

"We never doubted it," he replied. "Long day, Tess. Time to go home."

The wind currents outside the Flatiron Building swirled around her as she walked past, sending her skirts billowing. It amused her to see the men loitering nearby in hopes of getting a peek at an ankle or two. A policeman stood at the corner, ordering the oglers to move along, since nobody could do anything about the winds. They wouldn't need him once women got brave enough to shorten their dresses.

A man was standing on her stoop. Jack? She moved closer, and saw that

he held a cigarette in one hand and was restlessly combing back his gold-flecked hair with the other.

No, not Jack.

He saw her and smiled, and she caught her breath. Oh, she had missed that smile.

"Tess."

"Hello, Jim."

"Well, it's done."

"Yes, I know."

"I did what I had to do. I tried to tell you in advance, but I guess you knew by then what was up and decided you didn't want to see me." His eyes were guarded but steady: so deeply blue. "Anyway, now I'm here to ask what it cost me."

"Pinky told me you sent me a note, but I never got it," Tess said.

"You didn't?" He looked stunned.

"No," she said. "I don't know why I didn't—I thought you just forgot me. Or—"

A light was dawning in his eyes. "Or I had talked to Pinky for her story without telling you?"

"Yes."

"All I wanted to do was give you a ride around the park in one of those fancy carriages," he said gently. "And tell you I was going to Washington but coming back."

"I would have liked that," she said.

He gave her a rueful smile. "I kept hoping you would show up—those horses knew me pretty well by the time I left. My guess is the Duff Gordons intercepted my note. But at least I know you didn't stand me up."

"I owe you more—that wouldn't happen," she said quickly.

"Would you have understood? That I had to testify?"

She needed no time to form an answer. "You said what you honestly believed, and that's more than the others did." She reached out her hand. "It hasn't cost you my friendship, if that's what you mean."

The look of relief on his face cut through to her heart. She did not want to move, even as he reached out and their fingers touched. Not even when, standing there, he slowly drew her hand to his face, kissing it with undisguised

tenderness. Gently, she disengaged, her mind in turmoil.

"Can we walk awhile? Maybe through another park in your nice but less fancy new neighborhood?" His eyes were alight now, not quite dancing but warm with relief.

"Of course," she said. Her hand had felt so good, held inside the curve of his fingers. She hadn't anticipated that.

Jim had a long stride, but so did she, when she put her mind to it. He was talking quickly, giving her his impressions of Washington, talking in the rapid way of someone who has been storing up tidbits to share. He stopped as they entered a park and leaned down to pick up a rolling chestnut, then, laughing, tossed it toward a racing squirrel. They had to talk soon.

"I've stayed with Lucile," she said.

"I know. And I don't blame you."

Her face flushed and she looked away.

"Stop accusing yourself, Tess."

"I'm torn—"

"You think you're the only one? Torn between choices? We all were."

"Jim, the committee has called her to testify."

"I guess I'm not surprised. Is she making you choose sides?"

"Why did it have to go this way?" she burst out, her eyes filling with tears.

Jim tossed another chestnut without looking at her. "If you need to pull away from me to keep your job, I'll understand," he said. "I can take anything, as long as I know you're my friend."

"I am," she said fervently. "I am, I always will be."

They walked in comfortable silence until Jim stopped and turned her toward him.

"I've got good news," he said. "Really good news." He suddenly seemed almost shy.

"What is it?"

"Mrs. Brown, your ally in the lifeboat?"

Tess nodded, waiting.

"She saw me whittling away at the hearing in Washington, and started praising my work, very over the top. I thought she was a bit daft."

"She's not daft at all," Tess said quickly.

"I'm trying to be modest, okay?" He grinned and tossed another chestnut, sending the industrious squirrel in fast pursuit. "Anyway, she liked what she saw, and commissioned me to do a piece especially for her." He glanced sideways at Tess, teasingly. "A bigger version, to tell the truth, of the one I carved for you. She wanted the whole ship—why, I don't know."

"You mean a model of the *Titanic*?" Tess wasn't sure how she felt about that.

"Yes."

"That's wonderful, Jim. But—doesn't it give you nightmares, revisiting the ship?"

"No," he said slowly. "It's a bit healing, actually. Anyway, she came up with something even better." He cleared his throat and faced her squarely. "My dear Miss Collins"—he made an elaborate bow—"you are looking at somebody described as a master craftsman by an excitable lady who can make anything happen. Best of all, for me, a job."

"That's fantastic," she said, laughing. "Absolutely fantastic."

"So—and do remember you are looking at a *future* 'master craftsman'— this whittler from London now has a job in a woodworking shop—a great place, good money." He was talking faster now. "The place is brilliant. They've got the best carving knives I've ever seen, and I'll be doing some specialty work for them—relief carving, on mirrors and the like. To pull out from the wood a face or a picture—I love that. What—" He stopped dead and slapped his forehead. "What am I thinking of? It's nearby. Want to come and see it?"

An instant of hesitation; then Tess nodded, caught up in his excitement and pride. He quickened his pace, and she almost had to run to keep up with him now. "Guess what? Lucile is letting me design a dress for her show," she said breathlessly. "I'm working with wonderful material and it's exciting—"

He stopped suddenly, turned, and lifted her by the waist, swinging her around. "That's great news. Look at

us—we're both finding what we want! God, it *is* exciting, isn't it?"

"Yes," she said, laughing, still breathless, not wanting him to let go. How could she feel this so intensely—what about Jack?

He lowered her gently, taking her hand again as they resumed walking. The memory of the first time they had touched hands on the *Carpathia* flashed, the intimacy shared without words.

"Does the woodworking shop mean you're staying here? Not heading West?" she asked.

"I'm here for now. Maybe later, who knows? I'm in a union shop, so I can do union work here. It's good to be flexible, especially when you've got reasons not to leave." He flashed her a quick grin, then looked around, as if only now noticing where they were. "I've heard of this place," he said. "They call it Union Square. Lots of speeches and demonstrations. A good place in a good country." He barely broke stride. Finally, a few yards farther on, he

stopped and pointed. "There it is," he said.

Tess saw a somewhat shabby building tucked between two boarding houses. Jim grabbed her hand, opened the door to the shop, and stopped as they stepped inside, inhaling deeply. "Smell the sweet wood?" he said. "I love that smell."

Tess nodded. It was such an aromatic, earthy smell—comforting, really. No tinge of wetness or coldness; no hint of sea or salt. The floor was covered with shaved scraps of wood, some tissue-thin, some crunched together like a woman's curls. A soft, powdery substance coated a long, battered oak table that held a jumble of tools, the likes of which she had not seen before.

"You can do anything with these tools," Jim said, picking one up. He nodded toward a smooth slab of wood. "It's the frame for a mirror," he said. "I'm working on it now." He nodded toward an elaborately detailed Baroque mirror hanging next to the table. "That's my model."

"Where is the *Titanic*?"

"In the back room." He took her hand again and together they walked to the back of the shop, Jim nodding and joking with a few of the woodworkers. He clearly already felt comfortable here.

"There it is. I've only begun, really. Got a lot of work to do on it yet."

Almost fearfully, Tess stared at the ship. The four smokestacks, carved bold, gave her a shiver. How grand and enthralling they had been.

"Go ahead, Tess. Touch it. It's all right."

With one finger she followed the curve of one of the finished lifeboats. Tiny and still, but a perfect replica. The slender ropes tied tightly, not swirling and slipping across the deck. The delicately molded steps leading to the lookout's station, where no binoculars waited . . . She touched the stern, the last part of the *Titanic* any of them had seen.

What did I learn? she wondered. What did it teach me?

"I've got a lot more work to do to get it right," Jim said, standing at her shoulder.

"Jim, it's wonderful." She couldn't take her eyes off the model. "Where were we standing when we met?"

He pointed to a place near one of the lifeboats. For a moment, they both looked in silence, saying nothing. Then Jim spoke quietly.

"I once said to you I didn't think we were so different, and I saw in your eyes that you didn't agree. I hope that's changed."

Straightforward and honest. Regardless of the tumult in her heart, she must be, too. But how? What could she say?

He laid his hands gently on her shoulders and turned her around to face him. "I need to see your eyes," he said with such tenderness, she could say nothing else. "I'm going to kiss you, Tess Collins. Something I've wanted to do since our walk through the park."

She couldn't help herself. His arms around her, his lips on hers, the powerful, sensual feel of him—for a long, slow moment, she met his hunger with her own, winding her arms around his neck, touching his soft, unruly hair. He whispered into her ear, then met her lips

again. What was she doing? She pulled away.

"No, no. Jim, I'm too confused."

"I'm sorry—was this too fast?"

"No, that's not it."

"Tess, there's so much I want to say." He was talking rapidly again. "All I've been able to think about for days is the idea of building a new life in this country with you." He held up his hands, palms out. "These are my tools, my passport to better things, just like yours are. Tess, we have our futures right here." He touched her chin, looking into her eyes with an expression so hopeful, it was painful. "Can you give at least some consideration to it being the two of us together?"

And there it was, like a warming light, and so much in her wanted to respond, to say yes. But another part of her held back, looking in another direction. How could she know—how could she be sure of anything right now? "I think all this is wonderful, and you're wonderful, and I have a bond with you that I'll share with no other in my life," she managed. And then stopped.

It took a long moment, but the color slowly left Jim's face. "Are you saying no?" he said.

"I'm saying I'm not sure."

He stood very still, looking as if he had been slapped in the face. "It sounds like no to me. Is it because I testified?"

"No, no, I admire you—I meant that."

"I would never compromise you, Tess. Maybe I was assuming too much, too fast? I'm sorry, I can wait."

She tried to think of what to say.

"Or—is there someone else?"

She nodded slowly.

A pause. "Did I miss a signal?" His voice shook slightly. "I never knew. Have I been wrong about that?"

"There wasn't anyone before, please know that. But—"

"But there is now."

"Yes," she whispered.

He stepped back, looking so stunned that she had to stop herself from reaching for his hand. She couldn't have reached him anyway. Heartsick, she saw the light in his eyes fade. He was retreating from her—how could she

have expected anything different? His hands remained at his sides.

"Forgive me for taking too much for granted."

"I'm very confused, and I don't want to hurt you," she said. Stupid, meaningless words that meant nothing. She had done precisely that.

"I don't think that's in your control anymore."

"I still feel it."

"That won't do either of us any good," he said. "Look, I presumed too much."

"No, it's that so much happened so fast. Oh, Jim—"

"It's all right," he said mechanically. "But I should go now." He shoved his hands into his pockets, stepping through the doorway. "Look, I'll walk you home. It'll be dark soon, and you shouldn't walk alone."

"No, it's all right if you need to go. I can find my way."

He looked away, silent for a moment. A breeze had sprung up, moving softly through the trees, ruffling his hair. When he spoke, it was in a tone simultaneously flat and curious. "I might as well

ask, I guess. You really think I'm just a village boy?"

"How—"

"How did I know? Your Lady Duff spread it around on the *Carpathia*." He shrugged. "It doesn't matter anymore. I wouldn't want you to be ashamed of me. Makes for an awkward setup."

"I'm not, and I never could be," she managed.

"Nice to hear, I guess."

"Please, Jim. We have something important between us, a friendship—let's not destroy it."

This time he looked at her in total disbelief. "Are you really asking for that? Just—snap my fingers and change how I feel about you?"

"No, no, that was stupid."

"I think I need to walk somewhere. I wish you well," he said. He turned his back to her, his shoulders bent under a mountain of hurt, and strode away.

Look around, she thought. Please. But he didn't. She turned and walked slowly in the opposite direction, stepping over the wood chips, smelling the sweetness of this place. She had just

lost something huge, leaving a hollowed-out space that felt as if it could swallow her up. If she had only had more time to think it through. And what did that mean? The only thing she knew for sure right now was that she could no longer hold these two men in separate compartments in her heart.

------

Jack was waiting outside her building in a dark-blue Buick, the engine running impatiently, its silver headlamps glowing. How long had he been waiting? Tess walked slowly, both relieved to see him and yearning for time alone. She wasn't ready; she needed to go into her flat, close her door, and catch her breath.

He stepped from the car, leaned forward and kissed her cheek, eyes watchful. "Maybe you don't want to explain anything," he said. "But I need to know where I am."

So courteous. Jack always treated her as someone with dignity; already she felt calmed.

"You saw me with the man from Life-boat One who wanted to go back," she said.

"He must be a very brave man."

"He is." Again her eyes were filling up.

"And he loves you—am I right?"

She nodded.

"Why are you crying, Tess?" His voice was so gentle. Not anxious, not angry, not probing.

"I'm not. It all happened too fast."

"Perhaps you could explain."

"I refused him." Such a cloaked, old-fashioned word.

Jack's shoulders, visibly tensed, began to relax. "Are you sure?" he said. "I saw the way you looked at him. I won't stand in the way of something you want, but I have to know."

"I'm sure." Listening to her own voice, so thin. Nothing coming out of her mouth sounded clear-cut and certain.

"You may just want to be."

She covered her face with her hands. "How are you so wise?" she asked.

He sighed. "Experience. Too much,

actually." He paused, then went on. "Uncertainty isn't a bad thing. I wish I could slow everything down, but I can't. May I hold you?"

She needed to know more, to take time. But in his arms everything seemed to disappear. It felt so good to float above the ground, to put aside her worries.

"Am I invited?" he murmured, touching the pulse in her neck with his lips.

"Yes."

"There is something I want to propose," he said. "Marry me."

Tess froze.

"I know it's fast, but I've looked long enough and made enough of my share of mistakes to know when it's right."

"But you're still married," she said.

"The divorce documents were ready for our final signatures when I stepped onto the *Titanic*. You are a cautious one, Tess." His smile was warm and kind. "If I allowed myself to be timid, I wouldn't be who I am today."

"I'm not timid, I'm just—just surprised."

He raised an eyebrow. "So where is

the brave and adventurous girl I met on the *Titanic*?"

"I don't want to be married, not yet," she burst out. She could see her mother's face, hear her cautionary words. "I know what happens. I've told you, I want to work, I want—"

Jack laughed. "I'm not asking you to choose," he said. "I'm one of the few men you'll know who can give you the life I know you want to lead. You can have it all. Do you doubt that?"

She shook her head.

"Then what's the problem?"

It was too easy, that was the problem. She pulled him closer, unable to say the words.

"I have to think about it," she whispered.

## 13

Pinky squinted through a soup of fog and rain as she waited outside the imposing offices of Dunhill, Brougham and Picksley on Fifty-seventh Street. Stakeouts were the most boring part of her job, but this one shouldn't last much longer.

The massive front door of the establishment suddenly swung open. Out stepped three men.

I knew it, Pinky thought triumphantly.

Sir Cosmo was dressed, as usual, in an impeccably perfect suit, his mustache as manicured as ever. He was

speaking hurriedly to the pair—one wearing the same horn-rimmed glasses she remembered from the courtroom. They shook hands as she watched, and Cosmo walked away.

Pinky approached the two men. The one in the glasses stiffened as he saw her.

"Hello there," she said cheerfully. "I know about your plan, fellas. I guess the only thing I don't know yet is how much the Duff Gordons are paying you."

------

Tess heard the rain drumming on her bedroom window and buried her head back under the covers, wishing for sleep without the wild pitch of dreams that had consumed her all night. No use. She sat up in bed, thankful now for being given a day off. She needed it. But Jack's voice, his persuasiveness, remained in her head as she finally rose and put the kettle on to boil. She could hear shouting from the next apartment, a man and a woman fighting. Last night,

when she crept into her own bed past midnight, she had heard their bed-springs squeaking urgently through the wall. She might as well have been back home. She didn't want to live a life like that, all anger in the day and sex in the dark, and many babies and no money.

What if there was plenty of money? What was wrong with marriage then?

She poured her tea and sat down to sip the fragrant brew. Jack could teach her about this new country, navigate her through the trials ahead; he would be there to protect her and make good things happen. He lived on top of his world, not fighting for a place within it. She could relax for the first time in her life. And if it had all happened in too breathtakingly short a time, that couldn't be helped. Don't think of Jim. Simplify. He was right; in a way, they were alike— poised on the brink of new things, thirsty and ready. But neither was each other's navigator. And wasn't that what she wanted now?

Slowly, she dressed. She would take a walk uptown, maybe to Central Park. Anything, somewhere to be around

people; such a dreary day. She wished she would hear from her mother, but nothing yet. It did bring home the realization that in this vast new country, there was no one in whom she could confide.

Tess pulled on her gloves and took her umbrella and set out, slamming the door loudly, which silenced her quarreling neighbors. She shivered in her thin coat and pulled it closer as she stopped at the grocery for the newspaper. She couldn't break her habit now of scanning the stories, bracing for the sight of Lady Duff Gordon's name in some newly shocking context.

Her eye stopped and fixed on a small two-paragraph story. There was a memorial service today for Isidor Straus— the co-owner of that amazing store in Herald Square—at Carnegie Hall. A special farewell for a man of distinction, the paper said, whose wife chose to stay on the ship with him, rather than leave him to die alone.

She closed the paper. That's where she would go today. She would pay homage to someone she didn't know,

whose fate had been tied to her own. He and she existed in a common fraternity now, dead or alive, one none of the people on the *Titanic* would choose, but there it was. It made—what an odd, bleak thought—for a sense of belonging to something.

It was a long walk, but it soothed her spirit. By the time she reached Forty-second Street, the rain had stopped and the sun was breaking through. A garden of red-and-white striped umbrellas suddenly came into view. Women in spring hats and men in Sunday suits were clustered around flower stands and vendors selling sausage and peppers, while groups of children sat on the street, watching a puppet show. Of course, it was a street festival, complete with a band, the violinist wearing a red cap with a drooping tassel that bounced against his cheek as he played. A woman in a yellow apron was spooning out an ice-cold confection in different flavors and colors. Curious, Tess came closer.

"Gelati," the woman said, smiling,

seeing her interest. "Better than ice cream."

Tess smiled back and opened her purse. She took a bite from the small cup the woman handed her; the smooth, light chocolate was delicious. So she would pretend she was Italian for a little while, shedding all thoughts of deadlines and doubt and hurt.

At Carnegie Hall, the crowds clustered on the sidewalk turned quiet and somber. She joined them, asking a man, "When do we go in?"

"Do you have an invitation?" he said.

"No, I didn't know I needed one."

"Heavens, madame, everyone knew that." But he said it kindly. "Never mind; here comes the mayor."

A large black carriage drawn by horses was pulling up to the curb, and two policemen began pushing the crowd back. Tess watched as a portly man dressed all in black stepped down from the carriage, then turned and helped a middle-aged woman descend. She took his arm, and the two of them walked past the crowd and into the hall. More carriages and automobiles were

pulling up, all in a long, black line. The crowd was silent, except for the sound of a woman crying.

After the last guest entered the hall, a guard left the outer doors wide open, a kindness, people whispered, to allow them to hear the prayers and eulogies. No one tried to enter.

A soft chanting came from the hall. "They're reciting Kaddish," the man next to her said, obviously assuming that she wouldn't be familiar with the Jewish prayers.

But she was. A memory of what she had heard out on the sea in that flimsy lifeboat was spilling forth. Someone, in another boat, had been reciting this mournful prayer, his voice caught and held in the still, freezing air. She lowered her head, surprised at the solace it gave her now.

"Tess?"

She looked up. Pinky stood there holding her canvas bag close to her chest, wearing a limp hat that still dripped with drops of rain.

"You're covering this?" Tess said. Her voice might sound cold, but she couldn't

help it. Pinky always came with noise and tension, and right now she was thrusting herself into Tess's one calm moment in many days.

"Not on assignment. I just thought I'd come by. I knew him."

Tess felt a twinge of shame. "I feel a little like I know him, too," she said.

They stood together silently, listening to the rhythm of the Hebrew prayers. When the service ended, the mayor and other dignitaries climbed back into their automobiles and carriages and drove away.

Pinky broke the silence. "So you have to boil silkworms to make silk?" she said off-handedly.

"What?" Tess said, startled.

"You know. Silk. I'm reading up on design and stuff. Got Van Anda to assign me to Lady Duff's big fashion show. That's tough on the silkworms, don't you think?"

"I suppose we could cut everything out of linen and wool," Tess said with a smile, reaching for her handkerchief. "But think of all those shorn, shivering

sheep. Give me that hat of yours—I'm going to try and blot up the water."

"Do I look too sad?" Pinky said, handing it over. "I have to say, you do."

Tess stopped walking, concentrating on her blotting task before she answered. "I am a bit," she said before handing back the hat.

"Because of what you told Jim. Yesterday."

"Do you always know what's happening?" Tess said with a flash of irritated surprise.

"No, not everything. Who's the other man? And I'm not going to apologize for being intrusive—I'm just asking, and you don't have to answer."

"No, I don't. And I won't. Sorry, Pinky."

Pinky shrugged. Nothing ventured, nothing gained. "How is it going at Lady Duff's studio?"

"Are you asking me is Lucile all distraught and frantic about having to testify in two days?"

"I'd be surprised if she were. I figure she's looking forward to putting on a

grand performance. New York is happily waiting."

"Then what are you asking?"

"How about how things are for you, or am I just digging for gossip?"

Tess smiled, relenting. "She's letting me design a dress, and if it's good enough she'll put it in her show. It's done, except for a tuck in the sleeves. I'll show it to Lucile tomorrow, and truly, I'm proud of it. I think she will like it." Much more than that, she *prayed* that Lucile would like it.

"Silk?"

"Yes."

"Too bad—I wanted to write about cruelty to silkworms."

They both laughed, and continued walking, but Tess found herself slipping back into a melancholy mood. She was about to make some excuse so that she could break away and be alone again when Pinky spoke.

"My father isn't doing too well. The woman who takes care of him during the day said he's too cranky for her; I'm crossing my fingers she won't quit."

"I'm sorry, I hope not." It was easy to

forget that Pinky's brash spirit hid real troubles.

"I figured I would pick up some tomatoes for him at the street market after old Mr. Straus's memorial." Pinky took off her hat, changed her mind, and crammed it on her head again. "Thanks for getting some of the water out of this thing."

"If it starts raining again, I have an umbrella." The words were out so quickly, she couldn't pull them back. Now Pinky would expect her to keep walking.

"That's good, thanks." And then, as if she had just thought of it: "Why don't you come home with me? I'll make us some lunch. You might like meeting my father; he's basically a good person, just thinks that the whole world should revolve around him. But then that's the way it always was, I guess. I've got cheese and salami, fresh."

So Pinky wanted to talk. What was there to say? She wanted to talk, too.

The stairwell smelled faintly of urine, and Tess tried to hold her breath as

long as she could as they climbed up to the fourth floor.

"We take turns scrubbing the floors, my neighbors and me. Usually it smells fine, but I'm the one who didn't do it yesterday. Sorry about today."

"I've smelled worse," Tess said lightly. And she had. She just didn't like to admit it.

Prescott Wade was propped up on several pillows, staring out the window with an open book in his lap, when they entered his bedroom. He was a smaller figure than Tess had envisioned, more frail. But his thin, bony fingers grasped her hand firmly when Pinky introduced them.

"Pinky talks about you," he said. "You're the girl working for the big designer, right? Only in America, that kind of thing?"

"I'm trying." She liked his brusqueness.

"Good, don't settle. Sarah here, she's a good reporter. But she wants to be Nellie Bly." His eyes traveled toward Pinky. "She can't do it with me around. I guess I clipped her wings." His eyes

closed and he turned his head to the wall.

Pinky gave his shoulder a swift pat and beckoned Tess to follow her out of the bedroom. She began hacking into a head of lettuce, frowning slightly. "He's not himself, but then he never is anymore."

"Do you think of yourself as Nellie Bly?"

Pinky paused, her knife hovering above the vanquished lettuce. "I would like to travel around the world the way she did. Meeting people, riding camels, shooting rapids—" Her eyes turned dreamy. "I could do it, and I could do it with just clean underwear, same as she did. No luggage."

"Why?"

"Why did you want to come to America? Because I want to have adventures and see the world, that's why. But, to tell you the truth, I'd settle for more money."

"Can you get that?" Tess asked curiously. In her experience, it simply didn't happen.

"Women don't get raises at newspa-

pers. Just lots of praise, if you're lucky, but no money. Here, slice the bread." She shoved a loaf of bread and a butcher knife toward Tess.

"What's wrong with your father?" Somehow, as she sliced bread and Pinky made the salad, the question didn't seem intrusive.

"He's had several heart attacks, and each time he gets weaker." Pinky kept her head down as she cut into a tomato.

"I'm sorry."

When Pinky looked up, her eyes were unusually bright. "He's not always easy, but he's a pretty good father. I give him morphine for the pain. Do you like your salami thick or thin?"

"I like it whichever way you choose to slice it."

"Thin it is."

The next few moments passed in relative silence as the lunch was laid out on a table covered with oilcloth. That task done, Pinky put her hands on the back of a chair and looked straight at Tess.

"Sit down. I have something to tell you," she said.

"About what?"

"About Jim. He's in trouble."

Tess lowered herself into a chair, not taking her eyes off Pinky.

"The people who want him out of the way have been digging around in his past, and they've discovered an old indictment from the coal-strike demonstrations."

"What?" Tess almost knocked the bread tray off the table.

"I'm told the police were arresting everybody in sight, clubbing a lot of heads, things like that. When the mine workers fought back, a cop got slugged. Jim was one of the crowd, and a union organizer to boot. Don't be too shocked; the charges were dismissed a few days later."

Her hands began to tremble. "So why is Jim in trouble?"

"Because someone managed to reactivate the indictment against him."

"Someone? Who?"

Pinky didn't answer directly. "Did you

know he's been subpoenaed for the British hearings?"

"No, he didn't tell me that yesterday."

"I guess he had more important things on his mind."

Tess winced. "Please, Pinky. Don't."

"I'm sorry, Tess. But you know how you hurt him."

Tess nodded.

"Okay. Anyway, that means he'll have to go back. He'll be arrested the minute he steps on English soil, and that 'scandalous' development will get full play in the British newspapers, shooting down the credibility of his testimony here. Voilà, he'll no longer be a threat to the Duff Gordons, because who wants to believe a criminal? After the hearings are over, Lady Duff skips off to the next fashion show, the charge will be dropped again, very quietly. Neat package, actually."

"How do you know all this?"

"I've got sources. I'm a reporter, remember?" Pinky's grin wasn't quite as easy as usual. Neither of them had touched the food.

"So, Lucile is out to discredit Jim any way she can."

"Sure. Nobody stands to profit the way she does. And it turns out it *was* her lawyers coaching those crew members when Jim testified. Big law firm here. I checked them out."

Tess blinked, trying to absorb the news. First, disbelief—then anger—and now, deep inside, fury. Yes, Lucile was capable of this. It was outrageous, imperious—everything. "Does Jim know?" she managed.

"He found out last night; he's surprised, but kind of stalwart. You know, the British thing about the stiff upper lip."

"Are you writing a story?"

Pinky paused before replying. "I'm waiting. The minute I write it, it does exactly what she wants it to do. I'd rather wait and see what tricks she'll try to pull testifying here."

"You are sure about this?"

"I'm positive, or I wouldn't be telling you. Eat something." Pinky shoved a slice of salami between two slices of

bread and handed it to Tess. "There's another possible outcome."

"What is it?" Tess took the sandwich and bit into it; she couldn't taste a thing, not with the hard knot of anger engulfing her.

"If somebody with better lawyers on the job than Lady Duff—not an easy find, mind you—manages to quash the indictment before it gets publicized. Stomp it back into the past where it belongs. Guess who's working on that?" This time her grin was authentic.

"All right, who?"

"The terrific, smart, rich Mrs. Brown. She's furious. She's got big plans for Jim, and she doesn't want to lose him. How's the sandwich?"

"I can't taste it." Tess pushed it away and stood. She paced, unable to stay still.

"You're pretty upset."

"Did you think I wouldn't be? Playing such a dirty trick on Jim, trying to ruin him? I'm furious that she would hurt him."

Pinky pushed back from the table,

too. "Somebody already has," she said quietly.

They fell into a momentary silence.

"I'm sorry," Pinky said again. "I guess I like to think you don't deserve him."

Tess was too shaken to mount a defense. "I don't," she said.

"So what are you going to do?"

"I'm going to quit. I will not stay with that woman—I can't stay there one more day, not now." The shock of disbelief shredded away; she had no doubts. It wasn't enough to pay off those seamen for their testimony—no, Lucile was too controlling to settle for that. She wanted all criticism silenced. "I can't work for her anymore. I'd never trust her again."

"You can move in here," Pinky said. "I mean it, you know. You can start making dresses—I even have a sewing machine—and when you make some money you can get your own place."

"How would I find clients?"

"No problem," Pinky said buoyantly. "I'll send everybody I write about to you, and maybe even Van Anda's wife; she could use some fancier clothes.

Tess, it's a great idea. You don't need Lucile!"

Tess felt her smile falter. Pinky was so brashly American, all exuberance and confidence. She knew how to defy the rules; maybe there was something to learn from that. There had to be, because she was stepping into a void.

But there was Jack.

------

Her feet ached from the long walk home. Jack was waiting for her. She took the flowers he held out to her without seeing them. "She's done something terrible to Jim," she blurted.

He looked at the flowers, which she had unthinkingly dropped to the sidewalk. "All right, tell me," he said.

And she did, letting it all spill out, caring not a whit how it sounded, as he listened in silence.

"You care quite a lot about this man's welfare," he finally said.

"Of course, I do," she said. "How can Lucile do this? She's trying to ruin his life, just as everything is opening up for

him. Part of me can't believe it, and another part thinks, For goodness' sake, how naïve can you be, to be so surprised? I—"

"But what is your role in all this?" he asked with something of an edge to his voice. "What are you going to do, Tess?"

"I'm going to quit, of course," she said, surprised at his question.

"You would walk out before the show? Abandon the chance to show the gown you're so proud of?" He said it in such a gentle yet probing way.

"Does that make me sad? Yes. But I don't have a choice."

"There's always a choice, Tess. That's what makes life so complicated."

"Well, this one is mine."

Jack put out his arms and pulled her close. "Perhaps that means you're closer now to making a more important choice," he murmured.

She said nothing, just closed her eyes and waited for the comfort that came with his embrace. Tonight it was elusive, even when she finally noticed the flowers.

-------

Pinky sat in the kitchen for a long time after Tess left. She picked at the salad, rolled a piece of salami between her fingers. Well, she had done what she set out to do. She had set something in motion, and she would just have to see what came next.

"Sarah."

Oh, for God's sake, she had forgotten her father's lunch. She made a sandwich hastily, put it on a plate, and walked into his room. He wasn't fooled.

"Stale bread," he said.

"I was thinking."

"About that young man you've talked about?"

Pinky sank heavily onto the bed. "I wish you weren't so observant."

"So what's the problem?"

She hesitated, wondering why she should bother, knowing he was quite capable of falling asleep in the midst of what she wanted to say. "He's hurting because of Tess."

"So she dumped him for someone else."

"How did you know?"

"I didn't. Damn it, Sarah, it's always

the same story. Your generation didn't invent it, you know." His thin fingers brought the sandwich up to his mouth, then dropped it back on the plate. "I'm tired, think I'll go back to sleep."

"Sure." She stood, ready to leave. She just wanted out of this bedroom, out of this apartment, out of everything.

His hand reached for hers and squeezed, again with surprising strength. "I'm not so drugged up I don't know how you feel, kid."

With a rush of gratitude, Pinky squeezed back.

## 14

The morning light shone weakly through a window in need of washing, but even bright sunshine wouldn't have lifted Tess's spirits. She sat on the bed, brushing her hair, pulling through the tangles. One by one. There was no need to hurry. And there was no need to rehearse what she was going to say. She adjusted her hat, weaving the hat pin carefully through the straw, then walked out into her future, whatever it was going to be.

The doors of Lucile's private elevator opened, inviting her into its exclusive

domain. How laughable it was, the idea that being allowed inside a cranky, slow elevator was a mark of privilege. She lifted her skirt slightly, ignored the elevator, and took the stairs.

"Tess, where have you been? Come here!"

Lucile's voice rang through the loft, turning every head toward Tess as she entered. Billows of silk and wool puffed up from the humming sewing machines, catching the light now streaming through the windows—a wonderful, shimmering sight. A catch in her throat—how she loved this place. She didn't allow herself to linger. Only a few wondered why, as she walked through the loft to the runway set up for the show, she did not immediately take off her hat.

"My goodness, dear, I'm been dying to see you. Why are you so late? Never mind, just look!" Lucile pointed at a model, who, as if on cue, began to stroll down the runway toward Tess. She was wearing Tess's finished gown. The richly hued cream silk looked even better than it had two days ago. With a shorter

skirt, it bounced, catching the light, tossing it back into the room, catching it again. It was as she had imagined. Her dress. She had done this.

"It's absolutely *marvelous!*" Lucile said, clasping her hands. "I fixed that little tuck in the sleeve for you this morning, is that all right?" She didn't wait for an answer. "Perhaps it's a bit shorter than it could be, but my clients can order it any length they want. Tess, you've done a fabulous job. It will absolutely be in the show."

Tess kept staring at her gown, even as Lucile's praise grew more elaborate. The dress didn't work, not fully. She stared critically at the bodice, and decided that not only should she have angled the darts more; a square-cut neckline would have been better. It had almost worked.

"It isn't as good as it should be," she said.

"Spoken like a true designer, dear. Of course it isn't perfect, but it's got a fresh feel to it, and I'm happy. Don't be so hard on yourself. Why do you look so dour?"

"May we talk in your office?"

Impatiently, Lucile shook her head. "No time—we have much to do. What is it you want?"

It wasn't an easy thing to open one's mouth and shatter the lively, bustling mood. "I'm sorry it had to happen this way, but I am quitting," Tess said quietly.

"What? You are *what*?" Lucile almost shrieked the words.

Tess felt as if she had lifted a knife and plunged it through a crowd. Why would her leaving matter? But heads were turning, eyes wide. A hush fueled by quick whispers flew through the loft.

Tess pointed at her dress. She couldn't trust herself to pick it up.

"Letting me make this was a bribe, pure and simple. You were buying my loyalty."

"What are you talking about?" Lucile said.

"You knew money would be too blatant. Money was for those sailors, so they would lie about Jim Bonney at the hearings. But a bribe it was."

Lucile's face turned gray. She

clutched at her heart, and James came running out of the office to hold her up.

"I didn't need a bribe. I would have stayed because I wanted to. But not now, not for anything."

*"What are you talking about?"*

"Oh, Lucile, please stop pretending. You're plotting to paint Jim Bonney as a common criminal in England—that's what I'm talking about. To actually get him arrested on a false charge. Why? Was he that much of a threat to you?"

"I couldn't care less about that sailor."

"What happened in your boat?"

Lucile stared at her, features frozen. She turned away. "You're hysterical. I do not know what you're talking about."

"It's easy to deny, I guess. But I can't believe how easily you would try to ruin a man." Tess's voice was cracking now.

Lucile stood braced against a cutting table, her eyes dark as brackish water. "I have nothing to do with any absurd scheme to send your sailor to jail. Do you understand?"

Of course she would deny it, that was her nature. This woman in front of her, her mentor, the woman who had

so casually plucked her from a life of service and opened up the world to her, was perfectly ready to bluff this one through. She no more cared what happened to Jim than she cared what happened to the people who could have—who *should* have—been in her lifeboat. All this, all this around her—the fabrics, the clothes, the dreams—everything was built on selfishness. The only thing built on anything admirable was Jim's behavior after the ship sank.

"I would respect you more if you admitted the truth. But it doesn't matter; I can't work for you anymore."

"That's just simply not possible, Tess. I want you here, and I know nothing about any plot to destroy that sailor."

"I don't believe you."

Lucile thrust out her chin, her lips pulled thin. "Then you are breaking your promise to *me.*"

"Goodbye." Tess turned to leave.

"Just what do you think you're going to do, Tess? Make beds and clean toilets again?" Lucile said defiantly.

"I don't know, but I'll find out."

"What about your dress? Don't you

want it in the show?" It was the last ar-
row in her quiver.

Tess turned back, aware that all eyes
were on her, caught by this unprecedented act of self-immolation. "I don't
care," she said slowly. "Call it your own,
if you wish. Or throw it away."

"Perhaps I'll get some pillowcases
out of it—is that what you want?" Lucile was playing to her audience now,
desperately.

"That would be fine." Tess turned
toward the paralyzed workers in the
room and smiled. "Thank you all, you
were wonderful to me," she said, and
then marched out of the loft, leaving
only silence in her wake.

------

## SENATE OFFICE BUILDING
## WASHINGTON, D.C.

William Alden Smith greeted the visitor
to his Washington office in the Senate
Office Building with weary courtesy.

"My goodness, Senator, you look
very down in the mouth," his visitor said

as she walked into the room, filling it with her girth and her hearty voice.

"Hello, Mrs. Brown," he said. If she was here to once again push her case for going on the stand, he would have to discourage her firmly this time.

"Not having much fun, are you?"

"Of course not, this is a serious matter."

"You've not had a great run in the British papers, I see."

"Being called 'a born fool' because of my lack of nautical expertise is a weary experience," he snapped.

Mrs. Brown laughed. "Oh, come now, Senator. When you asked Officer Lowe if he knew what an iceberg was made of—"

"Yes, yes, I know." Did she have to repeat it?

"And he said, with a straight face, 'Ice,' can't you smile a bit at yourself?"

"I am more concerned with serious issues. Do you realize the man who told us there were no binoculars on the ship is being ostracized by all the surviving officers? Nobody will talk to poor Fleet, which is outrageous. He won't come

out of his room at the boarding house, not even to eat. I'm worried about him."

"Quite properly, of course. But you're doing a good job," Mrs. Brown said, settling herself cheerfully into a chair, not appearing a bit in awe of his quite imposing office. "It's a thankless one, and you haven't pretended to knowledge of ships or the sea. I like an honest man."

Mollified, Smith allowed himself a smile. "I do have trouble remembering which end is the bow and which is the stern," he admitted. "But when my investigation is complete there will be a strong, comprehensive body of information for the public to digest."

"With no one admitting to anything, of course. Isn't that the way of the world?"

"Indeed it is."

She wiped her forehead with a wrinkled handkerchief. "My, it's hot in here, I would think politicians wouldn't like the heat too much," she said absentmindedly. "You're wondering why I'm here, right? Well I'm not here to persuade you to put me on the stand, if

that's worrying you. But I sure could use some help."

"What about?" he asked, caught off guard.

"That obnoxious couple, the Duff Gordons. Not a very nice pair, I'd say. I think they're out to crush that sailor who testified about their behavior on the lifeboat. You know who I mean, right?"

Smith remembered the sight of Jim Bonney's long legs striding away from the Senate Office Building. "Yes, I do," he said.

"Well, I found out from the *Times* reporter, Pinky Wade, that he's about to be caught in a nice little trap they've set up." She swiftly filled Smith in on the details, then sat back, folding her hands over her ample stomach. "Can you pull some strings? Get somebody paying attention to what they're trying to do?"

"I don't have much leverage with British officials," Smith said dryly. "They seem to think I'm some kind of comic figure."

"I know that—Lord's sake, the same

is true for me. Don't let it get you down. But you have contacts over there; I know you do. A couple of old classmates, I hear? In the House of Commons?"

He wondered how she happened to know this, and peered at her more closely. She must be more keenly intelligent than she appeared.

"All it would take is for somebody to check the records and block any attempt to reactivate a dead charge. Just a little fresh air on what's going on, you know?"

"I will make some inquiries," he said carefully. "All I can do is raise interest among the right people and see if they're willing to follow up."

"Good enough." She beamed. "Bonney is a very talented man, you know. An artist. He'll do well here, if he can shake the *Titanic* off his back."

"I believe that may be true for many of us," Smith said, feeling his weariness descend again.

"Well, Senator, my feeling is, none of us ever will get free of it all the way."

"Indeed," he said with a sigh. "We

go back to New York this afternoon to hear more testimony tomorrow."

"So I hear. With Lady Duff Gordon as a star witness. Do you think we will learn anything more of the truth in Lifeboat One?"

"I will at least have this beleagured woman on the record, whatever she says."

"A modest goal, Senator."

"Mrs. Brown, you may be surprised."

------

Lucile threw open the door of the hotel suite just as Cosmo, standing in front of the sideboard, was pouring a glass of bourbon from a crystal flask.

"I'll take one of those," she said, tossing her handbag onto the sofa. "I've had a terrible day. That ungrateful girl has quit on me, accusing me of all sorts of things. I never should have brought her here, I can see that now."

Cosmo poured a second glass and turned, holding it out to her. His gaze was calm and steady. "For you, dear. You are going to need it."

"What does that mean?" she said, walking forward and taking the glass.

"I've had the report on what happened today. I thought Tess might make a little noise, but she acted quite rashly. Too bad."

"What are you saying?" She was holding the glass now, staring at him.

"Can we pass on the indignant part of the scene? You wouldn't have wanted to know, and I'm quite weary of hysterics."

"Wanted to know *what*?"

"You already know, I think."

For a moment, there was silence.

"Cosmo, what did you do to me?" Her voice had an authentic quaver.

"I have done nothing *to* you. I have done something *for* you. That sailor will no longer be a threat. I do hope you still understand the difference." He drained his glass with a quick toss.

"Tess denounced me and quit. I don't quite see how that was beneficial to me."

"For God's sake, you can do without her. If my plan goes through properly, the British press will have reason to

treat us much more kindly. We can't stop what Bonney might say, but we can change how reporters react to him. Think of it as a chess maneuver, Lucy."

"And he goes to jail?"

"Briefly. Just long enough for public opinion to exonerate us for being victims of a deceitful rabble-rouser."

"But I have lost Tess."

"Your substitute daughter, of course. For the one you actually lost."

In the silence that followed, the mantel clock seemed to tick louder than usual.

"You were not happy about the pregnancy, as I recall."

"I would have adjusted."

"Nonsense. A child would have drastically complicated our lives."

"Let's see. What was it? Respectability and money for you and—let's see, what was there for me? I've forgotten."

"Don't sneer at me."

"I'll tell you what I got. The woman I loved. Or so I thought."

"This is such a tiresome story," she said, taking off her jacket, turning her face away. "As for this sailor, you must

find another way, Cosmo. I can't tolerate this. Several more clients canceled this afternoon, and I think it's because Tess's tirade is making its way around town. I don't know who will come now."

"That's a price you may have to pay to stave off a worse disaster back home."

"Is that all the sympathy I get from you?"

Cosmo slowly poured himself a second shot of bourbon and stood holding it, staring at the glass. "I'm afraid there's more. I will be with you for your testimony, Lucy. But I'm going back to London tomorrow night."

She felt her first jolt of fear. "You're leaving me here alone? Not staying for my show? Whatever is so important that it takes you away at this crucial time?"

"I'll stand by you for the inquiries, here and at home. But that's all I can promise."

"My God, Cosmo, what are you saying?"

"I believe things have changed for us—quite significantly, I'm afraid," he

said. "I've enjoyed over the years being the quiet supporter who could make things work for you. But not anymore. It isn't just this caterwauling American press tearing my reputation apart. It's the fact that you see me far more as a servant than as a husband. Just one more obedient follower doing the bidding of the great Lucile." He looked at her fully for the first time in a long while. "I've made the mistake of letting you get away with it for too long."

Lucile swayed, the bourbon sloshing to the rim of her glass, spilling onto the carpet.

"Hold yourself up, dear. I'm not going to grab you." Once again, he drained his glass. "You will have to fend for yourself here, I'm afraid. As I said, I will stay by your side through the inquiries. After that, I don't know."

"You would leave me? *Abandon* me?"

In the long silence that followed, she looked as if she might truly faint.

"I said, I don't know."

"Then I will be thinking of alternatives myself."

He smiled faintly. "That's my Lucy. I

like your instinct to fight back, always have."

"Then you surely aren't serious?"

"Yes, I am. Never more serious about anything in my life." He nodded toward Lucile's bedroom door. "Elinor is in your room, waiting for you."

She turned, white-faced, and walked unsteadily through the parlor to the bedroom door. It opened as she reached out to turn the handle. Elinor, her eyes pitying, stood there, holding out her arms.

------

The day's light was fading when Pinky heard a sharp knock on the apartment door. Probably a neighbor complaining about the smell of her burned brisket again. Why did she keep overcooking the bloody roast? Too much on her mind, that was why. Braced, she opened the door and found herself staring at Jim Bonney.

"Got some soap and water and a mop?" he said.

"I'm sorry about the smell, I'm just so lazy—"

"Just get me the bucket of soap and water and throw in some bleach." He patted her on the shoulder, reached behind her, and pulled out a mop leaning against the wall.

"I keep it there because I'm always just about to clean the hall." Stop apologizing, she told herself as she hurried into the kitchen for Fels-Naptha and water. Within a few minutes, Jim was scrubbing the stairs with ferocious energy.

"You shouldn't be doing this," she protested.

"What do you think I did on that ship? I'm better at it than you are, I'd say."

"Not better, just faster." She bit her lip. There she was, firing off again.

"Suit yourself. Smell anything?"

He was at the bottom of the stairs, leaning on the mop and grinning up at her.

She sniffed. "No," she said delightedly. "Well, just the bleach."

"Then my job is done."

She reached out for the bucket and

mop and stood aside for him to come in. "Now you have to stay for dinner," she said. "That's my thank-you."

This time it was Jim who sniffed the air. "Burned meat, right? Smells delicious. I accept."

Now, close up, she saw how worn his face looked. This was no social call, much as she wished it was. "Come join me in the kitchen," she said.

He sat down heavily, rubbing hands turned red with laundry soap. "You haven't written anything about this indictment?"

She put a pot of water on to boil and began peeling potatoes. "I want to see if Mrs. Brown can turn it around. I told Tess."

"You did? What did she say?"

"She quit. Denounced Lady Duff and walked out."

Jim went still. "She quit?"

Pinky glanced at him, long enough to see the astonishment in his eyes. "She did it for you, nobody else. She has nothing to gain, and that's the truth."

He dropped his head, then lifted it

quickly. "She shouldn't have done that. I don't need empty gestures."

"Gestures?" Pinky turned fully to him, astonished. "That's no *gesture,* that's a genuine *protest,* and you should know it better than anyone."

"I'm grateful. But Tess is giving up what she loves; I don't want her to do that. And it isn't going to change anything. That's done, over with."

"I'm sorry, but you don't sound as if you believe a word you're saying."

"I have to make it true," he said quietly.

"Just get this straight. She sacrificed hugely for you today."

"She's in love with someone else. That's the fact of it."

Why was she working so hard at this? It was her big mouth again. "Maybe you think that, but you don't know for sure."

He lifted his head. "What an optimist," he said with the shadow of a grin.

"I fake it pretty well. Are you braced for Lady Duff's testimony tomorrow?"

"She'll say what she wants to believe."

"With plenty of theater thrown in."

He laughed, then looked around the kitchen. "Look, can I help? Put together a plate for your father? Better get that brisket out of the oven."

"Oh, yes, I'm forgetting it again." She opened the oven door and pulled out the roasting pan, her face flushing from the heat. He wasn't asking her to be his advocate with Tess. No hints about carrying messages. Had he really given up? She didn't believe it.

------

Dinner this time was in a restaurant with walls that glowed like a fine glass of Burgundy. Tess could only pick at her food—richly marbled roast beef, currants whipped into a soft cheese soufflé—unable to muster the energy to eat, not even such fare as was before her. She listened distractedly to Jack, barely hearing him.

He threw down his napkin. "You've got only one thing on your mind right now," he said, and then fell silent.

Tess barely heard him. "I kept de-

fending her. What was wrong with me? I should have realized that everything had to be done her way. I did what I had said I would never do again. I kept my head down, tried to please—" She put her fork down; it was no use. Again, she could hear her father's voice. Yes, she had been a foolish girl, but not by doing what he warned against. She had been foolish *not* to speak up, *not* to step forward.

"You are here with me now. You've left Lucile. Isn't that enough?"

With effort, she shifted attention. "No, not while Jim is in trouble."

"He isn't caught in their trap yet. Who's working on it?"

"Mrs. Brown, from the ship; she spotted his talent in carving and is starting him in business here."

"Ah yes, Mrs. Brown. The indomitable, unsinkable Margaret." He smiled. "We've had some business dealings over the years. Quite a formidible woman, and she knows how to pull strings. So you've quit in protest. Now what?"

She could hear the clock ticking be-

hind her. "I don't know. I know what you're asking me, but I just don't know yet."

"A sensible response. In many ways, I'm a stranger to you." He sat back in his chair, gazing at her thoughtfully. "I'm asking too much, I'm afraid."

She straightened up in her chair. "Then tell me who you are."

"The product of a fairly predictable life with more privileges than most, but I earned them myself. A slow learner, which probably explains two divorces." A silence fell between them. "Not enough?" Ruefully, he touched his sideburns. "Turning gray," he said. "I'm sensitive about that. Does that help?"

"A little."

"Well, you don't seem to have as much hesitation over your bond to that sailor. And how long have you known *him*?"

"That's different," she said, startled.

His face clouded. "Maybe you love him, Tess. Maybe that's what's holding you back."

He looked so profoundly sad, she couldn't sit still. Silently, she pushed

the table aside and moved close, her arms encircling him. He had a right to know where he stood.

"Please give me time," she whispered. He cradled her head with one hand, and they both held on.

15

"I'm ready." Lucile stood in the bedroom doorway, dressed all in black, surveying her face in the boudoir mirror. "Do I need more powder?"

"You're fine," Elinor replied. "Cosmo said to make sure you review those briefing papers before we go downstairs."

"I don't need them," Lucile said with a faint echo of her usual haughty manner. "And why isn't Cosmo here to tell me that himself? He's a coward, that's what he is—"

"Stop it, Lucy, he's not a coward.

This is going to ruin him, and you know it. They're already making 'doing a Duff-Gordon' slang for bribery back home."

Elinor's face was almost as pale as her sister's.

Lucile said nothing at first, pulling a white lace handkerchief from her glove and dabbing her eyes. "We've both been maligned, and I'll not let them get away with it. And Cosmo won't leave me; it would only deepen the scandal." She looked directly at her sister. "I'm right, aren't I?"

Elinor forced a smile. "I hope so."

Again, a silence.

"We need to go downstairs soon."

Lucile sighed. "Is the white handkerchief against the black dramatic enough? Or should I wear a white lace collar, too?"

"Save the collar for London."

"I can handle this just fine, Elinor, stop looking at me that way."

Elinor, for once, was neither jaunty nor flippant. "Of course. And I will do my best to pick up the pieces."

-------

The East Room was filling rapidly. Pinky stood near the back of the room, scanning faces so intently that she didn't see Jim making his way toward her through the crowd until he touched her shoulder. His cheeks were high with color and he was smiling.

"What are you doing here?" she said, drawing him to a corner. "You'll be swarmed by reporters, if they see you."

"I had to take that chance. I have news," he said. "That indictment? Withdrawn this morning. Don't know why, don't know how, but it's dead."

Pinky slapped her pencil against her notebook triumphantly. "I knew it! I knew Mrs. Brown would find a way to set this right. How did she do it?"

"She didn't. She told me this morning neither she nor Senator Smith could get any help from the British government."

"So what happened?"

"I don't know. Neither does she. A mystery—how about that? But now I don't have to go back to England and

prove I'm not a criminal. That might not be what most people think is good news, but it sure is mine. I probably won't even be subpoenaed now for the inquiry, since I've got a job here."

A man, mopping his brow vigorously in the intensifying heat of the crowded room, shouldered past them, mumbling something about the impossibility of finding a seat. Angry shouts were coming from the doorway; once again, people who wanted in were having trouble pushing into the room.

"Thanks for the brisket," he said soberly. "And for being on my side."

And then he was gone, leaving her to stand there wondering what had happened to her journalistic objectivity. Because he was right.

No, he wasn't gone. He had stopped still as a woman approached him, and now they were facing each other, inches apart. It was Tess, and Pinky drew in her breath. What was *she* doing here, after quitting yesterday? Were they both crazy?

------

Jim appeared so quickly that Tess had no chance to prepare herself. He looked different somehow. He was dressed in new clothes, a crisp shirt and sweater, but that wasn't it. No, there was more— a different kind of energy to him, a focus. She felt suddenly awkward.

"Hello, Tess." His smile was bright but carefully impersonal, his manner calm. He didn't look flustered at all. "I hear you quit your job with Lady Duff."

Tess nodded, not trusting her voice.

"You didn't need to do that, not for me. It was your big opportunity, and I don't want that to be lost to you."

"She wanted to damage you, and I had to fight back."

"So when she went right ahead—"

"I had to quit. You mean more to me than the job," she said simply.

His steady gaze faltered. Behind them, the grandfather clock in the Waldorf's lobby began to strike the hour, heavily and ponderously. She counted. It took him eight strokes before he responded.

"I don't understand. Not given what changed between us."

"It was the only thing I could do. My only power." She laced her fingers together, pressing them tightly in front of her.

He looked at her, both baffled and cautious. "Explain, please. Why, for me?"

She wavered. If she could only reach down inside herself and pull out the right words. If she could yank them forth, cup her hands around them, offer them—what were they? She thought of Jack. His steadiness, his confidence. And then the moment passed, lost somewhere in the seconds marked by the ticking clock.

He shrugged. "I guess you don't know why. Punishing yourself like that for a village boy was probably a bad move."

She turned her head away. "Jim, please."

"I'm sorry, Tess. That was petty of me. It just came out, I guess."

"You're angry."

"Because you tossed me over?" He shrugged and shoved his hands in his

pockets with a touch of swagger. "Yes, I guess I am. But I don't want you hurt."

"Jim, I'm so sorry, I want us—"

The sad, steady look he gave her silenced her. They both stood for a moment, neither able now to find any words, let alone the right ones. Then Jim nodded toward the rapidly filling rows of chairs. "Better grab yourself a seat before they're all gone. I assume you're not here to offer Lady Duff your moral support?"

"No." She had found her voice. "I saw you."

This time he was the one who hesitated before speaking. "Tess, the indictment was withdrawn this morning. I'm clear to stay."

"Oh, my goodness, what wonderful news," she gasped. Her hands flew to her mouth. "I am so relieved, so glad. Who did it? Was it Mrs. Brown?"

"No, it wasn't. I don't know how it happened, but it did." He smiled, differently this time. There was a glint of something in his eyes, but he blinked it away, then turned to make his way through the crowd and out the door.

------

By ten o'clock, the East Room and lobby were jammed with people packed together more tightly than ever. Tess tried to make her way out of the crowd, planning to listen from the doorway, but she couldn't move. She sank into the only seat left, near Pinky, as Senator Smith banged his gavel once again.

"Our first witness this morning will be Lady Lucile Duff Gordon," he announced. "Please make way for the witness to move forward."

And, in almost eerie obedience, the crowd parted.

Lucile walked slowly through the opening space to the front of the room, a tiny figure all in black, wearing a large black hat with a veil covering her eyes. In one hand she clutched a snowy white handkerchief. The room went almost completely still as she settled into the witness chair.

Senator Smith glanced at his fellow committee members a bit uneasily. This was no frightened, illiterate crewman. And all Britain would be ready to pounce if he didn't handle it right.

"Lady Duff Gordon, tell us about how you and your husband came to be in Lifeboat One. Let's start there," he said.

"Of course, Senator," she said with calm hauteur. "I had quite made up my mind that we would be drowned, and then suddenly we saw this little boat in front of us—a tiny thing—and I said to my husband, 'Ought we not to be doing something?' My husband asked if we might get into that boat, and the officer said in a very polite way indeed, 'Oh, certainly, do; I will be very pleased. And then we were helped in.'"

Tess glanced at Pinky, who raised an eyebrow. What sort of singsong manner was this?

The questions continued, becoming less general; Lucile went on answering in a strong, haughty voice, painting an almost ludicrous picture of politeness and gentility in Lifeboat One, dabbing periodically at her eyes with the handkerchief.

"Now I must ask you, after the *Titanic* sank did you hear the cries of the people who were drowning?"

"No, after the *Titanic* sank, I never heard a cry."

"You did not hear any cries at all?" Smith asked, incredulous.

She looked at him, matching his own tone of incredulity. "Wouldn't I know, Senator? My impression was there was absolute silence."

It was said with such serene certitude that the room exuded hushed awe. A good performance deserved appreciation. Everyone knew it wasn't true, but this small woman on the stand was, by the strength of her will, determined to make it true.

"Did you hear anybody shout out in the boat that you ought to go back, with the object of saving people?"

"No."

"You knew there were people in the water, did you not?"

"No, I don't think I was thinking anything about it."

"Did you say it would be dangerous to go back, that you might get swamped?"

"Heavens, no."

Senator Smith held up a copy of the

*Sunday American* with Lucile's interview. "You speak in this interview of hearing agonizing pleadings for help. Which is it, madam?"

She never hesitated. "That so-called interview is a total invention," she said. "A disgusting journalistic invention."

Tess could hardly sit still. Was she really saying all this?

"And what about the rumors that your husband paid off the crew members so they would not go back to help the dying?"

"He can speak for himself, of course. But all he offered was a little help for them to get started again." Her voice was becoming more brisk and impatient.

"Your testimony quite drastically differs from that of the seaman Jim Bonney."

"Well, of course it does. He is a menace, as far as I am concerned. And, if I may say so, a liar."

Tess found herself rising to her feet, staring at Lucile, oblivious of the eyes now turning in her direction.

"I assumed that's what you thought,"

another committee member murmured. "But we need you on the record. What do you have to say to his charge that people were pushed away from Lifeboat One? That some were close enough to be pulled into your almost empty boat?"

"Total nonsense."

Tess could stand no more. She began pushing her way out of the room, not caring who watched or who knew her identity. But she felt Lucile's eyes following her. It struck her that one always knew when Lucile was watching.

Lucile turned to Smith, her voice wobbling slightly. "How much more of this, Senator? I really am a busy woman."

"Madam, we are dealing with life and death here," Smith retorted. "Your lack of patience is disturbing."

"I'm sorry I do not meet your expectations. May I go now?"

The panel was silent; the room was silent.

"You are dismissed," Smith finally said. "But"—he raised a hand as the crowd began to stir—"after a short

break, we have another witness this morning." He paused for added effect, then said, "Mrs. Jordan Darling, who was also on Lifeboat One."

Lucile's hat slipped, her startled eyes suddenly visible. She gripped the edges of her chair, stumbling slightly as she rose. A lively murmur immediately swept the room. The widow, yes, the widow of the man who disguised himself as a woman and then, publicly exposed, committed suicide. Can you believe it? Why would she want to face the public after her husband's cowardly behavior?

Pinky was already squeezing her way through the crowd, trying to reach Tess. But Elinor reached her first.

"I must talk to you this afternoon," she said. "Truly, it's urgent."

"About *what*?" Tess replied angrily. "About your sister's lies?"

"I've not lied to you, Tess. I'm saying talk to me. Please."

Tess took a deep breath, replying just as Pinky, breathless, reached her side. "I'll decide after I hear what Jean Darling has to say."

Senator Smith was quite pleased with himself as he surveyed the crowded room. Lady Duff Gordon had made a mistake if she thought her arrogance would win the day in an American inquiry. No one could accuse him of having hog-tied a member of the British upper class; the silly woman did it to herself. *Entitlement,* that was the right word. He would be glad to be done with the lot of them.

"Our next witness is not here under subpoena," he began. "She has specifically asked for this opportunity to put on the record a few thoughts on the frailty of human character in the face of tragedy." He stared out across the quiet room, relishing the reaction to his modest note of suspense.

"Will Mrs. Jordan Darling please take the stand?"

Tess swiveled in her seat, watching the graceful, lithe figure of Jean Darling as she threaded her way through the clutter of chairs to the front of the room. She wore a gray jacket and skirt, with a string of tiny pearls at her throat. She held her head high. The lights from

above glittered off her impeccably arranged hair, which was now almost pure white. A flash of memory took Tess back to the moment when she saw the Darlings dance, all poise and lightness, onto the *Titanic*. A delicious, airy moment filled with ripples of delighted laughter and applause. Gone forever.

------

"It is not necessary for you to offer testimony," Senator Smith began. Would she break down? You never knew with women, and the more genteel they were, the less predictable. "I want to emphasize that your appearance here is purely voluntary, at your request. I want that noted for the record. Is that correct?"

"Yes, Senator."

"We are all aware of your husband's unfortunate demise, and I wish to offer my condolences."

"Thank you."

"Can you tell us why you wished to come here today?"

Jean Darling appeared quite calm as she gazed out at the room. Her demeanor was serene—that of a woman who had asked to do this and was not going to indulge in qualms now. Even if it meant being burned again in the ferocious gaze of the newspapers or subjected to more jeers and derision.

"I am in awe of the stories of bravery I've heard during these hearings," she began. "The man who took off his life belt and put it on his wife's maid? I know my husband would have wanted to be that man." She paused, the crispness of her usual ladylike tone softening. "But I must tell you, only part of me regrets that he wasn't. Another part would still snatch a cloth from a table and throw it around his shoulders, anything to save his life. Even though"— her voice was shaking now—"I as much as killed him with that gesture. I will be haunted all my life by three things: the fact that I did not let my husband die the way he would have preferred, and the fact that it did not occur to me to join him. The third, and worst, is that perhaps the lives of two children could

have been saved by our both standing back."

Tess closed her eyes, brought back again to the shrieking cacophony of breaking glass, grand pianos tipping into the sea, beds, chamber pots, luggage, people clawing up the deck as the ship sank. Acts of bravery, accusations, stupid behavior—it was all in this room.

"You don't have to do this, Mrs. Darling," Senator Smith interrupted gently.

"Yes, I do. I won't be long, Senator." She opened her small handbag and drew forth a white linen handkerchief.

"I thought at first that speaking out would help clear my conscience, but that won't ever happen. I've given that idea up," she said, clutching the handkerchief tightly. "What I believe now is that accepting the reality of my decision is what is important. I can't forgive my actions, or the actions of another. The rashness of a moment changed my life and my husband's, and there were probably other quick decisions that changed the lives of other people on that ship. When my husband died, I

wanted to place blame. I wanted to *avoid* blame. Not anymore. I want to acknowledge that my character was not strong enough to be brave, and if any others secretly feel the same please know you are not alone. I only hope that, if tested again, I would be up to the task."

The room was preternaturally still. Tess could hear the breathing of people sitting in the row of chairs nearest to her. If they didn't want to understand, it didn't matter. Jean Darling had pointed plain and clear to the sad heart of it all. She had done it, alone.

"Is there more you want to say, Mrs. Darling?"

She straightened her back. "I thought not, when I asked to come, Senator. But I have changed my mind."

The room stirred.

"What would you like to tell us?"

"It is in reference to Lady Duff Gordon's testimony." She drew a ragged breath. "There were opportunities to be brave in that lifeboat that were not taken. We had room, we had plenty of

room. But we were all driven by fear. No, that's wrong."

"What do you mean, Mrs. Darling?"

"There was one brave man, and anybody in that boat who denies it is still driven by fear."

So at least some pieces of this sad puzzle were going to fit together, Senator Smith told himself. "And who was that?" he asked.

"Jim Bonney. And *that* is reality. I'm finished, Senator."

"Just one moment." Senator Bolton's raspy voice cut in, sending a ripple of surprise through the room. "You are not an official witness, madam, and you can refuse to answer. But, given the charges and countercharges about what happened on Lifeboat One, I wonder if you can fill in some of the gaps. Were people trying to get in your boat? Was anyone pushed off? What did you see, exactly?"

Mrs. Darling sat back, a startled look on her face. But when she spoke her voice was composed. "People were calling to us from the water. I saw one

man grab the side of the lifeboat to pull himself in."

"What happened then?"

"I heard a scream, a woman's scream. I saw a man stand up, holding an oar above his head. Mr. Bonney swore and stood up, wrestling with the man who raised the oar, and got it away from him."

"Why was it raised?"

"To knock that poor soul off the boat."

A tingling sensation spread across Tess's head and neck, as hot as fire, even as her hands turned to ice. Hardly a breath was drawn in the crowded room. This was the truth of what happened in Lifeboat One.

Senator Smith stirred uneasily. This was more than he had bargained for. If he asked now who that person was who raised the oar, he would lose control of these hearings. It would, quite possibly, be seen as the final straw by the British, who were already convinced that he was on a witch hunt.

"Do you have more to say?"

A long silence. "No," Mrs. Darling said. "It's over."

"Thank you, you may step down." Senator Smith looked out over the array of quiet, stunned faces before him. "Please allow Mrs. Darling to leave before we clear the room."

Pinky joined Tess, and together they walked out with the almost silent crowd.

"Look," Pinky said, nodding in the direction of a woman standing, unrecognized, by the open door.

It was Lucile. She had removed her lipstick. Her face was still, lips fading into pale skin, and the black hat had been discarded in favor of a scarf. Without her usual color, she looked like a bird that had been stripped of its plumage—so much so that no one seemed to recognize her. She was suddenly, surprisingly, impossibly small.

Not a word was exchanged as they walked by.

Outside, Tess said quietly to Pinky, "I have to leave now. I have to go pack my things."

The walk home was peaceful. She felt the warmth of the late-afternoon

sun on her neck and took off her hat to lift her face to its rays, taken fleetingly back to the moment that she and Jim stood over the bodies of the mother and baby on the *Carpathia.* I turn my face to the rising sun; O Lord, have mercy.

All the losses. Left with a lifetime of shame and dishonor, Jean Darling had mustered the courage to acknowledge her mistakes, a voluntary action that would be foreign to Lucile. She would never break out of the silky cocoon she had woven for herself. She would most likely rather march grandly over a cliff.

A hoarse shout to look where she was going as a driver clattered by. Tess stepped quickly back from the curb.

It was over, this particular dream. But the Duff Gordons had been stopped from ruining Jim's life, and that was all that mattered. So she walked now on the streets of New York, once again just a servant girl from Cherbourg without a job. That mattered, too. But not as much. And why did she feel a strange serenity about it all?

------

"My goodness, Tess, you *are* in a fog. You were ready to walk right by me," a voice said with light amusement.

"Elinor," Tess said in surprise. Lucile's sister stood on the street corner, her always present parasol—a green one, this time—shading her eyes from both the sun and the glances of passersby.

Elinor gestured toward a waiting car, which Tess hadn't noticed.

"Have you decided to talk to me?"

"I know you'll want me out of the flat very soon, and if you could give me a week more I would appreciate it. I will repay you for your kindness."

"Oh, for God's sake, Tess, get in the car."

"Why? What do you want from me?"

Elinor thrust a copy of the *New York World* toward Tess, her light manner evaporated. "This afternoon's paper, a little late with the story, but it will be read with some relish around town. If you will just read the headline, please?"

Tess took the paper and held it with both hands, a faint wind rippling the pages. She squinted and read, "Lady

Duff Gordon's 'Loyal' Secretary Abandons Ship."

"Not the front page, mind you. But just wait until tomorrow. I can imagine the headlines now: 'Secretary Walks Out During Lady Duff Gordon Testimony.' Things like that. Did you plan it? No, I thought not."

"Here's the headline, Elinor: 'Brave Sailor Vindicated of Vicious Duff Gordon Charges.' Do you really want to play this game?"

Elinor sighed. "They're all nails in Lucile's coffin, my dear. Especially, if you recall, since the spring show is tomorrow. Please talk to me."

Tess folded the paper and stepped into the car, with Elinor following. A fleeting thought occurred: for the first time in her life, she had been referred to as a "secretary." Not as a maid.

Elinor rapped on the window that separated the passengers from the driver. "Just drive around, Farley," she commanded. "Anywhere. Show us some of the sights of New York." She settled back into her seat, turned to Tess, and wasted no time.

"Cosmo is leaving her. Heading back for London. And over half the reservations for her show have been canceled. She's slipping, Tess."

"Cosmo is leaving?" Tess couldn't believe it.

"She ordered him around one time too many, I'm afraid. That last fight over the sailor cracked things open."

Tess just stared, puzzled.

"Oh, of course, you don't know about that. God, I need a cigarette. Do you mind?"

Tess shook her head, waiting.

A match flared, and Elinor's meticulously manicured fingers touched it to the end of her cigarette. She inhaled deeply. "That's better," she said, sighing.

"Will you explain, please?"

"You put on quite a show, denouncing her. But Lucile wasn't the one trying to get your sailor friend arrested. It was all Cosmo's idea."

"Without her knowledge—is that what you're saying? How could that be?"

"Oh, my dear, you really don't know

how things work in our world, do you? Cosmo is in charge, always has been. There have been a few unfortunate financial setbacks for Lucile's competitors over the years—nothing that could be tied to him, of course, but he has been devoted to paving the way for her. That's what he was doing this time."

Tess covered her mouth with one hand, staring straight ahead. "I was wrong?"

"Don't overreact," Elinor said airily. "Remember, Lucy doesn't want to know the mechanics of how Cosmo gets things done, which isn't quite the same as being totally innocent. You understand that, don't you?"

"Yes, I do. And after what she had to say today, don't even *think* of asking me to go back."

Elinor seemed to crumple, the air and lightness disappearing. "I know, I know. She is so stubborn and wrong, and if she loses her business *and* Cosmo, I fear for her. Everything that's been building up has finally culminated. A rich man can open up the world for

you, but he can also close it down. Lucile forgot that, I'm afraid."

Tess could not hold back what was
probably a useless, naïve question.
"She's done such arrogant things. But
you are her sister. Do you still love her?"

"Love?" Elinor inhaled, then exhaled
a slow spiral of smoke before answering. "I'm not sure what that means.
People talk a lot about love, and most
of it is rubbish. My sister and I are
bonded, and always will be. We're a
pair, and we understand each other. If
life doesn't offer happy endings, we
know how to manufacture them."

"What do you mean?"

"I've rewritten my life more than
once, you know. And Lucy does the
same thing, only with fabric. Romantic,
ephemeral clothes that create fantasy—
what a lovely way to float through life.
But one has to be quick to change direction in order to make it work. She
isn't quick." Elinor paused, then added
quietly, "Do I love her? Yes."

The two women sat in silence as Farley swung around a corner and drove

past Union Square. Tess stared out the window, recognizing the path where she and Jim had walked when she told him about Jack. Just one more hole in her heart that wouldn't heal.

"What do you want me to do?"

"Just show up for the show. Let the reporters know that the 'secretary' changed her mind and stayed loyal."

"I'm not going back, Elinor. I can't. I may owe Lucile an apology for accusing her of trying to get Jim arrested, but I can't work for her anymore."

"Just for the one day. Please. Don't forget, your sailor got out of that trap."

"How did you know that?"

"Tess, I make a point of knowing *everything*."

Jean Darling's words swam through Tess's head, not quite absorbed yet, looking for a place. Not forgiving, not excusing. This wasn't about forgiving; it was about accepting what couldn't be changed. Offering a helping hand from the lifeboat, perhaps, futile as it might be for both of them.

Did she want Lucile to fail? Yes. She

deserved it. No. It would ruin her life and those of the people who worked for her. One last gesture; maybe it would teach Lucile something. She would move forward from that.

"She'll probably throw me out," she said.

Elinor smiled. "Maybe—thanks for taking the risk. But my bet is you'll save her from full humiliation. By the way, I'm paying the rent on your flat until you're able to do it yourself."

"Is that supposed to be a bribe? You saved it for last." She realized once again that she still liked Elinor.

"I don't do bribes, dear. A waste of time."

------

Pinky sat on the edge of her father's bed, stirring a cup of tepid soup, waiting for him to wake up so she could coax a little food into him. Bad days, good days. This—according to the always complaining Mrs. Dotson—had been a bad day. She wished he would

be up for talking tonight. She needed to talk to someone. Lady Duff's testimony was ludicrous, but it was Jean Darling who made it a smashingly good story. And how did that indictment get dropped? Maybe Jim didn't care, but she did. And what happened when Jim and Tess confronted each other? She dipped a finger delicately into the bowl of soup and tasted it. Chicken broth with carrots, his favorite, but it was getting cold. Why did she feel so weary?

"So here you sit, moping over cold soup."

She jumped. Prescott Wade was awake, a remnant of his familiar grin on his face.

"I'll heat it up," she said,

"Don't bother, I'm not hungry anyway."

"You have to eat."

"So what happened today?"

She told him about the hearing—about Lucile, about Jim. He was actually listening, unlike those many evenings when he drifted away and she ended up talking to herself. She hated

that feeling of being in an echo chamber.

"Whoever got that indictment quashed knew what they were doing," he said, breaking into her recounting. "Maybe somebody worried about what Tess would do. Lucile's sister, the Hollywood gal?"

"Elinor? I don't think so. She's in a different kind of world."

"Who did Tess dump the sailor for?"

She started. He must have heard Jim telling her what happened. "I don't know."

"Has to be someone connected with the hearings or the dress shop. She hasn't been here long enough to meet anyone else."

She sighed, and put the bowl of cold soup down on the table next to her father's bed. "I don't know why I care," she said.

"Work and your feelings are getting all mixed up, aren't they, kid?"

She nodded numbly.

"Well, it's not a crime to lose objectivity, even in our business. Who mat-

ters more to you, Sarah? Jim or Tess? It sounds complicated, and you may have to choose."

His voice was stronger than she expected—and so was her answer. "They're both my friends," she said.

He knew when to stop talking. The two of them sat in silence until Pinky groped for a handkerchief in her skirt pocket and blew her nose with vigor.

"You're shaking the bed," he said, and chuckled.

She flashed him a grin and tucked the handkerchief back into her pocket. "I'll go fix us both a decent dinner," she said, getting up.

"You know what I think?" he said as she started to leave the room. "I think I see your future, Sarah. It's a good one. A happy one."

"What do you see?"

"You're going to put on your hat and travel the world. You're going to dance across the moon. I'll bet on it." His face crinkled into a smile.

"I don't want you gone," she whispered.

"I know, kid. I love you, too." His smile

broadened. "By the way, I have a hunch about who killed that indictment."

"You do?" Startled, Pinky almost dropped the bowl of soup. "Who?"

"You're a good reporter. You figure it out."

# 16

Tess paced the floor of her flat, counting the steps back and forth. Anything to pass the time. Lucile's show would begin with high tea at two in the afternoon, a little early for teatime, but in America it apparently didn't matter. She would show up just before the show began, and who knew how Lucile would react? Was she crazy to have agreed to this?

She stopped pacing and briefly closed her eyes, thinking of what was now going on in that magical loft. The lighting was being adjusted, the cur-

tains arranged, the programs—she had seen the design, and it was quite striking—were being arranged at the door. The music stands—for Lucile's favorite string quartet—were being set up next to the catwalk. All of this, now, today, farther away from her than ever before.

Slowly she looked around her small room, memorizing its contours. Goodbye to all this, and don't waste time feeling sorry for yourself—ups and downs and all that. And there would be work; she would design and stitch and do what she did best. She would be afraid, but she could do it. She sat down on that thought and stared out the window, willing herself to look beyond the obvious: to see what was hidden in the trees, behind the buildings; the small markers of what came next, discreetly etched. Look for them.

------

"Move, move, everybody move!" Lucile clapped her hands, surveying the frenetic activity in her loft, now magically transformed to the House of Lucile,

caught up in the last-minute frenzy of preparation, giddy with pleasure.

"The gowns are *spectacular,*" Elinor murmured as her eye took in the scene.

"Indeed, they are. The mannequins, of course, are American—not quite up to British standards but reasonably sophisticated all the same," Lucile said. "If they only had the discipline to walk for two hours each morning with books balanced on their heads, they would have decent posture, but no, Americans like to slouch." She rolled her eyes, then clapped her hands. At her order, each model obediently strolled the runway, taking a practice turn for Lucile's inspection. Good, lips were rouged properly, hair arranged the way she wanted—then she frowned.

"What happened to the boutonniere I wanted on that girdle?" she demanded of one of the mannequins.

"The flowers were soiled, Madame," the girl answered nervously. "I took them off."

Lucile impaled her on an icy stare. "Then why didn't you speak up so new

flowers could be made? I fear you have no brains in your head. Just feathers."

Elinor tapped her sister on the arm. "Not worth a scene," she said. "You don't want a mannequin crying."

Lucile turned away with a dismissive exclamation, stalking over to the tea tray and picking up each cup for inspection. "These are not clean," she announced loudly.

"They are, Madame. I think you're seeing a slight discoloration," said James quickly. "But we'll have them rewashed immediately."

Lucile returned to her sister, pulling her to a corner of the room. "Is Mary Pickford coming?" she asked in a low voice.

"She promised, for what that's worth," Elinor replied. "She might want something modern—"

"*Why,* for heaven's sake? What is wrong with these actresses? Don't they understand that they look sensual and beautiful in my gowns? Hollywood is so vulgar. Really, Elinor, I don't know how you can live and work there."

Elinor smiled a bit tightly. "It pays,

dear sister. And a vulgar movie star who doesn't bother reading the newspapers is just what you need today."

Lucile deflated instantly, as limp and flat as a punctured balloon.

"I know, I know—I'm just being cruel." Even Elinor couldn't bring up the absence of Cosmo's comforting, supportive presence.

"Is it going to be a disaster?" Lucile asked.

"Not with a little bit of luck." There was no use telling Lucile of the dozens of last-minute invitations hand-delivered last night to second-tier members of New York society. Lucile would scorn many of them, but that was a problem for later. All she needed to do was fill the damn room.

Lucile lifted her chin high. "I will see it through with dignity."

Elinor patted her arm. "Said with a minimum of drama, dear. I'll be here, whatever happens. Remember, no tears. You can't risk swollen eyes today. Not pretty."

------

The sun was high when Tess left her room and walked out to the street to make her way to 160 Fifth Avenue. She would walk slowly and wait within a few yards of Lucile's studio until the clients had arrived. Recognition was not a problem; she was just a name in the papers, no more than that.

"Tess? What are you doing here?"

She turned to see Pinky's astonished face. "Showing up one last time," she said as calmly as she could.

Pinky's eyes widened. "After quitting? You're backing out of that?"

"No." How to explain? "I'm not going to stomp on her. She has too much at stake today."

Pinky looked genuinely baffled. "This is a cruel woman who was ready to ruin Jim. And you're going to support her today?"

"She wasn't the one doing that; it was Cosmo. I'm not here to defend her." Tess wanted Pinky to understand. "I'm paying back a debt, in the only way I can. She brought me here."

"Pretty expensive passage, I'd say."

Tess tried to smile. "I agree. But re-

member what Jean Darling said? Pinky, don't always be a reporter."

"I'm not, that's part of my trouble," Pinky said with a sudden wistful smile. "Tess, I've got news, too. The *World* offered me a job. More money."

"That's wonderful. Aren't you happy?"

"Not really. It's a rag. Well, at least compared to the *Times*."

"But—"

"I know. I don't have much choice."

"Are you sure?"

Pinky was too surprised to answer. They stood together in silence, watching as the first black town car rolled up in front of the House of Lucile. It was half past one o'clock.

"How many? Maybe I've miscounted." Tess hoped she had.

"Ten cars, fifteen women. Plus a few reporters I know, all ready to write about the death of the House of Lucile. How many was she expecting?"

"Over fifty. Please don't rub your hands in glee."

"Look, I hate her pretensions, but I saw how defeated she looked yester-

day. I'm not completely hardened, you know."

"Who is that?" Tess pointed at a woman emerging from one of the automobiles. "She's beautiful."

Pinky followed her gaze to a carefully dressed woman wrapped in a feathery silk coat. "That's Jack Bremerton's *first* ex-wife—big scandal when he divorced her," she said. The statuesque Mrs. Bremerton stood, immobile and queenly, waiting for the doorman to open the door of the building.

Pinky turned and saw the bright flush spreading across Tess's face as she stared at the woman. "Tess?"

Slowly, Tess transferred her gaze back to Pinky. "Sorry, I wasn't paying attention," she said.

More cars were drawing to the curb. A sudden flurry of aides tumbled from them, bowing and murmuring obsequiously, holding out their hands to assist the brightly lipsticked women emerging like gauzy puffs of color from their limousines.

"The stars have arrived," Pinky said,

pulling out her notebook. "I've got to get over there. See you inside."

"Who is it?"

"First one is Pickford. Second one is Duncan, the one with the scarf."

"I didn't think they would come."

Pinky gave her a slightly exasperated look. "With all these reporters here, why wouldn't they show up? What actress wouldn't?" And she was gone, hurrying toward the door as the silver heels of a tiny Mary Pickford disappeared inside.

Tess prepared to enter herself as three more cars drew up and stopped. Several women emerged from each car, straightening hats and tugging at their wraps, then stood somewhat awkwardly on the sidewalk as if awaiting orders.

Just then Elinor emerged from the building, nodded briskly, and ushered them in, whispering instructions. She glanced up, saw Tess, and nodded in the direction of the women.

"Shopgirls hired to fill the room. Are you coming?" she asked with a smile.

Tess nodded, marveling at Elinor's

resourcefulness. She would do anything to get her sister through this. And
if agreeing to show up was some sort
of trap for Tess, it was too late to back
out now.

The loft was transformed. Even
though she had been part of the preparations, Tess felt swept away by the
elegant results. The chiffon-draped
stage was lit from beneath by hidden
spotlights that cast a glow as soft as
candlelight. It was all dazzling and
magical, just as she had known it would
be. To the side, partly hidden, Lucile's
musicians were playing something
beautiful. She wished she knew what it
was. There was so much to learn.

James and a couple of aides were
quietly removing the two back rows of
chairs, the noise masked by the music.
Servants in black dresses and crisp,
white linen aprons were serving tea,
while reporters, including Pinky, stood
along the walls, relegated to the sidelines.

Lucile, dressed in a plum-colored
Grecian tunic, her brilliant red hair piled
high and a queenly smile on her face,

was greeting each guest with just the right combination of warmth and hauteur. Watching her, Tess realized that she was seeing the full magical creation of "Madame Lucile" for the first time.

James spied her, his eyes widening in shock. It occurred to Tess that he might think she was here to cause a disruption. And she might, without intending to, if Lucile, the ever-mercurial Lucile, spotted her and ordered her to leave. She could only hope Elinor was right—that the one thing Lucile craved today was to avoid humiliation.

The musicians paused as Lucile mounted the stage, a spotlight on her determinedly calm face. "My dear friends, you are about to see an *extraordinary* collection; I would venture that it is the best of my career. I am sure you will all agree." She nodded slightly to a secretary holding the all-important order book. Tess knew the message: the secretary was to watch reactions to each gown. After the show, she would quietly approach clients whose interest seemed most likely to

translate into a purchase. Very discreetly, of course.

Elinor, sitting near the front, glanced back at Tess, raising a questioning eyebrow. But Tess couldn't get her legs to move.

"And now—" Lucile lifted her arm, palm up, facing the catwalk. "The first piece in the 1912 spring collection of the House of Lucile! I call this gown, my dear friends, the Sighing Sound of Lips Unsatisfied. Listen to the whispers of the chiffon as it moves, and you will know why it is so named."

A murmur spread among the reporters, punctuated by a titter, but Lucile's guests clapped politely as a mannequin swathed in powder blue strolled out of the shadows, turned slowly to reveal the gown, and then vanished from the stage.

"Next is this lovely tea gown, quite appropriately named a Frenzied Song of Amorous Things," Lucile announced as another mannequin in a shimmery mixture of tulle and brocade took to the catwalk.

The titters from the reporters were

louder this time. Tess winced inwardly. No number of suggestions had deterred Lucile from continuing to name her dresses.

"Could be that dressing gown of hers that went down with the ship," chuckled one reporter, a bit too loudly.

The tiny but regal Mary Pickford lifted a small gloved hand to her lips, as if to suppress a titter herself. Lucile's lips were pulled tight now, her expression still.

Tess could leave her alone up there no longer. Without a thought of what she would do when she got there, she approached the stage.

Lucile glanced swiftly in her direction, her face pale as clear ice. Tess braced for a scene, an order to leave. She was probably walking into a disaster.

But there was no surprise in Lucile's eyes. None. Tess's suspicion was true; this was a programmed drama. Elinor had hatched it with her sister's full knowledge, knowing that nobody got away with surprising Lucile. It was a waste to be indignant, Tess told her-

self. Lucile could get through this now, appearing to be vindicated, and it didn't matter if it wasn't true; it just had to appear to be true—until the show was over.

"My dear friends, I want to introduce to you a promising new young talent whom I have been mentoring," she said, turning toward her seated guests. "And here she is, Tess Collins!"

Again, scattered applause. Close up, Tess could see the lines curving deep across Lucile's brow and the dark shadows under her eyes. Even if she was a pawn here, she could still give Lucile this one last thing. She smiled out at the audience.

Lucile hardly paused. "And just in time, too," she said with a flick of more than triumph. "The next gown you will see, ladies and gentlemen"—her gaze flickered as she glanced at the reporters—"is the creation of Miss Collins. A quite elegant confection in silk—without a name, unfortunately."

The spotlight swung to the catwalk entrance, allowing Tess's surprise to go unnoticed. Elinor had persuaded Lucile

to keep her gown in the show? Lucile surely would have tossed it in a bin. And yet here it was.

The mannequin moved forward, not as languorously as before, the lights dancing off the fabric, deepening its texture. As the model turned, the shortened skirt flipped up, revealing a quick display of skin above her boots. A murmur went through the room, but no titters.

"Miss Collins, tell us about it," Lucile said suddenly. "This is your creation."

Tess looked out at the crowd, hesitating, wondering what she could possibly stammer out. "This is a dress designed to move naturally, that is uninhibiting," she began. "But I wanted it to be practical and modern, so a woman could get out of carriages and motor cars quickly, walk fast on sidewalks; run without tripping over her skirt. Everything is changing, and women's clothes have to change, too." She paused. A few heads nodded slightly, and she felt encouraged. "Within a few years, for example, we won't be fussing with dozens of buttons on our

gowns; we'll have new kinds of clo-
sures, and that's just one thing. But
right now, even though it may seem
daring, we can shorten our skirts. We
don't need to be sedate anymore." Was
she actually saying these things? The
mannequin had completed her turns
and was moving backstage. Tess
watched her go, her critical eye in full
operation. Maybe the bodice worked,
after all. But it was so plain, nobody
would want it. The applause was lively.
She saw in Lucile's face a flash of surprise: the audience actually liked that
boringly simple gown.

"My young student and I will now alternate the introductions," she suddenly
announced. She bowed to Tess, seemingly enjoying her startled look. And
probably also the fact that the rude tit-
tering had stopped.

------

Pinky stirred restively in her seat as the
show progressed. She couldn't think of
a less likely event for her to be covering, apart from the fact that she was

here to follow the drama of it all. Sitting for a couple of hours staring at dresses filled with furbelows and ribbons was not her idea of a good time, although Tess's contribution looked easy and comfortable. She looked around at the women in the room. Hard to believe they could be so fascinated by clothes, of all dreary things. Their faces looked waxen, carefully powdered; their lips various shades of cherry pink. They sat erect, probably held up by corsets.

Her eyes continued to travel around the room, her gaze stopping finally on the tall Mrs. Bremerton, who somehow managed to look totally fascinated and totally miserable at the same time. Getting the combination right must take a lot of practice. Why had Tess looked so upset at the sight of her? Idly, Pinky doodled with her pencil on a copy of the program, then stopped, pencil poised in the air.

Of course. That's who the other man was. It fit. Tess had asked about him, talked about him—and then, not a word. What an idiot she was! Her father had guessed it immediately; he

hadn't lost his sharpness for reporting. For her, it had to hit her in the face. So what did she do with this one? She shifted her gaze to Tess, almost wishing she hadn't figured it out.

-------

The show was almost over. The model wearing the wedding gown—the pièce de résistance of Lucile's design work—swept down the catwalk with full drama, the dress sparkling as its intricate beading danced in the light. A burst of appreciative applause filled the room as Lucile signaled the lights to rise. The quartet, on cue, switched to a livelier tune. The guests began to stir, smoothing down their dresses, chatting in low tones with one another, smiling at Madame Lucile, some with genuine admiration.

With Elinor hovering, Mary Pickford chose one of Lucile's gowns, dictating the changes she wanted in a lightly musical voice. "No tulle under the skirt, please," she instructed. "And would you shorten it—oh, maybe seven or eight

inches? I like shorter skirts." She did not order Tess's dress, but really, that was too much to expect.

After the audience members sipped tea and ate tiny lemon biscuits, effusively thanking Lucile as they drifted toward the door, Tess realized that there had been only two more orders for gowns—one from, of all people, the cool ex-Mrs. Bremerton.

"There will be more orders later," Elinor said at her elbow. "My bet is, someone will order your dress." She sighed. "Still, things are changing. It's in the air, really, and I wish Lucile would heed it. Or at least stop giving her dresses these ridiculous names."

"Why didn't you tell me Lucile was in on this little ruse?"

"That you were coming? My dear, with her volatility, I wouldn't dare leave that to chance. And if I had told you, you wouldn't have come. Anyway, it's just as well; she knows it was a performance."

"And I was one of the players." What did it matter anymore? She could walk away from the deception. But she felt

compelled to offer something else. "I don't think I've fully understood before today how much talent she has. Her gowns are gorgeous, truly beautiful, but, more than that, their structure is so artful."

"It's true," Elinor replied quietly. "But her time is gone."

Slowly Tess walked toward Lucile. Madame was standing straight as a rod of iron at the entrance, chatting brightly in her throaty voice, saying goodbye to the last of her guests, waving the reporters out with a well-manicured hand. For just a moment, after all were gone, she stared after them, her face unreadable.

"Lucile?"

Lucile started, then turned around. "Ah, Tess, now I'll learn your true motives for showing up today." Her bright smile was back in place. "Wasn't this fun? That silly Isadora Duncan, always complaining about gaining weight. But did you notice she didn't hesitate to ask for hot chocolate instead of tea? Really, these actresses. And did you see that poker-faced Mrs. Bremerton?

She obviously came out just fine from her divorce; that's apparent from her pick. There is just so much to do now. We—"

"Lucile, please."

A pause. "Ah, as I suspected. You haven't changed your mind, have you? This was—how best to put it? An *acted* show of support."

"I hear you expected that." Tess felt very calm. "But in another way I'm not acting at all. You didn't know about the scheme to arrest Jim, and I'm sorry I denounced you."

"I don't forgive you, Tess."

"I'm not asking for forgiveness, Lucile."

"You are being outrageously—"

"Rude? Impudent? Arrogant?"

"Beyond your station."

She looked so fierce and, yes, fragile. "I don't work for you anymore," Tess said gently.

"Then why are you here?" Lucile demanded.

"I came back to help you through this day. I want no part of ruining you or your business."

"Well, that's appropriate, I'd say."

"You really are a masterly designer, Lucile. And this is a superb collection."

"I'm glad you realize that."

"I'm sure it will sell."

"Well, it will, of course." Lucile's voice was slightly thin. Suddenly she reached out a hand and rested it on Tess's arm. "Stay with me," she said quickly. "I'll train you, if you want to stay in this country. Or you can come back to England with me. I'll take very good care of you, give you every opportunity. That's a promise."

Slowly but firmly, Tess shook her head. Lucile's nature wouldn't change. It would always be to praise and criticize and goad and condemn, ensnaring everyone into a constant dance of trying to please, running harder, doing anything to please Madame. Not only could she *see* the web; she could *feel* it, and she'd not let its sticky pleasures catch her again.

"We would end up hating each other," she said.

For a long moment, Lucile said nothing. "Well, that's a decision made," she

finally managed. Nothing soggy now. Crisp, crisp as a cracker. "Perhaps you're right."

She patted her hair and began to turn away, then stopped, as if making a decision. She turned, pointing to her office. "Please come into my office—I have something to tell you privately."

There was nothing private about that glass-encased box, although it might seem to be so to a woman who lived always in the public eye. Without comment, Tess followed Lucile.

The door closed. A pungent, slightly acrid smell filled the room, even though the wilted flowers had all been removed. Lucile's desk was a chaotic jumble. Unused invitations, a spilled box of face powder, scissors, even a wad of used chewing gum—one of Lucile's vices, according to Cosmo—wrapped in paper. Lucile seemed to notice none of it. She folded her arms together, turning partially away from Tess, not looking at her as she spoke. "You called me regal once. Remember?"

"Yes, I remember."

"I'm not, of course. I came from a

family as impoverished in its way as yours. I scrabbled up the ladder, dear, breaking a fair number of rules along the way. But I came from nothing to something. I like the taste of success, however unattractive in a woman. Do you understand?"

"Yes."

"Of course, you do. When I met you, you were ready to fight your way up that ladder. I saw me in you." She turned to face Tess squarely. "I lost a child at birth, long ago. She would have been about your age. Am I to lose her again?"

"Are you talking about *me*?" Tess managed, astonished.

"Of course."

Tess tried to regain her voice, but the silence was awkward; she saw that in Lucile's eyes. "I'm sorry you lost your child," she finally said. "I had no idea—"

"I can see that. Well, I thought I would try. But you must know that risking humiliation is not something I do lightly." Lucile began picking at a small tray of tea cakes balanced precariously, amid all the jumble, on the edge of the desk. "I suppose you have reason to be glad

you aren't my daughter. I would have been a terrible mother."

"Lucile, I am truly sorry."

"Never mind, I can see by your reaction that it's done." And yet she made no move to leave the office. She began picking off bits of frosting from a cake, absentmindedly dropping them back on the tray.

"I'm not one who likes to revisit traumatic events, as you know," she said, not quite in control of her voice. "But there is something else to clear up."

"What is that?"

She straightened her shoulders resolutely. "What happened in the lifeboat."

Tess caught her breath and waited.

"I did the exact right thing in ordering those men not to go back, and I stand by that. I don't care what people have to say about an empty boat—one takes care of oneself first." She paused. "There is something, I suppose, to what Jean Darling was saying. About avoiding blame. About the impossibility of forgiving oneself." She waved her hand distractedly. "That kind of hand-wringing isn't for me, but I might as well tell

you, somebody did grab at my leg in the lifeboat. Quite a shocking, frightening thing, really."

"What did you do?" The close air in the room was making Tess faintly ill.

"Will you let me finish? You might want to. I told you, someone grabbed me. I couldn't see who was pawing me." It was almost as if she were talking only to herself now. "I thought it was some clumsy seaman. So I pushed him away, as hard as I could. And then I heard a splash."

Silence. It was several seconds before Tess could respond. "What happened next?" she finally said.

"I called for assistance, of course. He grabbed at me again, and one of the men pushed him away."

"With an oar?"

"Yes."

"My God, Lucile."

"I don't know who did it, if that's your next question. It was dark."

The convenience of night. "You must have some idea."

"If you're asking if it was Cosmo, I could hardly believe *that*. And you'll be

happy to know it wasn't your sailor, because he got up and fought the man who was trying to help me. Almost capsized us. I've told you all I know."

"Why didn't you say all this when you testified?"

"Are you serious? I would be accused of murder." Lucile began pacing. "I wasn't the only one," she said. "You stand there, looking so shocked; why did I tell you this? There were other . . . splashes, but I could see nothing. We wanted to survive—what is wrong with that? What are you going to do now? Tell the world?"

"Oh, Lucile." She wanted to cry and scream at the same time.

Lucile's voice was rising, her words coming faster. "Why are those of us who survived to blame? Did we cause that calamity? Do you remember what it was like to watch that ship go down? My God, I couldn't believe it. Tipped onto its bow like a toy, a toy of nature, a sight like none anyone has seen, and we're supposed to come out of it unscathed? Go back to civility, men tipping their hats to women, saying 'after

you' when getting into the lifeboats—
what a joke! If there is a God, surely he
was amused—how stupid are we to
sail the ocean on something built out of
toothpicks? *We* were the toys! What is
going on in this world?"

And with that cry she stopped pacing. "I find it hard to believe that I was
the only one pushing him away, but
maybe I was."

"You weren't trying to kill the man."

"Of course not. I simply didn't want
to be touched. At least, that's what I
tell myself." Her back was to Tess now.
That proud, rigid spine, straight—in-
flexible.

"There was no time to think," Tess
managed.

"Yes, yes, but you notice, of course,
that I never told anybody. My character
wasn't any stronger than Jean's."

"So why *are* you telling me?"

"Oh, just to clear the air, I suppose.
Things always have been a bit murky
between you and me."

"Complicated," Tess said softly.

Lucile turned at that and gave her a
quick, hard smile. "My dear, *all* my re-

lationships are complicated. Good luck to you."

Tess was suddenly blinking back tears. "You brought me here," she said. "You gave me a chance. You pointed the way, and I thank you for that."

"Oh, for goodness' sake, don't get weepy. Really, that's enough. Goodbye, Tess."

"Lucile—"

But Lucile turned to the door, opened it, and walked away, leaving Tess in midsentence.

"James!" she cried out, clapping her hands angrily. "Where are you? Get somebody to clean up that tea table, will you? And let's get these curtains down tonight. Isn't anybody going to do any work around here except me?"

Tess left the office, walking slowly toward the elevator and Elinor, who was waiting at the door.

"So she told you what happened," Elinor said calmly. "She did say this morning she wanted the chance to do that."

"Maybe she's blaming herself for something she couldn't have done on

her own. She couldn't have had the power to push that man off the boat."

"She told me it was Tom Sullivan who wielded the oar."

"On Cosmo's order? Or hers?"

"We'll never know. My guess? That sneaky oaf did it on his own. See how we piece our stories together? To redeem ourselves, I suppose."

"Why did she want me to know?"

"She decided after listening to Jean Darling's testimony. Said it was something she had to do. I know she didn't ask you to keep this private, but I hope you will."

Tess could only nod. Another choice.

"By the way, Lucile asked me to give you this." Elinor held out a small velvet bag and put it in Tess's hand. "She called it a memento. Something about keeping you safe and soothing the heart. She said you would know what she meant."

Tess slowly undid the strings, her eyes stinging. The moonstone earrings.

"Please don't say you can't take them—please don't do that to her."

Tess slowly nodded again. "Thank her for me," she said.

"I hope you know she's dreadfully sad about losing you."

"There was much more I wanted to say."

"So did she, I suspect." Elinor sighed for a second time. "But what is done is done. You read the future right, if that's any consolation. My sister can't change. Do you have any plans? What are you going to do?"

"I don't know."

"Well, good luck. You know you're in a small category of people—you survived Lucile." Elinor said this almost tenderly, taking the harshness out of her words. "Stay in touch, and if you ever need any help look me up. That is, if you ever get out to California." She paused. "I'll speak to a few people about finding you a job. I hear the one who calls herself Coco Chanel is hiring. Moving beyond hats quite quickly. You obviously have a future in—what is that expression Lucile hates? I remember— the 'rag trade.'"

Tess smiled. "I'm still very good at

buttons, though they'll soon be out of date."

"Follow up—it's a start, anyway. Oh, before I forget—" She pulled an envelope from her bag. "This came for you yesterday."

Tess's heart leapt when she looked at the handwriting, each letter so carefully, painstakingly drawn. So her messages home got through. She pictured her mother squinting under the light of a candle as she wrote. Home, a connection to home. She tucked the letter into her pocket to read later, when she was alone.

She stepped into the elevator, catching a last glimpse of Lucile pacing the aisles of the shop, her hair slightly askew, giving orders right and left as the elevator doors closed.

Just as she had begun to understand, it was over. Her thoughts flashed back to the grand woman who had walked the deck of the *Titanic* as if she owned the world. Madame Lucile. Walking beside her, hearing the silky rush of awed whispers left in her wake. Do you know who that is? The most famous,

the best, couturiere in the world. To wear her clothes was to be at the pinnacle. And it had all dissolved—all a fantasy.

Tess closed her eyes, opening them only as the doors drew apart on the ground floor. No one hovered—no yelling reporters, no clients. She stepped out of the elevator, feeling herself leaving one dream and entering another. The only reality of the moment was her mother's letter.

17

Pinky stood on the sidewalk, looking uncharacteristically diffident as Tess stepped out of the building. All the society guests had vanished, but there were still clusters of hired shopgirls waiting for the town cars, bubbling with giggles about the posh event to which they had been invited at the last minute, with payment, no less.

"You stayed," Tess said with a rush of gratitude.

"Oh, I thought maybe I'd wait for you. Didn't think you were going to hang

around up there. Want to come to my place for dinner?"

Maybe it was the kindness of the offer, maybe she would have let go anyway, but the tears came.

Pinky looked a little alarmed, but that didn't stop her from awkwardly patting Tess on the back. "I can't say I understand what you were trying to do, but you gave better than she deserved," she said.

"I had to give back something. I owe her a great deal."

"Was it hard to walk out again? Were you tempted to stay?"

Tess shook her head. "No. I'm not making those compromises anymore."

"You don't have to tell me; I can see how she eats everybody up. But your dress looked nice."

Tess managed a shaky smile; any fashion comment from Pinky had to be a novelty.

"I'm wondering why you got all flustered when you saw Mrs. Bremerton," Pinky ventured. "Something was happening, and I think I know what." Maybe that was too blunt, but there it was, out

in the open. Things were always better out in the open. Most of the time, anyway.

"You're a good observer," Tess said.

For an awkward moment, neither of them spoke.

"I don't know what you're doing tomorrow, but would you like to come to the suffragist parade? It starts in Washington Square, under the arch. Have you seen it yet? It's a beautiful arch." Changing the subject was not Pinky's strength, and she was stumbling over her words now in a rush. "Remember I told you about the white horse? It's beautiful, and the woman riding it has this incredible long hair, so it will be very dramatic; photographers like that. I'm hoping for the front page. Especially if the women raising money for a memorial to the men of the *Titanic* show up. They're furious because the suffragists are saying the *Titanic* women shouldn't have been so quick to let the men die instead of themselves. Quite a juicy little story."

"Pinky, it was chaotic," Tess said

wearily, not wanting to relive it all once more.

"Well, equality cuts all ways. Everything gets political, that's all I know. So there will be jeers and jokes, but it's a good thing when women pull together."

"Thank you, I'll think about it," Tess said. Suddenly she envied Pinky. It was easy for her, seeing everything so simply; it must be comfortable to be so confident of choices.

"Why Bremerton instead of Jim?" Pinky said unexpectedly.

"It's not like that. They're very different."

"What does that mean?"

"Are you asking as a reporter or as a friend?"

Pinky had already decided, somewhere around the time that fancy wedding dress upstairs floated past her stupefied vision. "A friend," she said.

"Jack is—" She groped for the right words. "He's a magical man from a magical world."

Pinky looked honestly puzzled. "Where do you go with that?"

"That's what I'm trying to decide."

"Well, he's rich and must be in love with you, so I guess you think you'd be crazy to pass him up. I suppose you want to get married. I thought about that once, and there was this man. . . ." Pinky's voice turned wistful. "But I couldn't do it. I don't want marriage— I'd feel like a mouse in a trap."

"It doesn't have to be like that."

"Usually it does." Pinky wasn't sure how to tell Tess what she couldn't bear to lose: the thrill of walking into a room, knowing that, as a reporter, she carried an identity that commanded attention, if not respect, knowing the job shielded her from being dismissed or ignored, knowing it gave her access to such a wide variety of worlds, even though sometimes they scared her. "I couldn't give up my job for anything," she said.

"You have, and that's brave."

"What are you saying?"

"You gave up your job for Jim." And this time Pinky had the sense to say no more. She had seen the look on both their faces yesterday.

The two women stood in silence for a long moment.

"I've got a big chicken ready to go in the oven," Pinky finally said shyly.

"Thank you. But not tonight. I have things I have to do." Impulsively, Tess hugged her.

"Maybe I'll see you tomorrow?" Pinky asked.

"Maybe."

"If you come, it'll mean something."

"Oh? What would it mean?"

"Just an instinct. Bye, Tess." Pinky turned and walked slowly up the block in the direction of her office, wondering if she was right or wrong. And maybe it wasn't true that she would give up anything that threatened her job. That didn't make her safer. Maybe the only thing that mattered was giving up the idea that there was a place to hide. She inhaled deeply; maybe it was time for her to take a risk. Tess had.

------

Van Anda eyed Pinky as she made her way across the newsroom to his desk. Even with plenty of practice, he couldn't quite read her mood. She had lost a

little of her bounce lately, and he knew the signs—she was getting bored with the *Titanic* beat. But hell, she was still churning out great stories.

"So, what've you got for me from the fashion show?" he said with a grin, but she didn't seem to be in a joking mood.

"They had to pack the room with women salesclerks to make it look respectably full," she said. "Not a good day for the House of Lucile."

"How much can you give me? And get something in there about the clothes, for God's sake. Women want that."

"There was a nice yellow dress. Silk."

"You have an eye for fashion, I see."

It was their usual comfortable back-and-forth. But Pinky couldn't leave it at that, not today. "Carr, the *World* offered me a job."

Van Anda straightened fast, his chair creaking under him. "Job? What sort of job? They don't use women."

She stared him in the eye. "Yes, I know. Just good reporters."

Van Anda cursed silently; he had flubbed that one. "They can't have of-

fered you much. You're not considering this, are you? You'd be crazy to leave the *Times*."

There it was, her opportunity. All the way back from Lady Duff's loft, she had been rehearsing what she would say. She could do anything—dive into any story, ask any outrageous question, pursue a lead or a source with total persistence—and she didn't give up until she got what she wanted. She was proud of what she did, and proud of how she did it. She was all of this. And she had the respect of other reporters and her editor. So what was tying her tongue?

"Look, maybe you need a break from disaster stories. I can put you on a team investigating the mayor's cronies— some good stuff there. We—"

"I want a raise."

"What?"

"I want more money. I deserve it."

"You get good money, for this business."

"The typesetters get fifty cents an hour, and I get less." She smiled at his

expression. "Didn't think I knew that, did you?"

Van Anda groaned, leaning forward. "Pinky, you're a smart woman. But things are tight in this business right now."

"They're always tight."

"I wish I could help you on this." She had to be bluffing—she would never leave the *Times*. No sane reporter would leave the classiest paper in the city.

But her courage was growing. "I want a raise. I want a dollar an hour."

"You've got to be kidding." Van Anda was stalling now. Lose one of his best reporters? Not a good idea. "Why don't we talk a few months from now, and I'll see what I can do."

Pinky tried to swallow past the dryness in her throat. Here she was, walking the plank, sawing it off behind her. "No, sir, I need a raise *now*."

Van Anda leaned back in his chair, staring at her. "You would actually go work for that rag?"

She thought of her father, of her constant money dance with Mrs. Dotson. "Yes."

"Go write your story; let me think about this."

"I would rather settle it now. Get that off my mind, which will let me write a better story."

Here she stood, demanding to be paid almost the same as his other reporters and, truth be told, she was worth it. That much money for a woman? It wasn't done. But times were changing. Lord, who knew what was next with women like this. She wasn't backing down, or smiling, or trying to win him over. She was setting the bar. Amazing.

"What are they offering you?"

"A dollar an hour."

"Jesus, where do they get the money?"

"Beats me."

"Okay, kid. Seventy-five cents an hour. Best I can do."

"One dollar."

They stared at each other. If there was ever a time when she mustn't break eye contact, it was now.

Van Anda threw his pencil down on

the desk. "Okay, one dollar. You better be worth it."

She grinned wide, but her legs were trembling. "You already know I am, Carr."

"Yep. Do me a favor, will you? Keep this under your hat or all the men will want more money, too." He was scratching his ear, looking a bit shocked at himself; they would joke about it later, maybe tomorrow.

Pinky sailed back to her desk, humming. She had done it; she had good news to bring home to her father. Forget the chicken. Tonight it would be fresh corn and a flank steak. Today, she felt she could see the future. It was all right. And she would, as her father said she would, somehow, herself, someday, dance on the moon. Or, at least, see Africa.

------

The solid click of the lock on her apartment door was an incredible relief. Alone, Tess sank into a chair and pulled her mother's letter from her pocket.

Just the sight of the familiar handwriting gave her a sudden longing for home, so much so that the first words on the page were shocking:

**My dear daughter,you've survived a terrible tragedy, but above all, don't think about coming home.**

She read on, her hands holding the paper so tightly, it almost tore:

**You have done a brave thing, and I want you to find your place in that new world of New York, whatever it might be. We both know that if you were here you'd be cleaning parlors and mending dresses for the rest of your life. I lie in bed at night staring at the ceiling and trying to imagine what it must be like. I can almost imagine it being me.**

There was more, mainly news about her father and her brothers and sisters,

and about the neighbors and the price of cheese and meat and the bad year for potatoes. She read eagerly, starved for the plainness of her past life. And then at the end:

**I've told you to look for opportunity, dear Tess. Keep your head up, not down. Don't settle for safety. Push forward—you are not foolish to try.**

Tess folded the letter smooth, staring at it on the table in front of her.

*You are not foolish to try.*

Try for what? Jack would open the whole world for her. Not only that, he could help her open up the world for her mother. To think of it, to think of her mother freed of the grinding labors of her life, of having some ease and comfort, was overwhelming.

What an extraordinary thing to have a man like that love her. It made her feel valued in a way she had never known, as if she danced inside a fairy tale. She had dreamed about him, and had then found herself gently enfolded

into his version of the world. But perhaps the same had been true of the second Mrs. Bremerton. And the first.

She could allow herself to think of Jim, too. To remember the energy and excitement of life bursting from him, surrounding her, making her laugh and dream and think—that's what he represented. Not security, just hope.

There was no more time to avoid the only question that mattered. Why was she thinking of choosing a man who could make her whole? How could she do that when she didn't yet know who she was in this new world?

She stood and walked over to the dresser, where she had placed Jim's lifeboat, picking it up, tracing its lines and curves with her finger, wondering suddenly if it would float. She carried it to the washbasin, drew water, and placed it gently inside. It rocked a bit on its slightly rounded bottom, then moved forward, bumping against the side of the basin. How skillfully it had been carved. She thought of Jim's deft fingers, his excitement when he took her to the carpentry shop. She waited.

Why did this matter? It didn't, of course. But it did float. And she found herself yearning to hope.

------

The sky was fully dark when she knocked on the door of Jack Bremerton's office. She waited, it seemed for a long time, before she heard the rattle of the chain inside as it was unhooked.

The man named Mr. Wheaton— Jack's secretary—opened the door, his eyes widening. "He isn't expecting you."

"I know, but I have to talk to him."

"Oh, dear." He hesitated, as if debating whether to let her in. "Well, he's not here at the moment, but please come in. He's with Mr. Ford at dinner. Is something wrong?" He was watching her carefully.

"I do need to talk to him, Mr. Wheaton."

"Of course. Would you like a sherry?" He moved to a sideboard, picked up a crystal decanter, and poured a glass of the wine-red liquid, giving a quick little bow as he handed it to her. "You mean

a great deal to him, you know. I do hope nothing is wrong."

Tess sipped the sherry, wishing Jack would appear. She didn't want to talk with Wheaton, not now.

"I'm happy to hear the seaman who rowed Lifeboat One escaped the trap set by the Duff Gordons," he said.

"It was a great relief," she replied in surprise. She wondered how he knew.

Wheaton turned and placed the decanter on the sideboard. He seemed to make a sudden decision. He looked at her, his features sharpening. "You know who arranged that, I presume?"

It took a second or two before she realized what he was telling her. "It was Jack?"

"Yes."

"Oh, my goodness." He had done that for her. He had saved Jim from shame and trouble. He had done that, taking a burden of worry from her shoulders. The fact that he was powerful enough to do it so quickly was amazing. What an act of tremendous charity.

"He doesn't want you to know."

"Why?" she asked. She wished he would come in the door right now, this minute, so that she could thank him to his face immediately.

"He didn't want it to influence you. He didn't want you to marry him because you were—grateful. It wouldn't be enough."

"No, it wouldn't."

"I'm guessing by your manner why you're here. I realize Jack is impulsive and all this has happened quickly. But I must say, if you have concerns he is a fine, upstanding man."

"I know that—I truly have never doubted it," she said.

Together they heard the click of the lock on the front door.

"Goodbye, Miss Collins." Wheaton smiled faintly and disappeared through another door, closing it gently behind him.

And now Jack was standing in front of her. He blinked, startled, then seemed to know, without a word being spoken, why she was there.

"Let me hold you first," he said.

"I can't, I just have to say it."

"No, I will. You aren't going to marry me."

"You are an amazing, quite wonderful man. But no, I can't."

"Why not?"

"I don't feel what I want to feel." It hurt to say it; his eyes widened.

He strode to the sideboard and poured himself a glass of sherry. His voice, though still relaxed, had an edge. "Tess, I love you. I will make you happy, you can do anything. There's plenty of money. I told you, if you want a design shop, I will give you one. What do you want? I'll get it for you. I want to spoil you."

Tess's thoughts flew to Cosmo and Lucile. "I don't want to be spoiled."

"It's perfect, you and me. Where is your courage?"

"I'm trying to exhibit some now."

"Go ahead, then. I'm listening."

There was no way to express her doubts gently. "I feel borne along on your enthusiasm and certainty, but it isn't real enough for me."

Jack seemed back in total control of himself. "Tess, do you think I'm under

any illusions about the source of your attraction to me? May I say it bluntly, dear? It's all right to want money and security; women have their reasons for marrying older, established men. It's the way the world works." He flashed one of his calm, wry smiles. "We each have our bargaining chips."

"I wonder if we both are acting on what we *want* to be real. You've had two wives already." She thought of the first Mrs. Bremerton, standing at Lucile's doorway, as hard and contained as a marble statue.

He blinked. "That's cruel of you. I can't undo my past mistakes."

She swallowed. "You might eventually want a fourth one."

"So *that's* what this is all about."

"The fear of that might make me become someone different. But that's not why, Jack. It's much more."

"What *matters*? What matters besides us? I adore you. What more do you want?"

What more, indeed? She would have comfort beyond her dreams. But not to be able to give back in similar mea-

sure—to love him equally—would leave an emptiness that couldn't be filled. And then, eventually, she wouldn't try. She would take; she wouldn't give. She would be left with a tepid heart.

"To be wholly myself first," she whispered.

"If we all waited for that, we'd do nothing."

"I want to try."

His eyes wavered. He rubbed a hand through his hair as he drained the glass, then stood and stared at the wall. "Well, at least you're telling me to my face. I tend not to do that in my life. So there's my character flaw, dear. I'm a coward. But good at chess."

"Jack, you saved Jim, and I thank you for that from the bottom of my heart. It was a selfless act."

"That damn Wheaton!"

"I'm glad I know."

"Well, it wasn't selfless. I just wanted you, with unencumbered emotions. It was the easiest way to guarantee it. And I suspect Jim has something to do with your change of heart."

"Yes, he does. But he doesn't know it."

"Well, perhaps you should let him know."

"I'm afraid it's too late for that."

His reply was almost kind. "Perhaps not."

"In a way, it doesn't matter." She could tell that he didn't understand, so she switched the subject. "Why did you do something so enormously generous?"

"Because I like having the power to get what I want—that's what it's about. I enjoy winning. It was just one more thing I could do."

"I don't believe it's only that."

He sighed. "All right, Tess. I don't like people like the Duff Gordons who casually ruin other people's lives, and I'm happy to thwart them. And I don't like companies like White Star. Lord knows, I've made a lot of money off their kind, but that doesn't mean I believe their delusions. When they get in trouble, they'll offer up anybody to save themselves. Here's the joke—companies like White Star end up believing their own

boasts. World's grandest ship, inde-structible—that kind of thing. That's when they get in trouble. And they don't see it. So they do it again and again. And people like me find ways to profit."

"That sounds—very American."

"It is. Look," he added slowly, "you're afraid I'll get restless and move on; that's what my wives said. You could change that."

"Not by myself."

"Maybe that's what I wanted most. Your faith in me. It's obviously not there." He looked at her sadly, tenderly. "You are so fresh and young, my dear. Perhaps I would kill that with my own cynical take on life."

There was nothing more to say. They stood apart, strangely relieved, without grief. "I wish you well," she said. "Jack, I'm trying to be the person I believe I am, because if I don't do that, if I play a role, any role, I'll end up making us both unhappy."

"Like the famous Lucile?"

"Perhaps."

He let out an almost derisive snort.

"She certainly proved a powerful role model."

Tess turned to go. She had done it, snipped her second lifeline in this new country. Yet there was no uncertainty, no anguish, just that same pervasive sadness that had taken her out of Lucile's loft and brought her here.

"What made up your mind?"

"My mother, in part. Mostly my own common sense."

He paused, absorbing her words. "And I don't fit into that." He raised a hand when she started to reply. "I guess that proves I can't start making more out of my life by shaping yours." He moved forward, giving her a gentle, brief embrace. "Goodbye, Tess."

She hugged him back. "Goodbye, Jack." She opened the door, then squeezed the knob tightly as she closed it behind her.

------

The morning was cloudy, with a soft wind blowing, bending the fragile tulips that grew in clusters along the edge of

the flower beds at Union Square. Tess, her loose hair blowing in the wind, gazed across the park to the short, nondescript building that held Jim's woodworking shop. She had no reason to think she would see him, and certainly no intention of approaching him, but somehow she had found herself here, waiting for something to come clear. Perhaps she was just here to say a silent goodbye. She would soon know.

And then she saw him. His lanky figure, slightly hunched forward, his gait loose and springy—a young man hurrying toward his future. She couldn't make out his features under his cap, but she knew that man, those hands. I know how he feels, she told herself. Everything is open; everything is possible. How can I interfere with that?

As he reached the shop, he turned in her direction. She lifted her arm and waved slowly.

For a few seconds he stood still, poised on the step. Then he lifted his hand and waved back; waved for a long, sweet moment. Then he turned, disappearing into the shop.

So it was, indeed, goodbye.

She made her way toward Washington Square Park, inhaling the sweet smells of spring in the air. Her step was steady. Everything was ahead.

------

The park was a sea of patriotic color, with flags of red, white, and blue waving amid an array of women dressed in dazzling white. Tess walked through the crowd, amazed at the energy and excitement. Women were pushing wicker prams with swaddled, bored-looking babies in them, while others laughed and shouted to one another, some of them singing songs she had never heard. They all wore hats—silk bonnets, straw boaters—and banners across their chests proclaiming VOTES FOR WOMEN. One group was raising a large sign, a sheet inked with the words WE DEMAND EQUALITY. How many were here? Pinky's story had said this morning they expected twenty thousand people, women from the home, the the-

ater, women's clubs; even Quakers would be on the march.

She looked around, craning her neck to see above the crowd, and spotted a graceful stone arch. This must be what Pinky had been talking about. Getting to it was taking some elbowing. "You going to the tallyho parade, lady?" shouted a man cheerfully as she tried to squeeze by him. "All the way up Fifth Avenue? You ladies have the strength for that?"

It was a carnival. Breathtaking. All this activity for the vote? Young girls in pinafores were running around with canvas newsbags selling suffrage magazines or twirling parasols with WE WANT THE VOTE scrawled across their cotton surfaces. Young men stood on the sidelines, poking one another and laughing.

Tess's eye was caught by one small knot of women, looking quite grim, waving a banner that read YOU DISHONOR OUR BRAVE MEN. A woman in a gray serge coat was shouting at a stout suffragist in white. As Tess moved closer, she

saw that the woman in white was Mrs. Brown.

"How could you betray us by supporting these people?" yelled the woman in gray. "You were with us on that ship! What was wrong with saving women and children first?" Her voice spiraled into the wail that was so familiar to Tess; remembering it made her shiver.

"Honey, it cuts both ways," Mrs. Brown replied in a firm voice. "We had good men and some rotten ones. Same for women—don't get your bloomers in such a frenzy."

That only provoked more shouting. Another woman in white thrust her face full at the woman in gray. "Accepting male chivalry just weakens us," she said urgently. "Don't you understand?"

Mrs. Brown spotted Tess and gave her a hug. "Well, dearie, now you're seeing how we do things in America," she said. "I kind of wish my suffrage friends had left this particular argument for equality off the books. It's cutting down on the numbers today." With a

wave, she began to drift back into the crowd.

"Tess! Tess!"

Pinky had spotted her, and was jumping up and down to get her attention. "You came!" She elbowed through the crowd and grabbed Tess's hand. "Isn't this incredible?" she said. "Everybody is here—mothers and housewives, milliners, librarians, social workers, laundry workers. Tess, everybody is for it; we're going to get the vote!"

"I've never seen so many different kinds of women in one place," Tess said. She briefly wondered how they had all been able to get permission to leave their jobs for the march.

"We've got Chinese women here. Their feet are bound when they're babies and they can barely hobble around, so they will ride in a carriage. But *they* can vote in their country—what do you think of that?" Pinky pointed in the direction of a carriage covered in flowers. "Our oldest suffragist is ninety-four; she'll ride in that. And we've got thousands of men joining us. Isn't that something?"

Tess nodded, not trying to talk above the din.

"We're organizing now. Come over here—I want to show you the white horse. I get my chance to ride it before we start; it'll be a good picture for the *Times*."

"Who rides it in the parade?"

"A woman lawyer, believe it or not."

Pinky was greeted exuberantly as she joined the crowd around the horse. "Your turn, Pinky!" someone shouted.

Tess reached out to stroke the animal's nose. It was a beautiful mare, tall and strong, with intelligent eyes, as dazzlingly white as the dresses on the women gathering for the march. Its gaze seemed to rest on her, offering pride. She liked that.

"Up you go!"

Pinky, helped by two other women, swung herself up into the saddle. She felt filled with excitement, and it wasn't just because of her chance to play this little part in history. Last night she had feared that Tess was about to vanish, but something had changed even as

they talked. She had felt it then; she knew it now.

She clutched the saddle horn, feeling strong and powerful. She could see everything from up here. "This is wonderful!" she shouted, scanning the crowds fanning out throughout the square.

"Be sure to hold on," Tess said.

"Hold on? I want to gallop around the park!" She glanced down at Tess. "Come on, you've got to get up here." She slid her way down the flank of the horse and jumped to the ground. She grabbed Tess and put the reins in her hands. "Climb on!"

"Why not?" Tess said, laughing. And up she went, swinging her leg over the back of the magnificent animal, pulling herself tall.

The view was breathtaking. Her gaze swept out across the splendid, exciting square. Yes, she could see the horizon, the view so much more sweeping than she had expected. She saw now what Jim had seen, what had been there all the time. So much to do and know, and yes, she could do this.

And then she saw something else. A familiar figure, cap pushed back, walking toward her. She saw him moving closer, saw those clear, blue eyes. She heard a laugh—whose? Her own. And it was all right. She could be right or wrong, but her vow to herself was clear now. She would be strong and not always too careful, not settle for a smaller life, and face what was true.

What was true? Perhaps it was here, staring her in the face.

"May I help you down?" Jim said. He was standing beneath her now, his hands on the bridle, looking up, his eyes alight.

Palms up, arms stretched out, she reached toward him.

"Yes," she said.

Much of the testimony in this book is taken directly from the transcripts of the U.S. Senate hearings in the aftermath of the sinking of the *Titanic.*

The basic bones of the story are true: Lady Duff Gordon, a world-famous designer, escaped with her husband and secretary in a lifeboat that, according to various reports, could have held between forty and fifty people instead of only twelve. She adamantly opposed going back for survivors. Cosmo Duff Gordon did offer the crewmen money— whether as a bribe to obey his wife's demands or as an act of gratitude, no one really knows.

Cosmo and Lucile were vilified in the

press on both sides of the Atlantic. Although in my story Lucile testifies in the United States, she and Cosmo actually escaped that ordeal. However, they drew heavy attacks when they were forced to testify in England.

The public scorn and ridicule took a toll.

In the aftermath of the hearings, the House of Lucile—yes, she did give romantic names to her gowns—began its long decline, and Sir Cosmo and Lady Duff Gordon eventually separated.

Senator William Alden Smith delivered his final, emotional report on the U.S. *Titanic* hearings in a crowded Senate chamber on May 18, 1912. At the heart of the disaster, he said, was a reckless "indifference to danger" at several key points.

He listed them: The *Titanic* was moving too fast through an iceberg field. The crew was inexperienced. There were no binoculars on board. Wireless communication was inadequate. There had been no lifeboat drills, and there were not enough lifeboats for all the people on the *Titanic*.

He successfully urged Congress to pass legislation that would mandate sufficient lifeboats on all ships.

And the great Margaret Brown—later remembered as the "unsinkable Molly Brown"—was a true oar-wielding heroine of the *Titanic.*

All else is fiction, with the exception of a puzzle at the heart of this tragedy for which there is no single answer: why did only one lifeboat make an attempt to save those dying in the water? It is on that question that my story is built.

And finally, Millvina Dean, the last survivor of the *Titanic,* died at the age of ninety-seven on May 31, 2009. This was exactly ninety-seven years to the day after the *Titanic* was launched from Belfast.

*Kate Alcott*

## ABOUT THE AUTHOR

KATE ALCOTT is a journalist who has covered politics in Washington, DC, where she currently lives.

**About the Editor**

EDGAR LEON NEWMAN is Associate Professor of History at New Mexico State University, Las Cruces. He has previously edited *Proceedings of the First and Eighth Annual Meetings of the Western Society for French History* and has written articles for the *Journal of Modern History* and *Nineteenth-Century French Studies*.

## ACKNOWLEDGMENTS

Good friends read and read . . . how many versions? My thanks to you all— Ellen, Irene, Judy, Linda, Margaret, and my sister, Mary.

Esther, you are a stand-out, stand-up friend and agent. And Melissa, your ideas and enthusiasm were just what a writer hopes for from a good editor.

And Frank, you gifted me with my magnificent replica of the *Titanic,* betting mine wouldn't sink. Thank you.

*To Frank, always.*

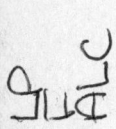
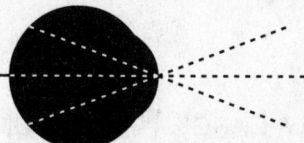

*The Dressmaker*

A NOVEL

KATE ALCOTT

DOUBLEDAY LARGE PRINT HOME LIBRARY EDITION

DOUBLEDAY
NEW YORK    LONDON    TORONTO
SYDNEY    AUCKLAND

was during routine combatives training. I could show you a scar on my elbow where I had to have surgery because of something he did. I would never say a cross word to the man otherwise, because he's the finest commander this country currently has. Of course, I'm biased.

Kurt shook my hand and apologized for interrupting the team's training. I shrugged it off. "Thanks for throwing in the trailer. It caused a little high adventure."

Kurt grinned and said, "You guys need a wrinkle every once in a while. A few more days and you'd have figured out what he was doing."

"We didn't wait. We took him down. Would have had both targets if you hadn't paged."

"You took him down? He just entered the exercise today. Where is he?"

"In the parking garage."

Kurt was flabbergasted. "Jesus, Pike! You brought him here?"

I held up my hands. "Sir, don't worry. He's blindfolded in the back of a van inside a dog kennel. He has no idea where he is."

Kurt turned to one of the men with him and barked out instructions. I watched him get the van keys from Bull, then scurry out of the room. The way I was looking at it, *Return ASAP* meant get my ass here as soon as possible, so I wasn't too upset at the breach in security. Kurt knew me pretty well, so he

45

shouldn't have been too surprised. More like business as usual.

Years ago, Kurt had been my first troop commander at a Special Mission Unit on Fort Bragg, and pretty much kept me from letting my arrogant attitude get me fired. He looked past the arrogance to the raw talent, and while everyone else wanted to get rid of me as trouble, he managed to channel my energy until I had sloughed off the bad and kept the good. Well, mostly.

Kurt shook his head and said, "We'll talk about this later. Have a seat."

After getting the team's attention, Kurt said, "Sorry for cutting your culmination exercise short, but there's been a significant change to the mission profile. Your target, Mustafa Abu Azzam, is currently traveling to Tbilisi, Georgia. This is his third trip, and, yes, he has always returned to Jordan, but we think we've finally figured out what he's been doing in Tbilisi. Intelligence indicates that he's been attempting to purchase a quantity of radioactive waste from some contacts in Chechnya. Apparently, he's been successful, and is planning on conducting the transaction within the next few weeks."

He paused to let that sink in, then continued. "Now, obviously, Azzam getting material for a dirty bomb isn't something we can allow, so things have sped up a bit. We can't be sure he'll return to Jordan with the material, so we have to stop him before he gets it, which is where you come in."

I didn't have to be told why we were the ones who were going to Tbilisi instead of the team in Jordan. The cover plan used by Johnny's team, the same cover plan that we were going to fall in on, was specifically built for that region of the world, down to a particular commercial sector in a specific city. The cover wouldn't transfer to Tbilisi without a significant chance of compromise.

"What's our status in Tbilisi? We've all been prepped for Jordan."

Blaine answered, "Alias shop is working that now. Luckily, we had built a plan for Tbilisi, so we just need to dust it off. Your new documents will be ready by the time you fly."

Knuckles spoke up. "What sort of support package can we expect? We haven't done any infrastructure development in Tbilisi. Seems we're going to be running the ragged edge on this."

"Believe it or not, we're sitting pretty good. We began some preliminary infrastructure development on Azzam's first trip to Tbilisi as a precaution, so we aren't starting from ground zero. The support team that was flying to Jordan tonight will divert to Tbilisi. You'll have a complete package."

I cut to the chase, asking the question on everyone's mind. "Are we at Omega now?"

47

Kurt said, "No, not officially. Since the target's changed location, I have to brief the Oversight Council tomorrow, but I can't wait on their approval to get your team moving. Worst case, I should have an answer before you land. Given the ramifications of what he's trying to do, I see no issue."

The Taskforce called each stage of an operation a different Greek letter, starting with Alpha for the initial introduction of forces. Being at Omega — the last letter in the Greek alphabet, symbolizing the end — meant we were ready to execute the mission. The missions themselves could take anywhere from three months to a year. Getting to Omega was hard work, with an enormous infrastructure behind it. There were generally three or four different missions canceled for every one that made it to Omega. It was the crown jewel of our profession, the gold at the end of the rainbow.

"Good enough," I said. "When do we leave?"

Kurt said, "Well, your team'll be flying with the support package tonight, along with Blaine. The flight plan's already been filed, so a few extra people won't cause a spike. *You*, however, will deploy on Monday, as scheduled." He grinned. "Don't worry, you'll get the leave I promised."

I heard what he said, my face betraying the struggle going on inside. Kurt noticed my discomfort but didn't ask for my opinion. "Okay, before I turn it over to Blaine, remember, we don't have execute authority on this. I expect it but don't have it yet. Don't go Rambo on me."

# 7

It would have made things a hell of a lot easier if Kurt had simply ordered me to go. Now I would have to make a choice about whether to leave the team on the night they deployed, or abandon my family after I had promised I would be home for my daughter's birthday. Nothing was more important to me than Heather and Angie, but as the team leader the mission took priority. It was an impossible choice.

My deployment was nothing new for my family. I had married Heather after I was accepted into the Special Mission Unit on Fort Bragg, so she was used to frequent absences. Even so, leaving is like twisting a knife each time I do it, especially now that Angie is old enough to know I'm gone. Our last night together before the culmination exercise hadn't been a very good one.

I had been out grilling steaks when I heard a thump inside the house, like something had crashed. I went inside to find Heather staring at the thermostat on the wall, clearly upset. I asked her what had fallen.

"That was me kicking the damn wall. The air conditioner's broken again. That's just great. Right before you leave. Perfect. Something else I'll have to deal with."

This wasn't a good way to start our last night together for at least six months. I tried to mollify her. "I'll have Paul handle it. I'll call him right now."

Paul was our next-door neighbor. He was a good guy, but I really didn't care for him. He was always upbeat, always helpful, to the point where it was sickening. I'm probably jealous because he spends more time with my family than I do. He's the one that Heather turns to for any immediate help, and that hurts. But that's not his fault, it's mine.

Heather waved her hand. "Paul couldn't fix a leaky faucet. Don't bother. I'll get Tim to help. He's a lot better with his hands, and he's home now."

She started to say something else but held her tongue.

I could tell she wanted to get something out but wasn't sure I wanted to hear it tonight. I needed to avoid a fight at all costs. While I, personally, didn't really fear what the future held, I couldn't predict what would happen on a deployment, and couldn't allow Heather's last memory of me to be a fight. We both knew the job was dangerous. We never talked about it out loud, but the potential consequences were there all the time. Tonight it was worse, because I was leaving. It was like a heavy presence that surrounded everything in the room. I took a gamble, hoping whatever she wanted to tell me would be a simple thing that I could smooth over before I left.

"What? What were you going to say?"

"I've said it before." She sighed, brushed a strand of hair out of her face, then let it out. "Why do you have to go? Why is it always you? You've been gone since 9/11. Isn't it someone else's turn?"

*Shit. That gamble hadn't paid off.* "We've been over this. I can't just up and leave. I'm the team leader. It takes time to train a replacement. This is my last tour. I promise."

Task Force tours were a little different than anything I had done before. They were six months long, followed by three months of downtime, followed by a three-month ramp-up prior to deploying again. During the last month of the ramp-up, we deployed permanently to D.C. and dropped all contact with our past, so for the family it was more like a seven-month rotation. The final month was lockdown. It was when we were completely cleaned from our past and prepped to become whatever was called upon by the mission. Tonight was the last night before the lockdown in D.C., the last night before my final seven-month absence. I was stepping down after this tour, something I had promised Heather I would do.

She gave me a bitter look. "Yeah, just like your last rotation at the Unit. And then you go and volunteer for this new thing. What'll it be next, Pike? At least when you were with the Unit I had other wives to talk to, people I could call who knew what I was going through. Now I don't even have that. I have to run around telling everyone you're some sort of communication technician in the Eighteenth Airborne Corps. Do you know how stupid that makes me sound? You're never here, and when you are, you never put on a uniform. It's ridiculous."

"Honey —"

She continued, speaking so fast her sentences began to run together. "Angie's learned how to swim and you've never been in a pool with her. The damn next-door neighbor's teaching her to ride a bike. She's going to be six in a month and you haven't been to a single birthday she can remember."

She stopped, clearly wishing she hadn't said these things on the night before I deployed. She began to cry. "It's not fair. Why is it always you? Tim left the Unit. Why can't you do the same?"

Tim was a friend who had just retired from the military and started his own security consulting business. It would do me no good to tell her that Tim was still conducting dangerous work — maybe more so because he no longer had the backing of the U.S. government. I embraced her, whispering in her ear, "It's not always me. There're plenty of guys like me. I've told you I'm done. This is my last tour."

She began to sob. "You've said that before. . . . I worry all the time. . . . I'm afraid when the phone rings. It's always the same man telling me you're okay. I think to myself, *Why would I think he's not okay?*, then realize the call is because someone else is dead. One of these days he's going to tell me you're dead. I can't do this anymore. . . ."

I knew then that something had broken; something inside Heather had collapsed under the strain. She had always known the importance of my work, and had given me unwavering support through absences at Christmas, birthdays, and anniversaries. She had been my biggest cheerleader, but something had changed. It sank in for the first time that this really was my last tour. I love the mission with a passion. More than just a job, it defines who I am. But make no mistake, I love my family more.

I held her close, stroking her hair. "Shhh. That's not going to happen. Look, I'll talk to Kurt, see if I can get a weekend at home after the lockdown, so I can be at Angie's birthday. That'll be a start, won't it?"

Heather looked at me, her face softening. I had hoped that night that committing to come home for Angie's birthday would be the first step toward Heather's believing in our new future.

Before I could say anything else, Angie came scampering in from outside. "Dad! The food's on fire!"

Heather broke the embrace and looked into my eyes. "I'm sorry. I shouldn't have said any of that." She sniffled and wiped the tears from her face. She gave me a halfhearted smile. "Go save the steaks. You can save the world tomorrow. We'll see you in a month."

I smiled back, kissed her on the lips, and jogged out to the grill.

After dinner, Heather went to clean the kitchen and I took Angie to her room on my back. I turned out the lights and lay next to her.

"Dad, did you know Mr. Paul's going to teach me to ride a bike?"

"Mom told me that. I can't wait to see you do it."

I answered nicely but wanted to leap out of bed, run next door, and punch good ol' Mr. Paul in the mouth. Maybe I wanted to punch myself, I don't know.

"Will you watch me when you get back?"

"Of course I will, doodlebug. Go to sleep."

She closed her eyes but kept talking. "How long are you going to be gone this time?"

I felt an acid bile in my stomach. "Same amount of time, but this will be the last time for a while."

"How come you always have to go? Mr. Paul never goes away. How come he gets to play with Megan all the time?"

Angie was old enough to make connections between my life and the lives of others. Looking at her by the glow of the nightlight, I felt more torn than I ever had in my life, pulled in opposite directions by forces outside of my control. It was almost a physical pain.

I stroked her hair. "You know why I have to go."

"To keep the bad men away?"

I leaned over and gave her a kiss. "That's right, to keep the bad men away."

# 8

Memories of that night, and the commitment I had made to Heather, were interrupted by Blaine Alexander moving to the front of the table. He addressed the group. "Well, I'm lucky to be working with my favorite team on this one."

The comment caused the team to laugh. Whenever he became involved, the endgame had begun, so whatever team he was working with became his favorite team. Blaine and I had worked together on multiple operations in the Taskforce. He was a pretty switched-on guy, politically savvy and tactically sound. He had to be to keep the job. Before he could continue, I raised my hand. "Sir, I need to talk to Colonel Hale. Can you start without me? It won't take a minute."

He nodded, knowing what it was about. "Yeah, go ahead."

I left the room at a jog, seeing Kurt talking to his deputy commander, George Wolffe, outside of the Ops Center. George had come over from the CIA's National Clandestine Service. I don't know him near as well, but from what I've seen, he's calm and level-headed. Unlike a lot of the folks at the CIA, Kurt said he was a meat-eater, so that was good enough for me. I didn't mind talking in front of him.

"Colonel Hale. Hey. Hold up. I need to talk to you."

"What's up?"

"I need to go with the team. I need to fly tonight."

Kurt looked at me like I was nuts. "What are you talking about? You're the one who begged me to break protocol and let you go home for your daughter's birthday. I broke every rule in the book to make that happen. People jumped through hoops to get you clean for the trip. Now you want to go to Tbilisi?"

"Sir, things have changed. The trip was planned because of our deployment schedule. The team's now deploying early. I need to go."

"You need to go home to your family. Come on, Pike, nothing's going to happen between now and when you get there. They'll just be building a pattern of life. This thing won't kick off for at least a week."

"You don't know that. We could be in a world of shit in twenty-four hours. I *need* to go. It's *my* team."

"Pike, think about this. You're the one who told me you haven't been to a single birthday of your daughter's since the first one. Go home. Azzam will wait. Even if this pops, there'll be other targets. Take the leave."

"No. This is it. I told you before. This is my last rotation. There won't be any other targets for me. My team's leaving. I need to go. We're at Omega, for Christ's sake. Don't do this to me."

Kurt said nothing for a beat, staring at me, mulling over the request. "Okay. You can go. But if you're flying tonight, you don't have time to get to a non-attrib phone for a call. Heather's going to get the usual notice from the Alias Shop after you're gone."

Heather had gotten this kind of impersonal phone call from operations plenty of times, updating her on my status. This time would be particularly difficult, but I knew she would understand.

"Good enough. She'll get over it. She knows this is my last tour. After this, it'll be Pike 24/7."

When I reentered the conference room, Knuckles gave me a look. I nodded, bringing a smile to his face. After that, we both focused on the man talking, spending the next four hours getting an in-depth briefing on the target, his templated actions, the Tbilisi environment, and the cover we would use to get the mission done.

Later, as we were packing our kit for the flight in the fourth-floor locker room, Knuckles broached the subject. "Heather's going to murder you for this. You promised her. It's the only reason she let you do this tour."

"She'll understand. The guy's trying to get a fucking dirty bomb. It's what I'm here for. It's not like I did this for a boondoggle to Hawaii or something." I started packing, saying again, "She'll understand."

Knuckles finished what he was doing and walked out of the room, saying, "That's what I said before my divorce."

I shouted at his back, "You married a stripper when you were nineteen! She left you three months after you tied the knot! Heather will understand."

Knuckles had already left the room, leaving me to say the last part as more of an affirmation than a fact. I stared at my kit, wondering if I was making a huge mistake. Knuckles was good. He was ready. I had been training him to take over after this tour anyway. I truly believed he could do it, but I also knew that the transition was six months early, and while he had the raw talent, he hadn't been a team leader inside the Taskforce. An Omega operation wasn't the time for him to figure out what that meant. The risks were too great. On top of that, the team — any team — develops its own personality, driven by the team leader. The members weren't plug and play. We were clicking because of my leadership style. I'm not saying it was perfect, or even the best, but that was irrelevant. They were used to me, and now wasn't the time to switch horses. It was one more birthday, but after this, I would be at them all.

*Tbilisi, Georgia*
*Four Days Later*

I heard my earpiece crackle, then the words I was waiting for: "Pike, Hedgehog is on the move. Should be passing you in about one minute."

I was sitting on a patio just off Rustaveli Street in downtown Tbilisi, sipping my coffee like the seven other patrons around me. I had to physically fight to suppress a smile. I absolutely loved this work and would have done it for free. I looked at my watch, realizing with a pang of guilt that today was Angie's birthday. I consoled myself that I had made the right call. Kurt had been wrong. Azzam was going down tonight or not at all. If I had stayed behind, the team would have been forced to either conduct the operation without its full complement of people, including their team leader, or miss the opportunity altogether. Given the stakes, they might have attempted it, but odds were they would have decided to pass, wasting a year's worth of work.

"Roger. Break — break. Knuckles, this is Pike. Hedgehog's headed home. You have execute authority."

"Roger all. About time."

Muslim names are always long, drawn-out, impossible-to-say things. Being the Ugly Americans, we usually gave a nickname to whoever we were tracking just to clean things up. Sometimes it's simply his initials, as in UBL for Usama bin Laden, or AMZ for Abu Musab al-Zarqawi. Other times, it's because the guy reminds us of someone. We had taken to calling Azzam the "Hedgehog" due to his remarkable resemblance to the porn star Ron Jeremy.

Azzam was currently conducting a complicated Internet dance of challenge and counterchallenge with the Chechen who was providing the radiological material to ensure that each was who he said he was, and that neither was the enemy. The Chechen himself had entered Georgia through the contested Pankisi Gorge, with onward travel into Tbilisi. Intelligence indicators showed they were planning on conducting the transaction no earlier than a week from now, which ordinarily would have given me plenty of time to plan a detailed operation.

Unfortunately, the Georgian interior police, with the help of a few choice pieces of intelligence from the United States, were set to arrest the Chechen tonight. This forced us to take down Azzam as well, as he would flee once he got word that the Chechen had been captured. You'd think we could just tell the Georgians to hold off, but the truth was that, while Georgia was a staunch ally of the United States, my team was inside the country without their knowledge. The Georgians had no idea about Azzam, and I'd just as soon keep it that way. Let them have the Chechen. Azzam would lead to much bigger fish.

The patio I was on sat at an intersection, giving me a commanding view down three of the four streets in front of it. Azzam should be walking toward my café, moving straight at me. It was still fairly early in the night, but the streets were already starting to pick up with partygoers hitting the bars and nightlife.

A rowdy group exited the Irish pub down the block, obviously already drunk. As soon as they cleared the sidewalk and crossed the street, I saw Azzam. I looked away. Call me superstitious, but from past experience, I'm positive that staring at someone somehow causes them to know you're there.

"Knuckles. I've got him. He's on schedule. No deviation."

"Roger."

Over the past four days we had developed a pattern of life on Azzam, and determined that

the best time to snatch him was after his dinner meal, before he got back to his hotel. Each night, Azzam had eaten in the same restaurant, then walked the half mile back to the small, local inn he had found. He stayed on main thoroughfares through most of his route but took one shortcut down a narrow, one-lane road in order to avoid walking the extra four hundred meters the main road would have forced on him. This was where we intended to take him down.

I continued to sip my coffee like all the folks around me, without staring at the pedestrians to my front. I caught a flash of light out of the corner of my eye. Looking back to Rustaveli Street, the main four-lane thoroughfare that ran through Tbilisi, I saw a police car pull up on the opposite side, lights flashing.

*Shit. That's going to cause a deviation.*

# 10

It had been two days since the phone call with the robotic-sounding man telling Heather that Pike would be unavailable to come home this weekend. He had been unfailingly polite, but it had done nothing to blunt the hurt she felt. She hadn't had the courage to tell Angie her father wouldn't be here for her birthday. But then Angie had yet to ask. In truth, she would probably take it better than Heather herself.

It was already past one, and she still hadn't picked up Angie's birthday cake at the supermarket. Before she did, though, she needed to go to Tim's to pick up the piñata. She had asked him to help with the birthday party when she found out Pike wouldn't be home, and he'd readily agreed. She had an ulterior motive for the favor: She intended to convince Tim to put some pressure on Pike to retire. Or at least find a less dangerous job. She wasn't even sure what it was that Pike did, but it had to be worse than the SMU,

and that was bad enough. While not best friends, Pike and Tim got along well, and Tim was the only one with any experiences like Pike's. The only one Pike would listen to. In her heart, she secretly hoped Tim would offer him a job at his consulting company.

She hadn't told Angie about the piñata, but like children everywhere, Angie had picked up that there were secrets afoot and was sitting expectantly in the backseat. She rounded the corner to Tim's house and parked on the street. She recognized Tim's Blazer in the driveway, but not the two unfamiliar sedans behind it.

Angie asked, "Whose cars are those?"

Heather had no idea, and hoped she wasn't interrupting a meeting Tim had scheduled.

"I don't know. Probably salespeople."

Before Heather could stop her, Angie jumped out, racing to the back door, shouting, "Maybe it's Daddy!"

"Angie! Wait!"

Heather felt a pang of guilt. In keeping the piñata secret she had hoped to lesson the blow of her father's absence. Now it appeared she had only exacerbated it, as Angie had surmised her father was the surprise. Rehearsing what she would say as she walked up the driveway, she saw that the back door was open, with shards of glass on the ground. She heard Angie shriek and felt adrenaline fire into her body.

Heather's eyes dilated and her muscles became engorged with blood in a fight-or-flight response. She chose to fight, running into the kitchen through the back door. She saw a large man holding Angie by the hair twenty feet away.

Without conscious thought, Heather snatched a paring knife from a block on the counter and charged the man with a primal scream. She registered him flinging Angie away like a rag doll as he prepared to defend himself. Before she reached him she was knocked to the ground from behind, disarmed, and jerked to her feet. She noticed blood all over the room. Great washes of it, as if someone had slopped a bucket haphazardly about. Looking for the source, she saw Tim lying on the floor, wicked gashes all over his body, his intestines slopping out from a hole in his stomach. She felt faint, unable to assimilate the slaughter.

The man holding her said, "What the fuck are we going to do now?"

"Well, we can't take them with us."

She faced the voice and saw a handsome blond-haired man, his hands covered in blood up to his elbows. His eyes were purple and flat. Dead. Unbidden, a memory of her childhood dog came to mind — a large husky that had been hit and killed by a car. When Heather had found him, his lifeless eyes looked like those of the man in front of her.

The man restraining her said, "Whoa, Lucas, I didn't sign on for killing a woman and a kid. They're not on the target list."

Lucas said, "No shit. I fucking get that, but we need to get out clean. I didn't ask them to come here. Look at the bright side: It'll help confuse the authorities. It'll play right into our cover of random violence. They'll have so many threads to run down, it'll cover our tracks."

Another man Heather hadn't noticed, now holding Angie, said, "I ain't doing that. No way. No amount of money's worth this."

Lucas snarled, "The mission takes priority. Don't go soft on me. I'll do the work. Just hold them still."

Heather spoke for the first time. "Please. We won't say anything. Please don't hurt my baby girl."

Lucas looked at her with something bordering compassion and said, "I'm truly sorry about this. Just the wrong place at the wrong time. Unfortunately, I can't make it painless. It's got to look like something crazy happened here."

Before she could say anything else, Lucas shattered her jaw with a vicious right cross. She hit the ground on her hands and knees, feeling the blood spill out of her mouth. She heard Angie scream, "Mommy!" then felt something smash into her spine. She rolled over and surprised the men by rapidly crawling to her purse. Lucas grabbed her legs and jerked her back, but not before she had her cell phone. She hit 911 before he could stop her. He smacked the cell phone out of her hand, towering over her.

"You bitch. You just lost any sympathy from me."

He hammered her broken jaw again. Everything went black.

Three hundred miles away, inside the Taskforce Headquarters, a computer started bleating.

## 11

The Tbilisi police car remained where it had stopped.

"Knuckles, this is Pike. Stand by for a FRAGO. Azzam's about to deviate his line of march."

"Roger. You want me to stand down?"

I thought for a second. Ordinarily, unlike our training exercise, this would be an automatic rollover, as the chance of compromising the team far outweighed any hasty plan that we came up with. But with the Georgians taking out the Chechen tonight, a rollover wasn't possible. We would take him tonight, or start all over, waiting another six months to a year to get him — if we could even track him again.

"No, don't stand down. I'm going to pick up a follow. We know he's headed to his hotel. We just don't know the route. Keep the same plan. Pick your guys up and get ready to drop them off somewhere else. I'll see what road he commits to. Once I give you that call, do a

71

map analysis and see what the most logical route would be to the hotel. Position on that route. If he takes it, take him down. If he doesn't, we'll wait for another day. You copy?"

"Yeah. I got it. I'm moving the assault team now."

I should have called Blaine before changing the plan, but things were moving quickly, and we didn't have time for a bunch of questions going back and forth. I knew the intent: Get the terrorist without compromising the team. I didn't need a call to HQ to confirm that.

I watched Azzam out of the corner of my eye. He rounded the turn in front of the café, paused for a second or two when he saw the police car, then began walking again. I threw some money on the table and left the café, holding thirty feet behind him. Before I reached Rustaveli, Azzam turned left.

"Knuckles, he's headed south down Rustaveli. I'm betting he'll cross at the next light — the street we couldn't figure out the name. You remember?"

"Yeah, I remember. It had that kindergarten school on it?"

"That's it. I'm thinking he'll walk up the street past the school, then head east toward the hotel."

"Got it. Doing the map reconnaissance now. Looks like he'll come straight up that street and get on his original route at the top, hanging another left. The only place to get him is at that turn. The road does a little zigzag up front, allowing us to snag him without anyone seeing the action from down the street."

"Sounds good to me. If there is any chance of compromise, let him go. Understand?"

"Yeah, I got it."

I looked at the kindergarten street, the one Azzam would use after crossing Rustaveli, hating what I was about to say. I said it anyway. "I'll trigger him crossing Rustaveli, but I'm going to have to stay on the west side or I'll get burned. From there, he's your target."

This was a major flex. I was supposed to follow Azzam up to the planned kill zone. That road was a well-traveled thoroughfare, the sidewalks on both sides used extensively by the local population. In the original plan, once he had committed to the shortcut, away from the pedestrians, I would prevent him from escaping the way he had come and provide command and control for the team during the assault.

The new road he was on was a thin, narrow hardtop without sidewalks and devoid of anyone at this time of night. I stood a good chance of compromising the operation by attempting to follow him, especially since his antennae were probably up looking for a threat. I would miss the assault, which sucked beyond words. It also put the entire assault in Knuckles's hands.

There was a pregnant pause before Knuckles responded, "Good to go. Standing by."

I knew Knuckles was now feeling the pressure, but decided that saying nothing conveyed more trust in him than any hokey attaboy I could give.

I watched Azzam stop at the next intersection, waiting for the light to change. I kept going, passing within five feet of him and continuing south down Rustaveli as if I had a different destination. I found a sidewalk food vendor about seventy meters away and got in line, awaiting my turn and watching Azzam.

I waited until Azzam was across Rustaveli and committed to the school street before calling Knuckles. I stepped out of line and brought my cell phone to my face so I wouldn't look like a nutcase talking to the air.

"Knuckles, Hedgehog's across. He's about five minutes out. I'm headed to my car."

"Roger all. We're set. If he takes this route, we have him."

"Roger. Once you have him, revert back to the original plan. Link up with me at my car and I'll run interference back to base."

"Got it. Next call will be jackpot or dry hole."

## 12

Knuckles sat in his van, his mind working at warp speed. He was parked on the zigzag road just to the east of the kindergarten street, facing the kill zone, the three-man assault team in position, but the plan was now going to shit. He had picked the zigzag road as the perfect kill zone based on Pike's following Azzam and triggering the assault as the team leader, something that was crucial to prevent the team from taking out the wrong person. They wouldn't have the time to identify Azzam before assaulting. They needed to positively know that the next man in the kill zone was the target, and Knuckles was now the man who would have to make that call.

Unfortunately, the zigzag road worked for the actual hit but caused problems with the trigger. From where he was parked, Knuckles couldn't see through the kill zone to the school street to alert the team, hidden in the shadows. The first he would see of anyone was when they were through it and in front of the van. He cursed silently. *Fucking Pike. Always winging shit.* He could abort, but the thought never crossed his mind. He turned to the teammate driving the van.

"Where's the Remington ball? We're going to have to trigger with remote video."

"In the small Pelican case right behind my seat."

Knuckles reached behind the driver's seat and found the box. Opening it, he pulled out what looked like a black, rubberized baseball. They called it a "Remington ball" because it was sold by the Remington Arms Company, the same people who make firearms. Invented and built in Israel, it was basically a hardened camera that could be rolled, dropped, or thrown. Knuckles had absolute faith in it, mainly because he had tried very hard to break it in the past. No matter how roughly he had treated it, the ball faithfully transmitted video to a handheld screen up to one hundred and twenty-five meters away — farther than he could throw it. What he found really unique — in fact a little creepy — was that the ball would right itself after it stopped rolling, putting the camera into operation as if it had a mind of its own. Once it did that, Knuckles could make the camera rotate a full three hundred and sixty degrees, seeing anything in the vicinity by remote control. In this case, they would only need to see down the street Azzam was walking up, allowing him to trigger the assault team when Azzam turned the corner.

But they'd need to get the ball into position. They drove as fast as they dared, hitting the street and doing a U-turn. Knuckles dropped the ball against the curb as the driver headed back to their original spot. Before Knuckles could orient the camera, Pike called and said Azzam was across the road and five minutes out. Knuckles cursed Pike again, taking a deep breath. Success or failure now depended on his actions alone. He didn't dwell on it. He confirmed the linkup plan with Pike and banished any fears, mentally preparing for the assault. He got the camera under control and began peering at the video screen, patiently waiting. Eventually he saw a fuzzy figure advancing on the camera ball.

"Two minutes out."

"Roger."

He watched the man get closer and closer, until he took up the entire display. The picture was clear enough for him to recognize Azzam. Knuckles rotated the ball as he passed, now watching the target's back moving into the first hitch.

"Thirty seconds."

"Roger."

Knuckles nodded to the driver, who started the van, pulling into the street at a slow pace.

He rounded the first hitch in the road and saw Azzam bathed in the glow of the headlights. They were late. The driver inched the gas pedal forward just as the assault team deployed.

Knuckles saw one man move to Azzam's front, while the other two advanced from the rear. One held a Taser X26 stun device. He pulled the trigger from a distance of five feet. Firing two projectiles attached to wires, the Taser caused Azzam to instantly lose neuromuscular control. He fell to the ground with only a sharp exhale of breath, quivering, unable to move. The other men from the assault element fell on him, flex-tying both his hands and legs with zip ties much like those used on garbage bags, only much, much thicker.

The driver pulled the van up parallel to the downed terrorist, while Knuckles threw open the sliding side door. Two men outside heaved the terrorist into the van while the third kept the voltage going, preventing Azzam from doing anything but twitch. They climbed in behind him, sliding the door shut. Knuckles breathed a sigh of relief, feeling the clammy sweat on his body for the first time. They'd been working toward this moment for what seemed like years, but the entire operation had taken less than the planned five seconds. The van sped out of the area, only stopping momentarily to allow Knuckles to recover the Remington ball.

■ ■ ■ ■

It had been almost seven minutes, and I was growing a little antsy. Maybe I should have had Knuckles confirm his plan. I was itching to break radio silence but wouldn't, mainly because I'd never hear the end of it from Knuckles. I knew better than to bug the team. He would do the right thing. I hoped. Finally, I got the call.

"Pike, Pike . . . this is Knuckles . . . Jackpot. I say again, Jackpot." Knuckles spoke in a calm monotone, as if he had just awakened from a nap.

I knew this was an act. He was probably hyperventilating when he put the handset down. I matched his cadence, because that's what cool commandos do, and replied, "I copy Jackpot. What's your ETA to my location?"

"Two minutes."

"Roger. Standing by."

I cranked the car and waited. Two minutes and fourteen seconds later they pulled up, not that I was looking at my watch. Knuckles was grinning like a teenager who had just egged the principal's house. He gave me a thumbs-up, and we pulled out of the parking lot with me in the lead. My car would now be a buffer vehicle for any contingencies that might happen en route.

Within minutes we were out of Tbilisi proper and headed toward a warehouse the support team had rented, not a single bit of evidence left that anything at all had occurred.

I called in the mission, alerting the reception team we were en route. Twenty minutes later, the car and van pulled into a vacant warehouse, the rolling door closing behind us.

I left the packaging of the terrorist to the support team, knowing he wasn't being flown out until tomorrow. In the meantime, he would be given a complete physical to make sure he wasn't on the verge of a heart attack, then sedated for the trip. My part of the mission, the fun part, was over. I grinned when I saw Blaine Alexander come out of the small office we were using for a tactical operations center.

"Another good one. No issues whatsoever."

I noticed that Blaine's face was grim.

"What's up? Did something go bad on the Chechen hit?"

"No. It's personal. Can I see you alone?"

My first thought was that he was pissed that I had altered the plan and taken Azzam without talking to him. I followed him into the office. "Yeah. Sure. What's up?"

Blaine closed the door. "Pike, I don't know how to tell you this. It's about your family."

After the first sentence I could no longer

hear him. All I could hear was my daughter saying I kept the bad men away.

# PART TWO

# 13

*Guatemala*
*Nine Months Later*

Professor John Cahill gave an exasperated sigh and sat down, sinking into the fetid jungle soil. Sometimes he felt like he was trying to run a race in knee-deep mud. He was deep within Guatemala's Reserva de la Biosfera Maya — the Maya Biosphere Reserve — in the northeastern department of El Petén, and for some reason his workforce had decided to quit. He had been doing this sort of excursion into the heart of the Yucatán going on thirteen years now, all in a quest for his mythical Temple of Priests. He had been robbed by bandits, contracted malaria, and almost killed by an asp, but never had his workforce refused to continue.

Once a rising star in the Latin America department of the University of North Carolina, he was now teaching undergrads basic anthropology theory at the College of Charleston, his fall from grace complete. The school itself was a pretty good liberal arts college, but it didn't have a major in archaeology and didn't give a rat's ass about his theories of the Mayan demise, forcing him to fund these expeditions out of his own pocket.

As always, he had hired local Mayan laborers without going through the required steps with the Guatemalan government. Nobody had cared before, and surely nobody would now, but an unhappy labor force could bring unwanted scrutiny. The Biosphere, one of the last remaining uncharted rain forests on earth, was dotted with Mayan archaeological treasures. Because of this, his activities would not be looked upon as a prank. Disgusted, he called over the native leadership, determined to find out what on earth could cause his hires to give up a new set of thirty-cent rubber sandals.

The natives themselves couldn't articulate to the professor exactly what it was they feared, only that they wouldn't go any farther on this specific route. In the end, they were torn between their instinct and the bounty the professor represented. They weren't stupid. They still wanted a new set of rubber sandals. They just didn't want to pay for it with their lives.

While the professor argued with the leadership, Eduardo and Olmec, two of the younger members of the expedition, were having their own parley. Eduardo, a spindly nineteen-year-old, was sure this halt was an opportunity not to be missed. All he had to do was convince his partner.

"Olmec, now's our chance! The Elders still believe in the old ways too much. We can find this temple, take something of value, then get back here before dark. Tomorrow, at least we'll have something to show for it besides the professor's quetzals."

Olmec, one year younger than Eduardo, but rooted in a much earlier time, responded, "We don't even know where it is. Only the professor knows. He never tells anyone more than the next hundred meters. There's no way we're going to find that temple by ourselves. If we could, why has our village signed on for these trips every year? We'd have done it by ourselves a long time ago. I'll tell you why — because there is no temple. There's only the curse."

Unlike Olmec, Eduardo had lost all semblance of Mayan instinctual heritage and saw such hesitation as complete idiocy. He was one of the few from his village who had made the trek as a migrant worker to the fabled United States. Some said that he did more than simply make the trek, but was in reality tied in to the illegal transport of workers into the United States.

"There is no curse. It's just an old wives' tale used to keep kids from wandering away in the jungle. Have you ever heard of anyone dying from some strange ailment out here or disappearing completely? Anyone at all?"

Olmec didn't say anything, prompting Eduardo to continue. "I saw the map on the professor's computer with the markings showing where the temple is. You could read the map and lead us to it."

Two years ago, while Eduardo was away, working in the U.S., a Presbyterian church from Santa Fe, New Mexico, had sent a "mission" to their village, spending a month building houses, wells, and sewage. One of the gringos was a scoutmaster. He loved his scouting job, and spent his evenings teaching the village boys scouting skills such as using a map, compass, and GPS. Olmec had paid attention.

Eduardo knew he was close to hooking his superstitious friend. All he needed to do now was convince him of the simplicity of the idea.

"I've been watching where the professor puts his GPS. I'll go take it. He won't miss it now, since we aren't going anywhere anytime soon. The maps too. He doesn't keep a good watch on either, because he thinks nobody knows how to use them."

Olmec sighed, then said, "If you get the equipment, I'll lead the way."

Eduardo slipped off, returning in minutes with a map, compass, and GPS.

Olmec reluctantly turned on the GPS and

took a little time orienting the map.

"According to this, we're only five hundred meters from the temple, basically due north."

Eduardo said, "Let's get going. We've got about an hour of daylight left."

With Olmec leading, the young men slipped into the jungle. After thirty minutes of fighting through the foliage, Olmec called a halt. He had been diligently keeping his pace count, a method to measure distance by counting the number of times his left or right foot hit the ground, and had hit four hundred meters.

"We're pretty close to the professor's spot on the map," Olmec said. "Keep your eyes open from here on in. If the temple's here, we could walk right over it and never know."

They continued for no more than five minutes when Olmec hissed at his friend. He saw something in the jungle. A hump that didn't fit. A tangle of vines and shrubs that didn't seem natural. The gathering gloom was making him jumpy, like a child in bed at night who imagines the towel on the rack is a burglar. He was ready to return to the camp.

"We've gone far enough," he said. "Let's go back."

Eduardo nodded in agreement. "Okay. Let's just fan out a little and see if we can find anything."

Olmec had walked less than ten feet when he heard Eduardo trip and fall. He saw him sitting down next to a rectangular stone.

"Look!" Eduardo said. "This is man-made. The temple is here!"

Olmec, once reluctant to continue, became infected with the thought of discovery. He quickened his pace toward the hump he had seen. It was about eight feet tall and appeared to be a solid mass of earth. As he got closer, he saw that draping vines gave an illusion of mass, but that it was actually some sort of cave. Setting down the GPS and map, he moved the vines aside. A few meters inside the opening, just at the edge of light, was a gallon-sized sack made of woven grass encased in stucco.

"Eduardo! Get over here! I think we've found what we were looking for!"

"What is it? Is it gold? Jade? What?"

Olmec moved toward the sack, sure that it contained something of wealth.

## 14

The professor grew tired of the back-and-forth discussion among the men in the local Mayan dialect.

He addressed the shaman, who acted as the villager's spiritual leader. "Speak in Spanish. What's the problem?"

"There is no problem. We simply will not go any farther. The area you're leading us into is full of blackness and death."

This was the third time the shaman had made such a statement, without any elucidation of what he meant. The professor was about to explode into a tirade when it struck him that this could be proof of the temple's existence. He wished he had asked thirteen years ago where they didn't want to go.

He had always been fascinated by the Mayan civilization, and was convinced that all theories of their demise were incorrect. The Maya had reached their height at about 900 A.D., and had a civilization that rivaled any in Europe, the Middle or Far East. For reasons known only to Maya ghosts, they had simply ceased to exist. It was one of the enduring mysteries of human existence, and many theories attempted to explain their downfall, ranging from outlandish alien invasions to the more mundane. The professor thought that everyone was looking at the problem backward. In his mind, it wasn't outside influences that had caused the people to disappear, but something in the cities themselves that caused them to leave.

The professor's theory revolved around his interpretation of a fairly new Maya codex called the Grolier Codex. The last of four known Maya codices, it was found under suspicious circumstances in 1965 and was considered by many to be a fake. Others had determined it to be authentic and maintained that it detailed the Maya calendar as it related to the planet Venus.

The professor had reached an altogether different conclusion. At the time of the Mayan decline there were two ruling elites in competition with each other: the political royalty and the religious shamans. Both continually fought for control of the population of the Mayan city-states, and both were equally bloodthirsty. He believed the shamans had developed a weapon, mystical in the eyes of the average Mayan, which was used to seize power. He extrapolated that this weapon had somehow gotten out of control and had caused one or two dramatic wipeouts of various cities, which in turn led to an evacuation of other cities in a superstitious panic, and a wholesale destruction of the civilization.

He was convinced that the Grolier Codex detailed the location of a temple, restricted to shamans alone, that housed this weapon. He had no idea what the weapon could have been, and cared only about finding the temple. He dealt in a world of history, of dangers long since dead. It never entered Professor Cahill's mind that, if his theory were true, he was trying to find a weapon that the world was ill prepared to deal with.

Eduardo reached the entrance of the cave in time to see Olmec pick up the sack. A fine cloud, not unlike flour, puffed out, encircling Olmec.

"This isn't worth anything," Olmec said. "It's a bag of dirt."

Eduardo began to dig through some scattered pottery, looking for something else of value, when he heard Olmec trip and fall. He was about to ask if Olmec was all right when what he saw caused him to stumble back and fall himself. Olmec had dropped the sack and was thrashing around as if hooked to an electrical generator. His head was growing lumpy and distorted and his breathing sounded as if he were drawing air through a swizzle stick. As his metamorphosis continued, he began to froth at the mouth, gasping for air. All of his exposed skin appeared to be rippling, as if a band of cockroaches were running through his veins. Before Eduardo could recover from his initial shock, Olmec's eyes bulged obscenely, his mouth cranked open farther than any human's should, and he ceased to move. Eduardo screamed, finding that deep in his soul he was still a Mayan, and ran out of the temple.

He sprinted about fifty feet and stopped, torn between helping his friend and getting the hell out of there. He decided that his friend was beyond help.

The professor asked the shaman if he could speak to the men as a group, intent on overcoming their superstition with gold, like an age-old explorer from Spain. As the men gathered around they heard an awful shriek to the north of their position, then a desperate thrashing sound. They began to rumble, looking at each other as if their neighbor could explain the noise.

The racket grew in strength until it appeared to be just outside the camp itself. The men began backing up, moving away from the sound, like a herd of antelope one step removed from full-scale panic, tenuously waiting to see who would be the first to start the stampede.

Exasperated, the professor advanced to the

edge of the camp, convinced the noise was man-made.

He saw the boy and shouted, "It's Eduardo! Someone get the first aid kit!"

Eduardo broke into the clearing of the camp, torn and bleeding from his pell-mell run through the jungle gloom. He fell to his knees, gasping for air. The men gathered around him, all shouting questions at once. The professor noticed that Eduardo was clutching his GPS in a bloody hand.

He snatched it away, shouting above the cacophony, "Where'd you get this, you little thief! Where'd you go?"

Eduardo looked up at the panic-stricken faces around him, eyes wild, showing more white than iris, and blurted out in Mayan, "The curse is real! It has consumed Olmec! He's been taken!"

That was enough to penetrate the thin veneer of modern logical thought, the words lancing the ancient suspicions hidden deep within each man. The tripwire broke. The men began to flee in all directions like a pile of leaves caught in a hurricane gale.

Within seconds the professor was alone. He slowly moved in a circle, dumbfounded by the turn of events. Listening to the stampede grow fainter and fainter, he mumbled, "What did Eduardo say?"

The question was swallowed by the vast expanse of jungle.

# 15

Eighteen hundred miles away, inside Task-force Headquarters, Knuckles zipped up his kit bag in preparation for his upcoming deployment. Unlike his last deployment, this trip was going according to plan, with no mad rush or changes in the mission. Now a team leader, his team had finished their culmination exercise this morning and was due to leave the next day.

He looked at the empty locker to his right, the dusty space bringing back memories of the last time he had done this, with Pike packing next to him. Knuckles couldn't help but smile. That mission had been pure Pike. *Talk about pulling success out of your ass.* Knuckles shook his head, thinking of the actual assault, remembering the final few seconds of absolute chaos. *"I'm not going to be able to cross. The target's all yours. . . ."* Looking back, Knuckles knew that Pike had just been coaching and mentoring, making sure he was ready to take over the team. Only Pike would do that on a live mission. The trust Pike had placed in him made him feel proud, but the circumstances made him chuckle. *What an asshole. Blaine would have ripped his head off at that decision if it had gone bad.* Knuckles wished he could talk to Pike before he deployed, let him know who they were chasing and get a little verbal encouragement. That last mission had been almost a year ago. Since then, Pike had dropped off the face of the earth. Knuckles loved being a team leader but would have gladly given that up — and more — to have his friend back.

Pike had taken the loss of his family harder than anyone Knuckles had ever seen. He seemed to blame himself from the moment he found out. Knuckles had hoped that he would go through the grieving process and rebound, and had even told Kurt Hale that he would remain a 2IC in order to let Pike keep the team, hoping that would help him recover. Kurt had agreed, but it hadn't worked. Pike had just grown increasingly bitter, with anger being his primary emotion. His judgment as team leader had begun to falter, with him lashing out at any small mistake and constantly fighting with his superiors. It had come to a head when Pike irrationally took the initiative on a simple exercise and subdued a Rabbit through force, shattering his face in full view of a group of tourists at the Country Club Plaza in Kansas

City, Missouri.

Knuckles felt like kicking himself every time he thought about it. He had known Pike was acting strangely. The final radio calls had been a clear warning that Pike was on the edge. He should have seen it. Should have stopped it.

The consequences of Pike's actions could have been severe. Besides the simple fact that he had harmed someone who had been recruited to help them train, the incident put the cover of the Taskforce in jeopardy. The Taskforce managed to prevent that, but Kurt pulled Pike from the team. Knuckles fought the decision, purely on loyalty grounds. The transfer only caused Pike to sink lower. Three months later he had demanded to be cut free from the military, and Kurt had granted his request.

After Pike left, Knuckles had called him twice a month just to check up, but two months ago the cell phone number had come back disconnected. Knuckles now had no idea where Pike had gone or how to contact him.

He finished packing and left the locker room, going down to the Ops Center on the second floor. He saw Kurt Hale and George Wolffe across the room gathering up data and talking with analysts. He knew they were leaving shortly to give the quarterly update to the Oversight Council. He was glad someone did it, or he wouldn't have a job, but he didn't think he could put up with the bullshit. Kurt waved him over.

"You guys ready? Any issues?" Kurt said.

"Nope. We're good to go. Hopefully we can get to Omega on this go-around. Don't worry about us. You should be worrying about the Oversight Council."

"No problems there," Kurt said. "They know we're doing the right thing. All I need to do is keep them up to speed. You do the work and I'll get the Omega authority. Lord knows we've chased this guy enough."

"I know. I can't wait to take this fucker out. This should be Pike's target. He's the one that found him years ago. I'm thinking of tattooing Pike's name on his ass before I turn him over to the support team."

Kurt laughed. "I was thinking that exact thing this morning. Not the tattooing, the fact that Pike's the one that got us here. You still talk to him? How's he doing?"

"I have no idea. His cell phone's disconnected and I don't know what he's doing now. I keep hoping he'll give me a call. I'm afraid that one day I'm going to see him on the news, peeking out the window of a house surrounded by SWAT guys."

"Come on. That shit won't happen. Pike's still Pike. Don't worry about him. He'll turn up. He just needs some time. Focus on the mission."

"I know, I know. I'm on the mission. One hundred percent."

"Good to hear. Look, I've got to go. The Oversight Council won't wait. I probably won't see you before you deploy." He stuck out his hand. "Good luck."

Kurt Hale and George Wolffe crossed the Potomac River, entering into the District of Columbia. George was driving, giving Kurt time to reflect on what Knuckles had said. He had put on a brave face and told Knuckles not to worry, but the truth was that Kurt was very concerned. He wished there were something he could do to bring Pike back into the fold, but he had tried everything at his disposal, from simple downtime to in-depth therapy. Nothing had worked. Kurt knew Pike's days as an operator were over but didn't think there was any way he would end up like Knuckles had said. Pike just wasn't made that way, no matter how bad it got.

The shame of the whole thing was that he knew the Taskforce wouldn't have been where it was without Pike. It had been a long, hard fight to get the unit established, and Pike's initial successes had guaranteed its survival.

George broke him out of his thoughts, asking, "What are you brooding over? You look like someone just shit on your birthday cake."

"Nothing. I was just thinking about how far we've come. If Knuckles gets to Omega, it will be like closing a circle. Missing that terrorist four times is what caused me to quit the first attempt at the Taskforce and build what we have now. Dumb bastard doesn't even know he's the reason so many of his friends are now dead or captured."

"Yeah, I know. I'd like to be there to see him go down. That ain't it, though. I know you better. What's up?"

Kurt paused, then said, "Pike. Once we turned him loose we started taking out terrorists like they were delivered to our door. I don't know . . . I guess I feel like I used him, then threw him away."

"Cut that talk out. Pike was good, but even you said he was a handful. He was always going off on his own. He never asked for permission to do anything. Just did what *he* thought was right. In my mind, we're lucky he didn't cause an incident while he was here. Shit, we *did* have an incident. We're just lucky it was during training."

Kurt knew that was bullshit. The Taskforce had existed for only three short years but in that time had executed over twelve Omega operations, all perfectly. A third of those successful operations were done by Pike's team, a number twice as big as the next most successful team's. Other team leaders said it was simply luck — being at the right place at the right time — but Kurt had worked with Pike long enough to know it was something else.

Most of the success was due to hard skills, but a crucial part was simply an ill-defined talent that couldn't be explained. Pike just made things happen. Yeah, he was a handful, but you couldn't argue with success.

George saw him bristle and backed off. "I'm not saying he wasn't good. I'm just saying that this effort is greater than one man. You can't let an individual — any individual — supersede what we're doing."

"Yeah, I know. I get it. I don't need my own speeches thrown at me."

Kurt had used the "greater good" argument to convince President Warren to begin with. He wasn't sure anymore it was right. The greater good had been used to defend a lot of actions in the past, including Pol Pot and Hitler. In contrast, the constitution of the United States itself was based on the individual — every individual. *When does the greater good become evil? When was it okay to kill one innocent to protect many? When the many said so? Or when the one has a vote?* It wasn't a trivial question, because Kurt and President Warren had managed to create an organization that, in the wrong hands, could be very evil indeed. He was walking a slippery slope, trying to keep his perspective on what was truly in the greater good against men, like that asshole Standish from the council, who didn't understand the meaning of the term.

His thoughts were broken by their sedan pulling up to the security gate for the Old Executive Office Building next door to the White House. The imposing granite structure housed some of the most important offices in the U.S. government, including the office of the vice president and the National Security Council. It was also where the Taskforce Oversight Council convened.

George parked the car. "Hey, I know how you feel about Pike. I didn't mean that the way it came out."

Kurt smiled, letting him off the hook. "Don't worry about it. I know what you meant. Let's go get this brief over with."

# 16

Within his palatial estate a few miles outside of Guatemala City, Miguel Portilla addressed the two Arabs in English. "To ensure I understand, you're offering me a retainer to move items across the border into the United States for a period of three years. These items can range from human beings to boxes no larger than three feet by three feet and weighing no more than two hundred pounds. Is this correct?"

"Yes. We're willing to pay you a handsome fee regardless of whether we bring you something to ship or not," stated the taller of the Arabs in heavily accented English. He appeared to be the spokesman, with the other Arab simply looking on and listening.

Miguel was a smuggler, although applying that term to him was like saying Bill Gates was a computer salesman. He was the undisputed leader of high-end smuggling into the United States. First earning his reputation with the Cali cartel in Colombia, he now worked exclusively with Los Zetas, a ferocious drug cartel made up of former Mexican Special Forces currently at war with the Mexican government.

"If I agree to do this, it'll cost much more than you've offered, as I believe the implications will have a traumatic impact on my business. In addition, I'll get your items into the United States, but I won't travel more than forty miles across the border. I have no interest in being associated with your enterprise."

Miguel was no fool. He knew that he was being asked to smuggle people and equipment that would be used solely to inflict death and destruction on the United States. In so doing, he also knew that the United States would react in a frenzy of fear, turning its porous borders into an airtight Tupperware container that an ant would have trouble infiltrating. He cared not a whit about the damage and destruction, but was concerned a great deal about the future of his industry. He also knew that in this day and age, the one thing that could destroy him was being named as an associate of a terrorist group. He could bribe his way out of any smuggling charge or connection to Los Zetas, but he couldn't stand up to the pressure the United States would bring to bear if he was seen as helping terrorists who murdered innocent American civilians. Drugs and death in Juarez were one thing. Death on American soil was something else entirely.

Before the Arab could answer, one of Miguel's ever-present personal security detail came in and whispered in his ear.

"Show him in," said Miguel.

The door opened, and Eduardo was led into the room. He appeared healthy enough but still bore the scars of his jungle panic. He looked timidly at Miguel, then at the two Arabian men. Miguel made a big show of friendship toward the young Mayan, seeking to put him at ease. "Eduardo! How're you doing? I thought you'd still be on the professor's expedition. Don't worry. You can speak freely. These ignorant foreigners don't speak Spanish."

Eduardo was afraid to say the wrong thing to this powerful man. He had worked for Miguel in the past as a high-end coyote, smuggling migrant workers into the United States. Miguel was one of the few coyotes who could get you into the U.S. in style, not packed like cattle in the back of a non-air-conditioned U-Haul, destined to die of heatstroke in the middle of the desert. Of course, this service cost much more than the migrants could afford, so the first few years of their wages, instead of being sent back to the family, were mailed to Miguel. Failure to mail the wages guaranteed that there wouldn't be a family in need of funds in the future. Miguel had earned the moniker of "The Machete" by his methods of ensuring compliance.

"Sir, you told me to tell you if the professor found anything. Well, he found something."

Eduardo explained the entire expedition in detail, telling of his and Olmec's actions, the discovery of the temple, Olmec's death, and his subsequent journey here.

Miguel was intrigued. "Tell me again how Olmec died. What was it he found?"

Eduardo went through the description of the bag and Olmec's symptoms, reliving the terror again as he told the story. Miguel failed to notice the increased interest of his two guests in the description of the death.

"And you know where this temple is? You can take some of my men there?"

"No, sir. Olmec read the map, and he's dead. The only one who would know where the temple is would be the professor. I wish I could take you there, but I can't."

Miguel's demeanor turned cold. "But you said you had a GPS. Surely that would make this simple. Where is it? Are you hiding something from me?"

Eduardo felt sweat pop on his forehead. "Sir, the professor took the GPS back. I promise I don't know where the temple is, but I do know where the professor is. He's staying at a hotel in Flores waiting on a flight home. He's got the GPS. I promise I'm not hiding anything."

Miguel began smiling again. "I believe you, Eduardo. You've always been true to your word. So I understand, only two people have been to the temple, you and Olmec, and only one person knows the location, the professor?"

Eduardo visibly relaxed. "Yes, sir. I'm the only living person who's seen the temple, and the professor is the only one who can find it."

"Good. Very good. Please head home and speak nothing of the temple or the professor." He handed Eduardo a wad of cash and showed him to the door.

Miguel saw an opportunity that he would have to seize immediately. If he could get to the temple before the government or UNESCO found out, he could ransack it, use his smuggling network to get the pieces inside the U.S., and sell them at a handsome profit. If he did it quickly enough, the government or UNESCO would never know it existed. First, he had to locate the temple. That meant finding the professor. Second, he had to eliminate anyone else who knew about it and was in a position to talk.

Miguel motioned to the security man who had shown Eduardo in. "Kill him once he reaches the bus station. Take his body into the jungle. Oh, and don't forget to get my money back. Send in Jake."

The security man nodded and went about

his tasks as if he had been told to bring a glass of water.

Miguel spoke to the Arabs in English. "I'm sorry, but something of urgency has come up. You're welcome to stay in the guesthouse. I'll send someone for you when we can continue our conversation."

The taller Arab nodded and said, "I hope it won't interfere with our transaction, but we understand the demands of your business."

The head of Miguel's security entered the room just as the Arabs were leaving. A large man, at six feet four inches, Jake walked with the grace of a cat. The only gringo on the detail, he was also the only one with any true security experience. He had been expelled from the British Special Air Service for activities that he wouldn't elaborate on. The rumor making the rounds was that he had enjoyed interrogating suspected terrorists a little too much, using force long after the subject had spilled his guts. Since then, he had hired out to numerous organizations, finally landing as Miguel's head of security.

"You wanted me?"

"Yes. I need you to go to Flores and find a man named Cahill. He's an American professor staying in a hotel in the town. Probably a flop-house. Don't hurt him. Bring him back here with all of his equipment. Pay particular attention to any electronic items such as computers or GPS. I need him in the next forty-eight hours. Take my plane to the airfield at Santa Elena."

Jake simply nodded and left the room. That was another reason Miguel liked him. He never asked questions. Given some guidance, he simply executed, unlike all of the other pipe-swingers he employed, who would ask a thousand questions to ensure they didn't screw up. Jake was fire and forget, and just like a guided missile, once he locked on there was little that could be done to stop him.

# 17

In the fourth-floor conference room of the Old Executive Office Building, Harold Standish glared at Kurt Hale, infuriated. The man was arrogant to a fault. The Oversight Council meeting was winding up, and Standish had been stiff-armed on every question he had asked. It didn't help his mood that nobody else on the council seemed to think Kurt was being insubordinate. In fact, most seemed to agree with him. Tall, at six feet six inches, Standish looked like a cross between Ichabod Crane and Christopher Plummer, with a head of close-cropped salt-and-pepper hair and the sour disposition to match. At the official conclusion of the meeting, he closed his portfolio, stood up, and stalked out of the room before anyone could stop him.

He went down to his NSC office on the third floor, flew through the anteroom without addressing his secretary, and fell into his chair. Staring at his computer, he began to calm down. He was still, after all, a very powerful man. A political strategist of rare skill, he had risen from the trench warfare of American politics by mastering the art of manipulating information. He was the go-to guy when it came to playing dirty. By the time he was thirty, he was richer than he'd ever thought he would be. By the time he was forty, he was the undisputed master of political destruction. By the time he was forty-five, he was becoming aggravated at how he was treated. How could he be so rich, and yet still feel like the boy with the dirt between his toes, begging for scraps?

He vividly remembered the victory party for the previous president's second term. He was celebrating with the rest of the campaign staff when the president-elect motioned for his top advisors to follow him into his suite. Standish, who had been standing in the group, went along as well. Once the doors closed he found everyone looking at him like he was a turd in a punch bowl. The silence was extremely uncomfortable. The president-elect finally broke it.

"Harold? Is there something I can do for you?"

"Sir? Uh . . . no. I thought you had asked me to come in here."

"No, Harry, the campaign's over. Your job's done. We have real work to do now." Standish vividly remembered the president's patronizing smile. "If it wasn't for you we wouldn't even be having this meeting. I mean that."

*We have real work to do now.* The words had hit Standish as hard as a physical slap. He had seen some of the advisors fighting to suppress a smirk. He left feeling a burning shame. He realized at that moment that money wasn't the Holy Grail. Power was.

Standish began putting his talents to use getting a key to the doors of power. He had worked hand in hand with the same people who had smirked at him in that suite and he knew he was just as intelligent as they were. Someday he'd jam that smirk straight up their ass. He didn't have the experience or backing to join the political fray, but there were other ways to get on the inside. When Payton Warren began his first run for president, Standish had eagerly signed on. Simultaneously, he began his research, looking for a position to which the president could appoint him, should he win. He found it in the National Security Council.

Created by the National Security Act of 1947, the same act that had created the Air Force, Central Intelligence Agency, and the Joint Chiefs of Staff, the NSC was designed to help the executive branch synchronize political and military affairs. What Standish found attractive was that the statute dictated who would be on the council by law, but, unlike other organizations such as the CIA and the DOD, it didn't specify any congressional oversight. It was one of the most powerful entities in the U.S. government, but the legislative branch had no control over its activities. In effect, it served one man: the president. Outside of the members mandated by law, the president could appoint anyone to the council for anything. *Perfect.* Since its creation in 1947, Standish saw that the NSC had evolved into a byzantine organization that fluctuated every time administrations changed, making it hard to ascertain who was doing what — exactly what he needed.

He had read about the NSC under President Reagan, and had become fascinated at how a mere lieutenant colonel in the Marine Corps named Oliver North, working as a junior staffer at the NSC, had managed to create a complete clandestine infrastructure and manipulate foreign policy on a grand scale. The fact that it had eventually unraveled, splashing into the history books as the Iran-Contra affair, did little to temper him. Clearly, the people involved weren't his caliber.

He had worked hard on the president's campaign, proving to be more indispensable than ever before, with his information critical in the political fight. After the election, he asked for and received an appointment as a do-nothing member of an inconsequential subcouncil on the NSC's statutory Committee on Foreign Intelligence. He went to work, using his skills to build what he wanted. In three short years he had managed to create the Deputy Committee for Special Activities, and had slowly but surely been included in the mission planning for all covert operations. If it was a secret operation on foreign soil, he knew about it. And knowledge was something he knew how to use.

He had come a long way since that late-night meeting. The memory still made his face flush, but that would fade. Soon, it would be him asking people to leave the room.

Standish was startled out of his thoughts by a knock on his door, followed by the president's national security advisor, Alexander Palmer, entering the room.

"Hey, Harold, you got a minute?"

Standish stood up and put on his kiss-ass face, wondering why his boss was here unannounced.

"Sure, sir. All the time you need. How can I help you?"

Palmer took a seat without being asked. "It's about the Taskforce meeting we just left. Kurt has some concerns about your line of questioning, and frankly, so do I."

*That fucking crybaby,* Standish thought, *what did he say?*

"Okay," he said, waiting on Palmer to continue.

115

"I let you on the Oversight Council because it seemed to fit the office here, but your primary purpose is simply to absorb what's said so you can see how it affects other activities going on. I don't expect you to weigh in on any decisions."

He picked up a paperweight off Standish's desk and twirled it around in his hands. "The council is well versed on the ramifications of these types of things. It seemed as if you were questioning our judgment."

*Shit. I'm being frozen out. What did Kurt say?* Still wearing a smile, Standish said, "Got it, sir. I just thought that Kurt and the council were being a little timid on everything. We have quite a few opportunities here that we could seize right now if we wanted. I don't think the council understands how important —"

Palmer interrupted. "Look, I know you don't have a lot of experience in government, and I see that as a good thing, but these activities are very, very, volatile. The combined experience of the council is probably over a hundred years dealing with national security issues. You have to trust that we know what we're doing."

*Maybe that's why nothing ever gets done, you pompous ass. You've worked so long inside the government you don't even realize you're a chickenshit. The entire council thinks that talking about doing something is the same*

116

*as action.*

"Sir, I meant absolutely no disrespect. I know I have less time in the government than other folks, but I *have* worked inside the NSC for the last three years. I've seen how things run. We seem to make more charts and briefings *about* doing something than actually doing something. I just think the Taskforce could be better utilized."

Palmer replaced the paperweight and stood, indicating the meeting was over. "I hear you. Sometimes I think the same way, and admire your attitude, but you've only been on the Oversight Council for six months. Give it some time before you decide we're all hand-wringers. See a few operations go down, then begin to contribute. Okay?"

"Sure. Yes. I don't want to get a reputation as a know-it-all. I'll sit back and watch for a while."

"Good. That's what I hoped you'd say. You're a valuable contributor and I don't want to lose you."

Standish watched the door close, thinking, *Valuable contributor, huh? Not yet, but I will be, you patronizing asshole.* He had seen the sausage factory of decision-making by the inner circle of the U.S. government and determined it was a recipe for failure. What was needed was decisive action, without a bunch of quibbling from Congress, or, heaven forbid, from the great unwashed of the

American electorate.

Since Al Qaeda had started this war in 2001, Standish had seen the U.S. take a daily beating on everything it did in its defense. The public just didn't seem to understand that there was a threat. *Christ, even global warming is seen as a bigger danger.* After watching all of the timid, halfhearted measures employed by the United States, he was convinced that something more aggressive needed to occur, outside of the public eye. The Taskforce was the perfect tool for the job. If he could get control of the Taskforce, the nation could get serious about terrorism. He couldn't order around the CIA or the military, but he could definitely find a use for an organization that had no official affiliation with the U.S. government. *Shit, even Ollie North could do that.*

# 18

The Arabs had retired to Miguel's guesthouse and were embroiled in a heated conversation. Far from being ignorant, both had spent countless hours with a Rosetta Stone Spanish software program in preparation for this trip. While they couldn't pass as natives, they were now fairly fluent — something they had kept hidden from their host.

The shorter of the two went by the *kunya* of Abu Sayyidd, after Sayyidd Qutb, the Egyptian member of the Muslim Brotherhood, whose rabid proselytizing and interpretation of the Quran were, before his execution in 1966, milestones in future Islamic fundamentalist thinking.

The taller one, and the one who had done all the talking earlier, went by the *kunya* of Abu Bakr, after the first caliph who ruled following Muhammad's death, and the first caliph leading to the split between Shia and Sunni.

Ordinarily a *kunya* is a nickname meaning

"the father of," as in Abu Abdullah meaning "the father of Abdullah," and is commonly used in Arabic countries. In actual practice it's a method for fanatics wanted by authorities to take an alias with a hidden meaning. The naming conventions in Arabic countries made it very hard to keep track of individuals, as a person's recorded name could be any variation of full name or *kunya*.

Unlike their heroes of 9/11, neither Bakr nor Sayyidd had been radicalized in modern Europe, where Mohammed Atta and his ilk were treated as inferior beings and outsiders, leading them to turn inward toward Islam. Abu Sayyidd and Abu Bakr heard the calling from the mosques in their own home towns in Saudi Arabia, a radical influence unstemmed by the ruling House of Al Saud because of the simple fact that the threat led outside the kingdom, and thus was something to be encouraged no matter how much the United States protested.

In the Saudi government's thinking, if the radicals were given something greater to hate than the ruling class, so much the better. Not to mention that many in the ruling class sympathized with the cause anyway. Let the radicals leave the kingdom and get killed. It was a win-win situation.

Like many of the men who had made the trek to Iraq, Abu Bakr and Abu Sayyidd didn't start out as rabid ideologues. They were simply looking for a little adventure in support of a worthy cause. Their plan was to go to Iraq, fulfill their romantic notion of the fight to support Islam for a few months, and then return to their life in Saudi Arabia, working a normal job and telling stories of their heroic actions to their grandkids years later.

The naïve illusion of jihad was broken quickly. Most actions were accomplished by snipers shooting their targets in the back, improvised explosive devices hidden in the dark of night, or suicide missions that left dozens dead and dozens more brutally mangled with little discrimination between the infidel and the believer. One walk through the bloody devastation of a suicide bomber was enough to take away any idealistic notions of jihad.

Abu Bakr and Abu Sayyidd were lucky in that they weren't chosen for a suicide "martyr" mission. At the time, the terrorist pipeline had enough *shahid,* and thus they were allowed to fight, with IEDs and rifles. Once they had killed, their mindset began to change. They had to justify within themselves the murders they committed, and their psyche simply couldn't accept that they had done wrong. The answer was simple: The cause was just, no matter what reality they saw on the ground that refuted the propaganda.

Sayyidd and Bakr, like many other radical-ized fighters, had become nothing more than weapons of the most dangerous kind. Literal smart-bombs. Living, breathing, thinking weapons willing to trade their lives for their nihilistic goals, without any moral restraint remaining against taking innocent life. Had they the means, they would slaughter their enemies on a massive scale. The leadership of Al Qaeda had striven mightily to obtain such a capability. Sayyidd believed he may have found it in the story told by the native boy. All he had to do was convince Bakr.

# 19

Inside his fleabag hotel, the professor twitched at every noise he heard in the hallway outside, wondering how long he had before he was arrested. He couldn't believe the debacle that had occurred. The Mayans had come out of the darkness one by one, chopped to ribbons. So far only eight of the twelve original members had made it home. Counting Olmec, he could be looking at charges of manslaughter or murder of four people. He regretted the deaths, he truly did, but the real shame was that no one would care that he was correct about his theory.

After spending the night by himself, it had taken him a full day to get out, and that was mainly due to his GPS. Without it, he'd probably be trying to suck water out of vines right now. He had hotfooted it to Flores, a small town on an island in the Petén province, with access to the airport at Santa Elena. At fifty-eight, he was weary down to the center of his bones, and wanted nothing more than to return to his calm life in Charleston. He hoped that the news of the travesty wouldn't make it to this town before he could catch a plane out. Meanwhile, to keep his mind off his impending doom, he collated his information on the temple. Maybe, just maybe, he could get out of this alive and return with a real expedition of scientists.

As he always did, he maintained his level of secrecy, only this time he wanted to get all traces of the location of the temple out of his immediate possession. He downloaded the waypoint data and tracks from the GPS to his computer. Then he wiped the memory of the GPS so that it showed no trace of where he had been. He opened his laptop and booted up a very powerful encryption program by means of a sequence of keystrokes. The program itself couldn't be found by a cursory examination. He pulled the drop-down menu and selected the steganography feature.

The professor had first heard of steganography, or the hiding of messages in otherwise innocent carriers such as pictures or letters, while still an undergraduate student. He had read about the ancient Greeks, where Herodotus tells of hiding a message of Xerxes' planned invasion underneath the wax of a writing tablet to avoid scrutiny, and the legends of the pirates, where the head of a man was shaved and tattooed with a treasure map that was concealed when the hair grew back.

Later on, while on a dig with a savvy undergraduate of his own, he had been shown the modern usage of the technique. Every computer file, such as JPEG, MP3, or WAV, has unused data streams within itself, basically empty pockets that serve no purpose. The steganography program simply fills up this empty space with the data that one wishes to hide. Thus, while the picture of Aunt Sally still looks like a picture of Aunt Sally, someone who knows there is hidden information within the picture can extract and reconstruct it.

After the program booted up, the professor was asked what he wanted as his carrier file, or the file that would hide the data. He selected three MP3 songs from his hard drive. When asked what he wanted to hide, he selected the GPS data. He continued by selecting AES 256 encryption and the password key. Now, even if the data were to be separated from the songs, it would be encrypted in an algorithm that had never been cracked, and thus would be secure.

In thirty seconds it was done. He was asked if he wanted to create a physical key, and selected "yes." When prompted, he put a blank thumb drive in the USB port and the computer churned for a few more seconds.

He now had his data securely encrypted

and could extract the data both virtually with a password on his computer, which held the steganography program, and physically by inserting the thumb drive into whatever computer held the carrier file, regardless of whether that computer contained the stego program or not. Once the thumb drive registered, it would self-extract the data.

The professor plugged in the phone line and dialed the closest ISP given to him by the front desk. It never failed to amaze him how far and deep the Internet had penetrated. It seemed like it was in more places than indoor plumbing. Once he was connected, he logged onto Hotmail.com and pulled up his account. He typed a short note and e-mailed the songs to his niece in Charleston, South Carolina. Jennifer was an anthropology student, so it wasn't outside the realm of possibility that she would appreciate the local Mayan music. Still, even if she thought it a little odd, she'd have no idea the information she was helping her uncle to hide.

Three minutes later the e-mail completed sending. He closed out of the Internet, then used a shredding program to erase all traces of his stego activities. Nothing related to the expedition remained on his hard drive.

He gave a sigh of relief and leaned back in his chair. Maybe he should get himself a giant margarita and relax a little bit. As he cataloged the bars in the small town he heard a knock on his door, and his name called out. He nearly passed out in shock. Just as his mind spun into overdrive, with fantasies about the tortures he would experience along with the ludicrous choices he faced, such as jumping out of the third-story window, it dawned on him that the man outside the door was speaking with an English accent. He must be an expat who worked for the hotel. When he had signed in, the professor had tipped handsomely to generate goodwill, so perhaps the man was here to warn him about something he had heard on the street. In the span of seconds the professor went from doom to giddy excitement. He rushed to the door, intent on seeing who was there.

There was no peephole, forcing him to crack the door. He found himself looking up into the ice-blue eyes of a man a full head taller than himself. His clothes didn't indicate that he worked for the hotel. In fact, he was dressed like he was going into the jungle. His face was expressionless, giving no hint as to why he had knocked. The only indication of why he was there was a section of pipe held in his right hand. Maybe he was a plumber.

"Yes?"

"Professor Cahill?"

"Yes. Can I help you?"

In response, the man kicked in the door, knocking the professor to the floor. The last thing the professor saw was the section of pipe coming at his head.

128

# 20

Jennifer Cahill opened her eyes and watched the ceiling fan above her rotate for half a minute. *This isn't going to cut it. I need to find something to do or I'm going to go nuts.* At first, she had enjoyed sleeping in. Waking up whenever she felt like it or rolling over and going back to sleep had been a nice reprieve. Now, with spring break almost over, she was beginning to feel a little restless. As an anthropology major herself, she had asked her uncle to let her go with him to Guatemala, but he had refused. She hoped he was having some luck, although she knew it was a long shot. Everyone else had written him off as a crackpot, but she believed in him, if for no other reason than because he had been so kind to her.

She threw off the covers and padded into the kitchen. She had a one-bedroom apartment in a row house on Pitt Street about two blocks from the College of Charleston, in the heart of downtown. The house had been turned from a regal antebellum statement of the past history of Charleston into a rat maze of individual apartments for college students. She was the only one still at home. Everyone else had left the city for party time at some spring break location. She didn't miss that. At twenty-eight, she wasn't that much older than her peers, but she was a world apart in maturity. She'd had enough of the spring break bullshit and *Animal House* lifestyle on her first try at getting a degree.

She put on a pot of coffee and went to open the front door to get some fresh spring air. It was only March, and the weather was already starting to warm up. The swelter was something that she enjoyed. She couldn't see how anyone could live in cold weather. She got cold in a movie theater — forget about living permanently in the snowbelt. Having grown up as a tomboy on a ranch outside of Dallas, Texas, where she had spent most of her time outdoors, she had become used to the heat. It was muggier here, but still pretty close. If she couldn't live in Texas, at least she could sweat like she did.

She turned to check her coffee and found a flyer at her feet. It was for a live band at a bar called the Windjammer on the Isle of Palms, a barrier island about thirty minutes from her house. She picked it up and saw writing at the bottom: "You should be going stir crazy by now. The offer still stands —

you can stay with us. Meet us at the Windjammer tonight. If you don't like it, you can always go home." It was signed by her girlfriend Skeeter.

Jennifer thought about it for a second. She was looking for something to do, and maybe it was time to get out a little. Yeah, she'd have to fight off all the ogling boy-men who only wanted to get drunk, then get laid, but she could handle that. She just wasn't sure it would be fun anymore. Those situations always made her think of her past. *Shit, who am I kidding? I think about the past no matter what happens. The damn weather makes me think about it.*

She poured herself a cup of coffee and was reading the flyer again when her cell phone rang.

"Hey, you're up. Let me guess. You're in your pajamas studying for a test that might come after spring break. Did'ja get my flyer?"

Jennifer smiled. "Hello, Skeeter. No, I'm not studying. I had a man over here last night. He's an exchange student from Nigeria. He's still asleep because we were up pretty late watching C-Span. I'm not sure what you mean by flyer."

"Bullshit. I left a flyer on your doorstep. Go get it. I'll wait."

"I got the stupid thing. It's in my hand right now."

"Well, what do you say? Come on out. The

condo's already paid for, so it won't cost you a thing."

"Skeeter, you know how I feel about that scene."

"Jesus, Jennifer! When are you going to let go? I get you had a rough time, but come on. This is your last year of college! Your final spring break. You'll be able to sit in a cubicle and slave away to your heart's content in a little bit. Think about it. I'll call back and bug you later."

Jennifer was going to reply when she realized that Skeeter had hung up. The truth of the matter was not a day went by when she didn't think about her ex-husband and what he had done. Not a day without feeling sweat break out over the memory, wondering what her life would have been like if she had stayed in school the first time.

She had dropped out of the University of Texas after her junior year to marry the iconic frat boy son of a Texas oil tycoon, who had just graduated. Things had been fine for all of ten minutes before she realized he was sleeping around on her. It was as if her husband was trying desperately to hold on to his frat boy lifestyle while walking up the corporate ladder. Nobody held him accountable, least of all his trophy wife. Thinking about it now, she had been very shallow. She had been raised poor, but proud. The Cahill name had been drilled into her from an early age as something that mattered beyond wealth. She had believed it, then had thrown it away.

They held on for four long years, mainly because divorce wasn't accepted by the in-laws. She made do with the finer things in life, all the while knowing that everyone was laughing at her behind her back. On the surface she had everything a girl could want, or at least anything that could be acquired with cash — cars, trips to St. Lucia, jewelry, you name it. She was only missing the things that money couldn't buy, like respect. For a Cahill, this was worth more than wealth. She tried hard to get her husband to stop, then tried to adjust her pride to accept her lot, but neither worked.

It finally came to a head when she arrived home to find him in bed with his secretary. Cheating at a sleazy motel was one thing, but doing it in her bed was another. The scene was branded into her soul, still as raw as the day it had happened. The secretary covering up her obviously fake breasts, a small smile on her face, no fucking shame whatsoever. Her husband taking control, not even acting as if he had done anything wrong.

She had begun to pack her bags, telling him that it was finally over. He told her to stop. She told him to screw himself. He slammed her against her dresser and punched her viciously in the stomach, causing her to fall onto the floor. He calmly told her to unpack her things and left the room. She remembered lying on the floor in her own spit and vomit, gasping for air, the fake-tit whore stepping over her with a sheet around her body.

She fled the marriage with the clothes on her back, returning to her mother's house in McKinney, Texas. The next few weeks were a nightmare. The punch seemed to have done something internally. She had cramps so bad she was left doubled over in pain. Her period came early, and very heavy. She went to the doctor and in the same breath he told her that she had been pregnant — and had had a miscarriage.

Jennifer shook herself. The memories always caused her to sweat, making her heart palpitate. *That fucker . . . I should have . . .* She took three deep breaths. *Quit thinking about it. Think of anything else . . . Think of positive things. . . .*

After the miscarriage, her family had been her anchor. She had lost her way, but they didn't care. They had rallied around her as soon as she had come home. She didn't tell her family about the miscarriage, fearful of her brothers' possible retaliation. Sometimes, when the darkness came, she toyed with the idea of letting them in on the secret, knowing they would kill that sorry sack-of-shit with a cheese-grater. Looking back, she was glad she never did, but a part of her waited for the

134

day when she could get retribution. On days like today, when she was left clutching a counter, taking deep breaths to control her fear, she wanted nothing more than to cause him the same agony.

In the end, while it wasn't a pleasant thought, she knew that the attack was the best thing that could have happened. She had understood that she could never win any legal battles in a system owned lock, stock, and barrel by the family, and that it was the fight alone that they were afraid of. It never entered their minds that something bad would happen to their son. They just didn't want the embarrassment of the publicity. So, as they had been doing since robber baron times, they bought her off. They gave her an impressive little nest egg of two hundred thousand dollars, telling her never to talk about what had happened. She agreed. She remembered the moment well, thinking she should have crossed her fingers behind her back because if she ever got the opportunity, she would bury the family and sow their graves with salt.

Now, standing in her kitchen a thousand miles away, she had had enough of the hate and fear. Maybe a night out would help. Just because the Windjammer had a bunch of drunken college men didn't mean they were all like him.

She glanced at her computer screen and

noticed she had an e-mail from her uncle. She forgot about the Windjammer. *He's not supposed to come out of the jungle for at least three days.* Obviously, once again he had failed to find the temple. She smiled to herself, thinking of him hacking his way through the jungle on yet another attempt. No matter how many times he failed, Uncle John remained optimistic. She admired that in him. Then again, she knew she'd find anything her uncle did something to admire. He had gone out on a limb to help her, getting her a fresh start at his own university based solely on the fact that she was his niece, telling white lies that could have cost him tenure. She would never forget that.

She opened the e-mail and saw that it was nonsense. It said nothing at all about his trip, or his return. It was just a few MP3s containing some local music. She found this strange, but not unduly so, as her uncle was always doing goofy stuff. *Last time he came home he gave you a real shrunken skull. Be thankful this is just music.* Whatever had happened, he would give her the full story on his expedition when he got back. She hooked up her MP3 player and began downloading the songs. Her uncle must have thought they were some pretty good tunes if he'd e-mailed them to her instead of just waiting until he returned. With the music downloading, she went to pack an overnight bag.

# 21

Abu Sayyidd was electrified by the story they had heard. "Did you listen to that? The boy found some sort of ancient weapon in the jungle. A weapon that can be used to kill the infidels. What we've been sent here to do, we can accomplish in half the time, a month instead of years."

Abu Bakr wasn't so sure Sayyidd was right. He was a pragmatic planner, a man who had escaped death precisely because he had predicted and counteracted contingencies before they occurred. This mission had taken close to a year to develop, and he was reluctant to simply throw it away on the story of a native boy.

"Sayyidd, please. We don't have the time or equipment to go foraging through the forest for some sort of mythical weapon. We don't even know if that boy was telling the truth. We've worked too hard to get where we are."

Their purpose was to set up a mechanism to infiltrate the United States using the illegal immigrant pipeline already established. Once the cells were in place, they would conduct synchronized acts of terror that would dwarf September 11, 2001. The hope was for a sustainable, repeatable mechanism that would cause the U.S. to crack down harshly on all things Arabic (and even Sikh, Hindu, whatever was seen as "strange"), which would in turn plant a seed of jihad inside the U.S.

Sayyidd persisted. "You heard the description of the death. The weapon is something like the poison weapons we learned about in the camps. Something The Sheik has tried mightily to obtain. We might now have the ability to do what no other has done."

"What on earth makes you think there's a weapon in the jungle?" Bakr said. "I've heard children with more logical skepticism than you."

"Have you never heard of the medicines that are found in the rain forest? It's said to be a wonderland of ancient plants simply waiting to be discovered. What's the harm of looking? If we find it, we may truly bring the far enemy to his knees! We were chosen for this mission based on our skills and judgment. We need to use both."

Never having worked with Sayyidd before, only trusting that his superiors had selected the right man, Bakr was suspicious of Sayyidd's eagerness to abandon all they had worked for up until now. He took a different tack. "Why is your idea, even as fleeting as it is, better than what we're already doing? The only difference is time, and the fact that the original plan allows multiple blows against our enemy. How will your blow of one time outweigh the ability to strike repeatedly?"

Abu Sayyidd inwardly smiled. He was making headway. He had been thinking about their mission for a long time, and saw the fatal flaw within the jihad as currently waged.

"Tell me, what's the greatest problem facing the jihad today? Is it truly the far enemy? His transgressions on the land of Mecca and Medina spit in the face of all true Muslims everywhere, yet he is allowed to continue. Why is that? It's because the true Muslim has been seduced by Satan, choosing Big Macs over the purity of the Quran.

"The average Muslim doesn't understand the threat of the far enemy. We need the man on the street to take up arms. The grocer, shoe salesman, and barber. If all Muslims would throw one rock, we would succeed. The only way to do this is to show the far enemy's true colors, to prove that they want to dominate and rule over a Christian empire."

Al Qaeda's doctrine, developed by Bin Laden and his leadership, stated that the only way to return to the ways of the Prophet was to destroy the "far enemy" that supported, and in some cases propped up, the godless regimes that had come to power in the nations of the Middle East, the so-called near enemy. The United States was first on the list of the far enemy for its support of the Kingdom of Saudi Arabia, Israel, Egypt, Jordan, and a host of other countries.

Bakr sighed. "Okay. So what. You sound like any imam in our mosques. What's that got to do with this mystical weapon? How can a single blow get what you want? It takes multiple blows against the far Satan to get him to do anything. The people of the U.S. have no memory. How will you cause this to change?"

Sayyidd held up his hands. "Please. Let me finish. We need to force the United States to attack all of a Muslim faith, without discrimination. To force the average Muslim to take up arms — either for faith or survival. I think we can cause this to happen if we *don't* attack the far enemy in his homeland. We'll attack him through his Zionist proxy. If we unleash this weapon against the murderous occupiers of Palestine, we can guarantee that they'll react in a frenzy. It would be a catalyst of war against their neighbors, which will cause the far enemy to choose between his Zionist son or the pure Muslims. It's no question who he will side with."

Abu Bakr was impressed with the logic of Sayyidd, and actually a little surprised, but still didn't think simply attacking Israel would be enough, even with a weapon of mass destruction. He was intrigued, though, and mulled the idea over in his mind. The more he thought about it, the more he thought it might succeed, with an additional twist.

"I don't think the weapon alone would be a sufficient catalyst. We need to ensure the Zionists will attack another. A bomb, no matter how great, may simply cause them to slaughter Palestinians, and that is an old story."

Baker paced back and forth a minute, then said, "Why not kill two birds with one stone? If we were able to bring about the attack you envision and blame it on the Persians, we could use the United States to eliminate those infidels while accomplishing exactly what you want. The United States has already forgotten about Iraq and begun to rattle their sabers toward Iran. With the Persians constantly talking about driving Israel into the sea and their current nuclear ambitions, it wouldn't take much evidence to convince the Zionists of their culpability. The attack would cause a major conflict, forcing all to choose sides."

Abu Sayyidd thought the idea was a good one but impossible to execute.

"But how will we implicate the Persians? We have no contacts with the Shia dogs, and I don't think they'd volunteer."

Sayyidd had a point. While Iran did indeed

141

provide support to various terrorist groups, most notably Hezbollah, the regime had little affinity for the Sunni-based Al Qaeda. Bakr knew there were ways around this. "One step at a time. We're assuming such a weapon exists. I'm not averse to seeing if we can find the weapon, provided it doesn't jeopardize our long-term efforts. For now, let's focus on simply getting the weapon. If that fails, we can still continue on our original task. That remains the priority."

Bakr gave Sayyidd a stern look. "You understand that, correct?"

Pleased at the new path, Sayyidd said, "Yes. Of course. I wouldn't do anything foolish."

Abu Bakr went to the back of the room and opened a box. They had brought with them a test case — a collection of items that were not illegal individually but, put together, were sure to be confiscated. If the package made it to the contact inside the U.S., then AQ would continue to the next step with Miguel's network. Inside the box was a Canon Rebel XTi digital camera, four Garmin 60CS mapping GPSs, four 3M P100 medical respirators, a box of glass test tubes, and two remote control garage door openers. Fairly innocuous items by themselves, but if the box were searched, the items together would trigger a response, which would allow the terrorists to judge the integrity of the smuggling network.

Abu Bakr was disappointed in the packing

list. "Where's the police scanner? The GPS and respirators will be useful for finding the weapon, but we need the police scanner right now."

"Ahh . . . I did some research on the American laws, and the police scanner we obtained had the ability to scan in the American cell phone spectrum. It's illegal to import those to America, so I took them out. I didn't think we'd really be using any of this equipment. It was just to see if the network was good."

Bakr was flabbergasted. "You took something out of the box because it was illegal? Something that we were illegally trying to smuggle in? What in all that's holy —"

"Don't begin to attack me!" Sayyidd said. "We were specifically told not to include illegal items so that if the box was found there would not be a legal reason to pursue its owners. It would simply get confiscated. I didn't know we would use the equipment."

Bakr waved his hand. "What's done is done. I won't mention it again, but if you wish to proceed on this path we need to find a scanner."

He pointed to the suitcase holding their laptop computer and Thrane M4 satellite phone. "Get on the Internet and find a local store that sells scanners. One that can scan in the nine-hundred-megahertz range that the cell phones here use. We need to hear what's

143

being said from inside this room. It's the only way we can stay ahead of Miguel."

# 22

The professor woke up bouncing on the backseat of an old Toyota Land Cruiser, having no idea how long he had been unconscious. He was covered in a musty blanket that stank of horse sweat and moldy hay. He heard the Englishman talking on a cell phone.

"He's not permanently injured, but he's going to have a headache. I took everything with him and checked him out of the hotel. Outside of some ratty clothes and a few maps of the biosphere, all he had was a laptop, an American cell phone, and a GPS. He had no return plane tickets."

The professor tried to move and realized that both his legs and hands were shackled like those of a death row inmate, which he was beginning to believe he had become. He was convinced that he was headed to some dank prison deep within Guatemala, to be held on the charge of murder and antiquities theft.

The man on the phone continued. "No, he

didn't have anyone else with him. He looked like he was about to flee. I didn't want to try to smuggle him past airport security, so I'm driving back. I'll be there in about seven hours. I'll see you then."

Eight and a half hours later, the professor sat in absolute panic. He was tied naked to a chair with a cloth bag over his head. He could make out light, but nothing else. He felt he had been sitting for at least forty-five minutes but in truth had lost all track of time. He heard a door open and felt a breeze on his naked chest. He made one final attempt to raise whatever dignity he could muster.

"I am an American citizen and a famous archaeologist. The embassy knows I am here, and in fact sponsored my expedition. They will come looking for me, and when they find me, they will punish you."

The only response he received was two alligator clips clamping onto his nipples. His heart began to hammer in his chest. He thought he was going to piss himself or throw up. A voice with a heavy Spanish accent stated, "You are Professor Cahill, a known antiquities thief and potential murderer. Far from sponsoring your expedition, the American embassy will more than likely sponsor your extradition to Guatemala to stand trial. Spare me your theatrics and you may yet walk out of here. I want to know where the temple is located. I've been through your computer and GPS and could find no reference to it. I have very little patience. Tell me what I want to know and I'll let you go."

It finally dawned on the professor that he wasn't in the hands of anyone remotely associated with the Guatemalan government, and that his overwhelming fears twenty-four hours ago paled in comparison to his present predicament. For all of his eccentricities, at his core the professor was a very intelligent man. In an instant, he computed that the only thing that would keep him alive was the fact that he alone knew where the temple was located. The minute he gave this up, he would be discarded with as much fanfare as a used condom.

As he began to form a plan, a searing jolt of electricity rocked his body, causing him to lock up in a rictus of pain, screaming out his soul. As rapidly as it came, the pain left.

The disembodied voice spoke again. "I can see you're thinking of ways to lie to me. Trust me, the longer you sit and think, the more I believe what you say is a lie. You have exactly three seconds to start talking, or I'll flip this switch and leave it on for an hour."

The professor gasped for air, sweat running freely over his body, his mind racing. He didn't have a plan. He didn't know what to say. His heart was palpitating, skipping irregularly.

"Three, two, one . . ."

"*Wait.* I'm trying to talk. Please . . . Dear God, don't do it again. I'll tell you whatever you want. I have two GPSs. I FedExed the one I used in the jungle to my niece in Charleston, South Carolina, from Flores. I don't have the information here, but I can get it. Please . . . Please . . . Please . . . I want to help you."

The professor couldn't believe how ridiculous this sounded. Why on earth would he do that? It made no sense whatsoever, but if he told them the truth, he would simply be made to retrieve the data from his Hotmail account. It was still in the sent folder. Once he gave that up, and he was sure he wasn't strong enough not to, he would be dead. He had to buttress the argument, so he began babbling to stem the punishment that was sure to come.

"You know what happened. A man died at the temple. I was not on a sanctioned expedition. The government would arrest me. I had to get rid of the data without losing it. I was afraid of getting arrested. I wanted to keep the location but didn't want to have any evidence on me. You have to believe me!"

He was met by silence. The disembodied voice circled around behind him. "Professor, that story is so ridiculous it insults my intelligence. I'm a smuggler. I know every single way to get something into the United States. I know there is no FedEx office in Flores.

Why on earth would you think I would believe that?"

The professor now believed he would die. The man had freely told him he was a criminal. Obviously, he had no intention of letting him go. In a panic, the professor began to expand on his story, making it more unlikely, grasping at straws.

"I gave it to an American who was leaving yesterday. We had become friends drinking at the bars, and I didn't want any evidence on me if I was stopped at the airport. He promised to FedEx it as soon as he landed in the United States. You must believe me! I'm telling the truth!"

"All right. I'll give you the benefit of the doubt. What was this man's name?"

"His name? It was . . . Uhh . . ."

With that, the pain returned like a lightning bolt. The professor jumped out of the chair, his entire body bowed out in an attempt to get away from the agony, his ankles and wrists holding him in place. He let loose a keening wail, then collapsed back into the chair, his bowels releasing onto the floor.

"Why'd you shut it off?" Miguel asked.

Jake said, "I didn't. He's still got megavoltage going through him."

"Wake him up," said Miguel.

Jake shut off the juice and felt the professor's pulse. "We can't. He's dead."

"What the fuck do you mean, dead? We

barely got started."

"Maybe he had a bad heart. We usually do this to men and woman much younger than him. Whatever, it's irrelevant. He's stone-cold dead."

"Shit. What do you suppose the odds are that he was telling the truth?"

Jake grinned. "As a matter of fact, probably pretty good. He didn't say anything that we can contradict, and people who follow the law usually panic when they realize they might be caught doing something illegal. The story is so damn stupid it just might be true. If you want to continue with this, it wouldn't hurt to simply check it out."

"Perhaps. I suppose it's worth following through. I'll give our friends in the U.S. a call. They owe me a favor, and this won't take much effort. In the meantime, I saw that our friends from overseas brought some computer equipment with them. Please go get them. Maybe they can take a look at his computer and find something we missed."

Jake left the room to go to the guesthouse while Miguel dialed an unlisted number.

"Let me speak to Vincent." He waited while the phone was handed off. "Yes, it's your southern helper, and it's time to repay the favor owed. I'd like you to get a package for me that's been mailed. It's coming by FedEx to a woman named Cahill in Charleston, South Carolina. She's the niece of a profes-

sor at the College of Charleston under the
same name and may very well be going to
the school. You don't need to be polite to
her."

## 23

Sayyidd stared at the laptop he had been asked to examine, wanting to shout in triumph. The thumb drive he had found among the belongings next to the computer had come to life, asking if he would like to use something called "cryptmaker" to extract data. He had been right. The computer was hiding a steganography program. He hit "yes" and waited for the work to be accomplished. Three of the twenty JPEG pictures he had cut and pasted from the laptop had dissolved, leaving behind a notepad file welcoming him to the cryptmaker family and giving him a troubleshooting guide. He realized that these were probably the example photos that came with the software package, allowing a new user to play with the software without fear of losing any valuable data.

Two hours earlier, when Jake had asked if either Bakr or Sayyidd could help with a computer problem, he had jumped at the chance. After meeting Miguel's computer expert, a man introduced only as José, he had been led into a room containing a table heaped with clothes, a laptop computer, cell phone, and GPS. While examining the computer, he began to suspect that it held a covert partition used for a steganography program due to the large amount of random digital photos and MP3s. José might have been an expert at typical computer problems, but he hadn't spent a life on the run with the world's greatest superpower chasing him. While serving as the media chief for his cell in Iraq, Sayyidd had used steganography quite a bit. He knew the signs. He also knew that he had no chance on earth of figuring out the keystrokes for a hidden program. His only hope was a physical key, something missed by Miguel's men. He had asked José for a glass of water to get him out of the room. As soon as he had left, Sayyidd had searched the clothes on the table. To his absolute surprise, he had found a thumb drive missed by the computer expert and had loaded it on the computer.

He was now sure he was only seconds away from finding the temple's location. One of the pictures on the hard drive would hold the data. He only needed to find the right one.

He was about to go back to the photo files when he heard José returning down the hallway. He deleted all of the files from the thumb drive, palmed it in his hand, and backed away from the computer.

José handed him the water and said, "You ready to continue?"

Sayyidd shook his head. "Not really. I've found nothing in two hours. I can't do anything more than what you've already done. I think this is a waste of time but will continue if you wish."

José said, "I knew this was folly to begin with. Miguel appreciates you trying anyway. You may go."

Sayyidd hurried back to the guesthouse with the thumb drive. He knew that Bakr would be livid at his theft. If Miguel realized what had taken place, they would both be dead. Sayyidd was counting on nobody knowing the thumb drive existed. He told Bakr of his experiences and what he had found. As expected, Bakr initially flew into a rage at Sayyidd's risks, but calmed down when told of the manner the thumb drive had been taken and the fact that Miguel's computer expert hadn't searched it. There was nothing to be done about it now anyway. The thumb drive was theirs. Risking returning it would be worse than keeping it.

The stego program itself made no sense to Bakr, given Miguel's previous phone call. They had obtained a Bearcat scanner earlier in the day, and both had heard the conversation between Miguel and his friends in the U.S. describing a FedEx package. Why would

Miguel be searching for a package if the temple location was on the computer? Bakr told Sayyidd to check the Web for a FedEx office in Flores, the last place the professor had been. Within minutes, Sayyidd answered that the only FedEx was in Guatemala City.

Bakr digested this. The facts didn't make sense. Let Miguel waste his time and money searching for answers in America. Bakr was sure that the data was hidden somewhere on the professor's computer, and that maybe they were as close as Sayyidd thought to pleasing Allah as no man had before.

# 24

The old man had been watching the boat-pretender for close to two months, waiting on him to do something interesting.

He called the man the pretender because he didn't act like anyone who owned a sailboat. He had seen plenty of people rich enough to own such a luxury in his job at the marina, and this man didn't fit the profile in any way whatsoever.

For one, the old man had never seen the pretender's boat leave the dock. Ever. Truthfully, he was unsure if the pretender even knew how to sail.

For another, boaters were a partying, gregarious bunch. When they docked, it was all about margaritas, bragging, and laughter. The old man had never seen the pretender smile. Never seen him talk to a single captain of another boat.

He'd figured out early on that the pretender was living on the boat. Something that wasn't allowed long-term, but the old man said nothing. Working dawn until dusk pumping gas at the marina, the old man had studied the pretender just to break the monotony. Every other day the man would punish himself with a workout routine on the deck of the boat, working until total exhaustion in the South Carolina heat, seemingly trying to kill himself, the sweat rolling off his body in rivers. He would then leave for a run that lasted about an hour. When he returned, the old man would watch him stagger behind the Dumpsters and vomit, sometimes on his knees. He didn't understand why until the pretender had passed by him finishing a run. The man stank of liquor, the foul smell wafting out of his pores like a fog.

After that, the old man began to lose interest, not wanting to waste his time on a drunk. Then one day the pretender had surprised him. Buying fuel for his boat, he had recognized the U.S. Army Second Division patch on the old man's hat and had asked if he had been in the Army.

The old man had grown wary, not wanting to be patronized as he had been by all the other rich folks who treated him like a piece of furniture, fulfilling their duty of patriotism with a pat on the head before demanding gas.

He had said, "Yes."

"Korea?"

"Yes. During some bad times."

The pretender had nodded with understanding. "Nobody can take that away from you. Even when you wish they could."

The old man was shocked. *He knows.*

A long time ago, on another continent, nobody had cared about the color of his skin. Rednecks and racists alike had learned that combat was color-blind. All that mattered was skill, and the old man had found that he inherently possessed something that others did not. Once upon a time he had been regarded as a savior, a man who could keep you alive, if you were lucky enough to be near him. He had been held in awe by better men than those who now demanded his gas. He was reminded of this by the nightmares that still caused him to lose sleep. He both loved and hated that time in his life, and somehow the pretender *knew.*

He began watching the pretender with renewed interest. The next time they met, he had asked, "Were you in the service?"

"Yes. The Army."

"Been to Iraq? Afghanistan?"

"Both at one time or another."

"Seen some bad shit?"

"Not really. The bad shit's here at home."

The answer had confused the old man. He continued to watch, waiting on the pretender to do something interesting. Eventually, he began to believe he had been wrong. The pretender held no secret truth. He was simply a drunken loser, dealing with the same demons as the old man. That is until the day the pretender disappeared and the old man had found two dead bodies behind the Dumpster, both killed by hand. That caused him to rethink the pretender's status for sure.

I woke up in my king-sized bed and rolled over to kiss my wife. My arm hit the pylon holding the foldout twin bed, and I returned to the reality of my existence like I had done every morning for the last nine fucking months. Each day, in the brief moment between being asleep and awake, I had one split second of happiness before remembering what had become of my family. If I could bottle each split second, I'd give the remainder of the day to God, or the Devil, or whoever else was having a party out of my pain. Twenty-three hours, fifty-nine minutes, fifty-nine seconds, and some change for each split second. It would be a good trade.

I relive the grief process every single day, like clockwork. I'm still waiting for it to be a dull ache at the back of my soul, like all the doctors promised would happen. Instead, each morning the pain is as strong as that night in Tbilisi almost a year ago.

I sat up in bed and looked at the picture of Heather and Angie on my counter. I felt the pain begin to turn to rage. That also happened like clockwork. It's hard to explain the level of the anger. It's like trying to explain color to a blind man. I'm afraid to really put into words the dark thoughts that come to me. I want to rip someone apart while they're still alive, to destroy something so completely that nothing identifiable remains. Sometimes the thoughts scare me.

I hate the rage, but there's nothing I can do about it. It won't go away. I've tried. I've seen doctors and gone to support groups, but nothing quenches it. I've talked to guys who say they used to be in the same boat as me, who lost their wife to cancer, or their family in a plane crash, and they say the pain will dull, the rage will dissipate. They mean well, but they're wrong. It hasn't dulled one bit. I think it's because they aren't in the same boat as me. They had their pain thrown on them without being asked. I earned every sorry bit given to me. They lost their family to fate or God. I killed mine.

If I had listened to Heather and hadn't done that final tour, they'd be alive. Shit, I could have done the tour and simply come home for Angie's birthday — *like I promised* — and they'd be alive. Simple as that. Because of it, my punishment is a rage that's hard to quantify. A blackness that wants to eat me. Wants to eat everything, spreading its rotting hatred until the entire world is burning. I don't think it will ever go away. It's hard enough just to control. It sits just below the surface, a beast looking to run free.

Sometimes I fantasize about letting it loose, about completely giving in to it. I haven't yet, but it's hard. Very, very hard.

My residence is my latest attempt to get rid of the pain. I took our savings and bought a sailboat. An extreme fixer-upper. I had this idiotic fantasy that I'd spend my days sanding wood, working on the engine, and live like some dumb-ass hermit at a monastery. In my imagination, the blackness would slowly dissipate the further along I got, until I was some sort of mystical sailor who finally understood the meaning of life. Apparently, that shit only works in the movies.

So far, I haven't done a single thing with the boat. Well, at least nothing positive. I have managed to turn the galley into a giant garbage can. There are enough pizza boxes and beer cans to keep it afloat if it springs a leak. Last night, I had decided that today would be the day I would begin work on the top deck, sealing it and doing other maintenance. Now, in the morning light, I really didn't give a shit about my crumbling deck. I'd rather go get a beer. It was my day off from physical training, so I didn't have anything I really needed to do. I kissed my finger and touched the picture of my family. *Who am I kidding? I never have anything I really need to do.*

## 25

Jennifer and Skeeter, along with six other girls, entered the front door of the Windjammer a little after eight at night. The floor was already crowded, but nowhere near as crowded as it would be in a few more hours. At least at this hour they could move around without pushing and could hold a conversation without leaning in and yelling into each other's ears.

Jennifer had shown up at Skeeter's condo on the Isle of Palms a little over two hours ago. Skeeter appeared surprised that Jennifer had shown up, and went out of her way to make sure she was settled in, kicking out the coed currently sleeping in one of the guest rooms and giving Jennifer the bed. Surrounded by the other girls having a good time, Jennifer began to feel glad she had come. Now, standing inside the Windjammer, she wasn't so sure.

Four frat boys stood in the middle of the large dance floor, loud and obnoxious. Jenni-

fer recognized the ringleader. His name was Tad, and he reminded Jennifer of her ex-husband both in looks and attitude. *Great. Just what I need to ruin the evening.* Tad himself seemed to think it was his destiny to sleep with Jennifer and came on to her at every opportunity. *Just ignore him. He's not your ex-husband. He's just a loudmouth.* She felt a tap on her shoulder.

"Hello . . . are you listening?" said Skeeter.

"Yeah. Sorry. What did you say?"

"What do you want to drink? I'll go fight the bar."

Jennifer laughed at that, because she knew Skeeter's idea of "fighting" the bar entailed "accidentally" brushing up against a man with her breast, saying excuse-me, then scooting through the gap made when the man turned around.

"I'll come with you. Maybe we can get a stool."

Skeeter moved through the crowd like she owned the place, using her hand or breast to part the crowd, depending on gender. When she reached the bar only one man separated her from her goal. Seated on one of the few available stools, he was holding a beer and staring unfocused at the bar top, apparently deep in thought. He was clearly easy pickins, as he was here on his own and probably looking for a date. Skeeter brushed his upper arm with an ample breast and said, "Excuse me, can I get in here?"

Jennifer waited to see his reaction when he saw Skeeter. It was always funny watching a man's face turn from a normal expression to a drooling mass of testosterone upon looking into her eyes.

In this case, the guy looked up at her with no more expression than if he were talking to a cabdriver. Saying, "Yeah, go ahead," he scooted over, giving her space at the bar. As Skeeter moved forward he locked eyes with Jennifer, nodded, then returned to his beer. His stare made Jennifer want to take a step back. It wasn't exactly mean, just annoyed, as if they had interrupted something important. Older than most in the bar, wearing a simple T-shirt and sporting a day-and-a-half beard, he had a white scar that ran through his cheek, charting a path through his stubble.

Skeeter ordered a couple of margaritas and moved back from the bar. "What's up with that guy? He looked at us like he was wondering if we owed him money. I've had more interest paid to me by a transvestite. He'd better watch himself, or he's going to find himself on the short end of the Skeeter Slam."

"Come on. Leave him alone. He doesn't look like someone with a very good sense of humor."

"Yeah, I know. It's easier to screw with Tad anyway. Let's go make those guys drool."

164

"Can't we just stay here? I don't feel like putting up with Tad's shit."

"What's the big deal? He's just a blowhard. If he gets obnoxious we can leave. How about —"

Before she could finish, they both heard Tad's raised voice. He and his little group had surrounded another college student and were in a face-off. She heard Tad telling the student to get the hell out of the bar on his own two feet or leave in an ambulance. *Friggin' great. Now there's going to be a bar fight. Why did I come out here?*

From the other side of the group, the man from the bar suddenly stood up and walked over to Tad, saying, "Leave him alone. He's been sitting there listening to your shit for a half hour. You're even."

Jennifer stared at him, surprised. The penetrating gaze was gone, replaced by an unfocused alcoholic haze. She must have been imagining things, because this guy was clearly drunk. No wonder he hadn't hit on them. He probably hadn't even been able to focus on them. She knew that he was in trouble, because Tad would kick his ass just to make his night, and no matter how good a fighter the man might be sober, now he was swaying back and forth and would be lucky to land a punch. Jennifer saw Tad look at the drunk, sizing him up. She could tell that Tad had come to the same conclusion she had.

Tad said, "You know what makes me sick? Shitbags like you who come into the Jammer stinking up the place instead of hanging out at the VFW next door with the rest of the winos."

With that, he threw a hard right punch, catching the drunk full in the face.

To his credit, the man didn't fall, but he had no coordination to protect himself. Tad waded in, throwing right after left, almost all of them connecting in one way or another. The drunk staggered back, protecting his face and feebly throwing a succession of worthless jabs that Tad batted away. He finally fell over, whereupon Tad set about kicking him relentlessly in the ribs.

Tad's sycophant friends wasted no time jumping on the other college student, all of them falling to the ground and rolling around. The bouncers came screaming in, focused on the three-to-one fight, flinging bodies left and right to separate them, not realizing there were two fights occurring, and leaving Jennifer to watch the punishment Tad was dishing out. She flashed back to her ex-husband and snapped. Without thinking, she dropped her drink and ran the ten feet to the fight. She grabbed Tad's arm and jerked him back, screaming, "Leave him alone! You're going to kill him!"

Tad shook her off, intent on continuing the assault. Jennifer threw herself onto the man, shielding his body with hers. Tad stopped, looking at her in a murderous rage as if he was considering kicking her as well. Instead, he made a hasty exit out the back onto the deck. In seconds, the bouncers had control of the other fight and proceeded to escort the offenders to the door.

Jennifer helped the bloodied, pathetic fighter to his feet, talking to the bouncer headed their way. "I have him. I'll get him out of here."

"You'd better. Before I have him arrested."

She didn't know why, but she began leading him out of the bar, apologizing to the bartender as she walked. Maybe she saw herself on the floor four years ago. Maybe she just wanted an excuse to leave. *Maybe this just wasn't such a great idea. . . .*

Skeeter ran over to her. "Where are you going? You didn't do anything! You need to stay. All the assholes are gone now and the music hasn't even started."

"Skeeter, I appreciate it, but I'm no longer in the mood. I'm going to get this guy wherever he needs to go and head on back to the condo for some sleep. I'll pack up and go home tomorrow."

Skeeter watched her leave. Another sorority sister asked, "Where's she going with that loser? Is she desperate? She can do better than him."

Looking at her friend, Skeeter replied,

"She's just saving another lost puppy. Like every other time this happens, that puppy is going to end up doing nothing but peeing on her floor. I've seen his type. He'll give her nothing but grief."

# 26

Jennifer led the man to her car, a beat-up Mazda RX-7, which she had left at the end of Ocean Boulevard. He shuffled along a half a step behind her, making no effort to talk. She asked him repeated questions, but he just mumbled in response. She couldn't even get him to tell her his name. *Great. He really is a drunk. Maybe I'll just give him some change and point him to the nearest park bench.* When they finally got to her car, he attempted to wave her off, saying he was fine and could get home on his own. She was surprised by the sudden apparent sobriety. He was no longer swaying, and his eyes were fairly clear, although it was hard to tell with the swelling. *What was with this guy? He was a drunk one minute, and sober the next? Why fake being drunk?*

She said, "Look, don't act like you're putting me out. You're really doing me a favor. If you go off on your own, I'll have no excuse for not going back in there. I'm headed home anyway, so you might as well let me give you a ride — that is unless you live somewhere other than the Isle of Palms. I'm not running a taxi service to Charleston."

"I live at the marina, but I don't need a ride. My bike is down the street. I'm sober enough to drive."

"Are you nuts? Even if you were stone-cold sober, you'd probably wreck from the beating. Come on. I'm offering a ride for free. No strings attached."

"I don't need a ride. Worst case, I'll just walk. It will do me some good."

The penetrating gaze was back, forcing her to glance away.

"Walk? It's like five miles away. Quit bitching and get in."

He closed the gap between her and the car. With the car preventing her from moving away, he leaned into her personal space.

"Why do you feel compelled to help me out? You don't know anything about me. The world is full of monsters, why do you think you're immune from them? Do you think that just because you made some pathetic attempt at 'helping' me out I won't rape you? How long do you think it would have taken the bouncers to get to me? About a half second after you did? Don't flatter yourself. I didn't need the help then, and don't need it now."

He was towering over her, his eyes radiating anger. For a split second she was afraid,

170

wanting to bolt, wondering if she had made a terrible mistake. But her fear quickly gave way to irritation. What the hell was this all about? All she was trying to do was to help him out. He definitely wasn't a charmer, but he didn't seem like the type who would smack someone around just for the hell of it. After living with her husband for four years, her antenna for that sort of thing was fairly well tuned. Either way, she'd had enough. *Ungrateful son of a bitch.*

"Back off! What the hell is your problem? If I thought you were going to attack me I'd have let Tad crush your ass. If you planned on raping me, why on earth would you tell me beforehand? Oh, and yeah, I did save your ass. In case you didn't notice, Tad was giving you a beating that was about to be the difference between a ride in my car and a ride in an ambulance. Thanks for your appreciation, now get the hell out of my way and start hoofing it to the marina, superman."

She pushed him back from the door, yanking it open and banging her head as she tried to get inside the small cockpit of her car. She reached over to close the door when he leaned in and stopped her.

"My name's Pike. Pike Logan."

"Pike? What, are your parents Romanian vampires or something? Thanks for the information, but at this stage I really don't give a shit. Please let go of my door."

"That's just what I'm called. Look, I apologize. I haven't had a good day and took it out on you. I could use that ride."

When she looked back up at his face, she saw the intensity had been replaced by pain and confusion. Maybe shame. She was left with the impression that he hadn't apologized to anyone in a long time, and he was waiting to see if the gesture was worth it. *Shit. I know I'm going to regret this.*

"Get in. I'll take you home." Once he was settled in the passenger seat, she stuck out her hand and said, "I'm Jennifer Cahill. What's your real name?"

He took it, saying, "I told you, it's Pike. Pike Logan."

She started the car and pulled out of the parking lot, keeping the conversation going. "Really? If I were going to book you for assault, that's what I'd write down? What was the name written on your birth certificate?"

"I've been called Pike for a long time. It's my name now."

They rode in silence for a few minutes before she tried again.

"If you live at the marina, you're either passing through or working as a sailor. Which is it?"

"Neither. I moved here about two months ago. I don't like paying rent and couldn't afford a house. A guy was selling a beat-up thirty-seven-foot boat that needed a lot of work. The plumbing was okay, and the slip was paid for a year. I bought it, and now I live there."

"Wow, that's pretty romantic."

"It puts a roof over my head."

Jennifer waited for more, but he said nothing.

"That's it? Nobody buys a boat just to live on. They buy it for a reason. Come on, what's yours?"

She saw him grimace at the question.

"I told you why. There isn't any deep meaning. It's just a damn boat. A place to live. Do we have to keep talking about it?"

She let it go. Luckily, they had turned onto Forty-first Avenue and were only seconds from the marina. The rest of the ride was spent in silence.

"All right, we're here. Where do I go?"

"Just park it anywhere. I can walk in from here. What do I owe you for the ride?"

Jennifer hesitated, and then said, "Does your boat have a bathroom? I really have to go."

She regretted saying it as soon as it came out. She really just wanted to use the bathroom but was sure he would take it a different way. She didn't want him to think she was attracted in any way. When she saw his face, she realized that he was embarrassed as well.

"Ahh . . . yes . . . I do have a bathroom,

but it's a dinky thing that requires you to pump it to get it to work, sort of like a floating outhouse. You're welcome to use it, if you want. Just don't complain about the mess."

"Okay. If you don't mind, I'll use it and go on home."

Jennifer walked down into the galley of the boat and was repulsed by the mess. *Doesn't this guy know that underwear doesn't wash itself? Man, how could he live in this filth?* She was really wondering what the toilet would be like, and figured she'd be doing the squat-and-hover like she was at a sleazy truck stop in between Mississippi and Louisiana. She looked around in an attempt to find something to talk about to break the awkward silence. She was just about to ask him if dirty socks were commonly used as insulation when she saw a picture of a very pretty woman on the shelf above the foldout bed.

"Is that your girlfriend? She's gorgeous."

"That's my wife. She's dead, and I don't want to talk about that either."

The words hit Jennifer like a cold shot of water. Next to the woman in the picture was a small child. She wisely decided not to ask who that was. Pike showed her the toilet, which was surprisingly clean, and how to operate the pump that flushed it. After she finished, she came out, trying to look cool leaning against the doorjamb, saying, "Thanks. I guess I'll head out now."

There was another moment of awkward silence. It looked to her like Pike didn't know what to say. She was wondering if he was going to spit out some sort of Tourette's syndrome rant when he finally said, "Well, I appreciate your help tonight. Thanks again for the ride."

With a wry grin, Jennifer said, "You don't lie very well. Thanks for the use of your bathroom."

Pike gave her a smile that reached his eyes for the first time. The effect diminished his Halloween mask appearance. *He ought to do that more often.*

"You don't lie very well either," he said. "I meant it."

Jennifer left the boat, wondering if she would ever see Pike again. She also wondered why she cared. He was attractive enough in a weird, Grizzly Adams sort of way, but he had a personality that seemed to swing between outright asshole to limited tolerance. He had moments of humor and kindness that almost seemed to be fighting their way out.

She had reached the front of her car before she saw the two men standing behind it.

She stopped where she was, immediately feeling unease and toying with running back to Pike's boat. "Can I help you guys?"

The taller of the two moved to the driver's side. "You can help yourself, that's for sure."

The shorter man, surprisingly fast, circled around behind her.

## 27

I pulled out my bed and sat down, thinking about Jennifer. *What in the hell was that all about? Who throws their body on a complete stranger in a bar fight? And then offers to take them home afterward? Especially someone like me?* That took a lot of guts — or stupidity. I wasn't sure which, but I was leaning toward guts. She didn't act stupid. I was starting to feel a little bad about the way I had treated her. I thought about the vile things I had yelled at her by her car and felt a wash of shame. *Jesus, what an asshole.* I was surprised she'd let me in her car.

I looked in my small mirror and felt the anger come back at the sight of my beaten face. Lately, after I get a few beers in me, I begin thinking about beating the hell out of someone just to release a little of the pain. I hadn't sunk so low as to simply punch the first person I saw, but I could usually count on some blowhard to be around as the night wore on. I had found out early on that I must look like a mean bastard, because blowhards usually backed down when I confronted them. I solved that dilemma by acting like I was too drunk to brawl. The problem with this cycle was that some sort of switch goes off after I pick the fight and I end up taking an ass-beating. I just can't bring myself to crush whoever I'm fighting. That's probably a good thing. All it would take is one fight to get out of control, and I would then be viewed as a menace to society, the fall from grace complete.

Outside, I heard, "Pike!"

*What now?*

Scrambling up onto the deck, I saw Jennifer running flat out down the gangway to my boat, followed by two other men.

Before I could say anything, she ran right by me, shouting, "Help me!" as she went down into my boat. I turned back around and faced the men.

They had reached the deck of my boat and stopped. They looked completely out of place for a marina. One was squat, with a bullet head and no neck. He had a ridiculous hoop earring in one ear. The other was taller, and more distinguished, with glasses and a little gray at the temples. Both were wearing suits.

The taller one spoke. "This is none of your business. Just step aside. We're her cousins. We told her some bad news about her uncle, and she took it the wrong way."

They both advanced onto my deck as he spoke, with the Neanderthal guy circling to my left.

"Get the fuck off of my boat."

Neanderthal spoke for the first time. "No, you get off. I promise, I'm much worse than that pissant college boy that kicked your ass. I'm not going to stop with a couple of punches. Step aside."

From Neanderthal's position I was having a hard time keeping both men in sight. They clearly had done this before, and I could almost smell Neanderthal's eagerness to tear into me. The fight was coming, because there was no way I was getting off my own fucking boat. I gave one attempt to stop it, since it wasn't really fair for Neanderthal to think the frat boy had won on skill.

"Look," I said, "I don't want any trouble. Just leave and there won't be any need to call the police."

Neanderthal said, "You've already got trouble," then swung a hard right cross. *Idiot.*

I raised my left arm, forming a triangle against my head in order to protect it. I took the brunt of the blow and wrapped my left arm around the man's right, trapping his elbow. I brought my right arm underneath the elbow and wrenched against the joint with great force, causing it to splinter upward, against the direction it was intended to go. Before the damage had even registered in

179

Neanderthal's brain, I put his head between my arms at waist level in a guillotine choke, preventing him from harming me while I tried to determine what the other man was doing, an unknown threat still on the loose.

While we danced around, the taller man pulled out a double-edged Gerber Mark I boot knife.

"Let him go, or I'm going to carve you up."

I stared at the knife to make sure it was real, feeling a perverse sense of joy. In fact, it was more like elation, as if I had just rubbed off a winning lottery ticket. He had pulled out a lethal weapon, which legally allowed me to escalate to lethal force. *I can let the beast loose.*

I locked eyes with the knife-wielding man and grinned. Instead of cutting off the blood flow in the Neanderthal's carotid arteries and simply causing him to pass out, I jerked upward with all of my strength, snapping his neck cleanly. I continued to pull until I felt his vertebrae separate and his neck begin to stretch like a weak rubber band.

I dropped that lifeless sack of shit and took off at a dead sprint toward the tall man. He looked at me in amazement and brought his knife hand up, preparing to rip me open. I faked in, causing him to slash early. I dodged the sweeping blade and trapped his knife hand in between my own two hands. Controlling the blade, I ducked under his arm, bringing the knife with me and turning his arm into a pretzel. I continued to rotate until his joints gave, first at the elbow, then at the wrist. It sounded like a kid twisting bubble wrap. I completed the circle and ended up facing him head on, still holding his knife arm, which had turned into a useless piece of bone and gristle. I looked deep into his eyes and rammed the blade straight into his fucking skeevy heart.

He remained standing for a full second, his mouth a perfect O, looking down in disbelief at the knife sticking out of his chest, still held by his own destroyed arm, his hand facing the opposite of where it should be. He fell over backward onto the deck.

I looked around for other threats and found none, either on the boat or on shore. All I saw were the two people I had butchered. My rage disappeared. I knew that I had crossed the final threshold. *I've just killed two people in cold blood. I'm a fucking psychopath. I'll be put down like a rabid dog, and I deserve it.*

I wasn't sure what to do. I figured I'd better call 911 but decided to check on Jennifer first. I called her name and descended into the galley. She came flying out of the forward hold, hugging me and crying uncontrollably. She stopped sobbing and began babbling something about her uncle and the danger he was in.

I held on to her arms and pushed her back a little until I could see into her eyes, saying, "Whoa. Slow down. It's okay now. What did those guys want?'

"I don't know. They said that my uncle was in trouble, and that if I wanted to help him I had to give them a package he had sent. I don't know what they're talking about. I never got a package, but when I told them that, they said that it was going to be very painful for me if I continued to lie. The shorter one began talking about what he was going to do to me if I didn't give them the package."

I already knew something screwy was going on, because Neanderthal had mentioned my fight at the Windjammer. These guys must have had Jennifer under surveillance, and an effort like that meant that somebody wanted something very badly from her. I found it hard to believe she was completely in the dark. *Great. Just perfect.* I had broken up some sort of sleazy criminal exchange.

"Who are those guys, and don't give me 'I don't know.' Bad guys hunting you for no reason only happens in the movies. What are you into? Drugs or something?"

Jennifer shook her head violently. "I'm not into anything. I don't know what they're after. Something about my uncle, I guess."

"Who's your uncle?"

"He's on a research expedition in the

182

Guatemalan rain forest. I have no idea what they could want with him, or with me. I'm telling the truth. They were definitely after me because they knew my uncle's name. I don't know what's going on."

She broke down again and began to sob, sinking into a chair. I didn't buy a single bit of what she'd said. I didn't think the crying was an act, because they probably had threatened her with all sorts of vile shit, but I was sure she was lying about not knowing what was going on. After interrogating hundreds of suspected terrorists, I had a cynical view about a person's innocence when the facts didn't jibe. You wouldn't believe the number of times I have heard a terrorist say something stupid like, "I swear, I didn't know that the car in my garage had four hundred pounds of TNT in it. I just took it in for an oil change. . . ."

I figured Jennifer and her uncle were involved in some sort of drug smuggling scheme, and would leave it at that. *Research expedition. Yeah, right. Researching how to get some product across the border.*

Whatever she was into, I now had a new concern. I had just whacked a couple of unsavory individuals. These types of thugs had bosses who remained in power by being the biggest badasses in the jungle. They wouldn't let this go, but would be coming for me to make sure everyone knew what happened to somebody who interfered. On top of that, there was no way the cops would believe that I had nothing to do with whatever was going on.

I thought about my options, which is to say I realized I had very few. I could simply get on my boat and start sailing somewhere, getting someplace safe and starting over, but in the two months I had owned the boat, I had done absolutely nothing with it. It was less seaworthy now than when I'd bought it. Not that that really mattered, since I barely knew how to sail and had about four hundred dollars to my name. That pretty much eliminated the water option. I could leave the boat and do the same thing on land, but my finances made this even more unattractive. At least with the boat I'd be taking my house with me. Without it, I'd either be sleeping outdoors or running out of money in a matter of days.

I cursed and punched a bulkhead, the anger coming back with a vengeance. Jennifer recoiled at the violence, but I didn't give a shit.

"You're going to tell me what's going on before the cops get here. I'm not going to get rolled up into whatever bullshit, amateur-hour scheme you and your uncle are into."

"I don't know! Jesus, I'm supposed to be on spring break! If you don't want to talk to the cops, fine, I won't mention you. I'll just say somebody yelled at the jerks and they panicked and ran away. You've done your good deed, you don't have to worry about any police activity, since I'm sure that you've got an arrest record a mile long. In fact, I'm pretty sure I don't want any police officer to think that you and I are somehow involved in something either."

*Is she drunk?* I looked at her in amazement, then remembered that she hadn't been around for the finale of the fighting. "It's a little bit late for that. The two apes up top are dead. I killed them. I'm involved whether you like it or not, and I don't like to be involved in something I have no control over. Tell me what's going on."

Jennifer looked at me, stunned. "You *killed* them? How? Why on earth would you do that —"

"Because the assholes that wanted to talk to *you* pulled a knife on *me*. It's done, and now I'm involved in a mess I want no part of. Who's your contact? Who sent those guys?"

Jennifer simply sat there.

I backed off. Scaring the shit out of her wasn't going to get me anywhere. I leaned back, thinking about what I knew. My gut was suddenly saying she wasn't lying. When I thought about it, I realized the woman who'd helped me tonight didn't seem like the type involved in anything like drug smuggling. It just didn't add up. Someone like that would have waited until I was unconscious, then picked my pocket. I stopped that line of thought. *Don't be fooled by the package. You don't know her at all.*

Either way, it wasn't my problem. I needed to figure a way out of this mess and quit worrying about whether she was guilty. I went back to the deck, feeling the clock ticking rapidly. It was a miracle that nobody around the marina had heard the ruckus, but it was only a matter of time before someone wandered by. Thinking it through, I realized that it would be much, much better if I called the police, or if Jennifer did. Every second of delay was going to look suspicious.

I searched both bodies. The only things of value were a couple of wallets with driver's licenses from New York and New Jersey and a couple of cell phones. I checked the contact list of both phones. They were empty, which indicated in and of itself that these guys had something to hide, although that was blatantly obvious at this point. I switched to the call history of the phones, hoping that these guys weren't that diligent with their operational security. The shorter man — Anthony from his driver's license — had no incoming calls, and about twenty calls to 1-900 numbers on the outgoing list, thus was little help. The taller man, or Edward, had two incoming calls, one from overseas by the look of the number. His outgoing-calls list only

contained two numbers, one of them matching up to the overseas incoming number. I
went back to Jennifer.

"Do you know the country code of Guatemala?"

"I think so. It's either 520 or 502."

"Well, one of the guys has an international
phone number starting with 502, so he's calling Guatemala. Does your uncle have a GSM
phone that works outside the U.S.?"

"No. He always communicates over the
Internet. Most of the places he goes don't
have cell phone service, so he doesn't bother."

I hit redial on the phone, wondering who
was paying the bill for this call.

Jennifer stood up. "What are you doing?
Who are you calling?"

"I don't know who's going to answer, but
I'm getting my ass out of trouble with whoever is after you. You might want to do the
same. I'll pass the phone to you when I'm
done."

I stood waiting for the connection to be
made. Finally, a man with a heavy Spanish
accent answered in English. "So good of you
to call. I assume that it's done? Do you have
some good news?"

"Uh, no. We don't have the package. And
the guy who owns this phone won't be getting the package. He's now out of the picture
for the long term."

I had no idea who this was, but there was a

better-than-even chance that whoever he was, he was being monitored. I didn't want to incriminate myself on some DEA tape.

"I'm sorry, my English isn't that good. Could you please explain yourself?"

"Yeah, I'll try to make it as plain as I can. Your messenger acted like an asshole and I took him off the project. I'm not involved in any way, and just want to make sure that you know that I don't have the package, don't want the package, and don't even know what it is."

## 28

On his Guatemalan estate, Miguel cursed
under his breath. *Those damn amateurs.* He
should have known they would screw this
up, but he was on a tight time schedule, and
they were the only ones who could have reacted in time. His calculator brain began assessing courses of action. The guy on the
other end of the phone, whoever he was, was
clearly no innocent bystander, as he'd had
the presence of mind to call and had fairly
good operational security on the phone. Tony
and Ed must have said too much, and now
this guy wanted a piece of the action. On the
other hand, why would he start out by saying
he wanted nothing to do with it? Of course,
he could be the police, but if that were the
case it really didn't matter. Miguel wasn't
tied to whatever antics Ed and Tony had
pulled. The only loss was the package itself,
and if this was the police, the whole operation was over anyway. He needed to determine who this guy was, and maybe turn this

to his advantage.

"I'm beginning to think you have a wrong number. I'm sure I don't know what you are talking about, but am curious. If you don't know anything about the package, then how do you know there is one? That seems a little illogical."

"Look, the person who was supposed to get the package is sitting right here. She told me about it. I'm not involved and just want to make sure you know that I'm not trying to get the package, whatever it is. Your business is with her, not me."

Miguel had the opening he wanted but was still not sure this wasn't a trick. "All right, because I'm curious and have nothing else to do right now, I'll talk to her. Put her on."

"I will, but before I do, are we good? I'll get her on the phone, and I'm out of it? I didn't mean to do anything, but your messengers were insistent."

"Sure, you're good. Put her on. Since I don't know about a package or any messengers, I certainly won't be upset at you for anything."

Miguel waited a few seconds, then heard a female's voice. "Hello? Who's this?"

He was surprised, but pleasantly so. This seemed to be the real deal, and it didn't look like the entire operation had been brought to a halt. He still needed the package, but maybe you wish, you can run. It'll just increase the pain of your death. Put on the girl."

"Hang on, hang on. I'll get your package. We don't have it here. I just met the girl, and she's been out here all week."

"I'll make this plain, as I'm not sure my English would be able to get across any subtle nuances. Bring me the package or I will kill your uncle in a very slow, painful manner."

"Yeah, yeah, I get it. I don't speak Spanish, so I'll talk slow as well. It's not my uncle and I don't give a shit about him."

I saw Jennifer snap her head around, looking at me like I was a piece of dog shit on her shoe. I held up a finger and continued. "The package is probably at her house in town. We'll go see if it's there."

I waited a beat, hearing only silence. "You still there?"

"Yes. I'm now trying to decide if I want the package more than the pleasure of killing you. Let's get something straight: I will slaughter you and anyone you have ever known if you speak to me in such a manner again. Do you understand?"

*Oops. I guess that wasn't so smart.* "Yes."

"You and Jennifer call me when you have the package. If you don't call in the next six hours, you can start the clock ticking on your life. Tell the girl her uncle will be skinned alive."

I hung up the phone and looked at Jen-

194

he could get it through her. He dropped his innocent pretenses. "Is this the niece of John Cahill?"

"Yes, this is Jennifer. What do you want? How do you know who I am?"

"I'm a business associate of your uncle's. He told me that he mailed you a package by FedEx yesterday. Unfortunately, he mailed you something that he had promised me, and I need to get it back. My two friends were sent there to get it from you, but apparently you would prefer to steal what is rightfully mine."

The phone went silent. After a pregnant pause, the woman spoke.

"I don't know what to say. I don't have a package from my uncle. If you would let me talk to him, maybe I can sort this out."

Miguel knew he had to manage this carefully. His only lead was the phone call going on right now, and both would likely flee as soon as they hung up. He didn't even know the man's name. He needed to turn this to his advantage, bringing the mountain to Muhammad, as his foreign guests would say.

"I'm not sure what else your uncle could add to the conversation. He told me he sent you a package, the method it would arrive, and the date. What I need is that package, and since you have seen fit to prevent my men from collecting it, I'm going to need you to bring it to me."

191

"I'm telling the truth. I didn't kill your guys, Pike did."

*What the fuck did she just say?* I jumped up in a spasm, trying to get the phone out of Jennifer's hands. She turned around in a circle, batting my hands away and continuing the conversation.

"I'm the person they threatened. I don't want to be a part of this either. Whatever my uncle owes you, I'll help him to repay. Whatever is in the package, I'll make sure you get a replacement. If you would just get my uncle on the phone, we can sort this out."

I saw Jennifer's face go white at whatever the man was saying. I quit trying to get the phone.

"Please, please don't hurt my uncle. . . . I'll do what you want. . . . Whatever you want . . ."

She looked me in the eye, her expression pleading for help, and said, "Pike wants the phone. . . . I don't know. . . . Please . . . Here's Pike."

She held out the phone with her hand over the microphone and said, "Talk to him. Please . . . do something. I don't know what to tell him. I don't know anything about a package. Don't let him hurt my uncle."

I snatched the phone and put my own hand over the microphone. "Why in the hell did you give him my name and tell him his men

192

were dead? I'm trying to help us out and you're sitting there digging a grave for both of us. Focus on your own damn grave and leave me out of this!"

"Please . . . Talk to him." The fear on her face cracked my anger.

*Shit. She's telling the truth.* I looked at her for a second, making up my mind.

I removed my hand and said, "This is Pike."

"I didn't know the extent of the damage to my operation. Is what she says true?"

I gave up any pretense of operational security. If someone was recording this, I was already screwed.

"Yes, it's true, but I only reacted to what they did. The assholes came on my boat and tried to knock me out. When I stopped that, they pulled out a knife and tried to gut me. I have no idea what this is about, but I'm not going to be held accountable for your team losing their cool. I really didn't want anything to do with this. They escalated, not me."

"I don't give a shit about your excuses. I only care about the fact that your interference will cost me profits. I don't have my package because of you. I'll give you a choice. Either get the package and deliver it to me or I'll take the profits out of your skin."

Shit. That was the last thing I wanted t hear. What in the world had this girl gotte involved in?

He continued. "Don't test my patience

193

nifer's ashen face. *Yeah, I'll be sure and relay that bit of sunshine.*

## 29

It took relatively little time for us to determine that there was no package waiting at Jennifer's apartment. She went to her computer to see if she had a FedEx tracking number, or anything to indicate something was on the way, but came up empty.

Jennifer said, "What the hell am I going to do now? I don't even know what's supposed to be in the package, so I can't even fake it."

I needed to get some background before I offered any advice. "What was your uncle doing in Guatemala? I mean for real, no bullshit?"

Jennifer sighed again, like she didn't think I would believe what she had to say, which was smart, because if it was some sort of Indiana Jones bullshit, I wouldn't.

"My uncle has a theory about the demise of the Mayans. He thinks the Mayan priests created a weapon a long time ago that got out of control. For the last twenty years he's gone down to Guatemala to find a temple that he thinks will prove his theory." She saw the skepticism on my face and raised her voice. "I know it sounds ridiculous, but it's true. That's what he's doing in Guatemala."

This was getting downright stupid. "So, your uncle believed that the Mayans had invented or found the world's first WMD? Did he look for crop circles during Christmas break?"

Jennifer's eyes clouded with a scowl. "I never said anything about WMD. I said a weapon. Many, many respectable scholars believed his theory."

I chuckled and held up my hands in a gesture of surrender. "WMD stands for weapon of mass destruction. It's a military term meaning any weapon that can kill a lot of people, like a nuke, or biological weapon. They're pretty hard to make. I'm not trying to get you mad, but is there a chance that your uncle was doing something besides looking for this temple?"

Jennifer shook her head adamantly. "No. No way. He was obsessed with the temple. He spent all year using every spare minute to research possible new sites. Nobody was paying for the trips anymore, so he had no reason to pretend."

"Was there anything about this trip that was different from the other trips? Did you talk to him at all?"

"Not really. He didn't have the money for a

satellite phone. The only contact I had with him after he went into the jungle was an e-mail he sent a couple of days ago."

Jennifer paused a moment as a look of realization crossed her face.

"Actually, I did think it was a little odd, because it came before he was supposed to be out of the jungle. I just figured it meant he hadn't found anything."

"What did it say?"

"It was nothing. He had found some local music and sent it to me. He didn't even say anything about his trip."

"Let me see it."

Jennifer pulled up the e-mail. "See, it's nothing. The music isn't even that good. It sucks."

"Did he send you music on every trip? What was special about this music?"

"Nothing, now that you mention it. It was just some local music."

"Yet he'd been going to the same place for years and just now noticed the local music? That doesn't make any sense."

"Well, it might not make any sense, but that's what it is. My uncle is eccentric, so I wouldn't put it past him. The bottom line is that it's just a bunch of MP3 music. Nothing more."

"Pull up the properties of the music. Right-click on it."

Jennifer did as I asked, showing that the

song she clicked on was about ten megabytes.

"Click on the next one."

It was nine megabytes.

"These files have been altered."

I was pretty well versed in various terrorist communication methods. I had come across steganography on multiple occasions from the computer equipment my team had confiscated, usually because some analyst with a fifty-pound head deep in a basement found it.

"I think your uncle sent you something hidden in these songs. The average MP3 song is about three to five megabytes. These songs are all twice that size, but not twice the length. I think he hid something in here, and whatever it is, it's what the man on the phone wants."

"Are you serious? How do we get it out? What do we do?"

"Whoa. Calm down. It might be nothing more than a bad copy of an MP3. If he got it from some corrupted server in Guatemala it could just have a bunch of extraneous stuff attached, or even some malicious software like a virus or Trojan horse. I'm just saying that steganography is a possibility. He might have embedded some message inside the songs."

"How can we tell?"

"We can't, without the program that created it. Whatever is in there will be encrypted and hidden."

I watched Jennifer deflate again. She said, "So what do we do now? That doesn't help us out at all."

*What do you mean, "we?"* I wanted to ask.

Instead, I thought about it for a minute, then said, "This might be enough. What we know is that the guy on the phone thinks your uncle mailed something. We also know he doesn't understand how it was sent or exactly what it was. I'm going to assume that he knows it was some sort of computer data, and he just doesn't know the form it's coming in."

"Okay, so? How does that help my uncle?"

"Well, you could plausibly tell the guy on the phone that you got the package, and that it was an MP3 player. You can see where it goes from there. If he seems to think that's okay, you take it to him, then use the stego portion as leverage to get your uncle back. In other words, let him get the MP3 player and see if he honors his part of the deal. If he doesn't, tell him the stuff is encrypted and you'll decrypt it when you get your uncle back."

"What do I do if I can't decrypt the files? This sounds like a dangerous game you're playing with my uncle's life. We don't even know if this is stegocryptography or whatever you called it."

"Yeah, it's a game, but the alternative is to

say, 'I don't have the package. Feel free to send me my uncle's skin when you're done. I'm making some boots.' I'm offering some alternatives. If it is stego, your uncle made it and should be able to decrypt it. If it's not stego, you don't have a hand to play anyway. The fact remains that he thinks you have a package from FedEx, and you don't."

Jennifer looked at me in disgust. "Jesus, do you work at being such a jerk, or does it come naturally? I'm just trying to figure out the best thing to do, not questioning your manhood."

I let that go and watched her pace back and forth for a couple of seconds.

She said, "Trust me, it's painful to say this, but I can't see a better way." She stopped pacing and looked me squarely in the eyes. "Will you help me with this? Will you fly to Guatemala with me and help me get my uncle back? I'll pay the way. I have money. Please . . . I don't have anyone else to turn to. My uncle's a good person."

*Shit. I knew that was coming.* She didn't stand a chance in hell of getting this done. If left on her own, she would be eaten alive. Even so, getting involved was sure to be a dead end. I figured that if I left right now I could get out of here clean. I had dumped the bodies in the woods behind the marina Dumpster, so they probably wouldn't be found until morning and wouldn't be tied to me, at least not right away. The problem was that I didn't have the means to just up and leave. On top of that, I had the asshole on the phone who just might try to track me down. If I left now I would be looking over my shoulder for the next few years.

I felt squeezed by my lack of choices. I wanted to punch a wall again. *Maybe I should just dial 911 and haul ass.* That wouldn't do the uncle any good, but it would keep Jennifer from getting killed, no matter how much she thought otherwise. The uncle probably deserved what he got. It would also probably dissuade the man on the phone from hunting me down.

I prepared to give her the bad news. She was staring at me like I was a firefighter that was going to pull her baby from a burning building. *Jesus. Did she practice that look?*

I steeled myself, thinking that this really was in her best interest, and said, "Uhh . . . Yeah. I'll help you."

*Huh? Where did that come from? You idiot.*

Jennifer's face broke into a radiant smile. "Should I call or you?"

I thought about retracting my statement but didn't have the courage. "I'll do it. Let him know you aren't coming alone. Maybe he'll rethink any shenanigans he's planning."

I pulled out the cell phone, said, "Here goes nothing," and hit the last-call button.

# 30

Inside the guesthouse, Bakr turned off the police scanner. He had heard the entire conversation between Pike and Miguel and was puzzled by it. He gave Sayyidd a questioning look. "Are you sure there wasn't a FedEx location in Flores?"

"I'm sure. There was nothing like that, DSL, UPS, anything. I searched for all of them."

"Then what was that all about? Why are they talking about an MP3 player? What do you think's going on?"

Sayyidd thought about it, then decided it didn't matter. "The answer is simple: Allah is leading the way, praise His name. The explanation is irrelevant. We may not know why, but we do know what. The MP3 player has the data. We have the key. We just need to get the player and extract the data. It is being delivered right to us."

Bakr didn't really care for Sayyidd's blind faith but let it go. "Maybe. Maybe not. Either way, we need to inform The Sheik that we might be altering the plan. He should know that we've come upon an opportunity that we wish to seize. Let him give us further guidance."

Bakr was concerned that this new direction was outside the intent of his masters, and thus wanted to make sure he wouldn't be blamed for acting irresponsibly. To do so would endanger his status as a martyr when he died. As much as he mistrusted Sayyidd's simple belief in God's will, he still dealt in the world of religious fervor and wanted the blessing before continuing. This meant a risky message, something that was specifically forbidden on this mission. They had a file of six different e-mail accounts that could be used only once. Al Qaeda didn't know what was being monitored or who was being watched, and thus were treating every communication as compromised as soon as it was sent.

Bakr scribbled a message onto a notepad.

"Boot up the M4 and send this to the first address. You remember it, correct?"

"Of course. I've memorized all six."

Once the connection was established, Sayyidd typed in the message:

Praise be to God, prayer and peace be upon the Prophet of God. Operation Badr has taken a turn for the better. We are no longer looking to strike the far enemy in his homeland. We have found a catastrophic weapon that will wipe the Zionists into the sea at the same time it causes the far enemy to destroy the Persians. In the name of God, the Merciful, the Compassionate, we will rejoice in the destruction of all infidels, leaving the Caliphate assured. Please respond with a blessing for this new mission, or tell us the path to take.

The message went out to a Yahoo! address, where it would sit for a day, then be forwarded to another address, then another, before being transferred to a thumb drive and driven across a border to another Internet café, sent again to another account, transferred via cell phone verbatim, then copied to a CD, and eventually find its way into the hands of Al Qaeda leadership. Just as Al Qaeda feared, along this path it would be intercepted by U.S. intelligence, and end up in a massive pile of "chatter" to be sorted through for relevance, where it would sit at the bottom, waiting to be viewed by some low-level analyst in the depths of a windowless building.

# 31

After hanging up the phone with Pike, Miguel said, "They're bringing the package down here. They've agreed to meet us to deliver it, but I don't trust that. Get in touch with our people at the department of immigration. Have them be on the lookout for Jennifer Cahill from the United States."

"There's no visa requirement to get here from America if they come as tourists," Jake said. "We won't get any warning before they land."

"I know. We'll only have a small window to control the situation, but luckily all flights from the U.S. fly straight here into Guatemala City. We should be able to blanket every flight coming from America for the next three days."

Jake agreed, then added, "Should we build a net inside the local hotels as well? There's a small chance that they could get through customs without us being alerted."

"Yeah. That makes sense. Have it done.

Stick to the tourist hotels."

"What do you want me to do when I find them?"

"Whatever it takes to bring them in to me. I want to get them in our hands before they have a chance to make any sort of plans or change their minds and talk to the authorities. Let's not inadvertently kill anyone else before we have our information."

Jake grinned. "I'll do my best."

The humidity hit me like a wet rag as soon as we exited the airplane, causing immediate sweat to pop out. It did little to add to any misery. I had tried to get as much sleep on the plane as I could, but thirteen hours of flying or waiting around airports for connecting flights did nothing but make you feel tired. My mouth felt like someone had polished my teeth with dryer lint, my hair had a greasy feel, and I was dehydrated from the in-flight dry air. Jennifer didn't look that much better.

The man on the phone had given us directions to his house, telling us which roads to use to get out of Guatemala City. Once in the hills to the east of the city, we were supposed to simply stop and ask the first person we saw for the house of El Machete.

There wasn't any way I was going to make it that easy.

We had landed at the Santa Elena airport

in the north of Guatemala after connecting through Cancún. I didn't want to land in Guatemala City, since I was pretty sure that Machete would have that covered, so we had purchased two sets of tickets. It would be a seven-hour trip down south, but at least we would make it through whatever initial net he had established without getting caught right off the bat. We picked up our Jeep CJ-5 we had rented over the Internet and wasted no time heading to Guatemala City on Highway 5.

I had never been to Guatemala before, and after talking to Jennifer, I learned she hadn't either. The sum total of her knowledge was wild-ass stories told by her uncle. None were of any help. My knowledge was limited to the fact that Guatemala had the distinction of being one of two countries — Iran being the other one — that the CIA had managed to overthrow in the 1950s. I wouldn't even have known that, except the story was a damn clown-fest and pretty funny to read about, with CIA agents mistakenly attacking British ships and revolutionaries attempting to ride into battle in beat-up station wagons. Funny except the fallout was a thirty-six-year civil war that left thousands of innocent people dead. I suppose it kept Guatemala out of Commie hands, so it was worth it. As long as you weren't Guatemalan.

■ ■ ■ ■

Jake was in the process of building his net inside the tourist hotels when his phone rang with the special tone reserved for his boss.

"Have you heard anything from our friends downtown?"

Jake told him no, but that he hadn't been checking in with them. He'd been too busy with the hotels.

"I'm wondering if they slipped through customs."

Jake swore under his breath. Miguel was as ruthless as anyone he had ever seen, but sometimes he had the patience of a four-year-old. "It's only been about twenty hours. Give it some time. They'll be here."

"I don't trust the people we've paid. I want our own people on every flight coming in. Make that happen."

"Sir, doing that now risks missing them both ways. I haven't finished with the hotels. We need to stick with the plan."

"Jake, hear what I'm saying. Do as I ask. Now."

Jake acknowledged the task, then hung up, cursing. Why come up with a plan if you're going to change it because you're impatient? Give the plan a chance to work. *Jesus, why did I come down here?*

Pulling out now meant a risk he didn't want

to take, as it would split the detection efforts before either one was complete. Nothing he could do about it. When Miguel made up his mind, it was done. In other assignments Jake would try to convince his boss of the correct path to take, but Miguel was different. Jake had seen Miguel do things to other humans that would have shocked Stephen King. He wouldn't admit it to anyone, but Miguel had the ability to scare him. Jake would do as he was told. He would just have to make sure he covered both the hotels and the airport as well as he could.

He looked at his list of hotels and called both team leaders, telling one to continue with the mission of the hotels and giving the other the redirection to the airport. The second team leader acknowledged the task and began calling his men.

Two of the members of the second team were pulling into the parking lot of a midrange hotel just outside of Zona 10 called Casa Bonito Clara when the driver's cell phone rang. The pair was preparing to go inside and spread around some cash when they were stopped by the team leader's call. The driver told the team leader where he was and the other hotels they had already visited. The team leader made a note of the hotels, then gave the driver his next instructions. The driver motioned to his friend to get back in, started the car up, and pulled into traffic, headed for the airport. As they left, they failed to notice the old CJ-5 being driven by two gringos pulling into the parking lot.

## 32

Pike had told her to stay away from the chain hotels and to find a small discreet hotel somewhere in the tourist areas. It looked like she had succeeded and she hoped Pike would be happy with the choice. She was still unsure about him. He seemed constantly on edge, like he would lose his temper if the traffic light didn't turn green soon enough. And he wasn't much of a conversationalist. He refused to talk about anything involving his past. When she had asked him how he was able to kill two men with his bare hands, he had gone into asshole mode, telling her not to look a gift horse in the mouth. In fact, the only time he had opened up was when they were preparing to leave, showing a small window into his inner self.

While she bought the airline tickets online, he had gone back to his boat to pack. She had to wait until he came back because she couldn't reserve the flight without knowing his real name. The ticket needed to match his

ID. When he returned, she asked him for his passport.

"So you've finally figured out a way to get my name." He had reached into his pocket and pulled out a pristine tourist passport, tossing it to her. "Here you go."

She was surprised at its new appearance.

"I thought by the way you talked you were some sort of world traveler. This thing hasn't ever been used."

"I've traveled quite a bit, but not on that passport. You'll be the first to use it."

She opened the passport and looked at his personal information.

He said, "Yeah, I know, it's a damn strange name. Just get the tickets."

She went through the procedures for buying the tickets, typing in "Nephilim Logan."

"You don't have a middle name?"

"No. Before you ask, my parents were good people, but children of the sixties. When I was born, they had a lot of New Age, weirdo crap going on in their heads. When they married, they were full of hopeful ideas about how they were going to change the world. They ended up owning their own house-painting business, but I was stuck with the name."

"What's Nephilim mean? Something out of Norse myth or a type of laundry detergent?" Seeing him scowl, she backed up, saying, "I'm just kidding. Surely it has some special meaning."

"Yeah, it's from the Old Testament. It's supposed to be the name of a race of half god/half man people who roamed the earth during Adam and Eve times. They were supposed to be some sort of badass heroes, but all the name ever got me was a fight as I grew up. I've always hated it."

Jennifer had had no answer to that.

Now that they were actually in Guatemala, she wondered if she was placing too much faith in a complete stranger. *Complete stranger? That's putting it mildly. He slaughtered two people with his bare hands. What do I do if he goes off his rocker with me?*

She watched him pace the room, finally peeking out the window, causing her to wonder if she'd made a bad choice.

"Is this place okay?"

"Yeah. Just like I asked for. I'm just concerned that this place is some sort of local gem and will be under the eye of whoever was on the phone. Nothing we can do about it now, since we had to hand over our passports to check in. If he has this place under his thumb, we're made. At any rate, we don't have a lot of time before he starts to wonder where we are. Every minute takes away from your uncle's chances, so I think we had better get moving."

"Are you sure that going to his house is smart?"

■ ■ ■ ■

*Is she really questioning my judgment?* I couldn't believe it. In the past, I had hated dealing with people who had no idea what they were doing in situations such as this, but I would tolerate it because I was forced to. I had dealt with country teams in American embassies all over the world who always asked the dumbest questions imaginable. Usually diplomats concerned with worst case scenarios or intelligence personnel worried about the impact to their operations; both looking for any reason to cancel a mission, but neither having the expertise to even ask the right questions. Now I didn't need to get anyone's approval. I decided to nip this in the bud right away.

"Look, let's get something straight right now. I'm the one who knows what to do here. I'm the one who can get your uncle back. I'd appreciate it if you wouldn't start questioning me at every turn. I know you're putting yourself out on a limb and want to feel some semblance of control, but that ain't gonna happen. You don't have a clue about what you're doing, and you're a damn menace to this whole operation just by being here."

I saw Jennifer recoil at my outburst, which made me feel like an asshole. Like I did outside her car at the Windjammer. My anger

215

wilted, and for the second time in nine months, I felt like apologizing instead of ripping off her head. Before she could say anything, I held up my hands.

"Okay, okay. Sorry. That was a little overboard. I want to conduct a recce" — seeing Jennifer scrunch her eyebrows at my terminology, I scratched the shorthand — "reconnaissance of his house just to get a feel for who we're dealing with. He told us how to find his house on the last phone call, and we would be stupid not to use that information to get some insight into the enemy. All I want to do is a drive-by."

She didn't look convinced.

"Look, we're wasting time. Can we talk about this as we go?"

Jennifer backed down. "All right. Let's go."

# 33

The contact from Santa Elena said, "She came through here. She and her companion rented a Jeep here about ten hours ago. No information on where they were headed."

Jake swore, aggravated that he had missed the Santa Elena embarkation point. While no flights from the U.S. landed there, plenty of flights from neighboring countries did. He had thought there was little chance his targets were smart enough to transfer at another country and didn't like being outwitted.

Intent on getting any information he could on his prey, he asked, "Did you get the name of her companion?"

"No. He didn't speak and didn't fill out any paperwork. They paid in cash and the girl used her license. I did get a description. The rental man remembered him pretty well because he said the guy scared him. He's a white guy, about six foot two, one hundred and ninety to two hundred pounds, brown hair cut short, and blue eyes. He said he looked hard. He has a scar on his face that cuts down his right cheek. The rental guy said he didn't look like someone who took a lot of shit."

Jake took this in. This man was shaping up to be a greater threat than they had anticipated. He was smart enough to have figured out a route that would evade Jake's net and had been strong enough to kill Miguel's men in the U.S. He was someone to watch out for. Jake decided to quit underestimating the man. He called Miguel.

"I found them. They came in through Santa Elena. They rented a Jeep and are now probably inside Guatemala City. Current whereabouts are unknown." Jake then relayed the description of Pike, ending with his assessment of the threat.

Miguel said, "I knew that fucker wouldn't call when he arrived. He might be as dangerous as you say, but look on the bright side: He's no professor — he'll live a long, long time before his body quits. I assume that since you know they're inside the city, it'll only be a matter of a few hours until you bring them to me."

"Consider it done. If you would do me the favor I ask that you leave the man alive long enough for me to kill him."

"Of course. He is yours."

Abu Bakr noted the information they had just

overheard and thought through the ramifications.

"This man Pike doesn't sound like someone to trifle with. I'm inclined to forget about the treasure hunt and execute the mission given to us by The Sheik."

"Please," Sayyidd said, "he's only one man. An infidel at that. We can defeat him just as we defeated the soldiers of the Great Satan. We now know what he looks like. God willing, the rest will be easy."

Bakr didn't believe it would be as simple as Sayyidd said. They still had to beat Miguel's enterprise to the punch.

"We'll need to be quicker than Jake. Once he finds the location of the package we'll have little time to intercept it. Does this scanner work on batteries?"

Sayyidd said, "No, it doesn't, but it has an adapter for a car cigarette lighter."

"That'll work. Let's wait inside the car Miguel gave us. Once we hear the location, we'll need to move immediately while Miguel and Jake are coming up with a plan. You'd better pray that Allah is really looking out for us, or we'll be the ones begging for the pain to end."

# 34

I looked closely at the chain-link Cyclone fence, trying to determine if it was electrified or wired with sensors. After convincing Jennifer that this recce wasn't stupid, it would suck to get caught like an amateur before even observing anything of value. I saw nothing to indicate that the fence had any electronic monitoring at all.

Following the directions from the man on the phone, we had driven out of the city and into the countryside, leaving all traffic behind. We had found the road leading to his estate, the pavement winding away into the hills behind a ten-foot gate. I realized that the only way I was going to get any intel was on foot, so I pulled up another quarter of a mile and hid the Jeep on the side of the road in a turnout. I left Jennifer in the woods and told her I would be gone no more than an hour. She just about lost her mind, but I didn't give her enough time to protest before moving off into the cover of the woods. Hopefully, she wouldn't get in the Jeep and leave me stranded.

I approached the fence and sat for another couple of minutes, watching the road on the inside that paralleled its path. Satisfied that I was alone, I vaulted over the top and raced across the road into the wood line on the other side. I continued moving uphill until I came to a large open field falling away from the high ground. In the center was the house of El Machete.

*House* wasn't the right word. This was a gigantic fortress-like compound protected by an eight-foot brick wall. All it needed was a moat with a drawbridge. The centerpiece was a three-story mansion fronted by a circular drive. Next to the main building was a one-story bungalow that looked like a residence or guesthouse. Adjacent to the guesthouse was some sort of warehouse or garage, with multiple vertical doors and several chimneys. All told, the compound inside the walled area was probably three hundred by five hundred meters, with several other outbuildings. Machete clearly had money.

I glanced at my watch, thinking I'd better start heading back before Jennifer got antsy. When I looked back up, I saw a man round the corner of the wall dressed like a modern-day ninja. I thought my eyes were playing tricks on me. He looked like he had gone to Commandos Are Us and bought out the

221

store. He was outfitted from head to toe in every conceivable type of black Velcro tactical gear, complete with a black balaclava hiding everything but his eyes. All of his equipment was state of the art, including the Heckler and Koch 416 rifle he had slung over his shoulder. The 416 had been developed jointly with H&K and U.S. Special Operations as a replacement to the M4 carbine, the shortened version of the M16 A2. Both fired 5.56mm, looked the same, and in fact, the H&K was designed the same to cut down on any learning curve for soldiers who were used to the ergonomics of the M4. It also allowed any components used on the M4 to directly transfer to the 416. The primary difference was that the 416 operated with a push rod piston instead of a gas tube like the M4, making it much more reliable. The weapon was fairly new and very expensive.

The 416 was outfitted much like the man, with every conceivable gadget attached to the rail systems, including an EOTech holosight and an AN/PEQ-15 laser attached to the rail system behind the front sight post. The PEQ-15 housed both an infrared and visible laser aiming module, and was a controlled export item from the United States.

This information alone told me a great deal about my adversary. On the downside, the fact that this guard in Guatemala had such exorbitant kit meant that his boss had serious money, serious contacts inside the arms world, and the intelligence to buy the best. *So much for the phone threats being a bluff.* On the plus side, the fact that the target looked like the Michelin man with all of that kit on told me that he wasn't a professional.

Anyone who used such kit for a living found quickly that less was more. Attempting to climb buildings or enter narrow rooms with ten tons of accessories flopping around usually ended in catastrophic failure. I had learned early to pare down my kit to the absolute essentials, leaving the rest of the Velcro for the wannabes who did more showing off than fighting. *Like this loser.*

I watched him as he continued walking down the wall and turned the corner out of sight. About ten seconds later, another guard rounded the corner to the south of the compound, opposite where the first guard had disappeared. Obviously, they maintained a roving foot patrol outside the residence and probably had a mounted patrol along the fence line.

I felt a split-second burst of fear as I realized I had been too hasty on my sensor analysis at the fence. Whoever was here had enough money to wire the entire jungle and could buy the expertise to monitor it. I then realized that if it had been wired, I would've already been caught. I decided not to test my theory and began moving as swiftly as I dared back down to the Jeep and Jennifer.

Jake pulled into the parking lot of the Casa Bonita Clara with a head of steam, hammering the brakes hard enough to cause a slight skid in the gravel. He had just finished talking to one of his team leaders and had discovered that the Casa Bonita hotel had been missed during the shift to the airport. *Because of incompetent idiots who couldn't follow simple instructions.* The team had reported their location at the hotel, and the team leader had assumed they had gone inside and established contact. They hadn't, and now he had a gap in the plan that might prove fatal. He felt like he was leading a bunch of children, forcing him to check and recheck everything to get the smallest task accomplished.

Walking to the front desk, he tapped his hand on the counter, waiting on the woman behind it to finish with a balding German complaining about his bill. Once he was gone, Jake addressed the woman.

"Hi. I'm looking for some friends of mine. They were supposed to arrive today, but I haven't heard from them. I was wondering if you could look and see if they've checked in?"

The woman smiled warmly. "I'm sorry, I'm not allowed to reveal any information on our guests. If you'd like, you can leave me a mes-

sage for them with your contact information, along with their name. I'll ensure that they get it."

Jake smiled back, attempting to be as friendly as the woman, but failing because his smile did nothing but bare his teeth, giving him all the warmth of a great white shark.

"Perhaps I wasn't clear. The bloke who wants to find them is El Machete. I would hate to be the person who refused his request."

The woman's smile faded, replaced with a look of fear. She glanced around to see if her manager was in sight, then said, "What are their names?"

"Jennifer Cahill and a man."

The woman tapped on the keyboard and said, "They're here. Second floor, second room on the right. Room eight." Visibly shaking, she said, "Please leave now."

Jake grinned, thanked her, then went back to his SUV. He dialed Miguel's number.

Miguel answered after the fourth ring. "What've you found? Please tell me you have some good news."

"I have their location. I'm pulling in the teams and heading back to the compound. I'll be there in twenty minutes."

Miguel wasn't satisfied with that answer. "Well, don't make me beg. Where are they?"

"They're staying in a hotel inside Zona Ten called the Casa Bonito Clara. It poses some

additional challenges due to its small size, but nothing insurmountable."

Miguel smiled for the first time in over twenty-four hours. "Good. Very, very good. I'm looking forward to meeting this Mr. Pike. Come on back. We'll figure out how we're going to skin this cat. Shouldn't take long. Once we have the package, I want you on the road tomorrow looking for the temple."

"Okay . . . Got it. We're coming home now. See you in a few minutes."

Sitting inside the loaned Chevy Suburban, Bakr and Sayyidd heard the entire exchange. Bakr started the giant SUV and drove down the winding road toward the highway while Sayyidd booted up the M4 satellite phone to search for the hotel.

Sayyidd said, "You're going to have to stop and give me five minutes before I can get the connection. This thing doesn't work very well on the move."

Entering the close-packed concrete land-scape of Guatemala City proper, Bakr began to look for a place to pull over. Finding one, he waited while Sayyidd achieved a satellite signal. Seconds later, Sayyidd found the hotel's Web site.

"I have it. We're only minutes away. What do you want to do?"

# 35

Jennifer and I crossed the lobby of the hotel and headed to the stairs. I had made it back to her and the Jeep without incident, although she was spitting mad. I had found her hiding in the bushes, apparently unsure if the racket I made while approaching wasn't a bad guy or a jaguar. I had pulled a bush aside and found her staring up at me in fear, which had immediately turned into anger.

"You think you could give me some warning that it was you coming? What the fuck are we doing out here? Jesus Christ! I can't believe I let you talk me into this."

"Hey, calm down. It was worth it. Nothing bad happened."

She had continued on, and I had let her. I took the tongue-lashing, because she was right. That *was* a pretty shitty thing to do. I should have simply left her in the hotel room, like I was going to do now.

"I've got about forty-five minutes before I need to head out. You can do whatever you like, but I'd ask that you don't leave the hotel until I get back. We're getting close to wrapping this up, and I don't want to have any hiccups."

"Where're you going tonight? Do you have an idea?"

"Not really, but there are always tourist markets around the big hotels. I'll wander around a little bit until I find one that meets our needs. I want one that's open enough to require a large amount of manpower to cover it and give us multiple options for escape, yet small enough for us to see the exchange people before they spot us."

"I'd like to come with you."

I paused, acting like I was considering it, then said, "It'd be better if you just waited here. I'm not going to be gone that long."

"Are you trying to hide something? I'm getting a little sick of being stuck in the corner like a five-year-old. I might even be able to help you. Wouldn't it be better for both of us to know what the site looks like in advance?"

"Look, I appreciate the offer, but I'm going alone. Just stay here."

I walked to the door, now just wanting to get out of the room before she convinced me to let her come. I had my hand on the doorknob when she came back at me.

"Wait, I thought you said you had forty-five minutes before you had to leave. It's only been about two, or was that a bunch of crap just to keep me thinking you had some sort of incredible plan?"

*Man alive, she tries hard to piss me off.* "Look, I'm trying to save your uncle's life. I'm not going to fight you on this. Just sit down. Please. I'll be back soon."

"Well, you won't need the MP3 player for this, will you? Leave it here with me."

"What, now you think I'm trying to fuck you over or something? Jesus, *you* asked *me* to come here. To help you. If I wanted to cut my own deal, I'd do it without sneaking around. How about a little trust?"

She threw her handbag onto the bed, "Okay, fine. I do trust you. So you won't mind leaving the MP3, will you? Unless you plan on doing something with it while I'm sitting here twiddling my thumbs."

She was right, there was no reason to keep the MP3, but there was no way I was going to admit that now. I left without another word. For whatever reason, my rage had yet to show itself, and I wanted to get out before that changed and I lost control.

Exiting the hotel, I wondered what brain disease had caused me to fly down here in the first place. All I had to look forward to was a murder rap when I got back home, no matter how this turned out. *What the hell am I doing? Who gives a shit about someone's uncle?* I considered simply getting on a plane and going back to the U.S. I'd have to get

229

Jennifer to buy the ticket, but I figured she'd do it. She clearly didn't like me being in charge.

I flagged down one of the unregulated taxis that regularly cruised the city. I asked where I could take my girlfriend to see some sights downtown. The driver said he knew just the place, called the Plaza Mayor, and set out toward the historic district.

He let me out at an open air market and pointed toward a towering, ornate cathedral a few blocks away. After walking west, I came upon a large open parade field with a fountain in the center. It did look like a great tourist stop, but it sucked for an exchange. There weren't any crowds to hide within, and it had a clear field of view from all directions. I stopped a woman and asked about the parade ground. The woman didn't speak English, and shrugged apologetically.

Another person standing nearby taking pictures must have overheard me because he said, "You from the United States?"

I told him I was.

"Me too. This is the central plaza or Plaza Mayor in Guat talk. It really gets hopping on the weekends. I was here last Sunday and there must have been a thousand people around here, all out to have a good time. It's the best time to be here. If today wasn't Sunday, you'd see nothing at all." The man was younger than me, with a four-day growth of beard, a stuffed backpack at his feet.

I moved on with a wave, acknowledging his help, silently giving thanks for Birkenstock-wearing, dope-smoking granola-eaters. *Quite possibly America's number one export.* Crossing to the other side of the parade ground, past the large fountain in the center, I came upon a small Plexiglas monument containing a single flame burning from a hidden gas source. The inscription read, *"A los héroes anónimos de la paz"* — the anonymous heroes of peace — a monument to the peace accords of 1996 that ended the civil war here. If the place got as crowded as the backpacking college student said, I had found my exchange location.

I began to walk away from the monument, back toward the taxi stands. Moving through the packed streets full of vendors, I got sick of being accosted by every single one and turned into an alley as a shortcut.

I walked for thirty seconds before realizing it was a dead end. Turning back, I faced two local nationals moving in my direction. I pushed through them with a halfhearted excuse-me, getting a quick feeling that something wasn't right by the way they stared at me. As soon as my back was to them, I was thumped hard on the head and hit in the kidney. Rolling with the blow I turned to face the pair, only to be tackled. They were uncoordinated, simply hitting and kicking me all over like in a schoolyard fight. I lashed out with a backfist and connected with one of them. He rolled off and shouted at his friend. I turned my attention to the other man on top of me, preparing to wrap my legs around the man's waist in a guard mount that would prevent him from pinning me down and allow me to finish the fight. Before I could do it, his friend jerked him off of me, and both ran back down the alley.

I stayed still for a few seconds to catch my breath, then laughed at how easy it had been for a couple of local pickpockets to take me down. As I sat up, it dawned on me that the first man had shouted to his friend in Arabic. I couldn't speak the language but had listened to it almost more than English in the past few years, and had no doubt that's what I heard. *What the hell? Why would a couple of rag-head toughs be running around Guatemala?*

I had seen stranger things and let it go. I checked my watch and wallet and saw that I still had both, so they had failed in their attempts. I picked up my backpack and looked through it. All appeared to be there. I honed in on the small outside pocket, torn open by the assault. A shock went through me. The MP3 player was gone. I ripped through the rest of the knapsack looking for the device. It wasn't there. I searched the ground around me, seeing nothing. I ran back the way I had come, scanning left and right, but still came up empty. I stopped searching. *What the hell am I going to tell Jennifer? How are we going to make an exchange? How on God's green earth have I managed to lose the device?*

I flagged down a taxi, gave him directions, and sat back for the ride. Before I knew it, I was back at the hotel. I exited the cab and dragged myself up to our room, not wanting to tell Jennifer what had happened, knowing she would hate me for the incompetence that would cost her uncle his life.

I unlocked the door. She wasn't in sight, so I checked the bathroom. It was also empty. I was surprised, and felt the anger rise. I remembered I had said not to leave, but I could see her going out just to spite me. I was working myself into a fine, justifiable rage, building up an argument to counter the sting of losing the MP3 player, when I noticed a piece of paper on the bed. I picked it up and got the second shock of the day.

*You said you would call when you arrived. If you would like to see the girl in one piece, please call immediately.*

# 36

I stared at the note for a heartbeat and then sat heavily on the bed, holding my head in my hands. I had failed all the way around. I had misjudged the opposition and misjudged my own capabilities. *I'm a fucking fraud. I should've never come down here.* Nothing good was going to come out of continuing now. I ran through my options and settled on the best course of action: *Get the fuck out of here, right now. Get back to the United States.* I could fly back and relocate to another part of the country, starting over again. I wasn't without skills, although they had proven worthless here. I could hire on with a security firm. I had the credentials. They were hiring twenty-five-year-olds with only basic training on their résumé. I could go overseas and make some money, let this entire fiasco blow over, and build a nest egg at the same time.

I stood up and began packing my things. I wouldn't even check out. Let Jennifer's credit card handle the bill. She wouldn't need it anymore anyway. After packing my rucksack, I looked around the room to see if I could use anything of Jennifer's before I left. I dug through her purse, searching for cash. I pulled out her passport, seeing her face inside. I paused. From out of nowhere I thought about my family. Heather and Angie.

I squeezed my eyes shut, rubbing them hard with my hands. *This isn't the same. I didn't ask to be here. I failed Heather by omission. There's nothing I can do here.* Staying was stupid. Trying to do anything about Jennifer was dumber still. All it would do was cause more death, most notably my own. *What the hell can I do? I have no money, no equipment, no men, no support, no nothing. The man on the phone has everything.*

I opened my eyes and found myself looking into the mirror across the wall, a hollow, empty soul staring back. *What the fuck have I become?*

I was sickened by my own reflection, ashamed of my previous thoughts. *Heather would have left the man in the mirror.* I sat still, thinking of my family, then thinking of Jennifer. I had no doubt that she would have tried to help if the roles had been reversed, no matter the risk to herself. The thought caused a wave of disgust at what I had planned. *I can't go back like this. I have to do something. If I die, I die. Better than dying in an IED attack*

235

*guarding a shipment of Baskin-Robbins ice cream in a war zone somewhere.*

I felt better right away. Even though the odds almost guaranteed my failure, I felt at ease.

I left the luggage, taking only the small backpack. I left the room as I had found it, with the note lying on the bed. I was surprised that I hadn't been attacked yet, since Machete clearly knew where we were staying. I took it as a good sign. I ran to our Jeep.

I merged onto 2 Calle and headed in the direction of the man's house, wondering just what the hell I was going to do. Thinking through my courses of action, I decided to simply continue with the plan. While the end state had changed, not much in the plan had been altered.

My original idea had been to find a place that would facilitate multiple exits, forcing Machete to spread out in an attempt to cover all bases. Since I was now about to attempt an assault on his house, I needed to get as many men out as possible to even up the odds. Plaza Mayor worked either way. The only difference was that I had to keep Jennifer in the house while the hired guns came to find me. I hoped I would accomplish that through a phone call. *I'm hoping for a lot to happen. Not a great way to plan.*

My first order of business was to get a

236

weapon, and I was pretty sure I knew where to get one that was top of the line. Stopping the Jeep at the same pullout I had used earlier for my recce, I exited and raced through the woods to the chain-link fence surrounding the compound. I sat still for a few minutes to make sure I was alone, then pulled out the cell phone I had taken off the dead man in Charleston. I dialed Machete's number, using the lighted keypad to see in the darkening gloom.

He answered the phone on the first ring. "Hello, Mr. Pike. I'm so glad you decided to call. I was beginning to wonder what to do with Jennifer."

I fought to control my anger, needing to play a role. "Look, let's skip the small talk. I'm sorry I ever came down here. I want to give you the package right away. I'm located at the Plaza Mayor. I'll meet you at the peace monument with the flame. I'll be in the crowd. One man, and one man alone, should stand at the monument every half hour starting at eight P.M. You got that so far?"

"Yes. I understand. We'll meet you then?"

"No. The man should light a cigarette with his right hand. When I see that, I'll throw the MP3 player to him sometime between eight and ten. I won't come close enough for anyone to identify where the MP3 player came from. If I suspect that you're more intent on getting me than the device, I'll disappear and you won't hear from me again."

"And the girl?"

I paused, knowing that I was about to put Jennifer into extreme danger, but also knowing that I had to ensure she remained behind.

"I don't care about the girl. I just want to get you off my back. I thought about leaving the package in the hotel and hauling ass, but I want to make damn sure you get it. Once you get the player, we're through."

"Smart man. I'm good with that. We'll be at the monument. If I don't get the player, I'm going to find you. Don't fuck with me."

I gritted my teeth at the threat, thinking I would enjoy killing this asshole. "Understood. You only have about forty-five minutes, so you'd better get moving."

Jennifer, lying on the floor shackled and gagged, saw Miguel hang up and waited to hear what he said to Jake.

"He's pretty smart. He has a good plan to keep himself in one piece, although I'm sure you'll find a way to defeat it." Miguel then relayed Pike's demands.

Jake said, "That makes it harder, but not impossible. The Plaza Mayor will be jammed with a thousand locals. I'm going to need everyone for this, or he'll get away. Security here will be a little light while we're gone."

"Take whoever you need. I want him almost as much as the package."

Jennifer saw Jake glance her way. "What about the girl? Are we taking her?"

She perked up, waiting to hear the exchange plan.

"No. He's a man after my own heart. He doesn't give a shit about her. He only wants out. I'll give her to the remaining guard force as compensation for missing out on tonight's fun."

*What?* Jennifer's brain refused to compute what she had just heard. She watched in a daze as Jake left the room, barking out orders as he went. Her mind finally clicked. *Jesus Christ. I'm going to die.* It failed to register that death was the least of her concerns.

She heard Miguel talking to the remaining guard. "Take her to the interrogation room. Pick four men who deserve a reward and give her to them."

Her predicament began to sink in. She tried to talk through the gag in her mouth, to get Miguel to understand there was some mistake. She was ignored. The guard grabbed the manacles around her wrists without even giving her a chance to stand up. *No, no, no. This isn't happening.* She was dragged kicking from the room.

# 37

After hanging up, I vaulted the fence and raced to the vantage point I had found earlier. Crouching in the woods, I waited, trying to see one of the guards patrolling the exterior grounds. I focused my eyes on the brick wall surrounding the compound, vaguely lit up enough to allow me to make it out. I used my peripheral vision to pick out movement, knowing that it was better in the night than my primary eyesight. Soon, I spotted a guard moving down the wall.

I moved in a crouch on a path to intersect the guard, covering the terrain as rapidly as I could without making enough noise to alert him. I closed within fifteen meters of his back and began stalking my prey. When I was five feet away, I closed the distance at a sprint. I wrapped my right arm around the guard's neck and pressed my shoulder into the back of his head, forcing it down. Kicking the back of his knee, I flung myself backward, pulling him horizontally toward the ground. Our bodies separated like a pair of scissors. We both hit the earth at the same time, the guard on his back and me on my stomach. The force of the fall generated enormous leverage applied through my shoulder directly into the man's neck, snapping it cleanly. I sat up, grabbed the dead man by his equipment vest, and dragged him thirty feet into the darkness. I began stripping the body, ripping away all of the junk to get to the ammunition for the 416.

Jennifer lay on her stomach inside the warehouse. She was still clothed, but her shoes had been removed to hamper any escape attempt. She could see the implements of torture in the gloom, along with dark brown stains at irregular intervals along the walls. In the corner she saw a pile of clothes and recognized her uncle's shirt. She began shaking uncontrollably. *What the fuck am I going to do? Something . . . there's got to be something.* Up until now, she had managed to maintain a semblance of self-control because she felt certain that the police or Pike would be arriving to help. People like her didn't end up shackled in a drug lord's house. At least not for long. Pike's comments to Miguel had popped that bubble; she now knew she was on her own. *Think . . . Think . . . Think. Gotta be a way out. . . .* The door opened, and she saw five Guatemalan men enter the room, all staring at her and smiling. *Oh, my God.*

The thumb drive worked perfectly, surprising Bakr. In his heart, he hadn't thought they would actually get the data, and in their rush to get to the hotel, he hadn't planned a next step.

As soon as they had arrived, they had seen a red Jeep driven by a man matching the description given by Jake. They watched him and a woman enter the hotel and had barely begun to discuss their options when the man exited alone less than five minutes later, giving them an opportunity they couldn't ignore.

Now they had the GPS location to the temple, but they didn't have a GPS. Bakr didn't want to return with the data to Miguel's house, but somehow they needed to get one of the GPSs inside their test package, along with the 3M respirators. While mulling the options over dinner, Bakr decided he would be the only one who went back. Sayyidd would remain in the restaurant with the data, waiting for him to return.

I finished kitting up and conducted a functions check on the weapon, relieved when it appeared to work fine. I had stripped the man of his assault vest, then stripped the vest of the clutter it held. To my surprise, the guard had a plate-hanger underneath his vest, complete with front and back Level III armor plates, rated to stop everything up to 7.62 × 51mm, the primary round used in NATO sniper rifles and light machine guns. *What the hell is he wearing this for?* I wasn't going to question it. I was fairly sure I would need the protection.

I ditched just about everything the man had, throwing away a ton of bullshit accessories that might be useful on Batman's utility belt but would do me no good. The one thing I wanted that the guy didn't have was a radio, but that in itself gave me some relief about Machete's security posture. *Body armor and no radio? He's wearing the kit as a costume.* I kept only the three magazine pouches, each holding two magazines loaded with thirty rounds of Hornady match grade 5.56mm boat-tail hollow points.

For weapons I took the H&K 416 and a Cold Steel push knife, a nasty instrument with a three-and-three-quarter-inch double-sided cutting edge and a "T" handle perpendicular to the blade.

Satisfied that I had all I wanted from the dead guard, I began to move toward the front gate, using the wall as cover, all the while scanning for cameras or other early warning devices. So far, no alarm had been raised, but it was only a matter of time before the guard I had killed was missed.

I held no illusions of what I was about to attempt. The standard operating procedure of my last unit prohibited entering a room as an individual. Two people could enter for extreme situations, otherwise three was the minimum, with four or five preferred. I was now going to assault the *entire fortress* on my own, using a weapon I had never fired, that might not even be zeroed, and certainly wasn't zeroed for me. I would be lucky if the wannabe I had killed had bothered to sight-in the weapon at all. I had no idea if the weapon had been properly maintained. Should it fail at any time, I would be a dead man.

As bad as that was, it was the least of my problems. Depending on how many men had left to go chasing shadows at the Plaza Mayor, I was outnumbered upward of twenty to one. In order to succeed I would have to maintain what we called relative superiority, attacking each man individually, or at most two at a time. Should an alarm go up, forcing me to fight a concentrated mass, I would lose.

Continuing down the wall toward the front gate, I heard a commotion on the other side. A man with a UK accent was shouting instructions in English against the background of multiple vehicles being loaded. I grinned. *Fuck, yeah. Get 'em all out of here.*

I waited until all the vehicles had left and was about to scale the wall when I heard movement to my right. I pressed against the

244

brick, trying to squeeze into the shadows. Another guard came sauntering down the wall, moving without a purpose, his weapon slung and his hands in his pockets. I started breathing in a shallow pant, hoping he couldn't hear it, even though it sounded like an industrial fan to me. He came within five feet, then stopped and turned around, as if he was going back to the gate. *What the hell's he doing?*

Before he could make up his mind about where he was going, I closed on him, trapped his head, and stuck the push blade into the left side of his neck, slicing to the right and ripping out his windpipe and both carotid arteries. I held him upright, aiming the jet of blood away from me, then lowered him to the ground.

I quickly scaled the wall and raced to the first door I could see, a side entrance away from the massive, ornate entryway in the front of the mansion. I tried the knob and saw that it was unlocked. I paused, mentally preparing for what was to come, my conscious mind screaming for me to flee. Taking a couple of deep breaths, I knew that my next step, like a parachutist jumping out of an airplane, would be irreversible. *I can walk away now and live.* Not long ago I was one of the most highly skilled practitioners of armed combat on earth. There were maybe eight or ten people in the world who could equal my talent. I used that to psych myself up but knew in my heart it was a lie. Those skills had long since faded, and I didn't stand a chance in hell of rescuing Jennifer. I was going to die before I got through the first floor.

*Fuck it.* I raised my weapon to the position of high ready and turned the knob.

# 38

Lying on the floor, Jennifer stared warily at the men who had entered. So far, none of them had done anything against her, apparently because they were waiting on the word to start the fun. She had no idea what she should do. *Should I fight, or simply give in? If I fight, will that only bring on an ass-kicking before the rape, or will they back off?* She knew she couldn't keep up a fight for long, and that they could simply hold her down while battering her into submission. She might sustain enough damage to kill her outright. *But if I put up enough of a fight, they might be forced to hold me down while they rape me. Maybe I won't have to take on two or three guys at once.* She closed her eyes at the thought; her new definition of success being not all five men raping her at the same time. *Dear Lord, help me. Don't let this happen. Please . . . Please . . .*

I entered a small room that appeared to be a

butler area, stuffed with shelves holding all sorts of kitchen utensils. Swinging my weapon in an arc, I attempted the impossible task of covering three hundred and sixty degrees simultaneously. A frightened man dressed as a servant stood up, throwing his hands high above his head. He clearly wasn't a threat, but I had no way of detaining him and didn't have the time even if I could. My success rested primarily on my ability to keep the enemy from knowing an assault was under way, but speed was a close second. If an alarm was raised, the only thing that would keep me alive was keeping the enemy from knowing where to orient their efforts. If I maintained enough momentum, going as fast as I possibly could, the enemy wouldn't be able to pinpoint my position and would hopefully attack areas after I was through them.

I squeezed off a double tap to his head and raced to the next door before he even hit the ground. I suppose I should have felt some pity, but there was only relief at the fact that the weapon I held had hit what I aimed at. He was collateral damage. Nothing more. He knew who he was working for. *Fucker should have picked a better employer.*

I entered the next room and dropped a man in military kit racing for a weapon propped against the wall. I scanned the room for other targets, settling my sights on another man sitting in a large wing-backed chair smoking a cigar. Apparently a study, the room was paneled with dark wood and lined on one side by a giant bookshelf. The other side housed a fireplace, with the husks of a long dead fire sitting on an iron grate like a blackened skeleton. The man was dressed in a business suit, smiling, with his hands outstretched, the Cuban cigar wafting smoke toward the ceiling.

"You must be the infamous Mr. Pike. Jake was right — you are full of surprises. I'm assuming you've come to bring me my package."

I eased off of the trigger. "Where's the girl?"

"All in good time. She's fine. First, where's my package?"

I felt the time slipping away, like lifeblood flowing from an open wound. "Where — Is — The — Girl."

The man leapt up in a rage, shouting, "Who the fuck do you think you are? You think you can enter *my* house, attack *my* people, and walk away unscathed? You think —"

Before he could finish his sentence, I blew out the back of his head with a high-velocity hollow point, watching him fall backward into the chair. *Who do I think I am? I'm the man with the gun, dumbass.*

I moved on, clearing room after room. The majority of the mansion was unoccupied, which made the clearing fairly fast. My assault was only into minute number twelve by the time I had cleared the first and second floors, encountering only two more men, killing both. I went to the third floor, clearing it and finding no trace of Jennifer. I couldn't believe I was still alive and felt my luck evaporating by the second. *Where the fuck is she?* Exiting the last room, I moved at a light jog in the direction of the stairs. While I was still twenty feet away, a servant appeared at the top. Seeing me, he whirled around and began racing back down the stairs, screaming at the top of his lungs. I snapped off a couple of rounds but missed. *Shit. Now the race is on.*

## 39

The lead guard bent down to unlock the shackles on Jennifer's ankles. She lashed out with both feet, hitting him squarely in the chest and knocking him flat on his back. She hadn't made a conscious decision to fight, reacting only by instinct. She decided her instincts were correct. Given a choice, she'd rather be beaten to death. *Motherfucker's going to work for this.* She rotated on her back, feet out toward the group.

The other guards laughed at the man she had kicked even as they moved in on her. Two circled around her. She tried to stay with them by spinning on her back, but it was impossible. One slapped her hard in the face with an open hand, stunning her. Two other guards grabbed her manacled arms, holding her down. The lead guard got back up, dusted himself off, and walked back to her. Standing over her, he spit into her face, then stomped on her stomach with his full weight, taking the wind out of her and causing her to double up. He bent down and unlocked the manacles on her legs without a further fight. Grinning at her pain, he pulled out a tactical knife and sliced off her clothes. She curled up in a ball, wondering how long her body had left before it was shattered.

Stairwells were the worst area to fight through. There was no cover at all and only one way to move. It was a funnel that required several men working as a team to successfully clear. I had a choice, either sprint down the stairs in an attempt to beat anyone setting up at the bottom, or wait for them to attempt to come up. I split the difference, deciding to wait for them on the second floor. It was a calculated risk, as it would allow the alert to reach everyone in the compound, but I didn't like the odds of beating the enemy down three flights of stairs. If anyone was at the bottom by the time I got there, I would be easy to pick off. Better to let them do the hard work.

The stairs had one advantage in that it would limit the men coming up to two abreast, thus preventing them from bringing their total firepower to bear, and allowing me to fight no more than two at a time.

As I reached the second-floor landing I heard the rush of men on the hardwood floor below. I switched magazines, replacing the one in the weapon with a full thirty rounds. I waited in the darkness, my back to the wall, the stairwell opening up five feet to my right. I heard the shouting of the men below as they attempted to organize a collective response, then the pounding of feet on the stairs. I waited for a couple of heartbeats, getting control of my adrenaline. *Here we go. . . . Don't miss. . . . Don't miss.* I checked that my holosight was still functioning, then turned into the stairwell, flipping my weapon from safe to semiautomatic.

I saw seven men rushing up the stairs, the first three with a look of shock when they saw me coming. They were all outfitted like the guard outside. Without conscious thought, I shifted my aim to their heads to avoid any body armor. I began firing controlled pairs, pulling the trigger so fast the weapon sounded like it was on automatic. The first three men died instantly, two perfect holes appearing like magic between their eyes. One fell backward, blocking my shot at the remaining men. The four were firing wildly back at me.

Like inexperienced soldiers everywhere, their initial shots went high, but with this much lead coming my way, the odds were against all of them continuing to miss. I clipped one in the shoulder and was turning to move back to the cover of the second floor hallway when one of the wild rounds struck me directly over my heart. The armor plate saved my life, but the force from the kinetic energy of the bullet still knocked the shit out of me, causing me to fall backward. Lying back, momentarily stunned, I poured fire down the stairwell in an effort to suppress the guards, desperate to finish the fight before one of them could calm down enough to shoot straight.

Realizing I was dead meat if I remained on the floor, I forgot about the cover and launched myself straight into them. The one I had wounded was holding his shoulder and crawling back to the first floor in an effort to escape. Of the other three, one was changing magazines and two continued to shoot ineffectually. One of the guards, shooting wildly at my charge, apparently thinking the noise alone would stop me, hit the man standing in front of him in the back of the head, killing him. Deadeye quit shooting, shocked at what he had done. *Nothing like a little luck.* I killed him while moving at a dead run down the stairs, close enough to see the look of shock on his face as his soul fled his body.

Continuing to move, I reached the third man before he could work the bolt release of his weapon. I jammed the barrel of the 416 into the man's forehead, causing an imprint of the flash suppressor on his skull and knocking him out. I double-tapped the unconscious man's head as I vaulted over him, feeling the weapon lock open on an empty magazine. Intent on stopping the man with the shoulder wound from getting away, I wasted no time trying to reload.

The man was on the ground floor and on his feet, moving toward a door off the huge, cathedral-like den at the base of the stairs. He was shuffling along like Quasimodo, looking back over his shoulder as if he was being chased by the devil, his shattered arm dangling uselessly beside him. I caught him just as he reached the door. Dropping the 416 on its assault sling, I reached across the man's face, pulling his head back by digging my fingers into his eyes and yanking upward. I hammered his windpipe above the thyroid cartilage with my other hand, crushing it. I let the man fall, his mouth working like a fish out of water, his lungs pumping to get air in through his destroyed windpipe.

I had now cleared the entire house and seen no sign of Jennifer. *Shit. Maybe they took her.* I knew I was running out of time. If I was still here when the men from the Plaza Mayor returned, I would be dead.

Jennifer was yanked up from the floor by her hair. On her knees, her hands cuffed to her front, her face swelling from the earlier blows, she looked up at the lead guard before her. He leered down, holding on to her head by her hair.

He drew his finger across his throat and

255

said, "You no bite."

He then unbuckled his pants, dropping them to his knees. The rest of the guards giggled like they were on a school outing to an amusement park, anticipating their turn on the ride.

Jennifer looked into the man's eyes, saying, *"Por favor . . . Por favor . . . Por favor."*

The man only laughed. She lost all hope. She was nearly catatonic, resigned to the atrocities about to occur. The man let go of her head and began to lower his dingy, stained underwear. She looked up at him again, praying to see some sign of humanity, some shred of decency that would make him rethink what he was doing. Instead, she saw his head explode like a burrito in a micro-wave. She stared uncomprehendingly as the man fell over backward.

Before his death could register, a cyclone of violence erupted around her, the head of man after man exploding as if touched by the hand of God. The local standing behind her grabbed her around the neck and jerked her to her feet, shielding his body with hers. He placed a knife against her throat and whirled her around toward the door. Her eyes focused on a man advancing toward them holding a rifle pointed directly at her.

# 40

I placed the crosshairs on the head of the man holding Jennifer. He was about thirty-five feet away, far enough that I didn't trust the zero of my weapon to make the surgical shot required to kill him without risking Jennifer.

When I had initially entered I had seen Jennifer on her knees with nothing on but bra and panties, five men surrounding her, one facing her with his pants down. I had come very close to leaving the zone I had been in since starting the assault, my rage exploding from the depths of my soul. *No, no. Not helping.* I suppressed it and set about killing the men as rapidly as possible, with all of the emotion of someone mowing the lawn. All were focused on Jennifer. None had a gun within arm's reach. They stood no chance. I killed the first four as easily as shooting a Bianchi Cup at an IPSC match, squeezing the trigger in an easy rhythm as the men scattered like roaches caught by a light.

Before I could complete the string, the fifth man had managed to put Jennifer in front of himself, using a knife to control her. He was shouting something in Spanish. Unfortunately for him, I didn't have a clue what he was saying.

I moved forward at a fast walk, closing the distance to her, my weapon raised and ready. The man became shrill, shouting the same thing over and over, his eyes getting wide, attempting to drag Jennifer backward. When I was five feet away, I aimed for the eye orbit and pulled the trigger, knowing that when the bullet tore a channel through his brain it would sever the medulla oblongata, reducing his body to a useless sack of flesh and removing the risk of the knife reflexively jerking and hurting Jennifer. Blood and brain matter sprayed out, coating the right side of Jennifer's face in a fine mist. She sank to the floor, staring vacantly at nothing. The violence she had just witnessed, in addition to the trauma of her kidnapping, had caused her to shut down. I just prayed that I had gotten to her in time to prevent any assault.

I left her sitting down and searched the bodies on the floor until I found the keys to the handcuffs on her wrists. After unlocking her, I shook her shoulders, constantly talking to her. Eventually, she looked at me with recognition.

"We have to get out of here. Can you walk?"

She nodded in a vacant way. I realized that I had to get her some clothes and shoes. We still had to get to the jeep, and Jennifer would be ripped to shreds moving through the jungle at night nearly naked.

I helped her up, continuing to talk in a calm, deliberate manner. "We're still in danger. I'm going to have to continue clearing rooms as we leave. We'll find you some clothes as soon as possible. Stay behind me, but I want you to stay in the last room we're in, only coming in when you hear me call. Can you do that?"

She nodded again, this time with more focus. I smiled at her, encouraging her to engage me.

"I'm going to lead the way. When we get to a door, I'm going to be aiming at it to prevent any surprises. I can't turn around to find you. I want you to keep your hands on my assault harness. When you're ready for me to proceed, squeeze my shoulder. Can you do that?"

She spoke for the first time. "Yes. Just get me the fuck out of here. Please, please, get me out of here."

I smiled again, lying through my teeth. "Don't worry, the hard part's over. You have nothing to worry about now. Let's get going."

I moved back to the open door, scanning the courtyard between the mansion and the warehouse facility. To the left I saw the guesthouse. Maybe it would contain some clothing.

"When we leave here, I'm going to focus my attention to our right, on the main house. I need you to focus to the left. If you see anything at all, jerk my harness and I'll reorient. I can't see three hundred and sixty degrees simultaneously, so you'll be the only thing keeping us from getting smoked from the left. Can you do that?"

When she nodded, I said, "We're going to run to that house over there. Do you see the door in the front? I'm going to stop on the left side of that door. Are you ready?" She nodded again. "Okay. Let's go."

I exited the warehouse and sprinted forward, my weapon moving wherever my eyes went, training on every window and door I could see as I ran by them. I fully expected to spot a muzzle flash at any second. *What the hell am I doing? Continuing an assault with my 2IC dressed in a bra and panties. I've lost my mind.* We reached the building without getting shot at, which was a damn miracle. At the door, I waited until I felt Jennifer squeeze my shoulder, then turned the knob and entered.

# 41

Jennifer jumped when she heard gunfire erupt in the bungalow. She pressed herself up against the wall, her mind racing. The room had gone quiet, and she realized she didn't know what to do if Pike never called. *He could be dead. Maybe there's a bad guy about to come out. No way are they getting their hands on me again.* She was on the verge of racing across the courtyard when Pike called her in, telling her not to look at the floor. Relief flooded through her. She entered, seeing a man dressed in black sprawled on the floor in the foyer, his arms splayed out as if he was about to be crucified. She saw Pike crouching next to a door up ahead, his weapon at the ready. She wasted no time running up behind him and giving his shoulder a squeeze. She watched him splinter the door open with a kick, then disappear. She heard no gunfire. After a pause, she heard him say, "Someone's living in this room, and I don't think it was the guy I killed in the foyer. Check out the closet and luggage and see if you can find something to wear."

Jennifer entered and went straight to the closet. She began going through the luggage, finding men's clothing. She pulled out a long-sleeved shirt and a pair of sweatpants. Digging deeper, she found a Quran, heavily worn and thumbed through, but didn't find any shoes. She moved to a box in the corner of the room, finding some kind of gas mask and a Genie garage door opener, just like the one she'd grown up with. She held them up, saying, "Pike, what do you think these are for?"

Pike turned from the door and said, "I don't know. Did you find some clothes?"

"I found a top and bottom, but no shoes." She dropped the gear back into the box, moving to the other piece of luggage. Digging through it, she didn't see any shoes. Nearing the bottom, inside a pocket on the side, she found two passports. She flashed quickly to her uncle, but both had pictures of the same stranger.

"Pike, what's going on here? Two passports for the same guy. One's from Saudi Arabia and the other's from the U.S. for some guy named Carlos. The picture's the same in both. What do you suppose these are for?"

Pike blew out the air in his cheeks. "I really don't know, and our time's running out. Please keep looking."

Jennifer dropped the passports and moved

into the bathroom. Here she discovered a pair of ratty leather sandals, four sizes too big for her. She tried them on and found they would just about stay on her feet.

"Okay, I found something, but I'd probably be better off wrapping my feet in newspaper."

"Good enough. It's time to go. After you dress, we're going out the same way I came in, through the woods down to the Jeep. We'll be moving fast. If you have any trouble keeping up, say something. Otherwise, I'll assume you're good to go. Any questions?"

Jennifer paused, then said, "Yeah, actually, I do. Why don't we steal one of their vehicles right here instead of running through the jungle? They've got a bunch of Suburbans in the warehouse where you found me."

"That sounds like a plan. Do you know exactly where they are?"

"Yeah. Head back to the place where you found me, but go into the door on the end of the warehouse. I saw the vehicles when they dragged me through there."

"Okay. Get dressed. When you're ready, we'll go."

I covered the outside of the room, waiting on her to put on the clothes. I was running contingencies through my mind when it dawned on me that I hadn't done a single thing to find her uncle, the only reason we'd come down here in the first place.

"Jennifer — I've been in just about every

room on this compound looking for you. I didn't see any indication of your uncle."

I felt sure the uncle was dead and didn't want to spend a single second hunting for him. I looked her in the eyes, knowing if she wanted to search, I'd do it. *Please, don't ask. We need to leave.*

Her answer surprised me. "He's dead. That fat bastard who runs this place told me so. If we get out of here alive, I'm going to do everything in my power to cause him a slow death."

On her face I saw a little of the rage I keep hidden inside me. "I killed him, but it was quick. After seeing what they were doing to you, I wish I had taken my time."

She looked up from putting on the sweatpants, a weak smile on her face. "Don't beat yourself up. If I didn't know better, I would have thought you were waiting outside for the perfect moment. You came in the nick of time. They didn't do anything to me."

I couldn't believe the relief that washed over me. I felt a valve release. "I'm sorry about your uncle. I wish I could have done something to help him."

"It's done," she said, finishing dressing. "Let's get the fuck out of here."

Following her instructions, we had no trouble finding the vehicle bay. Two Suburbans, each with the keys in the ignition. Seconds later we were out of the compound, heading down to the highway. A quarter mile after leaving we saw a single set of headlights approaching. Since we were still on the compound road, it had to be someone related to Miguel. I tensed up, telling Jennifer to hold on tight. My entire assault on the compound had lasted a little over an hour, which, with driving time, meant that Machete's men had only attended two of the meet times at the Plaza Mayor. With any luck, they had another hour before the men grew tired. Whoever this was probably had no intention of trying to stop us. We passed the vehicle at a high rate of speed, the headlights masking whoever was behind the wheel.

# 42

Abu Bakr watched the vehicle recede in his rearview mirror, wondering why it was going so fast. He passed through the inner gate, seeing it open, something that had never happened in the week that they had been there. He parked at the end of the drive and went to the front door. Entering, he advanced cautiously into Miguel's study. First he saw Miguel apparently asleep in his chair, then a body on the floor, hands outstretched toward a weapon against the wall.

Bakr paused, catching the familiar slaughterhouse smell of bodily fluids slowly crusting. Somebody had hit Miguel's enterprise, but how on earth had they gotten past Jake and all the rest of the security? He approached Miguel, stopping short five feet away. The back of his head was a raw crater, the wall splattered with bone and brain matter, reminding him of the martyrs he had seen die in Fallujah.

It looked like Sayyidd was going to get what

he wanted after all. Now that Miguel was dead, their original mission was destroyed. The long-term infiltration into the U.S. had depended on his smuggling network. No doubt, someone would rise up and take charge of the massive organization, but it would be years before the infighting was done and someone was crowned king. No matter what Bakr had thought of the idea initially, getting to the temple and finding the weapon appeared to be the best course of action now.

Bakr raced from the room to his bungalow, seeing it had been ransacked, with their belongings thrown about haphazardly. He went straight to the box designed to test Miguel's network and grabbed the GPS systems, test tubes, and the respirators, leaving the rest of the equipment. He then packed their clothes as fast as he could. He found everything but his favorite sandals. He looked under the bed and in the bathroom but couldn't find them. Why would someone want those? They were old, worn out, and nasty, but had great sentimental value, as he had worn them on the hajj. He had no answer but had wasted enough time looking for them.

He grabbed the luggage, returned to the car, and raced out of the compound, heading back to the restaurant. Right after making the turn onto the main highway, he passed a caravan of Suburbans led by Jake. There was one answer: Jake hadn't been on the compound. When he found out what had happened, Guatemala City was going to turn into a bloodbath.

Abu Bakr returned to the restaurant, relaying to Sayyidd everything he had seen. Sayyidd was fascinated by the story, seeing it as another example of Allah's will. "Now we're the only ones looking for the temple. Everyone else is dead. If that isn't a sign of God's plan, then nothing is. We're going to succeed."

Bakr wondered how Sayyidd had managed to live as long as he had when he deferred all decisions to blind faith. "That may be true, but we still need to be careful. Allah guides the righteous but turns his back on fools. We need to get rid of Miguel's vehicle and get out of Guatemala City. We need to plan our next move, not simply run into the jungle half prepared."

With that, he stood up, throwing some money on the table to pay for dinner. Sayyidd followed him outside. They unloaded the Suburban and took a cab to the main bus station in Zona 1. Sayyidd moved to a corner and loaded the GPS data from the thumb drive into the Garmin.

Moving back outside to allow the GPS to see the sky, Bakr waited for it to lock on to the satellite signals. It eventually beeped and showed them their current location.

Bakr went to the waypoint manager and looked at the waypoints now stored in the GPS. They numbered fifteen, without any special labels. He frowned. This gave them the general location, but without knowing which waypoint was the location of the temple, they would be thrashing around the jungle for months.

"This isn't going to work. We don't have the time or experience to go treasure hunting."

Sayyidd took the GPS. "Let me look at something."

Sayyidd went to the main menu and pulled up "tracks," a setting on the Garmin that left a bread-crumb trail wherever the GPS went. The latest track stored went generally straight, weaving here and there, passing through all of the waypoints. When it hit waypoint fifteen, it began a looping journey, moving north, then back south, continuing back crazily through the jungle before ending at the start point of the expedition.

Sayyidd smiled. "The boy Eduardo didn't put a waypoint at the temple, but the professor ran the GPS with the track feature on. It shows everywhere they went. It looks like waypoint fifteen was the last camp where the boys took the GPS. All we need to do is mark another one at the farthest location, where the track loops back onto itself."

Within seconds he did exactly this, labeling

it sixteen. "Now, we simply need to move to this location."

Sayyidd smiled broadly at his partner. "We can be there in a day or less."

# 43

We'd been driving for close to an hour before Jennifer asked where we were going.

"We're headed to Belize. I'm going to a place called Puerto Barrios on the eastern edge of Guatemala. From there, we'll take a ferry to a town called Punta Gorda."

"What're we going to do there? Maybe we should just fly out from here."

"Maybe, but I've been to Belize a few times, so I know it better than this place. I don't want to be in this country when the word gets out about what I did. I'm sure a lot of people lost their livelihood tonight."

Jennifer leaned over and placed her hand on my arm.

"Hey, I never thanked you for saving my life. I'm sorry that I caused this mess, but I'm glad you were here." She smiled.

I felt an enormous wash of shame at what I had planned earlier. What was I going to say to that? *Yeah, I'm a great guy. By the way, I was within a split second of leaving you to get gang-raped so I could save my own ass.* I shook her hand off and told her the truth.

"Look, I'd like to say I came to help you because I'm a nice guy, but I'm not. You were rescued by the memory of a dead woman. I'm not a hero. I thought I was one once, but that stupid fairy tale was killed nine months ago."

We sat in silence for a moment. An incredibly uncomfortable silence. I wished I hadn't opened my mouth. *Just take the thank-you and let it go.*

"You can't expect me to sit here with that answer. What do you mean? Why'd you come back for me?"

I sighed, debating whether to continue. I decided to get it all out. "Nine months ago I was in a special unit in the military. I had been deployed at war since 9/11. My wife had borne the brunt of the deployments. While I was off doing exactly what I wanted, she had to stay home and pay the bills and raise our daughter. She asked me to quit, to not go on my next deployment, but I pulled on her patriotic heartstrings, giving her a pack of lies about how I was needed to save America. She let me go. A month into it, my wife and child were beaten to death by some sorry son of a bitch looking to rob a house."

I stopped, lost in thought, unsure of why I was talking about this. Jennifer said nothing.

Eventually, I continued, feeling a little catharsis.

"Because I wanted to keep doing a bunch of bullshit stuff in the name of the United States, my wife and child were killed. If I'd stayed home they'd be alive. And nobody was making me go. The unit was voluntary. Because of my selfishness, I killed my family. That's the only reason I came for you. I was reminded of my wife, nothing more. I'm not a good guy."

Jennifer was shocked by the story. She thought she might be hearing something that hadn't ever been said aloud. She looked at Pike, gripping the steering wheel like he was trying to choke it to death, and didn't know how to respond. She knew that what he'd said wasn't true. *Nobody with those character flaws would do what he just did. Nobody else on God's green earth would even attempt it, saint or otherwise.*

She asked a simple question. "Would you have come for me if your wife was still alive? Would you have attacked that place all by yourself?"

Pike considered the question, reflecting on it for a few moments. "Yes. It's what I used to do. It's what I used to be when I believed in a lie. But I'm not that man anymore."

Jennifer smiled to herself in the darkness. She gave a simple response, not realizing the implications of the words. "Well, I don't think it was a lie. Welcome back."

I'm sure she made the comment simply to break away from the awkward conversation, but it struck a chord deep inside. Back when I was operational, I had a quote from George Orwell hanging inside my Taskforce locker that defined the essence of what I believed I was: *People sleep peacefully in their beds at night only because rough men stand ready to visit violence on those who would do them harm.*

The death of my family had shattered that illusion, leaving me believing my life was nothing more than an act in a play that others directed. I had turned my back on everything I once held as sacrosanct, convinced that I had been used like a puppet because all of the terrorists I had killed had done nothing to prevent the death of all that I held dear.

Even so, deep in my soul, I desperately wanted to believe again. I wanted to feel the faith of my past, to be what I once was. Jennifer's comment sliced through the pain, opening up a window, albeit small, to the hope beneath. I liked the feeling. *Is it really that simple?*

I glanced over at her and squeezed her hand, choking out two words that meant far more than she could possibly realize. "You're welcome."

# 44

Passing through a small town, really just a collection of huts spanning the highway, I began to look for a vehicle to trade for our Suburban. I needed one that appeared mechanically sound but was old enough to allow me to carjack it without too much trouble. Something built before all the newfangled computers, laser keys, and complicated steering-wheel locks. On the outskirts of the village I saw a Ford Fiesta parked in the yard of a house that looked like it had been made from flattened beer cans. The car itself was at least twenty years old, dented and patched many times, with a coloring consisting of mottled spray paint covering the original finish like a bad rash. I drove past it a hundred meters and pulled over.

"I'm going back to get that car. You get behind the wheel here. When I start it, I'll pull out and flash you with the headlights. Let me pass you, then pull in behind me. We'll go about a mile down the road, then pull over and swap cars."

"Are you sure you can steal it?"

"Yeah. I've done it before. Shouldn't be too hard."

I pulled out the little Suburban tool kit from the glove box, consisting of a pair of pliers, a small hammer, and both a Phillips and flathead screwdriver. Leaving the car, I fell into a light jog down the darkened highway to the Fiesta.

Using the giant side mirror of the Suburban, Jennifer watched Pike approach the vehicle and peer through the driver's side window. She watched him rear back with the hammer, shielding his face from potential flying glass. Saw him shatter the window, only to be met by an ear-splitting alarm. Saw him running back toward her like a scalded dog.

She jammed the SUV into drive and hit the gas as he jumped in. She threw a rooster tail of dirt, fishtailing back onto the highway, weaving left and right. She started laughing uncontrollably, tears in her eyes, fighting to stay on the road.

Pike first looked indignant, moving on to aggravated, and ending with plain angry. "What're you laughing at? Christ! Watch where the hell you're going!"

Between hitches of laughter, Jennifer gave a poor impression of Pike's baritone. "I can rip that car off. Shouldn't be any trouble."

Pike shook his head, looking out the window. Jennifer continued to laugh, unable to stop, letting off pent-up emotion. The laughter was genuine but had a little bit of a brittle edge. She finally calmed down enough to look at him. Seeing his annoyance, she tried to mollify him. "Come on. You have to admit that was funny. You looked like a teenager caught in the girlfriend's bed by her father."

I tried hard to maintain my annoyance, but it was a losing battle. Running through what had happened, I broke down with an embarrassed grin.

"Who in the hell puts an alarm on a vehicle like that? Who would steal that piece of shit out here?"

"Maybe there's a huge market for twenty-year-old American-made cars in Guatemala. Or maybe a lot of commandos come through here after blowing the hell out of Guatemala City and he's sick of them taking his cars for a getaway."

"Okay, okay. Let's find another car."

"Are you sure? Maybe we should stick with the Suburban while we're ahead. I'm not saying you can't do it. If you say you can, then I'm sure you can. I just don't want you to be forced to kill half the village to prove it."

She looked at me mischievously. "I'll bet you never ask anyone for directions, either, huh?"

She saw me grimace and said, "I'm just teasing. We'll do whatever you think we need to."

"We need it, and I won't kill anyone to get it. I *have* done this before. Trust me."

She lightly touched my arm. "I do trust you."

I didn't know what to say to that. I was completely unused to being on the receiving end of someone's trust, and it did nothing but embarrass me. Before the silence could grow uncomfortable, I saw a Chevy Cutlass ahead on the left side of the road, circa 1984.

"All right, mission number two. Same plan. This time, if an alarm goes off, wait for me to get inside the vehicle before you act like Dale Earnhardt, okay?"

"You got it. You want me to honk when we pass it? See if I can save us some time with the alarm?"

*Man, she's got some balls.*

"Please just pull up a hundred meters."

I exited the vehicle and cautiously moved up to the Cutlass. The doors were unlocked. This was more like what I expected from the backwoods of Guatemala. Opening the door, I sat down behind the wheel. I took out the hammer and began smashing at the base of the turn indicator on the left side of the steering wheel stalk, attempting to get at the mechanism underneath the sheath of alloy steel. I opened up the steering column, with the cheap alloy coming off in quarter-inch flakes. I jammed a screwdriver into the mechanism usually rotated by the key and yanked backward. The car sputtered, coughed, finally catching itself as it warmed up. Satisfied that the vehicle would run, I took the wheel and began forcefully yanking it left and right, breaking the lock holding the steering wheel in place.

I hit the lights to warn Jennifer I was on the way, pulled onto the deserted highway and picked her up, and transferred the weapons and assault kit to the Cutlass. Within seconds we were back on the road to Puerto Barrios, leaving the Suburban abandoned on the side of the road.

Jennifer spent the next couple of hours staring out the window, savoring the fact that she was still among the living. She couldn't control the thoughts and images flying through her head — her kidnapping, how close she was to being violently gang-raped by a bunch of savages, the vivid punishment Pike had brought to those same savages, the murder of her uncle — all competing for attention in her conscious mind. She turned on the radio of the Cutlass, looking for an outside diversion. She got nothing but static or Spanish music. *That figures. What I wouldn't give for an iPod right now. Wait a minute . . .*

"Hey, you still have my MP3 player? I'd

like to use it if it's handy."

She saw Pike look out the window and waited for him to answer. After a few seconds, she thought maybe she'd said something wrong, but couldn't figure out why.

He finally said, "I don't have it. I'll buy you a new one."

"Huh? Where is it?"

"Man, who gives a shit about the MP3 player? In the end, it didn't matter what was on that thing. I said I'll buy you a new one, for Christ's sake."

"You don't have it? Seriously? What happened to it? Did you sell it or something?"

Pike sighed. "I was mugged, okay? It was stolen. I don't want to talk about it."

*What? That's absolute bullshit. . . . There's another story here.* She waited to hear it. After a moment of silence, she said, "Really? Are you telling the truth? *You* got mugged?"

"More like an attempted mugging. A couple of Arabs attacked me at the central market. Probably trying to get enough money to pay for some flight lessons. I chased them off pretty quickly, and they didn't get my wallet or watch or anything else valuable. All they got was the MP3 player. Let it go. I'm pissed off enough."

Jennifer started to ask another question, then thought better of it. "Hey, I don't care. I wasn't trying to get you mad. Let's drop it."

A lost thought tickled the back of her brain.

Something about the theft of the MP3 that she wanted to follow up on, but hadn't. Like a person who just set her keys down and now can't find them, it tugged at her subconscious, an itch begging to be scratched.

# 45

Exiting the bus in Flores, Sayyidd was anxious to start looking for the temple. After checking in, he set about cataloging the belongings that Bakr had packed. He began to search at a faster pace, clearly upset about something.

Bakr said, "What's wrong? What're you looking for?"

"I'm missing a shirt and a pair of American workout pants. Didn't you pack them?"

"I didn't have time to search the entire room. I took what was in front of me. I didn't see any other clothes, but they might've been there. I myself couldn't find my sandals. Don't worry about your Western disguises. We can replace them."

Sayyidd debated telling Bakr why he was concerned. In the end, Allah would either protect them or not. Did it matter whether he said anything? *Insha'Allah* guided his life. If God wasn't willing, then He wasn't willing. Nothing Sayyidd could do would alter that. Even so, it wasn't in his nature to hide things.

"I understand that I can purchase more clothing, but there's something in the shirt that we'll need. I had a scrap of paper in the pocket with the emergency e-mail addresses on it."

Abu Bakr's face contorted in anger.

"You *wrote down* the e-mail addresses? What were you thinking?"

"I know — it was stupid, but we aren't in the Land of Two Rivers, and nobody is actively hunting us. I did memorize them, but this mission was too important to rely on memory. I knew we wouldn't have the opportunity to conduct a meeting if we forgot them. They were our lifeline! Either way, didn't you say everyone was dead at Miguel's? It shouldn't matter. Allah has guided us to this point, and He will still guide us."

"You're proving to be an idiot. One of the dumb little neophytes who believe everything told them, driving a truck full of TNT because they're told they're delivering groceries. They make good martyrs but are not of Allah's chosen. Allah guides those who show they are worthy, not those who spit on his favor. Please tell me you didn't have the passwords with them."

Sayyidd couldn't bring himself to tell the truth. He thought Bakr was acting like an old woman, afraid of his own shadow, but didn't want to cause him to question the mission. He didn't believe he had the strength or courage to succeed by himself. Years ago, before giving himself to the jihad, he might have been up to the task, but his experiences in Iraq had paradoxically given him an Achilles' heel — his complete trust in Allah had left him with no faith in himself. He longed to be like men such as Bakr, but in his heart knew he wasn't. He held a secret shame that tore at the fabric of his being, an individual weakness that corroded the essence of his capability: He didn't believe he had the courage to be a *shahid.*

A suicide bomber's detonator wasn't pressed by Allah. It was pressed by the man wearing the bomb. A man who executed Allah's will by his own action. A man like Bakr. Deep inside, Sayyidd questioned whether he had that same strength, afraid of the answer he would find when put to the test. He told Bakr a small white lie to protect the larger one festering in his soul.

"Of course I didn't keep the addresses with the passwords. I'm not that stupid. They're just e-mail addresses. They won't mean anything to anyone at Miguel's estate. Even if someone goes to them, they'll get nothing."

Bakr appeared to be mollified and let it go.

"We need to figure out how we're going to get to the temple and package the weapon. From Eduardo's description, it sounded like anthrax or ricin, only it acts instantly. Judging by the way Eduardo described the victim's distress, I'm almost positive it must be drawn into the respiratory tract and doesn't act on contact with the skin. Since it's not made by modern man, it should have particles large enough to be filtered by the 3M masks we brought."

Sayyidd had some training on WMD, but very little. Bakr had specialized in them at training camps in the Bekaa Valley of Lebanon, and thus Sayyidd deferred to him.

"If you say so."

Bakr smiled at Sayyidd's trusting ways. "I said I *believe* it must get into the respiratory tract, but I'm not sure. It could just as easily be some sort of nerve toxin that kills on contact. Are you willing to risk that?"

"If it's Allah's will that we die, then we die. I don't believe He would get us this far only to kill us deep in the jungle. I'm willing to risk it. Are you having second thoughts?"

Bakr internally cringed. Sayyidd's blind faith left him wondering how Sayyidd had lived for three days in Iraq, much less three years.

"No. This path isn't any more dangerous than what I've done in the past. I believe I'm correct. We should be protected."

Sayyidd pulled out the GPS.

"It looks like the temple's only twenty kilometers from here. We should be able to rent a four-wheel drive and get within ten kilometers before traveling on foot. If all goes well, we should have the weapon within a day. The only thing we're missing is food for the trip."

"We need more than simply food," Bakr said. "We need to purchase some equipment that will allow me to decontaminate whatever we find. Start thinking about what we're trying to do. We aren't going out to pick flowers. You don't follow my instructions exactly, we'll both be killed."

# 46

I woke early the next morning, while it was still dark. I was disoriented for a minute before remembering where I was. I snapped completely awake. I hadn't thought I was in my own bed, at my old house. I hadn't thought my family was still alive. I had no split second of happiness. I also had no gut-wrenching letdown. *I've lost my happiness.* I wasn't sure what to make of the trade-off. I didn't want to lose Heather, and that split second was all I had left.

I lay in bed thinking about the shift that had just occurred. Before I could get too melancholy, the last twenty-four hours of my life came back with a vengeance. I thought about the absolute insanity of what I had done, and the fact that I was still walking. It made no sense to me. How I had been allowed to live when I had practically begged God to kill me in the maelstrom of Machete's compound? Why had my family been taken when they'd done nothing more than go

288

about their daily lives? It wasn't fair. *I should be dead.* I looked over at the other bed, watching Jennifer snoring softly. *We should both be dead.* I watched her roll over and felt a weird twinge, an unfamiliar pang. *Maybe it's payback for Heather.*

Dawn was starting to break. I slipped silently out of bed and went to our small bathroom. I splashed water on my face and stared in the mirror for a half minute. *Well, I'm up now. What to do?*

I went to the door and looked at Jennifer's slumbering form again. The twinge came back, making me feel uncomfortable. Making me think about Heather. Like a magnet repulsed, I wanted out of the room, away from the feeling. I went through the sliding door to our little outside courtyard, watching the sun break the horizon.

I sat down, enjoying the view for no other reason than it allowed me to focus on something else. I lost track of time and was startled out of my reverie by the sliding glass door opening. Jennifer came out, still dressed in the long-sleeved cotton shirt and sweatpants. She'd cleaned up the blood but still looked pretty ragged.

"How're you feeling?" I said.

"Better than I would have been, I'm sure."

She stood there for a moment, then said, "I've got something I want to talk to you about."

"Okay . . ."

She said nothing, clearly wrestling with the issue in her mind.

"Well? You have to speak if you want to talk to me."

She hesitated a second more, then said, "I think something bigger is going on than just us running from El Machete. I meant to bring it up last night on the drive, but it slipped my mind."

I walked to the door of our room. "What do you mean?"

She said, "Uh, well, how do you know that Arabs took the MP3 player?"

*Please. Not this again. She must have really loved that thing.* "I thought we were dropping that. I'll buy you a new one."

"No, no. It's not that. I just think that something's going on. I don't want you to think I'm crazy, and maybe it's nothing."

I shrugged. "I heard them talking. They spoke Arabic. No doubt in my mind. Now, what's the big secret?"

Jennifer hesitated, like she was embarrassed to say what was on her mind.

"Come on. Spit it out. What's up?"

"Well, don't laugh, but I don't think it was a random mugging. I think those guys attacked you for the MP3 player so they could find the temple. So they could ransack it and steal what my uncle rightfully discovered."

I looked at her like she had a second head.

I figured she was going to have some stupid theory on how her uncle had survived and was now being held by terrorists in Beirut.

"Huh? What're you talking about?"

"While I was held, Miguel — El Machete — told me the story of my uncle finding the temple. He said that a native entered first, but died from being exposed to the contents of some type of sack protecting the entrance. This fits my uncle's theory exactly. The story had to have come from my uncle, because Miguel wouldn't know to make that up."

I didn't hide my disdain, forcing her to race to get the rest out. "Wait, I know it sounds crazy, but the room where I got my clothes had a Quran and two different passports for the same guy. One passport was from Saudi Arabia with an Arabic name, and one was issued by the United States to some guy named Carlos. Now, you tell me that you were mugged by Arabs in Guatemala. What are the odds of that?"

I considered that. I had thought it just about as strange as getting mugged by a couple of Girl Scouts but put it into the category of "strange things happen." I knew there was no way that WMD had been created by the Mayans, and even if it had, it wouldn't have lasted for a thousand years.

"Look, I don't know why I was mugged by Arabs. Maybe they got stranded and needed some cash. Maybe they thought they were doing their part for the jihad. It really doesn't matter. We have no proof whatsoever of a giant plot, and even if it's true, there's nothing we can do about it."

"Why would Machete lie to me? He was about to kill me. There was no reason to lie. Why did the Arabs quit as soon as they got the MP3 player?"

"They didn't quit because they wanted to, they quit because I was about to rip their heads off. As for Machete, he may believe what your uncle told him, but we have no idea what yarns your uncle was spinning. He lied about the FedEx package for starters, he may have lied about some mythical protection simply to keep Machete from going after the temple. Don't build this up into some giant terrorist conspiracy. Our first priority is to get back to the U.S."

"I'm *not* saying they're terrorists, but those guys are up to no good. Staying as guests of Machete is proof enough of that. Just think about it some, okay? All I want to do is tell someone. My uncle spent his entire life looking for that temple, only to get murdered when he succeeded. I don't want a couple of thieves to steal what he found. It's not fair. If I'm wrong, we only look like kooks, but if I'm right, we might be preventing something bad from happening."

"Stop. I know you want your uncle's death to mean something — trust me, I've been there — but sometimes bad shit just happens. He got killed by a sick fuck, and we dealt with that. End of story. Let it go."

She jerked like I had slapped her. "That's not it. That's not what I think. Nobody but my uncle believed the temple even existed. Now he's found it, and it's probably full of archaeological treasures. People have been trying to determine what happened to the Mayans forever. *I've* had to study about it with two different professors who both had different theories. That temple may hold the truth. It would be priceless, but now that history's going to be lost to a couple of grave-robbers who'll destroy the find for some paltry money. I can't let that happen. All I'm asking is that we consider how we could get the information to the right people."

I really didn't give a shit about the Mayans, but a part of me did identify with her determination.

"All right, I'll mull it over. In the meantime, let's go get you some normal clothes, get our passports stamped, and get on a ferry. We can't do anything on the run anyway."

Two hours later we were on the first ferry headed to Belize and safety. Once under way, I felt a huge weight leave my shoulders. I didn't want to scare Jennifer, but I had felt we were in very real danger every minute we were in Guatemala. Now that there was nothing to stop us from entering Belize, I felt our chances of survival had gone from about 60 percent to almost 100 percent. I relaxed for the first time in over thirty-six hours, enjoying the sun and balmy weather.

My mind began to drift, thinking about what Jennifer had said earlier in the morning. I still thought the entire WMD scenario was crazy, but I had to admit that the Arabs' attempt to rob me inside Guatemala City, and the fact that they only took the MP3 player, was a coincidence that didn't stand the light of day. Coupled with the passports and Quran, I began to think Jennifer was onto something. She simply thought someone was going to rob her uncle of what he had dedicated his life to find, but maybe there was something more.

I hadn't said anything to Jennifer about what she had seen inside Miguel's compound, not wanting to build up the conspiracy theory, but the items in the box at the back of the room had all of the hallmarks of terrorist equipment. The 3M respirators were used to protect first responders against inhaled threats, but could be used just as easily to protect terrorists from harming themselves while constructing nuclear, biological, or chemical weapons. The garage door opener was benign on the surface, but I had seen it used plenty of times as a triggering device for improvised explosive devices. Put together with everything else, I began to think that

Jennifer's instincts might be right. There was no way that the two guys who ambushed me were on the way to finding a thousand-year-old WMD, but I was beginning to believe that Machete was helping a terrorist enterprise, and that this enterprise was still on the loose. *Maybe I've destroyed more than a simple criminal syndicate.* The only question was whether the two Arabs still had the capability and the will to do anything now that El Machete was dead.

■ ■ ■ ■

# PART
# THREE

■ ■ ■ ■

# 47

Abu Bakr opened the door to their hotel room in Flores, completely spent from their ordeal. It had taken two days to get in and out of the jungle, much more time than he had thought. He was dehydrated, hungry, sliced up, and sore, but still felt a sense of urgency. He didn't know how long they had before Miguel's men found them. Being inside Guatemala was downright dangerous, with the risk increasing every minute.

They packed up hurriedly, checking out and taking a cab to the airport. Inside one of their pieces of luggage was the fruits of their jungle trek: a Tupperware container secured with duct tape and plastic sheeting. It protected the material they'd found next to a dead native boy deep in the jungle; something bad had happened out there, Bakr was certain. Something that might be the result of the weapon they dreamed of, and Bakr was looking forward to finding out.

They were about to purchase tickets on one

of the local small planes when Bakr pulled Sayyidd out of line.

"What's wrong?"

"Take a look at what they're doing to the bags. They're putting each one through an X-ray."

"So? That's a result of our glorious victory against the Great Satan. We have no weapons. The X-ray will show a container of dirt. What are you afraid of?"

"I saw a man's bag searched after the X-ray. They weren't looking for weapons. They're looking for artifacts. This isn't for security; it's to prevent looters from taking treasure from the country."

"I say again, who cares? We have a bag of dirt."

"We can't chance it. Our package will look like a blob on X-ray. They'll be forced to check it out. We can't risk having them open the container, releasing the weapon. We can't fly out of here."

"What do you want to do? What else can we do?"

"We need to get to another country, where there's less security. Either Mexico or Belize. Let's get out of here and find a bus station."

Catching a cab, they made the short trip to the Santa Elena bus station. After a brief investigation, they found a bus heading to the Yucatán in Mexico at four in the afternoon, and another one heading to Melchor de Mencos on the Belizean border within the hour. Finding out that they could take a further bus into Belize City, and from there an airplane out, they bought the ticket.

Bakr, not sure if Sayyidd would remember, asked, "You have your American passport, right? Without that, you'll need a visa to enter Belize. I don't want to be embarrassed."

Sayyidd scowled, saying, "Yes, chosen one, I have the passport. I traveled the long way to get here as well. I haven't forgotten what to do."

"I meant no disrespect. I'll continue to ask questions, the same way I did in battle. It's why I'm still alive. I would expect the same from you. Please, let's talk about the mission."

"What do you mean?"

"I've been thinking," Bakr said, "and I believe we need to test the weapon. Now. Before we fly out. We don't even know if it's deadly. I put a sample in a test tube, hoping maybe we'd get a chance to analyze it with our specialists before we employ it, but really there's no reason for that. We test it here, and we'll know."

"You told me you saw the dead boy in the temple. Isn't that proof enough? Why risk letting the weapon out now?"

"Yes, I did see the boy, but we don't know what killed him. He might have had a heart attack or something else. I know it's a small

301

chance, but we should be sure that the effort we're going through will be rewarded. We need to know the weapon is real. On top of that, I need to see how the weapon works. That's the only way I'll be able to determine the optimum method of deployment. Otherwise, I'll just be guessing."

They heard their bus being called. Getting up, Bakr said, "When we get off at the Belizean border, we'll find a place to test it."

Two hours later, Bakr was bouncing along inside the ancient converted school bus, roasting in the heat. The fan in the roof did little to provide any relief, although the local nationals riding with him didn't seem to mind. Looking around, he began to get an idea. He asked the man sitting in front of him how far they were from the border, speaking Spanish for the first time. When he heard they were only about ten minutes away, he told Sayyidd in Arabic, "We're getting off right now. When we stop, let me go up top to get the luggage."

"Why? We'll have to walk the rest of the way."

Bakr pulled out the test tube he had filled in the temple. "We're going to test the weapon right here, while the bus is still out in the middle of nowhere."

He moved to the front, gave out a lame excuse to the driver, and convinced him to pull over. Climbing on the roof, he pretended to mess with their luggage, passing one bag down, then pretended to struggle with the other. The driver killed the bus, not wanting to waste the gas, something Bakr was waiting for. Working swiftly, he securely taped a piece of twine to the test tube, then measured out the length of one of the fan blades in the roof of the bus. He cut the twine, tied the loose end at the hub of the fan, then laid the test tube on the edge of the mount. Now, once the bus started back up, the fan would jerk the tube off the mount and smash it against the frame, shattering the vial. Once that happened, Bakr hoped the poison would be blown into the bus by the rotation of the fan.

He retrieved his bag, climbed down, and called the driver to him — wanting to make him walk back to the bus to give them more time to increase their distance before it was started. He gave the driver a tip and thanked him, then began walking back the way they had come. The driver shook his head and moved back to the bus, muttering about crazy foreigners as he went.

Bakr and Sayyidd were walking as fast as they could when they heard the bus start up. Turning around, they watched it begin driving away. It moved about forty yards down the road before it began weaving back and forth. Then it lazily crashed into the wood line on the edge of the road, never getting up over twenty miles an hour. Nothing happened for a long five seconds, then the back door exploded open and two people fell out, clawing at their necks and writhing on the ground as if they were trying to scrape off ants covering their bodies. From the inside of the bus Bakr could hear what sounded like a group of pigs grunting, and could vaguely see arms and legs thrashing about, like a nest of snakes.

"Allah the Merciful," Bakr said in a subdued whisper. "It works better than I would have ever dreamed. And faster too."

# 48

Jennifer and Pike checked into their rustic villa in the small village of Punta Gorda, Belize. With Pike gone to sniff around the town, Jennifer was finally able to take off the filthy clothes she'd stolen. She filled the sink with cool water, soaked a rag, and blotted her face. She felt a sharp sting on her right cheek. She jerked her hand away like she'd touched a hot stove. *Damn, that hurt.* She leaned forward and looked at her cheek in the cracked mirror above the sink, seeing two small gouges ripped out, each about the size of a popcorn kernel. She had no recollection of how she'd sustained them, and hadn't even noticed the cuts when she'd cleaned off at the hotel in Guatemala last night. She leaned in closer. *Shit . . . that's going to leave a scar. Matches my nose.*

She was the only one who could still see the small white line across the bridge of her nose, a trophy from her childhood of competing with her older brothers. She thought of the tree she had fallen out of. Like lightning jumping from pole to pole, her thoughts went from that summer day, to her brothers, to her mother, ending with her uncle. And what had happened to him.

*Uncle John's dead.* Up until now, she hadn't had the luxury of dwelling on his loss. The thought hammered home for the first time. She felt the grief roil her like a wave, fighting to take control. She closed her eyes and leaned forward, resting her head on her arms. *Not now. Later. Think about this later, when you're home.* She took off her sweat-soaked undergarments and washed them in the sink, a mindless chore to keep her busy. She then stepped into the shower, trying to keep moving to prevent her mind from returning to the sorrow. Ten minutes later she toweled off and put on the simple floral print dress and leather sandals she had purchased. Picking up the stolen pants and shirt, she turned to throw them in the trash when a small bit of paper fluttered to the ground. Curious, she picked it up.

I came back from exploring the town and entered our room, calling out to Jennifer. She came out of the bathroom freshly scrubbed and wearing her new clothes. I was a little surprised by the transformation. She had a couple of cuts on her cheek and a little swelling around her left eye, but she certainly

wasn't ragged anymore. *Huh. She's a damn hammer. How'd I miss that before?*

"What're you looking at?"

"Uh . . . nothing. I was just surprised to see you without those Arab rags on."

"Well, speaking of Arabs, have you thought about what we talked about earlier?"

*And she's crazy. . . . What is it with her family and conspiracy theories?*

"Man, you're like a dog with a bone. I told you I'd think about it, but we can't do anything until we get to the U.S. anyway. Let's focus on that right now."

"I found something in the shirt. A bunch of e-mail addresses and passwords. I think we need to tell someone sooner rather than later. They may have already robbed the temple and smuggled out the artifacts."

I paused, torn because I wanted to stomp this latest request, but intrigued by the find.

"How many addresses?"

I knew that terrorists used hundreds of e-mail addresses to communicate, a move and countermove continually fought between intelligence agencies and Al Qaeda. AQ switched addresses so frequently it made me wonder how they knew which ones to use, but somehow they did.

"Six different addresses, with six different passwords."

"Well, that will be something we want to turn over to whoever we talk to in the States.

*When* we get there."

"Pike, please, I think this is important. We need to tell someone now. Can't we go to the U.S. embassy? Won't they do something with it?"

I shook my head. "Unfortunately, no. They would listen to us, but they wouldn't do anything with the information. It'd be put into some report and buried in a ton of other information. You wouldn't believe the amount of reports that embassies get on crime and terrorism. We'll get quicker action by flying to the States first."

I could tell she didn't believe what I'd said. "Nobody in the embassy deals with crime? Who gets called when an American citizen is a victim of something?"

"The legal attaché. He's the representative of the FBI at the embassy, and if we go to him, he's going to be more concerned with the death and destruction we've done than any story of a temple vandalism. They'd listen to us for about five seconds. Then they'd put us in handcuffs. Remember, we don't have any proof of what you think. The only thing we have in concrete is that I've killed folks both in the U.S. and in Guatemala. Going to them isn't going to get the action you want. It's just going to get us in trouble."

"Well, couldn't we talk to the CIA? Wouldn't they listen to us?"

"Jennifer, trust me on this. I have a lot of

experience working with country teams. We wouldn't even get in to see the CIA. They won't have a sign out front saying, 'Spying Done Two Doors Down.' They aren't acknowledged publicly. If we went to the embassy and said, 'We'd like to talk to the head spy,' we'd be shown the door."

"Look, how about this? We go to an Internet café and check out these e-mail addresses. If we see something in them that leans toward some type of illegal activity, we take that to the embassy. How does that sound?"

I gave up. "Okay, fine. We're safe here. We can either take some time out walking the beaches and seeing the sights, or we can waste our time trying to figure out this giant conspiracy theory. First can we get some lunch?"

"Sure. I'm hungry."

We practically ran to the first taco stand Jennifer could find, where I watched her suck down fish tacos like she was in some kind of competition. We finished in fifteen minutes, with Jennifer tapping her foot while I paid the bill. A little later, we found a tourist store with two ancient computers in the back. For the small price of twelve U.S. dollars per five minutes, we were allowed access. Sitting down, Jennifer went to the first e-mail account listed, at Yahoo.com. Putting in the password, we saw that the account was empty. Looking in the sent file, Jennifer saw one entry. She clicked on it, pulling it up.

"Look! It's in Arabic! This account is used by the guys staying at Miguel's."

"Great. We already know they're Arabs. All this proves is that they're e-mailing their family to tell them what they bought as tourists."

"Hang on, let me check the other accounts."

She did so but found nothing else. Every other account was empty. *Okay. Maybe she'll let this go now.*

She began typing on the computer, pulling up the Google search engine.

"What're you doing now?"

"I'm going to try and translate the Arabic. I have to do this kind of research all the time at school. I've never translated anything before, but trust me, there's a Web site that'll tell us what this says."

*Jesus Christ. Stick a fork in it and call it done.*
"Come on. This is getting ridiculous."

"Just a second. We paid for five minutes. Let's use it."

She found a dozen translation sites and clicked on the first one that came up. Copying the Arabic from the Yahoo! mail, she pasted it into the translation box, then clicked on the "GO" button. We sat and waited for the slow Internet connection to work. Eventually, it timed out. She went back to the Google search page and clicked on the next one, trying again. Before this one timed out, it presented the translation of the Arabic text.

Jennifer, clearly disappointed, said, "Looks like you're right. A drunk must've sent this message. Let's go."

The pasted Arabic had turned into a translation in English, reading:

*Praise be to Allah, peace and prayers be upon the Prophet of God. Trip took our rotary [for good]. We have sight to the enemy hits far in country his. We established weapon that the Zionist inside the searching will wipe the poison he causes the enemy far to the Persians destroy. In Allah's name, the Merciful, the Compassionate, we will rejoice in the destruction from all [['iynfydls]], Hope responds with blessing to new task, or says us the path to takes.*

I stared at the screen. *I'll be damned. She found something.*

## 49

Jennifer said, "What? What're you looking at?"

"We need to print this and the original Arabic. Don't say anything else in here. We'll talk back at the room."

Jennifer was about to respond when I cut her off, looking at the woman manning the trinket counter. "Please, I know it sounds paranoid, but I'd rather do this somewhere else."

She printed both pages and we left, returning to the hotel. Along the way, I told Jennifer what I thought.

"It looked like a drunk had written the passage because it's a free Internet translation. Basically, it's a cheap-ass computer giving you exactly what it sees. The point of those things is to get you to buy a better translation. It's like you said, 'Last one home is a rotten egg,' and that was translated into Arabic as 'The long dead dropping from the bird is owned by the man who has the last house.' We don't know what idioms they used that the computer doesn't understand, but the direct translation says some things that support the fact that those guys are up to no good."

"Really?" Jennifer looked at me in surprise. "What did you see?"

"Let's get back to the hotel and I'll show you."

Twenty minutes later we sat at the cheap desk in our room, the translated printout in front of us. I pointed at what I had seen. "Look, ignoring the bad grammar, you find the following words: *weapon, Zionist, Persians, destroy,* and *infidels.* On top of that, you've got all the "Praise Allah" stuff. I'm starting to believe your crazy theory. At the least, I'm starting to believe that there might be some terrorists, and *they* believe your theory."

"Terrorists? Seriously? What do you make of the translation? Can you figure anything out from it?"

"Well, taking it at face value, I can make some assumptions. Rearranging it a little bit we get something that appears a little clearer." Working with the translation, I ended up with:

*Trip took our rotary [for good]* (No Idea). *We have sight to the enemy hits far in country his.* (We have the sight to hit the far enemy in his country). *We established weapon that the*

*Zionist inside the searching will wipe the poison he causes the enemy far to the Persians destroy.* (We have a poison weapon that the Zionists were searching for which will cause the far enemy to destroy the Persians.) *In Allah's name, the Merciful, the Compassionate, we will rejoice in the destruction from all [['iynfy-dls].,* (Praise Allah, we will rejoice in the destruction of all infidels.) *Hope responds with blessing to new task, or says us the path to takes.* (We hope you respond blessing our new task, or tell us the path to take.)

Putting it together, I came up with:

*Praise be to Allah, peace and prayers be upon the Prophet of God. We have the sight to hit the far enemy in his country. We have a poison weapon that the Zionists were searching for which will cause the far enemy to destroy the Persians. In Allah's name, the Merciful, the Compassionate, we will rejoice in the destruction of all infidels. We hope you respond blessing our new task, or tell us the path to take.*

Jennifer read it, asking, "I don't get it. Who's the far enemy? Jewish people?"

"We're the far enemy. It's what Al Qaeda calls the United States and anyone who supports us. Basically, the West."

"So this is saying that they're going to attack us? What's the Zionist-Persian thing?"

"*Zionists* in Arabic would translate into Israelis. Persians are Iranians. Looking at

314

what I came up with, I'm sure it's not right. There's no way that the Israelis are looking for a Mayan poison weapon." I paused, thinking, "Unless your uncle was Jewish. They could mean that *he* was looking for it. Was he Jewish?"

Jennifer shook her head. "No. If anything, he was atheist. I don't have any Jewish relatives as far as I know. What's up with all the 'Praise Allah' stuff? It sounds fake, like someone stereotyping an Arab. Do they really talk like that?"

"Not every Arab, but devout Muslims do — which by definition, a jihadist is. All those guys use about ten sentences for every one that means anything. You can't ask them the time of day without them spouting off four sentences kissing Allah's ass before they look at their watch."

I pushed back from the table. "Okay. I think we ought to stick with what we know out of the message. The fact that they mention kicking Persian ass means they're probably not supported by Iran. That knocks out Hezbollah and the Shiites, and since they talk about the far enemy, they probably believe in the doctrine of Al Qaeda. So . . . I'd say they're Sunni Arabs affiliated with Al Qaeda. They're also asking for a blessing on the mission, so whatever they're doing is not what they were sent to do. They're basically asking permission."

I leaned back, putting my hands behind my head. "So, we have a couple of AQ terrorists sent to Guatemala to do some sort of evil activity, who then got sidetracked by the story of the weapon, and are now trying to get the weapon to do something horrible against the U.S., the Israelis, the Iranians, or all three."

Jennifer halfway nodded. "Okay. What do we do now? Go to the embassy or wait until we get to the U.S.?"

"Well, I think we should try the embassy. I think I can get us in to the CIA. If not, we can always fly home. The key will be talking to the Agency. They'll be the only shop that won't care about the path of destruction we've left in our wake. Sound good?"

"I thought you said we couldn't find the CIA."

"I'm not saying it'll work. But I know how embassies operate, and how to find the CIA in the maze. If we get to the right guy, and I can get him to send a cable to headquarters, I can guarantee that the cable will be read."

"Okay. If you say so. What do we do now?"

"We take the first bus out of here to Belmopan. That's where the embassy is. I've been there a few times."

The shadows created by the dropping sun told me we weren't going anywhere today. I looked at my watch. "It's past seven now, so we've probably missed the last bus, but we can check the schedule for tomorrow."

She didn't look convinced but followed me out the door. Before I could lock it, Jennifer backed into me, her face ashen.

"The asshole that kidnapped me is in the lobby. He's talking to the clerk."

# 50

The hotel had only six rooms. A simple establishment built around an old colonial house, it had a balcony that extended out past our room and overlooked the front desk, with stairwells coming up left and right to our floor. Looking down I saw a Caucasian and a native discussing something with the clerk. The clerk pointed in our direction, and before I could move, the men were looking right at Jennifer and me. Time froze for a fraction of a second. Jennifer broke it, racing down the hallway toward the access to the roof veranda. The men immediately sprang into action, taking the far stairwell to cut her off.

*Shit.*

It wasn't the course of action I would have chosen, but I didn't bother yelling. Too late for that. Jennifer had committed us, and I had no choice but to follow, although going to the roof was possibly the worst choice. We couldn't jump off a three-story building.

We raced up the small stairwell and broke out onto the roof. I slammed the door shut and jammed a deck chair up against it. Jennifer kept going to the railing, looking down. I surveyed the area, determining what I had to fight with, which was pretty much nothing. We were on a small ten-foot-by-ten-foot veranda. No weapons, no room to dodge and fight two men.

Jennifer shouted over her shoulder, "You can climb down this, can't you? You've had some type of badass commando training, right?"

I couldn't believe how stupid that question was.

"Yeah, I can, but I sure as shit can't do it with you on my back. Get over here in the corner and stay down."

Jennifer bent down and tore off her sandals, throwing them over the side, followed by the knapsack she was using as a purse. "Don't worry about me."

Before I could stop her, she vaulted the balcony and disappeared. I ran over to the railing. Jennifer was already at the second level and scampering down the building like a monkey.

I was about to vault the railing myself when I heard the men hammer the door from the inside. The deck chair gave a foot. There was no way I could make it to the bottom before they reached the rail, and I'd be an easy target. I raced back, stopping on the side of the foot-long crack held in place by the deck chair, waiting on the men to break through.

They hammered the door twice more, finally causing the deck chair to fly off. The first man ran out with his pistol extended in one hand, breaking into the darkness of the deck and silhouetted by the light of the stairwell.

As soon as he was clear of the door, I grabbed the hand holding his pistol and used his own momentum to slingshot him up and over the railing of the deck, letting him fall the forty feet below. Turning, I saw the second man, the Caucasian, coming through the door, pistol at the ready. The sudden darkness from the light of the stairwell gave me an edge, as the man searched the gloom for a target he couldn't yet see. I kicked out hard and launched his pistol over the railing.

The force of the kick caused me to rotate slightly, getting rid of the immediate threat but exposing me to a counterassault. He wasted no time, giving me a roundhouse kick to my upper thigh that damn near crippled me. I went to a knee, collapsing my arms around my head to protect it. He followed with a snap-kick. My arms absorbed the blow, but it knocked me over. Hitting my back, I saw him close in for the kill, my position vulnerable for an endgame. I rose up on my arms like a crab and lashed out for his nearest leg with my foot, forcing him to back up and allowing me to regain my base. Back on my feet, we circled each other.

"I'm glad you got rid of the weapon," he said. "I'd rather beat you to death for the trouble you've caused. You should have hidden the Suburban. Not too many ways to go on that highway."

*English accent.* I said nothing, simply watching his technique. He had his hands raised chin high, balled into fists with his palms facing the ground. He bounced lightly on his feet, alternating between right and left, with one always poised to snap out and strike. A Muay Thai stance, so he had some training. *But Muay Thai's a stand-up game. Get his ass on the ground, and he's mine.*

He continued. "Where'd the little honey go? I'm looking forward to spending a little time with her. Once I get rid of you, she and I are going to get very well acquainted."

I ignored his banter, wondering why he wasn't forcing the fight. It dawned on me what he was doing. *He's stalling. He's got backup on the way. No time to fuck around.*

I waited for him to dance forward again, then shot inside his striking range, blocking a palm strike and following up with a right cross to the side of his head. I clinched him, grabbing his left biceps and controlling that arm, but before I could get my head into his chest he clocked me with a wicked elbow from the right, hammering right above my eye and causing an explosion of my vision. The blow broke the weak dam holding my blackness back, letting the beast loose. I now no longer wanted to escape. I wanted to destroy. I collapsed into him, protecting my head by pressing into his chest and completing the clinch. He gave me a useless blow to my back, and I was where I wanted to be.

I stretched my lower body back and drilled my knee into his inner thigh, hitting the tangle of nerves there, causing him to jerk in an attempt to escape. He raised his knee to attempt the same on me, but I was twisted away from the strike and waiting. I grabbed underneath the raised knee and launched forward with all of my might. He instinctively rotated to absorb the fall with his upper body, and I obliged, driving him full-force into the deck.

I ended up on his back in a rear-mount, his body facing the deck, the most vulnerable position I could ever imagine. He continued to fight furiously, trying to achieve dominance, but he had little skill on the ground. I pinned his arms with my legs and wrapped my right arm around his head, putting his forehead in the crook of my elbow and locking my hands together. *Good night, asshole.*

I bent his head back, listening to his rasping breath. When I got as far as I could, I hopped up onto the small of his back with my knee, freeing up his arms. Before he could react, I yanked to the rear, keeping his back pinned with my knee. He gave a guttural scream, then I felt his spine snap. The sensation sickened me a little, breaking my rage.

I rolled off him, gasping for air, a little ashamed of what I had done. Maybe a little afraid. *You didn't have to kill him.* I heard movement and immediately rotated into a fighting crouch, only to see Jennifer in front of me.

"Jesus Christ!" she said. "Are you okay?"

I relaxed and wiped the sweat from my brow. When my hand came away, it was coated in blood. *The elbow strike.*

"Yeah. Just a small cut. Head wounds bleed a lot."

"What about him?"

I looked at the body, maybe lifeless, maybe not, and couldn't bring myself to tell the truth. "I knocked him out. He's not a threat."

I walked over to the body and ripped a section of shirt, pressing it into my forehead to stop the bleeding. "Did you see anyone in the lobby? Anyone else coming up?"

"Huh?"

"The hotel lobby. Did you see anyone? Can we go out that way?"

"I didn't go through the lobby. I climbed back up."

*Is she fucking kidding?* "You climbed back

323

up here? On the side of the building?"

"Yeah. There was a guy who came over the rail. I guess you threw him. He hit the ground hard, but he was still moving. I knocked him out with a rock and then waited on you to come down. When you didn't, I figured maybe I could help."

She was looking at me like she had done something wrong. I was having a hard time getting my head around the story.

"Well, get ready to go back down. This guy was waiting for backup, and they're going to be here any second. Can you get down a second time?"

She smiled with relief — whether it was because I hadn't chastised her or whether she thought we were on the way to getting clear, I wasn't sure.

"See if you can keep up," she said.

She repeated her monkey maneuver and was halfway down the building before I even cleared the railing, scampering over balconies and using drainpipes like a kid on a playground.

By the time I jumped the last six feet to the ground, she had her sandals back on and was ready to run.

"What do we do now?"

"Get the fuck out of here."

The hotel was situated on the eastern edge of town, right on the beach. I decided to go north, along the beach for a few hundred meters, before cutting back into town. After passing several buildings, I cut west through an alley, heading to the bus station. When I reached the edge of the building, I crouched and peered around the corner. Jennifer closed up right next to me, so near I could feel her trembling.

We slipped across the street and began working our way westward. It dawned on me that the trembling wasn't just from the recent action. Her experiences in Machete's house had scarred her deep inside, and seeing the Englishman had brought it ripping back out. She was barely coping. I decided to get her mind off Machete. "Where'd you learn how to be a monkey? I've never seen anyone climb that fast."

"I got in a lot of trouble as a kid. My mom got me started in gymnastics to focus me. I kept at it for quite a while."

"Hmm. This is probably the first time in history that all the money flushed for some kid's activities actually paid off in the real world. You should thank your mom."

I grinned to show I was kidding. She scowled back, which was okay because that was better than the fear.

"It was a little bit more than that. When I dropped out of college the first time I had a bit of a bad stretch. Broke up with a guy and had the usual 'trying to find yourself' thing. I auditioned for Cirque du Soleil and was accepted. I trained up in Montreal for three months, learning all sorts of crazy things. That building was nothing."

I had seen several Cirque du Soleil shows, and the feats that were performed were unreal. Literally mind-bending. I'd watch an acrobatic trick and wonder if my eyes were deceiving me, if it wasn't a trick done with mirrors. The focus and dedication required rivaled anything in professional sports, or my world for that matter.

I stopped walking and turned around. We were inside another dark alley, which caused Jennifer to bump into me. I looked at her with a new appreciation.

She said, "What? It's not some French circus. It's a pretty well respected —"

"I know what it is. You were in it? For real?"

"I sort of was. I was accepted and finished the apprenticeship, but right before I was slotted for a show I decided it wasn't for me. I was pretty screwed up back then."

"Still, that's pretty amazing."

"Yeah, well, I decided to go back to college. That decision's worked out well so far, don't you think?"

She grinned at her joke. *Success.*

# 51

In Belize City, waiting at their gate for the flight to Cancún, Bakr said, "We've got some time. Let's see if The Sheik has responded."

Sayyidd moved to a secluded space within the terminal that had a look angle to the satellite. He went through the laborious process of getting online with the M4 satellite phone, then checked the first Yahoo! address they had used.

Bakr said, "What're you doing? That's the first address. They won't respond to that. They'll respond to the second address."

He looked closer at the screen, becoming livid. "Is something in the sent file? Is that the message we sent earlier? You didn't erase it?"

Sayyidd gave an embarrassed shrug. "We did this together. I forgot to delete it. You forgot to tell me to delete it. It's a mistake."

Deleting the message from both the sent and trash files, he said, "It's gone."

Bakr rubbed his forehead. He now saw that

he would have to look over his shoulder for everything.

"Please check the other address."

Going to the other Yahoo! account, Sayyidd glowed with anticipation when he saw four messages in the in-box. Three were for penile implants and counterfeit Viagra; one was an e-mail for them. Opening it, he read a simple paragraph, written in Arabic:

Praise be to Allah and all thanks to Allah, your message brings hope to the breasts of true believers. Travel with the weapon to Imam Walid abdul-Aziz. Meet and discuss together the path to success. Peace be upon you in your journey. Imam Walid will send you a message in his own good time for the meeting. May Allah make this a day of pride and success for the Muslim Ummah.

Sayyidd looked up in confusion. "Who's Imam Walid? Where's he located? Are we supposed to guess?"

"Don't worry, my friend. He's a man that'll help the plan you've come up with, just as he's helped hundreds of other true believers in Europe. I know he lives in Norway, but don't know his actual address. We'll go to Cancún and catch a flight to Oslo. Send a reply to The Sheik telling him of the successful test. Before we leave, delete both messages."

Sayyidd did as he was told, saying, "I don't need to be treated like a child. I can learn from my mistakes."

## 52

I looked at the list of agencies, trying to smoke out the cover name the CIA was using at this particular embassy. I was looking for the name of an agency that sounded legitimate but was so innocuous it had no specific mandate. A name that nobody would call for anything. I knew most of the legitimate organizations, such as USAID, and focused on the ones I didn't. Finally, my eyes settled on the pompous-sounding Office of Southern Hemispheric Relations. That sounded like what I was searching for. The title was so broad that nobody would call them unless they had been given the number.

Jennifer asked, "How will we get to the CIA? You're right, I don't see them listed."

*She didn't just say that.* I looked left and right, relieved to see that nobody was within earshot. Trying to remain calm, I said, "Please don't say that name again. In fact, please don't say anything."

Chagrined, Jennifer lapsed into a sullen silence.

We had made the last bus to Belmopan without any other trouble, and had crashed in the nearest hotel we could find. Waking up this morning, it had taken little time to find the embassy and get through the outer security. Now was the hard part — how to get past Marine Post One. I would need to get someone from the CIA to meet me in the lobby, because I wasn't on any approved access roster that Post One maintained.

I waited for the young Marine behind the bulletproof glass to finish what he was doing and ask me my business. I asked for the number to the office, moved to the phone provided, and gave them a call, Jennifer standing expectantly beside me. A man answered on the third ring. It took a little bit of convincing, made harder since I didn't want to say anything specific on an open phone line, but I finally managed to get him to meet us in the lobby. I gave him my description and hung up the phone.

Jennifer looked at me with a question.

"Someone's coming down. We'll see if it's the right guy or not."

Eventually, a young man came out of the elevator, dressed in chinos and a button-down shirt, looking like he would start to shave in a few years. He glanced nervously around the lobby, passing over me and focusing on Jennifer. He smiled at her, then continued to look around. *Great. An idiot.* I stood up and walked over to him.

"Looking for someone?"

He showed a spark of surprise, quickly covered up by bluster.

"I'm Eric. You apparently had some information you wanted to pass?"

"Yeah, can we go to your office?"

"No. Let's go over to the couch and you can tell me what you have."

I'd figured he'd do that and agreed. I was in a little bit of a quandary, since I didn't know if this guy was really in the CIA, and knew there was no way he would admit to it, so I would either have to dive in headfirst, or walk away.

Eric pulled out a notebook and pen, turning to me to speak when he noticed Jennifer walk up. He went into a random diatribe about the weather. I relaxed. *He's a flunky, but he's a spook.* Nobody else would have flexed at the approach of a stranger.

I interrupted the soliloquy. "She's with me. Don't worry about her."

He stopped talking, looking from me to Jennifer and back. I took the initiative, telling him why we'd come. As I went through the story, conveniently leaving out a majority of the death and destruction, I noticed that Eric kept stealing glances at Jennifer's chest and had failed to write down a single thing. I stopped talking.

Eric, smiling yet again at Jennifer, finally felt the silence and turned back to me. I leaned into his personal space.

"Look. You had better start writing some of this stuff down. There's going to be a cable coming out of this that I expect you to send. Understand?"

That flustered him. "Hold on a minute. *You* asked *me* to come down here, not the other way around. I'll decide what we do with your information, not you. Let's get that clear right now."

My rage began to bubble up, catching me by surprise, an unwelcome enemy determined to show who still owned my soul. Jennifer put her hand on my arm, probably seeing the signs and trying to blunt the edge. It worked, at least a little. I no longer wanted to kill him, just hurt him.

"Give me your pen and paper."

"Why?"

"Because I'm going to write your cable. I'm close to ripping off your head and shitting down your neck. To save us both the embarrassment, I'm going to tell you what to send."

Eric handed me the pad and backed away. Jennifer glared at me, clearly upset at the way this was turning out.

I took the paper and wrote a one-paragraph note. At the end of the note, I wrote, "PrometheusPike." Handing the pad back to

Eric, I said, "Send that in a cable. I don't care who you route it to, as long as you include the crypt at the bottom. Do you understand?"

Eric nodded, completely subdued. "Is there some way I can contact you here? If I need to?"

I thought for a second. "Yeah, get me a hotel with an embassy rate and you'll know where we're staying."

"Okay, okay, I can do that. Give me a few minutes. I'll be right back."

Five minutes later, he returned with the confirmation number, the address to the hotel, and a little bit of his confidence back.

"Here's where we send all of our TDY folks. It's on my credit card right now. You need to put it on your card, or your cable's going in the trash."

I stared at him in silence until he began to falter, glancing over his shoulder at the Marine in Post One for help. He finally held out the address and confirmation number with a slight tremor. Jennifer shook her head and took the Post-it note, thanking him for his time. Then she turned without a word and began walking at a brisk pace out of the embassy.

Catching up to her outside, I said, "Well, that went better than expected. We very well might get a cable out, and as a bonus, we got a cut-rate hotel room."

Jennifer turned so quickly I ran into her. "Do you have to be such an asshole to everyone? He was just trying to help. We'll be lucky if he uses your note to blow his nose."

She was as mad as I'd ever seen her, slightly trembling but looking me in the eye and daring me to bark back, waiting on the inevitable rage she knew I had.

Instead, my anger not only disappeared, as it had in the past, but it reversed. For some idiotic reason I wanted to calm *her* down. To make her smile. *Jesus. I want her to like me.* I was so conflicted I wasn't sure what to do. I hadn't given a shit about any person on earth since Heather, and that's the way I had liked it. *What the hell? Am I going crazy?* Crazy or not, she had something that seemed to stop my slide into the abyss. Kept me human. Or at least reminded me of what human was. An innocence I wanted back.

"You're right. I shouldn't have done that. He pushed my buttons. I don't want to be a prick, but it just happens sometimes. I'm working on it. Can we forget about it?"

She looked confused, then suspicious. "Well . . . okay."

She waited a second, as if she expected a trick. When none came, her anger deflated a little bit. "Let's just hope he does something with what we told him."

I smiled, relieved. "He'll send the cable. It's too volatile not to send in this day and age.

Easier to pass the responsibility to someone else."

# 53

Eric returned to his office, still flustered by the encounter with Pike. On the one hand, he didn't want to send the cable precisely because Pike had demanded he do so. *Yeah, maybe I was a little distracted by Pike's companion, but that's no reason to act like such an asshole.* On the other hand, if he did nothing and Pike's wild story proved to be true, there would be hell to pay.

Today was one of the few times he could send a cable out on his own. Ordinarily, he just wrote the cables for release by the chief of station, but Belize had been without a chief for six months, and would probably be without one for the foreseeable future as the CIA pulled experienced hands to fill the gaps created by dealing with a substate threat that couldn't be seen by satellites. With the deputy chief on leave, and Steve, the only other case officer, out doing what he was paid to do, he was now left alone at the wheel.

A year out of college, six months out of

training, Eric had the requisite skills for his position of collating reports and sending cables but had little to no experience in the rough and tumble world of covert operations. He decided it would be better to send the cable and get scolded for clogging up the pipe than not send it and get hammered for missing a terrorist attack.

He typed up Pike's paragraph, adding some of his own observations, and launched it out, including the Counterterrorism Center on the distro, along with the usual Latin American Affairs desks. He included the crypt that Pike had given him.

The cable traveled at the speed of the internet, instantly residing in the in-boxes of the people he had put on the distro. Because of the crypt, it was rerouted to several select boxes as well.

Seconds later, alarms began to go off in some of the most powerful offices in Washington, D.C. Some had official titles; others were simply oak doors with no indication of what was behind them. The crypt that Pike had given was unique to his last unit, and was guaranteed to get attention. It was a verification, sometimes a distress code that allowed operators working in deep cover to send a message through "ordinary" CIA channels during extreme situations, when established communications had failed. It had never been used. It was designed to get attention, and within a second or two of Eric's finger depressing the button on his computer's mouse, it had done its job.

Inside Taskforce Headquarters, the duty officer sat staring at a computer screen, bored out of his mind. The man was dressed in casual business attire, but like everyone else in the office, except the little old ladies downstairs, he looked like an athlete. He always wondered if maybe they shouldn't change their cover to something with professional sports. *Maybe be Jerry Maguire's D.C. office or something. Maybe hire Kelly Preston to roam around here, solidifying the cover.* Before his mind could wander to something less savory, the computer at his desk signaled an incoming message. He stood up and printed it out, giving a low whistle when he saw the crypt.

He took the cable directly to Kurt Hale's office. He knew Kurt was in the process of packing up to go on a date night with his wife, something they hadn't done in over six months. He saw Kurt's expression change when he walked in, Kurt recognizing that his night might be shot.

"What's up, Mike?"

"We got a Prometheus message five minutes ago."

Kurt stopped what he was doing, running

through his mind the two active operations currently ongoing. Only Knuckles was anywhere near an endgame. The other operation was still in the formative stages, laying the groundwork for execution two or three months from now. A Prometheus alert meant something had gone very badly for someone.

"Which Team?"

"Well, that's what's strange. I think it's from Pike. It's not from anyone active here."

"Pike? Pike Logan?" Before Mike could respond, Kurt realized he was asking questions that Mike couldn't possibly answer. He reversed himself and said, "Okay. Let me see the cable. And holler down the hall at George."

"You got it. Here's the message."

Kurt read the cable, a short, simple paragraph. Skipping through the usual disclaimers about walk-ins, no established reporting record, and the ominous "Contact may have been attempting to influence as well as inform" trailer, he read:

Contact stated he had information regarding a potential WMD terrorist attack. Contact had no concrete information about the attack, but stated that he had intercepted Internet traffic implying an Al Qaeda involvement in procurement of WMD for the application against United States, Israeli, or Iranian interests. Contact stated that he believed the WMD was not radiological. Contact stated that two unknown subjects of Arabian descent were in the process of procuring the WMD. Contact became evasive when questioned on his knowledge of the afore-mentioned WMD, refusing to state how he knew this information. Contact firmly believes that the procurement is time sensitive, and that the AQ members are actively pursuing this aim.

It was impossible that anyone on earth would know the Prometheus alert crypt unless Pike had told them, and in Kurt's mind, it was equally impossible that Pike would have told anyone such a secret. On the other hand, the Pike he knew might no longer exist. *Maybe he's slipped down completely, and is selling plasma on the street for his next bottle of Mad Dog 20/20, babbling secrets to anyone who will listen.* Kurt rejected that, as it didn't explain how a stranger was able to contact the CIA in an overseas embassy, then send the message. Everything pointed to its being Pike, however bizarre it appeared. Even so, they would need to confirm the identity before proceeding. Kurt turned at the knock on the door, seeing his friend and deputy commander.

"How long's it been since you made a trip to Central America?"

George looked puzzled by the question. "Well, not since we were supporting the Contras back in the good ol' days. Are they now the next terrorist threat? We going down to take them out?"

Kurt chuckled, filling him in on what he knew, then saying, "Call the station down there and let them know we're coming. Tell them to contact whoever's calling himself Pike. If it's him, we'll figure out what's going on. If it's not, we'll figure out where the breach occurred. Either way, this is too big of a problem to ignore. We should be able to get down and back in one day, two at the most."

"Easy enough. I assume we're leaving tomorrow morning?"

"Yeah, I've got a date tonight that I can't miss."

# 54

A few miles away, Harold Standish sat at his desk in the Old Executive Office Building, silently reading the Prometheus cable. He saw an opportunity. A way to get America back on war footing, and get control of the Taskforce at the same time. A way to strengthen the defense of the United States. *If the whiners on the Oversight Council are too timid to preempt an attack, maybe they need to see one up close.*

The more he thought about it, the more he liked the idea. America had lost its focus on terrorism precisely because it hadn't been attacked in close to a decade. The stupid electorate had the memory of a bovine, conveniently forgetting the threat, instead lambasting the very government that provided their protection. *A WMD going off would wake them the fuck up, that's for sure.* There would be a feeding frenzy just like 9/11. All the politicians would be screaming for action. The Oversight Council would have to bend

343

with the pressure. The Taskforce would be turned loose. *With any luck, the council will be too busy doing their day jobs to look closely at Taskforce activities. I'll be the man left at the wheel. It's not like my day job takes up a lot of time.*

Standish paused, realizing he was thinking about the slaughter of untold innocent civilians, not simply numbers in a news report. He pondered the cost and benefits. He decided the deaths were necessary. *Great leaders throughout history have had to make hard choices such as this.* He knew that Truman himself had made the decision to drop the atomic bomb based on this very same principle. *Hundreds of thousands of Japanese civilians killed to save millions of Americans. This is no different. There's a greater good here.* He, of course, would need to go on vacation for about a month to ensure he was out of the blast radius, should Washington be in the crosshairs. *This town could stand to lose a little deadweight anyway.*

He called his in-staff intelligence officer and asked him to run down any "chatter" on terrorist threats within the last three days involving the words *Israel, WMD, Iran,* and *poison weapons.* Within thirty minutes, the man arrived with fourteen NSA reports that had some tangential relationship to the search criteria. Most were clearly not what Standish was looking for, only detailing vague information of little value. Using the Prometheus cable, he necked down the reports until he found an NSA cut describing a WMD attack against Israel. He didn't have the background in terrorism to understand the reference to the far enemy, and was unsure why the intercept mentioned the historical state of Persia instead of the modern nomenclature of Iran, but since this was the only bit of intelligence that talked of pushing the Zionists into the sea via a single weapon — something that anyone could understand — he honed in on it, noting the reference to something called Operation Badr. He was pleased to see the intel was raw, meaning nobody had analyzed it yet, and thus nobody knew it existed.

"Ken, run a search on Operation Badr. Bring me what you find immediately."

Five minutes later Ken returned with a single message. "This is the only thing that's come in with those search terms."

Standish read the report, which simply said that Operation Badr was progressing and that a device had been tested successfully. He connected the dots. "Okay, do an open-source search on anything strange happening in Belize. Focus on a group of unexplained deaths. See if anyone in the press has reported anything like that."

After another wait, Ken returned, saying,

"There was nothing in Belize. The only thing I could find was a bus crash on the border, but it was on the Guatemalan side."

"What's so fucking strange about that? I told you unexplained deaths."

"Well, everyone on the bus died, but nobody died from the crash." He handed the press report to Standish. "Apparently, they all died of some strange illness."

Standish read the news report and smiled. *The weapon's real.* "Ken, I want you to destroy any mention of these two intercepts about Operation Badr. Figure out who else got them, and erase them. Do it without their knowledge. Those reports never existed. Understand?"

Ken, a sycophant cut from Standish's mold, didn't question the directive. "Easy enough. I'll do it as soon as I get back to my office."

"Good. In addition, I got a cable from Belize today. Rescind that cable as well. Ensure it also doesn't exist." He gave the intelligence officer the cable cite number.

Ken asked, "What about the station in Belize? Won't they ask why it was rescinded?"

"I'll handle the station when they come in to work tomorrow. Just get rid of the cable right now."

"Okay — I'm on it."

Standish reflected on what he knew. On the one hand, it was a golden opportunity to accomplish exactly what he believed was neces-

346

sary. On the other, while not out of control yet, it was an opportunity that had quite a few leaks. He had managed to stop the raw intel from being spread but couldn't be sure about the Prometheus cable. *If that thing's not rescinded in time, I'll never be able to deny I knew about it.* Luckily, it had come from Belize. CTC would probably shunt that cable to the back of the pack, focusing on Pakistan, Iran, and whatever else was brewing right now. *They won't give a shit one way or another about a rescinded cable from Central America.*

His primary problem was the Taskforce. They would get the Prometheus alert and would act on it. He had to shut them down right away. There was no love lost between himself and the unit, but they would listen to him, since they were still on shaky ground and couldn't afford an enemy of his stature. He could bring them down with a well-placed leak, and they knew it.

He called the Taskforce duty officer, went secure on his STE telephone, identified himself, and asked if the unit was planning any new movement in the next twenty-four hours.

On the other end, the duty officer Mike, knowing who it was, stated no. He didn't literally lie, as his bosses were traveling truename as part of their true affiliation — Kurt as a member of J3 SOD, and George as a

TDY member of the Office of Southern Hemispheric Relations — thus they weren't traveling under any of the covers used by the Taskforce. His answer was technically correct — there was no Taskforce movement. Standish next asked to speak to the commander and was told that he was out.

Standish hung up after leaving a message for Kurt to call first thing in the morning. He was satisfied that he was good for the time being. The cap was in place.

# 55

I woke up to the phone ringing, answered and perked up, replying quickly and ending the call. I saw that Jennifer was awake and leaning on an elbow, wearing a cheap tourist T-shirt with her hair sticking out all over the place, making me grin. Rubbing her eyes, she asked who was on the phone.

"It was the embassy. They want to see us at ten o'clock. The cable must have worked, because we've been invited behind the green curtain. We get to talk to the wizard."

Waking up fast, Jennifer tried to brush her hair in place, asking, "What's that mean? Who'd you talk to?"

"That was the asshole Eric." *Shit . . . Be nice. . . .* "Sorry. That was the nice man from the embassy, Eric. He asked us to come back."

"That's good news, isn't it? Do we need to do anything before we go?"

"No. I'm not sure what the cable caused. We'll just see how it goes. Either way, we got some action, so that's good."

She looked at me like I was hiding something, and I was, but she let it go. "Okay, Jason Bourne, I'll follow your lead."

When we got to the embassy, even I was surprised at who was waiting.

Standish called the Taskforce first thing in the morning, early enough to get Mike before his twenty-four-hour shift as the duty officer was over. Going secure on his STE, Standish asked to speak to Colonel Hale.

"Sir, he's gone TDY this morning."

"*What?* I thought you told me last night that he was out with his wife. Where is he?"

"Sir, he was out with his wife last night. Today he left."

*Who does he think he's talking to?* "Tell me where he is right this minute."

"Sir, I can't give you that information on this phone."

Standish was on the verge of frothing at the mouth. "I'm on a fucking secure line. You will tell me where he is, right this minute. Do you understand me? Is that clear?"

"Sir, I'm not trying to be difficult, but I must follow security procedures. Colonel Hale's location is top secret. Your phone is only certified up to secret message traffic. I'm not allowed to tell you his location on this line. Not my rule."

Standish realized he was done. The STE

secure phone was only certified by the NSA to pass information up to the secret level. He couldn't order the man to break classification rules, since he would be on record violating the safeguard of national secrets. He also knew that he was being stiff-armed on purpose by the duty officer, but couldn't fight it. *At least not right now. You mess with the bull, you get the horns.*

"Listen to me Mr. *Duty Officer.* Pick up a fucking pen. Write this down. I want Kurt Hale and George Wolffe in my office within twenty-four hours or I will go to the president and have all unit operations canceled pending an investigation of improper actions. Is that understood?"

"Yes, sir. I have it."

"Don't test me on this. If you value your mission, you won't push me. I *will* see Hale and Wolffe or you'll cease operations."

Standish slammed the phone down. *When I get control of that unit, he'll be out greeting people at Walmart.*

Done with the Taskforce, he turned his attention to the next problem: dealing with the CIA station in Belize. He couldn't call the station directly because they weren't in his chain of command and wouldn't have a clue who he was. He would have to do it through the Latin America Division in the headquarters at Langley. Luckily, he knew the chief of LA and could use him to clamp down on Belize. All he had to do was control the conversation correctly. Satisfied with his strategy, he picked up the phone and dialed the chief of LA on his gray line, a direct secure connection into the CIA.

# 56

"Holy shit! What're you doing down here?" I said.

After giving me a handshake and an embrace, Kurt verbally poked me, saying, "Well, I've got nothing better to do than chase phantom Prometheus cables. It's what I do on my off-time."

I got out, "Sir —" before he cut me off with a hand.

"Just kidding. How're you doing?"

I figured the question held more than it seemed, and that he wasn't asking how I was doing *this* morning. I answered truthfully, "Well, honestly, sir, I'm doing better now than I was a week ago."

"Still blocking punches with your face, huh?"

I smiled and touched the cut above my eye. "Long story, sir." Turning to Jennifer, I continued. "This is Jennifer Cahill. She's the reason I'm down here, and also the one who figured out what's going on."

He greeted Jennifer politely, then said, "Okay, how about letting me in on the secret."

I laid out the whole story, with the exception of the discovery of the e-mail addresses. After the bullshit shenanigans, I didn't trust Eric as far as I could throw him. There was no telling what the station here would do with that information.

After about an hour of give and take, Kurt got to the bottom line. "Given your lack of ability to do anything, I get the Prometheus alert, but, really, is there any proof that such a weapon exists? What do you want me to do now?"

I had known that was coming and, in reality, agreed with his skepticism. "Sir, I'm with you. I've been struggling with the whole Mayan WMD thing since this started. Whether that weapon is real or not is an open question. In my mind, what's not a question is that two intelligent terrorists with multiple passports *believe* it's there, and are trying to get it to kill as many people as possible."

"Okay. I can see that. Sounds like something that's happening all over the world every five seconds. Why bring us in? You know this isn't what we do."

"I didn't intend for you guys to fly down here to see me. I just wanted to talk to the chief of station. Sorry, but I played the only card I had. I think someone needs to check this out, to see if something strange happened on an expedition in the Petén region. If not, no harm. If so, investigate further."

Kurt looked at Eric, who said, "That makes sense to me. It's very little work to run this to ground. I'll give the station in Guatemala a call and have them check it out."

Kurt thanked him for the support, then asked George if there was anything else they were missing.

George said, "No, Pike's right. Let the station get some assets on the ground. We'll figure this out pretty quickly."

Satisfied, Kurt wrapped up the meeting. He told us to come on back at nine the next morning to see where we stood. I walked with him out the door, stopping to allow him to retrieve his cell phone from the cubicles outside the station spaces. Since the cell phones could be used as eavesdropping devices, they weren't allowed inside any secure government facility.

Turning on his phone, Kurt said, "Well, I'm not going to blow smoke up your ass. I don't think there's much chance of some secret Mayan weapon being out there, but since we're here, might as well play the hand. No harm done by poking around a little bit."

He stopped when his phone chirped. "Jesus. I got six calls while I was inside there."

He closed the phone. "Let's get some dinner tonight. I'm sure you've got some things you want to tell me that you didn't want to say in there."

*Smart man.* "You read my mind. I held some cards back. There's a great little fish stand near our hotel. Give me a call at the hotel when you're ready to go."

I watched him walk off, dialing his phone.

Inside the station, Eric finished his coordination with his compatriots in Guatemala to check out Pike's story. Talking to the deputy, he was disappointed to hear that it would be a couple of days before they could get on the ground at Flores, but was satisfied when he said they could make some calls to contacts up there for an initial snapshot. Eric thanked him, asking him to call back tomorrow at eight A.M. with any results, and hung up.

The phone rang with his hand still on it, startling him. Picking it back up, he was startled again when he found out that the chief of the Latin America division was giving him a personal call from Langley. Listening intently, he began to take notes.

When Jennifer and I got back to our room, I noticed the red light blinking on our old-fashioned phone. Jennifer went to the bathroom, leaving me to get the message.

Coming back out, she asked, "Who was that? Kurt? Is he going to take us out to a nice dinner instead of the taco stand?"

"I wish. Kurt's been called back to D.C. Something important came up, and he's got to get back immediately. He said to send him a message through Eric, and he'd take it from there."

"Well, he seemed like a pretty busy guy. I'm surprised he even flew down."

She could see that I was disappointed, and tried to make a joke. "He clearly knew better than to mess with you. I'm sure if you send another cable, he'll do something with it. Maybe you should tell him to meet us in the Caribbean, and that he needs to give us some tickets to get there."

"He'll do something with it, but cables are never as good as face-to-face. Whatever called him back will take front seat. It'll be hard to pry him away from that now."

I was surprised at the level of my disappointment, and wondered if I was more upset at our theories taking a backseat to something else, or that this adventure was drawing to a close. I hadn't realized how much I had wanted to go to that meeting tomorrow, and to continue on with this excursion. I think in my heart I was hoping Kurt would take me with him to figure out what was going on. *What a fantasy.*

I said, "Let's go get a flight out of here for tomorrow. No sense hanging around here now. Whatever we find out at the meeting tomorrow morning, the rest of this will be in someone else's hands."

"That sounds good to me. I'm ready to get back to my simple college life."

Her words gave me another kick in the gut. *I hear you. Boy, am I ever ready to get back to being a worthless fucking bum.* Once we left the embassy tomorrow, she would go back to her life and I'd go back to mine. All I had to look forward to was waking up in a rage every morning. I could already feel my self-worth eroding. The thought was depressing and must have showed on my face.

"What's wrong? Are you really that worried about the cable doing nothing? I thought Kurt was the Wizard of Oz."

I lied, "Yeah, I'm worried about the cable. You're probably right, though. No sense in crying over it now. Let's see what happens tomorrow. Come on. I'd like to get a plane that doesn't allow goats in the aisle."

"Palmer," President Warren said, "can you hang on a second?"

Alexander Palmer stopped at the door to the Oval Office, letting the other members of the president's national security team leave.

"Sure, sir. What's up?"

Warren stood up and leaned against his desk. "The Taskforce got a Prometheus alert, but I never saw it."

"Oh, yeah. Standish told me about it. He's run it to ground already. Some sort of misfire.

It wasn't Prometheus material. Sorry if I didn't bring it to your attention, but it was nothing."

"What do you think about him?"

"Standish? Ahh . . . I think if he wasn't around you wouldn't be president, but he's not really giving us much in the administration. He's just taking up space on the NSC. Is that what you mean?"

Warren had been thinking about what Kurt had said months ago. About some unknown terrorist with the skill and patience to really do some damage. The thought scared him. As president, he'd created the Project Prometheus at significant risk and let them run at full throttle. He had thought they were winning, that the risk had been worth every penny. But the commander didn't. Kurt thought they had just been lucky — as if the Taskforce was no match for a smart terrorist, and that that man was out there right now, planning. The revelation had caused him to lose sleep.

President Warrant was a political infighter. A winner. He took no quarter and wasn't above dirty tricks to win — just like every other politician at this level. He had a lot on his plate — the economy, global trade issues, the constant bickering between parties — but only one issue really scared him: the loss of American lives because of something he had failed to do. And not in a political way either.

It scared him in a personal way. He couldn't imagine being president on 9/11, watching the bodies fall from the burning towers. It was the one issue where politics had no business. And probably the one thing that allowed him to relate to Kurt Hale. Everything else he did in the name of democracy would make Hale's stomach turn.

He had reviewed his national security team and begun to wonder if he'd ceded too much control. Everyone had become complacent when it came to terrorism, himself included. He'd allowed Palmer to run the NSC as he saw fit, but after hearing about Standish's questions at the last Taskforce Oversight Council meeting, he was beginning to believe the man was dangerous.

He said, "No, I don't mean what he's contributing to the administration. You put him on the Taskforce Oversight Council, and I'm wondering if that was wise. You work with him. I'm asking if he can be trusted. NSC business is one thing, but the Taskforce is something else. There's no room for error."

"Well, he has managed to work his way on the inside a hell of a lot quicker than I would have thought possible, but he's doing a good job. He keeps me abreast of all the secret things going on. He's pretty good at collating information."

"That doesn't answer the question. Is he a threat? Standish's answer for anything is brute force. He doesn't understand the complexity. Doesn't have the experience or background."

Palmer reflected for a moment. "No, I think he's okay. We both know he loves the feeling of being on the inside. He's like a political groupie, but that's about it."

President Warren locked eyes with him. "Palmer, don't let him become a threat. This isn't about payback or politics. I won't tolerate American deaths. That's got nothing to do with politics."

Palmer smiled. "Sir, don't worry about that. He's a coward at heart. He likes playacting. He doesn't have the balls to do anything for real."

# 57

Lucas Kane fiddled with his PDA, waiting on Standish to finish with a phone call. He played the keys with manicured fingers, looking like any other successful power broker in Washington, D.C. Actually, he looked like an actor in a beer commercial portraying a successful power broker in Washington, D.C. He had sandy-blond hair, an athletic build, and a face that belonged in a weekly Hollywood tabloid. From across the street, women were automatically drawn to him. Up close, when they could look into his eyes, the attraction would usually wilt. His eyes were dead. Not unintelligent, just lacking in any warmth. His last date, after saying she would rather not see him again, commented that they reminded her of a three-day-old bruise. Purple and rotting.

Lucas didn't give a shit, as long as the date paid him back for the dinner and a movie once they returned to his apartment, which this one had, even if a bit reluctantly. *If the eyes are a window into the soul, I guess a bruise is pretty damn close.*

Standish hung up the phone, saying, "They're on the way over. Should be here in about five minutes. You sure you can do this?"

"Yeah, I'm sure. It's not brain surgery. The key is the information you gave me. If the phone's a different model, or the pager information is incorrect, it might not work."

"That intel's good. I've seen them myself."

"Shouldn't be an issue, then. We'll know shortly."

He left the office and positioned himself on a bench in the marble hallway within view of the entrance to Standish's office, but far enough away as to be inconspicuous. He opened a magazine.

He didn't have to wait long. Two men approached Standish's office. He focused on the one matching the description of his target. They stopped and placed their two-way pagers and cell phones in the ubiquitous cubicles provided outside every government office that whispered the nation's secrets. He noted which cubicle his target used. He waited until they passed through the cipher-locked door, then waited an additional few seconds. When nothing happened, he walked at a quick pace and pulled both the pager and cell phone from the cubicle. He raced down the stairs to the equipment he had left in his vehicle parked outside.

His task was to clone the cell phone with a sophisticated Trojan horse virus, which would allow a separate cell phone to act exactly like the original. Anytime the target phone rang, the other would ring too. Anytime it dialed out, his would dial out. It would be like a three-way call every time the target used his phone, except that he wouldn't suspect it.

In addition to manipulating the phone, he was going to reverse the pager the target wore. Using the information given to him by Standish, Lucas knew that the device was specially constructed, capable of worldwide coverage through a satellite network, and equipped with a "panic button" that would send out a signal based on Global Positioning System satellites. Once triggered, it would give a grid reference to its location worldwide. Lucas was going to ensure that the pager sent a signal without the button being pushed, in effect, making the pager a beacon without the target even knowing it. The trick would be ensuring the signal didn't enter the normal channels and thus cause an alert. Instead, it would be visible only to someone who knew it was broadcasting. Lucas didn't yet know exactly why this target needed to be tracked, but something told him that Standish wasn't finished using him on this particular assignment.

Standish left Kurt and George sitting in the

anteroom for five more minutes, just because he felt like being a prick. Eventually, he closed out the solitaire game he was playing and told his secretary to show them in.

He heard them enter, pretending to work on his computer. He let them stand for a few seconds before turning around. He pointed to the chairs in front of his desk and started right in, skipping any pleasantries.

"You received a Prometheus alert two days ago, yet you didn't notify anyone at all. If I remember your initial information briefings to me, those were supposed to trigger a response, but when I called the Taskforce, I got an idiotic duty officer who acted as if nothing was wrong. Either you're running an organization that isn't the caliber you so eloquently brag about in your brief, or you're attempting to hide things from a member of the council that oversees your activities. For your sake, I hope it's incompetence."

Standish watched both of them squirm a little, clearly not expecting to be attacked. *Good. They need to know who's the boss here.*

Kurt said, "Sir, we did get an alert, but it wasn't what you think. Neither of your reasons is accurate — the alert came from an old unit member. It didn't involve an active mission and thus didn't require a response from the Taskforce.

"As for you not getting any word about it, I apologize, but if you remember the brief you were just talking about, we get oversight solely on which target to attack and our method of engagement, based on potential second- and third-order effects that might be generated from the action. Once we get the go-ahead to proceed against a target, there is no further oversight, unless one of those variables changes."

*Is he giving me a lecture? Like I'm slow?* "Colonel Hale, don't treat me like a child. I understand how the Oversight Council works. I'm one of the members. Perhaps it's you that needs a refresher on who you work for."

Kurt backpedaled. "Sir, we meant no disrespect, but the Prometheus alert is a tactical control measure used solely by us in the Taskforce, and we didn't realize a report to you was necessary."

Standish steepled his fingers. "Well, maybe I should speak to the president about relooking at this little experiment's rules of engagement. It sounds to me like you think you get to decide what does or does not occur within your little secret world."

George broke in. "Sir, he's not trying to tell you that you had no right to know, he's explaining why you didn't initially get any feedback. We're here specifically to provide that feedback. Kurt and I just came from meeting the man who sent the cable. He has an interesting story to tell, and while it may have some merit, the odds of it being true aren't that great."

George continued, giving Standish a broad sketch of Pike's story, knowing that Standish had read the original message. He finished by telling Standish the coordination made with Guatemala and the way ahead.

"So, what's the Taskforce going to do with this? Anything?"

Kurt said, "Well, it depends on what the CIA finds out. Right now, there isn't a whole lot we can do and, with the information we have, not much we should be doing. This is more of a CIA issue. Unless you want us to start focusing on it, we're going to let them take the lead. We have enough on our plate without this."

*Perfect. Just what I wanted to hear.* "No, that sounds right."

Looking at his watch, Standish said, "I've got another meeting coming up. I appreciate you two taking the time out of your day to come down. We don't have to be looking across the fence at each other all the time. I want to work with you. All I ask for is a little courtesy and respect."

He paused. "Trust me — if I don't get it, you will cease to exist."

## 58

After the door closed behind Kurt and George, Standish buzzed his secretary and told her to show Lucas in as soon as he arrived. After a minute and a half, Standish saw him coming through the door and was embarrassed to feel his pulse rate go up. He wouldn't admit it to anyone, but Lucas scared him. *Bastard looks like he belongs in Alaska killing baby seals.* He was a cousin of Standish's wife, and extremely useful for certain tasks, but Standish didn't like being alone with him for any length of time. He watched Lucas plop down in a chair as if he were in his own office.

"No issues," Lucas said.

"Will it work?"

"No. You pay me just to pretend." He tossed the phone to Standish, reached into his pocket and pulled out another phone, dialing a number. The phone rang once before the one in Standish's hand began ringing.

Standish heard Kurt Hale answer after the

fourth ring. Lucas said, "Can I speak to Betty?"

Through the phone he held, Standish heard Kurt say, "Sorry, wrong number."

Lucas hung up.

Standish grinned. With any luck, not only would he get all information relating to the Mayan weapon, but he might also get other useful information relating to the Taskforce, or even Kurt's personal life. *I should have done this a long time ago.*

"Can you tell anything was done?"

"Not at a casual look-over. If the phone's software is scrubbed, they'll see it was manipulated."

"We're good there. No way they'll suspect this office of doing anything. What about the pager?"

"The pager's a little different. That panic beacon attempts to transmit on any signal it can find, like cellular, FM, you name it. With that much stuff blasting out on a constant stream, there's a chance someone will pick up the signal. It'll also run the batteries down about four times as fast, which might spike the target. I figured it would be better to restrict it to satellite only, so that's what it will transmit on. The batteries will still burn more quickly, but not enough to spike."

"Okay. What's that mean to me?"

"You'll only get a location when the beacon can see the sky. If the beacon loses signal, it'll just show its last known location."

"That's fine by me. The pager was just a benny anyway. I'll cut a check to the same account for your time. Is that acceptable?"

"Yeah. Same account."

Standish paused, internally making a decision. "Before you go, I need to read you on to something that might require your attention."

"All right. I'm still on your retainer. What's up?"

Standish's only weak link now was Pike himself. He had already gleaned both his and Jennifer's passport information from the station in Belize and had fed that into the gigantic, bureaucratic Homeland Security database, ensuring they would be stopped at whatever port of entry they attempted to use. His only purpose was to tie them up until the terrorists could set off their weapon. Getting arrested as a terrorist associate should do the trick. By the time they got an apology and a pat on the back, the bomb should have gone off. Still, Standish hadn't gotten to where he was by not planning, and he wanted to ensure he had a contingency in place. He'd play nice first but had no compunction about turning nasty.

"I have a couple of individuals I might need you to deal with."

Standish gave him a brief rundown on Pike and Jennifer, leaving out the reasons he wanted them stopped. Lucas didn't ask why or what they represented. It wasn't part of the mission and thus wasn't something that concerned him.

When he was finished, Lucas said, "What do you want me to do with them?"

"Nothing right now. I'll call you if I need you."

Lucas let the silence extend out a bit to show what he thought of that answer, then said, "Yeah, I get that. That wasn't my question. What do you want me to do with them if you call? What's the mission?"

"Get rid of them."

Lucas sat forward in his chair, looking a little agitated at the verbal dance. "What the fuck does that mean? Tell me what you want done. I'm doing the work. The least you could do is actually say it. You want them locked up, sent to the hospital, what?"

*Let him know you aren't afraid to get your hands dirty.* "Kill them. Or do you have an issue with that?"

Lucas stared into Standish's eyes. "I'm pretty sure you know the answer to that."

Standish recoiled in his chair, mentally trying to distance himself from Lucas without appearing to do so.

"Yes. I guess I do."

A year ago, Lucas had been a SEAL serving in Afghanistan, where he had been accused of intentionally killing civilians. That in

371

itself wasn't remarkable, since not a day went by without Standish's reading some bullshit report of Americans killing civilians. Ninety-nine point nine percent of those reports were propaganda put out by the enemy to stir up a little Islamic fury. The difference with the accusations against Lucas was they hadn't been brought forward by some unknown local with an ax to grind, but by his own teammates. Just before the investigation began in earnest, the two teammates died violently in an IED attack. The investigation took a new tack, now looking into the deaths of two American servicemen as well as the deaths of the Afghanis. Before it could build up enough steam, as a favor to his wife, Standish pulled Lucas out of the fire with a few well-placed words, allowing him to leave the military at fifteen years, his only true punishment being the loss of retirement pay. Now he was wondering if using Lucas might be a mistake. *He's liable to kill two hundred people to get this done.*

Standish decided to deal with that possibility up front. "I don't care how you do it, and don't need it to look like an accident or anything stupid like that, but you have to do it in such a way that it won't lead back to me. Ever. And don't kill a ton of civilians just to get them. Understand?"

"What's your definition of 'a ton'?"

*Jesus. He's a cold-blooded son of a bitch.*

"I'll understand a collateral damage number of five or less. More than that and you've exceeded the rules of engagement."

"I can do that. You got anyone you want killed right now, or is this it?"

Standish punched his secretary's buzzer. *Get him the fuck out of here.*

## 59

The next morning at 0815 we were both in
the lobby of the embassy, with the same
Marine flipping through the clearance sheets.
Ten minutes later, after checking the massive
amount of rosters at his disposal, the lance
corporal turned to me and said, "I'm sorry,
sir, but you're not listed."

I asked for the number to the office and
called up. Getting Eric, I was told to hold
fast, and he'd come down to me. I hung up
the phone, a sick feeling in the pit of my
stomach.

"Something's up. I think we're about to get
the blow-off."

Eric exited the elevator and walked over to
us with a big smile.

*Shit. This is going to be bad.*

"Hey, I guess you didn't get the word. The
meeting's off."

Seeing me scowl, he said, "Hold on, now,
it's not my call. My bosses in D.C. told me
to cease and desist. Even the guys you

brought down left last night."

"Fine. Got it. At least tell us what you found out from Guatemala."

"Well, the guys in Guatemala couldn't get to the Petén region for a couple of days. They were set to go when HQ stopped that as well. They did make some phone calls and found out that there was an expedition, which ended badly. Of course, they couldn't confirm anything. All they could find out was that one boy apparently was consumed by some sort of ancient curse and another disappeared after the expedition. Nobody knows what happened to them for real."

*What the hell? Why would they have been called off?* "So, preliminary investigation concurs with what we say, but it's not worth following up on? What's up with that?"

I knew Eric was just the messenger, and that he didn't like giving us this news. He continued in a calm voice. "Pike, please, all we have is that some sort of 'ancient curse' caused the disappearance of a boy. If we ran after every rumor like that, we'd be spending all of our time chasing Bigfoot."

"Okay. Fine. I'd like you to send a cable out to that effect. Can you at least do that?"

Eric shook his head. "Pike, I'd really like to help, but we've done more than we should have already. I'm not going to send out any more unsolicited cables. If HQ asks for clarification, I'll do so, but I'm not sending anything else out on your say-so."

I turned and walked away before I did something I'd regret, not even bothering to say good-bye to him. Jennifer caught up with me outside.

"What are we going to do now?"

"Nothing. We're getting on a bus to Belize City and going home. We're done."

I said the last two words with more force than necessary, causing her to look up sharply. I covered up the slip, speaking softer. "Look, this is over. Nobody cares and we can't do anything with it by ourselves. We gave it our best shot and got further than I thought we would. Let's just get home and see if we're going to be arrested for murder. We're in enough trouble already without pushing this any further."

"Well, I just don't think we should quit."

She saw me start to react and held up a hand. "Wait — before you go into asshole mode — hear me out. We believe that these guys are up to no good. Nobody else does, and maybe they're right, but what if they're not? Can't we do something else? You're the expert. Have we exhausted all our options?"

I thought about what she said, feeling a little slimy that I wanted to continue more for the sense of mission than saving anyone's life.

"Well, if you want to foot the bill, we can go to D.C. and contact Kurt again. We don't have a lot, but we do have a few things he hasn't seen. We can give him the e-mail addresses for further tracking, get a real translation of the initial message, and tell him that the superficial investigation in Guatemala supports what we said. Is that what you want to do?"

*This isn't right. I'm convincing her to chase shadows so I don't have to go back to my boat. So I don't have to face my life. If she's dumb enough to say yes, give her the truth.*

We walked in silence for a minute. She said, "Yes."

*Man, is she stubborn.* "Are you nuts? You're going to flunk out of school. Our own government doesn't give a shit about this. Even if we do go to D.C., we don't have a clue where the terrorists are, or what they have. We won't get anywhere, and you'll just get a lighter bank account from paying the way."

Jennifer crossed her arms. "Yeah. I *know* that. But my family has a long history of doing stupid shit. Just ask my uncle." She looked hard at me. "What if someone like us existed before 9/11? Would you have wanted them to quit?"

*Gee, thanks. I really feel slimy now.* "No, I guess not."

After exiting our flight in Atlanta, we proceeded down the narrow gateway funneling us into the customs complex of the United

States. We had a connecting flight into Washington but still had to pass through U.S. Immigration to continue. We moved up to the counter together, where I showed my passport. The man behind the counter ran the bar code and stiffened.

I watched his expression turn to stone. He asked Jennifer, "Are you traveling together?"

She said yes and handed him her passport. He ran it through the scanner, his face showing no emotion. Turning back from the computer, he became pleasant.

"I'm afraid that I'm going to have to ask both of you to follow me. We're going to need some additional information about your trip."

I felt the hair stand up on the back of my neck. *Shit. We've been flagged because of the dead guys in Charleston.*

Remaining pleasant, I asked, "Questions about what? We were only gone a few days. We can answer them right here."

The customs agent remained deadpan, giving me no indication that he was a threat, but also no indication that he was friendly. "Sir, this won't take but a couple of seconds. We've had some trouble with U.S. citizens coming back from Central America. All we want you to do is take a little survey to help us facilitate future travel. I don't want to hold up the line here to do that. Once you're done, you'll be on your way."

As we moved down the hallway to the

secondary interrogation rooms, I dismissed the Charleston angle, since suspected murderers would have been arrested and handcuffed immediately. We were walking free and clear behind the customs official. I relaxed, thinking that maybe Kurt had set up a method to contact us, since he had left Belize before I could give him a phone number.

Entering the secondary interrogation area, I stood behind the customs official, listening to him tell the man at the desk who we were and where we were going. I waited while the man typed in the information. I saw a reflection of the computer screen on the windowpane to the man's right. In it were the passport photos of both Jennifer and me, surrounded by words that were inverted due to the mirror image. I couldn't make out what the paragraph underneath our pictures said, but did decipher the words above them: "WANTED FOR QUESTIONING ON SUSPECTED TERRORISM ACTIVITIES." A spurt of adrenaline jolted my body.

Projecting an outward calm, I asked, "Can we use the bathroom before we do anything else? We haven't had a chance to go since we landed."

The agent said, "This won't take a minute. Once we give you the surveys, you can do whatever you would like."

I nodded, my mind racing. I knew what was about to happen. We would be separated and taken to different interrogation rooms. We would be locked in and questioned for hours. The interrogators would compare notes on the answers that we gave to see if they matched up. Using that information, they would continue the questioning. Since I hadn't bothered to develop a cover story with Jennifer, it would do me no good to lie. Whatever I said wouldn't match what Jennifer said. On top of that, Jennifer would more than likely tell the truth, believing that the truth would be the best course of action. Unfortunately, our story was so unbelievable that it would cause the customs agents to become *more* suspicious, not less.

I had no idea why we were flagged in the Homeland Security system, but had no doubt that the second Jennifer mentioned two Arab terrorists with a WMD, we would be locked up until we could prove we weren't associated with them. We could be detained for days, if not weeks.

*We need to break out of here right now, before we meet the interrogators. The fewer people the better.*

To compound matters, I had to do it without harming the agents. This wasn't their fault. They got paid to intercept terrorists. *I'd do the same thing.*

The agent at the desk said, "Good to go. Rooms seven and thirteen. Rob and Kenny are tied up right now, but they'll be down in ten minutes. They'll meet you there."

The first agent nodded, telling us, "Follow me." He turned and punched in the code to the cipher lock of the door leading into the interior hallway, and presumably the secondary interrogation facilities. I checked out the man behind the computer, seeing that he had taken off his equipment belt and hung it on the wall behind him. *Mistake number one.*

I knew why they were acting so pleasant — it was to prevent a scuffle in front of any passengers or other civilians. What I didn't understand was why they had used only one agent to do this. They should have a man behind me and a man in front, preventing me from taking out both at the same time. *Mistake number two.*

Before the man could open the door, I threw my left arm around his neck and drew the Glock 19 from the holster on the agent's right hip. I raised my right leg and racked the slide of the Glock on the edge of my boot. I kicked the back of the agent's leg hard enough to cause him to lean backward, with me supporting his weight. I rotated the agent away from the door, placing the front sight of the Glock on the agent behind the desk. The action happened in a blink of an eye, quick enough to prevent the agent behind the desk from getting to his feet. He held up his hands, a look of terror on his face, convinced he was face-to-face with an insane suicidal maniac.

I barked out orders quickly, intent on dominating the confrontation. "Don't fucking move. I don't want to hurt anyone. Put your hands on top of your head."

## 60

Jennifer stood dumbfounded by Pike's actions. *Jesus Christ, he's gone nuts. He's flashed back to some sort of Rambo scene getting tortured by the Vietcong.*

"What in the hell are you doing! Have you lost your *mind?* My God! Pike! Put down the gun!"

Pike bared his teeth at her and said, "Take a look at the computer monitor."

The agent Pike was holding tried his hand at negotiation. "Look, we only have a few questions. Nobody's saying you're a terrorist. Put the gun down and we can sort this out peacefully."

Pike laughed. "I suppose this whole hostage-taking thing would be forgotten, huh? If I give you the gun, we can start over like this never happened? Promise?"

Jennifer cut in, turning back from the monitor. "What's this mean? Why are we on the screen as terrorists? What's going on here?"

Pike said, "I don't know. Something's

screwed up, and we don't have the time to sort it out here."

He addressed the customs agents. "Both of you listen to me. We aren't terrorists, and I can't have you arrest us. I'm going to have each of you take off your clothes. I'm then going to tie you both up. I'm not going to hurt either one of you. Please don't do anything to escalate this situation. I really, really don't want to hurt you. Do you understand my instructions?"

They both nodded. "Okay. You at the desk, take off your clothes. Once you're done, lie down on your stomach with your ankles crossed."

The man at the desk complied, lying down with nothing on but a T-shirt and underwear.

Pike spoke to Jennifer. "Go outside and wait for me. Alert me if someone's coming this way."

Jennifer started to leave, then paused. *He wants me out of the way. . . . He's going to hurt them . . . maybe kill them. . . .* Before she could say anything, the agent on the floor became agitated, looking wildly at Pike and Jennifer, apparently making the same mental leap that Jennifer had.

"Stop what you're thinking. I'm not going to harm you, but I *am* going to embarrass you. I'm sending Jennifer outside because I'm about to make you take off your underwear. That's it. Do you want her to stay? Will that prove I'm not about to cut your throat?"

The agent thought about it, then shook his head.

"Okay. Jennifer, please go outside."

Jennifer left the room. She thought she'd made a mistake, turned back to reenter, and saw the cipher lock on the door. *Damn. He's going to do something bad. This isn't right. Stopping the terrorists isn't worth hurting innocent people.*

A short time later Pike came out, holding the agents' clothing and equipment belts, looking queasy and sweating. *Shit. He hurt them. I'm going to hell.*

"Come on. We've got to move. We're about to have every policeman in the city of Atlanta trying to find us."

Jennifer put a hand on his chest, stopping him.

"What did you do in there?"

Pike was brought up short by the ferocity on her face.

"Hey, easy. I just tied them up butt-naked. Nothing else. Made me sick to my stomach doing that to good guys." He looked up and down the hallway. "We need to go, *now.*"

She felt an enormous weight leave her shoulders. *Thank God.* Then she felt a little shame at what she had thought previously.

She said, "What do you think's going on? We're terrorists now?"

He started moving at a fast walk back the way they had come, toward the passport area, shoving the agents' equipment and clothing into the first garbage can he came across.

"I don't know, but we need to get the hell out of this airport. The tricky part is going to be getting out of the customs and immigration area. With any luck, we can bluff our way through. Just remember to project an air of calm confidence. Customs agents smell fear like a bloodhound. Walk like you own the place, and we should be good to go."

She caught up to him, saying, " 'Smell fear like a bloodhound' . . . that's just great. It's exactly what I thought I'd be worried about at this stage in my life. When I said this trek was the right thing to do, I didn't mean I wanted to wear a prison jumpsuit. There is a limit."

He jerked his head around as he fast-walked up the hallway. "What's that supposed to mean? We're getting arrested one way or another. I just postponed it a little bit. Hopefully a great bit."

"I know . . . I know. It's okay. I told you we Cahills do stupid shit too. Of course, I'm pretty sure you've just set a record. . . ."

Pike cut her off by raising a finger to his lips. They had reached the double doors that led back into the customs area. Pike poked his head out, then said, "This is it. A new flight's in and the place is buzzing. You ready?"

Realizing what she was about to do, Jennifer's bravado left her. "Pike, I don't know if I can do this. We just broke the law in a big way. We held a gun on federal agents and threatened them with death. I don't think I'm going to be able to remain calm."

"I hate to break this to you, but we don't have a choice."

# 61

We slipped into the flow of people headed to the baggage claim.

"Remain calm. We're going to walk right to the man over there taking the customs forms. He'll let us through as long as we don't look like we're hiding something."

I gave her a reassuring smile. "You ready?"

She nodded weakly, looking like she'd rather go back to the interrogation room. *Don't worry about that. If this doesn't work, we'll be there soon enough.*

We got in line behind a family of four. Acting like I was a newbie tourist, I held up our blue-and-white cards and said, "Do we give these to you?"

The man nodded, saying, "No luggage?"

"Yeah, we have luggage. It's somewhere between here and South America. Don't get me started."

The man smiled and waved us through. We entered the security checkpoint and made it to the far side without any issues, now back into the airport proper inside concourse E.

"All right, we need to get out of here and get lost in the city. Unfortunately, we're at the last terminal in this damn airport. We're going to have to cross all five concourses to get out of here. We need to start moving faster. Sooner or later they're going to lock this place down."

We jogged down the escalator to the underground trains, with one pulling up as we hit bottom. I ignored it, pulling Jennifer to the moving sidewalk in front of me.

"What are you doing? We get on that and we can be at the entrance in minutes."

"Yeah, I know, but it's too risky. They pull the trigger on an alarm and that train's going to stop, with us inside it and no way out. We need to run it to the end."

We started walking like we were missing a plane, fast, but not fast enough to cause someone to stare. I noticed that the camera systems here in the tunnel were only clustered around the train entrances and exits.

Right after passing the escalators to Concourse C the trains ceased running, with an alert flashing that they were having mechanical issues.

"Good call," Jennifer said. "Looks like you were right."

"Yeah, but if the trains have stopped, we're out of time. They know we're loose. They'll try to camouflage it for a couple of minutes to keep everyone calm, but eventually, this place is going to be covered in cops."

As we moved toward Concourse B I saw the trains start to move again. *Huh. What's that about?*

We reached the escalator entrance to the B Concourse just as another train stopped, exploding out with about twenty police officers. *Oh, shit.*

Instead of running past Concourse B, I pushed Jennifer to the escalator, going up into the concourse. Glancing back, I saw half of the force coming up with us, apparently not recognizing we were ahead of them. *No pictures out yet.* We reached the top and went left, away from the direction the police were headed. Unlike the tunnel, in the concourse the cameras looked like something out of a Vegas casino, one little dome sticking out of the ceiling every thirty feet. *Shit.*

I hugged the wall, attempting to cross the concourse to the down escalators on the far side, getting back to the tunnel while there was still a gap in the police presence. Before we reached it, a group of police crossed over, headed our way. I turned into an alcove, rotating in front of Jennifer and shielding her face with my body.

"Tell me when they've passed us. If they start walking toward us, the game is up."

I saw Jennifer's face blanch. "Shit," she

said. "One's moving directly toward us. What do we do? Should we run?"

"Stay calm. If he's headed to us, we're done. Don't assume that's what he's doing, though. We wait until he asks us a question."

"He's still coming. He's walking right to us."

"Okay . . . okay. Bend down and mess inside your bag. Anything to hide your face. Act like you're looking for tickets or something."

Squatting down, I began to rummage through my carry-on next to her. I could hear Jennifer muttering under her breath.

"Shit. I'm going to prison. . . . Mom's going to love this. . . . Uncle's fucking dead. . . . I'm a terrorist . . . the only man I know's a nutcase. . . . All I try to do is the right thing. . . . Why does this stuff happen to *me*. . . . Who'd I piss off. . . ."

I saw the cop out of the corner of my eye. I waited for the tap on the shoulder. He moved right past me and kept going into the alcove. For the first time, I noticed it was a men's room. *Whew. Too close for comfort.* I reached over to get Jennifer's attention when I caught the tail end of her rambling.

". . . Why don't you just tie the fucker up butt-naked? Right here . . . get us out of this the same way you got us into it. . . ."

*What a crybaby.* "You going to bitch all day, or can we get the hell out of here?"

She snapped out of it, saw we weren't under arrest, and looked up at me with a sheepish grin. I saw her eyes focus on the sign above my head.

"Yeah. He went in to take a piss. We should go before he's done."

"Sorry. I didn't mean any of that. Just letting off a little steam."

I began walking down the concourse toward a restaurant, saying, "Well, you'll have plenty of time for that, because we're fucked. We can't get out without getting to the far end, and I'm pretty sure there's a platoon of cops at baggage claim by now. We need a way out that normal passengers don't use."

"I know a way."

I looked at her face and saw she was serious. "What do you mean?"

"There's a pilots' lounge down below Concourse A. Get down there, and we can get on the Delta employee bus. It takes us right out of the airport grounds."

"How do you know that? Are you sure?"

"My dad was a pilot for Delta. He was also a deadbeat sack-of-shit that I haven't seen since I was seven. After my parents divorced, his idea of quality time was dragging me through here while he worked. I've spent plenty of time in that lounge."

She had just earned her weight for the entire trip. "Can you find it? How do we get in? What's the procedure?"

"I can find it, but that was way, way before 9/11. I have no idea about the procedure now."

"You said A Concourse? That's the next one up. Let's go."

We saw that the escalator was now free of police, and hurried to get to the tunnel below before they returned. The escalator was a long one, about sixty feet down to the ground. Halfway down, a cop sauntered over and positioned himself at the bottom, his back to us. He acted a little bored until he turned around and glanced up. Then he looked like he was going to shit his pants. *Damn. Pictures are out.*

## 62

The cop pulled his weapon and aimed it up at us while we glided relentlessly toward him. Jennifer was in front of me, preventing any action. He was an older guy, about sixty, and I saw the pistol barrel shake with his adrenaline. *He's liable to shoot out of reflex.*

"Jennifer, raise your hands."

We both did, and continued our glide, with him shouting all sorts of commands at us and into a radio. Every time he moved his other hand to key the mike on his shoulder, the gun hand would quake violently. *Right handed.* He backed up as we reached the end of the escalator, both hands back on his weapon, screaming at us to keep our hands in the air. I slipped in front of Jennifer at the end, attempting to calm him.

"We're done. We're done. Please don't shoot."

Once we were on the ground with him, and seeing our acquiescence, he seemed to grow more confident, saying, "Up against the wall. *Now.*"

He barked out orders like an overweight Dirty Harry. I turned to face the wall, making sure that Jennifer was to my left, away from the barrel I was about to move. I waited on him to key his mike, leaving one hand on his weapon. I heard him start talking. *Please be strong enough to take this.*

I rotated to my left, pushing his gun hand away from me while grabbing on to the wrist. I drove a light, stunning palm strike into his nose with my right hand, then closed it over my left, controlling the pistol. I rotated the wrist, locking up the joints in his arm like a twisted rubber band. I didn't move fast enough to destroy his arm but did move with enough speed to force his body to react, literally doing a flip to prevent his arm from being damaged. He hit the ground hard, the wind knocked out of him. I felt like shit.

"Sorry about that."

I picked up his weapon, ripped his radio from his belt, and took off in the direction of Concourse A, leaving him gasping for air on the ground. Jennifer stumbled after me.

"Holy fuck. We are definitely going to jail now."

"Yeah, probably so, because if we face another police officer, I'm not doing that again. We give up."

I shoved the weapon into the first trash can I could find but kept the radio. I saw Concourse A ahead, and the cops moving around it. *Need another way up.*

Luckily, the lack of trains had caused everyone to use the walkway, so the tunnel was starting to swell with people still attempting to go about their daily lives. We intermingled with a group headed toward the concourse, listening to them talk about terrorists on the loose. I saw a handicapped elevator ahead, without any police presence. When we came abreast of it, I stopped and pressed the button, the door opening while the group still flowed around us. As we rode up, the cop's radio crackled with the news that we were at Concourse B. *Perfect.* Within seconds we were standing outside of Gate A19, no police in sight, looking at the entrance to the pilots' lounge. The news wasn't good. *Fuckin' bin Laden.*

"That figures. Everyone has to swipe their badge before keying in a code."

The good news was that the door was down a small hallway, so we wouldn't be seen doing something unless someone was in the hallway with us. The bad news was that Delta Airlines was serious about security. Nobody entered the door without badging in. Not even when someone already had the door open. Everyone waited, one at a time, to key in their code. *Fucking pilots never listen to anybody. Why now?*

"We need a reason for someone to hold

open the door. And we need to do it quick, before the police realize we aren't at Concourse B. They'll be back in force."

"What are we going to do?"

I watched a purser push an old man down the concourse in a wheelchair, and came up with an idea. *It worked on the exercise before Tbilisi. Nobody suspects the disabled.*

"Follow me."

I hugged the walls, staying out of the fisheye of the cameras every thirty feet. Getting to a smoking lounge, I found what I was looking for.

"Get in."

"What?"

"Get in and act like you need this chair."

Jennifer scrunched up her eyes, clearly wondering if maybe we weren't now on the desperate side of things, which we were. She sat down in the wheelchair.

"I'm going back to the ATM next to Gate 19. I'll mess around there until someone goes into the hallway. If he's alone, I'm going to wait until he opens the door, then holler at him to hold it."

"This will never work. Delta doesn't have pilots in wheelchairs."

I began pushing. "Yeah, you might be right, but you'd be surprised at the number of times ridiculous shit I've pulled out of my ass has worked."

"Ahh . . . no. I don't think I would. Pulling

stuff out of your ass seems to be your way of life."

We reached the ATM just as a single pilot began walking down the hallway. I pushed her forward.

"It's worked out pretty well so far."

# 63

"Hey! Hold that door, please. Let me get her through and I'll badge in."

The pilot looked at me, trying to decide, then held it open.

"Thanks. I appreciate it. Just let me get her inside."

I could tell he was wondering why a guy in civilian clothes wanted to take a female in a wheelchair into the pilots' lounge, but his chivalry took precedence.

He said, "You sure you're in the right place? You know there's no elevator in here, don't you?"

I pushed Jennifer through, saying, "Yeah, I know. She can walk short distances. She'll be okay. We're just catching the bus."

I saw the door close and said, "Give me a hand with her leg braces, will you?"

He came to the front of the wheelchair, where I was fiddling with the leg platforms. I stood up and grabbed the conveniently thick polyester collar of his uniform and cut off the blood flow to his brain. Once he was down, I ripped off his badge and stuffed him into an empty closet designed to hold the carry-on luggage of pilots coming and going.

"Okay. What now? Where do we go?"

Jennifer was stunned, looking at me like I was the Terminator.

"Come on! Where do we go?"

She snapped out of it, saying, "Down. There's a stewardesses' lounge on the right and a pilots' lounge on the left. Once we get in there, we need to move straight to the exit. There's a bus stop underneath the concourse."

Two minutes later we were waiting with a bunch of other Delta employees for the shuttle to the Delta parking lot, me wearing the pilot's badge around my neck with the picture side conveniently against my chest. After the longest three minutes of my life, we were on the next bus headed out of the airport. We sat in the back, away from anyone else, Jennifer still trembling from our narrow miss.

She said, "I don't think I'm cut out for this law-breaking stuff. It's going to give me a nervous breakdown."

I said, "Trust me; I didn't think it was fun either. You get used to it."

"What do we do now? Are we still going to D.C., or are we headed to Mexico to find a cheap house to spend the rest of our lives?"

"If you're game, I think we should continue on to D.C. Still want to do that?"

"Well, shit, we're outlaws now. It looks like the choices are turn ourselves in, run for the rest of our lives, or try to solve this thing. That's probably the only way to get any mercy. Maybe cut the jail term to half of our lives."

"Okay. I'm game. The folks looking for us know we're in Atlanta, so we need to do all preparations here, while it won't give anything away."

"What preparations do we need to do? How are we going to get to D.C. with the cops chasing us?"

"We have to disappear. We can't use any credit cards, cell phones, anything tied to either you or me. Right now, the police know we're in Atlanta, so it won't do any harm to use your ATM or credit cards here. It'll just reinforce what they already know. Once we leave here, we can't use anything that will trigger an alert with the authorities. First thing we need to do is go to an ATM and take out your max amount of money. Next, we need to get to a place that sells prepaid credit cards and cell phones. We also need to get a rental car for local use."

Something dawned on me. "You don't have your cell phone with you, do you?"

"Yes. I turned it back on when we hit the U.S. It works now."

"Turn it off and take out the battery."

"I haven't called anyone. Nobody knows it's on."

"Doesn't matter. Your phone talks without you using it. It constantly sends out a signal to make sure it has a tower it can talk to. This signal leaves a trail, essentially telling anyone who wants to check that your phone talked to such and such tower at such and such time. They can track the city you're currently in and neck it down to which tower you're near. Depending on the concentration of towers, it can put you within a couple of city blocks. That's *without* using any special gear. Trust me, turn it off and take out the battery."

I had intimate knowledge of the power within the U.S. government and knew that any slip-ups would cause us to be caught fairly quickly. Despite all that, the federal government wasn't omnipotent. Most fugitives were caught by doing something stupid, like returning to the scene of the crime, or going to a family member for help. Smarter fugitives managed to evade the law for extended periods of time, no matter how much effort was put against them.

A buddy of mine in the FBI had chased a man named Eric Rudolph, a homegrown terrorist who had murdered at least three people and wounded upwards of a hundred because of his twisted beliefs, including the 1996 bombing during the Atlanta summer Olympics. He'd managed to evade the FBI and local police for five years, despite a million-dollar bounty on his head and being on the FBI's top-ten most wanted list. *Great. You're hoping you're as good as that sick bastard. Perfect.*

# 64

Harold Standish slowly hung up his phone. Disappointed at the failure at the Atlanta airport, he wasn't overly surprised. Pike and Jennifer were proving to be more resourceful than he would have thought, but knowing Pike's background now, he should have anticipated it. He quickly punched in Lucas's private number.

"It's Standish. Remember what we talked about yesterday? I need you to execute. Come by the office and I'll give you the phone you worked on. They're headed here but I don't know when they'll arrive. I'm sure they'll make contact on the cloned phone."

After listening for a few seconds, Standish replied, "I'll be here. See you then."

Before the Atlanta incident, he'd had doubts that using Lucas was the best course of action. He'd contracted Lucas many times before for simple break-ins to gather information on opponents, but he had never asked him to do anything violent. After hearing what had happened in Atlanta, he saw Lucas as the only solution. *Let's see them get away from someone who doesn't play by the rules.*

Seven hours after we had exited the Metro at Five Points, we pulled into the Sheraton, in Greensboro, North Carolina — about halfway to Washington, D.C. We had robbed Jennifer's bank account of about five thousand dollars and converted that to pay-as-you-go credit cards and prepaid cell phones. Once that was accomplished, we found a "rent-a-wreck" car place and rented a nondescript sedan for in-town use, telling the man behind the counter our car was getting repaired. Finally, we'd stopped yet again to buy some clothes. Jennifer was probably getting sick of leaving our bags at every hotel we stayed at.

After checking in, as we rode up in the elevator, Jennifer asked a question that apparently had been bouncing around in her head.

"Are you sure you're not a drug dealer or something? How come you know all about hiding from the authorities? I know you didn't learn that stuff at basic training."

"I had to learn it for some other things we did. I've never had to do it as a real fugitive."

I could tell she didn't buy that answer.

"Sure. I bet. I can't wait to get back to Charleston. You're going to save me a bundle when you set up my free cable. I'm looking forward to it."

"I'm telling the truth. I'll be running out of tricks soon, trust me."

The door opened on our floor. Jennifer exited, muttering, "I doubt that."

Bakr and Sayyidd exited their plane in Oslo, Norway, exhausted from the trip. Given the seven-hour time difference from Belize, they landed at ten o'clock at night, almost twenty-four hours from the time they had left. Bakr had found them a small hotel on the outskirts of Oslo that catered to Muslim immigrants. Going through customs without issue, they flagged a cab and gave the driver an address.

For security reasons, Bakr had them exit the cab three blocks from the hotel. While they walked, Sayyidd asked about Walid abdul-Aziz, and why on earth they were in this country. It didn't make any sense to him. The place was frigid and full of blond-haired, blue-eyed infidels. It seemed the last place they should be.

"Norway is one of the few countries in Europe that allows us to blend in without undue scrutiny from the authorities," Bakr told him. "Believe it or not, it has a very large Muslim population. Larger than the people here realize, so there isn't a backlash yet. God willing, we'll own this country before they realize we're here."

"What do you mean? Own the country?"

"The faithful have been flooding into Europe for decades. We're the minority now, but we'll eventually outpace the native people. Sharia law has already been allowed in some countries. If we can't win by fire, we might win by simple numbers."

"So, we're safe here? The *Ummah* are all true believers?"

Bakr scoffed, "No. No way. Most of the Muslims came here to escape their life at home. They were told about the free welfare and decided to join in. Don't trust them just because they pray to Mecca. They'll turn you in simply to prove they aren't a threat."

Wearily unpacking their bags, Bakr checked to ensure the weapon was still intact in its duct-tape cocoon. Seeing no signs of a breach, he asked Sayyidd to set up the M4 satellite phone and check the e-mail account.

Sayyidd demurred. "Let's get some sleep first. The message will be waiting for us when we get up, and there's nothing we can do with it right now anyway."

Bakr started to argue but didn't have the energy. He was growing weary of his partnership with Sayyidd, wanting to be on his own again. He was unsure why his leadership had chosen Sayyidd for their original mission, but was becoming convinced it had been a mistake. A mistake that he would more than likely have to rectify. Crawling into bed, he turned out the lights.

## 65

Finished cleaning up, I gave Jennifer's door a light knock. I sensed her looking through the peephole, then saw the door swing open. Jennifer was smiling, standing barefoot while finishing buttoning the top of her shirt, her hair wet and smelling of shampoo.

"Hey, you're early. Let me get my shoes."

She moved away from the door without waiting on a response, which was lucky, because seeing her like that made me about as comfortable as a snail crossing salt flats. *Don't knock like this again. Call first.*

She came back to the door wearing a ball cap, her wet hair stuck through the hole in the back. The effect floored me. Heather had worn her hair the same way almost every weekend. *Jesus. I can't do this.* I knew it wasn't Jennifer's fault, but the combined effect cut me to the quick. She noticed me stiffen and looked at me with concern.

"Are you all right? What's wrong?"

I had no idea why my brain had made that

connection. Heather looked nothing like Jennifer. It was just a ball cap — a stupid connection that passed quickly, like the jolt you feel when a car starts crossing into your lane on the freeway, then swerves back.

"Nothing. Let's go. I did a recce of the north lobby and found the business center."

Eight minutes later we were sitting in the The Link, a pseudo–business center, pseudocafé, with me on one computer and Jennifer on another. I logged on to the Embassy Suites Web site in Old Town Alexandria and proceeded to get us a couple of rooms.

I was finishing up the reservation, asking for adjoining rooms, when Jennifer whispered, "Pike. There's another message. It's in a different e-mail account. The first account's empty. The message we printed in Belize is gone."

I closed out my system. "Print it out."

After she hit print I said, "Scoot over. Let me try something."

I got behind the keyboard and typed www .whatismyipaddress.com.

"What're you doing?"

"Well, we can't read the message itself, but with a little luck, we can determine where it came from. All I have to do is get the full header of the e-mail and paste it into this Web site. It should have the originating IP address, which, if we're lucky, is tied to an actual location. Sometimes it's good to go, other times it doesn't work, but it's worth a shot."

I clicked "get source" and waited for the computer to quit churning. The screen loaded with an analysis of the message.

Jennifer asked, "What's that telling us? Do you understand any of that?"

"No. The normal human language is at the bottom."

I scrolled down the screen until I saw "source." I felt Jennifer leaning over my shoulder, reading the screen:

Country: Norway
City: Oslo
Lat: 59.54.45
Long: 10.44.19

"You're a genius!" she exclaimed.

She got a stranglehold on my neck, giving it a hug. She pecked my cheek with a light kiss.

*What the hell was that?* I leaned away from her.

"I can't believe you just did that! It's like black magic or something. Why don't you raise your hands and say, 'Behave, and I'll bring back the sun'?"

"Hold on. All this really says is that the message went through Norway as a first gate. It doesn't mean it came from Norway. There's a good chance of that, but it isn't absolute proof. It's easy to fool this type of thing."

"All right, all right. It's still pretty cool. You're a walking library of cool stuff."

I didn't let it show, but I was secretly pleased with the attention. If I'd had a tail, I'd have been wagging it like a dog getting a pat from his owner. *I'm pathetic.*

"I'm going to delete this completely. If nothing else, it'll slow down the terrorists."

Making sure the message was gone from both the in-box and the trash file, I said, "I got a couple of rooms in D.C. Tomorrow, I'll give a friend from my old unit a call. He's an Arabic speaker and can decipher both this message and the one before. Sound like a plan?"

"Sounds like a good plan."

We headed back to our rooms to rack out. Jennifer opened her door, then turned around.

"Hey, Pike?"

I stopped working my key. "Yeah?"

"I'm sorry for that thing in the business center. I didn't mean anything by it."

She couldn't have made me more uncomfortable if she had asked to borrow a condom. Why bring it up?

"That's okay. You didn't do anything wrong. I'm just still a little touchy about that sort of thing, I guess. Not your fault."

"That's what I mean. I could tell I made

you uncomfortable. I wasn't trying to . . . to . . . make you think of your wife. Anyway, I just wanted to make sure we're still on the same sheet of music. I shouldn't have done that." She broke into a smile. "But you do have some neat tricks."

Abu Bakr awoke before Abu Sayyidd. He could feel the endgame in his bones and was itching to bring it about. Quietly setting up the M4, he logged on to the Internet and checked the next address on the e-mail list. Two messages were in the in-box, both supposedly from Nigeria telling him he had been named in a rich man's will. All he needed to do was wire some money to get his inheritance. Disappointed, Bakr checked the other addresses. None contained the message he was looking for. This was getting a little annoying. Working at a snail's pace was fine when one had that luxury, but they needed to get moving. It had been over forty-eight hours since their last message.

He woke up Sayyidd.

"We have no new message."

Sayyidd rubbed the sleep out of his eyes, secretly happy that his desire to go to bed earlier had proved to be the right call.

"How long should we wait? What do we do if he never contacts us?"

"I think we should send another message to The Sheik. If that doesn't work, we head out on our own. I think I can get some SEM-TEX explosives from some helpers in the Balkans, but we won't be able to implicate the Persians. God willing, we'll still accomplish our mission."

Sayyidd was pleased that Bakr was now getting impatient, and was willing to strike out together with or without the message.

"Let's send the e-mail," he said.

Bakr turned back to the computer and typed a simple message:

*We have successfully entered the country of Walid. He hasn't contacted us. We wanted to ensure that he knew we were ready to meet. God willing, please give us the path to take.*

Bakr closed the laptop. "Now we wait."

## 66

Lucas leaned back from his computer with a new appreciation for his adversary. His research/administration assistant had sent him a data dump on his assigned targets. On the screen was the enlisted record brief for Nephilim Logan, the man he knew as Pike. The ERB was a one-page document used by the U.S. Army to encapsulate a soldier's career. In Pike's case, his assignments read like a who's who of the military elite. Initial assignment to the 3rd Ranger Battalion, on to Special Forces, with two years in Okinawa in 1st Bn, 1st Special Forces Group, followed by eleven years in 1st Special Forces Operational Detachment — Delta. His last assignment had been as some do-nothing communications technician on Fort Bragg. *Retirement job.*

His military schooling had produced more badges than he was allowed to wear at any one time on his uniform, to include a Combat Infantryman's Badge with a star, indicating combat in two different conflicts. He would clearly not be an easy target. *Another time, another place, and we'd be drinking beers together.*

Jennifer Cahill, on the other hand, had proven to be exactly as advertised: a college student. The only thing remarkable about her was her picture, since even the passport photo couldn't hide her good looks. Other than that, she had spent most of her adult life as either a student or a housewife.

Lucas was a careful, meticulous planner. He would become obsessed with the research on his targets prior to conducting a mission. It was what made him successful on assignments that were way outside the bounds of U.S. law. In truth, it was no different than what he'd done while in the military. Learn about the enemy in the hopes of exploiting a weakness and avoiding enemy strengths. To this end, he'd found it useful in his work to subscribe to various data mining Web sites available on the Internet. It never failed to amaze him how much information was free for the taking to someone who wanted to look.

He was broken out of his thoughts by the phone ringing. Looking at the caller ID, he saw it was Standish. *Shit. Just what I need.*

"Hello?"

"Hey. Standish here. Have you heard anything yet?"

*Why the hell is he bothering me?* Standish had no expertise at all in man-hunting. His skills were in personal destruction from the shadows. Cowardly stabbing people in the back. The truth of the matter was that Lucas respected the target Standish had given him much more than he did Standish himself. But Standish *was* paying the bills. *I just need to cut out this micromanaging bullshit.*

"Standish. Listen to me. You gave me the phone less than twenty-four hours ago. I'm not sure what you think's going to happen, but your target is a hard, hard man. This isn't going to be easy. I'll get it done, but I won't be answering to you every five minutes. I'll call you when the mission's accomplished. If you don't hear from me, assume it hasn't been done. You got that?"

"Whoa. *I'm* the one paying for this. If I want information, you'll give it to me. I'm not going to throw money at you just to have you blow it without oversight. Do *you* have *that?*"

"Yeah. I got it. Fuck this. I quit."

"What? You can't quit. You owe me."

Lucas snarled, "I owe you *nothing.* You push that button one more time and you're going to see firsthand what I owe you. Understand? I don't want to hear that *ever* again."

Lucas waited a few seconds, hearing nothing but breathing.

"Call me when you have something."

"Fine."

Lucas was sick of hearing what he owed Standish. *Fucking politician.* A weasel like every other politician. *No honor. No belief in something greater than himself.* Just whatever favor could be gleaned based on which way the wind was blowing. Yeah, Standish had possibly helped him out, but the truth of the matter was there wasn't any proof that he had done anything wrong. The only people who could prove he had killed civilians were dead in an IED attack. He'd eventually have gotten off anyway.

He regretted having killed his teammates, but they had lost their way. *It was war, God-dammit.* He had killed the civilians to get information on terrorist attacks. It had worked. The team broke up a terrorist cell that had murdered at least thirty Americans and would have murdered thirty more. He didn't understand why his teammates had chosen to turn him in, but he couldn't let it stand. He had done the right thing. Two noncombatants for thirty Americans. *How could that not be seen as a good thing?*

He had been working the civilian side of the defense industry for over a year now, and was beginning to hate it. Everything was about the almighty dollar. Nothing was about a cause, a goal greater than the individual. It disgusted him, and he wanted out. Even his actions in Afghanistan, while others might not understand them, were for something larger than money. At the least, it saved American lives, even counting the two who had died at his hand. The sacrifice was for a larger effort. Now his work did nothing but cause money to exchange hands.

It wasn't that he disliked the work. Truth be told, he'd never minded killing, any more than the average big game hunter. He didn't draw any particular pleasure from the act itself but did enjoy the hunt. Now, though, the purpose was gone.

Since he had started contracting out, most of his employment had been nothing more than gleaning sleazy information for Standish, the greatest "success" coming when he found a political rival with a young boy. It disgusted him. He'd done only one violent act since leaving the Navy, on behalf of a foreign corporation looking to gain an inside advantage on a classified defense contract. Their only competition was a small outfit at Fort Bragg, something the foreign entity should have been able to outbid. The problem was that the competition was U.S. based, and thus the foreign company was convinced they were going to lose. Lucas had smoked the CEO of the U.S. contractor, securing a foreign win. The money had been extremely lucrative. Worth the woman and child he'd been forced to kill as well. The money Standish was throwing around was even better. *Enough to quit this shit forever.* He looked at this target as a blessing. The fact that two people would die caused him no angst at all. It was just work.

Lucas returned to the problem at hand. He had a pretty good background on both of his targets now and began to build a plan of attack. He would need his best folks for this one, as he was fairly sure a mistake against Pike had the potential to be catastrophic. He ran through his Rolodex of employees — all of whom worked for him on a contract basis — picking ten that fit the bill. He purposely left out the two who had worked with him at Fort Bragg. When push came to shove, they had balked at killing the woman and child. He had no idea where this would go and didn't need anyone who might hesitate.

He gave each of the men a call, telling them he had a job and the time to show up at the office if they were interested. He then began building a target package on both Jennifer and Pike. In the back of his mind, he thought about the money he'd make and the chance to get out. To get away from people like Standish. *Maybe I'll get my check and smoke him for free. Help out the country.*

## 67

I waited until I was outside of Fredericksburg, on Interstate 95 about forty-five minutes south of Washington, D.C., before I made the call. I had Jennifer dial the number on our new TracFone, then hand it to me. A man answered on the third ring.

I said, "Ethan, hey, it's Pike Logan. How're you doing?"

There was a pregnant pause. I'm sure he was getting over the initial shock of hearing my voice. I looked over at Jennifer, raised my eyebrow, and tilted the phone so she could hear.

"Pike? What's up? How're you doing?"

"Hey, nothing like a call from the past. I'm fine. I'm going to be in D.C. tonight, and I thought I'd drop by for a visit."

Ethan was an analyst inside the Taskforce. As such, he was support. Ordinarily, there was an unofficial separation between opera-tors and direct support personnel, but I had always thought the distinction was bullshit, and had hit it off with Ethan. Being a geographic bachelor whenever I was in D.C., I had dinner with Ethan's family about twice a month. The last time I had seen him was in the mission brief for the operation in Tbilisi.

Since my implosion, Ethan hadn't said two words to me. It would do him no good to take sides on my demise, and so he had taken the route of discretion being the better part of valor. I didn't blame him, although I could hear the wariness in his voice as I finally convinced him to let us come by.

Jennifer, having heard my end of the conversation, said, "That's a friend? Don't get mad, but out of curiosity, how bad were you when you left? What happened?"

"About as bad as I was when we first met. You can expect everyone to look at me funny, like a cancer patient who might or might not be in remission. Everyone will be afraid to ask how I am."

I was surprised to find I was comfortable talking about it. That was a first.

"There wasn't any big blowout, like a drunk finally killing a carload of kids or something. I just sort of . . . fell apart. The Force did everything they could to help me, but it was all based on me wanting to get better. I didn't. Eventually, I just left."

Jennifer appeared lost in thought. She finally said, "You ever think about fate, or destiny? You ever think that God makes things happen for a reason?"

"I think about that all the time. In fact, it tears me up. Why'd you ask?"

She suddenly looked embarrassed and uncomfortable. "Nothing. Nothing at all. I just sometimes wonder."

I let the silence go for a second, then prodded her. "Wonder what? What were you going to say?"

"Well, what're the odds of me picking you up at the Windjammer? Me, someone who's about to get killed, picking up you, the one person with the skills to prevent it? Think about it, what are the odds that we'd collide at all? Given the entire United States? Shit, given just the city of Charleston? It's just weird, is all. It's a perfect storm. It makes me think."

"So what's the reason for this? Besides my company, I mean?"

"Maybe saving a lot of lives."

# 68

Later, after the settling in at the hotel, I decided it was time to get moving. "It looks like we have a few hours before we need to link up with Ethan. I'm going to the Task-force Headquarters to leave a note for Kurt along with our cell phone numbers." I paused, not wanting a fight. "No offense, but I can't take you there. I have to go alone."

She smiled. "Come on. I'm not that big of a jerk, am I? I understand. I'll just hang around here. No big deal."

No way was I going to resist that opening. "No, no. That's not what I meant. Jerk isn't what I'd call you. Anyway, what you could do —"

"What's that mean?" She flicked her hand and backhanded my stomach. "Would you like to see me be a jerk? I don't think you'd enjoy it."

"Oww. Jesus. I don't like it right now." I snatched her hand out of the air to prevent her from hitting me again. "I was just kidding. What I was going to say was it would help if you went out and bought a laptop. One with wireless so we don't have to keep searching for Internet business centers. Can you do that?"

She squinted at me, the touch of a grin on her face. Waiting a beat, she said, "Sure. Gives me something to do, anyway. We'll just meet back here?"

I realized I was still holding her hand and dropped it like a piece of hot iron. "Yeah. I should be gone no more than an hour. Get your stuff. We can walk to the Metro together. If you get off two stops after Reagan National you'll be at a pretty big mall. The stop's Pentagon City."

When she saw my embarrassment, Jennifer's little grin threatened to break into a smile, causing a clash of confusing feelings. I dealt with it the usual way — by getting pissed off.

"What? What're you grinning about? Can we go?"

She rolled her eyes, holding her hand in front of my face and making me feel like an ass. "Yeah. Let me get my purse before your head explodes."

We headed to the Metro station and hopped on the first train in, the Blue Line. We sat in the back, away from anyone else, and rode silently past the first two stops. One minute out from the Pentagon City stop I remembered what we were doing, and the fact that Jennifer wasn't a professional. I kicked myself for having taken her precautions for granted. She was going out by herself, into a world where someone wanted both of us very badly. A world full of invisible predators.

"Hey, the next stop is yours. Look, I don't want to scare you, but please be very, very careful. I've racked my brain about the Homeland Security alert, and can't come up with any reason whatsoever for that to have occurred. One name might be a coincidence, but both our names together is outside the realm of believable. I think that the alert has something to do with what we know."

"You said that was just a mistake. Why would anyone do that on purpose?"

I held up my hands. "I don't *know* it was done on purpose. On the one hand, it could simply be a mistake, some crossed wires from our visit to the embassy in Belize. There is also the very, very slim chance that it was sent by Kurt, and once we were in the interrogation rooms they would have simply put us in contact with him."

"And if it's not?"

"Well . . . the other reasons aren't that good. It could mean that someone knew we were traveling together, and so knew *why* we were traveling. Whoever that someone is wanted us to get arrested so that we're out of the picture."

Jennifer pondered a bit, asking a question softly: "You really think that alert was done intentionally to get us out of the way?"

"I honestly don't know. In my heart, I don't believe that, but I want you to act as if it's true. Treat the entire mall trip as if you're walking through a crack slum. Check out anyone coming near you. Avoid any contact with strangers. Someone stares at you the wrong way, get the fuck out. Go back to the hotel room. You tracking?"

She nodded.

I continued. "As soon as you're off the train, call my cell phone so you can simply hit redial in an emergency. Call me every thirty minutes. If you don't get through, if I don't answer, get out. Go straight to the hotel. Lock the doors and wait. I'll get in touch. If I don't hear from you, I'm coming straight here, to the mall. If anything happens, try to stay in the area, create a scene, whatever you can do to give me a clue on finding you."

"Whoa — are you serious? You think it's that bad? I can't believe this. All right . . . I'll try to leave a bloody napkin or maybe a finger for you to find."

"Come on. That's not funny. I don't think it's that bad, but it doesn't hurt to be prepared."

"Okay, okay. I can handle myself. I'll stay in crowded areas and scream my head off if someone tries anything. What about you? You're going straight to the one place that has people like you, the one place that can hurt you. What if they're the ones that did it? Maybe we should just call your unit."

I shook my head. "They change numbers every three months. I can't call. Even if I could, it's not the Taskforce. No way. That's not what they do. If anything, they can figure out what's going on."

The train pulled into Pentagon City.

"This is you. Don't get hurt."

Jennifer smiled. "I'll be okay. Trust me; I can deal with a shopping mall."

She jumped out just as the doors were closing. I continued to stare out the window, seeing her pull out her phone to call me. My phone rang as the train pulled away. I gave her one more admonishment about being alert, then hung up. I was wondering if splitting up was such a hot idea. The cell phone contact plan was of more psychological help than anything else. It would allow me to know she was safe but wouldn't do anything to help me find her. If she didn't call, I knew there would be very little I could do.

I put myself at ease with the thought that nobody had paid us a second's worth of attention on the drive up here, and both hotels had checked us in without question. While the police were probably ripping my boat apart in Charleston, we hadn't been on any

427

news programs I had seen. I'd just have to hope our luck continued.

## 69

Lucas assessed his assembled team, satisfied that they could get the mission done. He had called ten men, needing at least five for the mission. Four of the ten were already contracted on another assignment. Out of the remaining six who answered his call, four were ex–U.S. Navy SEALs and two were ex–U.S. Army Special Forces. All were ruthless, intelligent, and very highly trained. After thanking them for coming, he started the PowerPoint slideshow, giving them the background on the targets.

He began with Jennifer, getting juvenile comments on her looks and heckling about why their skills were needed.

The demeanor changed when he got to Pike. The men became serious, taking notes and asking questions.

After the background, he gave them the mission statement.

"Both of these targets are to be terminated. There are no specific constraints on the termination. The only rules of engagement are that they are both out of the picture, and the act cannot be traced back to us. Collateral damage is acceptable as long as it is restricted to five or less.

"We know they're coming here, to D.C. In fact, they may already be here. Through information from other sources, we believe they'll make contact with an individual or individuals here in Washington. One of those individuals is tied to this phone."

He held up the cloned handset. "This is our only lead. We'll set up a duty roster, with this post manned 24/7. During the day, you'll stay here, just like that mission against the defense contractor six months ago. The bunks are still in the back, Xbox and cable still hooked up. At night, if you're not on duty, you're free to do what you want, as long as you can get back here in thirty minutes on a recall, sober and ready to work. Along with the man minding the phone, half the team will bunk here each night on a rotating basis.

"The actual mission will be fluid, no set plans or rehearsals. The Fort Bragg op was a pretty good template to use. Get this done, and we get a pretty good paycheck."

He turned to the SEAL directly to his right. "Mason, you're the team chief. Set up the duty roster however you see fit. Assign positions and issue out the necessary kit. Sean's out front with your beepers and cell phones, all new and clean."

Lucas paused. "All of you look at me."

He waited until he had their undivided attention, "This Nephilim character's picture is next to the definition of *badass* in the dictionary. Do not underestimate him. We need to take him out quick. If you get him in your sights, and can meet the rules of engagement, take him down. We can deal with the girl at our leisure, but make a mistake against this guy, or let him know he's being hunted, and he'll kill you. Any questions?"

Lucas spent the next thirty minutes answering a barrage of queries on everything from the title trace of the cars they would drive to the response time of EMS vehicles at an automobile accident. Holding true to the ethos of the special operations units they had come from, Lucas let the planning evolve from the bottom up. He gave out the guidance and let them sort through the gritty details.

Forty-five minutes later, they had the skeleton of an operational plan, with various straw man scenarios rehearsed on whiteboards and individual assignments dictated. They could now execute a multitude of plans on a moment's notice, with only the actual location of the operation unknown.

Sayyidd watched Bakr pace back and forth in their small hotel room, clearly impatient that a message hadn't arrived. Sayyidd had checked the account every hour on the hour, but they'd received nothing. Bakr stopped pacing and walked to the door.

"I'm going out. I need to get some air. This is driving me crazy."

"Allah has shown us the way throughout this journey. He'll continue to do so. There's no reason to worry or get angry. He'll speak again when He's ready."

When Bakr didn't respond, Sayyidd thought maybe he was getting through to him. He had convinced Bakr to choose this path, and now wondered if Bakr himself had the courage to believe in their destiny. Maybe he was looking for a reason to fail. Sayyidd had seen it before. Otherwise brave, righteous men cracking under the pressure placed upon them by the word of God. Not wanting to fail, but unable to simply leave, they ended up doing foolish things to ensure their place in heaven. He needed to prevent that with Bakr. He knew his limitations. Sayyidd had proven time and time again that he could accomplish missions against all odds, but always as a member of a team. Never as a leader. Or, in this case, on his own. Without Bakr, he knew he would fail.

He booted up the M4, praying that Walid had answered. He checked the next Yahoo! address and immediately deflated. It was empty. Behind him, he heard Bakr say, "Still nothing?"

Before Bakr could get angry again, Sayyidd said, "Let me check the other addresses. Maybe it went to the wrong one."

Sayyidd went to the next address on the list, watching anxiously as the new Web page loaded. There were two messages, one spam and the other from The Sheik. A shiver ran through him. Finally, an answer. He opened the message. It was short, and to the point.

*Praise Allah, my pilgrims have made it to the land of Walid. I have passed your message, and Walid has replied that he gave you instructions, which you did not follow. He will contact you again, but requests that you send the e-mail address you wish to use to ensure there are no more mistakes. May Allah smile on your mission. All are aware of your journey, and all praise your quest. Wait for his contact, then smite the infidels with his help.*

Sayyidd breathed a sigh of relief. It had all been a simple mistake. He felt a huge weight leave his shoulders. Everything was going to be okay. He turned away from the computer, smiling, only to see Bakr, his face drained of blood, staring at the screen as if he had seen his own death. Sayyidd had had enough.

"What is it now, you old woman? Can't you be happy about anything? Thirty minutes ago you were whining like a dog about not getting a message, now you're mad about getting one."

Bakr sat in silence. He finally said, "I'm taking the weapon in the morning. We've been discovered."

Sayyidd was stunned. "Taking the weapon? Have you lost your mind?"

"Walid sent us a message, but we didn't get it. Now we get the next message on the *next* e-mail address. Why? Why didn't The Sheik send the message in the order he dictated us to use? It's because there was a message, and he thought we had received it, thus that e-mail address was no longer usable. We didn't get it because someone else retrieved it. Someone has that e-mail address, and might have the others. I have no idea of the technology the Great Satan employs, but it's not impossible."

Left unsaid was the mistake that Sayyidd had made in Guatemala.

"Quit it," Sayyidd said. "You're constantly afraid of your own shadow. Why does everything have to be some evil plot against us? Why can't you trust in Allah to protect us? Just once?"

Bakr spoke in a dangerously quiet tone. "Dog, it's because of my caution that I live. I have killed more infidels in a month than you have in your life. I have no idea why Allah has shined a light on you and allowed you to survive with the mistakes you make, but I'm not going to repeat them."

Sayyidd felt a chill. Bakr was not a man to

test, and Sayyidd could sense the mission falling apart, with Bakr about to make a decision that would leave him alone. Without any support. Forcing him to face his fears. He held his tongue, awaiting Bakr's decision.

"I'm leaving tomorrow with the weapon," Bakr said. "Whatever happens here, we can't let the infidels steal the means of victory. It may simply be a mistake, but we should act as if it isn't. You will remain behind here to wait for Walid's message. Once you have that, meet him and finish the final planning."

"But where will you go? What'll I do once I meet Walid?"

"I'll head to Bosnia. There are plenty of old fighters there willing to help. You do exactly what we were going to do all along. Give him our request for evidence to blame the Persians, and figure out how we'll get into Palestine. Once you know that, contact me with the plan. God willing, we'll meet again and continue our journey together."

"But if you're right, I'll be arrested. I'll be the one who dies without striking a blow against the infidels. Maybe we should both go."

Sayyidd's voice cracked. He hoped Bakr took it as concern for the mission, and not a fear of being exposed as a fraud. It must have worked, because Bakr didn't sugarcoat anything, choosing instead to give him the hard facts.

"You may very well die here, or at the least be put in prison, but your part of the mission is worth that risk. Without you and Walid, I'll be forced to go on my own, with little chance of starting the catalyst that you envisioned. I need your help to make this work. Even so, we can take steps to protect ourselves."

"How? What should I do?"

"It's time for you to become what you were going to become in America: a simple college student, without any political aspirations. If they suspect us, the far enemy will focus on this section of the city. Check out of this Muslim hotel. Find one in the city that doesn't stand out and allows you to blend into the local tourist scenery. Set up your meeting with Walid away from known hotbeds and radical mosques. That should protect you more than any security procedures I could devise."

Sayyidd calmed down, feeling more secure. After all, Bakr had the weapon. Bakr would be the *shahid.* Sayyidd wouldn't have to push the button. He would be the facilitator, and with Allah's help, they would succeed.

"All right. I'll stay and meet Walid. How will you get to Bosnia?"

"Well, I can't fly, since they might be watching the airports. I'll take a ferry from here to Germany. From there, I'll take trains and buses until I join up with our Muslim brothers in Tuzla. It'll take a little longer but will be more secure."

"Give me five minutes and I'll get that set up."

Before he could boot up the M4 satellite phone, Bakr stopped him. "Wait. We need to ensure we can communicate first. I want you to establish a separate e-mail address, known only to you and me. Every twenty-four hours, I want you to send me a message. Include the town of Fallujah in the message somewhere. If I don't hear from you every twenty-four hours, or I get a message without the mention of Fallujah, I'll assume you've been captured or killed. I'll then immediately take the weapon and attempt to use it to the best of my abilities."

He stopped, waiting for Sayyidd to look up. When he had Sayyidd's undivided attention, he began again. "Sayyidd, I don't want to make you mad, but the only way that splitting up will be a mistake is if you fail in this task and inadvertently send me to my death. Once I believe that you're discovered, I'll immediately flee to stay out of the hands of the authorities. There'll be no turning back. Do you understand?"

Sayyidd said, "I understand. Don't worry. I won't fail you."

Bakr relaxed, satisfied that he had made his point. "From here out, we must act as if we were still in the Land of Two Rivers. Watch around you. Look for the infidel with the knife. We've come very far in a short amount of time. God willing, we'll finish our journey in victory, but it will require diligence, and I'm sure we'll both be tested before this is through."

Sayyidd felt sick to his stomach at the thought of being left alone.

## 70

I called Jennifer as soon as I stepped off the Metro at King Street, asking her to meet me in the lobby. I had managed to leave my number at Taskforce Headquarters, but it hadn't been smooth. I was no longer a member of the elite little club. I didn't have the badges or passwords to get me into the inner sanctum, so I had to make a fuss. Even then, after getting through the first gate, and begging to simply leave a number for Kurt, I was ignored because Kurt officially didn't exist. I was politely asked to leave by Abigail, a gray-haired lady from whom I had bought Girl Scout cookies for years. I'd bought enough to put her grandkid through college, yet she acted like she'd never seen me. Eventually, the internal security force had shown up, giving me the not-so-subtle hint to get the fuck out. Before they pitched me headfirst out the door, Abigail finally broke through her stupid cover and said she'd take my number. I knew she'd get it to Kurt, so I

guess I had succeeded.

By the time I reached the lobby Jennifer was already downstairs, carrying our new laptop.

Less than an hour later we were at Ethan's house. I took the lead to the front door, looking at my watch before I rang the doorbell. *Close enough for government work.* I rang the bell and waited.

Immediately, a dog began barking like his fur was on fire. I smiled. "Sounds like a rabid wolf, but he's really a teddy bear."

I heard Ethan tell the dog to shut up before opening the door. I waited, a little anxious at the response I would get.

Ethan gave me a big grin, holding his arms open. *Whew.* After embracing me, he noticed Jennifer for the first time.

"Who's this?"

"A friend of mine. Jennifer Cahill, this is Ethan Merriweather. Otherwise known as Haji."

Ethan shook her hand, then invited us both inside.

I bent down to ruffle the fur of a brown-and-tan mutt that looked like a cross between a bulldog and miniature collie. The dog began to jump all over me, slobbering.

"Hey, Eddie, how ya been?" Looking up, I asked, "Kathy around? I'd like to say hello."

"No, unfortunately, she's not. She really wanted to see you as well, but Emily and Rachel had a big Girl Scout thing tonight. It's been planned for a month."

I nodded, relieved at the answer. It would be pretty hard for Kathy to decide at the last minute to attend something like that, and I knew that Ethan wouldn't outright lie to me.

Standing up from Eddie, freeing him up to run over to Jennifer and begin slobbering all over her, I said, "That's too bad. I'd really like to see her and the kids. I don't know how long I'll be in D.C., but maybe I'll get the chance later."

"How about coming by for dinner tomorrow night? I know we're out here in the boondocks, but she'll make your favorite — chicken pot pie."

I couldn't help but laugh because chicken pot pie was what Kathy always served when I came to dinner, whether I wanted it or not.

"You want some home-cooked food?" I asked Jennifer.

"I think that would be great, if one extra is okay."

I knew Jennifer's coming was implied. "Sounds like a date." I paused, then got to the point. "Can we go to your study? I've got some stuff to show you."

"You know the way. I'll grab some beers."

Once Ethan entered, I spread out both e-mail messages, one repeatedly folded and stained, the other a fresh computer printout.

"Haji, this is what we need translated. We

got these from two different e-mail accounts. It's terrorist related, but we don't really know how."

He picked up the first sheet, spending a few minutes studying it. Placing it down, he picked up the second sheet. After about fifteen seconds, he placed it back down and returned to the first sheet, walking around the room and studying it.

I finally got fed up. "Well, what's it say?"

Ethan snapped out of his trance, looking at us like he didn't know where we'd come from. After a pause, he said, "Okay, one is clearly some sort of terrorist message. It talks about killing infidels and other things. The other is simply an invitation to coffee, with an address."

I already knew that one was terrorist related but was surprised at the other translation.

"What's the address? Is it in Norway?"

"It doesn't have a country listed, but it's a coffee shop somewhere in Europe. The verbiage is a direct phonetic translation, and isn't American. The meeting occurred today at thirteen hundred."

"What's the other message say? The first one?"

"Well, it's pretty ominous, but it's something I read every single day in chatter we get fed, so don't freak out."

"Yeah, yeah. The difference here is that I've met them; I know they're trying to kill people. I just don't know how. What's it say?"

"Here's what I *think* it says: 'Operation Badr will exceed our expectations. We no longer will strike the far enemy in his homeland. We came upon a weapon that will push the Zionists into the sea at the same time it causes the far enemy to destroy the Persians. Praise Allah, we will rejoice when all infidels are destroyed because of this, leaving us with the assurance of the Caliphate. Please reply, telling us this path is blessed, or tell us what to do next.' Is that what you expected?"

"Yeah, something like that. What do you make of it? What's an Arabic mind saying when it says that?"

"Well . . . I'm not an Arab. I'm not really keen on telling you what I think because I'm probably wrong."

"Haji, cut the shit. I'm not a robot. I already know what *I* think. I'd like to hear what *you* think. I'm not going to run off shooting people because of it. You're an analyst, for Christ's sake. This is what you do."

Ethan held up his hands. "Okay, okay . . . Starting right off, they reference the Battle of Badr, the first significant defeat of Meccan forces by Muhammad, which led to Islam taking over the Arabian Peninsula way back when. Going further, this is clearly an AQ message. The references to the far enemy and the Caliphate point to that. Getting to the meat, in my mind, these guys have a weapon and they intend to use it on Israel. That, in itself, isn't unusual. Every Arab with a firecracker says that sort of thing. In this case, I don't think these guys believe they have a firecracker. I think they have a weapon that is dangerous enough to cause a phenomenal re-action, something designed to cause the Israelis to really, really go nuts.

"Okay. So far I'm tracking. That's about what I thought. What about the Persian com-ment? I couldn't make heads or tails of that. What do you think he's saying there?"

"Honestly, that part's a little disturbing. I'm not sure, but it could mean that the weapon will be blamed on Iran, causing Israel to attack them. The second order of effect for that, of course, would be that we would support Israel, drawing us in to a war with Iran. The end result, in the mind of the guy who wrote this . . ." He paused, looking at me. "Understand, I'm not saying this would happen, but I think they want to start the clash of civilizations everyone blabs about. They want to start a true holy war, using Israel as the bad guy. We'd be forced to defend Israel in any attack against Iran; and all other Arab states, because it's Israel doing the attacking, would be forced to choose sides. There's no question whose side they'll choose."

Ethan stopped, thinking about what he had

just said. "Man, this could actually work. If they could blame the Iranians for a serious attack, especially with the nutcase in charge constantly talking about destroying Israel, it probably would start a chain reaction that would lead to a global fight between the Christian and Muslim worlds."

He paced back and forth for a second. "Do you really think that such a weapon is real? Do you think these guys really found something in Guatemala?"

"I don't know. I'm inclined to think they did, since a couple of indigs died on her uncle's expedition, and these guys have made arrangements to meet someone to continue on whatever journey they think they're on. If they failed in finding a weapon, or if the weapon wasn't real, why continue?"

"Shit, this is bad news. What're you going to do?"

"I'm not going to do anything. I'm going to pass everything you just said to the Taskforce. Kurt should contact me tomorrow. What you could do, if you don't mind, is simply reinforce what I'm going to say. I'll tell Kurt everything I have, but you know what my reputation is. He might blow me off, and I wouldn't blame him. Either way, this is a problem for the Taskforce, not for me."

Ethan mulled over his options. Finally, he said, "Yeah, I can do that. I don't know how soon I'll see the boss — you remember his schedule — but I'll certainly tell him when I see him."

Ethan stood at the door until they drove off. Once they were out of sight he went to the telephone to call Domino's for the second time that week. Before he dialed, he thought about Pike's visit. He picked up the handset, calling the Taskforce duty officer instead.

## 71

Mason hung up the cloned cell phone. Picking up the clean duty phone, he called Lucas.

"We got a hit. Pike was visiting a guy named Ethan Merriweather tonight."

"Is he still there?"

"No. He left. The man on the phone says that Pike talked about interesting stuff, and just wanted to relay that. Want to do anything with this?"

"Yeah. Alert the team. Tell them to get in as fast as possible. While we're inbound, figure out everything you can on this Ethan Merriweather. Find out where he lives and do a quick analysis of the area. I don't want to waste any time when we get to the office. Give us a target dump on both the man and his location."

"You got it. Anything specific you want me to hone in on?"

"Yeah, figure out if this guy's a badass as well. Check his military background. I guarantee he has one."

"Roger that. See you in thirty minutes."

It took Mason all of ten minutes to get a complete background on Ethan, to include his address, family members, and the last time he had paid his electric bill.

Thirty-two minutes later he was briefing the assembled team.

"The target is a thirty-four-year-old Caucasian male. His MOS is 96B, intel analyst. He is currently working in J3 Special Operations Division at the Pentagon. He's airborne qualified, but that's it as far as specialized schooling we care about. Basically, he's your standard intel weenie. No known firearms, no bills being paid to 'Johnny's house of jujitsu,' nothing dangerous at all.

"He has a wife and two children, both girls; ages eight and eleven. Of note, he does have a dog, but I couldn't determine a breed. All I could find were some vet bills for various things, which leads me to believe the dog is getting on in years."

Moving to the next slide in the presentation, Mason continued the briefing, covering the neighborhood and the house where Ethan lived in detail. When he finished, he turned the briefing over to Lucas.

Standing up, Lucas said, "This is pretty straightforward. We simply need this Ethan to tell us where to find Pike. Once we have that information, terminate whoever is in the house. Don't do it before we have the information, since you might need to use the wife or children for persuasion on the target."

Randy, one of the SF men, cut in. "What's our authorized level of persuasion? What if he refuses to talk?"

"There is no limit. Make him talk. Does anyone here have any qualms about that?"

The team looked around at each other, but nobody said a word.

"If you look at the team, you'll see the only two missing from the Fort Bragg op are Carl and Alan. When push came to shove, they didn't have the stomach for the work. Almost caused mission failure right when we were culminating."

Lucas made eye contact with each member of the team. "Does anyone have any qualms about terminating the wife and kids? No judgments here, not everyone can do this kind of work. If that's you, say so now, before we launch."

Once again, nobody said anything.

"Okay. Spend ten minutes figuring out how you want to tackle this problem. No more than that. It's pretty straightforward and the trail's getting colder every second we sit here. For all we know, Pike and the girl are already driving to another city. I expect you guys to be on the road in fifteen minutes."

# 72

I rolled over, groggy and unsure of what had awakened me, the noise blending in to my semiconscious dream. I realized my cell phone was ringing and snatched it up before whoever was calling could hang up, knowing it was either a wrong number or Kurt.

"Hello?"

"Pike, is that you?"

"Yeah, who's this?"

"It's Kurt. We need to meet. You went to Ethan Merriweather's house last night?"

"Yes, sir, I did, but it was simply to get all the facts before I talked to you today. I didn't do anything —"

"Ethan's dead," Kurt said, "I need to talk to you right now."

I was wide-awake now. "What? What the fuck are you talking about? I just saw him."

"I'm not going to talk on a cell phone. Let's do this face-to-face."

I stopped my questions. "When and where?"

"It's now about nine forty-five."

I fumbled for my watch, thinking that surely couldn't be right, but it was. Jennifer and I had decided just to sleep in until we woke up, but I never figured we'd both be out until this late in the morning. I must have been more tired than I thought.

Kurt continued talking. "I have to clean up a few things and make sure efforts are tracking over here. Meet me at eleven at Four Courts."

"I'll be there."

"Don't be late. I won't have a lot of time and I need to figure out what the hell's going on."

"I won't be late. I'm staying a hundred feet from a Metro stop."

I hung up the phone, my head spinning over what I had just heard. *Haji dead? He was healthy as a horse. Did he have a heart attack or something? Get hit by a car? Surely this had nothing to do with our visit. Did it?*

There wasn't any sense in trying to figure it out without any facts. I could sort it out with Kurt in an hour.

As I began putting on my clothes, the ramification of what Kurt had said finally hit home. *Haji was dead.* Having had multiple friends die in combat since 9/11, I understood the grieving process at the graduate level, but it didn't make it any easier. I had a hollow feeling inside, something I knew would bounce around for a long time, slowly diminishing until it only appeared when something triggered a memory of Ethan.

I remembered Kathy and the kids, wishing I had seen them last night. They would need support right now. I was sure the Taskforce was on that. They were very, very good about taking care of the families of fallen soldiers. Even so, I wanted to help, and wished the first time I was to see Kathy would not have been in the wake of Ethan's death.

In Crystal City, Lucas's team was gearing up for another run at Pike and Jennifer. Even though last night hadn't paid off immediately, it looked like it had worked in the end.

Lucas's research assistant was furiously working the computer to gather all data on "Four Courts" and hotels near Metro stops in the D.C. area.

Lucas was giving instructions while the men got their kit on and equipment organized.

"We know they're taking the Metro, which means they'll be walking to the linkup. We'll need a trigger position outside. We'll set up two shooters at Four Courts" — Lucas paused, staring at his research assistant — "wherever the hell that is — hurry the fuck up, Jerry."

"I got it, I got it. It's an Irish pub in Clarendon, right across from the Arlington Courthouse. I'm doing a quick scan of the surrounding area."

Lucas continued. "The two shooters there will be the primary killers. They'll be located at the nearest cover and concealment from the pub. Two others will be mounted in a vehicle. On the trigger's call, they'll approach and conduct a random drive-by shooting. The intent is twofold: One, camouflage the killing of the girl and Pike. To that end, you need to spray rounds loud and long. Two, to drive Pike and the girl into the real shooters. At the first shot of the drive-by, Pike will immediately take cover, moving to the nearest alley or other protected position. That's where the primary shooters will be located.

"Make sure you all take the same caliber of weapon. I don't expect a full-on ballistics check, but the cops will think something's funny if three innocent civilians are killed by a nine-mil in a random drive-by, while two others are dead from forty-cal fire."

Mason cut in. "Why not just smoke them with the drive-by? Make it simple?"

"If you can kill them from the car, so much the better, but I'm not counting on it. This guy's good and will probably be able to get out of the line of fire. I'm counting on his survival instincts to get his ass. Mason, you're the trigger. You need to pick them up at the Metro and follow them to Four Courts. More than likely that means the Orange Line stop by the Arlington Courthouse. Don't get compromised. Remember, this guy probably has spider sense. Do everything by the book. Use your judgment on when to make the call for the drive-by team. Jerry, you ready? We need to do some timing analysis."

Jerry turned on the overhead. "Yeah, I'm ready."

He pulled up a Google Earth image of Clarendon, Virginia, with several markers embedded. Using a laser pointer as if he were about to discuss stock prices, he began, giving a complete overview of the target area. From there, the team spent the next fifteen minutes coming up with a hasty plan, using the skeleton they had created the day before. Once all the questions and answers had been exhausted, and everyone was comfortable with his respective role, Lucas took back over.

"We're out of time. Any other questions? I know this is fast, but that's why you guys are making the big money." When no one spoke, he said, "Let's saddle up."

# 73

Hearing a soft knock on her door, Jennifer woke up. She saw Pike standing in the connecting doorway, the light from his room showing he was dressed.

She stretched, saying, "Where're you going? What's up?"

"Kurt called. He wants to meet right now."

"Well, that's good, isn't it?"

Pike hesitated, not sure how to break the news. He decided just to say it.

"Ethan's dead. He died last night."

Jennifer brought her hand to her mouth. "Oh, my God. What happened?"

"I don't know. I'm hoping to get some answers from Kurt. I'm headed to Clarendon to see him." He paused again. "I have to go alone. I'm going to be talking about a lot of old unit business. Kurt won't talk with you there."

"That's it? You tell me a man I met last night is dead, then switch gears to the meeting with Kurt? What about Ethan's family?

Have you talked to them?"

"I haven't talked to anybody. I just found out ten minutes ago. Anyway, nobody will contact the family until the family lets the Taskforce know it's okay. I've been here before. Some wives want a lot of support; some just want to be left alone. Once that's sorted out, we can do whatever we think's best. I've got to go."

"Don't you think we should be doing something to help out his family? I don't even know them and I feel like I should help."

"Please don't fight me on this. There's nothing we can do right now. I'm not doing anything until I talk to Kurt. This might have something to do with our visit."

"*What?* What do you mean by that?"

Pike backtracked, sitting next to her on the bed. "It's just a big damn coincidence, is all. Look, you have to trust me on this. I can't stay. I'm running behind as it is. Please don't leave the hotel. I'll be back in probably two hours."

Pike exited to the hallway through her door, not returning to his room. Jennifer sat on the bed in a little bit of a daze, still absorbing what he had said. It didn't seem real. Outside of going to a funeral for her grandmother, and one high school friend who died in a car crash, Jennifer had had little experience dealing with mortality. Now it seemed like death was stalking her everywhere she went. Whatever she touched turned to ash. *Why would Ethan be dead?* It wasn't fair. He had a wife and a family. He didn't do anything to deserve this. *But neither had Uncle John. Or Pike when he lost his family.* She closed her eyes. *Please don't let it be because of me. Please, please.*

Her mind clicked on where Pike was headed, snapping her eyes back open. He might think Kurt was a peach of a guy, but she wasn't so sure. Yeah, Pike was a one-man wrecking crew, but what if he was moving into a trap laid by a bunch of guys just as good as him? He wouldn't even recognize it because of the trust he placed in the Taskforce. She grabbed her phone and dialed his number. She listened to it ring in her ear, then realized she could hear it ringing in his room as well. She jumped out of bed and went to his room through the connecting door. She saw his phone on the nightstand next to his bed.

"Damn it!"

She ran back to her room, ripping through her clothes in an attempt to get dressed before he got on the elevator. She left the room barefooted, running to the foyer, but Pike had already gone down.

Heading toward Clarendon, I realized I had run out of the hotel so hastily I'd left without my cell phone. *Stupid, stupid mistake.*

Not only could Kurt not contact me for anything, such as changing the meeting time or location, but I couldn't make sure that Jennifer was safe. I thought about returning for it, but knew I didn't have the time. If I missed this meeting with Kurt, I might not get another chance.

By the time I got to the Orange Line I saw I was running late, causing me to worry about missing Kurt. He had stressed he had little time. *Should've never gone into Jennifer's room.* I paced back and forth, staring at my watch every few seconds like that would speed things up. Finally, the train arrived.

Luckily, the Court House stop was the first one past Rossyln. I exited the train at a trot. Glancing at my watch, I saw it was 11:03. *Shit. Kurt's probably already called. Probably leaving Four Courts right now.* I broke into a run.

Exiting the Court House stop I could see the Four Courts pub about a hundred meters away on Wilson Boulevard. Two people were outside it, neither of them Kurt. If he had left in the last couple of minutes, I should be able to see him. *Maybe he's still there.* I waited for the light to change, allowing me to cross the street. After two seconds, I had had enough of waiting. A break in traffic presented itself, and I sprinted across. I continued to the entrance at a fast walk, straining to see if Kurt left the pub.

My attention was jerked to the street by a car swinging onto Wilson Boulevard at a high rate of speed, tires squealing fast enough to produce smoke. I saw the car immediately slow down, the right side window lowering.

I watched a man wearing a ski mask stick his head out, looking like an IRA terrorist in Belfast. *What the hell?* I stopped walking, processing the scene and preparing to react. The man stuck a Heckler and Koch MP5 out the window, aiming it at a couple to my front. He let the MP5 rip, spraying the front of Four Courts with rounds. Both the man and woman were hit instantly, spinning and falling to the ground.

Time stretched out, moving at half speed. I assessed my options and realized I was in serious trouble. I was standing in front of the plate-glass window of Four Courts with no protection in sight, nothing at all to stop the rounds that were about to tear into me. I knew my best bet was an alley to my rear about thirty feet away, but from the time of the first round until now, I computed that I wouldn't make it there before I was hit.

The man was still spraying rounds on full automatic, the bullets shattering the plate glass to my front, stitching toward me like a sewing machine. I saw the man's gun hand begin to lose control from the recoil, giving me a sliver of hope. The car continued forward at a slow rate of speed, only fifteen feet away. *Take him head-on.* If I was wrong, I was dead. I launched myself at the vehicle, watching the man's eyes widen as he saw me coming. He tried to swing the weapon directly at me instead of shooting rounds at the front of the building. I beat him by the blink of an eye. Just as the weapon was about to cross my body, I closed my hands on it.

Jerking upward, I tried to rip the MP5 out of the man's hands, the weapon cycling with the rounds blasting skyward, inches from my head. The man fought me to regain control, and almost succeeded, when his driver decided to accelerate, causing the weapon to be wrenched out of his hands. The car hurtled forward with its tires squealing again.

I watched the vehicle race away, then scanned for any other danger. I caught movement over my right shoulder and trained my weapon on the threat. A man was exiting the alley I had passed on my way to the pub. The same alley I had been going to use for cover. He had a pistol in his hand and was looking for a target. I let loose with the remaining rounds in the MP5's magazine, chipping the bricks around him and forcing him to retreat back down the alley.

The air was split by the sound of sirens approaching. I looked at the couple shot earlier, seeing the man sitting up holding his shoulder. The woman lay on her back, rolling left and right, her abdomen sprouting a red stain, dripping on the concrete. I knew I should help them, but had to make a hard choice. My conscience screamed for me to stay, but the man in the alley told me this wasn't random, and that I was the target. I decided to leave the scene. I dropped the weapon and took off at a dead sprint back to the Metro station across the street.

## 74

Two blocks away, Lucas was on an encrypted radio trying to get a handle on what had occurred. "What's the status? What happened?"

Mason came through first. "The target came alone. The girl wasn't with him. He didn't give me time to set up. He came out of the Metro at a dead run. I didn't have time to give the mounted team a warning order. By the time I called, he was almost at the pub. The mounted team was forced to rush, alerting the target that they were coming before they could engage."

The mounted team cut in. "The psycho didn't run for cover like you said. He ran right at us. He grabbed my weapon right out of my fucking hand. We were forced to exfil."

Lucas cursed. If they were lucky, Pike would think it was a random drive-by. That would be a break, but wasn't assured. The hope was crushed by the next call.

"This is shooter one. I saw what occurred with the mounted team. I tried to get a clean shot but was compromised. He suppressed my fire with the weapon from the mounted team." Shooter one's clinical description broke down. "He came close to fucking killing me. I didn't get off a shot."

Lucas dropped his mike in frustration. Pike definitely knew it was a setup now, and that he was being hunted. *Shit. This operation just went from easy to almost impossible.* Picking up his cell phone, he called Jerry. "Did you find the hotel they're at? Next to the Metro?"

"Lucas, there are about five hundred hotels next to Metro stations. There's no way I can neck it down without more information."

Kurt tore out of the Four Courts pub, trying to ascertain what had occurred. Seeing no sign of Pike, he moved immediately to the wounded civilians, honing in on the woman as the most seriously hit.

"You'll be okay. Help's on the way," he said, conscious of approaching sirens. He began initial first aid, checking her airway and putting direct pressure on her wounds as an ambulance screamed to a halt beside them. Paramedics leapt out to conduct triage.

Kurt told them what he knew, then walked away before he got tied up by the police. He pulled out his cell phone and called Pike's number. At the sound of a woman's voice, he was about to disconnect, thinking he had a wrong number. Then he remembered.

"Jennifer?"

"Yes. Who's this? Where's Pike?"

"This is Kurt. I don't know where Pike's at. Where are you? You're not with him?"

Jennifer's voice grew alarmed. "No, I'm at the Embassy Suites. Pike left to meet you alone over forty-five minutes ago. What did you do to him?"

"Me?" He was shocked by the question. "For Christ's sake, why would I do anything to him? Jennifer, listen to me. Get out of the hotel now. Don't even bother packing. Get out — go somewhere safe. Do it now. Write this number down" — he read out his cell number — "call me when you're safe. Let me know where you are."

It took several more attempts before she took him seriously, testing his patience. "Get out, Jennifer," he repeated, "every second is dangerous."

"But Pike —"

"Leave him a note that only you and he would understand. But get out. *Now!*"

Jennifer's voice grew cold. "I hear you. I'm leaving. I'll do as you say, but if you've done anything to Pike . . . if he's hurt . . . I'm going to fucking *destroy* you. I don't know how, but I will."

Lucas had regained control of his team, reconsolidating in an empty parking lot eight miles away from the failed hit. He was running his options through his mind when his phone rang.

"Yeah, what do you have?"

Jerry was breathless. "They're staying at the Embassy Suites in Old Town Alexandria. The girl's there now but was just told to leave. Pike doesn't have his cell phone. The girl has it. He doesn't know she's been told to leave. I'm sure he's headed back there, but he only has the Metro. If you hurry, you can get both of them. Worst case, you'll only get him."

Lucas grinned, immediately barking out commands. "They're at the Embassy Suites in Old Town. Mounted team go there immediately. Stake out the lobby and try to find the girl. She's probably already gone, but it's worth a shot. You other four head to the King Street Metro station. Pike's headed back. Pick him up when he gets off the Metro. Once you have him in sight, call the Embassy Suites team. He'll be headed that way. Close on him and finish the job. We can find the girl later, if necessary."

Riding back on the Metro, my mind was running nonstop, trying to figure out what had just happened. I could come up with only one answer: Dr. Evil did exist and his name was Kurt Hale.

Earlier I had decided that didn't make sense, because Kurt wouldn't kill Ethan. I then realized that I didn't even know if Ethan was dead. All I knew was that Kurt had said so. Now it looked like he had said it to keep my mind occupied on Ethan's death instead of looking for threats. Every other fact pointed to Kurt.

Only one person knew where I was going, and that was Kurt. In fact, it was Kurt who had set the meeting up. Kurt had said he needed to straighten out some things because of Ethan's death, but if Kurt really had set this up, then Ethan was alive, and Kurt had used that time to set up his trap instead.

The thought sickened me to my core. The Taskforce was an anchor I had placed my entire trust within. If Kurt could do this, then there was no such thing as good. The world was just a mess of gray. I knew that Kurt wasn't inherently evil, but nothing else explained what had occurred. It wasn't a bunch of amateurs who had attacked me, but guys who knew what they were doing. I had to have been under surveillance to trigger the drive-by, surveillance that I had failed to notice because I was conveniently thinking about Ethan's death and the meeting with Kurt. The shooter in the alley was the final touch. It was clear that the drive-by shooter was simply the sweeper, designed to push me into the alley, and certain death. It was a miracle it hadn't worked. Had I been five feet closer to the alley, I would have immediately sought it out, looking backward at the drive-by shooter, not forward into the alley.

The more I thought about it, the more I began to build into a rage, feeling the anger grow white-hot. For the first time, wanting it white-hot. Savoring the feeling.

Kurt must have set us up in the Homeland Security database. When that didn't work, Kurt had used my loyalty to the Taskforce as a weapon to kill me. Kurt must have also turned off the CIA from investigating anything further in Belize. Few people in the U.S. government had the power to do all of that, and Kurt Hale was one of them. I was just lucky I had come alone. If Jennifer had been there, I would have reacted differently, and we'd probably both be dead.

I felt an electric jolt of adrenaline. *Jennifer's alone at the hotel.* I racked my brain, trying to remember if I had told Kurt where we were staying. I didn't think so, but I might have. I looked at my watch, wishing the train would move faster. I settled back into the seat, letting the rage flow through me, raw and thumping. If Kurt did anything to Jennifer, I was going to burn the Taskforce down.

The four men Lucas had assigned to the Metro station entered and fanned out to positions that allowed them to dominate the platform without being seen. One, surveying the crowd simply out of curiosity, honed in on a woman across the tracks, waiting for the

467

Metro going the other way. He keyed his covert radio.

"Brandon, look at the woman to your three o'clock. I think it's the target."

Brandon studied the woman. She was acting antsy and pacing back and forth. She carried a laptop case and a backpack that looked stuffed. "Yeah, that's her. Stand by. I'm calling for guidance."

Brandon dialed Lucas's cell. "Sir, this is the Metro team. I've got the female target here preparing to board a train. Do you want us to remain behind for the male, or follow her?"

Lucas paused a moment, considering. He went with the bird in the hand. "Follow her. As soon as you get the chance, terminate her. Make sure you can get out clean before you pull the trigger."

"Roger that. Train's coming. Gotta go."

Brandon called the team. "Board the northbound train. She's the new target. We stick with her until we can smoke her. Hurry, I can see the train approaching. Get to the other side."

They raced back downstairs, moving under the tracks, then back upstairs to the northbound side. All four members just managed to board before the doors closed. None noticed Pike exit the train on the southbound side.

■ ■ ■ ■

In the lobby, Mason had just answered a call
·from Lucas when he saw Pike blow by him
to the elevator.

Lucas was finishing up telling Mason the
new plan. ". . . so they won't be able to give
you early warning. They're on the girl now.
When he gets there —"

Mason interrupted. "He's here. He just
went by me to his room. We can't do anything
in here. All the rooms look into a giant
atrium. We can't even get to his room without
anyone seeing us, much less break in. We're
going to have to wait."

Lucas thought for a moment. "Okay. That's
not bad. He'll either head to the other target,
or she'll come back here. I'm betting he
heads to her. Hold what you got and tail him.
I'll coordinate with the other team. If you
guys meet in the middle we can finish this
thing. Don't wait for that, though. You get a
chance, kill that bastard."

# 75

I went through my room into Jennifer's. It was empty. All of her clothes were gone and so was the laptop. I went back to my room. For the first time, I noticed that all of *my* clothes were gone as well. I saw my cell phone where I had left it, only now it was sitting on a piece of paper. Picking it up, I read,

> Kurt called. I'm going to the place I went to yesterday. I'll be getting a bite to eat. Call me when you get this.

I smiled for the first time that morning. *Smart girl.* She was going to the most crowded place she could find, and she had managed to tell me exactly where without writing it down. She would be in the food court at the bottom of the mall. I didn't like the fact that Kurt had called, but hopefully she would be safe until I could get there. Kurt clearly just wanted to get her out of the hotel so he could kill her. He probably didn't count on me still being alive.

I picked up the phone and dialed Jennifer. She answered on the first ring. "Pike? Is that you?"

*Thank God.* More relief than I thought I had in me coursed through my body. I put on a calm voice.

"Yeah. How're you? Are you okay?"

"I think so. I just got off the Metro. Kurt called and told me to get out of the hotel. He left his number and told me to call him when I was out and safe somewhere."

*That fucker.* "You haven't called, have you?"

"No, not yet."

"Don't. Just go where you told me you were going. I'm on my way. Do not call Kurt."

"Pike, what's going on? I'm scared. I think someone's following me. I keep seeing the same guy. He jumped on the Metro at the last minute, and now he's been thirty feet behind me ever since. I don't want you to think I'm paranoid, but I think it's real."

I spoke slowly and clearly. "I think it's real too. Stay in crowded areas. Don't pay him any attention. If he thinks he's burned, he'll either do something drastic or be replaced by someone else. Better to know who's following you than to have to figure it out. Move to where you said you would meet me. Anybody tries anything, kick them as hard as you can in the balls, then run off screaming. Run in a zigzag pattern. I'm on the way. Can you do that?"

I heard her take a deep breath. "Yeah . . . Yeah, I can do that. I'm not going to ask why the zigzag pattern. I don't want to know what you're going to say."

"Don't worry. I'm coming. Hold tight. I'll be there in minutes."

In the courtyard of the atrium, Mason saw Pike leave the room three floors up. He called his teammate. "Get ready. He's coming down."

The man was just outside the elevator exit, waiting. He watched Pike exit and head to a stairwell.

"He's not going to the Metro. I say again, he's not going to the Metro."

Mason cursed. "Stay on him."

"He's going to the parking garage. If I go into the stairwell with him, I'm burned."

"Hold on. Sit tight. Let him go. He spots you and we're going to have a gunfight right here. Don't take him on one-on-one. Remember, he took an MP5 from the mounted team this morning."

Mason thought about his options. He decided he needed to punt to his higher headquarters. He called Lucas and relayed the news.

In the Crystal City office, Lucas took the call, feeling punched in the gut with the latest report. *Jesus. Predicting this guy's actions is proving impossible.* He knew that he was now going to have to earn his salary. The hard way. It pissed him off. *Screw drinking a beer with him. Prima-donna SMU asshole. When I get him I'm going to castrate his sorry ass.*

"Let him go. Head back to the office. We need to regroup. This seat-of-the-pants shit isn't working."

I parked the rental and entered the mall. Standing at the railing of the first level, I looked down into the basement level of the food court, spotting Jennifer. I knew that if she'd seen one man, there were several more. Nobody with any training tried to conduct surveillance alone, and these guys had training. I gave her a call, watching as she answered.

"Hello?"

"It's me. I'm in the mall. Don't look around, but I'm looking at you right now." I saw her raise her head and couldn't resist teasing her. "I said don't look around! . . . Just kidding. . . . Listen, I need you to —"

"Jesus, Pike, this isn't a joke!" she said, speaking in a fierce whisper. "Come get me! The man I saw is directly behind me. He's been sucking on that small Coke for twenty minutes."

I spoke in soothing tones. "Okay, okay, slow down. Everything's just fine now. I need to identify who else is with that guy. I need you to get up and walk toward the stairwell to your left front. Just casually get up and walk that way, going up the stairs. Don't rush."

I watched the crowd. As soon as Jennifer began moving, a man to her right front stood up, moving with her, slightly behind. *One.* I watched Coke man. Coke man looked over at another man, who rose as well, moving toward the stairs ahead of Jennifer. *Two.* Jennifer was halfway up the stairs, one man in front, one man behind, when Coke man rose. *Three.* He must be the last one. I faded into a store.

I called Jennifer. "You have three of them on you. We've got to slim it down. I need to get you with just one guy. Go into a store for a little bit to give me time to set up. I'll call back in a minute."

I heard a little panic in her voice. "Wait! Don't hang up. I don't know who they are. They might kill me here."

"Jennifer, trust me. They won't do anything here. If they were going to, they would've already done so. As long as they think you don't know they're on you, they'll be content to follow. If you push them, they might try something to keep you from running. You'll be all right. It's almost over. Go drool over some shoes or something."

She waited a second before answering. "Pike, you're an asshole. Don't wait too long to call, or I might run just to make you work."

"I'll only be a minute. I'm sure they're

wondering who you're talking to, so act like this's nothing. One more call and we're done. Hang in there."

I hung up and sprinted to the nearest anchor store, a Macy's. Taking the escalator stairs two at a time, I exited on the second level. Looking around, I thought it would work. I could put my back to the elevator next to the escalator exit and not be seen by anyone coming up.

I gave Jennifer a final call.

"Hey, here we go. This is the endgame. I need you to go to Macy's. Take the escalator up to the second level. The escalator will act as a funnel. They'll hang back, so that by the time you exit you should have only one man on you, with the other two staggered behind. Exit the escalator and turn left. I'll be right there, so don't jump. Just walk on past into the store. I'll do the rest. Got it?"

"Yeah. I got it. I act like I'm shopping and you kick their ass. I think I can do that. You sure this'll work? What if two follow?"

"Then I'll improvise, but these guys are pretty switched on. I don't think they'll pull any amateur shit. Key here is to move naturally. These phone calls have got to be making them antsy. Don't act like you've got some sort of instructions to do something. Whatever you do, don't look down while on the escalator or look back while walking. You ready?"

"Yeah. See you in a couple of minutes. I'm moving now."

I pressed myself into the small opening for the elevator door and waited. Four minutes later, Jennifer exited, walking by me at a natural pace, looking like a shopper who didn't have a care in the world. She didn't so much as give me a glance, making me think she had missed me. Then I noticed she was giving me an "A-OK" sign with her hand, her arm still swinging easily. I blinked. *Huh. Cool as a cucumber.*

I moved into a slight crouch, resting on the balls of my feet. Nine seconds later, I could hear the man following talking to someone on a radio. ". . . no, don't wait on me. If you have a clear opportunity to kill her and get away, take it."

*Damn. I missed someone. They must've had a floater in the mall.*

## 76

The man exited the escalator still giving instructions on his concealed radio, looking a little strange babbling into thin air. ". . . we'll link back up at the garage. Just remember, no gunfire. . . ." It was Coke Man. He saw me, the recognition causing his eyes to widen. ". . . holy shit . . ."

*Great last words.* I grabbed him by his shirt and whirled him around, pinning him against the elevator door. He immediately began to struggle, trying to tie up my arms. Before he could, I reached up with both hands and grabbed his head by the hair. I slammed it as hard as I could against the steel elevator support, hearing his skull crunch. I dropped him and took off in the direction Jennifer had gone, hitting redial as I went.

"Hey, I screwed up," I said. "They had a floater running around the mall and he's on you now. Get to a crowded area as fast as you can."

"I'll try. I took the first left and I'm in some

baby section. Nobody's here." She paused, then said, "Oh, shit. Pike, I looked back . . . I saw him . . . he knows I saw him . . . he's walking right at me. I can't get out of here without going by him."

I turned the corner and spied her about seventy-five meters away. The man following her was closing in at a fast walk, giving up any pretense of being a shopper. She was right. The only way out was through him. She was pinned in by a corner wall that opened up to a balcony on the third floor. Unfortunately, no shoppers were up there looking down. The killer would feel safe.

"I see you. I see you." *Too far away. I'm not going to make it.* At least the man hadn't started running at her yet, giving me precious seconds.

She said, "Get ready. I'm going to set this guy up for you."

*Huh? What the hell is she talking about?* "Jennifer, listen to me —"

Before I could say anything, she dropped our backpacks and the laptop and took off running toward the wall below the third-level balcony. The killer began sprinting, rapidly closing the distance to her. I dropped the phone and followed suit, running flat out, as fast as I could. *What the hell is she doing?* There was nowhere for her to hide or defend herself. The killer closed the distance to five feet just as Jennifer veered directly at the corner. *Now she zigzags.*

I was thirty feet back, unable to do anything to prevent the man from catching her. I was just about to scream to distract the man when Jennifer launched herself in the air. She planted one foot on the left wall of the corner and pressed off, rising another four feet. She repeated the sequence with her right foot and got high enough to grab the railing of the third-floor balcony. She pulled herself over the rail, leaving the killer looking up, stunned. *And alone.*

I sprinted right at him. He was two feet off the wall, his head cocked back, completely unaware that I was coming. *Wow. This is going to leave a mark.* I hit him just below the shoulder blades like an NFL linebacker, snapping his head straight back and driving him completely unprotected into the wall. I heard his ribs crack like dry kindling and felt a spray of blood from something damaged. When I dropped him, I saw his face was a gory mess. *Ouch.* I looked up and saw Jennifer, white as a bedsheet but smiling.

I smiled back, showing her that I thought this was just business as usual, although my face was probably white too. *Jesus, that was close.*

"Get your ass down here, spider monkey."

"I can't get down from here. Only up. Keep heading around the corner. There's a stairwell in back. Meet me there."

I ran back and gathered up my phone and our luggage, then ran in the direction she had indicated. I met her coming out the door. Knowing we were about five seconds from being seen by the other guys tracking her, I grabbed her hand and began dragging her toward the nearest exit.

"Come on, we aren't out of the woods yet."

We made it to the garage and the rental without getting spotted. I jumped into the driver's seat while Jennifer ran to the passenger side.

After closing her door, Jennifer leaned over and wrapped her arms around me in a fierce squeeze. She was trembling, adrenaline still coursing through her.

She said, "I thought you were dead or in the hospital. What happened? Why did Kurt call?"

I said, "Let's get the hell out of here while we still can. I'll tell you while we drive."

I started the car and exited the parking garage. "Before that, though, what on God's green earth was that Flying Wallendas bullshit back there? What were you going to do if you missed? Fall on top of his head?"

"No way was I going to miss. I told you, I used to do that stuff for a living. And somebody had to do something after your brilliant plan went to shit."

"Touché. So we had to flex a little bit. All

480

part of the strategy." I grinned at her. "I will say that was some pretty switched-on thinking back there. Scared me to death, but worked out very well."

I told her what had happened and my fears about the Taskforce.

Jennifer didn't seem to buy the theory. "You were the one that said it couldn't be the Taskforce. Now you think it is?"

"I can't come up with any other explanation."

"Why on earth would the Taskforce do that? What possible good would it do?"

"I have no idea, which is why I'm going to call Kurt right now. Where's his number?"

Jennifer got out the number and dialed the phone, handing it to me.

I heard Kurt answer and said, "Guess you missed, huh, asshole?"

"Pike, is that you? What happened at Four Courts? Where are you?"

"You'll find me soon enough, you son of a bitch. I still want to meet, but on my terms."

"What's your problem? What's going on?"

"My problem is that you tried to fucking kill Jennifer and me. I'm willing to meet so you can tell me why. I'm sure there's an incredibly good reason."

"Have you lost your mind? Why the fuck would I do that?"

"Cut the shit. You were the only one who knew where we were meeting. You fed me that

481

bullshit story about Ethan, then laid out the trap. I want to know why."

"Pike, Ethan is dead."

Kurt waited for me to say something, but his tone threw me off. He didn't sound like he was playing a role. When I didn't say anything, he continued.

"His whole family is dead. His older girl . . ."

"Emily."

"Yeah, Emily, was tortured to death. Both her eyes were punctured and four fingers were cut off from her right hand. Ethan himself was missing an ear and had all of the skin flayed from both of his thighs. The wife and other daughter were tied up and shot in the back of the head. This wasn't random. It had something to do with what you talked to him about."

What he said left me speechless. I tried to process it but couldn't.

"Pike? You still there?"

I refocused. "That's still just a story from you. I don't know it's true. All I know is that only one person on earth knew where I was going, and I walked into an ambush."

"There's another explanation. Either your phone or my phone is being monitored."

I considered this. "You still want to meet?"

"Yeah. Name the place."

"Meet me in ten minutes at the last place we saw Billy Donatelli. You aren't there in

482

ten minutes I'm gone. You come to that place, alone. If you're still a warrior, you'll feel a set of crosshairs on your skull. If I see anything strange at all, anybody attempting to set up a long-range shot or ambush, I'm *not* going to just leave. I'm going to let you get in position and then blow your head off. After you're dead, I'll leave. Is that understood?"

"Yes. It's understood. I'll be there. Don't turn the maintenance guy into the bogeyman."

I pulled into our destination, parking the car and hanging up the phone.

Jennifer looked around, confused. "What are we doing at Arlington National Cemetery? Where's the last place you and Kurt saw Billy?"

"Here. I was his troop sergeant major, Kurt was the commander of the Unit. He died in Iraq in 2004."

## 77

Kurt hung up the phone, realizing that Pike had picked the perfect meeting location. One, the reference to Billy was something that only he and Pike would know. Two, it was close enough to the Taskforce — only a mile as the crow flies — that Pike could force a very short timeline, thereby preventing Kurt from setting up any type of trap if he was so inclined. Three, Billy's grave would be in the middle of a vast expanse of white stones, no cover or concealment anywhere to hide a hit team. Four, the reservation was blanketed by patrols of either National Park rangers or military police, all investigating anything out of the ordinary in an attempt to prevent vandalism to the hallowed ground. Fifth, and perhaps most important, the location was sacred to both Pike and Kurt, and Billy's headstone would send a message that some things were worth more than whatever politics Pike believed Kurt was involved in.

Kurt grinned in spite of himself, wondering

how long it had taken Pike to think of it. *He's still the best under pressure.*

He hit the timer of his watch and set out at a trot to his car, yelling at the duty officer that he would be back in an hour.

Lucas and his team heard the entire exchange at the Crystal City office. Lucas knew there was no way to figure out where both of these guys last saw the man named Billy Donatelli. He would have to rely on the beacon embedded in Kurt's pager. One thing was for certain: With two men in the hospital for a cracked skull and broken ribs, and two failed attempts, he wasn't going to launch out of here at the first opportunity. Pike had proven that he could thwart even well-laid plans. Now that he knew he was being hunted, he would be treated like the threat he posed. *Should've pushed Standish on the collateral damage. Should've used a car bomb.*

I stood still, looking but not seeing the cross bearing Billy's name, my mind a thousand miles away on a combat action years ago.

When I looked up, Jennifer asked, "How did he die?"

"On an assault. Nothing big, nothing fancy. It was an assault like hundreds of others. This one happened to be a hornet's nest."

I changed the subject, not wanting to talk about it. "We need to find a hiding place so we can watch Kurt and whoever else might come in."

I saw a knoll with a copse of trees about eighty meters away. It looked down on the site of Billy's grave, with unobstructed views three hundred and sixty degrees. It would work.

"Come on, Kurt should be here soon. If anyone else is coming, they'll be first, and we need to be hidden."

Eight minutes later we watched a single individual advance to Billy's grave. I recognized Kurt's walk. Rolling over, I winked at Jennifer and said, "You see me drop, get out of here."

She rolled her eyes, muttering, "Asshole. If I had any sense . . ."

I lost the rest, running out to meet Kurt. Within two minutes, he convinced me that he was telling the truth, which gave me no small amount of relief. Finding out he had turned would reset what I knew about the United States government and what we stood for, and that would have been as bad as the trauma I felt when my family died. I was just now beginning to believe again that what I had done with my life was worthwhile. A betrayal by Kurt would have crushed that forever.

After calling Jennifer, we got in the rental and exited Arlington. I asked Jennifer to drive, letting Kurt and me sit in the back and sort out what the hell was going on.

Once outside of the Arlington complex, I told Kurt everything I knew. I ended with Ethan's analysis and the attempts on our lives.

"So, we definitely have two terrorists, probably still in Norway, who think they have a catastrophic weapon and are intent on using it. On top of that, some sorry sons of bitches here in the U.S. want to ensure they succeed." I waited a beat, then said, "Well, I'm finished. I think that's enough information to work on. I'm ready to get out of this business. How soon before you can launch the Taskforce?"

Kurt's expression gave me a sinking feeling. He appeared to be considering what to say, which meant it probably wasn't going to be good. When he finally spoke, it was like cracking open a rotten egg.

"Pike, look, I don't think there's anything the Taskforce can do about this. I can't just launch willy-nilly, whenever I feel like it. There's the Oversight Council to think about. This is more of a problem for one of the Special Mission Units."

I was speechless. I'd thought he was going to say he couldn't do anything for two or three weeks, not that he *wouldn't* do anything *at all*. I finally spit out, "What the hell are you saying? Terrorists are about to kill hundreds, if not thousands, of people. We may be on the verge of World War Three. Ethan was skinned alive for this information, and you're worried about some pissant council oversight?"

Out of the corner of my eye I saw Jennifer flinch at my statement, then stare into the rearview mirror trying to catch my eye. I ignored her.

Kurt caught the look, apparently realizing we were now treading on classified information in front of a civilian. He held up his hands. "Pike, calm down. You know how it works. That's the way it is, and I'm not going to talk about it here."

"Fuck that. Read her on later. She's lost her fucking uncle and about lost her own life for this. She's not going to run around spouting at the mouth, and I want an answer. I've earned an answer."

He said nothing for a minute, making up his mind. "All right. You *know* the answer. Our unit was not designed for and is not capable of a rapid-alert scenario. That's why the damn Delta Force exists. It takes us months to develop the infrastructure and cover to penetrate a sovereign country and take down a target without it being exposed as an American operation. We can't simply pick up and haul ass to Norway like an invasion force. It would compromise the unit."

"Who gives a shit? Jesus, what's more important? Four people have died already.

Two more were shot attempting to stop me from seeing you. I can't believe you wouldn't gladly throw the unit away to do this. I can't understand where you're coming from."

"Pike, it's more than the Taskforce. If we get compromised it will bring down the president. Not only that, but his entire administration, and would literally shock the nation to its core. Do-gooders would seize the opportunity to muzzle every other action against the terrorist threat. You think Internet wiretaps are hard to do now? After this, they won't exist at all. In fact, it's not hyperbole to say the best thing that could happen for Al Qaeda is for the Taskforce to be discovered in a foreign country killing terrorists. It would make Lillehammer look like a mild error in judgment."

I knew all about Lillehammer, and the irony wasn't lost on me that these terrorists had gone to the same country that caused Israel's Wrath of God operation to blow up in their face. In June of 1973, Israel had sent a hit team to the small town in Norway to kill Ali Hassan Salemeh, otherwise known as the Red Prince, the man responsible for the 1972 Munich Olympic massacre of Israeli athletes. Instead of getting him, they killed an innocent Moroccan waiter by mistake. Rapid police work uncovered the Israeli connection, with several of the agents being arrested before they could get out of the country. The repercussions were immediate and profound, starting with the permanent dismantling of the Wrath of God teams and ending with Israel being vilified on the world stage, compared to the very terrorists they sought to kill.

I didn't buy the argument. "Sir, I get where you're coming from, but there's a higher purpose here. Israel was simply conducting an attack based on revenge. We're trying to preempt a WMD attack, to save countless lives, for Christ's sake. It's not the same thing, even if we get compromised. The repercussions are worth it. Would you rather have World War Three or some egg on the president's face?"

"Pike, we don't even know if the WMD is real. All you have is what Ethan gleaned from a single paragraph. It doesn't make it fact." He paused for a moment, then his tone softened. "Look, I get that there's a threat out there, but the Taskforce isn't the correct tool to use against it. Let me get this information into the system. Let the CIA and the Special Mission Units handle it. That's what they do."

"Jesus Christ! You sound like all the jackasses that said the Taskforce doesn't need to exist. You *know* what happened with the first effort to create our unit. You put this information into the system and we're going to get our wheels spinning for weeks, until someone believes it's a true, distinct threat. You said it yourself. It's just a paragraph on a piece of paper and the word of a discredited operator. Nobody is going to take that seriously, and we don't have time to prove it. We can't waste a week developing corroborating evidence to convince the National Command Authority to launch. That bomb's going off before then."

I looked at Kurt to see if anything I said was registering. When I didn't get a response, I threw out my final trump card.

"In fact, because the Taskforce operates without constitutional constraints, we're the *only* element that can execute. Everyone else will be waiting on DEPORDS and presidential findings. Please. I'm begging here. Think about what you're saying."

"Pike, I have a greater obligation to the nation. If you had something besides simple extrapolation of what you *think* is going on, I might do something. I simply can't jeopardize the entire presidential administration and the future defense of the nation based on what you *think*."

I grunted, sick of the conversation.

"Get back to Arlington. Drop Kurt off," I said to Jennifer.

Turning back to Kurt, I said, "I'm not the only one who believes there's a bad fucking event coming. Someone tried very hard to keep me from talking to you. I guess they

491

could have spared all the death and destruction, since you don't give a damn in the first place."

I could tell the words stung, but Kurt held firm.

"What're you going to do now?"

"I'll go to Norway and save the fuckin' world by myself — without any help from your Taskforce."

"You can't get on a plane. You'll be arrested from the Homeland Security database."

That answer caused me to start swearing like a sailor and punching the seat in front of me.

Kurt put a hand on my shoulder. "Hold on. Look, I can't launch a force, but I can support you from here. I'll get you to Norway on one of our aircraft. Give me those e-mail addresses. I can have them monitored 24/7. You said you deleted the meeting message, right?"

That mollified me a little. "Yeah. It's gone. They couldn't have made that meet, so I'm thinking they're still hanging around waiting."

"Good. I'll keep an eye on the e-mails. When they set up a new meet, I'll relay the information to you. Give me an e-mail address."

I didn't have one. Jennifer turned around. "I have one. Will any address do?"

"Yeah, I don't care what it is."

Jennifer gave him a Hotmail address.

Kurt said, "Good enough. We'll monitor this 24/7 as well. If you need any analytical help, send us an e-mail."

Kurt reached into his pocket, pulling out his worldwide pager. "Here. If you find them, and confirm there is a weapon, use this. You remember how, right?"

"Yeah. I remember."

"You alert us back here, and I'll assume you've found something. I'll launch a team your way."

He held the pager in his hands, not yet passing it over. "Pike, I meant what I said. Don't press this button just because you believe something's going on. Don't use it for your own personal vendetta. Once I launch, and we get compromised, there's an even chance that the U.S. government is going to go through a seizure. Make sure it's worth it."

## 78

Kurt gave me the pager, saying, "One more thing. You really will be on the Impossible Mission Force for this one. You get caught, and you're going to be hung out to dry. You won't get any official sanction from here."

"I didn't expect it. I won't get caught. I haven't been yet."

We pulled into Arlington and switched to Kurt's car. We spent the majority of the time it took to drive to the Dulles FBO listening to Kurt set up an aircraft for me. Finally, it was done, and I got to ask about the men who had tried to kill us.

He said, "I've been thinking about that quite a bit, but really have no idea. Whoever it is has a lot of power, but all the people with power like that simply wouldn't do it. It doesn't make any sense to me. I can't even figure out why they would want a terrorist attack to occur in the first place. The whole thing is screwy. Anyway, it's no longer your concern."

"Huh? It's exactly my concern. They aren't trying to kill you. They're trying to kill Jennifer and me."

Kurt's face became hard. "That's not what I meant. You focus on the terrorists. I'll find out who killed Ethan and tried to kill you. Don't worry about them. They have ceased to exist. I can't bring back Ethan's family, but I promise you the men who did that will pay."

Out of the corner of my eye I saw Jennifer visibly blanch. I'd purposely not told her the grisly details of Ethan's family to spare her feelings, but she had now connected the dots between the body count and who was dead. Maybe realizing for the first time that doing the right thing had consequences outside of our control, and that the good guy doesn't always win.

Kurt continued, pulling into the general aviation section of Dulles, "Whatever you do, don't call my cell phone until I have it scanned. Those assholes are tracking either you or me, and I don't trust my own equipment at this stage. I've got the thing dismantled in my pocket right now."

We pulled into Signature Air at the Dulles FBO. He parked the car and turned around. "Well, I couldn't get you a junky airplane. All we have available at short notice is the rockstar bird."

I grinned. "Perfect. Nothing like riding in style."

Jennifer looked from me to Kurt, asking, "What's the rock-star bird? Are we flying on a Greyhound tour bus?"

"Better than that. It's a Gulfstream IV. Just like the rock stars use."

Then the second part of her question hit me.

"And 'we' aren't flying on it. I am. You need to head on back to Charleston and go back to school."

She was silent for a second, the words not sinking in. When they finally did, she exploded. "What? Bullshit! I'm going with you."

I glanced at Kurt for support.

He gave her a look I'd seen a hundred times. "We appreciate everything you've done, but let's face it, you're not capable of providing help here. Pike will work better alone, without having to worry about you. You don't have to go back to Charleston if you don't want to. I have some safe houses here in D.C. you can use for a while. You'll have the protection of the Taskforce until this thing is over."

That seemed to really piss her off. "You didn't even believe the story in the first place. You have all of this talent and resources at your disposal and you're sending Pike by himself. You don't have the right to even talk to me. I'm the one that figured this thing out.

496

I'm the one that got Pike to start this hunt. Me. Not you. All you've done is spit on our efforts, cloaking yourself in some bullshit tale of higher patriotism."

She ignored Kurt, turning her back to him and facing me. She looked into my eyes the same way she had when she asked me to go to Guatemala. I could see the hurt on her face, like I had broken her trust. *Surely she can understand that she's completely unprepared for this. It's not like we're going on a roller coaster ride and she's a quarter inch too short.* Her expression caused the twinge again, much stronger than before, making me want to end her pain. *Stop that . . . stay focused.*

She said, "I haven't been a liability. I've earned it. You can use me on this and you know it. They won't suspect a woman of anything."

I said nothing, conflicting emotions churning away. I considered the question, trying to leave my confusing, sorry-ass feelings out of it. Looking at it dispassionately, the truth of the matter was she had a point. I was already at a disadvantage for the work ahead. I had seen what the terrorists looked like when they mugged me, which meant they also knew what I looked like. *But they haven't seen Jennifer.* And she was right — the Arab's inbred prejudice against women might help us.

True, she wasn't a badass counterterrorist

commando, but she had the raw talent. Beyond the physical ability, which she had in spades, she was very good at solving problems under pressure. She had proved that less than an hour ago with her circus stunt in the mall. This trait, above all others, was prized in the Taskforce, and was the cut line that kept otherwise outstanding soldiers at the level below. With a modicum of internal talent, you could teach anyone to surgically shoot, run all night, or do hand-to-hand combat, but the ability to think on your feet and solve problems in real time was the prize. She had the mettle necessary for operations, only lacking the experience. She was a quick learner, though, and had gotten quite a bit of experience over the last few days. I made up my mind.

"She's not a liability. She's going."

Jennifer gave me a radiant smile, then turned and glared at Kurt.

Kurt exploded. "Have you lost your mind? She can't go. She's a damn civilian. She'll compromise the whole operation!"

"Sir, I appreciate your support, and your opinion, but you've already told me I'm hanging my ass out on my own. I'm also a civilian. It's my call, and I say she goes. I need the help. Unless you want to launch a team with me, that is."

Kurt grimaced but backed down. "You're going to be the man on the ground. Your call."

"Thanks. We'll contact you when we get in-country. What's the name of the corporation we're supposed to be flying with?"

He gave us both a down-and-dirty dump of the cover of the aircraft we would be on, ending with a caveat.

"Remember, you don't work for the corporation. You have nothing to do with the corporation. The plane is only stopping to refuel. You get off, and the plane flies away. You simply hitched a ride because you know someone who knows someone who got you a free seat. Happens all the time. You only need the cover story when you land. Once you're in-country, never mention the corporation again. You're tourists, or whatever else you want to be, but you're not connected to me."

Moving through the FBO to the flight line, I grinned. "Like old times. Except for that little 'you're on your own' thing."

Kurt wished us luck, holding his hand out to Jennifer. She graciously returned the shake.

He shook my hand, saying, "Look, I want to stop this as much as you do. Do what you do best and we can both rest easy."

I returned the handshake, feeling a little embarrassed at my outbursts earlier. "Sorry about yelling at you. I understand your position. I won't let you down."

I held his hand a little longer than necessary and locked eyes with him.

"Don't let me down either."

# PART
# FOUR

## 79

Inside his Crystal City office, Lucas closed out the tracking Web site in disgust. It had grown dark outside, and he wondered if he had missed the opportunity to take out his prey. The pager beacon had gone to Arlington National Cemetery, then had driven aimlessly about for the next couple of hours. It had finally stopped at the Dulles Fixed Base Operations center, where it had remained ever since. That meant one thing: the beacon, and presumably whoever was carrying it, had flown somewhere. Due to the length of time it had remained stationary, that flight was taking some time, either going across the country or out of it.

He picked up the phone to relay the bad news. When Standish answered, Lucas went secure and got right to the point.

"We missed both targets. The beacon signal itself has become stationary at Dulles, which leaves me to believe the targets are airborne moving to another location. Do you wish to proceed?"

For a moment he heard nothing but breathing on the other end, disgusting him. *Weasel can't make a decision. He'd last about eight seconds in combat.*

"Well, yes, I guess so," Standish said. "We need to get it done."

"Even if it means going to a foreign country? You willing to risk that?"

"Is that what they're doing?"

"I won't know until the beacon lands, but the last report was over four hours ago, so they're flying a long ways. What do you want me to do?"

"What have you done so far?"

Lucas proceeded to tell him about the lead they had gleaned from Ethan's phone call the night before, clinically using terms such as *asset information* and *neutralizing further exposure.* Before he could continue with the morning's events, Standish put two and two together and interrupted the conversation.

"Whoa! Wait a minute! Don't tell me you're involved in that multiple murder in Herndon. Lucas —"

"Yeah, that was me."

"Jesus Christ! They're calling it a Charles Manson copycat killing, for God's sake! They think a psycho gang's on the loose. Are you insane? Four people were fucking slaughtered. Tortured to death."

504

Lucas wanted to reach through the phone and rip out Standish's heart. *You coward. Just like everyone else. Want to get the job done, but don't have the balls for the work.*

"Listen to me, you self-righteous blowhard, you gave me my mission parameters and I'm still within them. I'm accomplishing the fucking mission. You don't like how I'm doing it, then you should've specified some restrictions beforehand. Now shut the fuck up and let me finish my situation report."

On the other end of the line, Standish felt sick to his stomach. Not because of the deaths in Herndon, but because of the possible exposure to himself. He was barely listening to the rest of Lucas's situation report, frantically going through all of the ties that connected them, when something Lucas said clicked, bringing him back into the conversation.

". . . So we were forced to exfil without terminating either target. From there we regrouped, waiting on contact from the asset's phone you gave me . . ."

*Holy shit. He did the drive-by shooting in Clarendon as well? That can't be right. No way is that right.*

"Wait . . . wait. Are you telling me you're also responsible for the shootout across from the Arlington Courthouse? You actually opened fire on a bunch of civilians?"

505

This time Lucas didn't shout. He spoke in a calm, deliberate manner. Standish recoiled from the venom he felt coming from the phone.

"I'll say this one more time. You gave me my parameters and my mission. I'm executing. You told me to ensure the hit wasn't traced to you, and *that's* why we did the drive-by. I'm following your lead. Don't question my methods again."

*He thinks he's in charge. I'm losing control.*

"Bullshit. You've *exceeded* my parameters. I told you that collateral damage had to be five or less. You killed four at the house in Herndon, then shot at least two at the courthouse, maybe more. You're *outside* my guidance, and my guidance stands. Is that understood?"

"Standish . . . there are two targets. A collateral damage of five per. That means I still have four to work with. Anyway, two of my guys are in the hospital because of your target, so I really don't give a shit about your damn *guidance* anymore. It's getting personal."

Standish couldn't believe how quickly the violence had escalated. He thought about telling Lucas to stand down but was afraid of his response. *He might ignore me altogether.*

"Okay, okay. I can see the miscommunication, but I'm the one in charge. I'm still the one funding this. You want to get him, the

506

only way you'll do it is with my money — and that comes with my oversight. Got it?" He waited on a response, the silence making him wonder if he'd already lost control.

"All right," Lucas answered, "as long as we understand each other."

"Continue with your report."

After Lucas had finished, Standish gave him the go-ahead to execute — even on foreign soil — but told him that no more collateral damage was to be tolerated. He hung up the phone, wondering if Lucas would bother to listen to him. *I'm going to have to do something about him when this is over. Too much exposure. Too much of a threat.*

## 80

After a solid day and night of heading inexorably eastward, Bakr exited the train station at Tuzla, Bosnia-Herzegovina. Weary down to his bones, he gathered his meager possessions and walked to the first taxi he could find. Speaking in halting English, Bakr asked for a cheap hotel somewhere downtown. The driver held up a finger, saying he knew just the place.

Driving east, toward the heart of downtown, the taxi traveled about two miles before stopping in front of a nondescript four-story concrete building with a Cyrillic sign in the front.

"Here. They treat you well here," he said.

Bakr thanked him and was surprised when the man butchered the phrase *Allahu Akhbar* in return.

Bakr stared at the man, smelling of liquor and smoking a cigarette, thinking surely he was not one of the faithful.

"Are you a man of the book?"

"Yes, yes."

Bakr said, *"Allahu Akhbar,"* and exited the cab. He knew that the horrific civil war that had occurred in Bosnia during the 1990s had been primarily between the Serbian Christian population and the Bosniak Muslim population, but had never stopped to think that a "Muslim" in Bosnia was as far removed from his version of Islam as the far enemy itself.

Bakr entered the lobby of the hotel, seeing an establishment dating back possibly to the 1940s, solidly built of quarry stone, decorated with heavy drapes and dreary colors. The long registration desk, complete with old-fashioned boxes mounted on the wall behind for the guest to place his or her key, was manned by a thin, acerbic-looking man wearing the ubiquitous black leather jacket found all over Bosnia. Bakr checked into his room, happy to see that, although old, it was clean and tidy. The primary concern he had was that the door had a shabby, cheap lock, without a secondary locking mechanism. That would force him to take the weapon everywhere he went.

His first order of business was to check the prearranged e-mail account with Sayyidd. He had made initial contact twenty-four hours ago after leaving the ferry in Kiel, Germany, but that e-mail had been disappointing, with Sayyidd saying he was still waiting on a message from Walid. On the plus side, at least he appeared to be following instructions. The message referenced Fallujah and said that he had checked out of the Muslim section and moved closer to the city center.

Getting directions from the front desk, he found an Internet café four blocks away. Logging on to the account known only to him and Sayyidd, he was relieved to see the reference to Fallujah, then excited when he saw that Walid had sent the instructions for the next meet. It would occur at one o'clock today at a coffee shop in Oslo. Sayyidd ended by saying he would relay what had occurred later on, as soon as he was done.

Bakr leaned back in his chair, satisfied that their planning was still on track. His shift to Bosnia might have been unwarranted, but it was still the prudent thing to have done. It might also have removed one burden from Walid's back, as he thought he could get explosives and detonating material from a contact inside this country. He wasn't convinced that Sayyidd had the expertise to ensure the correct materials were taken from Walid, and there was no way they would return to Norway to remedy any mistakes. Better for him to see if he could gather the materials here.

While still a fighter in Iraq, he had been given the name of a person who was very active helping out Chechen rebels in their fight against the Russian infidels. All he knew was his name, Juka Merdanovic, and that he lived somewhere around Tuzla. He had never met the man but had been told he wouldn't turn away a Muslim in need.

# 81

As I was pulling into my fourth parking spot, my phone rang.

"Yeah, what's up?"

"Pike, he's waiting at a bus stop. I think he's going to get on. What should I do?"

*Shit.* I couldn't believe I had failed to plan for a Metro or bus scenario. That was absolutely what would be expected, since the terrorists more than likely didn't have a car. *Chalk one up to fatigue. You'd better pull your head out of your ass, or you're going to fail.* I told her to hang on a second, rapidly running through courses of action in my mind.

"All right, board the bus with him. When you see him get up to leave, give me a call. You stay on the bus. Getting on with him can be a coincidence. Getting off is asking to get burned. You exit at the next stop and head back to the one where he got off. I'll call you when I either find out where he's going, or I lose him."

"Okay. I can do that. Sorry I didn't see this

coming and call earlier."

I smiled at her taking the blame. "*I'm* the one who should have seen this coming. Don't worry about it. We're still good to go."

We had landed in Oslo a couple of hours ago and had immediately checked Jennifer's e-mail account for a message from the Task-force. Sure enough, the terrorists had received another message directing a meeting at a coffee shop at one o'clock in the city center, which didn't give us a lot of time to set up. We located the shop with only thirty minutes to spare. I'd put Jennifer inside, with me outside as a spotter, since I was the only one who knew what they looked like. Of course, that meant I couldn't conduct the actual surveillance because they would spot me.

When Jennifer found out she'd be in the coffee shop alone, she seemed to realize for the first time this was for real. I had reassured her, reminding her of the surveillance classes I'd given on the flight over, stressing again that it wasn't some arcane skill reserved for spies, but just common sense. She didn't seem to buy it, but she'd exited the car. At precisely one o'clock I'd recognized the shorter of the two guys who'd mugged me in Guatemala. I'd almost missed him, because I was looking for a pair. His friend was nowhere in sight, which could mean he was conducting countersurveillance like I had in the mall. No way to tell and nothing I could do about it anyway. I called Jennifer and triggered the surveillance.

After the meeting broke up, Jennifer had managed to track him for five blocks to the bus station, but she was now out of play. That was going to leave me doing the dismounted work, which would be hard to do without getting burned. I pulled out, driving slowly until I saw the bus ahead of me. Picking up the pace, I trailed the bus to the next stop, seeing both Jennifer and the terrorist waiting to board. Four stops later, she called.

"He's standing up. He's getting off."

"Got it. You go to the next stop and head back here."

I immediately scanned for a parking spot, whipping the car around and cramming it into a space barely large enough to hold a moped. I waited for the terrorist to commit to a direction before falling in behind him. The sidewalks in this area were much less congested than in the city center, with only a few couples using them. I knew that if he turned around there was no way he would miss me, but there was nothing I could do about it. I stayed as far back as I dared, praying the terrorist had no reason to feel he was being followed and would walk straight to his destination.

Luckily, that's exactly what he did. Striding with a purpose and ignoring his immediate surroundings, he entered a five-story building. I gave him a few minutes, then approached.

It was a youth hostel, a cheap hotel catering to college students and wandering backpackers. It was clean and neat, although a little threadbare, with a throng of young men and women coming and going.

I went across the street to a small restaurant/bar, took a table in the corner that had a view of the entrance to the hostel, and gave Jennifer a call, telling her where to find me.

Sayyidd flew up the stairs of the youth hostel at a rapid clip, anxious to e-mail Bakr the good news. Walid had not only told him he could get "proof" of Iranian complicity for the WMD attack, along with the necessary explosive material, but he could get them into Israel proper with little trouble at all. In fact, he wanted Sayyidd to come with him tomorrow to the hinterlands of Norway to meet the man who would facilitate their travel. Unfortunately, the location of the facilitator was outside the footprint of the satellites for the Thrane M4 phone. While they covered a broad swath of the world, it wasn't 100 percent coverage. It meant he would be out of e-mail contact with Bakr for forty-eight hours, but he felt that was of little consequence.

Booting up the M4, he typed a jubilant

message, giving Bakr the details of the meeting, including the fact that he might not get any further message in the next twenty-four hours. He reassured Bakr that he would attempt to locate an Internet café, but that the M4 would probably not link up with the satellite.

As he leaned back with a sense of satisfaction, Sayyidd's reflections on his meeting with Walid were interrupted by a growling in his stomach. He didn't bother to shut down the computer, since he would be gone less than forty-five minutes and wanted to see Bakr's reply as soon as he returned.

Absently looking at the menu on the table, I was running through our next potential steps when Jennifer found me and sat down with a big grin on her face.

"Told you — you're a natural," I said.

"It was really sort of fun. I could get into doing that stuff."

"Well, that's good to hear, because I'm pretty sure you're going to get another chance at it."

I gave her a rundown of what I knew, telling her that we needed to figure out, before we did anything else, whether the other terrorist was with his partner. In the end, we had to have positive proof these idiots had a weapon of mass destruction, or, equally, that they did not, which might mean breaking into

516

their room. I couldn't risk that unless I knew the room was empty, and knocking on the door wasn't a preferred technique.

"What do you think?" I asked. "Any idea how the two of us can maintain 24/7 surveillance on this place?"

"You're asking me? Why? You're the expert."

"Hey, I told you this wasn't rocket science." I glanced out the window. "I have some ideas, but I don't have a monopoly on smarts. If you —"

I saw the terrorist leave the hostel across the street.

Jennifer said, "What? What is it?"

"The guy you followed is on the move."

"Already?" Jennifer leaned over trying to see out the window.

"Shit, he's headed this way," I said.

I looked around for another exit, but we were out of luck. Short of running through the kitchen, the front door was the only way in or out. I saw the man halfway across the street and moving with a purpose directly toward our restaurant.

"He's coming in. Hide your face."

Jennifer picked up a menu and pretended to read it. I did the same, but my angle was horrible. At least Jennifer had her back to the guy. I was facing the entrance with the small menu the only thing hiding my features. I heard the front door open and tried to become invisible. I waited for some indication that he had walked deeper into the restaurant but heard nothing. *Why's he standing at the entrance? Move, dammit. Go to the bar.* The bell on the front door chimed again. Without lowering the menu, I glanced back out the window, seeing someone running toward the hostel. With a start, I realized it was the terrorist.

"Shit! We're burned! We need to stop him before he gets to his buddy!"

I raced past a group of startled patrons and flew out the door. I ran as hard as I could, slowly closing the distance. I saw him look back, fear etched into his face. He put on a final burst of speed, taking the steps to the hostel three at a time. He blasted through the front door, bowling over a couple at the entrance.

I came through the entrance right behind him, in time to see him fling open a stairwell door. I followed, a flight-and-half of stairs behind, then narrowed it to one flight. I heard him open the door above me. I reached the fourth floor and exited the stairwell, catching a glimpse of a man entering a room midway down the hall. I had no idea if it was the terrorist or not, but had no other options. I took off at a dead sprint.

I reached the door just as it was slammed shut, jamming my foot in the opening and letting it bounce harmlessly against the sole of my boot. Drawing back, I threw my full weight against the door, causing it to explode inward, flinging whoever was behind it against the wall.

I followed the open door into the room and recognized the terrorist on the floor. I reached out to grab him, but he scrambled away, putting the bed between us.

For a split second, we just stared at each other in a standoff, both of us panting. I saw the look of fear on his face turn to determination. I moved into a fighting crouch, preparing for the assault that was coming.

It never came.

Instead he shouted, *"Allahu Akhbar!,"* then turned and launched himself headfirst out of the window, shattering the glass with his momentum. The scream continued for four long floors, growing fainter, like a passing train whistle, until it was abruptly cut off when his body impacted the street below.

Before I could assimilate what had happened, I heard someone else at the door and whirled around, seeing Jennifer, out of breath from her run. She looked around the empty room, then at me.

"Where'd he go?"

## 82

Bakr exited the back of a pickup at the end of a rutted dirt drive leading to a crumbling two-story farmhouse. He thanked the driver for the lift, staring at the house as the man drove away. The people here and in the surrounding hills existed at the poverty level, barely scraping a living out of the hardscrabble ground. The residence was built entirely of stone and had been frequently patched with homemade masonry, with the residue of a past fire visible. Moving listlessly about in a pen next to the farmhouse were a couple of skinny goats and a small flock of chickens, all digging in the dirt to find a bit of greenery that had long since been eaten.

It had taken Bakr the better part of the day to track down Juka's residence, and he still wasn't sure this was it. Before walking up to the house, Bakr reviewed in his mind the tale he would spin to obtain Juka's help. Bakr had learned of Juka's existence through a Chechen who had come to Iraq to glean IED techniques that he could take back to his fight against the Russian invaders of his homeland.

Bakr knew that Juka was a supporter of Muslim causes, but not because of the religion. That just happened to be the common denominator between himself and others like him. Before the summer of 1995, it was unlikely that Juka had even considered his religion as something that defined him. In July of that year, the Serbian army had surrounded Juka's town of Srebrenica and set about on an orgy of violence, wantonly killing men, raping women, and burning everything touched by a Muslim hand.

Bakr knew he would need to play on Juka's emotion of Muslim unity, steering clear of any mention of Al Qaeda and the Great Satan. Far from wanting to harm the United States, Juka actually liked America, since it was American airpower, under the guise of NATO, that had come screaming in to punish the Serbians when the truth of Srebrenica reached the world. It disgusted Bakr, but he was sure that Juka didn't hold America to blame. Because of this, Juka would have to be handled carefully.

Bakr rapped on the rough-hewn door, hearing movement on the other side.

"Yes? Can I help you?"

Bakr was unsure about the man before him. His face held deep wrinkles, made more pronounced by the dirt ground into the crevices, his eyes sunken with large black circles underneath. The age fit, but Bakr had expected more of a sense of purpose, a little more fire in the person he was seeking. What he saw was a man stooped by a lifetime of eking out a living from the ground, not a man steeled by a lifetime of fighting.

"Yes, I'm looking for a Bosnian named Juka. I'm on my way to Chechnya, and I was told by a friend that he may be able to help me."

Bakr watched the man go through a small transformation. He straightened up, giving Bakr a penetrating stare with pale blue eyes, apparently measuring his mettle with the gaze alone. He leaned against the doorjamb, now projecting a sense of confidence where before there had only been defeat.

"Really? And what would this friend's name be?"

"Milan Petrovic. He knew I was coming this way, and asked for me to pick up some things for him en route to Chechnya. Things that a Bosnian named Juka Merdanovic could provide."

The man stepped away from the door, holding his arm open in a gesture of welcome. "I am Juka. I'm at the service of any man befriended by Milan. Come inside and tell me how I may help."

An hour later, Bakr stepped out of Juka's

decrepit Lada in front of his hotel in downtown Tuzla, carrying a small wooden box, a gift from Juka.

"Milan will be forever grateful for your attention to his wishes," Bakr said.

Juka waved his hands, washing away the compliment. "I'm the one who will forever be grateful to Milan. I owe him my life. Beyond that, he's taking up arms to protect his people. Helping you help him is a small measure, and I'm glad to do it."

Juka leaned over to the open window.

"If you have any trouble finding the house, or getting in, call this number."

He handed Bakr a scrap of paper with a Bosnian international number written on it.

"The phone is located in a clean house near the one with the supplies you need. Nobody will answer, but the messages are checked every day. Don't say who you are. Just tell them what you need. It'll be provided."

Bakr took the number and waved good-bye, watching the Lada jerk forward, belching smoke. Juka had served his purpose. He had given him the location of a safe house on the northern side of Sarajevo. Inside this house were all the necessary components to fabricate any type of explosive device he desired. Bakr hadn't needed to prove his Chechnya credentials or state his requirements at all. Juka had taken it on faith that he was there on behalf of Milan, and had stated that Bakr could take anything he wished from the house. At one point in the conversation, while describing the inventory of the house, he stood up.

"I have just the thing for you. Something special that I don't keep in the house in Sarajevo. In fact, it's the only one I have ever seen."

Leaving Bakr alone in the rustic den, he rummaged around in a hall closet, returning with a wooden box. Inside was a wireless remote detonation device. Covered in Cyrillic lettering on the outside, it was small, with the receiver about half the size of a pack of cigarettes, and the transmitter slightly larger than a baby dill pickle. It was a state-of-the-art device used to clandestinely fire explosives from a distance. How Juka had ended up with it was anybody's guess.

While Bakr was happy with the option to remotely fire the weapon from up to two hundred meters away, he knew the detonator's true benefits lay in its channel-hopping capability and the fact that it used a separate signal for both arming and detonating.

Having played the IED game extensively in Iraq, Bakr understood that these features would defeat the average countermeasure employed against radio-controlled improvised explosive devices. Known as a "jammer," the countermeasure basically broadcast a louder signal than the IED transmitter, preventing the receiver from getting the command to detonate, thus "jamming" it. A simple concept, it was analogous to a person listening to a radio station in the middle of nowhere. One second, the channel's putting out country music, the next Gothic rock, as the radio itself relayed whichever signal was strongest. The IED jammer worked the same way. It blasted out huge amounts of white noise on the transmitter's frequency, preventing the receiver from hearing the command to detonate.

The channel-hopping feature on Juka's device meant that the transmitter and receiver, synchronized together, frenetically hopped frequencies from the moment it was turned on, never transmitting on the same frequency for more than a millisecond. This ensured that the average jammer wouldn't be able to defeat it, as it wouldn't be able to sufficiently track which frequency the detonator was using, and thus couldn't override the signal. The second feature, the separate signals used for arming and detonation, meant that the weapon wouldn't be inadvertently set off by someone opening his garage or playing with a remote-controlled airplane. In order for the device to explode, it would take one signal, linked to a security code, to arm the bomb, and another, also linked to a code, to detonate it.

Juka had placed the detonator reverently in

Bakr's hands, beginning to fidget once he realized that he had given it away. He made Bakr promise that he would save it for use on a special target, using all of the other mundane detonators he would find in the Sarajevo safe house for everyday terrorist attacks.

Opening the door to his hotel room, Bakr grinned at the memory. Yes, he would save this detonator for a special occasion. The perfect occasion. Placing the detonator on the nightstand, he went to the Internet café to check on the meeting with Walid.

Opening the latest message, it appeared that Sayyidd had done everything he had asked, and more, giving him a little guilt over his previous thoughts about his partner. He was a little concerned by the lack of e-mail contact in the next twenty-four hours, but seeing that this e-mail had arrived within the last hour, he was sure Sayyidd would check his account one more time before leaving, and reply. He typed a quick response, describing his successful meeting with Juka. He hit send, finally beginning to accept that everything was working out.

# 83

Jennifer asked again, "Where is he?"

I ran to the window, the broken glass crackling under my feet like popcorn.

"He jumped out the fucking window."

"He jumped? Are you sure he —"

"No, I didn't throw him out. As much as I would have liked to, I'd have to be the Incredible Hulk to chuck his ass out the window from across the room."

I saw a crowd gathering around the broken body, most looking down, but some looking up at my location, the drapes swinging gently in the breeze providing an instant point of reference. I snapped my head back before they saw me.

"We have about one minute before we'll be asked a lot of questions. Start packing up his stuff. We'll look at it back in the hotel."

"What about the other guy? What are we going to do about him?"

"I think he's here alone. There's no evidence of another person, no additional luggage, toothbrush, nothing."

Stuffing passports and any other paper I could find into my backpack, I said again, "Come on, pack that computer up. We need to move."

When I didn't notice any movement, I said, "What's up? We have *got* to go."

"An e-mail just came in, from a different Yahoo! account. He's still logged on and connected to the Internet."

"Close it all up," I said. "Don't turn anything off, just close it up for travel. Maybe we can duplicate it at our hotel, but we don't have time to mess with it now."

Finishing up, I held the door open for Jennifer. Just prior to letting it close forever, she grabbed my arm.

"Wait." She ran to the nightstand and grabbed a thumb drive. Holding it up, she said, "No telling what's on this thing."

"Good catch. That's probably got their whole diabolical plan."

She squinted like she was debating on whether to kick me in the nuts. Before she got the chance, I left the room. Once outside I turned left, choosing the opposite stairwell to the one by which we had arrived. We exited out the back, but were forced to walk through all the gawkers on the east side of the hotel to get to our vehicle. The smashed body hadn't been moved, appearing just as it had when I'd looked out the window minutes before. We pretended to be just as shocked as everyone else until we were clear of the crowds and could sprint to our car. Fifteen minutes later we were back in our hotel room.

I set the laptop on the coffee table and brought it out of sleep mode. The last e-mail was still on the screen.

"Toss me that thumb drive."

Putting it in the computer, I saw it was empty. *So much for finding the diabolical plan.* I copied the Arabic text from the e-mail onto the thumb drive, followed by the e-mail header information, then took the drive over to Jennifer, who had booted up our computer and was getting online.

"The thumb drive had nothing on it. Here's the last e-mail that was on the screen, along with the header. Can you send this to the Taskforce? Kurt said he'd have analysts standing by. Time for them to earn their pay."

"Sure. You think they'll be able to get anything out of this?"

"I don't know. I'm going to try to get back into the Yahoo! server and get all his e-mails before his password times out."

She sent the e-mail, then asked me, "What was that Web site that did the magic stuff?"

"What is my IP address dot com. You remember how to use it?"

"Yeah, I think so. I'll let you know if I get stuck."

I was pulling up the wireless toolbar on the

terrorist's computer, attempting to get on-line, when Jennifer said, "The other guy, if that's who sent the e-mail, is in Tuzla, Bosnia-Herzegovina. Does that make any sense?"

"Yeah, actually it does. That's where all the muj went to during the Bosnian war. He's probably got some contacts there."

I tried to connect to the hotel wireless network but failed, being told it was "in use." "Will this hotel network handle two comput-ers with the same password at the same time?"

She was staring at our computer and gave me an absentminded answer. "I don't know."

"His damn password is going to time out. We're going to lose the messages. Get off the Internet and let me go."

"Wait. I'm getting a message. Don't cut it yet. Why don't you try using the Ethernet cable? That's not tied to the wireless."

I felt the press of time and was about to rip her computer out of the wall when what she'd said rooted home. *Damn . . . little brainiac might be right again.* I plugged into the cable and began reconfiguring the terrorist com-puter, asking what the latest message said.

"It looks like that last message was from the other terrorist. He's found some explosive material and is ready to meet the first guy — I guess the guy that jumped out the window."

I continued messing with the other com-puter, only half listening to what she said.

"He's ready to build the bomb, and the window-jumper here in Oslo has some connection who can get them into Israel. The guy in Tuzla is thanking him for the work."

I saw the little wireless icon show a green connection. "Yeah! I'm online, and his account's still open."

"Didn't you hear what I just said?"

"Yes. I did. Give me the thumb drive. I want to copy all the messages in the sent-and-received files."

She passed it over, allowing me to load the new messages.

"Send that to them. See what they say."

She did as I asked, saying, "Pike, what are we going to do? I guess I had hoped that at some point we'd figure out we were wrong, especially since nobody else wanted to believe us. Every time we find something new, it tells us we're still right."

"Hang on. Let's see what the rest of the messages say. We can figure it out from there. Let's face it, everything said so far could be for a single suicide attack into Israel. It may be nothing more than that. One bad guy is dead, and the other has no idea. We're still on the offensive here."

One hour later we got the answer from the Taskforce. It didn't get any better. The man who had jumped to his death had been very sloppy with his operational security. He had saved every e-mail sent and received, allowing the analysts at the Taskforce to build a pretty good picture. In a clinical report, the analytical transcript summarized what the e-mail exchanges contained. In general, it gave the strongest backing yet to Ethan's original take, buttressing the theory that the overarching goal was to deploy a weapon in Israel and blame the Iranians. The report read in a clinical, unemotional manner:

A. Terrorist A, having suspected that the pair was under surveillance, fled to parts unknown as a preventative measure.

B. Terrorist A, to ensure a self-healing operation, enacted a negative tripwire, whereby a penalty would be incurred if a code is not sent. Terrorist A will immediately cease all communication, assume the plan is compromised, and conduct the event at the earliest convenience, most likely at a target of opportunity. The penalty is reset every 24 hours. The code itself is undetermined, but most likely is some combination of words within each e-mail sent.

C. Terrorist A has coordinated for explosives at his present location but has not physically obtained them. The explosives themselves are held at a safe house, exact location undetermined. Along with the explosives he has obtained a complex detonation mechanism, type unknown.

D. Terrorist B has coordinated for transportation to Israel and coordinated for evidence to implicate Iran in the attack. Exact details and facilitation measures are unknown.

E. Terrorist B is going to finalize coordination for transportation methods and routes today, and will be out of e-mail contact for 48 hours. Terrorist B asked Terrorist A for an additional 24 hours before incurring a penalty.

F. Terrorist A has agreed to the additional time, with the caveat that Terrorist B make every attempt to make contact.

It is the consensus of the analysts that together, both terrorists have the means at their disposal to introduce an explosive device inside the borders of the State of Israel. It is further believed that they have the means to blame the attack on the State of Iran, at least initially. It is impossible to ascertain from the e-mails presented whether this blame will withstand rigorous forensic and investigative scrutiny, although it is the opinion of the analysts that such scrutiny may not occur, as the politics of the event will more than likely supersede any attempt at determining the actual facts, with initial reports becoming the perceived truth.

On the question of whether the event

will be WMD related, the analysts could not reach a consensus. There is no evidence that the device is a WMD, as neither terrorist refers to it as such, and a review of worldwide all-source intelligence for the last thirty days does not reveal any new indications of recent WMD activity. It may simply be a conventional terrorist operation with little second- and third-order repercussions. On the other hand, it is unusual for this much preparation, coordination, and infrastructure development be used to support a single suicide attack.

"Not good. Looks like we have forty-eight hours to play with. The muj motherfucker's going on a suicide run after that. No telling where."

Jennifer's face was pale. "We can't do this alone. Can't Kurt go get that guy now? Isn't this enough proof?"

"No. You heard his dilemma in D.C. That hasn't changed. It's sad to say, but a simple suicide attack won't cut it. He's not going to risk political upheaval on an event that occurs every day all over the Middle East. He's also not going to launch based on our hunch, especially when his own analysts can't agree that it's a WMD. We have to prove it."

"How on earth are we going to do that?"

"Same way we were here. He's obviously

got the device, if there is one. We didn't find one here, so we need to go there, find him, then check out what he has."

"Where's 'there'?"

"Tuzla, Bosnia. Pack your stuff. We need to leave right now. We have a little over forty-eight hours before he goes nuts. Once he's convinced they're compromised, there's no telling where he's going to go."

Jennifer remained seated. "Are you serious? Where are we going to go? How are we going to find this guy? At least here we had the message about the coffee shop. How are we going to find him in an entire city?"

"Pull up that e-mail trace again. It should have come with a map. It's not that accurate, but I've been to Tuzla. It's not that big of a place and probably doesn't have that many Internet cafés. It's a long shot, but we go to Tuzla, find the closest café to the map location given, and see if we can find him."

"What happens if we don't find him?"

"He blows up a bunch of people. Not much we can do about it. All we can do is try."

"Shit, Pike, we can't do this. We're going to fail. *Fail.* Can't you see that? Why isn't anyone else helping. . . ."

She put her head in her hands. I sat down next to her and rubbed her back.

"Look, this will all be over, whether we like it or not, within the next forty-eight hours. All we can do is try our best. Hang in there for a couple more days and it will end one way or another."

She sat up. I was relieved to see a spark back in her eyes. "Okay. Forty-eight hours. But when we get home I am kicking somebody's ass in the United States government."

# 84

Five thousand miles away, Kurt Hale sat at his desk with the latest intel reports from Pike. He rubbed his eyes, not liking the choices he faced, or the repercussions if he chose incorrectly. He wasn't surprised by the fact that there was no black-and-white description of the terrorists' intentions or capabilities. It was just the way of intelligence. From past experience, he knew there was never a smoking gun. You always had to make a judgment call, read the tea leaves, and hope you came close.

He knew that Pike would take the commander's intent he had given seriously, and wouldn't send an alert unless he proved there was WMD involved. Unfortunately, according to this last batch of e-mails, waiting until Pike's call might be too late. The team wouldn't have time to launch from the U.S. to wherever Pike ended up before the terrorist fled on his suicide mission, killing thousands and possibly starting World War III.

On the other hand, if Kurt did launch a team, he would quite possibly bring down the president of the United States of America and irreparably harm the future defense of the nation, whether the threat was real or not. Once he pulled that trigger, there would be no going back.

Kurt knew that hunting a human being was hard enough, especially one who knows he's the prey. Accomplishing the mission in another sovereign country, without leaving any fingerprints — the way the Taskforce operated — was exponentially harder.

Before starting up the Taskforce, Kurt had studied any and all operations that had a hint of being the same as what he would be called upon to conduct. He had learned — through others' mistakes — that just getting the guy wouldn't qualify as a success. The most glaring example post 9/11 that Kurt had seen was a rendition operation of a radical Egyptian cleric called Osama Moustafa Hassan — or Abu Omar — from Milan, Italy, by the CIA in 2003.

The operation itself was conducted successfully, with Abu Omar captured and flown to parts unknown, but the ensuing police investigation uncovered the entire plot, to include the specific names of CIA operatives involved. Using cell phone records, car rental receipts, hotel guest logs, and other old-fashioned police work, the Italians dissected the entire operation from start to finish. His abduction was ruled an illegal kidnapping, with most of the CIA operatives named in an arrest warrant. Since Italy is a member of the European Union, the warrants were valid in every other EU member nation. The end state was an enormous embarrassment for the CIA, with scores of operatives no longer able to set foot on the European continent.

The point was driven home to Kurt that the actual capture or killing was the easy part. He decided that the Taskforce would never attempt an operation without the requisite groundwork laid first, which took time. If a target presented itself before they could conduct the operation without compromise, it was passed up to wait for a better day.

Now the Taskforce had no time to prepare, no infrastructure in place. Kurt had no doubt that they could successfully snatch or kill the terrorist currently in Bosnia, but knew that it would take little police work to unravel that Americans had been involved. Once word reached back that a capture/kill operation had occurred involving American forces, the press and the U.S. government itself would unwittingly help the Bosnians in their investigation, with the Taskforce exposed as a paramilitary organization operating outside the bounds of U.S. law. The president would have no choice but to step forward and accept responsibility.

He would have liked someone to talk to, someone to bounce ideas off of, but he had purposely kept his support of Pike a secret from his own men, including George Wolffe. If it blew up, at least they would be protected as unwitting. The only one he trusted above him was the one man who would bear the brunt of the decision — the president — and he was currently on a European goodwill tour. Contacting him meant going through the White House communications room. Using that, with everything recorded and God knows who else listening, would be the same as announcing Prometheus in the newspaper.

He thought about the Oversight Council and decided against discussing the problem with them. He had never called an emergency session, and after his last meeting with Standish, he didn't trust his ability to control the direction of the conversation without presidential support.

The irony wasn't lost on him that he was contemplating becoming what he feared the most — a single man making Prometheus decisions. *My fear of Standish has made me Standish.* He was at the top of the slippery slope, looking down. *What will the reason be next time?* It was his decision, and he was running out of time to make it.

## 85

Bakr awoke and rolled over to ensure the weapon was still in place underneath his bed. Seeing the Tupperware container, he smiled. He wouldn't need to worry about losing the weapon much longer. Today was the day that Sayyidd was to finalize both their method of entry into Israel and the means by which they would implicate the Persian infidels. He quickly dressed, anxious to see what Sayyidd had sent. He knew it would be another thirty minutes before the café opened, but he didn't have the patience to sit around in his hotel room. He decided to get a bite to eat at a coffee shop across the street from the café. He felt like breaking into a run after leaving the hotel, but forced himself to walk at a natural pace.

The service at the coffee shop was rapid, since there were only two other customers: a woman who was clearly closer to paradise than the usual Bosniak unbeliever, as she had her head covered in a scarf, and, on the other of the room, a small man who looked like he spent most of his nights on the street, with a frayed black leather jacket and dirt-encrusted shirt, his gnarled hands holding the steaming cup of coffee as if he had purchased it more for the heat it provided than the coffee itself.

Bakr fidgeted until he saw the owner flip the Cyrillic sign in the window of the café, signaling the start of business for the day. He threw some money on the table and rapidly crossed the street.

Two minutes later, Bakr leaned back in his chair, disappointed by the fact that Sayyidd hadn't e-mailed him back. There was nothing to be done about it. He would just have to wait until tomorrow for the news.

He left the Internet café, walking toward his hotel at half the speed he had used to get there. Caught in his own thoughts, he failed to notice the Muslim woman from the coffee shop match his pace on the opposite side of the street.

Jennifer let the terrorist get a hundred yards away before picking up surveillance behind him. Learning all the time, she now stayed on the other side of the street, knowing it gave her a better ability to keep him in sight without his suspecting he was being followed.

Pike had been wrong on the number of Internet cafés. There were, in fact, seven within the radius of the e-mail trace. They had driven by each one and had discarded several, one because it was located next to a police station, a few that catered solely to tourists, and those that had their interiors monitored by cameras.

The process of elimination left two cafés, although Jennifer knew they were wishing away alternatives that might, in fact, be used. Luckily, both she and Pike knew what this terrorist looked like, allowing them to split up. The window-jumper wasn't the man that Jennifer had seen in the passport in Guatemala, which meant that she would recognize the remaining terrorist.

One location could be watched from a coffee shop situated across from the café. The other had no convenient location from which to view the entrance other than from a parked car on the same street. Not wanting to repeat what had happened in Oslo, with the terrorist recognizing him, Pike had given Jennifer the coffee shop location, buying her a quick disguise of a multicolored head scarf, a set of large, cheap sunglasses, and an ankle length peasant's dress of the type that was ubiquitous in downtown Tuzla. She had dyed her hair black to complete the transformation, and now looked like one of a hundred Bosnian women roaming the city center.

Jennifer had been sitting in the coffee shop for only a few minutes, barely enough time to think through her surveillance plan, when a man resembling the passport photo came in. She wasn't sure, since the guy in the passport had a beard, and this man didn't. When he left the coffee shop and entered the Internet café, all doubt fled her mind. *That's him.* She called Pike and told him. Before Pike could find her, she saw the terrorist leave. *Showtime. You can do this. Not that hard.* Jennifer started window-shopping across the street, keeping pace within a football field of him, all the while running through her mind what she was going to do next.

Her mission was simple: Figure out where he was staying, right down to the hotel room. *And I need to be right behind him to do that.* She started to close the distance before she realized her dilemma. *What if he walks for the next four miles? I can't stay right behind him. He'll wonder what the hell I'm doing.* The longer she walked, the more she wanted to close the gap. *Fuck. This sounded easy on the airplane. He's going to turn into a hotel and I'm going to lose him.*

After three blocks, seeing the sidewalks beginning to swell with noontime shoppers that would give her some cover, she decided she'd pushed her luck for long enough. She crossed over, her fear of missing the opportunity now overpowering.

She picked up a position about thirty

meters behind him, keeping him in sight through the crowds, but just barely. She called Pike and gave him an update, referring to the terrorist with the name she had seen in his American passport in Guatemala.

"Carlos has gone about four blocks from the café. I'm still on him. He appears to have a destination, but he's not moving with a purpose. Are you nearby?"

"Yeah, I'm right outside your Internet café. I'll be within a couple of blocks of you at all times. How're you holding up?"

"I'm okay. I'm about to fall asleep on my feet, but I'm okay. Nothing like exhaustion to tamp down stress."

"I hear you. I just about ran over a kid five minutes ago. Look — I'm having second thoughts about how far we should push this today. I think you should just pinpoint his hotel. We can find some other way to figure out his room. I think we're risking too much by you going in."

*Why's he changing the plan now?* "Would you think this was too risky if you were walking behind him, or is it because you're afraid of me getting hurt? We only have another twenty-four hours, and I don't think we'll get another chance. I'm going to finish this."

"Damn it, this isn't a *game*. There's no trophy at the end. If he figures out what's going on, he's liable to freak out and launch the device right in the hotel. Yeah, I'm worried about you, but I'd be just as worried about any teammate."

She watched Carlos pause outside of a hotel, looking left and right. She saw him glance at his watch like he was trying to decide what to do. She vaguely heard Pike continue.

"I'm just saying that I'm not sure a plan hashed out on an airplane after four days without sleep is the one we should go with. Let's figure out where he's staying and take a long, hard look at our options."

She didn't reply, focused on the terrorist. She saw him turn to the hotel entrance. *Holy shit. This is it.*

"Hello? Jennifer, you still there?"

"He just went into a hotel. I have to go."

"No! Jennifer, wait —"

Jennifer hung up the phone and rushed forward, reaching the door in time to see Carlos moving to a stairwell inside. Focusing on the backpack he was wearing, she gave a half-thought of quitting, Pike's warning reminding her of the stakes. *Stop that. Get it done.*

To her right she saw a wizened old man at the front desk, reading a newspaper and paying her no mind. Crossing quickly to the stairwell, she heard footsteps above her, separated by a single landing. *How am I going to figure out his floor if I can't see him?* It dawned on her that she would only need to listen. When she heard his footsteps cease, she would simply exit on the next floor.

No sooner had she come up with the plan than she realized she was hearing nothing but the echo of her own footsteps. Carlos had exited the stairwell.

I flung the phone against the dash. *What the hell is she thinking? What was I thinking coming up with this dumb-ass plan?* I didn't even know where she was. From where I was parked outside the café I could see about forty different ways the terrorist could have gone. *Calm down. Think.* From what Jennifer said, they were somewhere within a four-block radius. How many hotels could there be inside that? Logically, they were probably west, toward downtown. I threw the car into drive and headed deeper into the city. *Please don't get hurt. Please, please.*

Hurrying to the next floor, Jennifer paused outside the stairwell doorway, listening for any sign that someone was just beyond. Hearing nothing, she gathered her courage and opened the door.

Carlos stood directly in front of her, fumbling with his key and softly cursing the old lock. At the sound of the stairwell door, he turned. Jennifer stumbled back, preparing to

547

flee into the stairwell in a fight or flight response. *Get a grip. He doesn't know who you are.* Her eyes locked with the terrorist's. He smiled, nodding hello before returning to work his key. She smiled back and moved past him, seeing the hallway end about fifty feet away at a men's room. *What am I going to do when I reach that? Shit. I've got no reason to be here. Should've turned around.*

She kept walking, feeling his eyes on her back, wondering what the hell was taking him so long. *Get in your damn room.* As she approached the bathroom, her mind began to work in overdrive. *What if this is a men-only hotel? Or has floors separated by gender? He's going to know something's up. He's going to kill me.* She envisioned him stalking right behind her, knife raised to strike. With a superhuman effort, she kept walking forward, fighting the urge to turn around and look. She reached the end of the hall. *Now what? He's going to see you standing here doing nothing.* She turned to the last door and did the only thing she could think of, giving it a soft knock while stealing a glance back the way she had come.

The hallway was empty. She felt her knees begin to buckle and threw her hand up to the doorjamb for support. *Jesus, why don't I listen to Pike?* Leaning against the frame with her eyes closed, taking quick, shallow breaths, she didn't even notice that the door had opened until she heard someone speak.

Standing in front of her in his underwear, black socks held up by garters on his skinny legs, wearing a stained wife-beater T-shirt, was a man of about sixty. The man looked at her suspiciously and said something in Serbo-Croatian.

Feeling nauseous, Jennifer said, "Sorry, wrong room."

She speed-walked back down the hallway, taking care not to make any noise as she opened the door to the stairwell. Reaching the street outside, she walked as fast as she could without breaking into an overt run, not conscious of the direction she was going or the people she bumped into in her haste to put some distance between herself and the hotel. She made it about ninety feet before the enormity of the close call hit home. She stopped, reaching toward the nearest wall for support. She leaned over and threw up, splashing vomit on her legs and causing people on the sidewalk to immediately avoid her.

Racked with dry heaves, she sank to her knees. A crowd began to gather around her, with several people asking her questions in Serbo-Croatian. *Get out of here. You're making a scene. You're going to blow this whole thing.* She stood up, brushing off the help and looking for an escape route. She heard a man on the street yelling something, then recognized it was Pike. *Thank God.*

She ran to the SUV as Pike opened the passenger door. She leaned back into the seat, shaking and gasping for air as if she had just run a marathon. Pike gunned the engine, pulling away from the hotel.

"You all right? What the fuck happened?"

"I'm okay." She closed her eyes, breathing deeply, repeating the phrase as if to prove it to herself.

"I'm okay."

## 86

In his Crystal City office, Lucas pinched the bridge of his nose, wanting more than anything to smash his computer into little pieces. No sooner had his team landed in Norway then the beacon had shown up in Tuzla, Bosnia-Herzegovina.

Through Standish he had confirmed that Kurt Hale was still in D.C., which led him to surmise that Hale had passed the device to Pike. This was a net positive, provided he could keep a bead on the pager and get his team in position quickly. The first update of its location had been Oslo, causing an immediate launch of the team. Now the damn thing was saying it was in Tuzla. *This is turning into a wild goose chase.*

On top of that, someone here in the States was making inquiries about the death of the analyst and the shooting at the Four Courts pub. He hadn't been able to determine who it was but knew it wasn't official law enforcement. Someone had made a connection between the two and was closing in on his operation.

Regardless, he still had a mission to accomplish. He gave the order for the team in Oslo to redirect to Tuzla at their earliest opportunity. He then turned to his Rolodex and compiled a list of names for a backup team. There was no telling where this was going to lead. He needed the flexibility to launch from inside the European continent while maintaining a reserve. He would fly with the backup team, directly coordinating the mission on the ground. It was becoming impossible to command and control the complex twists of the operation from five thousand miles away, and getting out of the country right now had a certain appeal. Not to mention the chance of getting out of the office and into the hunt.

I waited for Jennifer to finish brushing her teeth before continuing the debriefing. When she returned to the bedroom, she looked a little bit like her normal self, the fear of her close call receding.

"Are you burned? Did Carlos suspect anything? Do anything when he saw you?"

"No, not really. I think I'm fine there. I'm pretty sure he thought I was a local. I didn't say anything, and neither did he, so I didn't give him any reason to think I was anything but a Bosnian."

"Good. I think we drive on with the plan. We wait for him to check his e-mail tomorrow. While he's in the café, I'll crack into his room and see if I can spot the device, or come up with anything else that screams WMD. Run me through what you saw for security. What were the door locks like, did you see any cameras, was there a lot of traffic, basically anything you can think of that might interfere with me getting in."

Jennifer sat for a moment, collecting her thoughts. When she was ready, she gave me a fairly detailed description of everything she had seen. I expected her to have tunnel vision, focusing on her survival after the contact with Carlos like most civilians would have, but she was able to clearly describe the exact number of doors in the hallway, the type of lock, the direction the doors opened, and even give a fairly good description of the old man she had inadvertently run into, to include what she could see of the layout of his room. I had gotten less information from trained operators in the past.

"So, you're positive you didn't see any cameras? Anything being fed to the front desk?"

"No. There's nothing like that. I'm sure of it. The hotel's fairly run-down. The only thing I saw was an old guy at the front desk, and he didn't even look up when I entered."

"You're positive that there was only one

lock, and it was like ours here in the hotel room?

"Well, I'm positive that's true about the guy's room at the end of the hall. I can't say for sure about Carlos's room, since he was standing in front of his door when I went by, but if all of the rooms are the same, then it has a lever, and a keyhole above the lever. That's it."

"And it looked just like our door lock?"

She pointed at our hotel room door. "Down to the engraving on the plate."

"Okay. I think I can get in with our key."

"How? Just because it looks like our lock doesn't mean our key will fit. I mean, really, I've seen enough *Magnum PI* episodes to know that won't work."

"If our key will fit into Carlos's keyhole, it will work. It won't open it, you're right, but I'm going to take our key and make a 'bump key.' If I do it right, we should walk right in." I grinned. "Trust me."

## 87

We attempted to have a normal evening at a local restaurant. Jennifer was subdued throughout the meal and I could tell that something was eating at her. When we got back to the hotel, she asked, "What are we going to do if you don't find any WMD in his room?"

"Honestly, I don't know. I've been thinking about it, and don't have an answer. Let's take it one step at a time. Right now, I just want to build the bump key and go to sleep. We're both exhausted, and it might be the only rest we get for a while."

Jennifer nodded absently. "Yeah, I could use the sleep."

"Look, quit worrying. We can't do anything right now and it'll just keep you awake all night."

"I know, I know, but . . . Pike, I'm scared. I really thought I was going to die today. I have never been so terrified. This guy plans to kill a lot of people. I don't think I realized what that meant until I thought he was going to kill me."

*Here it comes. She's seen the elephant. Need to give her some confidence.* "Quit it. Fear isn't bad. You just have to manage it, like you did today. This guy is going to *try* to kill a lot of people. We're going to stop it. Right?"

She stared at me, like she wanted to say something but wasn't sure how. I'd seen it before. Soldiers who had a near-death experience and wanted to talk, but didn't know what to say. Her next question threw me completely off.

"What was Heather like?"

I sat in silence for a second or two, wondering where this was going.

"I . . . I can't sum that up in a sentence. Why'd you ask?"

She didn't answer the question. Didn't appear to even hear it. "You know what I was thinking about at the end of that hall? I mean besides the scared shitless feeling that I was going to die? I thought that if Carlos killed me it would destroy you."

"Come on. That's not going to happen. You're not going to die and I'm not going to self-destruct."

She ignored me. "I felt so selfish. I had run into the hotel because we needed to get the information and it was *my* life. But it's more than my life."

"Jennifer, it's never just your life. There's

always someone else who'll be hurt. That's just the way it is."

She was staring at me now, making me uncomfortable. The twinge had come back with strength unlike anything I had felt since I had lost Heather. It was almost unbearable, a confusing mishmash of emotions that made me want to flee the room. *Stop it. Remember the mission. Focus.*

She continued. "I understand that my death would affect others. I mean, my death would also crush my mother, but I didn't think about her. This was different. The fear of dying wasn't as bad as the fear of causing you pain."

*Where is this going?* I had intended to give her a little support, a shot of confidence, like I had done many times to other soldiers in the past, but I was no longer on familiar ground. "Well, I'm glad I'm good for something. If pity gets the mission done, then I guess I'm a pathetic loser who'll fall apart at the drop of a hat. Can we talk about something else?"

"That's not what I meant. I . . . I don't know what's going to happen tomorrow and I just wanted you to know. . . ."

"What?"

She leaned in and kissed me.

"You're a good man. Much better than you give yourself credit for. Maybe better than anyone I've ever met. You didn't kill your family. You should let it go."

I sat still, frozen by her actions.

Jennifer laughed. "Wow. I finally made you speechless. I should have done that days ago."

"Jennifer . . . I . . . uh . . ."

She put a finger to my lips. "Shhh. I'm not looking for any deep thoughts. I just wanted to say that . . . in case . . . you know."

*In case one of us dies.*

I remained silent for a second, not wanting to dwell on tomorrow's potential consequences.

"You asked about Heather," I said. "She was . . . a lot like you."

The words seemed to bring a sense of calm to her. She put her hand over mine.

"Thank you. I think that's the best compliment you could ever give."

"You're welcome. Now, enough of the soul-searching." I stood up, locking my churning emotions away and trying to concentrate on the mission. "We need to get some sleep. We have a big day tomorrow."

She remained seated, saying nothing, but with a different glint in her eyes.

"What?"

"I . . . I'd rather you didn't sleep on the floor tonight. Is that all right?"

The question took a moment to sink in. When it did, it separated my confusing emotions like oil and water. *Jesus, you want to.* The thought made me feel like a traitor, disgusting me to my core. *I can't sleep around on Heather.* The notion was ridiculous, but overwhelmingly there nonetheless. *Shit. What do I say now?*

Jennifer had just been through a harrowing event, and had now opened herself up in the most vulnerable way possible. The close call itself may have been to blame. I didn't want to hurt her. I sat down again, taking her hand.

"Jennifer . . . I . . . I . . . can't do that. . . ."

She blinked and looked at the floor. When she looked back at me, she was smiling, like I had confirmed something.

"I know. I just meant you could use a good night's sleep. Off of the floor. The bed's big enough."

We both knew what she really meant, but somehow my answer had avoided giving her pain. I smiled back, relieved. No matter what happened tomorrow, tonight I had done something right.

## 88

At seven A.M. Bakr got out of bed and completed sunrise prayers, wishing for the thousandth time that he were allowed the small dignity of a prayer rug as part of his cover.

At seven-thirty, he walked to the end of the hall for his shower. He fidgeted in his room for another forty-five minutes, playing with the remote detonator and going through linkup options with Sayyidd in his mind. At eight forty-five, he packed up the weapon. Stepping onto the street, he looked left and right, then proceeded at a slow pace to the Internet café so as to arrive after it had opened.

Jennifer sat in her peasant's dress with a different colored scarf in place on her head. The scent of vomit still occasionally wafted from her dress like the odor of a dead animal in the attic, the stench floating about with no clear source no matter how hard you walked around sniffing the room. She had done her best to clean the dress but had missed a spot somewhere.

She'd awakened before their alarm went off, the room artificially dark due to the heavy drapes, the corners showing the feeble light of dawn creeping in. Raised on an elbow, gazing at Pike's slumbering form, she could barely pick out his features. *This isn't fair. Why are we all alone out here? Why can't we just go home and forget about terrorists and WMD? Let someone else stop him.* She had lain in bed feeling a sense of impending doom, as if she had been convicted at trial and today was the day she reported to jail.

That feeling had remained throughout the morning, and persisted still. Sitting in the back of the coffee shop, she jumped when her cell phone rang, spilling her cup of coffee halfway to her mouth. She heard two simple sentences.

"He's on the move. He's going slow, so it'll probably be five minutes before you see him."

She acknowledged the call and hung up, the sense of dread building in her gut. Four minutes later she saw Carlos down the street, walking at a leisurely pace toward the café. It would take him a couple more minutes to get there, but that would only be more time for Pike inside the hotel. She picked up her phone and dialed, wishing it were still yesterday, not wanting to set things in motion.

561

■ ■ ■ ■

Outside of Bakr's hotel, one of Lucas's team members from Norway sat looking at a map, trying to determine if he was in the location dictated by the computer plot of the beacon. He glanced up to get his bearings on the street, looked back at his map, then did a double take when he saw Pike exit a Pajero SUV fifteen feet to his front.

He had pulled into the parking spot five minutes before merely to pinpoint his location, one of several sites being reconnoitered by Mason's team based on the trail left by Pike's pager. This was supposed to be just a familiarization day, necking down possible locations and getting a feel for the area. Fumbling with his cell phone, he calmed down enough to dial, ducking to prevent Pike from seeing him.

"Mason? Yeah, I've got Pike. He's fucking right in front of me. The girl's not with him. He just went into a hotel."

He paused, listening. "I don't know if he's staying here or not, but if you want him, I need to get the team here ASAP. I'm not going to try take him out on my own. I haven't seen the girl, but let's face it, he's the threat. Get rid of him, and she'll be easy."

He listened a few more seconds. "Yeah, I get that we can't track the girl, but this guy's been pretty damn dangerous from the beginning. You sure you want to attempt a capture?"

Hearing Mason's reasoning, he relented. "Okay, I can do that. If you get a team here, I should be able to close on him fast enough to prevent him from doing anything."

He listened a moment.

"If he gives me any trouble, I'll smoke him right here. If not, he can tell us where to find the girl. I don't recommend going in after him. We can ambush him when he comes out. Maybe we'll get lucky and they'll both come out."

I entered the hotel like I belonged there, carrying the bump key and a small mallet I had purchased the day before. I moved straight to the stairwell, the distance and direction exactly as described by Jennifer. Exiting the third floor, I paused in front of Carlos's door. I strained my ears, listening for any movement behind it or from the rooms down the hall. Hearing none, I placed the key in the lock. It slid in easily. I moved it forward, feeling the clicks of the pin tumblers through the key. When I went past the last tumbler, I pulled the key back out until it clicked once. Looking left and right, ensuring I was alone, I raised the mallet and gave the key a sharp rap, applying torque as soon as the key seated past the pins. The lock broke free, the cylinder turning. I rotated the key and turned the lever, pushing the door. It didn't budge. I paused a half second and pushed again. The door was still locked. Puzzled, feeling the press of time, my instinct was to simply kick in the door. *Hold on. Solve the problem.* I went through possibilities in my mind. I remembered that European locks sometimes go two full rotations to open. I repeated the procedure with the bump key, feeling a sense of relief when the lock cylinder turned again, releasing the door. I entered the room.

Once again, Jennifer's description was spot on. The room was small, consisting of a single floor lamp, an end table, a chair, and a twin-sized bed. No closet and no bathroom. I went to a duffel bag on the chair first, sifting through the clothes. Finding an American passport, I saw that Jennifer had been right. The name inside was Carlos Menendez. *Hispanic. Very smart.* I wrote down the name and passport number for future reference. I saw nothing else of interest. I moved to the nightstand, opened a drawer, and found a wooden box inside. I pulled it out, setting it on top of the end table.

## 89

Bakr sat at his usual table, staring at the in-box for the e-mail account between him and Sayyidd. The box was still empty. Bakr felt drained, cheated of the gift for which he had so patiently waited. What the hell was Sayyidd up to? Why hadn't he e-mailed? Bakr couldn't bring himself to think the unthinkable — that Sayyidd had been captured or killed. Surely he was just hung up on his trip with Walid. They were too close to paradise for something to happen now.

He calmed down, mentally chastising himself for his pathetic wheedling. The forty-eight hours were up, and he had told Sayyidd he would immediately leave, but he decided to give his partner more time. Too much was riding on Walid's coordination. If Sayyidd didn't send an e-mail by this afternoon, he would begin looking for routes into Israel on his own, planning his next steps. He would return tomorrow morning and check again, giving Sayyidd an extra twenty-four hours. If there was still no response, he would assume the worst and leave Bosnia, heading perhaps toward Turkey, then onward into Syria.

Leaving the café, Bakr chastised himself again for his weak constitution, purposely picking up his gait to get away from the thoughts of self-pity.

Inside Carlos's hotel room, I was carefully checking the box for any indications of booby traps when my phone rang.

"Yeah? How long? Okay. I'm headed out. No, I haven't found anything, but I really haven't had time to check it out completely."

I started the chronograph feature of my watch, figuring I had about two minutes to finish up. Sure the box was clean, I lifted the lid and found my first indication of terrorist activity. I pulled the remote detonation device out of the box and turned it over in my hands, considering what I should do with it. I looked for some way to disable it without Carlos being aware, but quickly dismissed the idea, since I couldn't read the Cyrillic writing and didn't know enough about its operational capability to ensure I did it correctly without his knowing. I placed it back in the box and returned it to the drawer exactly as I had found it.

Before I closed the drawer I noticed a scrap of paper with an international number written on it. I copied it down, assuming it had been placed there by Carlos, since the end table and room were completely barren, without a trace of rubbish.

I searched the rest of the room but found nothing at all. I had confirmed the detonation device the terrorist had referred to in his e-mail, but still could not prove or disprove any connection to WMD. I looked at my watch, seeing one minute and forty-three seconds had passed since Jennifer's call. *Out of time. I need to go.*

I left the room, getting as far as the stairwell before I remembered I hadn't relocked the door. I ran back and inserted the bump key, gave it a whack, and attempted to turn the cylinder. It refused to move. I repeated the procedure with the same results. A gunfighter's mantra floated through my head. *Slow is smooth and smooth is fast.* Ignoring the clock, I started over, carefully feeling the pin tumblers and setting the key perfectly. I gave it another whack, breaking the cylinder free. I turned it over once, feeling the cylinder lock up again. *No more time to mess with it.*

Trotting rapidly down the stairs, I considered my next move. I had no proof of WMD, but I was personally convinced that Carlos had it and was carrying it around on his back. I contemplated taking out Carlos by myself but quickly tossed that idea. It would be impossible for me to get close to him without being recognized and I had no idea if the device was armed and ready to explode, inside a glass container that could be thrown, or simply in a Ziploc bag that would break in a scuffle. The idea of wrestling Carlos for control of a device that could kill hundreds by just being released into the atmosphere was best left in the category of last resort.

I reached the second floor landing and made a decision. *Alert the Taskforce.* I hated to do it, and knew I had promised I wouldn't without positive proof of WMD, but I decided that the circumstances warranted action. I pulled out the pager/beacon and hit the series of keys necessary to trigger the emergency signal. Nothing outward changed. It beeped once, returning to show the time. Reaching the first floor, I placed it back in my pocket and exited the stairwell.

Nodding to the old man behind the desk, I left the hotel and walked straight to my SUV, purposely not looking in the direction of the Internet café. I unlocked the driver's side door, looking down and hiding my face from anyone coming down the street. I was about to sit down when I felt the barrel of a pistol jammed into my kidney.

"You make a single fucking move, and I'll kill you right here. I know your capabilities, so trust me I won't be guessing about your intentions. You understand? Nod if you do."

I did as he asked.

"Raise your hands where I can see them, but don't make it look like you're surrendering." The man jammed the barrel again. "Don't do anything stupid. I can kill you and get out of here clean."

I placed my hands on the door and roof of the car, feeling the press of time. I was facing the direction Carlos was coming from and would be impossible to miss. I didn't mind the gun in my back but needed to speed this up.

I turned my head slightly, about to say something when I was cut off angrily by the man with the gun, "Keep facing forward! Don't move a fucking muscle until my partner arrives."

I attempted to hide my face, saying, "Look, I'm willing to do whatever you want. I'll come quietly. Can we just get moving?"

"What the hell are you looking at? Raise your head."

I continued looking down.

"Raise your fucking head or you're dead. Do it now."

I sensed the fear in the man and could almost feel his finger tightening on the trigger. I reluctantly raised my head, seeing another man approaching out of the corner of my eye.

The man gave me a wide berth. "Car's on the way. Should be here in five seconds."

"Good. This guy scares the hell out of me."

I ducked my head again, counting out the seconds. I reached to five with no car when the man with the gun said, "I tell you to raise your head again, and we'll be throwing a body in a car. I'm not sure you can feel it, but that's a fat barrel in your back. There will be no noise."

I raised my head, hearing a car pull up.

I looked up the street, trying to see anyone resembling Carlos in the distance. Spotting no one, I scanned the people closer to me. I saw a man resembling Carlos approaching, no more than twenty meters away. I was about to push my luck and lower my head again when the man met my eyes. I recognized the terrorist at the same time he recognized me.

## 90

Jennifer picked up a loose follow as soon as Carlos left the Internet café, staying on the opposite side of the street. When he increased his pace to a fast walk, closing in on the entrance to his hotel, Jennifer felt the anxiety in her stomach begin to skyrocket. *Why hasn't Pike called? What's he doing?* Carlos was one block away and about thirty seconds from getting so close that Pike couldn't possibly leave without being seen. She kept his pace, almost forced to break into a trot, the speed of events ratcheting up her anxiety even further. She pulled out her cell phone, preparing to call Pike again, when she saw Carlos abruptly stop. She paused, watching closely. She saw Carlos spin around and take off running the way he had come.

Stunned, Jennifer looked down the street, trying to identify what had caused the reaction. She saw Pike standing next to his car talking to two other men, a second car idling next to him. She turned back to the terrorist, seeing him in a wild run, his pack flopping crazily on his back as he dodged through the foot traffic.

She watched him for a split second longer, then returned to Pike and the two strangers. She saw Pike drop his keys out of view of the men, then move toward the sedan in the middle of the street.

She felt light-headed, the crowds around her fading into the background, the pressure to make the right decision crushing her like a physical thing. Pike had said he hadn't found the WMD, which meant that Carlos must be carrying it. *And Carlos has seen Pike. He knows we're after him.* He was now running to parts unknown with a massive deathtrap on his back, under pressure to use it sooner rather than later.

She saw Pike get in the back of the sedan. She knew that the men who had him intended to kill him. Would kill him, possibly in the next few minutes. She watched the door close, frozen in place. *What can I do about that? Nothing.* In fact, they wanted her as well. Showing herself now, attempting some pathetic action to stop three trained killers from driving away with Pike, would only guarantee both their deaths. She felt a burning sense of helplessness.

She ran the choices through her mind, her brain working at the speed of light. *What would Pike do? He wouldn't dither back and forth. He'd make a decision and execute.*

She began a fast walk in the direction of Carlos, knowing what Pike would tell her to do. *Go after the terrorist. Save the many. Screw the few. Do what was best overall, not what you would like to do.* She broke into a run, going through in her mind what she should do next, evaluating options for the surveillance and tracking of Carlos. She looked back the way she had come, watching the car make a U-turn and begin driving away from her.

She continued running, straining for a glimpse of Carlos to her front. She glanced back one more time, seeing the taillights of the car flash, watching it make a right turn out of sight. Her conviction faltered. Unbidden, she had a vision of Pike lying in a roadside ditch. Her mind superimposed the graphic violence she had witnessed in Guatemala over Pike's visage, a nightmare flash in her mind of Pike's head exploded open, brain matter and bone splattered on the ground, his eyes looking skyward, unseeing.

The image hit her with a physical blow, causing her vision to blur, her breath to catch in her chest. She slowed to a walk, the image burning into her soul. She turned around and began sprinting toward the Pajero. *Fuck the terrorist. Someone else can stop him.* She knew the decision might mean hundreds of people died, but there was only one death she cared about, and she would do what she could to stop it, no matter how insurmountable the odds.

Pike had talked of saving the many as the best course of action, that numbers alone decided the value of the effort, but that didn't seem right anymore. It wasn't just about numbers. Jennifer knew beyond a shadow of a doubt that someone would die today. Probably a great many people, including her. If Pike was standing when the smoke cleared, the sacrifice would be worth it.

Bakr paused to catch his breath, leaning against the corner of a building. He had run flat out for ten or eleven blocks, randomly turning left and right to lose himself in the city. So far, he hadn't noticed anyone chasing after him — in fact he hadn't seen a single reaction to his flight whatsoever. He believed he was momentarily safe.

Clearly, it was no coincidence the man from Guatemala was now in Tuzla. He was here because of Bakr. But if that was so, why hadn't the man chased him? Why let him run away without a single response? Maybe the man didn't recognize him. Maybe they knew that the partner of Sayyidd and Walid was in Tuzla but didn't know exactly who he was. If that was the case, he was still invisible. He needed to get back into his hotel, retrieve the detonator, and head to Sarajevo. That would be a complete break from everything the enemy knew. He would once again be on the offensive, safe in his anonymity.

He considered the hotel room. It would be a great risk to return there, since the enemy could be waiting for him. On the other hand, he hadn't told Sayyidd where he was staying, and the very fact that he had seen them nonchalantly hanging around out front indicated a coincidence, since they would never have been so brazen had they thought he was staying there. The detonator was worth the risk. He would just have to be very careful in his approach, ensuring the hotel didn't contain a trap.

# 91

The men in the sedan had the presence of mind to handcuff me, but luckily they had done so after I was in the car, leaving my hands to my front. I would never have made that mistake, but I wasn't going to complain. *Hopefully, they'll learn this lesson the hard way.*

In front of us was another sedan holding three men, leading the way out of town. I was sandwiched between the two guys who had taken me off the street, both of them hard looking with a military air. The man known as Mason, sitting on my left, was the only one who spoke.

"Pike, listen, this is nothing personal. I'm sure you understand. It's just a professional mission. You're going to die. That's a given. The choice you have is how. We need to know where the woman is. Tell us that, and we'll simply put a bullet in your head."

*Well, there you go. Nothing personal about it. They just want to kill me.*

"Go fuck yourself."

Mason nodded. "Yeah, okay. I figured my little speech wouldn't convince you. That's no problem. We have plenty of time."

We had left Tuzla and were headed south on a twisting two-lane road, the view alternating between rugged hillside and steep drop-off. The lead car was occasionally lost from sight around the sharp curves. After five minutes, we made a right turn on to a narrow blacktop that followed the ridgeline, heading deeper into the rugged terrain, away from the heavily trafficked main road.

Mason continued. "Look, I'll give you something to think about while we drive, just to ensure you know I've got the stomach for the work: I'm the one who talked to your friend Ethan. Trust me, it wasn't pleasant. I took no joy in it. The conversation lasted a long, long time."

*You little coward.* I stared deep into Mason's eyes, causing him to look away. "You should have kept that to yourself. I would've only killed you in self-defense. Now I'm going to kill every fucking one of you purely for the pleasure of it."

The driver gave a nervous laugh and said, "We'll see how tough you are in thirty minutes, asshole. Your buddy thought he was pretty hard, too, right up until we punctured his daughter's eyes."

Before I could respond, he jerked the wheel to the left, shouting, "Shit! Hang on!"

We were slammed back into our seats by a collision from the rear. The car swerved lightly right, then left, coasting to a stop on the side of the road.

Mason looked out the back window, saying, "What the hell happened?"

"We got rear-ended by some Bosnian bitch. Wait a sec and I'll get rid of her."

"Hurry up," Mason said. "We lost our escort. Assholes kept going around the curve without even looking back."

"Yeah, yeah. I'll throw some money at her. Give me a minute."

I turned around and felt a shock slap through my body. Jennifer was walking slowly to the back of our car, stooped over with a hand at her back, giving the impression of an injury.

Both Mason and the man to my right were focused on the activity to the rear. I didn't have a clue what Jennifer was doing but knew instinctively it was going to be borderline insane. *She has no idea what she's up against.* Before I could even come up with a half-baked plan, I heard Mason shout.

"What the fuck is that bitch doing! Jesus Christ!"

I looked back again and saw the driver doubled over holding his genitals. I watched Jennifer wind back up and kick him again, apparently attempting to drive the man's balls up into his neck. He fell over onto the ground. Jennifer proceeded to kick him in the head with all of her might. *Jesus, she's lost her mind.* His body was now on the ground and hidden from view, but Jennifer's leg pistoning back and forth like a jackhammer was not.

Mason threw open the door, screaming, "Watch Pike!"

The man to my right was still fixated on the beating the driver was receiving. The situation clicked — one man exiting the vehicle, the other focused on the fight. Neither one paying attention to me. *Big mistake.*

I drew my head back and slammed it full force into the face of the guy to my right, the hard, thick portion of skull right above my eyes caving in the brittle bones of the man's nose and eye sockets with a sickening crunch. Rotating toward Mason, I used every bit of strength I had to kick out with both feet, catching him halfway out of the door and launching him out of the car like I'd strapped his ass into an ejection seat. I ripped the Glock out of the lifeless hands of the first man and dove out the other passenger door just as Mason recovered and began firing into the back of the car, missing me but killing his unconscious partner.

I heard Jennifer scream, "Pike!," then the sounds of gunfire. *Shit. Move faster. She's gonna get hit.* Rising up on a knee, I saw Jennifer running to the back of our rental SUV with Mason standing up trying to get a clear shot.

I raised the weapon in a two-handed grip, smoothly settled the front sight post on Mason's head, and squeezed the trigger.

"Good-bye, motherfucker."

The force of the round threw Mason into the ditch beside the road, his head cratered open with bits of bone and brain matter oozing slowly onto the ground, his eyes looking skyward, unseeing.

Seeing no other threats, I said, "Jennifer! Come out! It's okay."

I ran to the passenger side of the Pajero. "Hurry up. We need to get out of here before that second car comes back, and I can't drive with handcuffs on."

Jennifer jumped inside and turned the key. The starter ground over but failed to catch.

"Shit! I didn't hit you guys that hard."

"Forget this thing, get out and go to the sedan." I jumped out just as the other carload of men came flying back around the mountain curve at a high rate of speed.

"Too late," I said. "Come out this side. Get behind the Pajero."

Jennifer crawled across the seat, exiting the passenger side and ending up on the ground next to me. Before I would lose the chance, I ran in a crouch to Mason, ripping the spare magazines for the Glock 19 from his belt.

The car came to a stop, both doors flying open, the men crouching behind them preparing to fire. The air grew silent, with the occasional whisper from the men carrying across the roadway.

I peeked around the Pajero, talking over my shoulder to Jennifer. "What in the hell was that all about?"

"Beats me," Jennifer said, breathing hard. "I was winging it, but it worked."

I pulled back around. "Man, I've seen some seat-of-the-pants shit before, but this is an absolute record."

I saw her laugh, apparently completely confident that everything would now turn out perfect. *She doesn't get it. She's used to miracles happening.* I knew the truth. I was facing three trained killers with two magazines of 9mm and shackled hands. I looked to our rear for an escape route and saw a hill rise about seventy-five feet. *We go that way and we'll be cut down for sure.* I knew what I would do if the roles were reversed — put suppressive fire on our position while maneuvering a force to flank us. Once they got on the high ground, with no cover between us and another gunman to our rear, we would be dead. There wasn't a lot I could do about it, since the odds of killing all three while they used the car for cover were just about nonexistent. *Shit. We're going to need another miracle.*

## 92

I poked my head up to get another read, immediately drawing a fusillade of fire. In that glimpse I had seen two men preparing to flank us. In order to do so, they would have to cross the road, traversing about forty feet of open ground. I leaned around the front of the SUV, keeping low, and saw them begin to move. I snapped off a few rounds, driving them back, but drew fire on my new position in return, forcing me to jerk back behind the Pajero.

Jennifer, still oblivious to our peril, asked, "What are we waiting for? What are we going to do?"

"Jennifer . . . we're in deep shit. I'm not sure what we're going to do. Once they get to the high ground in back of us, we're dead. The only thing that runs through my head is the ending of *Butch Cassidy and the Sundance Kid.*"

Jennifer's smile faltered, the predicament finally getting through. "How are we getting away?"

I peeked around the front of the Pajero again, seeing the two men making another break, both armed with assault rifles. I was able to snap off three rounds before being driven back, thinking I had winged one of the men, but ultimately unsure. They made it across the open ground. I rolled back around, leaning against the frame of the Pajero. *Fuck. We're done.*

"This is it. I want you to crawl underneath the SUV. They're going to reach the high ground in about a minute. From there, they'll kill us both. Once I start shooting, I want you to roll out the other side and run across the road, into the underbrush. Run down the hill as fast as you can. With any luck the other guy will be focused on the firefight and won't be able to get a clean shot at you. Once you're in the woods, keep going. Don't stop for anything. Run until you hit another car or a town."

Jennifer sat still, the implications of the plan sinking in.

"What about you?" she said. "What are you going to do?"

I couldn't meet her eyes. "I'll find you in the town. Okay?"

"No, no, *no*. I'm not doing that. Let's both run."

*Please don't make this hard.* "Look, someone has to pin them down so the other can make the run. Since you can't shoot, that leaves

583

me. Please, get underneath the damn truck. We're out of time."

Jennifer's face flushed. She started to say something else but thought better of it. She leaned close and gave me a peck on the cheek. I saw her eyes begin to water.

She said, "I'll see you in the town."

I leaned back, resigned to what was coming. Make no mistake, I wanted to live. But I had a greater responsibility to Jennifer. There was no way I was going to let her die. I was disappointed at how my life would end, but not tragically so. I had had a good run. My only shame was the mess I had become over the last year. *Just when I crawl out of the sewer, I get killed. What a waste.* God seemed to enjoy knocking me around. I just hoped my death would be enough entertainment. *Let Jennifer live. You're getting me. You'll have my entire fucking family. Isn't that enough? Please let her get out of here.*

I looked at the sky, seeing the contrails of a jet high overhead, wondering where it was going. I thought about Carlos, running loose with a device that would kill hundreds, if not thousands, hoping someone else would be able to stop him. I saw a helicopter in the distance, lazily circling as if looking for something. I felt a spring breeze against my face, light and warm, rustling the tree branches. *Why have I never taken the time to enjoy that before?* I wondered if my life had been good enough to earn the right to see Angie and Heather in heaven. I checked my weapon, saying another silent prayer for enough speed to give Jennifer a chance to escape. *Don't let them kill me quickly.*

I scanned the hillside and picked up a glint of metal in the sunlight at the top. *It's time.*

I dropped the half-empty magazine from the Glock, loading in a full one and laying out the other full one on the ground. I waited for the fight.

"They're at the top of the hill. Hold for about five rounds before running. Once you start, do not stop. Don't look back at me. Don't worry about the gunfire. Do you understand?"

I could hear Jennifer sobbing, ripping into my soul. *Jesus. Don't cry. It's okay.*

"Yes . . . I understand. Pike . . . don't die. I . . . I . . . Please don't die."

As I formed my answer, knowing that these words would be my last on earth, my pager began to vibrate. *What the hell?* The screen said: *Mark your position. Mark your position. Coming in hot.* I stared at the pager for a split second before the truth sank in.

"Get out from underneath the truck! Take off your headscarf and start waving it. *Hurry.*"

She wiggled out, ripping off the scarf and waving it back and forth like she was in a lifeboat in the middle of the ocean.

"What's up? Why am I doing this?"

*Someone else is God's entertainment. Someone who fucking deserves it.* "It's the cavalry. Stand by. These assholes are dead."

The pager vibrated again with a single word: *Marked.*

The world had returned to level, all doubt and fear banished by that simple message. I had been given an incredible gift. *A miracle.*

The feeling of relief was short-lived as the air around us snapped with supersonic rounds puncturing the steel of the Pajero. *Shit. We're out of time.*

"Get back underneath the truck. *Move!*"

I shoved Jennifer bodily backward, then began raking the hillside with the Glock, hitting nothing but hoping to suppress the incoming fire. Bullets were chewing up the ground around us, causing a feral fear to surface. *So fucking close. Not fair.* I got Jennifer behind the wheel well, jammed underneath the axle, and turned to fight. The two men were coming fast, one firing while the other moved, flip-flopping down the slope. I snapped off the remaining rounds in the first magazine and reloaded, traversing the hillside to draw the fire away from Jennifer's position. I dove behind the cover of a large tree, the ground around me exploding in pops like someone was working a Weed Eater against the trunk. *Where's the fucking cavalry?*

I could tell who was moving and who was

shooting because there was a pregnant pause in the fire each time they transitioned. I waited for it, then rolled to the right, attempting to keep them from flanking me or closing on Jennifer. I knew it was ridiculously stupid, but if I didn't even up the odds, we were both dead, and the small gap was all I had in my favor. If I did it right, I'd be facing the man on the move, and he'd block the shot of the guy providing the suppressive fire.

As soon as I aimed the Glock, I knew I was dead. I had picked the wrong side. The man to the left was moving, and I was facing the barrel of the man to the right, aimed directly at my head fifty meters away. Too far to hit with the pistol, but easy for the assault rifle. *Fuck.*

No rounds came my way. Instead, the man turned and aimed at the crest of the hill. For the first time I felt the deep thump of rotor blades. A Bell 427 helicopter sliced across the top of the hill, incongruously painted in bright yellow and white, with a logo emblazoned on the side reading Epeius Oil Exploration. The helicopter's blades bit into the air as it rotated violently, the open door facing the earth. I could see the team inside, held in place by the centrifugal force of the rotation, three holding SR-25 sniper systems at the ready. I couldn't hear the gunshots due to the rotor blades but saw the muzzles flash, two times each.

"Yeah, motherfuckers. Eat that."

The helicopter immediately circled around to the other side of the car hiding the single man. He jumped up and began to run, only to be cut down by the precision fire of the men inside, the 7.62 match-grade rounds flying unerringly toward his head as if it was a giant magnet.

Finished shooting what it could see from the air, the helo hovered over the road, its right door sliding open and a man hooking a thick fast-rope to the rescue hoist hanging off the side. Once attached, he threw out a kick bag holding the remaining coils. It fell to earth, the fast-rope snaking out of the bag on the way down. No sooner had the rope hit the ground than men began sliding down it, controlling their descent by hand and foot pressure alone, like a fireman sliding on a pole. One after another they exited the aircraft, until a total of five men were on the asphalt, fanning out and looking for targets.

When the last man hit the ground, the crew chief dropped the rope, allowing it to fall harmlessly to earth. The helicopter banked and flew out of sight.

I stood up, manacled hands in the air, saying, "You got them all."

The lead man turned, smoothly training his weapon on me. There was no overt threat in the gesture. The weapon simply moved as naturally as if the man were pointing.

I stared, mute at first, before words finally found me.

"Holy shit, *Knuckles?*"

# 93

Knuckles was trying very hard to remain serious, but he couldn't stop a giant grin from creeping over his face.

"Hello, Pike. Seems like I'm always bailing you out of trouble."

I was grinning like a schoolboy, too, but I didn't give a shit. "Hey, Knuckles. It's really good to see you."

Knuckles came over while the rest of the men fanned out, clearing the immediate area and searching the dead men and vehicles.

I stuck both of my cuffed hands out for a handshake, which Knuckles ignored. Instead he gave me a powerful embrace.

He held my shoulders. "It's really good to see you too. Alive, I mean."

"Man, you ain't lying. Ten more seconds and you'd be scraping us off the street."

"Who's the babe?"

Jennifer scowled, but I knew Knuckles was just kidding, trying to figure out what was going on.

"This is Jennifer Cahill, my partner in crime."

Knuckles smiled warmly, disarming her anger, and shook her hand.

I asked, "How in the hell did you get here so quick? I tripped my beacon less than an hour ago."

"Yeah, I know," he said. "It caused us to shit our pants. We were alerted by Kurt a day and a half ago. We're over in Tunis, doing 'Oil Exploration.'"

Knuckles raised his hands, making quotation marks.

"We were told simply to get our ass to Tuzla with the total package and link up with you. We got to Sarajevo this morning from Italy, refueled, and were heading in to Tuzla when your beacon went off. We homed in on it and saw the gunfight going on down here. The beacon wasn't precise enough to tell us who was who on the ground, so we paged you."

I couldn't believe how close we had come to dying. *I've used up my luck for the rest of my life. Or maybe it wasn't luck.*

One of the men came up with the keys to the handcuffs on my wrists. I gave him an embrace as well, like it was old home week. I waved in the direction the chopper had left.

"What's up with the helo? That's new."

Knuckles grinned. "Yeah, we got that since you left. It's a Bell 427. State of the art. You know the motto of the Taskforce — 'Money's

591

no object.' Anyway, we were tracking your favorite guy over in Tunis and about to pull the trigger when we got the redirect to here."

He paused, looking around at the battle site they had just entered.

"Enough about my story. What in the hell is going on here? Who are these guys?"

"I have no idea about the assholes here, but there's a terrorist in Tuzla that needs to be killed. We gotta get moving."

One of the men hollered at Knuckles, standing over the driver Jennifer had beaten into submission. He was awake and scared.

"Hey," I said, "I forgot about him. I guess there is someone who can tell us what's going on."

I pulled Jennifer out of earshot of the other men.

"Listen, I need you to get into the car across the street. Sit in the back and close the doors."

She looked at me warily. "Why? What are you going to do?"

"Well, I'm not asking you to leave because I'm going to make him take his clothes off."

"Pike . . . are you sure? I don't think this is right."

"Jennifer, he told me in the car that he blinded Ethan's daughter. You don't have to like it, but I'm going to make him tell me what's going on."

Jennifer's eyes widened, but she stood firm.

"And then you're going to do what? Kill him? Just like that? In cold blood?"

"We don't have time for this. Carlos is still running loose."

"I get that, Pike, I really do, but I don't want you to kill him. You'll be just like him. You'll become him. Is that what you want?"

*Can't she see he deserves to die?* I thought about what had happened today. Who was alive and who was dead. And the gift. *Shit. Maybe she's right.* "Okay, look, I won't kill him. Just get in the car."

Jennifer hesitated, then jogged away to the car without looking back.

Knuckles and I walked to the man on the ground, now sitting up and staring at us, fear radiating off of him, his face swollen and bloody from where Jennifer had kicked the shit out of him.

I squatted down to his level, tapping his forehead with the barrel of my Glock. "Hey, tough guy. Didn't quite work out like you wanted, did it?"

He began babbling instantly. "Don't kill me. I'll tell you everything I know, but I swear, it isn't much. I'm just a contractor for a company called Trident Global Threat Analysis. Please . . ."

"Trident Threat Analysis, huh? How original. Let me guess, you're a SEAL."

The man nodded.

The Trident was the nickname given to the

593

badge awarded after successfully completing Basic Underwater Demolition/SEAL, the arduous selection and training course that produced the Navy SEALs. Not too hard to figure out.

"How about that," I said to Knuckles. "He's a fuckin' retard. I can't believe a SEAL came that close to killing me."

Knuckles, an ex-member of SEAL Team Six, chuckled and said, "Maybe we should cut him a break for choosing the right branch of service."

"He's on the team that tortured and killed Ethan's family."

Knuckles's smile faded. "Maybe you should let me take a crack at him."

I returned to the driver, staring into his eyes, conveying no mercy. "Maybe I will. Depends on my man here. What's your mission? Who hired you? Who's the boss?"

Six minutes later I had all the information I could get from the guy. It wasn't much. He knew that the company was owned by a former SEAL named Lucas and that the mission had been to simply kill Jennifer and me. The good news was they were the only team on the ground, and the Taskforce had killed or captured everyone in it. As to how the team had found us, the man only knew that it was by electronic means. Somehow, Mason seemed to have an accurate picture of where

Jennifer and I had been both in Oslo and in Tuzla.

Knuckles asked, "How could he get a beacon on you without you knowing?"

"I have no idea. It could be our cell phones, but I don't see how. We've had three different sets since this started, and bought each one with cash. The only other thing I've been carrying is Kurt's personal pager. It hasn't been out of my hands since he gave it to me, so it can't be that."

"You don't have anything else they could have altered?"

"No. We've been living like vagabonds. Doesn't matter now, anyway. The team's dead and we need to get moving. We can figure it out later."

Knuckles pressed a hidden switch on his thumb, giving his men commands through what looked like an ordinary Bluetooth cell phone earpiece. They coalesced around us, all reaching out and shaking my hand or giving me an embrace.

Knuckles gave a brief warning order of what was about to happen, then split the team between the two functioning sedans. After they began loading, he looked down at the driver, asking, "What about this guy?"

*Fuck turning the other cheek.* "Well, I promised Jennifer I wouldn't kill him, so I guess he stays. Doesn't mean I can't make it hard for him."

I aimed the Glock at the man's knee and pulled the trigger, shattering the patella. I ignored his scream. *You're lucky you didn't kill Jennifer. Nothing would've stopped me from carving you up.*

"Come on," I said, "let's go. We can talk as we drive."

I left the man writhing on the ground in pain, blood jetting out from the wound. Four steps to the car, I glanced at the sky. *No lightning. Must be Old Testament Day.*

We got in the car with Jennifer. Having heard the gunshot, she gave me a questioning look.

"Don't worry, I didn't kill him. If he's smart, he'll come out alive."

She said nothing.

I headed back to Tuzla, the other car following. "Before I begin, give me a rundown on what you've got here. What are the assets available?"

"Well, we were at Omega in Tunis, so we've got the total package on the ground. You saw the 427. We can use that in a pinch, but only to exfil whoever we get. We have no cover for status here, so I can't let that thing be seen doing anything operational. Dropping in here was pretty damn risky, but the gunfight sort of overcame that. It's supposed to only be passing through. Obviously, we have the team you just saw, but we have the same issues.

We're all employees of Epeius, supposedly exploring for oil in Tunisia. We're really hanging it out here. There'll be no plausible deniability if this falls apart."

Knuckles was gently reminding me of the potential sacrifice should things go wrong.

"Sounds like you guys were about to pull the trigger. Sorry for the change of mission, but, trust me, it's worth it."

Knuckles said, "You'll be sorrier about it when I tell you who the target is."

"Who?"

"Your old pal Crusty."

"Crusty? That bastard's still around? You guys haven't taken him off the board?"

"Yeah, he's still around, and he's moved up in the world. He's no longer just a low-hanging fruit to whack for the hell of it. His security ain't getting any better, though. We can fall right back into it, as long as we don't blow our cover over here."

*Shit. He's not going to like what I have to say.* "Well, it's going to be sticky. Our target knows he's being hunted. It's going to be very hard to take him off the board without a firefight. Whatever happens to your cover, it'll be worth it."

"Let me guess, you've found Bin Laden and he's here with a nuke on his back."

"Close. It's not Bin Laden."

He didn't need a map drawn out. "You're tracking someone with WMD? For real?"

"Yeah. He's going to deploy it soon. Maybe in the next few hours. And I don't know where the fuck he went."

## 94

We planned our next moves in a parking lot a block down from Carlos's hotel. It had been a little strange at first, since out of the five folks on the ground, four of them had been my guys — including Knuckles. I could tell he was unsure how to handle the situation, so I had deferred to him and simply fallen in as a team member. He didn't say anything, but I knew him well enough to see he was greatly relieved. I also knew he'd let me take over the team if I'd asked. But I wasn't ready. These men had worked and trained relentlessly for a very long time to hone their skills to a razor's edge. Part of that was individual, and part was teamwork. Either way, I was on the low end of the stick for both. *Taking charge would just be an ego trip. Knuckles is the man now.*

And he had grown quite a bit while I was gone. I watched him with the team and could see they were clicking. It was painful to admit, but my taking over would just make them less effective. I was satisfied with providing the intelligence, letting Knuckles handle the assault. I knew he'd defer to me if it came to that.

Knuckles finished giving instructions, wasting little time on fancy planning. "All right, remember we're dealing with WMD. Take that seriously. Pike's going to lead the way. We get to the room and scan it for heat. If we see a source, we go in hard. If the room's clean, we take it slow. No sense alerting the rest of the hotel if we don't have to."

I'd be lying if I said I didn't get a kick out of the mission brief. It was like nothing had changed, and I was sitting on the patio at Tbilisi. *About to save the world.* Maybe that's a bit much, but it *was* a good feeling. Knuckles finally got to us. "Jennifer, I want you to engage the man at the front desk. Keep him focused on you until we're in the stairwell. We're going to enter in two groups, three seconds apart. Once the second group is in the stairwell, you can head on back to the cars here."

Jennifer nodded, apparently comfortable in her role.

"Pike, I want you to lead so we don't make a mistake on the door, but once you've pinpointed the objective, I want you to pull security while we're in the room. Okay?"

*Security? That sucks.* I didn't push it. "No issues. It's all yours. You got any kit for me?"

Knuckles grinned, obviously relieved that I hadn't demanded to be with the entry team.

"Of course," he said. "I knew you wouldn't have anything. You never did." He turned to a man carrying a civilian pack. "Give him the kit we brought."

Inside the bag was some communications equipment and an H&K UMP, just like everyone else was sporting. It was a small, lightweight submachine gun built primarily of space age polymer, which made it easier to break down and hide from X-ray inspection. While it lost the power of the cartridges chambered in carbines and rifles, the UMP had the appeal for the Taskforce of being easily concealable. There were other automatic weapons that were smaller, but the UMP chambered the more powerful .45 caliber instead of the ubiquitous, but less powerful, 9mm. The .45 had a much greater knockdown power and was a subsonic round, thus making the UMP easy to suppress without the need for special rounds. I pulled it out and did a functions check, knowing it was unnecessary, but doing it anyway out of habit.

Once he saw I was ready, Knuckles started the ball rolling, telling Jennifer, "Showtime. We'll be thirty seconds behind you."

She glanced at me with a question. No fear, just unsure of whether she should leave. Wanting my approval before she followed the orders of a stranger she'd just met.

I said, "Time to put your money where your mouth is."

She broke into a smile and started walking, saying, "Please. I'm just wondering if I should stay behind so I can pull your ass out of the fire."

Knuckles let her get out of earshot before saying, "Is she good to go? What was that all about?"

"Nothing," I said. "She's just good at winging shit. And proud of it too."

"Fucking great. Just what I need. You guys must be the perfect couple."

Two minutes later, the entire team was stretched out along the hallway of Carlos's room. I pulled security the way we had come, the team prepared to enter, with various team members covering the other hotel room doors. One man turned on a sophisticated thermal viewer that allowed him to see heat sources through a variety of construction materials. It couldn't determine if the source was a man, but it would alert us if a large mass in the room was putting out more heat than the ambient temperature. Short of a space heater being operational, it would be a human, since the device wouldn't register such things as candles or lighters. The man swept the room quickly, then shook his head. Knuckles turned to the next man, twisting his hand as if he were using a key.

The man immediately dropped to a knee,

pulling out a much more sophisticated version of my homemade bump key. It looked like a key on one end, with a baseball sized lump on the other. He inserted it into the lock, pressed a button on the baseball, and swung the door open, leaning back as the entry team blew by him into the room. Five seconds later we were all in the room, discussing what to do next.

"He came back and took the detonator," I said. "Ballsy guy, I'll give him that."

Knuckles said, "You got any idea where he went, or are we now at the 'let's go fishing' stage?"

"I only know he has a safe house somewhere in Bosnia, presumably around here, but it could be anywhere."

"That's not much of a help."

Then I remembered. "Wait. I copied a phone number while I was in here. I'm positive it was something of his. It might only be his contact here, but it might also be the safe house. Either way, we hit that thing and we'll get something out of it."

"We've both hit jackpot with less in the past," Knuckles said. "Let's get the hell out of here before the locals start sniffing around."

Back on the street we linked up with Jennifer at the parking lot. I told her what we had, then read off the phone number to Knuckles.

She asked, "What're you going to do, try to

call that and trick him?"

"No," I said, "we're going to try to pinpoint it. The landline infrastructure here was pretty much demolished during the war, so this number is probably a cell phone. Just about every single cell phone built now comes with a GPS feature. What we're going to do is try to turn it on and have it send us its location. It might not work, because we need a digital network to slave on, and the phone needs a GPS. If we have both, we can dial the phone without it ringing and do some black magic."

While I was talking one of the team had pulled out a normal looking cell phone, telling it to boot up a hidden program. He said, "We're good. We have a digital signal."

He dialed the number, watching the screen. "It's a cell."

He spent thirty seconds thumbing the keypad as if he were texting a friend.

"Got a GPS."

He continued to work it for another half minute.

He looked up with a smile. "We're in business. Got a grid."

He read the grid reference out to another man working a laptop computer with a world mapping program.

"It's a house in Sarajevo," he said, "north of the river about middle way through the city."

"That's outside the Republic of Srpska part

of Sarajevo. It'll be a Muslim neighborhood,"
I said. "That fits. We need to get moving. He's
got a few hours' head start."

Knuckles said, "Well, unless he's flying, we
can beat him. We sent the 427 to the old
Eagle base. No Americans there now, since
SFOR left, but it is an operational airport.
We can probably beat him to Sarajevo. The
key question is whether that's where he's going."

"Won't know that until we get there. Let's
load up. You can follow me. I still remember
the way to Eagle base."

An hour and a half later we were flying
south, with me fuming over the bureaucratic
nightmare of getting the helicopter fueled up
and ready to go at the old air base. *Third-
world bullshit. Maybe we should chase Carlos
right into that damn terminal. Give 'em a sense
of urgency.* Watching the ground race underneath, I relaxed. It would take less than forty-
five minutes to get to the Sarajevo airport,
even taking into account more bureaucracy.
We should be very close behind him.

My mind wandered to the team we had
killed, and how they had managed to find
Jennifer and me. Eliminating everything I
could think of, I was left with one possibility:
They had somehow managed to track Kurt's
pager. I couldn't see how on earth that would
be true, since the pagers were treated as
sensitive items in the Taskforce, but there

605

simply wasn't any other explanation. Short of some miraculous new technology, it was the only weak point I could find, and if Kurt's pager was compromised, they were all probably vulnerable. With the team dead or bleeding on the side of the road, it was no longer a threat on this operation, but the compromise would need to be explored after we finished here.

## 95

Bakr waved his arms at a cloud of smoke spewed out by the departure of an inner-city bus. He surveyed the area, getting his bearings. Juka had given him directions to the house from the Sarajevo bus station, and Bakr had researched the city while waiting on Sayyidd to answer, but the image he had created in his mind didn't fit the reality on the ground. Finding a map on the wall, he quickly located the tram that would take him to the city center.

The trek back to his hotel room had been little trouble; the man from Guatemala and his henchmen were nowhere to be seen. He hadn't pushed his luck, spending less than three minutes in his room, packing up his things and taking the detonator. The bus ride itself had been inside a bouncing, belching machine that should have been retired years ago, but that was quickly forgotten in his eagerness to find the safe house.

Riding the tram parallel to the Miljacka

River, he could still see the scars of war throughout the city, with mortar impacts slashing the street and bullet holes pocking the walls of older buildings. As the tram closed in on the old section of the city known as Bascarsija, he began to notice a healthy security presence. Pulling into his stop inside the old market area, he saw an overwhelming number of police. Too many for simple tourist protection.

His first thought was that he had already been tracked and was now on the verge of getting captured. Frozen in place for a second, the panic rising, he debated whether he should simply keep riding. He was broken out of his thoughts by someone else trying to exit.

Speaking in English, Bakr asked, "Why're all the policemen here?"

The Bosniak smiled and said, "Big ceremony today. It's the fifteenth anniversary of the Markale massacres during the war. They're just here to keep the peace."

Hoping the relief didn't show on his face, Bakr exited with the man, asking what the massacre was about.

"During the siege here the Serbians launched three separate mortar attacks on the Markale Market right up the road there. Killed a lot of people. They're putting up a memorial today. Something more formal than a Sarajevo Rose."

Bakr thanked the man and moved on. He hadn't known the name of the market but had read about the actions there, as well as the siege itself, in his research earlier. The Markale was the largest outdoor market in Sarajevo, and the attacks had killed hundreds of civilians who were simply trying to survive. He knew a "Sarajevo Rose" was the impact of the mortars themselves, now filled in with red paint and left as they were the day they were fired as a reminder of the callous act. Ultimately it had convinced the Western world to intervene in the bloody conflict.

It disgusted Bakr that the Muslims here would turn to the West as their savior, going so far as to put up a monument commemorating their weakness. Maybe if they didn't act so much like the infidel, they wouldn't have needed the help of the infidel.

He walked through the old section of the city and entered into the close-packed neighborhoods to the north. Using Juka's directions, he approached what he thought was the safe house. It was hard to tell, since all the buildings looked the same, but this was the only house with a large concrete planter in the front yard, looking like a horse trough filled with dirt. Juka said it had been put up after a mortar round had landed in the street, but that it now served to keep people away from the front of the house. He could always call the number Juka had given him for the clean safe house somewhere nearby, but preferred to use that as a last resort.

Bakr glanced around, seeing nothing more than a couple of pedestrians walking away from him and a woman beating a rug on an upstairs balcony down the street. He went around the left side of the house and jumped the waist-high concrete wall of the courtyard. He moved to the northeast corner and squatted down. Looking closely at the ground, he searched for a length of twine coming out of the neglected patch of flower garden. Pulling gently, he followed it for a foot and a half, eventually pulling up a key. He smiled. He had the right house.

Bakr unlocked the back door and swung it open without going inside. He stood and listened for thirty seconds. Hearing nothing, he walked slowly into the house, smelling the musty, cloying odor of a space rarely used. He searched throughout the downstairs and upstairs, slowly walking and listening for anyone or anything. Eventually he was satisfied that the house was empty.

He moved to the front and peeked out the window, getting a clear view up and down the street. He saw nothing out of the ordinary. The woman continued beating her rug, dust swirling around her head, giving her a halo in the afternoon light, but nothing else was moving. He found the basement door and went downstairs, fumbling a second before finding a light. He took a moment to let his eyes get used to the dazzle.

Against the back wall, stacked from the dank floor to within a foot of the ceiling, were enough explosives to take out an entire city block. He saw blasting caps, AK-47s, blocks of Semtex, ball bearings, remote-control aircraft components, cotton vests, wiring, and anything else he might need to build his suicide weapon. It would take him some time to integrate his special detonator, but he had the expertise to make it work.

Lucas waited on his men outside of the Sarajevo customs area, where he was the first to make it through. The team didn't have to worry about anyone in customs searching their bags — they were using black diplomatic passports secured by Harold Standish through contacts inside the National Security Council.

He hung up his cell phone for the third time. For some reason he had no contact with Mason at all. The phone simply rang and went to voice mail. He chalked it up to a sorry cell network. He watched the first team member come through the customs hallway, carrying his duffel bag covered in military patches. *Way to go, 007. Real inconspicuous.* He reflected again on the fact that he was dealing with the second tier. They were all special operations guys, but not the cream of the crop. They were good enough at executing simple missions, with specific instructions, but would not do well at contingencies or thinking on the fly. *They sure as shit aren't as good as Mason's team. Why won't that guy answer the phone?*

# 96

On final approach to the Sarajevo airport, I could see a flurry of activity on the tarmac. Instead of airport workers in yellow vests, I saw a bunch of guys in business suits casing the place. Getting on the headset, I asked the pilot what was going on.

"Some sort of ceremony in town today. They got dignitaries coming in from all over Europe."

Knuckles cut in. "That's great. Should make our illegal exfil with a captured terrorist that much easier."

I grinned at him. "Come on. What's the point of living on the edge if you don't lean over a little?"

He just shook his head.

The pilot said, "Might work out better for us. We're being directed to land at the old military side of the airport — away from all the security. Should be able to come and go freely from this end."

The Taskforce team exited the Bell 427

while the rotors were still turning, the whine of the engines slowly growing weaker. I was itching to get started. "We need some vehicles. Anyone know anything about this airport?"

One of the pilots responded, "Yeah, there're a couple of car rental places inside. The terminal's small, so it shouldn't be too hard to find."

I wanted to start barking out orders but held back, waiting on Knuckles.

"Okay," he said, "pilots stay here, ready to move. Keep the helo on strip alert, because we're probably coming back fast. Be prepared to flex to Tuzla. If I see the security's too tight, we'll exfil from there with the package. Retro, you and Jennifer go find a couple of rental cars. Something big enough to carry up to two more men than we have. You know what we're looking for."

Jennifer and the man called Retro had started to leave when one of the pilots shouted, "Wait. I'll go with you." Jerking a thumb over his shoulder at Knuckles, he said, "He always wants 'strip alert,' but we usually end up sitting around for days, begging for food from anyone who passes by. I'll get a car for us as well."

After they left, Knuckles asked me, "Well, what do you think? What's the play? Go in hard right now?"

He was doing all the right things, taking

input from everyone, making me a little proud for no reason whatsoever.

"No. I think we should get the cars and conduct a recce to get a feel for what we're dealing with. From there we can make a plan."

Knuckles nodded. "Yeah, I agree." He started giving orders. "Break out the visor cams. We don't have a lot of time to go pure clandestine, so don't worry about a deep install."

Jennifer and Retro returned in two beat-up sedans within twenty minutes, with the pilot right behind them. No sooner had they exited the cars than four men began rigging one for clandestine surveillance. Using four cameras the size of lipstick tubes, they hid them in the upholstery and fed the lines into a digital recording device. The cameras would give a three-hundred-and-sixty-degree view around the chassis, allowing detailed planning against the target.

While the car was being rigged, Knuckles and I studied a map of the target area with Bull, the man he had selected to conduct the reconnaissance. Knuckles had picked him because he most closely resembled the indigenous population, and I'd given him the leather jacket I'd bought as additional camouflage.

Knuckles asked me, "You ever been here? What're the neighborhoods like? Is it like

Fallujah where everyone knows you don't belong?"

"I haven't been in that neighborhood, but you know the city's a significant tourist attraction, at least as far as Bosnia goes. I'd say that most of the tourist stuff is centered on the sights downtown but they probably see strangers quite a bit all over the place. It's probably not suspicious to drive by, especially just once."

An idea hit me. "Hey, why don't you take Jennifer as some eye candy? She's pretty good under stress, and she's already dressed like a Bosnian woman. She'll lower the profile if she's in the car. If they have some sort of early warning going on, they won't suspect a couple."

Knuckles chewed the idea over for a few seconds. "Yeah, that'll work. Bull, you got an issue with that?"

"No. It's not like we're going into a gunfight. She'll be much more of an asset than a liability."

I saw Jennifer getting a little aggravated with the talk going back and forth, as if she weren't there or didn't have a vote.

"You game for that?" Knuckles asked her. "All you'd have to do is ride and keep your eyes open."

She said, "Yes. I can do that. Thanks for asking. I figured you were just going to tie me to the front seat no matter what I said."

Knuckles looked at me like he was going to scrub her participation.

"She's good to go," I said, smiling at her. "She just likes to be the one telling people what to do. She doesn't listen to me either."

Jennifer purposely ignored me. "You're Bull, right?"

"Yeah."

"What do you want me to do?"

Bakr placed the finishing touches on his explosive package, attempting to make it as unobtrusive as possible. Ordinarily he would have embedded the entire device in ball bearings and nails in an effort to create as much death and destruction as possible. In this case, all he wanted to do was disperse his Tupperware container of death without destroying it. He opted not to build a suicide vest but to utilize the backpack he already had.

His biggest challenge was creating enough of an explosive effect to distribute the toxin over as large an area as possible without actually destroying it in the fire and pressure of the explosion itself. It was a delicate Catch-22. Go too large, and all he would get was an explosion that consumed the toxin. Go too small and he would kill very few people. Luckily, he'd had in-depth instruction on how to tamp the material and protect it from the fire of the explosion as well as how to maximize the downwind hazard once the poison was airborne.

Taping down the blasting caps, he heard a vehicle approach down the road. He had been in the house for over an hour and hadn't heard a single car yet. He paused his work and went upstairs to the window. He relaxed, seeing a beat-up sedan pass by with a Bosnian man and woman inside. They paid his house no attention whatsoever. He returned to the device, connecting his special detonator to the blasting caps.

## 97

Lucas wondered how far he could push his second-tier team. He decided to opt with their strengths: full-on frontal assault. Hopefully, it wouldn't come to that, as he had to assume that Mason's team was on Pike right this moment, tracking him for the kill. He asked his tech man what was taking so long for a beacon fix, only to be told for the third time that the pager track download was locked up. He took a deep breath and let it out, asking again, "How much longer is this going to take?"

"It's rebooting now. Shouldn't be but a few more minutes."

Lucas walked in a small circle, physically forcing himself to remain patient. The men returned from the rental agency, driving an SUV and a sedan. Together, they were large enough to hold the team plus equipment and perhaps one more person. The vehicles blended into the traffic around the airport, pleasing Lucas with the selection. *Figured they'd bring back a convertible mustang or a two-seater Porsche. Maybe I'm selling them short.*

One of the drivers said, "Somebody just beat us to the counter. This is all they had available, but they should work."

Lucus mentally rolled his eyes. *So much for thinking they made a conscious decision.*

Knuckles paused the video at the target house, seeing the same two-story style with a courtyard in the back that appeared all over the area. The front of the house was clean, with a clear path to the door. No parked cars or fences to worry about. It was located on the east side of the street, with houses on both sides and behind it.

"What were the atmospherics of the neighborhood?"

"Quiet," Bull said. "In fact, we didn't see a single automobile. A couple of pedestrians and a few folks tending gardens, but definitely not a hopping place."

Knuckles stared at the still image. "All right. I don't want to do a mounted assault. We do an offset on the main thoroughfare to the east, then conduct a dismounted movement to the target from the south, the opposite direction of the recce drive-by. We move in two groups. One takes squirter control in the rear, the other enters the house from the front."

Knuckles paused for questions, then continued. "Remember, we don't know what's in this house, so we can't treat it as a hostile force. Discriminate on every target. We don't want to end up killing some old housewife."

Knuckles finished the briefing by splitting the team, putting me on squirter control. *Out of the fight again.* I didn't argue, knowing he was right.

I moved off to the rear of the lead car, checking my weapon and spare magazine placement, working to ensure I could reload in a minimum amount of time. Jennifer walked over, tentatively asking, "Hey, I'm not trying to bug you, but I didn't understand any of that."

I continued working on my kit. "Based on what you guys are saying about the traffic in the area, we don't want to drive right up to the target. We'll park on the main road to the east, then walk there. It should help us remain undetected. Me and another guy will move to the back to catch what we call squirters — really just a name for anyone trying to run. We'll lock down the back of the house while the team enters from the front."

Jennifer nodded absently, looking distinctly uncomfortable at how fast this was progressing.

"Relax," I said. "Your job's over. Don't worry about us. We do this for a living."

I heard the other men beginning to load

the cars. "See you in a few minutes."

She locked eyes with me, saying, "Please be careful. Let them do the hard stuff. Don't do anything heroic. Don't let Carlos blow you up."

"Cut that shit out. You should be worrying about him."

I started to get in our car when she grabbed me by the arm, "Pike, I'm serious. You might have nine lives, but you've been going through them like a chain-smoker. A life can only have so much luck. We're both working on credit now. I can feel it. Promise you'll be careful."

I looked at her, realizing she was deeply worried.

"I'll be careful. This'll be all right. Trust me."

"I do trust you," she said, with a hint of a smile. "A little, anyway. It's just that you're acting different. I can't put a finger on it, but it's like you now think you're invincible. You used to be an asshole about everything, sure it was failure. Now you act like this is all just a ride at Disneyland."

"Hey, this is what I do. I've been killing terrorists a helluva lot longer than I've known you. Sorry if I get a kick out of it, but don't tell me to go back to what I was. You don't like it, I'm sorry. But *this* is who I am."

She recoiled, and I knew I had missed the point. The hurt and pain in her expression reminded me of Heather the last night I had seen her. I remembered what I had said after Jennifer had thought Carlos was going to kill her in the hotel — *It's never just about you.*

"Jennifer, listen to me. Carlos is about to kill a lot of people. We're the only ones who can stop him. And I mean *we* are the only ones who can stop him. You and me. You saved my life, and I don't mean just today. There's got to be a reason for that. I don't want to die any more than you do, but I'm the one that's here, and I'm the one that's got the skill to kill that asshole. You know I can't promise nothing bad's gonna happen, but if it does, you need to believe it was worth it. Okay?"

She sighed. "Yeah, okay. Just don't do anything stupid. Please. Before you jump off of a building, remember you can't fly. Can you do that? For me?"

"Sure. But you need a better analogy, because I *can* fly."

"Smartass," she said. "Good luck."

## 98

The tech man got Lucas's attention. "He's right here in Sarajevo. About three klicks from the airport and moving east."

*About fucking time.* He addressed the entire team. "Listen up. We aren't going to do any fancy work over here. If we execute, it'll be a simple frontal assault, but hopefully it won't come to that. Mason's team's in-country, and presumably tracking Pike right now. The last thing I want to do is screw up an operation he's already executing."

One of the men cut in. "So we're just backup for Mason?"

"Maybe, maybe not. I can't get in touch with Mason or his team, and I don't want to lose the targets again. If we can't link up with them, we'll get a fix on the beacon and hit Pike and the girl ourselves."

He saw the team start to grin, apparently anticipating an easy kill and the bonus that went along with it. "Don't get a hard-on yet. I've told you what happened in D.C. Remember that. This isn't a cakewalk. We close in on him and take him out with overwhelming force. I'm not risking another complicated operation. We smoke him and the girl, then immediately head back here and catch the first thing flying home."

Lucas gave the team a minute to break their weapons out and kit up, then said, "All right. Let's move. Remember what I said. You might think you're a killer, but this guy really is."

Twenty minutes later, Lucas's team idled in the parking lot of a restaurant on the northern end of Sarajevo. They had traveled the entire length of the city, the cars spreading out on the surface roads in an attempt to contact Mason and his team by both cell phone and radio. They had failed, and now Lucas had a choice to make. *I can spend my time trying to find Mason, or I can spend my time trying to kill Pike.*

He decided to execute the mission with the second-tier team, since he had no idea how long Pike's beacon would last. *Batteries might be going dead while I sit here with my thumb up my ass. Lose that, and the whole game's over.* He'd worry about Mason later. In fact, he wouldn't worry about Mason at all. He'd failed, and now, as in the past, Lucas would be forced to clean up the mess. He liked to think he was being logical, but the truth was he *wanted* Pike. Wanted to be the one who twisted the knife. And make no mistake, Pike wasn't going to die easy. Not anymore. As he saw it, all of his troubles centered on one man. The ongoing investigation that had forced him to flee the U.S. was precisely the result of this asshole's evading Lucas's net. The thought rankled him. Made him eager for the hunt.

He watched the beacon track on the computer in his lap and committed the team.

"Target's on the move. He's headed this way. By the speed of the beacon, he's mounted. We'll wait here until he dismounts. Once he's stationary, we'll roll. This car will lead, passing up his location. The trail car will follow, stopping short. On my command — I say again, on *my* command — we'll execute the mission. Nobody, and I mean nobody, will fire until I give the command. Once that command is given, everyone with a shot needs to fire. Is that understood?"

Lucas waited, hearing confirmation from every member of the team. "Okay. Good. I'll call once he stops. We'll take a look at the terrain, form a quick plan, then move."

Superimposed over the satellite image of the neighborhood, Lucas watched the beacon inch closer, seeing it stop short about a kilometer from their location. Within a minute, he saw the dot move again at a much slower speed.

"Stand by. He's now on foot."

Lucas felt the tension grow. The endgame was approaching. Pike was a dangerous man, someone to fear, but he couldn't possibly stand up to the concerted effort of the entire team. *Maybe he can kill one or two, but there's no way he can kill us all.*

He saw the blip stop inside the courtyard at the back of a house on the east side of a small street. This was it.

"All right. Team leaders get over here."

He pointed out the house, dictating where the vehicles would stop and where they would dismount and set up fields of fire.

"We wait until he comes out, all night if we have to. Once he's out, we open up, killing him. Pretty simple. Any questions?"

One team leader asked, "What about the girl? Isn't she part of the mission?"

"Yeah, she is, but I can't predict whether she's with him or not. If she's with him, smoke her. If not, we'll find her later. I'm through messing around with this guy."

Retro and I covered the back door and a corner window from the courtyard at the back of the house, waiting on the call from Knuckles. My earpiece gave a hollow echo, Knuckles speaking in a calm monotone, "Execute, Execute, Execute." The call brought back memories of assaults past. I tensed up, waiting to see if someone would attempt to run from the rear of the house. My mind's eye ran through what was occurring in the house, the team flowing like water through the rooms looking for a threat. I heard no gunfire, which could be either good or bad.

Five minutes later I heard the all-clear given, and the back door was opened by Knuckles.

"What did you find?" I said.

"Nothing. We found the cell phone, but it's the only thing here right now. No other targets. The house looks like it's lived in, but there's nobody home."

"Great. That figures."

"What do you think? A stay-behind?"

"I don't know. I suppose that's the best course of action. We don't have anything else. I could stay, you could give me another couple of guys, and we could sort it out when the owner returns. How's that sound?"

"I'm good with that, but maybe we're getting ahead of ourselves. Let's turn this place upside down first. Maybe we'll find something of interest. In the meantime, maybe whoever owns this phone will return while we're still here."

"Let's get busy. I'll start upstairs."

A hundred meters down the street, Bakr had finished with the device and was sitting before his dinner of moldy bread and nuts when he perked up at the sound of another car, only the second one he had heard all day.

Lucas pulled past the target house, parking on the east side of the narrow street. The position gave him a full view of the right side of the street and clear fields of fire to the front door of the target. His satellite imagery display showed the beacon superimposed directly over the house. Pike had moved inside. He waited until he saw the follow vehicle stop short on the other side of the target about a hundred meters away before telling the team to deploy into firing positions. He watched one man exit the follow vehicle and move nonchalantly to the corner of the house where his car was parked, taking cover behind a concrete planter. Another man sauntered across the street, attempting to cover the back of the target house.

Bakr peeked out the front window. His heart skipped a beat when he saw a car stop right in front of his house with three Caucasian men inside. That was not natural at all. He continued watching from the corner of the window, wanting to believe his paranoia was getting the better of him, but feeling the adrenaline start to flow. He saw one man with a rifle walk to the corner of his house and take a knee, peering over the planter out front. The man made an attempt at hiding the weapon under his jacket, but the barrel could still be observed poking out under the hem. Bakr had seen enough.

He raced to the basement, taking the stairs two at a time. Grabbing an AK-47 and four loaded magazines, he sprinted out of the basement and up to the second floor. Peering out a bedroom window, he saw the gunman directly below him.

The man was obviously preparing to assault the house with the other men from the car. Bakr knew he had to go on the offensive, and quickly. He could attempt to run out of the back of the house, but feared it was already covered with men he couldn't see. He could run out the front, but that would send him straight into at least three men. Either plan of escape would be better if he seized the initiative while they were still getting ready. He slowly opened the window, praying it didn't squeak.

## 99

The sound of an AK-47 rocking on full automatic caused me to hit the floor. *What the fuck?* It wasn't in our house, so it wasn't directed against the team. I peeked out a window, trying to identify the source of the fire, the upstairs vantage point giving me an unobstructed view down the road. I saw a man crumpled on the front lawn of a house across the street, two doors down. I leaned forward to identify the shooter, calling, "Contact — house to the northeast about seventy-five meters away. One man down. Unsure of shooter location."

Knuckles responded, "Not directed at us. Everyone stay cool. Probably some sort of gang fight or leftover animosity. We don't want to get dragged into that. Get eyes out three-sixty. Call in to let me know your position."

Bull called from downstairs, "Two vehicles to the front of the house on the east side. Three men. One man at the vehicle to the north, two men at the vehicle to the south. All are armed and focused on us. They're using the cars for cover. What's the call?"

Knuckles came back, cold and calm. "Stand by. Develop the situation. We don't know if they're police, criminals, or what. If they display hostile intent, take them out."

I was about to call my position when a hail of bullets shattered the window to my front. I dropped flat to the floor. "Contact, contact. North side of house. Fire directed at me."

I rolled to my left, coming up underneath the second window of the room.

I peered out the corner of the window, looking back toward the house with the fallen man. I caught a glimpse of a man jumping out of the back courtyard and sprinting away. Before I could process what I had seen, I caught movement directly below me and refocused. I saw a man crouched and running toward the back courtyard of the house next door. I called Knuckles, raising my H&K at the same time.

"One man, armed, moving toward cover. Not the original shooter from across the street. He's holding an MP5, not an AK. He's the guy that shot at me."

I tracked the guy until he paused at the courtyard wall, preparing to vault over it. I ignored Knuckles's radio calls, squeezing off three rounds during the split-second pause. The man tumbled down.

"North side's clear. One squirter from the original house moved north."

"Roger. Bull, continue to hold fire out front unless they fire first. I don't want to kill some psycho neighborhood watch. What do we have in the rear?"

The team members covering the back courtyard began to report. The immediate threat gone, I thought about the squirter I had seen. *A man with a backpack. Carlos.*

I cut in on Knuckles getting status reports. "Break — break. Squirter is the precious cargo. I say again, squirter is PC."

Knuckles came back immediately. "Still in sight?"

"No," I said, "he's running north. I don't know who these clowns are, but we need to clear out of here quick."

"Shit . . . Roger that. All elements, all elements — anyone with a weapon is now designated a hostile force. Engage at will."

Lucas heard the first AK-47 rounds and snapped his head toward the sound. He saw the team member at the corner of the house two doors down doing a macabre dance, rounds stitching him throughout his torso. He saw two arms holding an AK out of a second-story window, the weapon rocking back and forth on full automatic. He was momentarily stunned. *What the hell is going on?* He shook off the confusion, rapidly analyzing his current options. He decided to withdraw. All element of surprise was lost. The police were more than likely on the way. They needed to get the hell out of here.

He keyed his radio to speak but was interrupted by more gunfire erupting out of his sight, on the north side of the target house. He recognized the sound as an MP5.

"Cease fire! Cease fucking fire! Who's shooting?"

"Sir, it's Sanford. I had a clear shot at Pike in the target house. I think I got him."

"I said don't shoot until I gave the command! Jesus! Everyone listen up. We're getting out of here. Move back to the —"

Before he could finish, another burst of fire came from the north side of the house. It wasn't an MP5.

He swore under his breath. *This is turning into a fucking debacle. What is it with this guy?* He was like a curse.

"All elements check in."

He saw the driver of the vehicle to his rear give him a thumbs-up, on a knee and covering the house the AK fire had come from. He saw the final man from his vehicle running back across the street from the south of the target house, hearing him in his headset. "This is Copfeld. I'm coming across right now."

With the dead man shot from the window, and including himself and his driver, he had everyone but Sanford.

"Sanford, this is Lucas. You copy?" He paused and tried again, "Sanford, Sanford, this is Lucas. You copy?"

When Copfeld reached his position he said, "We need to get the fuck out of here. I want you to run back to the other vehicle and get a view down the north side of the house. See if you can find Sanford. Don't penetrate across the street. If he's there, get him here. If you don't see him, he's on his own. Watch that house to the rear. You understand?"

"Yeah. Give me some cover while I move."

Lucas grabbed his sleeve before he left. "You do anything different from what I just said, and I'm going to kill you myself."

Copfeld stumbled back from the ferocity on Lucas's face. He began running toward the other car as fast as he could. He made it about twenty meters before Lucas saw his head explode and his body crumple to the ground, twitching from the impact of multiple rounds. Lucas had barely registered his death when bullets began slicing the air near him like a buzz saw. *What in the hell is inside that house? An army?* He immediately collapsed behind his car, trying to make himself as small as possible, the bullets shattering the glass and puncturing the sheet metal all around him. The drivers of both vehicles rolled out, rapidly bringing their weapons to bear on the men shooting from the house.

The fight lasted a total of fifteen seconds. The drivers returned fire to the best of their ability, but couldn't compete with shooters safely ensconced behind cover. First one, then another fell over as a hail of bullets pummeled their bodies like an invisible meat tenderizer. The other targets gone, the bullets began to focus on Lucas's specific position, chewing up the concrete of the street, the dirt around him, and the metal of the car. He knew he had seconds to live. He thought about returning fire and going out with his guns blazing, valiantly trying to accomplish the mission. A bullet clipped his arm, making the decision for him. He felt explosive rage at his failure, knowing that Standish had kept vital information from him. *Just another retired soldier, my ass.* He suppressed his anger, wanting to fight another day. Wanting the chance to bring some pain to the Honorable Harold Standish. He raised his weapon by the barrel and waved it back and forth over the roof of the car. The firing ceased. He stood up, laying the weapon on the roof of the car and raising his hands.

He saw the front door open and two men come out, both holding weapons and scanning the area before running to his location. They drove him facedown into the ground and flex-tied his hands behind his back.

Bakr ran until his lungs felt like they would

burst. He didn't look back, didn't attempt to blend in, didn't try to hide his fear from other pedestrians. He just let his legs churn away, running deeper and deeper into the Bosnian neighborhood. Eventually, he stopped, bent over, his hands on his knees, gasping for air. He heard nobody following. Once again, he was confused by the reaction of the enemy. Why did they never chase him down? They obviously had some method to track him, but continually made blatantly amateur moves whenever they closed in. He could still hear the crackle of gunfire from the direction he had come. What on earth were they shooting at? Were they so pathetic that they would continue shooting an empty building long after he was gone? Was he misreading the whole thing? He couldn't believe that.

His next move boiled down to two choices: He could attempt to hide here, in Sarajevo, until the heat died down, or he could get out right now. Staying was appealing, since it would allow him to put some thought into his next move, and perhaps come up with a solid plan instead of simply running on a wing and a prayer. On the other hand, he had to assume that the enemy had some method of finding him, since they kept showing up all over the globe, from Guatemala, through Oslo, to here.

He decided he needed to run, to go to the station and get on the first thing leaving, whether that was a train or a bus. If they could find him, it would be better to be a moving target. The greatest risk was the station itself. If something wasn't leaving immediately, he would be vulnerable while waiting around. It was a chokepoint that he'd have to risk.

# 100

I crushed Kurt's beeper underneath my boot, having just confirmed that's how we'd been tracked. The man known as Lucas had pretty much spilled his guts in an effort to keep his ass from getting torn apart, and the beacon information had come as an unwelcome surprise. I didn't need any more. I squatted down, getting eye-to-eye with the man.

"You guys are like a bad rash. You keep coming back no matter how much I think you're done. Is there anyone else in this country looking for us? Anyone else we have to worry about?"

"No. Nobody else. Trident Global Threat Analysis is my company. I'd know if someone else was here. You killed everyone I had over here."

"All right, shithead. We're leaving here. If you're lying and we get in a gunfight, I'm going to pretend you're a principle I'm protecting so that I can kill you in my own sweet time later. Do you understand what

I'm saying?"

Lucas nodded, but he didn't look particularly scared. *Hmm . . . need to keep an eye on him.* I stood up, talking to Knuckles.

"I don't know where Carlos ran off to, but he can't possibly have a ton of different safe houses here to choose from. My bet is he's either running to a hotel, or running to the bus station. Either way, the station's our first priority. If he's not there, we can stake it out to ensure he doesn't show up later, then begin working the hotels. What do you think?"

"What about the airport?"

"I don't think he'll go there. He won't risk being on some watch list after he's seen me."

"Sounds good to me. We need to get moving, though. We can't prove a negative. If he gets on a bus or train before we get there, we'll never know it and spend the next month trying to find him here in Sarajevo."

I bent down and jerked Lucas to his feet, showing little compassion for his discomfort. Knuckles called the team into the foyer and gave them the next potential mission at the station. I took over, giving the best description I could of Carlos, to include the pack he carried.

We left through the back of the house, the men falling into an easy perimeter around Lucas. We reached the vehicles just as four police cars, sirens screaming, flew by us to the location of the firefight.

Bull opened the trunk of one. I told Lucas to climb in. Lucas hesitated for a brief moment, starting to say he wasn't a threat and would behave. I gave him a straight punch right into his mouth, splitting his lips against his teeth. Before he could recover, I grabbed him by the throat and shoved him into the trunk. Bull slammed the lid.

Riding the tram back to the bus station, Bakr scanned outside, looking for a threat. Pulling into the station, he saw two cars drive into the parking lot out front. One continued to the far side of the parking lot, the other stopped short about seventy-five meters from the entrance. He saw the men from the cars fanning out, two headed toward the train station up the street and two headed into the bus station. He saw the man from Guatemala. He began to believe the man was the devil. He began to sweat.

He told the tram driver he had forgotten something at his hotel, then sat in the back, behind the crush of people boarding. Riding back to the city center, he considered his options. Beyond anything else, he didn't want to waste the device. Using it here would only kill several hundred, mostly Bosnians or other Eastern Europeans. He'd be lucky to kill a single Zionist. The impact would be minimal. Even so, the thought was growing in his mind. It was an eventuality that had to be considered. The man from Guatemala wasn't going to stop, and somehow he seemed to know wherever Bakr went.

He left the tram one stop early and proceeded north into the city, pulling out the number Juka had given him. Maybe someone would answer and get him out of here. He listened to the phone ring, then go to voice mail. He hung up without leaving a message.

He reached a walking promenade filled with people, all moving to the west, and remembered the ceremony. A germ of an idea began to form.


"Any ideas?" Knuckles asked.

"Not really. Maybe it's time to pull in the Bosnian authorities."

"How the hell are we going to do that? And not give up the Taskforce? What are we going to tell them? 'Be on the lookout for a swarthy man with a backpack'? We don't have a picture and we don't even know his real name."

We had finished our search of the bus and train station, and Carlos was nowhere to be found. I was certain he hadn't come here, and now we didn't have a thread to pull.

Knuckles said, "Maybe he went to the airport after all."

"Maybe, but once he got there he'd see all

of the security for the dignitaries and go away."

We both stopped and looked at each other, a terrible truth dawning on us.

"Shit — he's got a perfect target right here. We need to find out about that ceremony."

Knuckles called the pilots and had them get on the SATCOM to the rear for some answers. Within minutes, his phone rang. When he hung up, I knew it was going to be bad.

"It's a formal ceremony for the fifteenth anniversary of the Markale mortar attacks. They're putting up a monument. France, England, and Germany will all have representatives here."

*Great. A perfect target.*

Knuckles continued. "Worse than that, the secretary of state is representing the United States. He's on the ground now."

"What? How could you guys deploy here and not know that? Jesus."

"He wasn't supposed to come here. He's supposed to be with the president on a goodwill tour. I've got that schedule and this isn't on it. Apparently, it just came up."

"Is it just him? Is the president here as well?"

"No, it's an entourage, but the SEC-STATE's the biggest name."

"If this is someone's late-breaking good idea, the Secret Service didn't have a lot of prep time for security. When's the ceremony?"

"It's going to happen within the next hour."

Before I could say anything else, the phone we had taken from the safe house began to ring inside Knuckles's backpack.

Bakr stopped a passerby, asking, "Who's coming to the ceremony?"

"A lot of people. President Silajdzic is going to speak."

"So it's all Bosnians? Why all the security?"

The man looked at Bakr with contempt. "Of course not. France and Britain have representatives here. The American secretary of state is speaking. The world understands the importance of this day."

All Bakr heard was the guest list, his mind now working in overdrive. He began following the crowds to the west on the Ferhadija promenade, plotting his options. He knew that the odds of crossing into Israel were now slim. They were probably on high alert. Even if he could make it, he had no way to implicate the Iranians. He would make the news, but little else.

The deciding factor was the man from Guatemala. He was relentless, and Bakr felt in his heart the man would find him sooner rather than later.

He made up his mind. An attack here would have more symbolism. He could strike at least three leaders of the far enemy. His weapon would mainly kill Bosniak Muslims at the ceremony, but that in itself would be symbolic. They were cozying up to the far enemy and literally thanking the Great Satan for his so-called help. Because of this, they invited *takfir,* and would feel the repercussions. The attack would show what happens to Muslim *kafir* who stray from the path. It might even fracture the relationship between the West and this Muslim community, forcing them to embrace their true heritage. Forcing them back onto the path.

He reached within eyesight of the market and saw a crowd of about five hundred. Eighty meters away rested the raised platform the guests would use. A wall of security was checking everyone that entered into the inner ring. He recognized the security perimeter for what it was: standoff protection from a conventional man-packed explosive device. The distance was certainly good enough to thwart his blast, but the perimeter would provide no help at all against his poison.

Knuckles dug out the safe house phone from his backpack.

I said, "Don't answer it. That's got to be him."

Once it registered with a number, Bull began working to find its location with his special phone. Wthin seconds, he had a grid.

Plotting it with a GPS, he said, "He's downtown."

I pulled out a tourist map, marking the location, then found the Markale Market. "He's in that area. He's going to hit the ceremony."

Knuckles said, "Maybe. Maybe not. If we go in right now and get compromised, we may spook him into using the device. Maybe we should wait and see if he beds down tonight, then hit him with his guard down."

Knuckles had a point. We could make this a self-fulfilling prophecy if we screwed up. We now had a way to track him, as long as he kept that phone. It would be much, much easier to take him down in a hotel room than on a crowded street. On the other hand, any moment could bring a mushroom cloud. *Decision time.*

## 101

Bakr surveyed the wind patterns of the open air market. The entire area was covered by a high overhead roof of galvanized steel, but a slight breeze could still be felt coming out of the east. That is where he would set the weapon off. He moved around the crowd until he was situated as close as he could be to the security perimeter without gathering any undue curiosity. He stood for a few minutes, trying to appear as if he were just passing the time, when he noticed one of the security personnel glance his way a third time. He began to walk away, looking for somewhere he could wait that was close enough to allow him to get in position rapidly. Finding nothing, he kept moving. Eventually, he came upon a public restroom. It wasn't nearly close enough, but would have to do as a staging point. He was sure he would be able to hear the announcements when the ceremony began. Moving into a stall, he sat down and locked the door, waiting to hear the Great Satan's secretary of state taking the stage.

In the end, the potential for a massive amount of civilian deaths — at a ceremony commemorating the murder of civilians from a previous heinous act — made up my mind. The symbols of power from the United States and other European countries provided a target for Carlos to use, but as always, it would be the innocents who paid the price.

"We need to take him out. Now. It's a risk, but I don't think he's going to wait. The target's too juicy, and he's on the run."

Knuckles nodded. I knew he would see it my way. "Let's load up."

We drove along the river toward downtown Sarajevo, then cut in north to the grid of Carlos's last-known location. We were only allowed to go a short distance before hitting a roadblock, with all cars being turned away.

"Should've expected this," Knuckles said. "No way are they going to let a potential VBIED near the ceremony."

"At least they have some sort of security going on. Turn around and park it on the river. That'll only be about three blocks south."

After we had parked the vehicles, while Bull worked to get a new grid for Carlos, I said, "What about Lucas?"

"What about him?"

"We can't leave him alone. He's no push-over and a slippery bastard to boot. Someone needs to cover him, or he'll screw this whole thing up."

"I agree," he said, "but we can't afford to leave a teammate to babysit his ass. We need every man on this."

"Call the pilots. Get one of them to come here and swap cars."

Knuckles grimaced. "Pike, I can't do that. I can't risk the cover of the bird. Those guys are pilots, period. You know that."

"Shit, man, that guy's running around with a damn bomb on his back! Fuck the damn rules." I stopped, holding up my hands. "Okay, okay. I'll tell Jennifer to come get him. She can switch cars and take him back to the 427. The pilots can guard him until we get there. Can they at least do that?"

"Yeah, they can do that."

I called Jennifer and gave her instructions, a little piqued at Knuckles's rigid adherence to procedures. *This is one time he should be flexing like Gumby.* I let it go, knowing he had a point. Compromise the pilots and we wouldn't be able to fly out of here. *Jennifer's switched on enough to get the job done.* For the first time I realized that I trusted her as much as the Taskforce members themselves.

By the time I hung up the phone, Bull had pinpointed the new location. "He's just south of the market. Maybe one hundred and fifty meters away from it."

I looked at the map and said, "That's straight north from here. He's about two blocks up."

Knuckles gave final instructions, splitting the team into two-man elements. "Bull, you and Retro come in from east to west. Pike and I will come up from south to north. The rest of you box in from west to east. Hopefully we'll pin him in. Everyone, remember he's got a WMD. Whatever you do, don't hit the pack or his chest. If you have to shoot, go for the head."

The problem with the cell phone track was that it only gave us a snapshot in time. We couldn't do any real-time tracking, so whatever we had was only as good as the time we had it. Knuckles and I began walking up the sidewalk to the north, scanning the crowds. The other men were quickly lost from sight as they began their part of the mission.

Without any traffic, the streets were teeming with people going toward the ceremony. *Great. Rush hour.* The crowds were a definite problem. For one, it forced me to hide the UMP under my jacket, the folding stock jammed into my armpit. *I'm not going to be the fastest gun in the West running around like this.* For another, I could be walking right by the terrorist and not see him. Moving closer to the market, Knuckles and I both heard the loudspeakers signaling the start of the ceremony.

Bakr heard the announcer droning on and on about the significance of the day, first in Serbo-Croatian, then in English. Bakr waited, straining to hear any announcement that the dignitaries had arrived. He couldn't afford to leave and return. The man from Guatemala was somewhere close. He could feel it. When he left this bathroom, it would be straight to the eastern corner of the security perimeter. Once there, he'd continue on, past any demands that he halt. Only when someone drew his weapon would he trigger the device.

He heard a different voice, then the words he was waiting for: the introduction of the guests of honor. He squeezed his eyes shut and said a silent prayer. Pulling the detonator from his pack, he conducted a self-test of the system. When it registered green, he opened the door and stepped into the light.

He was shocked by the number of people who had shown up in the time he had spent in the bathroom. He would have to fight his way through the crowd to get close enough to ensure a successful strike. Setting off the device this far away would kill a lot of people but would most likely miss the targets, as they would vacate before they were hit with the downwind hazard. Pushing his way east, he continually scanned for anyone not focused on the stage. His confidence grew as the crowd cheered the speaker, with no threat in sight. He saw the perimeter fence with the security personnel ahead. Even the guards were staring at the stage. He pushed around a happy group, clearly having started the celebration early, and saw two men at the edge of the perimeter, both scanning the crowd as if they were looking for a friend.

He studied them before continuing, looking for anything out of place. They wore jackets, which wasn't unusual, but the bulges on their hips told a different story. Panic began to close in again. How had they tracked him so successfully? He backed up into the group and turned around, considering his options. Before he could decide, one of the drunks in the group pushed him, demanding he get out of the way. He bumped into another man, who pushed him back again. The scuffle was drawing attention he didn't need, making his choice for him.

He fought his way clear and went back the way he had come, attempting to get out of the crowd and circle to the west just to get close to the perimeter. He felt sweat popping out all over his body, thinking about what he was going to do if he was seen. Should he simply run? Attempt to make it inside the perimeter? No. They would kill him. He had heard the gunfire and seen the rifles from earlier. The only thing worse than killing a few measly hundred Eastern Europeans with his device would be dying with it strapped to his back, unfired.

He pulled the remote detonator out of his pocket, holding it tightly in his hands. Breathing deeply, he skirted the crowd. He saw the bathroom he had used to hide. He saw the door open about fifteen meters away. He instantly recognized the person exiting. The man was looking away, but he would soon turn and see him. Bakr frantically searched but there was nowhere to run, no way out through the crowds. Swiveling back, he met the eyes of the devil. Time slowed. The man reached underneath his jacket, bringing something out. Bakr raised the detonator, whispering, *"Allahu Akhbar."* He pressed the button.

I felt a shock of adrenaline fire to my soul. I was staring straight into the face of the terrorist. I began to draw the H&K UMP, seeing the terrorist raise his hands with the detonator I had seen in the hotel room. *Why the fuck didn't I smash that thing?* My weapon snagged on the interior lining of the leather jacket. I knew I was dead. I might survive the blast, provided the man hadn't embedded the device with shrapnel, but couldn't get away from the poison, whatever it was. I yanked the weapon, tearing the lining, watching the terrorist with morbid fascination, like a man stuck on the tracks and seeing the train bearing down on his car. I saw him press the detonator, but nothing happened. *The idiot forgot to arm it first.* The terrorist realized it as well, frantically working the buttons on the device.

I brought the weapon up to shoulder height, slowed my breathing, and drew a focused bead on the man's head, squeezing the trigger. I saw a blossom of red appear between his eyes just as his finger frantically probed for the button a second time, and he toppled over backward, landing on the pack.

# 102

Jennifer had made the rental car switch at the river three blocks away when she heard an explosion, loud enough to vibrate her car. She saw a cloud of smoke rise up the street. Then she saw that it wasn't smoke, but some sort of dust. It wasn't rising, but hovering, gently floating about, segments slowly falling to earth, reminding her of videos she had seen after the towers fell on 9/11. She floored the vehicle, driving as fast as she could to get out of the area.

She rolled into the airport exceeding the speed limit by thirty kilometers an hour. She had passed what must have been every police car and fire engine in Sarajevo, all headed to the explosion. She slammed on the brakes and ran to the Bell 427.

"The terrorist blew up the market. The WMD is out!"

For the first time, she noticed that the rotors were turning and the pilots were going through preflight. One said, "We know. The embassy's already been alerted and is request-ing military support. We're getting out of here."

"What? You're leaving? What about the guys at the market?"

"We can't do anything about that. Our higher knows the situation. It's in their hands now. Our orders are to get the hell out of here."

"Are you serious? What about Pike and Knuckles? You can't just leave."

The pilot stopped what he was doing and fixed her with an icy stare.

"Ma'am, Knuckles was a teammate. More than that, he was my friend. I understand the situation. There's nothing I can do about it. If anyone on the team is alive, they know what they need to do. We have a procedure for this type of contingency. My mission is to protect what I can at this point. I'm sorry, but that's it."

He turned back to his preflight. Jennifer stood in shock, unsure of what to do. She remembered the man in her trunk.

"Wait. I have the guy I was supposed to get. What about him?"

The pilot stopped. He turned to his partner and said something. Both exited the helicop-ter. One took the keys from Jennifer, the other drew a pistol and aimed it at the trunk. Swinging it open, they found it empty. The pilot gave the keys back to Jennifer without saying a word. He had finished preflight and was preparing to crank up the rotors for good, when he exited one more time.

"Look, I'm not sure what your whole story is or who you belong to, but let me give you some advice: I'd get on the first plane out of here. I'm sorry we can't take you. I would if I could."

Still trying to process what was occurring, Jennifer simply nodded her head. She stood still until she was driven back by the rotor wash of the helicopter. She saw it take off, and continued to watch it until it was a speck in the sky. She walked in a circle, unsure of what to do next. On the far side of the airport, she could see a beehive of activity around the dignitaries' planes.

She went into the terminal and bought a ticket on a Bosnian airline headed to Frankfurt, Germany. It was due to leave in four hours. She went back to the rental car and tried to drive back into the city. She saw the lights flashing a mile out. She got within a half of a mile of the downtown before being stopped at a police checkpoint. The man spoke little English. All he could say was, "Go, Go. Poison." She turned around and headed back the way she had come.

She located the only hospital in the city and went to it. The place was a madhouse, with people in white running back and forth, and the wounded being brought in. She found someone who spoke English and asked about Americans. He told her he had not seen any Americans at all.

She drove back to the airport. She didn't feel grief. She didn't feel anything except exhaustion, both physically and emotionally. The flight to Frankfurt was a blur. While she waited for her connecting flight, the event began to sink in. *How had everything gone so bad so quickly?* She had cautioned Pike on the danger, but in her heart she had really thought he *was* invincible. He'd survived time and time again, pulling out miracles as ordinary events. If anyone was going to die, it should have been her. *How is this supposed to be justice? Where's the destiny now?* She put her head in her hands, trying to stop her thoughts. She heard someone talking to her and glanced up, seeing a Lufthansa Airlines ticket agent.

"Ma'am, are you all right? Can I help you?"

Because Pike had drilled it into her over the last four days, her first thought was she was making a scene. *Act like the other passengers. You're going to get burned.* She was then hammered with the futility of the thought. *What a joke. None of that helped in the end.*

"Yeah," she said, "I'm fine."

The agent looked as if he wasn't convinced but left her alone.

Thirty minutes later, he came back.

"Ma'am, are you on this flight?"

For the first time it registered that everyone had left the gateway.

"Yes. Sorry. I wasn't paying attention."

"No problem, but we're about to close the door. Are you sure you're okay? Is there anything I can do for you?"

*Can you bring back the dead?* "I'm all right. Sorry for the trouble."

She landed at Dulles International Airport completely spent. She had no idea what she was going to do next. She had a connecting flight to Charleston but didn't feel like getting on it. She felt like curling up in a ball and forgetting everyone and everything. She instinctively thought she should be crying or grieving over the loss of Pike, but all she felt was hollowness inside.

She joined the immigration line, moving forward like sheep to a trough. She saw CNN on a TV across the immigration area. She caught the flash of Bosnia-Herzegovina and focused on the story. She couldn't hear what was being said but saw a video of the market, men and women wandering in a daze, police waving the cameras back, firemen running holding bleeding bodies, and an incongruous single individual in a space-age bio-suit. The screen cut to a photo, the name Harold Standish beneath it. She had no idea what that was about and didn't have the energy to care. She waited to see something about the president admitting the Taskforce's existence or some other catastrophic news conference, but the story ended.

She handed her passport to the man behind the counter. He scanned it and stiffened. She felt a stab of adrenaline, remembering what had happened in Atlanta, followed immediately by resignation. She had no strength to fight the bogus terrorist charge. *At least it solves my problem of what to do next.* Before the man could say anything, she said, "I'll come with you. Just take me wherever you need to."

He looked at her suspiciously, saying, "Follow me."

He led her down a hallway to a small room that contained two folding chairs and a table. He told her to wait, then left, locking the door behind him.

She sat for a half hour, mostly in a daze. She tried to remember her time with Pike, but her subconscious refused to engage. She was having a hard time seeing his face. She remembered the last thing he had said to her, and didn't believe it. *It wasn't worth it. We should have let him get away.* She laid her head on the table and began to cry. Sobs racked her body in convulsions. They slowly faded away, leaving her with the same drained, hollow feeling. She heard the door open and looked up, eyes red. She saw a man enter and smile.

"Jennifer Cahill?"

"Yes."

"I'm Mike. I'm from the Taskforce. You're not in any trouble. I was waiting on you to land. Kurt Hale wanted to see you as soon as you hit U.S. soil. I'm supposed to take you to him."

She showed no emotion. "Okay. How'd you know I'd be coming here?"

"We didn't. We have folks at every major embarkation point in the U.S. We left the terrorist alert in place. Sorry."

She waved it away and stood up. "I could really give a shit about that. Let's go get this over with."

As they left the immigration area he asked about her luggage. She shrugged. "It's in Bosnia. I don't have any."

They walked in silence for the rest of the way, exiting the airport. Getting to the car, he tried one more time to draw her into a conversation.

"I understand you ended up finding and stopping the terrorist."

She looked at him like he was an idiot. "I guess so, if you believe forcing him to blow everyone up early is stopping him."

He put the car in drive and didn't say another word. The rest of the trip was spent in silence. As they got onto the toll road, the weather turned sour, with rain beating the metal of the car. The only sound was the windshield wipers flipping back and forth.

Jennifer gazed out the window, ignoring the drive. Eventually, the car pulled into a checkpoint. She registered that the car had stopped, then realized where they were.

"Why are we here?"

"This is where Kurt is at the moment. I was told to bring you straight to him."

The guard waved them through to the West Wing parking area of the White House.

After a short walk, Jennifer stood outside the White House situation room, waiting to be asked to enter. The door opened and she saw a long table surrounded by wood-paneled walls with multiple plasma screens. She immediately recognized the president of the United States at the head of the table. He stood and approached her.

"Hello, young lady, we've been waiting for you. I'm Payton Warren," he said, extending his hand.

Jennifer didn't even begin to know what to say so she simply shook his hand, mute.

To his left was Kurt Hale. She looked around, recognizing the secretary of state and the secretary of defense. She saw other faces that she didn't know, but felt she should, vague recollections from Sunday news shows. *What's this all about? Why am I here?* She went from face to face, waiting on someone to tell her what to do. At the far end she saw a man with a horrendous visage. His face was scabbed, without any eyebrows. His arm was in a sling, a set of crutches to the side of his chair. He was smiling at her. The smile was real and familiar.

## 103

I saw Jennifer look from face to face, waiting for her to get to me, wanting to see the same glow I had experienced when she entered the room.

It dawned on me that I had been subconsciously holding back, protecting myself from the meat-cleaver of disappointment if it was a case of mistaken identity and someone else was at the Dulles Airport. Maybe secretly protecting myself against the trauma of having the newly formed scab covering the loss of my family ripped out raw had the unthinkable happened. In that moment, I realized that Jennifer had been right in Bosnia: Her death would have destroyed me completely. Left me broken beyond repair.

I watched Jennifer continue to search for some indication of why she was here or someone she recognized. She looked like shit. Like she'd spent the last twenty-four hours sleeping on park benches and knew the next twenty-four hours held nothing but the same.

She finally got to me. I saw her face change from a lack of recognition to one of shock, then she fell backward into a chair. *Not exactly what I expected.*

From behind her, Knuckles jumped up, saying, "Whoa! Hang on there. You okay?"

I could tell she recognized him, but she simply stared like she was seeing a ghost.

He asked again, "Jennifer? You all right?"

Something clicked within her, and without a word, she jumped up and raced over to me.

*Holy shit, she's going to hug me.* It would hurt, but I didn't want to stop her.

She stopped short, smiling, tears running freely down her face. She leaned over and gingerly kissed my forehead on the crew-cut of singed hair.

"You bastard. I guess you do have ten lives."

I grinned. "Yeah, I guess so. Took you long enough to get home. I was starting to worry."

She ignored everyone else in the room, simply taking my hands into hers and staring at me. After a second, she seemed to remember where she was, and what had led to this meeting. She asked, "What happened? What's going on? Why isn't everyone dead?"

Kurt said, "Well, we ended up being very, very lucky. Scientists are still studying the material, but it looks like the WMD was only deadly to those genetically predisposed."

"What's that mean?"

I took over. "The weapon they found was

an ancient sack of spores from a plant that's probably extinct. It causes major anaphylactic shock in people predisposed to be allergic to it. Basically, it causes the same reaction as in someone allergic to bee stings, only a hundred times worse."

"Okay . . . that still sounds pretty bad. Isn't it?"

"Yeah, it is, but I managed to kill Carlos before he could set off the device. He fell on top of it, which somehow caused it to go off. His body tamped down the explosion, like a soldier jumping on a grenade. On top of that, it looks like folks from Europe aren't nearly as susceptible to the spores as guys from Guatemala, where they came from. Luckily, I fall into that camp."

Jennifer processed that, coming to the natural conclusion, "So, the whole thing was a waste of time? All that death and destruction for nothing? Ethan's death —"

The president spoke. "No, not at all. The bomb killed close to fifty people, but the team forced the terrorist to set it off far enough away from the ceremony that the representatives attending were able to escape before they were contaminated. Because of our unique security relationship with Bosnia, we were immediately asked for help. Most of the deaths *were* caused by the spores, but we were able to alleviate any concerns of a WMD rapidly, taking the emotion out of the attack.

There'll be conspiracy theories for years about it, but the majority of the world thinks it was a conventional attack."

Kurt interjected, "Mainly because the terrorist put all his faith in the spores and didn't embed any shrapnel in the explosive. He also knew what he was doing. He kept the explosive power low to prevent burning up the WMD material, which worked in our favor, especially when his own body lessened the blast radius. If he had set off a conventional bomb with higher explosives and shrapnel, we probably would have had the same amount of casualties, so the story's plausible."

The president continued. "If he had made it to Israel, and had been able to implicate the Iranians, it would have caused immediate retaliation. He would've killed hundreds, and Israel would have feared a second strike. Unlike Bosnia, they wouldn't have asked for our help or listened to any pleadings of restraint. Trust me, the WMD was real. Real enough to get us into World War Three."

"Okay . . . I guess that's good news. . . . Wait, that didn't come out right. I mean I'm glad the effort was worth it. I couldn't live with Ethan's death on my conscience if this was all for nothing."

She squeezed my hands, her face now alive, the broken look gone. "Ahh . . . this is a bit much to take in all at once. I'm not sure why I'm here. What do you need from me?"

The president spoke again. "Nothing. We were meeting here to discuss the repercussions of the whole affair when you landed. I asked for you to come here simply to thank you. You have immeasurably helped the country, and quite possibly the world. Your perseverance deserves my thanks as the representative of the American people." He gave his winning campaign smile. "That's all I wanted to say. If there's any way I can help you, don't hesitate to ask."

Jennifer winked at me, then smiled at the president with all the charm she could muster — which was substantial. *Uh-oh.*

"Well, sir, I appreciate it. I really do. Unfortunately, I promised Pike I was going to kick someone's ass in the U.S. government for leaving us hanging out there. I suppose I should start with you. Can you help with that?"

I closed my eyes. *I cannot believe she just said that.* When I opened them again I saw a roomful of the most powerful people on earth looking anywhere but at her. I could tell she was enjoying this immensely. She continued. "Then again, you guys did do the right thing in the end, so maybe I'll let it go. I guess all's well that ends well."

I squeezed her arm a little harder than was necessary, trying to shut her up before she did some real damage.

"Hey, guess what?" I said. "The folks you

want to beat up took care of our little problem in Charleston. We don't have to worry about that anymore."

I thought she was going to rip into the rest of the group just for the enjoyment, and prayed she wouldn't. She grinned at me and said, "Okay, then, how about a nice hotel room?"

The room broke into relieved laughter. The president said, "I think I can manage that."

He grew serious again. "Ladies and gentlemen, I appreciate your time, but I have a press conference in an hour. I can't thank you enough for your service."

The meeting broke up with people shaking hands and saying good-bye. Shortly we found ourselves outside, me hobbling along on my broken ankle with Jennifer trying unsuccessfully to help. Eventually, everyone was gone and it was just us. She looked around, noticing we were alone.

"Where are we going? Better yet, how are we getting there?"

I said, "I guess we go hail a cab."

"Wow," she said, "that thank-you didn't last very long."

Jennifer began walking toward the gate with me hobbling along beside her, when someone shouted behind us.

"Jennifer . . . Pike?"

"Yes."

"The president asked me to give you guys a

ride to the Hay-Adams Hotel here in D.C. You have the Presidential Suite, compliments of the White House."

"All *right*," she said. "That's more like it."

Thirty minutes later Jennifer was admiring the view from the living room of our suite, the White House majestic in the last glimmers of twilight. Now that we were alone, she brought out the questions she knew nobody but me would answer.

"Hey, what happened to all the bullshit threats about the Taskforce bringing down the administration? Everyone kept saying we had to do all the work because using it was too risky. Why isn't there the big disaster everyone talked about?"

I knew what she was asking was highly classified, but it never crossed my mind to tell her a story. More than anyone else, she had earned the truth.

"It turns out that Dr. Evil is a guy in the National Security Council. He hired all of the trained killers. Their attempts in Bosnia gave the Taskforce a way out. We've blamed the whole thing on them, saying that a Lone Ranger hired a bunch of mercenaries to stop a terrorist. He's going to be indicted as a reluctant hero."

"That's the guy I saw on the news? Standish something-or-other?"

"Yeah. With all the press talk of the U.S.

outsourcing combat power to independent contractors, it's plausible. The Taskforce is good to go."

She bristled. "Good to go? Are you kidding? What's going to happen to him? He tortured and killed a whole family. He tried to kill *us*. He should be strung up from the nearest tree. Now he's going down in history as 'helping America'? How's that justice?"

I didn't want to go there. I wanted to leave all of this behind for others to sort out. I tried to soothe her. "He'll get what's coming to him."

Jennifer squinted at me, her expression alone telling me she didn't think that was good enough. After what she had said to me on the hillside in Bosnia, I wasn't going to elaborate on what that meant. She wanted justice for the man's actions but probably couldn't stomach the Taskforce version. Luckily, she let it go.

"Okay. I guess in Washington getting indicted and suffering humiliation is what constitutes the worst that can happen."

I crawled onto the bed, trying to find a comfortable position that didn't rub my burns. "Why don't you get cleaned up? Maybe we can go get a bite to eat at a real restaurant for a change."

For the first time, Jennifer seemed to realize she was wearing the same peasant clothes she had worn for days. She ran a hand through her greasy, black-dyed hair.

"Yeah, that sounds good. Great, actually. What am I going to do about clothes?"

"We can go shopping first. Maybe put it on the president's tab."

"Even better. He owes me more than a hotel room. Give me thirty minutes."

She went inside the bathroom and I heard the sink start to run.

Jennifer hadn't asked the obvious question of why on earth Standish had wanted a bomb to go off in the first place. I had seen his initial FBI interrogation and it had made me sick to my stomach. Made me want to jump through the two-way mirror and slice him open with the broken shards. Of course, the Taskforce would have frowned on that. Not because I had killed him, but because I had done it in front of everyone. Bad form. I'd have to be satisfied with someone else delivering justice.

Standish had been completely unrepentant, shouting at the interrogators that his actions were necessary to protect American lives. He seemed to firmly believe that his efforts were not only legitimate, but good for the nation. The thought disgusted me. He sounded just like all of the terrorists I had ever chased. The only thing missing was him shouting, "It's God's will!" Like every other psychopath who justified his actions as nothing more than destiny.

I knew there was no such thing. "Destiny" was a tool used by the vicious or weak to explain a tragedy — nothing more. If God controlled our destiny, then wouldn't the good guy always win? Where was God when Hitler killed the Jews? Where was He when the planes hit WTC one and two? In the genocide in Bosnia or Rwanda? Was mass rape a destiny? Or just fucking evil? *Where was the destiny in my family being murdered?*

Jennifer had asked about the chances of us colliding, thinking that it was meant to be because the odds were astronomically against it, but I knew better. I had seen the truth. God, or fate, or destiny — whatever the hell you wanted to call it — had never crossed my path. *You make your own luck. Just like I did in Machete's compound.*

The thought sounded like a cracked bell as soon as it came into my head. *No way should I have survived that.* The more I reflected on the last couple of weeks, the more it seemed there *was* some invisible hand looking out for Jennifer and me. Every time we were on the verge of failing, something happened that spurred us forward. It made me wonder. *Maybe there is a purpose. Maybe Jennifer's right.*

I didn't like the thread I was working, didn't want to stare too hard into the looking glass, because believing in one meant I had to believe in the other. That the loss of my family was for a reason, which was something I could never embrace.

I heard the shower stop, blessedly bringing me back to the present, or more precisely, my future. Kurt had offered me a job back at the Taskforce. A recall to active duty. The offer was compelling and conflicting at the same time. I could go back to being a rough man protecting our way of life, but the choice would mean losing Jennifer.

After all we had both been through together, I had become as close to her as any other teammate I had known. A part of me, I knew, wanted more than that. Another part, much more powerful, was repulsed by the notion. It would be a very, very long time before I could ever let go of Heather. Maybe never.

Even so, I wanted to continue working with her. She was as switched on as anyone I had operated with before, and we clicked as a team. I had toyed with an idea the whole flight home and now had the beginnings of a plan on how to make that happen. Jennifer held the key. She'd be graduating soon and looking for employment, but I knew she'd no longer be happy doing something boring. She'd tasted what it was like to work for something greater than personal gratification, and while she'd probably get the same satisfaction doing her anthropological work, she'd miss the thrill. The question was whether she'd admit that to herself. I couldn't tell her what I had planned, because it was classified, not to mention she'd think it was nuts, but that was okay. I'd see if she was willing soon enough, and could get her the clearance if she was agreeable — later, after the ground-work was laid. All I needed was some start-up funds — and I had a good idea how to get those.

Minutes later Jennifer came out in a plush robe, smelling freshly scrubbed but looking puzzled.

She said, "Okay, I got it on Standish, but what about the other guy? The one in the trunk? He did the actual killing. What's the Taskforce doing about him? Just let him go free?"

Truthfully, in the aftermath of the explosion and the exfiltration, I had forgotten about Lucas. "He's in the same boat. He'll get what's coming to him."

"So they found him?"

"What?"

"They found him after the bomb went off?" She could see the puzzlement on my face. "You didn't know?"

"Know what? What the hell are you talking about?"

"Pike, Lucas wasn't in the trunk when I switched cars. He got away."

## 104

Thirty miles away, in the swank Chevy Chase section of Washington, D.C., a nondescript sedan pulled into the circular drive of the Honorable Harold Standish. Three men exited. They had already done their reconnaissance earlier and knew Standish was home alone. One manipulated the alarm system while the other two worked the lock on the door. All three entered. They moved directly to Standish's study, finding him facedown on his desk, a spreading pool of blood beginning to leak onto the floor.

The team leader called directly to the Taskforce Ops Center on his secure cell phone. "Someone beat us to him. He's already dead."

"How?"

"Gunshot wound. This guy must have made quite a few enemies."

"Can you still make it look like a suicide?"

The team leader studied the dead man for a few seconds. "Possibly. He's been shot in the temple at close range, and there's no exit wound, so it was a small-caliber weapon. That works." He pulled out the .22 rim-fire hand-gun they'd taken from Standish's bedroom earlier in the day. "The problem is that a bal-listics check will show the bullet inside his head didn't come from the gun I'm going to leave in his hand."

"We can work that issue. Just make sure there aren't any other anomalies that give them a reason to look."

"Okay. I'll have to build a bullet trap, then squeeze off a round in his hand to get gunshot residue on him, but that's not an issue. He'll just be missing a phone book."

"Get it done."

Eight minutes later the sedan pulled away, the alarm reset, no evidence at all of a break-in. Only a dead man and a suicide note.

I was awakened by Jennifer insistently poking me in the thigh.

"Pike, wake up! Look at the TV."

I cracked my eyes open, seeing a breaking news story about someone committing sui-cide.

"It's that National Security guy. He killed himself."

*Big surprise. Couldn't see that coming.* "Wow. I guess he couldn't live with the shame."

Jennifer looked at me suspiciously. I thought she was going to say something, but she must

677

have thought better of it.

She turned off the TV. "Well, what now? Are we headed home?"

*That depends on you.*

"Kurt asked me to come back to the Task-force," I said.

I saw her face fall and felt the tension leave my body. *This might actually work.*

"That's great," she said, without a lot of conviction. "I know it means a lot to you. Are you going to do it?"

"I think I have a better idea. Go to my jeans and check the front right pocket."

She did as I asked, pulling out a thumb drive.

"Is this the window-jumper's drive?"

"Yeah. The Taskforce guys looked at it. Turns out it's a physical key for a steganography program. You still have your uncle's e-mail?"

She nodded.

"You want to go find a lost temple?"

# ACKNOWLEDGMENTS

First and foremost, this book is a work of fiction. There is no such thing as the Taskforce, the Oversight Council, or Omega operations, contrary to what Hollywood and some reporters want you to believe.

Pike Logan, however, is real. He represents a small fraternity that, more than anything else, is the catalyst of this book. I had the honor of serving with many, many Pike Logans, but make no mistake, I am not he. I owe them a debt of gratitude, not only for what you're holding in your hand, but for allowing me to serve alongside them. Greater still, the nation owes them a debt of gratitude for successful operations that will never see the light of day.

When I first put pen to paper, this was, of course, the finest novel ever written. Family swooned over it. Friends begged to read it. Fortunately, it didn't take long to realize it needed massive work to reach a level worthy of publication. Through a series of fortuitous events, I met Caroline Upcher, a freelance editor and published novelist in her own right. She has the distinction of being the singular reason you're reading these words. She not only helped me frame the story, but literally taught a knuckle-dragger like me how to write. If any new writers are reading these words for a clue of how I managed to get published, there's your big black X.

Even after all the work, someone still had to be willing to take a risk on an unknown. I'm indebted to John Talbot of the Talbot Fortune Agency for doing just that. When nobody else seemed willing to even want to open the Word document, he decided to see where it would go. Hopefully, it was worth the look.

As for the book itself, a huge thank-you to Major Beau Spafford, of the South Carolina Army National Guard and a James Island Redneck, who's currently getting shot at in Afghanistan. You won't find anyone with more common sense. Well, I should say more common sense who's willing to use the book as an excuse to go drink beer. He corrected innumerable inconsistencies.

To select people from my former life: thank you. The special mission world is close-knit and very unique. Writing for publication of any sort is frowned upon, but some friends agreed to read the manuscript to make sure I hadn't said anything that would compromise the safety of those still in harm's way — namely themselves. I say agreed, not supported, because my name on the cover is irritating enough.

A huge thank-you goes out to Dutton publishing and my editor, Ben Sevier. Honestly, I was worried when I signed the contract that I'd also sold my soul. I had visions of this big-name publisher ordering me to change everything in it that I held dear. Far from it, Ben took the manuscript to the next level, coaching, mentoring, and providing invaluable guidance. Again, I found myself learning.

Unlike what I originally naively believed, getting a book published entails more than just hitting print. Although that's certainly an option, I'm grateful that the Dutton team chose not to take that route and have relentlessly supported the effort to see this succeed.

Finally, I'd like to publicly thank my wife, Elaine. One, for not losing her mind at the risk of leaving the military for a writing career, and two, for fixing all of my knuckle-dragging mistakes before anyone else had a chance to read them. When we were first married, she started a tally of what I owed her for various deployments and problems she was forced to solve in my absence, all based on the size of a diamond. I'm up to forty-three carats, which is roughly the size of the

Hope diamond. So, if you see me in the Smithsonian "researching diamonds" for my "next book," you'll know why. Just don't turn me in when it comes up missing. I love you.

# ABOUT THE AUTHOR

**Brad Taylor** served for more than twenty-one years in the U.S. Army, retiring as a Special Forces Lieutenant Colonel. During that time he held numerous infantry and special operations positions, including eight years in 1st Special Forces Operational Detachment — Delta where he commanded multiple troops and a squadron. He has conducted operations in support of U.S. national interests in Iraq, Afghanistan, and other classified locations. He holds a master's of science in defense analysis with a concentration in irregular warfare from the Naval Postgraduate School in Monterey, California. When not writing, Brad serves as a security consultant on asymmetric threats to various agencies. He currently lives in Charleston, South Carolina, with his wife and two daughters.

The employees of Thorndike Press hope you have enjoyed this Large Print book. All our Thorndike, Wheeler, and Kennebec Large Print titles are designed for easy reading, and all our books are made to last. Other Thorndike Press Large Print books are available at your library, through selected bookstores, or directly from us.

For information about titles, please call:

(800) 223-1244

or visit our Web site at:

http://gale.cengage.com/thorndike

To share your comments, please write:

Publisher
Thorndike Press
10 Water St., Suite 310
Waterville, ME 04901